THE NEW INTERNATIONAL COMMENTARY
ON THE
NEW TESTAMENT

General Editors

NED B. STONEHOUSE
(1946–1962)

F. F. BRUCE
(1962–1990)

GORDON D. FEE
(1990–2012)

JOEL B. GREEN
(2013–   )

The Epistle to the
HEBREWS

GARETH LEE COCKERILL

WILLIAM B. EERDMANS PUBLISHING COMPANY
GRAND RAPIDS, MICHIGAN

Wm. B. Eerdmans Publishing Co.
2140 Oak Industrial Drive NE, Grand Rapids, Michigan 49505
www.eerdmans.com

23 22 21 20 19 18 17   2 3 4 5 6 7 8

Library of Congress Cataloging-in-Publication Data

Cockerill, Gareth Lee.
The Epistle to the Hebrews / Gareth Lee Cockerill.
pages   cm.   — (The New international Commentary on the New Testament)
Includes bibliographical references and indexes.
ISBN 978-0-8028-2492-9 (cloth: alk. paper)
1. Bible. N.T. Hebrews — Commentaries.   I. Title.

BS2775.3.C625   2012
227′.8707 — dc23

2011052836

To Rosa,
to our children by birth and by marriage,
to our grandchildren,
and to Dave

CONTENTS

CONTENTS

CONTENTS

EDITOR'S PREFACE

It is with considerable mixed emotions that I (gladly) introduce this commentary to the reading public. On the one hand, this work represents a signal end of an era for this commentary series, since it is both replacing a commentary by the second general editor (F. F. Bruce) and is the final editorial task of the third general editor, whose onsetting bout with Alzheimer's disease has necessitated his relinquishing this task, even though a few additional replacement volumes are still in the mill, as it were. I have had the privilege of working with Gary Cockerill quite closely over the past several years, and am pleased heartily to commend this commentary to the primary intended readership of this series — the proverbial "busy pastor" and biblical students in colleges and seminaries. The reader will quickly recognize that the author is not only well acquainted with the secondary literature on this great biblical book, but has also brought his own deep love for the author of Hebrews and his work to the task so that it shines throughout these pages. I am glad to be able to commend it to one and all.

GORDON D. FEE

AUTHOR'S PREFACE

Hebrews is a literary work from the first-century Hellenistic world. Yet the exposition that follows in this commentary does not treat this book at a distance as if it were a laboratory specimen. My intention is to do more than explicate an ancient document within its context and then draw some analogies for contemporary believers. I would enable modern readers to enter the Christian world of Hebrews and allow that world to reshape their hearts and minds. I hope this commentary will help those who approach this ancient but ever-relevant text to hear the word God has spoken in his Son, enter the divine presence through the cleansing he provides, and persevere through obedient faithfulness in fellowship with the people of God. Richard Hays has reminded the church that the purpose of biblical exposition is to enter the biblical narrative and allow it to transform the hearer's perspective and behavior.[1] There is no better book for carrying out this mandate than the Letter to the Hebrews.

In our initial conversations concerning this book Professor Gordon Fee asked me to justify issuing a new volume on Hebrews in this series. I suggested that developments over the past decades in the study of ancient rhetoric, in the analysis of Hebrews' structure (particularly through discourse analysis), and in intertextual studies warranted such a venture. I am grateful that he agreed. No NT book is more diligent in presenting the OT Scripture for its Christian hearers than this book, which begins by declaring: "God, who spoke in the prophets, . . . has now spoken in One who is Son." None of-

---

1. Richard B. Hays, *First Corinthians,* Interpretation (Louisville: John Knox, 1997), 173: "One of our fundamental pastoral tasks is to teach our congregations to find themselves in the stories of Israel and the early church. . . . Our pedagogy has failed miserably to teach this skill because we have usually tried too hard to make the text 'relevant.' Rather than seeking to make the text relevant, Paul seeks to draw his readers *into* the text in such a way that its world reshapes the norms and decisions of the community in the present. That is the task of biblical preaching."

fers a higher degree of rhetorical sophistication. One does not have to embrace all of the methodology advocated by various practitioners of these disciplines to be enriched by their work.

First of all, then, this commentary is based on a fresh analysis of the structure and rhetorical shape of Hebrews. Each individual passage is interpreted with sensitivity to the role it plays within the author's overall strategy for persuading his hearers to embrace the truth he presents and to act accordingly. I believe you will benefit significantly from engaging the full presentation of this structural analysis in the Introduction before proceeding to the exposition of your favorite passage. The opening paragraphs of each section and subsection of the exposition also situate the particular portion of the text under consideration in relation to the whole. It may seem audacious to present yet another structural analysis of Hebrews. I offer this analysis humbly, only after carefully listening to the text of Hebrews, and with deep appreciation for all that I have gained from other analyses. I ask you, the reader, to judge this analysis on the basis of its ability to enrich your understanding of individual passages and of Hebrews as a whole.

This commentary also offers fresh insight into Hebrews' use of the OT. The author of Hebrews understands the relationship between God's word in the Son and previous revelation as one of continuity and fulfillment. His approach has much that can enrich contemporary Christian biblical interpretation. My understanding of this subject as given in the Introduction to this commentary informs the exposition of the commentary proper.

When people discovered that I was writing a commentary on Hebrews they would almost invariably ask, "Well, who wrote it?" One certainly can and must study Hebrews within its first-century environment. In my judgment, however, the evidence available is insufficient to determine with certainty the name of the author or to be overly precise about the location, specific identity, and situation of the recipients. Thus those who base their interpretation on an unduly specific reconstruction of Hebrews' origin are likely to skew their understanding of the book in proportion to the idiosyncrasy of their proposal. Nevertheless, each proposal highlights some aspect of Hebrews. Thus we will survey various proposals in the Introduction not so much to determine which one is correct as to benefit from the insight each provides.

It is necessary to say something about translation, textual variants, and secondary sources. I have done my own translation of Hebrews so that I would not be under obligation to critique a particular version and so that I could make stylistic features and various emphases of the Greek text more readily accessible to the English reader. Many commentaries on Hebrews provide extensive analysis of textual variants. I have addressed textual issues only when they significantly impact interpretation and as part of the exposition itself rather than in a separate section. Due to the increased volume of scholarly publication, one can no longer claim to have mastered all of the literature on Hebrews. I have tried to be as comprehensive as possible and to interact with the sources that seemed most helpful. I am glad that the fine commentary by Peter O'Brien appeared just in time for consideration. I regret that my friend David Allen's commentary came just a bit too late.

I owe a great debt of gratitude to many for their help and encouragement. First of all, I am indebted to Professor Fee for giving me this opportunity and especially for his clear feedback on my initial draft of the opening chapters. That feedback set the direction for the whole. I would be amiss to omit my appreciation for my doctoral mentor, Professor Mathias Rissi, although this is not the commentary on Hebrews that he would have written. He first sparked my academic interest in Hebrews and guided my study with both insight and encouragement. My thanks to Ron Smith and Ray Easley, former President and Dean, respectively, of Wesley Biblical Seminary, for arranging my schedule and providing other resources that facilitated this project. Dan Burnett, Director of Library Services for Wesley Biblical Seminary, has graciously responded to my many requests for interlibrary loans. I am especially grateful to Kenneth Elliott, Director of the Library at Reformed Theological Seminary, Jackson, Mississippi, and to John McCarty, the Circulation Director. They cheerfully provided me with bibliographical resources, with a research room that greatly facilitated the completion of this project, and with collegial camaraderie. Milt Essenburg, of Eerdmans Publishing, has given me the encouragement in these final months that he has given to so many other commentators before me.

I am profoundly grateful to my friend since graduate school days, Dave Steveline, without whose encouragement this book would never have been begun. I wish to thank my daughter Allene and two sons-in-law, Carey Vinzant and David O'Donnell. Carey not only read the manuscript of this commentary with the eye of both a stylist and a theologian but also prepared the indexes. Allene and David provided extensive help with the Bibliography. I am grateful to my three daughters, Allene, Ginny, and Kathy, for their encouragement over the years, and, most of all to my wife of more than forty years, Rosa, who has patiently, graciously, and lovingly lived these past years for the time "after commentary." It is to her, to our children by birth and by marriage, to our grandchildren, and to Dave that I would dedicate this volume.

GARETH LEE COCKERILL

ABBREVIATIONS

I. BIBLICAL TEXTS AND TRANSLATIONS

CEV	Contemporary English Version
ESV	English Standard Version
HCSB	Holman Christian Standard Bible
KJV	King James Version
LXX	Septuagint (Old Greek Old Testament)
MT	Masoretic Text (Standard Hebrew Old Testament)
NA^{27}	*Novum Testamentum Graece.* Nestle-Aland, 27th ed.
NAB	New American Bible
NASB	New American Standard Bible
NJB	New Jerusalem Bible
NKJV	New King James Version
NLT	New Living Translation
NRSV	New Revised Standard Version
REB	Revised English Bible
RSV	Revised Standard Version
T/NIV	Today's New International Version/New International Version
TEV	Today's English Version
TNIV	Today's New International Version
UBS^{4}	*The Greek New Testament.* United Bible Societies, 4th ed.

II. JOURNALS

AUSS	*Andrews University Seminary Studies*
BBR	*Bulletin for Biblical Research*

Bib	*Biblica*
BR	*Biblical Research*
BSac	*Bibliotheca sacra*
BT	*The Bible Translator*
BZ	*Biblische Zeitschrift*
CBQ	*Catholic Biblical Quarterly*
CTJ	*Calvin Theological Journal*
CurBS	*Currents in Research: Biblical Studies*
EvQ	*Evangelical Quarterly*
ExpTim	*Expository Times*
GTJ	*Grace Theological Journal*
HTR	*Harvard Theological Review*
Int	*Interpretation*
JBL	*Journal of Biblical Literature*
JETS	*Journal of the Evangelical Theological Society*
JSNT	*Journal for the Study of the New Testament*
JTS	*Journal of Theological Studies*
NovT	*Novum Testamentum*
NRTh	*La nouvelle revue théologique*
NTS	*New Testament Studies*
RevBib	*Revue biblique*
RevExp	*Review and Expositor*
RevQ	*Revue de Qumran*
SBLSP	*Society of Biblical Literature Seminar Papers*
SJT	*Scottish Journal of Theology*
SPhilo	*Studia philonica*
TJ	*Trinity Journal*
TynBul	*Tyndale Bulletin*
TZ	*Theologische Zeitschrift*
WTJ	*Westminster Theological Journal*
ZNW	*Zeitschrift für die neutestamentliche Wissenschaft und die Kunde der älteren Kirche*

III. REFERENCE WORKS

BDAG	W. Bauer, F. W. Danker, W. F. Arndt, and F. W. Gingrich, *Greek-English Lexicon of the New Testament and Other Early Christian Literature.* 3rd ed. Chicago, 1999
BDF	F. Blass, A. Debrunner, and R. W. Funk, *A Greek Grammar of the New Testament*

DLNTD	*Dictionary of the Later New Testament and Its Development.* Edited by R. P. Martin and P. H. Davids. Downers Grove: InterVarsity Press, 1997
L&N	*Greek-English Lexicon of the New Testament: Based on Semantic Domains.* Edited by J. P. Louw and E. A. Nida. 2nd ed. New York, 1989
LSJ	H. G. Liddell, R. Scott, H. S. Jones, and R. McKenzie, *A Greek-English Lexicon*
MHT	*A Grammar of New Testament Greek,* by J. H. Moulton (vol. 1), W. E. Howard (vol. 2), and N. Turner (vols. 3-4)
MM	J. H. Moulton and G. Milligan, *The Vocabulary of the Greek New Testament*
OTP	J. H. Charlesworth, ed., *Old Testament Pseudepigrapha*
PG	*Patrologia graeca* (= *Patrologiae cursus completus: Series graeca*). Edited by J.-P. Migne. 162 vols. Paris, 1844-64
Str-B	H. Strack and P. Billerbeck, *Kommentar zum Neuen Testament*
TCGNT	B. M. Metzger, *A Textual Commentary on the Greek New Testament*
TDNT	*Theological Dictionary of the New Testament.* Edited by G. Kittel and G. Friedrich. Translated by G. W. Bromiley. 10 vols. Grand Rapids: Eerdmans, 1964-76

IV. SERIES

AB	Anchor Bible
ACCS: NT	Ancient Christian Commentary on Scripture: New Testament
AnBib	Analecta biblica
ANTC	Augsburg New Testament Commentary
BU	Biblische Untersuchungen
BZNW	Beihefte zur Zeitschrift für die neutestamentliche Wissenschaft
CBQMS	Catholic Biblical Quarterly Monograph Series
HNT	Handbuch zum Neuen Testament
JSNTSup	Journal for the Study of the New Testament: Supplement Series
KEK	Kritisch-exegetischer Kommentar über das Neue Testament (Meyer-Kommentar)
LCL	Loeb Classic Library

LNTS	Library of New Testament Studies
MNTC	Moffatt New Testament Commentary
MTS	Marburger Theological Studies
NCBC	New Century Bible Commentary
NIBCNT	New International Biblical Commentary: New Testament
RNT	Regensburger Neues Testament
SB	Sources bibliques
SBLDS	Society of Biblical Literature Dissertation Series
SNTSMS	Society for New Testament Studies Monograph Series
TNTC	Tyndale New Testament Commentary
WBC	Word Biblical Commentary
WUNT	Wissenschaftliche Untersuchungen zum Neuen Testament

V. APOSTOLIC FATHERS

Barn.	*Barnabas*
1-2 Clem.	*1-2 Clement*
Did.	*Didache*
Herm. *Mand.*	Shepherd of Hermas, *Mandate*
Herm. *Sim.*	Shepherd of Hermas, *Similitude*
Herm. *Vis.*	Shepherd of Hermas, *Vision*
Ign. *Eph.*	Ignatius, *To the Ephesians*
Ign. *Magn.*	Ignatius, *To the Magnesians*
Ign. *Phld.*	Ignatius, *To the Philadelphians*
Ign. *Trall.*	Ignatius, *To the Trallians*
Mart. Pol.	*Martyrdom of Polycarp*
Pol. *Phil.*	Polycarp, *To the Philippians*

VI. CLASSICAL SOURCES

Ann.	Tacitus, *Annales*
Claud.	Suetonius, *Divus Claudius*
Cyr.	Xenophon, *Cyropaedia*
Diatr.	Epictetus, *Diatribai (Dissertationes)*
Enn.	Plotinus, *Enneades*
Ep.	Seneca, *Epistulae morales*
Eth. Nic.	Aristotle, *Nichomachean Ethics/Ethica nichomachea*
Hist.	Herodotus, *Histories/Historiae*

Inst.	Quintilian, *Institutio oratoria*
Inv.	Cicero, *De inventione rhetorica*
Mem.	Xenophon, *Memorabilia*
Mor.	Plutarch, *Moralia*
Off.	Cicero, *De officiis*
Onir.	Artemidorus, *Onirocritica*
Onom.	Pollux, *Onomasticon*
Rhet.	Aristotle, *Rhetoric/Rhetorica*

VII. CHURCH FATHERS

1 Apol.	Justin Martyr, *1 Apology/Apologia I*
Civ.	Augustine, *The City of God/De civitate Dei*
Dial.	Justin Martyr, *Dialogue with Trypho/Dialogus cum Tryphone*
Epist.	Jerome, *Epistulae*
Haer.	Hippolytus, *Refutation of All Heresies/Refutatio omnium haeresium*
Hist. eccl.	Eusebius, *Ecclesiastical History/Historia ecclesiastica*
Hom. Heb.	Chrysostom, *Homiliae in epistulam ad Hebraeos*
Mart.	Tertullian, *To the Martyrs/Ad martyras*
Pan.	Epiphanius, *Refutation of All Heresies/Panarion (Adversus Haereses)*
Peregr.	Lucian, *The Passing of Peregrinus/De morte Peregrini*
Pud.	Tertullian, *Modesty/De pudicitia*
Vir. ill.	Jerome, *Lives of Illustrious Men/De viris illustribus*

VIII. JOSEPHUS

Ag. Ap.	*Against Apion/Contra Apionem*
Ant.	*Jewish Antiquities/Antiquitates judaicae*
J.W.	*Jewish War/Bellum judaicum*
Life	*The Life/Vita*

IX. APOCRYPHA AND PSEUDEPIGRAPHA

Bar	Baruch
1-2 Esd	1-2 Esdras
1-4 Macc	1-4 Maccabees
Jdt	Judith
Sir	Sirach/Ecclesiasticus
Sus	Susanna
Tob	Tobit
Wis	Wisdom of Solomon
Apos. Con.	*Apostolic Constitutions and Canons*
As. Mos.	*Assumption of Moses*
Ascen. Isa.	*Martyrdom and Ascension of Isaiah 6–11*
1 En.	*1 Enoch (Ethiopic Apocalypse)*
2 En.	*2 Enoch (Slavonic Apocalypse)*
3 En.	*3 Enoch (Hebrew Apocalypse)*
2 Bar.	*2 Baruch (Syriac Apocalypse)*
3 Bar.	*3 Baruch (Greek Apocalypse)*
4 Ezra	*4 Ezra*
Jos. Asen.	*Joseph and Aseneth*
Jub.	*Jubilees*
L.A.B.	*Liber antiquitatium biblicarum* (Pseudo-Philo)
L.A.E.	*Life of Adam and Eve*
Let. Aris.	*Letter of Aristeas*
Liv. Pro.	*Lives of the Prophets*
Mart. Isa.	*Martyrdom and Ascension of Isaiah 1–5*
Mart. Pet. Paul	*Martyrdom of Peter and Paul*
Pss. Sol.	*Psalms of Solomon*
Sib. Or	*Sibylline Oracles*
T. Benj.	*Testament of Benjamin*
T. Dan	*Testament of Dan*
T. Iss.	*Testament of Issachar*
T. Jos.	*Testament of Joseph*
T. Jud.	*Testament of Judah*
T. Levi	*Testament of Levi*
T. Mos.	*Testament of Moses*
T. Reu.	*Testament of Reuben*
T. Sim.	*Testament of Simeon*

X. PHILO

Abraham	On the Life of Abraham/De Abrahamo
Agriculture	On Agriculture/De agricultura
Alleg. Interp.	Allegorical Interpretations/Legum allegoriae
Cherubim	On the Cherubim/De cherubim
Confusion	On the Confusion of Tongues/De confusione linguarum
Creation	On the Creation of the World/De opificio mundi
Decalogue	On the Decalogue/De decalogo
Dreams	On Dreams/De somniis
Drunkenness	On Drunkenness/De ebrietate
Embassy	On the Embassy to Gaius/Legatio ad Gaium
Eternity	On the Eternity of the World/De aeternitate mundi
Flaccus	Against Flaccus/In Flaccum
Flight	On Flight and Finding/De fuga et inventione
Giants	On Giants/De gigantibus
Good Person	That Every Good Person Is Free/Quod omnis probus liber sit
Heir	Who Is the Heir?/Quis rerum divinarum heres sit
Joseph	On the Life of Joseph/De Iosepho
Migration	On the Migration of Abraham/De migratione Abrahami
Moses	On the Life of Moses/De vita Mosis
Names	On the Change of Names/De mutatione nominum
Planting	On Planting/De plantatione
Posterity	On the Posterity of Cain/De posteritate Caini
Prelim. Studies	On the Preliminary Studies/De congressu eruditionis gratia
QE	Questions and Answers on Exodus/Questiones et solutiones in Exodum
QG	Questions and Answers on Genesis/Questiones et solutiones in Genesin
Rewards	On Rewards and Punishments/De praemiis et poenis
Sacrifices	On the Sacrifices of Cain and Abel/De sacrificiis Abelis et Caini
Sobriety	On Sobriety/De sobrietate
Spec. Laws	On the Special Laws/De specialibus legibus
Unchangeable	That God Is Unchangeable/Quod Deus sit immutabilis
Virtues	On the Virtues/De virtutibus
Worse	That the Worse Attacks the Better/Quod deterius potiori insidari soleat

XI. DEAD SEA SCROLLS

Gen. Apoc.	Genesis Apocryphon (1QapGen[ar])
1QH	*Thanksgiving Hymns*
1QM	*War Scroll*
1QpHab	*Pesher Habakkuk*
1QS	*Rule of the Community*
1QSa	*Rule of the Congregation* (Appendix a to 1QS)
1QSb	*Rule of the Blessings* (Appendix b to 1QS)
4QAmram[b]	*4Q Visions of Amram[b]* (4Q533)
4QBer[f]	*4QBlessings[f]* (4Q280)
4QCatena[a]	*Midrash on Eschatology[a]* (Catena)
4QDeut32	*4QDeuteronomy32* (4Q44)
4QFlor	*Midrash on Eschatology[b]* (4QFlorilegium)
4QShirShabb[a-b]	*Songs of the Sabbath Sacrifice[a-b]* = 4Q400-4Q401
4QTest	*4QTestimonia*
11QMelch	11QMelchizedek (11Q13)
CD	Cairo Genizah copy of the *Damascus Document*

XII. RABBINIC LITERATURE (TARGUMS)

Frg. Tg.	*Fragmentary Targum*
Gen. Rab.	*Genesis Rabbah*
Tg. Neof.	*Targum Neofiti*
Tg. Onq.	*Targum Onqelos*
Tg. Ps.-J.	*Targum Pseudo-Jonathan*

BIBLIOGRAPHY

I. COMMENTARIES

These commentaries are cited by last name, volume number where appropriate, and page.

Andriessen, Paul, and A. Lenglet. *De Brief aan de Hebreeën.* Roermond, Netherlands: Roman and Zonen, 1971.

Attridge, Harold W. *The Epistle to the Hebrews.* Hermeneia. Philadelphia: Fortress, 1989.

Bénétreau, Samuel. *L'Épitre aux Hebreux.* 2 vols. Commentaire Évangélique de la Bible. Vaux-sur-seine: Édifac, 1989-90.

Bleek, Friedrich. *Der Brief an die Hebräer erläutert durch Einleitung, Übersetzung und fortlaufenden Commentar.* 2 parts in 3 vols. Berlin: Ferdinand Dümmler, 1936-40.

Braun, Herbert. *An die Hebräer.* HNT 14. Tübingen: Mohr, 1984.

Bruce, F. F. *The Epistle to the Hebrews.* Rev. ed. The New International Commentary on the New Testament. Grand Rapids: Eerdmans, 1990.

Buchanan, George Wesley. *To the Hebrews.* AB 36. New York: Doubleday, 1972.

Calvin, John. *The Epistle of Paul the Apostle to the Hebrews and the First and Second Epistles of St. Peter.* Edited by David W. Torrance and Thomas F. Torrance. Translated by William B. Johnston. Calvin's Commentaries 12. Grand Rapids: Eerdmans, 1963.

Cockerill, Gareth L. *Hebrews: A Bible Commentary in the Wesleyan Tradition.* Indianapolis: Wesleyan Publishing House, 1999.

Delitzsch, Franz. *Commentary on the Epistle to the Hebrews.* 2 vols. Translated by Thomas L. Kingsbury. Edinburgh: T&T Clark, 1878.

deSilva, David. *Perseverance in Gratitude: A Socio-Rhetorical Commentary on the Epistle "to the Hebrews."* Grand Rapids: Eerdmans, 2000.

Dods, Marcus. "The Epistle to the Hebrews." In *The Expositor's Greek Testament*, Vol. 4. W. Robertson Nicoll. New York: Dodd, Mead, 1910.

Ellingworth, Paul. *The Epistle to the Hebrews: A Commentary on the Greek Text.* New International Greek Testament Commentary. Grand Rapids: Eerdmans, 1993.

Fudge, Edward William. *Hebrews: Ancient Encouragement for Believers Today.* Abilene, TX: Leafwood, 2009.

Gooding, David. *An Unshakeable Kingdom: The Letter to the Hebrews for Today.* Grand Rapids: Eerdmans, 1989.

Gordon, R. P. *Hebrews.* 2nd ed., previously published by Sheffield Academic Press, 2000. Readings: A New Biblical Commentary. Sheffield: Sheffield Phoenix Press, 2008.

Grässer, Erich. *An die Hebräer.* 3 vols. Evangelisch-Katholischer Kommentar. Neukirchen: Benziger, 1990, 1993, 1997.

Guthrie, Donald G. *The Letter to the Hebrews.* Edited by Leon Morris. TNTC 15. Grand Rapids: Eerdmans, 1989.

Guthrie, George H. *Hebrews.* The NIV Application Commentary. Grand Rapids: Zondervan, 1998.

Hagner, Donald A. *Hebrews.* Edited by W. Ward Gasque. NIBCNT 14. Peabody, MA: Hendrickson, 1990.

Heen, Erik M., and Philip D. W. Krey, eds. *Hebrews.* ACCS:NT 10. Downers Grove, IL: InterVarsity Press, 2005.

Héring, J. *The Epistle to the Hebrews.* Translated by A. W. Heathcote and P. J. Allcock. London: Epworth, 1970.

Hughes, Philip Edgcumbe. *A Commentary on the Epistle to the Hebrews.* Grand Rapids: Eerdmans, 1977.

Johnson, Luke Timothy. *Hebrews: A Commentary.* New Testament Library. Louisville: Westminster/John Knox, 2006.

Kistemaker, Simon J. *Exposition of the Epistle to the Hebrews.* New Testament Commentary. Grand Rapids: Baker, 1984.

Koester, Craig R. *Hebrews: A New Testament Translation with Introduction and Commentary.* AB 36. New York: Doubleday, 2001.

Kuss, Otto. "Der Brief an die Hebräer." Pages 11-127 in *Der Brief an die Hebräer und die Katholischen Briefe.* Edited by Otto Kuss and Johann Michl. RNT 8. Regensburg: Friedrich Pustet, 1953.

Lane, William L. *Hebrews.* 2 vols. WBC 47a-47b. Dallas, TX: Word Books, 1991.

Lenski, R. C. H. *The Interpretation of the Epistle to the Hebrews and of the Epistle of James.* Columbus, OH: Wartburg, 1946.

Lightfoot, Neil R. *Jesus Christ Today: A Commentary on the Book of Hebrews.* Grand Rapids: Baker, 1976.

Michel, Otto. *Der Brief an die Hebräer.* 12th ed. KEK 13. Göttingen: Vandenhoeck & Ruprecht, 1966.

Mitchell, Alan C. *Hebrews*. Sacra Pagina 13. Collegeville, MN: Liturgical Press, 2009.

Moffatt, James. *A Critical and Exegetical Commentary on the Epistle to the Hebrews*. International Critical Commentary. New York: Charles Scribner's Sons, 1924.

Montefiore, Hugh. *A Commentary on the Epistle to the Hebrews*. Harper's New Testament Commentaries. New York: Harper & Row, 1964.

Morris, Leon. "Hebrews." In *The Expositor's Bible Commentary with the New International Version of the Holy Bible,* Vol. 12. Edited by Frank E. Gaebelein. Grand Rapids: Zondervan, 1981.

O'Brien, Peter T. *The Letter to the Hebrews*. The Pillar New Testament Commentary. Grand Rapids: Eerdmans, 2010.

Pfitzner, Victor C. *Hebrews*. ANTC. Nashville: Abingdon, 1997.

Riggenbach, D. Eduard. *Der Brief an die Hebräer.* 2nd-3rd ed. Kommentar zum Neuen Testament 14. Leipzig: Deichert, 1922.

Robinson, Theodore H. *The Epistle to the Hebrews*. MNTC. London: Hodder and Stoughton, 1933.

Scott, E. F. *The Epistle to the Hebrews: Its Doctrine and Significance*. Edinburgh: T&T Clark, 1922.

Spicq, Ceslas. *L'Épître aux Hébreux*. 2nd ed. 2 vols. Études biblique. Paris: Gabalda, 1953.

———. *L'Épître aux Hébreux*. Sources bibliques. Paris: Gabalda, 1977.

Stedman, Ray C. *Hebrews*. Downers Grove, IL: InterVarsity Press, 1992.

Thompson, James W. *Hebrews*. Paideia. Grand Rapids: Baker Academic, 2008.

Walters, John. "Hebrews." Pages 1139-69 in *Asbury Bible Commentary*. Edited by Eugene E. Carpenter and Wayne McCown. Grand Rapids: Zondervan, 1992.

Weiss, Hans-Friedrich. *Der Brief an die Hebräer.* KEK 13. Göttingen: Vandenhoeck & Ruprecht, 1991.

Westcott, B. F. *The Epistle to the Hebrews: The Greek Text with Notes and Essays*. Repr. Grand Rapids: Eerdmans, 1951.

Wilson, R. McL. *Hebrews*. NCBC. Grand Rapids: Eerdmans, 1987.

Windisch, H. *Der Hebräerbrief.* Tübingen: J. C. B. Mohr, 1931.

Witherington III, Ben. *Letters and Homilies for Jewish Christians: A Socio-Rhetorical Commentary on Hebrews, James and Jude*. Downers Grove, IL: IVP Academic, 2007.

II. GENERAL BIBLIOGRAPHY

Adams, Edward. "The Cosmology of Hebrews." Pages 122-39 in *The Epistle to the Hebrews and Christian Theology*. Edited by Richard Bauckham, Daniel R. Driver, Trevor A. Hart, and Nathan MacDonald. Grand Rapids: Eerdmans, 2009.

Adams, J. C. "Exegesis of Hebrews VI.1f." *NTS* 13 (1966-67): 378-85.

Aitken, Ellen Bradshaw. "Portraying the Temple in Stone and Text: The Arch of Titus and the Epistle to the Hebrews." Pages 131-48 in *Hebrews: Contemporary Methods — New Insights*. Edited by Gabriella Gelardini. Biblical Interpretation Series 75. Atlanta: Society of Biblical Literature, 2005.

Allegro, John N. "Fragments of a Qumran Scroll of Eschatological *Midrāšîm*." *JBL* 77 (December 1958): 350-54.

Allen, D. L. "The Authorship of Hebrews: The Lukan Proposal." *Faith & Mission* 18 (2001): 27-40.

Allen, David M. *Deuteronomy and Exhortation in Hebrews: A Study in Narrative Re-Presentation*. WUNT 238. Tübingen: Mohr Siebeck, 2008.

Andriessen, Paul. "La communauté des 'Hébreux,' était-elle tombée dans le relâchement?" *NRTh* 96 (1974): 1054-66.

————. "L'eucharistie dans l'épître aux Hébreux." *NRTh* 94 (1972): 269-77.

————. "Das grössere und vollkommenere Zelt (Hebr. 9,11)." *BZ* 15 (1971): 76-92.

————. "Renonçant à la joie qui lui revenait." *NRTh* 97 (1975): 424-38.

————, and A. Lenglet. "Quelques passages difficiles de l'épître aux Hébreux (5,7; 7,11; 10,20; 12,2)." *Bib* 51 (1970): 207-20.

Aschim, Anders. "Melchizedek the Liberator: An Early Interpretation of Genesis 14?" Pages 243-58 in *SBL 1996 Seminar Papers*. Atlanta: Scholars Press, 1996.

Attridge, Harold W. "God in Hebrews." Pages 95-110 in *The Epistle to the Hebrews and Christian Theology*. Edited by Richard Bauckham, Daniel R. Driver, Trevor A. Hart, and Nathan MacDonald. Grand Rapids: Eerdmans, 2009.

————. "The Psalms in Hebrews." Pages 197-212 in *The Psalms in the New Testament*. Edited by Steve Moyise and Maarten J. J. Menken. London and New York: T&T Clark International, 2004.

————. "'Let Us Strive to Enter That Rest': The Logic of Hebrews 4:1-11." *HTR* 73 (1980): 279-88.

————. "Paraenesis in a Homily (λόγος παρακήσεως): The Possible Location of, and Socialization in, the 'Epistle to the Hebrews.'" *Semeia* 50 (1990): 211-26.

————. "The Uses of Antithesis in Hebrews 8–10." Pages 1-9 in *Christians among Jews and Gentiles: Essays in Honor of Krister Stendahl on His Sixty-Fifth Birthday*. Edited by G. W. E. Nickelsburg and G. W. MacRae. Philadelphia: Fortress, 1986.

Auffret, P. "Essai sur la structure littéraire et l'interprétation d'Hébreux 3,1-6." *NTS* 26 (1979-80): 380-96.

Aune, David. *The New Testament in Its Literary Environment*. Philadelphia: Westminster, 1987.

Bachmann, M. "'. . . gesprochen durch den Herrn' (Hebr 2,3): Erwägungen zum Reden Gottes und Jesu im Hebräerbrief." *Bib* 71 (1990): 365-94.

————. "Hohepriesterliches Leiden: Beobachtungen zu Hebr 5:1-10." *ZNW* 78 (1987): 244-66.

Backhaus, K. "Das Land der Verheissung: Die Heimat der Glaubenden im Hebräerbrief." *NTS* 47 (2001): 171-88.

Barrett, C. K. "The Eschatology of the Epistle to the Hebrews." Pages 363-93 in *The Background of the New Testament and Its Eschatology*. Edited by W. D. Davies and D. Daube. Cambridge: Cambridge University Press, 1956.

Bateman IV, Herbert W. *Early Jewish Hermeneutics and Hebrews 1:5-13*. American University Studies, Series VII: Theology and Religion 193. New York: Peter Lang, 1997.

————. "Two First-Century Messianic Uses of the OT: Heb 1:5-13 and 4QFlor 1.1-19." *JETS* 38 (1995): 11-27.

Bauckham, Richard. "The Divinity of Jesus Christ in the Epistle to the Hebrews." Pages 15-36 in *The Epistle to the Hebrews and Christian Theology*. Edited by Richard Bauckham, Daniel R. Driver, Trevor A. Hart, and Nathan MacDonald. Grand Rapids: Eerdmans, 2009.

————. *Jesus and the God of Israel*. Grand Rapids: Eerdmans, 2008.

Baugh, S. M. "The Cloud of Witnesses in Hebrews 11." *WTJ* 68 (2006): 113-32.

Beale, G. K. *The Temple and the Church's Mission: A Biblical Theology of the Dwelling Place of God*. New Studies in Biblical Theology 17. Downers Grove: InterVarsity Press, 2004.

Berényi, Gabriella. "La portée de διὰ τοῦτο en He 9:15." *Bib* 69 (1988): 108-12.

Bieder, Werner. "Pneumatologische Aspekte im Hebräerbrief." Pages 251-60 in *Neues Testament und Geschichte*. Festschrift for O. Cullmann. Edited by H. Baltensweiler and B. Reicke. Tübingen: Mohr-Siebeck, 1972.

Black, David Alan. "Who Wrote Hebrews? The Internal and External Evidence Reexamined." *Faith & Mission* 18 (2001): 3-26.

Black II, C. Clifton. "The Rhetorical Form of the Hellenistic Jewish and Early Christian Sermon: A Response to Lawrence Wills." *HTR* 81 (1988): 1-18.

Bligh, John. "The Structure of Hebrews." *Heythrop Theological Journal* 5 (1964): 170-77.

Blomberg, Craig L. "'But We See Jesus': The Relationship between the Son of Man in Hebrews 2.6 and 2.9 and the Implications for English Translations." Pages 88-99 in *A Cloud of Witnesses: The Theology of Hebrews in Its Ancient Context*. Edited by Richard Bauckham, Daniel R. Driver, Trevor Hart, and Nathan MacDonald. LNTS 387. T&T Clark, 2008.

Bodinger, M. "L'Énigme de Melkisédeq." *Revue de l'histoire des religions* 211 (1994): 297-333.

Bornkamm, G. "Das Bekenntnis im Hebräerbrief." *Theologische Blätter* 21 (1942): 56-66.

Bowman, Thorleif. "Der Gebetskampf Jesu." *NTS* 10 (January 1964): 261-73.

Brandenburger, Egon. "Text und Vorlagen von Hebr. V 7-10: Ein Beitrag zur Christologie des Hebräerbriefes." *NovT* 11 (July 1969): 190-224.

Brawley, R. L. "Discursive Structure and the Unseen in Hebrews 2:8 and 11:1: A Neglected Aspect of the Context." *CBQ* 55 (1993): 81-98.

Brooks, Walter Edward. "The Perpetuity of Christ's Sacrifice in the Epistle to the Hebrews." *JBL* 89 (1970): 205-14.

Bruce, F. F. *Biblical Exegesis in the Qumran Texts.* Grand Rapids: Eerdmans, 1959.

———. "'A Shadow of Good Things' (Hebrews 10:1)." Pages 77-94 in *The Time Is Fulfilled: Five Aspects of the Fulfillment of the Old Testament in the New.* Grand Rapids: Eerdmans, 1978.

Bulley, Alan D. "Death and Rhetoric in the Hebrews 'Hymn to Faith.'" *Studies in Religion* 25 (1996): 409-23.

Caird, G. B. "Exegetical Method of the Epistle to the Hebrews." *Canadian Journal of Theology* 5 (1959): 44-51.

Caneday, Ardel B. "The Eschatological World Already Subjected to the Son: The Οἰκουμένη of Hebrews 1.6 and the Son's Enthronement." Pages 28-39 in *A Cloud of Witnesses: The Theology of Hebrews in Its Ancient Contexts.* Edited by Richard Bauckham, Daniel R. Driver, Trevor Hart, and Nathan MacDonald. LNTS 387. T&T Clark, 2008.

Casey, J. M. "Christian Assembly in Hebrews: A Fantasy Island?" *Theology Digest* 30 (1982): 323-35.

Clements, Ronald E. "The Use of the Old Testament in Hebrews." *Southwestern Journal of Theology* 28 (1985): 36-45.

Coats, George W. "Lot: A Foil in the Abraham Saga." Pages 113-32 in *Understanding the Word.* Edited by James T. Butler, Edgar W. Conrad, and Ben C. Ollenburger. JSNTSup 37. Sheffield: JSOT Press, 1985.

Cockerill, Gareth Lee. "The Better Resurrection (Heb. 11:35): A Key to the Structure and Rhetorical Purpose of Hebrews 11." *TynBul* 51 (2000): 214-34.

———. "Building Bridges to Muslims: A Test Case." Pages 323-43 in *Contextualization and Syncretism: Navigating Cultural Currents.* Edited by Gailyn Van Rheenen. Evangelical Missiological Society 13. Pasadena: William Carey Library, 2006.

———. *Guidebook for Pilgrims to the Heavenly City.* Pasadena: William Carey Library, 2004.

———. "Heb 1:1-14, *1 Clem.* 36:1-6, and the High Priest Title." *JBL* 97 (1978): 437-40.

———. "Hebrews 1:6: Source and Significance." *BBR* 9 (1999): 51-64.

———. "The Melchizedek Christology in Heb. 7:1-28." Ph.D. diss., Union Theological Seminary in Virginia, Richmond, 1976.

———. "Melchizedek or 'King of Righteousness.'" *EvQ* 63 (October 1991): 305-12.

———. *"The Melchizedek Tradition,* a Review." *Int* 31 (July 1977): 328-29.

———. "Melchizedek without Speculation: Hebrews 7:1-25 and Genesis 14:14-24." Pages 128-44 in *A Cloud of Witnesses: The Theology of Hebrews in Its Ancient Context.* Edited by Richard Bauckham, Daniel R. Driver, Trevor Hart, and Nathan MacDonald. LNTS 387. T&T Clark, 2008.

———. "Structure and Interpretation in Hebrews 8:1–10:18: A Symphony in Three Movements." *BBR* 11 (2001): 179-201.

———. "To the Hebrews/to the Muslims: Islamic Pilgrimage as a Key to Interpretation." *Missiology* 22 (1994): 347-59.

———. "A Wesleyan Arminian Response to a Moderate Reformed View." Pages 415-29 in *Four Views on the Warning Passages in Hebrews.* Edited by Herbert W. Batemann IV. Grand Rapids: Kregel, 2007.

———. "A Wesleyan Arminian View." Pages 257-92 in *Four Views on the Warning Passages in Hebrews.* Edited by Herbert W. Batemann IV. Grand Rapids: Kregel, 2007.

Cody, Aelred. *Heavenly Sanctuary and Liturgy in the Epistle to the Hebrews.* St. Meinrad, IN: Grail Publications, 1960.

Collins, John J. *The Apocalyptic Imagination: An Introduction to Jewish Apocalyptic Literature.* 2nd ed. Grand Rapids: Eerdmans, 1998.

Cortez, Felix H. "From the Holy to the Most Holy Place: The Period of Hebrews 9:6-10 and the Day of Atonement as a Metaphor of Transition." *JBL* 125 (2006): 527-47.

Cosaert, Carl P. "The Use of ἅγιος for the Sanctuary in the Old Testament Pseudepigrapha, Philo, and Josephus." *AUSS* 42 (2004): 91-103.

Cosby, Michael R. *The Rhetorical Composition and Function of Hebrews 11 in Light of Example Lists in Antiquity.* Macon, GA: Mercer University Press, 1988.

———. "The Rhetorical Composition of Hebrews 11." *JBL* 107 (June 1988): 257-73.

Craigie, Peter C. *Psalms 1–50.* WBC 19. Waco, TX: Word Books, 1983.

Croy, N. C. *Endurance in Suffering: Hebrews 12:1-13 in Its Rhetorical, Religious, and Philosophical Context.* SNTSMS 98. Cambridge: Cambridge University Press, 1998.

———. "A Note on Hebrews 12:2." *JBL* 114 (1995): 117-19.

Currid, John D. *A Study Commentary on Genesis.* 2 vols. Webster, NY: Evangelical Press, 2003.

D'Angelo, Mary Rose. *Moses in the Letter to the Hebrews*. SBLDS 42. Missoula, MT: Scholars Press, 1979.

Dahl, N. A. "'A New and Living Way': The Approach to God according to Hebrews 10:19-25." *Int* 5 (1951): 401-12.

Davidson, Richard M. "Christ's Entry 'within the Veil' in Hebrews 6:19-20: The Old Testament Background." *AUSS* 39 (2001): 175-90.

————. "Inauguration or Day of Atonement? A Response to Norman Young's 'Old Testament Background to Hebrews 6:19-20 Revisited.'" *AUSS* 40 (2002): 69-88.

————. "Typology in the Book of Hebrews." Pages 121-86 in *Issues in the Book of Hebrews*. Edited by Frank B. Holbrook. Springfield, MD: Biblical Research Institute, 1989.

Davies, W. D. *The Gospel and the Land: Early Christianity and Jewish Territorial Doctrine*. Berkeley: University of California Press, 1974.

Davila, James R. "Melchizedek, the 'Youth,' and Jesus." Pages 248-74 in *The Dead Sea Scrolls as Background to Postbiblical Judaism and Early Christianity*. Edited by James R. Davila. Leiden: Brill, 2003.

De Jonge, M. *The Testaments of the Twelve Patriarchs: A Study of Their Text, Composition and Origin*. 2nd ed. Van Gorcum's Theologische Bibliotheek. Assen: Van Gorcum, 1975.

De Young, James Calvin. *Jerusalem in the New Testament: The Significance of the City in the History of Redemption and in Eschatology*. Kampen: Kok, 1960.

Deichgräber, R. *Gotteshymnus und Christushymnus in der Frühen Christenheit: Untersuchungen zu Form, Sprache und Stil der frühchristlichen Hymnen*. SUNT. Göttingen: Vandenhoeck und Ruprecht, 1967.

Deissmann, G. Adolf. *Bible Studies: Contributions Chiefly from Papyri and Inscriptions to the History of the Language, the Literature, and the Religion of Hellenistic Judaism and Primitive Christianity*. 2nd ed. Translated by Alexander Grieve. Edinburgh: T&T Clark, 1909.

Demarest, Bruce. "Hebrews 7:3, a Crux Interpretum Historically Considered." *EvQ* 49 (1977): 141-62.

————. *A History of Interpretation of Hebrews 7,1-10 from the Reformation to the Present Day*. Beiträge zur Geschichte der Biblischen Exegese 19. Tübingen: Siebeck, 1976.

deSilva, David A. *Despising Shame: Honor Discourse and Community Maintenance in the Epistle to the Hebrews*. SBLDS 152. Atlanta: Scholars Press, 1995.

————. "Hebrews 6:4-8: A Socio-Rhetorical Investigation (Part 1)." *TynBul* 50 (1999): 33-57.

————, and Victor Matthews. *Untold Stories of the Bible*. Lincolnwood, IL: Publications International Ltd., 1998.

Dey, Lala Kalyan Kumar. *The Intermediary World and Patterns of Perfection in Philo and Hebrews.* SBLDS 25. Missoula, MT: Scholars Press, 1975.

Dibelius, Martin. "Der himmlische Kultus nach dem Hebräerbrief." Pages 160-76 in *Botschaft und Geschichte: Gesammelte Aufsätze II: Zum Urchristentum und zur hellenistischen Religionsgeschichte.* Tübingen: Mohr Siebeck, 1956.

Docherty, Susan E. *The Use of the Old Testament in Hebrews: A Case Study in Early Jewish Bible Interpretation.* WUNT 2/260. Tübingen: Mohr Siebeck, 2009.

Dolfe, Karl-Gustav E. "Hebrews 2,16 under the Magnifying Glass." *ZNW* 84 (1993): 289-94.

Dörrie, H. "Ὑπόστασις, Wort- und Bedeutungsgeschichte." *Nachrichten (von) der Akademie der Wissenschaften in Göttingen* 3 (1955): 35-92.

Dumbrell, W. J. "The Spirits of Just Men Made Perfect." *EvQ* 48 (1976): 154-59.

Dunnill, J. *Covenant and Sacrifice in the Letter to the Hebrews.* SNTSMS 75. Cambridge: Cambridge University Press, 1992.

Dussaut, L. *Synopse structurelle de l'épître aux Hébreux.* Paris: Cerf, 1981.

Ebert, Daniel J. IV. "The Chiastic Structure of the Prologue of Hebrews." *TJ* 13 n.s. (Fall 1992): 163-79.

———. "Wisdom in New Testament Christology, with Special Reference to Hebrews 1:1-4." Ph.D. diss. Trinity Evangelical Divinity School, 1998.

Edwards, Jonathan. *A History of the Work of Redemption.* First published Edinburgh. W. Gray, 1774. Edinburgh: Banner of Truth Trust, 2003.

Eisele, Wilfried. *Ein unerschütterliches Reich: Die mittelplatonische Umformung des Parusiegedankens im Hebräerbrief.* BZNW 116. Berlin and New York: Walter de Gruyter, 2003.

Eisenbaum, Pamela M. "Heroes and History in Hebrews 11." Pages 380-96 in *Early Christian Interpretation of the Scriptures of Israel: Investigations and Proposals.* Edited by C. A. Evans and J. A. Sanders. JSNTSup 148. Sheffield: Sheffield Academic Press, 1997.

———. *The Jewish Heroes of Christian History: Hebrews 11 in Literary Context.* SBLDS 156. Atlanta: Scholars Press, 1997.

———. "Locating Hebrews within the Literary Landscape of Christian Origins." In *Hebrews: Contemporary Methods — New Insights.* Edited by Gabriella Gelardini. Biblical Interpretation Series 75. Atlanta: Society of Biblical Literature, 2005.

Ellingworth, Paul. "Hebrews and *1 Clement:* Literary Dependence or Common Tradition?" *BZ* 23 (1979): 262-69.

———. "'Like the Son of God': Form and Content in Hebrews 7:1-10." *Bib* 64 (1983): 238-41.

———. "The Unshakable Priesthood: Hebrews 7.24." *JSNT* 23 (1985): 125-26.

Elliott, J. H. *A Home for the Homeless: A Social-Scientific Criticism of 1 Peter, Its Situation and Strategy.* Minneapolis: Fortress, 1990.

Elliott, J. K. "Is Post-Baptismal Sin Forgiveable?" *BT* 28 (1977): 330-32.

Emerton, John A. "Riddle of Genesis 14." *Vetus Testamentum* 21 (1971): 403-39.

Emmrich, Martin. "'Amtscharisma': Through the Eternal Spirit (Hebrews 9:14)." *BBR* 12 (2002): 17-32.

———. "Hebrews 6:4-6 — Again! (a Pneumatological Inquiry)." *WTJ* 65 (2003): 83-95.

———. "Pneuma in Hebrews: Prophet and Interpreter." *WTJ* 63 (2002): 55-71.

———. *Pneumatological Concepts in the Epistle to the Hebrews: Amtscharisma, Prophet, and Guide of the Eschatological Exodus.* Lanham, MD: University Press of America, 2003.

Enns, P. E. "Creation and Re-Creation: Psalm 95 and Its Interpretation in Hebrews 3:1–4:13." *WTJ* 55 (1993): 255-80.

Fanning, Buist M. "A Classical Reformed View." Pages 172-219 in *Four Views on the Warning Passages in Hebrews.* Edited by Herbert W. Bateman IV. Grand Rapids: Kregel, 2007.

Fee, Gordon D. "Wisdom Christology in Paul: A Dissenting View." Pages 251-79 in *Way of Wisdom: Essays in Honor of Bruce K. Waltke.* Edited by J. I. Packer and Sven K. Soderlund. Grand Rapids: Zondervan, 2000.

Filson, Floyd V. *"Yesterday": A Study of Hebrews in the Light of Chapter 13.* London: SCM, 1967.

Fitzmyer, Joseph A. "Melchizedek in the MT, LXX, and the NT." *Bib* 81, no. 1 (2000): 63-69.

———. "The Melchizedek Tradition, a Review." *CBQ* 39 (July 1977): 436-38.

———. "'Now This Melchizedek. . . .'" *CBQ* 25 (July 1963): 305-21.

France, R. T. "The Writer of Hebrews as a Biblical Expositor." *TynBul* 47 (1996): 245-76.

Frankowski, J. "Early Christian Hymns Recorded in the New Testament: A Reconsideration of the Question in the Light of Hebrews 1,3." *BZ* 27 (1983): 183-94.

Fretheim, Terence E. "The Book of Genesis: Introduction, Commentary, and Reflections." Pages 319-674 in *The New Interpreter's Bible.* Nashville: Abingdon, 1994.

Friedrich, Gerhard. "Das Lied vom Hohenpriester im Zusammenhang von Hebr 4,14–5,10." *TZ* 18 (March/April 1962): 95-115.

Gager, J. G. *The Origins of Anti-Semitism: Attitudes toward Judaism in Pagan and Christian Antiquity.* Oxford: Oxford University Press, 1984.

Gelardini, Gabriella. "From 'Linguistic Turn' and Hebrews Scholarship to *Anadiplosis Iterata:* The Enigma of a Structure." *HTR* 102 (2009): 51-73.

———. "Hebrews, an Ancient Synagogue Homily for *Tisha Be-Av:* Its Function, Its Basis, Its Theological Interpretation." Pages 107-27 in *Hebrews: Con-*

temporary Methods — New Insights. Edited by Gabriella Gelardini. Biblical Interpretation Series 75. Boston: Society of Biblical Literature, 2005.

————. *"Verhärtet eure Herzen nicht": Der Hebräer, eine Synagogenhomilie zu Tischa be-Aw.* Biblical Interpretation Series 83. Leiden and Boston: Brill, 2007.

Gheorghita, R. *The Role of the Septuagint in Hebrews: An Investigation of Its Influence with Special Consideration to the Use of Hab 2:3-4 in Heb 10:37-38.* WUNT 2/160. Tübingen: Siebeck, 2003.

Gilbert, G. H. "The Greek Element in the Epistle to the Hebrews." *American Journal of Theology* 14 (1910): 521-32.

Gleason, Randall C. "The Eschatology of the Warning in Hebrews 10:26-31." *TynBul* 53 (2002): 97-120.

————. "A Moderate Reformed View." Pages 336-77 in *Four Views on the Warning Passages in Hebrews.* Edited by Herbert W. Bateman IV. Grand Rapids: Kregel, 2007.

————. "The Old Testament Background of Rest in Hebrews 3:7–4:11." *BSac* 157 (2000): 281-303.

————. "The Old Testament Background of the Warning in Hebrews 6:4-8." *BSac* 155 (1998): 62-91.

Gnilka, Joachim. "Die Erwartung des messianischen Hohenpriesters in den Schriften von Qumran und im Neuen Testament." *RevQ* 2 (1960): 395-426.

Goulder, M. "Hebrews and the Ebionites." *NTS* 49 (2003): 393-406.

Gourgues, M. "Remarques sur la 'structure centrale' de l'épître aux Hébreux: A l'occasion d'une réédition." *RevBib* 84 (1977): 26-37.

Grässer, Erich. *Der Alte Bund im Neuen: Exegetische Studien zur Israelfrage im Neuen Testament.* WUNT 35. Tübingen: Mohr/Siebeck, 1985.

————. *Der Glaube im Hebräerbrief.* MTS 2. Marburg: Elwert, 1965.

————. "Der Hebräerbrief 1938-1963." *Theologische Rundschau,* Neue Folge, 30 (1964): 138-236.

————. "Das Heil als Wort: Exegetische Erwägungen zu Hebr 2,1-4." Pages 261-74 in *Neues Testament und Geschichte.* Edited by Heinrich Baltensweiler and Bo Reicke. Tübingen: Siebeck, 1972.

————. "Mose und Jesus: Zur Auslegung von Hebr 3:1-6." *ZNW* 75 (1984): 2-23.

————. "Das Wandernde Gottesvolk: Zum Basismotiv des Hebräerbriefes." *ZNW* 77 (1986): 160-79.

Greenlee, J. Harold. "Hebrews 11:11 — Sarah's Faith or Abraham's?" *Notes on Translation* 4 (1990): 37-42.

Gregory, Andrew. "Disturbing Trajectories: *I Clement,* the *Shepherd of Hermas* and the Development of Early Roman Christianity." Pages 142-66 in

Rome, the Bible, and the Early Church. Edited by P. Oakes. Carlisle: Paternoster, 2002.

―――. *"I Clement:* An Introduction." *ExpTim* 117 (2006): 223-30.

Grelot, Pierre. "Le texte du Psaume 39,7 dans la Septante." *RevBib* 108, no. 2 (2001): 210-13.

Grogan, Geoffrey W. "Christ and His People: An Exegetical and Theological Study of Hebrews 2:5-18." *Vox Evangelica* (1969): 54-71.

Grudem, Wayne. "Perseverance of the Saints: A Case Study from the Warning Passages in Hebrews." Pages 133-82 in *Still Sovereign: Contemporary Perspectives on Election, Foreknowledge, and Grace.* Edited by Thomas R. Schreiner and Bruce A. Ware. Grand Rapids: Baker, 2000.

Gudorf, Michael E. "Through a Classical Lens: Hebrews 2:16." *JBL* 119 (2000): 105-8.

Guthrie, Donald G. *New Testament Theology.* Downers Grove, IL: InterVarsity Press, 1981.

Guthrie, G. H., and R. D. Quinn. "A Discourse Analysis of the Use of Psalm 8:4-6 in Hebrews 2:5-9." *JETS* 49 (2006): 235-46.

Guthrie, George H. "The Case for Apollos as the Author of Hebrews." *Faith & Mission* 18 (2001): 41-56.

―――. "Hebrews." Pages 919-95 in *Commentary on the New Testament Use of the Old Testament.* Edited by G. K. Beale and D. A. Carson. Grand Rapids: Baker Academic, 2007.

―――. "'Hebrews' Use of the Old Testament: Recent Trends in Research." *CurBS* 1 (2003): 271-94.

―――. "Old Testament in Hebrews." *DLNTD* (1997): 841-50.

―――. *The Structure of Hebrews: A Text-Linguistic Analysis.* Repr. Grand Rapids: Baker, 1998.

Gyllenberg, Rafael. "Die Komposition des Hebräerbriefs." *Svensk Exegetisk Årsbok* 22-23 (1957-58): 137-47.

Hagner, Donald Alfred. *The Use of the Old and New Testaments in Clement of Rome.* Supplements to *Novum Testamentum* 34. Leiden: E. J. Brill, 1973.

Hahn, Scott W. "A Broken Covenant and the Curse of Death: A Study of Hebrews 9:15-22." *CBQ* 66 (2004): 416-36.

―――. "Covenant, Cult, and the Curse-of-Death: Διαθήκη in Heb 9:15-22." Pages 65-88 in *Hebrews: Contemporary Methods — New Insights.* Edited by Gabriella Gelardini. Biblical Interpretation Series 75. Atlanta: Society of Biblical Literature, 2005.

Hamm, Dennis. "Faith in the Epistle to the Hebrews: The Jesus Factor." *CBQ* 52 (1990): 270-91.

―――. "Praying 'Regularly' (Not 'Constantly'): A Note on the Cultic Background of διὰ παντός at Luke 24:53, Acts 10:2, and Hebrews 9:6, 13:15." *ExpTim* 116 (2004): 50-52.

Hanson, A. T. *Jesus Christ in the Old Testament*. London, 1965.

Harnack, Adolf von. "Probabilia über die Adresse und den Verfasser des Hebräerbriefes." *ZNW* (1900): 16-41.

Harris, Murray J. "The Translation and Significance of Ὁ ΘΕΟΣ in Hebrews 1:8-9." *TynBul* 36 (1985): 129-62.

Hay, David M. *Glory at the Right Hand: Psalm 110 in Early Christianity*. Society of Biblical Literature Monograph Series 18. Nashville: Abingdon, 1973.

Hays, Richard B. *First Corinthians*. Interpretation. Louisville: John Knox, 1997.

———. "'Here We Have No Lasting City': New Covenantalism in Hebrews." Pages 151-73 in *The Epistle to the Hebrews and Christian Theology*. Edited by Richard Bauckham, Daniel R. Driver, Trevor A. Hart, and Nathan MacDonald. Grand Rapids: Eerdmans, 2009.

Helyer, L. R. "The *Prōtotokos* Title in Hebrews." *Studia Biblica et Theologica* 6 (1976): 3-28.

Hengel, Martin. *Crucifixion*. Philadelphia: Fortress, 1977.

Herron, T. J. "The Most Probable Date of the First Epistle of Clement to the Corinthians." *Studia patristica* 21 (1989): 106-21.

Hoekema, Anthony A. "Perfection of Christ in Hebrews." *CTJ* 9 (1974): 31-37.

Hofius, Otfried. "Eine altjüdische Parallele zu Röm. IV.27b." *NTS* 18 (1971-72).

———. "Das 'erste' und das 'zweite' Zelt: Ein Beitrag zur Auslegung von Hbr 9 1-10." *ZNW* 61 (1970): 271-77.

———. "Inkarnation und Opfertod Jesu nach Hebr 10, 19f." Pages 132-43 in *Der Ruf Jesu und die Antwort der Gemeinde: Festschrift für J. Jeremias*. Edited by E. Lohse. Göttingen: Vandenhoeck & Ruprecht, 1970.

———. *Katapausis: Die Vorstellung vom endzeitlichen Ruheort im Hebräerbrief*. WUNT 11. Tübingen: Siebeck, 1970.

———. *Der Vorhang vor dem Thron Gottes: Eine exegetisch-religionsgeschichtliche Untersuchung zu Hebräer 6, 19f und 10, 19f*. WUNT 14. Tübingen: Siebeck, 1972.

Hollander, H. W. "Hebrews 7:11 and 8:6: A Suggestion for the Translation of *Nenomthetētai Epi*." *BT* 30 (1979): 244-47.

Holmes, Stephen R. "Death in the Afternoon: Hebrews, Sacrifice, and Soteriology." Pages 229-52 in *The Epistle to the Hebrews and Christian Theology*. Edited by Richard Bauckham, Daniel R. Driver, Trevor A. Hart, and Nathan MacDonald. Grand Rapids: Eerdmans, 2009.

Holwerda, David E. *Jesus and Israel: One Covenant or Two?* Grand Rapids: Eerdmans, 1995.

Hooker, Morna D. "Christ, the 'End' of the Cult." Pages 189-212 in *The Epistle to the Hebrews and Christian Theology*. Edited by Richard Bauckham, Daniel R. Driver, Trevor A. Hart, and Nathan MacDonald. Grand Rapids: Eerdmans, 2009.

Hoppin, Ruth. *Priscilla's Letter: Finding the Author of the Epistle to the Hebrews.* Fort Bragg, CA: Lost Coast Press, 1997.

Horbury, W. "The Aaronic Priesthood in the Epistle to the Hebrews." *JSNT* 19 (1983): 43-71.

Horning, Estella B. "Chiasmus, Creedal Structure and Christology in Hebrews 12.1-2." *BR* 23 (1978): 37-48.

Horton, Fred L., Jr. *The Melchizedek Tradition: A Critical Examination of the Sources to the Fifth Century A.D. and in the Epistle to the Hebrews.* SNTSMS 30. Cambridge: Cambridge University Press, 1976.

Howard, F. W. "The Epistle to the Hebrews." *Int* 5 (1951): 80-91.

Hughes, Graham. *Hebrews and Hermeneutics: The Epistle to the Hebrews as a New Testament Example of Biblical Interpretation.* SNTSMS 36. Cambridge: Cambridge University Press, 1979.

Hughes, John J. "Hebrews IX 15ff. and Galatians III 15ff.: A Study in Covenant Practice and Procedure." *NovT* 21 (1976-77): 27-96.

Hughes, Philip E. "The Blood of Jesus and His Heavenly Priesthood in Hebrews, Part I: The Significance of the Blood of Jesus." *BSac* 130 (1973): 99-109.

———. "The Blood of Jesus and His Heavenly Priesthood in Hebrews, Part II: The High-Priestly Sacrifice of Christ." *BSac* 130 (1973): 195-212.

———. "The Blood of Jesus and His Heavenly Priesthood in Hebrews, Part III: The Meaning of the 'True Tent' and 'the Greater and More Perfect Tent.'" *BSac* 130 (1973): 305-14.

Hurst, Lincoln D. "Apollos, Hebrews, and Corinth: Bishop Montefiore's Theory Examined." *SJT* 38 (1985): 505-13.

———. "The Christology of Hebrews 1 and 2." Pages 151-64 in *The Glory of Christ in the New Testament.* Edited by L. D. Hurst and N. T. Wright. Oxford: Clarendon, 1987.

———. *The Epistle to the Hebrews: Its Background of Thought.* SNTSMS 65. Cambridge: Cambridge University Press, 1990.

———. "Eschatology and 'Platonism' in the Epistle to the Hebrews." In *Society of Biblical Literature Seminar Papers.* Atlanta: Scholars Press, 1984.

———. "How 'Platonic' Are Heb. Viii.5 and Ix.23f.?" *JTS* 34 (1983): 156-68.

Irwin, J. "The Use of Hebrews 11:11 as Embryological Proof-Text." *HTR* 71 (1978): 312-16.

Isaacs, Marie E. "Hebrews 13.9-16 Revisited." *NTS* 43 (1997): 268-84.

———. *Sacred Space: An Approach to the Theology of the Epistle to the Hebrews.* Edited by Stanley E. Porter. JSNTSup 73. Sheffield: JSOT Press, 1992.

Ito, A. "Concerning the θυμιατήριον (Heb 9:4) [in Japanese]." *Exegetica* 10 (1999): 149-65.

Jeremias, J. "Hebräer 10:20: τοῦτ' ἐστιν τῆς σαρκὸς αὐτοῦ." *ZNW* 62 (1971): 131.

Jobes, Karen. "The Function of Paronomasia in Hebrews 10:5-7." *TJ* 13 (1992): 181-91.

———. "Rhetorical Achievement in the Hebrews 10 'Misquote' of Psalm 40." *Bib* 72 (1991): 387-96.

Johnson, Luke Timothy. "The Scriptural World of Hebrews." *Int* 57 (2003): 237-50.

Johnson, R. W. *Going outside the Camp: The Sociological Function of the Levitical Critique in the Epistle to the Hebrews.* JSNTSup 209. Sheffield: Sheffield Academic, 2001.

Johnsson, William G. "Defilement and Purgation in the Book of Hebrews." Ph.D. diss., Vanderbilt University, 1973.

———. "Defilement/Purification and Hebrews 9:23." Pages 79-103 in *Issues in the Book of Hebrews.* Edited by Frank B. Holbrook. Silver Spring, MD: Biblical Research Institute, 1989.

———. "The Pilgrimage Motif in the Book of Hebrews." *JBL* 97 (1978): 239-51.

Jones, E. D. "The Authorship of Hebrews XIII." *ExpTim* 46 (1934-35): 562-67.

Joslin, Barry C. "Can Hebrews Be Structured? An Assessment of Eight Approaches." *CurBS* 6 (2007): 99-129.

———. *Hebrews, Christ, and the Law: The Theology of the Mosaic Law in Hebrews 7:1–10:18.* Milton Keynes: Paternoster, 2008.

Kaiser, Walter C. "The Promise Theme and the Theology of Rest." *BSac* 130 (1973): 135-50.

Käsemann, E. *The Wandering People of God: An Investigation of the Letter to the Hebrews.* Translated by R. A. Harrisville and I. L. Sundberg. Minneapolis: Augsburg, 1984.

Kilpatrick, G. D. "Διαθήκη in Hebrews." *ZNW* 68 (1977): 263-65.

Kistemaker, S. J. "The Authorship of Hebrews." *Faith & Mission* 18 (2001): 57-69.

Kittel, G., and G. Friedrich, eds. *Theological Dictionary of the New Testament.* 10 vols. Translated by G. W. Bromiley. Grand Rapids: Eerdmans, 1964-76.

Kobelski, Paul J. *Melchizedek and Melchiresha': The Heavenly Prince of Light and the Prince of Darkness in Qumran Literature.* CBQMS 10. Washington, DC: The Catholic Biblical Association of America, 1981.

Koch, D. A. "Der Text von Heb. 2.4b in der Septuaginta und im Neuen Testament." *ZNW* 76 (1985): 68-85.

Koester, Craig R. "Conversion, Persecution, and Malaise: Life in the Community for Which Hebrews Was Written." *Hervormde Teologiese Studies* 61 (2005): 231-51.

———. *The Dwelling of God: The Tabernacle in the Old Testament, Intertestamental Jewish Literature, and the New Testament.* CBQMS 22. Washington, DC: The Catholic Biblical Association of America, 1989.

Kooij, Arie van der. "The Ending of the Song of Moses: On the Pre-Masoretic

Version of Deut 32:43." Pages 93-100 in *Studies in Deuteronomy: In Honour of C. J. Labuschagne on the Occasion of His 65th Birthday*. Edited by F. García Martínez. Supplements to *Vetus Testamentum* 53. Leiden and New York: Brill, 1994.

Kögel, J. *Der Sohn und die Söhne: Eine Exegetische Studie zu Hebr 2:5-18*. Gütersloh: Bertelsmann, 1904.

Kurianal, James. *Jesus Our High Priest: Ps 110,4 as the Substructure of Heb 5,1– 7,28*. European University Studies. Frankfurt am Main: Peter Lang, 2000.

Laansma, Jon. "The Cosmology of Hebrews." Pages 125-43 in *Cosmology and New Testament Theology*. Edited by Jonathan T. Pennington and S. M. McDonough. London: T&T Clark, 2008.

———. *"I Will Give You Rest": The Rest Motif in the New Testament with Special Reference to Mt 11 and Heb 3–4*. WUNT 98. Tübingen: Siebeck, 1997.

Laub, R. *Bekenntnis und Auslegung: Die paränetische Funktion der Christologie im Hebräerbrief*. BU 15. Regensburg: Pustet, 1980.

Layton, S. C. "Christ over His House (Hebrews 3:6) and Hebrew אשׁר על־הבית." *NTS* 37 (1991): 473-77.

Lee, John A. L. "Hebrews 5:14 and ἕξις: A History of Misunderstanding." *NovT* 39 (1997): 151-76.

Legg, John D. "Our Brother Timothy: A Suggested Solution to the Problem of the Authorship of the Epistle to the Hebrews." *EvQ* 40 (1968): 220-23.

Lehne, Susanne. *The New Covenant in Hebrews*. Edited by David Hill and David E. Orton. JSNTSup 44. Sheffield: JSOT Press, 1990.

Leithart, P. J. "Womb of the World: Baptism and the Priesthood of the New Covenant in Hebrews 10.19-22." *JSNT* 78 (2000): 49-65.

Leschert, Dale F. *Hermeneutical Foundations of Hebrews: A Study in the Validity of the Epistle's Interpretation of Some Core Citations from the Psalms*. National Association of Baptist Professors of Religion Dissertation 10. Lewiston, NY: Mellen, 1994.

Lescow, Theodor. "Jesus in Gethsemane bei Lukas und im Hebräerbrief." *ZNW* 58 (1967): 215-39.

Lewis, T. W. "'And If He Shrinks Back . . .' (Heb. 10:38b)." *NTS* 22 (1975-76): 88-94.

Lincoln, Andrew T. *Hebrews: A Guide*. London and New York: T&T Clark, 2006.

———. "Hebrews and Biblical Theology." Pages 313-38 in *Out of Egypt: Biblical Theology and Biblical Interpretation*. Edited by Craig Bartholomew, Mary Healy, Karl Möller, and Robin Parry. Scripture and Hermeneutics Series 5. Grand Rapids: Zondervan, 2004.

———. "Sabbath, Rest, and Eschatology in the New Testament." Pages 197-220 in *From Sabbath to Lord's Day: A Biblical, Historical and Theological Investigation*. Edited by Donald A. Carson. Grand Rapids: Zondervan, 1982.

Lincoln, L. "Translating Hebrews 9:15-22 in Its Hebraic Context." *Journal of Translation and Textlinguistics* 12 (1999): 1-29.

Lindars, Barnabas. *New Testament Apologetic: The Doctrinal Significance of the Old Testament Quotations.* London: SCM, 1961.

———. "The Rhetorical Structure of Hebrews." *NTS* 35 (1989): 382-406.

———. *The Theology of the Letter to the Hebrews.* Edited by J. D. G. Dunn. New Testament Theology. Cambridge: Cambridge University Press, 1991.

Linnemann, E. "A Call for a Retrial in the Case of the Epistle to the Hebrews." *Faith & Mission* 19 (2002): 19-59.

Lo Bue, Francesco. "The Historical Background of the Epistle to the Hebrews." *JBL* 75 (1956): 52-57.

Loader, W. R. G. *Sohn und Hoherpriester: Eine Traditionsgeschichtliche Untersuchung zur Christologie des Hebräerbriefes.* Wissenschaftliche Monographien zum Alten und Neuen Testament 53. Neukirchen-Vluyn: Neukirchener, 1981.

Löhr, Hermut. "Anthropologie und Eschatologie im Hebräerbrief: Bemerkungen zum theologischen Interesse einer frühchristlichen Schrift." Pages 169-99 in *Eschatologie und Schöpfung: Festschrift für Erich Grässer zum siebzigsten Geburtstag,* vol. 89. Edited by M. Evang, H. Merklein, and M. Wolter. BZNW 89. Berlin and New York: de Gruyter, 1997.

———. "Reflections of Rhetorical Terminology in Hebrews." Pages 199-210 in *Hebrews: Contemporary Methods — New Insights.* Edited by Gabriella Gelardini. Biblical Interpretation Series 75. Atlanta: Society of Biblical Literature, 2005.

———. "Thronversammlung und preisender Tempel: Beobachtungen am himmlischen Heiligtum im Hebräerbrief und in den Sabbatopherliedern aus Qumran." Pages 185-205 in *Königsherrschaft Gottes und himmlischer Kult im Judentum, Urchristentum und in der hellenistischen Welt.* Edited by M. Hengel and A. M. Schwemer. WUNT 55. Tübingen: Siebeck, 1991.

Longenecker, Richard N. *Biblical Exegesis in the Apostolic Period.* Grand Rapids: Eerdmans, 1975.

———. "The Melchizedek Argument of Hebrews: A Study in the Development and Circumstantial Expression of New Testament Thought." Pages 161-85 in *Unity and Diversity in New Testament Theology.* Edited by R. A. Guelich. Grand Rapids: Eerdmans, 1978.

Luck, Ulrich. "Himmlisches und irdisches Geschehen im Hebräerbrief: Ein Beitrag zum Problem des 'historischen Jesus' im Urchristentum." *NovT* 6 (July 1963): 192-215.

Lührmann, D. "Der Hohepriester ausserhalb des Lagers (Heb 13,12)." *ZNW* 69 (1978): 178-86.

Lust, Johan, Erik Eynikel, and Katrin Hauspie, comps. *Greek-English Lexicon of the Septuagint.* Stuttgart: Deutsche Bibelgesellschaft, 2003.

McCormack, Bruce L. "'With Loud Cries and Tears': The Humanity of the Son in the Epistle to the Hebrews.'" Pages 37-68 in *The Epistle to the Hebrews and Christian Theology*. Edited by Richard Bauckham, Daniel R. Driver, Trevor A. Hart, and Nathan MacDonald. Grand Rapids: Eerdmans, 2009.

McCown, Wayne Gordon. "Ο ΛΟΓΟΣ ΤΗΣ ΠΑΡΑΚΛΗΣΕΩΣ: The Nature and Function of the Hortatory Sections in the Epistle to the Hebrews." Th.D. diss., Union Theological Seminary in Virginia, 1970.

McCullough, J. C. "The Old Testament Quotations in Hebrews." *NTS* 26 (1979-80): 363-79.

Mackie, Scott D. "Confession of the Son of God in Hebrews." *NTS* 53 (2007): 114-29.

―――. *Eschatology and Exhortation in the Epistle to the Hebrews*. WUNT 223. Tübingen: Mohr Siebeck, 2007.

McKnight, S. "The Warning Passages of Hebrews: A Formal Analysis and Theological Conclusions." *TJ* 13 (1992): 21-59.

MacLeod, David J. "The Cleansing of the True Tabernacle." *BSac* 152 (1995): 60-71.

McNair, Bruce G. "Luther, Calvin and the Exegetical Tradition of Melchizedek." *RevExp* 101 (2004): 747-61.

McNamara, Martin. "Melchizedek: Gen 14,17-20 in the Targums, in Rabbinic and Early Christian Literature." *Bib* 81 (2000): 1-31.

MacRae, George W. "'A Kingdom That Cannot Be Shaken': The Heavenly Jerusalem in the Letter to the Hebrews." *Tantur Yearbook* (1979-80): 27-40.

―――. "Heavenly Temple and Eschatology in the Letter to the Hebrews." *Semeia* 12 (1978): 179-99.

Malone, Fred A. "A Critical Evaluation of the Use of Jeremiah 31:31-34 in the Letter to the Hebrews." Ph.D. diss., Southwestern Baptist Theological Seminary, 1989.

Manson, T. W. "The Argument from Prophecy." *JTS* 46 (1945): 129-36.

―――. "The Problem of the Epistle to the Hebrews." *Bulletin of the John Rylands University Library of Manchester* 32 (1949-50): 1-17.

Manson, William. *The Epistle to the Hebrews: An Historical and Theological Reconsideration*. London: Hodder & Stoughton, 1951.

Manzi, Franco. *Melchisedek e l'angelologia nell'Epistola agli Ebrei e a Qumran*. AnBib 136. Rome: Pontifico Istituto Biblico, 1997.

Marrow, S. B. "*Parrhēsia* and the New Testament." *CBQ* 44 (1982): 431-46.

Martin, R. P., and P. H. Davids, eds. *Dictionary of the Later New Testament and Its Development*. Downers Grove: InterVarsity Press, 1997.

Mathewson, D. "Reading Heb 6:4-6 in Light of the Old Testament." *WTJ* 61 (1999): 209-25.

Maurer, Christian. "'Erhört Wegen der Gottesfurcht,' Hebr 5,7." Pages 275-84 in *Neues Testament und Geschichte: Historisches Geschehen und Deutung im*

Neuen Testament, Oscar Cullmann zum 70. Geburtstag. Edited by Heinrich Baltensweiler and Bo Reicke. Zürich: Theologischer Verlag, 1972.

Meier, John P. "Structure and Theology in Heb 1,1-14." *Bib* 66 (1985): 168-89.

———. "Symmetry and Theology in the Old Testament Citations of Heb 1,5-14." *Bib* 66 (1985): 504-33.

Ménégoz, E. *Le théologie de l'épître aux Hébreux.* Paris, 1894.

Metzger, Bruce M. *A Textual Commentary on the Greek New Testament.* Stuttgart: Deutsche Bibelgesellschaft/United Bible Society, 1994.

Miller, James C. "Paul and Hebrews: A Comparison of Narrative Worlds." Pages 245-64 in *Hebrews: Contemporary Methods — New Insights.* Edited by Gabriella Gelardini. Biblical Interpretation Series 75. Atlanta: Society of Biblical Literature, 2005.

Mitchell, Alan C. "The Use of πρέπειν and Rhetorical Propriety in Hebrews 2:10." *CBQ* 54 (1992): 681-701.

Moe, Olaf. "Der Gedanke des allgemeinen Priestertums im Hebräerbrief." *TZ* 5 (1949): 161-69.

Moo, Douglas. Review of *Hebrews as Pseudepigraphon: The History and Significance of the Pauline Attribution of Hebrews. BBR* 20 (2010): 295-96.

Morris, Leon. "The Biblical Use of the Term 'Blood.'" *JTS* 3 (1952): 216-27.

Mosser, Carl. "Rahab outside the Camp." Pages 383-404 in *The Epistle to the Hebrews and Christian Theology.* Edited by Richard Bauckham, Daniel R. Driver, Trevor A. Hart, and Nathan MacDonald. Grand Rapids: Eerdmans, 2009.

Motyer, Stephen. "The Psalm Quotations of Hebrews 1: A Hermeneutic-Free Zone?" *TynBul* 50 (1999): 3-22.

———. "The Temple in Hebrews: Is It There?" Pages 177-89 in *Heaven on Earth.* Edited by T. Desmond Alexander and Simon Gathercole. Carlisle, Cumbria, UK; Waynesboro, GA: Paternoster, 2004.

Nairne, Alexander. *The Epistle of Priesthood: Studies in the Epistle to the Hebrews.* 2nd ed. Edinburgh: T&T Clark, 1913.

Nanos, Mark D. "*New* or *Re*newed Covenantalism? A Response to Richard Hays." Pages 183-88 in *The Epistle to the Hebrews and Christian Theology.* Edited by Richard Bauckham, Daniel R. Driver, Trevor A. Hart, and Nathan MacDonald. Grand Rapids: Eerdmans, 2009.

Nardoni, E. "Partakers in Christ (Hebrews 3.14)." *NTS* 37 (1991): 456-72.

Nauck, Wolfgang. "Zum Aufbau des Hebräerbriefes." Pages 199-206 in *Judentum–Urchristentum–Kirche: Festschrift für J. Jeremias.* Edited by Walther Eltester. Berlin: Alfred Töpelmann, 1960.

———. "Freude im Leiden: Zum Problem einer urchristlichen Verfolgungstradition." *ZNW* 46 (1955): 68-80.

Nel, P. J. "Psalm 110 and the Melchizedek Tradition." *Journal of Northwest Semitic Languages* 22 (1996): 1-14.

Newsom, Carol. *Songs of the Sabbath Sacrifice: A Critical Edition*. Harvard Semitic Studies. Atlanta: Scholars Press, 1985.

Neyrey, J. H. "'Without Beginning of Days or End of Life' (Hebrews 7:3): Topos for a True Deity." *CBQ* 53 (1991): 439-55.

Nicole, R. "Some Comments on Hebrews 6:4-6 and the Doctrine of the Perseverance of God with the Saints." Pages 355-64 in *Current Issues in Biblical and Patristic Interpretation*. Edited by G. Hawthorne. Grand Rapids: Eerdmans, 1975.

Nissilä, K. *Das Hohepriestermotiv im Hebräerbrief: Eine exegetische Untersuchung*. Schriften der Finnischen exegetischen Gesellschaft 33. Helsinki: Oy Liiton Kirjapaino, 1979.

O'Neill, J. C. "'Who Is Comparable to Me in My Glory?' 4Q491 Fragment 11 (4Q491C) and the New Testament." *NovT* 42 (2000): 24-38.

Oberholtzer, T. K. "The Warning Passages in Hebrews, Part 2 (of 5 Parts): The Kingdom of Rest in Hebrews 3:1–4:13." *BSac* 145 (1988): 185-96.

Osborne, Grant R. "A Classical Arminian View." Pages 86-128 in *Four Views on the Warning Passages in Hebrews*. Edited by Herbert W. Batemann IV. Grand Rapids: Kregel, 2007.

Owen, H. P. "The 'Stages of Ascent' in Hebrews V.11–VI.3." *NTS* 3 (1957): 243-53.

Partin, H. B. "The Muslim Pilgrimage: Journey to the Center." Ph.D. diss., University of Chicago, 1969.

Peterson, David G. *Hebrews and Perfection: An Examination of the Concept of Perfection in the Epistle to the Hebrews*. SNTSMS 47. Cambridge: Cambridge University Press, 1982.

———. *Possessed by God: A New Testament Theology of Sanctification and Holiness*. Grand Rapids: Eerdmans, 1995.

———. "The Situation of the 'Hebrews' (5:11–6:12)." *Reformed Theological Review* 35 (1976): 14-21.

Pietersma, Albert, and Benjamin G. Wright, eds. *A New English Translation of the Septuagint, and the Other Greek Translations Traditionally Included under That Title*. New York and Oxford: Oxford University Press, 2007.

Pilhofer, P. "KREITTONOS DIATHEKES EGGYOS. Die Bedeutung der Präexistenzchristologie für die Theologie des Hebräerbriefs." *Theologische Literaturzeitung* 121 (1996): 319-28.

Polen, Nehemia. "Leviticus and Hebrews . . . and Leviticus." Pages 213-25 in *The Epistle to the Hebrews and Christian Theology*. Edited by Richard Bauckham, Daniel R. Driver, Trevor A. Hart, and Nathan MacDonald. Grand Rapids: Eerdmans, 2009.

Preisendanz, Karl, ed. and trans. *Papyri graecae magicae: Die griechischen Zauberpapyri*. 2nd ed., 2 vols. Stuttgart: B. G. Teubner, 1973-74.

Proctor, J. "Judgement or Vindication? Deuteronomy 32 in Hebrews 10:30." *TynBul* 55 (2004): 65-80.

Rahlfs, Alfred, ed. *Psalmi cum Odis*. Vol. 10 of *Septuaginta Vetus Testamentum Graecum Auctoritate Academiae Scientiarum Gottingensis editum*. Göttingen: Vandenhoeck & Ruprecht, 1979.

Rainbow, Paul A. "Melchizedek as a Messiah at Qumran." *BBR* 7 (1997): 179-94.

Rapske, B. *The Book of Acts and Paul in Roman Custody*. Grand Rapids: Eerdmans, 1994.

Rhee, Victor. "Chiasm and the Concept of Faith in Hebrews 11." *BSac* 155 (July-September 1998): 327-45.

————. *Faith in Hebrews: Analysis within the Context of Christology, Eschatology and Ethics*. New York: Peter Lang, 2001.

Rissi, Mathias. "Die Menschlichkeit Jesu nach Hebr. 5.7 und 8." *TZ* 11 (1955): 28-45.

————. *Die Theologie des Hebräerbriefes*. WUNT 41. Tübingen: Mohr/Siebeck, 1987.

Robertson, A. T. *A Grammar of the Greek New Testament in the Light of Historical Research*. 3rd ed. New York: Hodder & Stoughton, 1919.

Robertson, O. Palmer. *The Books of Nahum, Habakkuk, and Zephaniah*. New International Commentary on the Old Testament. Grand Rapids: Eerdmans, 1990.

Roloff, Jürgen. "Der mitleidende Hohepriester: Zur Frage nach der Bedeutung des irdischen Jesus für die Christologie des Hebräerbriefes." Pages 143-66 in *Jesus Christus in Historie und Theologie: Neutestamentliche Festschrift für Hans Conzelmann zum 60. Geburtstag*. Edited by Georg Stecker. Tübingen: Mohr, 1975.

Rooke, D. W. "Jesus as Royal Priest: Reflections on the Interpretation of the Melchizedek Tradition in Heb 7." *Bib* 81 (2000): 81-94.

Rose, C. *Die Wolke der Zeugen: Eine exegetisch-traditionsgeschichtliche Untersuchung zu Hebräer 10,32–12,3*. WUNT 60. Tübingen: Siebeck, 1994.

Rothschild, Clare K. *Hebrews as Pseudepigraphon: The History and Significance of the Pauline Attribution of Hebrews*. WUNT 12/235. Tübingen: Mohr Siebeck, 2009.

Sabourin, Leopold. *Priesthood: A Comparative Study*. Studies in the History of Religion (Supplement to *Numen*) 25. Leiden: E. J. Brill, 1973.

Salevao, Iutisone. *Legitimation in the Letter to the Hebrews: The Construction and Maintenance of a Symbolic Universe*. JSNTSup 219. New York and London: Sheffield Academic Press, 2002.

Salom, A. P. "*Ta Hagia* in the Epistle to the Hebrews." *AUSS* 5 (1967): 59-70.

Sarna, N. M. *Genesis*. Jewish Publication Society Torah Commentary. Philadelphia: Jewish Publication Society, 1989.

Schenck, Kenneth L. "Keeping His Appointment: Creation and Enthronement in Hebrews." *JSNT* 66 (1997): 91-117.

———. "Philo and the Epistle to the Hebrews: Ronald Williamson's Study after Thirty Years." *SPhilo* 14 (2002): 112-35.

———. *Understanding the Book of Hebrews: The Story behind the Sermon.* Louisville and London: Westminster John Knox, 2003.

Schenk, W. "Hebräerbrief 4,14-16: Textlinguistik als Kommentierungsprinzip." *NTS* 26 (1979-80): 242-52.

Schierse, Franz Joseph. *Verheissung und Heilsvollendung: Zur theologischen Grundfrage des Hebräerbriefes.* München: Zink, 1955.

Schille, Gottfried. "Erwägungen zur Hohepriesterlehre des Hebräerbriefes." *ZNW* 46 (1955): 81-109.

———. "Katechese und Taufliturgie: Erwägungen zu Hbr 11." *ZNW* 51 (1960): 112-31.

Schmidt, T. E. "Moral Lethargy and the Epistle to the Hebrews." *WTJ* 54 (1992): 167-73.

Scholer, John M. *Proleptic Priests: Priesthood in the Epistle to the Hebrews.* JSNTSup 49. Sheffield: Sheffield Academic Press, 1991.

Schröger, F. *Der Verfasser des Hebräerbriefes als Schriftausleger.* BU 4. Regensburg: Pustet, 1968.

Silva, Moises. "Perfection and Eschatology in Hebrews." *WTJ* 39 (1976): 60-71.

Simcox, G. A. "Heb. XIII; 2 Tim IV." *ExpTim* 10 (1898-99): 430-32.

Simpson, E. K. "The Vocabulary of the Epistle to the Hebrews, II." *EvQ* 18 (1946): 187-90.

Skarsaune, Oskar. "Does the Letter to the Hebrews Articulate a Supersessionist Theology? A Response to Richard Hays." Pages 174-82 in *The Epistle to the Hebrews and Christian Theology.* Edited by Richard Bauckham, Daniel R. Driver, Trevor A. Hart, and Nathan MacDonald. Grand Rapids: Eerdmans, 2009.

Smillie, G. R. "Contrast or Continuity in Hebrews 1.1-2?" *NTS* 51 (2005): 543-60.

———. "'ho logos tou theou' in Hebrews 4:12-13." *NovT* 46 (2004): 338-59.

———. "'The One Who Is Speaking' in Hebrews 12:25." *TynBul* 55 (2004): 275-94.

———. "'The Other Logos' at the End of Heb. 4:13." *NovT* 47 (2005): 19-25.

Son, Kiwoong. *Zion Symbolism in Hebrews: Hebrews 12:18-24 as a Hermeneutical Key to the Epistle.* Paternoster Biblical Monographs. Waynesboro, GA: Paternoster, 2005.

Songer, Harold S. "A Superior Priesthood: Hebrews 4:14–7:27." *RevExp* 82 (1985): 345-59.

Sowers, G. *The Hermeneutics of Philo and Hebrews: A Comparison of Interpretation.* Richmond: John Knox, 1965.

Spicq, Ceslas. "L'Épître aux Hébreux: Apollos, Jean-Baptiste, les Hellénistes et Qumran." *RevQ* 1 (1958-59): 365-90.

Sproule, John A. "Παραπεσόντας in Hebrews 6:6." *GTJ* 2 (1981): 327-32.

Stanley, Steve. "Hebrews 9:6-10: The 'Parable' of the Tabernacle." *NovT* 37 (1995): 385-99.

———. "A New Covenant Hermeneutic: The Use of Scripture in Hebrews 8–10." Ph.D. diss., University of Sheffield, 1994.

———. "The Structure of Hebrews from Three Perspectives." *TynBul* 45 (1994): 245-71.

Stegemann, Ekkehard W., and Wolfgang Stegemann. "Does the Cultic Language in Hebrews Represent Sacrificial Metaphors? Reflections on Some Basic Problems." Pages 13-23 in *Hebrews: Contemporary Methods — New Insights.* Edited by Gabriella Gelardini. Biblical Interpretation Series 75. Atlanta: Society of Biblical Literature, 2005.

Sterling, G. E. "Ontology versus Eschatology: Tensions between Author and Community in Hebrews." *SPhilo* 13 (2001): 190-211.

Stott, Wilfrid. "The Conception of 'Offering' in the Epistle to the Hebrews." *NTS* 9 (1962): 62-67.

Stökel Ben Ezra, Daniel. *The Impact of Yom Kippur on Early Christianity: The Day of Atonement from Second Temple Judaism to the Fifth Century.* WUNT 163. Tübingen: Mohr Siebeck, 2003.

Strobel, August. "Die Psalmengrundlage der Gethsemane-Parallele Hebr. 5, 7ff." *ZNW* 45 (1954): 252-66.

Swetnam, James. "Christology and the Eucharist in the Epistle to the Hebrews." *Bib* 70 (1989): 74-94.

———. "The Context of the Crux at Hebrews 5,7-8." *Filología Neotestamentaria* 14 (2001): 101-20.

———. "The Crux at Hebrews 5,7-8." *Bib* 81 (2000): 347-61.

———. "Form and Content in Hebrews 1–6." *Bib* 53 (1972): 368-85.

———. "Form and Content in Hebrews 7–13." *Bib* 55 (1974): 333-48.

———. " 'The Greater and More Perfect Tent': A Contribution to the Discussion of Heb. 9:11." *Bib* 47 (1966): 91-106.

———. "Hebrews 10,30-31: A Suggestion." *Bib* 75 (1994): 388-94.

———. *Jesus and Isaac: A Study of the Epistle to the Hebrews in the Light of the Aqedah.* AnBib 94. Rome: Pontifical Biblical Institute, 1981.

———. "Jesus as Λόγος in Hebrews 4,12-13." *Bib* 62 (1981): 214-24.

———. "On the Literary Genre of the 'Epistle' to the Hebrews." *NovT* 11 (1969): 261-69.

———. "Τῶν λαληθησομένων in Hebrews 3,5." *Bib* 90 (2009): 93-100.

Synge, F. *Hebrews and the Scriptures.* London: SPCK, 1959.

Tasker, R. V. G. "The Integrity of the Epistle to the Hebrews." *ExpTim* 47 (1935-36): 136-38.

Theissen, Gerd. *Untersuchungen zum Hebräerbrief.* Studien zum Neuen Testament 2. Gütersloh: Gerd Mohn, 1969.

Thiessen, M. "Hebrews and the End of the Exodus." *NovT* 49 (2007): 353-69.

Thomas, Kenneth J. "The Old Testament Citations in the Epistle to the Hebrews." *NTS* 11 (1965): 303-25.

Thompson, James W. *The Beginnings of Christian Philosophy.* CBQMS 13. Washington, DC: The Catholic Biblical Association of America, 1982.

Thornton, T. C. G. "The Meaning of αἱματεχυσία in Heb. IX.22." *JTS* 15 (1964): 63-65.

Thurén, Jukka. "Gebet und Gehorsam des Erniedrigten (Hebr. V, 7-10 noch einmal)." *NovT* 13 (April 1971): 136-46.

———. *Das Lobopfer der Hebräer: Studien zum Aufbau und Anliegen vom Hebräerbrief 13.* Åbo: Akademi, 1973.

Thyen, Hartwig. *Der Stil der Jüdisch-Hellenistischen Homilie.* Forschungen zur Religion und Literatur des Alten und Neuen Testaments, n.s. 47. Göttingen: Vandenhoeck & Ruprecht, 1955.

Torrey, C. C. "The Authorship and Character of the So-Called 'Epistle to the Hebrews.'" *JBL* 30 (1911): 137-56.

Toussaint, S. D. "The Eschatology of the Warning Passages in the Book of Hebrews." *GTJ* 3 (1982): 67-80.

Trudinger, L. Paul. "The Gospel Meaning of the Secular: Reflections on Hebrews 13:10-13." *EvQ* 54 (1982): 235-37.

Übelacker, Walter G. *Der Hebräerbrief als Appell: Untersuchungen zu Exordium, Narratio und Postscriptum (Hebr 1–2 und 13,22-25).* Coniectanea Neotestamentica or Coniectanea Biblica: New Testament Series 21. Stockholm: Almqvist & Wiksell International, 1989.

van der Horst, P. W. "Sarah's Seminal Emission: Hebrews 11:11 in Light of Ancient Embryology." Pages 287-302 in *Greeks, Romans, and Christians: Essays in Honor of Abraham J. Malherbe.* Edited by D. L. Balch, E. Ferguson, and W. A. Meeks. Minneapolis: Fortress, 1990.

Vanhoye, Albert. "Le Dieu de la nouvelle alliance dans l'Épître aux Hébreux." Pages 315-30 in *Le notion biblique de Dieu,* vol. 41. Edited by J. Coppens. Bibliotheca ephemeridum theologicarum lovaniensium 41. Gembloux: Duculot, 1976.

———. "Discussions sur la structure de l'Épître aux Hébreux." *Bib* 55 (1974): 349-80.

———. "Esprit éternel et feu du sacrifice en He 9,14." *Bib* 64 (1983): 263-74.

———. "L'οἰκουμένη dans l'Épître aux Hébreux." *Bib* 45 (1964): 248-53.

———. "Longue marche ou accìs tout proche? Le context biblique de Hébreux 3,7–4,11." *Bib* 49 (1968): 9-26.

———. *Old Testament Priests and the New Priest according to the New Testament.* Petersham, MA: St. Bede's Publications, 1986.

———. "'Par la tente plus grande et plus parfaite (He 9:11).'" *Bib* 46 (1965): 1-28.

———. "La question littéraire de Hébreux XIII.1-6." *NTS* 23 (1977): 121-39.

———. *Situation du Christ: Épître aux Hébreux 1–2.* Paris: Cerf, 1969.

―――. *Structure and Message of the Epistle to the Hebrews.* Subsidia Biblica 12. Rome: Editrice Pontifico Instituto Biblico, 1989.

―――. *La structure littéraire de l'épître aux Hébreux.* 2nd ed. Paris: Desclée de Brouwer, 1976.

―――. "La 'teleiôsis' du Christ: Point capital de la christologie sacerdotale d'Hébreux." *NTS* 42 (1996): 321-38.

Verbrugge, V. D. "Towards a New Interpretation of Hebrews 6:4-6." *CTJ* 15 (1980): 61-73.

Vögtle, A. "Das Neue Testament und die Zukunft des Kosmos. Hebr. 12:26f. und das Endschicksal des Kosmos." *Bibel und Leben* 10 (1969): 239-54.

Walker, Peter. "Jerusalem in Hebrews 13:9-14 and the Dating of the Epistle." *TynBul* 45 (1994): 39-71.

Wallace, Daniel B. *Greek Grammar beyond the Basics: An Exegetical Syntax of the New Testament.* Grand Rapids: Zondervan, 1996.

Wallis, I. G. *The Faith of Jesus Christ in Early Christian Traditions.* SNTSMS 84. Cambridge: Cambridge University Press, 1995.

Walters, J. R. "The Rhetorical Arrangement of Hebrews." *Asbury Theological Journal* 51 (1996): 59-70.

Wansink, C. S. *Chained in Christ: The Experience and Rhetoric of Paul's Imprisonments.* JSNTSup 130. Sheffield: Sheffield Academic, 1996.

Webster, John. "One Who Is Son: Theological Reflections on the Exordium to the Epistle to the Hebrews." Pages 69-94 in *The Epistle to the Hebrews and Christian Theology.* Edited by Richard Bauckham, Daniel R. Driver, Trevor A. Hart, and Nathan MacDonald. Grand Rapids: Eerdmans, 2009.

Wedderburn, A. J. M. "The 'Letter' to the Hebrews and Its Thirteenth Chapter." *NTS* 50 (2004): 390-405.

―――. "Sawing Off the Branches: Theologizing Dangerously *ad Hebraeos.*" *JTS* 56 (2005): 393-414.

Weeks, Noel. "Admonition and Error in Hebrews." *WTJ* 39 (1976): 72-80.

Welborn, L. L. "On the Date of First Clement." *BR* 29 (1984): 35-54.

―――. "On the Date of First Clement." Pages 197-216 in *Encounters with Hellenism: Studies in the First Letter of Clement.* Edited by C. Breytenbach and L. L. Welborn. Arbeiten zur Geschichte des antiken Judentums und des Urchristentums. Leiden: Brill, 2004.

Wenham, Gordon J. *Genesis 1–15.* WBC 1. Dallas: Word Books, 1991.

Westfall, Cynthia Long. *A Discourse Analysis of the Letter to the Hebrews: The Relationship between Form and Meaning.* LNTS 297. London: T&T Clark, 2005.

Wider, David. *Theozentrik und Bekenntnis: Untersuchungen zur Theologie des Redens Gottes im Hebräerbrief.* Edited by Erich Grässer. BZNW 87. Berlin and New York: Walter de Gruyter, 1997.

Wiid, J. S. "The Testamental Significance of διαθήκη in Hebrews 9:15-22." *Neotestamentica* 26 (1992): 149-56.

Wilcox, Max. "The Bones of Joseph: Hebrews 11:22." Pages 114-30 in *Scripture: Meaning and Method*. Edited by Barry P. Thompson. Hull: Hull University Press, 1987.

Williamson, Clark M. "Anti-Judaism in Hebrews?" *Int* 57 (2003): 266-79.

Williamson, Ronald. "The Eucharist and the Epistle to the Hebrews." *NTS* 21 (1975): 300-312.

———. *Philo and the Epistle to the Hebrews*. Arbeiten zur Literatur und Geschichte des hellenistischen Judentums 4. Leiden: Brill, 1970.

———. "Platonism and Hebrews." *SJT* 16 (1963): 415-24.

———. "Hebrews 4:15 and the Sinlessness of Jesus." *ExpTim* 86 (1974): 4-8.

Wills, Lawrence. "The Form of the Sermon in Hellenistic Judaism and Early Christianity." *HTR* 77 (1984): 277-99.

Wolmarans, Johannes L. P. "The Text and Translation of Hebrews 8:8." *ZNW* 75 (1984): 139-44.

Worley, David A., Jr. "God's Faithfulness to Promise: The Hortatory Use of Commissive Language in Hebrews." Ph.D. diss., Yale University, 1981.

Wray, Judith Hoch. *Rest as a Theological Metaphor in the Epistle to the Hebrews and the Gospel of Truth: Early Christian Homiletics of Rest*. SBLDS 166. Atlanta: Scholars Press, 1998.

Wuttke, Gottfried. *Melchizedek, der Priesterkönig von Salem: Eine Studie zur Geschichte der Exegese*. BZNW 5. Giessen: Alfred Töpelmann, 1927.

Young, Norman H. " 'Bearing His Reproach' (Heb 13:9-14)." *NTS* 48 (2002): 243-61.

———. "The Day of Dedication or the Day of Atonement? The Old Testament Background to Hebrews 6:19-20 Revisited." *AUSS* 40 (2002): 61-68.

———. "The Gospel According to Hebrews 9." *NTS* 27 (1981): 198-210.

———. "Τοῦτ᾽ ἔστιν τῆς σαρκὸς αὐτοῦ (Heb. x.20): Apposition, Dependent or Explicative?' " *NTS* 20 (1973-74): 100-114.

———. " 'Where Jesus Has Gone as a Forerunner on Our Behalf' (Hebrews 6:20)." *AUSS* 39 (2001): 165-73.

———. "Αἱματεκχυσία: A Comment." *ExpTim* 90 (1979): 180.

Zerwick, Max, and Mary Grosvenor. *A Grammatical Analysis of the Greek New Testament*. 4th ed. Rome: Editrice Pontificio Instituto Biblico, 1993.

Zimmermann, Heinrich. *Die Hohepriester-Christologie des Hebräerbriefes*. Paderborn: Ferdinand Schöningh, 1964.

INTRODUCTION

The purpose of this Introduction is to facilitate a deeper and more comprehensive understanding of Hebrews and of the commentary that follows. Part I, entitled "Hebrews in Its Environment," is concerned with the origin of Hebrews and with relevant features of the cultural, linguistic, literary, and religious world in which it was written. Thus this first part begins with a section on the often-asked question concerning the author's identity, entitled "The Pastor Who Wrote Hebrews." Four sections follow: "The Pastor's Sermon," "The Pastor's Congregation," "The Pastor's Worldview," and "When Did the Pastor Write This Sermon?" Part I gives close attention to what Hebrews reveals about the skills, background, values, and goals of its author as well as the situation of its recipients and the nature of the author's concern for them.

The four sections of Part II, "The Message of Hebrews," are particularly crucial because they focus on Hebrews' use of the OT, its rhetorical shape, and its abiding message. First, the section entitled "The Sermon's Use of the Old Testament" argues that the author had a well-thought-out understanding of how Christ fulfilled the OT that continues to be relevant for modern Christians. The next section, entitled "The Sermon's Rhetorically Effective Structure," draws on the flourishing literature concerning Hebrews' structure and relation to ancient rhetoric. It presents a comprehensive analysis of the way in which the author has structured Hebrews in order to inspire his readers/hearers to persevere in faith and obedience through the provision of Christ, their "Great High Priest" (4:14). The reader will receive particular benefit from perusing this section because the following commentary uses this structural analysis to elucidate each passage. The overviews at the beginning of each major section of the commentary are also helpful. Part II concludes with sections entitled "The Sermon's Abiding Message" and "The Sermon's Outline." This final section distills the structural analysis already given into a clear outline that serves as a basis for the commentary that follows and thus as a helpful map for the reader.

1

Use of terms like "pastor" and "sermon" in these titles reflects a certain understanding of Hebrews' nature and purpose. This way of describing Hebrews has also been chosen with the hope that it will make this material more accessible to the modern reader. I owe a deep debt of gratitude to the many great interpreters who have preceded me in this task. I have sought to listen to them with care and have been immeasurably enriched by their insights. My desire is, by God's grace, to pass on to the reader what insight has been given me.

I. HEBREWS IN ITS ENVIRONMENT

A. THE PASTOR WHO WROTE HEBREWS

Although the text of Hebrews does not disclose the name of the author, it does reveal much about his ability, his concerns, and his relationship to those he addresses.[1] He was a master of elegant Greek who understood the principles of rhetoric and oral persuasion as taught in the ancient world. He had a thorough knowledge of the OT and a clear understanding of how it should be interpreted in light of its fulfillment in Christ. He was well acquainted with the past history of the people to whom he was writing (2:3-4; 6:10; 10:32-34; 13:22-25) and was deeply concerned lest they fail to persevere in their devotion to and public confession of Christ (3:1; 4:14; 10:23). Thus he warns them against laxity or carelessness in their adherence to the Son of God (2:1-4; 5:10-14; 6:1-3), against the attractions of the unbelieving world (12:14-17), and especially against yielding to the social pressure of the larger society that did not accept Christ (3:7–4:11; 10:32-39; 12:1-13). Continued inattention to the Son of God coupled with acquiescence before ungodly opposition might lead to apostasy (6:4-8; 10:26-31; 12:14-17). The full sufficiency of the Son of God as the effective High Priest of God's people is the author's antidote against these dangers. Through Christ's definitive removal of sin God's promise of a future eternal "City" is certain and his power for present perseverance is real (4:14-16; 10:19-25). The Son of God thus incarnate as Savior and High Priest is the final revelation of God (1:1-4), who fulfills all

---

1. The masculine pronoun will be used throughout for the author of Hebrews, not merely for convenience but because of the masculine participle διηγούμενον ("tell") with which he describes himself in 11:32. Ruth Hoppin, *Priscilla's Letter: Finding the Author of the Epistle to the Hebrews* (Fort Bragg, CA: Lost Coast Press, 1997), has tried unsuccessfully to revive Harnack's proposal of Priscilla as author (Adolf von Harnack, "Probabilia über die Adresse und den Verfasser des Hebräerbriefes," *ZNW* [1900]: 16-41). See Mitchell, 5.

that the old order anticipated. The author does not claim direct apostolic authority but bases his appeal both on the Gospel as acknowledged by his hearers' own confession of faith and on the authority of the OT Scripture.[2] His deep concern for the spiritual welfare of his hearers, his preoccupation with the OT, and the sermonic shape of his book (see pp. 11-16 below) justify our referring to him as "the pastor."

Although, due to the paucity of evidence, attempts to identify the author of Hebrews with any NT person must be, at best, inconclusive, the discussion of this issue is not without significance.[3] First, during the Patristic period the identity of the author was closely tied to the acceptance of Hebrews into the canon. A look, then, at the Patristic discussion is important in understanding Hebrews' place in the list of approved NT books. Second, the attempt to identify the author underscores the uniqueness of Hebrews among NT writings and thus reminds the modern reader of Hebrews' distinctive contribution to the church's understanding of the gospel.

1. Authorship and Canonicity

Hebrews appears between Romans and 1 Corinthians in $\mathfrak{P}^{46}$, a collection of Pauline epistles dated c. A.D. 200. It already bears the title "To (the) Hebrews" in this manuscript.[4] In Vaticanus, Sinaiticus, and Alexandrinus, the great codices from the fourth and fifth centuries, Hebrews occurs after Paul's letters to churches but before his letters to individual persons.[5] Beginning with the sixth-century Codex Claromontanus, Hebrews assumes the place it has in contemporary English Bibles after the other letters of Paul. In the minds of most contemporary Christians it is canonical but no longer Pauline. It has thus become the first of the "General Epistles" (James; 1 and 2 Peter; 1, 2, and 3 John; Jude). As will become evident below, these changes in location reflect the differences between East and West concerning authorship and canonicity.[6]

---

2. On the "confession" (3:1; 4:14; 10:23) of those receiving Hebrews see Scott D. Mackie, *Eschatology and Exhortation in the Epistle to the Hebrews* (WUNT 223; Tübingen: Mohr Siebeck, 2007), 226-29, and those cited on 227, n. 54; similarly Scott D. Mackie, "Confession of the Son of God in Hebrews," *NTS* 53 (2007): 125-28, esp. 126, n. 44.

3. Ellingworth, 3, lists a total of thirteen proposed authors.

4. This title may have been given to Hebrews by analogy with the titles of the Pauline letters (Bruce, 3). The letter conclusion in Heb 13:22-25 may have suggested association with Paul. Clement of Alexandria also seems to have known Hebrews by this title (Eusebius, *Hist. eccl.* 6.14.3-4).

5. Also in manuscripts C, H, I, K, and P. In some manuscripts Hebrews also occurs between 2 Corinthians and Galatians. See Weiss, 117-18, esp. nn. 13, 14.

6. $\mathfrak{P}^{46}$, Vaticanus, Sinaiticus, and Alexandrinus come from the East; Claromontanus, from the West.

They are also in accord with Hebrews' final acceptance in the list of canonical books, despite doubts about its Pauline authorship.[7]

The earliest known use of Hebrews was in the western Roman Empire, where it was quoted by and echoed in *1 Clement,* written from Rome around the end of the first century.[8] There are echoes of Hebrews in Polycarp (c. A.D. 69-155), and it is quoted by Irenaeus (c. A.D. 180), Tertullian (c. A.D. 155-220), and Gaius of Rome (c. A.D. 200).[9] None of these writers, however, cites Hebrews as canonical or attributes it to Paul. Nor is Hebrews included in the Muratorian Canon (c. A.D. 175?). Although Hippolytus (died c. A.D. 236) quotes Hebrews extensively in his *Commentary on Daniel,* he appears to deny its canonical status by excluding it from the thirteen recognized Pauline epistles.[10] The only suggestion from these sources for the authorship of Hebrews comes from Tertullian, who attributes it to Barnabas.[11] This silence may indicate that the West knew that Hebrews was not Pauline and thus did not consider it apostolic and canonical.[12]

In the East, however, the situation was different. At the end of the second century Pantaenus (c. A.D. 180), the founder of the great catechetical school in Alexandria, Egypt, claimed that Hebrews was both Pauline and canonical. As noted above, this affirmation is supported by the way in which $\mathfrak{P}^{46}$ locates Hebrews between Romans and 1 Corinthians. Pantaenus, however, recognized the lack of a normal Pauline introduction as an impediment in need of explanation: Paul had not affixed his name because he was only the apostle to the Gentiles, while "the Lord" was the "apostle" (cf. Heb 3:1) to the Jews (*Hist. eccl.* 6.14.4).[13] Pantaenus's successor, Clement of Alexandria (c. A.D. 200), continued to affirm the tradition of Pauline authorship and canonical status, though he expanded the explanation against possible objec-

---

7. For a helpful survey of the interpretation of Hebrews up to 1750 see Koester, 19-40.

8. See "When Did the Pastor Write This Sermon?" pp. 34-41 below.

9. In *Phil.* 12:2 Polycarp calls Christ "the eternal high priest" (cf. Heb 6:20; 7:3). For Irenaeus and Gaius of Rome's use of Hebrews see Eusebius, *Hist. eccl.* 5.26.3; 6.20.3. For Tertullian see *Pud.* 20. Cf. S. J. Kistemaker, "The Authorship of Hebrews," *Faith & Mission* 18/2 (2001): 58.

10. Kistemaker, "The Authorship of Hebrews," 58. See Hippolytus, *Haer.* 6.30.9.

11. In *Pud.* 20, Tertullian describes Barnabas as one who "learned his doctrine from apostles and taught with apostles" (Kistemaker, "The Authorship of Hebrews," 59). One does not hear of Barnabas's authorship again until Jerome, *Epist.* 129, *Vir. ill.* 5.59, mentions him as a suggestion made by some. For older commentaries who support Barnabas's authorship see Spicq, 1:199-200, n. 8.

12. David Alan Black, "Who Wrote Hebrews? The Internal and External Evidence Reexamined," *Faith & Mission* 18/2 (2001): 19; Andrew T. Lincoln, *Hebrews: A Guide* (London/New York: T&T Clark, 2006), 3.

13. Kistemaker, "The Authorship of Hebrews," 58.

tions (*Hist. eccl.* 6.14.3). He attributed the omission of Paul's name to Paul's desire not to offend the Jews to whom he had addressed this epistle. Moreover, he said that Paul wrote in Hebrew and that Luke translated Hebrews into Greek. This claim appears to acknowledge not only the absence of a Pauline introduction but the significant difference between the style of Hebrews and that of the Pauline letters.

For several reasons it is worth quoting Origen (c. A.D. 185-254), Clement's successor, as recorded by Eusebius (*Hist. eccl.* 6.25.11-14). First, he names two other persons whom some considered candidates for the authorship of Hebrews — Clement of Rome and Luke. Second, he expresses his own doubt concerning Pauline authorship without denying Hebrews' canonical status:

> If I gave my opinion, I should say that the thoughts are those of the apostle, but the diction and phraseology are those of someone who remembered the apostolic teachings, and wrote . . . down at his leisure what had been said by his teacher. Therefore, if any church holds that this epistle is by Paul, let it be commended for this. . . . But who wrote the epistle, in truth, God knows. The statement of some who have gone before us is that Clement, bishop of the Romans, wrote the epistle, and of others that Luke, the author of the Gospel and the Acts, wrote it.[14]

By the fourth century the West began to join the East in affirming both the Pauline authorship and the canonical authority of Hebrews. Heb 1:3 and 13:8, in particular, were widely used in the Arian controversy to substantiate orthodox Christology.[15] Thus it is no surprise that Athanasius's influential festal letter of A.D. 367 included Hebrews, locating it between 2 Thessalonians and 2 Timothy, in accord with Codices Sinaiticus and Vaticanus. Hilary, Bishop of Poitiers (c. A.D. 315-67), helped to bring the West into line with the East by affirming both the Pauline authorship and the canonicity of Hebrews.[16] Both Augustine (A.D. 354-430) and Jerome (A.D. 342-420) lent their support to this movement.[17] The councils of Hippo (A.D. 393) and Carthage (A.D. 397) included Hebrews, but listed it after the thirteen Pauline epistles as "one to the Hebrews." The fifth Council of Carthage (A.D. 419) in-

---

14. As quoted in D. L. Allen, "The Authorship of Hebrews: The Lukan Proposal," *Faith & Mission* 18/2 (2001): 27.

15. See Athanasius, *Four Discourses against the Arians* 1.4.12; 1.36; 2.48; Gregory of Nazianzus, *Oratio in laudem Basilii* 38.1; Cyril of Jerusalem, *Catechetical Lectures* 12.17; Heen and Krey, 232-34; O'Brien, 3; Johnson, 6.

16. *De Trinitate* 4.11. See Kistemaker, "The Authorship of Hebrews," 58.

17. See Augustine, *Christian Instruction* 2.8.12-13; *Civ.* 10.5; 16.22; Jerome, *Vir. ill.* 5; *Epist.* 53.8; 129.3, 7.

corporated Hebrews within the canon as the fourteenth epistle of Paul without further comment.[18] As noted above, this is the place it occupies in the sixth-century Codex Claromontanus. Hebrews was recognized as apostolic and canonical, though hesitation over its Pauline authorship continued. To the quotation from Origen above one should add the witness of Jerome:

> The Epistle which is inscribed to the Hebrews is received not only by the Churches of the East, but also by all Church writers of the Greek language before our days, as of Paul the apostle, though many think that it is from Barnabas or Clement. And it makes no difference whose it is, since it is from a churchman, and is celebrated in the daily readings of the Churches. (*Epist.* 129)[19]

Although Hebrews is first attested in the West *(1 Clement),* the West appears to have accepted it as Pauline and canonical only in the fourth century under the influence of the East. The significance of the silence of Clement of Rome, Polycarp, Irenaeus, and Hippolytus concerning the authorship of Hebrews remains a mystery. They may have been ignorant of the author's identity, or they may have had a tradition that Hebrews was written by someone other than Paul. It is doubtful, however, if their failure to accept Hebrews as Pauline and canonical can be explained entirely in light of the Montanists, who used it to substantiate the impossibility of restoring those who renounced the faith under persecution. Even Tertullian *(Pud.* 20), who used Hebrews to oppose such restoration, claimed neither Pauline authorship nor canonical status. Thus, both the hesitancy of the West to accept Hebrews and the need felt in the East to posit an intermediate scribe or translator attest the un-Pauline character of this work. It is clear that Pauline authorship was defended in order to sustain Hebrews' canonical status. In the end, however, the greatest biblical scholars of the ancient church (Origen, Jerome) affirmed Hebrews' worth and canonical status despite doubts over Pauline authorship.

2. Candidates for Authorship — A Review

The distinct contribution of Hebrews stands out sharply when compared with the Pauline letters. In contrast to Paul, Hebrews' primary picture of the situation of its readers is as the people of God entering his presence and on pilgrimage to their eternal destiny. Furthermore, Hebrews' exposition of

---

18. Black, "Who Wrote Hebrews?" 19.

19. Kistemaker, "The Authorship of Hebrews," 59. In *Vir. ill.* 5.59, Jerome repeats the suggestion first made by Clement of Alexandria that Paul wrote Hebrews originally in Hebrew (Mitchell, 3). Aquinas also accepted Luke as the translator of an original Pauline Hebrew letter (Allen, "The Authorship of Hebrews," 28).

Christ's high priesthood finds no parallel in Paul. Hebrews differs from Paul in its stress on Christ's work as cleansing/sanctifying the people of God so that they can enter God's presence.[20] Christ's high-priestly ministry provides the pilgrim people of God grace for endurance and assurance of final entrance. Hebrews' universal custom of introducing OT quotations with terms denoting speaking rather than writing creates a sense of the immediacy of God's word absent in Paul. While Paul and Hebrews both refer to the New Covenant (2 Cor 3:4-11; Heb 8:6-13; 10:15-18), Hebrews' comparison of the Old and New is distinct from the Pauline treatment of this subject.

These basic differences in perspective are further supported by differences in style. The pastor, for example, unlike Paul, interweaves exposition and exhortation in order to move the hearers to perseverance through appropriation of what is theirs in Christ.[21] Whereas Paul may occasionally use the less-to-greater argument (Rom 5:12-21) since it was widespread in the contemporary world, this manner of argumentation is fundamental to the way Hebrews relates the Old and New Covenants.[22] These major differences are supported by many differences in imagery (e.g., the ship in 2:1; the anchor in 6:19) and vocabulary (Hebrews uses 169 words that appear nowhere else in the NT).[23] Paul had not received the gospel from any human being (Gal 1:12). Both the author and recipients of Hebrews had received the good news from "those who heard" the Lord (Heb 2:3).[24] These many ways, therefore, in which Hebrews differs from the Pauline letters in style, vocabulary, and content all but rule out Pauline authorship.[25]

Despite the striking differences between Paul and Hebrews, which he acknowledges, David Alan Black has contended for a modified version of Pauline authorship. He would explain these differences by arguing that Paul

20. O'Brien, 6.

21. *Pace* Black, "Who Wrote Hebrews?" 4; Rom 6:12-14 and Gal 4:12-20 afford no real parallel with the way this blending of exposition and exhortation forms the very body of Hebrews.

22. *Pace* Black, "Who Wrote Hebrews?" 4, who cites Rom 5:12-21 as parallel to Hebrews.

23. On the difference between the terminology of Hebrews and Paul see Ellingworth, 7-12; Attridge, 2-3.

24. Clare K. Rothschild, *Hebrews as Pseudepigraphon: The History and Significance of the Pauline Attribution of Hebrews* (WUNT 12/235; Tübingen: Mohr Siebeck, 2009), has claimed, on the basis of the letter ending and other similarities with the Pauline writings, that the late first-century author of Hebrews was presenting himself as Paul. However, the way in which the author refers to himself in 2:1-4 and his failure to claim or even allude to apostolic authority make Rothschild's contention untenable. For further criticism see Douglas Moo, Review of *Hebrews as Pseudepigraphon: The History and Significance of the Pauline Attribution of Hebrews, BBR* 20 (2010): 295-96.

25. Attridge, 2-3; Ellingworth, 7-12.

dictated Hebrews to Luke, who was allowed considerable latitude in recording what Paul said.[26] He argues that the quotation from Origen above supports this theory: "But who wrote *down* the epistle, in truth, God knows."[27] Thus, by "who wrote *down*," Origen is not referring to the author but the penman who took dictation from Paul. It is not likely, however, that Origen was referring to a penman.[28] Origen says that some think Clement or Luke wrote Hebrews at a later time based on what they remembered of Paul's teaching. It will be argued below that the pastor has used the principles of Hellenistic rhetoric with consummate skill to produce a well-crafted homily or sermon. Content and form have been so intimately wed by one brilliant mind that they cannot be separated.[29] Hebrews is not translation Greek. Differences in style, vocabulary, and theology render both direct and indirect Pauline authorship most unlikely.[30]

1 Clement and Hebrews differ so vastly in style and content that one need give no further attention to the suggestion that Hebrews was written by Clement of Rome. A look at the way the two books use the OT and understand the Aaronic priesthood is sufficient to set them apart from one another.[31] However, there have been contemporary advocates for both Luke, suggested by Origen, and Barnabas, suggested by Tertullian and mentioned by Jerome. There is little to commend Barnabas beyond the facts that he was

---

26. In order to mollify the many significant acknowledged differences between Paul and Hebrews, Black attempts to show similarities. Many of these similarities, however, are superficial or very general. There is, for instance, little commonality between "sword" as the word of God in Eph 6:17 and its use in Heb 4:12-13. In the former it is part of the armor that the believer should put on and use. In the latter it refers to God's probing the depths of the human psyche (*pace* Black, "Who Wrote Hebrews?" 7). Nor is there much significance in the fact that both Paul and Hebrews use alpha-privative words and genitive absolutes (*pace* Black, "Who Wrote Hebrews?" 4-16).

27. Black, "Who Wrote Hebrews?" 20, cf. 18, translates the substantive participle ὁ γράψας not as "who wrote" but as "who wrote *down*."

28. *Pace* Black, "Who Wrote Hebrews?" 20, the use of γράφω for Paul's secretary Tertius in Rom 16:22 proves nothing except that this word could be used for a penman as well as for an author. In this regard it has the same range of meaning as the English word "write." It is important also to note that Origen's statement is found in Eusebius, who often prefers a compound form of γράφω when referring to a penman (see Mitchell, 2-4, for examples).

29. As Kistemaker ("The Authorship of Hebrews," 61) has observed, Paul often breaks off in the middle of a sentence or follows a diversion. The pastor, however, has composed Hebrews so that "[e]very sentence . . . is complete and contributes to the flow of his argument."

30. For a different attempt to revive Pauline authorship see E. Linnemann, "A Call for a Retrial in the Case of the Epistle to the Hebrews," *Faith & Mission* 19/2 (2002): 19-59.

31. Clement uses the Aaronic priesthood as a model for a Christian priestly hierarchy (see *1 Clem.* 40:5; cf. Ellingworth, 13).

associated with the Pauline circle, that his name (meaning "son of consolation") echoes the designation of Hebrews as a "word of consolation" (13:22), and that he was a Levite. There are, of course, no genuine writings of Barnabas with which one might compare Hebrews.

David Alan Black's suggestion that Luke took dictation from Paul has been discussed above. David Allen, on the other hand, has vigorously defended direct Lucan authorship. The linguistic evidence he presents, however, is less than impressive. The fact that there are forty-nine words unique to Hebrews and the Lucan writings compared with fifty-six unique to Hebrews and Paul provides no support for Lucan authorship.[32] The linguistic sophistication of both authors adequately accounts for the appearance of 67.6 percent of Hebrews' vocabulary in Luke-Acts. While it is true, for example, that only Acts and Hebrews among NT writings call Jesus "Pioneer" (Acts 3:15; 5:31; Heb 2:10; 12:2),[33] this term occurs in the *sermons* that Luke has recorded and plays no further role in his presentation. Thus, none of Hebrews' theme words are prominent in Luke and Acts. The literary form of Hebrews is a decisive argument against Lucan authorship. Hebrews is a masterful sermon. As noted above, Luke records the sermons of others, yet there is nothing in Luke-Acts to indicate that Luke himself had a significant preaching ministry.[34]

The Church Fathers never identify Apollos as the author of Hebrews. Dissatisfaction with other possibilities, however, led Martin Luther to propose his candidacy.[35] The description of Apollos in Acts 18:24–19:1 is a description of the kind of person who wrote Hebrews. The superior education of the writer of Hebrews is evident from his rhetorical skill. Its writer was steeped in Scripture and a competent expositor of its meaning, just as was Apollos. The book of Hebrews is the work of a powerful preacher with a deep pastoral concern for his hearers. Apollos's skill in demonstrating Christ's messiahship from the OT is in accord with the pastor's Christological exposition. Apollos's ability to confound Jews who did not acknowledge Christ fits well with the apparent Jewish-Christian elements in the recipients' background.[36] Though Apollos was from Alexandria, the home of

---

32. Allen, "The Authorship of Hebrews," 29, says there are fifty-three words uniquely common to Hebrews and Luke. However, this fifty-three contains four proper names, whereas proper names have been excluded from the fifty-six words uniquely common to Hebrews and Paul.

33. In both Acts 5:31 and Heb 2:10 ἀρχηγός ("Pioneer") is also connected with σωτηρία ("salvation").

34. George H. Guthrie, "The Case for Apollos as the Author of Hebrews," *Faith & Mission* 18/2 (2001): 50.

35. Guthrie, "The Case for Apollos as the Author of Hebrews," 43-44.

36. Guthrie, "The Case for Apollos as the Author of Hebrews," 50-52.

Philo, his authorship is not dependent on the supposed neo-Platonic character of Hebrews.[37] The growing recognition of Hebrews' rhetorical sophistication has lent support to the case for Apollos's authorship.[38]

The proposed authorship of Apollos requires a date for Hebrews before the destruction of the Temple in A.D. 70. In the NT Apollos is associated with Ephesus and Corinth. Thus those who assert Apollos's authorship often suggest these cities as either the destination or the place of origin. For example, Apollos wrote Hebrews from Rome after Paul's death to a group of wealthy Jews in the Ephesian church who had become discouraged due to persecution,[39] or Apollos wrote Hebrews from Ephesus to a Jewish faction in the Corinthian church,[40] or Apollos wrote Hebrews from Corinth to the Lycus valley in order to counter the same heresy addressed by Colossians,[41] or Apollos wrote Hebrews to Rome after Paul's death but before the destruction of the Temple. That is why he relayed the greetings of "those from Italy" (13:24).[42] The suggestion that Hebrews counters the heresy of the Lycus valley assumes an unlikely apologetic purpose for the comparison with the angels in 1:4-14. There is no other evidence of a wealthy Jewish minority in the Ephesian church. Hebrews addresses discouraged believers rather than the triumphalistic Corinthians who were fascinated with earthly wisdom and with spiritual gifts.[43] Nor is it likely that Heb 13:19 describes one who refused to go to Corinth (1 Cor 16:12). However, such speculations about destination do not negate the considerable evidence given above for Apollos's authorship. Of course his authorship cannot be confirmed.[44] The mere suggestion, however, that the person described in Acts 18:24–19:1 might have been Hebrews' author directs the reader's attention to the rhetorical skill and pastoral concern that have shaped this book. Thus we turn next to the literary genre of Hebrews.

---

37. None have argued more vigorously for Apollos on the basis of Hebrews relationship to Philo than Spicq, 1:209-19. This introduction will argue below that Hebrews does not share the neo-Platonic worldview of Philo. Nor does Hebrews practice the allegorical exegesis so characteristic of Philo's work.

38. Ellingworth, 21; Hagner, 23; and Pfitzner, 26.

39. F. W. Howard, "The Epistle to the Hebrews," *Int* 5 (1951): 80-91.

40. Francesco Lo Bue, "The Historical Background of the Epistle to the Hebrews," *JBL* 75 (1956): 52-57.

41. T. W. Manson, "The Problem of the Epistle to the Hebrews," *Bulletin of the John Rylands University Library of Manchester* 32 (1949-50): 1-17.

42. Guthrie, "The Case for Apollos as the Author of Hebrews," 44, lists Lenski, Lane, Ellingworth, Hagner, Pfitzner, and himself in support of a Roman destination.

43. L. D. Hurst, "Apollos, Hebrews, and Corinth: Bishop Montefiore's Theory Examined," *SJT* 38 (1985): 505-13.

44. Attridge, 4, objects that there may have been others like Apollos in the first-century church. More telling is the query raised by Bruce, 12: Would the church at Alexandria have forgotten that the Alexandrian Apollos was the author?

B. THE PASTOR'S SERMON

One of the more fruitful endeavors of contemporary scholarship has been the attention given to the oral character of Hebrews.[45] Even the English reader can observe the lack of an epistolary introduction, the predominance of first person plural pronouns (we, our, us), and the prominence of verbs of saying and hearing (2:5; 5:11; 6:9; 8:1; 11:32). The pastor announces themes ahead of time in order to alert his hearers and build expectation before returning for their fuller development (e.g., Christ's high priesthood in 2:17-18). He weaves together exposition and exhortation in order to maintain his hearers' attention.[46] Recognition of this oral character has led many to compare Hebrews with Hellenistic rhetoric, as taught by Aristotle, Quintilian, and Cicero, and with what has been called the "synagogue homily."[47] Hebrews gives much evidence of exalted rhetorical style by its use of the following: grandly constructed periodic sentences (1:1-4; 2:1-4; 5:7-10; 7:26-28; 10:19-25), alliteration (e.g., the repeated "p" sound in the Greek text of 1:1; cf. 2:1-4; 4:10; 11:17), internal rhyme (5:8; 6:20), wordplays (5:8; 7:9; 9:16), and chiastic structure in which the first and last elements of a passage balance one another (2:18; 3:4).[48] *Anaphora,* or the repetition of a term, such as the "by faith" of 11:1-31, is also an indicator of exalted speech.[49] In harmony with ancient oratory Hebrews is replete with legal (6:16; 7:7), athletic (12:1-2, 12-13), and pedagogical (5:11-14; 12:4-11) metaphors.[50] Its author also uses the language of logic, appropriateness, and necessity common in rhetorical argument.[51] He was also wont, as were the orators of the day, to compare the one being extolled with the great of the past (1:1-14; 3:1-6; 4:14–5:10;

45. On the oral nature of Hebrews see David Aune, *The New Testament in Its Literary Environment* (Philadelphia: Westminster, 1987), 212-14. See also Steve Stanley, "The Structure of Hebrews from Three Perspectives," *TynBul* 45 (1994): 248-50.

46. See O'Brien, 21; Johnson, 10.

47. C. Clifton Black II, "The Rhetorical Form of the Hellenistic Jewish and Early Christian Sermon: A Response to Lawrence Wills," *HTR* 81 (1988): 5, cites Aristotle, *Rhet.* 1.2.1358b; Cicero, *Inv.* 2.3.12-13; 2.51.155-58, 176; 2.58.176-77; and Quintilian, *Inst.* 3.4.12-16; 3.7.1-28; 3.8.1-6; 3.9.1.

48. Thompson, 6; Johnson, 8.

49. Thompson, 6.

50. Thompson, 6.

51. Hermut Löhr, "Reflections of Rhetorical Terminology in Hebrews," in *Hebrews: Contemporary Methods — New Insights,* ed. Gabriella Gelardini (Biblical Interpretation Series 75; Atlanta: Society of Biblical Literature, 2005), 199-210, argues that the terms κεφάλιον ("main point," 8:1), ἀναγκαῖον ("necessary," 8:3); πρέπειν ("to be appropriate," 2:10; 7:26), ἀδύνατον ("impossible," 6:4; 10:4; 11:6), and λόγος τῆς παρακλήσεως ("word of exhortation," 13:22), suggest that the author was influenced by the type of logical argument characteristic of ancient rhetoric.

7:1–10:18) and to impress the hearers with appropriate example-lists from history (6:13-20; 11:1-38). It appears that Hebrews as a whole, like the oratory prized by the ancient world, was constructed to influence its hearers by reinforcing their perspective and values and/or by urging them to pursue a particular course of action.

Ancient rhetoric was normally divided into three categories: "judicial" was used to convince a jury that a past action was true or false, blameworthy or commendable; "epideictic" was used for the praise of famous people on public occasions with the purpose of instilling or reinforcing certain virtues and values; and "deliberative" was used to persuade a legislative assembly to take a certain course of action.[52] Some contend that Hebrews is closer to epideictic rhetoric; others argue that it favors deliberative rhetoric.[53] Identification as epideictic tends to put emphasis on the comparison of the Son of God with the heroes of old in the expository parts of Hebrews and thus on the book's theological content.[54] Identification as deliberative rhetoric gives pride of place to the hortatory parts of Hebrews and thus to its practical appeal for perseverance. However, the debate between epideictic and deliberative rhetoric is misplaced.[55] One cannot force Hebrews into the context of public celebration appropriate for epideictic rhetoric or into the legislative assembly appropriate for deliberative rhetoric. Hebrews is best under-

---

52. On the types of rhetoric see Aristotle, *Rhet.* 2.3.2-9; Quintilian, *Inst.* 3.4.1-16.

53. Attridge, 14; Harold W. Attridge, "Paraenesis in a Homily (λόγος παρακήσεως): The Possible Location of, and Socialization in, the 'Epistle to the Hebrews,'" *Semeia* 50 (1990): 214; Pfitzner, 8, 21-22; Pamela Eisenbaum, *The Jewish Heroes of Christian History: Hebrews 11 in Literary Context* (SBLDS 156; Atlanta: Scholars Press, 1997), 11-12, and others identify Hebrews as "epideictic" rhetoric; Barnabas Lindars, "The Rhetorical Structure of Hebrews," *NTS* 35 (1989): 383; K. Nissilä, *Das Hohepriestermotiv im Hebräerbrief: Eine exegetische Untersuchung* (Schriften der Finnischen Exegetischen Gesellschaft 33; Helsinki: Oy Liiton Kirjapaino, 1979), 74-78, 143-47, 230-44; and esp. Walter G. Übelacker, *Der Hebräerbrief als Appell: Untersuchungen zu Exordium, Narratio und Postscriptum (Hebr 1–2 und 13,22–25)* (Coniectanea Neotestamentica or Coniectanea Biblica: New Testament Series 21; Stockholm: Almqvist & Wiksell International, 1989), 214-29, are among those who consider Hebrews "deliberative" rhetoric. Johnson, 13, describes Hebrews as "deliberative rhetoric with epideictic features."

54. Although Attridge calls Hebrews "epideictic," he affirms the parenetic purpose of the whole (Attridge, "Paraenesis," 223).

55. Koester, 52-54. Cf. Lane, 1:lxxxix; deSilva, 46; Johnson, 13; and George H. Guthrie, *The Structure of Hebrews: A Text-Linguistic Analysis* (repr.; Leiden: Brill, 1994; Grand Rapids: Baker, 1998), 32-33. See Thompson's succinct statement: "Thus one can conclude that Hebrews has elements of both deliberative and epideictic rhetoric, for it contains both praise for the work of Christ and a call for action by the reader" (Thompson, 12).

stood as an example of the kind of homily or sermon typical of the synagogue and thus used in early Christian worship.[56] Such homilies appear to have been characterized by both OT exposition and exhortation. After all, the purpose of a homily was to interpret an inspired and authoritative text, show its relevance for the present, and urge the hearers to obey its teaching.

Hebrews bonds exposition and exhortation to form a close-knit appeal. In fact, our author calls what he has written a "word of exhortation" (13:22). This is the same term used to describe Paul's sermon or homily at the synagogue of Pisidian Antioch (Acts 13:15). Beginning with Paul's speech mentioned above, Wills contends that such synagogue homilies evidenced a tripartite structure: (1) an "exemplary section" that contained such material as Scriptural quotations, OT examples, and exposition; (2) a second section that drew conclusions from the first and showed its relevance for the hearers; (3) an exhortation, using the imperative and hortatory subjunctive, urging action appropriate in light of the first two sections.[57] He acknowledges that this pattern was often repeated in the same work and sometimes accompanied by various digressions as, in his opinion, it is in Hebrews.[58]

56. Hartwig Thyen, *Der Stil der Jüdisch-Hellenistischen Homilie* (Forschungen zur Religion und Literatur des Alten und Neuen Testaments, n.s. 47; Göttingen: Vandenhoeck & Ruprecht, 1955), 10-23, 43-50, 62-72. Thyen bases his study on Philo's commentary on Genesis, *1 Clement,* and 4 Maccabees; Stephen's speech in Acts 7; *Barnabas,* Hermas, the Wisdom of Solomon, and Hebrews. Thyen refers to Hebrews' use of first and second person pronouns, to the way it introduces OT quotations with words that denote "saying," and to other rhetorical features. Joseph A. Swetnam, "On the Literary Genre of the 'Epistle' to the Hebrews," *NovT* 11 (1969): 261-69, summarizes Thyen. See also Franz Joseph Schierse, *Verheissung und Heilsvollendung: Zur theologische Grundfrage des Hebräerbriefes* (Münich: Zink, 1955), esp. 207, and the earlier interpreters he cites who spoke of Hebrews as a sermon. Gabriella Gelardini, "Hebrews, an Ancient Synagogue Homily for *Tisha be-Av:* Its Function, Its Basis, Its Theological Interpretation," in *Hebrews: Contemporary Methods — New Insights,* ed. Gabriella Gelardini (Biblical Interpretation Series 75; Boston: Society of Biblical Literature, 2005), 107-27, identifies Hebrews as a synagogue homily for *Tisha be-Av* according to the Palestinian Triennial Cycle. See also Gabriella Gelardini, *"Verhärtet eure Herzen nicht":* Der Hebräer, eine Synagogenhomilie zu Tischa be-Av (Biblical Interpretation Series 83; Leiden and Boston: Brill, 2007). Her proposal is interesting, but the evidence she cites from the Babylonian Talmud and the Mishnah is late (Mitchell, 16).

57. Lawrence Wills, "The Form of the Sermon in Hellenistic Judaism and Early Christianity," *HTR* 77 (1984): 277-99, finds this threefold pattern in a variety of sources: *1 Clement* (283-85); the speeches in Acts (286-88); 2 Cor 6:14–7:1 (288); various Pauline passages (288-899); 1 and 2 Peter (289-91); Ignatius; and *Barnabas* (291-92). He also references Jewish sources such as Susanna, the Epistle of Jeremiah, and *Testaments of the Twelve Patriarchs* (293-96). Wills's case is somewhat weakened by his own acknowledgment that this "form" appears to be flexible (Wills, "The Sermon in Hellenistic Judaism," 279).

58. Wills, "The Sermon in Hellenistic Judaism," 277-99.

The sermons identified by Wills have adapted the resources of classical rhetoric to the new situation of the synagogue.[59] C. Clifton Black shows how the opening of Paul's speech at Pisidian Antioch in Acts 13:16b can be understood as the introduction or *exordium* of classical rhetoric. He finds three further parts of the classical oration in Wills's "exempla" section of this homily: the *narratio* or narrative statement of the facts (vv. 17-25); the *propositio* or proposition to be proved (v. 26); and the *probatio,* or proof of the proposition (vv. 27-37). These are then followed by an appropriate epilogue (vv. 38-40).[60] It should be no surprise that the synagogue developed the available rhetorical resources for the purpose of explaining and applying Scripture within the context of worship.[61]

Some are hesitant to describe the literary form of Hebrews as a "synagogue homily" even though they admit the features of the text described above.[62] Nonetheless, these features seem to justify referring to this book as a sermon whatever their historical origin. The way Hebrews begins without epistolary introduction, the sustained exposition of Scripture, the repeated concern with, and weaving together of, exposition and exhortation, the oral character of the material, the way the author has skillfully arranged his material to persuade his hearers, and his deep pastoral concern all betray the presence of a master homiletician.

An immediate benefit of grasping the sermonic character and shape of Hebrews is a reinforcement of the close relationship between exposition and exhortation.[63] Thus the author's exposition of Christ's High Priesthood is no ad hominem argument. By this presentation he would confirm the finality of Christ in general and the continuing legitimacy of the OT as the word of God.[64] At the same time, he would use exhortation both to prepare his hearers

---

59. Black II, "Rhetorical Form," 1-18.

60. Black II, "Rhetorical Form," 7-11. See Black's summary on 15-16.

61. Black II, "Rhetorical Form," 5; Attridge, "Paraenesis," 217. Cf. Guthrie, *Structure,* 32-33.

62. For instance, Gordon, 22, acknowledges that Hebrews contains "homiletic features," but thinks that calling Hebrews a "homily" is an overstatement. Bénétreau, 1:26, still prefers the term "letter."

63. The discussion below, entitled "The Sermon's Rhetorically Effective Structure," will confirm this fact.

64. Note the statement by Ronald E. Clements, "The Use of the Old Testament in Hebrews," *Southwestern Journal of Theology* 28 (1985): 37: "The whole theme and character of these quotations is designed to show how richly valuable the Old Testament remains for the Christian in order that the whole fullness of God's revelation may be known." Cf. G. B. Caird, "Exegetical Method of the Epistle to the Hebrews," *Canadian Journal of Theology* 5 (1959): 45. Graham Hughes, *Hebrews and Hermeneutics: The Epistle to the Hebrews as a New Testament Example of Biblical Interpretation* (SNTSMS 36; Cambridge: Cambridge University Press, 1979), 108, argues that the pastor had proba-

to grasp this teaching and to urge them to act upon it. One cannot separate theological exposition from exhortation nor diminish one in favor of the other. Their integration is necessary to achieve the author's pastoral purpose.

It is not sufficient, however, to stop with the identification of Hebrews as a synagogue homily or to point out that it is exposition and application of Scripture. Hebrews is a Christian synagogue homily. The synagogue homily adapted ancient rhetoric for the purpose of interpreting and applying an inspired and authoritative Scriptural text. Hebrews, however, presents a Christological interpretation and application of that text. This Christological orientation has extended Hebrews' adaptation of rhetoric beyond both the Hellenistic world in general and the synagogue in particular. For instance, the Son of God is not merely praised by comparison with the greats of the past so that the hearers will imitate his virtue, as was the custom of epideictic rhetoric. Nor is Christ one more hero in the ongoing history of the people of God narrated in Jewish hero-lists.[65] He is shown to be the consummation and fulfillment of all God's previous saving work, and thus he surpasses the heroes of old not merely in degree but in kind. He is the "Pioneer and Perfecter of the faith" (12:2), who alone enables the faithful to persevere in obedience and finally to enter God's eternal blessing. The interpreter, then, must be sensitive to the way in which Hebrews has used the resources of Hellenistic rhetoric and of the synagogue without neglecting the particular shape given to those resources by the Christological orientation of this sermon.

The pastor did not begin this sermon with the typical letter-introduction found in Paul lest he diminish the full force of his oratory. The letter ending he has attached in 13:22-25, however, does nothing to dissipate this sermon's power. In light of this ending, many would call Hebrews a "homily" or "sermon" sent as a letter to be read in the assembled worship of

bly developed his understanding of how Christ fulfilled the OT before composing this sermon. In the sermon, however, he uses what he has already developed as motivation for appropriate action.

65. The differences we have suggested between Hebrews as a "Christian homily," the "synagogue homily," and Hellenistic rhetoric are reminiscent of the differences Eisenbaum has found between the example list in Hebrews 11:1-38, Jewish example lists, and the use of example lists in the Greco-Roman world (Eisenbaum, *Jewish Heroes, passim,* with her conclusions are on 225-27). Greco-Roman lists usually draw assorted examples from the recent past without regard for continuity between them. Since the Jewish works, like Ben Sirach 44–50, draw their examples from Scripture, those examples come from the ancient past and depict the historical continuity of Israel. In light of the fulfillment brought by Christ, however, the examples in Heb 11:1-38 depict the history not of ethnic "Israel" but of the people of God who have always anticipated his coming. See the comments on 11:1-40. In short, the Jewish lists differ from the Greco-Roman because they are interpreting Scripture; Heb 11:1-38 differs because it is interpreting Scripture in light of Scripture's fulfillment in Christ.

the congregation about whom the pastor was concerned.[66] This understanding of Hebrews accounts for its careful composition as a written document, its oral character, and its letter ending.

C. THE PASTOR'S CONGREGATION

1. What the Sermon Reveals about Its Hearers

The hearers must have been followers of Christ who could appreciate the elegance of the pastor's Greek and thus were at home both linguistically and culturally within the Hellenistic world. The pastor's sending the greetings of "those from Italy" (13:24) confirms the fact that both he and his hearers moved in a circle that included people living outside Palestine. The pastor is obviously addressing a specific group of people. Yet he does not call them a "church" or designate the city in which they live. These features suggest that he is addressing a house church rather than all the believers of a particular locality. This possibility is substantiated by the way he exhorts his hearers to "greet" *all* their leaders (13:24) and to be concerned for "all the saints" (10:25).[67] The mention of "our brother Timothy," along with other features of the letter closing (13:22-25), suggests that the community addressed by Hebrews was closely connected with the Pauline circle and perhaps with other groups of first-century believers as well. The members of the congregation to which Hebrews is addressed were obviously well versed in the OT and had been followers of Jesus for some time (2:1-4; 5:11-14).

Yet they were also in danger of compromising their commitment to Christ. They appear to have suffered from lassitude and from a tendency to neglect the gospel they had received (2:1-4). They had become spiritually dull and thus slow to grasp the full significance of what Christ had done and of his continuing relevance as all-sufficient Savior (5:11–6:8). In fact, they were in danger of reverting to a spiritual immaturity totally inappropriate for experienced believers. The pastor fears that this lassitude, neglect, and regression might lead to apostasy from Christ (6:1-8; 10:26-31).[68]

This lassitude and resulting danger of apostasy were clearly exacerbated by the resistance of the unbelieving world. Many, at least, in this con-

---

66. Koester, 81, lists Attridge, Grässer, Hagner, Lane, Long, Pfitzner, Übelacker, Backhaus, Cody, Vanhoye, and Wray in support of this position. See also Weiss, 40-41.

67. See Weiss, 75.

68. Ellingworth, 78-79, categorizes the dangers facing the addressees as passive (lassitude, neglect, immaturity), active (apostasy), and external (the pressure of ostracism and persecution). The present exposition assumes that these were not separate but related problems.

gregation appear to have been intimidated by the disdain and marginalization that they suffered as a result of their loyalty to Christ (10:32-34; 11:1-40; 12:1-11). They had received the gospel from those who "heard" Christ (2:1-4) and had been believers long enough to have successfully braved an earlier time of persecution (10:32-34). That persecution had included public harassment, imprisonment, and the confiscation of property, but had fallen short of martyrdom (12:4). Now, however, in their discouraged state they shrink back from their Christian commitment due to present marginalization and to fear that more, perhaps life-threatening, persecution may soon come (10:36; 13:6).[69]

Their anxiety at present marginalization, anticipated suffering, and perhaps impending martyrdom may have been exacerbated by disappointment that Christ had not yet returned (1:14; 10:36-39) or by their failure to realize and appropriate his full sufficiency as Savior. Thus some, at least, were neglecting to attend the community's times of worship (10:24-25; cf. 3:13-14). Under these circumstances it was only natural for them to be attracted by the privileges and respect that would be theirs by abandoning their commitment to Christ and identifying with the unbelieving world (see 12:14-17 and comments).[70] The pastor is concerned that they persevere in the life of faith and obedience. He wants them to continue to live as if God's promise for the future is certain and his power for the present is real (see on 11:1-6). Thus he would have them avail themselves of the cleansing from sin and access to God provided by the Son, their all-sufficient High Priest (4:14–10:25; esp. 10:19-25). This High Priest is also the "Pioneer" (12:2) through whom they can be certain of entering God's future promised "rest," the eternal "City" that has always been the destiny of the people of God (11:8-10, 13-16; 12:22-24).

In order to understand the context of the recipients' situation more fully modern readers need to grasp the role of honor and shame in the first-century Hellenistic world.[71] People received honor when they were given

---

69. R. W. Johnson, *Going outside the Camp: The Sociological Function of the Levitical Critique in the Epistle to the Hebrews* (JSNTSup 209; Sheffield: Sheffield Academic, 2001), has attempted to determine the situation and purpose of Hebrews by using Mary Douglas's group/gird analysis of societies. He concludes that the ideal society envisioned by Hebrews is one that would be willing to incorporate new people into their fellowship. As Lincoln, *A Guide*, 53, says, this proposal runs counter to the obvious concern of the author to promote perseverance in the face of opposition. Furthermore, the very evidence Johnson provides shows that Hebrews is "strong group"/"weak grid," not "weak group"/"weak grid" as he proposes. An analysis of "strong group"/"weak grid" fits well with Hebrews' concern for perseverance.

70. See the fine discussion of the recipients' situation in Lincoln, *A Guide*, 52-68.

71. See the monograph by David A. deSilva, *Despising Shame: Honor Discourse*

public recognition that their attitudes and conduct conformed to what was socially expected. Shame resulted from public rejection due to lack of conformity. It was crucial to have a sense of what was shameful since a person's identity and reputation were closely identified with the honor and recognition given one for appropriately fulfilling his or her place in society. Furthermore, one shared the honor — or shame — of one's social group. Thus it was honorable to act in such a way that one protected the honor and public approval of those groups to which one belonged. Moreover, a culture of honor and shame was carried out within a patron/client relationship. Patrons were those who were socially superior and who controlled the benefits of life through wealth and the ability to bestow position and influence. The socially inferior client looked to a patron for the necessary benefits of life. It was the honorable thing for the patron to generously grant these benefits and, correspondingly, for the client to be loyal to his or her patron by supporting them in various endeavors but most of all by praising them publicly and acknowledging their beneficence. It was the epitome of shamefulness for the patron to withhold generosity or for the client to be slack in public praise or to fail in supporting the patron in public matters. This relationship between patron and client was intended to be permanent. Furthermore, some people served as brokers mediating between clients and patrons, thus enabling clients to receive patronage and patrons, praise.

The past suffering, present marginalization, and possible future persecution of those addressed by Hebrews entailed a great loss of honor and a source of shame before the larger community. Heb 11:37-38 describes the epitome of disgrace through total exclusion of the faithful from human society. The pastor seeks to show his hearers that this very shame suffered at the hands of the unbelieving world is a mark of great honor before God, their ultimate Patron. This God has mediated to them the inestimable beneficence of eternal salvation through the brokerage of his Son and their Patron, Jesus Christ. Indeed, Jesus has provided these benefits through suffering the vilest of shame (12:1-3) and has thus been given the highest honor by God through being exalted to his right hand (8:1-2). They honor Father and Son both by persevering in loyalty and by their perpetual offer of praise and gratitude for the benefits they have received (12:28). By taking his place with the suffering and thus dishonored people of God, Moses (11:25-26) became an example of such behavior second only to the example of the Son of God himself (12:1-3). The Son assumed the shame of God's people (2:5-18) in order to bestow upon them the benefits of "such a great salvation" (2:3).

---

and Community Maintenance in the Epistle to the Hebrews (SBLDS 152; Atlanta: Scholars Press, 1995), and his commentary in which he expounds Hebrews in terms of honor/shame and the patron/client relationship. See also the summary in Lincoln, *A Guide,* 48-51.

2. Were These Hearers Jewish or Gentile in Background?

The above description of the recipients of Hebrews has not addressed the question of their Jewish background. Were they attracted to the practices of the synagogue as a means of escaping persecution and shame or of addressing some other felt need? One can understand Hebrews without identifying either the name of its author or the location of the recipients. One cannot, however, interpret Hebrews without taking a position as to whether the recipients were Jewish or Gentile believers.[72] Were they ethnic Jewish followers of Christ who were either hesitant to make the necessary break with the synagogue or in danger of a relapse into Judaism? If so, they may have feared disgrace at the hands of their fellow Jews or been concerned about rejection by the larger community at the loss of the protection afforded by the synagogue.[73] The Roman historian Tacitus would call Christianity, which he distinguished from Judaism, a "pernicious superstition" (*Ann.* 15).

Attraction to the synagogue may also have been the result of a felt spiritual need or of an inadequate theology. Lindars, for instance, argues that they were attracted to the synagogue meals associated with the sacrificial ministry of the Temple in order to find continuous cleansing for post-baptismal sin.[74] Goulder suggests that the whole of Hebrews' Christology is an apologetic against an Ebionite Christianity that took Christ as no more than an archangel (cf. Epiphanius, *Pan.* 30.16.3-4). The proponents of this diminished view of Christ of necessity looked to Jewish rituals for fulfillment of spiritual needs.[75] Others have proposed that Hebrews presents the sufficiency of Christ's sacrifice in order to address a lack felt due to the destruction of the Temple.[76] Or, on the other hand, was the pastor addressing a mixed or Gentile audience fatigued from the length of the road, marginalized by unbelieving society, and beginning to lose confidence in Christ? Perhaps they were disaffected by the delay of Christ's return.[77]

---

72. The recent popular commentary by Fudge demonstrates the fallacy of attempting to avoid this question. His refusal to address this issue becomes a de facto decision to interpret Hebrews as if it were *not* written to Jewish believers.

73. Bruce, 382; Ellingworth, 78-80; Bénétreau, 1:28-29; W. R. G. Loader, *Sohn und Hoherpriester: Eine Traditionsgeschichtliche Untersuchung zur Christologie des Hebräerbriefes* (Wissenschaftliche Monographien zum Alten und Neuen Testament 53; Neukirchen-Vluyn: Neukirchener, 1981), 258. Koester, 71, however, thinks that identification with the synagogue may not have provided much protection.

74. Barnabas Lindars, *The Theology of the Letter to the Hebrews,* ed. J. D. G. Dunn (New Testament Theology; Cambridge: Cambridge University Press, 1991), 4-15; cf. Bruce, 382; Ellingworth, 78-80; Donald G. Guthrie, 31-38.

75. M. Goulder, "Hebrews and the Ebionites," *NTS* 49 (2003): 393-406.

76. Cf. Mitchell, 9, 11.

77. Gordon, 15.

Several important considerations are often overlooked when examining this issue. First, Hebrews is completely free from any kind of ethnic distinction.[78] The author never differentiates Jews from Gentiles or Greeks from barbarians. Thus when interpreters take the term "Jewish Christian" in an ethnic sense, they immediately introduce confusion. If one is going to use the term, it must be understood in a religious sense: "Jewish Christian" means those followers of Christ who have been acculturated into and continue to be attracted by Jewish religious practices regardless of their ethnicity.[79] Such acculturation may have happened to Gentiles after their conversion since many of their fellow followers of Jesus were Jewish. It may have occurred by identification with the synagogue as proselytes or God-fearers before their conversion to Christ. In any case, "Jewish Christian" describes both Jews and Gentiles who give allegiance to Christ while insisting on or feeling the need of various Jewish associations or practices.[80]

Second, there is no direct polemic in the first twelve chapters of He-

78. Clark M. Williamson, "Anti-Judaism in Hebrews?" *Int* 57 (2003): 276, anachronistically introduces ethnic distinctions foreign to Hebrews when he says, "Hebrews gives no indication that the renewed people of God is anyone other than Israelites." There is nothing in Hebrews that either overtly or implicitly defines the people of God in terms of ethnicity. Furthermore, Williamson's further affirmation that "the sacrificial system" was "the only issue of the old covenant that was superseded" is misleading. This assertion appears to be based on a faulty interpretation of Heb 7:11-14. Moreover, it minimizes the difference that this change entails. The reality of cleansing from sin and access to God anticipated by the Old Covenant has now come to fruition in Christ.

79. See Goulder, "Ebionites," 395, n. 6. Cf. Koester, 48, who emphasizes that the hearers' relationship to Greco-Roman culture, to the Jewish subculture, and to the Christian community is more important than ethnicity.

80. Some argue that the "parting of the ways" between Judaism and Christianity had not yet occurred when Hebrews was written. See Susan E. Docherty, *The Use of the Old Testament in Hebrews: A Case Study in Early Jewish Bible Interpretation* (WUNT 2/ 260; Tübingen: Mohr Siebeck, 2009), 1, and the sources cited in her note 1. Thus, according to this view, it is anachronistic to speak as if Christianity and Judaism were understood as separate religions at that time. Assuming, for the moment, that the recipients of Hebrews were "Jewish Christians" as defined above, they may not have thought of themselves as "Christians" of Jewish background but simply as followers of the Jewish religion who acknowledged Christ. In the final analysis, however, this distinction is not as significant for the interpretation of Hebrews as some would claim. The whole burden of Hebrews is that fulfillment in Christ reveals the true purpose of the Old Covenant — a purpose very different from that embraced by practicing Jews who did not believe in Christ. Thus, even if the recipients thought of themselves as adherents of the Jewish religion who followed Christ, they would still be sharply distinguished from other Jews in both belief and practice. This situation might lead to ostracism and persecution or to felt need and nostalgia for former practices just as much as if the recipients thought of themselves as "Christians" who had formerly practiced Judaism.

brews. This situation casts doubt on any comprehensive interpretation of Hebrews that rests primarily on opposition to false teaching.[81] In these chapters
the pastor never compares Christ with contemporary Judaism but only with
the institutions of the Old Covenant and priestly system as described in the
Pentateuch.[82] Christ stands in continuity with this system by fulfilling it.
Third, from the beginning the writer envisions one people of God spread out
through history. Those who have responded to God's call by faith have always been his people (though it has always been possible to fall through unbelief).[83] The faithful of old and the faithful since Christ belong to this one
people.[84] Those God addressed in the "prophets" are the "fathers" of those he
has now addressed in "one who is Son" (1:1). Contrary to what many suggest, Hebrews envisions no "break" in salvation history.[85] Christ has fulfilled
what those OT institutions always foreshadowed and has provided what was
needed to bring the faithful people of God — whether they lived before or after his coming — to their God-intended goal (11:39-40).

In Heb 13:9-10, however, the pastor contrasts himself and his hearers
(the "we" is inclusive) with "those who serve in the Tent." As argued in the
commentary on these verses, this phrase is not a reference to OT people but
to contemporaries who lived according to the old order after the coming of
Christ. Thus here, at last, the pastor appears to tip his hand. The purpose of
his long discourse on how the all-sufficient Son of God has fulfilled and thus
demonstrated the merely typological nature of the old is revealed. The pastor's intention has been to encourage his hearers clearly to distinguish themselves from those who still live by the provisions of that former order. To go
"outside the camp" (13:13) is to separate from these people. There are features of the earlier chapters, particularly the section dealing with Christ's
high priesthood (4:14–10:18), that provide supporting evidence. It is true that
any follower of Christ who accepted the OT would eventually be forced to in-
quire concerning the continuing role of the Aaronic priesthood. However, the

81. Weiss, 56-57. *Pace* Goulder, "Ebionites," 393-406.
82. *Pace* Iutisone Salevao, *Legitimation in the Letter to the Hebrews: The Construction and Maintenance of a Symbolic Universe* (JSNTSup 219; New York and London: Sheffield Academic Press, 2002), who often argues as if the pastor's interaction with
the OT was direct interaction with contemporary Judaism.
83. See pp. 43-45, "Fundamental Assumptions," under "The Sermon's Use of the
Old Testament" below.
84. Eisenbaum, *Jewish Heroes,* 3, 142, *passim,* contends that the pastor has "denationalized" OT history so that it no longer refers to Israel but to the people of God in
general who find fulfillment in Christ. Her position assumes that the pastor began with
something like the nationalistic hero list of Sirach 45–50. If so, this supposed process of
"de-nationalization" occurs completely outside the text of Hebrews.
85. *Pace* Salevao, *Legitimation,* 404.

way the pastor so forcefully challenges the saving sufficiency of that priesthood and sacrificial system (7:11-19) appears to be more appropriate for people who had at least a residual suspicion that it was effective.[86] His argument that Christ's coming has "abolished" (7:18) the old and rendered its sacrifices unnecessary (10:18) suggests that his readers thought some form of participation in the old order appropriate. One might also argue that Gentile believers tempted to abandon Christ would not be moved by appeals to a Scripture they had accepted only when they identified with Christ.[87] The author's concern that his hearers not "fall away from the living God" (3:12) is no objection to their Jewish roots.[88] The pastor is convinced that rejection of fulfillment in Christ is rejection of all that God has ever spoken and thus a rejection of God himself.

It seems most likely that the pastor's concern that his hearers rely on Christ rather than take refuge in the synagogue or maintain vestigial Jewish religious practices was part, but not all, of his reason for composing this sermon labeled "To the 'Hebrews.'" The very fact that the pastor makes no mention of these Tent-worshipers until the end suggests that more is at stake. Note particularly the examples of faith in Heb 11:1-40. Moses, for instance, did not abandon the Jewish way of life, but Egypt, the unbelieving world of his day (11:27), just as Noah "condemned" the entire unbelieving world of his day (11:7). The pastor is concerned about his hearers' standing firm against the pressure of and thus separating from unbelieving society and its values, whatever form that unbelieving society may take. Furthermore, by showing how Christ fulfilled the old order he not only establishes Christ's sole sufficiency in relation to that order but in relation to all claimants. Hebrews clearly affirms God's speaking in his Son as the fulfillment of all God has said before (1:1-4) and the only source of "such a great salvation" (2:3). The pastor earnestly desires his hearers to appropriate Christ's abundant provision within their daily lives.

Several important suggestions concerning the location of the recipients are discussed below (pp. 34-41). Before leaving the present discussion, however. it is necessary to address the question of supersessionism. This issue is closely associated with the Jewish background of Hebrews' recipients. It has also received much discussion in scholarly circles.[89] Does Hebrews

86. Bruce, 6-7; O'Brien, 11. One might think or modern converts from animism or other religions in various parts of the world who keep a charm or talisman hidden away "just in case."

87. Bruce, 6.

88. *Pace* Weiss, 71. See Ellingworth, 24.

89. *The Epistle to the Hebrews and Christian Theology,* ed. Richard Bauckham et al. (Grand Rapids: Eerdmans, 2009), a book of essays delivered at the 2006 St Andrews Conference on Hebrews and Theology, contains five essays and seventy-five pages on this

teach that Christianity "supersedes" Judaism or that the church "supersedes" Israel? Concern over this matter has been motivated by a legitimate desire to oppose the mistreatment of Jews in the modern world. However, it has also been fueled by the pressure of contemporary pluralism against the absolute claims of Christ.

As noted above, Hebrews *never* compares Christianity with Judaism, the church with Israel, nor, apart from 13:9-10, those who follow Jesus with those who follow Jewish practices. According to Hebrews, the people of God are, and always has been, the people who *hear* the word of God and respond with faith and obedience. There is nothing in this sermon that would demean or marginalize Jews as a people. As will be elaborated below (pp. 52-53), the Old Covenant, while not an effective means of *salvation,* retains a very positive role as the God-intended type that finds fulfillment in Christ.[90] Hebrews was written to encourage its readers/hearers in the face of persecution and provides no basis for the mistreatment or persecution of anyone. Hebrews does, however, without equivocation, affirm the sole-sufficiency of Christ as Son/High Priest and Savior.[91] Furthermore, its author substantiates this claim on the basis of God's previous revelation in the OT and thus in relation to the saving efficacy of the Mosaic Covenant.[92] One does violence to the text of Hebrews if one forces it to speak otherwise.[93]

---

subject: Richard B. Hays, "'Here We Have No Lasting City': New Covenantalism in Hebrews," 151-73; Oskar Skarsaune, "Does the Letter to the Hebrews Articulate a Supersessionist Theology? A Response to Richard Hays," 174-82; Mark D. Nanos, "*New* or *Re*newed Covenantalism? A Response to Richard Hays," 183-88; Morna D. Hooker, "Christ, the 'End' of the Cult," 189-212; Nehemia Polen, "Leviticus and Hebrews . . . and Leviticus," 213-25. For a helpful discussion see also Williamson, "Anti-Judaism in Hebrews?" 268-69, and esp. Gordon, 24-29, 36-53.

90. *Pace* J. G. Gager, *The Origins of Anti-Semitism: Attitudes toward Judaism in Pagan and Christian Antiquity* (Oxford: Oxford University Press, 1984), 180-84, cited by Williamson, "Anti-Judaism in Hebrews?" 268-69, there is no hint of a Marcionite rejection of the OT in Hebrews.

91. In this sermon the pastor is not concerned with those who have never heard of Christ. He is quite clear, however, that there is no salvation for those who are clearly confronted with but reject Christ (6:4-10).

92. Thus Gordon, 53, is correct when he writes, "The implication [of Heb 6:6 and 10:29] is that it is the recognition or rejection of Christ that determines whether one stands within the biblical faith continuum and that, from a Christian point of view, becomes constitutive of the breach between nascent Christianity and Judaism."

93. This is apparently what Hays, "New Covenantalism," 167, attempts to do when he says, "Would not the logic of Hebrews' own symbolic world allow us to propose that [Jews who do not recognize Jesus as Mediator of the New Covenant], too, insofar as they continue to trust in the God of Abraham, Isaac, and Jacob, greet the promises from afar?" The weakness of this assertion is attested by the last five words, "greet the promises from afar." Those described in Heb 11:13 by this phrase could not enter into those prom-

D. THE PASTOR'S WORLDVIEW

1. The Pastor's Dependence on the Christian Tradition

The most significant aspect of the pastor's worldview is his fundamental dependence on common Christian tradition. The pastor is committed to the Son's eternal preexistence (1:1-3); incarnation (2:5-18; 8:1–10:18); crucifixion (5:7-10; 9:11-14; 10:5-10; 12:1-3); and exaltation (1:13; 8:1-2; 10:11-14), including belief in his resurrection (13:20-21). He joins the other NT writers in his conviction that Christ has sufficiently dealt with sin and is, therefore, God's definitive provision of salvation (4:14-16; 10:19-25). No one is more convinced than he that Christ is the fulfillment of God's OT revelation (1:1-4). He would have his hearers persevere until the coming Judgment (12:25-29), when they will receive final salvation at Christ's return (9:28).

Similarities between Hebrews and Paul are due largely to their shared dependence upon this tradition.[94] There are, however, some commonalities between the distinctives of Hebrews and the particular emphases of other NT writers. W. Manson has identified parallels between Hebrews and Stephen's speech in Acts 7.[95] Both seem to envision the people of God on the move and to question the finality of OT institutions.[96] Heb 1:1-4 is reminiscent of the opening verses in John's Gospel (John 1:1-5). Both Hebrews and John put great emphasis on Christ as the Son or the Son of God.[97] Hebrews and 1 Peter are often compared because both were written to encourage perseverance in the face of persecution. Both refer to the pilgrim people of God (Heb 11:8-16; 12:22; 13:14; 1 Pet 1:1; 2:11). Both call Jesus a "Shepherd" (Heb 13:20; 1 Pet 2:25; 5:4).[98]

Hebrews' development of Christ's high priesthood, however, is a unique contribution to NT theology. There are intimations of Christ's high-priestly role in other NT writings. In Rev 1:13 Christ appears in high-priestly attire.[99]

---

ises apart from "us" and the work of Christ that "we" enjoy (see the commentary below on 11:39-40). See the critique of Hays in Skarsaune, "Supersessionist Theology," 174-82.

94. For an extensive list of points of contact between Hebrews and Paul see L. D. Hurst, *The Epistle to the Hebrews: Its Background of Thought* (SNTSMS 65; Cambridge: Cambridge University Press, 1990), 108. For a briefer summary see Lincoln, *A Guide,* 41.

95. William Manson, *The Epistle to the Hebrews* (London, 1951).

96. See the evaluation of Manson in Hurst, *Background,* 89-106. Lincoln, *A Guide,* 42, notes that while Stephen rejects the Temple, which Hebrews does not mention, he seems to approve of the wilderness Tent, which Hebrews considers provisional.

97. On Hebrews and the Johannine literature see Spicq, 1:109-38.

98. On the similarity with 1 Peter see Attridge, 30-31, and Ellingworth, 15-17.

99. Bruce, 29, n. 125.

His intercession in Rom 8:34 suggests a high-priestly ministry. A number of passages affirm the sacrificial nature of his death (Matt 26:27; John 1:29, 36; Rom 3:25; 8:3; 1 Cor 5:7; 1 Pet 1:19-21; Rev 5:12).[100] Hebrews develops such ideas by showing how the eternal Son's obedient self-offering has fulfilled all that the Aaronic priesthood anticipated.

2. The Pastor and the Heavenly/Futuristic Eschatology of Apocalyptic Writings

While Hebrews is not an apocalypse,[101] yet our author's commitment to the common Gospel tradition includes his use of the futuristic two-age eschatology characteristic of the apocalyptic writings.[102] The OT prophets looked forward to a new saving act of God in which he would establish his rule. Apocalyptic writers emphasized the evil nature of the present age of injustice dominated by Satan and the cataclysmic, world-changing nature of God's coming salvation that would inaugurate the new age of divine rule.[103] Hebrews agrees with the rest of the NT in its affirmation that this ultimate intervention by God occurs in two stages: at his first coming Christ fulfilled all that the old sacrificial system anticipated by definitively dealing with sin; at his second coming he will usher his own into the final gift of salvation (1:13; 2:5-9; 9:26-28).[104] His second coming will be the occasion for the resurrec-

---

100. On Rom 3:25 as a reference to the Day of Atonement see Hooker, "'End' of the Cult," 205.

101. For example, *1 Enoch, 4 Ezra,* and *2 Baruch.* Note the following widely accepted definition of an apocalypse: "An apocalypse is defined as a genre of revelatory literature with a narrative framework, in which a revelation is mediated by an otherworldly being to a human recipient, disclosing a transcendent reality which is both temporal, insofar as it envisages eschatological salvation, and spatial insofar as it involves another, supernatural world" (John J. Collins, *The Apocalyptic Imagination: An Introduction to Jewish Apocalyptic Literature* [2nd ed.; Grand Rapids: Eerdmans, 1998], 4-5; cited by Mackie, *Eschatology and Exhortation,* 31). Such writings were distinctive in the vividness with which they described the heavenly world, populating it with angels and other beings around the throne of God.

102. Lincoln, *A Guide,* 43. The following phrases are typical of such thinking: "the world to come" (τὴν οἰκουμένην μέλλουσαν, 2:5), "but now once for all at the consummation of the ages" (νυνὶ δὲ ἅπαξ ἐπὶ συντελείᾳ τῶν αἰώνων, 9:26), and esp. "the powers of the age to come" (δυνάμεις τε μέλλοντος αἰῶνος, 6:5). See Mackie, *Eschatology and Exhortation,* 35-36.

103. See *1 En.* 17:15; *4 Ezra* 7:50, 112-13, 119; *2 Bar.* 44:8-15; 83:4-9; *T. Levi* 10:2; and the discussion in Mackie, *Eschatology and Exhortation,* 30.

104. Lincoln, *A Guide,* 43, argues that Hebrews makes use of this two-age paradigm. See also Michel, 58; Koester, 100-104; deSilva, 27-32; Mathias Rissi, *Die Theologie des Hebräerbriefes* (WUNT 41; Tübingen: Mohr/Siebeck, 1987), 125-30;

tion, the final Judgment, the overthrow of the present world order, and final entrance into God's eternal kingdom (12:25-29). The time between Christ's first and second comings is often described as a time of overlap between the old and new ages. One might argue that the continuation of the "old age" is evident in the way in which the faithful both before and after Christ live as aliens in the world (11:1-21), subject to persecution by, and exclusion from, unbelieving society (11:22-27; 35b-38). On the other hand, the new has come because the faithful now experience cleansing of the conscience (9:11-14), access to God's presence (4:15-16; 10:22), and the provisions of the New Covenant (10:15-18).

Hebrews' interest in the heavenly world which Christ has entered (3:1, 13, etc.) and to which the recipients have been called (1:3) suggests even closer ties with the world of Jewish apocalyptic.[105] Apocalyptic writers such as *1 Enoch, 2 Baruch,* and *4 Ezra* tended to combine belief in an already existing heavenly eternal world with commitment to a future, world-shaking in-breaking of the kingdom of God.[106] The Dead Sea Scrolls confirm this combination.[107] Hofius and others have compared Hebrews and *4 Ezra* be-

---

C. K. Barrett, "The Eschatology of the Epistle to the Hebrews," in *The Background of the New Testament and Its Eschatology,* ed. W. D. Davies and D. Daube (Cambridge: Cambridge University Press, 1956), 363-93; and James C. Miller, "Paul and Hebrews: A Comparison of Narrative Worlds," in *Hebrews: Contemporary Methods — New Insights,* ed. Gabriella Gelardini (Biblical Interpretation Series 75; Atlanta: Society of Biblical Literature, 2005), 250.

105. deSilva, 27-32; Hurst, *Background,* 38-42; Caird, "Exegetical Method," 45; Graham Hughes, *Hebrews and Hermeneutics,* 63; Barrett, "Eschatology," 393. Lincoln, *A Guide,* 42.

106. The earliest apocalyptic texts, such as *1 Enoch* 1–36, 72–82, emphasize the spatial distinction between heaven and earth; later apocalyptic writings such as *4 Ezra* and *2 Baruch* give more weight to temporal eschatology (Mackie, *Eschatology and Exhortation,* 31-32). On the shaking of the universe at the Judgment compare *4 Ezra* 10:25, 28; *2 Bar.* 32:1-4; and *Sib. Or.* 3:675-80 with Heb 12:25-29 (Koester, 103). "What is significant for the interpretation of Hebrews is that in this literature vertical and horizontal dimensions are found side by side, so that a restored Jerusalem and its Temple can be depicted both as the heavenly Jerusalem and Temple and as the Jerusalem and Temple which are to come to earth at the end" (Lincoln, *A Guide,* 43).

107. Note the heavenly world in 1QS 11:8 and the establishing of God's reign on earth through the overthrow of this present evil world in 1QM 11:5-10. There are a number of other parallels between Hebrews and the scrolls: The writers of the scrolls understood themselves as a "New Covenant" community (1QS 1:16-18). Their separation from the Jerusalem Temple (1QHab 8:9; 9:9) parallels Hebrews' rejection of the OT sacrificial system. They, too, conceived of prayer as a "spiritual sacrifice" (4QFlor 1:6; 1QS 8:6-8; 9:3-11). Their expectation of a priestly as well as a royal messiah (1QSa 2:1-21) is reminiscent of Hebrews' emphasis on Christ's high priesthood. Yet they were obsessed with laws of purity that Hebrews rejects (1QS 1:11-12; 6:17-22) and anticipated the re-

cause *4 Ezra* describes both the state of souls in heaven (*4 Ezra* 7:88-101) and the final salvation yet to come (*4 Ezra* 7:26, 36) as "rest" (cf. Heb 3:7–4:11).[108] This author's vision is complete with a description of the place and state of the damned (*4 Ezra* 7:36-44). Both the heavenly world and the future age were often used to vindicate the righteousness of God. Although the faithful suffer in this evil age, they enter the heavenly world at death and will be vindicated in the coming age of salvation. Such apocalyptic writers developed OT teaching about the eternity of God, the transitory nature of the world, and coming judgment. They also drew on ancient ideas that pictured God's heavenly dwelling place as his throne room or Temple.[109]

In order, however, to understand Hebrews well one must also observe the aspects of its thought that distinguish it from the worldview found in these writings. These differences are due to the pastor's purpose and to his conviction that Christ has fulfilled the OT. His belief in the heavenly world itself is not merely dependent upon apocalyptic tradition but is Christologically and exegetically established. He knows that there is such a heavenly world because Christ has "sat down at the right hand of the throne of the Majesty in heaven" (8:1) in fulfillment of Ps 110:1. First, then, Hebrews refrains from speculative descriptions of the heavenly world. There is, for instance, no depiction of a place reserved for the unfaithful as in *4 Ezra*.[110] The pastor is writing a sermon, not an apocalypse. Thus he bases everything on his own careful interpretation of the OT and tailors all that he says to encourage his hearers in perseverance. Second, the pastor has his own reason for introducing the eternal heavenly world. He is not concerned, for example, as are *4 Ezra* and *Joseph and Aseneth,* with the place of departed souls.[111] Rather, he uses the heavenly world to clarify the benefits that Christ has *already provided* for the faithful. Through the work of Christ the people of God have ac-

---

establishment of a purified Temple sacrificial system. See Hurst, *Background,* 43-66, and the literature he cites. See also the commentaries by Bruce, Hughes, and Buchanan. There have been many studies that compare various passages in or aspects of Hebrews with the scrolls. See, for instance, the references given in the commentary below on Heb 7:1-10.

108. Otfried Hofius, *Katapausis: Die Vorstellung vom endzeitlichen Ruheort im Hebräerbrief* (WUNT 11; Tübingen: Siebeck, 1970), 60-63.

109. See the comments on 8:1-2 and 9:23-24 below.

110. Thus one must be wary of reading everything the pastor says from the perspective of apocalyptic without contextual warrant. Michel, 204-5, for instance, argues that "passed through the heavens" in Heb 4:14 is a description of the multiple heavens (usually three or seven) characteristic of Jewish apocalyptic. As already noted above, Hebrews refrains from such speculations. See also Edward Adams, "The Cosmology of Hebrews," in *The Epistle to the Hebrews and Christian Theology,* ed. Richard Bauckham et al. (Grand Rapids: Eerdmans, 2009), 132.

111. In this commentator's judgment, however, he does believe that the "spirits of the" departed "righteous" are with God in heaven. See the comments on 12:23.

cess *now* into the presence of God in heaven. Through this access they receive the "mercy" and "grace" (2:17-18) they need *now* for perseverance in faithfulness until final entrance at Christ's return (9:28; 12:25-29).

Finally, despite the influence of the two-age schema, these ages cannot be equated simply with the times of the Old and New Covenants. In particular, the Old Covenant must not be identified with the old age dominated by evil that continues until Christ's return. First, Hebrews does not picture the era of the Old Covenant as the time of evil's dominion but as the time of anticipation.[112] God was not absent, for he "spoke" through Moses and the other "prophets" (1:1-2; 3:1-6). The Old Covenant may not have provided salvation, but it foreshadowed and typified the salvation to come. Second, the time of the Old Covenant does not continue until Christ's return. Since Christ has fulfilled what that covenant anticipated (7:11-19; 10:5-10), the time for participating in its institutions has come to an end. The Old Covenant retains force not as an era but as a Scriptural type and as a word of judgment on those who reject Christ (see on 12:18-21). Thus, in light of both the positive value given to the time of the Old Covenant and the definitive nature of Christ's fulfillment, history can, from the covenantal point of view, be divided into three ages: the past age that anticipated the work of Christ; the present age of "drawing near" through the work of Christ; and the future age that will be initiated by final entrance into God's presence at the return of Christ. Failure to recognize these distinctions has often caused interpreters to assume that the Old Covenant had not yet passed away when interpreting Heb 8:13 or to pose an undue overlap between the two covenants in Heb 9:8-10.

3. The Pastor and the Influence of Neo-Platonism

It is well known that the apocalyptic writings combine belief in a heavenly world with the hope of a future age of salvation. Furthermore, belief in this heavenly world as the Most Holy Place of God's dwelling is rooted in the OT and the ancient Near East.[113] Yet many have argued that the apocalyptic worldview does not provide an adequate background for Hebrews' fusion of these two concepts. They usually concede that Hebrews received the idea of the present and future ages from apocalyptic or from apocalyptic influence mediated by the Christian tradition. Yet Hebrews has joined the spatial heavenly/earthly dualism of neo-Platonism with this temporal dualism. There is

---

112. See pp. 41-59, "The Sermon's Use of the Old Testament."

113. G. K. Beale, *The Temple and the Church's Mission: A Biblical Theology of the Dwelling Place of God* (New Studies in Biblical Theology 17; Downers Grove: InterVarsity Press, 2004), 31-50.

an absolute metaphysical distinction between the material world of perpetual change and the permanently changeless heavenly world of ideas. The first is a never-ending copy of the second.

It is the Hellenistic character of Hebrews and its affinities with the Alexandrian Jewish exegete and philosopher Philo (c. 20 B.C. to A.D. 50) that have suggested Hebrews' dependence on neo-Platonism.[114] This comparison with Philo was both natural and appropriate. Both Philo and Hebrews evidence a knowledge of sophisticated Greek and the principles of Hellenistic rhetoric. Both interpret Scripture for the contemporary situation. Both refer to a heavenly world. Both attest several textual variants not found in the standard LXX or in other writers.[115] Both draw on the literary vocabulary and figures of speech common to the educated of the time.[116] Furthermore, the two writers are roughly contemporary with one another. Advocacy for an affinity between the worldviews of Philo and Hebrews reached magisterial proportions in the masterful commentary of Spicq.[117] It has had its most devoted protagonist in the works of Thompson and thus has been given contemporary currency in his recent commentary.[118] Käsemann, Theissen, Grässer, Braun, and especially Eisele have attempted to buttress the influence of this spatial dualism on Hebrews by adding a broad selection of Gnostic and neo-Platonic sources to the standard comparison with Philo.[119]

114. Hurst, *Background,* 7, nn. 1-2, lists Grotius in 1646 as the first to suggest similarity between these two writers and E. Ménégoz, *Le théologie de l'épître aux Hébreux* (Paris, 1894) as the first to fully develop this comparison.

115. In the quotation from Gen 2:2, "And <u>God</u> rested <u>on</u> the seventh day" (καὶ κατέπαυσεν ὁ θεὸς ἐν τῇ ἡμέρᾳ τῇ ἑβδόμῃ), only Philo (*Posterity* 64) and Hebrews (4:4) attest the underlined words. Only in Philo, *Confusion* 166, and Heb 13:5 does one find the following quotation conflated from Josh 1:5 and Deut 31:8: "I will never leave you nor forsake you" (οὐ μή σε ἀνῶ οὐδ' οὐ μὴ σε ἐγκαταλίπω). The other commonalities suggested by K. L. Schenck, "Philo and the Epistle to the Hebrews: Ronald Williamson's Study after Thirty Years," *SPhilo* 14 (2002): 128, are less significant.

116. For instance, both use athletic and pedagogical language for moral development. Compare Heb 5:11-14; 12:1-3, 12-13 with *Agriculture* 9.160. See Schenck, "Philo and the Epistle to the Hebrews," 127. Cf. R. Williamson, *Philo and the Epistle to the Hebrews* (Arbeiten zur Literatur und Geschichte des hellenistischen Judentums 4; Leiden: Brill, 1970), 296.

117. Spicq, 1:39-166.

118. Thompson, 21-26. Cf. Johnson, 15-21.

119. For the most extensive collection of these sources with translation into German see Wilfried Eisele, *Ein unerschütterliches Reich: Die mittelplatonische Umformung des Parusiegedankens im Hebräerbrief* (BZNW 116; Berlin and New York: Walter de Gruyter, 2003), 135-368. There are, of course, significant differences between Philo and the speculations on "rest" found in the Gnostic literature of the second to fourth centuries. See Jon Laansma, *"I Will Give You Rest": The Rest Motif in the New Testament with Special Reference to Mt 11 and Heb 3–4* (WUNT 98; Tübingen: Siebeck, 1997), 154-58.

Opinions differ as to the degree of neo-Platonic influence. Barrett is representative of those who admit neo-Platonic elements but affirm the dominance of apocalyptic.[120] The advocates of neo-Platonism usually contend for a synthesis of the two but offer various proposals as to the nature of their combination. Older commentaries often postulate an awkward amalgamation.[121] Weiss thinks that Hebrews makes use of a Jewish Hellenistic synthesis of these elements to carry out his Christological agenda.[122] Some have explained the tension by distinguishing between the eschatologies of the pastor and of his audience.[123] Thompson admits little more than a vestigial residue of futuristic eschatology.[124] Eisele would exclude its presence altogether.[125] Many suggest that the pastor makes use of the heavenly world in order to counter his hearers' discouragement at the delay in Christ's return. This ap-

---

Hofius and Laansma have exposed the weakness of Käsemann's derivation of the supposed "wandering-people-of-God" motif (Heb 3:1–4:13) from Gnosticism. See E. Käsemann, *The Wandering People of God: An Investigation of the Letter to the Hebrews,* trans. R. A. Harrisville and I. L. Sundberg (Minneapolis: Augsburg, 1984), esp. 17-96; Hofius, *Katapausis, passim;* and Laansma, *Rest Motif, passim.* Yet Grässer, 1:209-11, 218-20; and Braun, 90-93, who retain sympathy for Käsemann's proposal, often loosely associate Philo, *Joseph and Aseneth,* and Gnostic sources. See also Gerd Theissen, *Untersuchungen zum Hebräerbrief* (Studien zum Neuen Testament 2; Gütersloh: Gerd Mohn, 1969), 124-26. There may be some justification for this association if all are taken simply as witness to the metaphysical dualism in question. In speaking thus, however, one must be wary of anachronism and of overgeneralization. Hebrews lacks many features characteristic of Gnostic literature such as the creation of the world by a demiurge, human beings' possessing a spark of the divine, and salvation by knowledge (Lincoln, *A Guide,* 47).

120. Barrett, "Eschatology," 363-93. Cf. Koester, 283; Schenck, "Philo and the Epistle to the Hebrews," 114, 119; and Mackie, *Eschatology and Exhortation,* 6.

121. Moffatt, liv, xxxiv; Scott, 102, 109-12, 120.

122. Weiss, 96-114, distinguishes between what he calls "(Jewish) apocalyptic eschatology" and "(Jewish) Hellenistic eschatology." The first is linear in that the future age of salvation follows the present evil age. The second is a Hellenistic Jewish modification of the first in which the contrast between a heavenly and an earthly world is combined with the contrast between the ages. Hebrews, then, uses various currents from this "Hellenistic eschatology" to demonstrate the present effectiveness of Christ.

123. See George W. MacRae, "Heavenly Temple and Eschatology in the Letter to the Hebrews," *Semeia* 12 (1978): 179-99; G. W. MacRae, "'A Kingdom That Cannot Be Shaken': The Heavenly Jerusalem in the Letter to the Hebrews," *Tantur Yearbook* (1979-80): 27-40; and G. E. Sterling, "Ontology versus Eschatology: Tensions between Author and Community in Hebrews," *SPhilo* 13 (2001): 190-211.

124. See, for instance, James W. Thompson, *The Beginnings of Christian Philosophy* (CBQMS 13; Washington, DC: The Catholic Biblical Association of America, 1982), 41-52. Cf. Lala Kalyan Kumar Dey, *The Intermediary World and Patterns of Perfection in Philo and Hebrews* (SBLDS 25; Missoula, MT: Scholars Press, 1975), 123.

125. Eisele, *Ein unerschütterliches Reich,* 64-133.

proach finds ultimate expression in Eisele, who argues that entrance into the heavenly realm of changeless "rest" at death has replaced entrance into final "salvation" at Christ's return (9:28).[126]

Because of their common heritage in the Hellenistic world Philo can be helpful in understanding Hebrews at the level of semantics and imagery. A brief glance, however, at Philo's worldview reveals the essential gulf between the two. Philo conceives of a noumenal world of ideas grasped by contemplation. The physical world is an eternal but changeable and ever-changing copy of the unchanging noumenal world of permanence and inactivity. Between the two stands the logos that is an image of God (*Alleg. Interp.* 3.96) and the pattern for the created world.[127] Salvation is the freeing of elect souls from the flesh in order that they might return to this noumenal world that was their home before they descended into the world of change. The individual soul achieves this salvation by meditation on the logos as revealed in the order of the created world. By such meditation the soul is able to rise above sense perception and passion to the contemplation of the Pure Being that is God (*Creation* 151–79; *Alleg. Interp.* 1.53-55, 88-89, 90-96).[128]

Thus Philo affirms the immortality of the soul, not the resurrection of the body (*Joseph* 264). He believes in the eternity of the ever-changing material world and fervently rejects the Stoic doctrine of its future conflagration (*Eternity* 75–76). The addition of other neo-Platonic sources may be impressive but adds little to the debate, for they reveal the same kind of dualism found in Philo. Further pursuit of this question, then, focuses on the text of Hebrews. References to the heavenly world or sanctuary and related issues in 6:19-20; 8:1-5; 9:1-14; 9:23-24; and 10:1 have been especially important. It has also been argued that the "rest" of 3:7–4:11 refers to a state of changeless repose entered in the heavenly world at death, and that 12:25-29 betrays the pastor's belief in a heavenly changeless and an earthly changeable world. Furthermore, Eisele goes to the ultimate extreme and would remove reference to Christ's return from Heb 9:27-28; 10:25; 10:36-39; and 12:25-29.[129]

Williamson, on the other hand, has shown that the disparity between the worldviews of Philo and Hebrews is accentuated by attention to detail. Even when Hebrews and Philo use similar terms to describe the heavenly world and related subjects, they invariably use these terms in different

126. Eisele, *Ein unerschütterliches Reich,* 64-133.

127. Schenck, "Philo and the Epistle to the Hebrews," 129.

128. See the concise summary of Philo's worldview in Montefiore, 6-7.

129. For his exegesis of the relevant passages see Eisele, *Ein unerschütterliches Reich,* 64-133. He admits the tenuousness of his own argument when he says, in regard to 9:27-28; 10:25, 36-39, that he had to establish his position from "sparse evidence and from cross references within the context" (Eisele, *Ein unerschütterliches Reich,* 124). Eisele follows the lead of Grässer, 2:88, 206-7.

ways.[130] Williamson's work has been supplemented and substantiated by Hurst.[131] Furthermore, Laansma has demonstrated conclusively that the "rest" in 3:7–4:11 refers to the ultimate destiny of God's people at Christ's return.[132] Edward Adams argues cogently that Hebrews affirms a concrete heavenly world entered by Christ and open to the people of God rather than a neo-Platonic world of ideas.[133] The exposition in the commentary below on the passages cited in the previous paragraph provides further evidence for the absence of significant neo-Platonic influence. It is important also to note the fundamental difference between Philo's allegorical interpretation of the OT in accord with Greek philosophy and Hebrews' Christological understanding.[134]

130. Williamson, *Philo and Hebrews, passim.* Even Mackie, who would leave room for neo-Platonic influence, speaks of the author operating "loosely" within "Middle Platonic cosmology." Mackie (quoting Barrett, *Eschatology,* 309) goes so far as to say that the author "redefines the structure and the very nature of the cosmos with his proclamation 'that what lies between heaven and earth, God and man, is not the difference between the phenomena of sense-perception and pure being, but the difference between holiness and sin'" (Mackie, *Eschatology and Exhortation,* 119-20). Finally, "the author's use of terms and concepts common to Middle Platonic cosmology is extremely limited" (Mackie, *Eschatology and Exhortation,* 120).

131. Hurst, *Background,* 7-42. Schenck, "Philo and the Epistle to the Hebrews," 112-35, presents no evidence that detracts from Williamson's main thesis.

132. The pastor does not even describe this "rest" as heavenly lest he divert his hearers' attention from the fact that it is *future* and from the resultant need for perseverance (Laansma, *Rest Motif,* 282-83). This is no cessation of activity but a joyous future "Sabbath celebration" (4:9) anticipated by the picture of such a celebration in 12:22-24 (Laansma, *Rest Motif,* 273, 281-83). Furthermore, the pastor's belief in the resurrection of the dead preempts entrance into final blessedness at death. See the comments below on 11:17-19, 35 and the more extended argument in Gareth L. Cockerill, "The Better Resurrection (Heb. 11:35): A Key to the Structure and Rhetorical Purpose of Hebrews 11," *TynBul* 51 (2000): 215-34.

133. Adams, "Cosmology," 122-39. There can be no question, in Adams's view, of 12:25-29 describing the created world as a changeable and ever-changing copy of an unchangeable heavenly world. Indeed, he believes that Hebrews anticipates the re-creation of the material world (Adams, "Cosmology," 136-38). Whether or not this is true, one can say that the "inhabited world" to come (2:5) promised as an inheritance to the faithful, the "heavenly Jerusalem" (Heb 12:22), is just as "concrete" as the Jerusalem that comes down from heaven in Rev 21:9-27.

134. These differences are well illustrated by the way both authors handle Melchizedek. See the exposition of 7:1-25 below and Gareth Lee Cockerill, "Melchizedek without Speculation: Hebrews 7:1-25 and Genesis 14:14-24," in *A Cloud of Witnesses: The Theology of Hebrews in Its Ancient Context,* ed. Richard Bauckham et al. (LNTS 387; T&T Clark, 2008), 128-44, esp. 134-36. Schenck's attempt to find traces of Philonic allegory in Heb 7:1-3 and 9:5 is unfounded (Schenck, "Philo and the Epistle to the Hebrews," 125). Furthermore, *pace* Schenck, "Philo and the Epistle to the Hebrews," 124, the fact

Finally, misplaced reliance on metaphysical dualism has led to serious misinterpretations that have no support within the context of Hebrews. For instance, Thompson and others assume that the identification of something as "better" because it is heavenly implies metaphysical dualism.[135] In fact, Hebrews does not speak this way as often as some would suggest. The sacrifice of Christ, as will be demonstrated below, does not take place in "heaven."[136] Rather, it brings access to heaven because it provides present purification for sin. This sacrifice is thus "better" (9:23-24) because it consists of the earthly, incarnate obedience of the eternal Son of God (see on 9:11-15; 10:5-10). The New Covenant is "better" (13:6) because it promises and provides forgiveness of sins and heart transformation (see on 10:15-18). The fact that Christ ministers in the "true Tent" (8:2) is evidence for, but not the cause of, his superior high priesthood.[137] Only the "home" sought by God's people can be said to be "better" because it is "heavenly" (11:16) — it is the eternal dwelling place of God.[138] The oft-repeated assumption that the Old Covenant and the Mosaic Tent were symbols of the transitory physical world has no basis whatsoever in the text itself.[139] Finally, the argument that the invitation to go "outside the camp" (13:13) is an exhortation to abandon the physical world for the heavenly runs roughshod over the immediate context. "Outside the camp" cannot be the heavenly world because it is the place where Christ suffered and thus the place of bearing "his reproach."[140]

Hebrews, then, gives every evidence of being a unique and profound development of the gospel tradition on the basis of careful OT interpretation. The pastor makes use of, but cannot be explained by, perspectives drawn

---

that Philo occasionally practices literal interpretation is without significance for his relationship to Hebrews. It was normal for many interpreters to practice such interpretation when it suited their purpose.

135. Note Thompson's statement: "The author not only contrasts the old with the new; he claims that the new is ontologically superior to the old because it belongs to the transcendent world" (23).

136. There is no support for Johnson's statement, 20, that "Jesus' priestly act is one that is 'once for all' because it takes place in the realm of 'true being,' namely heaven (9:26)." This assertion brings neo-Platonic assumptions to the text.

137. See the commentary below on 8:1-5.

138. The fact that heaven is superior because it is God's dwelling place has deep OT roots that are maintained in the literature of Second Temple Judaism and is thus no sign of neo-Platonism (*pace* Johnson, 19).

139. *Pace* Käsemann, *Wandering,* 58-60. Hebrews says that the Old Covenant and Tent could not provide access into the place of God's presence (9:1-10). It attributes the impotence of the Mosaic Tent to the fact that it was earthly and dependent on mortal humanity (7:11-19; 9:1-10). However, it never presents that Tent as representative of the earthly.

140. See the commentary on 13:13.

from the apocalyptic understanding of a present heavenly world that will be manifest as a future reality after judgment. He "is an independent and creative theologian who has set about interpreting the OT with his own agenda and in his own fashion."[141]

E. WHEN DID THE PASTOR WRITE THIS SERMON?

1 Clement's dependence on Hebrews confirms the first-century composition of this sermon.[142] *1 Clem.* 36:1-6's use of Heb 1:1-14 is especially clear.[143] The context of *1 Clem.* 36:1-6 provides no rationale for the association of Pss 2:7; 104:4; and 110:1 other than dependence on Hebrews.[144] This author reveals his indebtedness to Hebrews by the way in which he associates these quotations directly with Christ's high priesthood. *1 Clem.* 36:1-6 follows Hebrews by introducing these quotations as the direct speech of God. Though characteristic of Hebrews, this mode of introduction is otherwise absent from *1 Clement.* The mention of Timothy in Heb 13:23 is the most concrete internal evidence for the date of Hebrews, suggesting a time within the lifetime of Paul's younger associate.[145]

Attempts to date Hebrews more precisely usually involve suggestions

141. Laansma, *Rest Motif,* 356.

142. *1 Clement,* it should be noted, can no longer be dated with certainty to A.D. 96; it may have been written as early as the 70's or 80's (Andrew Gregory, "*I Clement:* An Introduction," *ExpTim* 117 [2006]: 227–28). It was known and still read in Corinth as a letter sent to that church from the church at Rome in the middle of the second century (Eusebius, *Hist. eccl.* 3.16; 4.22-23). See L. L. Welborn, "On the Date of First Clement," *BR* 29 (1984): 35-54 [repr. in *Encounters with Hellenism: Studies in the First Letter of Clement,* ed. C. Breytenbach and L. L. Welborn [Arbeiten zur Geschichte des antiken Judentums und des Urchristentums; Leiden: Brill, 2004], 197-216); T. J. Herron, "The Most Probable Date of the First Epistle of Clement to the Corinthians," *Studia patristica* 21 (1989): 106-21; and Andrew Gregory, "Disturbing Trajectories: *I Clement,* the *Shepherd of Hermas* and the Development of Early Roman Christianity," in *Rome, the Bible, and the Early Church,* ed. P. Oakes (Carlisle: Paternoster, 2002), 142-66.

143. Compare *1 Clem.* 9:3 with Heb 11:5; *1 Clem.* 10:7 with Heb 11:17; *1 Clem.* 17:1 with Heb 11:37; *1 Clem.* 21:1 with Heb 12:1; and *1 Clem.* 27:2 with Heb 6:18. For a thorough discussion of *1 Clement*'s use of Hebrews see Donald Alfred Hagner, *The Use of the Old and New Testaments in Clement of Rome* (Supplements to *Novum Testamentum* 34; Leiden: E. J. Brill, 1973), 179-95.

144. For more detailed argumentation see Gareth Lee Cockerill, "Heb 1:1-14, *1 Clem.* 36:1-6, and the High Priest Title," *JBL* 97 (1978): 437-40. See also P. Ellingworth, "Hebrews and *1 Clement:* Literary Dependence or Common Tradition?" *BZ* 23 (1979): 262-69.

145. For the account of Paul selecting Timothy as his assistant see Acts 16:1-3 (ca. A.D. 49).

concerning its specific purpose, literary genre, recipients, and the circumstances of its composition. Thus this section on dating forms an appropriate conclusion to the previous considerations of authorship, genre, recipients, and religious background. Such proposals have been legion and have appeared to engender almost as much confusion as the biblical demoniac by that name (Mark 5:1-20). At the risk of oversimplification, I offer the following paragraphs to provide perspective by grouping proposals into three broad categories. First, there are those who argue that Hebrews was written to a Gentile audience late in the first century with little or no concern for the destruction of Jerusalem. Second, some recognize Hebrews' affinity with Judaism but date its composition shortly after Jerusalem's fall in A.D. 70. A third group contends for the traditional position that Hebrews was written to a largely Jewish-Christian audience before the fall of Jerusalem.

The first group argues that Hebrews was written later in the first century to an audience unconcerned with the Jewish/Gentile distinction. In their varied opinions, these authors suggest that the recipients of Hebrews were discouraged by societal pressure, held an insufficient view of Christ, and/or were disillusioned by the delay of Christ's return.[146] Some have even suggested that Hebrews was a treatise written as a general appeal to the second/third-generation church.[147] The interpreters in this group usually emphasize Hebrews' dependence on the neo-Platonic dualism exemplified by Philo or even on the more radical dualism of Gnosticism.[148] Moffatt is typical when he says that Hebrews identifies the Old Covenant with the phenomenal world of change and the New with the transcendent eternal world.[149] The true situation of the hearers is found in the pastor's warnings and other exhortations. Hebrews' exposition of the OT is just that — Scriptural exposition without any anti-Jewish apologetic purpose.[150] More recent advocates of this position are likely to explain Hebrews' comparison between Christ and representatives of the old order by reference to Hellenistic rhetoric: ancient orators compared the person being praised to heroes of old not to denigrate the old

---

146. Käsemann, *Wandering,* 24-25; Moffatt, xxiv, xxvi; Braun, 2; and Weiss, 72-73, are representative statements of this position.

147. See Grässer, 3:30, 57-59. Pamela M. Eisenbaum, "Locating Hebrews within the Literary Landscape of Christian Origins," in *Hebrews: Contemporary Methods — New Insights,* ed. Gabriella Gelardini (Biblical Interpretation Series 75; Atlanta: Society of Biblical Literature, 2005), 229-32. This approach minimizes the personal references in Hebrews and casts doubt on the integrity of 13:22-25. For refutation see Mackie, *Eschatology and Exhortation,* 9-11; Weiss, 72-74; and the comments on 13:22-25 below.

148. For the latter see Windisch, 131-33, *passim;* Braun, 1, *passim.*

149. Moffatt, xxxi-xxxiv. Cf. Käsemann, *Wandering,* 59, who claims that the Jewish cult is "a specific representation of what is earthly."

150. Weiss, 58-60.

but to extol the person described and to promote the values that person exemplified.[151]

Both groups two and three date Hebrews in relation to the destruction of the Jerusalem Temple. For various reasons those in group two propose a date shortly after the Temple's destruction. Kistemaker argues that it would have been dangerous to contend for the insufficiency of the old order before the Temple's demise.[152] Mitchell suggests that such an argument would have been inconceivable while the Temple stood.[153] Some scholars think Hebrews was written to deal with the shock of the Temple's destruction.[154] Those who propose a date shortly after the Temple's ruin are freer to suggest that the congregation addressed was composed of Gentiles as well as Jews or perhaps of Gentiles with Jewish connections.[155]

Those, however, who argue for a predestruction date often contend that the recipients were Jewish Christians who failed adequately to separate themselves from, or were tempted to return to, the synagogue. The recipients may have feared the rejection of their fellow Jews or mistreatment by society at large once the protection of the synagogue was removed. They may have felt a spiritual need for the rituals of the synagogue or been confused by a teaching that denied the sufficiency of Christ apart from these rituals.[156] Many who affirm an early date emphasize the influence of the futuristic eschatology characteristic of apocalyptic writings rather than the spatial dualism of neo-Platonism.[157] An early date fits well with the identification of He-

151. Thompson, 36, 41; cf. Aristotle, *Rhet.* 1.9.39.

152. Kistemaker, 15-16, however, belongs with group three in his belief that the recipients were attracted to Judaism.

153. Mitchell, 26-27, appears to fear admission of a predestruction date lest he be forced to concede an "anti-Jewish" element within Hebrews' argument.

154. Marie E. Isaacs, *Sacred Space: An Approach to the Theology of the Epistle to the Hebrews,* ed. Stanley E. Porter (JSNTSup 73; Sheffield: JSOT Press, 1992), 223; Ellen Bradshaw Aitken, "Portraying the Temple in Stone and Text: The Arch of Titus and the Epistle to the Hebrews," in *Hebrews: Contemporary Methods — New Insights,* ed. Gabriella Gelardini (Biblical Interpretation Series 75; Atlanta: Society of Biblical Literature, 2005), 131-48; and Gelardini, *"Tisha be-Av,"* 107-27. It is doubtful whether Hebrews was written to address the shock of the Temple's fall felt by a *Gentile* house church in Rome (*pace* Mitchell, 26-27; cf. Koester, 53).

155. Thus deSilva, 1-32, argues for a mixed Jewish-Gentile house church in Rome shortly after Jerusalem's fall. Like those who locate Hebrews later in the first century, he thinks the problem faced by the recipients is societal pressure and fatigue rather than attraction to Judaism. Yet he would not affirm the dominance of neo-Platonic dualism as many of them do.

156. Bruce 3-21; Ellingworth 21-33; Hagner, 1-8; Hughes, 10-32; Bénétreau, 1:21-23; Lane, 1:li-lxvi; George H. Guthrie, 19-23; O'Brien, 9-20; and many others.

157. Spicq's magisterial commentary, on the other hand, was the premier defense

brews as a synagogue homily. While the exhortations are important, the OT exposition itself should not be neglected when determining the situation of those addressed.

The discussion of authorship above has already mentioned some who suggest that Apollos wrote Hebrews to either Corinth or Ephesus before the fall of Jerusalem. Most of the other suggestions for a predestruction date and a Jewish-Christian audience can be further divided into two categories. Some identify the recipients as a house church that was part of the larger Christian community in Rome.[158] Others locate the recipients in Palestine, perhaps in Jerusalem.[159] The early ascription of the title "To the Hebrews" and the subscriptions at the end of chapter 13 in various manuscripts suggest that early copyists affirmed a Palestinian destination.[160] The pastor would have his

---

of Hebrews' close relationship to Philo. Yet he advocated a predestruction date and located Hebrews' recipients in Jerusalem. While not denying the influence of neo-Platonism, he saw Hebrews' association with Philo as evidence that it was directed to Jewish Hellenists like those associated with Stephen (Acts 6–7). See Spicq, 1:4-6, 221-31, 243-44, 254-57. He thought these Jewish Hellenists had been priests and were longing to return to their former role. Later he altered his position, affirming that they were of Essene background (Ceslas Spicq, "L'Épître aux Hébreux: Apollos, Jean-Baptiste, les Hellénistes et Qumran," *RevQ* 1 [1958-59]: 365-90). Johnson, 17-21, 41, also argues for an early date (A.D. 45-70), but for the influence of Philo.

158. Bruce, xxiii-xxxv, 14, 267-69; Lane, 1:liii-lx; Ellingworth, 23-33; Koester, 49-50; O'Brien, 14-15; George Guthrie, 9-23; and Pfitzner, 31-32. Some who affirm a postdestruction date and a mixed or Gentile audience also favor a house church at Rome (deSilva, 2; Weiss, 76; cf. Attridge, 11). In addition, several listed above in favor of a date soon after Jerusalem's destruction favor this position (Aitken, "Portraying the Temple"; Mitchell; Kistemaker).

159. Delitzsch, 1:4, 20-21; 2:46, 140, 332, 414; Westcott, lxii-lxxix; Hughes, 19; Buchanan, 255-56; Spicq, 1:220-52. For a list of earlier interpreters who held this position see Spicq, 1:234, n. 4. See also the various articles by Randall C. Gleason ("The Old Testament Background of the Warning in Hebrews 6:4-8," *BSac* 155 [1998]: 2-91; "The Old Testament Background of Rest in Hebrews 3:7–4:11," *BSac* 157 [2000]: 281-303; and "The Eschatology of the Warning in Hebrews 10:26-31," *TynBul* 53 [2002]: 97-120]. Carl Mosser, "Rahab outside the Camp," in *The Epistle to the Hebrews and Christian Theology*, ed. Richard Bauckham et al. (Grand Rapids: Eerdmans, 2009), 383-404; and Peter Walker, "Jerusalem in Hebrews 13:9-14 and the Dating of the Epistle," *TynBul* 45 (1994): 39-71, argue that the call to go "outside the camp" in Heb 13:13 was a call to leave Jerusalem. See the commentary on that verse.

160. These subscriptions read, "to the Hebrews" (ℵ, C, I, Ψ 33); "to the Hebrews written from Rome (Italy)" (A, P); "to the Hebrews written from Italy through Timothy" (1739, 1881, many others); "to the Hebrews written from Rome by Paul to those in Jerusalem" (81); "to the Hebrews written in Hebrew from Italy anonymously through Timothy" (104); "an epistle of Paul to the Hebrews written from Italy through Timothy" (0285). Jerome, *Vir. ill.* 5, and Chrysostom, *Hom. Heb.* 2, argued for a Jerusalem destination due to Hebrews' interest in the Jewish sacrificial system.

hearers make a clear break with the synagogue so that they would not suffer the judgment that was going to come upon Jerusalem when it was destroyed. The recipients, however, were fearful of the reaction of their Jewish co-religionists. Those who hold this view often identify the earlier persecution suffered by the recipients with the persecutions in Acts (cf. Acts 8:1-3) and the impending persecution with events surrounding Jerusalem's destruction.

Those who believe Hebrews was written to a house church at Rome often begin with the fact that it was first quoted by *1 Clement* in Rome. They note that the pastor sends the greetings of "those from Italy" (13:24). This statement, they contend, makes best sense if the pastor is referring to expatriate Italians who send greetings to their homeland. They note that the word Hebrews uses for "leaders" was frequently employed at Rome.[161] They point to various features of Hebrews mentioned above that suggest it was written to a smaller group within the larger fellowship.[162] The attraction of the synagogue was causing members to withdraw from the larger fellowship of Christians in the city. The expulsion of the Jews from Rome under Claudius (A.D. 49) may have been the persecution they had endured; the one coming under Nero (A.D. 64-68) fulfilled the pastor's concern about future suffering.[163]

The arguments for a late first-century date, though varied, are subjective and unconvincing. These arguments usually focus on the "second-generation" character of the recipients; the institutional nature of the church in Hebrews; the supposed dependence of Hebrews on other NT documents; the sophistication of Hebrews' theology; concern with the delay of Christ's return; and Hebrews' affinity with other supposed late documents such as 2 Peter and *1 Clement*.[164] However, the fact that the recipients had received the gospel "from those who heard" (2:3) and had been followers of Jesus for some time (5:11-14) neither requires nor suggests a late first-century date. Hebrews is clearly free of that concern with structure, church office, and tradition supposedly characteristic of the late first century.[165] There is less

---

161. ἡγούμενοι ("leaders") in Heb 13:7, 17, 24. Cf. *1 Clem.* 21:6; Hermas, *Vis.* 2.2.6; 3.9.7.

162. Lane, 1:lix-lx; O'Brien, 15. Rom 16:2-5, 14, and 15 suggest the existence of house churches at Rome by A.D. 60.

163. For the expulsion of the Jews in A.D. 49 see Suetonius, *Claud.* 25.4.

164. Eisenbaum, "Locating Hebrews," 232-37, argues that, like 2 Peter and *1 Clement*, Hebrews lacks the seeming anti-Jewish polemic characteristic of both the earlier NT books and works from the mid-second century such as *Barnabas* and the writings of Justin and Tertullian. She suggests that this indicates a late first- or early second-century time when there was a strong sense of commonality between Jews and Christians in face of the common enemy, Rome.

165. It is significant that Weiss, 57, 95, admits this fact since he persists in dating Hebrews late.

"moralistic" exhortation than in many of the Pauline letters. There is no clear evidence of Hebrews' dependence on the synoptic Gospels or other NT literature.[166] To argue that it must have taken some time for the development of Hebrews' sophisticated theology is merely to beg the question.[167] Concern with the delay of Christ's return, if present, need not indicate such a late date. Hebrews' theological sophistication distinguishes it from both 2 Peter and *1 Clement* as well as from Christian literature of the early second century.

On the other hand, three arguments are often proffered for a pre–A.D. 70 date: the pastor's use of the present tense when describing the sacrificial ritual, his failure to mention the destruction of Jerusalem, and his insistence on the demise of the old order.[168] The third of these is the strongest. As to the first, it is true that the pastor's arguments in Heb 8:4 and 10:2 may have been more forceful if the sacrificial ritual were still being conducted in Jerusalem.[169] Yet Josephus, Clement of Rome, and others use the present tense to describe the sacrificial ritual long after the destruction of the Temple.[170] Montefiore is one of the most enthusiastic advocates of the Temple's destruction as determinative for the dating of Hebrews: "The best argument for the supersession of the old covenant would have been the destruction of the Temple."[171] Thus the assumption is that, since the author does not use this approach, the Temple must still be standing.[172]

The pastor's use of Scripture, however, makes it unlikely that he would have used the Temple's destruction as evidence for the demise of the old order. More is involved than the oft-mentioned fact that the pastor bases his exegesis on the descriptions of the priestly ritual and the wilderness Tent in the Pentateuch. As Eisenbaum has pointed out, he studiously avoids reference to Israel's life in the Promised Land, and to the institutions that charac-

166. *Pace* Eisenbaum, "Locating Hebrews," 228-29, there is no reason to suppose dependence on the synoptic tradition of the torn curtain (Mark 15:38; Matt 27:51; Luke 23:44). Mitchell's suggestion that Hebrews develops theological motifs from Mark is interesting but tenuous (Mitchell, 10-11).

167. O'Brien, 19, for instance, compares Hebrews' Christology with the Christology of Paul in 1 Cor 8:6 and with the pre-Pauline tradition evident from Phil 2:6-11 and Col 1:15-20.

168. Note the use of the present tense in 7:28; 8:3; 9:7; 9:25; 13:11.

169. Gordon, 32-33; Bruce, 32; O'Brien, 19; Johnson, 39.

170. *1 Clem.* 40-41; Josephus. *Ant.* 4.6.1-8 (102-50); 4:7.1-7 (51-87). Josephus uses the past tense in *Ant.* 4.9.1-7 (224-57). See Attridge, 8, n. 58; Kistemaker, "The Authorship of Hebrews," 63, n. 27; and Koester, 53.

171. Montefiore, 3. Cf. Bénétreau, 1:21.

172. Moffatt, xxii, is typical of late-date advocates who explain this omission by arguing for the Gentile nature of the recipients and by distancing them both temporally and geographically from this event.

terized that life.[173] The pastor pictures the situation of his hearers as analogous to God's people of old who had *not yet* entered the Promised Land (3:7–4:11; 11:1-31).[174] Furthermore, even they were seeking the heavenly "City" rather than an earthly country (11:8-16).[175] Thus, the *irrelevance* of the earthly Temple's destruction to the author's argument eliminates the pastor's failure to mention this event as a means of dating this sermon.[176] It also makes it unlikely that he was writing to warn believers of the Temple's demise.

According to Hebrews, Christ's coming in accord with prophecy has demonstrated what was already implicit in the Pentateuchal text: first, the Old Covenant with its sacrificial system was never adequate as a means of approaching God; second, that same covenant has always been and continues to be valid as a type or anticipation of Christ.[177] The pastor's contention, therefore, that the old must now be "abolished" (7:18; cf. 10:18) does not mean that the old has *become,* or merely that the old has now been *revealed* to be, insufficient. It cannot mean that the old has ceased to be a divinely revealed type of Christ. It must mean that the old must no longer be *practiced* (13:10-13). To practice the old before Christ was to anticipate his fulfillment; to practice it after, however, is to deny his sufficiency.

This concern, then, that the people of God abstain from the practices of the old order fits well with, though it need not require, a time before the Temple's demise. Hebrews appears to fit the description often attributed to it by those who contend for a pre–A.D. 70 date and a Roman destination. It is best understood as a Christian adaptation of a synagogue homily or sermon dedicated to moving its hearers through exposition and application of OT Scripture. It is likely that the pastor's hearers experienced some attraction for

173. Eisenbaum, *Jewish Heroes,* 140-42, 170-75, *passim.*

174. See J. Dunnill, *Covenant and Sacrifice in the Letter to the Hebrews* (SNTSMS 75; Cambridge: Cambridge University Press, 1992), 141-43, who argues that Hebrews pictures its recipients as parallel to Israel in Deuteronomy on the verge of crossing into Canaan.

175. Braun, 109; Ellingworth, 68-69; Hofius, *Katapausis,* 178, n. 337; Laansma, *Rest Motif,* 275. Since the pastor shows virtually no interest in the earthly Promised Land (Grässer, 1:209; Weiss, 281; Ellingworth, 235, 254; Hofius, *Katapausis,* 56), one can hardly say that he saw it as a "partial" but not the "true fulfillment" of the promise (*pace* Rissi, *Theologie,* 18; Westcott, 100; Bruce, 105, 109). At best one might say, on the basis of Heb 4:1-11, that he saw it as a "type" of that "true fulfillment." See "The Sermon's Use of the Old Testament," pp. 41-59 below.

176. Thus *pace* Steve Motyer, "The Temple in Hebrews: Is It There?" in *Heaven on Earth,* ed. T. Desmond Alexander and Simon Gathercole (Carlisle, Cumbria, UK; Waynesboro, GA: Paternoster, 2004), 177-89, it is unlikely that references to the Mosaic Tent were intended as veiled references to the Temple.

177. See "The Sermon's Use of the Old Testament," pp. 41-59 below.

the synagogue and/or for Jewish religious practices. Hebrews makes excellence sense when read in terms of the heavenly world/futurist eschatology of Jewish apocalyptic. Both its early citation by *1 Clement* and mention of "those from Italy" (13:24) are in accord with a Roman destination. The evidence is insufficient, however, to narrow the time of Hebrews' composition with certainty beyond a range of A.D. 50 to 90.[178]

Indeed, some of the evidence cited by those who hold a late first-century date has important implications for the interpreter. Concern with attraction to the synagogue or with lingering Jewish practices, while present, is not alone sufficient to account for Hebrews. The pastor has a broader agenda related to the unique sufficiency of Christ, spiritual maturity, and faithful endurance in the face of rejection and persecution. Furthermore, the pastor's exposition of the OT is more than apologetic against an interpretation that denied fulfillment in Christ. It is, in itself, a demonstration of the OT's relevance for followers of Christ and a defense of his uniqueness as the only sufficient Savior.

II. THE MESSAGE OF HEBREWS

A. THE SERMON'S USE OF THE OLD TESTAMENT

1. Introduction

The OT is the "bone and marrow" of Hebrews.[179] From beginning to end this book is an expository "sermon" that rests on careful OT interpretation.[180] The pastor quotes the OT, alludes to the OT, summarizes OT passages, recounts events from the lives of OT persons, and often echoes the idiom of the Greek OT.[181] For the sake of clarity, this commentary normally reserves the word

---

178. Cf. Koester, 50; Attridge, 6-8.

179. George H. Guthrie, "'Hebrews' Use of the Old Testament: Recent Trends in Research," *CurBS* 1 (2003): 272.

180. R. T. France, "The Writer of Hebrews as a Biblical Expositor," *TynBul* 47 (1996): 246.

181. The rhetorical style of Hebrews and the quality of the pastor's Greek suggest that the recipients as well as the author were most at home in the Greek language. Thus it was only natural for the pastor to use the Greek text of the OT accepted by his hearers. See Guthrie, "Hebrews' Use of the Old Testament," 275; R. Gheorghita, *The Role of the Septuagint in Hebrews* (WUNT 2/160; Tübingen: Siebeck, 2003), 2. For a visual summary of the quotations, allusions, etc. in Hebrews, see the helpful chart in George H. Guthrie, "Old Testament in Hebrews," in *DLNTD* (1997): 846-49. In this chart Guthrie omits the quota-

"quotation" for places where the pastor uses an introductory formula and closely follows the wording of the OT text.[182] He quotes the following twenty-eight OT passages, listed here in canonical order:[183] Gen 2:2 (Heb 4:4); 21:12 (Heb 11:18); 22:16-17 (Heb 6:14); Exod 24:8 (Heb 9:20); 25:40 (Heb 8:5); Deut 9:19 (Heb 12:21); 31:6 (Heb 13:5); 32:35 (Heb 10:30a); 32:36 (Heb 10:30b); 32:43 (Heb 6:1); 2 Sam 7:14 (Heb 1:5a); Ps 2:7 (Heb 1:5b; 5:5); 8:4-6 (Heb 2:5-10); 22:22 (Heb 2:12); 40:6-8 (Heb 10:5-10); 45:6-7 (Heb 1:8-9); 95:7-11 (Heb 3:7-11); 102:25-27 (Heb 1:10-12); 104:4 (Heb 1:7); 110:1 (Heb 1:13); 110:4 (Heb 5:6; 7:17, 21); Ps 118:6 (Heb 13:6); Prov 3:11-12 (Heb 12:5-6); Isa 8:17 (Heb 2:13a); Isa 8:18 (Heb 2:13b); Jer 31:31-34 (Heb 8:7-13; 10:15-18); Hab 2:3-4 (Heb 10:37-38); Hag 2:6 (Heb 12:26).[184] The pastor quotes twenty-five of these passages once, two of them (Ps 2:7; Jer 31:31-34) twice, and one (Ps 110:4) three times, making a total of thirty-two OT quotations.[185] The pastor's OT quotations contribute to the rhe-

---

tion of Ps 110:4 in Heb 7:17, but appears to rectify this oversight in George H. Guthrie, "Hebrews," in *Commentary on the New Testament Use of the Old Testament,* ed. G. K. Beale and D. A. Carson (Grand Rapids: Baker Academic, 2007), 968.

182. Guthrie, "Hebrews' Use of the Old Testament," 273.

183. The LXX differs from the Hebrew/English OT in the chapter-verse numbering attributed to many of the passages quoted by Hebrews: Ps 8:4-6 = 8:5-7(LXX); Ps 22:22 = 21:23(LXX); Ps 40:6-8 = 39:7-9 (LXX); Ps 45:6-7 = 44:6-7(LXX); Ps 95:7-11 = 94:7-11(LXX); Ps 97:7 = 96:7(LXX); Ps 102:25-27 = 101:26-28(LXX); Ps 104:4 = 103:4(LXX); Ps 110:1, 4 = 109:1, 4(LXX); Ps 118:6 = 117:6(LXX); and Jer 31:31-34 = 38:31-34(LXX).

184. This reckoning takes Isa 8:17 and 8:18 in Heb 2:13 as two different quotations. It does the same with Deut 32:35 and 36 in Heb 10:30. It also includes Hab 2:3-4 (Heb 10:37-38), although this quotation has no introductory formula because the pastor clearly implies that God is the speaker of these words. On the other hand, this list excludes Gen 14:17-20 (Heb 7:1-10); Ps 97:7 (Heb 1:6); and Isa 26:20-21 (Heb 10:37-38). The first of these has no introductory formula; the second is a quotation of Deut 32:43 rather than Ps 97:7; and the third is insufficiently clear. Guthrie's chart, mentioned above, also lists five quotations from Ps 95:7-11 or some part thereof (Heb 3:7-11; 3:13, 3:15; 4:3-5; 4:7) and two from Ps 40:6-8 (Heb 10:5-7; 10:8-9). It is difficult to determine just how many times the pastor quotes from these two psalms because of the way he comments on them in midrashic fashion immediately after their initial quotation. Why, for instance, does Guthrie list Heb 4:3, 5 as one quotation from Ps 95:11 and not two? The same question could be asked about Ps 40:6-8 in Heb 10:8-9. One gets a truer picture by omitting the recitations from Pss 40:6-8 and 95:7-11 in the interpretations that follow the full quotation of each.

185. While all agree on the principal quotations used by Hebrews, it can be difficult to distinguish between quotations, allusions, and other references to the OT. Thus it is not surprising that various interpreters differ in their count. For instance, L. T. Johnson, "The Scriptural World of Hebrews," *Int* 57 (2003): 239, finds forty-one quotations; R. N. Longenecker, *Biblical Exegesis in the Apostolic Period* (Grand Rapids: Eerdmans, 1975),

torical structure of this sermon.[186] They form the basis for his teaching on Christ and salvation.[187] They undergird his warnings.[188] In accord with the NT pattern, Hebrews may allude to or echo other literature but quotes only from the canonical books of the Hebrew OT.[189]

2. Fundamental Assumptions

The pastor's authority rests on the gospel message (2:1-4) that he holds in common with his hearers and on the persuasive quality of his exegesis.[190] Heb 1:1-4 enunciates the fundamental principles that underlie his interpretation of the OT. First, the God who "spoke" through the OT has now "spoken" in one who is Son.[191] The inclusion of the OT under the rubric of "the prophets" (1:1)

164, thirty-eight; Spicq, 1:331, thirty-six; Michel, 151, thirty-two; Caird, "Exegetical Method," forty-seven, and Westcott, 472, twenty-nine. The difficulty here is illustrated by Guthrie, who on one occasion lists thirty-six quotations, thirty-five allusions, eighteen instances where OT material is summarized, and fourteen where an OT name or topic is mentioned without specific OT context (Guthrie, "Old Testament in Hebrews," 843); but on another occasion lists thirty-five, thirty-four, nineteen, and thirteen, respectively (Guthrie, "Hebrews' Use of the Old Testament," 274); and on yet another occasion thirty-seven, forty, nineteen, and thirteen (Guthrie, "Hebrews," in *Commentary on the New Testament Use of the Old*, 919).

186. See Caird, "Exegetical Method," 44-51; Longenecker, *Biblical Exegesis*, 175-85; R. T. France, "The Writer of Hebrews as a Biblical Expositor," *TynBul* 47 (1996): 245-76; J. R. Walters, "The Rhetorical Arrangement of Hebrews," *Asbury Theological Journal* 51 (1996): 59-70; and the discussion of Hebrews' structure below.

187. See on 2 Sam 7:14; Pss 2:7; 45:6-7; 102:25-27; 104:4; 110:1 in Heb 1:5-14; Pss 8:4-6; 22:22; and Isa 8:17-18 in Heb 2:5-18; Ps 110:4 in Heb 7:1-28; Ps 40:6-8 in Heb 10:5-10; and Jer 31:31-34 in Heb 8:7-13; 10:15-18.

188. See Deut 32:35-36 in Heb 10:30; Ps 95:7-11 in 3:7–4:11; Prov 3:11-12 in Heb 12:4-11; Hab 2:3-4 in 10:36-38; Hag 2:6 in 12:25-29.

189. *Pace* Gelardini, *"Tisha be-Av,"* 117, use of the Greek Bible does not indicate acceptance of noncanonical books.

190. Stephen Motyer, "The Psalm Quotations of Hebrews 1: A Hermeneutic-Free Zone?" *TynBul* 50 (1999): 8. "The author *reports* the words of Scripture as the evidence supporting his contention that Christ is far greater than the angels. The style of the argument is not revelatory, but argumentative, appealing to evidence and reason" (Motyer, "Psalm Quotations," 5, italics original).

191. Graham Hughes, *Hebrews and Hermeneutics*, 5-31. This declaration distinguishes what God has spoken in his Son from his previous speaking. Therefore, *pace* Ellingworth, 41-42, 351; A. T. Hanson, *Jesus Christ in the Old Testament* (London, 1965); Barnabas Lindars, *New Testament Apologetic: The Doctrinal Significance of the Old Testament Quotations* (London: SCM, 1961), 210-13, and others (see Erich Grässer, "Der Hebräerbrief 1938-1963," *Theologische Rundschau*, Neue Folge 30 [1964]: 207), the preexistence of the Son is not the key to the pastor's use of the OT. The OT quotations that God addresses to the Son (e.g., Pss 2:7; 110:1, 4) or the Son to God (Pss 22:22; 40:6-8; Isa

indicates that it anticipated God's ultimate self-revelation. Thus this final word in the Son is both continuous with, and the fulfillment of, all that God said before the Son assumed humanity. Second, to the continuity of the divine Speaker one must add the continuity of the human recipients. Those to whom God spoke through the prophets were the "fathers" of those he addresses in his Son (1:1-2). God's people have always consisted of those who hear, embrace, and persevere in the word of God.[192] Both those who live before and after Christ have received the same call, the same promise, the same "gospel," and are on pilgrimage to the same heavenly "city," which all the faithful will obtain through Christ.[193] There is one God and one people of God.

This firm confidence in the continuity of the divine speaker and of the human addressees underlies the pastor's sense of the immediacy of God's word. Thus it is no surprise that he prefers OT passages that are in the form of direct address and that he introduces them with verbs denoting speech rather than with "it is written."[194] What God has said in the past is of more than anti-

---

8:17-18) pertain to the Son's incarnation, suffering, and exaltation, not to the time of his preexistence. See Motyer, "Psalm Quotations," 7-10 and Guthrie, "Hebrews' Use of the Old Testament," 286. On the other hand, the fact that the Son becomes incarnate (2:5-18; 10:5-10) presupposes his preexistence.

192. "The community does not precede the divine speech. . . . God's speech is that which calls and constitutes the community" (John Webster, "One Who Is Son: Theological Reflections on the Exordium to the Epistle to the Hebrews," in *The Epistle to the Hebrews and Christian Theology,* ed. Richard Bauckham et al. [Grand Rapids: Eerdmans, 2009], 77-78).

193. Graham Hughes, *Hebrews and Hermeneutics,* 43, mentions all of these continuities save the last. The fact that all will attain the ultimate goal only through the Son (11:39-40) clenches the identity of those both before and after Christ as the one people of God. According to Heb 2:5-18, Christ assumed the humanity of God's already existing people in order to bring them to this goal. See the commentary on 3:1-6 and 11:1-40. Cf. Webster, "One Who Is Son," 76: "the relation of Israel and the church is not a matter of the history of religion but of the history of revelation." Yet to speak of "Israel" and "the church" as separate is to go outside the pastor's frame of reference.

194. "With God as the understood subject, Hebrews introduces citations with expressions such as 'He said' (1:5), 'He says' (1:6; 2:12; 8:8; 10:15), 'by saying' (3:15), 'He has said' (4:3), 'the one who said' (5:5), 'He has promised' (12:26), and 'He swore by saying' (6:13-14)" (Johnson, "The Scriptural World of Hebrews," 240). The Son answers God's declarations to him by "saying" Ps 22:22; Isa 8:17-18; and Ps 40:6-8 (Heb 2:12-13; 10:5-7) (Harold W. Attridge, "God in Hebrews," in *The Epistle to the Hebrews and Christian Theology,* ed. Richard Bauckham et al. [Grand Rapids: Eerdmans, 2009], 104-6). Hebrews introduces Ps 95:7-11 with "the Holy Spirit says" (3:7). See the commentary on "the Holy Spirit testifies to us" in 10:15. The indefinite introduction of Ps 8:4-6 in Heb 2:5-10 ("one has testified, saying") keeps the focus on God (Guthrie, "Hebrews' Use of the Old Testament," 274-75). Cf. "it is testified concerning him" (7:17). Γέγραπται ("it has been written," Heb 10:7) is part of the quotation.

quarian interest. God "speaks" to his people in the present both by the words
that he spoke to his people of old (Heb 3:7–4:11; 10:36-39) and by his conversations with his Son concerning the Son's incarnation and exaltation (1:1-
14; 2:11-13; 7:1-28; 10:5-10). God's final revelation embraces more than
what the Son has said. God's final revelation is found in the fully adequate
Savior he has become through his incarnation, obedience, self-offering, and
session.[195] The work of the Son enables God's people to grasp his previous
revelation more clearly and obey it more diligently.

3. The Psalms and Related Passages — "God Has Spoken"

If one would understand the pastor's approach to the OT one must observe
the selection and source of his quotations and how he uses different types of
biblical materials.[196] As noted, the OT is the speech of God that anticipates
his final revelation in the Son. Even words originally spoken by another to,
about, or on behalf of God have become divine speech by being included in
Scripture.[197] Thus the pastor's most significant quotations come from the
psalms, prophets, and passages like the Song of Moses in Deut 32:1-43, since
these parts of the OT are conversational in nature.[198] There are, however, two
deeper reasons for this selection. First, in these passages God announces the
future coming of the ultimate High Priest and promises the New Covenant.
Second, God's OT words of warning take on even deeper significance in light
of the fulfillment that has come in God's Son.

First, the Divine Proclamation and the Promise of a New Order.
God's proclamations to his Messiah/Son in Ps 2:7; 2 Sam 7:14; Ps 45:6-8; Ps
102:25-27; and Ps 110:1 (Heb 1:5, 8-14) reach their climax in Ps 110:4 (Heb
5:5-6; 7:1-25).[199] God himself attests the sufficiency of his high priesthood
by affirming his divine sonship (2 Sam 7:14; Ps 2:7) and sovereign deity (Pss

195. Webster, "One Who Is Son," 77, quotes Michel, 95, "His coming to earth and
his exaltation, his word and his way are *God's speaking* to us" (italics original).

196. This section has been divided according to the different parts of the OT
canon for convenience. It is, however, the typical content of the various sections and the
type of material they contain more than a rigid division of the canonical books. Thus Deut
32:43 and 2 Sam 7:14 come under this section though they are found in the Pentateuch
and the historical books, respectively.

197. See Docherty, *Old Testament,* 197, *passim.*

198. In fact, since Deuteronomy is framed as direct address, it is not surprising
that Hebrews contains as many quotes from Deuteronomy (9:19; 31:6-8; 32:35, 36, 43) as
from all of the rest of the Pentateuch together (Gen 2:2; 21:12; 22:17; Exod 24:8; 25:40).

199. On the Messianic nature of Ps 2:7; 2 Sam 7:14; Ps 45:6-7; and Ps 110:1 see
the commentary on 1:5-14 below. Ps 45:6-7 (Heb 1:8-9) addresses the King/Messiah as
"God." On this basis the pastor ascribes to the Son the praise offered God in Ps 102:25-27
(Heb 1:10-12).

45:6-8; 102:25-27); by inviting him to be seated at his right hand (Ps 110:1); and finally by affirming the high-priestly nature of that session (Ps 110:4).[200] These quotations, climaxing in the proclamation of Ps 110:4, function as the divine promise that God's exalted Son will fulfill and replace the Aaronic priesthood (Heb 7:11-19). The Son uses the words of Scripture to answer the Father. He has confirmed his acceptance of the divine invitation and the fulfillment of this promise through his incarnation (Isa 8:17, 18 in Heb 2:13), faithful obedience (Ps 40:6-8 in Heb 10:5-10), and resultant vindication (Ps 22:22 in Heb 2:12).[201] Thus the sufficiency of the Son's high priesthood is substantiated by the promise of God and by the affirmation and obedience of the incarnate, now exalted, Son. It is in this capacity that the Son is the ultimate self-revelation of God.

God's New Covenant promise in Jer 31:31-34 (Heb 8:7-13; 10:15-18) is closely related to this divine conversation and especially to God's declaration of priesthood in Ps 110:4. God's proclamation of a new priest substantiated the ineffectiveness of Aaron's high priesthood (Heb 7:11-14) and the full competency of Christ's (Heb 7:15-25). The New Covenant promise shows the insufficiency of the Old Covenant (Heb 8:6, 13) and the efficacious character of the new (Heb 10:15-18). It is by his high-priestly work that God's Son has established and continues to mediate/guarantee this New Covenant (Heb 7:22; 8:6; 9:15; 10:11-18). Thus Ps 110:4, the climax of God's conversation with his Son, and Jer 31:31-34 are the key divine proclamations upon which the pastor builds his case for the fulfillment accomplished by Christ's first coming and subsequent session (Ps 110:1a in Heb 1:13).[202] God's promise of final judgment in Hag 2:6 (Heb 12:26) will be fulfilled at Christ's return when God makes the Son's "enemies" his "footstool" (Ps 110:1b in Heb 1:13).

Second, the Intensified Urgency of Obedience. By demonstrating that

200. God's words to his Son are reinforced by the Scriptural injunction to and description of the angels in Deut 32:43 (Heb 1:6) and Ps 104:4 (Heb 1:7). These verses command the angels to worship the Son and affirm their created malleable, as opposed to his eternal, nature. The ambiguity as to whether God or his Son is the one speaking these words to the angels only heightens the difference between them and the Son.

201. Cf. Attridge, "God in Hebrews," 104-6. On the pastor's rationale for attributing these passages to the Son, see the relevant portions of the commentary below. The praise of the psalmist in Ps 8:4-6 (Heb 2:5-10) becomes the word of God which the pastor uses to explain how the Son obtained the exaltation affirmed in Ps 110:1 (Heb 1:13) through suffering and death.

202. Steve Stanley, "A New Covenant Hermeneutic: The Use of Scripture in Hebrews 8–10" (Ph.D. diss., University of Sheffield, 1994), as summarized by Gheorghita, *Septuagint,* 18-19, calls the fulfillment of these passages in the high priesthood of Christ and the New Covenant "prophetic" fulfillment. Unfortunately, Stanley's dissertation was unavailable to this commentator.

the present is the time between fulfillment and final Judgment the divine speech in the first category of quotations above provides the context for God's warnings and exhortations to his people in the second. First, since God's desire for faithful obedience is unchanging, his words of exhortation to his people of old continue to address his people in the present (Ps 95:7-11 in Heb 3:7–4:11; Hab 2:3-4 in Heb 10:37-38; Hag 2:6 in 12:25-29; Deut 31:6 in Heb 13:5).[203] Furthermore, since all Scripture is from God, even exhortations by his messengers, such as Prov 3:11-13 (Heb 12:5-6), continue in force. Second, God's final revelation in his Son has intensified rather than nullified the urgency of these exhortations. The privileges God's people now enjoy only reinforce the importance of heeding these OT warnings (cf. 2:1-4; 10:26-31; 12:25). However, God's last word to his people is one of promise: "I will never leave you nor forsake you" (Josh 1:5 in Heb 13:5). As noted above, the OT contained the appropriate answers for the obedient Son. It also contained a fitting response for the obedient people of God: "The LORD is my helper; I will not fear. What can a human being do to me?" (Ps 118:6 quoted in Heb 13:6).[204]

4. The Pentateuch — Moses Bears "Witness to the Things That Would Be Spoken" (3:5)

In the psalms and prophets and related material God (1) promises the fulfillment that has come in Christ and (2) urges his people to faithful perseverance. The pastor, however, has not forgotten the five Books of Moses which are the foundation of the Old Testament. God's final speech in his Son is, as one would expect, what defines their true function. Through describing the Old Covenant and through relating the early history of God's people Moses bears "witness to the things that would be spoken" by God in his Son (3:5). Moses' witness functions in at least four different ways. The first two support all of the pastor's other uses of the OT. The third and fourth correspond to and supplement the two ways in which Hebrews uses the psalms and related material as described above.

A Context for the Drama of Salvation. First, three interlocking Pentateuch images — Sinai, the Promised Land, and the wilderness Tent — provide the categories for describing Christ's all-sufficiency and the resulting situation of God's people. Sinai is fundamental, since it was the defining mo-

203. These appear to be the passages that Stanley, "A New Covenant Hermeneutic," describes as having "universal" fulfillment (cited in Gheorghita, *Septuagint,* 18-19).
204. Harold Attridge, "The Psalms in Hebrews," in *The Psalms in the New Testament,* ed. Steve Moyise and Maarten J. J. Menken (London and New York: T&T Clark International, 2004), 210-12.

ment of God's self-revelation when he brought his people into fellowship with himself. The God of Sinai called his people to pursue their pilgrimage to the place where they would enjoy this fellowship. God's Sinai revelation also provided the Tent and its priesthood as a means of approaching him while on their journey. This pattern prefigures the coming of God's Son. God's self-revelation in his Son has fulfilled the intention of God's self-disclosure on Sinai (1:1–2:18; 12:4-29). By its provision God's people can enter the heavenly homeland that has always been the goal of their journey (3:1–4:13; 10:19–12:3).[205] In the meantime they have daily access to God in the true Most Holy Place through the high priesthood of the Son (4:14–10:18).[206] The heavenly homeland and the true Most Holy Place represent the same reality — the true dwelling place of God.[207] Thus present access is both the means of perseverance and a foretaste of what awaits the faithful pilgrim at journey's end. The imagery of Sinai, Promised Land, and Tent play an important role in the structuring and rhetorical effectiveness of Hebrews.

Supporting Quotations and Allusions. Second, since the Mosaic books provide the context for the pastor's interpretation, it was natural for him to use short quotes or allusions from the Pentateuch to clarify his descriptions of OT institutions or examples (see below) and to explain quotations taken from elsewhere in the OT. Thus he quotes Exod 24:8 (Heb 9:20); Exod 25:40 (Heb 8:5); and perhaps Deut 9:19 (Heb 12:21) to clarify the descriptions of Old Covenant institutions. Note also the allusion to Num 12:7 in Heb 3:2. He quotes Gen 22:16-17 (Heb 6:14) and Gen 21:12 (Heb 11:18) in

---

205. Dunnill, *Covenant,* 135, 141-43, misses the fine nuance of Hebrews when he suggests that the writer envisions his hearers "on the Edge of the Land." The pastor does not want his hearers to suffer the fate of the wilderness generation who "rebelled" on the verge of entrance at what should have been the conclusion of their pilgrimage. Furthermore, the pastor would insist that the time for obedience is now. Yet it is more accurate to say that the recipients are, like the faithful of chapter 11, in need of endurance because they are on pilgrimage to their heavenly destiny. Allen has pointed out many helpful connections between Hebrews and Deuteronomy, yet his attempt to present Hebrews as a re-presentation of Deuteronomy also fails to take adequate account of Hebrews' *dominant* concern for perseverance amid suffering. Furthermore, the faithful of Hebrews do join the people of old before Sinai. They stand before the fulfillment Sinai only typified. They do not stand on the verge of entering Canaan; they stand before the heavenly home which the faithful of old also anticipated. See David M. Allen, *Deuteronomy and Exhortation in Hebrews: A Study in Narrative Re-Presentation* (WUNT 238; Tübingen: Mohr Siebeck, 2008).

206. Dunnill's suggestion that the hearers are "at the door of the Tent of Meeting" is also misleading (Dunnill, *Covenant,* 135, 146-48). Through Christ the faithful are able to enter.

207. Both from the fact that Christ has taken his seat at the right hand of God (1:3, 13) and from many indications within the OT itself the pastor is convinced that the reality typified by land/city/Most Holy Place is nothing less than the heavenly abode of God.

order to elucidate the example of Abraham. The list of examples in Heb 11:1-40 is filled with biblical allusions. Finally, the pastor quotes Gen 2:2 (Heb 4:4) in order to explain Ps 95:11, and alludes to Gen 14:17-24 (Heb 7:1-10) in order to explain Ps 110:4.

The Typological Nature of the Old Order. Third, the Pentateuchal descriptions of the old order provide both the basis for its correspondence with the work of Christ and the signs of its own inadequacy to provide salvation (Heb 5:1-3, 7-9; 8:3-5; 9:1-10, 16-22; 12:18-21). For example, the old order foreshadowed Christ by showing that salvation consisted of entrance into the presence of God through cleansing from sin by an effective sacrifice and a competent high priest who would administer a covenant. On the other hand, its inability to provide the salvation it prefigured was adequately demonstrated by the fact that it provided entrance to only an earthly Tent, only once a year, and only for the high priest. These features are coordinate with God's declarations to the Son and promises of a new order discussed under the psalms and related material above. The promises of the new confirmed the ineffectiveness of the old already apparent in the Pentateuchal descriptions. They also pointed to fulfillment of the pattern established by the old in the person of God's Son. Thus together the promises of the psalms and prophets and the descriptions in the Pentateuch establish the typological relationship between the old order and the new.[208] That earlier work of God foreshadowed the fulfillment that it was not able to provide.

Old Testament Examples of Faithfulness and Disobedience. In addition to descriptions of the old order, the Books of Moses provide a record of God's dealings with his faithful people from Abel through Abraham to Moses (Heb 11:1-40). They also describe the disobedience and ultimate loss of Esau (12:14-17) and of the faithless wilderness generation (3:7–4:11). The faithful of old provide more than an example of persevering obedience; they embody the people of God with whom the pastor would have his hearers identify. The disobedient are the apostate whose company they must avoid. Scripture is the ongoing conversation of God with his people. Thus examples from the Books of Moses join exhortations from the psalms, prophets, and related literature in urging obedience with redoubled intensity since the coming of God's Son.

5. The Historical Books (Joshua through Nehemiah)

2 Samuel 7:14 (Heb 1:5) and (probably) Josh 1:5 (Heb 13:6) are the pastor's only quotations from the historical books. Both of these quotations function

---

208. This appears to coincide with the "typological" fulfillment advocated by Stanley, "A New Covenant Hermeneutic," according to Gheorghita, *Septuagint,* 18-19.

as part of the Psalms and related passages discussed above. The pastor mentions the fall of Jericho (11:30), Rahab (11:31), Joshua (4:8), Gideon, Barak, Samson, Jephthah, David, and Samuel (11:32; cf. 4:7). Some of the acts of faith recorded in 11:32-38 may have come from these books. Pamela Eisenbaum, however, has done interpreters of Hebrews a service by demonstrating that the institutions characteristic of Israel as a nation in the land play no role in Heb 11:1-40.[209] The ultimate goal is the *heavenly* city. Thus even if the faithful deeds of 11:32-38 occurred in the land of Canaan, they are no different than those recorded in 11:1-31 and done by the faithful outside Canaan. Eisenbaum's insights are relevant to the absence of the earthly Promised Land, earthly Jerusalem/Temple, and the Davidic kingship throughout Hebrews despite their centrality to the OT historical books. God's words regarding the son of David in Ps 2:7 (Heb 1:5a), 2 Sam 7:14 (Heb 1:5b), and Ps 110:1 (Heb 1:23) are fulfilled directly in the exaltation of the eternal Son at God's right hand without intervening explanation or remainder.[210] The pastor never uses the term "Promised Land" for the ultimate goal of God's people.[211] With one verse (4:8) he dismisses any fleeting notion that Joshua may have given God's people ultimate "rest" by entering that earthly entity. The closest the pastor gets to using any of these earthly institutions typologically is when he calls the eternal city the "heavenly Jerusalem" (12:22). The pastor has probably omitted mention of these institutions for both theological and rhetorical reasons.[212] First, if he would demonstrate the finality of Christ, he must focus on the Pentateuch so that he can show how Christ fulfills the covenant upon which the people of God were founded. Second, reference to the land and its institutions would only have distracted from his insistence that the people of God have always been on pilgrimage to the true promised "rest." He has no room for the illusion of earthly permanence that those earthly institutions, or the hope of their restoration, might engender. Any turning aside to deal with earthly land, temple,

209. Eisenbaum, *Jewish Heroes,* 187-88, *passim.*

210. Ps 2:7; 2 Sam 7:14; Ps 45:6-7; and Ps 110:1 were probably applied to Jesus as David's heir (see Motyer, "Psalm Quotations," 13-17, and many commentaries). However, the fulfillment of these passages by the exalted eternal Son of God has become so axiomatic that mention of David would be both unnecessary and distracting.

211. The translation of πατρίδα in 11:14 as "homeland" may remind the English reader of the term "Promised Land." The two expressions, however, have nothing in common. The first does not include the Greek word for "land" and can mean "home city" as well as "homeland." See on 11:14 in the commentary below. The only time the pastor mentions the earthly Promised Land is when he says that Abraham lived "in the land of promise, as in a foreign land" (11:9). The commentary below suggests that this statement might be paraphrased, "the so-called land of promise."

212. See the discussion on pp. 34-41 of the date when Hebrews was written.

or city would only have distracted from the rhetorical unity and persuasive force of his sermon.

6. Hebrews 3:7–4:11; 7:1-10; and 12:18-24

In addition to the principles enumerated above, three passages deserve individual attention. The interpretation of Ps 95:7-11 in Heb 3:7–4:11 is a unique blend of several features already mentioned. First, it is an exhortation to God's people of old drawn from the psalms because of its continuing relevance. It is also, however, an example taken from the Pentateuch. It has been prepared for by the allusion to Num 12:7 in Heb 3:2, echoes Num 14:1-45, and is elucidated by the quotation of Gen 2:2 in Heb 4:4. The pastor draws two crucial deductions from the fact that this psalm originated in the time of David long after the demise of the wilderness generation. First, God's OT exhortations have continuing relevance for the people of God "today" (Heb 3:7). Second, the true destiny of God's people has always been a future heavenly "rest" and not an earthly Promised Land (Heb 4:1-11). By demonstrating this fact Ps 95:7-11 takes on the eschatological character of Ps 110:1, 4 and Jer 31:31-34. Thus this passage is not merely exhortation but exposition fundamental to the pastor's understanding of fulfillment in Christ.

The allusions to the account of Melchizedek in Gen 14:17-24 (Heb 7:1-10) also require our attention. The Melchizedek of Genesis stands above both the history of the faithful and the institutions of the Old Covenant. Thus the role he plays in the OT fits none of the categories above: Melchizedek is neither an example to be followed nor an institution of the old order now antiquated by the coming of God's Son. His function in Hebrews is determined by Ps 110:4 (Heb 5:6, 10; 6:20; 7:17, 21). His appearance in Genesis explains the eternal nature of the coming priest addressed by this psalm and provides a historical basis for that priest's superiority over the Levitical priesthood. Aaron is the type which Christ has fulfilled. Melchizedek provides the Scriptural evidence for Christ's fulfillment of the Aaronic priesthood. Thus the Melchizedek of Ps 110:4 and Gen 14:17-24 is crucial to the pastor's entire enterprise. Without him there would be no adequate Scriptural substantiation for the high priesthood of the Son.

If Melchizedek is the seed that makes the pastor's interpretation possible, then Heb 12:18-24 is its full fruition. The "Sinai" of 12:18-21 and the "Zion" of 12:22-24 represent what Sinai has become first for the apostate, then for the faithful.[213] Because the Son of God has fulfilled the type given on

---

213. Since Sinai and Zion are opposites, they do not represent the Old and New Covenants, as Graham Hughes, *Hebrews and Hermeneutics,* 44, and others contend.

Sinai (recorded in the Pentateuch) in accord with the OT promises (Ps 110:1, 4; etc.), the faithful enjoy the presence of God on "Zion." On the other hand, because he has fulfilled that type the moral demand of the Old Covenant has been intensified (2:1-4). Therefore the apostate stands before a "Sinai" of exclusion from God's presence reserved for those who have rejected the Son — Sinai without grace. This warning climaxes the pastor's use of Ps 95:7-11 (3:7-4:11) and other OT exhortations as noted above. Christ's fulfillment of the old order has clarified the typological nature of its sacrificial ritual but intensified its demand for faithful obedience.[214]

7. *Continuity and Typology*

This study of the pastor's use of the OT has provided a basis for explaining the word "typology" and for addressing the related issue of continuity/discontinuity. The above paragraphs have recounted two ways in which the pastor's use of the Pentateuch dovetails with his use of psalms, prophets, and other parts of the OT. First, the Pentateuchal descriptions of the old order of salvation join the promises/prophecies of the new in establishing a typological relationship between the old order and Christ. Second, the examples of faithfulness/unfaithfulness drawn largely from the Pentateuch, join the divine exhortations, taken mostly from other parts of the OT, in urging obedience. These principles encapsulate the essence of the pastor's Christological approach to the OT.

The second pair of interpretive principles given above clearly affirms the continuity of the people of God. Christ's coming has only added urgency to the exhortations and examples from of old. God's people both before and after Christ have the same need of obedience if they would enter God's eternal City (11:13-16; 12:22-24) and "rest" (4:1-11). Graham Hughes, however, represents many who would argue that the first pair of principles given above establishes discontinuity between the old and the new.[215] After all, the Pentateuchal descriptions of the old priesthood and covenant demonstrate the *in*adequacy of the old. The promises of a new priesthood and covenant from other parts of the OT affirm the all-sufficient *adequacy* of the new. This ap-

---

Hughes admits that the continuity between the two has been reduced to a bare minimum. In fact, it has been reduced to zero.

214. Thus we can agree with Lincoln, *A Guide,* 78, that the change in the law brought by Christ's fulfillment is a change in the whole law — including the moral law. It does not, however, change all in the same way. Performance of the rituals is no longer necessary, the ethical demand is intensified.

215. Graham Hughes, *Hebrews and Hermeneutics,* 68-71. The continued popularity of this continuity/discontinuity contrast is evidenced by the recent studies of Lincoln, *A Guide,* 79-81, and Hays, "New Covenantalism," 155.

proach, however, fails to hear Hebrews on its own terms.[216] The typological relationship established by the first pair of principles above is one of continuity. These principles do not show that the Old Covenant has been invalidated, but that, on the basis of its own testimony, it was never intended to be final. That covenant and its priesthood have always been typological and anticipatory, even if their true nature was not fully realized until the coming of Christ. They continue to have the same validity today that in principle they have always had.[217] Moses continues to be a "witness" to the things that would be and have been "spoken" in God's Son (3:5). What Hebrews says about the finality of Christ would only be in tension with an interpretation of the OT that affirmed the sufficiency of the Old Covenant.[218] Thus, the relationship between Christ's high priesthood and the old is best described as continuity and fulfillment rather than continuity and discontinuity.[219] The pastor's assertion that the old priesthood has been "abolished" (7:18) by fulfillment in Christ does not contradict this conclusion. By this statement, as noted above, the pastor means that the faithful must no longer practice the sacrifices of the old order since Christ has fulfilled what they anticipated. To continue these practices would be to deny the continuity that Christ has established with the old through its fulfillment.

This relationship that Hebrews establishes between the old and new covenants and priesthoods falls within the definition generally given to the term "typology": OT institutions, persons, and events through which God re-

---

216. Hughes admits that the author shows no embarrassment at this supposed tension between continuity and discontinuity within his work. Stanley, "A New Covenant Hermeneutic," as summarized in Gheorghita, *Septuagint,* 18-19, appears to have corrected this inappropriate contrast between continuity and discontinuity.

217. Thus Graham Hughes, *Hebrews and Hermeneutics,* 71, is mistaken when he distinguishes between the texts that continue to address the community and those no longer valid. The descriptions, for instance, of the Mosaic Tent and its ritual as summarized in 9:1-10 continue to be valid as the Word of God that affirms the typological nature of the old order.

218. Thus the objections of A. J. M. Wedderburn, "Sawing Off the Branches: Theologizing Dangerously ad Hebraeos," *JTS* 56 (2005): 393-414, are misdirected. The pastor does not destroy the basis for the superiority of the New Covenant by establishing the ineffectiveness of the Old. He does not simply abolish the Old or reject its categories. Rather, he argues that it was a God-intended type that would be fulfilled by and give meaning to the New Covenant.

219. "In the first place the author believed that the old covenant was a valid revelation of God. It had been superseded and fulfilled but not abrogated. It contained a genuine foreshadowing of the good things to come, not a Platonic illusion of ultimate reality" (Caird, "Exegetical Method," 46). Long ago Westcott perceived the positive place that the OT occupies in Hebrews (Westcott, lviii, lxxxii-lxxxiii, 4, 480-86). See also Lane, 1:cxxx-cxxxv.

deemed his people were types that foreshadowed what he would accomplish in Christ.[220] There is a correspondence between what God accomplishes through the type and its fulfillment. Yet the fulfillment by its very nature is superior to the type. These types provide a pattern or structure and a vocabulary for comprehending Christ and the salvation he brings. One must not, however, apply a predetermined definition of typology without a careful analysis of Hebrews' use of the OT like the one given above. In Hebrews, for instance, the types are revelatory and anticipatory, but devoid in themselves of ultimate saving efficacy. Furthermore, as has been noted above, Aaron, not Melchizedek, is a type of Christ. It is because the Son is "like" Melchizedek (Heb 7:15-19) that he is superior to Aaron and fulfills what Aaron foreshadowed. To use the word "typology" for both of these, all but opposite, relationships introduces naught but confusion. It is also misleading to call the OT people of God a type of the new. As noted above, the pastor assumes that there is one people of God throughout history whose destiny has always been the eternal Mount Zion.[221] The faithful of 11:1-40 are not *types* but *examples* drawn from the earlier history of that one people.

8. Hebrews and Contemporary Jewish Use of the Old Testament

The preceding analysis of OT exposition provides the basis for a brief comparison with contemporary sources.[222] Most interpreters recognize a number

---

220. See Guthrie, "Hebrews' Use of the Old Testament," 288-90, and Motyer, "Psalm Quotations," 12-13. Graham Hughes, *Hebrews and Hermeneutics,* 101-10; Salevao, *Legitimation,* 345-83, esp. 345-57; Susanne Lehne, *The New Covenant in Hebrews,* ed. David Hill and David E. Orton (JSNTSup 44; Sheffield: JSOT Press, 1990), 13, 97-98, and others affirm a typology in Hebrews where there is correspondence, contrast, and superiority between a type and its fulfillment. Richard M. Davidson, "Typology in the Book of Hebrews," in *Issues in the Book of Hebrews,* ed. Frank B. Holbrook (Springfield, MD: Biblical Research Institute, 1989), 121-86, is helpful but fails to adequately distinguish the different ways in which OT figures, etc. prefigure Christ.

221. See the commentary, esp. on 2:5-18; 3:1-6; 3:7–4:11; and 11:1-40.

222. See the summaries in Guthrie, "Hebrews' Use of the Old Testament," 279-83 and Docherty, *Old Testament,* 63-82. Bateman has compared Hebrews to the rabbinic rules of exegesis and to the catena at Qumran (Herbert W. Bateman IV, *Early Jewish Hermeneutics and Hebrews 1:5-13* [American University Studies, Series VII: Theology and Religion 193; New York: Peter Lang, 1997]; H. W. Bateman, "Two First-Century Messianic Uses of the OT: Heb 1:5-13 and 4QFlor 1:1-19," *JETS* 38 [1995]: 11-27). Williamson's massive study includes comparison of the use of Scripture in Philo and Hebrews (Williamson, *Philo and Hebrews*). F. Schröger, *Der Verfasser des Hebräerbriefes als Schriftausleger* (BU 4; Regensburg: Pustet, 1968), focuses on the particular methods used by Hebrews and contemporary sources. Eisenbaum, *Jewish Heroes,* compares Heb 11:1-40 with contemporary hero lists such as that found in Sirach 45–50.

of general parallels between Hebrews and contemporary Jewish practice. Hebrews is fond of arguing from the lesser to the greater (in Hebrew, *qal wayyomer;* e.g., 2:1-4; 10:26-31; 12:25-29).[223] Hebrews sometimes associates verses that contain the same word or words (in Hebrew, *gezera shawa;* e.g., "son" in 1:5 or "rest" in 4:1-11). Some have suggested that Hebrews puts special emphasis on the first mention of something in Scripture (e.g., "rest" in Gen 2:2/Heb 4:1-11; "priest" in Gen 12:14-27/Heb 7:1-10) or that Hebrews argues from the silence of Scripture (e.g., the absence of Melchizedek's genealogy in Gen 14:17-24/Heb 7:1-3). Heb 1:5-14 (like 4QFlorilegium, 4QTestimonia, and 4QCatena) strings a number of quotations together in order to sustain a particular point.[224] The roll call of the faithful in Heb 11:1-40 is reminiscent of hero lists in Sirach 45–50 and other sources. The merits of these suggestions will be evaluated as they arise in the commentary below.

Susan Docherty's helpful study makes several observations that underscore the unique features of Hebrews' OT interpretation. She justifies comparison with the admittedly later rabbinic sources on several grounds. First, she argues for the Jewish character of the NT.[225] Second, she notes the presence of rabbinic practices in earlier sources. Her study is also justified by the fruitfulness of the insights it provides. Her work is built on the conviction that the traditional lists of rabbinic exegetical rules do not adequately describe rabbinic exegetical practice.[226] Thus she uses Arnold Goldberg's systematic analysis of what the rabbis actually did when they interpreted the OT.[227] According to Docherty, both Hebrews and the rabbis demonstrate their commitment to the OT as God's word by the care with which they quote its text.[228] Both indicate their belief in the coherence of Scripture by the way

223. Docherty does not mention the argument from less to greater, probably because she focuses on the quotations in Hebrews chapters 1, 3, and 4 where it does not occur. Despite this lack, her selection of the quotations in these chapters as representative is not without justification (Docherty, *Old Testament,* 7-8, 143).

224. Hebrews 1:1-14, however, does more than string the text together. As the commentary below will demonstrate, the pastor skillfully joins these quotations in order to advance his argument. See Docherty, *Old Testament,* 152.

225. Docherty, *Old Testament,* 81-82, 119.

226. See Docherty, *Old Testament,* 89-90. Such lists were attributed to Hillel, Ishmael, and Eliezer ben Yose. For the list of Hillel's rules see Bateman IV, *Early Jewish Hermeneutics,* 9.

227. Docherty, *Old Testament,* 102-20, refers to Arnold Goldberg and those who have followed him — Alexander Samely and Philip Alexander. Her discussion of Hebrews appears to depend most on the work of Samely.

228. Docherty, *Old Testament,* 140-41, 177 (i), 180, 194 (i), 196-97, thinks that the author of Hebrews has seldom altered the LXX text he received. She attributes many of the ways in which he deviates from our standard LXX text to the fluidity of the LXX

they associate texts from various parts of the canon.[229] Both carry out their interpretation by putting their quotations within a new context.[230] Yet both often show an awareness of the larger context from which the cited text is taken.[231] Both highlight key words or phrases for comment.[232] Perhaps one of her more significant contributions is to point out that Hebrews, like the rabbis, is concerned with the particular features of the text itself, including ambiguities within the text and questions which the text itself raises.[233]

What Docherty fails to see, however, is the way in which the pastor's use of these very methods distinguishes him from the rabbis. These procedures implement and give legitimacy to his Christological interpretation.[234] First, the new context into which the pastor puts OT quotations is a Christological context: the God who spoke *of old* has *now* spoken in one who is *Son* (cf. Heb 1:1). These quoted passages once anticipated the incarnation and exaltation/session of the Son of God. They have now found their fulfillment in those events. Thus Hebrews has a sense of historical sequence, progression, and fulfillment absent from the rabbis.[235] Second, the pastor uses the particular features of the text and the questions they raise to facilitate his Christological interpretation. For instance, the way in which Ps 45:6-7 (Heb 8:8-9) addresses the Messiah as "God" was in perfect accord with his agenda. Third, the expressions Hebrews highlights are central and crucial to the OT passages from which they are drawn ("son," "rest," "priest forever," "new covenant"). They are never peripheral, as in some rabbinic interpretation. Fourth, the way in which all quotations are drawn into this Chris-

---

text in the first century and thus to alternate readings (Docherty, *Old Testament,* 121-42). In this way she argues a reverence for the text characteristic of later rabbinic interpretation. Bateman would allow the author of Hebrews more leeway in editing his received text. He, however, thinks this in accord with contemporary Jewish practices (Bateman IV, *Early Jewish Hermeneutics,* 121-48).

229. See Docherty, *Old Testament,* 197-98, and her discussions of the wider context of each quotation studied.

230. Docherty, *Old Testament,* 177 (ii) and often.

231. Docherty, *Old Testament,* 178 (xi, xii), 195 (iii, iv), and often.

232. Docherty, *Old Testament,* 180, 195 (v, viii), *passim.*

233. Docherty, *Old Testament,* 178 (xiv, xv), 196 (xi). For instance, the occurrence of "son" in 2 Sam 2:7 (Heb 1:5) and its openness to eschatological interpretation may have been a problem for others, to which Hebrews had a ready answer (Docherty, *Old Testament,* 153-54). The apparent attribution of deity to the king or messiah in Ps 45:7-8 may also have been a problem for some. Such examples could be multiplied from most of the quotations Docherty examines.

234. See, for instance, Motyer, "Psalm Quotations," 11, 15-20.

235. Docherty's suggestion that this sense of progression is due to Hebrews' eschatological orientation is true but insufficient as an explanation (Docherty, *Old Testament,* 197-98). Eschatology finds its fulfillment in Christ.

tological focus gives Hebrews a unified perspective lacking in rabbinic sources. The final divine revelation that fulfills all previous revelation is not in the written prophetic text but in the person of the Son — eternal, incarnate, obedient, and now exalted. Thus *pace* Docherty, for the writer of Hebrews the OT can never be the linguistic "artifact" that it was for the rabbis.[236] It is not, for interpretive purposes, a mere collection of graphic signs and letters that can be pressed for multiple meanings. Its meaning is Christologically determined. It is "exalted speech," the living record of the actions and the voice of God.[237]

Docherty acknowledges that Hebrews differs significantly in literary form from rabbinic midrashim.[238] She does not, however, seem to realize the full significance of this fact.[239] The way in which this synagogue sermon draws on the resources of ancient rhetoric to arrange all of its material in a unified, persuasive whole sustains, and is sustained by, the pastor's unified vision of the OT's Christological fulfillment.

9. Contemporary Relevance

What relevance do the exegetical methods of Hebrews have for OT interpretation today? Some have condemned the pastor's exegesis as conditioned by the limitations of his time and thus judged that it was no longer acceptable.[240] Others have suggested that the pastor's OT interpretation rests on a *sensus plenior* or "fuller sense" absent from the text as originally given but now revealed by the Holy Spirit.[241] Graham Hughes, however, has found a firmer basis for the pastor's exposition. He argues that the OT intimations of something better yet to come plus the specific ways in which Jesus has fulfilled these intimations give "permission" for the pastor to develop his interpretation.[242] Hughes is ready to admit that the OT might "invite" or "suggest" the

236. Docherty, *Old Testament,* 180, 192, 197.
237. Docherty repeatedly notes that Hebrews not only sees the OT as God's speech but, by emphasizing the "oath" of God, identifies it as exalted speech. See Docherty, *Old Testament,* 149, 178 (ix), 193, 195 (vii), 197.
238. Docherty, *Old Testament,* 179 (xix).
239. In all fairness, she does suggest that the relationship between Hebrews' literary genre and its use of Scripture should be a matter for further study (Docherty, *Old Testament,* 205).
240. Weiss, 181; Moffatt, xlvi; Schröger, *Der Verfasser,* 71, *passim.* Cf. Longenecker, *Biblical Exegesis,* 184-85.
241. Spicq, 1:337-38, 349. See Guthrie, "Hebrews' Use of the Old Testament," 284. For Emmrich's claim that the pastor practices "pneumatological" exegesis see the comments on 3:7-11; 9:6-10; and 10:15-18 below (M. Emmrich, *"Pneuma* in Hebrews: Prophet and Interpreter," *WTJ* 64 [2002]: 55-71).
242. Graham Hughes, *Hebrews and Hermeneutics,* 104-7, 118; Guthrie, "He-

interpretation advocated by Hebrews but insists that such an interpretation was not "necessary."[243] That is, if one approaches the OT without faith in Christ other interpretations are equally valid.

If one were to put Hughes's position in terms more congenial to the writer of Hebrews, one might say, "If God has not now spoken in one who is Son, other interpretations of the OT are valid." To put the issue in this way demonstrates how far this question is from the mind of one who is absolutely confident of the Son's vocation as the ultimate revelation of God. The pastor who wrote Hebrews is convinced that his OT interpretation is not only based on this fact but in turn substantiates it. God's word in his Son is the key to the OT; on the other hand, God's previous revelation substantiates the fact that he has now spoken in his Son. The discussions above of how the pastor uses different types of OT material have shown how he establishes common ground with others by beginning with the OT apart from Christ. On the basis of the OT alone he argues not merely for the "futurity" (to use Graham Hughes's term), but for the *futility* of the old order as a means of salvation.[244] Thus on the basis of the OT alone the pastor would exclude any interpretation affirming that the old priesthood and covenant had ever been an adequate way of approaching God.[245] He then seeks to substantiate God's revelation in his Son by showing how it coherently fulfills what the old order both intimated and lacked.[246] His is no *pesher* interpretation of mysteries revealed only by esoteric revelation.[247] The pastor does not present a revision of God's OT word, but its God-intended fulfillment.[248] He would demonstrate the full relevance of the OT for those who have accepted God's word in his Son.[249]

---

brews' Use of the Old Testament," 297. See the discussion of "Continuity and Typology" on pp. 52-54 above.

243. See Graham Hughes, *Hebrews and Hermeneutics,* 63-64, 98-107; Hughes uses the word "invite" on p. 63, "suggest" on p. 107.

244. See Graham Hughes, *Hebrews and Hermeneutics,* 63-64.

245. Lincoln, *A Guide,* 76, acknowledges Hebrews' assertion that the old order was never effective, though he does not fully develop the significance of this fact.

246. On the care with which the pastor interprets the OT and the respect he gives to the context and logic of the text see Motyer, "Psalm Quotations," 7-8; Guthrie, "Hebrews' Use of the Old Testament," 284; Dale F. Leschert, *Hermeneutical Foundations of Hebrews: A Study in the Validity of the Epistle's Interpretation of Some Core Citations from the Psalms* (National Association of Baptist Professors of Religion Dissertation 10; Lewiston, NY: Mellen, 1994), 15-20, *passim.* Cf. also Gheorghita, *Septuagint,* 57; Ellingworth, 41.

247. For the historical and chronological approach to the OT that distinguishes Hebrews from the *pesher* interpretations of Qumran see Docherty, *Old Testament,* 196 (xiv, xv). See also Motyer, "Psalm Quotations," 11, and Weiss, 66.

248. *Pace* Salevao, *Legitimation,* 404, Bénétreau, 1:40, and many others, there has been no break or fissure in God's revelation.

249. Clements, "Old Testament," 36. "I should like to suggest that, so far from be-

On the basis of the preceding discussion we can now summarize the abiding hermeneutical principles that underlie the pastor's interpretation of the OT. First and most fundamentally, God's word in the incarnate, obedient, now exalted Son fulfills all that God has said. Therefore the Son stands in complete continuity with and fulfills all previous revelation. Second, the Old Covenant with its priesthood and sacrifices has always been and continues to be a type and foreshadowing of the full sufficiency of Christ as Savior. It was never meant to be an adequate means of salvation in itself. This relationship between old and new is demonstrated both by the descriptions of the old order in the Pentateuch and by the promises and intimations of fulfillment in Christ found mostly in the psalms, prophets, and related literature. Third, those who live by faith in the word of God constitute the one people of God throughout history. Their goal has always been and continues to be final entrance into God's eternal "rest." Thus the examples of both the faithful and the unfaithful along with God's promises, warnings, and words of encouragement to his people of old retain their validity with increased urgency because of what Christ has done. To be faithful today is to join the faithful of all time.

These principles of interpretation provide continuing guidance for those who confess that God has now "spoken in one who is Son" (1:2). They do not, however, provide liberty for contemporary Christians to "critique and relativize" teachings of Scripture they might find objectionable. The argument that Hebrews provides such warrant is invalidated by the fact that the pastor would not have admitted to critiquing and relativizing Scripture.[250]

---

ing an example of fantastic exegesis which can be totally disregarded by modern Christians, Hebrews is one of the earliest and most successful attempts to define the relation between the Old and New Testaments, and that a large part of the value of the book is to be found in the method of exegesis which was formerly dismissed with contempt" (Caird, "Exegetical Method," 45).

250. Andrew T. Lincoln, "Hebrews and Biblical Theology," in *Out of Egypt: Biblical Theology and Biblical Interpretation,* ed. Craig Bartholomew et al. (Scripture and Hermeneutics Series 5; Grand Rapids: Zondervan, 2004), 333-34, contends that contemporary Christians can "critique and relativize" objectionable teachings in the NT as well as the OT on the basis of the same tradition about Christ that Hebrews used. This contention contains several further inconsistencies in addition to the definitive objection given in the text above. It minimizes the fact that the only access one has to such tradition is in the NT. Thus critiquing the NT on the basis of the tradition about Christ comes very close to critiquing the tradition itself. Interpreters who do this make themselves, not the NT, the standard. Hebrews explains but does not critique this tradition. The writer of Hebrews who put such a premium on the OT as the word of God would never have agreed that the books of the NT were nothing more than "culturally conditioned, witnesses to the eschatological fulfillment in Christ" (Lincoln, "Biblical Theology," 333, n. 22). Finally, Lincoln's contention that the "not yet" aspect of fulfillment in Christ gives legitimization to such critique of Scripture is little more than rhetoric. The "not yet" of Hebrews does noth-

B. THE SERMON'S RHETORICALLY EFFECTIVE STRUCTURE

1. Introduction

It was fashionable at one time to suggest that Hebrews was a collection of disparate expositions of Scripture.[251] Significant progress in several areas of New Testament study over the past fifty years offers the prospect of a much more holistic interpretation. This Introduction has already noted the ways in which Hebrews has been compared with ancient rhetoric and with the preaching of the synagogue. Thus it comes as no surprise that some have analyzed its structure in accord with the recognized divisions of epideictic or deliberative rhetoric.[252] Others, as noted in the preceding section, have suggested that the pastor has structured Hebrews in accord with the main OT quotations.[253] Still others have made notable strides in analyzing Hebrews on the basis of formal criteria. This last approach was given prominence by Vanhoye's attempt to delineate the structure of Hebrews on the basis of literary features alone.[254] His work has been followed by George Guthrie's and Cynthia Westfall's application of discourse analysis.[255]

Although each of these analyses has its values, none of them appear to be fully satisfactory. Vanhoye's insistence on using literary features alone seems artificial. His attempt to force Hebrews into a chiastic mold breaks down in the central section of the book.[256] Westfall's insistence that Jesus is

---

ing to relativize the finality of the fulfillment already achieved by Christ. It refers simply to his return "for salvation" (9:28) at the Judgment.

251. In his 1991 commentary Weiss, 79, still felt it necessary to deny this atomistic approach. See France's concise comments on the unity of Hebrews (France, "Biblical Expositor," 248-49).

252. Übelacker, *Appell;* Koester, 79-86; Thompson, 13-20.

253. Caird, "Exegetical Method," 44-51; Longenecker, *Biblical Exegesis,* 175-85; France, "Biblical Expositor," 245-76; and Walters, "Rhetorical," 59-70.

254. A. Vanhoye, *La structure littéraire de l'épître aux Hébreux* (2nd ed.; Paris: Desclée de Brouwer, 1976). The first edition was published in 1963. See also A. Vanhoye, "Discussions sur la structure de l'Épître aux Hébreux," *Bib* 55 (1974): 349-80, and A. Vanhoye, *Structure and Message of the Epistle to the Hebrews* (Subsidia Biblica 12; Rome: Editrice Pontifico Instituto Biblico, 1989).

255. Guthrie, *Structure;* Cynthia Long Westfall, *A Discourse Analysis of the Letter to the Hebrews: The Relationship between Form and Meaning* (LNTS 297; London: T&T Clark, 2005). For a summary of suggested structural analyses before Guthrie see Lane, 1:lxxxiv-xc, and Guthrie, *Structure,* 1-23. For a favorable and concise summary of Guthrie's work see Lane, 1:xc-xcviii. See brief summaries of both Guthrie and Westfall in O'Brien, 30-34. See also Barry C. Joslin, "Can Hebrews Be Structured? An Assessment of Eight Approaches," *CurBS* 6 (2007): 99-129.

256. For evaluation of Vanhoye see James Swetnam, "Form and Content in He-

the speaker of Psalm 95 in Heb 3:7–4:11, while essential to her structural analysis, finds no support in the text.[257] Guthrie's insightful work would have been more helpful had he analyzed the expository and hortatory sections as a unity.[258] As the paragraphs below in particular and the text of this commentary in general hope to demonstrate, each hortatory section has been crafted to fit a particular place in the discourse.[259]

Here, then, is a brief overview of the structure advocated below. The parallel character of Heb 4:14-16 and 10:19-25 provides the initial impetus for dividing the main body of Hebrews into three large sections — 1:1–4:13; 4:14–10:18; and 10:19–12:29.[260] Even though the high priesthood of Christ

---

brews 1–6," *Bib* 53 (1972): 368-85; James Swetnam, "Form and Content in Hebrews 7–13," *Bib* 55 (1974): 333-48; M. Gourgues, "Remarques sur la 'structure centrale' de l'épître aux Hébreux: A l'occasion d'une réédition," *RevBib* 84 (1977): 26-37; and Guthrie, *Structure,* 11-17. Vanhoye's analysis obscures the close parallels between 4:14-16 and 10:19-25 (O'Brien, 29). The segmentation of Hebrews that we will propose below demonstrates how the chiastic balance between 1:1–4:16 and 10:19–12:29 serves the linear progression of the pastor's appeal.

257. Instead of recognizing that the salvation provided by Jesus the High Priest is the word of God proclaimed by Jesus as Apostle, Westfall insists on arbitrarily keeping the roles of High Priest and Apostle separate from each other simply because they come from different semantic domains (Westfall, *Discourse Analysis,* 112). Furthermore, she mistakenly insists that there are two houses of God in 3:1-6, one pertaining to Moses and one to the Son (Westfall, *Discourse Analysis,* 117). These two mistakes contribute to her arbitrary assertion that Jesus is the speaker of Ps 95:7-11 in 3:7–4:11 (Westfall, *Discourse Analysis,* 115). However, even if one granted these assumptions, there is no direct indication in the text that 3:7–4:16 "develops Jesus' role as a messenger/apostle" (Westfall, *Discourse Analysis,* 110).

258. On the division between the expository and hortatory passages see Guthrie, *Structure,* 112-45. When Guthrie, *Structure,* 126, says that Christ's sacrifice "finds its superiority in its heavenly locale (9:11, 23-24)," he confuses, as is common among many, the evidence for the *superiority* of Christ's sacrifice with its *cause*. Christ's sacrifice provided him with entrance into heaven as High Priest, but it was not offered in heaven (see on 9:11-15). This mistake has led Guthrie to an unfortunate attempt at dividing the expository parts of Hebrews between heaven and earth (Guthrie, *Structure,* 121-24). Thus, 7:1-28 takes place on earth, but 8:3–10:18 (following a transition in 8:1-2) in heaven. Heb 7:1-28, however, pertains to the exaltation and eternal nature of the Son; on the other hand, the incarnate obedience that constituted Christ's effective sacrifice in 10:5-10 is at the heart of 8:1–10:18. Guthrie's comment that "spatial orientation is not primary" in 7:1-28 actually applies to much of Hebrews (Guthrie, *Structure,* 122).

259. It is often difficult to determine if a passage is expository or hortatory. Westfall, for instance, criticizes Guthrie's identification of Heb 11:1-40 as hortatory (Westfall, *Discourse Analysis,* 19-20).

260. Guthrie, *Structure,* 79-82. Cf. Wolfgang Nauck, "Zum Aufbau des Hebräerbriefes," in *Judentum-Urchristentum-Kirche: Festschrift für J. Jeremias* (ed. Walther Eltester; Berlin: Verlag Alfred Töpelmann, 1960), 200-203. Weiss, 46-47, criticizes Van-

is the pastor's main theme, it predominates only in the central of these three sections. The first section proclaims God's revelation in the Son and warns against disobedience. The second presents Christ's high priesthood as the fulfillment of his sonship and the content of God's self-disclosure in the Son.[261] Through this ministry God's people have both the unprecedented privilege of entering his presence and an intensified obligation for obedience. Thus the third section urges faithful endurance until Christ's return, enabled by the sufficiency of his high priesthood.[262] Although the comments below will show a reverse or chiastic parallelism between sections one and three, these sections are not equal. They relate to one another as preparation to fruition. The divine sonship of the first section is the pastor's foundation. The high priesthood of the Son in the second is his main theme. The perseverance of the people of God in the third is his ultimate goal.

The analysis that follows is sensitive to the formal features of the text, to its use of Scripture, and to its rhetorical shape. However, it puts considerable emphasis on the pastor's imagery and on the concrete way in which he has arranged his material to motivate his hearers. The introductions to the various sections placed appropriately throughout this commentary, as well as the exposition of individual passages, provide further linguistic, rhetorical, and conceptual substantiation. The final justification for this structuring is the insight it provides into the individual parts and total impact of this sermon.

---

hoye for neglecting the significance of these two passages. Westfall, *Discourse Analysis,* 137, acknowledges them but also fails to give them due place. Gelardini's attempt to make 3:1–6:20 a unified section is unconvincing (Gabriella Gelardini, "From 'Linguistic Turn' and Hebrews Scholarship to *Anadiplosis Iterata:* The Enigma of a Structure," *HTR* 102 [2009]: 63; Gelardini, *"Verhärtet eure Herzen nicht,"* 249-87). Her arguments for the semantic coherence of this section are weak. The idea that Christ's high priesthood is paralleled by the intercession of Moses in Numbers 13–14 is unjustified. Heb 3:5 makes it clear that Moses is not "faithful" as a priest but as a "witness to things that would be said." Furthermore, 4:14–5:10 only begins to explicate the faithfulness of the Son. His faithfulness is defined by his incarnate obedience, explicated in 8:1–10:18 (10:5-10). Finally, "Unbelief of the Sons" and "Sinful People Need the High-Priestly Ministry" are less than appropriate titles for Heb 4:14–6:12 and 4:14–5:10 respectively.

261. "The logic is that God has 'spoken' through a Son, who not only uttered God's word but who *was* God's word, since he communicated God's will through his life, death, and exaltation" (Koester, 104-5).

262. Weiss, 52-54, rightly affirms the importance of high priesthood in section two for the author's appeal in section three.

2. Hebrews 1:1–2:18 and 12:4-29: God Has Spoken from the Mountain

Ancient orators chose their imagery with care in order to address their hearers' emotions *(pathos)* as well as their reason *(logos)*.[263] The preceding discussion of Hebrews' use of the OT has underscored the important role played by three interlocking Pentateuchal images — Sinai, Promised Land, and Mosaic Tent. The pastor has structured Hebrews in accord with the way the Son fulfills the pattern established by these categories. When the pastor would urge his hearers to perseverance in 3:1–4:13 and 10:19–12:3 he uses Promised Land imagery to describe God's dwelling place as the heavenly "homeland" (11:13-16), the eternal "City" (11:9-10; 12:22-24), or the divine "rest" (4:1-11).[264] When he would urge them to approach God even now for the grace necessary for perseverance, he describes it as the heavenly Most Holy Place typified by the Tent (4:14–10:18). The pastor begins and ends by comparing God's ultimate self-revelation in the Son with his self-disclosure on Sinai. What God has said (1:1–2:18) and continues to say (12:18-24) through the incarnate, exalted, eternal Son will reach consummation in God's final declaration at the Judgment (12:25-29). Because it typifies God's final revelation in his Son, the Mount Sinai theophany is foundational to the other two images employed by Hebrews.

In 1:1–2:18 the pastor contrasts the "so great salvation" that God has "spoken" in his Son with the Sinai "word" spoken through angels (2:1-4). God's proclamations to the Son affirm both his preexistent deity and his exaltation to God's right hand (1:1-14). The Son's response to the Father affirms his assumption of humanity and suffering as the means to his exaltation as sufficient Savior (2:5-18).[265] By describing the Son's incarnation and suffering in 2:5-18 the pastor discloses the content of the "salvation" that was "so great" by comparison with the angelic Sinai "word" (2:1-4). Übelacker describes Heb 1:1-4 as the *exordium* or introduction to an ancient speech and 1:5–2:18 as the *narratio* or narration of the facts the speech would present.

263. Along with the arousal of emotions *(pathos)* and the use of reason *(logos),* ancient orators would also attempt to move their audiences by *ethos* or "character." It was essential that the hearers believe in the integrity and competency of the speaker. The author of Hebrews says little about his own character but emphasizes the faithfulness of God, who speaks both in the prophets and in his Son (1:1). See the discussion of *logos, pathos,* and *ethos* in Koester, 87-92. Cf. Johnson, 14.

264. Mackie, *Eschatology and Exhortation,* 208-11, is correct when he contends that "drawing near" through Christ the High Priest refers to a true experience of cleansing and entrance into God's heavenly presence. *Pace* Mackie, however, this fact does not negate but provides the resources for persevering as the pilgrim people of God.

265. Mackie, "Son of God," 114-29; Mackie, *Eschatology and Exhortation,* 216-30.

This *narratio* climaxes in 2:17-18 with the thesis the orator would establish, called the *propositio* or proposition.[266] The way in which 1:1–2:18 introduces the incarnation and suffering of the eternal, now exalted, Son lays a foundation for both the high-priestly Christology of Hebrews and for the writer's concern that his hearers persevere through suffering. If 2:17-18 introduces the pastor's central thesis that the Son is the all-sufficient High Priest, 2:10 introduces the subsidiary theme of the Son as the Pioneer and example par excellence of endurance (12:1-3; cf. "forerunner" in 6:20; "Great Shepherd" in 12:20). The first (High Priest) will dominate the central section of Hebrews (4:14–10:18); the second (Pioneer) surfaces again at the center (12:1-3) of the final section (10:19–12:29). It is through his high-priestly ministry that the Son as Pioneer enables his own to enter their ultimate destiny.

The pastor returns to the vision of God's speaking from Sinai in 12:14-29.[267] The God who spoke through the incarnation and exaltation of the eternal Son (1:1–2:18) now speaks through that same Son from the heavenly "Zion" (12:14-24).[268] God's revelation through the incarnation and exaltation of the Son provided the benefits of salvation (1:1–2:18). His continuing revelation through the incarnate, now exalted Son makes those benefits available in time of need (12:14-24). God, however, will speak once more. The pastor concludes the main part of this sermon by contrasting God's final universe-shaking word at the Judgment with his earth-shaking voice once heard by those who stood at the foot of Sinai (12:25-29). Only those who avail themselves in the present (12:14-24) of what Christ has accomplished in the past (1:1–2:18) will be able to stand before that theophany. The initial contrast in 1:1–2:18 anticipated Christ's fully sufficient high priesthood (4:14–10:18). The concluding contrasts in 12:14-29 assume the full explanation of this sufficiency and the need of perseverance through appropriation of its benefits.

Although the Sinai imagery does not begin before 12:14 and is not absolutely clear before 12:18, it is appropriate to begin this final section with 12:4. The coming of Jesus in 12:1-3 marks the turning point between the people of God past (11:1-40) and present (12:4-24). One need only observe the correspondence between the individual subsections of 1:1–2:18 and 12:4-29. God's word spoken in his Son according to 1:1-4 finds ultimate vindication in the word he will speak at the Judgment according to 12:25-29. It is

---

266. Übelacker, *Appell,* 106-9, 185-97.

267. Heb 12:14-17 is included with this section because it echoes the covenantal language intrinsic to Sinai and characteristic of vv. 18-24.

268. Because the finished work of Christ climaxed in his session, the God who spoke at Sinai now offers salvation from Zion. In 12:22-24 all three images coalesce — land/City; Most Holy Place, and the Mount of God's self-disclosure.

through the eternal, now-exalted Son, who is superior to the angels (1:5-14), that God now speaks his gracious word of salvation from the heavenly "Zion" (12:18-24). The intervening explanation of "such a great salvation" (2:3) makes it clear that the "neglect" of 2:1-4 leads to the apostasy of 12:14-17.[269] Finally, the suffering that marks the legitimacy of God's true "sons and daughters" in 12:4-13 is formative in their appropriation of salvation. The suffering appropriate for the Son in 2:5-18 is the means by which he provided that salvation.[270]

God Has Spoken in His Son (1:1–2:18)
In His Son (1:1-4)
   Through the Eternal Son (1:5-14)
      Don't Neglect "So great salvation" (2:1-4)
      By the Suffering Son (2:5-18)

God Speaks/Will Speak in His Son (12:4-29)
      The Suffering of Legitimate Sons and Daughters (12:4-13)
      Don't Fall into Apostasy (12:14-17)
   Through the Son from Heaven (12:18-24)
At the Judgment (12:25-29)

3. Hebrews 3:1–4:13 and 10:19–12:3: On Pilgrimage to the Promised Home

As noted above, when the pastor urges his hearers to persevere until final entrance into God's presence at Christ's return, he employs imagery associated with pilgrimage to the Promised Land. According to Heb 1:1–2:18, God's revelation in his Son has fulfilled the great theophany at Sinai. It was natural to follow this assertion with a warning against identifying with the wilderness generation who stood at Sinai but failed to enter God's promised dwelling place through disobedience (3:1–4:13). This warning finds its sequel in the pastor's invitation of 11:1–12:3 to join the obedient on pilgrimage to the promised City.

Thus after warning his hearers to shun the wilderness generation (3:1–4:13) the pastor proclaims the full sufficiency of Christ their High Priest (4:14–10:18) before urging them to join the faithful (11:1–12:3). He knows

---

269. The warning in 2:1-4 anticipates the example of the wilderness generation in 3:1-19. The example of Esau in 12:14-17 is the foil or opposite of those enrolled in the catalogue of the faithful according to 11:1-40.

270. If the Sinai imagery is not yet apparent in 12:4-13, it is only inferred in 2:5-18 by the contrast with the angels.

that it is more effective to put what he would have his hearers avoid before what he would have them embrace. The location of the means of perseverance between the two is also strategic. The warnings will make his hearers anxious to receive this means of perseverance. On the other hand, how could they effectively accept his urgings to emulate the faithful without comprehending the resources that are theirs in Christ?

It will be necessary to extend the beginning of the section describing the faithful of old from 11:1 back to 10:19. Heb 4:14-16 and 10:19-25, as noted above, are crucial transition points in the pastor's sermon that exhibit many similarities of structure and content. Although a case can be made for attaching both of these passages to the central section describing Christ's priesthood, it is rhetorically more effective to join each to what follows.[271] In 4:14-16 the pastor is whetting the appetite of his hearers for what he is about to say concerning the high priesthood of Christ. By his description of its benefits as the means of perseverance in 10:19-25 he is directing them forward to the life of faith soon to be described.[272] In fact, 10:19-39 as a whole is best understood as a three-link chain binding the history of the faithful in 11:1–12:3 to the sufficiency of Christ as High Priest in 4:14–10:18. The first link urges perseverance based on the great benefits available in Christ (10:19-25); the second warns of the dire consequences for neglecting these benefits (10:26-31); and the third is an invitation to exercise such perseverance by joining the faithful people of God (10:32-39) as described in 11:1–12:3.

The correspondence between the warning in 3:1–4:13 and the invitation in 10:19–12:3 is substantiated by detailed analysis. The paragraphs above have drawn attention to the affinities between 10:19-25 and 4:14-16. The warning of 10:26-31 parallels the warning of 4:12-13; the invitation to join the faithful people of God in 10:32-39 echoes the exhortation to enter God's "rest" in 4:1-11; thus the history of the faithful of old in 11:1-40 stands in opposition to the history of the disobedient wilderness generation in 3:7-

---

271. Michel, 8, and Wolfgang Nauck ("Zum Aufbau des Hebräerbriefes," in *Judentum–Urchristentum–Kirche: Festschrift für J. Jeremias,* ed. Walther Eltester [Berlin: Verlag Alfred Töpelmann, 1960], 199-206) both divide Hebrews into three major sections, as we have done, although both include 13:1-25 in the third major section. Nauck would end the second section at 10:31 because of the parallels between 4:14-16 and 10:19-25. In the 1936 edition of Michel's commentary (p. v) he ended the section at 10:18. However, on p. 8 of the 1966 edition he ends the second section after 10:39 (i.e., 1:1–4:13; 4:14–10:39; 11:1–13:25). Rafael Gyllenberg, "Die Komposition des Hebräerbriefs," *Svensk Exegetisk Årsbok* 22-23 (1957-58): 137-47, is mistaken when he includes 4:14-16 with the previous section. See the discussion in Weiss, 47-48, who also insists that one cannot begin the last section at 11:1.

272. The internal structure of each of these passages sustains this arrangement. See the commentary below.

19. Finally, the introduction of Christ as the faithful Son in 3:1-6 sets a trajectory toward the climactic presentation of Christ as "the Pioneer and Perfecter of the faith" and example par excellence of suffering in 12:1-3. Observe the diagram below:

Avoid the Disobedient (3:1–4:13)
The Faithful Son (3:1-6)
   The Unfaithful Generation (3:7-19)
      Avoid Them (4:1-11)
         Warning (4:12-13)
            [Prepare for Christ's high priesthood] [4:14-16][273]

Christ's High Priesthood (4:14–10:18)

Join the Faithful (10:19–12:3)
            Appropriate Christ's high priesthood (10:19-25)
         Warning (10:26-31)
      Join Them (10:32-29)
   The Past Faithful (11:1-40)
The Exalted Son (12:1-3)

The crucial exhortation to join the faithful of old in 10:19–12:3 is Christologically determined. The pastor begins this exhortation by encouraging his hearers to avail themselves of Christ's high-priestly provision (10:19-25). He concludes by urging them to emulate the sufferings of the faithful Son of God (12:1-3), who as "Pioneer" enables them to pursue the race of faith to the finish line.

4. Hebrews 1:1–4:13 and 10:19–12:29: The Disobedient and the Faithful

It is now possible to appreciate the skillful way in which the pastor has arranged 1:1–4:13 and 10:19–12:29 to encourage perseverance. Heb 1:1–4:13 is "A Short History of the Disobedient"; Heb 10:19–12:29 is "A History of the Faithful People of God from Creation to Consummation." One might summarize the first as follows: the God who revealed himself at Sinai through angels has now disclosed the final revelation of himself in his Son (1:1-14). Thus those who neglect the "great salvation" now revealed are more

273. This section, 4:14-16, is in brackets because it is actually, as noted above, the introduction to 4:14–10:18 rather than the conclusion of 3:1–4:13. Yet it is chiastically parallel to 10:19-25, the introduction to 10:19–12:29.

certainly liable to dire loss than those who received the Sinai revelation (2:1-4). The magnitude and content of this salvation are evident from the way the Son became incarnate and suffered for its procurement (2:5-18). All who have received the Son are "one house" with those who received God's revelation at Sinai (3:1-6). Thus all who confess Christ must not lose God's eternal "rest" through rebellion, as did the wilderness generation (3:7-19) before them. They must persevere until they enter what the rebellious forfeited (4:1-11), realizing the extent of their accountability before God (4:12-13).

The pastor has carefully constructed this "Very Short History of the Disobedient" to maximize its impact. The paragraphs above have noted how the pastor moves from comparing the Son with Sinai (1:1–2:18) to comparing those who hear God's word in the Son with the wilderness generation (3:1–4:13). Heb 1:1–2:18 provides the basis for the Son's high priesthood (4:14–10:18) as well as for comparison with the disobedient wilderness generation in 3:1–4:13. Heb 3:1-6 smoothes the transition from 1:1–2:18 to 3:7–4:13. The eternal Son of God's (1:1-14) assuming the humanity of God's people (2:5-18) confirms them as part of the "household" of God past and present (3:1-6).[274] This identification is fundamental to the use of the wilderness generation as an example (and to the examples of 11:1-40). While the hearers are one with those who have gone before, the privileges provided by this high priesthood give them an advantage over their spiritual ancestors.

The seemingly effortless flow of "The History of the Faithful People of God from Creation to Consummation" (10:19–12:29) reveals the pastor's skill at its best. He urges his hearers to make use of the privileges now theirs through Christ's high priesthood (10:19-25) and warns against rejecting them (10:26-31) in order that they might take their place among God's faithful people (10:32-39) whose history he describes in 11:1–12:29. Heb 11:1-40 relates the history of God's faithful from creation (11:2) to Christ. His coming in 12:1-3 is the grand turning point. Heb 12:4-24 describes the present situation of God's people: they experience the discipline of suffering within the world (12:4-13), but also the joy of fellowship with God and his people in the heavenly City (12:18-24). The pastor would help them endure the suffering by focusing their attention on this present experience of joy. He inserts a semifinal warning between these two realities (12:14-17). The main part of his sermon concludes with a description of the final Judgment and an exhortation to the life of gratitude and awe that should characterize those who anticipate God's "unshakable kingdom" (12:25-29).

The history that began with creation (11:2) and found its turning point in Christ (12:1-3) has reached consummation in the Judgment (12:25-29). The pastor arranges these two histories in order to turn his hearers from dis-

274. See Mackie, *Eschatology and Exhortation*, 216-26.

obedience (3:7-19) to persevering faithfulness (11:1-40). He directs their gaze through what God has said in the incarnation and exaltation of the Son (1:5–2:18) to the invitation he now gives through the incarnate, exalted Son (12:4-24) and toward God's future earth-shaking self-disclosure (12:25-29). He would enable his hearers to endure present and anticipated suffering by turning their attention to present and future eternal joy.

The following diagram should be read from bottom left to top right. (For more detail on I and III, see the diagrams on pp. 65 and 67 above, and on II see the diagram on p. 72 below.)

III. A History of the Faithful People of God from Creation to Consummation (10:19–12:29)

A¹. God Speaks/Will Speak in His Son (12:4-29)

B¹. Avoid the Disobedient (3:1–4:13)

II. The Son's All-Sufficient High Priesthood (4:14–10:18)

I. A Very Short History of the Disobedient People of God (1:1–4:13)

B. Join the Faithful (10:19–12:3)

A. God Has Spoken in His Son (1:1–2:18)

The pastor begins in "A" by presenting the foundation of what he will teach about Christ and salvation. He follows this foundation in "B" with the example he would have his hearers avoid. After explaining the high priesthood of Christ ("II"), he presents the grand history of the examples he would have them emulate ("B¹"), followed by the ultimate destiny of the people of God ("A¹"). Thus "A"/"B" under "I" and "B¹"/"A¹" under "III" are chiastic but not equal. The first pair are given for the sake of the second. Christ the only effective High Priest at the center ("II") is the turning point that is crucial to the whole. It is as High Priest that the Son — eternal, incarnate, exalted — fulfills the role of all-sufficient Savior as introduced in 1:1–2:18 ("A"). The salvation he thus provides clarifies the severity of the warning in 3:1–4:13 ("B") and provides the means to emulate the faithful through endurance in 10:19–12:3 ("B¹"). It is only as High Priest that he provides God's people with present access to God and brings them to their intended eternal destiny as depicted in 12:4-29 ("A¹").

The commentary below will exploit the theological and practical implications that arise from these chiastic parallels. These implications are usually more clearly significant when discussing 10:19–12:29, the second half of the chiasm. But one should note here how this arrangement demonstrates the tight integration between the supposed expository and hortatory parts of Hebrews.

5. Hebrews 13:1-25: The Peroration (and Letter Ending)

The above discussion has neglected Heb 13:1-25. Heb 13:1-21(18?) can be appropriately described as the *peroratio* or peroration with which ancient orators were wont to conclude their speeches.[275] This section is the pastor's final attempt to make his message concrete in the lives of his hearers. The letter-ending in 13:22(19?)-25 shows that this sermon was sent to be read to the congregation and thus confirms its use in the worship of modern Christians.

6. Hebrews 4:14–10:18: Entering the Most Holy Place

The vital central section of Hebrews describes the theme that was first introduced in 2:17-18, the sole sufficiency of Christ as High Priest. He alone can cleanse the people of God from sin and bring them into the divine presence. His high priesthood is the fulfillment of his divine sonship (see on 1:1-4).[276] As noted above, Heb 1:1–4:13 prepares the hearers for this subject. When describing the grand history of the faithful in 11:1–12:29, the pastor assumes a knowledge of the Son's high priesthood. The resources this Priest provides enable believers to faithfully take their place in that history (10:19-39). This central section shows the same structural care and rhetorical skill revealed in the analyses of 1:1–4:14 and 10:19–12:29 above. The introduction in 4:14-16 is carefully crafted to mention the as yet unexplained benefits of Christ's high priesthood in order to arouse the hearers' curiosity and desire. For people steeped in the OT the very assertion of Christ's high priesthood would necessitate comparison with the Aaronic priesthood. It would also require Scriptural evidence for the replacement of Aaron by Christ. Thus it is no surprise that immediately after the introduction in 4:14-16 the pastor provides a comparison/contrast between the Aaronic priest and Christ (5:1-10). This compar-

275. Cf. Koester, 554; Thompson, 273-74.
276. "Son" is clearly the fundamental designation with which the pastor begins and the overarching designation that sustains his entire argument. The pastor develops sonship in terms of Christ's high priesthood and "pioneership." "Son" is associated closely with God's ultimate self-disclosure; "High Priest," with Christ's sacrifice and with his ability to cleanse from sin; "Pioneer," with his resulting ability to bring God's people to the ultimate goal of their pilgrimage in God's presence. Thus the title "Pioneer" is introduced (2:10) well before the failed pilgrimage of the wilderness generation (3:7–4:11) and reasserted in 12:1-3 at the climax of the roll call of faithful pilgrims (11:1-40).

ison/contrast shows how Christ conforms to the requirements of priesthood. It also begins to explain how the Son has fulfilled what the Aaronic high priest only foreshadowed. At the heart of this comparison/contrast in 5:5-6 the pastor presents the biblical evidence for Christ's replacement of Aaron — Ps 110:4. At the conclusion of this passage he returns to this verse: Christ "has become a high priest forever after the order of Melchizedek."

The pastor is urgently concerned that his hearers not only understand but embrace Christ as the fully sufficient High Priest and Savior. Thus before continuing with his explanation of Christ's high priesthood he seeks to awaken them from their laxity and spiritual regression. He first shames them for their immaturity (5:11–6:3); then he warns them of the dire consequences awaiting the once "enlightened" who fall away (6:4-8). Having thus aroused their anxiety, he assures them that he does not believe they have thus fallen (6:9-12). Finally, he urges them to join those like Abraham who live trusting in the certainty of the oath-backed promise of God now fulfilled by Christ's high-priestly entrance into God's presence (6:13-20).

Having thus prepared the soil, the pastor returns to the biblical evidence for Christ's high priesthood. The God who invited him to "sit" at his "right hand" in Ps 110:1 (Heb 1:3, 13) pronounced him "a priest forever after the order of Melchizedek" in v. 4 of the same psalm. In Heb 7:1-10 the pastor turns to Gen 14:17-24 in order to show that Melchizedek was greater than Levi, the father of Aaron. In 7:11-19 he shows how Ps 110:4 substantiates the replacement of Aaron by the eternal Son. In 7:20-25 he outlines the certainty and sufficiency of Christ's priesthood because it is based on both the oath of God and the eternity of the Son. Thus Ps 110:4 makes it clear that the eternal and exalted Son is the Priest that fulfills what the Aaronic priesthood only foreshadowed. The pastor, however, must demonstrate how the eternal Son has become such a High Priest through his suffering and self-offering as intimated in 2:5-18. Thus in Heb 7:26-28 he summarizes what he has already said and introduces this theme of sacrifice.

Hebrews 8:1–10:18 is the pastor's grand "symphony" on the sacrifice of Christ. This symphony consists of three movements (8:1-13; 9:1-22; 9:23–10:18), in each of which the pastor repeats the same three themes in the same order — sanctuary (8:1-2; 9:1-10; 9:23-24); sacrifice (8:3-5; 9:11-15; 9:25–10:14); and covenant (8:6-13; 9:16-22; 10:15-18).[277] The purpose of this symphony is progressively to reveal the ultimate quality of Christ's sacrifice. The first movement initiates this process by focusing on the OT prophecies

---

277. Bruce, 180, entitles 8:1–10:18, "Covenant, Sanctuary, and Sacrifice." For a more detailed analysis of this section see the introduction to 8:1–10:18 on pp. 345-48 below, and G. L. Cockerill, "Structure and Interpretation in Hebrews 8:1–10:18: A Symphony in Three Movements," *BBR* 11 (2001): 179-201.

of the new. The second carries this concern further by looking at both the foreshadowings revealed by and the inadequacy inherent in the descriptions of the old order within the OT. The third concludes by giving a full description of the sufficiency of Christ's sacrifice and the reasons for its effectiveness. Note the increasing size of the sacrifice section at the center of each movement (8:3-5; 9:11-15; 9:25–10:14). These sacrifice sections present Christ's self-offering as the true Day of Atonement sacrifice that has fully provided for the removal of sin. Because it has removed sin, it is also the sacrifice of high-priestly consecration through which he has taken his seat at God's right (8:1-2; 9:1-10; 9:23-24) and the sacrifice by which he has established and become Guarantor/Mediator of the New Covenant (8:6-13; 9:16-22; 10:15-18). Observe the diagram below:

II. The Son's All-Sufficient High Priesthood (4:14–10:18)
   A. Introduction: "We have such a High Priest" (4:14–5:10)
      • Introducing the Son's High Priesthood (4:14-16)
      • The New High Priest and the Old (5:1-10)
   B. Preparation: Don't Fail to Grasp This Truth (5:11–6:20)
      • Reverse Your Unnatural Regression (5:11–6:3)
      • Avoid the Danger of Apostasy (6:4-8)
      • Shun Apostasy and Embrace the Community of the Faithful (6:9-12)
      • Trust God's Promise Verified by God's Oath (6:13-20)
   C. His Legitimacy and Eternity (7:1-28)
      • Melchizedek Greater than Levi (7:1-10)
      • The Son after Melchizedek's Likeness Replaces Aaron (7:11-19)
      • The Benefits of the Son's Priesthood (7:20-25)
      • The Surpassing Majesty of the Son as High Priest (7:26-28)
   D. His All-Sufficient Sacrifice: A Symphony in Three Movements (8:1–10:18)
      • First Movement: The New Promised (8:1-13)
      • Second Movement: The Old Antiquated; the New Foreshadowed (9:1-22)
      • Third Movement: The New Explained (9:23–10:18)

7. The Rhetorical Shape of Hebrews and Its Use of the Old Testament

The section on Hebrews' use of the OT above has demonstrated the importance of the quotations taken from psalms, prophets, and related parts of the OT. The pastor's strategic use of these quotations confirms the structural analysis given above. The discussion that follows asserts the unifying role played by Ps 110:1 and examines the use of these other key quotations in the three major sections of Hebrews: 1:1–4:13; 4:14–10:18; 10:19–12:29.[278]

The pervasive influence of Ps 110:1 is in accord with the pastor's dependence on early Christian tradition.[279] This verse is central to the foundation that the pastor lays in 1:1–2:18. It returns in 8:1-2 to play a crucial role at the heart of the central section on Christ's high priesthood (4:14–10:18). It surfaces again in 12:1-3 at the turning point in the concluding history of the faithful (10:19–12:29). "Sit at my right hand" in 1:13 at the center of the introduction (1:1–2:18) anticipates "You have come to Mount Zion" in 12:22, at the center of the conclusion to the main body of this sermon (12:4-29). In a stunning but most effective way the pastor replaces the expected reference to this verse in the peroration with Jesus' suffering "outside the gate" (13:12). The pastor's explanation of Ps 110:1 in terms of Ps 110:4; Ps 40:6-8; and Jer 31:31-34 is in harmony with the way he develops Christian tradition in terms of Christ's high priesthood and the New Covenant.

Since 1:1–2:18 lays the foundation for what follows, it is no surprise that this passage is dominated by Ps 110:1. The pastor alludes to this verse in 1:3; quotes it at the climax of chapter 1 (1:13); and uses Ps 8:5-7, Ps 22:22, and Isa 8:17-18 to explain its significance in 2:5-18.[280] The time between the

278. France, "Biblical Expositor," 261, affirms the centrality of Psalm 110 though he does not develop its importance for the structure of Hebrews. Buchanan's (xix) designation of Hebrews as a "homiletic midrash" on this psalm may not be as exaggerated as France supposes. See Lincoln, *A Guide,* 13, 69.

279. Ps 110:1 is the OT text most often cited by the NT (Richard Bauckham, *Jesus and the God of Israel* [Grand Rapids: Eerdmans, 2008], 21-23). In addition to Hebrews see Matt 22:44; 26:64; Mark 12:36; 14:62; 16:19; Luke 20:42-43; 22:69; Acts 2:33-35; 5:31; 7:55-56; Rom 8:34; 1 Cor 15:25; Eph 1:20; 2:6; Col 3:1; 1 Pet 3:22; Rev 3:21. See also Attridge, "Psalms," 198, and David M. Hay, *Glory at the Right Hand: Psalm 110 in Early Christianity* (Society of Biblical Literature Monograph Series 18; Nashville: Abingdon, 1973).

280. Caird, "Exegetical Method," 47, argues that Psalms 8, 95, and 110, and Jeremiah 31 "are the dominant passages that control the four main sections of Hebrews." However, he discusses only Ps 110:4, never Ps 110:1. This is a glaring omission in his otherwise very helpful study. This omission leads Caird to make Psalm 8, rather than Ps 110:1, the dominant passage in 1:1–2:18. Although France, "Biblical Expositor," 261, affirms the central importance of Ps 110:1, neither he nor others who have developed Caird's approach (Longenecker, *Biblical Exegesis,* 175-85; Walters, "Rhetorical," 59-70) have corrected Caird's deficiency by affirming the significance of Ps 110:1 in 1:1–2:18 or showing how it unifies the other major quotations. France follows Longenecker in identifying 1:1–2:4 as a separate exposition of a catena of OT quotations on a par with the later expositions of Psalms 8, 95, and 110, and Jeremiah 31(LXX 38). Furthermore, France and Walters both add Hab 2:6 as central to 10:32–12:2(3) and Prov 3:11-12 as central to 12:4-13 and 12:3–13:19, respectively. France finds an additional exposition of "Mount Sinai" in 12:18-29. Caird, "Exegetical Method," 47-49, thinks the pastor has chosen the main passages of his exposition because

session of Christ in the first half of this verse and his return in the second provides the context for the warning from Ps 95:7-11 in Heb 3:1–4:13.

The central section on Christ's high priesthood (Heb 4:14–10:18) attests the high-priestly nature of the session to which the Son was invited in Ps 110:1 (Heb 8:1-2). The first half of this section (4:14–7:28) is dominated by Ps 110:4; the second (8:1–10:18), by Ps 40:6-8. Ps 110:4 proves that the eternal, exalted Son is the true High Priest. Ps 40:6-8 explains how he became this exalted High Priest through his incarnate, obedient self-offering. Jer 31:31-34 (Heb 8:7-13; 10:15-18) provides the foundation for the argument of Heb 8:1–10:18, but Ps 40:6-8 (Heb 10:5-10) is its goal.[281] As the Son answered the invitation of Ps 110:1 with the words of Ps 22:22 and Isa 8:17-18 in Heb 2:5-18, so he answers the proclamation of Ps 110:4 with the words of Ps 40:6-8 at the heart of Heb 8:1–10:18.[282] Yet the pastor returns to Ps 110:1 in 10:11-14 in order to focus his hearers on the sufficiency of the Son seated at God's right as mediator of the New Covenant (10:15-18).[283]

The "History of the Faithful People of God from Creation to Consummation" in 10:19–12:29 affirms the adequacy of the one seated at God's right according to Ps 110:1 and the exemplary nature of the suffering through which he achieved this adequacy (Heb 12:1-3). The first half of this history (10:19–12:3) is dominated by Hab 2:3-4 (Heb 10:37-39) — ". . . my righteous one will live by faith."[284] Heb 10:19-39 prepares the hearers for this invitation to identify with God's righteous people. Heb 11:1-40 describes the righteous of the past whom the hearers are to join. In 12:1-3 the pastor rein-

---

they point to the self-confessed inadequacy of the old order. According to Longenecker, *Biblical Exegesis,* 185, these passages also were understood as speaking of the Messiah and/or "God's redemption in the last days." The pastor was also influenced in his choice of passages by other concerns, such as the hortatory character of Psalm 95(LXX 94):7-11.

281. Some scholars, such as Bruce, 28, have identified Psalm 40 as the dominant passage in this part of Hebrews. The studies by Caird, Longenecker, France, and Walters cited above all opt for Jer 31:31-34. Walters goes so far as to say, "Psalm 40 turns out to be of little more importance to the argument of this section than are Exodus 24:8, which is quoted in 9:20, and Deuteronomy 32:35 and Psalm 135:14, which are quoted in 10:30" (Walters, "Rhetorical," 65). Caird appears to be attracted to Hebrews' use of Jeremiah 31 because it is "a perfectly sound piece of exegesis" (Caird, "Exegetical Method," 47). I would not deny the importance of Jeremiah for Heb 8:1–10:18. However, I would affirm the crucial importance of Ps 40:6-8. As will be demonstrated in the exegesis below, the pastor argues from Jer 31:31-34 to Ps 40:6-8. This psalm passage is the pinnacle of his argument for the superiority of Christ.

282. Attridge, "God in Hebrews," 104-6.

283. Note how Ps 110:1 and 4 unite Heb 4:14–10:18. The pastor begins this central section of Hebrews with Ps 110:4 (Heb 5:5-6). He joins it to Ps 110:1 at the pivotal center of this section (Heb 8:1-2), and then concludes with Ps 110:1 as he approaches the end (Heb 10:11-14). See Attridge, "Psalms," 197-98.

284. France, "Biblical Expositor," 257. Cf. Walters, "Rhetorical," 65-66.

troduces Christ, once having suffered but now exalted in accord with Ps 110:1. Through his suffering/exaltation this "Jesus" has paved the way of faith trod by the heroes of 11:1-40. He has become the supreme example of the endurance enjoined in the final part of this history as recorded in 12:4-29.

The last half of this history features both the exhortation to endure suffering as God's formative discipline in Prov 3:11-12 (Heb 12:4-17) and the promise of final Judgment from Hag 2:6 (Heb 12:25-29). Note the pastor's declaration at the center of this section: "You have come to Mount Zion" (12:18-24). Christ's obedience and subsequent session at God's right according to Ps 110:1 is the means by which his people have come into his presence on "Mount Zion."[285] Thus this final section of the history brings to fruition the foundation that was laid in 1:1–2:18.[286] The diagram below illustrates the way in which Ps 110:1 unifies the pastor's exposition of the OT:

I. A Very Short History of the Disobedient (1:1–4:13)
    A. God Has Spoken in His Son (1:1–2:18)   **Ps 110:1**
    B. Avoid the Disobedient (3:1–4:13)   Ps 95:7-11
II. Christ's All-Sufficient High Priesthood (4:14–10:18)
    A. His Legitimacy and Eternity (4:14–7:28)[287]   Ps 110:4
                               Heb 8:1-2 ———————— **Ps 110:1**
    B. His All-Sufficient Sacrifice (8:1–10:18)   Jer 31:31-34/
                                        Ps 40:6-8

285. In my judgment it is more accurate to see this indirect reference to Ps 110:1 in 12:22 than to argue that 12:18-29 is an exposition "on Mount Sinai," as advocated by France, "Biblical Expositor," 259. Heb 12:18-21 does not even name Mount Sinai. Furthermore, the pastor's emphasis is on the "Mount Zion" to which his hearers "have come." He directs their attention to the "mediator of a new covenant" (v. 24) who has accepted God's invitation, "Sit at my right hand" (Ps 110:1).

286. Just as Ps 110:1 was supported by a catena of quotations in chapter 1 and explained by Ps 8:6-8, Ps 22:22, and Isa 8:17-18 in chapter 2, so "you have come to Mount Zion" is preceded by the exposition of Prov 3:11-12 in 12:3-13 and followed by the use of Hag 2:6 in 12:25-29. Ps 8:6-8 showed why the Son must suffer (2:5-10). Prov 3:11-12, why the "sons and daughters" must suffer (12:4-13).

287. Ps 110:4 (Heb 5:5-6; 5:10; 6:20; 7:1-25) gives 4:14–7:28 a certain coherence. At its very heart (5:5-6) the comparison/contrast between Aaron and Christ in 5:1-10 announces the theme of 7:1-28. Furthermore, the exhortation in 5:11–6:20 leads directly into 7:1-28. Yet 5:1-10 also announces themes that will be developed in 8:1–10:18. The exhortation in 5:11–6:20 has relevance for what the pastor will say in these chapters as well. Thus, while recognizing the coherence that is there in 4:14–7:28 it is helpful when expounding this central section of Hebrews to divide it into four main parts as we have done in the discussion above and the outline at the end of this introduction (4:14–5:10; 5:11–6:20; 7:1-28; 8:1–10:18). See further discussion in the introduction to 4:14–10:18 on pp. 218-20 below. One must not forget, however, that the central point of the unit comes at 8:1-2.

III. A History of the Faithful People of God from Creation to Consummation (10:19–12:29)

B[1]. Join the Faithful (10:19–12:3)[288]   Hab 2:3-4

          Heb 12:1-3 ———————— Ps 110:1

A[1]. God Speaks/Will Speak in His Son (12:4-29) (Ps 110:1)[289]

                           "You have come

                           to Mount Zion"

8. The Rhetorical Shape of Hebrews and Ancient Rhetoric

The above analysis is in full accord with the suggestion that the author of Hebrews has drawn on the resources of ancient rhetoric in order to communicate the truth and move his hearers to action. Suggestions as to the relationship between various sections of Hebrews and the parts of an address described by contemporary handbooks on rhetoric vary.[290] The structuring proposed above is in accord with Übelacker's identification of 1:1–2:18 as the pastor's *exordium* or introduction (1:1-4); *narratio* or conceptual foundation (1:5–2:18); and *propositio* or main "proposition" (2:17-18).[291] It has also identified 13:1-21(18) as the *peroration* or concluding appeal. The above

288. The introductory material in 10:19-39 is closely associated with and flows into the history of the ancient faithful in 11:1-40. The coming of Jesus in 12:1-3 brings this history proper to a climax. Yet in a broader sense 10:19-39 introduces the entire concluding main section of the book. The judgment intimated by the "coming one" in 10:36-39 does not come to fruition until 12:25-29. Thus, in order to recognize the introductory and transitional role of 10:19-39, the outline at the end of this introduction has put a major break between 10:39 and 11:1 as well as at the pivotal point after 12:3. See the introduction to 10:19-39 on pp. 460-63 in the commentary below.

289. As noted in the text above, "You have come to Mount Zion" describes the results of Christ's session. Thus we have here put Ps 110:1 in parentheses.

290. Thompson, 19, for instance, calls 1:1-4 the *exordium;* 1:5–4:13 the *narratio;* 4:14–10:31 the *probatio;* and 10:32–13:25 the *peroratio.* Koester, ix-xii, 83-86, on the other hand, describes 1:1–2:4 as the *exordium,* 2:5-9 as the "proposition," 2:10–12:27 as a series of "arguments," and 12:28–13:21 as the "peroration." He divides the argument into three series (2:10–6:20; 7:1–10:39; and 11:1–12:27). While acknowledging the importance of 2:5-9, in my judgment it is better to follow Üeblacker's identification of 2:17-18 as the pastor's "proposition" (Übelacker, *Appell,* 193-95; cf. O'Brien, 26). Furthermore, Koester's analysis misses the key importance of 4:14-16 and 10:19-25. It may also be somewhat misleading for many that he identifies 5:11–6:20 and 10:26-39 as "traditional digressions." This designation may be correct in terms of the technical language of ancient rhetoric. However, one must not suppose that these sections are "digressions" in the sense that they fail to carry forward the pastor's purpose. There is virtually nothing in this "sermon" that is superfluous to its rhetorical or persuasive impact.

291. Übelacker, *Appell,* 214-29. Cf. Nissilä, *Hohepriestermotiv,* 74-78, 143-47, 230-44.

analysis, however, does more than identify similarities with ancient rhetoric. It provides a basis for understanding how the pastor has effectively carried out his program of persuasion.

C. THE SERMON'S ABIDING MESSAGE

The above structural analysis of Hebrews has been a presentation of its argument and thus an exposition of its teaching. We conclude with a brief summary of Hebrews' message and an affirmation of its continuing validity. Hebrews has a message for the people of God who live in a world that refuses to acknowledge God: God has spoken. The words of Scripture are valid. The incarnation, suffering, obedience, self-offering, and exaltation of God's eternal Son are the ultimate self-disclosure of the divine character fulfilling what has gone before. They are also the all-sufficient provision for entering God's presence through cleansing from sin. This revelation of God and these benefits are now mediated through the incarnate, exalted, eternal Son seated at God's right. Through this word in the Son, God invites his people into his presence. He also provides for the cleansing from the sin of unfaithfulness and for the renewal of the heart in obedience that are necessary for entrance. He invites them to receive these benefits by drawing near. He calls them to a life based on the certainty of his promise of future salvation and the reality of his power for present victory over sin. They are to persevere in this life of faith despite the opposition of the world through the resources that are theirs in Christ until final entrance at Christ's return. For those who turn aside in rebellion and unbelief due to a desire for the world's approval or fear of its ire, the divine word of invitation will become a word of ultimate judgment.

God's people cannot afford to reject the message of Hebrews as no longer valid. Because high priesthood is intrinsic to the Son's identity as both all-sufficient Savior and Revealer, it cannot be reduced to a rhetorical device useful for addressing the hearers.[292] Aaron is the metaphor; the Son is the *true* "Great High Priest" (4:14). The pastor establishes the reality of the Son's high priesthood by basing it on Scripture (7:1-28). The significance of his priesthood is demonstrated by the way in which it encompasses the full scope of his work — incarnation, obedience, and exaltation (7:1–10:18, esp.

---

292. On this subject see both Ekkehard W. Stegemann and Wolfgang Stegemann, "Does the Cultic Language in Hebrews Represent Sacrificial Metaphors? Reflections on Some Basic Problems," in *Hebrews: Contemporary Methods — New Insights,* ed. Gabriella Gelardini (Biblical Interpretation Series 75; Atlanta: Society of Biblical Literature, 2005), 13-23, esp. 18; and Stephen R. Holmes, "Death in the Afternoon: Hebrews, Sacrifice, and Soteriology," in *The Epistle to the Hebrews and Christian Theology,* ed. Richard Bauckham et al. (Grand Rapids: Eerdmans, 2009), 229-52, esp. 248-49.

10:5-10). As High Priest the Son provides a full repertoire of benefits — deliverance from the covenant curse, forgiveness, cleansing, God's law implanted in the heart, present access to God, ultimate entrance into his presence.[293] As High Priest he fulfills the sacrifices of the OT in multiple ways by atoning for sin and confirming himself as efficient High Priest and Guarantor/Mediator of the New Covenant (8:1–10:18). He alone accomplishes what high priesthood was meant to accomplish. The force of the author's argument depends on the Son's being the High Priest par excellence.

Furthermore, the pastor's appeal would lose its effectiveness if the people of God could not experience an authentic cleansing from sin and a true entrance into the divine presence through the Son's genuine high priesthood.[294] As Aaron was a metaphor for Christ's high priesthood, so the ritual defilement of the Old Covenant was a metaphor for the moral and spiritual defilement of the heart or conscience. This defilement characterizes humanity and threatens the professed people of God with ultimate loss. Ritual impurity debarred people from joining the congregation in worship at the Mosaic Tent.[295] In an infinitely more profound way a disobedient and rebellious heart hardened and insensitive to God's word is defilement that separates one from the congregation and prevents present and final entrance into the divine presence.[296] By his obedient self-offering Christ the High Priest that "we have" (4:14; 10:21) has redeemed his people from the covenant curse acquired by their sin (9:16-22); "cleansed their consciences from dead works"

---

293. The fact that no other NT writer develops Christ's high priesthood is insufficient reason to deny its intrinsic nature. Furthermore, the intrinsic character of Christ's high priesthood does not exclude other complementary ways of describing the reality of his person and work. No one description can exhaust the reality of Christ.

294. Mackie, *Eschatology and Exhortation,* 200-201.

295. Koester, 119-23, with justification, argues that the OT makes a distinction between purification/cleansing (καθαρισμός, καθαρίζω) as the removal of uncleanness and sanctification (ἁγιάζω, ἁγιασμός) as being made holy or being set apart for God. A layperson could be purified or ritually clean without being set apart for God by sanctification. A priest, however, not only had to be clean but sanctified or set apart for God in order to enter the Holy Place. See also Mackie, *Eschatology and Exhortation,* 192; David G. Peterson, *Possessed by God: A New Testament Theology of Sanctification and Holiness* (Grand Rapids: Eerdmans, 1995), 34; and deSilva, 202. This distinction, however, is of minimal importance when applied to moral defilement. Moral defilement is what prevents one from entering the presence of God. By its removal one is set apart for God with the privilege of such entrance. Hebrews also refers to perfection (τελειόω). This term emphasizes the privilege of entering God's presence as a result of purification/sanctification. See on 7:19; 9:9; 10:1, 14; 11:40; and 12:23 below.

296. Some argue that Hebrews conceives of sin as both "defilement" and "unfaithfulness" (Pfitzner, 43-44). However, unfaithfulness or disobedience is defilement. A rebellious person is a defiled person.

(9:10-14) so that they can approach God with "true hearts" and purified lives (10:22); and empowered them for persevering obedience under the new covenant by inscribing God's law on their hearts (10:15-18). The pastor's great concern is that all who hear his voice continue to persevere by availing themselves of the grace provided by drawing near to God through this effective High Priest (4:14-16; 10:19-25).

D. THE SERMON'S OUTLINE

An outline of Hebrews based on the above structural analysis is given below as an aid to the reader of this commentary. The exposition that follows is organized according to this outline. The numbers in parentheses following the sub-headings of Part III designate the corresponding sections in Part I (and Part II, A, 1) with which the subheadings of Part III are chiastically parallel.

I. A Very Short History of the Disobedient People of God (1:1–4:13)
   A. Sinai Revisited: God Has Spoken in the Eternal, Incarnate, Now Exalted Son (1:1–2:18)
      1. God Has Spoken through His Son (1:1-4)
      2. The Incomparable Majesty of the Eternal, Exalted Son (1:5-14)
      3. The Urgency of Attending to God's Son-Mediated Revelation (2:1-4)
      4. The Crucial Importance of the Incarnate, Suffering Son (2:5-18)
   B. Tested at Kadesh-Barnea: Avoid the Congregation of the Disobedient (3:1–4:13)
      1. Consider Jesus, A Son over the House of God (3:1-6)
      2. Avoid the Company of the Faithless Generation (3:7-19)
      3. Pursue the Blessing Lost by the Faithless Generation (4:1-11)
      4. You Are Accountable before the Word of God (4:12-13)
II. The Son's High Priesthood — Resource and Urgency for Perseverance (4:14–10:18)
   A. The Life of Faith and the High Priesthood of the Son (4:14–5:10)
      1. Embrace This Great High Priest (4:14-16)
      2. The New High Priest and the Old (5:1-10)
   B. Don't Be Unresponsive But Grasp What Christ Has Provided (5:11–6:20)
      1. Reverse Your Unnatural Regression (5:11–6:3)
      2. Avoid the Danger of Apostasy (6:4-8)

79

3. Shun Apostasy and Embrace the Community of the Faithful (6:9-12)
4. Trust God's Promise Verified by God's Oath (6:13-20)
  C. Our High Priest's Legitimacy and Eternity (7:1-28)
    1. Melchizedek Is Greater than Levi (7:1-10)
    2. The Priest in "the Likeness of Melchizedek" Displaces Aaron (7:11-25)
    3. This Priest Is Exactly the Kind of Priest We Need (7:26-28)
  D. Our High Priest's All-Sufficient Sacrifice: A Symphony in Three Movements (8:1–10:18)
    1. First Movement: The New Promised (8:1-13)
    2. Second Movement: The Old Antiquated; the New Foreshadowed (9:1-22)
    3. Third Movement: The New Explained (9:23–10:18)
III. A History of the Faithful People of God from Creation to Consummation (10:19–12:29)
  A. The Life of Persevering Faith and the High Priesthood of the Son (10:19-39)
    1. Avail Yourselves of This Great Priest (10:19-25) (II, A, 1)[297]
    2. You Are More Accountable because of This High Priest (10:26-31) (I, B, 4)
    3. Pursue the Blessing Promised the Faithful (10:32-39) (I, B, 3)
  B. The Past History of the People of God until the Coming of Jesus (11:1–12:3)
    1. Join the Company of the Faithful of Old (11:1-40) (I, B, 2)
    2. Keep Your Eyes on Jesus, Seated at God's Right Hand (12:1-3) (I, B, 1)
  C. The Present History of the People of God until the Consummation (12:4-29)
    1. God's True Sons and Daughters Endure the Discipline of Suffering (12:4-13) (I, A, 4)
    2. Don't Sell Your Birthright, As Esau Did (12:14-17) (I, A, 3)
    3. God's Firstborn Enter His Presence through the Exalted Jesus (12:18-24) (I, A, 2)
    4. God Will Speak "Once More" at the Final Judgment (12:25-29) (I, A, 1)
IV. Instructions for the Life of Gratitude and Godly Fear (13:1-25)

---

297. The numbering in parenthesis following each of these sections designates the parallel section in part I (and part II, A, 1) above. See the structural-rhetorical analysis of Hebrews on pp. 60-79 above.

A. The Community of the Faithful and the Life of Gratitude and Godly Fear (13:1-6)
B. The Unbelieving World and the Life of Gratitude and Godly Fear (13:7-17)
C. A Sermon Sent as a Letter (13:18-25)

The Epistle to the
HEBREWS

Text, Exposition, and Notes

I. A VERY SHORT HISTORY OF THE DISOBEDIENT PEOPLE OF GOD (1:1–4:13)

As the pastor begins his appeal, he invites his hearers to envision God's people once again gathered around Sinai (1:1–2:18) and to recall their subsequent rebellion in the wilderness (3:1–4:13). The God who spoke at Sinai has now spoken in his Son, providing the "great salvation" (2:3) anticipated by that earlier angel-mediated revelation (1:1–2:18). The comparison/contrast between the Son and Moses in 3:1-6 reinforces the superiority of God's Son-mediated word and provides a transition to the post-Sinai rebellion of the Moses-led wilderness generation (3:7–4:13). Those who receive God's word in his Son must avoid imitating that generation's unfaithfulness (3:7-19) in order to enter the "rest" that generation forfeited (4:1-11), as people accountable before God's inescapable word (4:12-13).

Thus this privileged wilderness generation embodies the history of those who have experienced God's redemption but refuse to live in trust and obedience. Their experience puts before the pastor's readers the dire consequences of joining them in rebellion. Present accountability is greater because God has now spoken in his Son. Yet this speaking is a "great salvation" (2:3) that opens the possibility of life with God in union with the faithful whose history is recounted in 10:19–12:29.

A. SINAI REVISITED: GOD HAS SPOKEN IN THE ETERNAL, INCARNATE, NOW EXALTED SON (1:1–2:18)

In these two chapters the pastor introduces God's ultimate revelation (1:1-4) by inviting his congregation to overhear the conversation between God (1:1-14) and his Son (2:5-18). God addresses the Son by using the words of Scripture to affirm his eternal sonship and inviting him to the place of all authority at his right hand (1:5-14). The Son answers by affirming his identity with the people of God, confirming his faithfulness, and accepting God's invitation (2:5-18). The Son is superior to the angelic mediators of the Sinai revelation both through his exaltation as the eternal Son (1:5-14) and through the incarnate obedience that facilitated his exaltation as Savior (2:5-18). The initial emphasis on the eternal, exalted Son finds immediate application in the warning of 2:1-4.[1] This warning anticipates and is reinforced by the Son's provision of such a "great salvation" (2:3) as described in 2:5-18. These first two chapters climax in 2:17-18 with a word of encouragement that announces the main theme of Hebrews — the eternal Son is the all-sufficient High Priest. In summary: the Son is the fulfillment of God's OT revelation (1:1-4). Since he is far superior to the angels through whom the Old Covenant was revealed (1:5-14), it is urgent to heed God's salvation mediated through him (2:1-4). He has procured this salvation and assumed his place of preeminence through his incarnate obedience and death (2:5-18).

1. God Has Spoken through His Son (1:1-4)

> 1 *At various times and in various ways of old God spoke to the fathers by the prophets,* 2 *but at the end of these days he has spoken to us by one who is Son, whom he established as heir of all things, through whom he also made the worlds.* 3 *As the radiance of God's glory and the exact representation of God's very being, and as the one who bears all to its intended end by the word of his power, the Son, by making purification for sins, sat down at the right hand of the Majesty on high.* 4 *Thus he became as much superior to angels as the name he has inherited is more excellent than theirs.*

Although Heb 1:1-4 is an integral part of chapters 1 and 2, it is also carefully constructed to introduce the pastor's sermon. Thus these verses are fundamental to all that follows.[1] The pastor begins by announcing his basic prem-

---

1. Thus there is a tight coherence in 1:1–2:4 (see Cynthia Long Westfall, *A Discourse Analysis of the Letter to the Hebrews: The Relationship between Form and Meaning* [LNTS 297; London: T&T Clark, 2005], 89-99). It is important, however, to recognize the way in which 2:5-18 both reinforces 2:1-4 and completes 1:5-14.

1. For Heb 1:1-4 as the *exordium* or introduction to this sermon see Walter G. Übelacker, *Der Hebräerbrief als Appell: Untersuchungen zu Exordium, Narratio und Postscriptum (Hebr 1–2 und 13,22-25)* (Coniectanea Neotestamentica or Coniectanea Biblica: New Testament Series 21; Stockholm: Almqvist & Wiksell, 1989), 106; A. Vanhoye, *Situation du Christ: Épître aux Hébreux 1–2* (Paris: Cerf, 1969), 52-54; Thompson, 18-19; the commentaries cited in Koester, 174-75; and the Introduction to this

ise: God's self-disclosure in his Son is the climax and fulfillment of all previous revelation. This premise lays a solid foundation both for what the pastor will say about the Son's high-priestly ministry and for his urgent exhortations to faithful endurance.[2] He calls his listeners to attention through the elevated style of this passage and by building anticipation for the coming disclosure of what God has now said in his Son (1:2). Through the Scriptural quotations in 1:5-14 God himself attests the significance of this premise by affirming the grandeur of the Son.

Verses 1-2a describe God's revelation in his Son as the fulfillment of — and thus in continuity with — his OT revelation.[3] These verses climax in the declaration that God "has spoken to us in one who is Son." Verses 2b-3 underscore the ultimacy of this revelation by showing the Son's participation in the nature of God and by affirming his exaltation/session as the culmination of his saving work. Verse 3 climaxes with, "[the Son] sat down at the right hand of the Majesty on high." Verse 4 provides a transition whereby the ultimate greatness of the Son is further elaborated through comparison with the angels (vv. 5-14).

Like the two halves of a bean, the two climactic statements noted above are the seed of the pastor's theological vision: (1) God "has spoken to us in one who is Son" (1:1-2a); (2) "by making purification for sins, [the Son] sat down at the right hand of the Majesty on high" (1:3).[4] This making

---

commentary above (pp. 63, 76-77). Koester's identification of 1:1–2:4 as the *exordium* gives inadequate consideration to both the unique character of 1:1-4 and the close association between 1:1–2:4 and 2:5-18.

2. Although these verses do not mention Christ's high priesthood, they still (*pace* Westfall, *Discourse Analysis,* 98-99) introduce what follows by laying a foundation for that priesthood.

3. G. R. Smillie, "Contrast or Continuity in Hebrews 1.1-2?" *NTS* 51 (2005): 543-60, makes several important observations. On the one hand, the pastor uses none of the words in this opening section that he so skillfully uses elsewhere to depict contrast (e.g., ἀλλά, "but"; κρείττων, "better"; μεῖζον, "greater," etc., Smillie, "Contrast or Continuity," 550-52). There are also other features that affirm continuity between God's word in the prophets and in the Son (Smillie, "Contrast or Continuity," 552-56). Most of these are noted in the commentary below. These facts suggest that the element of contrast in 1:1-4 has often been overdone. On the other hand, one cannot remove all contrast because of the elevated diction with which the pastor describes the Son as the agent of God's revelation in vv. 2-3 (Smillie, "Contrast or Continuity," 558). When one sees fulfillment as an affirmation of continuity, then the unity of God's word throughout history is in complete harmony with the superiority and finality of what he has said in Christ. Both what God has said in the prophets and what he has said in his Son are valid as revelation, though the latter provided the "great salvation" (2:3) typified by the former. See "The Sermon's Use of the Old Testament" in the Introduction to this commentary (pp. 41-59, esp. 52-54).

4. The importance of these statements is highlighted by the fact that "he has spo-

purification and subsequent session will be explained in terms of high priesthood. They are the full disclosure of his sonship and thus the final and complete Son-mediated revelation of God.[5] The pastor intends his hearers to focus upon this Son exalted at God's right hand and the benefits he provides (8:1; 12:1-3).

1-2a   Even in English one can appreciate the balance and compactness of the two clauses in vv. 1-2a. These clauses articulate the basis for any sound biblical theology by affirming the continuity between God's OT revelation with its focus on Sinai and his final revelation in Christ. At the same time they anticipate what will soon be elaborated: Christ is God's final word that fulfills and thus surpasses his previous revelation. This initial focus on both continuity with, and eschatological superiority over, earlier revelation is fundamental to all that the pastor will say about the sufficiency of Christ for his hearers' perseverance. Thus in these opening words the pastor lays the foundation of the appeal for faithfulness that characterizes his sermon. It will be helpful to set the comparative elements of 1:1-2a in columns:

1. At various times and in various ways of old[6]	At the end of these days
2. God	(he)
3. spoke	has spoken
4. to the fathers	to us
5. by the prophets	by one who is Son

Items two through four emphasize the continuity of God's revelation: the one people of God has always been established by the word of God. The same God has spoken twice: "to the fathers" and "to us." The term "fathers" affirms the familial connection between those addressed by God's word of old and those now confronted by his word in the Son.[7] Those who have re-

---

ken" (1:2) and "he has sat down" (1:3b) are the main verbs in the Greek text of vv. 1-2 and 3-4 respectively (Lane, 1:3-9).

5. See Vanhoye, *Situation*, 52-54.

6. Vanhoye argues that "at various times and in various ways" is separate from "of old" and without parallel. Vanhoye, *Situation*, 56-57. When these words are included, this opening phrase that describes "of old" has eleven syllables and thus corresponds well with the ten syllables of its contrasting counterpart that begins with "at the end of these days."

7. A few manuscripts, probably including $\mathfrak{P}^{12}$, have ὑμῶν, "our," after πατράσιν, "fathers," thus making the connection between the "fathers" and the present Christian readers explicit. However, the use of "fathers" without a qualifier "marks the relation of 'the fathers' to the whole Church" (Weiss, 138 [translation mine]). Cf. Vanhoye, *Situation*, 57-58.

ceived God's revelation in the Son are the true descendants of the people of God in the OT. While it is true that some of the latter failed (3:7-16), others (see 11:1-38) were faithful to the end. The pastor's concern is that all who hear what he has to say about God's Son-mediated word be like the latter, not the former.[8]

Elements one and five in these columns reinforce the continuity of God's revelation by emphasizing the ultimate nature of his self-disclosure in the Son. Verse 1 begins emphatically with "at various times" and "in various ways." Each of these expressions translates a single Greek word. These two words sound alike and are almost indistinguishable in meaning.[9] By their sonorous combination the pastor embraces the bounty of the various times, places, ways, and methods used in God's OT revelation. Furthermore, "of old" affirms the antiquity and thus in the ancient mind the integrity of Scripture.[10] Yet these very terms that describe the rich diversity and venerable authority of God's OT revelation expose its incomplete and preliminary role when compared with God's final word spoken "at the end of these days" (v. 2).[11] The diversity and fragmentation of the old have been given focus and fulfillment by God's self-disclosure in "one who is Son." As will be explained in the following chapters, the old has been shown to be typological and anticipatory of the "great salvation" (2:3) he has provided.[12]

The Greek for "at the end of days" is one of several related phrases commonly used in the LXX to describe the prophesied time of God's coming judgment and salvation.[13] Many assume that this expression reflects a Hebrew form of speech in which the qualifying noun, "of days," is the main

---

8. The pastor uses a complementary participle, "having spoken" (λαλήσας), to describe God's address in the prophets (1:1), but the finite verb "has spoken" (ἐλάλησεν) in reference to the Son (1:2a). See Übelacker, *Appell,* 79. Though most English versions translate the participle as complementary, the pastor's emphasis is on what God has said in the Son. Compare the attributive construal of this participle in the NKJV ("God, who spoke . . .") with the temporal interpretation of the NASB ("God, after he spoke . . .").

9. These two words, πολυμερῶς and πολυτρόπως, both begin with the morpheme πολυ. No other extant pre-second-century author uses them in combination. πάλαι, "of old"; πατράσιν, "fathers"; and προφήταις, "prophets," also begin with a "p" sound and thus give an aural cohesion to this verse.

10. See Josephus, *Ag. Ap.* 1.29; 1.37-42. Cf. Mitchell, 35, 41.

11. For multiplicity as incompleteness see 7:23-24, 27; 9:25-28; 10:1-3, 11-14; Bénétreau, 1:66; and Riggenbach, 5. What might have been thought richness before Christ is now seen as the preliminary revelation that it was.

12. See Hughes, 36. *Pace* Ellingworth, 91.

13. See ἐπ' ἐσχάτου τῶν ἡμερῶν in Jer 23:20; 49:39 and the variants ἐπ' ἐσχάτῳ τῶν ἡμερῶν (Deut 4:30) and ἐπ' ἐσχάτων τῶν ἡμερῶν (Jer 30:24, Ezek 38:16, Dan 2:28, Dan 10:14, Hos 3:5, and Mic 4:1). These phrases translate the Hebrew באחרית הימים, "at the end of days."

idea, and thus understand it to mean "the days of the end" or "the last days."[14] By adding "these" the writer of Hebrews affirms that the present time is the time of prophetic fulfillment. These "last days" began with Christ's session and will end with his second coming, when his "enemies" will be made "a stool" under his "feet" (1:13).[15] They are also the time in which the recipients of Hebrews are urged to be faithful and to avail themselves of the benefits of God's redemption in the Son.[16] A more literal "at the end of these days," however, focuses our attention on the event of Christ's coming at the conclusion of the days of prophetic revelation.[17] Revelation in the Son is the "consummation of the ages" (9:26).

This opening sentence, which began with "at various times and in various ways," reaches a climax with the word "Son." God's word in the Son brings together all the pieces of that earlier fragmented revelation by fulfilling the salvation it anticipated. The NRSV's "a Son" accurately reflects the absence of the Greek definite article. This omission emphasizes the quality of sonship. God's final word is through "one who is" nothing less than his "Son." The pastor describes the entire OT revelation as given through "the prophets" in order to affirm both its validity and its anticipatory character.[18] If one likens God's word through the prophets to hearing someone over the radio, then his word in the Son is like meeting the speaker in person.

God did not speak merely "by" but "in" the prophets and preeminently "in" the Son.[19] Jeremiah shows us how intimately the prophets were involved with the word of God (Jer 8:18–9:3; 12:1-4). Hosea's life embodied his message (Hos 1:2-11). In their very persons God addressed their hearers. In a much more profound sense God's revelation was in the person of the Son. As the pastor will show, the Son fulfills his role as the ultimate revelation of God by becoming our fully adequate Savior seated at God's right hand (see esp. 2:5-18 below).[20]

---

14. Ellingworth, 93, refers to the Hebraic influence shown by the adjectival use of a noun in the genitive case. See also Riggenbach, 3.

15. Bénétreau, 1:65-66.

16. Weiss, 139.

17. On this interpretation Hebrews' use of the singular ἐσχάτου rather than the more common LXX plural ἐσχάτων is purposeful. Compare also 1 Pet 1:20: ἐπ᾽ ἐσχάτου τῶν χρόνων, "at the end of the ages."

18. Cf. Luke 24:25 and John 6:45. Both Moses (*1 Clem.* 43:1) and David (Acts 2:30) can be called prophets.

19. Here ἐν with the third inflectional form is the locative of sphere ("in the prophets"/"in the Son") rather than the instrumental of agency ("by the prophets"/"by the Son"). The quality of the author's Greek prohibits limiting ἐν to the significance of the Hebrew preposition ב (Riggenbach, 4). Nor, *pace* Braun, 19, is it necessary to draw on Hellenistic speculation about God's spirit displacing the personality. Cf. Weiss, 134.

20. Spicq, 2:58.

The pastor will use the finality of God's Son-revelation in two inter-locking ways. When he urges perseverance in faith he will remind his hearers that the responsibility of those who hear God's word in the Son is much greater than that of those who received earlier revelation (see 2:1-4; 10:26-31; 12:25-29). When he describes Christ's high priesthood he will contend that Christ has procured an effective salvation that exposes the typological, rather than salvific, role of the Old Covenant order (4:14–10:18). The finality of this salvation, in turn, provides the grace for and undergirds the urgency of perseverance (10:19-31).

2b-3 In these verses the pastor uses three relative clauses to describe the grandeur of this "Son" (v. 2a) in order to establish the magnitude of the revelation he mediates. Some have suggested that these relative clauses with descriptive participial phrases betray the presence of a familiar hymn or con-fession. This kind of construction belies a poetic style similar to that of other purported NT liturgical pieces (Phil 2:6-11; Col 1:15-20; 1 Tim 3:16) that also speak of the Son's preexistence, incarnation, and exaltation. The pastor's sophisticated vocabulary is appropriate for hymn or confession.[21] It is more likely, however, that the pastor composed these lines. The only unique terms are the words translated "radiance" and "exact imprint." These expressions are in full accord with the way his vocabulary reflects the sophisticated Jew-ish Alexandrian milieu represented by the Wisdom of Solomon and Philo.[22] The pastor differs from the NT parallels above both in the vocabulary he uses to describe and the order in which he recounts the Son's pre-existence, incar-nation, and exaltation.[23] Finally, these relative clauses are integral to the pas-tor's argument as evidenced by the way he uses the biblical quotations in vv. 5-14 to substantiate their validity and elaborate their significance.[24]

2b-c Comparison with the other supposed liturgical passages men-tioned above might lead one to expect that the pastor would begin by describ-ing the Son's preexistence or his role as agent of creation. He begins, how-ever, with heirship, both because it is rhetorically effective and because it is determinative for the meaning of sonship. This beginning is rhetorically ef-

---

21. For studies which affirm the use of a hymn see Koester, 178-79.

22. John P. Meier, "Symmetry and Theology in the Old Testament Citations of Heb 1,5-14," *Bib* 66 (1985): 524-28; J. Frankowski, "Early Christian Hymns Recorded in the New Testament: A Reconsideration of the Question in the Light of Hebrews 1,3," *BZ* 27 (1983): 183-90.

23. Nor is *1 Clem.* 36:1-6 witness to a preexisting tradition quoted by both He-brews and *1 Clement,* as claimed by J. C. O'Neill, "'Who Is Comparable to Me in My Glory?' 4Q491 Fragment 11 (4Q491C) and the New Testament," *NovT* 42 (2000): 33-35. For *1 Clement*'s dependence on Hebrews see the Introduction and the literature there cited (p. 34, n. 144).

24. Meier, "Symmetry," 524-28. See also Thompson, 33.

fective because it focuses the attention of the pastor's hesitant hearers on both the central theme and the ultimate concern of Hebrews:[25] the exalted Son/High Priest who is able to succor the faithful amid every distress (8:1; 12:1-3) and the great value of the inheritance that awaits the persevering people of God through him (cf. 1:14; 6:12, 17; 9:15).[26] However, the pastor's most important reason for beginning this way is that of the relationship between inheritance and sonship. Inheritance is the logical extension and fruition of sonship.[27] "Whom he made heir of all" stands in chiastic parallel with "he sat down at the right hand of the Majesty on high" (1:3d).[28] The Son entered the fulfillment of his sonship as universal heir at the heavenly session. His full exercise of that inheritance will become evident at his second coming "when his enemies are made a footstool for his feet" (1:13; 2:5-10; 9:28) and the faithful enter their inheritance with him (1:14).[29] Hebrews will demonstrate, then, that the eternal Son fulfills his role as Son and Heir only through his incarnation, earthly obedience, self-offering, and exaltation. His all-sufficient high priesthood and all that he did to become the "source of eternal salvation" (5:9) are intrinsic to what he is as "Son."[30] The Son fulfills

25. John P. Meier, "Structure and Theology in Heb 1,1-14," *Bib* 66 (1985): 176-77.

26. See Bénétreau, 1:66-67; Spicq, 2:5; Vanhoye, *Situation,* 62-64; and Koester, 178.

27. Bénétreau, 1:66; Riggenbach, 6; Thompson, 39.

28. As both Daniel J. Ebert IV, "The Chiastic Structure of the Prologue of Hebrews," *TJ* 13 n.s. (Fall 1992): 163-79; and Meier, "Structure," 168-89 agree. Ebert argues for the following chiastic parallels: the prophets/Son in 1:1-2a and the Son/angels in 1:4; "whom he made heir of all" (v. 2b) and "he sat down at the right hand of the Majesty on high" (v. 3d); "by whom he made the worlds" (v. 2c) and "by making purification for sin" (v. 3d). The central focus is on "being the radiance of his glory and the express image of his nature; and bearing all things by the word of his power." Ebert's weakest link is the relationship between 1:1-2a and 1:4. Meier, "Structure," 188-89, avoids this problem by beginning at v. 2b. "Whom he made heir of all" is parallel both to "he sat down at the right hand of the Majesty on high" and to the Son's superiority over the angels in v. 4. Note "heir" in 1:2b and "inherited" in 1:4. "By whom he made the worlds" (v. 2b) corresponds with "bearing all things by the word of his power" (v. 3b). The central emphasis falls on "being the radiance of his glory and the express image of his very being." Meier does not adequately account for "by making purification for sin" (v. 3c). Ebert's link between "by whom he made (ἐποίησεν) the worlds" and "by making (ποιησάμενος) purification for sin" is worth consideration (Ebert, "Chiastic Structure," 170-71).

29. Riggenbach, 6-8.

30. "[B]ut the author's assumption is that high priesthood is a part of the role of Jesus as Son" (Harold S. Songer, "A Superior Priesthood: Hebrews 4:14–7:27," *RevExp* 82 [1985]: 348, citing Robinson, 59-60, in support). Cf. also, ". . . One through whom the world was made, the One who is the 'exact imprint of God's very being' is not the 'eternal Son' (if by that is meant a Son whose identity is abstracted from the humanity he would

beyond all expectation the promise of universal dominion given to David's heir in Ps 2:8.[31]

What could be more fitting than for the one "whom he made heir of all" to be the one "through whom he created the worlds"? The Greek word translated "worlds" (cf. 11:3) can also mean "ages" (6:5; 9:26). Through the Son God created the temporal ages of the world and all that they contain — "the universe and everything in it" (NLT).[32] God's revelation in the Son is final because it comes through the one who is God's agent in creation as well as the God-designated universal heir. The attribution to the Son of both creation and ultimate sovereignty shows clearly that he is included within the unique identity of God. These functions are divine prerogatives never delegated to another.[33]

3   For ease in reading, the T/NIV, like most English translations, begins a new sentence at v. 3 — "The Son is the radiance of God's glory. . . ." In Greek, however, vv. 3-4 are one long relative clause that continues the description of the Son begun in v. 2b-c. God's self-revelation affirmed in vv. 1-2 is fulfilled in the person and work of the Son as described in vv. 3-4.[34]

---

assume in the incarnation) but the Son whose identity is already established in that he is appointed heir of all things" (Bruce L. McCormack, "'With Loud Cries and Tears': The Humanity of the Son in the Epistle to the Hebrews,'" in *The Epistle to the Hebrews and Christian Theology,* ed. Richard Bauckham et al. [Grand Rapids: Eerdmans, 2009], 59).

31. Note the quotation of Ps 2:7 and 2 Sam 7:14 in v. 5 below, along with Ps 45:6-7 in vv. 8-9 and Ps 110:1 in v. 13. Although these verses find their fulfillment in David's heir, they are attributed directly to the exalted Son who shares in the universal reign of God without reference to David. This omission is in accord with Pamela Eisenbaum's observation that Hebrews avoids reference to the earthly institutions so closely associated with kingship — land, Jerusalem, and Temple (Pamela Eisenbaum, *The Jewish Heroes of Christian History: Hebrews 11 in Literary Context* [SBLDS 156; Atlanta: Scholars Press, 1997], *passim*). Hebrews speaks only of a "heavenly" home, a "heavenly" Jerusalem that is identical to the "heavenly" Most Holy Place where the Son sits enthroned at God's right hand as heir of all things. The session of the Son, affirmed so clearly in the immediately following verses, sets the stage for these heavenly realities. In this light, then, the pastor is probably not consciously arguing that Jesus is both a Priest like Aaron and a King like David.

32. Vanhoye, *Situation,* 66. αἰῶνας refers to "The sum of the 'periods of time' including all that is manifested in and through them" (Westcott, 8). Many would also include the coming eternal world of salvation. See Ellingworth, 96; Hughes, 40, n. 10; Koester, 178; and Meier, "Structure," 178, n. 40. Vanhoye is probably correct, however, when he argues that "made" restricts reference to the temporal created order.

33. Richard Bauckham, "The Divinity of Jesus Christ in the Epistle to the Hebrews," in *The Epistle to the Hebrews and Christian Theology,* ed. Richard Bauckham et al. (Grand Rapids: Eerdmans, 2009), 15-18. The terms for "all things" and "the worlds" are "monotheistic language designed to distinguish God from the whole of the rest of reality" (Bauckham, "Divinity," 21).

34. Wider is correct in observing the theocentric basis of these opening verses,

Thus, a more literal rendering of v. 3 reads: "who being the radiance of his glory and the exact representation of his very being, and bearing all by the word of his power, having made purification for sins, sat down at the right hand of the Majesty on high."

"Being the radiance of God's glory and the exact representation of God's very being" is the heart of this description of the Son as the final revelation of God.[35] God's "glory" is the revelation of his nature (Lev 9:23; Num 14:21-22; Isa 40:5), often pictured as resplendent with light (Exod 24:16-17; 40:34-35; 1 Kgs 8:11). As "the radiance of God's glory" the Son is the "out shining" of who God really is. Although evidence from contemporary usage is indecisive, the close identification of the Son with God in the immediate context prohibits reduction of "radiance" to mere "reflection" (NRSV).[36]

The Greek word translated "exact representation" was used for the impression left by a seal and for the "impress, reproduction, representation" on a coin.[37] This term signifies an exact correspondence between the impression and the seal that made it.[38] Thus the Son is a perfect "imprint" of the "very being" of God.[39] These two complementary expressions, "the radiance of God's glory" and "the exact imprint of God's very being,"[40] preserve the distinctness of the Son while affirming that the finality of his revelation is based on his identity with the God he reveals.[41]

---

even if he draws conclusions unwarranted by the text. David Wider, *Theozentrick und Bekenntnis: Untersuchungen zur Theologie des Redens Gottes im Hebräerbrief,* ed. Erich Grässer (BZNW 87; Berlin and New York: Walter de Gruyter, 1997), 12-13.

35. Ebert, "Chiastic Structure," 167-74, and Meier, "Structure," 188-89. See the summary of their arguments on p. 92, n. 28 above.

36. Braun, 25; Bénétreau, 1:68-69. The Greek term ἀπαύγασμα can be active, "radiance," or passive, "reflection." It is active in Philo's *Spec. Laws* 4.123; and *Creation* 146, but passive in *Planting* 50. It is difficult to tell whether ἀπαύγασμα is active or passive in Wis 7:26, where wisdom is "the radiance/reflection (ἀπαύγασμα) of everlasting light." "A pure emanation of the glory of the Almighty" (NRSV) in 7:25 supports the active; "a spotless mirror of the working of God" (NRSV) in 7:26b, the passive. Origen, Chrysostom, Basil, Theodoret, and Gregory of Nyssa affirmed the active, as did the orthodox Fathers during the Arian controversy. See Spicq, 2:6 and Hughes, 42.

37. See Philo, *Drunkenness* 133.

38. Bénétreau, 1:69.

39. For χαρακτήρ, "exact imprint," see BDAG, 1078, 2. Although ὑπόστασις may be used otherwise in Heb 3:14; 11:1, there can be no dispute that here it refers to the essence or actual being of God.

40. Since "the radiance of God's glory" and "the exact imprint of God's very being" both complement the participle ὤν ("being"), they are to be taken together as complementing one another (Spicq, 2:8).

41. Bénétreau, 1:70. Braun, 26-27. According to Hughes, 44, the first phrase emphasizes identity with God's nature; the second, the separateness of the Son's person.

"Bearing all by the word of his power" also affirms the close identity of the Son with God. The universal heir and agent of creation is also the one who sustains the universe. The neuter plural "all" is as comprehensive as the "all" the Son inherited or the "worlds" he created (1:2). "By the word of his power," or, more smoothly, "by his powerful word,"[42] reinforces the sovereignty of the Son. The Son sustains the world by the same word through which it was created (compare 11:3). The ambiguity as to whether it is the Son's or God's word only highlights the close identity between the two.

The Son through whom God created the world and its ages (1:2a) does more than "sustain" them; he also "bears" or "directs" those ages to their God-intended goal.[43] The pastor is not propounding an abstract doctrine of predestination. The immediate context suggests that the Son accomplishes God's ultimate purposes by his making purification for sins and by his subsequent session. The broader context would add his second coming.[44]

It is necessary to examine the relationship of the two closely related present participles, "being" and "bearing,"[45] to the main verb of the sentence, he "sat down." The ESV is typical of the many English versions that translate these two participles as descriptive of the eternal Son without reference to his session: "He is the radiance of the glory of God and the exact imprint of his nature, and he upholds the universe by the word of his power." Koester, however, goes to the opposite extreme by arguing that these participles describe what the Son does at his session and thus apply only to the exalted Son: He "sat down at the right hand of the Majesty on high as the radiance of his glory and the impress of his substance, bearing all things by his word of power."[46]

The truth lies between these extremes. The Son has been the "radiance of God's glory" from eternity and the one "bearing all by his powerful word" since creation.[47] The separation of these participles from the main

---

Spicq, 2:6-9, takes the opposite position. Both are guilty of overinterpretation. *Pace* Koester, 180, however, the finality of revelation in the Son is dependent on his identity with God.

42. "The word of his power" is a Hebraism in which the possessive "power" is used as an adjective and "his" qualifies "word" (Bénétreau, 1:72).

43. Hughes, 45, n. 22; Westcott, 13-14; and Meier, "Structure," 182. Although Ellingworth, 100-101, claims that contemporary evidence for this usage is scarce, Spicq, 2:9-10, finds examples in the LXX, Philo, and rabbinic literature. Hughes, Westcott, and Spicq cite Patristic support.

44. Note the reference to the second coming in "until I make your enemies a stool for your feet" (Heb 1:13 quoting Ps 110:1). See also the exposition of Ps 8:4-6 in 2:5-9 below.

45. As noted above, Ebert, "Chiastic Structure," 167-74, sees these two participial phrases as the central focus of vv. 1-4.

46. Koester, 176, 178.

47. Meier, "Structure," 182-83.

verb by the aorist participle, the way they are closely joined,[48] the previous reference to the Son's role in creation (1:2c), and the following affirmation of his eternity (1:10-12) all affirm that this is a general description of the eternal Son. "Bearing all by the word of his power" is a natural description of deity not easily limited to the exalted Son.

However, these article-less participles also qualify "he sat down."[49] The "timeless" description of the Son in v. 3ab is brought into relationship with the once-for-all acts of atonement and exaltation in v. 3cd. Riggenbach's suggestion of a causal relationship is not far from the mark: "Because he was the radiance of God's glory . . . he sat down at the right hand of the Majesty on high."[50] The translation given above is less specific: "As the radiance of God's glory and the exact representation of his very being and as bearing all by the word of his power . . . he sat down." What the Son has been from all eternity comes to fruition and full expression in his exaltation and session. Thus God's people look to the exalted Son for the full revelation of the divine nature.[51]

The third participial phrase — "having made purification for sins" — is an aorist of specific action rather than a present of general description. The instrumental significance of this participle is substantiated by the many passages that identify Christ's sacrifice as the means of his session (Heb 9:11-14; 9:23–10:4; 10:11-14). "By making purification for sins" the Son sat down at God's right hand as High Priest of his people. "Purification" anticipates the description of Christ's atoning work in terms of a sacrifice that provides inner cleansing from the pollution and dominion of sin (9:13-14) and consequent removal of the barrier that separates humanity from God (9:23-24).[52] The middle voice of "having made" suggests that this purification was achieved in Christ's own person and thus lays the foundation for his self-sacrifice. A few late manuscripts add "through himself" and thus suggest that later copyists understood the text in this way.[53] The one through whom God

48. These participles are bound together by the particle τέ (Riggenbach, 8).

49. According to Weiss, 144-45, this description of the Son is "beyond time" and yet underlies all.

50. Riggenbach, 8. Lane's (1:5) concessive rendering, "Although he was the radiance . . . and although he bore all things," pits the Son's roles as revealer and sustainer against his exaltation.

51. Spicq, 2:8. Note Lane's evaluation: "although Jesus was the preexistent Son of God, . . . he entered into a new dimension in the experience of sonship by virtue of his incarnation, his sacrificial death, and his subsequent exaltation" (Lane, 1:26).

52. See BDAG, 488, 3, b, c; Friedrich Hauck and Rudolf Meyer, "καθαρός, καθαρίζω, καθαίρω, καθαρότης," TDNT 3:412-26.

53. Instead of τῆς δυνάμεως αὐτοῦ, καθαρισμὸν τῶν ἁμαρτιῶν ποιησάμενος, "of his power, having made purification for sins," uncial 0243 and minuscules 6, 424 (cor-

"made" the worlds (v. 2c) is the one who has "made" purification in his own person.[54]

This introduction to the pastor's sermon reaches the climax toward which it has been moving with the pastor's declaration of the eternal Son's session "at the right hand of the Majesty on high." This statement is a clear allusion to this sermon's key verse — Ps 110:1.[55] "He sat down" underscores the finality of the Son's session. "Right hand" is the place of ultimate authority where the Son shares God's "power without limitation, though always with the subordination implied in the fact that it is God who gives, and the Son who receives this supreme status."[56] "The Majesty on high" is a reverential way of exalting God and thus also of emphasizing the supreme greatness of the Son's position.[57] The pastor has composed this sermon in order to keep his hearers focused on this exalted Son as the only one adequate to sustain them in faith (12:1-3). With the aid of Ps 110:4 (Heb 5:6, 10; 6:20; 7:1-25) he will explain the unique sufficiency of this exalted one in terms of high priesthood. Heb 2:1-4, however, gives the immediate purpose for the grand description of the Son in these opening verses: the pastor seeks to impress upon his hearers the inexhaustible greatness of the Son of God, so that they will attend to God's ultimate self-manifestation with obedience and deepening understanding.

4 Verse 4 is closely bound to vv. 1-3 in that it tells what happened to the Son when, as v. 3d affirms, "he sat down" at God's right hand.[58] It is also a bridge to the son/angels comparison/contrast in vv. 5-14.[59] This contrast substantiates and expands the picture of the Son's supremacy already given in vv. 1-3 and thus adds weight to the pastor's appeal in 2:1-4.

---

rected), 1739, and 1881 (original) have τῆς δυνάμεως, δι᾽ ἑαυτοῦ καθαρισμὸν τῶν ἁμαρτιῶν ποιησάμενος, "of power, through himself having made purification for sins." 𝔓⁴⁶ is in essential agreement but reads δι᾽ αὐτοῦ instead of δι᾽ ἑαυτοῦ.

54. Compare "through whom he made (ἐποίησεν) the worlds" with "having made (ποιησάμενος) purification." Ebert, "Chiastic Structure," 170-71, argues that the pastor has deliberately replaced the more common καθαρίζω ("purify") in this last clause with καθάρισμον . . . ποιησάμενος in order to establish this parallel.

55. See "The Rhetorical Shape of Hebrews and Its Use of the Old Testament," pp. 72-76 in the Introduction above.

56. Ellingworth, 103. The Son's session at the right hand makes his sharing in the divine majesty and dignity absolutely clear. See Riggenbach, 12 and Spicq, 2:11. Bauckham, "Divinity," 32, reminds the reader that the Son does not sit on a second throne beside God's but "on the righthand part of the one heavenly throne."

57. See Bénétreau, 1:73; Weiss, 151; and Attridge, 46, n. 139.

58. The participle γενόμενος, "having become" (v. 4), qualifies the finite verb of v. 3, ἐκάθισεν, "he sat down."

59. George H. Guthrie, *The Structure of Hebrews: A Text-Linguistic Analysis* (repr.; Leiden: Brill, 1994; Grand Rapids: Baker, 1994), 100-102.

Verse 3 has just described what the Son has always been from eternity — "the radiance of God's glory and the exact representation of God's very being"; or from creation — "bearing all to its intended end by the word of his power." Verse 4 goes on to describe what he became when he "sat down" at God's right hand (v. 3d) — "as much superior to angels as the name he has inherited is more excellent than theirs." How can the agent of creation and the "radiance of God's glory" "become" greater than the angels? This *ambigua* deepens as we realize that the one already described as the eternal "Son" now inherits the "name" which, in light of v. 5, can be nothing other than "Son."[60]

It is gratuitous to contend that the writer is making use of diverse unreconciled traditions — that is, one affirming eternal sonship and another affirming sonship obtained by adoption at the exaltation.[61] A proper understanding of the pastor's theology provides the best answer to this seeming contradiction. The exposition of 2:5-18 below will make clear what has already been anticipated in these opening verses: through his incarnation, death, and exaltation the eternal Son became the fully adequate savior of his people. The angels have no such salvific function (see 1:14). Thus he who was superior to them as the eternal Son became superior to them in a new way at the exaltation by procuring human salvation.[62]

At the same time, as argued above, the exaltation is the fulfillment of what the eternal Son has always been. He enters into the full exercise of his sonship at the Father's right hand and consequently its significance is revealed to his people.[63] Thus it is quite appropriate and reflects no limitation or defect of language for the Father to say at the occasion of his session, "You are my Son; today I have fathered you" (1:5).

60. Bauckham, "Divinity," 21-22, argues that the Son inherits the divine name YHWH, translated as κύριος ("Lord") in the Greek OT, rather than the name "Son." This suggestion is supported by the opening words of Ps 110:1, "The LORD said to my Lord." This important psalm verse is alluded to in Heb 1:3 and quoted in 1:13. "Lord" is also the title given to the exalted Christ in Phil 2:9-11. Cf. Johnson, 73. In my judgment, however, this interpretation faces two obstacles. First, Bauckham is forced to take the "today" of Ps 2:7, "You are my Son; today I have begotten you," as a timeless "today" (Bauckham, "Divinity," 33-34). Second, it is as "Son" that Christ is contrasted with the angels in the following verses. See esp. v. 5. Nevertheless, Meier may be overconfident when he says, ". . . to try to avoid taking *onoma* [name] as the title Son is an exercise in avoiding the obvious" (Meier, "Structure," 187).

61. *Pace* Attridge, 54-55; Braun, 32-33; and Pfitzner, 39.

62. He became "better" than the angels because he had become the fully effective Savior by offering a "better" sacrifice (9:23) which established a "better" priesthood (7:18-19) and covenant (7:22; 8:6) through which the faithful enter the "better" (i.e., heavenly) homeland (11:16). In these references "better" is a form of κρείττων, which within Hebrews denotes superiority in kind, not degree.

63. Hughes, 54-55.

Thus the exalted Son upon whom the pastor would focus attention is also the eternal Son. There is no reason, as Schenck and a few others have suggested, to reduce the description of the eternal Son to figurative status because it is derived from personifications of Wisdom in Hellenistic sources. The Son's preexistence is not merely functional but personal.[64] The pastor may use expressions reminiscent of the references to Wisdom scattered throughout the Wisdom literature.[65] Upon closer scrutiny, however, Hebrews evidences neither the close verbal nor the convincing conceptual parallels with these sources that some have claimed. The only striking verbal echo of the relevant wisdom passages is the occurrence of "radiance" in Heb 1:3 (cf. Wis 7:26). "Wisdom" was the first thing God created and his companion (Sir 24:9; Prov 8:22-30). Hebrews can attribute creation directly to the Son (1:8-12). While "Wisdom" may be described as seated beside the divine throne (Wis 9:4), the Son assumes his place on God's throne in fulfillment of Ps 110:1 and thus shares the divine sovereignty. Wisdom sources never describe "Wisdom" as the agent of redemption or the ultimate heir of all. The rest of Hebrews shows no interest in wisdom speculations.[66] The pastor is not dependent on Wisdom speculation but uses language drawn from the Hellenistic environment shared by the Wisdom literature. He uses this language to include the Son within the identity of God by affirming his role as Creator,

64. Schenck argues that Hebrews did not believe in the personal or actual preexistence of the Son any more than the Wisdom tradition, upon which Hebrews is dependent, affirmed the personal or actual preexistence of "Wisdom" (Prov 8:22-31; Sir 24:1-22; and Wis 6:1–9:18, esp. 7:12, 22; 8:4-5; 9:1-9). The Son was "preexistent" only as a function of God. See Kenneth Schenck, "Keeping His Appointment: Creation and Enthronement in Hebrews," *JSNT* 66 (1997): 115; Kenneth Schenck, *Understanding the Book of Hebrews: The Story behind the Sermon* (Louisville and London: Westminster John Knox, 2003), 17, nn. 24-25. One might note that Schenck's method of argument is a classical case of reductionism — descriptions applied to Christ can mean no more than they did in the contemporary world in spite of their new context (cf. Vanhoye, *Situation,* 65-70; cf. 112-17).

65. Emphasis should be placed on the word "scattered." According to Bar 3:37, Wisdom lived on earth; according to *1 En.* 42:1-2, Wisdom was exalted to heaven; according to Wis 9:4, Wisdom is seated beside the divine throne. These kinds of statements each serve a particular purpose in their individual contexts and are not brought together to form a comprehensive picture of personified "Wisdom." For a discussion of relevant references in the Wisdom literature see Craig R. Koester, *The Dwelling of God: The Tabernacle in the Old Testament, Intertestamental Jewish Literature, and the New Testament* (CBQMS 22; Washington, DC: The Catholic Biblical Association of America, 1989), 108-12.

66. On this subject see Daniel J. Ebert IV, "Wisdom in New Testament Christology, with Special Reference to Hebrews 1:1-4" (Ph.D. diss., Trinity Evangelical Divinity School, 1998), 40-111 (cited in O'Brien, 53, n. 64). Cf. Gordon D. Fee, "Wisdom Christology in Paul: A Dissenting View," in *Way of Wisdom: Essays in Honor of Bruce K. Waltke,* ed. J. I. Packer and Sven K. Søderlund (Grand Rapids: Zondervan, 2000), 251-79.

Sovereign, and agent of redemption.[67] Such passages as Heb 1:8-12 clearly affirm the preexistence of the Son and contrast his eternity with the temporality of creation. Heb 5:8 and 10:5-10 assume the existence of the Son before the incarnation.[68] It was the preexistent Son who was "made lower than the angels" (2:9). Heb 1:2 indicates that the Son's preexistent role in creation is as real as his being universal heir.

God has indeed addressed his people. His speaking has a long history that has found fulfillment in one who is God's Son, eternal, incarnate and exalted. These affirmations elicit the question, "What has God said in his Son?" The pastor, however, will not give a premature answer. First, he must continue pressing upon his hearers the eminent majesty of the Son (1:5-14) in order to secure their proper attention to the "great salvation" (2:1-4) effected and revealed in his fulfilled sonship.

2. The Incomparable Majesty of the Eternal, Exalted Son (1:5-14)

5 *For to which of the angels did God ever say, "Son of me you are; today I have fathered you," or again, "I will be to him a Father, and he will be to me a Son?"* 6 *And again, when he introduces the Firstborn into the world, he says, "Let all God's angels worship him."*

7 *And on the one hand in regard to the angels he says, "The one who makes his angels winds, and his ministers a flame of fire."*

8 *But on the other hand to the Son he says, "Your throne, O God, is forever, and the scepter of uprightness is the scepter of your kingdom.* 9 *You have loved righteousness and hated lawlessness; therefore, O God, your God has anointed you with the oil of gladness beyond your companions."*

10 *And "You, from the beginning, Lord, founded the earth, and the heavens are the works of your hands.* 11 *They will perish, but you remain, and they will all wear out like an article of clothing,* 12 *and as a cloak you will roll them up, and as an article of clothing they will be changed. But you are the same, and your years will never cease."*

13 *And to which of the angels has he ever said, "Sit at my right hand until I make your enemies a stool for your feet."* 14 *Are they not all ministering spirits sent out for service on behalf of those who are about to inherit salvation?*

Comparison with the angels was the most effective way of substantiating the supremacy of the Son and his identity with God as affirmed in 1:1-4, and thus

---

67. See Bauckham, "Divinity," 22, n. 13. Cf. Johnson, 68-69.
68. Meier, "Structure," 186, n. 60.

of securing obedience to God's revelation in him (2:1-4).[1] There were none greater with whom the Son could be compared. Many believed that angels stood in God's heavenly presence worshiping around his throne and serving as his attendants awaiting his bidding.[2] To them was committed the governing of the nations, and through them God directed the forces of nature.[3] Some thought angels had authority over the world to come.[4] Furthermore, angels were believed to have been present as intermediaries on Mount Sinai.[5] Thus it was natural to contrast the Son who embodies God's final revelation with those angelic mediators of his earlier disclosure. As ancient orators praised a ruler by comparing him with great rulers of the past, so the pastor magnifies the Son by comparison with the angels.[6] This contrast substantiates the eternity, sovereignty, and exaltation of the Son. Its continuation in 2:5-18 confirms the saving significance of the Son's incarnation and death.

The pastor bases this comparison on the firm foundation of Scriptural authority. All but two of his quotations (Deut 32:43; 2 Sam 7:14) come from the Psalter (Ps 2:7; Ps 104:5; Ps 45:7-8; Ps 102:25-27; Ps 110:1).[7] Deut 32:1-43 is also a psalm, the "Song of Moses," which is repeated in the Greek OT as the second of fourteen odes joined to the Psalter.[8] Most of these quotations (Ps 2:7; 45:7-8; 102:25, 27; 110:1) are the word of God directed to his Son, who himself becomes the object of the psalmic language of worship and praise.[9]

1. Bénétreau, 1:95; Weiss, 158-60.
2. See *1 Enoch* 39; *2 Enoch* 17, 20–23; *3 En.* 1:12; 27:2; *Jub.* 2:2; *T. Levi* 3:5; 1QSb 25–26; 4Q400 (4QShirShabb[a]) (cited in Scott D. Mackie, *Eschatology and Exhortation in the Epistle to the Hebrews* [WUNT 223; Tübingen: Mohr Siebeck, 2007], 214, n. 5).
3. See Deut 32:8-9; Dan 4:10, 13, 20; Sir 17:17; *Jub.* 35:17; and *1 En.* 20:5.
4. See the comments on v. 7 below.
5. Acts 7:53; Gal 3:19; *Jub.* 1:27, 29; 2:1; and Josephus, *Ant.* 15.136.
6. Thompson, 41. *Pace* M. Goulder, "Hebrews and the Ebionites," *NTS* 49 (2003): 393-99, there is no anti-angel polemic in Hebrews. Note the positive references to angels in 1:14, 2:5, and 12:22. See Weiss, 158-60; Meier, "Symmetry," 522, n. 56; and Koester, 199-200. There is no sign that Hebrews was combating the veneration of angels (Mackie, *Eschatology and Exhortation,* 214-15).
7. Thus it is misleading to say, as Koester, 197, does, that these quotations "are taken from each of the major categories of OT writings."
8. The LXX title ascribed to this second ode, "Ode of Moses in Deuteronomy," demonstrates that it is an intentional duplication for liturgical use. See Lane, 1:28.
9. Several of these passages were originally addressed to the King/Messiah. Ps 2:7 and 2 Sam 7:14 occur in 4QFlor, a collection of Messianic proof texts from Qumran. John N. Allegro, "Fragments of a Qumran Scroll of Eschatological *Midrāšîm*," *JBL* 77 (December 1958): 350-54. Ps 2:7 is applied to Christ in Acts 4:26-27; 13:33-34 (cf. Rev 2:27; 12:5; 19:15) and alluded to at his baptism (Matt 3:16-17; Mark 1:10-11; Luke

Heb 1:5-14 falls naturally into three parts, vv. 5-6, 7-12, and 13-14. In vv. 5-6 and 13-14 the author moves from the Son (vv. 5, 13) to the angels (vv. 6, 14). Both pairs of verses are introduced with "to which of the angels?"[10] The first pair begins with Christ's sonship followed by the obeisance of the angels. The second begins with his exaltation followed by the servant-nature of the angels. This parallel arrangement frames the whole — the nature of the Son (v. 5), the position of the angels (v. 6), the position of the Son (v. 13), the nature of the angels (v. 14).[11]

The comparison in vv. 7-12 begins with what God spoke about the angels (v. 7) followed by what he spoke to the Son (vv. 8-12). This section focuses on the Son's deity and divine sovereignty. The first of the passages applied to the Son, Ps 45:6-7, was addressed to the King/Messiah in the OT; the second, Ps 102:25-27, was directed to God himself.

All these quotations were carefully chosen and arranged to substantiate and clarify Heb 1:2-4 and to prepare for the following argument.[12] For instance, Ps 2:7, quoted in v. 5, gives biblical support for the designation "Son" in 1:2; and Ps 110:1, already alluded to in 1:3d, provides Scriptural justification for the Son's exaltation/session.[13] This careful structuring of vv. 5-14 to suit the writer's purpose makes it very unlikely that he took these quotations from a traditional list such as one finds in 4QFlorilegium.[14]

3:21-22). On the Messianic use of these verses, see Spicq, 2:16, and Koester, 199. For a detailed comparison between 4QFlor 1:1-19 and Heb 1:5-13 see H. W. Bateman, "Two First-Century Messianic Uses of the OT: Heb 1:5-13 and 4QFlor 1.1-19," *JETS* 38 (1995): 11-27 and Herbert W. Bateman IV, *Early Jewish Hermeneutics and Hebrews 1:5-13* (American University Studies, Series VII: Theology and Religion 193; New York: Peter Lang, 1997), 149-206. See the section on Hebrews' use of the OT in the Introduction (pp. 41-59, esp. 45-46).

10. Τίνι γὰρ . . . τῶν ἀγγέλων (v. 5) and πρὸς τίνα δὲ τῶν ἀγγέλων (v. 13) are stylistic variations similar in meaning. For the emphasis added by the second phrase see on v. 13 below.

11. The attentive eye will also note another element of form here in that the pastor presents the nature and position of the Son and of the angels in a chiasm; thus: the Son's *nature,* the angels' *position,* the Son's *position,* the angels' *nature,* a substratum elegant in its subtlety.

12. Meier, "Symmetry," 523, finds exaltation in 1:2b, 5-6; creation in 1:2, 7; "preexistence, divinity, and eternal rule" in 1:3a, 8bc; creation and governance in 1:3b, 10-12; and exaltation again in 1:3d, 13. He omits vv. 3c and 9. His interpretation of the Son as Creator in 1:7 is strained (Meier, "Symmetry," 511-13). Koester, 197, and Weiss, 156, affirm general agreement between 1:5-14 and 1:1-4.

13. Notice how the author allows the importance of Ps 110:1 to come into focus. He alludes to this verse in 1:3, quotes it at the climax of his catalog of quotations in 1:13, and expounds it with the help of Psalm 8 in 2:5-9.

14. See Meier, "Symmetry," 530. *1 Clem.* 36:1-6 is quoting Hebrews and is thus

We turn now to the first comparison/contrast between the Son (v. 5) and the angels (v. 6) and to the quotations which justify Christ's inheritance of the all-important name "Son."

5 The central focus of v. 5 is the father/son relationship established between God and the one he addresses in Ps 2:7 and 2 Sam 7:14. These combined quotations move from sonship ("Son of me you are") to fatherhood ("today I have fathered you") and from fatherhood ("I will be to him a Father") to sonship ("and he will be to me a Son"). In the Greek text they begin and end with "Son." It is "Son" that first strikes the ear, and "Son" that the author leaves reverberating in his hearers' hearts. The Son described in 1:1-4 is the true recipient of God's OT declarations of filiation.[15] In him Ps 2:7 and 2 Sam 7:14 have found a fulfillment that far surpasses God's relationship to the merely human descendants of David.

The magnitude of this fulfillment is underscored by the fact that God never made such declarations of sonship to angels. The singular, "to which of the angels?" is significant. Occasionally the angels as a group were called "sons of God."[16] However, God never singled out an angel for a special relationship with himself by declaring, "You are my Son."[17] The magnitude of Christ's filial relationship and its superiority to the angels' relationship with God will be underscored by the obeisance of the angels in v. 6.

"Today I have fathered you" calls for further explanation. Various interpreters have suggested that this "today" is the "today" of the incarnation, or the exaltation/session, or the second coming. Some have tried to detemporalize the term by suggesting that it is the "today" of the eternal generation of the Son.[18] But vv. 3 and 4 would seem to identify this "today" with the exaltation/session, for it was when he "sat down at the right hand of the Majesty on high" that the Son inherited the superior name "Son."[19] The words of Psalm 2 addressed to the descendant of David find their ultimate

---

no evidence for the derivation of these quotations from a traditional list. For the dependence of *1 Clement* on Hebrews see the Introduction and the literature there cited (p. 34, n. 144).

15. See Vanhoye, *Situation,* 139, 143-44.

16. "Sons of God" occurs in the MT of Gen 6:2, 4; Pss 29:2; 89:7-8; Job 1:6; 2:1; and 38:7. In Deut 32:8 an original "sons of God" has been emended to "sons of Israel." The LXX retains "sons of God" in Gen 6:2, 4 and Ps 29:2 and 89:7. In Deut 32:8 and Job it substitutes "angels of God" (Job 38:7, "my angels"). When "sons of God" is used for a class of heavenly beings, it would be better if it were translated as "sons of the divine."

17. Vanhoye, *Situation,* 130-31.

18. See the discussion in Vanhoye, *Situation,* 139-42.

19. Attridge, 53-55; Bénétreau, 1:79; Bruce, 54; Braun, 35; Ellingworth, 114; Hughes, 54; Lane, 1:24-26; Koester, 191; Westcott, 21; Weiss, 160-61; Meier, "Symmetry," 504-5; and Vanhoye, *Situation,* 142-43.

fulfillment in the heavenly enthronement of Christ.[20] Furthermore, a declaration of sonship at the exaltation is in accord with the pastor's desire to keep the eyes of his hearers fixed on the exalted Son at the right hand (8:1; 12:1-3). The "today" of the exaltation is the "today" in which they are called to "hear his voice" (3:7, 13, 15; 4:7). Thus, as noted above (v. 4), at his exaltation and session the Son entered his inheritance as Son and the fruition of a sonship that had always been his. His identity is revealed for all.

6 The obeisance of the angels is corollary to God's proclamation of sonship in Ps 2:7 and cements the categorical distinction that separates them from the Son. Thus this angelic homage was rendered at the Son's exaltation/session[21] rather than at the incarnation[22] or second coming.[23] Elsewhere in Scripture angels never worship the Son at either of these events.[24] Angelic acclaim attends his triumphal entrance into the eternal "world" of sal-

---

20. Spicq, 2:23, argues that the Son is enthroned as heavenly king in fulfillment of Pss 2:7 and 110:1, originally addressed to the Davidic King at his enthronement. Westcott, 3, contends that in these opening verses of Hebrews the Son fulfills the roles of prophet, priest, and king. Braun, 31, however, shows the paucity of references to Davidic kingship. According to Hebrews, it is as High Priest that the Son is enthroned on high as God's complete self-revelation.

21. Lane, 1:26-27; Attridge, 55-57; Weiss, 162; Ellingworth, 117; O'Brien, 69; and Vanhoye, *Situation*, 155-57.

22. By putting "again" with "brings," a translation like the NKJV implies a re-entry and thus prevents reference to the incarnation: "But when He again brings the first-born into the world." Since δέ, "but," is always translated as if it were at the beginning of the sentence, the combined expression δὲ πάλιν, "but again," probably qualifies "he says" rather than "he brings in." "But again (δὲ πάλιν) he says . . . 'Let all the angels of God worship him,'" parallels "and again (καὶ πάλιν), 'I will be to him a Father . . .'" in v. 5. See Meier, "Symmetry," 509, and Bénétreau, 1:82. Thus "again" provides no impediment to locating God's command to the angels at the incarnation. Neither, however, does it provide supporting evidence. For a defense of the incarnation as the occasion in view, see Spicq, 2:17; Montefiore, 45-46; and Moffatt, 10-11. Bateman IV, *Early Jewish Hermeneutics*, 222, lets the synoptic Gospels provide the context for his interpretation rather than Hebrews when he suggests that the pastor is referring to Jesus' baptism as the time when God brought him "into the world."

23. Riggenbach, 19-20; Braun, 37; Michel, 113. Contrary to what is sometimes suggested, the aorist subjunctive of εἰσαγάγῃ, "he brings in," does not indicate future time but time coordinate with that of the main verb. See MHT, 3:112. Wallace is mistaken when he groups ὅταν, "when"/"whenever" with ἕως, ἄχρι, and μέχρι as terms which mean "until" and indicate action future in reference to the main verb. His own example belies his point: μακάριοί ἐστε ὅταν ὀνειδίσωσιν ὑμᾶς, "blessed are you whenever they revile you." The reviling precedes or is co-terminus with the blessing. See Daniel B. Wallace, *Greek Grammar beyond the Basics: An Exegetical Syntax of the New Testament* (Grand Rapids: Zondervan, 1996), 479.

24. At the first of these events they praise God (Luke 2:13-14); at the second they form the Son's entourage (Matt 16:26). Vanhoye, *Situation*, 155-57.

vation.[25] The same term is used of the coming "world" of salvation in 2:5. It often refers to the "inhabited world," and thus it accords well with the description in 12:22-24 of the world of salvation inhabited by God's faithful people, the angels, God, and Jesus the Mediator.[26]

"Firstborn" is an appropriate designation for the "Son" when he enters his inheritance at the exaltation/session.[27] Just as the Son fulfilled the Messianic promises of Ps 2:7 and 2 Sam 7:14, so he fulfills God's pledge: "I will make him my Firstborn, higher than the kings of the earth" (Ps 89:27).[28] Dominion over the nations is also dominion over the angels who direct their affairs (Deut 32:8-9).[29] The Son's exclusive relationship with the Father is affirmed by the use of "Firstborn" without a qualifier: he is not merely the "Firstborn" of angels or kings; he is *the* "Firstborn."[30] The absolute homage given the "Firstborn" by the highest and most exalted heavenly beings shows the magnitude of the sonship declared in v. 5 and the unprecedented nature of his relationship with God.

Both the pastor and his hearers acknowledged the Scriptural authority of v. 6b, "Let all the angels of God worship him," although this line is absent from the Masoretic Text (MT, the current standard text of the Hebrew OT). The discovery of 4QDeut32 confirms Westcott's belief that this quotation comes from Deut 32:43 in the pastor's Greek Bible.[31] This Qumran manuscript also provides evidence that the clause in question represents the primitive Hebrew text.[32]

---

25. Ardel B. Caneday, "The Eschatological World Already Subjected to the Son: The Οἰκουμένη of Hebrews 1.6 and the Son's Enthronement," in *A Cloud of Witnesses: The Theology of Hebrews in Its Ancient Contexts,* ed. Richard Bauckham et al. (LNTS 387; T&T Clark, 2008), 28-39. Cf. Lane, 1:27; Koester, 193; Weiss, 162-63; Johnson, 79; Mitchell, 48.

26. Cf. Meier, "Symmetry," 507. Note that the contrasting picture in 12:18-21 is bereft of fellowship.

27. On the "firstborn" as God's heir see Deut 21:15-17; cf. 2 Chr 21:3; Ps 89:28. Spicq, 2:18. For the combination "firstborn" and "heir" see Exod 4:2-23; cf. Rom 8:31 and Col 1:13-15.

28. This verse could easily have been in the writer's mind after quoting Ps 2:7 because Ps 2:8 is also a promise of universal dominion. Vanhoye, *Situation,* 157-59. Note also the perpetuity of the king's throne mentioned in Ps 89:29 and in Ps 45:6, cited in Heb 1:8. Cf. Weiss, 163.

29. Vanhoye, *Situation,* 157-59.

30. Compare Rom 8:29; Col 1:15; and Col 1:18, where πρωτότοκος, "firstborn," is used to show Christ's relationship respectively to Christians, creation, and those who are resurrected. For usage contemporary with Hebrews see Spicq, 2:17.

31. Westcott, 20.

32. This reading of Deut 32:43 is followed by the NRSV, the ESV, the NAB, and the NLT. See Arie van der Kooij, "The Ending of the Song of Moses: On the Pre-

As noted above, the song of Moses, Deut 32:1-43, is repeated as the second of fourteen odes attached to the Psalter in the Greek Bible. The Hebrew of 4QDeut32 reads, "Let all the gods (divine beings) worship him." Deuteronomy and the second ode represent alternate Greek translations of this Hebrew text: "Let all the sons of God worship him" (Deut 32:43) and "Let all the angels of God worship him" (Odes 32:43). The pastor's argument depends on the use of "angels" in this verse. Furthermore, a careful comparison of 4QDeut32 and the LXX with the MT suggests that "angels" was the initial and more accurate Greek translation of the original Hebrew text.[33]

Brenton's translation of Deut 32:43 (LXX)/Odes 2:43 is given on the left below.[34] Deuteronomy uses "sons of God" in line two and "angels of God" in line four; Odes uses "angels of God" in line two and "sons of God" in line four.[35] On the right is a translation of 4QDeut32.

Brenton's LXX Translation of Deut/Odes 32:43	A Translation of Deut 32:43 in 4QDeut32
Rejoice, ye heavens, with him, and let all the angels [Odes]/sons [Deut] of God worship him; *rejoice ye Gentiles, with his people, and let all the sons* [Odes] / *angels* [Deut] *of God strengthen themselves in him;* for he will avenge the blood of his sons, *and he will render vengeance,* and recompense justice to his ene-	Rejoice, O heavens, with him, worship him, all you gods (divine beings)![36] For he will avenge the blood of his sons, and take vengeance on his adversaries;

Masoretic Version of Deut 32:43," in *Studies in Deuteronomy: In Honour of C. J. Labuschagne on the Occasion of His 65th Birthday,* ed. F. García Martínez (Supplements to *Vetus Testamentum* 53; Leiden and New York: Brill, 1994), 93-100.

33. For a full discussion of v. 6b, see G. L. Cockerill, "Hebrews 1:6: Source and Significance," *BBR* 9 (1999): 51-64.

34. It is more difficult to use the Oxford translation of the LXX to show these parallels because it translates υἱοὶ θεού as "divine sons" rather than as "sons of God."

35. Odes 2:43b reads οἱ ἄγγελοι θεοῦ; 2:43d, υἱοὶ θεοῦ. Deut 32:43b reads υἱοὶ θεοῦ; and 2:43d, ἄγγελοι θεοῦ. There is almost no other textual variation between Deut 32:1-43 and Odes 2:1-43. Thus it appears that both texts represent the same translation of the original. It is clear, then, that, *pace* David M. Allen, *Deuteronomy and Exhortation in Hebrews: A Study in Narrative Re-Presentation* (WUNT 238; Tübingen: Mohr Siebeck, 2008), 49, this variation in the use of "angels"/"sons" was the result of scribal alteration — perhaps at the time of conflation.

36. The Hebrew word here is אלוהם, usually translated as "God," but occasionally used for "gods" or heavenly beings. The NRSV and ESV read "gods" in Deut 32:43, while the NAB and NLT read "angels of God."

mies, and will reward them that hate him; and the Lord shall purge the land of his people.

he will repay those who hate him, and cleanse the land of his people.

The italicized lines of the LXX are absent from 4QDeut32 and represent a Greek translation of an alternate Hebrew text.[37] This alternate Hebrew text appears to have some affinity with, though it is not identical to, the MT. Thus the standard text of the Greek Bible is a conflation of two translations, one representing the primitive text attested by 4QDeut32 (the non-italicized lines above) and one representing a text closer to the MT (the italicized lines).[38] When the italicized lines representing this alternate Hebrew text are removed from the LXX, the Greek translation of the primitive text of Deut 32:43 remains, and reads as follows:

> Rejoice, ye heavens, with him,
> and let all the <u>angels of God</u> worship him;
> for he will avenge the blood of his <u>sons</u>,[39]
> and recompense justice to his enemies,
> and will reward them that hate him;
> and the Lord shall purge the land of his people.

This Greek translation used "angels," not "sons" of God, for the "divine beings" of line two in order to avoid conflict with the mortal "sons" of God whose blood is avenged in line three.[40] Furthermore, "angels" was more

37. The first italicized line is a translation of the first line of the MT, which differs from the first line of 4QDeut32 only in the substitution of גוֹים, "gentiles," for שָׁמִים, "heavens"; and in an alternate pointing of עמו, the last three consonants of the line. The MT points עַמּוֹ "his people." They are unpointed in the text of 4QDeut32 and thus could just as easily have been pointed עִמּוֹ "with him," as represented by the first line of the LXX translation. Thus the first italicized line duplicates this first line of the LXX text. The next two italicized lines have no equivalent in the sparse MT, but the fact that they duplicate the second and fifth lines of the LXX text is apparent even in English.

38. Cockerill, "Hebrews 1:6," 51-57. It is more likely that conflation would occur between the two Greek translations because they differ more than the probable Hebrew texts upon which they are based (Cockerill, "Hebrews 1:6," 57).

39. The MT has not only omitted reference to the "divine beings" in line two but altered "his sons" in the next line to "his servants": "he will avenge the blood of his servants." See van der Kooij, "Song of Moses," 93-100.

40. In the text of Deut 32:43 as we have it in 4QDeut32, אלהים, "gods" or "divine beings," in line two, is followed by בינו, "his [God's] sons," in the next line. Pace Allen, Deuteronomy, 49, these two lines do not identify the "sons" with the "angels" by being parallel. The mortal "sons" whose "blood" God will "avenge" can hardly be identified with the "angels of God." Furthermore, "for he will avenge the blood of his sons" is clearly parallel to the two following lines.

in line with normal LXX translation practices.[41] Thus it appears that Hebrews follows an accurate Greek translation of the primitive Hebrew text represented by 4QDeut32: "Let all the angels of God worship him."[42]

Deuteronomy 32:43 calls on the angels to worship God because he has brought the salvation of his people to its conclusion. The pastor, however, is convinced that the exalted Son and "heir of all" (1:2) is the one through whom God has accomplished this salvation. Thus the angels are invited to worship him.[43] Angelic homage betokens his identification with God.

7 Who are these mighty ones whom God commands to bow before his "Firstborn"? The pastor describes them in v. 7, only to contrast them with the Son in vv. 8-12.[44] He continues to use the present tense of "say" in order to maintain the sense of immediate address established in v. 6.[45]

"Concerning the angels he says" introduces Ps 104:4 as God's description of these angelic beings.[46] The pastor will exploit the servant role of the angels as God's "ministers" in v. 14 below. Here, however, he underscores their finite nature. They are created, temporal, malleable beings whom God "makes" and "changes."[47] Furthermore, their temporality is emphasized by the fact that God changes them into "winds" or "a flame of fire."[48] Wind

41. The LXX never uses υἱοὶ θεοῦ to translate אלוהים. ἄγγελοι translates אלוהים in Pss 8:5 and 138:1 and ἄγγελοι αὐτοῦ in Ps 97:7. ἄγγελοι αὐτοῦ is closest to the (οἱ) ἄγγελοι θεοῦ of Deut 32:43 because the αὐτοῦ, "his," refers to God and has no Hebrew equivalent. See Cockerill, "Hebrews 1:6," 55.

42. See Cockerill, "Hebrews 1:6," 58.

43. Hughes, 60, n. 24; Vanhoye, *Situation,* 164-65; Ellingworth, 120; and Cockerill, "Hebrews 1:6," 60-61. In Deut 32:43 God will "vindicate" his "sons" and cleanse his land for his people. So in Hebrews the Son brings God's "sons" to "glory," and his sacrifice cleanses the heavenly homeland (Heb 9:23). Cf. Attridge, 57, n. 79.

44. Note the contrasting μέν/δέ ("on the one hand"/"on the other") in vv. 7 and 8, indicating the contrasting relationship between the angels (v. 7) and the Son (vv. 8-12). For Hebrews' frequent use of this μέν/δέ construction see 3:5-6; 7:5-6, 8, 18-20; 8:4, 6; 9:23; and 10:11-12. Weiss, 164, n. 32, and Spicq, 2:19.

45. "God," the subject of v. 5, continues to speak in vv. 6 and 7. One may assume that the pastor is able to attribute Deut 32:43 (in v. 6) and Ps 104:4 (in v. 7) to God because of his conviction that all Scripture is divinely inspired.

46. πρός with the accusative indicates the angels "about" which something is said in v. 7 and the Son "to" whom something is said in v. 8. See Attridge, 57, n. 80 and Ellingworth, 120.

47. The word for "makes" is also used in 12:27 to describe the created world which will pass away. Meier's suggestion that the Son and not God "makes his angels winds, his ministers a flame of fire," is interesting but questionable (Meier, "Symmetry," 512-13). The hearers would not have had sufficient clues to make this association.

48. *Pace* Koester, 193-94, and Vanhoye, *Situation,* 170-75, 220, the parallel with "a flame of fire" shows that πνεύματα should be translated as "winds" rather than as "spirits." See Bénétreau, 1:84; Riggenbach, 21-22, n. 45. The pastor prevents his hearers from

and fire are common descriptions of mutability in the rabbinic tradition, if not in the OT.[49] The pastor's substitution of "a flame of fire" for the LXX's "a flaming fire" may further emphasize the angels' ephemeral character.[50] When God spoke on Sinai he was accompanied by angels and surrounded by winds and fire (Exod 19:16-18; Deut 5:22-26).[51] As awesome as those manifestations were, they betokened the temporality of the angels in comparison to one more awesome.[52]

8   The transitory creatureliness of the angels, mighty as they are, is overshadowed by the Son's deity and eternal sovereignty affirmed by the quotation of Pss 45:6-7 and 102:25-27 in vv. 8-12. The God who addressed the Messiah as "Son" in Ps 2:7 addresses him as "God" in Ps 45:6-7: "Your throne, O God, is forever and ever."[53] This striking ascription of deity is repeated in v. 9 and is probably the chief factor in the pastor's choice of this psalm.[54] Like the

---

giving undue dignity to the "ministering spirits" (λειτουργικὰ πνεύματα) of v. 14 by calling them "winds" (πνεύματα) in v. 7.

49. *Yalquṭ Shim'oni* 2.11.3 seems to be a commentary on Ps 104:4: "God changes us [the angels] hour by hour . . . ; sometimes he makes us fire, and sometimes wind" (Bruce, 59, n. 81). For further references see Lane, 1:29; Bruce, 58; and Hughes, 62, n. 32.

50. The pastor may have written πυρὸς φλόγα ("a flame of fire") instead of the πῦρ φλέγον ("a flaming fire") found in the standard text of the LXX in order to balance πνεύματα ("winds") at the end of the previous line (Bateman IV, *Early Jewish Hermeneutics,* 129). The two expressions are parallel in meaning.

51. Vanhoye, *Situation,* 173-75; Westcott, 25.

52. Most English versions translate the Hebrew text of Ps 104:4: "He makes winds his messengers, flames of fire his servants" (NIV). Hebrews follows the LXX translation, "He makes his angels winds, his ministers a flame of fire," which is also a possible rendering of the Hebrew (note how the ESV translates the Hebrew text of Psalm 104). As Vanhoye has noted, the ancients probably did not make a great distinction between God's servants and the natural elements they directed (Vanhoye, *Situation,* 174-75).

53. There can be no question that the articular nominative ὁ θεός, "God," is used here to affirm the deity of the one addressed. This construction is the normal form of direct address to God throughout the Greek Bible. The literal translations of Aquila and Theodotion make this significance explicit by replacing the articular nominative with the vocative. See Riggenbach, 23, n. 50. Furthermore, the only other way this nominative could be construed would be something like, "God is your throne forever and ever." Such a statement is unparalleled in the OT. Unlike "God is my Rock," it makes the one addressed superior to God (Vanhoye, *Situation,* 180-81). Furthermore, "God is your throne" would be at odds with the Son seated at God's right hand (Heb 1:3, 14; 8:1; 12:1-3). See the argument in Meier, "Symmetry," 513-14, and compare Bruce, 59-60; Hughes, 64; Montefiore, 47; Michel, 118; and Vanhoye, *Situation,* 176-77. See Murray J. Harris, "The Translation and Significance of Ὁ ΘΕΟΣ in Hebrews 1:8-9," *TynBul* 36 (1985): 138-49, for a detailed defense of the vocative in v. 8. He, however, thinks that v. 9 is probably nominative and a reference to the Father (149-51).

54. Ellingworth, 125.

term "Son," this ascription has much greater significance when used to address the one at God's right hand than when applied to the Davidic King.[55] This affirmation of the Son's deity will be substantiated and augmented in vv. 10-12 by his identification as sovereign Creator and ultimate Judge.

This "God" is the one exalted to the Father's right hand whose rule is truly eternal, for his "throne is forever and ever."[56] "Scepter" underscores the sovereignty of the Son.[57] Hebrews' description of the Son's "scepter" differs slightly from that of the LXX. Hebrews reads: "And the scepter of uprightness is the scepter of your kingdom."[58] The LXX, following the MT, reads, "The scepter of your kingdom is a scepter of uprightness."[59] This slight shift in wording is significant: the scepter of the Son's kingdom is "the scepter of uprightness" *par excellence*. The rule of the divine Son now seated at God's right hand is righteous or upright in a way no other has ever been, for it is the exercise of God's own sovereign righteous rule so desired by the OT prophets.[60]

9 Ps 45:6-7 began by affirming the deity and sovereignty of the Son. It ends by reaffirming his deity and declaring the exaltation by which he entered into the exercise of his sovereign rule: "O God, your God has anointed you with the oil of gladness beyond your companions."[61] Anointing with the "oil of gladness" is a clear reference to exaltation.[62] This "oil of gladness"

---

55. Psalm 45 is the psalmist's address to the king. However, since all Scripture is from God, the pastor can join this passage to Ps 2:7 and 2 Sam 7:14 as the word of God (cf. Lane, 1:29). On the Messianic use of this psalm, see Riggenbach, 22, n. 47, and Spicq, 2:19. However, Justin's *Dialogue with Trypho* (56, 63, 86) would suggest that the Jews of his day did not accept its Messianic significance. Spicq, 2:19, says that while the title "God" was used metaphorically for the OT king, it is applied to the Son "in the proper sense (cf. v. 3)" ("au sens proper"). See also Weiss, 65.

56. εἰς τὸν αἰῶνα τοῦ αἰῶνος was used often in the LXX for eternity. See Spicq, 2:19.

57. See, for instance, Rev 2:27; 12:5; 19:13. Spicq, 2:19.

58. With most interpreters, the reading σου, "your" (singular) kingdom is to be preferred over the variant αὐτοῦ, "his" kingdom. See *TCGNT,* 592-93.

59. This change has been brought about by the transfer of the article from before the second ῥάβδος to the first and by the addition of the genitive article τῆς before εὐθύτητος. The LXX's ῥάβδος εὐθύτητος ἡ ῥάβδος τῆς βασιλείας σου: becomes in Hebrews ἡ ῥάβδος τῆς εὐθύτητος ῥάβδος τῆς βασιλείας σου.

60. Vanhoye, *Situation,* 185. Although εὐθύτητος is used nowhere else in NT, it has the sense of "moral rectitude" or "justice" in the LXX and often translates the Hebrew roots ישׁר or חם. Spicq, 2:19.

61. Attridge, 59; Riggenbach, 24; Ellingworth, 124; and Bruce, 60, agree that the Son is again addressed as "God" in v. 9.

62. Bénétreau, 1:86; Spicq, 2:19; Westcott, 27; Hughes, 65; Vanhoye, *Situation,* 192; Attridge, 60; Ellingworth, 124; Koester, 195. Meier's artificial attempt to restrict the reference of this psalm to the eternal deity of the Son is forced by his desire to make each

anticipates the "joy" set before Jesus in 12:2 and is a festive, joyful "anointing" suitable for the celebration described in 12:22-24. The Messianic nature of the psalm suggests a royal anointing, and the larger context of Hebrews invites us to see an anticipation of priestly consecration. "Beyond your companions" solidifies reference to the exaltation. The "companions" are probably not the angels who have been categorically distinguished from the Son.[63] They are God's people, the "sons and daughters of God" with whom the Son identifies in his incarnation (Heb 2:5-18) and thus owns as his "brothers and sisters" (2:11).[64] Thus these verses affirm the Son's deity, exaltation, and subsequent sovereign eternal rule. All of these elements have been implied in the prologue and are now made explicit and given Scriptural support.

The pastor also anticipates the earthly obedience of the Son when he says, "You have loved righteousness and hated lawlessness."[65] These verbs are aorists of past action and thus describe the Son previous to, and provide the basis for, his exaltation/"anointing." The way in which his loving "righteousness" is reinforced by his hatred of "lawlessness" aptly represents the Son's complete obedience unto death which the pastor will describe as the means of his exaltation in Heb 5:7-8 and 10:5-10.[66] By use of this psalm the pastor anticipates what he will begin to make explicit in 2:5-18 and will explain more fully in 4:14–10:18. The pastor never separates the exalted Son from all that preceded the exaltation. The exalted Son is the eternal Son who became human and was obedient unto death in order to enter into the full implementation of his gracious sonship and the open exercise of a sovereignty appropriate to his deity.

10 After affirming that the Son was "God," it was appropriate to ascribe Ps 102:25-27 to him. This psalm fits so seamlessly with Ps 45:6-7 that the pastor uses a mere "and" to connect the two.[67] He quotes Ps 102:25 in

---

of these verses in 1:5-14 parallel to specific elements in the prologue (Meier, "Symmetry," 515).

63. See Riggenbach, 24. *Pace* Meier, "Symmetry," 516, and Braun, 40-41.

64. The same Greek word, μέτεχοι, is used for "companions" in 1:9 and "partakers" or "companions" of Christ in 3:14. See Bruce, 61; Westcott, 27; Calvin, 14. Vanhoye, *Situation,* 192-94, thinks the reference is primarily to God's people without excluding the angels also present in 12:22-24.

65. Bénétreau, 1:86, and Weiss, 165-66, are representative of those who admit the anointing refers to the exaltation but deny that loving "righteousness" and hating "lawlessness" has any reference to incarnate obedience. However, even Bénétreau admits that incarnate obedience suits the immediate context. See Harris, "Hebrews 1:8-9," 159.

66. "By having 'loved righteousness and hated lawlessness' Christ has engaged his whole existence for the realization of God's design and the elimination of sin. This phrase of the psalm evokes the grand combat of the Passion in the spirit of the Christian" (Vanhoye, *Situation,* 188 [my translation]). Cf. Koester, 202.

67. Westcott, 28.

v. 10 to affirm the Son's creatorship and Ps 102:26-27 in vv. 11-12 to affirm his sovereign deity and role as final judge of all.[68] This Scripture confirms and amplifies the prologue's description of the Son as Creator, Sustainer, and universal Heir.

The pastor has put the pronoun "you" at the beginning of v. 10 in order to pick up the "your" at the end of v. 9.[69] The title "Lord" follows naturally from the "God" of vv. 8-9 and facilitates easy application of this psalm to Christ.[70] "From the beginning" is a clear reference to the time of creation.[71] "The earth" and "the heavens" encompass the whole created order. The attribution of creation directly to the Son goes beyond the agency of v. 2 and thus underscores the inclusion of the Son within the Godhead.[72] When Scripture speaks of the earth's "founding," it affirms the solidity of creation.[73] Thus use of this term in v. 10 emphasizes the sovereignty of the one described in v. 11 as "rolling up" this solid creation as if it were nothing more than a piece of cloth.

11-12 By continuing the quotation from Psalm 102 the pastor contrasts the eternity of the Son and the mutability of the creation over which he is sovereign. What he has made he also brings to its end.

The two ways in which the pastor deviates from the LXX text are important for determining his message. First, in v. 12a he appears to have substituted "you will roll [them] up" for "you will change [them]."[74] Second, in

---

68. For this two-part division of the quotation see Vanhoye, *Situation*, 196.

69. "Your companions" at the end of v. 9 is μετόχους σου in Greek. Verse 10 begins with the emphatic second person singular pronoun σύ, "you." Codex Sinaiticus follows the MT by omitting "you" (σύ) and "Lord" (κύριε). Codex Vaticanus reads, "from the beginning the earth *you, Lord* (σὺ κύριε), founded"; and Codex Alexandrinus, "from the beginning *you, Lord* (σὺ κύριε), the earth founded." The pastor follows Alexandrinus in the location of "Lord" but has moved "you" to the beginning to put emphasis on the one addressed.

70. Spicq, 2:20. κύριος, "Lord," emphasizes the sovereignty of the Creator. Hebrews uses this title for Jesus in 1:10; 2:3; 7:14; 12:14; and 13:20. It also uses "Lord" twelve times in reference to God when quoting the OT. Weiss, 167, n. 43.

71. κατ' ἀρχάς harks back to Gen 1:1. By putting the word "beginning" in this prominent place this psalm quotation becomes "a christological reading of the first verse of Genesis comparable with the christological reading of that verse at the beginning of the Johannine prologue" (Bauckham, "Divinity," 26).

72. The pastor was under no obligation to choose this psalm; thus there is no reason to argue that the Son's role as the direct agent of creation is due to the constraints of the OT text. *Pace* Meier, "Symmetry," 517-18.

73. See Prov 8:29; Isa 51:13; Jer 31:37; Job 38:4-7; and Vanhoye, *Situation*, 197.

74. The great majority of Greek manuscripts read ἑλίξεις, "you will roll [them] up," instead of] ἀλλάξεις, "you will change [them]." The few manuscripts which read the latter have been conformed to the LXX text. See *TCGNT*, 593.

v. 12b he has repeated the phrase "as an article of clothing" from v. 11.[75] The repetition of "as an article of clothing" adds grammatical smoothness.[76] It also changes the structure so that the first line of v. 12 becomes the center of a chiasm and the focal point of the passage: "and as a covering you will roll them up."[77]

> (a) They will be changed,
>> (b) but you remain;
>>> (c) and all as an article of clothing will become old,
> (d) and as a covering you will roll them up;
>>> (c¹) as an article of clothing they will be changed.
>> (b¹) But you are the same,
> (a¹) and your years will never cease.

The mutability of creation is announced in line (a), "they will be changed," continued in line (c) "and all as an article of clothing will become old," and concluded in line (c¹) by bringing the idea of "an article of clothing" and "change" together: "as an article of clothing they will be changed." These lines liken creation to a piece of clothing that becomes worn out and is thus "changed" in the sense of brought to an end.[78]

The eternity of the Son is introduced in line (b), "but you remain," continued in (b¹), "but you are the same," and concluded in the final line (a¹), "and your years will never cease" (cf. 13:8). The Son's role in creation makes it obvious that these verses refer to a life which is eternal and not merely endless.

Verse 12a (line d) brings both of these themes together. It is not just that the creation is temporal and the Son unchanging and eternal. He is the one who will bring the creation to its end: "As a covering you [the Son] will roll them [the heaven and earth] up."[79] The pastor's choice of "roll up" in-

---

75. The words ὡς ἱμάτιον, "as an article of clothing," are missing from the majority of manuscripts through conformity to the LXX, but they are strongly supported by a selection of the best manuscripts. See *TCGNT*, 593. Susan E. Docherty, *The Use of the Old Testament in Hebrews: A Case Study in Early Jewish Bible Interpretation* (WUNT 2/260; Tübingen: Mohr Siebeck, 2009), 136-37, attributes both of these variations in v. 12 to the Greek text used by the author of Hebrews. These variants are, however, admirably suited to the author's purposes.

76. The addition of ὡς ἱμάτιον, "as an article of clothing," means that ἀλλαγήσονται, "They will be changed," has its own complement rather than being dependent on ὡς περιβόλαιον, "as a covering," in the previous line.

77. Vanhoye, *Situation*, 198-99.

78. Cf. Weiss, 168, n. 45.

79. αὐτούς, "them," is masculine plural and thus takes the masculine plural οὐρανοί, "heavens," as its antecedent. The image of "rolling up" fits well with the "heav-

stead of the LXX "change" fits well with the clothing imagery. It will be no harder for the Son to remove this creation than for a human to fold up a coat or a blanket. Thus "as a covering you will roll them up" reinforces "whom he appointed heir of all things" from v. 2 as well as "bearing all to its intended end by his powerful word" in v. 3. This affirmation lays a foundation for the final judgment and shaking of the world in 12:25-29.

In vv. 5-12 the pastor has amplified and given Scriptural support to his description of the Son in the prologue. He has emphasized the divine sovereignty and eternity of the one who is "Son" (1:5), "God" (1:8), and "Lord" (1:10). In vv. 13-14 he concludes by reminding his hearers that, in accord with the divine invitation of Ps 110:1, this Son has been exalted to God's right hand. The "Lord" of v. 10 is the one to whom this psalm pertained.[80] Nothing is more fundamental to the pastor's concern than the truth divinely attested in this psalm.

13 As noted above, vv. 13-14 parallel vv. 5-6 and form the concluding bookend to this series of quotations. The quotation of Ps 110:1 in v. 13 parallels the quotation of Ps 2:7 and 2 Sam 7:14 in v. 5. Both vv. 6 and 14 describe the angels. "To which of the angels did God ever say?" in v. 5 is reechoed in "to which of the angels has he ever said?" at the beginning of v. 13. Yet this last introductory phrase is more emphatic than its counterpart, thus betokening the climactic importance of Ps 110:1. The pastor uses the perfect tense and locates both the verb and the adverb "ever" in the final, emphatic position of the Greek sentence. Psalm 110:1bc brings together the first and final descriptions of the Son in 1:2b-3 and encompasses all between: "Sit at my right hand" restates "he sat down at the right hand" (1:3d); and "until I make your enemies a stool for your feet" anticipates the final results of "whom he appointed heir of all" (1:2b).[81] Just as the prologue climaxed with an allusion to Ps 110:1 in 1:3d, so this chapter climaxes with its quotation.

By concluding this section with Ps 110:1 the pastor draws the eyes of his hearers to their exalted Lord (see 8:1-2; 12:1-3). It is in his exaltation that the eternal Son exercises his prerogatives as deity and fulfills the purposes of his sonship as the source of salvation for his people. Other NT writ-

---

ens." However, both the psalmist and the writer of Hebrews intend to describe divine sovereignty over the entire created order, "the earth" and "the heavens."

80. Ps 110:1a, "The LORD said to *my Lord,* sit at my right hand" (italics added; see Vanhoye, *Situation,* 209; Meier, "Symmetry," 519).

81. These "enemies" are certainly not the angels described in v. 14 as God's servants sent for the benefit of the faithful. Their number probably includes evil human beings, such as apostates (10:26-31) and persecutors (10:32-39; 11:35-38; 12:1-12). It may also have included the "devil" and other spiritual powers. The main point is that all opposed to the Son will be submitted to him. See Braun, 46; Meier, "Symmetry," 520, n. 48; Vanhoye, *Situation,* 218-20; and Bénétreau, 1:94.

ers recognized the importance of this verse, but the pastor alone used Ps 110:4 to develop the exaltation of 110:1 in terms of priesthood. As we will see, the importance of Ps 110:1 and 4 surpasses the frequency of their reference (Ps 110:1 in 1:3, 13; 8:1; 10:12, 13; and 12:2; Ps 110:4 in 5:6, 10; 6:20; 7:11, 17, 21).[82]

14 The lack of any contrasting citation in v. 14 allows Ps 110:1 to remain the final quotation and the pastor's definitive description of the present achievement and position of the Son.[83] Verse 7 has convinced the pastor's hearers that the angels are temporal created beings, God's "ministers," here called "ministering spirits." The hearers must, however, also understand the nature of angelic service. The pastor denies the popular belief that angels ruled the nations or that they performed a heavenly priestly ministry by insisting that "all" of them, in contrast to the sovereign, exalted Son, are "sent out."[84] The priestly connotation of the word "ministering" makes this denial more emphatic.[85] Furthermore, this use of "spirits" (see on 1:7) is unusual and probably indicates the "ethereal" nature of the angels. The Son is in charge of the nations (1:2-3) and, as the pastor will affirm, he alone is heavenly Priest. This vague description of angelic assistance to God's people draws attention to the all-sufficient ministry of the Son (cf. Acts 12:4-11; 27:23).

The pastor's opening declaration of the Son's divine appointment as "heir of all things" (v. 2) bears fruit in this concluding description of God's people as those "who are about to inherit salvation." The Son determines both their past and their future. Through him they are the heirs of the OT people of God and thus the recipients of all previous revelation. Through him

---

82. See "This Sermon's Use of the Old Testament" and "The Rhetorical Shape of Hebrews and Its Use of the Old Testament," pp. 45-46, 72-76, in the Introduction. Cf. Bénétreau, 1:89; Bruce, 63-64; and Ellingworth, 130.

83. Meier, "Symmetry," 519, n. 46, suggests that the pastor restricted himself to seven quotations. If so, then the fact that Ps 110:1 is the seventh quotation is further evidence of its climactic character.

84. Belief that the angels ruled the nations may have been based on the LXX of Deut 32:8: "When the Most High gave the nations their inheritance, when he separated the sons of Adam, he established boundaries for the nations according to the number of the angels of God." Lane, 1:45; Koester, 213; and Attridge, 70, n. 9. Bruce, 71, also refers to Dan 10:20-21; 12:1.

85. λειτουργικά is the word here translated "ministering." Words from the same root are used in relation to priestly service elsewhere in Hebrews: λειτουργός, "minister," of Jesus as priest in 8:2; λειτουργία, "ministry," of his priesthood in 8:6 and of the Aaronic priesthood in 9:21; λειτουργεῖν, "to minister," of the Aaronic priesthood in 10:11. λειτούργειν and λειτουργία are commonly used for the tabernacle/temple ministry in the LXX. λειτουργός is occasionally used of a priest in the Greek Bible (Isa 61:6; 2 Esd 20:40; Sir 7:30). See Vanhoye, *Situation,* 221.

and the fulfillment he has achieved they are "about to inherit" (1:14) the "salvation" he will bring at his return (9:28). The pastor would not have his hearers forget their past, but his emphasis is on their future. Above all he would have them live so that they will receive this inheritance through the exalted One who is "heir of all things." In order for them to understand both the privileges that are theirs and the gravity of their situation he will describe how the eternal Son became the fully sufficient, exalted Savior through his incarnation in 2:5-18. As noted above, these verses record the Son's obedient response to the Father's affirmations and invitation recorded in 1:5-14. These first two chapters serve as the basis for 4:14–10:18, the pastor's fuller explanation of the Son's sufficiency in terms of the high priesthood soon to be introduced in 2:17-18.

However, the pastor can restrain himself no longer. In 2:1-4 he must begin to exhort all who would hear to live as those "who are about to inherit salvation." The faithful perseverance necessary for reception of this inheritance is founded on giving their full attention and allegiance to "the great salvation" (2:3) the Son has provided. In vv. 1-14 the pastor has prepared his hearers to respond to this exhortation by describing the magnitude of the One through whom the salvation he would have them attend has been revealed and provided. In 2:5-18 he follows up this exhortation by beginning to describe the effective nature of this salvation and the means of its provision.

3. The Urgency of Attending to God's Son-Mediated Revelation (2:1-4)

1 *On account of this it is necessary for us to give much greater attention to the things heard, lest we drift away.* 2 *For if the word spoken through angels proved valid, and every transgression and disobedience received a just reward,* 3 *then how shall we escape if we neglect such a great salvation? This salvation had its beginning by being spoken through the Lord, and it was validated for us by those who heard him,* 4 *God adding his witness to theirs by signs and wonders and various miracles and apportionments of the Holy Spirit according to his will.*

With the inclusive "we"/"us" (2:1, 3) the pastor identifies with his hearers and draws them close in order to urge upon them the perseverance necessary to "inherit salvation." Heb 2:1-4 brings 1:1-14 to immediate application and is vital to all that follows.[1] In Heb 2:1 the pastor states the concern that has

---

1. *Pace* F. Synge, *Hebrews and the Scriptures* (London: SPCK, 1959), 44-52, and Hagner, 40, who calls 2:1-4 a "parenthetical exhortation." Because God has spoken in his

led him to address his hearers: "On account of this it is necessary for us to give much greater attention to the things heard, lest we drift away." "On account of this" indicates that the motivation for this exhortation is based on the superiority of God's self-revelation in the Son as elaborated in 1:1-14. The exhortations that follow (3:7–4:13; 4:14-16; 5:11–6:20; 10:19-39; 11:1-40; 12:1-29) flesh out what it means "to pay more earnest attention," and elaborate the nature and consequences of "drifting away." The theological teaching of Hebrews (2:5-18; 3:1-6; 5:1-10; 7:1–10:18) explains "the things heard."

Verses 2-3a reinforce the urgency of attending the "things heard" by comparing the preparatory and thus lesser OT revelation with God's final disclosure in the Son: if it was important to heed the former, how much more the latter. This less-to-greater argumentation was common in both rabbinic and Hellenistic circles and is fundamental to the pastor's strategy for moving his hearers to faithful obedience.[2] Verses 3b-4 support this comparison by demonstrating the certain validity of the new.

1 There are three key expressions in this verse: "to give much greater attention," "things heard," and "lest we drift away." The revelation God has "spoken" (1:1-14) is appropriately described as the "things heard" by his people. It cannot be distantiated from them as a text to be manipulated but engages them and requires their obedient response. By using this term the pastor anticipates the exhortation of Ps 95:7-11 (Heb 3:7–4:11): "Today, if you hear his voice," and the wilderness generation who heard but did not obey. Thus the pastor's first description of the gospel message underscores its divine origin and the urgency of obedience.

Failure to give "much greater attention" will result in "drifting away." These terms suggest a nautical metaphor: the hearers must attend to their course with diligence lest through neglect they drift away and miss their intended harbor.[3] It is not just that the hearers should give "greater attention" than previously given either by themselves or by those who received God's OT revelation (cf. the "wilderness generation" in 3:7–4:11). Their "attention" must correspond to the greatness of God's revelation in the Son.[4] Such

---

Son (1:1-14), it is imperative to give heed to what he has said (2:1-4) in order to inherit the "great salvation" (2:3) soon to be described (2:5-18). Note "Lord" in 1:10; 2:4; "salvation" in 2:3, 5; and the contrast with angels throughout. See Vanhoye, *Situation*, 252-54; Lane, 1:36, and Weiss, 182.

2. See Koester, 209, n. 68, the sources there cited, and "The Sermon's Use of the Old Testament" in the Introduction (esp. pp. 54-55).

3. προσέχω, "pay attention" (BDAG, 879-80), could sometimes be used for keeping a ship on course toward its intended port (LSJ, 1512, cited by Koester). This connotation is suggested here by the use of παρραρέω ("drift") below.

4. The "much greater" intensity of περισσοτέρως corresponds to the salvation

attention is the opposite of the "neglect" of v. 3. It involves holding "firm" to their confession of Christ (3:6, 14) and living in obedient faithfulness (11:1-38) with eyes fixed on Jesus (12:1-3).

Those who fail to give such attention "drift away."[5] This drifting is the opposite of "going on" in maturity (6:1) or of "drawing near" through what Christ has provided (4:16; 10:22), and thus of "running the course" to the heavenly goal (12:1).[6] Those who will not move toward God "drift away."[7] Careless drifting is culpable and, if unchecked, will lead to falling "away from the living God" (3:12).

This tendency to drift was evident from reluctance to identify publicly with the Christian community (10:25). It resulted both from moral and spiritual lethargy (5:11-14) and from the opposition of surrounding society.[8] Those who received Hebrews knew the meaning of persecution (10:32-39; 12:4-13; cf. 11:24-28). Present disdain from the larger community threatened greater hardship to come (11:35-38; 12:3-4). The pastor calls on believers to resist compromise despite social pressure and enticement. He urges them to truly "hear" the "things" that they have "heard." He will describe these things in v. 3a as "such a great salvation" and explain them in the chapters to come.

2   Every turn of phrase in this comparison between revelation in the Son and previous revelation drives home the urgency of obedient hearing. "Such a great salvation" far surpasses "the word spoken through angels."

The pastor, who began by describing God's previous revelation as "in the prophets" (1:1), can also describe it as "the word spoken through angels." His mention of angels is a clear reference to God's definitive revelation on

---

brought by Christ with its effective remedy for sin (9:14; 10:5-10). This salvation is, therefore, "better" in kind, not degree. Note the significance of κρείττων, "better," in 1:4; 6:9; 7:7, 19, 22; 8:6; 9:23; 11:16, 35, 40; 12:24. See Ellingworth, 135.

5. In the writer of Hebrews' usage, words that begin with the preposition παρα often connote disregard for God. "To drift away" (παραρρεῖν) in 2:1; "rebellion" (παραπικρασμός) in 3:8, 15; "to rebel" (παραπικραίνειν) in 3:16; "to be listless" (παρειμένος) in 12:12; and "to be carried away" (παραφέρειν) in 13:9. See Lane, 1:142.

6. Gareth Lee Cockerill, "A Wesleyan Arminian View," in *Four Views on the Warning Passages in Hebrews,* ed. Herbert W. Batemann IV (Grand Rapids: Kregel, 2007), 261.

7. Heb 11:8-13 shows that the Christian life is a pilgrimage to the heavenly homeland.

8. See pp. 16-18 above and deSilva, 2-70. Schmidt's exclusive emphasis on "moral lethargy" neglects the societal pressure and suffering described in 11:1-40 and other passages (T. E. Schmidt, "Moral Lethargy and the Epistle to the Hebrews," *WTJ* 54, no. 1 [1992]: 167-73). On the other hand, McKnight puts undue emphasis on the final, deliberate, public act of apostasy (S. McKnight, "The Warning Passages of Hebrews: A Formal Analysis and Theological Conclusions," *TJ* 13 [1992]: 40). Hebrews is concerned with the process of "drifting" that leads to apostasy.

Mount Sinai.[9] Contemporary Jewish sources bear witness to belief in angelic mediation on that occasion.[10] The rest of this sermon substantiates the pastor's focus on the Sinai covenant. "In the prophets" is a comprehensive expression that conveys the anticipatory nature of revelation before the incarnation. God's word "through angels" on Mount Sinai "encapsulates and epitomizes all pre-Son revelation."[11] It was the Sinai covenant that was fulfilled in the Son (3:6; 8:1–10:18). By recalling the awesomeness of that angel-mediated theophany (cf. 12:18-21) the pastor underscores the seriousness of disobedience. It was the disregard shown God's word spoken at Sinai by the wilderness generation that merited certain punishment (3:1-19). No revelation before the Son could be greater or more awesome than that foundational revelation mediated through these highest of heavenly (though created) beings on Sinai. "One who is Son," however, mediates a revelation that fulfills and thus is far greater than theirs (1:1-14).

As God's "word" the Sinai revelation was a disclosure of God's character that required human obedience.[12] The combination of "transgression" and "disobedience"[13] substantiates the legal validity of this revelation by affirming that absolutely every infraction was subject to punishment.[14] The

9. Ellingworth, 137-38; Attridge, 64-65. The article with "word" (ὁ . . . λόγος) and the aorist tense "he spoke" (λαληθείς) suggest that the pastor has a specific time and place in mind and thus accord with a reference to Sinai (Vanhoye, *Situation*, 233-34).

10. Ellingworth, 104. Although Paul used angelic mediation to show the inferiority of the law (Gal 3:19), for most sources angelic mediation demonstrated the unique character of the law (Acts 7:38, 53; *Jub.* 1:27, 29; 2:1; Josephus, *Ant.* 15.136). See Koester, 205. In Hebrews the greatness of the angel-mediated revelation points only to the ultimate superiority of the greater revelation in the Son.

11. Cockerill, "Wesleyan Arminian," 260, n. 6.

12. The pastor uses "word" instead of "law" for the Sinai revelation because he wants to emphasize its validity as a true revelation of God requiring obedience rather than its role as a type of Christ unable in itself to provide salvation (see this use of "law" in 7:19 and 10:1). Vanhoye, *Situation*, 234-35, agrees, *pace* Ellingworth, 138.

13. The similarity in both sound and meaning between παράβασις, "transgression," and παρακοή, "disobedience," is reminiscent of the similarity between πολυμερῶς, "at various times," and πολυτρόπως, "in various ways" (1:1). The verb παραβαίνω, "transgress," is used in the LXX to describe Israel's sin with the golden calf (Exod 32:8; Deut 9:12, 16) as well for other transgressions. παρακοή, "disobedience," corresponds to ὑπακοή, "obedience," in 5:8 and ὑπακούειν, "to obey" (5:9). These words for "obedience" and "to obey" come from the same root as the words for "hearing" (ἀκοή; 4:2; 5:11) and "to hear" (ἀκούω; 3:7, 15, 16; 4:2, 7; 5:9). It is appropriate to give "obedience" (παρακοή) to "the things heard" (τοῖς ἀκουσθεῖσιν, 2:1), as attested by "those who heard them" (ὑπὸ τῶν ἀκουσάντων, 2:3).

14. βέβαιος, "valid," is the first of several legal terms in these verses — ἔνδικος, "just" (v. 2); ἐβεβαιώθη, "was validated" (v. 3); and συνεπιμαρτυροῦντος, "adding his witness" (v. 4). Note words based on the same root as βέβαιος in Heb 3:6, 14; 6:19; 9:17;

pastor interjects a touch of irony when he says that such disobedience received its "reward."[15] The seriousness of obedience corresponds to the certainty of punishment.

3a There is, however, greater reason to heed the "great salvation" accomplished in Christ. This "great salvation" is more than a "word" that requires obedience and pronounces judgment. It is a provision for obedience that delivers from judgment and brings the faithful into fellowship with God. Thus this "great salvation" provided by a "Great High Priest" (4:14) is the main theme of Hebrews. By introducing this expression without explanation the pastor emphasizes the greatness of God's revelation in Christ and awakens curiosity about its content and meaning. He will show how God's revelation in the Son provides the effective salvation only anticipated by his previous self-disclosure.[16] The pastor's exhortation in these verses is intended to focus their attention on his description of the origin of this "great salvation" in Heb 2:5-18. That description, in turn, is meant to give immediate reinforcement to the pastor's exhortation. The better the hearers understand the exclusive sufficiency of this salvation, the more powerfully they will feel the urgency of "giving more earnest heed" and of "not neglecting" it.

The question "How shall we escape . . . ?" at the beginning of v. 3 brings the author's urgency to full focus. He leaves his reader to imagine what they will not escape if they "neglect" this "great salvation." To "neglect" this salvation is to despise God's revelation and treat it as inconsequential.[17] Subsequent exhortations will make it clear that such disregard for God's provision brings severance from its benefits, which results in eternal loss (6:4-8; 10:26-31).[18] The pastor is not arguing that the punishment for neglecting "such a great salvation" exceeds that for neglecting the angel-mediated message.[19] Even the wilderness generation suffered eternal loss

---

13:9. See BDAG, 172. This usage shows "that God's word is amply confirmed by the evidence of word and deed" (Ellingworth, 138). Legal terminology is particularly appropriate when making comparison with the Sinai revelation. See Lane, 1:37.

15. μισθαποδοσία ("reward") is used with its usual positive sense in 10:35 and 11:36. Note also μισθαποδότης ("rewarder") in 11:6. This word belongs to the often more sophisticated vocabulary of Hebrews not shared with the rest of the NT.

16. Vanhoye, *Situation,* 238-39. However, Heb 11:1-38 indicates that the OT faithful were obedient to God through trust in his promise even if they did not yet have the access to God's presence experienced through Christ by NT believers (11:39-40).

17. "Here neglect is tantamount to rejection of God's purposes (Jer 4:17; Wis 3:10; 2 Macc 4:14; Matt 22:5). Heedlessness is a trait of those who are overtaken by divine judgment (Matt 24:37-39; 25:1-17)" (Koester, 206).

18. "Though the menace which threatens the negligent is left imprecise, it is certainly perdition, as already suggested in 2:1, and it is presented as divine judgment in 10:27 and 31" (Bénétreau, 1:99 [my translation]).

19. *Pace* Bénétreau, 1:99, and many others.

(see on 4:1-11). He wants his hearers to feel that, if possible, the judgment of those faithless to the Son is even more _certain_ than the absolutely certain judgment of those disobedient under the OT revelation.

3b-4 God's angel-mediated word was shown to be valid by the inevitable judgment that fell on the disobedient. The "great salvation," however, was validated for the hearers by its origin in Christ, attestation by faithful witnesses, and confirmation by God.[20] The recipients of Hebrews have not been convinced by abstract argument but by credible testimony and their own experience of this salvation's reality.

The foundation for the validity of this "great salvation" is the fact that it had its beginning "by being spoken through the Lord."[21] The Son's incarnation, teaching, sacrificial death, exaltation, and session are the origin of this salvation and the content of its proclamation.[22] This salvation was certainly authoritative, because it was spoken through "the Lord" (compare 1:10).[23] "Lord" underscores the divine sovereignty of the one seated at God's right as

---

20. Vanhoye, *Situation*, 241. The initial participle phrase ἀρχὴν λαβοῦσα λαλεῖσθαι διὰ τοῦ κυρίου, "having a beginning to be spoken by the Lord," relates the communication of this great salvation to "the Lord" Jesus; the main verb ἐβεβαιώθη, "was confirmed," to those who heard him and relayed the message; and the concluding genitive absolute, συνεπιμαρτυροῦντος τοῦ θεοῦ σημείοις τε καὶ τέρασιν καὶ ποικίλαις δυνάμεσιν καὶ πνεύματος ἁγίου μερισμοῖς κατὰ τὴν αὐτοῦ θέλησιν, "God himself bearing witness with signs and wonders and various miracles and apportionments of the Holy Spirit according to his will," to God's confirmation of the message.

21. The construction ἀρχὴν λαβοῦσα λαλεῖσθαι is a bit strange (see Heb. 11:19; 2 Pet. 1:9). ἀρχήν must be taken as the object of λαβοῦσα and not the subject of λαλεῖσθαι for two reasons: first, if it were the subject of λαλεῖσθαι, then it would be necessary for the infinitive to complete the meaning of λαμβάνω, something that never happens in the Greek Bible; second, it is the "great salvation," not the "beginning," which is spoken and is thus the implied subject of λαλεῖσθαι. This infinitive is, then, an epexegetical explanation of ἀρχήν showing the means of the "beginning." Thus literally "having a beginning to be spoken through the Lord," or "having a beginning by being spoken through the Lord." The writer intentionally connects this revelation with Jesus. Cf. Koester, 211.

22. Lane, 1:39. It is better to understand "beginning" in this comprehensive way than to try to pinpoint the incarnation, exaltation, or some other point as the "beginning." See Erich Grässer, "Das Heil als Wort: Exegetische Erwägungen zu Hebr 2,1-4," in *Neues Testament und Geschichte,* ed. Heinrich Baltensweiler and Bo Reicke (Tübingen: Siebeck, 1972), 263-66 (cited in O'Brien, 88).

23. Bachmann's identification of "the Lord" in this passage with God and the word spoken with the prophetic word breaks the parallel with 1:1-4, weakens the significance of the comparison with angels in 1:5-14, underestimates the force of 1:10 for the meaning of "Lord," and removes the Son's incarnation and saving work from the central place in this passage which accords well with the rest of Hebrews. See M. Bachmann, "'. . . gesprochen durch den Herrn' (Hebr 2,3): Erwägungen zum Reden Gottes und Jesu im Hebräerbrief," *Bib* 71 (1990): 365-94.

the one who has accomplished God's ultimate revelation and thus provided a fully sufficient salvation.

The Gospel message was attested to the recipients of all NT books by "those who heard him."[24] Though it was God who confirmed his message, this divinely appointed human witness was essential to his purposes. Although the pastor reserves the word "apostle" for Jesus (3:1), he joins the rest of the NT in affirming the essential apostolic witness to Christ (see John 20:29-31).[25] This message was validated through those who heard "him."[26] It was through them that God communicated his revelation in the Son, and through them and their associates that he confirmed its validity with his own testimony. The readers probably knew the names of those who "heard him" and attested the gospel to them.

It was God, however, who used this human witness to confirm his message. He is the one who spoke it "through the Lord" in the beginning. He is the one who bore supporting testimony to the message of his witnesses by granting "signs and wonders and various miracles and apportionments of the Holy Spirit."[27] "Signs and wonders" was a set description of the great miracles by which God had delivered Israel from Egypt (Deut 4:34; 6:22; Ps 135:9; Jer 32:20-21). The same God bore witness to the ministries of Jesus (Acts 2:22), Paul (Rom 15:19), and the other apostles (2 Cor 12:12) through "signs," "wonders," and "miracles." Thus "signs and wonders" affirmed not only the validity of God's word in the Son but the continuity of this word with his Sinai revelation and with the gospel preached throughout the world. The pastor's argument would have been ineffective had his hearers not experienced such confirming events when they received the gospel (cf. Gal 3:5). He is so confident that he begins his letter and bases his appeal on the reality of this supernatural confirmation. Yet he makes no attempt to duplicate these events but bases his argument on their past occurrence as confirmation of the

24. *Pace* Weiss, 183-84. A preconceived idea of "early Catholicism" seems to lead Weiss and others to see in this description a reference to people who lived toward the end of the first century.

25. See Vanhoye, *Situation*, 243-44. This different use of the word "apostle" is no reason to deny that Hebrews affirmed the apostolic witness to Christ. Hebrews uses a terminology distinct from the rest of the NT.

26. English translations rightly supply this "him" lacking in Greek to show that the reference is to Christ. Bénétreau, 1:100-101, 104-5, gives an adequate critique of Attridge, Grässer, and others who argue that the reference is merely to the "message."

27. In this passage συνεπιμαρτυροῦντος, a compound of σύν, "with," and μαρτυρέω, "to bear witness," means that God has added his confirming witness to the testimony of those who "heard the Lord." Compare *1 Clem.* 43:1 and see references in Bénétreau, 1:102, n. 1. The emphasis given God's confirmation shows it to be decisive. In the following discussion "signs and wonders" is a translation of σημεῖα καὶ τέρατα, and "miracles" of δυνάμεις.

apostolic testimony. Thus he gives no encouragement either to those who would seek to replicate such "signs" or to those who would preclude God's providing such confirmation in the present.[28]

Throughout the NT "signs," "wonders," and especially "miracles" are the work of the Holy Spirit poured out on God's people through the exalted Christ (Acts 2:33; cf. Rom 15:19). Thus it is no surprise that these supernatural events were accompanied by "apportionments of the Spirit."[29] God's Spirit was given to his witnesses and was the agent of God's confirming miracles through them.[30] What God spoke through the Son he attested through the miraculous work of the Holy Spirit. The pastor may also be referring to the confirmation brought by his hearers' own reception of the Spirit.

The pastor uses the condition of fact in v. 2 and the question of v. 3 to involve his hearers and move them to action — "If God's word spoken through the angels was valid . . ."; to which they would certainly reply, "It was." Then, "How shall we escape . . . ?" to which they would unquestionably answer, "We shall not." The certainty of judgment under the Old Covenant makes judgment all the more certain on those who disregard the "great salvation" of the new. God spoke the first through angels. The second he has spoken in the Son and attested by the miraculous activity of the Holy Spirit. The pastor's appeal to fear is no cheap manipulation. He would awaken his hearers to the true condition of professed believers who discount God's "great salvation" in Christ. It is the promised blessings of salvation that are at stake. In 2:5-18 he begins to explore the nature and benefits of this "great salvation."

4. The Crucial Importance of the Incarnate, Suffering Son (2:5-18)

5 *For it is not to angels that he has subjected the world to come of which we are speaking.* 6 *For someone has attested somewhere, saying,*

---

28. However, Vanhoye's suggestion (*Situation*, 244) that the present participle, συνεπιμαρτυροῦντος, "bearing witness along with," indicates the continuation of the miraculous is weak. This participle qualifies the aorist verb ἐβεβαιώθη, "confirmed," and describes what was going on at the time of confirmation.

29. It seems best to take πνεύματος as objective genitive since God is the doer of the action. Bénétreau, 1:104-5.

30. In 1 Corinthians 12 the Spirit gives supernatural "gifts" (χαρισμάτων, 1 Cor 12:4) for the edification of the church. In Heb 2:4 God gives special "apportionments" (μερισμοῖς) of the Spirit to his witness in order to work his confirming miracles through them. The unusual character of those "gifts" and the miracles effected by these "apportionments" show that they were according to God's will (καθὼς βούλεται, 1 Cor 12:11; and κατὰ τὴν αὐτοῦ θέλησιν, Heb 2:4). See Vanhoye, *Situation*, 247.

*"What is man that you remember him,
or the son of man that you visit him?*[1]
7 *You have made him a little lower than the angels;
with glory and honor you have crowned him.
8 All you have subjected under his feet."*

*By subjecting everything, he left nothing unsubjected to him. But
now we do not yet see all things in a state of subjection to him. 9 But we
do see the one who has been made a little lower than the angels, Jesus,
because of the suffering of death crowned with glory and honor, so that
by the grace of God on behalf of everyone he might taste death.*

*10 For it was fitting to him, for whom are all things and through
whom are all things, in order to bring many sons and daughters*[2] *into
glory, to perfect the Pioneer of their salvation through suffering.
11 For both the one making holy and those being made holy are all
from one. For which reason he is not ashamed to call them brothers
and sisters, 12 saying, "I will announce your name to my brothers and
sisters. In the midst of the congregation I will praise you." 13 And
again, "I will put my trust in him." And again, "Behold, I and the children whom God has given me."*

*14 Therefore, since the children share blood and flesh, he himself
in like manner became a partaker with them, in order that through
death he might destroy the one who has the power of death, that is, the
devil, 15 and set free those who by fear of death throughout their lives
were subject to bondage. 16 For clearly it is not angels he has taken
hold of, but the seed of Abraham he has taken hold of. 17 Therefore, it
was necessary for him to be made like the brothers and sisters in every way, in order that he might become a merciful and faithful high
priest in things pertaining to God, to make atonement for the sins of
the people. 18 Because he himself has suffered when he was tested, he
is able to help those undergoing testing.*

Heb 2:5-18 completes the description of the eternal, exalted Son in 1:5-14 by
showing how his incarnation and suffering were the means to his exaltation
as all-sufficient Savior.[3] Thus this passage in turn reinforces the exhortation

---

1. On retention of the singular "man" and "son of man" see the comments on v. 6
below.

2. υἱός, "sons," is inclusive of all the faithful, "sons and daughters." "Sons" reinforces the parallel with "the Son." In the ancient world "sons" were heirs. Thus by affirming that all are "sons" the writer includes both women and men in the inheritance of salvation (compare 1:14).

3. Although the angels are not as prominent in 2:5-18 as they were in 1:5–2:4,

in 2:1-4.[4] Like its counterpart, 2:5-18 may be conveniently divided into three sub-sections: 2:5-9; 10-13; and 14-18, though the last two are closely bound to one another.

The conversation from chapter 1 continues. God concluded his address to his Son in Heb 1:5-14 with the invitation found in Ps 110:1: "Sit at my right hand." In Heb 2:5-9 the pastor uses Ps 8:4-6 to explain this invitation so that his hearers will understand the Son's answer given in 2:10-13.[5] Ps 8:4-6 shows that the eternal Son's exaltation/session at God's right as sufficient Savior was achieved only by his assuming humanity and suffering "death for every human being."[6] The Son's answer in vv. 10-13 confirms the suffering by which he became the "Pioneer" of his people's salvation as appropriate to the divine character and an expression of divine faithfulness. The Son joyfully accepts the Father's invitation (v. 12), affirms his human obedience (v. 13a), and owns God's "children" as his own (v. 13b). Verses 14-18 show the relevance of what the Son has affirmed for the hearers. The Son's incarnation and suffering in accord with the character of God were appropriate for the predicament of the "children" whom God had given him. Through his obedient suffering he fulfilled his sonship by becoming the High Priest able to deliver them from the sin that beset the human situation (vv. 17-18) and the resultant fear of death (vv. 14-16). With this reference to high priesthood the pastor introduces the theme of his sermon anticipated since the mention of "purification for sins" in 1:3.

Thus this section introduces the Son as the "Pioneer" (vv. 10-13) who

---

continued reference to them (2:5, 7, 9, 16) reinforces the complementary unity of these passages (Lane, 1:54; deSilva, 120; and Attridge, 94; *pace* Westfall, *Discourse Analysis,* 100).

4. Spicq, 2:29, and Weiss, 192, affirm the mutual relationship between 2:1-4 and 2:5-9. Mention of the "great salvation" in 2:1-4 anticipates the discussion of Christ's humiliation and death in 2:5-9. γάρ ("for") in v. 5 indicates that 2:5-18 provides additional motivation for the exhortation of 2:1-4 (*pace* Attridge, 69-70, n. 8) and thus confirms the connection with 1:1-14, which provided the initial motivation. Thus it is no surprise that γάρ also picks up the theme of submission from 1:1-14, as Westfall, *Discourse Analysis,* 101, contends.

5. Westfall's failure to see how Ps 8:4-6 expounds Ps 110:1 contributes to her failure to recognize the close connection between 2:5-18 and 1:1–2:4 (Westfall, *Discourse Analysis,* 106). See George H. Guthrie, "'Hebrews' Use of the Old Testament: Recent Trends in Research," *CurBS* 1 (2003): 281.

6. There is some validity to Koester's argument that 2:5-9 is the *propositio* or "proposition" that introduces the Son's suffering and death as the main theme of Hebrews underlying both his high-priestly work and his role as example of endurance (Koester, 219). Yet the high priesthood of Christ, introduced in 2:17-18, is the distinctive contribution of Hebrews. His eternal preexistence, assumption of humanity, suffering, obedience, and exaltation/session are all crucial to this priesthood.

leads God's people into the salvation they are "about to inherit" (1:14) at his return and as the High Priest (vv. 14-18) who has made the all-sufficient provision for their perseverance until they enter that inheritance. "Pioneer" (cf. 12:1-3) is the pastor's premier designation for Christ when he would urge perseverance amid suffering (10:19–12:29). "High Priest" (8:1-2), however, is his title of choice and his special preference when he would urge them to draw near and find the grace needed for perseverance (4:14–10:18). The "great salvation" (2:3) Christ provides is available only in union with the "Great High Priest" (4:14) he has become. The association with Sinai is maintained by the way in which Moses foreshadows the Son in his role as Pioneer just as Aaron typifies his high priesthood.

5-9 Verse 5 resumes the argument of 1:14 in order to introduce Ps 8:4-6 as the interpretation of Ps 110:1 (Heb 1:13).[7] The pastor quotes the relevant portions of Ps 8:4-6 in vv. 6-8a and then interprets them in vv. 8b-9.

5 The pastor extends the argument of 1:5-14 by contrasting the "angels" with the "man"/"son of man" described in Ps 8:4-6. When he identifies "the world to come" as the reality "about which we are speaking," he invites his hearers to look for its description in what he has already said.[8] It is the "world" in which the Son has been installed at God's right hand (1:6).[9] It is the "salvation" the faithful are inheriting (1:14).[10] It is the reality entered through the "great salvation" (2:3) the Son has provided.[11] Verse 5 is, in fact,

---

7. On this relationship between 2:5-9 and 1:5-14 see also R. L. Brawley, "Discursive Structure and the Unseen in Hebrews 2:8 and 11:1: A Neglected Aspect of the Context," *CBQ* 55 (1993): 84.

8. See G. H. Guthrie and R. D. Quinn, "A Discourse Analysis of the Use of Psalm 8:4-6 in Hebrews 2:5-9," *JETS* 49 (2006): 239. Blomberg's attempt to limit "about which we are speaking" to the coming quotation from Psalm 8 is forced and unconvincing (Craig L. Blomberg, "'But We See Jesus': The Relationship between the Son of Man in Hebrews 2.6 and 2.9 and the Implications for English Translations," in *A Cloud of Witnesses: The Theology of Hebrews in Its Ancient Context,* ed. Richard Bauckham et al. (LNTS 387; T&T Clark, 2008], 92-93). The identification of this "world" with the created world subjected to humanity finds no convincing support within the immediate or larger context.

9. οἰκουμένη, "world" (2:5), is used of the "world" the Son enters (1:6). See the comments on that verse. This world is the heavenly Most Holy Place (10:19-21) and homeland of God's presence (11:10-13), which is eternal (12:25-29). See Mackie, *Eschatology and Exhortation,* 42-44; F. F. Bruce, 71; O'Brien, 93.

10. Compare the "coming world of salvation" (τὴν οἰκουμένην τὴν μέλλουσαν) with "those who are about to inherit salvation" (τοὺς μέλλοντας κληρονομεῖν σωτηρίαν) in 1:14. "About to" in 1:14 and "coming" in 2:5 translate the same participle. One could translate 1:14: "those who are coming to inherit salvation." Compare 6:5 and 11:20.

11. The primary referent of "such a great salvation" in 2:3 is not final entrance into the coming "world" of salvation but God's provision in Christ for perseverance. *Pace*

a deduction from 1:13-14. First premise: the Son is seated at God's right hand (1:13). Second premise: the angels have been sent out to assist "those about to inherit salvation" (1:14). Conclusion: the angels, therefore, most definitively, are not the ones to whom this "coming world" of salvation "has been subjected."[12] The word "subjected" occurs three times in v. 8 below, first in the quotation of the last line from Ps 8:6 and twice in the interpretation of the psalm.[13] Thus its use here anticipates both the quotation from Psalm 8 in vv. 6-8a and its subsequent interpretation in vv. 8b-9.[14] Other NT writers also recognized "you have subjected all things under his feet" (Ps 8:6) as a reference to Christ.[15] Thus the pastor's use of this psalm may have been a creative development founded on common Christian tradition.[16]

6-8a   The initial position of "attested" in the Greek sentence emphasizes the solemnity and divine authority of Psalm 8.[17] "Someone somewhere" highlights the divine origin of Scripture by minimizing the identity of the human author, who addresses God through the power of divine inspiration.[18] "But" indicates that the one described in the psalm as "man"/"son of man" stands in contrast to the angels as the one in charge of the coming world of salvation.[19]

By beginning his quotation with Ps 8:4, "What is man that you remember him, or the son of man that you visit him?" the pastor intentionally

---

Brawley, "Discursive Structure," 90. The pastor's goal is to present the grandeur of this provision in all of its majesty.

12. Verse 5 begins emphatically with οὐ . . . ἀγγέλοις ("not . . . to angels").

13. See ὑποτάσσω ("subject") in both 2:5 and 2:8 (Ps 8:6).

14. Hebrews' use of this psalm has been facilitated by the LXX translation of אלהים, "God/gods" (Ps 8:5) as "angels." The OT context requires a translation like "gods"/"heavenly beings" (NASB, NRSV) or "angels" (TNIV, ESV). Compare Ps 82:1b. The Targums, Syriac translation, and many Jewish commentators support the LXX. Westcott, 44. See Bénétreau, 1:112, and Vanhoye, *Situation,* 270-71.

15. This verse could describe the subjection that occurred at Christ's session (Eph 1:20-23; 1 Pet 3:22) and that final subjection of all to him at his return (1 Cor 15:25-27; Phil 3:21). Hebrews integrates these two perspectives by affirming that the subjection that took place in principle at the exaltation would become a visible reality at Christ's return.

16. Compare the way in which he alone develops Ps 110:1 in the light of Ps 110:4.

17. διαμαρτύρομαι, "attest" (2:6), is an intensified form of μαρτυρέω, "to bear witness" (7:8, 17 and 10:15).

18. Philo occasionally used such indefinite formulas of citation even when he knew the speaker (*Unchangeable* 74, *Planting* 90, *Drunkenness* 61). See Hughes, 83, n. 60, and Koester, 213-14. Here, however, the use of this indefinite form is purposeful. It shows that Psalm 8 is not spoken by the Father to the Son (1:5-14) or by the Son to the Father (2:10-13). On the way Hebrews introduces Scripture see "The Sermon's Use of the Old Testament" in the Introduction (esp. pp. 44-45, n. 194).

19. Compare the δέ, "but," of 2:6 with the δέ of 1:6, 8.

injects an element of dissonance or ambiguity in order to stimulate the curiosity of his hearers. The resumption of the contrast with angels implies that this future world will be subjected to the eternal, now exalted Son of 1:5-14.[20] To whom could this world be in subjection other than the divinely designated "heir of all things" (1:2) now seated at God's right (1:3d, 13)? Yet by beginning with Ps 8:4 the pastor calls the one in charge of the future world "man" and "son of man." Whether or not "son of man" held Messianic overtones for those the pastor addressed, they recognized this term, in tandem with "man," as equivalent to "human being," just as the author of the psalm intended.[21]

As noted above, first-century Christians often applied Ps 8:6b, "You have subjected all things under his feet," to Christ. In fact, in accord with Hebrews, they sometimes associated this subjection with Ps 110:1.[22] No other NT writer, however, applies "what is man that you remember him, or the son of man that you visit him?" to Christ. The pastor, then, intentionally begins his quotation with this verse in order to assert Christ's *humanity*.[23] He has al-

20. Guthrie and Quinn, "A Discourse Analysis," 238-39.

21. Guthrie and Quinn, "A Discourse Analysis," 243-44, suggest that similarities between Stephen's speech in Acts 7 and Hebrews support a Messianic understanding. See also Bruce, 72-74 and Hughes, 84-85. Certainly it would not have been long before readers who were familiar with the Gospels might have heard Messianic overtones when reading Hebrews (R. T. France, "The Writer of Hebrews as a Biblical Expositor," *TynBul* 47 [1996]: 262). Yet "son of man" in Heb 2:6 lacks the definite article usually attached to it when Jesus uses it as a self-designation. Furthermore, the author of Hebrews gives no evidence of a Messianic understanding of this term elsewhere. See Dale F. Leschert, *Hermeneutical Foundations of Hebrews: A Study in the Validity of the Epistle's Interpretation of Some Core Citations from the Psalms* (National Association of Baptist Professors of Religion Dissertation 10; Lewiston, NY: Mellen, 1994), 104-5. In 2:5-18 the pastor is clearly asserting the humanity of Jesus. For critique of Käsemann's proposal that Gnostic, primal-man speculations have influenced this passage, see Attridge, 74-75 and Weiss, 197-98. Even Braun, 54, who affirms such influence on Paul, denies its presence in Heb 2:5-9.

22. Ps 8:6 is associated with Ps 110:1 in both 1 Cor 15:25-27 and Eph 1:20-23. Note the italicized portions of these verses: 1 Cor 15:25-27 (ESV): 25 For he must reign *until he has put* all *his enemies* (θῇ πάντας τοὺς ἐχθρούς, from Ps 110:1) *under his feet* [ὑπὸ τοὺς πόδας αὐτοῦ, from Ps 8:6). 26 The last enemy to be destroyed is death. 27 For "God *has put all things in subjection under his feet*" (πάντα γὰρ ὑπέταξεν ὑπὸ τοὺς πόδας αὐτοῦ; Ps 8:6). Eph 1:20-23 (ESV): 20 that he worked in Christ when he raised him from the dead and *seated him at his right hand* (καθίσας ἐν δεξιᾷ αὐτοῦ, from Ps 110:1) in the heavenly places, 21 far above all rule and authority and power and dominion, and above every name that is named, not only in this age but also in the one to come. 22 And *he put all things under his feet* (πάντα ὑπέταξεν ὑπὸ τοὺς πόδας αὐτοῦ, from Ps 8:6), and gave him as head over all things to the church." See Ellingworth, 150-51.

23. It is true that the pastor offers no interpretive comment on this opening line of

ready shown that the universal heir is the eternal, exalted Son (1:1-14). By quoting this clause he initiates his contention that the one in charge of the future world of salvation is also *human*. This enthroned heir is also one who became a *human* being.[24] There is no ambiguity as to the identity of the one to whom the future world of salvation has been subjected.[25] The question concerns the kind of person he is. No other early writer expounds both the deity and humanity of Christ more eloquently than the author of Hebrews. There was a certain appropriateness in using the term "son of man" to affirm the humanity of the eternal "Son."[26]

The pastor, then, quotes this psalm in vv. 6-8a because it is a description of humanity, but he does not intend to make a statement about humanity in general before applying the psalm to "Jesus" in v. 9.[27] Those who think the author begins by making such a statement usually interpret "we do not yet see all in a state of subjection to him" in v. 8c as a reference to humanity rather than to Jesus: the pastor is decrying the fact that fallen humanity has not lived up to its original position described in this psalm as the steward of creation. These interpreters often argue that "all," including the coming

---

the psalm (O'Brien, 96, n. 76, citing Attridge, 74; Lane, 1:47; Ellingworth, 149; L. D. Hurst, "The Christology of Hebrews 1 and 2," in *The Glory of Christ in the New Testament,* ed. L. D. Hurst and N. T. Wright [Oxford: Clarendon, 1987], 151-64, esp. 153). This fact, however, does not mean that he intends to make an independent statement about humanity in vv. 6-8 before applying this psalm to Jesus in v. 9. In v. 9 he identifies Jesus as the referent of the entire quotation.

24. Thus the way in which the TNIV and the NRSV render "man" and "son of man" respectively as "mortals" (TNIV)/"human beings" (NRSV) and "human beings" (NRSV)/"mortals" (TNIV) obscures the pastor's attribution of this passage to "Jesus." See Brawley, "Discursive Structure," 84, n. 13. Cf. deSilva, 108.

25. Thus we agree with Bruce, 72-74; Hughes, 84-85; and Weiss, 197-98, that the pastor's intention from the beginning is the application of this psalm to the Son. Brawley holds this position and lists a number of its supporters (Brawley, "Discursive Structure," 84, n. 13). For an effective defense using discourse analysis see Guthrie and Quinn, "A Discourse Analysis," 235-46.

26. Guthrie and Quinn, "A Discourse Analysis," 243. "Remember" and "visit" express God's "twofold regard of thought and action." In the LXX and the NT ἐπισκέπτεσθαι refers almost exclusively to a visitation for the benefit of the one visited. See Luke 1:68, 78; 7:16; Acts 15:14 (Westcott, 43). The pastor is not distracted with what is peripheral to his purpose in order to comment on these terms. When the text was applied to "Jesus," they may have suggested the gracious way in which God sustained him and exalted him to his right hand.

27. *Pace* Westcott, 41, 45; Moffatt, 21, 23; Riggenbach, 37-38; Montefiore, 55, 57, 58; Bénétreau, 1:109-10; and O'Brien, 97, who contend that the pastor does not apply the psalm to Jesus until v. 9 (or v. 8c). For a recent comprehensive statement of this position see Blomberg, "'But We See Jesus,'" 88-99. For others who support this interpretation see the literature cited by Blomberg.

world of salvation, will be subjected to humanity through Jesus, the representative human.[28] This interpretation of v. 8c faces several serious objections. First, in order to separate the "son of man" in v. 6 from the exalted, eternal Son some who hold this interpretation weaken the bond between 2:5-18 and 1:1-14 and thus obscure the close relationship between Ps 8:4-6 and Ps 110:1 (Heb 1:13). Second, there is no clear contextual evidence that substantiates the above interpretation of v. 8c. Thus this position lacks the kind of unambiguous substantiation provided by v. 9 for the identification of the "son of man" with Jesus. Third, the way in which the pastor absolutizes the "all" of v. 8a is in accord with the universal sovereignty of the Son (1:2, 13).[29] Fourth, although the pastor clearly affirms that Christ died for all (2:9), his focus is not on humanity as a whole but on the human people of God and their need for perseverance.[30] It is not humanity but the faithful who are destined for "glory" (2:10). Finally, Hebrews never says that the coming world will be "subjected" even to the people of God. The faithful will "inherit" (1:14), "enter" (4:1; cf. 3:18), or "receive" (12:28) God's ultimate salvation.

8b-c   The pastor's interpretation focuses on three statements from the psalm: "You have made him a little lower than the angels" (Ps 8:5a), Heb 2:7a; "with glory and honor you have crowned him" (Ps 8:5b), Heb 2:7b; and "All you have subjected under his feet" (Ps 8:6b), Heb 2:8a. The second and third refer to the exaltation and the second coming, respectively. Thus they are equivalent to Ps 110:1. When the Son accepted God's invitation, "Sit at

---

28. According to this interpretation of v. 8bc, the application of Psalm 8 to Jesus was based on belief in him as representative of humanity and thus the one through whom humanity obtains its destiny. Even some like Leschert, *Hermeneutical Foundations,* 119, still affirm this interpretation, though they note its weakness. The pastor clearly believes that God's purposes for the creation are fulfilled in the destiny of the people of God (1:1-4, 14). Elsewhere, however, he is not concerned with the salvation of humanity as a whole but with the perseverance of God's people. O'Brien, 105, would reconcile the idea of Jesus as the representative human and the pastor's narrower focus on the perseverance of God's people when he says, "The divine purposes for the whole of humanity, picked up from Psalm 8, find their fulfillment in the Son and those who belong to him." However, in vv. 14-18 below the pastor follows a very different line of argument. In these verses he does not say that the Son became human in order to represent humanity. He says that the Son became human because the people of God were human. He became human in order to represent the people of God as their High Priest.

29. Leschert, *Hermeneutical Foundations,* 109-10. Leschert also notes that the γάρ ("for") of v. 8 refers back to the subordination of the coming world in v. 5.

30. In an indirect way Blomberg, "'But We See Jesus,'" 99, admits this fact when he says that, if one misses the insights that come from interpreting 2:6-8a as the author's making a statement about the human condition, then one has "no other comparable passage in the letter from which to glean them." The anthropological interpretation is a foreign body in Hebrews.

my right hand" (Ps 110:1a), he was "crowned . . . with glory and honor" (Ps 8:5b). God will make his "enemies a stool for" his "feet" (Ps 110:1b) when he subjects "all . . . under his feet" (Ps 8:6b).[31] The main contribution of Psalm 8 is the way "you have made him a little lower than the angels" affirms the incarnation in relation to these other events.

The pastor reserves the first two of these clauses for v. 9. In v. 8bc he turns his attention to the third: "All you have subjected under his feet." He has prepared for what he wants to say about this clause by omitting Ps 8:6a and by ending the quotation before 8:7. In this way he has excluded the parts of the psalm that give specificity to the "all" that has been "subjected" to "man"/"son of man." Ps 8:6a identifies this "all" as the "works" of God's hands.[32] Ps 8:7, reflecting the authority given humans in the creation account (Gen 1:28), lists the animals — both domestic and wild — as under human subjection.[33] These verses would not have prevented but their omission facilitates the expanded inclusiveness of this "all" at the beginning of the pastor's interpretation in v. 8b: without further explanation he asserts that absolutely "nothing" was left "unsubjected to him."[34] The categorical nature of this statement is appropriate only for the one already identified as the universal heir of all at the beginning of this sermon (1:2). The next clause, "we do not yet see the all in a state of subjection to him," identifies the visible manifestation of this subjection with the return of Christ when his "enemies" will become a "stool for" his feet.[35] Christ will then usher the faithful into the final "salvation" (9:28) that awaits them at the Judgment (12:25-29).[36]

9 In v. 9 the pastor paraphrases the two remaining clauses from Psalm 8, represented by the italicized words in the translation below: "But *the one who has been made a little lower than angels* (cf. Ps 8:5a) we do see,

---

31. Compare the ἕως ("until") of Ps 110:1b with the οὔπω ("not yet") of Heb 2:8 in reference to Ps 8:6.

32. Ps 8:6a: "and you established him over the works of your hands." Although there is strong external evidence for including this line in Heb 2:7, it was probably added to conform with the LXX of Psalm 8. *TCGNT,* 593-94, and Vanhoye, *Situation,* 264-65.

33. Ps 8:7: "sheep and all cattle, and also the beasts of the field, the birds of the heavens and the fish of the seas, the things passing through the sea."

34. This forceful double negative ("nothing . . . unsubjected") indicates that this comprehensive "all" includes, but, *pace* Braun, 55, cannot be restricted to, the coming world of salvation.

35. "In a state of subjection" catches the nuance of the perfect passive participle ὑποτεταγμένα.

36. *Pace* Weiss, 193-94, and Brawley, "Discursive Structure," 84, 91, the pastor is not rebuking his hearers because they do not see what they should see with eyes of faith. This is shown by the way he associates himself with them in the inclusive "we." It is also substantiated by the way he subsequently affirms that they "do" see the incarnate and exalted Lord.

Jesus, on account of the suffering of death *crowned with glory and honor* (cf. Ps 8:5b)." By inserting the words "we do see, Jesus, on account of the suffering of death" between these two paraphrases the pastor interprets the first as a description of the incarnate Son and the second as a reference to his exaltation. By tracking the Greek word order, this somewhat awkward translation demonstrates the bold identification of the one "we see" as the incarnate one, the one "made a little lower than angels." "Jesus" is the pastor's favorite designation when speaking of the Son's humanity and suffering.[37] Thus the pastor has reserved his first mention of this name for this climactic position after his dramatic affirmation of the incarnation. This first use of the name "Jesus" opens the way for the first mention of Jesus' death: it is the incarnate "Jesus" who has been "crowned" "on account of the suffering of death" with divine "glory and honor" (cf. 12:1-3).[38] Only now can the pastor affirm the terrible and costly way in which the Son took his seat at God's right hand.

The pastor has used two perfect passive participles in his paraphrases of the two clauses from Ps 8:5: literally, "the one having been made lower than the angels" and "having been crowned with glory and honor." The first participle phrase is substantive, describing the one whom "we see" — the incarnate Jesus. The second is adverbial, describing the circumstances under which "we see" him — exalted, sitting at God's right hand, "crowned with glory and honor." Both participles are perfect, denoting a past act with continuing effect.[39] The son was made, and continues to be, "a little lower than the angels." He was crowned, and continues to be "crowned with glory and honor." The passive voice of the participles preserves the emphasis on God's initiative in the work of salvation.[40]

Thus there is no reason to deviate from the original intent of the psalm, both in Hebrew and Greek, by translating "a little lower" as "for a lit-

37. See 3:1; 4:16; 6:20; 7:22; 10:19; 12:2, 24; 13:12. Weiss, 197. According to Westcott, 45, "The personal name *Jesus* . . . always fixes attention on the Lord's humanity. . . ."

38. "On account of the suffering of death" qualifies "having been crowned with glory and honor." Throughout Hebrews Christ's suffering is the cause or means of his session (1:3; 9:12; 10:12). As 2:10 says, it is through this suffering that he is "perfected" as the savior of God's people. See Bruce, 75-76; Westcott, 45; and Spicq, 2:33.

39. Cf. Leschert, *Hermeneutical Foundations,* 112-13. Their use by the author is in full accord with his main contention that the High Priest of God's people is fully able to assist them in the present (4:14-16; 8:1-2; 10:19-25) because of the once-for-all sacrifice (7:12; 9:28; 10:10) by which he entered God's presence "once for all" (9:12).

40. As does διὰ τὸ πάθημα τοῦ θανάτου ("on account of the suffering of death"). διά with the accusative, "on account of," instead of διά with the genitive, "through" or "by means of." Elsewhere the pastor may say that Jesus achieves exaltation "by means of" his death (cf. 1:3). Here, however, he emphasizes that God exalts him "on account of" his death.

tle while lower."[41] It may sound paradoxical to say that the exalted Son to whom the angels pay homage (1:6) is still "a little lower than the angels," but this paradox is nothing other than the paradox inherent in the incarnation.[42] The pastor is affirming the continued humanity of the exalted and eternal Son as the representative of the people of God.[43] His full superiority over the angels as the Savior of God's people is the result of his eternity, his assumption of humanity, and his exaltation. He may not have been "taken from among human beings" (5:1), but he could only become the effective High Priest and Savior of the people of God by assuming their humanity (2:14-18). The Son's superiority to the angels as the one in charge of the coming world of salvation is the grand finale of the writer's Son/angels contrast (1:5-14).

These two perfect participles are integral to the pastor's argument because they describe the *present* sufficiency of the Savior resulting from his *past* assumption of humanity and obedient suffering. Nothing is more important than the fact that "we" do now "see" with the eyes of faith the incarnate Son of God in the state of ultimate exaltation because of his obedient suffering and death.[44] The pastor will explain Christ's high priesthood in order to

41. The Greek, but not the Hebrew, will allow this temporal rendering, which is followed by the NASB, RSV, NRSV, and ESV in both vv. 7 and 9. The NIV and NKJV are correct to use "a little lower" in both verses. By combining the temporal "a little while" with the plural "mortals" (v. 7), the NRSV incorrectly implies that being "lower than the angels" is a temporary state rather than a description of humanity. See Westcott, 44; J. Kögel, *Der Sohn und die Söhne: Eine Exegetische Studie zu Hebr 2:5-18* (Gütersloh: Bertelsmann, 1904), 25; and Vanhoye, *Situation,* 287.

42. See Westcott, 45 and Vanhoye, *Situation,* 287. Attridge, 76, n. 65, denies the continued humanity of the Son because he fails to see the nature of this paradox. His attempt (76, n. 64) to remove the force of the perfect is unconvincing. He argues that the temporal expression, "for a little while," limits the continuing effect of the perfect. However, the very point to be proved is that βραχύ τι is a temporal qualifier. In the other examples Attridge cites, 9:26; 10:14; and 11:5, temporal qualifiers do not negate the continuing effect implied by the perfect tense. Attridge cites the following in support of his position: Moffatt, 23; Michel, 139; W. R. G. Loader, *Sohn und Hoherpriester: Eine Traditionsgeschichtliche Untersuchung zur Christologie des Hebräerbriefes* (Wissenschaftliche Monographien zum Alten und Neuen Testament 53; Neukirchen-Vluyn: Neukirchener, 1981), 33; and David G. Peterson, *Hebrews and Perfection: An Examination of the Concept of Perfection in the Epistle to the Hebrews* (SNTSMS 47; Cambridge: Cambridge University Press, 1982), 214, n. 20.

43. "The exaltation is not understood here as annulment of the humiliation. It is only as the Humiliated One that Jesus is much more the Exalted One" (Weiss, 196, n. 14 [my translation]). Cf. Leschert, *Hermeneutical Foundations,* 112-13.

44. Thus the pastor contrasts the final consummation of all things that "we do not yet see" (v. 8b) with physical eyes, and the incarnate Jesus and exalted Son whom "we" do "see" with the eyes of faith. This distinction between two kinds of "seeing" comes from

demonstrate the full sufficiency of this Savior (4:14–10:18). He holds this Savior up as the example *par excellence* of endurance (12:1-3). Thus his whole purpose is to keep the eyes of his hearers fixed on none but this one whom "we" do now "see" (8:1-2; 12:1-3; cf. 4:14-16; 10:19-25; 12:22-24; 13:8). This High Priest alone is able to bring God's people into his presence and to enable them to endure until the end (4:14-16; 10:19-25). Whenever the pastor directs his hearers' gaze to the exalted Son, he is speaking of the eternal Son who assumed humanity and suffered to deliver the people of God.

One cannot overemphasize the importance of Jesus' death. Heb 1:3, "by making purification for sins he sat down at the right hand of the Majesty on high," anticipated this first mention of Christ's death as the cause of his subsequent glorification. In fact, everything has been moving toward this crucial introduction of his suffering. The pastor's biblical quotations have provided the context necessary for this assertion of its significance by affirming not only Christ's deity, exaltation/session, and second coming, but also his incarnation (made explicit by Psalm 8). It is crucial to note that the pastor speaks not merely of "death" but of identification with humanity in the "suffering" of death.[45] In fact, Hebrews normally speaks of Christ's death under the broader category of suffering (2:10, 18; 5:8; 9:26-27; 13:12). The Son's sufficient sacrifice was not a sanitary death but a perfect, continual obedience in the face of severe opposition and suffering that culminated in his death (2:10, 18; 5:8; 9:14; 10:5-10). At the heart of the pastor's message is the firm conviction that by this obedient suffering the Son has both provided for the salvation of his people (10:5-10) and left a most powerful example of endurance for the beleaguered people of God (12:1-3).

In his concluding clause the pastor asserts the purpose of all that he has been saying thus far. The incarnation, suffering, and exaltation of the eternal Son of God were all necessary "so that by the grace of God on behalf of all he might taste death" (Heb 2:9c).[46] Three aspects of this clause require

---

the context and not from the use of different Greek words (ὁράω in v. 8; βλέπω in v. 9). Cf. Brawley, "Discursive Structure," 85, n. 15.

45. "Stress is laid not upon the single historic fact that the Lord suffered death (διὰ τὸ παθεῖν θ.), but on the nature of the suffering itself (διὰ τὸ πάθημα)" (Westcott, 45-46). "The emphasis is on Jesus' suffering unto death rather than on the fact of death itself" (Montefiore, 58).

46. In a strictly grammatical sense, "so that by the grace of God for all he might taste death" qualifies "on account of the suffering of death" (Michel, 139). However, Attridge, 76, is correct: "The clause thus relates to the whole of what precedes and indicates the basic purpose of the savior's mission that culminates in his death and exaltation." Cf. Montefiore, 58; Westcott, 46; Spicq, 2:34; F. F. Bruce, 76; Ellingworth, 155; and O'Brien, 100. The exaltation was the "confirmation" and "empowering" of his death with "universal validity" (Weiss, 199).

comment. First, in accord with the clear statements of Ps 8:5-6, and with the passive participles earlier in v. 9, Jesus acted in accord with God's initiative and purposes. His saving death was accomplished by and was the outworking of "the grace of God."[47] Second, the benefits of his death in accord with God's initiative are available for every human being.[48] The pastor puts no limitation on the sacrifice of Christ, save the obedient faithfulness to which he urges his hearers.[49] It is important when reading Hebrews, however, to remember that the pastor has not addressed this sermon to humanity in general but to the faltering people of God. He is concerned that God's people persevere in faithful obedience through the provision made available by the Son's assuming their humanity and suffering death. Third, the expression "taste death" is fitting for one whom death could not hold.[50] Nevertheless, it is a Semitic expression that puts emphasis on Jesus' full experience of death with its bitterness and suffering.[51] The purpose of his incarnation, death, and exaltation was that he might fully experience death for every human being.

As in the above English translation, the Greek sentence ends emphatically and appropriately with the word "death." Verses 10-18 will show how Jesus' death was an expression of God's grace in harmony with both the character and saving purposes of God and the needs of God's people.[52]

47. Although the alternative reading "without God" (χωρὶς θεοῦ) occurs only in a few Syriac Peshitta manuscripts, one Vulgate manuscript, and a few Greek minuscules, it was known by Origen, Eusebius, Theodore of Mopsuestia, Theodoret, Jerome, Ambrose, and others. All the main Alexandrian and Western manuscripts, including 𝔓[46], support χάριτι θεοῦ, "by the grace of God." Despite this paucity of external evidence, Braun and Montefiore accept χωρὶς θεοῦ, "without God," as the most difficult and therefore preferred reading. Montefiore, 59, suggests that it accords with the pastor's preference for χωρίς, which occurs thirteen times in Hebrews. "Without God" means that Jesus suffered death without the comfort of God. Michel, 139-40, *TCGNT*, 594, and all who follow the better-attested reading, argue that χωρὶς θεοῦ was added as a marginal comment by a scribe under the influence of 1 Cor 15:27 to exclude God from the "all" for whom Christ died or the "all" subjected to Christ. A later copyist thought it a correction to χάριτι θεοῦ and thus emended the text. An original χάριτι θεοῦ is in accord with the way Hebrews attributes salvation to the divine initiative and is particularly fitting in light of the next verse's (2:10) affirmation of the appropriateness of Jesus's death to the character of God. See Weiss, 200-201; Spicq, 2:35; and Westcott, 46. Bruce, 70-71, n. 15, seems to think that χωρὶς θεοῦ was a scribal annotation later incorporated into the text by mistake and then "corrected" to χάριτι θεοῦ.

48. The masculine singular "for all" means "not only for 'all,' but 'for each'" human being (Westcott, 46). When "all" is neuter in Hebrews, it is usually plural (Spicq, 2:35).

49. Montefiore, 59. The ruler of all offers salvation to all. See Weiss, 200.

50. Vanhoye, *Situation,* 292.

51. Vanhoye, *Situation,* 292. O'Brien, 100, n. 102, refers to Isa 51:17; Jer 49:18; Matt 16:28; Mark 9:1; Luke 9:27; 14:24; and John 8:52.

52. Thus vv. 10-18 are the logical development of "the grace of God" in 2:9

10-13 The pastor's introduction of the Son's suffering in v. 9 enables him to resume the dialogue begun in 1:5-14. The Son's response to the Father attests that it was an appropriate expression of God's character and faithfulness for him to use suffering as the means of equipping the Son for his vocation as Savior. Verses 14-18 substantiate the Son's testimony by showing how the Son's assumption of humanity and subsequent suffering were appropriate for the situation in which God's people found themselves.

10 The pastor has already affirmed that the sovereign God, "for whom are all things and by whom are all things," achieves his purposes for all through his Son, "whom he appointed heir of all and through whom he made the worlds" (1:2).[53] Note that in both of these statements ultimate destiny precedes origin. The pastor is urgent that his hearers live in anticipation of this destiny because it encompasses God's purpose of bringing his "many sons and daughters into glory."[54] The beleaguered and humiliated people of God can take courage because they are nothing less than God's "sons and daughters" destined, if they remain faithful, to share the "glory" of his ultimate approval and of his presence.[55] Only the One who has been "crowned with glory and honor" (2:9) because of suffering and is thus the very "radiance" of God's "glory" (1:3) is able to bring them into this destiny.[56] Later the pastor will show the faithful that their own suffering corresponds to Christ's. It substantiates their legitimacy as God's "sons and daughters" who through perseverance follow the Son's example (12:4-11).

(Weiss, 204; cf. Lane, 1:55). The writer of Hebrews would have been astonished at any attempt to sever the saving work of the Son from the Father. He knows nothing of a wrathful Father opposed by a merciful Son.

53. δι' ὃν τὰ πάντα καὶ δι' οὗ τὰ πάντα ("on account of whom the all and through whom the all"). The article τὰ makes πάντα absolute (see v. 8). "The end of the creation, of the universe and of all history is the same One by whom all has come into existence" (Spicq, 2:37 [my translation]). The pastor underscores the deity of the Son by using the same διά (δι' οὗ) with the ablative of agency for both God (2:10) and the Son (1:2) (Westcott, 48).

54. The participle ἀγαγόντα, "bringing" or "leading," is accusative, modifying "God," the understood subject of the infinitive τελειῶσαι, "to perfect" (Lane, 1:56; Hughes, 102; O'Brien, 104). It is also telic, expressing the "divine design" (Vanhoye, *Situation,* 307, 309-10; Weiss, 206). The aorist tense of both participle (ἀγαγόντα, "bringing") and infinitive (τελειῶσαι, "to perfect") does not require simultaneous action (Montefiore, 60). God's intention of bringing his children to glory will not reach consummation until the return of Christ. Christ's being "perfected" was achieved at his exaltation/session.

55. For a discussion of "glory" as both receiving approval and entering God's presence see Koester, 228. "To enter God's glory (on the final day) is to enter the sphere where God's presence is manifest (Isa 60:19), and this signifies life everlasting with him (Rom 2:7; 5:2; 1 Cor 15:42-43; Eph 1:18; 1 Pet 1:21; 5:10)" (O'Brien, 105).

56. Spicq, 2:38, citing Westcott. See also Weiss, 205.

It is important that one not allow the complementary ways in which John and Paul speak of the children of God prejudice one's understanding of Hebrews. From Hebrews' perspective God's people are neither born (John 1:11-12) nor adopted (Rom 8:14-17) as his children through the Son. In Hebrews the Son brings the people of God who can already be called his "sons and daughters" to their God-intended destiny (see on vv. 11, 14 below).[57] By fulfilling his own sonship through providing redemption the Son brings theirs to fruition as well.

The pastor boldly asserts his shocking thesis: it was "appropriate" to the character and purposes of the sovereign God, the source, judge, and goal of "all," to use suffering to equip the Savior so that God could fulfill his purpose for his "sons and daughters." Christ's suffering was neither a logical necessity forced upon God nor a mere decision of his will, but an appropriate expression of the divine character.[58] Thus his incarnate suffering was integral to the Son's person as the ultimate revelation of God's nature. The pastor would persuade his hearers by enabling them to see and feel the way in which the suffering of the Savior was most appropriate to God's character in light of their need.[59] As the consummate verbal artist that he is, the pastor first sketches this appropriateness in vv. 10-18 and then expands his sketch into the full-blown mural of Christ's high priesthood in 4:14–10:18. This is his way of showing how the offense of the cross is the beauty of redemption that ravishes the soul.

It is as "the Pioneer of their salvation" that the Son brings God's children into their eternal destiny. A pioneer is one who, by entering a new land, enables others to follow.[60] By his incarnation, death, entrance into God's

---

57. Ellingworth, 647, is representative of many who miss this perhaps subtle yet important difference when he says, "Christ, by taking human nature and offering it to God as high priest, 'brings many sons to glory,' thus *making* them his brothers and children of God" (emphasis added).

58. Note the pastor's use of πρέπει, "it is fitting," rather than δεί, "it is necessary" (Vanhoye, *Situation,* 306). See Spicq, 2:36 and Westcott, 48. Cf. Philo, *Alleg. Interp.* 1.48; 3.203; and Josephus, *Ag. Ap.* 2.168 (cited by O'Brien, 103).

59. Alan C. Mitchell, "The Use of πρέπειν and Rhetorical Propriety in Hebrews 2:10," *CBQ* 54 (1992): 681-701, esp. 688-89, 694-97, has shown how the language of appropriateness (πρέπειν, "to be appropriate") was used in ancient rhetoric. The speaker would attempt to show how the course of action advocated was suited to the character of the speaker, the needs of the hearers, and the circumstances in which they found themselves. When hearers grasped this appropriateness with both their imagination and their feelings, they were much more likely to be moved, than by mere logical argumentation.

60. ἀρχηγός has a broad range of meaning such as "leader," "ruler," "instigator," and "founder" (BDAG, 138-39). "Pioneer" is most appropriate within the context of Hebrews. When people like Lane, 1:56-58, 62-63, interpret ἀρχηγός as the "champion" who delivers from death, they ignore the immediate context of v. 10 and interpret this word as

presence, and session at God's right hand the Son has opened the way for God's "sons and daughters" to enter the "glory" of the heavenly homeland prepared for them.[61] God's children are to follow their "Pioneer" (12:3), who is their "Forerunner" (6:20). This "Pioneer" is, then, the one through whom God "leads" his sons and daughters to glory.[62] This description of Jesus anticipates the coming comparison with Moses (3:1-6), who led God's people toward the earthly Promised Land.[63]

The plural "sufferings" includes all the temptations and trials that Jesus suffered as a human being (5:8), culminating in the bitter experience of death described in the previous verse.[64] It is the pastor's concern for his intimidated hearers that leads him to emphasize the importance of the way God used the "sufferings" of the incarnate Son to perfect him in his vocation as the "Pioneer" of his people's "salvation."[65] It is this suffering that validated his perfect obedience (5:8-10; 10:5-10) and provided the supreme example of endurance for God's oppressed people (12:1-3). The culminate aorist "to per-

---

if it occurred in vv. 14-15. Both Lane and Weiss are influenced by religious backgrounds alien to Hebrews. Lane thinks of the OT "Divine Warrior" and of Jesus as the "strong man" (Luke 22:28-30). Weiss (211-12) envisions the Gnostic redeemed redeemer, though he admits that there is no evidence for the association of ἀρχηγός with this myth. Loader's contention that ἀρχηγός was first used in relation to the resurrection is unsupported, nor do Acts 5:31, Heb 2:10, or Heb 12:1-3 refer to Jesus' "heavenly activity" (Loader, *Sohn und Hoherpriester,* 20).

61. See Hughes, 100, and Koester, 228.

62. The term ἀρχηγός (ἀρχή, ἄγω), "pioneer," is reminiscent of ἀγαγόντα (ἄγω), the word used in this verse for God's "bringing" or "leading" his sons and daughters to glory.

63. Geoffrey W. Grogan, "Christ and His People: An Exegetical and Theological Study of Hebrews 2:5-18," *Vox Evangelica* (1969): 54-71 and Leopold Sabourin, *Priesthood: A Comparative Study* (Studies in the History of Religion [Supplement to *Numen*] 25; Leiden: E. J. Brill, 1973), 210-11. ἀρχηγός, "Pioneer," is not used of Moses in the LXX. However, when the people rebelled at Kadesh-Barnea (3:7-19), they wanted to choose "another" ἀρχηγός to replace Moses (Num 14:4). Moses led God's "son" (singular) out of Egypt toward the Promised Land (Exod 4:21; Hos 11:1) just as this Pioneer leads the "sons and daughters" to glory (Vanhoye, *Situation,* 311).

64. διὰ τὸ πάθημα τοῦ θανάτου in v. 9, διά with the accusative singular, indicates cause: "because of the suffering of death" Jesus was "crowned with glory and honor." διὰ παθημάτων, διά with the genitive, indicates means: "by means of sufferings" he was "perfected" as Savior. The unqualified plural, παθημάτων ("sufferings"), refers not merely to Christ's death but to the lifelong process of suffering that culminated in his death. See O'Brien, 107; Bénétreau, 1:122; and Johnson, 97.

65. Peterson's contention that the whole series of events from incarnation to exaltation constituted the perfection of Christ as Savior is, in one sense, true (Peterson, *Perfection,* 73). Yet one must not obscure the pastor's emphasis on the centrality of the Son's suffering and on his obedience (10:5-10).

fect" refers to the completion of this process. Through this suffering God established Jesus as the "Pioneer" completely able to save God's people and bring them into their divinely appointed glory.[66]

"To perfect" can be used of the attainment of a goal, of achieving moral perfection, and in the LXX, in association with consecration to priesthood.[67] The vocational perfection of the Son as Savior incorporates and transforms all of these usages.[68] By his "perfection" the Son attained the ultimate goal, for he is seated at the right hand of the throne of God as the representative and fully adequate Savior of those who "draw near to God through him" (7:25). He did not reach this goal through a normal process of moral development, but through assuming human nature and living a life of complete obedience unto death despite suffering (5:5-10). This obedience unto death was a willing self-offering that did away with sin (9:11-14; 10:5-10) and thus consecrated him as the heavenly High Priest who alone can bring the faithful into God's presence (10:11-15). Thus the Son's vocation as Pioneer is fulfilled only through his high priesthood announced in 2:17-18.[69] Through that

66. Spicq, 2:39-40.

67. See the discussion in Lane, 1:57-58, and Ellingworth, 161-63. τελείουν was often used in the context of priestly consecration (Exod 29:9; 33:35; Lev 4:5; 8:33; 16:32; Num 3:3; 2 Macc 2:9; 4 Macc 7:15; Sir 34 [31]:10) even if alone it was not a technical term for this act (Peterson, *Perfection,* 29-30). Furthermore, the noun τελείωσις ("perfection") appears frequently within such contexts: Exod 29:22, 26, 27, 31, 34; Lev 7:37; 8:22 (21); 29 (28). Cf. Lev 8:26 (25), 31, 33. Philo, *Heir* 251; *Alleg. Interp.* 3.130; *Migration* 67; *Moses* 2.149 (Peterson, *Perfection,* 254, n. 6). Thus the Hebrews' context would make it virtually impossible for the hearers to miss the priestly associations of this term. Weiss's attempt, 209, to exclude the priestly by separating "perfection" and exaltation in 2:10; 5:9; and 7:28 is unconvincing. Even he must admit that these references are "near" the cultic sphere and that the cultic connotation is present when Hebrews refers to the inability of the law to bring perfection (7:11, 19; 9:9; 10:1, 14). On the priestly connotation of perfection in Hebrews see Gerhard Delling, "τελειόω," in *TDNT* 8:82-84; Martin Dibelius, "Der himmlische Kultus nach dem Hebräerbrief," in *Botschaft und Geschichte: Gesammelte Aufsätze II: Zum Urchristentum und zur hellenistischen Religionsgeschichte* (Tübingen: Mohr Siebeck, 1956), 160-76; Mathias Rissi, "Die Menschlichkeit Jesu nach Hebr. 5.7 und 8," *TZ* 11 (1955): 28-45; and Olaf Moe, "Der Gedanke des allgemeinen Priestertums im Hebräerbrief," *TZ* 5 (1949): 161-69.

68. Thus Peterson, *Perfection,* 66-73, is correct when he emphasizes the vocational nature of this perfection. However, one need not minimize the other connotations of this rich term that fit well with this vocational understanding and have an appropriate place within the context of Hebrews.

69. Similarity of sound helps the pastor associate these words: ἀρχηγός, "pioneer," and ἀρχιερεύς, "high priest," both begin with ἀρχή, "beginning," "first." ἀρχηγός is, as noted above, a combination of ἀρχή and ἄγω, the same word used in the participle ἀγαγόντα, translated above as "bringing" many sons and daughters into glory. The Son is the "arch-priest" and the "arch-bringer."

high priesthood the faithful have present access to God's throne in order that they might receive the grace (4:14-16; 10:19-25) necessary for perseverance and thus for following their Pioneer into the heavenly homeland (11:1-40).

There is no contradiction between Christ's eternal perfection as Son and his "being made perfect" in his vocation as the "Pioneer of our salvation." Every part of the NT declares that the Son's incarnation, death, resurrection, and ascension have equipped him to save. Note the words of the risen Christ in Matt 28:18, "All power has been given to me in heaven and on earth." When thus perfected, the Son fulfilled what he had always been as the "radiance of God's glory."[70]

11 Verses 11-13 show that the suffering of the Son was an appropriate expression of God's character, as v. 10 has asserted, because it was based on God's faithfulness to his people. It is clear that the "one making holy" is the Son of God and those "being made holy" are God's "sons and daughters." A proper understanding of this verse depends on the correct identification of the "from one" that unites them.[71] English translations rush to make this generic-sounding term more specific — "all have one origin" (ESV), all are "of the same family" (NIV), "all have one Father" (NRSV). The fundamental question is whether the unity of the sanctifier ("the one making holy") and the sanctified ("the ones being made holy") is based on their common humanity or on the saving purposes of God. There are several ways to understand this term as a reference to common humanity. First, those who take "one" as neuter (it can be construed as either neuter or masculine) understand it as a general reference to humanity.[72] Some who opt for the more likely masculine construal identify the "one" with a common human ancestor — Adam or Abraham.[73] Others identify it with God as the "Father" of humanity.[74] There is little if anything in the context that suggests a generic reference

---

70. See on 1:1-3 and cf. Moises Silva, "Perfection and Eschatology in Hebrews," *WTJ* 39 (1976): 60-71.

71. πάντες ("all") qualifies both οἱ ἁγιαζόμενοι ("those being sanctified") and ὁ ἁγιάζων ("the one sanctifying"), thus emphasizing their commonality derived ἐξ ἑνός ("from one"). Riggenbach, 51.

72. See Vanhoye, *Situation,* 334; Hughes, 105; and Pfitzner, 66.

73. For ἑνός ("one," ἐξ ἑνός, "from one") as a reference to Adam, see J. Héring, 19. For Abraham as the progenitor of humanity, see Buchanan, 32; Ellingworth, 165; Johnson, 97; J. Dunnill, *Covenant and Sacrifice in the Letter to the Hebrews* (SNTSMS 75; Cambridge: Cambridge University, 1992), 209-13; Mathias Rissi, *Die Theologie des Hebräerbriefes* (WUNT 41; Tübingen: Mohr/Siebeck, 1987), 60; and J. Swetnam, *Jesus and Isaac: A Study of the Epistle to the Hebrews in the Light of the Aqedah* (AnBib 94; Rome: Pontifical Biblical Institute, 1981), 132-34.

74. Spicq, 2:40-41. However, Spicq also says that "of one" corresponds to "by the grace of God" in v. 9 (Spicq, 2:41). deSilva's reference (114) to Stoic tradition of the common origin of humanity in God is irrelevant here.

140

to humanity. Hebrews never mentions Adam. A number of interpreters seem to opt for Abraham because he appears in v. 16. Yet he is mentioned in that verse as the progenitor not of humanity but of the people of God. The pastor has not provided his first hearers with sufficient contextual clues to make any of these identifications.

If "the one making holy" and "those being made holy" are the "Son" and the "sons and daughters" of v. 10, then the "one" from whom both spring is most naturally the God described in that verse as "the one for whom are all things and by whom are all things." Hebrews, however, never describes God as the universal Father of humankind.[75] The Son's solidarity with God's "sons and daughters" is rooted in God's redemptive purpose and thus was prior to and the basis for his becoming a human being (see the perfect tense in 2:9; the aorist in 2:14, 17). The pastor uses the generic "from one" both to emphasize their unity and because God is the Father of both in differing and complementary ways. After all, it is the Son who makes "holy" but the "sons and daughters" who are "being made holy." He is the eternal Son of God who has brought God's word to fulfillment (1:1-3). God's people, both before and after the incarnation, have always been God's "sons and daughters" because they responded to the divine word. The Son enters into the full exercise of his filial relationship through providing salvation and taking his seat at God's right hand (see 1:1-4). The "sons and daughters" enter the fullness of their filial relationship through the provision of the Son.[76] This correspondence reveals the fitting relationship between the Son and the "sons and daughters."

"The one who makes holy" and "those who are being made holy" anticipate both the priestly character of Christ's saving work and the corresponding need of God's people for deliverance from sin and death as described in vv. 14-18. In the OT it is often God who "makes holy" or "sanctifies."[77] Thus the Son's role in sanctification, as well as in creation and consummation (1:2, 8-12), confirms his deity. The way in which his priestly

---

75. Montefiore, 62.

76. Thus Lane, 1:58, is correct when he says, "Both the Son and those who are sons share a common familial relationship that is rooted in the gracious determination of God to bring his children to their destiny through the redemptive mission of the Son. . . ." So also Montefiore, 62, who affirms that God's people have the same "parent" because they are his "sons" but in a different way from the "Son." Westcott, 50; Koester, 230; Bruce, 81; Attridge, 89; and O'Brien, 109, agree that ἑνός ("one") refers to God. See R. Laub, *Bekenntnis und Auslegung: Die paränetische Funktion der Christologie im Hebräerbrief* (BU 15; Regensburg: Pustet, 1980), 77.

77. See the following passages in the Greek Bible: Exod 31:12; Lev 20:8; 21:15; 22:9, 16, 32, though God can also "sanctify" through an agent like Moses (Exod 19:34; 29:1; Lev 8:11-12). This term is also used with reference to Jesus in Heb 10:14; 13:12. See Lane, 1:58; O'Brien, 108.

ministry "makes holy" and thus transforms the "sons and daughters" of God is described in 9:11-14 and 10:15-22.[78]

Because God's "sons and daughters" were thus in need of being "made holy," the Son was "not ashamed" to identify with them by assuming their humanity with its suffering and death. In this way he confirmed the divine faithfulness by bringing God's gracious purposes to fruition. There is only one appropriate response to such generous beneficence: the "sons and daughters" must not be ashamed of Christ before a hostile world (10:32-39; 11:35-38; 12:3-11; 13:13-14).[79] God is not and will not be "ashamed" of those who persevere in loyalty to his Son (11:16).

12-13 ⌐By his threefold answer to the divine overture of 1:5-14 the Son acknowledges his relationship with the people of God and affirms his willingness to identify with them by assuming their humanity. The Son's three answers correspond to the Father's declarations in 1:5-14.[80] First, in v. 12 the exalted Son's quotation of Ps 22:22 (21:23 LXX), affirming God's people as his "brothers and sisters," corresponds to the Father's proclamation of the Son's divine Sonship in 1:5. Second, the Son's affirmation of his human faithfulness in v. 13a (2 Sam 22:3; Isa 8:17) complements God's declaration of the Son's divine sovereignty in 1:8-12. Third, in v. 13b (Isa 8:18) the Son accepts the Father's invitation to his right hand, given in 1:13 — on his own behalf and on behalf of "the children whom God has given" him. He has assumed their humanity in order to bring them to their destiny. His session will be the means of their entrance into God's presence. The brevity of the Son's answers in proportion to the divine declarations of chapter 1 does not detract from their importance but corresponds to the humble obedience that he affirms.⌐

At the exaltation God openly claimed the Son as his Son — "You are my Son" (Ps 2:7 in Heb 1:5). The Son responded by affirming his continuing

---

78. The term for "make holy" or "sanctify" (ἁγιάζω), introduced here in 2:11, is closely related to "cleanse"/"purify" (καθαρίζω, 9:14) and to "purification" (καθαρισμός, 1:3). While "make holy" may denote consecration to God (BDAG, 10, 2), it is a consecration brought about by cleansing from sin through the atonement provided by Christ's sacrifice (see Otto Procksch, "ἁγιάζω," *TDNT* 1:111-12). The old sacrifices could cleanse only "the flesh" but Christ's sufficed for the cleansing of "the conscience from dead works to serve the living God" (9:11-14). See the commentary on 10:5-10, 29 (cf. 13:12). This deliverance from sin is something the faithful have both experienced in a definitive way (10:10) and continue to experience (2:10).

79. deSilva, 115; Koester, 230.

80. This exposition develops Attridge's insightful suggestion that 2:12-13 contains the Son's answers to God's address in 1:5-14 (Harold W. Attridge, "God in Hebrews," in *The Epistle to the Hebrews and Christian Theology,* ed. Richard Bauckham et al. [Grand Rapids: Eerdmans, 2009], 104).

brotherhood with the people of God in the words of Ps 22:22: "I will announce your name to my brothers and sisters. In the midst of the congregation I will praise you."[81] This psalm of David and description of the righteous sufferer naturally finds its place on the lips of David's Son, who "tasted death" (2:9) for all. Jesus claimed it as his own by quoting its opening verse as he hung on the cross — "My God, my God, why have you forsaken me?" (Matt 27:46/Mark 15:34).[82] Verse 22 is the point in the psalm where complaint turns to thanksgiving. God has delivered. As Jesus cried out in dereliction, so he now announces his triumph at the exaltation.[83] As the perfected "Pioneer," the exalted Son praises God for the completed provision of salvation in the midst of his "brothers and sisters," the "congregation" of God's worshiping people in heaven and on earth (see 12:22-24).[84] This confession of his brotherhood is, in turn, an invitation for the sons and daughters to enjoy the benefits of their filial relationship with God now made available through their heavenly representative. To follow him in praise of God is the opposite of being "ashamed" of him before scornful humanity (cf. Luke 9:26; cf. 13:15-16). The Son's joyful acceptance of the exaltation as the Savior of God's people confirms the appropriateness of the suffering through which he attained this position.

As noted above, the exalted Son's proclamation of continuing brotherhood is followed by two more affirmations: "I will put my trust in him" (2 Sam 22:3; Isa 8:17) and "Behold, I and the children whom God has given me" (Isa 8:18). Although both declarations are found in Isa 8:17-18,[85] two

---

81. Hebrews quotes this psalm according to the standard LXX text except that it substitutes ἀπαγγελῶ, "proclaim," for διηγήσομαι, "tell, relate." For suggestions on the significance of this change see Ellingworth, 168.

82. NT writers, taking their cue from Jesus, saw how clearly Psalm 22 described his passion: his bones were not broken (John 19:31-36; Ps 22:16-17); his garments were divided by lot (Matt 27:35; John 19:23-24; Ps 22:18); and he was mocked by his tormentors (Matt 27:39-43; Ps 22:7-8). See Hughes, 107. "The ground of the application in the first case lies in the fact that the language used goes beyond the actual experience of David, or of any righteous sufferer" (Westcott, 50). deSilva, 116, adds, ". . . since the final word was spoken through the Son, the earlier words can frequently find their 'true' meaning when spoken by him as well." Thus Hebrews is using a passage that was widely understood by Christians as a reference to the Messiah (Johnson, 99).

83. Hughes, 108. It makes better sense of both the original psalmic and the present contexts if Christ proclaimed these words at his exaltation/session rather than at his second coming (Lane, 1:59) or incarnation (Attridge, 90).

84. See Bénétreau, 1:125-26. "Brothers and sisters" is clearly a designation for the people of God as evidenced by the parallel expression "congregation" in Ps 22:22b.

85. The way in which the LXX of Isaiah introduces Isa 8:17 with "and one shall say" (absent in the Hebrew text) has made it easy to apply Isa 8:17-18 to Christ. One might translate the LXX of Isa 8:17, "And one shall say, I will wait for God, . . . and I will

features of the text suggest that one should hear the first declaration as the word of David from 2 Sam 22:3 (LXX) before hearing it as the word of Isaiah from Isa 8:17.[86] First, the pastor has separated Isa 8:17, "I will put my trust in him," from Isa 8:18 by inserting "and again."[87] Second, the quotation from a Davidic psalm in v. 12 has already directed the hearers thoughts toward David. After hearing Isa 8:18 they would remember that Isaiah also spoke the preceding words. Thus "I will put my trust in him" gains redoubled force by its dual source in both the victorious king and the distressed prophet. This declaration of complete confidence in God by these two representatives of God's people finds absolute fulfillment in the Son's total abandonment to God proper for the human condition.[88] One cannot help but remember "Not my will, but yours be done" (Luke 22:42; cf. Matt 26:39 and Mark 14:36; see the comments on 5:7-8).[89] The Son's affirmation of his human obedience corresponds appropriately to God's attestation of his eternal divine sovereignty in 1:8-12 (Ps 45:6-7 and Ps 102:25-27). Together the Father's declaration and the Son's answer provide divine substantiation for the incarnation. The One whom the Father addressed as "God" was truly that One who in his obedient humanity "loved righteousness and hated lawlessness" (1:9a). In due time the Son will speak again, affirming the saving significance of his obedience (10:5-10), an obedience that was also crucial to his role as example of perseverance (12:1-3). This trusting obedience was the appropriate response of a human being to God. It was also appropriate for the one who would deliver God's people from disobedience.

"I will praise your name to my brothers and sisters" assures God's people that the exalted Son has not abandoned them. "I will put my trust in him" certifies the reality of his faithful human life. When the Son proclaims, "I, and the children whom God has given me" (Isa 8:18), he accepts God's invitation to sit at his right hand (Heb 1:13) on their behalf. He takes his seat in

---

put my trust in him (καὶ πεπιθὼς ἔσομαι ἐπ' αὐτῷ)." Compare the Hebrew text as represented by the NRSV/ESV, "I will wait for the Lord, . . . and I will hope in him."

86. The use of 2 Samuel 22 in Christian liturgy makes a reference to this passage all the more likely. See Lane, 1:59 and Vanhoye, *Situation*, 344-45. There is no reason to believe the author of Hebrews has Isa 12:2 in mind.

87. See Lane, 1:59-60 and Ellingworth, 169. Compare the way in which the pastor uses the same phrase, καὶ πάλιν, "and again," in Heb 10:30 to divide the quotation from Deut 32:35-36.

88. This emphasis on faithfulness implies the humanity of the Son (Bénétreau, 1:126-28). Thus it is unclear why Attridge, 91, doubts reference here to "the frailty of Christ in his human condition." See Vanhoye, *Situation*, 344 and Moffatt, 33. deSilva, 116, has been led astray by the patron/client relationship when he proposes that this is the Son's confidence in his people.

89. Compare "I will put my trust in him" (Isa 8:17) with "He trusted in God, let him deliver him" (Matt 27:43). Spicq, 2:42.

order to present them before God. He reminds them that his relationship with them is based on the "action of God."[90] God's gift to Isaiah of his children and disciples as a faithful remnant typifies the way in which God has committed the salvation of his people to the Son.[91] The one whom God owned as his Son at the exaltation (1:5) does not hesitate to acknowledge the people of God as his God-given "children" for whose redemption he is responsible. Nothing could bring more encouragement to the people of God. Nothing is more worthy of their highest praise.

There is no contradiction between God's people being Christ's "children" and God's "sons and daughters." The Greek word for "children" is often used as a general term for younger people with a close relationship to and respect for the one addressing them as "children."[92] Thus Christ's calling them his "children" preserves the uniqueness of the Son, affirms his solidarity with the "sons and daughters," and suggests that they are in need of his assistance. The term "children" is also fitting for those in need of instruction and thus anticipates the pastor's coming use of a verb and noun from the same root to describe the "training" appropriate for God's legitimate sons and daughters (12:4-11).[93]

How could the pastor affirm the Son's willingness to identify with God's people more forcefully? They are God's "sons and daughters," whom the Son acknowledges as his "brothers and sisters" and God-given "children." Although the Son acknowledged this relationship by his incarnation (v. 13a) and did not forget it in his exaltation (v. 12), it preceded both in the

90. This unity between the Son and his "children" is no evidence for the influence of the Gnostic redeemed-redeemer myth as argued by E. Käsemann, *The Wandering People of God: An Investigation of the Letter to the Hebrews,* trans. R. A. Harrisville and I. L. Sundberg (Minneapolis: Augsburg, 1984), 147-49, and supported by Braun, 63-64. See Bruce, 84; Lane, 1:60. Hebrews does not reflect Gnostic terminology, and the existence of this myth contemporary with Hebrews is highly problematic. The pastor's emphasis on the preincarnate relationship between Christ and God's people is more naturally explained by his conviction that Christ came to enable the people of God, already brought into existence through God's OT revelation, to attain their final destiny.

91. Spicq, 2:42, demonstrates that Isaiah is a type of Christ as God's faithful representative and the focal point of God's people. See also Westcott, 51-52. The "children" given once to Isaiah and now to Christ are the faithful people of God.

92. Note the risen Christ's use of this term, παιδίον, plural παιδία, to designate an affectionate relationship with his disciples (John 21:5). παιδίον is less encumbered by ideas of physical descent than its synonym, τέκνον, but both can be used in a figurative sense. See L&N §9.46, and Albrecht Oepke, "παῖς, παιδίον, παιδάριον, τέκνον, τεκνίον, βρέφος," *TDNT* 5:638.

93. As indicated in the note above, the word here translated "child" is παιδίον. Heb 12:4-11 employs the related verb form παιδεύω, meaning "to discipline," "to train," and the related noun, παιδεία, "discipline," "training."

145

character and saving purpose of God (v. 13b). In light of this divine purpose and his role as Savior it was most fitting for him to assume the humanity of God's people in order to deliver those who suffer from the bondage of their fallen human condition through his suffering (vv. 14-18).

14-18   The incarnate Son's suffering for the sons and daughters of God was an appropriate expression of God's faithfulness (vv. 10-13) because it corresponded to their fallen human condition captive through sin (vv. 16-18) to the fear of death (vv. 14-15). The remarkable degree of parallelism between vv. 14-15 and vv. 16-18 justifies treating them together as a subsection that explains the benefits of the Son's identification with and suffering for his people.[94] Each of these two sets of verses begins with a description of the people the Son came to save,[95] followed by an appropriate affirmation of the incarnation,[96] a description of the incarnation's purpose,[97] and an account of its desired effect on believers.[98] Furthermore, these verses are closely related because the terror of death is based primarily on the judgment incurred by sin (9:27). It is indeed a "fearful thing to fall into the hands of the living God" (10:31), who is a "consuming fire" (12:29). Thus the Son delivers from the "fear of death" (vv. 14-15) by removing the sin that brings judgment (vv. 16-18).[99] It is injudicious to argue that "fear of death" is an ad hoc intrusion into a book about atonement.[100] The pastor begins with the most acute human angst and moves to its root cause according to the biblical diagnosis of the human condition.[101] It is the subjection of God's people to the fear of death

94. Michael E. Gudorf, "Through a Classical Lens: Hebrews 2:16," *JBL* 119 (2000): 105-8, has suggested, on the basis of classical usage, that it is the "fear of death" from the last clause of v. 15 that has "taken hold of" the "seed of Abraham" in v. 16a. This suggestion is interesting, but it unnecessarily shifts the subject, which is Christ throughout these verses, and destroys the parallelism between vv. 14-15 and 16-18 by making v. 16a parenthetic.

95. "Therefore, since the children share blood and flesh" (14a); "For clearly it is not angels he has taken hold of, but the seed of Abraham he has taken hold of" (16).

96. "He himself in like manner became a partaker with them" (14b); "Therefore, it was necessary for him to be made like the brothers and sisters in every way" (17a).

97. "In order that through death he might destroy the one who has the power of death, that is, the devil" (14c); "in order that he might become a merciful and faithful high priest in things pertaining to God" (17b).

98. "And set free those who by fear of death throughout their lives were subject to bondage" (v. 15); "to make atonement for the sins of the people" (v. 17c).

99. See 4:15; 5:8; 7:26; 9:14; and Pfitzner, 67.

100. Thus, as Attridge, 75, n. 58, demonstrates, the Christology of vv. 14-15 is not derived from the Gnostic myth, as proposed by Weiss, 219-21, and others. Neither, however, is it dependent on a more undefined Hellenistic syncretism, as advocated by Attridge, 79-82.

101. *Pace* Attridge, 92, who denies that Hebrews attests the "Pauline" understanding of the relationship between sin and death.

that makes the Son's suffering of death such an appropriate way for him to deliver them in accord with the faithfulness of God. The pastor's concern with deliverance from death becomes quite evident in 11:1-40.[102] Verses 14-18 announce the main theme of this sermon — the Son's high priesthood — and lay a foundation for its anticipated development. Verse 18 shows the immediate relevance of this high-priestly ministry for God's struggling people. The encouragement in vv. 17-18 balances the warning of 2:1-4 and will be expanded in such passages as 4:14-16 and 10:19-25.

14-15 Because of the Son's God-given bond with the "children" (v. 13), he took on their human condition,[103] here described in all its frailty and brokenness as "blood and flesh." He was unique in his obedience, but fully one in sharing the kind of humanity that characterized the people of God.[104] The aorist tense of the verb translated "became a partaker" indicates that at a point in time and space he took on the fractured humanity that the children by nature "shared."[105] There is nothing in the aorist, however, that implies he later ceased to be human.[106] He assumed their broken humanity in order that it might be mended and glorified. The expression "blood and flesh" follows later Jewish tradition rather than the OT's "flesh and blood,"[107] but it fits well with the yet-to-be enunciated principle — "without the shedding of blood there is no removal of sins" (9:22).[108]

He took on this dying humanity in order that "through" his own "death"[109] he "might destroy the one who has the power of death, that is, the devil."[110] This is no Hellenistic speculation alien to Hebrews of a hero who

---

102. See the commentary below on this chapter, especially on 11:17-19, 35. Cf. also the comments on 5:7-10.

103. Ellingworth, 170-71, is correct in observing that the repetition of "children" underscores the inferential significance of οὖν, "therefore." Cf. Hughes, 110. *Pace* Attridge, 91.

104. Weiss, 217.

105. Thus μετέσχεν is inceptive aorist: the Son "began to share" in their humanity. On the other hand, κεκοινώνηκεν is the emphatic perfect emphasizing the present condition of God's people: they "share" the human condition. See Lane, 1:60; Bénétreau, 1:129; Spicq, 2:43; and Attridge, 92.

106. *Pace* Ellingworth, 171. See references in Spicq and Bénétreau cited in the previous note.

107. Ellingworth, 171. "Blood and flesh" also occurs in Eph 6:12. Cf. Matt 16:17; 1 Cor 15:50; Gal 1:16; *1 En.* 15:4.

108. So Spicq, 2:43, and Montefiore, 64.

109. The pastor is referring to Christ's death but omits the personal pronoun in order to emphasize that the intimidating power of "death" was destroyed by "death" itself. See Riggenbach, 55.

110. καταργέω, "destroy," can also mean "'to deprive something of its power' (Rom 3:31; Eph. 2:15)" (O'Brien, 115, citing L&N §76.26; Koester, 231).

conquers death.[111] Such heroes overcame death by a return to life. He conquers through death itself, though his victory was validated by his subsequent resurrection/exaltation. This fact is most simply explained by the assumption that the devil had the "power of death" because of the sinfulness of humanity.[112] Thus, although God's people must still die (9:27 again!), by removing their sin Christ has completely bereft the devil of his ability to intimidate them with death (see vv. 16-18).[113]

As in the English translation above, the Greek of v. 15 begins with "he might set free" and ends with "bondage." The rest of v. 15 depicts the result of this deliverance. The angst of the human condition is rightly described as a bondage to the "fear of death" that haunts every aspect of human life from beginning to end. This anxiety agrees with the biblical tradition, was widespread in the Hellenistic world, and is the perennial and universal human concern.[114] Thus the pastor strikes a chord of continual and contemporary relevance. There is no longer any need to practice the many ways in which humans deny or evade the reality of death, for by his incarnation and death Christ has set God's people "free" from its intimidating power.

16 Verse 14 began by asserting the need of God's people. Verse 16 begins by reaffirming the Son's commitment to them. By calling "those who are about to inherit salvation" through Christ (1:14) the "seed of Abraham" the pastor affirms that they are the heirs of God's promise to Abraham (see 6:12-20).[115] The Son fulfills God's covenant faithfulness by "taking hold of" this people of God in order to bring them into "glory" (2:10), just as God "took hold" of his people in order to bring them to the Promised Land.[116]

---

111. See Weiss, 219-21, Attridge, 79-82, and the sources they cite.

112. Spicq, 2:43-44. Gen 2:17: "for in the day that you eat of it you shall die." This connection between sin and death was native to the OT and widespread in the Hellenistic world. See Wis 1:13; 2:23-24; Montefiore, 65; and Bruce, 86.

113. For apocalyptic expectations of the Messiah's triumph over demonic forces see Attridge, 92, n. 153; O'Brien, 114, n. 161; and the sources they cite, including *As. Mos.* 10:1; *T. Levi* 18:2; *T. Dan* 5:10; *T. Jud.* 25:3; *Sib. Or.* 3:63-74; *1 En.* 10:13; *4 Ezra* 13:1; 1QH 6:29; 1QM 1:11, 13, 15, 17.

114. deSilva, 118. See also Attridge, 93, nn. 165-66, and Spicq, 2:44. Although the pastor refers to the common human preoccupation with death, what he has to say would certainly fortify his hearers against anticipated persecution (Lane, 1:54, 61). Johnson, 100; Koester, 232; and O'Brien, 116, n. 174, cite what contemporary philosophers like Seneca, Dio Chrysostom, Lucretius, Plutarch, and Cicero have to say about the fear of death.

115. Pfitzner, 68; Attridge, 94; O'Brien, 117. *Pace* Karl-Gustav E. Dolfe, "Hebrews 2,16 under the Magnifying Glass," *ZNW* 84 (1993): 290, the "seed of Abraham" does not refer to the Jews *per se*. As noted in the Introduction (pp. 20-21, 43-44), the pastor never distinguishes between an old and new people of God. "[S]uch a reading is impossible in this context" (Johnson, 102, n. 5).

116. See "In the day of my taking them (ἐπιλαβομένου μου) by the hand to lead

This "take hold" is present tense and describes all that the Son does from beginning to end to bring God's people into their eternal heritage.[117] He does not superintend their journey from a distance, but he "takes hold" of them and guides them by the hand.[118] What encouragement to disheartened hearers!

    17 If the Son was going to "take hold" of God's people and bring them to "glory," it was most fitting for him to become like them "in every way."[119] The pastor emphasizes this phrase by putting it first in the Greek sentence and thus underscores what he has said in v. 14: the Son did not assume an artificial or idealized humanity, but one characterized by the brokenness of the actual humanity which his people shared. The following purpose clause explains the appropriateness of this action. Since a priest by definition had to be part of the group he represented (Heb 5:1), it was necessary for the Son to assume the humanity of God's people "in order that he might become a merciful and faithful high priest" and do what priests do, represent them "in things pertaining to God" by removing their sin.[120]

    "Merciful and faithful" are inseparable as a comprehensive description of the effective High Priest that he has become. His "faithfulness" is both the source of his merciful beneficence and the constancy of its expres-

---

them out of Egypt," Jer 31:32 quoted in Heb 8:9. ἐπιλαβομένου is the aorist middle participle of ἐπιλαμβάνομαι. See O'Brien, 117 and Koester, 240. Hebrews, however, is not interested so much in past deliverance as in future perseverance. Thus Christ's high-priestly work is not pictured primarily as that which made them the people of God but as that which enables them to persevere as the people of God. This passage may have verbal reminiscences with Isa 48:8-10, which speaks of the "seed of Abraham (σπέρμα Αβρααμ) of whom God says, "I have helped (ἀντελαβόμην)." Compare also "my child" (παῖς μου, Isa 48:8) with "children" (παιδία, 2:13, 14), and "fear not" (μὴ φοβοῦ, Isa 48:10) with "fear of death" (φόβῳ θανάτου, 2:15) (cf. Lane, 1:63-64; deSilva, 119-20). These similarities, however, are no reason to assimilate the meaning of ἐπιλαμβάνεται ("take hold of") to the related verb ἀντιλαμβάνεται ("help"), as done in many translations (NIV, NASB, NRSV, ESV). See Vanhoye, *Situation,* 357-58, and Bénétreau, 1:131. Lane and deSilva, cited above, think Hebrews has substituted ἐπιλαμβάνεται for ἀντιλαμβάνεται under the influence of Jer 31:32.

    117. Several factors show that "take hold of" is not a reference to the incarnation, as suggested by Spicq, 2:45-46, and held by many Church Fathers and reformers: first, it is individuals, not human nature, that the Son "takes hold of." Second, those individuals are the people of God, not human beings in general. Third, if "take hold of" (v. 16) and "in every way made like his brothers and sisters" (v. 17a) both refer to incarnation, then Hebrews would be saying, "he became incarnate; therefore he became incarnate." See Hughes, 117-19.

    118. Vanhoye, *Situation,* 357-58.

    119. Ellingworth, 180, calls this identification a "moral obligation."

    120. τὰ πρὸς τὸ θεόν, "things pertaining to God," is a standard phrase in the LXX Pentateuch meaning "with regard to God" (e.g., Exod 4:16; 18:19). Lane, 1:65.

sion. He has become a merciful High Priest able to cleanse his people's sin and bring them into God's presence because of the faithful obedience to God that characterized his human life (5:7-10; 10:5-10). Furthermore, his people can rely on his faithfulness in the continuing administration of that mercy. Thus "faithful" encompasses both his loyalty to God and his trustworthiness as the savior of God's people.[121] The pastor reaffirms this faithfulness in 3:1-6 and explains it in his description of Christ's high priesthood (4:14–10:18; especially 5:7-10; 10:5-10), in order to portray Christ as the ultimate example of endurance in 12:1-3. The pastor also highlights the merciful benefits of this high priesthood in 4:14-16 and 10:19-25 (cf. 7:26-28). Here, at last, is the true and ultimate "faithful" priest that God promised in place of Eli's corrupt descendants (1 Sam 2:35).[122] His becoming such a high priest is the fruition of his sonship (see on 1:1-3) and the full revelation of a God who is characterized by "lovingkindness and faithfulness" (Exod 34:6).[123] Furthermore, by becoming such a Priest the Son was "perfected" in his vocation as the "Pioneer of our salvation."[124]

"To make atonement for the sins of the people" describes Christ's high-priestly ministry. The pastor probably has Christ's "once-for-all" sacrifice in view, though the present tense of this infinitive leaves room for the continuing application of the benefits of that sacrifice to God's people. Hebrews assumes the biblical doctrine that atonement is necessary because sin is an offense that separates from God and incurs his wrath (2:2; 3:16-19; 12:12-17, 29; 19:31). Thus, as here, the Bible often mentions the sin for which (Exod 32:30; Lev 5:10) and the person(s) for whom (Lev 1:4; 16:11) atonement is made. While the word here translated "to make atonement" is often used by Philo, Josephus, and Gentile writers of appeasing or conciliating another per-

121. For this dual understanding of πιστός ("faithful," "trustworthy") see, among others, Bénétreau, 1:133-34; Bruce, 88; Attridge, 95, nn. 189-90; and O'Brien, 121.

122. In 1 Sam 2:35 God promises: "I will raise up to myself a faithful priest . . . and I will build him a sure house" (καὶ ἀναστήσω ἐμαυτῷ ἱερέα πιστὸν . . . καὶ οἰκοδομήσω αὐτῷ οἶκον πιστόν). deSilva, 120, suggests that this mention of a "faithful house" may have led to the use of Num 12:7, in which Moses is "faithful" in all God's "house" (Heb 3:2, 5). Mary Rose D'Angelo, *Moses in the Letter to the Hebrews* (SBLDS 42; Missoula, MT: Scholars Press, 1979), 70-76, carries this argument further. She believes that the "royal priesthood" of Hebrews is based on both this oracle of a faithful priest and Nathan's oracle to David of a royal descendant (2 Sam 7:14-16/1 Chr 17:12-14). The clause "I will make him faithful in my house" (πιστώσω αὐτὸν ἐν οἴκῳ μου, 1 Chr 17:14) establishes a verbal link between the two. In fact, however, the pastor makes no overt use of 1 Sam 2:35. It would not have provided the justification for a non-Aaronic priest supplied by Ps 110:4.

123. See Vanhoye, *Situation,* 376-77, and Johnson, 104.

124. On the parallel between Christ's being "perfected" in v. 10 and his becoming High Priest in v. 17 see George Guthrie, *Structure,* 77-78.

son, in Scripture human beings do not "conciliate" God.[125] It is always God, often through his duly appointed representative, who "makes atonement" for sin. Thus it is no surprise that God's Son is the one who has made a fully adequate atonement. While the pastor has affirmed the benefits of Christ's death for all (2:9), it is God's "people" who receive those benefits.[126]

Those who would understand Hebrews receive a rich reward if they interpret "to make atonement" by listening carefully to the way Hebrews describes what Christ does with sin. The pastor will not allow his hearers to restrict this term either to the "propitiation" of God's wrath against sin or to the "expiation" of sin by its removal from the sinner. Nor does he distinguish neatly between the two. He speaks the language of covenant and Tabernacle. Thus his primary concern is the removal of impurity. As the typological old system removed outward impurity, so the work of Christ removes the impurity of the heart (9:11-14). An impure heart is a disobedient heart in rebellion against God. Thus the all-sufficient work of Christ transforms the kind of rebellious heart exemplified by the wilderness generation (3:12) into the obedient heart of the New Covenant characterized by joyous compliance with the will of God (10:11-18; cf. 10:22). Christ "cleanses the conscience from dead works to serve the living God" (9:14)! The old sacrificial system made it clear that impurity prevented access to God (9:1-10). Christ's removal of heart impurity dispenses with this barrier and provides access to the divine presence (10:19-22). His death can also be seen as propitiatory in that he took upon himself the covenant curse on the disobedient (9:16-22) so that God no longer "remembers" the disobedience of his faithful people (10:11-15). Those who "draw near to God through him" (7:25) find these benefits in union with their High Priest.

18 The pastor concludes his introduction of Christ's high priesthood by assuring his hearers of its immediate relevance for God's people as they face daily pressure to compromise their faith. This pressure is expressed by the word rendered "tempted" or "tested." Neither of these translations fully grasps the pastor's intent. His thinking includes general temptations to sin and testings by hard times, but his primary concern is with the pressures of the world that would lead his hearers to withdraw their loyalty and fall away from the faith.[127] The breadth of this term allows one to keep this main purpose in focus without failing to recognize a wider range of application to

125. Riggenbach, 61-62, n. 59.
126. The phrase "the people" is a common OT expression for the people of God and thus, like "sons and daughters," "brothers and sisters," "children," and "seed of Abraham," identifies the present hearers with God's people throughout history. See Vanhoye, *Situation*, 382-83.
127. Vanhoye, *Situation*, 384.

other situations.[128] Thus the pastor urges his hearers to persevere despite the scorn, disdain, and possible persecution of unbelieving society. He does not want them to seek that society's approval or be subverted by its rewards.

"Because he himself has suffered when he was tested" is to be preferred to "Because he himself was tested by what he suffered" (NRSV).[129] The pastor emphasizes the fact that Jesus "has suffered" in order to address the suffering his hearers experience from an unbelieving world (cf. 12:1-3).[130] Furthermore, the fact that Jesus "has suffered" implies that he passed the "testing." He did not let the severe opposition that culminated in the suffering of the cross deter him from absolute obedience to the divine will. The "testing" that reached its climax in the cross is over, but the benefit of his obedient suffering continues ever available for the people of God through identification with the High Priest he has become.[131]

Verses 17-18 bring this opening section of the pastor's sermon to a fitting conclusion.[132] God's Son with whom the pastor began in 1:1-4 fulfills his role as the ultimate revelation of God by becoming the all-sufficient High Priest described in these verses. Through his obedience despite suffering this High Priest has provided the "great salvation" of 2:3. By so doing he not only underscores the seriousness of the warning in 2:1-4 but provides the means for obedient perseverance. This announcement of the Son's high priesthood builds anticipation and whets the hearers' appetite for the fuller exposition of Christ's sufficiency to come.

128. Bénétreau, 1:135.

129. Vanhoye, *Situation*, 385-86. Interpreters differ on the relationship between the relative clause, ἐν ᾧ γὰρ πέπονθεν, "by/because of what he has suffered," and the participle, πειρασθείς, "having been tested," or "because/when he was tested." It is grammatically possible for the relative clause to qualify the participle; or the participle, the relative clause. The NRSV, given in the text above, follows the first option by translating the participle as causal and the relative as instrumental. The ESV follows the second, construing the relative as causal and the participle as temporal: "Because he himself has suffered when tempted." As explained in the text above, the context of Hebrews supports this second option.

130. This emphasis is shown by the fact that the relative clause is given the initial emphatic position, by the use of the perfect tense, πέπονθεν, "he has suffered," and by the intensive αὐτός, "he *himself* has suffered" (see O'Brien, 122-3). Weiss, 227, calls Christ's sufferings the prototype of trials faced by God's people.

131. The perfect tense of πέπονθεν ("he has suffered") not only puts emphasis on Jesus' suffering, as noted above, but it suggests that he successfully brought it to a conclusion (through obedience) and that its beneficial effects continue (cf. Spicq, 2:49).

⌜132. Note how the pastor opens this sermon in v. 1 with five "p" words — πολυμερῶς ("various times"), πολυτρόπως ("various ways"), πάλαι ("of old"), πατράσιν ("fathers"), and προφήταις ("prophets") — and closes this first section in 2:18 with three — πέπονθεν ("he has suffered"), πειρασθείς ("having been tested"), πειραζομένοις ("those who are being tested").⌟

B. TESTED AT KADESH-BARNEA: AVOID THE CONGREGATION OF THE DISOBEDIENT (3:1–4:13)

Heb 3:1–4:13 is the second half of "A Very Short History of the Disobedient" people of God that brings the story of their rebellion to its conclusion. In 1:1–2:18 the pastor announced that God's revelation in his Son had fulfilled, and was, therefore, in continuity with the revelation given to his people at Sinai. Thus it is not surprising that he would associate his addressees who had received God's word in Christ with the people who heard God speak at that mountain and then journeyed through the wilderness toward the Promised Land. It was also natural for him to begin this discussion by comparing the Son with Moses who was both mediator of the Sinai revelation and leader of the wilderness generation (3:1-6). Num 12:7-8, referenced in Heb 3:3-5, was an appropriate basis for this comparison because it described Moses as the unique agent of revelation and divinely chosen leader. The selection of this passage led naturally to the pastor's application of the wilderness generation's Kadesh-Barnea rebellion from Num 13:1–14:45 to his hearers in Heb 3:7–4:11.[1] The story of this generation encapsulated the short history of the disobedient. However, Ps 95:7b-11 had already used the Kadesh incident as a basis for exhorting God's people. Since this psalm was in the form of exhortation, the pastor found it more suitable for warning his hearers against imitating that generation's disobedience (3:7-19) and exhorting them to enter the "rest" the unfaithful forfeited (4:1-11). This history ends with a piercing reminder of the accountability of God's people before his penetrating word (4:12-13). This reminder reinforces the declaration of God's self-revelation with which this sermon began (1:1-3). Nothing less than such accountability would be appropriate for the word God has now spoken in his Son.

This carefully constructed section plays an essential role in the pastor's overall purpose of motivating his hearers to faithful endurance. Heb 3:1-6 establishes several facts that are essential to the pastor's skillful use of OT examples and that integrate 3:1–4:13 into the larger scope of his sermon: first and foremost, the Son and Moses both function in the *one* house of God composed of the wilderness generation led by Moses as well as those who have received God's word in his Son.[2] Because of this continuity God's OT people

---

1. Albert Vanhoye, "Longue marche ou accìs tout proche? Le context biblique de Hébreux 3,7–4,11," *Bib* 49 (1968): 18-19.

2. "The present situation of the readers is seen to virtually merge with the situation of the 'Fathers' at Kadesh" (Jon Laansma, *"I Will Give You Rest": The Rest Motif in the New Testament with Special Reference to Mt 11 and Heb 3–4* [WUNT 98; Tübingen: Siebeck, 1997], 264). One might also say that the situation of the "Fathers" has merged with that of the first recipients. Instead of contrast (1:1-2), or the argument from less to greater, the pastor uses comparison: "we have received good news just as they" (4:2;

serve as negative (3:7–4:11) and positive (11:1-40) examples for his people today. Second, the fact that Moses functions as a "steward" but Christ as a "Son" prepares for the typological relationship between the old and new orders of salvation in 4:14–10:18. Finally, the pastor reminds his hearers that the Son is "faithful." In a most effective way he turns them away from the wilderness generation who embodied "A Short History of Disobedience" (3:7-4:11) so that he can direct them to the glorious history of the faithful of old (11:1-40) who constitute the first chapter of the "History of the Faithful People of God from Creation to Consummation" (10:19–12:29). He builds anticipation by affirming the faithfulness of the Son in 3:1-6, but also by delaying its explanation until 4:14–10:18 (esp. 5:7-10; 10:5-10) so that it can be the turning point between the faithless (3:7–4:11) and the faithful (11:1-40). Having thus established the faithfulness of the Son, he is able to bring the history of the OT faithful whom his hearers must embrace (11:1-40) to a grand climax in the Son now revealed as the incarnate and exalted "Jesus" (12:1-3). By his faithfulness this "Jesus" has become both the supreme example of perseverance and the one fully sufficient to empower God's people for faithful perseverance.[3]

The continuity of God's people is of great importance for 3:7–4:11. The pastor deliberately delays any reference to the superior privileges given God's people in Christ in order to establish the strongest continuity between his hearers and the wilderness generation. That generation is an example for but not a "type" of Christian believers.[4] Both groups are part of the one peo-

---

Ellingworth, 214; *contra* Spicq, 2:71; Weiss, 256). The superiority of the Son in 3:1-6 does not anticipate a superior people of God (*pace* Bénétreau, 1:158) but the superior privileges brought by Christ that are ultimately beneficial for God's people both before and after the incarnation (cf. 11:39-40). Even Bénétreau (1:158) must admit "a strong bond of continuity." *Pace* Westfall, *Discourse Analysis,* 117, 121-22, there is nothing in this text that distinguishes a "house of Jesus" and a "house of Moses" (cf. her reference to "God's house" on p. 125).

3. Thus, the pastor does not prematurely introduce the Son as an example to be emulated in 3:1-6 or 3:7-19 (see Victor Rhee, *Faith in Hebrews: Analysis within the Context of Christology, Eschatology and Ethics* [New York: Peter Lang, 2001], 94-96). The strategic moment for the Son's example will not arrive until 12:1-3.

4. Once one realizes that there is *one* people of God, then it is misleading to speak of the "old" people as a type of the "new." The people of God in the past provide examples for the people of God in the present. See on typology under "The Sermon's Use of the Old Testament" in the Introduction (pp. 52-54). Many, such as Spicq (2:71-72) and Weiss (255-56), recognize a strong continuity between God's people before and after the incarnation but continue to speak of a "typological" relationship. Spicq can say that both Christians and Israel have "received the same *(mêmes)* promises, pass through analogous *(analogue)* tests, are exposed to the same *(mêmes)* danger of apostasy, are going toward similar *(sembles)* purposes, and are exhorted to faithfulness in identical *(identiques)* terms" (2:71-

ple of God called by his word to the same kind of faith and obedience in anticipation of the same "rest." Thus the wilderness generation's loss of God's "rest" poses the sternest warning to contemporary believers. On the basis of this continuity the pastor urges his hearers to separate themselves from their predecessors by persevering in faithful obedience.[5]

It is also crucial to identify the situation faced by the wilderness generation with whom the pastor would associate his hearers. Käsemann has argued that the pastor is drawing an analogy between his hearers and the forty years of wilderness wandering. However, Hofius, Vanhoye, and Laansma have shown that wilderness wandering is not the theme of this passage.[6] They have conclusively demonstrated that both the one who translated this psalm into Greek and the author of Hebrews would draw the attention of their hearers to the rebellion of the wilderness generation at Kadesh-Barnea as described in Num 14:1-45.[7] In fact, Vanhoye has argued that the Greek version of the psalm followed by Hebrews has suppressed virtually all reference to other wilderness events. Bénétreau has made a needed adjustment to this position.[8] He admits the prominence of the disobedience at Kadesh-Barnea, but argues rightly that this final refusal to enter the land is seen as the culmination of the wilderness generation's previous behavior. Thus the pastor is con-

---

72). Yet he calls the wilderness generation "the figure of the Christian people" (2:71). The key is, with Laansma, *Rest Motif,* 275, to recognize that God's people throughout history have *always* pursued the *same* "rest" (contrast Spicq's "similar [*sembles*] purposes"). The pastor simply does not think in terms of "Israel" and "the Church" (cf. Ellingworth, 216).

5. Thus while the difference "between the wilderness generation and the author's first readers is *formally* temporal . . . , in *substance* . . . ," it is the difference between unbelief and obedience (Ellingworth, 216, italics original). The exemplary use of the OT faithful (11:1-38), who have now through Christ (11:39-40) come with all the obedient to Mount Zion (12:22-24), assumes the unity of the people of God from Creation (11:1-3) to Consummation (12:25-29).

6. Even Grässer admits that Hofius has corrected Käsemann by showing that the theme of 3:7–4:11 is the crisis at Kadesh rather than the wilderness wandering (Erich Grässer, "Das Wandernde Gottesvolk: Zum Basismotiv des Hebräerbriefes," *ZNW* 77 [1986]: 167-69).

7. Otfried Hofius, *Katapausis: Die Vorstellung vom endzeitlichen Ruheort im Hebräerbrief* (WUNT 11; Tübingen: Siebeck, 1970), 117-39; Vanhoye, "Longue marche," 9-26. Laansma, *Rest Motif,* 263, lists twelve features of 3:7–4:11 that conclusively identify this incident with the Kadesh rebellion in Num 14:1-45.

8. Bénétreau, 1:160-63. Witness God's affirmation that their "hearts are always going astray" (Heb 3:10b, citing Ps 95:10b). This phrase in the psalm reminds the reader of God's charge (Num 14:22) that Kadesh was the climax of repeated disobedience. Bénétreau also reminds the interpreter that "testing" God was a common description of the wilderness generation's behavior. The rebellion at Kadesh was not just a rhetorical synecdoche in which a part is used for the whole of the wilderness period, as argued by Koester, 264, n. 124. It was the climax of Israel's rebellion in Hebrews just as it was in the OT.

cerned with the rebellion at Kadesh as the climax of the people's disobedience during the relatively short time since Sinai or perhaps deliverance from Egypt. Even if the Greek translation draws more attention to Kadesh, the Hebrew psalm also sees this rebellion as the climax of earlier refusals to follow the divine will. Heb 11:1-40 may describe the people of God on pilgrimage to the eternal City established by God (11:8-16).[9] In light of this focus on Kadesh, however, Heb 3:7–4:11 describes the people of God at what should have been the culmination of their pilgrimage.[10] The forty years of wilderness wandering was not a model for this pilgrimage but the fate of those who proved faithless at pilgrimage's end.[11]

Does the pastor envision a specific impending event in the lives of his hearers as their Kadesh of decision and judgment? Lane suggests that coming persecution would be a Kadesh-like test of their faith.[12] Yet such a crisis alone is hardly sufficient to explain the large and integral role that these chapters play in the author's pastoral strategy. Hofius argues that God's final revelation in Christ has brought the hearers to the ultimate place of decision and subsequent gain or loss.[13] Though none would wish to deny the influence of Christ's sufficiency on the pastor's urgency, this suggestion is less than fully adequate in a passage that makes only one reference to Christ (cf. 3:14). Neither of these suggestions sufficiently accounts for the way in which the rebellion at Kadesh climaxes a history of disobedience. The implied exhortations in 3:6 and 14 suggest that the pastor is not concerned merely about a specific crisis his hearers may face but about their perseverance until the end. The incident at Kadesh serves his purpose because it combines the ultimate disobedience that crowned a history of unfaithfulness with final judgment. Thus it brings into sharpest focus the nature of disobedience and of its inevitable consequences. In this way the pastor would awaken his hearers to the possible result of their present tendency to "neglect" the salvation God has provided and to "drift" away (2:1-4). If left unchecked, the unbelief incipient in such behavior leads to the kind of irreversible disobedience and ultimate loss experienced by their ancestors at Kadesh.[14] The pastor's "History of the

9. See the commentary on chapter 11, and esp. William G. Johnsson, "The Pilgrimage Motif in the Book of Hebrews," *JBL* 97 (1978): 239-51.

10. This lack of journey-motif in Heb 3:7–4:11 belies Käsemann's claim that the pastor's exposition of Psalm 95 is based on the Gnostic myth of the soul's journey through the cosmos to heaven (Käsemann, *Wandering*, 67-96, 240). See esp. Laansma, *Rest Motif*, 310-14.

11. *Pace* Lane, 1:90, Hebrews nowhere pictures the wilderness journey "as normative in the life of the people of God because it was a period of spiritual formation."

12. Lane, 1:90.

13. Hofius, *Katapausis*, 140-43.

14. Ellingworth's (222) attempt to reduce the force of this wilderness-generation

Faithful People of God from Creation to Consummation" in 10:19–12:29 concludes with the final "Kadesh" of entrance into or exclusion from God's "rest," there called the "Unshakable Kingdom" (12:25-29).

1. Consider Jesus, A Son over the House of God (3:1-6)

1 *Therefore, holy brothers and sisters, partakers of the heavenly calling, consider the Apostle and High Priest of our confession, Jesus, 2 as one faithful to the one who appointed him, just as Moses also was faithful in all his house. 3 For this one has been considered worthy of more glory than Moses to as great a degree as the one who establishes a house has more honor than the house. 4 For every house is established by someone, but the one establishing all things is God. 5 And on one hand Moses was faithful in all his house as a steward for a witness of things yet to be spoken, 6 but Christ as a Son over his house, whose house we are if we hold fast our boldness and our boasting in hope.*

The urgent invitation for the pastor's hearers to give Jesus their full attention in v. 1 sets the direction for the rest of this sermon. The pastor would have them "consider" the "Apostle and High Priest of our confession, Jesus" before he introduces the faithless wilderness generation (3:7-19). This exhortation, however, does not reach fruition until the pastor directs them to keep their focus on "the Pioneer and Perfecter of the faith, Jesus" (12:1-3) at the climax of the contrasting account of the past faithful. This latter description assumes what the former anticipates — Christ's sufficiency as both Savior and example of perseverance amid suffering.[1]

The pastor compares (v. 2) and contrasts (vv. 3-6a) this Person who is the proper Object of their concern with Moses. In this way he sketches the Son's connection with the "house" or household of God, his relationship to previous revelation, and his superiority as the Savior of God's people. Although this sketch anticipates further explanation, v. 6b provides immediate application and transition to the disobedient wilderness generation that follows. If the hearers persevere in their loyalty to Christ, they will continue to be God's "house" and avoid the fate suffered by their predecessors in the "house" of God during Moses' time (vv. 7-19).

1 Since the Son is "a merciful and faithful high priest" (2:17-18) able to sustain the faithful amid testing, the hearers are urged to give him

---

warning to a mere caution against passive lethargy is unconvincing. His interpretation of "to turn away from the living God" as "desertion" instead of "deliberate disobedience" is without support, especially in light of Num 14:11.

1. See pp. 153-57, the introductory comments on 3:1–4:13.

their fullest attention.[2] The pastor would encourage his hearers to obey this exhortation by the way he addresses them. "Holy brothers and sisters" reminds them of who they are as the people of God and of the divine initiative for their salvation. The Son who was not ashamed to own them as "brothers and sisters" before the Father (2:12) took on their humanity as the "one who makes" them "holy" (2:11) by cleansing them from sin (9:11-14).[3] "Brothers and sisters" (cf. 3:12; 10:19; 13:22) is, then, much more than a traditional designation used for others of the same religion.[4] The Son makes them "holy" so that they can truly be "partakers in the heavenly calling."[5] With this phrase the pastor orients them toward their destiny. This "calling" is an invitation to heaven and from heaven.[6] God's people are invited to enter the heavenly Most Holy Place (4:14-16; 10:19-25) in order to receive the grace necessary for perseverance. Their ultimate destination is the "heavenly homeland" (11:16), also described as the eternal city established by God (11:10) and the true "heavenly Jerusalem" (12:22). This invitation is also from "heaven" because it has been issued by God, made available through the mediation of the exalted Son (12:22-25), and offered through the proclamation of "such a great salvation" (2:3). They are "partakers" in this "heavenly" invitation because they are "partakers in" the one whom God invited to "sit" at his "right hand" (Heb 3:14; cf. 1:13). He is the one who enables God's people to hear the call and respond in obedience.[7] The pastor urgently

2. On the consequential nature of ὅθεν ("therefore") in v. 1, see Spicq, 2:64, and compare 2:17; 7:25; 8:3; 9:18; and 11:19. See also Weiss, 240, and Westfall, *Discourse Analysis,* 111.

3. The adjective "holy" (ἅγιοι) comes after "brothers and sisters" (ἀδελφοί) but before "partakers of the heavenly calling" (κλήσεως ἐπουρανίου μέτοχοι). Most translations take "holy" with the preceding expression, "holy brothers and sisters"; some construe it with what follows, "holy partners in a heavenly calling" (NRSV). Spicq, 2:64, understands it as an independent substantive, "brothers and sisters, holy ones, partakers of the heavenly calling." This adjective is often used substantively for the "saints" or "holy ones" in Acts, the Pauline letters, 1 Peter, and the Apostolic Fathers (cf. Heb 6:10; 13:24). It had already been used for Israelites in the LXX. See Braun, 77. Spicq is right in affirming that "holy" identifies these believers as the privileged people of God, but misled in excluding the personal moral transformation described in Heb 9:11. *Pace* E. Grässer, "Mose und Jesus: Zur Auslegung von Hebr 3:1-6," *ZNW* 75 (1984): 5-6, the future eschatological orientation of this call does not preclude, but rather implies, present moral and spiritual transformation.

4. For the use of such designations by early Christians, Jews, and other contemporary religious groups see Braun, 77.

5. Cf. P. Auffret, "Essai sur la structure littéraire et l'interprétation d'Hébreux 3,1-6," *NTS* 26 (1979-80): 381.

6. Koester, 242. Compare Phil 3:14; Eph 2:6; and 2 Tim 4:18.

7. See Weiss, 242. The Son "partook" (μετέσχεν) of his people's humanity (2:14)

desires his "brothers and sisters" not to imitate the wilderness generation, soon to be described, who through unbelief fell short of the heavenly destination offered them. He would have them persevere as the family of God (3:6).

This exhortation is supremely urgent because of the identity of the one to whom it directs their attention. He is none other than "the Apostle and High Priest of our confession, Jesus." John's Gospel often uses a verb related to the term apostle when it describes the Father's "sending" the Son into the world as his complete self-revelation and authorized representative (3:17, 34; 5:36-38; 6:29, 57; 7:29; 8:42; 10:36; 11:42; 17:3).[8] However, no other extant writer before Justin Martyr (A.D. 120) calls Jesus Apostle.[9] The NT uses apostle to describe the twelve Jesus chose, Paul, and a few other early church leaders. They were the accredited representatives of Christ "sent" by him and authorized to speak and act on his behalf.[10] On reflection, however, "apostle" is most appropriate as a summary of what the pastor has said in 1:1–2:4 about the Son as God's final and complete revelation.[11] It affirms his superiority to prophets (1:1), angels (2:2), and even to Moses (3:2), who was the supreme agent of God's revelation in the OT (see Exod 3:10; 7:16 and Num 16:28, 29).[12] God may have delivered messages through these other intermediaries,

---

so that they might be "partakers" (μέτοχοι) of the heavenly calling" (3:1). On the significance of the heavenly and the earthly in Hebrews see the Introduction (pp. 24-34).

8. Compare ἀπόστολος, "apostle," with ἀποστέλλω, "send." Similar ideas occur in such passages as Matt 10:40; John 13:20 and 14:9.

9. In the *First Apology* Justin calls Jesus "Son of God and Apostle" (12.9) and "Angel/Messenger [ἄγγελος] and Apostle" (63.5, 10, 14). In this last reference Justin appears to be dependent on Exod 23:20 LXX: "Behold, I send my angel [ἄγγελος] before you." Instead of "angel," the *Samaritan Targum* reads "apostle" in Exod 23:20 (and in Exod 20:23; 32:34). Thus Justin's reading might bear witness to a conflation of two textual traditions in Exod 23:20 — one that read "angel/messenger" (ἄγγελος); and one, "apostle" (ἀπόστολος). Lane, 1:75, suggests that if the author of Hebrews knew of such a variant reading, it might have influenced his use of "apostle" in this verse.

10. The NT understanding of ἀπόστολος as the accredited representative of another is unparalleled in contemporary Hellenistic Judaism but similar to the significance of the שׁלִיחַ or "apostle" in later rabbinic Judaism. Karl Heinrich Rengstorf, "ἀπόστολος," *TDNT* 1:420-24.

11. For the association of "son" with 1:1–2:4 and "high priest" with 2:4-18 see on those passages above and Bénétreau, 1:150, n. 1; Grässer, "Mose und Jesus," 8-9, and esp. Westfall, *Discourse Analysis,* 112.

12. It is probable that the use of "apostle" for Jesus was motivated by the contrast with Moses, who functioned as God's designated representative in the OT and in Hellenistic Judaism, even if he was not called by the title "apostle" in those sources. See Weiss, 244-48, and Ellingworth, 199. According to Rengstorf, "ἀπόστολος," *TDNT* 1:419, the rabbis referred to Moses (along with Elijah, Elisha, and Ezekiel) as God's "apostle" (שׁלִיחַ) because things took place through him such as water from the rock that were "normally reserved for God." Rengstorf, *TDNT* 1:421-22, and others have suggested that the

but the Son had full authority to speak and act on God's behalf (1:1). If "Apostle" encapsulates what the Son is as God's ultimate revelation (1:1–2:4), then "High Priest" portrays him as the one who has provided "such a great salvation" (2:3; cf. 2:5-18). "Apostle" contrasts the Son with Moses as the source of revelation; "High Priest" anticipates comparison with Aaron as the source of salvation (5:1-10).[13]

The close grammatical bond between these terms reflects the way in which the Son fulfills his role as the complete revelation of God (1:1–2:4) through his high priesthood (2:5-18).[14] As Apostle he acted on God's behalf by offering his obedient human life as a sufficient sacrifice for sin (5:7-10; 10:5-10). By this sacrifice he became the only High Priest fully competent to save God's people. The "so great salvation" (2:3) provided by this High Priest (5:9) is the ultimate revelation disclosed by God's Apostle.[15] Thus he has truly become the "Guarantor" of the New Covenant (7:25). As in 2:9 above, the pastor has reserved the name "Jesus" for the conclusion of his description. This ultimate revelation and all-sufficient salvation was achieved only through the Son's assumption of humanity as "Jesus." The pastor need use the term "apostle" no more, for he has invested Christ's high priesthood with its authority.

---

joining of "apostle" and "high priest" in Heb 3:1-6 reflects the rabbinic identification of the high priest as God's "apostle" (שׁלִיח). Heb 3:1-6, however, does not present Moses as a type of Christ in the capacities of both apostle/revealer and high priest as suggested by Spicq, 2:65. See the critique in Hughes, 127-28. The traditions about Moses' priesthood introduced by Lala Kalyan Kumar Dey, *The Intermediary World and Patterns of Perfection in Philo and Hebrews* (SBLDS 25; Missoula, MT: Scholars Press, 1975), 157-61, are alien to the text of Hebrews, which attributes no priestly function to Moses. Moses is a type of Christ as revealer (1:1–2:4) and leader of the wilderness generation (3:7–4:11); the Aaronic high priest is a type of Christ as high priest. Koester's attempt, 243, to connect ἀπόστολος, "apostle," with ἀρχηγός, pioneer" (2:10), is superficial and unconvincing.

13. If "Pioneer" (2:10) evoked Moses' role as leader of God's people toward the Promised Land, "Apostle" (3:1) reflects Moses' role as supreme OT agent of revelation.

14. The terms "apostle" and "high priest" are closely bound together by one article, τὸν ἀπόστολον καὶ ἀρχιερέα, thus designating two closely related aspects of the one described. Westfall, *Discourse Analysis,* 114, acknowledges the close relationship between these terms but fails to see that Christ's high priesthood fulfills his apostleship. This oversight is in agreement with her failure to see the close relationship between 1:1–2:4 and 2:5-18.

15. The suggestion that Apostle refers to Christ's earthly and High Priest to his heavenly ministry obscures the fact that the Son becomes the full revelation of God only when he has completed the work of redemption (*pace* Grässer, "Mose und Jesus," 9). These terms affirm the inseparable unity of revelation ("apostle") and redemption ("high priest"), not, as Spicq, 2:65, suggests, between incarnation and redemption. Bénétreau's (1:150) proposal that Christ represents God to us as "apostle," and us to God as "high priest" (cf. Johnson, 107; Pfitzner, 73), also fails to grasp the true interrelationship between the two.

This one is the "Apostle and High Priest whom we confess" (NIV; cf. 4:14 and 10:23) and to whom we bear witness. He is also the "Apostle and High Priest of our confession of faith" (NJB), that is, belief in him is the content of the faith affirmed by the people of God. It is virtually impossible to separate the act of confessing from the truth confessed.[16] The pastor may have reference to a formal confession used in the worship of the community to whom he is writing.[17] The freedom with which he uses the title "Son" indicates that the recipients were familiar with this title of widespread currency in early Christianity. It is more difficult to determine whether or not the recipients' confession referred to Jesus as "Apostle and High Priest." The phrase "Apostle and High Priest of our confession" suggests that it did. We have noted that ideas related to this use of "apostle" occur in John's Gospel and elsewhere, even if, as noted above, the term itself is not used for Christ before Justin Martyr.[18] However, even if the pastor did not introduce the high-priestly title to this congregation, his teaching on this subject was certainly new to them as evidenced by the fact that it required Scriptural justification (7:1-28) and was difficult for them to understand (5:11-14).[19] The pastor would reinforce his hearers' loyalty to the one whom they confess by using the Son's high priesthood to explain the significance of their affirmations concerning him (cf. 4:14-16; 10:19-25).

2 The pastor, as is his custom, has reserved the name "Jesus" for the emphatic position at the end of v. 1 (cf. 2:9) in order to rivet his hearers' attention on the incarnate Son of God. One should not translate the participial phrase with which v. 2 begins as indirect address: "consider that . . . Jesus was faithful."[20] Nor, however, should one relegate his faithfulness to a mere

16. O'Brien, 130, citing BDAG, 709, and L&N §33.274.

17. Compare the REB, "the faith we profess." See Hughes, 129. According to Koester, 243, the presence of the definite article favors reference to a formulated body of material with definite content. He also suggests that the exhortation to "hold" the confession "fast" in 4:14 and 10:23 indicates that its content could be "identified and grasped (cf. 4:14; 10:23)." Weiss, 243-44, thinks the pastor is referring to their baptismal confession.

18. References are given above. See Spicq, 2:64-65.

19. Attridge, 108, thinks the confession affirmed Christ as "Son" and perhaps as "Apostle" and "High Priest." O'Brien, 130, thinks that "Apostle and High Priest" would have been appropriate for the hearers' confession because they fit well with all the author has been saying. One would, however, have expected these terms to appear elsewhere in a confessional context (129, n. 20). Ellingworth, 199, would restrict the confession to "Son" alone. Bénétreau, 1:151, thinks the evidence insufficient to posit a fixed confession of any kind.

20. *Pace* O'Brien, 131, and the NRSV: "consider that Jesus, the apostle and high priest of our confession, was faithful to the one who appointed him. . . ." See also Lane, 1:71.

relative clause, "consider . . . Jesus, who was faithful." "Being faithful" is truly adverbial, describing the circumstances in which the hearers were to consider Jesus: "consider the apostle and high priest of our confession, Jesus, as being faithful." One might say, "in his faithfulness."[21] This faithfulness includes both the incarnate obedience of "Jesus" and the resultant continuing trustworthiness of the exalted "Apostle and High Priest."[22] The prominence the pastor gives to the name "Jesus" and the way he describes him as "faithful to the one who appointed him"[23] anticipate the way Christ describes the purpose of his incarnate life as "to do your will, O God" (10:7).[24] Such earthly faithfulness compares well with the faithfulness of Moses and contrasts appropriately with the unfaithfulness of the wilderness generation (3:7-19). The pastor, however, would not exclude the exalted "Apostle and High Priest" from this description. The deliberate use of the present participle, *being* faithful, encompasses both past earthly and present heavenly faithfulness in one continuous reality. The earthly obedience of Christ endures as the source of the exalted One's saving efficacy (10:5-10). That earthly faithfulness is the premier example for emulation (12:1-3) and the guarantee of Christ's present dependability as Savior.[25] Thus salvation is initiated by the God "who appointed him," accomplished through the faithful obedience of the incarnate Son "Jesus" (5:7-10; 10:5-10), and mediated through the ex-

21. Thus all of v. 2 is the object of "consider" (Auffret, "Essai," 382).

22. Hughes, 120; Westcott, 57; E. Grässer, *Der Glaube im Hebräerbrief* (MTS 2; Marburg: Elwert, 1965), 21-22; and I. G. Wallis, *The Faith of Jesus Christ in Early Christian Traditions* (SNTSMS 84; Cambridge: Cambridge University Press, 1995), 148, argue that πιστός applies primarily to the exalted Apostle and High Priest; Koester, 243; Montefiore, 67; and Moffatt, 37, among others, that its primary function is to describe Jesus' incarnate obedience.

23. ποιήσαντι, the aorist participle of ποιέω, should probably be translated "appointed" (1 Sam 12:6 LXX; Mark 3:14; Acts 2:36) and not "made." Hebrews distinguishes the Son from all created things (1:1-3). See Koester, 244, and Spicq, 2:65-66. Yet Grässer's suggestion ("Mose und Jesus," 12) that this term includes a reference to the "making" of Jesus' human body is interesting (cf. Johnson, 107). In 10:5-10 the Son does refer to the "body you prepared for me." Such an interpretation focuses the emphasis even more firmly on Jesus' faithfulness to God as a human being. It is probably going beyond what the context would warrant to join both connotations as an affirmation that the incarnation was the time of the Son's appointment as "Apostle and High Priest."

24. It makes more sense to say that he was "faithful" to God than that he was "accredited with God," as argued by A. Vanhoye, *Old Testament Priests and the New Priest according to the New Testament* (Petersham, MA: St. Bede's Publications, 1986), 96-98. After his initial presentation Vanhoye acts as if the text said "accredited" or "worthy of trust" by God's people. Jesus, however, is worthy of his people's trust because he has been faithful to God. See Koester, 243-44.

25. Thus since Christ was πιστός in the active sense of "faithful," he was also πιστός in the passive sense of "trustworthy."

alted "Apostle and High Priest," upon whom his people can depend without hesitation.

The faithfulness of Jesus and Moses is the formal basis for comparison.[26] Moses' faithfulness "in all God's house" was affirmed by God in Num 12:7, introduced here and quoted more fully in v. 5 below.[27] This "house" is God's people once led by Moses and now brought to glory by the Son (2:10, 14-18).[28] The pastor makes no use of Jewish speculations about Moses as a heavenly mediator.[29] Nor does he follow Philo by saying such things as that

26. The one who came to do God's will (10:5-10) and was "without sin" (4:15) was indeed more "faithful" than Moses. Such superiority is not, however, the pastor's point in this passage. Dey's critique of Spicq, whose title for this section is "The Faithfulness of Christ Is Superior to That of Moses" (my translation), is correct (Dey, *Perfection*, 156; Spicq, 2:63). Cf. Attridge, 109, n. 63; O'Brien, 131.

27. D'Angelo, *Moses*, 65-93, has argued that Heb 3:2 is a quotation of the Nathan oracle in 1 Chr 17:14 with only a secondary allusion to Num 12:7. 1 Chr 17:14 reads, "I will make him faithful in my house" (πιστώσω αὐτὸν ἐν οἴκῳ μου). According to this interpretation, the author uses the Nathan oracle to establish the faithfulness of Christ in v. 2 and Num 12:7 to affirm the faithfulness of Moses in v. 5 as a basis for comparing the two. See also Lane, 1:76-77. However, reference to 1 Chr 17:14 is very unlikely for several reasons. First, 1 Chronicles does not fit the syntax of this passage. It requires taking πιστόν with τῷ ποιήσαντι αὐτόν, "to the one who made [*or* appointed] him faithful," in order to make this phrase the equivalent of πιστώσω αὐτόν, "I will make him faithful" (1 Chr 17:14). It is much more natural for πιστόν to modify the Ἰησοῦν it follows. In any case, "I will make him faithful" is a questionable translation of πιστώσω αὐτόν in 1 Chr 17:14. See Johan Lust, Erik Eynikel, and Katrin Hauspie, comps., *Greek-English Lexicon of the Septuagint* (Stuttgart: Deutsche Bibelgesellschaft, 2003), 494. Second, reference to 1 Chronicles requires one to make "as was Moses" (ὡς καὶ Μωϋσῆς) a parenthesis and to take "in all his house" (ἐν [ὅλῳ] τῷ οἴκῳ αὐτοῦ) with Jesus. Even without the questionable ὅλῳ (all), this phrase clearly reflects Num 12:7 rather than any version of the Nathan oracle. Furthermore, it could not refer to Jesus because according to v. 5 he is not "in" but "over" God's house. Third, if the ὅλῳ (all) is original, reference to Num 12:7 is certain in v. 2. On the other hand, the addition ὅλῳ (all) by a later hand in conformity to Num 12:7 only underscores the way in which Heb 3:2 was heard as a citation of that verse. In fact, verbal similarity with Num 12:7 and dissimilarity with 1 Chr 17:14 make it difficult to imagine a reader hearing this verse in any other way. The pastor may well have withheld ὅλῳ (all) until the climax of his contrast between Moses and Christ in v. 5. At that point it enhances the superiority of Christ by exalting the one whom Christ surpasses. Cf. Grässer, "Mose und Jesus," 12, n. 49. Although external evidence for ὅλῳ (all) is evenly balanced, internal evidence favors scribal conformity of v. 2 to v. 5 and Num 12:7. See *TCGNT*, 594-95.

28. Both in Numbers 12 and in Hebrews "his house" refers to God's "house" (Ellingworth, 201). Dey, *Perfection*, 175-76, argues that in 3:3, 4 "his house" refers to the universe, in 3:6 to the human soul, and in 10:21 to the heavenly sanctuary in which God dwells. His interpretation of v. 6 is especially strained.

29. Various commentators refer to Jewish speculations about the exalted, heavenly status of Moses as mediator with God. See Attridge, 105. Even Grässer, who often

God gave Moses "the whole world."[30] His comments are based on the OT in general and on Numbers 12 in particular, a passage that describes Moses' unprecedented role as the channel of God's pre-Christian self-revelation. Moses saw the "glory" of God, and God spoke to him face to face. There is no indication that the pastor's discussion of Moses follows that on the angels because he believed Moses their superior.[31] The pastor first establishes the Son's preeminence in the most effective way by contrasting him with the highest heavenly beings. Then he turns to Moses because of Moses' role as premier agent of OT revelation, mediator of the Old Covenant, and leader of the people of God. It was Moses who established the priesthood and sacrificial system that foreshadowed Christ. Mention of Moses prepares the way for use of the wilderness generation he led (3:7–4:11).

3   The pastor emphasizes the demonstrative "this one" by locating it prominently toward the beginning of this verse. Although "Jesus," at the end of v. 1, is its closest antecedent, those English translations that insert that name "Jesus" here detract from the pastor's intended effect.[32] "This one" is both emphatic and broad. It includes all that the pastor has said about "the Apostle and High Priest of our confession, Jesus," yet it allows him to reserve the key term "Son" for the conclusion of his argument in v. 6. The "greater glory" due "this one" is sufficient reason for giving him one's full attention and allegiance as advocated in v. 1.[33] He is due greater "glory" than Moses in proportion to the greater "honor" due the builder of a "house" than the "house" itself.[34] His glory is superior not merely in degree but in kind. The use of "glory" in the first part of this comparison instead of the synonym "honor" is well suited to the immediate and larger context (cf. 2:9). The Son is worthy of more "glory" than others because of the way in which he reveals the "glory" of God. Moses may have been greater than the prophets because he saw the "glory" of God (Num 12:8 LXX) to such an extent that his face shone (Exod 34:29-30; 2 Cor 3:12-18). Yet, according to Exod 33:18, 22, his vision was limited. On the other hand, through his incarnation and death the exalted one at God's right is the very "radiance" and revelation of the "glory"

---

sees Hellenistic speculations as the source of NT Christology, argues that this passage is based on Moses' OT role as revealer and leader through the wilderness rather than on such speculations (Grässer, "Mose und Jesus," 14).

30. *Moses* 1.155-58; *Sacrifices* 9. See Koester, 251.

31. *Pace* Dey, *Perfection,* 155. See Lane, 1:79-80.

32. "For *Jesus* has been counted worthy of more glory than Moses" (ESV, italics added; cf. TNIV, TEV, NRSV).

33. The conjunction γάρ ("for") shows that vv. 3-4 give the motivation for v. 1 (Ellingworth, 203-4).

34. Lane, 1:77, is certainly correct when he asserts that this verse indicates the degree of glory by which the Son surpasses Moses. *Pace* Ellingworth, 203.

of God's very being (1:3) and the one who brings God's people into the "glory" of God's presence (2:10). "Has been considered worthy" is a divine passive. The same God who declared, "you are my Son" (1:5), has given validity to this valuation of the exalted Son as his complete self-revelation and fulfillment of all that was declared through Moses.[35] The perfect tense of the passive puts emphasis on this divine value judgment and underscores its continuing validity.[36] Faithfulness to one bearing such great honor brings encouragement to believers suffering the rejection and the shame heaped upon them by an unbelieving world.

In order to show the degree to which the Son surpasses Moses in "glory" the pastor appropriates what appears to have been a common proverb: "the one who establishes a house has more honor than the house."[37] He uses this proverb to describe a parallel relationship: the Son is to Moses as the builder of a house is to the house.[38] The one is superior in kind because he is the source of the other. The immediate context, however, suggests that the pastor is already thinking of the "house" as the people of God[39] and "the one who established it" as Christ.[40] Moses himself is part of this house (v. 5), which is brought into existence by God's self-revelation like that given at Sinai (2:1-4) or "in the prophets" (1:1).[41] Yet the pastor is not engaging in some

35. Koester, 244.

36. See Weiss, 247, n. 33, and O'Brien, 132. Cf. 1:2, 9; 2:9.

37. For examples of parallel proverbs see Koester, 245.

38. Dey, *Perfection,* 166-68, is correct when he argues that the writer of Hebrews is here expressing a parallel relationship. The immediate context, however, suggests the identification of the "house" with the people of God in a way not evidenced by the examples from Philo cited by Dey.

39. Ellingworth, 204. For "house" as a description of God's people see Exod 16:31; Hos 8:1; Jer 12:7; and Heb 8:8. According to *Targum Onqelos* (cf. *Fragmentary Targum*) Num 12:7 reads, "among my whole people" (Koester, 245). Grässer admits that this use of "house" for the people of God is based on Num 12:7 and the biblical tradition ("Mose und Jesus," 17-18). It is unclear why he goes on to insist that the "house" imagery in Hebrews is developed by the use of Alexandrian cosmology and anthropology when he admits that Hebrews differs significantly from Philo, who understands the "house" of Num 12:7 as the human soul in which God dwells (Grässer, "Mose und Jesus," 18-19). On Philo's use of house, see R. Williamson, *Philo and the Epistle to the Hebrews* (Arbeiten zur Literatur und Geschichte des hellenistischen Judentums 4; Leiden: Brill, 1970), 109-14. Nor does the "house" of Hebrews picture the people of God collectively as the dwelling place of God. Rather, it is God's "house" or people who enter God's heavenly dwelling place.

40. ὁ κατασκευάσας αὐτόν ("the one who established it") is parallel to οὗτος ("this one") at the beginning of v. 3, and thus to τὸν ἀπόστολον καὶ ἀρχιερέα . . . Ἰησοῦν, ("the Apostle and High Priest . . . Jesus") in v. 1. On this interpretation v. 4b affirms the deity — not the identity — of "the one who established" the people of God (*pace* Auffret, "Essai," 390).

41. Grässer, "Mose und Jesus," 17.

speculation about the preincarnate Son when he calls him "the one who established" this house.[42] As the fulfillment of revelation and the provider of redemption the Son brings God's people to their inheritance and intended end. Thus it is proper to call him "the one who established" the people of God. The pastor deliberately uses the word we have translated "establish" to express this relationship between Christ and God's people. This term can describe the "building" of a house (cf. Heb 11:7; Josephus, *J.W.* 6.191), but it can also refer to the completion of the house, to its being "furnished" or "equipped" for use (Heb 9:2, 6; Mark 1:2; Luke 7:17).[43] It is the salvation provided by Christ which completes and equips the people of God. Both those who lived before the incarnation, including Moses (compare 11:26), and those who live after, reach their goal through him (11:39-40). He is due greater "glory" because he surpasses Moses as the Redeemer surpasses the redeemed.

4 He also surpasses Moses as Moses' Creator. The conjunction "for" makes it clear that this verse is no parenthesis but an additional, concluding, even climactic argument for the superiority of the "Apostle and High Priest of our confession."[44] Read in isolation, the statement "Every house is established by someone" would be a truism, and the affirmation "the all-things establishing one is God" a self-evident tenet of biblical faith (cf. 11:3). Within this context, however, the first statement provides a transition from the "household" of God's people to the "household of creation."[45] The second affirms the deity of the Son as Creator. The pastor has already established the eternity of the Son and his role in both creating the world and bringing it to its intended climax (1:2b; 10-12). Thus it is no surprise when he calls the Son "the all-things establishing one" and reaffirms his deity.[46]

---

42. Contrast Justin Martyr's belief that it was the Son who spoke to Moses through the burning bush (*1 Apol.* 63, quoted in Heen and Krey, 52).

43. BDAG, 526-27; L&N §77.6; and Ellingworth, 204. Thus its use here in v. 3 prepares for its use in regard to creation in v. 4 (Isa 40:28; 43:7; Wis 11:24; 13:4; cf. Gen 1:2). For further examples of the use of this term see Spicq, 2:67.

44. According to Weiss, 247, γάρ joins v. 4 to v. 3. See also Lane, 1:77, and Koester, 252. Koester (252, n. 119) says Windisch, Moffatt, Spicq, Héring, and Hughes take v. 4 as a parenthesis. He cites Dey in support of the integral nature of this verse (Dey, *Perfection,* 166). Although Attridge, 104, thinks v. 4 parenthetical, yet he says that ". . . it seems to evoke the Son's association with God that ultimately renders him superior to any other intermediary between God and humanity."

45. Note the way *Targum Neofiti* translates Num 12:7, "In the whole world I have created, [Moses] is faithful" (Koester, 245).

46. The definite article ὁ with the substantive participle phrase ὁ δὲ πάντα κατασκευάσας, and the absence of a comparable article with "God" (θεός) shows clearly that "the all-things establishing one" is the subject of whom deity is predicated. Compare John 1:1.

"Establish" is the same word used in v. 3 with the same breadth of meaning. It encompasses the Son's role as Creator of all and as the universal "heir" who brings all to its intended end through redemption (1:2). Through bringing the "house" of God's people into its inheritance he fulfills God's purposes for the "house" of creation.

Failure to accept this verse as confirmation of the Son's divine creatorship leaves it a foreign body in the text.[47] When one accepts this verse as an affirmation of the Son's deity, it becomes a fitting introduction to the following verses which proclaim the divine Son's role over God's house in which Moses serves as "steward."

5-6a   These verses give content to the contrast between Moses and Christ and thus form the capstone of the author's argument for the latter's superiority. At the same time they affirm that the hearers are part of the same people of God who left Sinai for the Promised Land. Verse 5 begins with "And Moses on the one hand . . ."; v. 6 with, "Christ on the other hand." The term "Christ" avoids the emphasis on humanity inherent in the pastor's use of "Jesus" in v. 1, yet allows him to make sonship part of the contrast to be affirmed. Together "Jesus" and "Christ" frame this passage.[48] The elements of this contrast are given in chiastic order: "faithful in all God's house as a steward"; "as a Son over all God's house [faithful]."

The pastor does not denigrate Moses but magnifies his unique place in the divine economy as the one "faithful in all God's house as a steward" (quoting Num 12:7).[49] Hebrews affirms all that Num 12:1-16 has said about Moses' being the unrivaled channel of divine communication without equal before Christ. Moses alone "is faithful in *all* God's house" (emphasis added). The term "steward" bespeaks the unparalleled place of ministry granted him among the people of God.[50] Although this word can be translated "servant," it

47. Weiss, 248, n. 38, thinks it "completely unlikely" that this verse ascribes deity to Christ. He quotes Grässer approvingly, "With v. 4b it should not be said that Jesus is God, but that he belongs on the side of God, while Moses belongs on the side of human beings" (my translation). Grässer gives his case away when he admits that Jesus as Son and *Creator* is greater than Moses (Grässer, "Mose und Jesus," 16). In light of the way in which Hebrews has already affirmed the deity of the Son in 1:1-14, such denial reveals more about Weiss and Grässer's reluctance to concede this point than about the meaning of the text. See also the comments on Heb 7:1-3 below. Cf. James Swetnam, "Form and Content in Hebrews 1–6," *Bib* 53 (1972): 376-78. Weiss concedes that many early Christian interpreters understood this verse as an affirmation of Christ's deity.

48. See Attridge, 111. "Christ" appears in 5:5; 6:1; 9:11, 14, 24, 28; 10:10; 11:26; 13:8.

49. Contrary to Attridge, 111, who seems to think Hebrews belittles Moses. See Lane, 1:78.

50. In Jewish thought Moses was the most significant person in salvation history, sometimes even thought of as higher than the angels (Ellingworth, 194). The writer of He-

often denotes a high servant or minister, as evidenced by its use in the plural for the servants or "ministers" of Pharaoh.[51] From the beginning of Genesis to the end of Joshua only Moses is regularly called the "steward" of God (see Exod 4:10, 11; 14:31; Num. 11:11; 12:7; Deut. 3:24; Josh 1:2; 8:31, 33).[52] Even David, arguably the greatest post-Moses person in the OT, is never given this title.[53] There is no need to belittle Moses, for the greater Moses is, the more the Son's superiority will be magnified.

The pastor has prepared well for the reintroduction of the term "Son," withheld until now for contrast with "steward." "Son" invokes all that has been said about Christ as the one who "establishes" both the people of God and all creation. One who is "Son," Creator and Redeemer, cannot be described even as the highest servant "in" God's house. He takes his place with the Father "over" the household of God.[54]

Hebrews will explain the way in which the Son has "established" the people of God by describing his high-priestly ministry (4:14–10:18). However, immediate attention is given to Moses' contrasting role as "steward." His stewardship consists in being a "witness of things yet to be spoken." He bore faithful witness to God's future (from Moses' point of view) complete revelation that would be and now has been "spoken" in the Son (Heb 1:2 and 2:4).[55] His witness was especially clear in what he spoke about priesthood

---

brews, however, shows no interest in such speculations. Attridge, 111, warns against making too much of the θεράπων/δοῦλος ("steward"/"servant") distinction because the author takes θεράπων from Numbers 12. The pastor, however, has chosen to quote this passage for the very reason that it gives the highest evaluation of Moses in the OT. On θεράπων as "honored servant" see Lane, 1:78.

51. Exod 5:21; 7:10, 20; 8:3, 4, 9 (2x), 11, 21, 24, 29, 31, etc. God uses this term to speak of Job, "my servant," a number of times. See Lane, 1:78.

52. Otherwise Isaac is once called the "steward" of God (Gen. 24:44) and Joshua is once called the "steward" of Moses (Exod 33:11).

53. "Steward" is our translation of the Greek word θεράπων. David is called the δοῦλος, "servant" or "slave" of God.

54. S. C. Layton, "Christ over His House (Hebrews 3:6) and Hebrew אֲשֶׁר עַל־הַבַּיִת," NTS 37 (1991): 473-77, has suggested that the phrase "over his house" comes from an LXX expression for the royal steward — compare 1 Kgs 10:5 (οἱ ἐπὶ τοῦ οἴκου, "those over the house") and 15:5 (ἐπὶ τῷ οἴκῳ) and also in the LXX addition following 1 Kgs 2:46, ἐπὶ τόν οἶκον αὐτοῦ, "over his house." The interpretive significance of this observation is questionable. Christ is here the "Son," not a steward. The phrase arises in contrast to the description of Moses as "in" God's house. It associates the Son with God.

55. See deSilva, 138; Hughes, 136; and Auffret, "Essai," 385-86, 395. Some have suggested that Moses' witness consisted of "the things that would be spoken" by himself (Bénétreau, 1:154) or that he was a witness of the things that God would speak to him (Ellingworth, 208). Ellingworth argues that the OT context supports this last interpretation. Bénétreau thinks that reference to words spoken by Moses underscores the faithfulness of Moses emphasized in this passage. The larger context of Hebrews, however, is de-

(Heb 7:14). By establishing the sacrificial system Moses bore witness to the atoning sacrifice and high priesthood of Christ described in 8:1–10:18.[56] The pastor's insistence on the ineffectiveness of the Mosaic system as a means of salvation (7:18; 9:8, 11-14; 10:1-4) detracts nothing from its function as witness to the true source of "such a great salvation." As God's "steward," Moses — one-of-a-kind in the OT — is the chief witness to the unique person of the Son and to the finality of the salvation he provides.[57]

6b   This discussion of God's "house" is of vital importance to Christian believers like the recipients of Hebrews. "Whose house we are" identifies them as privileged members of this household over which Christ is Son and in which Moses serves as steward.[58] "If we hold fast our boldness and our boasting in hope" reminds them that those who enjoy this privilege must persevere in order to reap its blessings. The following account of the wilderness generation's rebellion shows the fate of the people of God when they fail to persevere. On the other hand, the faithful people of God in chapter 11 are to be emulated for their endurance.

Since Moses himself was a "steward" in God's house, there is no reason to limit this household to a supposed "new" people of God.[59] This inclusion of the wilderness generation and the OT faithful in the house of God over which Christ is the Son is in complete agreement with the rest of Hebrews. Heb 11:39-40 and 12:22-24 indicate that those who lived before Christ also enter God's heavenly homeland only through him. Thus, when

---

cisive for the future words that God would speak "in one who is Son" (1:1), who is immediately mentioned in v. 6a (Auffret, "Essai," 385). This interpretation detracts nothing from the faithfulness of Moses.

56. Swetnam argues that the words cited in 9:20 by which Moses established the Old Covenant bear witness to Christ's words of institution in the eucharist (James Swetnam, "Τῶν λαληθησομένων in Hebrews 3,5," *Bib* 90 [2009]: 93-100). Aside from other objections, this interpretation is far too restrictive. *All* that Moses did in establishing the old order bears witness to what God has spoken through the incarnation, obedience, suffering, and exaltation of the Son. That is why the old system is such a good type and foreshadowing of the new.

57. Thus, *pace* Grässer, "Mose und Jesus," 5, the contrast between the Son and Moses is significant for the doctrinal sections yet to come. However, as noted above, this contrast has little influence on the immediately following discussion of the wilderness generation (3:7–4:11). The Son may be superior to Moses, but the present people of God are one with the wilderness generation.

58. Verse 6b concludes the argument of these verses and is closely joined to what has gone before by the relative pronoun οὗ, "whose" (Auffret, "Essai," 382).

59. Ellingworth, 196. Nor is there any reason to take the "house" over which Christ is the "Son" in 3:6a as God's heavenly dwelling (*pace* James W. Thompson, *The Beginnings of Christian Philosophy* [CBQMS 13; Washington, DC: The Catholic Biblical Association of America, 1982], 92).

v. 14 below reiterates the same truth in more Christological terms, it is in full accord with this verse.[60] Because they are part of the one people of God, the wilderness generation and the faithful of chapter 11 are potent examples for contemporary believers.

In this concluding part of v. 6 the pastor returns to the greatest concern of his sermon (2:1-4), his urgent desire that the people of God persevere. Buist Fanning has made the most compelling case for the position that the author of Hebrews believed in the final perseverance of all true believers.[61] He has argued that this verse is an inferential use of the conditional construction in which a future condition will give evidence of a present reality: their present status as the "house" of God will be evidenced only by their future and final perseverance. He finds the same construction in the parallel exhortation of v. 14. Fanning gives a number of supporting examples for this construction that share two characteristics with v. 6b (and v. 14): first, the "then" clause usually precedes the "if" clause ("whose house we are"; "if we will hold fast . . ."); second, the verb in the "then" clause is present, while the "if" clause refers to the future. Thus, according to this interpretation, the pastor does not believe that those who are truly the people of God can fall away. He realizes, however, that while all those he is addressing may appear to be God's people, some of them are not. Only final perseverance will reveal who were and who were not genuine believers.[62]

While such use of the conditional is possible, the implications that Fanning would draw fit neither the larger nor the immediate context of this passage and are insensitive to the author's pastoral strategy. First, contrary to what Fanning maintains elsewhere in support of his position, the pastor *never* suggests that the full adequacy of Christ as Savior *guarantees* the perseverance of true believers.[63] On the contrary, his adequacy provides the sufficient *means* for them to persevere and the all-compelling *reason* for them to give

60. Verse 14 reads "for we have become partakers in Christ" instead of "whose household we are."

61. Buist M. Fanning, "A Classical Reformed View," in *Four Views on the Warning Passages in Hebrews,* ed. Herbert W. Bateman IV (Grand Rapids: Kregel, 2007), 172-219. See also Bruce, 94; Hughes, 138; George Guthrie, 134-36; and O'Brien, 135-36.

62. Fanning, "Classical Reformed," 207-18.

63. Fanning ("Classical Reformed," 197-99, esp. 198) cites Christ's permanent priesthood and consequent ability to save "forever" in 7:25 as an example of Hebrews' affirming the perseverance of believers. Yet he neglects to note that this benefit is specifically for "those who are drawing near to God through him." The present participle "drawing near" (προσερχομένους) describes an ongoing activity co-terminus with the receipt of Christ's benefits. The pastor seems to be concerned lest they cease to draw near and thus cease to receive the salvation Christ provides. Compare the exhortations to "draw near" (προσερχώμεθα) in 4:16 and 10:22. Fanning's neglect of this present tense verb is surprising in light of his close attention to syntax in Heb 3:6b.

diligence thereunto. Furthermore, Fanning must minimize the many and pervasive ways in which the pastor addresses his hearers in the strongest terms as true Christian believers.[64] What could be clearer than "brothers and sisters, holy ones, partakers of the heavenly calling" at the beginning of this chapter? They are members of God's "house" and "partakers of Christ" (3:14). They are Christ's "brothers and sisters" (1:11) and "children" (1:13), the "seed of Abraham" (1:16) who have a "great high priest over the household of God" (4:14; cf. 8:1) and "confidence to enter the holy place through the blood of Jesus" (10:19). They have been "enlightened," experienced the "heavenly gift," and become "sharers in the Holy Spirit" (6:4). They have experienced "the goodness of the word of God and the powers of the age to come" (6:5).[65] These are the people that the pastor urges in equally strong terms to persevere lest they suffer ultimate loss. The urgency of the author's exhortation assumes a surreal character if those who were already true believers inevitably would, and those who were only apparent believers inevitably would not, persevere.[66]

Guthrie, among others, confirms the force of this argument against Fanning's position by acknowledging that the pastor clearly describes *all* of his hearers as true believers in danger of failing to persevere, but takes refuge in the author's admission of ignorance as to their true spiritual condition. The author supposedly acknowledges this limitation when he says that he is "persuaded" of better things concerning them (6:8).[67] The fact, however, that the pastor does not know with certainty the spiritual condition of his hearers (what pastor does?) in no way implies that he believed some of them were true believers who would inevitably persevere while others were not genuine and thus inevitably would fall away.[68] Furthermore, the pastor did not say that he was "persuaded" of better things concerning them in order to affirm his ignorance but in order to encourage their perseverance. There is simply no positive evidence in the text of Hebrews that the pastor held such a view. Furthermore, this position introduces dissonance into the immediate context. The pastor clearly implies that Moses was a "steward" in the household or

64. Fanning, "Classical Reformed," 178-80.

65. Osborne comments, "The descriptions are incredibly powerful portrayals of real Christian experience" (Grant R. Osborne, "A Classical Arminian View," in *Four Views on the Warning Passages in Hebrews,* ed. Herbert W. Batemann IV [Grand Rapids: Kregel, 2007], 128; cf. also pp. 89-90).

66. For a more comprehensive evaluation of Fanning see my response to him on pp. 233-45 of the same volume in which his work appeared.

67. George Guthrie, 136.

68. The gratuitousness of this argument is demonstrated by the fact that it could be used to nullify *any* exhortation that seemed to imply believers could lose their eternal salvation.

people of God, which, in his time, consisted of the wilderness generation. However, since that generation was the example par excellence of those who do not persevere, they were obviously, on this proposed interpretation, never truly a part of God's people.

Both the order of the clauses in v. 6b and the selection of tenses are best explained on the basis of the immediate context and the author's pastoral intent. The "then" or result clause comes first, "whose house we are," in order to identify the hearers with the people of God discussed in 3:1-6. The conditional clause, "if we hold fast . . . ," follows in order to introduce the Kadesh rebellion of the Moses-led generation presented in 3:7-19 as the premier example of failure to hold fast.[69] The pastor omits the phrase "firm until the end" from v. 6 because he is about to describe that generation's failure to persevere. The inclusion of this phrase in v. 14 anticipates the endurance of the faithful that will dominate Heb 10:32–12:13.[70]

This construction with its selection of tenses reflects the pastor's concern with both the present and future dimensions of salvation. The pastor uses the present tense to describe what his hearers are now through the word of God ("whose house we are") as motivation for the appeal implicit in the contingent subjunctive ("if we hold fast"). This approach is in complete accord with the way he describes the privileges now theirs in Christ (note the "we have" in 4:14, 15; 10:19) as motivation for the perseverance necessary to receive final salvation (9:28). Furthermore, there is nothing that prevents taking the aorist subjunctive of the conditional clause, "if we hold fast," as a reference to the act of holding fast *per se* rather than as the completion of one's perseverance: "whose house we are (and continue to be) by virtue of the fact that we hold fast."[71]

In a similar way, the assumption that the hearers already have "boldness" and "boasting of the hope" to which they can hold reflects both the present and future dimensions of the life of faith to be described in Heb 11:1-40. First, through the work of Christ believers have been given "boldness" for present entrance into God's presence in order to receive grace necessary for

---

69. κατάσχωμεν, "let us hold fast," occupies the final emphatic position in the Greek sentence in anticipation of the example to be introduced in the following verses.

70. Thus although many early and widespread manuscripts include μέχρι τέλους βεβαίον, "firm until the end," in v. 6, its omission is substantiated by both authorial and scribal probability. In line with his focus on the wilderness generation, the author would be most likely to omit this phrase. However, in accord with v. 14, copyists would be most likely to supply its lack. See *TCGNT*, 595.

71. Thus this construction would represent a present general condition with a constative, rather than a culminative, aorist in the protasis ("if" clause). For a discussion of the present general condition see Wallace, *Beyond the Basics*, 696-99; of the constative aorist, 557-58.

perseverance (4:14-16; 10:19-25).[72] This "boldness" is not a mere feeling but the right or privilege of access to God provided and validated by Christ's high priesthood as described in 8:1–10:18. The grace regularly received through this access enables believers to boldly live their profession of Christ before an unbelieving world.[73] Second, they are to maintain their "boasting" in the "hope" of that future which will be theirs through Christ at his return (see 9:27-29; 12:25-29). This promised hope is of vital importance and is certain (see 6:11, 18; 7:19, and esp. 10:23). To "boast" in this future hope is the opposite of halfhearted belief. It denotes a life lived with a robust faith in God's future reward rather than in pursuit of the temporal, visible rewards offered by the present world. Contemporary believers are to live trusting in the present power of God, now more available than ever through Christ, and relying upon his promise of the future eternal reward in store for those who persevere (see comments on 11:1, 3, and 6). The following example of the wilderness generation further clarifies the nature and importance of this "holding fast" by describing the sin and fate of those who failed to persevere.

2. Avoid the Company of the Faithless Generation (3:7-19)

7 *Therefore, as the Holy Spirit says: "Today, if his voice you hear,* 8 *do not harden your hearts as in the rebellion, according to the day of testing in the wilderness,* 9 *where your fathers tested me with proving and saw my works* 10 *for forty years. Therefore, I was angry with this generation and said: They always go astray in heart, and they have not known my ways.* 11 *As I swore in my anger: 'They shall not enter my rest.' "*

12 *Be alert, brothers and sisters, lest there be in any of you an evil heart of unbelief through turning away from the living God.* 13 *But exhort one another day by day, while it is called "today," so that none of you might be hardened by the deceit of sin —* 14 *for we have become participants in Christ, if we hold the beginning of our steadfastness firm until the end —*

15 *while it is said: "Today, if you hear his voice, do not harden your hearts as in the rebellion."* 16 *For who, although they had heard, rebelled? Was it not all those who came out of Egypt through Moses?* 17 *And with whom was he "angry for forty years"? Was it not those who sinned? Whose corpses fell in the desert?* 18 *And concerning*

---

72. See Attridge, 112. For the use of παρρησία for boldness in approaching God see Philo, *Heir* 5–7; Josephus, *Ant.* 2.52; 5:38; and Lane, 1:79.
73. For this understanding of παρρησία, "boldness," see S. B. Marrow, "*Parrhēsia* and the New Testament," *CBQ* 44 (1982): 440-41.

whom did he "swear that they shall not enter into" his "rest," if not those who disobeyed? 19 *Thus we see that they were unable to enter in because of unbelief.*

Psalm 95:7-11 facilitated the pastor's desire to use the rebellion of the wilderness generation at Kadesh-Barnea (Num 13:1–14:45) as a warning against unfaithfulness.[1] The psalmist had already urged the people of God not to imitate the disobedience of their ancestors at Kadesh. Thus instead of beginning with Num 13:1–14:45, the pastor expounds the ready-made exhortation in this psalm, first as a warning against imitating the wilderness generation (Heb 3:7-19), then as encouragement to enter the blessing that generation forfeited (4:1-11).[2] The urgency of 4:11 highlights the warning character of the entire exposition.[3]

The exposition in 3:7-19 may be divided into three interrelated subsections: (1) the quotation of Ps 95:7-11 in vv. 7-11; (2) an initial interpretive application centering on the words "today," "heart," and "harden" in vv. 12-14;[4] and (3) an additional interpretation of the "rebellion" and its consequences in vv. 15-19. Verses 12-14 clarify the nature of the wilderness generation's sin and give instructions on how to avoid their downfall. Verse 14 expands the exhortation of v. 6.[5] Verse 15 reintroduces the citation of Ps 95:7, ending with the word "rebellion." Verses 16-19 expound this term showing the magnitude and consequences of the wilderness sin with a view toward deterring the hearers from a similar course. The author begins his explanation (vv. 12-19) by urging his hearers to "see" or give attention to what he would say. He concludes by telling them what they do "see" from the example of the wilderness generation — the awful consequences of unbelief.[6] The reader who would better understand the way in which the pastor's interpretation of Ps 95:7-11 is an integral part of his overall approach to the OT should consult

1. Use of the wilderness generation/Kadesh rebellion as the quintessential example of disobedience had a long history, both within the Bible and in Second Temple Judaism — Num 23:7-13; Deut 1:19-25; 9:33; Pss 95:7-11; 106:24-26; Neh 9:15-17; CD 3:6-9; *4 Ezra* 7:105; 1 Cor 10:1-12 (Weiss 256-57, nn. 11, 12; Lane, 1:85). The author of Hebrews, however, does not evince the particular influence of any other source, but has adapted the widespread use of this example to his own purposes.

2. See Laansma, *Rest Motif,* 283, 288-89.

3. In light of 4:11, Weiss correctly characterizes this entire exposition of Psalm 95 as "warning" (255-56).

4. In vv. 12-14 God's address to Israel has been applied directly to the addressees of Hebrews (Weiss, 254).

5. Ellingworth, 225.

6. Note βλέπετε, a second person plural imperative, "See!" in v. 12; βλέπομεν, "we see," in v. 19. In order to capture this nuance of concern we have translated the first of these verbs, βλέπετε, as "be alert."

174

the discussion of this text in the section of the introduction to this commentary entitled "The Sermon's Use of the OT."

7 The pastor uses Ps 95:7b-11 to support and explain the implied exhortation of v. 6.[7] "Therefore," if you would "hold fast" your "boldness," as instructed in v. 6, "do not harden your hearts" (v. 8). "As the Holy Spirit" even now "says" marks this psalm as the direct and unavoidable address of God to the hearers in the present.[8] "If you hear his voice" is rich in meaning. In one sense the recipients of Hebrews have, indeed, heard God's voice. This hearing is the occasion for choice between faithful action and heart-hardening disobedience.[9] Yet in the Greek of the psalm this clause is a contingent condition and thus an invitation to obey God's word. In this sense "hearing" his voice is synonymous with obedience and the opposite of hardening one's heart. "If you will hear his voice" is an appeal not to imitate the wilderness generation who rebelled at Kadesh, and whom God therefore condemned as those who "have not obeyed my voice."[10]

8 The most striking difference between the Greek version of this psalm as quoted in Hebrews and the Hebrew OT occurs in Ps 95:8. Note how

---

7. διό, "therefore," connects the exhortation in v. 8, μὴ σκληρύνητε, "do not harden your hearts," and thus the whole psalm, with v. 6 (Weiss, 258, n. 18; cf. Lane, 1:84; Ellingworth, 217; O'Brien, 140, n. 83). Riggenbach's (84-85) contention that the psalm is a parenthesis and that διό, "therefore," connects v. 12 to v. 6 is artificial (cf. Hofius, *Katapausis*, 127, n. 785). The pastor would not introduce this psalm of exhortation as the very word of God addressed to his hearers in the present and not include it as part of his own exhortation.

8. However, Emmrich introduces a distinction foreign to Hebrews when he contends that the author is referring to the Spirit's present role as the one addressing the hearers through Scripture to the virtual *exclusion* of his role as Scripture's author (M. Emmrich, "Pneuma in Hebrews: Prophet and Interpreter," *WTJ* 63 [2002]: 55-71; Martin Emmrich, *Pneumatological Concepts in the Epistle to the Hebrews: Amtscharisma, Prophet, and Guide of the Eschatological Exodus* [Lanham, MD: University Press of America, 2003], 27-32). As noted above, the pastor maintains a strong sense of continuity between the people of God old and new. The pastor can address this psalm of exhortation to his hearers because they are part of the one people of God to whom the psalm was originally directed. "Today" is always the time of urgent obedience for God's people (cf. Deut 4:1, 2, 26; 5:32; 6:2; Josh 24:17). The warnings God gave his people of old are not vitiated or replaced but only intensified by the coming of Christ (cf. 2:1-4 and comments on 12:18-21). Thus, it is misleading that Emmrich, "Pneuma in Hebrews," 58, calls the pastor's use of this psalm a "new oracle," even if "today" has been colored by the pastor's conviction that these are the "last days" (1:1).

9. Bénétreau, 1:158-59, calls this "hearing" of God's word the temporal and logical condition for hardening/not hardening the heart through disobedience/obedience.

10. Compare οὐκ εἰσήκουσάν μου τῆς φωνῆς, "they have not obeyed my voice" (Num 14:22), with ἐὰν τῆς φωνῆς αὐτοῦ ἀκούσητε, "if you hear his voice" (Ps 95:7b/Heb 3:7b).

the NRSV translates this verse: "Do not harden your hearts, as at Meribah, as on the day at Massah in the wilderness" (cf. Ps 95:8 in the ESV, RSV, NASB, and NIV). As is his custom, however, the author of Hebrews follows the LXX: "Do not harden your hearts, as in the rebellion, as in the day of testing in the wilderness" (Ps 95:8 in Heb 3:8). By transliterating the Hebrew terms our English versions retain "Meribah" and "Massah" as the place names found in Exod 17:1-7, but lose the significance of their meaning. On the other hand, Hebrews, following the LXX, retains the meaning of these terms by translating them as "rebellion" and "testing," but loses their local significance.

According to Exod 17:1-7, Moses gave the names "Meribah" ("rebellion") and "Massah" ("testing") to the place in the wilderness of Rephidim where the people "rebelled" and "tested" God soon after leaving Egypt. Because the people lacked water, they said, "Is the LORD among us or not?" (Exod 17:7b). After refusing to enter the Promised Land at Kadesh-Barnea (Num 14:1-12), the people again complained for lack of water, as recorded in Num 20:10-13. The place of this complaint is not given a new name but waters there supplied are called "the waters of Meribah" because of the people's rebellion. Thus those who read Psalm 95 in Hebrew would have recognized a reference to the "Meribah" and "Massah" of Exod 17:1-7, but only an echo of the "waters of Meribah" from Num 20:10-13.[11] They would have known not only that "Meribah" and "Massah" meant "rebellion" and "testing" but that they were the names Moses gave to the place of the people's rebellion soon after leaving Egypt.

Yet even in Hebrew the focus of this psalm was not on the event recorded in Exod 17:1-7, but on the refusal of the wilderness generation to enter the promised "rest" at Kadesh-Barnea as described in Num 14:1-45 and Deut 1:19-46.[12] "Swore in my wrath" is a clear echo of Deut 1:34: "And the LORD . . . was angered, and he swore."[13] It was after Kadesh that God swore this oath by which the rebellious generation was permanently excluded from

---

11. *Pace* P. E. Enns, "Creation and Re-Creation: Psalm 95 and Its Interpretation in Hebrews 3:1–4:13," *WTJ* 55 (1993): 265-66, the parallel character of Hebrew poetry detracts nothing from the fact that "Meribah" ("rebellion") and "Massah" ("testing") taken together recall Exod 17:1-7 rather than Num 20:10-13.

12. See the introduction to 3:1–4:13 (pp. 153-57), Lane, 1:85, and many others. Enns, "Re-Creation," 266, agrees. The psalm clearly does not concern God's refusal to let Moses and Aaron enter the land (Num 20:12; Deut 1:37), as suggested by Hofius, *Katapausis,* 33-35. That refusal referred to only two people and was accompanied neither by an oath nor by the strong condemnation evidenced in Ps 95:7-11. See Leschert, *Hermeneutical Foundations,* 158, 161.

13. Psalm 95:11, "I swore (שׁבע) in my wrath (באפי)," echoes Deut 1:34: "And the LORD . . . was angered (קצף), and he swore (שׁבע)."

God's "rest." The "hardening of the heart" by "testing" and "trying" God (Ps 95:8-9) better describes Kadesh than an earlier event for which the people suffered no reprisal.[14] Furthermore, the forty-year wandering was the direct result of the sin at Kadesh (Num 14:33-34).[15]

The LXX translators have retained and clarified this focus on Kadesh-Barnea.[16] It would have been almost impossible to have expressed the descriptive significance of "Meribah" and "Massah" while maintaining the geographical allusion present in the Hebrew text.[17] The LXX translators chose in accord with the psalmist's main emphasis when they translated these terms as descriptions of the wilderness generation's behavior.[18] The event recorded in Exod 17:1-7 sets the direction for their subsequent behavior and thus these names aptly described the course of their journey that climaxed in the rebellion at Kadesh. The psalm reverses the Exodus 17 order, putting "Meribah" ("rebellion") first in order to emphasize the gravity of the people's actions.[19]

14. See Laansma, *Rest Motif,* 263.

15. Leschert, *Hermeneutical Foundations,* 161.

16. Vanhoye shows many other connections between the Greek translation of this psalm and Numbers 14 as well as between Hebrews' interpretation and Numbers 14 (Vanhoye, "Longue marche," 10-11, 16-17).

17. In modern English one could try to bring out the place-name significance of these terms by capitalization: "Do not harden your hearts as at Rebellion, as on that day at Testing." The LXX translators had no such option. They could maintain these terms as place names by transliterating them as "Meribah" and "Massah," or they could communicate their meaning by translating them as "rebellion" and "testing." They chose the latter. As a result of this choice these terms have lost all association with the place of the people's rebellion in Exod 17:1-7 (Vanhoye, "Longue marche," 9-26). περιπικρασμός ("rebellion," Ps 95:8/Heb 3:8) appears nowhere else in the Greek OT (Vanhoye, "Longue marche," 13-14). Nor is πειρασμός ("testing," Ps 95:8/Heb 3:8) used elsewhere to translate "Massah." The cognate verb form, however, πειράζω ("to test"), is often used to describe Israel's persistent and characteristic disobedience in the wilderness. "The day of testing" is clearly a reference to the time, not the place, of an event (Vanhoye, "Longue marche," 15-16). "Where your fathers tested me" (Ps 95:9) is probably a reference to Num 14:22, where God speaks of the rebellion at Kadesh as the climactic tenth time of their testing him (cf. Vanhoye, "Longue marche," 14, 16-17).

18. The LXX consistently brings out the character of Israel's conduct in the wilderness by the way it translates the place names commemorating the people's disobedience. Compare Deut 6:16 in the Oxford translation of the LXX and in the NRSV translation of the Hebrew text: "You shall not tempt the Lord your God, as you tempted in the Temptation" (Deut 6:16 LXX); "Do not put the LORD your God to the test, as you tested him at Massah" (Deut 6:16 NRSV). Note also Deut 9:22: "And at the Burning also and at the Temptation and at the Graves of Lust, you were provoking the Lord your God" (Deut 9:22 LXX); "At Taberah also, and at Massah, and at Kibroth-hattaavah, you provoked the LORD to wrath" (Deut 9:22 NRSV).

19. Leschert, *Hermeneutical Foundations,* 155.

"Rebellion" appropriately describes the magnitude of the Kadesh event as the climax of their disregard for God.

This responsible choice by the Greek translators was doubly helpful in Hebrews' appropriation of the psalm. First, the removal of any allusion to place names gave the clear reference to Kadesh-Barnea in Ps 95:11 rightful dominance.[20] Second, translating "Meribah" as "rebellion" forcefully exposed the heinousness of the wilderness generation's conduct and thus strengthened the impact of the pastor's warning. This term fits those whom God described in Num 14:35 as "this wicked congregation congregated against me."[21] Their refusal to trust God's power and promise at Kadesh was the fatal climax of a history of disobedience.[22]

9-10 Mention of the forty-year period that those who came out of Egypt under Moses spent in the wilderness introduces consideration of the one significant way in which Hebrews' quotation of this psalm differs from the received LXX version.[23] The standard Greek translation lacks the "therefore" in v. 10. In this regard it conforms to the Hebrew original. The addition of this "therefore" appears to rearrange the relationship between the clauses of Ps 95:9-10 as quoted in Heb 3:9-10.[24] Compare the translations of these two verses as they occur in the received LXX and then with the addition of "therefore" in Hebrews:

20. The self-evident nature of the reference to Kadesh in Ps 95:7b-11 is attested not only by the LXX translation, but also by rabbinic literature and by the Targums (see Hofius, *Katapausis*, 42-47).

21. This translation brings out the wordplay between συναγωγῇ ("congregation") and ἐπισυνεσταμένη ("gather/congregate against") in the expression τῇ συναγωγῇ τῇ πονηρᾷ ταύτῃ τῇ ἐπισυνεσταμένῃ ἐπ᾽ ἐμέ.

22. See Bénétreau, 159-62, and the comments in the introduction to 3:1–4:13 (pp. 153-57) above.

23. Other ways in which his quotation of Psalm 95 differs from the standard LXX text are of little interpretive significance (Weiss, 259). (1) The standard LXX text of Ps 95:9 reads, "where your fathers tested me, proved me (ἐδοκίμασαν), and saw my works." Hebrews reads, "where your fathers tested me with proving (ἐν δοκιμασίᾳ), and saw my works" (variation underlined). Both the verb δοκιμάζω ("to prove, test") and the instrumental use of the related noun, δοκιμασία ("proving, testing"), emphasize the seriousness of the people's offense before God. Note Attridge's (115) comment: "In any case it ['with proving'] reinforces the note of accusation in the original text, since δοκιμασία has connotations of close and even skeptical scrutiny." Some translations, such as the NRSV and the ESV, omit "by proving" as superfluous and awkward in English. (2) Hebrews' use of "this" (ταύτῃ) generation in v. 10 instead of the LXX "that" (ἐκείνῃ) generation facilitates contemporary application of the wilderness warning. (3) Mere difference in spelling separates the second aorist of Heb 3:10, εἶπον, "I said," from εἶπα, the second aorist with first aorist ending found in the LXX.

24. Weiss, 259-60.

Ps 95:10-11 according to the LXX:
. . . where your fathers tested me, proved me, and saw my works. *For forty years* I was angry with that generation and said, "They always go astray in their hearts, and they have not known my ways."

Ps 95:10-11 according to Heb 3:9-10:
. . . where your fathers tested me with proving and saw my works *for forty years*. **Therefore**, I was angry with this generation and said, "They always go astray in their hearts, and they have not known my ways."

Without "therefore," "for forty years" (in italics) qualifies the following clause, as indicated by the underlining in the first translation above: "*For forty years* I was angry with this generation." This interpretation is in accord with the Pentateuchal understanding of the forty-year wilderness period as the time of divine judgment. It is also in accord with the pastor's interpretation of this verse in v. 17 below. When, however, "therefore" is added, the forty-year period qualifies the preceding clause, "and saw my works *for forty years.*"

Verse 17 below suggests that the pastor knew and interpreted this psalm in its standard form without the "therefore." This supposition is reinforced by the fact that this "therefore" does not occur in any known witness to the LXX.[25] Although the pastor appears to make few changes when quoting the OT text, he is not above minor interpretive paraphrases.[26] It is very possible, then, that he has purposefully inserted this "therefore" with the intention of stressing the causal connection between the people's "testing" God in v. 9a and the divine anger in v. 10a.[27] He would warn his hearers that such

25. Weiss, 260. This evidence, however, is qualified by the fact that Heb 10:30 and Rom 12:19 may follow an elsewhere unattested textual variant of Deut 32:35 LXX (Ellingworth, 542).

26. It is true, as Leschert, *Hermeneutical Foundations,* 191, n. 71, notes, that the author tends to cite a longer passage accurately and then treat it a bit more freely when he interprets it. Note, for instance, Jer 31:31-34, first quoted in Heb 8:8-12, then interpreted in 10:16-17; and Ps 40:6-8, quoted in 10:5-7 and expounded in 10:8-9. Yet the addition of διό ("therefore") is a very minor change comparable with the possible adaptations made by the pastor in the quotation of Ps 45:6-8 in 1:8-9, and even with variations in the quotation of Jer 31:31-34 in 8:8-12.

27. Riggenbach, 82-83. Others agree that the pastor is probably responsible for the insertion of διό ("therefore"), though evaluations of its significance vary (Attridge, 115; Lane, 1:88-89; O'Brien, 143; McCullough, "Old Testament Quotations," 371; and Docherty, *Old Testament,* 138). *Pace* Docherty, *Old Testament,* 138, 186, διό ("therefore") does not divide Psalm 95 into two distinct quotations. By its very meaning this term welds these clauses more closely together (see McCullough above).

refusal to trust God through disobedience *inevitably* brings the divine displeasure! The psalmist himself has already arranged his material in order to make this connection. Note that vv. 10 and 11 are in reverse chronological order. God actually "swore" that they would not enter his "rest" (v. 11) *before* he was angry with them "for forty years" (v. 10). This reversal, however, allows the psalmist to bring the anger of God (v. 10) into closer association with the faithlessness of the wilderness generation (v. 9). It also allows him to end his exhortation most powerfully with the oath of God by which the disobedient were excluded from God's rest.

Furthermore, the association of "for forty years" with the preceding "saw my works" can also be understood as reinforcing the same connection between wilderness-like disobedience and the threat of divine judgment.[28] The "works" of v. 9b ("and saw my works") are usually identified with the mighty works by which God delivered his people from Egypt and/or sustained them in the wilderness. This reading accords well with both the Hebrew and the standard (without the "therefore") Greek versions of the psalm: in both, v. 9 can be rendered, "when your fathers tested me . . . although they saw my works."[29] Thus the alternate reading brought about by the addition of "therefore" — they "saw my [God's] works for forty years" — has led some to suggest that the pastor believed in a forty-year period before the rebellion at Kadesh-Barnea during which the people experienced God's mighty "works" of deliverance/sustenance.[30] This supposition, however, is highly

28. Riggenbach, 83-84; Docherty, *Old Testament*, 138; and McCullough, "Old Testament Quotations," 371, suggest that the addition of διό ("therefore") identifies the forty years not only with the time of God's mighty "works" but also with the time of the people's disobedience: "they both tested me and saw my works for forty years." It is true that the wilderness generation continued to disobey God during the forty years that followed their exclusion from God's "rest" at Kadesh in Num 14:1-45. One need look no further than their complaints in Num 20:10-13 and 21:4-9 and the sin at Baal Peor in Num 25:1-15. The pastor's emphasis, however, is on the rebellion at Kadesh as the climax of previous disobedience and thus as the incident that brought definitive retribution.

29. The concessive nature of the Hebrew original is clear in most English translations of Ps 95:9: "your ancestors tested me . . . *though* they had seen my work" (NRSV, italics added). Since the people had seen God's mighty works of deliverance, they should not have "tested" him. The LXX translates the Hebrew גַּם, "though" or "although," as καί, usually translated as "and": "your fathers tested me . . . *and* they saw my works" (italics added). It is possible, however, for καί to have the sense of "although." See Bénétreau, 1:163. Cf. Weiss, 259.

30. Bruce, 99 n. 57, suggests that the pastor saw a typological relationship between the exodus, the forty-year wilderness wandering, and Kadesh on the one hand and Christ's death, a forty-year period, and the supposed imminent destruction of Jerusalem on the other. In addition to Qumran sources, he refers to the interpretation of Ps 95:10 in the Babylonian Talmud, *Sanhedrin* 99a, as a prophecy that the Messianic time would last

unlikely. Both this psalm itself and the way it is used by Hebrews threaten the hearers with judgment. Heb 3:7-19 ends with the bodies of the disobedient falling in the wilderness (v. 17). It is more probable that the pastor identified God's "works" not only with his acts of wilderness sustenance but also, perhaps even predominantly, with God's acts of judgment.[31] Thus one might render this verse, "when your fathers tested me . . . and [as a result] saw my works [of judgment] for forty years." This interpretation retains the identification of the forty years with the time of God's displeasure and reinforces again the certain causal link inherent in this psalm between human infidelity and God's wrath. Thus this "therefore," whether added by the pastor or found in the text he quotes, serves both directly, and by the way it rearranges the clauses of these verses, to reinforce the certainty, already present in the psalm, that divine displeasure will fall upon God's people who deliberately spurn his promise. Let the hearers awake from any lethargy that might lead them to such disobedience.

11 Both the pastor, and the psalmist he quotes, end most powerfully with God's oath that makes the exclusion of the unfaithful absolutely certain.[32]

---

for forty years. Enns, "Re-Creation," 273-75, on the other hand, thinks that the pastor is intentionally differentiating the forty-year period of his hearers from that of the wilderness generation. His hearers are experiencing a period of blessing in Christ (v. 10); the wilderness generation experienced forty years of judgment (v. 17). The pastor, however, gives no clear indication that he would establish a parallel between two forty-year periods. Connections with contemporary sources that speak of an end-time forty-year period are tenuous. See Spicq, 2:74; Attridge, 115; and Moffatt, 45, for further discussion and references. Enns's suggestion, in particular, fails to account for the fact that the pastor is committed to the unity of the one people of God throughout time. One wonders if the recipients would have recognized that something so subtle as the insertion of διό ("therefore") was intended to distinguish their situation from the forty-years' punishment of the wilderness generation. See O'Brien, 143. *Pace* Hofius, *Katapausis,* 127-30 (cf. Attridge, 115, and Lane, 1:88-89), there is no reason to believe that the author of Hebrews derived two forty-year periods from Ps 95:10 — one of blessing preceding, and one of judgment following, Kadesh.

31. A. Vanhoye, *La structure littéraire de l'épître aux Hébreux* (2nd ed.; Paris: Desclée de Brouwer, 1976), 93-94. The two, of course, are not mutually exclusive. After all, the mighty "works" by which God delivered his people from Egypt were acts of judgment upon the Egyptians. For the wilderness period as a time of experiencing God's wonders see Exod 16:35; Deut 2:7; 8:4; 29:5; Neh 9:21; and Amos 2:10; as a time of suffering his judgment see, in addition to Psalm 95, Num 14:33-34; 32:13; Deut 8:2; Josh 5:6. There is no hint in Hebrews of the wilderness period as a time of Israel's obedience (contrast Hos 2:14-15). The argument that the mighty "works" by which God delivered his people from Egypt, rather than his works of judgment, would form a more appropriate parallel with God's "works" of creation in 4:1-5 (see Attridge, 115, n. 28) or the works that confirmed the gospel in 2:4, cannot override the concerns of the immediate context.

32. Hebrews follows the LXX translation of God's oath in Ps 95:11, "if they

The pastor will use this oath both as the conclusion of his warning (3:17) and as the basis, in 4:1-11 (v. 3), of his assurance that "there remains a Sabbath rest for the people of God" (4:9). This oath that excludes the disobedient finds its counterpart in God's oath to Abraham (6:13-20) that underlies the history of the faithful in 11:1-40 and guarantees that all who persevere will have their place among the "firstborn" who inhabit the "heavenly Jerusalem" (12:22-24). This divine oath to Abraham will be fulfilled because it rests on God's oath to his Son in Ps 110:4. God has sworn that his Son will be an effective and eternal Priest "according to the likeness of Melchizedek" (7:15-16) and thus not merely the Mediator but the "Guarantor" (7:20-22) of a covenant by which God's people have genuine access to the divine presence. Thus God's people can be certain of the fate of the faithless (3:7–4:11), of the sufficiency of Christ (4:14–10:18), and of the destiny of the faithful (11:1-40), because all three truths are guaranteed by nothing less than the divine oath. To live "by faith" (11:2, etc.) is to live in accord with this reality.

12-14 By focusing on "today" (v. 7b; Ps 95:7b) and "do not harden your hearts" (v. 8; Ps 95:8; cf. "they always go astray in heart," v. 10), the pastor makes immediate application of this psalm to his hearers. God's words first spoken long ago address them in the "today" of their present. Now is the time to avoid the example of the wilderness generation who "hardened" their hearts and refused to trust God at Kadesh-Barnea.[33] The conditional statement of v. 14 reiterates the concern of v. 6 and shows that the specific exhortations of vv. 12-13 are given to facilitate the hearers' perseverance.

12 By addressing his hearers as "brothers and sisters" the pastor reminds them that they are part of the family (v. 6) of God acknowledged by the Son as his "brothers and sisters" (2:11-12). The present imperative "be alert" (or "see") bids them practice perpetual vigilance "lest" "an evil heart of unbelief" be present in any of them.[34] The unbelief of the ten spies showed how the faithlessness of a few (Num 14:36-37) could destroy the faith of many by turning their "hearts" away from God (Num 32:9b; Deut 1:28).[35]

---

should enter into my rest," εἰ εἰσελεύσονται εἰς τὴν κατάπαυσίν μου. The "if" clause of an oath requires a "then" clause in which the speaker normally invokes self-destruction: "if so and so, then I will die." Since the speaker of this oath is God, Bénétreau's suggestion is convincing: "If they should enter into my rest, then I would not be the living God" (Bénétreau, 1:163-64).

33. The exhortation not to harden one's heart was often used to warn people against repeating the sins of their ancestors (Neh 9:16-17, 29; 2 Chr 30:8; Jer 7:26; Acts 19:9). See Koester, 255.

34. The present imperative βλέπετε indicates "an enduring consideration: constantly guard . . ." (Spicq, 2:75). See BDAG, 179, and cf. Matt 24:4; Mark 13:5; Luke 21:8; Acts 13:40; 1 Cor 10:12; and Heb 12:25.

35. Thus the pastor is concerned not only that individuals within the church might

Thus the pastor would urge each of them to show familial care for the entire household.

The opposite of "an evil heart of unbelief" is a "true heart" characterized by the "full assurance of faith" (10:22) and thus an obedient heart upon which God has written his laws (8:10; 10:16). The heart against which the pastor warns his people is "evil" because it is characterized and directed by "unbelief."[36] This heart was evidenced when the "evil" wilderness congregation (Num 14:27, 35) refused to believe God at Kadesh-Barnea and thus to obey him (Num 14:11).[37]

"Unbelief" is the most comprehensive description of the sin of the wilderness generation. The pastor begins (v. 12) and ends (v. 19) his warning against following their example with this term. "Unbelief" encompasses disobedience, for it is both the refusal (or willing failure) to trust God and the consequent lack of faithfulness to God.[38] The "unbelief" of the wilderness generation reached breaking point when they refused to enter the land at Kadesh-Barnea. By this act they categorically denied the adequacy of God's power and the validity of his future but imminent promise to give them the "rest" for which they had left Egypt. Unbelief springs from the heart but becomes real in the concrete act of refusal to trust God (3:18). The pastor envisions no faith that does not lead to obedience, nor does he conceive of any obedience that does not stem from faith. The hostility faced by his hearers from unbelieving society precludes the hypocrisy bred when faith in Christ is popular.

The wilderness generation's act of "unbelief" at Kadesh stands in stark contrast to the deeds of the "righteous" in 11:1-38 who lived "by faith."[39] This clear parallel between the "unbelief" of one group and the "faith" of the other suggests that the "rest" lost by the wilderness generation

---

fall, but that their example and influence might cause the whole church, or a large part thereof, to follow the example of the wilderness generation (Hofius, *Katapausis*, 132-33, *pace* Michel, 188). Concern for the whole community and concern for the individuals it contains are mutually reinforcing. These concerns reflect God's own burden for his people (O'Brien, 145, n. 118; Lane 1:86).

36. "Of unbelief" describes the quality of the heart (Lane, 1:82i; Ellingworth, 222).

37. In Jer 16:12 and 18:22 an evil heart characterizes those who deliberately reject God and follow their own devices (O'Brien, 146).

38. Bénétreau, 165, n. 1, is correct when he criticizes those who would divide sharply between the two aspects of ἀπιστία's meaning. In Hebrews it refers first of all to "unbelief," to the refusal to trust God. Such unbelief, however, results in "unfaithfulness" to God's person and direction. In the same way πιστός ("faithful," 3:2. 5) describes the Son and Moses as those who trusted in God and thus were faithful to God.

39. The Greek words translated as "unbelief" (ἀπιστία), "faithful" (πιστός, 3:2, 5), and "faith" (πίστις, throughout 11:1-38) are from the same root.

is to be identified with the eternal "City" (11:10-11; 12:22; 13:14) and heavenly "homeland" (11:13-16) anticipated by the OT faithful. The way in which the pastor has coordinated both groups in his pastoral strategy, as outlined above and in the introduction to this commentary (pp. 65-70) reinforces this impression, as does the fact that both "rest" and "Promised Land" referred to the same reality in the OT.

The significance of an "evil heart of unbelief" is accurately conveyed by the phrase "to fall away from the living God."[40] Nothing less is adequate to describe the deliberate spurning of the power and promises of God through intentional and final disobedience. By this faithless action the people became "rebels against the Lord" (Num 14:9a LXX).[41]

The God of the OT is regularly described as the "living God" because, in contrast to the gods of the nations, he alone acts, demonstrating his power and keeping his word.[42] When the wilderness generation refused to enter the Promised Land, they denied the adequacy of God's power and the certainty of his promises. Thus by their refusal they were acting as if he were not "living." This denial took concrete expression in their question, "Is God among us or not?" (Num 14:11). God began his pronouncement of punishment by saying, "As I live" (Num 14:21, 28).[43] Thus their very exclusion from the land was proof that God was the powerful and trustworthy "living" God. To be without the "living God" is obviously to suffer ultimate loss. The pastor anticipates what he will say about those who "crucify again" (6:6) and "spurn" (10:29) the Son of God.

Thus "to fall away from the living God" is to act in such a way that one definitively rejects the reality of his power and the validity of his prom-

40. The articular infinitive phrase, ἐν τῷ ἀποστῆναι ἀπὸ θεοῦ ζῶντος, "in falling away from the living God" (the Greek infinitive becomes an English gerund) is epexegetical, defining "an evil heart of unbelief" (Ellingworth, 222; Bénétreau, 165; Weiss, 260; Koester, 158; Johnson, 117; O'Brien, 146, n. 125; and MHT, 3:146). *Pace* Spicq, 2:75-76, who thinks the infinitive shows the result of such a heart, "to the point of turning away from the living God." O'Brien, 146, n. 122, notes the similarity of sound that reinforces the connection between the Greek words for "unbelief" (ἀπιστίας) and "falling away" (ἀποστῆναι).

41. Compare ἐν τῷ ἀποστῆναι ἀπὸ θεοῦ ζῶντος ("in falling away from the living God") and Caleb's words in Num 14:9a: ἀλλὰ ἀπὸ τοῦ κυρίου μὴ ἀποστάται γίνεσθε ("but from the Lord do not become rebels"). ἀποστῆναι ("to fall away") is reminiscent of ἀποσταὶ γίνεσθε ("do not become rebels").

42. Weiss, 261-62. See, for example, 2 Kgs 19:4, 16; Isa 37:4, 17; Hos 2:1; Dan 6:21. Hebrews also speaks of the "living" God in 9:14; 10:31; and 12:22. For this expression in ancient Jewish writings see *Jub.* 1:25; 21:4; 3 Macc 6:28; and *Jos. Asen.* 8:5-6; 11:10. The NT makes free use of this OT description of God: Matt 16:16; 26:63; Acts 14:15; Rom 9:26; 2 Cor 3:3; 6:16; 1 Thess 1:9; 1 Tim 3:15; 4:10; and Rev 7:2; 15:7.

43. Cf. Weiss, 261-62.

ises. It is easy, however, to miss the shocking force of this phrase. There is little evidence that the recipients of Hebrews were tempted by idolatry.[44] Nevertheless, if they refuse to live by faith in God's power and in anticipation of his promises, they will be no better off than people who have turned "away from the living God" to worship dead idols.[45]

Nor does this phrase preclude the possibility that the hearers were in danger of abandoning their commitment to Christ by a return to the security and comfort of their pre-Christian Jewish practices.[46] From its opening verses (1:1-3) Hebrews has described Christ as the climax of all God has been doing through his people. Thus, to abandon him is to abandon the whole work of God and to identify with those who worshiped false gods. No amount of pious religious practice can avail for those who reject God's Son.

13 The pastor would give his hearers the antidote to this "evil heart of unbelief."[47] In order to avoid falling victim to its snare he would have them "exhort one another daily while it is called 'today.'" He provides them an example in this sermon, which he is sending them and which he calls a "word of exhortation."[48] The ten spies discouraged God's people from faithful obedience (Num 14:36; cf. Num 32:7, 9; Deut 1:28). The pastor's hearers, however, are to encourage one another in reliance on the power and promises of God. Yet the pastor is also urgent that they warn one another against developing a heart that refuses such trust.[49] Just as God addresses his own with both promises (4:14-16; 10:18-25, etc.) and warnings (2:1-4; 3:12-19; 4:12-13; etc.), so the mutual exhortation practiced by his people must encompass both encouragement to embrace the promises of God and warning lest his benefits be lost through disregard and disobedience.[50] Their mutual concern must not be casual or occasional, but "day by day," a regular and intentional part of their fellowship.[51]

44. See Bénétreau, 1:166, n. 1; Riggenbach, 86; and Weiss, 262.

45. The pastor makes no explicit contrast between the "living God" and idols (see Spicq, 2:75). Nevertheless, he and his hearers were certainly familiar with the way in which this term set God apart from idols both in the OT and in contemporary Jewish and Christian apologetic (see Weiss, 262, n. 31, and references in n. 42 above). It was this connotation that made the expression so appropriate. For examples of "falling away from the living God" as apostasy, see BDAG, 157-58, 2a.

46. *Pace* Weiss, 262. See Bruce, 99-100; Bénétreau, 166, n. 1.

47. The solution in v. 13 stands in contrast to the problem mentioned in v. 12. Note the "but" with which this verse begins (Ellingworth, 223).

48. See λόγος τῆς παρακλήσεως (Heb 13:22). Riggenbach, 87.

49. Ellingworth's (223) preference for "comfort" or "encouragement" in light of the broader context (6:18; 10:25; 12:5; 13:19, 22) and the LXX's preferred use of this term miss the urgency of the immediate context.

50. See O'Brien, 148.

51. καθ' ἑκάστην ἡμέραν is a stronger statement than καθ' ἡμέραν (10:25)

The urgency of this mutual warning/encouragement is intensified by the phrase "so long as it is called 'today.'" One cannot presume on the "'today'" of God's speaking. For the obedient the "'today'" of God's invitation lasts until the Judgment (12:25-29) or until their death.[52] However, an ultimate refusal to trust God resulting from a heart hardened through neglectful disobedience may bring an end to this time of opportunity (6:4-8; compare 9:27-28; 10:37-39). The pastor does not want his hearers to join the wilderness generation and thus to repeat their irreversible exclusion from God's "rest."[53]

The experience of the wilderness generation would suggest that the heart is "hardened" by repeated failure to trust and obey until people become so callous to God's voice that they refuse to heed his call.[54] "Sin," singular, is a besetting (12:1-2) power that deceives by causing people to see only the things of this world and not the invisible-to-the-human-eye possibilities of God.[55] This is exactly what happened to the wilderness generation.[56] They allowed the vision of Canaanite power to eclipse the amply demonstrated greatness of their God.[57] Thus, intimidated by the might of the land's inhabitants, Egyptian slavery seemed better than the promises of God (Num 14:1-4). As a result the wilderness generation refused to act with faith in God's power to overcome their enemies and with assurance in God's promise to give them the land. At its best sin gives only short-lived pleasure (11:25) before resulting in death (3:17).

(Ellingworth, 223). Thus it expresses the urgency of the exhortation but provides no sufficient grounds for assuming that the community addressed practiced daily meetings (Weiss, 262-63, n. 35; Bénétreau, 1:166; *pace* Windisch, 31; Michel, 188; and Hofius, *Katapausis,* 132).

52. The Syriac version of 10:25 describes "today" as lasting "until the Day of judgment (10:25)" (Koester, 259). See Ellingworth, 224.

53. Lane, 1:87. The pastor is aware that God now speaks his word of invitation through the exalted Son rather than through the prophets (1:1-3). However, in accord with his general emphasis in the interpretation of this psalm, he makes no distinction between the "today" of those who lived before Christ and of those, like his hearers, who live after (1:5). The invitation to obedience has not been changed — only enabled and intensified by the work of Christ. Thus Braun, 85-86, is mistaken when he tries to keep the "today" of Christ's exaltation (1:5) and the "today" of God's address (3:7-19) completely separate because the one is "Christological" and the other "paraenetic."

54. Unbelief is the origin, essence, and effect of this hardening (Riggenbach, 88).

55. Weiss, 263, compares this passage with Paul's reference to "sin" as a power in Rom 7:11. Cf. Riggenbach, 87. Sin deceives by offering something as more valuable, certain, and easily obtained than God's promises.

56. Hughes, 148, sees a reference here to the serpent deceiving Eve in the garden (cf. 1 Tim 2:14).

57. See Riggenbach, 81-82.

The pastor does not write so that his hearers will ask, "Have I been hardened and thus irrevocably lost God's rest?"[58] He writes, "Lest any of you be hardened." This phrase is a passive of permission — "Lest any of you allow yourselves to be hardened."[59] He says in effect, "Do not let the powerful opposition of the society around you, or the rewards it would give for conformity, blind you to the reality of God's power and the certainty of his promise so that you abandon him for temporal reward."[60] The deceptive power of sin is not an excuse for disobedience but an urgent call for vigilant resistance. "Instead of allowing sin to make them resistant to the word of God, the listeners are to allow the word of God to make them resistant to sin."[61]

14 The pastor has urged this mutual concern in vv. 12-13 as an aid for the perseverance enjoined in v. 6. He concludes this section of exhortation by returning to that need for perseverance. Such mutual concern is vital to the endurance in faithfulness necessary (v. 14b; cf. v. 6b) for believers to reap the benefits of the privileges they enjoy as described in vv. 6a and 14a.[62] According to v. 6a, the pastor and his hearers are united with the wilderness generation in God's "house." To be, however, part of this "house" over which Christ presides as Son is to be "participants" in Christ (v. 14). Thus calling them "participants in" Christ anticipates the privileges now theirs through Christ's soon-to-be-described high-priestly ministry (4:14-16; 10:19-25) without destroying continuity with the people of old. Although God's faithful OT people did not yet enjoy these privileges while on earth, they now participate in them, for they also are part of the house over which the Son presides.[63] It is as participants in Christ that the people of God from all time will enter the "rest" and heavenly "homeland" anticipated by the OT faithful (11:13-16).

---

58. Many sensitive consciences have been deeply depressed by misunderstanding the pastor's intention. The apostasy he envisions is as definitive and unmistakable as the wilderness generation's refusal at Kadesh. The perpetually unrepentant nature of their rebellion is demonstrated by their subsequent attempt to take the land on their own (Num 14:39-45) and by their behavior during the years of wilderness wandering. As God said, "They always go astray in heart" (Ps 95:10). Those seriously concerned for their spiritual welfare have not "fallen away from the living God."

59. Lane, 1:87.

60. Although it was the Canaanite threat that led to the wilderness generation's disobedience, the allure of earthly good was the occasion for Esau's profanity (12:14-17). For a further discussion of faith see the exposition of 11:1-6 below and Gareth L. Cockerill, "The Better Resurrection (Heb. 11:35): A Key to the Structure and Rhetorical Purpose of Hebrews 11," *TynBul* 51 (2000): 223-26.

61. Koester, 259.

62. For this understanding of "for" (γάρ) in "for we have become," see Bénétreau, 167.

63. See comments on Heb 11:39-40; 12:22-24 below.

The perfect tense of "we have become" describes the present reality that the author and recipients of Hebrews now enjoy in light of the past event of their conversion. When "we" believed we entered into a continuing participation in Christ. Some have translated "participants in" as "partners with." The Greek term can be used to describe business associates who share in a common profit or loss. Thus as "partners with Christ" persevering believers will enter with him into the inheritance of "rest."[64] The context of Hebrews, however, prohibits the restriction of this term to mere partnership. It is certainly no partnership of equals, for the benefits are all provided by Christ but enjoyed by his faithful people.[65] Believers are "participants" or "sharers in Christ" just as they are "participants" or "sharers" in the "heavenly calling" (3:1) and the "Holy Spirit" (6:4).[66] They participate in the Son who brings the "sons and daughters" to glory, who acknowledges them as his "brothers and sisters" and "children," even to the point of "partaking" of their humanity through the incarnation.[67] This is a much more intimate relationship than that depicted by the "house" of God (v. 6).[68] The "great salvation" Christ provides is enjoyed by those who participate in his exalted person at God's right hand (1:13; 8:1).[69] They can be described as "those who are about to inherit salvation" (1:14) because they are united to the one who is "heir of all things" (1:2). There is no salvation apart from union with the one who is its "source" (5:9) and with the "house" (v. 6) over which he presides. With this statement the pastor whets the appetite of his hearers for the fuller description to come of Christ the High Priest in whom they share. How important to maintain one's loyalty to Christ and identity with his people!

64. Bénétreau, 167; Koester, 260; Lane, 1:87; and Riggenbach, 88, would limit this term to the idea of "partners with" Christ.

65. "The egalitarian tone of 'partner' in English makes it less suitable to the point being made by Hebrews" (Johnson, 118).

66. Ellingworth, 227 (cf. Westcott; Hughes; Braun). Compare "for we have become participants in Christ" (μέτοχοι γὰρ τοῦ Χριστοῦ γεγόναμεν, 3:14) with "participants in the heavenly calling" (κλήσεως ἐπουρανίου μέτοχοι, 3:1) and "having become participants in the Holy Spirit" (μετόχους γενηθέντας πνεύματος ἁγίου, 6:4).

67. The noun μέτοχοι, "sharers," is from the same root as the verb used in 2:14 to affirm that the Son "partook" (μετέσχεν) of the humanity of God's people.

68. Weiss, 264. O'Brien, 150, n. 141 (citing Hofius, *Katapausis*, 133, 215, n. 820; Ellingworth, 226; and Koester, 260), notes that 2 Esd 7:28; 14:9 and *1 En.* 104:6 use the word μέτοχοι ("partners," "participants") for the companions of the Messiah and the residents of heaven. It is through being "sharers" in Christ that his followers realize their "heavenly calling" (3:1).

69. See E. Nardoni, "Partakers in Christ (Hebrews 3.14)," *NTS* 37 (1991): 456-72, though it is difficult to see how this participation, as described by Nardoni, is similar to the Platonic participation of the physical world in the reality of the noumenal, as he suggests.

Continuing participation in Christ is dependent upon, and therefore motivation for, the perseverance enjoined by the contingent conditional clause "if only we hold the beginning of our steadfastness firm until the end."[70] There is little support for the subjective reading "confidence" or "assurance" espoused by most English versions in place of "steadfastness" in the translation above.[71] The Greek term in question is often employed to denote the stable or unchanging reality that underlies appearances[72] and thus can be used to describe steadfastness understood as unchanging and therefore dependable resolve and conduct (Josephus, *Ant.* 18.24). Reference to the initial steadfastness evidenced by these believers after their conversion as described in 10:32-35 is well suited to the immediate context. Perseverance in such steadfast faithfulness until death or the return of Christ is the opposite of "falling away" and of the sin and disobedience of the wilderness generation.[73] This steadfastness is more than a reference to the original "frame of mind" espoused by the hearers at conversion.[74] The pastor is not concerned with a mere subjective attitude but with a way of life characterized by the "boldness" of witness to Christ enjoined in 3:6 above. The hearers are to hold their initial steadfastness "firm" because the saving revelation of God upon which it is based is utterly "firm."[75]

The term here translated "steadfastness" is used in 1:3 of the "very being" of God revealed in Christ's provision of "such a great salvation."[76] It is

---

70. Ellingworth, 227, suggests that ἐάνπερ may throw "more emphasis than ἐάν on the following condition." The translation "if only" (cf. NAB) attempts to catch this nuance.

71. "The beginning of our confidence" (NKJV), "our first confidence" (NRSV/RSV), "our original confidence" (ESV), or "the confidence we had at first" (NIV). *Pace* Spicq, 2:77-78, and Riggenbach, 90-91, Ruth 1:12 and Ezek 19:5 provide no support for such an understanding (Helmut Köster, "ὑπόστασις," *TDNT* 8:580-82). "Reality" is a better translation in the first of these references; "plan," in the second. Riggenbach's (90-91) objection to "steadfastness" or "endurance" because it is characteristic of the course but not the beginning of the Christian life is without force.

72. Köster, "ὑπόστασις," *TDNT* 8:580-86.

73. Weiss, 265-66. ὑπόστασις, "steadfastness," "reality," stands in contrast to ἀποστῆναι, "to fall away," in v. 12.

74. Ellingworth's "the confident frame of mind in which you began the life of faith" (228) misses this nuance. Cf. H. Dörrie, "Ὑπόστασις, Wort- und Bedeutungsgeschichte," *Nachrichten (von) der Akademie der Wissenschaften in Göttingen* 3 (1955): 39. The term "steadfastness" describes and gives content to the colorless "basic position we had at the beginning" espoused by Lane, 1:81. Cf. Bénétreau, 168.

75. βεβαία, "firm," is the feminine form of the adjective used to describe the certainty of God's word through the angels in 2:2.

76. Thus Köster, "ὑπόστασις," *TDNT* 8:585-88, argues that all three occurrences of this word (ὑπόστασις) in Hebrews (1:3; 3:14; 11:11) reflect the dualistic way it was used in Middle Platonism to describe the unchanging reality of God and the world of

possible that the pastor intends for it to have the same meaning in this present verse. Note the translation of the NAB: "if only we hold the beginning of the reality firm until the end." According to this understanding, the hearers are urged to hold steadfastly to the reality of God received in Christ at their conversion. This utterly dependable divine reality is, in turn, the foundation of steadfastness and source for the bold witness of 3:6.[77]

15 The pastor strategically reintroduces Ps 95:7. His introductory phrase, "while it is being said," underscores the urgency created by the present time of opportunity.[78] With "Today, if you hear his voice, do not harden your hearts" the pastor would impress his message upon his hearers by providing a final, memorable summary of the exhortation in vv. 12-14. With "as in the rebellion" he announces the dire gravity of the wilderness generation's disobedience that will be the theme of 16-19.[79]

16-19 In light of the wilderness generation's experience of God's grace (v. 16) the refusal at Kadesh-Barnea was justly called a "rebellion" which deserved God's wrath (vv. 17-18) and ultimate exclusion from God's blessing (v. 19). This rebellion (v. 16) is described as "sin" (v. 17), "disobedience" (v. 18), and finally as "unbelief" (v. 19).

The pastor makes skillful use of interrogation in vv. 16-18 to draw his hearers into the concluding statement of v. 19. Verses 16-18 each begin with a rhetorical question that focuses attention on the wilderness generation, the seriousness of their sin, and its dire consequences. In v. 16, and again in v. 17, a second question elicits affirmation of the proper answer to the first. The correct answer to the question in v. 18 is obvious and leads directly to God's exclusion of the wilderness generation due to unbelief as affirmed in v. 19. In this concluding verse the warning reaches its highest pitch in anticipation of what the pastor will say about apostasy in 6:1-8 and 10:26-31.[80] Yet

---

ideas. The clearest evidence for such influence is its use in 1:3 for the "very being" of God. Yet the "very being" of God revealed in the redemption of Christ is utterly unlike the transcendent God of Middle Platonism. Köster's contention that all three usages must be the same is obviously groundless.

77. See Attridge, 119; Johnson, 118.

78. "While it is being said" translates the articular infinitive ἐν τῷ λέγεσθαι. Attridge suggests that this infinitive should be taken as middle and instrumental rather than, as in the translation we have followed, passive and temporal. Thus he would translate it "by saying." The hearers are to warn one another and hold firm to the reality they have received (vv. 12-14) "by saying" to one another the words of the psalm: "Today, if you hear his voice, do not let your hearts be hardened." Attridge, 119-20. This suggestion is interesting but perhaps overly subtle.

79. Thus this verse is both a summary reminder of what has gone before (NASB; NIV; Lane, 1:88) and an introduction to what follows (REB; NJB; Ellingworth, 228; Koester, 261; Weiss, 266; Grässer, 1:192).

80. Lane, 1:89; cf. Hofius, *Katapausis,* 137.

this threat of exclusion forms the backdrop for the promise of entrance to be elaborated in 4:1-11.[81]

16 "For who, although they had heard, rebelled?" picks up "if you hear" and "rebellion" from the beginning and end of Ps 95:7. The pastor is clearly referring to those who disobeyed God at Kadesh-Barnea as recorded in Numbers 14.[82] They had "heard" God's promise that he would bring them into the promised "rest." They refused to heed Caleb's warning (Num 14:9) and "rebelled" against God (cf. Num 14:35). The aorist tense of "rebelled" underscores reference to this specific event. The concessive participle, "although they had heard," emphasizes the culpability of their disobedience.[83] The magnitude of God's promise brought awesome responsibility.

The identification of those who rebelled as "all those who came out from Egypt through Moses" certifies their identity as those who sinned at Kadesh and further accentuates their responsibility. Numbers describes them as "the whole congregation" (Num 14:1, 2, 5, 7, 10) and as "all the sons of Israel" (Num 14:2).[84] God refers to them as "all those who have seen my glory and my signs that I did in Egypt and in the wilderness" (Num 14:22). The fact that they had experienced God's great deeds of deliverance from Egypt and sustenance in the desert carried out through God's "faithful servant" Moses (3:1-6) left them without excuse.[85] God further describes this refusal to trust him as the climax of persistently willful unbelief (Num 14:22). Thus their disobedience at Kadesh deserved both the description of and the punishment due "rebellion." By assenting to the culpability of the wilderness generation the hearers admit their own awesome responsibility. The congregation addressed by the pastor could fall away just as did that "wicked congregation" at Kadesh (Num 14:35).

Many early interpreters have understood this verse as a clarification reminding the hearers that Moses, Aaron, Caleb, and Joshua were not among the rebels: "For some, when they had heard, rebelled, but not all those who came out of Egypt through Moses" (cf. KJV; Douay-Rheims; Geneva Bible). With a mere change in accent the first word of v. 16 can be construed as "some" instead of "who."[86] Nevertheless, the context lends strong support to

---

81. According to Riggenbach, 91, vv. 15-19 bring out the significance of the psalm as warning, and lay the foundation for its use as promise to follow.

82. Hofius, *Katapausis,* 135-36.

83. Taking the participle ἀκούσαντες ("having heard") as concessive (Lane, 1:82r) better suits the context than the temporal rendering of the NASB, "when they had heard," or the attributive interpretation of the NRSV, "Now who were they who heard?"

84. Compare the "all" (πάντες) of Heb 3:16 with "the whole congregation" (πᾶσα ἡ συναγωγή) and with "all the sons of Israel" (πάντες οἱ υἱοὶ Ἰσραηλ).

85. Hughes, 153-54, rightly emphasizes that the people who experienced this great deliverance were the last we would expect to rebel against God.

86. Compare τίνες, "who," with τινές, "some." This interpretation takes the parti-

the interrogative interpretation. The pastor would impress his hearers with the privileges and thus the great culpability of the wilderness generation. He has no concern to remind them of the unnecessary, because commonly known, details about Moses, Aaron, Caleb, and Joshua.[87] The parallelism with vv. 17-18 also supports this understanding.[88] Spicq reminds us that the word translated "some" seldom begins a clause.[89]

17 Like v. 16, vv. 17 and 18 each begin with an interrogative pronoun referring to the wilderness generation — "and with whom" (v. 17); "and to whom" (v. 18).[90] However, God, not the wilderness generation, is the subject of these verses. Verse 16 has described the grace the people had received and the resultant culpability of their rebellion; vv. 17-18 describe God's correspondingly appropriate, but frightening, response to their disobedience at Kadesh. Verse 17, citing Ps 95:10, affirms with absolute certainty the duration and finality of God's wrath. Verse 18, citing Ps 95:11, states the blessing from which God excluded the disobedient.[91]

This verse is an undisputed reference to those who "sinned" (note the aorist tense) at Kadesh-Barnea before the "forty years" of God's wrath (Num 14:33-34) and the subsequent falling of their "corpses in the desert" (Num 14:29, 32).[92] Although God sustained them during this forty-year period, his wrath was unrelenting until the death of the last rebel. Every year was a re-

---

ciple as temporal, "when they had heard." It also construes the οὐ in the second part of the sentence as a simple negative — it "was not all those who came out of Egypt," rather than as indicating a question expecting an affirmative response — it "was all those who came out of Egypt . . . , was it not?"

87. Spicq, 2:78-79; Weiss, 267, n. 12; Riggenbach, 92-93.

88. Attridge, 120, but cf. Ellingworth, 229-30. We have already noted above the way in which vv. 16-18 contain a series of questions. Verses 17 and 18 also begin with a form of τίνες: compare τίνες γάρ (v. 16) with τίσιν δέ (vv. 17, 18).

89. Spicq, 2:78-79. The strongest support for the translation "some" is the ἀλλ' which begins the second clause of v. 16: ἀλλ' οὐ πάντες οἱ ἐξελθόντες ἐξ Αἰγύπτου διὰ Μωϋσέως, "but not all of those who came out of Egypt through Moses." If this sentence is a question, then ἀλλ' must be taken as affirmative or as linking a series of questions without adversative force (Lane, 1:82). Ellingworth, 229-30, provides classical precedents for such usage.

90. Although the English translations differ, vv. 17 and 18 both begin with τίσιν δέ in the Greek text.

91. This verse shows clearly that the author of Hebrews is familiar with the standard LXX reading according to which this forty-year period is the post-Kadesh time of judgment, not a pre-Kadesh time of seeing God's wonders (Ellingworth, 232). See the comments on vv. 9-10 above.

92. The aorist substantive participle τοῖς ἁμαρτήσασιν ("those who sinned") is a clear reference to the sin at Kadesh-Barnea that preceded the forty-year wandering (Ellingworth, 233).

minder of their faithlessness and their forfeited blessing. The wilderness wandering of "those who sinned" did not find its end until "their corpses fell" like those slaughtered in battle. "Fallen corpses" describes a death appropriate for apostates (Isa 66:24).[93] Those who died thus suffered an accursed death (Gen 40:19; Deut 28:26; 1 Kgs 14:11; 21:24; 2 Kgs 9:10, 34-35; Jer 7:33; Ezek 29:5; 2) and were often left unburied (1 Sam 17:46; Lev 26:30). The tragedy of the wilderness generation's fate is made all the more poignant by the fact that, although they "came out of Egypt" bound for "rest," their dead bodies fell in the barren "desert." This awful place of death contrasts with what v. 18 is about to say concerning the blessing from which they were excluded.

18   The oath of God established with absolute certainty the irreversible exclusion of those who "disobeyed" at Kadesh from God's "rest" (Deut 1:34-35).[94] This yet to-be-defined "rest" was the ultimate blessing for which God had redeemed them from Egypt. The pastor directs his hearers' eyes toward the final and tragic consequences of their disobedience in preparation for his warnings against apostasy in 6:1-8 and 10:26-31.

Until now the pastor has been seeking to turn his hearers away from Kadesh-like unfaithfulness. Thus he has concentrated on the seriousness of the offense committed by the wilderness generation. Notice the breadth of vocabulary he has used to describe their conduct — "rebellion" (v. 16), "sin" (v. 17), and "disobedience" (v. 18). He has shown the resulting appropriate divine judgment on their behavior. And yet the very mention of the "rest" from which they were excluded anticipates the blessing God still offers the faithful (4:1). What follows will describe that "rest" as the goal and basis of their hope (4:1-11). Furthermore, the certainty of the divine oath, here established, also undergirds the adequacy of God's provision for entrance into his blessing (6:13-20). His oath (Ps 110:4) has made Christ the absolute "Guarantor" of salvation for those who faithfully persevere (7:20-22). The God who pronounces unremitting judgment on the faithless promises unfailing grace to the faithful.

19   The pastor brings his hearers to the main point and conclusion of the argument in vv. 15-18: the wilderness generation "could not enter in because of unbelief." "Unbelief," first introduced in v. 12 above, is the final description of their "rebellion" (v. 16) and "sin" (v. 17) at Kadesh-Barnea. The penultimate designation of their offense might be "disobedience" (v. 18), but the ultimate and comprehensive description of rebellion against God is "un-

---

93. Koester, 261.

94. Again the aorist participle τοῖς ἀπειθήσασιν ("to those who disobeyed") fits well as a reference to the commission of the specific sin at Kadesh-Barnea punished by God's oath.

belief."[95] As noted above, "unbelief" implies unfaithful behavior. It is rejection of the veracity of God's promises and the reality of his power.[96] Thus it is the source of, implies, and includes the kind of direct, climactic refusal to obey God exercised by the wilderness generation at Kadesh. By concluding this chapter with the word "unbelief" the pastor leaves his warning ringing in the ears of his hearers. The tragic result of this unbelief is stated in the terse phrase, "they could not enter in." The divinely established "could not" was absolute. It received empirical verification by the wilderness generation's failed attempt to enter the land after God's judgment (Num 14:39-45), an action that also confirmed their faithless rebellion.[97]

Some have argued that since the OT is referring only to the loss of physical Canaan the author of Hebrews is threatening the hearers with mere temporal punishment.[98] This argument introduces a distinction between temporal and eternal blessings not present in the OT text. The disobedient wilderness generation lost the entire promise for which they had been delivered from Egypt. By omitting the word "rest" in 3:19 the pastor invites his hearers to ask what it was that the wilderness generation "could not enter."[99] He answers this question in chapter 4 by affirming that the "rest" forfeited by that unfaithful generation as described in 3:15-19 was God's eternal "rest" promised to modern believers.[100] This news serves to encourage his hearers' faith-

95. Note the emphatic position of ἀπιστίαν, "unbelief," at the end of v. 19.

96. "The disobedience which is rebellion against God (4:6, 11) has its ultimate basis in the unbelief which does not trust the goodness and power of God (cf. 3:12)" (Riggenbach, 95, my translation). Cf. Bénétreau, 1:169.

97. Although v. 19, introduced by καὶ βλέπομεν, "and so we see," gives every evidence of bringing vv. 15-18 to a conclusion, the author may also be thinking of Num 14:39-45. Cf. Hofius, *Katapausis*, 137.

98. Cf. T. K. Oberholtzer, "The Warning Passages in Hebrews, Part 2 (of 5 Parts): The Kingdom of Rest in Hebrews 3:1–4:13," *BSac* 145 (1988): 188.

99. "The absolute or elliptical use of εἰσελθεῖν reflects the author's lack of interest in the earthly Promised Land (→ v. 18). He implies that in failing to enter Canaan, the wilderness generation thereby, or *a forteriori,* lost their place in God's final resting-place" (Ellingworth, 236).

100. There is no reason to think that the pastor uses "rest" for the earthly Promised Land in 3:12-19 but for eternal "rest" in 4:1-11, *pace* Leschert, *Hermeneutical Foundations,* 127-37, and Harold W. Attridge, "'Let Us Strive to Enter That Rest': The Logic of Hebrews 4:1-11," *HTR* 73 (1980): 286. Leschert claims that the focus on Kadesh-Barnea in chapter 3 indicates that the pastor's initial concern was with the physical Promised Land. However, the statement that Joshua did not give them "rest" in Heb 4:8 makes it clear that, even for the wilderness generation, this "rest" was no earthly inheritance. Heb 4:11b still has the Kadesh disobedience in view. The pastor had no need to define "rest" when discussing the sin and punishment of the wilderness generation in 3:12-19. Thus he effectively withheld that definition until 4:1-11, when he began urging his hearers to enter what that generation had lost.

fulness and to whet their appetite for the pastor's teaching on the high priesthood of Christ. The pastor will present the ministry of the incarnate and exalted Christ (1:3, 13; 8:1) as provision both for perseverance and for final entrance into this "rest."

3. Pursue the Blessing Lost by the Faithless Generation (4:1-11)

1 *Therefore, let us fear, since a promise remains of entering his rest, lest any of you should be found to have fallen short.* 2 *For we also have had good news proclaimed to us just as they, but the word that they heard did not profit them because they had not joined themselves to those who heard with faith.* 3 *For we are in the process of entering this rest, we who have believed. As he has said, "As I swore in my wrath, they shall never enter into my rest," although his works had been completed since the foundation of the world.* 4 *For he has spoken somewhere concerning the seventh day thus, "And God rested on the seventh day from all his works."* 5 *And in regard to this again, "They shall never enter into my rest."* 6 *Because, therefore, it was necessary for some to enter into it, and those who first had the good news proclaimed to them did not enter through disobedience,* 7 *he again designated a certain day as "today." He made this designation by speaking through David after so long a time, as it has already been said: "Today, if you hear his voice, do not harden your hearts."* 8 *For if Joshua had given them rest, he would not have spoken after these things concerning another day.* 9 *Therefore, a Sabbath rest remains for the people of God.* 10 *For the one who enters into his rest has himself rested from his works just as God rested from his.* 11 *Let us be diligent, then, to enter into this rest, lest anyone fall by the same example of disobedience.*

This section of the pastor's sermon is framed in vv. 1 and 11 by renewed warnings against emulating the wilderness generation whose tragic end has just been described in 3:16-19.[1] Their "unbelief" (3:19) is cause for "fear" (4:1), and their "disobedience" (3:18) must be avoided at all cost (4:11).[2] Yet the pastor would redirect his hearers' primary attention from the unbelief of

---

1. The references to "entering rest" (vv. 3, 11), "we who have believed" (v. 3a), and "the same example of disobedience" (v. 11) suggest that not only vv. 1 and 11 but also vv. 3a and 11 form an inclusion around this passage (Guthrie, *Structure*, 79). This observation reinforces the unity of vv. 1-3a.

2. Ellingworth, 237, argues that the "therefore" (οὖν) in 4:1 shows the dependence of these verses on 3:16-19. Weiss, 267, confirms the relationship between the "let us fear" of 4:1 and the "unbelief" of 3:19.

the wilderness generation to the "rest" they forfeited. In 3:12-19 he urged his hearers not to emulate that disobedient generation's unbelief. Now he urges his hearers to give all diligence so that they might enter the "rest" that generation forfeited. The concluding phrase of v. 11 makes it clear that the pastor will not let his hearers forget that former warning against unbelief. It provides the necessary background for his exhortations to enter God's "rest." Yet it has been his desire from the beginning that his hearers make every effort to enter that "rest."

If the pastor had begun in chapter 3 by defining God's "rest," it would only have distracted his hearers from the nature of the unbelief against which he warned them and its tragic consequences as described in the Pentateuchal narrative. Now, however, since he would urge his hearers to enter that once-forfeited "rest," he must establish both its nature and its continued availability for the people of God.

The pastor begins, then, in vv. 1-3a by affirming the relationship of his hearers with God's people of old.[3] In the divine economy they are one with God's ancient people because they too have received God's invitation to enter his "rest."[4] In their response, however, they are — and the pastor urges them to be — the opposite of the wilderness generation. They have "believed," so they are in the process of entering God's "rest."[5] In vv. 3b-10, then, the pastor must demonstrate both the nature and continued availability of this "rest" for the people of God before returning to the concerns of vv. 1-3a in the final exhortation of v. 11.

The course of the pastor's argument can be divided into two parts — vv. 3b-5 and vv. 6-10.[6] In the first section the pastor weaves the by-now-familiar Ps 95:7 together with Gen 2:2 in chiastic fashion as the Scriptural basis of his argument.[7] He begins by citing Ps 95:7 in full (v. 3b), and then cites the key term "works" from Gen 2:2 (v. 3c); he follows this hint with the

3. We have included v. 3a with vv. 1-2. Otherwise our segmentation of this passage (vv. 1-3a, 3b-10, 11) follows Laansma, *Rest Motif,* 285. Note the first person plural in vv. 1-3a and v. 11.

4. Compare Ellingworth: "Here, however, continuity is maintained between the people of God in the old and new dispensations: there is for the writer of Hebrews only one λαὸς τοῦ θεοῦ." Ellingworth, 255.

5. Note how the encouragement of v. 3a parallels the warning of v. 1.

6. Thus there is a dividing point between vv. 5 and 6. Nevertheless, it is crucial to note the distinctness of vv. 1-3a and to keep the course of the pastor's argument in vv. 3b-10 together. Thus the analysis above does not give the prominence to this dividing point attributed to it by Lane, 1:95-96, Pfitzner, 79, and Vanhoye, *La structure littéraire,* 96-97, who divide this section into two parts — vv. 1-5 and vv. 6-10.

7. Note the detailed chiasm that Laansma finds in vv. 3b-5 (Jon Laansma, "The Cosmology of Hebrews," in *Cosmology and New Testament Theology,* ed. J. T. Pennington and S. M. McDonough [London: T&T Clark, 2008], 288).

full citation of Gen 2:2 (v. 4), only to conclude with the key phrase from Ps 95:7 (v. 5): "if they will enter into my rest." In vv. 6-10 he draws out the implications of this Biblical evidence. The conclusion that some, then, must still enter God's "rest" (v. 6) is confirmed by Ps 95:11 (v. 7), and not contradicted by Joshua's entrance into Canaan (v. 8). The pastor restates this conclusion with clarity in v. 9.[8] In the process of this argument the pastor has clarified the nature of this "rest" as ultimate entrance into God's own place of "rest" and participation in the great eternal "Sabbath celebration" (v. 9) of the people of God. Thus God's people enter this "rest" only after ceasing from the "works" or struggles of this life (v. 10).

The pastor's argument, then, depends on these three Scripture citations: Ps 95:11; Gen 2:2; and Ps 95:7. First, God's oath of Ps 95:11 makes it certain that the wilderness generation did not enter God's "rest." Second, according to Gen 2:2, the rest in question was God's eternal "rest" prepared since the creation. Thus someone must enter it. Third, the availability of God's "rest" is confirmed by the invitation of Ps 95:7 to heed God's word "today."

As argued in the introduction to this commentary (pp. 63-70), the pastor uses two types of imagery to describe the place where God's people enter his presence. When he is urging them to persevere until final entrance at the return of Christ, he uses Promised Land language to describe that reality — "rest" (4:1-11); "homeland" (11:13-16); and "City" (11:9-10; 12:22).[9] When he encourages them to draw near in the present so that they can receive grace for perseverance, he speaks of the Most Holy Place that has been opened for the people of God through Christ's high priesthood (4:14–10:25). We noted how important this distinction is both for understanding the pastor's use of the OT and for grasping the structure of his sermon. We also noted its inherent logic. When the pastor would motivate his hearers to final perseverance, he draws his primary examples from those OT people who were anticipating entrance into the Promised Land (3:7–4:11; 11:1-40).[10] The ritual of the Mosaic Tent, however, which typified the high-priestly work of Christ, was the place of daily approach to God. Thus, al-

8. Note the inferential particles οὖν and ἄρα, both translated "therefore," in vv. 6 and 9 respectively.

9. *Pace* Judith Hoch Wray, *Rest as a Theological Metaphor in the Epistle to the Hebrews and the Gospel of Truth: Early Christian Homiletics of Rest* (SBLDS 166; Atlanta: Scholars Press, 1998), 91, the fact that "rest" language is limited to Heb 3:7–4:11 is no barrier to its obvious identification with the "city"/"homeland" language of chapter 11. Hebrews often uses the specific language of an OT text only when expounding that text. Compare the use of "the order of Melchizedek" only in 5:6, 10; 6:20; and 7:1-25.

10. See the commentary on 11:32-38 and pp. 49-51 in the Introduction for a discussion of the exemplary use of people who were already in the land.

though the pastor uses the imagery of Most Holy Place and "rest"/"home-land"/"city" in different ways, he is aware that they describe the same reality.[11] He brings the two together in the grand climactic picture in 12:22-24 of what is both the "City" that God's people will enter and the Most Holy Place to which they "have come" (cf. Rev 21:9-27).[12]

---

11. For further discussion and for the association of Land, City, and Temple/Most Holy Place in the OT and contemporary Judaism see pp. 651-53, and esp. p. 652, n. 49. It is particularly important to keep in mind both that the pastor uses Promised Land and Most Holy Place language in different ways *and* that he believes they describe the same reality. In fact, any anomaly caused by Jesus entering the Most Holy Place but his followers entering the heavenly Homeland/City/"Rest" (see Leschert, *Hermeneutical Foundations*, 137, n. 56) is clarified by the identity of the two in 12:22-24. His entrance is clearly the source of theirs. Instead of seeing all of these different descriptions as referring to the same entity, Hofius distinguishes between a heavenly Most Holy Place, within a heavenly Temple, within a heavenly Homeland. This causes him to err by insisting that the "rest" of God's people is not in the heavenly Homeland as a whole but only in the Most Holy Place that has been entered by Jesus. Since, according to 10:19, Christ has entered the Most Holy Place, then this place must be the "rest" his people will enter. See Hofius, *Katapausis*, 53-54. This position suffers from several fatal flaws. First, it ignores Hebrews' parallel use of the wilderness generation and "rest" with the faithful of chapter 11 and the "heavenly homeland." Second, it contradicts the evidence Hofius himself has presented. He has shown how rest, land, and sanctuary are identified in Jewish interpretation contemporary with Hebrews. Third, it ignores the *prima facie* association between "rest" and Promised Land in the OT. Fourth, it overlooks the fact that Hebrews does not make such clear distinctions between the terms it uses for the place of final fellowship with God. Abraham was seeking both "a city that has foundations" (11:10) and a "heavenly country" (11:16). Fifth, it is based on an inadequate interpretation of Heb 10:19. Heb 10:19 is not referring primarily to final entrance into God's "rest," but to present entrance in order to receive grace for perseverance. Furthermore, Hofius's contention (*Katapausis*, 37-41) that Psalm 95 in its original context already identified God's "rest" with worship in the Temple is both hypothetical and without relevance to the interpretation of Hebrews because it would not have been recognized by either the pastor or his hearers. See Laansma, *Rest Motif*, 42-45.

12. In light of the obvious identification between rest/homeland and the sanctuary of Christ's session established in the text above, one cannot limit this "rest" to a millennial kingdom centered in the earthly Promised Land (cf. 11:13-16), *pace* Buchanan, 64-74; Walter C. Kaiser, "The Promise Theme and the Theology of Rest," *BSac* 130 (1973): 135-50; S. D. Toussaint, "The Eschatology of the Warning Passages in the Book of Hebrews," *GTJ* 3 (1982): 70-74; and T. K. Oberholtzer, "The Warning Passages in Hebrews: The Kingdom of Rest in Hebrews 3:1–4:13," *BSac* 145 (1988): 185-96. For extensive critique of this position see deSilva, 156-63. Hebrews knows nothing of speculation about six world ages culminating in a millennial Sabbath, as found in *Barnabas* (C. K. Barrett, "The Eschatology of the Epistle to the Hebrews," in *The Background of the New Testament and Its Eschatology,* ed. W. D. Davies and D. Daube [Cambridge: Cambridge University Press, 1954], 369-73).

Laansma, following Hofius, has demonstrated conclusively that the "rest" of chapters 3 and 4 is both local and future.[13] It is the place where God's people will join him in his "rest" penultimately at death and finally at the Judgment.[14] The local nature of this "rest" is attested by its identity with the "homeland" and "City" of 11:9-10, 13-16, and 12:22-24.[15] Hebrews re-

13. Laansma, *Rest Motif*, 278-79. For more extensive discussion see Laansma, *Rest Motif*, 252-358. Hofius has demonstrated that Psalm 95 is referring to a "place" and not just a "state" of rest in the Hebrew original as well as in the LXX (Hofius, *Katapausis*, 33-41). This understanding is confirmed by rabbinic interpretation (Hofius, *Katapausis*, 42-43). Laansma agrees that both Psalm 95 and Hebrews use κατάπαυσις for a "place of rest," but shows that Hofius has gone beyond the evidence when he contends that this word has virtually become a technical term for such a place (Hofius, *Katapausis*, 48-50).

14. While Hofius, *Katapausis*, 59-90 (summaries on pp. 74, 90), may exaggerate Hebrews' commonalities with ancient Jewish apocalyptic, he is correct in his critique of the Gnostic origin for Hebrews' idea of "rest" propounded by Käsemann, *Wandering;* Grässer; Theissen; and Braun. Hebrews shares almost nothing with later Gnostic speculations about "rest" as a preexistent state lost by a cosmic fall into matter and restored by knowledge of its true origin. Gnostic sources use ἀνάπαυσις instead of κατάπαυσις for "rest," do not develop this concept in conjunction with the OT texts on the wilderness wandering, and, in complete variance with Hebrews (2:14; 10:5), are based on a dualistic view which rejects the body and the material world (Leschert, *Hermeneutical Foundations,* 142). Nor does Hebrews evidence significant similarity with Philo's understanding of "rest." Philo never refers to Psalm 95 in this regard, and his discussion of Gen 2:2 involves Pythagorean-like numerical speculations and discussion of the immutability of God (*Posterity* 64; *Alleg. Interp.* 1.6, 16; Leschert, *Hermeneutical Foundations,* 139-40). Furthermore, he allegorizes the wilderness wandering as "an ethereal journey of the virtuous mind returning from its temporary sojourn in an earthly body to its heavenly home" (Leschert, *Hermeneutical Foundations,* 138; cf. *Posterity* 64). If Philo is so distant from Hebrews, he can hardly bear witness to an earlier Gnosticism upon which Hebrews is dependent (Leschert, *Hermeneutical Foundations,* 143). Braun and others who maintain Gnostic influence are often characterized by two methodological flaws. First, they operate with an untenably broad definition of "Gnosticism" that includes everything from Philo to *Joseph and Aseneth* and the Nag Hammadi documents. Second, they argue for Gnostic influence on the basis of minimum similarity between this broadly defined Gnosticism and Hebrews. Thus Braun, 93, cites the fact that Hebrews locates God's resting place in heaven as evidence of Gnostic influence. Even he admits that Hebrews "does not develop the complete breadth of gnostic thought" about God's rest (Braun, 93).

15. This identification is substantiated by the way the OT identifies "rest" with the Promised Land (Deut 12:10; see also Exod 33:14; Deut 25:19; Josh 1:13, 15; 21:44; 22:4; 23:1). Cf. O'Brien, 163, and Leschert, *Hermeneutical Foundations,* 162-63. Furthermore, both rabbinic and apocalyptic literature interpreted "rest" and "land" as the final dwelling place of God's people in his presence (Hofius, *Katapausis*, 43-47, 59-74). In order to deny this connection between the "rest" and the "heavenly homeland" Wray must minimize the naturalness of this association based on both the OT and the parallels from contemporary literature. She must also downplay many other features of Hebrews 3 and 4. See Wray, *Rest as a Theological Metaphor,* 91.

peatedly speaks of this "rest" and those entities with which it is associated as things that can be "entered." The local nature of "rest" is confirmed by the use of this term in the LXX and in Second Temple Judaism.[16] Few books in the NT assert more emphatically the concrete nature of the ultimate destiny of God's people than does Hebrews. These factors that affirm its reality as a "place" and not merely a "state" also confirm that the entrance envisioned for the people of God is future. The failed entrance of the wilderness generation was to have been both future and decisive. The faithful of chapter 11 were looking forward to their future entrance into what God had prepared for them. Even though Christ has come, God's people still receive this entrance as a "promise" (4:1) that they must strive to obtain. In fact, this Promised Land imagery is particularly unsuitable as a description of present entrance because of the way it identifies contemporary believers with God's people of old. The pastor is convinced that God's people, past and present, have always anticipated ultimate entrance into his presence. Those who lived before Christ, however, did *not* enjoy the privileges of access during their lifetimes that are now available for the people of God through his high priesthood (2:1-4; 10:26-31; 11:39-40). Their experience, then, mirrors the future hope but not the present privilege of contemporary believers. Thus neither the wilderness generation nor the faithful of chapter 11 were appropriate examples of what every believer now has in Christ. There is, in fact, nothing in 3:1–4:13 that suggests present entrance besides the present tense verb of 4:3: "we are entering into rest." Every feature of the immediate and larger context indicates that this verb should be taken as progressive or futuristic, "we are in the process of entering into rest."[17] While the pastor believes that Christ provides present entrance into God's presence for the people of God, that is not what he is talking about in chapters 3 and 4. The attempt to introduce this idea in these chapters only begets confusion.[18]

1 The pastor began the previous section of this exhortation in 3:12 with the imperative "see" or "be alert lest." His hearers, however, have now "seen" (3:19) the horrible fate of the wilderness generation (3:16-19). Thus the pastor begins this new section of his exhortation with the much stronger "let us fear lest," softened only by the inclusion of the author himself with his hearers in the first person plural.[19] It is not only, however, the terrible fate of the wilderness generation but also the great value of what is offered the peo-

---

16. Laansma, *Rest Motif,* 106-11; O'Brien, 164.

17. See Laansma, *Rest Motif,* 306.

18. See also O'Brien, 165-66, for a collaborating summary of the arguments in support of the position taken above.

19. οὖν, therefore, draws out the implications of the example just given in 3:15-19.

ple of God, of what is at stake, that motivates this exhortation to fear. The pastor urges his hearers to a new level of caution and concern appropriate to both their peril and the opportunity that is theirs to enter God's own "rest."[20]

God's people stand at this point of opportunity "because a promise of entering his rest still remains" for them. One might translate the perfect passive participle, "is remaining," or "is standing." They are living in the reality of this ancient promise's continuing validity. Furthermore, the promise is not simply a promise of "rest" but a promise that *they,* the people of God, can "enter" that "rest."[21] Since the promise given the wilderness generation is still in effect, God's "rest" is available and its loss a true possibility.[22] In the following verses the pastor substantiates the availability of this promise, concluding with "there remains a Sabbath rest for the people of God" (v. 9). The perpetuity of the promise given the wilderness generation implies the eternal nature of the "rest" in question, as the pastor will explain below. The urgency of the pastor's exhortation gains additional impetus from the temporal force of the participle: not only "because" but "while a promise of entering his rest still remains."[23] It is possible to pass beyond the time of opportunity by forfeiting this promise through unbelief and disobedience.

God's promise is fundamental to biblical theology in general and to the thought of Hebrews in particular. This promise of entering God's "rest" forfeited by the wilderness generation is the promise of a heavenly homeland given to Abraham (11:9-10), guaranteed by God's oath (6:13-20), and certified to the faithful by Jesus' entrance into God's presence on their behalf (6:19-20; cf. 7:20-22). The fact that both God's "rest" and the homeland sought by Abraham are the object of this promise underscores their identity and substantiates the future, ultimate nature of entrance thereunto. Faith is conducting one's life on the assumption that this promise of God is certain and that his power to fulfill it is assured (11:1-6).

In light of this great promise, God's people should fear lest "any of you be found to have fallen short." This rendering is more in accord with the pastor's urgency than the more common, "lest any of you seem to have fallen short."[24]

---

20. The aorist hortatory subjunctive, φοβηθῶμεν, is ingressive — "let us begin to fear" in a way we haven't feared before (Lane, 1:93).

21. Laansma, *Rest Motif,* 285, n. 156.

22. This "promise" was for the people of God of all time. It finds its fulfillment in Christ. All of God's people, both from before and after Christ, will together receive the final fulfillment of this promise through Christ at the end (Laansma, *Rest Motif,* 303).

23. The present participle καταλειπομένης, "remaining," is a genitive absolute that modifies ἐπαγγελίας, "promise," thus literally, "a promise remaining." It can have both causal, "because a promise remains," and temporal, "while a promise remains," significance. Laansma, *Rest Motif,* 285, n. 156, affirms the temporal.

24. Bénétreau, 1:170; O'Brien, 160; cf. Michel, 191; Attridge, 124; and Weiss,

The pastor's concern is that they not be found by God to have come short of their eternal goal at the Judgment. The wilderness generation came all the way to the border of the Promised Land but "fell short" of entrance through refusal to trust God. Those who follow them in such rebellion are destined to forfeit what God has promised. The opposite of falling short is perseverance in the life of faith and obedience until final entrance into God's rest (cf. 11:1-38).[25] There is a finality to the perfect tense "have fallen short" reminiscent of the Kadesh generation's permanent exclusion (3:19) and anticipatory of the apostasy yet to be described (6:4-8; 10:26-31). "Lest any" reminds us that the pastor is concerned with every individual within the congregation he addresses.

2 The pastor reaffirms the oneness of his hearers with the wilderness generation in receiving the offer of eternal rest (v. 2a) while urging an opposite response to God's invitation (vv. 2b-3). God's promise "remains (v. 1), "for we [Christian believers] also have had the good news" of God's "promise" of eternal rest "proclaimed to us just as" the wilderness generation had that good news proclaimed to them.[26] The way this sentence is formed suggests that the wilderness generation received the original "good news" or "gospel." They too were offered God's eternal "rest." The revelation they received at Sinai through the angels was to be and has now been fulfilled in the "great salvation" provided by Christ (2:1-4) that it typified. Thus those obedient to that earlier offer were destined to enter God's eternal "rest" through Christ in company with those after him (11:39-40).[27] In the consummation God's faithful people of all time will enjoy his rest without distinction (12:22-29).

"We have had the good news proclaimed to us" is in the perfect tense. For the pastor's hearers the good news of God's "promise" has taken the form of the "great salvation" provided by Christ and proclaimed to them at the inception of their community (2:1-4). The proclamation of that good news,

---

275. Ellingworth, 239-40 and Laansma, *Rest Motif,* 285, n. 156, argue for "seem to have fallen short." Some would construe δοκῇ τις ἐξ ὑμῶν ὑστερηκέναι as "lest anyone should think that he or she has come too late" for the promise. This interpretation takes δοκῇ as "lest anyone should think" and ὑστερηκέναι as "to have come too late" (instead of as "to have fallen short"). The pastor, however, is concerned about impending unbelief, not about an eschatological misconception (see Attridge, 124).

25. The larger context and the use of both the wilderness generation and the faithful of chapter 11 as examples indicate that the opposite of "having falling short" is not "having attained" but perseverance in faith and obedience until final attainment.

26. The term εὐαγγελίζω ("preach the good news") is related to the word εὐαγγέλιον ("gospel") and is often used in the NT for its proclamation. The Greek reader would also have perceived a wordplay between εὐαγγελίζω and the related word ἐπαγγελία ("promise") in v. 1. The "promise" was the "good news" that was proclaimed.

27. Of course, since the faithful of old enter God's eternal blessing (11:9-10, 13-16), it makes little sense to argue that the unfaithful of old have forfeited anything less.

however, continues to address God's people in the present "today" of their opportunity. It summons them to enduring faithfulness. Thus the pastor warns his hearers to distance themselves from the unbelieving response of those who previously received the "good news" of God's eternal "rest."[28] The "but" which begins v. 2b sets the wilderness generation's rejection in contrast to the appropriate response: "but the word that they heard did not profit them because they had not joined themselves to those who heard with faith."[29] In the immediate context of the wilderness generation "those who heard with faith" is a reference to Joshua and Caleb (Num 13:25–14:10).[30] The pastor, however, is already thinking of the heroes of faith catalogued in 11:1-38. The "with faith" of this verse anticipates the many "by faith's" and "through faith's" of that chapter.[31] The wilderness generation did not join themselves

28. "Formally, the contrast is one of generations; in substance, it is between listening, believing, obeying, and holding fast on the one hand, and the failure to do so on the other." Ellingworth, 254.

29. "The word which they heard" is literally "the word of hearing" (ὁ λόγος τῆς ἀκοῆς). This interpretation takes "of hearing" as a descriptive genitive (see Hughes, 157 and Attridge, 125). Remember Ps 95:7, "Today, if you hear. . . ." Thus the reference is to the word of God that they actually did "hear," although without obedience. This allows "of hearing" to have the same connotation as "those who heard" (τοῖς ἀκούσασιν) later in the verse. Both words refer to the receiving of information, not to obedience. The idea of obedience is contained in the expression "by faith" (τῇ πίστει).

30. The Greek reads, συγκεκερασμένους ["having joined themselves"] τῇ πίστει ["by/with faith"] τοῖς ἀκούσασιν ["to those who heard"]. It is better to take τῇ πίστει ("by/with faith") with the following substantive participle τοῖς ἀκούσασιν ("to those who heard") than with the preceding adverbial participle ("having joined themselves"). Thus the text reads "not having joined themselves to those who heard with faith," rather than "not having joined themselves by faith to those who heard." In 3:16 "those who heard" refers to the rebels and thus needs the qualifying "with faith" here to clarify the referents as obedient hearers. Although τῇ πίστει would more clearly refer to τοῖς ἀκούσασιν if it followed the participle, Hebrews often brings words forward out of normal order for emphasis. Note the separation of τηλικαύτης ("such a great") from the word it modifies (σωτηρίας) in the phrase in τηλικαύτης ἀμελήσαντες σωτηρίας (2:3). This phrase is literally, "such a great" (τηλικαύτης) "having neglected" (ἀμελήσαντες) "salvation" (σωτηρίας). Consider also the way πίστει ("by faith") is given the initial position throughout chapter 11. However, even if the statement is construed as "not joining themselves by faith to those who heard," it still speaks of their identity with the people of God, though the association with chapter 11 is not as clear. For this interpretation of συγκεκερασμένους see Spicq, 2:81; Attridge, 126, n. 45; and Laansma, *Rest Motif,* 286.

31. The articular τῇ πίστει, "with/by faith," in 4:2 anticipates the anarthous πίστει, "by faith," in 11:3, 4, 5, 7, 8, 9, 11, 17, 20, 21, 22, 23, 24, 27, 28, 29, 30, 31. All of these uses are instrumental of means. When introducing the catalogue of faithful in 10:39 the pastor uses ἐκ πίστεως, "by faith," the ablative of means, in dependence on Hab 2:4. The pastor then uses the ablative of means διὰ πίστεως, "through faith," in 11:33 as a summary description of all those in the climactic compact section of his catalogue. Note the similar

"to those who heard with faith," but "we" do belong "to the people of faith" (10:39) enumerated in that catalogue.[32] The surface awkwardness of the Greek phrase we have translated "because they did not join themselves to those who heard with faith" appears to have given rise to several textual alterations. Nevertheless the way in which this statement reinforces one of the author's main concerns joins with the weight of manuscript evidence to attest its authenticity.[33] The pastor is not urging his hearers to mere mental assent or private obedience, but to enduring identification with the great company of those who live "by faith," despite the ridicule of and exclusion from unbelieving society. "Did not profit them" is deliberate understatement that only serves to sharpen the ominous "they could not enter in because of unbelief" at the conclusion of 3:16-19.

διὰ τῆς πίστεως in v. 39 used to summarize the entire catalogue. It is, perhaps, significant that in the first (τῇ πίστει, 4:2) and last (διὰ τῆς πίστεως) of these references the pastor uses the article as a pointer to the faith he will and then has described.

32. συγκεκερασμένους is the perfect middle or passive participle of συγκεράννυμι, to "mix" or "join," denoting an enduring identification with the people of faith. The middle fits well with the pastor's emphasis on the responsibility of the wilderness generation for their unbelief. In the UBS[4] and NA[27] editions of the Greek NT this participle is accusative plural masculine, modifying ἐκείνους, "those ones," "them" (the wilderness generation). Literally, "those ones not having joined themselves to those who heard with faith," or, as we have translated causally above, "because they had not joined themselves to those who heard with faith."

33. Some manuscripts read συγκεκερασμένος, nominative singular masculine, instead of συγκεκερασμένους, accusative plural masculine. In these manuscripts συγκεκερασμένος modifies λόγος — "the word which they heard did not profit them, not being joined by faith to those who heard." In a few of these manuscripts this reading is made smoother yet by substituting the genitive plural participle τῶν ἀκουσάντων, "of those who heard," for the dative plural, "to those who heard." The participle now qualifies τῇ πίστει, "not being joined to the faith of those who believed." Some manuscripts have taken another course, replacing the masculine plural aorist active participle τοῖς ἀκούσασιν, "to those who heard," with a neuter plural aorist passive, τοῖς ἀκούσθεισιν, "to the things they had heard." Thus the whole phrase would read, "not being joined by faith to the things they had heard." All three of these options remove the awkwardness of the wilderness generation's not being "joined" to "those who heard with faith," that is, to the believing congregation of God's people. In the first two variations, "those who heard" refers to the disobedient wilderness generation itself. In the third, the participle has been altered to refer to "the things they had heard." Nevertheless, as argued above, reference to "those who heard with faith" fits well with the pastor's emphases. Thus it has all the marks of authenticity — an appearance of awkwardness to copyists, appropriateness for the author's argument, and the strongest manuscript support. It is indeed the reading that can explain the others (Laansma, *Rest Motif,* 286, n. 162; Attridge, 125-26; Weiss, 278, n. 88; Lane, 1:93h). Thus there is no need, with Hughes, 157-58, Bruce, 103, n. 4, and others to postulate a primitive corruption of the text. For the manuscript evidence see *TCGNT,* 595.

3a By contrast, the pastor rushes to describe himself and his hearers: "For we are entering that rest, we who have believed." "We are entering rest" is a true continuous present that stands in opposition to the final dictum on the wilderness generation: "they could not enter in." The journey of the wilderness generation is over. "They could not enter in" (3:19) is the conclusion of their story. "Our" journey, however, is in progress. "We are in the process of entering rest."[34] It is for this very reason that the pastor urges perseverance. He is now ready to explain the nature of this "rest."[35]

The pastor would emphasize the importance of faith and spur his hearers to perseverance by reserving "we who have believed" for the end of the sentence. He is assured that his hearers are on the way to this eternal "rest" because, in contrast to the unbelievers (3:19) of the wilderness generation, they are those "who have believed." This relative clause translates a substantive aorist participle. The aorist is constative, asserting that a life evidencing trust in God's power and promises is characteristic of those who are on their way to "rest." The pastor would encourage his hearers by affirming that they are such people. This affirmation is a perpetual encouragement for all who are living the life of faith to continue therein.[36] Past belief is no guarantee of entrance but a spur to continued faithfulness, as v. 11 makes clear (cf. 10:32-39).

In vv. 3b-9 the pastor demonstrates from Scripture that God's promise of rest once offered to the wilderness generation is still valid (v. 1) and thus that "we who have believed" are indeed in the process of entering the place

---

34. Thus present continuous action fits naturally in the context of this passage. Cf. Montefiore, 83; Attridge, 126; and the extensive discussion in Laansma, *Rest Motif,* 305-10. Mitchell, 97, achieves the same effect by calling this verb an "ingressive" present, indicating "a present state that will be completed at a future time." As deSilva, 155, has pointed out, those who insist that "we who are entering" affirms present entrance treat this verb as perfective. Furthermore, the psalmist says nothing about entering God's rest "today"; rather, "today" is the time for obedience, the time when one must not "harden" one's heart. See the critique of Lane, 1:99 and Andrew T. Lincoln, "Sabbath, Rest, and Eschatology in the New Testament," in *From Sabbath to Lord's Day: A Biblical, Historical and Theological Investigation,* ed. Donald A. Carson (Grand Rapids: Zondervan, 1982), 212-13 in deSilva, 153-56. Wray's attempt to find at least a hint of present entrance in this verse reveals the lack of evidence for such a position (Wray, *Rest as a Theological Metaphor,* 73-85, cf. 34, 47).

35. The lack of a qualifying genitive (i.e., "my" rest) and the probable lack of the article, although it is present in all other uses of this noun in Hebrews, prepare for the writer's explanation of this rest as something more than the land of Canaan. See Ellingworth, 246.

36. *Pace* Ellingworth, 246, the "we-statement" format does not rob this statement of gnomic or general significance. Hebrews always uses the plural when speaking of believers' access to God, but the singular when addressing the possibility of apostasy.

of promised rest. The first step in his argument reaches its conclusion in the "therefore" of v. 6; the second, in the "therefore" of v. 9.[37]

3b-5 In these verses the pastor provides Scriptural evidence to substantiate what he has said about the continuing validity of God's "promise" (v. 1) and the present experience of his hearers as those who are entering God's "rest" (v. 3a) on the basis thereof. He carefully knits together his key verse, Ps 95:11, with Gen. 2:2. As noted above, he begins by citing Ps 95:11 (v. 3b), followed by an allusion to Gen 2:2 (v. 3c) that highlights the word "works." He then quotes Gen 2:2 in v. 4 and concludes by re-quoting the appropriate phrase from Ps 95:11 in v. 5: "if they will enter into my rest."

It is important to note the way the pastor emphasizes the continuing validity of these verses as the word of God, the basis upon which he has associated them, and the tension that he has created between them. The perfect tense used in introducing these quotations affirms their continuing validity as divine address. Note "as he has said" (v. 3b) introducing Ps 95:11. Since all Scripture is God's word, Gen 2:2 can also be introduced with the solemn "he [God] has said" (v. 4):[38] "for he has said concerning the seventh day thus, 'And God rested on the seventh day from all his works.'"[39]

The pastor has brought these two texts together because they speak of "rest." Yet he is not arbitrarily employing the widespread practice of associating passages containing the same term.[40] Since Ps 95:11 refers to God's ("my") rest, it was natural to explain that rest by reference to God's resting at the culmination of creation recorded in Gen 2:2.[41] Several Aramaic Targums

---

37. In v. 6 the pastor uses οὖν, "therefore," but in v. 9, ἄρα.

38. Lane, 1:100. Compare the "he" of the NIV, NKJV, NASB, and ESV in v. 4 to the "it" of the NRSV. It is unclear why Ellingworth, 247, thinks that "Scripture" is the subject in v. 4.

39. Hebrews, along with Philo, quotes Gen 2:2 as follows: καὶ κατέπαυσεν ὁ θεὸς ἐν τῇ ἡμέρᾳ τῇ ἑβδόμῃ ἀπὸ πάντων τῶν ἔργων αὐτοῦ, "and God rested on the seventh day from all his works." The standard text of the LXX omits ὁ θεὸς ἐν, thus reading "And he rested on the seventh day from all his works." The addition of ὁ θεός only emphasizes the obvious fact that "God" is the subject of this statement. τῇ ἡμέρᾳ τῇ ἑβδόμῃ is locative of time with or without the preposition ἐν. Ellingworth notes that ὁ θεὸς ἐν appears in the Hexaplaric manuscripts of the LXX. He also suggests that the retention of the superfluous καί at the beginning of the quotation evidences Hebrews' reluctance to edit the text he received. Thus it is unclear why Ellingworth (248) does not think Hebrews and Philo are witnesses to an alternate LXX textual tradition.

40. As suggested by many commentators. See Weiss, 269; Attridge, 128-29. The LXX text of Gen 2:2 uses the verb κατέπαυσεν ("he rested"; from καταπαύω); that of Ps 95:11 employs the related noun κατάπαυσιν ("rest"; accusative singular of κατάπαυσις). This practice of associating passages that contained the same term was traditional and not limited to the rabbis, as evidenced by its use in Philo (Attridge, 129, n. 77).

41. Leschert, *Hermeneutical Foundations,* 190, is correct when he says that this

associate these two texts despite the fact that Gen 2:2 and Ps 95:11 use different words for rest in both Hebrew and Aramaic.[42] The association is intrinsic:
if one wanted to understand what God meant when he said "my rest," one
must go to the place in Scripture that describes God's resting.[43]

The "although" at the beginning of v. 3c anticipates the tension that
the pastor will develop between these two verses. In good rhetorical fashion,
however, he begins by maintaining an element of suspense: the tension is initially introduced between God's oath prohibiting the wilderness generation's
entrance into his "rest" in Ps 95:11 (v. 3b) and the fact that "his works" have
been completed "since the foundation of the world." Only in v. 4, with the
full quotation of Gen 2:2, do the hearers discover that the completion of
God's works of creation inaugurated his own "rest."[44] Thus the tension is between God's prohibition against the wilderness generation entering his "rest"
and his own permanent entrance into that perpetual "rest" at the culmination
of creation. Yet this initial mention of God's "works" in v. 3c does more than
maintain an element of suspense. It provides a natural bridge to the quotation
of Gen 2:2 and highlights the idea of "works" to which the pastor will return
in v. 10. What, however, is the conflict between God's preventing the wilderness generation from entering his "rest" (Ps 95:11) and his own entrance into
eternal "rest" at the culmination of creation (Gen 2:2)? In v. 6 the pastor clarifies the nature of this tension and reveals its obvious and necessary solution.

6 "Therefore" indicates that the pastor is going to resolve the tension between and bring out the logical significance of the now-substantiated
facts: God has established his "rest" at the culmination of creation, but pro-
hibited the wilderness generation from entering it. The modern reader must
grasp the pastor's underlying assumption: if God established his eternal rest
at the culmination of creation and invited the wilderness generation into it,

---

practice "can be used in a perfectly legitimate manner where the meaning warrants a verbal connection." Attridge, 130, n. 92, thinks that the "again" (πάλιν) in v. 5 shows that the
writer of Hebrews is thinking of the "rest" in Ps 95:11 as a repeated mention of God's resting in Gen 2:2.

42. Ellingworth, 248, refers to *Targum Onqelos* and *Targum Pseudo-Jonathan.*
Lane, 1:100, says that Gen 2:1-3 was read after Ps 95:1-11 in the liturgy of the Greek-
speaking synagogue, though Attridge (129, n. 83) reminds us that this practice is not attested before the sixteenth century.

43. In a similar way the pastor will explain Ps 110:4 in Heb 7:1-10 by reference to
Gen 14:17-20.

44. "His works" is an allusion to the "works" of creation in Gen 2:2 rather than to
God's "works" of blessing and judgment mentioned in Ps 95:9 (Heb 3:9) and experienced
by Israel when leaving Egypt and traveling through the wilderness. Furthermore, he entered his "rest" after completing his works. Thus the "rest" must not be thought of as one
of his works (Lane, 1:99; deSilva, 165). See Attridge, 130, for the Jewish background of
the Sabbath as God's eschatological rest.

then he must have intended for his people to join him in his "rest." Since God's purposes will not be frustrated, the failure of the wilderness generation to enter is certain evidence that others will. If those to whom "the good news [of the promise] was proclaimed" did not enter, then surely the "promise remains" (v. 1) for those to whom that "good news" is now proclaimed.

"Because of disobedience" is homiletically effective though not logically necessary for the argument. The pastor would remind them that, although they are one with the wilderness generation in receiving good news, they must *not* imitate that generation's disobedience. Their inability to enter can be attributed both to their "unbelief" (3:19) and their "disobedience." The close relationship between the two has already been explained in the comments on 3:19 above. While the term "unbelief" might be more comprehensive, "disobedience" focuses on the deliberate act by which it is expressed. The pastor may have felt that this use of the more concrete expression was appropriate for the heightened emphasis expressed by both the "let us fear" (v. 1) with which he began and the "let us be diligent" (v. 11) with which he will conclude. Much is at stake in pursuit of God's "rest."

7 The invitation to enter God's rest issued in Ps 95:7 should be no surprise. "Because" (v. 6) God established his eternal rest with the intention that his people would enter it, but it was rejected by the wilderness generation, he "again" established a "day" of opportunity. This day was thus subsequent to the "day" of his offer to the wilderness generation. The "today" of Ps 95:7 is the establishment of this new opportunity: "Today, if you hear his voice, do not harden your hearts." This invitation is of continuing validity and thus remains open for God's people "today."

The pastor affirms that God spoke this psalm "through David" and "a long time" after the rebellion at Kadesh in order to show that it was subsequent to the invitation given the wilderness generation. The expression "through" or "in" David is identical to that used in 1:1-2a for God's speaking "in the prophets" and "in one who is Son." God is the primary speaker who acted through the psalm writer David.[45] Thus reference to David substantiates the new "today" of opportunity without compromising the divine origin of this invitation. Nor does the use of human agency limit revelation's effectiveness to the time of the agent.

With "as it has already been said" the pastor reintroduces Ps 95:7, a verse so central to his exhortation that it has "already" been cited in 3:7b-8 and 15.[46] This verse began as a warning against hardening "their hearts"

---

45. Thus Attridge, 130, may be right when he suggests that the reference might be to David as a prophet and not just to the book of Psalms, as argued by Moffatt, 52, and Bruce, 108.

46. For προείρηται, "as it has been said before" or "as it has already been said," as

(3:12-14). Next it exposed the gravity of the wilderness "rebellion" and thus the urgency of avoiding that generation's example (3:15). Finally, in 4:7, it confirms the continuing validity of God's "promise" (cf. 4:1) and summons his people to seize his invitation and persevere until they enter his "rest."[47] The pastor omits the ominous "as in the rebellion" that was so important in his second citation of this verse, because he anticipates better things of his hearers.

8   The pastor buttresses the above conclusion by answering a possible objection. Someone might say, "True, the wilderness generation failed to enter God's 'rest,' but did not Joshua lead the next generation into that 'rest' when he brought them into the Promised Land?" Ps 95:7 is the pastor's answer to this question as well: "If Joshua had given them rest (which he did not), then God would not have kept on speaking of another day" through Ps 95:7 after his people had entered Canaan. The imperfect tense, translated "would not have kept on speaking," has iterative force. God's invitation in Ps 95:7 has continued to be addressed to his people in their "today." The very existence of this invitation demonstrates that the promised "rest" was more than earthly Canaan.[48] *thus, the wilderness generation was barred also from eternal rest.*

Although in Greek the names for "Joshua" and "Jesus" are the same, the pastor develops no Joshua/Jesus typology.[49] His passing comment about

---

a reference to the pastor's previous citation of this verse in 3:7b-8 and 3:15 see Ellingworth, 252.

47. It is not clear why Ellingworth argues that Ps 95:11 is a direct promise of "rest" and thus removes the negative way in which it is used in this passage. This interpretation is unnecessary and appears to run contrary to the plain meaning of the text. Ellingworth, 250.

48. M. Thiessen, "Hebrews and the End of the Exodus," *NovT* 49 (2007): 353-69, argues that Hebrews sees the whole history of Israel up to the present as taking place during the exodus. He appears to understand this exodus period as the time between the literal exodus from earthly Egypt and final entrance into the heavenly homeland. This awkward pairing of one "earthly" event (the exodus) and one "heavenly" (entrance into the land) introduces confusion and causes him to miss the typological nature of OT institutions and events. He almost seems to understand the present verse not as a declaration that the earthly Promised Land was not the true "rest" but that Joshua did not bring the people into the earthly Promised Land: "Israel has been brought out of Egypt but has never, even up until his [the author's] own day, entered into the land that God had promised them" (Thiessen, "Exodus," 354-55).

49. There is really no evidence for Attridge's (130) suggestion of a possible Joshua/Jesus typology based on the ἀρχηγός, "pioneer," title used in 2:10. Leschert, *Hermeneutical Foundations,* 126, n. 13, cites others in support of such a typology. The pastor refuses to be distracted by the obvious similarity between these two names (Ellingworth, 253). When referring to "Jesus," the pastor usually puts this name in the final emphatic position, as in 2:9. However, he deemphasizes this reference to "Joshua" by denying the name either the first or last emphatic position in the Greek sentence.

Joshua merely serves to answer an objection, as noted above, and strengthen his argument for God's abiding promise of entrance into divine "rest."[50]

9 The pastor's opening (v. 1) and closing (v. 11) exhortations depend on the continued validity of God's promise inviting his people into his "rest." He established this validity in v. 6 on the basis of the Scripture cited in vv. 3b-5. Here in this verse, after the reinforcement and clarification found in vv. 6-7, he restates that conclusion in grander form: "Therefore a Sabbath celebration remains for the people of God."

If the word the pastor has been using for "rest" denotes the place of final "rest," the eternal "City" and "homeland," "Sabbath celebration" provides the hearers with some idea of what they will enjoy there.[51] This term, first attested by Hebrews, was probably derived from the verb "to celebrate the Sabbath." In the Church Fathers it "stresses the special aspect of festivity and joy, expressed in the adoration and praise of God" which was to characterize that holy day.[52] The pastor gives us a picture of such joyous celebration in 12:22-24. Thus "Sabbath celebration" describes the nature and quality of that "rest" without detracting from the fact that it is identified with and to be fully experienced in the yet-to-be-entered "heavenly homeland" (11:16).[53] Just as this rest was established by God as the climax of creation, so his people will receive final entrance at the culmination of creation (12:25-29), for it

---

50. Ellingworth, 253-54.

51. Laansma, *Rest Motif,* 278-79, has demonstrated conclusively that κατάπαυσις in this passage refers to the place of future blessedness. Attridge's contention (" 'Let Us Strive,' " 282-83) that κατάπαυσις ("rest") must be nothing more than a state because it is "defined" by σαββατισμός ("Sabbath celebration") is reductionistic. His argument that "rested from all his work" (v. 10) describes a state begs the question. "If we translate κατάπαυσις in v. 10 locally the sense is, 'the one who enters God's resting *place* rests from his works as God did from his.' The Sabbath celebration takes place in the resting place, and is made possible by resting from one's works. This is perfectly intelligible, and Attridge's objections (Attridge, 131, n. 108) are without force" (Laansma, *Rest Motif,* 281, n. 142, emphasis original).

52. Lane, 1:102. σαββατισμός occurs in Justin, *Dial.* 23.3 (born A.D. 168); Epiphanius, *Pan.* 30.2.2 (A.D. 315-403); *Martyrdom of Peter and Paul* 1 (end of third century); and *Apos. Con.* 2.36.2 (fourth century). All of these authors use this term to describe a Sabbath celebration of rest from normal work and joyful worship of God. Each uses the term σάββατον when referring to the Sabbath itself. See Hofius, *Katapausis,* 103-5. Thus Käsemann's contention that Hebrews' identification of this rest with σαββατισμός parallels the Gnostic identification of the final place of rest as the Sabbath/Seventh Heaven has no support. As "Sabbath celebration," σαββατισμός denotes neither the seventh day nor cessation and quietude. Hofius, *Katapausis,* 116-17.

53. There is nothing in the text to support Bénétreau's argument that "Sabbath celebration" describes present daily access to God parallel with the present weekly access of the Jewish Sabbath (Bénétreau, 183).

is God's promised "Unshakable Kingdom" (12:28). While the pastor's focus in 3:7–4:11 is on future final entrance, by the time he gets to his grand description of this "Sabbath celebration" in 12:22-24 he has abundantly described the present access to God available to believers through Christ (4:14-16; 10:19-25). Thus in that description the persevering faithful join the already victorious faithful in the great Sabbath celebration of God's rest. The pastor would give his hearers a glimpse of this glorious reality as the supreme encouragement for perseverance in faithful obedience. This "Sabbath celebration" is the ultimate blessing — but only for those who persevere as the "people of God," not for those who fall away through "unbelief."

10   This verse is intended to further clarify the "Sabbath rest" of v. 9. The text makes it emphatically clear that "the one who has entered God's rest," whoever he or she may be, has "rested from his works."[54] Some have identified this person with the Son, others with the faithful follower of Christ.

If "the one who has entered his [God's] rest" refers to the Son of God, it is an affirmation of his exaltation and an anticipation of the entrance language used to describe his access into the heavenly Most Holy Place (4:14-16; 6:19-20; 9:12, 24; 10:19-25).[55] According to this interpretation, Jesus "has rested from his works that provided salvation," which he accomplished through his obedient life and atoning self-sacrifice. This emphasis on completion fits well with what the pastor will say about Jesus' session as evidence that his saving work is complete and sufficient (10:11-14). Furthermore, it bears witness to the truth that redemption parallels creation: just as God rested from his works of creation, so the Son has now rests from his works of redemption. Thus Christ's provision gives a second reason for the accessibility of God's "Sabbath celebration": rest established by God, access provided through Christ. However, the pastor does not appear to have given his hearers sufficient clues to identify Christ with the enigmatic "one who has entered [God's] rest."

It is more likely, then, that this "one who has entered his [God's] rest" should be identified as a faithful member of "the people of God" whose perseverance is complete. The "works" from which this faithful person has rested are not the "dead works" from which Christ cleanses the believer (9:14). Such "dead works" are no fit parallel to God's "works" of creation.[56]

---

54. καὶ αὐτός is emphatic: "he himself even."

55. Attridge, 131, suggests this interpretation as a possibility and, in n. 110, cites Franz-Joseph Schierse, *Verheissung und Heilsvollendung: Zur theologischen Grundfrage des Hebräerbriefes* (Munich: Zink, 1955), 134-35; Leopold Sabourin, *Priesthood: A Comparative Study, Studies in the History of Religion* (Leiden: E. J. Brill, 1973), 204; and Vanhoye, *La structure littéraire*, 99-100, in its support. Ellingworth, 255-57, summarizes the arguments presented for this position in Andriessen and Lenglet, 75, who follow Vanhoye and Schierse. See also deSilva, 167-69.

56. See Attridge, 131, n. 110.

They are, rather, the "works" of one's earthly pilgrimage. Just as God entered his rest at the culmination of creation, so believers enter God's "Sabbath rest" at the culmination of their earthly pilgrimage, initially at death and finally at the return of Christ (9:28; 12:25-29). There is no suggestion here of earning salvation through "works." "Rest from works" suggests relief from the arduousness of the way, from societal pressure to conform, from ridicule and persecution.[57] Thus v. 10 underscores the future nature of entrance into this "Sabbath rest" as motivation for faithfulness and clarifies its character by placing it in stark contrast to the toils of an earthly believer.

What the pastor has said about the "rest"/"Sabbath celebration" helps us to understand his thinking about the relationship of the created world to the eternal world of salvation. After completing the works of creation, God established and entered into this "rest." When the created order passes away at the Judgment (12:26-27), this rest, now called the permanent "City" (11:10) and the "Unshakable Kingdom" (12:28), will remain. Thus this enduring "rest," "City," and "Kingdom" has received its eternal quality and ultimate reality through its establishment by God, but it is beyond the created order.[58] We might express this today by saying that it belongs to a different, that is, "eternal," dimension of reality.

11 In v. 1 the writer urged his hearers to "fear" lest they fall short of God's rest; here he urges them to "become diligent" in pursuit of entrance thereunto. Fear of loss should inspire greater diligence in pursuit.[59] The availability of the promise of entering God's wonderful "rest" and its quality as a great "Sabbath celebration" (vv. 3b-10) are more than sufficient motivation for this renewed effort.[60] Since this rest is God's own ultimate rest, the goal of creation, and the intended destiny of God's people, they must pursue it with a new diligence. The pastor would awake them from the lethargy implied by the "drifting" and "neglect" against which he warned them in 2:1-4 lest they fall into apostasy. He would replace slothfulness with zealous pursuit of entrance into God's rest through a life of faithful obedience. He has focused the hearers' vision on the magnitude of the goal and the dire conse-

---

57. The faithful "rest from the labors of a faithful life in this world" (Laansma, *Rest Motif,* 358). For a full discussion of alternatives see Laansma, *Rest Motif,* 296-300. He refers to promised deliverance from suffering in *4 Ezra* 7; Rev 14:13; and 2 Thess 1:3-10.

58. Hofius, *Katapausis,* 55, misses this distinction when he identifies God's "rest" as one of the works of creation.

59. Both φοβηθῶμεν ("let us fear"), as noted above, and σπουδάσωμεν ("let us be diligent") are ingressive aorists (hortatory subjunctive) urging the hearers to a new level of precautionary "fear" and diligence of pursuit (see Lane, 1:94).

60. οὖν ("then," "therefore") shows that this exhortation is dependent on the preceding argument.

quences of its loss. He will soon reinforce this argument by describing the great provision for its attainment through the high-priestly work of the Son (4:14–10:25).

The pastor who moved from "fear lest anyone fall short" (v. 1) to "give more diligence to enter" would conclude once more with a warning not to follow the wilderness generation — note the ominous word, "fall" (cf. 3:17): "lest anyone fall by the same example of disobedience." The pastor has moved the word for "the same" near the beginning of the Greek clause in v. 11b and deliberately reserved "disobedience" for the end.[61] Thus he draws his hearers' attention once more inexorably to the "same" fallen wilderness generation.[62] Note his continued concern for the whole congregation and for each of its members — "lest any of you." Their "diligence" must express itself in mutual concern for each other's perseverance. They must avoid both the concrete "disobedience" (4:11; cf. 4:6) of the wilderness generation and the "unbelief" (3:19) from which it sprang.[63] The pastor would leave this dire warning against Kadesh Barnea–type "disobedience" ringing in their ears.

With this final caution the pastor draws his discussion of the wilderness generation's failed pilgrimage to a close. After explaining the great benefits of Christ's high priesthood, he will return to the theme of pilgrimage in 10:36-39 and catalogue the great examples of faith in 11:1-38. As his hearers must avoid identification with the unbelieving and disobedient wilderness generation, so they are to identify with those who receive the "promise" (10:36) because they live "by faith" (10:38). This tragic history of disobedience will be countered by the glorious history of God's people of faith.

---

61. Note the word order in 4:11b: ἵνα μὴ ἐν τῷ αὐτῷ τις ὑποδείγματι πέσῃ τῆς ἀπειθείας. ἐν τῷ αὐτῷ, "in the same," has been brought forward and separated from the noun it modifies, ὑποδείγματι, "example," by the subject τις, "anyone." Furthermore, τῆς ἀπειθείας appears to have been separated from the ὑποδείγματι that it qualifies by the verb πέσῃ. It is possible, but not likely, that τῆς ἀπειθείας is an ablative of means qualifying πέσῃ, "fall through unbelief." Qualification of ὑποδείγματι is more likely because the pastor normally attributes "disobedience" (3:18; 4:6) or "unbelief" (3:19) to the wilderness generation. Thus by moving ἐν τῷ αὐτῷ forward and reserving τῆς ἀπειθείας for the end, the pastor appears to have used the liberty afforded by Greek syntax to emphasize these terms.

62. Ellingworth, 258-59, argues that ἐν τῷ αὐτῷ . . . ὑποδείγματι is instrumental of means or cause, "by means of the same example." It is difficult, however, to understand how observing this example would cause anyone to fall. Thus a locative makes better sense: lest anyone fall "into the same example," that is, into the same kind of disobedience experienced by the wilderness generation.

63. In fact, 𝔓46 reads ἀπιστίας, "of unbelief," in 4:11 instead of ἀπειθείας, "of disobedience."

4. *You Are Accountable before the Word of God (4:12-13)*

12 *For living is the word of God and active; and sharper than any two-edged sword; and penetrating until it divides life and spirit, even joints and marrow; and judging the thoughts and intentions of the heart.* 13 *And no created thing is hidden before him, but all things are naked and prostrate to the eyes of him to whom a word of reckoning is due from us.*

12-13 These verses bring this first section of Hebrews to its grand conclusion. Heb 1:1–4:11 has put great stress on God's speaking and on the commensurate accountability of his people. The God who spoke in the OT has now spoken his final word in one who is Son (1:1-14); thus it is urgent that God's people not "neglect" this final word (2:1-4), which is "such a great salvation" (2:3). In 2:5-18 the pastor has begun to describe the greatness of this salvation. He demonstrates the Son's superiority to God's preeminent OT agent of revelation, Moses, in 3:1-6, before confronting his hearers with the example of the Moses-led wilderness generation's tragic refusal to heed God's word (3:7–4:11). This first large section of Hebrews (1:1–4:13), which began with God's final revelation in his Son (1:1-4), ends with a compelling assertion of human accountability before the word of God (1:12-13) commensurate with such a revelation. The very fact that God's word provides such a great salvation (2:3) and promises God's eternal "rest" means that it is also a word of judgment on those who reject God's gracious offer.[1]

Verses 12-13 are not only a fitting conclusion to 1:1–4:13 as a whole but also to 3:1–4:11, the story of the faithless wilderness generation in particular.[2] The refrain of Ps 95:7 reechoes in the background: "Today, if you hear

---

1. See Pfitzner, 85.

2. Although Westfall, *Discourse Analysis*, 140-42, agrees that v. 11 concludes 4:1-11, she makes 4:11-16 a separate unit that concludes the first major section of Hebrews and introduces the second. She bases this on the thrice-repeated οὖν accompanied by hortatory subjunctives (σπουδάσωμεν, "let us be diligent"; κρατῶμεν, "let us hold fast"; and προσερχώμεθα, "let us approach") in 4:11, 14, and 16. Verses 12-13 support the exhortation of v. 11; v. 15 supports the exhortation of v. 14; and 5:1-10 supports the exhortation of v. 16. Verses 11-13 are supposed to summarize 3:1–4:11; vv. 14-15, 1:1–2:18; and v. 16 introduces what follows. However, the reintroduction of high priesthood in v. 14 divides it sharply from vv. 11-13. Verse 14 is no summary of 1:1–2:18. Westfall's analysis does not account adequately for "Having then a great high priest who has passed through the heavens, Jesus, the Son of God." As noted in the commentary below, these themes will be developed in what follows. The fact that this phrase precedes and provides motivation for the exhortation of v. 14 also suggests a significant break between vv. 13 and 14. On the coherence and function of 4:14-16 see pp. 218-20 below.

his voice. . . ."[3] The "word of hearing" (4:2) addressed to the wilderness generation was indeed the word which was heard and therefore brought accountability for obedience. Thus these verses add great force to the exhortation that concludes 4:1-11. The hearers must certainly "begin to give a new diligence" (4:11) to enter God's rest because they are utterly accountable before the word of God. The total effectiveness of the "word of God" as here described removes all doubt that God's address was limited to the wilderness generation or some other specialized group of people.

⌐It is important to compare this warning that concludes the opening section of Hebrews, with 10:26-31, the warning that (along with 10:19-25) introduces the final section (10:19–12:29). The arresting admonition of Heb 4:12-13 prepares the hearers to receive the benefits of Christ's high priesthood, affirmed in 4:14-16, so that they can avoid falling into the faithlessness of the wilderness generation. Heb 10:26-31, on the other hand, draws on those benefits explained in 5:1–10:18 and described in 10:19-25, as means and motivation for the hearers to identify with the great catalogue of the faithful in 11:1-38. Both warnings stress accountability. The first ends, "all things are naked and prostrate to the eyes of him to whom a word of reckoning is due from us" (4:13b); the second with, "It is a fearful thing to fall into the hands of the living God" (10:31). The first derives its urgency from the magnitude of the promised "rest"; the second adds greater urgency from the full adequacy of Christ's saving work as the only provision for entering that rest.[4]⌐

12   The first and emphatic word in the Greek sentence is "living." Like God himself (3:12; 9:14; 10:31), his word is "living" and thus "active" and absolutely effective in all it does.[5] This is the "word" of God by which he created the world (11:3).[6] It is the word once spoken in the prophets, but now spoken in the incarnate and exalted eternal Son (1:1-2).[7] God's word continues to address the people of God, even through the pastor's sermon, as the ex-

---

3. Cf. Lane, 1:96; Attridge, 133; Weiss, 284; O'Brien, 174.

4. See the section entitled "The Sermon and Its Rhetorically Effective Structure" in the Introduction (pp. 60-77).

5. Attridge, 134.

6. Although the term used for "word" in 11:3 is ῥῆμα rather than λόγος.

7. *Pace* J. Swetnam, "Jesus as Λόγος in Hebrews 4,12-13," *Bib* 62 (1981): 214-24, the context prevents limiting the "word of God" to the divine "logos" of John 1:1-14. This expression must embrace the word of God addressed to the people who lived before Christ, such as the wilderness generation just mentioned in this passage. However, this "word of God" finds its fulfillment and climax in what God has spoken through the Son. Hebrews knows nothing of a preincarnate revelation in the Son. By definition, God's ultimate revelation in his Son is encompassed in his incarnation and exaltation. See "The Sermon's Use of the Old Testament" in the Introduction (esp. pp. 41-47).

position of Ps 95:7-11 has just demonstrated.[8] The fate of the wilderness generation is evidence that his word comes to pass. One cannot evade the living word of God, for it penetrates and exposes the deepest recesses of the human person.

The word of God is described by phrases beginning with "sharper," "penetrating," and "discerning." Each description expands or explains the previous. The pastor wants his hearers to see the word of God as "sharper than any two-edged sword." He emphasizes its razor-edge sharpness by his next description, "penetrating until it divides life and spirit, even joints and marrow."[9] Whether this phrase means the division of "life from spirit" and "joints from marrow," as most affirm, or whether it means the division of each entity, "life," "spirit," "joints," and "marrow," as Ellingworth contends, is of little moment.[10] God's word is so sharp that it can divide the indivisible.[11] It has more than laser-like penetrating quality. This description gives the hearers a visceral feeling for the sharp, penetrating power of the word of God.[12] The desire to evoke this feeling accords well with the evidence Smillie has provided suggesting that the pastor is picturing the word of God as the surgeon's knife.[13] The pastor, however, does not develop such imagery lest he detract from the warning nature of this passage.[14]

8. On the role of God's word in creation see Gen 1:3; Ps 33:9; and Isa 55:11. On the judging function of God's word see Amos 1:2; Ps 51:6; and Jer 7:13. Often the OT prophetic books begin with the "word of the LORD" coming to the prophet (Isa 1:10; Jer 1:4; Amos 5:1; Mic 1:1; Joel 1:1; Hag 2:20; Zech 1:7; cf. also 1 Sam 15:24; 2 Sam 12:9; 1 Kgs 12:24; 2 Kgs 9:36; 1 Chr 10:13; 2 Chr 11:2). Wis 18:14-16 personifies the word of God as a warrior who exercises the sharp sword that represents God's decrees against the Egyptians who refuse to let Israel leave Egypt.

9. For the combined use of "soul" (ψυχή) and "spirit" (πνεῦμα) see Wis 15:11; Josephus, *Ant.* 3.260; Philo, *Worse* 80–83; *Heir* 55–57; *QG* 2.59. Hebrews appears to use both "soul" (10:39) and "spirit" (10:39) with little distinction (O'Brien, 177, n. 137).

10. Ellingworth's (263) argument that joints and marrow do not touch is worth consideration.

11. "Life and spirit" often occur together as a pair. See Wis 15:11; Josephus, *Ant.* 1.34; Philo, *Worse* 80–83; *Heir* 55–57; *QG* 2.59.

12. "For the ancients 'marrow,' deeply hidden inside the bones, served metaphorically for that which was most intimate in the body of a person" (G. R. Smillie, "'ho logos tou theou' in Hebrews 4:12-13," *NovT* 46 [2004]: 343).

13. Smillie, "Hebrews 4:12-13," 348-49. The word μάχαιρα is often used for a knife or dagger shorter than what is normally implied by the English word "sword" (Josh 5:2, 3; 24:31; Judg 3:16-22 in the LXX). Cf. Ellingworth, 282. Smillie references Wilhelm Michaelis, "μάχαιρα," *TDNT* 4:527, and the examples there cited, as evidence that this word could be used for a surgeon's knife. The fact that it is used to separate "joints and marrow" concurs with this proposal. Cf. Swetnam, "Jesus as Λόγος," 218-19.

14. Smillie must unduly minimize the warning character of 3:7–4:11 in order to argue that the pastor is here attributing a healing power to the word of God. Furthermore,

After making his hearers see and feel the precise, sharp, penetrating power of God's word, the pastor tells them what this penetrating power is: God's word penetrates and divides by "discerning or judging the thoughts and intentions of the heart." "Thoughts and intentions" is a comprehensive expression used to describe all that goes on in the human "heart."[15] It is possible with the KJV/NKJV to take "discerning" as a noun — "a discerner [judge] of the thoughts and intentions of the heart." This is the pastor's bottom-line statement.

God's word exposes what is in the human heart by confronting it with the claims of God. His address to the wilderness generation exposed the hardness of their hearts through unbelief (see on 3:8, 10, 12; 4:7 above). Their unwillingness to trust God's power and promise became evident to all. However, this penetrating word of God is a call to repentance. The pastor would expose any tendency to lethargy or unbelief in order that his hearers might turn from it.

13 God's word so accurately and penetratingly exposes what is in the human heart because the God who speaks his word already knows what is there.[16] There is no escape from his knowledge. For emphasis the pastor affirms the all-seeing knowledge of God first negatively, then positively. He begins with, "no created thing is hidden before him." Not only the human heart or person, but absolutely nothing in the creation he has made is beyond his penetrating gaze. The comprehensive reach of God's knowledge is emphasized by the opening words of the contrasting clause: "but all," absolutely

---

the contention that the following passage, 4:14-16, is a word of encouragement is no argument that the present passage should be so construed. Hebrews regularly follows warning with encouragement (see 6:1-8 followed by 6:9-12; and 10:19-25, by 10:25-31). Smillie, however, does provide a needed corrective. This present passage is not about the condemnation of the executioner's sword (*pace* Michel, 198-99, n. 3). It is, however, about the exposure of the human heart and therefore about the accountability, and, indeed, the absolute helplessness, of God's people before him (Lane, 1:102; O'Brien, 175). See Smillie, "Hebrews 4:12-13," 338-59.

15. The difficulty in making a clear distinction between ἐνθύμησις ("thoughts") and ἔννοια ("intentions") only emphasizes the penetrating power of the word of God, able to "judge" between them (Johnson, 135). See BDAG, 336, 337; Attridge, 136; O'Brien, 177, n. 138. The pastor, ever sensitive to the resonance of his words in the ear, has chosen two terms that begin with ἐν.

16. The idea that nothing is hidden from God was common in the OT. This concept was prominent in contemporary Judaism (*1 En.* 9:5; *Letter of Aristeas* 132–33; Sir 16:17; Philo, *Abraham* 104) and was not absent from the Greco-Roman world (Seneca, *Ep.* 83; Epictetus, *Diatr.* 2.14.11). For further references see Attridge, 136, nn. 48, 49; Koester, 274; Lane, 1:103. The pastor, however, has used this imagery with renewed force and specificity in light of all that he says about the word of God and its final disclosure in the "great salvation" (2:3) provided by God's Son.

"all" things and persons are known to him. That they are "naked and laid bare to his eyes" affirms the depth of his knowledge. He knows all persons and things, and he knows them totally and completely. The word translated "laid bare" is derived from the Greek word for "throat" and was sometimes used of a wrestler "taking" his opponent "by the throat" and "overthrowing" him.[17] Smillie, however, has suggested that it was also appropriate as a description of the patient whose head was pulled back on the operating bench.[18] Ellingworth is probably correct when he argues that the word is too rare for it to be a dead metaphor unrecognized by the hearers.[19] Thus Montefiore catches the precise nuance, "naked and prostrate" before his eyes.[20] The pastor would have his hearers realize their total helplessness and defenselessness before the inescapable eyes of God.

It is none other than this God "to whom a word of reckoning is due with reference to us." The Greek sentence ends with "the word." A wooden translation of this statement enables us to see the intended wordplay: "to whom in reference to us the word."[21] This passage ends with the answering "word" of accountability that the hearers must give to the all-penetrating "word" of the all-knowing God.[22] This most powerful ending is intended to leave the hearers almost shaking with trepidation at their awesome responsibility. How can they make adequate response. In the immediately following verses (4:14-16) the pastor begins to reassure them by affirming the great blessings that are theirs through Jesus, the Son of God. Without this knowledge of their responsibility they would not be able to adequately appreciate and grasp what Jesus has done for them.

II. THE SON'S HIGH PRIESTHOOD — RESOURCE AND URGENCY FOR PERSEVERANCE (4:14–10:18)

The pastor has used the history and fate of the unfaithful, and the awesome statement of accountability with which that history concluded (4:12-13), to

---

17. See Spicq, 2:90-91.
18. Smillie, "Hebrews 4:12-13," 347-48.
19. Ellingworth, 264-65.
20. Montefiore, 89
21. πρὸς ὃν ἡμῖν ὁ λόγος. This translation takes ἡμῖν, "us," as dative of reference, "to whom the word [must be given] in reference to us." It could also be instrumental of agency, "to whom the word [must be given] by us."
22. See G. R. Smillie, "'The Other Logos' at the End of Heb. 4:13," *NovT* 47 (2005): 19-25. This forceful statement of accountability before God echoes the common idiom, "to give a word," meaning "to give account."

underscore the importance of faithful obedience to the word of God. In this way he has been preparing his hearers to receive his teaching about the high priesthood of the Son of God. As their High Priest the Son is both the fulfillment of God's previous revelation and the God-provided way for his people to avoid the fate of the disobedient. Thus in Heb 4:14–10:18 the pastor describes the Son as the all-sufficient High Priest and the fully adequate resource for perseverance in faithful obedience. Those who take advantage of God's marvelous provision not only avoid the fate of the faithless, but they join the grand company of the faithful whose story is told in 10:19–12:29, and who are destined to receive an "Unshakable Kingdom" (12:28). Thus, the pastor would urge his hearers not only to shun the unfaithful of old (1:1– 4:13), but, through the all-sufficiency of the Son their High Priest (4:14– 10:18), to take their rightful place among those who persevere in obedience (10:19–12:29).[1]

The reader will remember that the pastor opened his sermon with an exposition of the Son's grandeur (1:1–2:18). In fact, he allowed his hearers to overhear a grand conversation between God (1:5-14) and his Son (2:5-18) so that they would better comprehend the Son's identity and appreciate his key role in providing "such a great salvation" (2:3). The pastor now returns to that conversation and brings it to a climax in order to explain the Son's all-sufficiency as the High Priest who alone provides for the removal of sin and for access to God. This section is best divided into four parts — 4:14–5:10; 5:11–6:20; 7:1-28; and 8:1–10:18 — that can be grouped into two pairs.[2]

---

1. See "The Sermon's Rhetorically Effective Structure" in the Introduction to this commentary (pp. 60-77).

2. In the Introduction this commentary (pp. 70-71) has noted the cohesion given Heb 5:1–7:28 by the quotation of Ps 110:4 (5:5-6, 10; 6:20; 7:1-25). Guthrie, *Structure*, 82, argues for a high-level cohesion shift at 5:1, a median-level shift after 7:28, and an inclusion between 5:1-3 and 7:26-28. His analysis has been followed most recently by O'Brien, 187-88. James Kurianal, *Jesus Our High Priest: Ps 110,4 as the Substructure of Heb 5,1–7,28* (European University Studies; Frankfurt am Main: Peter Lang, 2000), has dedicated his dissertation to proving the unity of this section. Yet Kurianal's attempt to expound 5:1–7:28 as one section fails to account adequately for the fact that the comparison/ contrast between Aaron and the Son in 5:1-10 introduces 7:1–10:18 as a whole (see Kurianal, *Jesus Our High Priest*, 263-68, for a summary of his arguments). He recognizes that 5:5-6 announces the theme of 7:1-28, but fails to see that 5:1-3, 7-10 establishes a typological relationship between the priesthoods of Aaron and the Son that is then developed in 8:1–10:18. The themes from 5:1-3, 7-10 reappear in 7:26-28, not merely as an inclusion but also in order to introduce the following section. Thus it is clear that 5:1-10 introduces not only 7:1-28 but also 8:1–10:18. The "entity of Melchizedek" may be "deactivated" after 7:28 (Westfall, *Discourse Analysis*, 188), but other aspects of 5:1-10 come to the fore. Moreover, the exhortation in 5:11–6:20 is not without relevance for 8:1–10:18 as well as for 7:1-28. The break between 7:28 and 8:1 is hardly more pronounced than the

The first pair (4:14–5:10; 5:11–6:20) brings the hearers back to the divine conversation of 1:1–2:18; introduces the high priesthood of Christ as the main topic for discussion, and prepares the hearers to fully embrace the Son as their High Priest. The second pair (7:1-28; 8:1–10:18) expounds the majesty and sufficiency of this High Priest by bringing the conversation between God and his Son to its conclusion.

The pastor, always concerned for his hearers' faithfulness, returns to the high priesthood of Christ by urging them to take advantage of its soon-to-be-described benefits (4:14-16). To this exhortation he joins a comparison/contrast that establishes a typological relationship between Aaron's high priesthood and that of the Son of God (5:1-10). This typology is fundamental to the argument of both 7:1-28 and 8:1–10:18. However, the pastor is concerned lest his hearers not realize the great value of embracing and the dire consequences of neglecting God's ultimate word revealed in the Son as High Priest. Thus he uses the exhortation of 5:11–6:20 to arouse and encourage them to enthusiastically embrace his teaching on this subject before he expounds Ps 110:4 (6:20) and explains the nature of the Son's high-priestly ministry. In 7:1-28 the pastor expounds Ps 110:4, God's confirmation of the Son in his eternal high priesthood. This divine declaration legitimizes the Son's high-priestly vocation by providing its Scriptural support and reveals his character as the eternal and exalted High Priest. In 8:1–10:18 the pastor develops the comparisons/contrasts between the Aaronic high priest and the Son that were enumerated in 5:1-3, 7-10. In this way he is able to show how the Son became such an exalted high priest through his human obedience. At the heart of this section is Ps 40:6-8 (Heb 10:5-10): the Son accepts the Father's appointment to high priesthood (Ps 110:4) by affirming his incarnate obedience (Ps 40:6-8). With this affirmation of total submission to the divine will the Son fulfills the sonship declared by the Father at the conversation's beginning (Ps 2:7; Heb 1:5).

Thus 7:1-28 and 8:1–10:18 relate to one another much as 1:1-14 related to 2:5-18. In 1:1-14 the Father addressed the Son as his eternal and exalted Son. In 2:5-18 the Son replied by affirming his incarnate obedience as the means of his exaltation. In 7:1-28 the Father addresses the Son as the eternal, exalted High Priest. In 8:1–10:18 the Son answers by affirming his incarnate obedience (10:5-10) as the means by which he has accepted this Father-given vocation and become such an all-sufficient, exalted High Priest.

---

breaks after 5:10, 6:12, or 6:20. Guthrie, *Structure,* 83-84, finds high-level cohesion shifts after both 5:10 and 6:12. Thus, despite a degree of formal unity in 5:1–7:28, it is more helpful to divide this section as in the commentary above. For the inclusion of 4:14-16 with this section see "The Sermon's Rhetorically Effective Structure" (esp. pp. 61-62; 67, n. 273; and pp. 70-71).

A. THE LIFE OF FAITH AND THE HIGH PRIESTHOOD OF THE SON (4:14–5:10)

The pastor introduces this section by urging his hearers to take advantage of these yet-to-be-described benefits. This initial exhortation raises the readers' expectations and whets their appetite for the pastor's fuller explanation to follow.[1] By boldly asserting the ultimacy of Christ's high priesthood, the pastor appears to question the perpetuity of the Aaronic high priesthood affirmed by the Old Testament (2 Chr 23:13). Thus it is no surprise that he follows the introductory invitation (4:14-16) with a comparison/contrast between Christ and the Aaronic high priest, in which he claims Ps 110:4 as Scriptural support for his position (5:1-10). The pastor follows this comparison/contrast with an exhortation (5:11–6:20), carefully crafted to awaken his hearers so that they will embrace the full significance of what he has to say about the Son as all-sufficient High Priest.

1. Embrace This Great High Priest (4:14-16)

14 *Therefore, because we have a great high priest who has gone through the heavens, Jesus, the Son of God, let us hold firmly to our confession. 15 For we do not have a high priest who is unable to sympathize with our weaknesses, but we have one who has been tempted in every way, just as we are, yet without sin. 16 Therefore, let us approach the throne of grace with confidence, so that we may receive mercy and find grace to help us in time of need.*

Heb 4:14-16 resumes the theme of Christ's high priesthood first mentioned in 2:17–3:1,[1] and introduces the grand exposition of that theme in 5:1–

1. On the importance of the parallel exhortation in 4:14-16 and 10:19-25 for the structure and effectiveness of this sermon see "The Sermon's Rhetorically Effective Structure," esp. pp. 61-62; 67, n. 273; and pp. 70-71.

1. Heb 4:14 repeats the terms "Jesus," "high priest," and "confession" from 3:1. A number of expressions in 4:15-16 concur with terms used in 2:17-18: "To sympathize" and "tempted in every way, just as we are" from 4:15 correspond to "merciful" and "made like his brothers in every way" in 2:17. The phrase "find grace to help us in time of need" in 4:16 corresponds to "able to help those who are being tempted" in 2:18. *Pace* both Vanhoye, *La structure littéraire,* 104-7, and Braun, 85, the repetition of these terms in 4:14 does not form an inclusion with 3:1. The theme of Christ's high priesthood has not been discussed in the intervening verses. Rather, v. 14 resumes the theme introduced in 2:17-18, 3:1. Thus it is to be taken as an introduction to the following exposition of that theme rather than as the conclusion to the previous section. Vanhoye would add v. 14 to what precedes and join vv. 15-16 to 5:1-10. However, the cohesion of this unit is demon-

10:18.[2] The pastor establishes what he is going to say about the high priesthood of Christ on what he has already said about the "Son of God" (4:14; cf. 1:1-14) and the fully human, sympathetic "Jesus" (4:14; cf. 2:5-18). This "High Priest" is "great" (4:14) because as the "Son of God" (7:1-28) he became the human "Jesus" who by his self-offering "passed through the heavens" and sat down at God's right hand as the representative of God's people (8:1–10:18). The exposition below explains vv. 14-16 in light of what the pastor will say about Christ's high priesthood in the following chapters. It is important to remember, however, that he does not intend these verses to be a full explanation. He wishes simply to impress his hearers with the magnitude of Christ's high priesthood and to intensify their interest in what is to come.

It is easy to follow the author's thought in this passage. With three sentences he offers the people of God two similarly structured arguments, taking the form "Since *we have* . . . , therefore *let us* . . . (i.e., basis and appeal).

> v. 14 "Because we have a great high priest . . ."
> (therefore) "let us hold fast to our confession."
> Vv. 15-16 (Because) we also have a fully sympathetic High Priest, therefore let us come with confidence to find help in time of need.

The order in which the pastor presents these two arguments shows the relationship between what he has said and what he is about to say. The first picks up the theme of holding fast (3:6, 14) from the story of the wilderness generation and thus reminds the hearers not to turn away from God, as they did. It is no surprise that the second is longer, for it points forward to the description of this High Priest in the following chapters and to the provision he has made for coming into God's presence. This provision is the means by which the people of God "hold fast" and avoid the tragedy of disobedience. The pastor will reverse these two themes in the coordinate exhortation in 10:19-25 that introduces the next section. He will make this reversal in order to lead his hearers from the all-sufficient high priesthood of Christ to victorious perseverance in identification with the faithful of all time as described in 11:1-40.[3] The pastor's explanation of Christ's high priesthood is thus no

---

strated by the parallel structure, unity of theme, and hortatory nature of v. 14 and vv. 15-16. Comparison with the corresponding exhortation in 10:19-25 reinforces this conclusion. See the discussion in "The Sermon's Rhetorically Effective Structure," esp. pp. 61-62; 67, n. 273; and pp. 70-71.

2. See Guthrie, *Structure,* 102-3.

3. Compare ἔχοντες οὖν ("therefore, because we have") in 4:14 and 10:21;

theological speculation, but the all-important Christological foundation for his exhortation.[4] The type of high priest that God's people have is both the source of victorious Christian living and the motivation for Christian responsibility.

14 With a resumptive "therefore"[5] the pastor offers a twofold appeal to his readers: "Retain your confidence in Christ by making use of the grace he provides." The "therefore" itself goes back to 2:18–3:1 in particular, with its first mention of Jesus as High Priest, but at the same time it presupposes everything that has been said to this point.[6] In typical "pastoral" style, the writer uses the inclusive "we" throughout, thus identifying himself with his readers and with all who are called to be God's faithful people. "We" as the people of God have this great High Priest.

The *basis* of this first appeal is the "high priest" that the people of God "have." The adjective "great" sets the tone for this verse. Everything in this description is used to emphasize the immeasurable superiority of this High Priest. In the Greek Old Testament *great priest* is equivalent to *high priest*.[7] Thus there is redundancy in the expression "great high priest": one might say, "great great priest" or "high high priest."[8] This redundancy underscores the unspeakable greatness of this High Priest, who is far superior to the Levitical priests because he is "powerful to save."[9] The pastor reinforces Christ's high-priestly superiority by adding in terse, compact form, "who has gone through the heavens, Jesus, the Son of God."

προσερχώμεθα μετὰ ἀληθινῆς καρδίας ἐν πληροφορίᾳ πίστεως ("let us come with true hearts in full assurance of faith," 10:22) with προσερχώμεθα οὖν μετὰ παρρησίας τῷ θρόνῳ τῆς χάριτος ("therefore, let us approach the throne of grace with confidence," 4:16); and κατέχωμεν τὴν ὁμολογίαν τῆς ἐλπίδος ("let us hold fast to the confession of hope," 10:23) with κρατῶμεν τῆς ὁμολογίας ("let us hold firmly to our confession," 4:14).

4. Weiss, 292-93.

5. The resumptive force of οὖν is likewise picked up by the "then" of the NRSV, NASB, etc.

6. Weiss, 292-93. See the opening introductory paragraph above.

7. For ὁ ἱερεὺς ὁ μέγας, "great priest," see Lev 21:10; Num 35:25, 28, 32; Hag 1:1, 12, 14; 2:3; Zech 3:1, 9; 6:11. Before the Maccabean period ἀρχιερεύς, "high priest," occurs only in Lev 4:3 and Josh 22:13. See Johnson, 139.

8. The author of 1 Maccabees uses the full term μέγας ἀρχιερεύς, "great high priest," in reference to Simon Maccabaeus (1 Macc 13:42), and Philo uses it to describe Melchizedek (*Abraham* 30) and the Logos (*Dreams* 1.214, 219; 2.183). See Ellingworth, 266. Both authors employ this term to emphasize the greatness of the high priest in question.

9. Spicq, 2:91. The pastor announces the superiority of Christ's high priesthood in 4:14-16 by using the term "great high priest." He concludes his discussion of this theme in 10:19-25 with the term "great priest." In between these two references he has expounded "the incomparable majesty of His person" (Riggenbach, 118) and the saving efficacy of his priestly work. Compare 13:20, "the great Shepherd of the sheep."

This High Priest is so great because he has "gone through the heavens" and sat down at the right hand of God (1:3).[10] Just as the Aaronic high priest went through the veil into the earthly Most Holy Place, so Christ has entered into the very presence of God in heaven itself (9:1–10:18). "Who has gone through" translates a Greek perfect participle and signifies the continuing validity of Christ's having entered God's presence. The access to the Father that he has obtained is a present and continuing reality for his people![11]

Christ, however, was able to enter God's presence as our High Priest only because he was the eternal "Son of God"[12] who became the fully human "Jesus"[13] and offered himself to "provide purification for sins" (1:3). In 7:1–25 the pastor will explain how Christ's divine sonship empowers his high priesthood, while in 8:1–10:18 he will show how "Jesus'" sinless humanity and self-offering provide access into God's presence. Christ's full identification with humanity and his divine sonship are the basis upon which he surpasses every other mediator.[14]

Since this High Priest alone can meet our needs, "let us," the people of God, "hold fast to our confession." In saying "hold fast," the writer urges tenacious endurance in Christian profession.[15] The NIV translates the Greek word rendered "confession" (cf. 3:1) by "the faith we profess" (cf. 3:1). This

10. The plural "heavens" does not commit the author to a Hellenistic or rabbinic belief in a series of three or seven heavens (*pace* Spicq, 2:91), but indicates that Jesus has penetrated through whatever levels of heaven there may be into the place where God dwells. Nor is it likely that this is a reference to a two-part heaven parallel to the Holy Place and Most Holy Place of the earthly sanctuary (see Braun, 124; Bénétreau, 1:197). The varied usage of "heavens"/"heaven" (οὐρανοί/οὐρανός) in Hebrews militates against a precise cosmology of multiple heavens (Weiss, 294). In 1:10 the plural refers to the part of the temporal, created universe that is above the earth, and in 8:1 and 9:23 to the transcendent, never-ending dwelling place of God. In 11:12 the singular refers to the temporal, and in 9:24; 10:34; 12:12, 25; and probably 12:26 to the transcendent heaven.

11. "His entrance has been achieved and the results are immutable" (Spicq, 2:91). See Hughes, 170, and Attridge, 139.

12. "Son" in 1:2, 5, 8 and 3:6 means "Son of God." Here, however, the pastor uses the full title for clarity and to highlight the contrast with the name Jesus. Our High Priest's humanity and deity are put side by side. The pastor also uses "Son of God" for clarity and emphasis in 6:6; 7:3; and 10:29.

13. The pastor uses the name "Jesus" when he wants to direct our attention to the earthly life and humanity of our Lord (see 2:9; 3:1). "Jesus" is also used in connection with high priesthood in 6:20; 7:22; 10:19; 12:24; 13:12 (Donald Guthrie, 121).

14. Contrary to Spicq (2:92), there is no indication that the writer is comparing Jesus to contemporary high priests or religious leaders.

15. The present subjunctive, κρατῶμεν, shows that the pastor is encouraging his readers to continue holding faithfully to what they already posses. The difference between κρατῶμεν ("Let us hold firmly," 4:14; cf. 3:14; 4:14; 6:18) and κατεχῶμεν ("Let us hold unswervingly," 10:23; cf. 3:6) is stylistic rather than semantic. See Ellingworth, 267.

term refers first of all to the content of our confession, the substance of "the faith" we profess — belief in the uniqueness and saving efficacy of Jesus Christ; and, secondly, to our public profession of that faith.[16] The pastor is going to explain Christ's high priesthood to his readers in order to fortify their belief in Jesus as God's Son and fully effective High Priest so that they will continue to live a life that professes faith in him.

15 The description of "our" High Priest in v. 14a suggests the comprehensive scope of that high priesthood: this High Priest is the Son of God who became the human Jesus and has entered God's presence on behalf of God's people through the offering of himself for sin. The description in v. 15 is explicit rather than suggestive, and specific rather than comprehensive. In this verse the author elaborates one aspect of that high priesthood — the identification of the incarnate "Jesus" (v. 14a; cf. 2:5-18) with his people. Because Jesus has experienced and overcome every kind of temptation to which humans are subject, he is able to empower his people in their human weakness. Jesus' victory over temptation is all the more reason why "we" should "hold firmly to the faith we profess" (v. 14). His victory is the basis of our "confidence" to "approach the throne of grace" in times of testing and temptation (v. 16).

This High Priest is so great that he is truly able "to sympathize with our weaknesses." The writer's description takes the form of a vivid contrast: "we do not have, . . . but we have." The first half of this contrast asserts what our High Priest can do, "sympathize with our weaknesses." The second half tells why he is able to do it: he "has been tempted in every way, just as we are, yet without sin." The pastor counters any doubt his hearers may have with an emphatic double negative,[17] "we do not have . . . who is unable": this High Priest is most assuredly the One who is able "to sympathize with our weaknesses."

The underlying Greek word often denotes a bond stronger than the English "to sympathize" (cf. 4 Macc 13:23). This is a "sympathy" that leads to active assistance. It finds expression and is embodied in the grace of forgiveness and victory over temptation that this High Priest ministers to those who come to God through him. His sympathetic help empowers us in the midst of all those inherent human limitations that make us vulnerable to temptation, here called "our weaknesses."[18] The Aaronic high priest, on the

16. See the discussion of this term in 3:1 above.

17. Spicq, 2:92; Westcott, 107.

18. Spicq, 2:92. Although the term ἀσθένεια has a breadth of meaning roughly equivalent to the English "weaknesses" (compare Luke 8:2; Rom 6:19; 8:26; 1 Cor 8:7-10; 15:43; 2 Cor 11:30; Gal 4:13; 1 Tim 5:23; Jas 5:14), its use here is more specific. Compare the related word ἀσθενής, "weakness," in 7:18. Christ sympathizes with "our weaknesses," but he was not determined by "weakness" as was the Aaronic high priest. See the comments on 5:2 below.

other hand, was able only "to deal gently with" sinners, to put up with and excuse their sin, because he was "subject to weakness" and thus sinful himself (5:2).[19]

The perfect tense of the participle "has been tempted" indicates that Jesus endured temptation through his entire life until its completion at/in his death (see Luke 22:28, 31), when he "resisted to the point of shedding" his blood (12:4).[20] It also attests that the benefits of his overcoming are still available to the people of God. The accomplishments of his earthly life are the basis for his heavenly ministry through which he enables his people to overcome temptation.[21]

The pastor has an urgent concern that his hearers hold firm despite their impending experience of shame and persecution.[22] Nevertheless, the emphatic "in every way, just as we are" makes it impossible to restrict Jesus' temptation to the fear of suffering. Every enticement to disobedience is a temptation to faithlessness. The author wants his hearers to be steadfast in their faith whether they are tempted by the deceitfulness of sinful pleasures (11:25) or by the fear of hardship.

However, Jesus' full experience of human temptations would have been useless had he not been "without sin." The pastor is not describing his preincarnate sinlessness but pronouncing a verdict on the course of his incarnate human life.[23] He experienced temptation as we do, but he did not re-

19. For the significance of the contrast between συμπαθεῖν (4:15), "to sympathize," and μετριοπαθεῖν (5:2), "to deal gently with," see W. Michaelis, "μετριοπαθέω," *TDNT* 5:938. The etymology of these two words gives some indication of the difference. Both are based on the root παθεῖν, meaning "to suffer," "experience," or "feel." The prefix συμ means "with," and the prefix μετριο means "measure." Thus συμπαθεῖν suggests "suffering or feeling with" someone; μετριοπαθεῖν, "measuring or restraining one's feelings toward" another. Yet Lane (1:114) is right when he says that συμπαθῆσαι "extends beyond the sharing of feelings (i.e., compassion). It always includes the element of active help (cf. 10:34; 4 Macc 4:25; 13:23; *T. Sim.* 3:6; *T. Benj.* 4:4). In this context the stress falls on the capacity of the exalted high priest to help those who are helpless...." See also W. Schenk, "Hebräerbrief 4,14-16: Textlinguistik als Kommentierungsprinzip," *NTS* 26 (1979-80): 242-52.

20. Spicq, 2:93.

21. Lane, 1:114.

22. See 10:32-39; 11:32-38; 12:4-13; and 13:11-14. On the role of "shame" and "honor" in Hebrews see deSilva, 58-71, who argues that the writer urges his readers not to be discouraged by the "shame" they receive from the outside world but to seek "honor" from God through Christ, the most effective "Patron."

23. Thus, in a sense, Ronald Williamson, "Hebrew 4:15 and the Sinlessness of Jesus," *ExpTim* 86 (1974): 7, is correct when he says that the "sinlessness" to which Hebrews refers was not something that Jesus "possessed when he began his struggle with temptations, a kind of built-in pre-disposition against sin which would have infringed the

spond as we do — he never yielded.[24] Thus we can be certain that he is able to give us victory. Jesus, the incarnate Son of God, lived a completely obedient and therefore sinless human life. By this obedience he has been perfected as our Savior and thus has become the "source of eternal salvation" (Heb 5:8-10; cf. 2:18).

16 Because "we," as God's people, have this kind of high priest, the pastor urges us to "approach the throne of grace with confidence" in order to receive the help we need for victorious living. Under the Old Covenant none could "approach" God's "throne," the Ark of the Covenant in the Most Holy Place, save the high priest, and he but one day in the year.[25] This annual approach was with great fear because God's throne was the place of judgment against sin.

Now, however, God's people are urged to draw near to the true heavenly "throne" of God "with confidence" because their High Priest has made that "throne" a throne "of grace," a true "mercy seat," for those who approach God through him.[26] God is no less holy than he was in the OT (cf. 4:12-13;

---

reality of his humanity." He is wrong, however, when he thinks that Jesus began by sinning but overcame that sin by persistent obedience culminating in his death. The writer of Hebrews believes that Jesus lived a completely obedient life culminating in his death. Of course, the verdict "without sin" could not be affirmed of this life until its completion. Thus in this sense he "became" sinless, that is, he presented his Father with a completely sinless human life, only at his self-offering. See on 5:1-10 and 10:5-10 below.

24. This understanding of "without sin" allows the interpreter to take χωρὶς ἁμαρτίας, along with κατὰ πάντα ("in every way") and καθ᾽ ὁμοιότητα ("according to likeness," "like") as qualifying the participle πεπειρασμένον ("tempted"). The process of temptation was without sin because Jesus never yielded. Spicq (1:93) argues that χωρὶς ἁμαρτίας qualifies ὁμοιότητα and thus restricts the way in which Christ's temptation was like ours. Lane (1:114) is certainly correct when he says that Christ's being without sin "does not restrict the likeness of the testing but relates exclusively to its outcome." It is possible to take καθ᾽ ὁμοιότητα not as "like our temptations" but "according to his likeness to us" (Peterson, *Perfection,* 78); Bruce, 116, n. 65; O'Brien, 184. However, *pace* O'Brien, the pastor is not concerned with, though he would not deny, the uniqueness of Christ's temptation, either in the wilderness or on the cross. He would have seen Christ's refusal to turn stones into bread (Matt 4:3, 6) or to come down from the cross (Matt 27:40) as examples of the kind of faithful obedience his hearers should imitate.

25. προσερχώμεθα, "let us approach," is often used in the LXX for entering covenant relationship with God and approaching him in worship. See Attridge. 141. It can be used of priestly ministry (Lev 9:7; 21:17; 22:3) or of congregational worship (Exod 16:9; Lev 9:5). This word is rare elsewhere in the NT, but is a favorite in Hebrews for describing the access to God won by Christ for his people (7:25; 10:1, 22; 11:6; 12:18, 22). For an extensive study of προσέρχομαι see John M. Scholer, *Proleptic Priests: Priesthood in the Epistle to the Hebrews* (JSNTSup 49; Sheffield: Sheffield Academic Press, 1991), 95-149.

26. Ellingworth, 270. The term ὁ θρόνος τῆς χάριτος ("the throne of grace") occurs nowhere else in the NT, the LXX, or the Apostolic Fathers (Braun, 128). Riggenbach

12:25-29), but Christ's obedient sacrifice has taken away the sin of the faithful and "cleansed" their "consciences from dead works" (9:14) so that they can come into the presence of this holy God. Thus the "confidence" (3:6; 10:19-23, 25) with which God's people approach is more than a feeling. Through the work of Christ they have received authorization to enter God's presence.[27] As God's people the recipients of Hebrews and we as their heirs can be sure of God's gracious acceptance.

The combination of "mercy and grace" powerfully pictures the total adequacy of the benefits God's people receive when they enter God's presence through this "merciful" (2:17) High Priest. "Mercy" is reminiscent of God's covenant love and unfailing faithfulness demonstrated in the history of Israel and culminating in Jesus Christ.[28] Through God's "mercy" the faithful are forgiven and released from their sins. The words translated "find grace" are often used in the Greek OT of finding "favor" in someone's eyes.[29] As noted above, this "throne of grace" is a place where God's people meet with God's favor and acceptance. "Grace," however, is much more than passive divine acceptance. "Grace" is the new reality of redemption freely available for God's people through the death of Christ (2:9) and mediated by God's Spirit (10:29). God's "grace" provides the power to overcome temptation and to live faithfully in all the circumstances of life.[30] God's "help" is "timely" because it is available twenty-four hours a day — whenever his people face trials and temptations. His "help" is sufficient to enable his people to "hold firmly to the faith" they "profess" despite opposition and persecution.

These two exhortations, the first in v. 14 and the second in vv. 15-16, mutually support one another. Because our "great High Priest" (the one who is "the Son of God" and has entered heaven on our behalf) is also "Jesus" (v. 14a), who sympathizes "with our weaknesses" (v. 15), we, as God's faithful, both can and should draw near to God confident of acceptance and of finding the "help" (v. 16) needed to "hold fast" the "faith we profess" (v. 14b NIV).

(122, n. 21) cites rabbinic sources in which the "throne of grace" is contrasted with the "throne of judgment." The MT of Prov 20:8 uses the phrase כסא־דין, "throne of justice," but this reference is obscured by the LXX.

27. Bénétreau, 1:200. See H. Schlier, "παρρησία, παρρησιάζομαι," *TDNT* 5:884.

28. In the LXX ἔλεος, "mercy," usually translates a form of the root חסד, which denotes God's faithful covenant love. See, for example, Josh 2:14; 2 Sam 2:6; 15:20; Pss 24:10 LXX; 60:8 LXX; 83:12 LXX; 84:11 LXX; 88:15 LXX.

29. This usage of χάριν ("grace") with some form of εὑρίσκω ("find") occurs twelve times in the LXX of Genesis alone (Gen 6:8; 18:3; 30:27; 32:5; 33:8; 33:10; 33:15; 34:11; 39:4; 47:25; 47:29; 50:4). The manuscript support for εὕρωμεν ("let us find") in Heb 4:16 is overwhelming despite its omission by B.

30. Bénétreau, 1:201.

2. The New High Priest and the Old (5:1-10)

1 *For every high priest taken from among human beings is appointed for human beings in things pertaining to God, in order that he might offer gifts and also sacrifices for sin.* 2 *He is able to deal gently with those who are ignorant and going astray because he himself is also beset with weakness.* 3 *Because of this he must offer for sins on his own behalf as well as on behalf of the people.* 4 *And no one takes this honor for himself but is called by God, just as also Aaron was called.*

5 *Thus also Christ did not glorify himself to become High Priest, but the one who said to him, "You are my Son, today have I begotten you,"* 6 *also spoke thus in another place, "You are a priest forever, according to the order of Melchizedek."*

7 *In the days of his flesh he offered both prayers and petitions to the one who was able to save him out of death with loud cries and tears, and he was heard because of his godly fear.* 8 *Although being One who is Son, he learned obedience through what he suffered.* 9 *And having been perfected, he became to all who obey him the Source of eternal salvation,* 10 *having been designated by God High Priest according to the order of Melchizedek.*

The brief description of Christ's high priesthood in 4:14-16 has given the hearers a taste of what is to come and thus made them hungry to know more about the benefits that priesthood provides. However, it has also raised questions in their minds. If the Son of God is the kind of High Priest intimated in these verses, how does he relate to the God-established Aaronic priesthood? Furthermore, what biblical authority does the pastor have for Christ's priesthood in light of the perpetual character attributed to that earlier priesthood instituted by Moses at God's direction? Thus it is no surprise that the pastor begins his extended discussion of Christ's high priesthood by comparing and contrasting this new High Priest with the old.[1]

Verses 1-4 describe the OT high priesthood; vv. 5-10 the high priesthood of Christ. The description of the former begins with "every high priest" and concludes with "Aaron."[2] The description of the latter shows that

1. Since A. Vanhoye, "La 'teleiôsis' du Christ: Point capital de la christologie sacerdotale d'Hébreux," *NTS* 42 (1996): 334, n. 19, fails to see that these verses contrast as well as compare, he puts 5:1-10 in the larger section 3:1–5:10, which supposedly compares the two priesthoods. On the other hand, Kurianal's (*Jesus Our High Priest,* 49-83) exclusive emphasis on contrast obscures the way in which 5:1-3, 7-10 establishes the typology developed in 8:1–10:18.

2. *Pace* Ellingworth, 272, the Son of God is not included in the "every high priest"

"Christ" (v. 5) is "High Priest according to the order of Melchizedek" (v. 10). Verses 1-4 are characterized by the present tense of general description; vv. 5-10 use the aorist for the acts and events through which Christ fulfilled his high priesthood.[3] The pastor shows no concern with priesthood in the Gentile world and gives no evidence of polemic against corruption in the Jerusalem Temple.[4] He carefully shapes his account of the OT high priest in order to show how that priesthood prefigures the Son's high-priestly ministry. The ineffectiveness of the old contributes to this prefigurement by establishing the necessity and effectiveness of the new. Finally, the pastor initiates his description of the new in vv. 5-6 by quoting Pss 2:7 and 110:4 as its biblical substantiation.

Most interpreters acknowledge the chiastic structure of this passage in which vv. 1-3 parallel vv. 7-10 and v. 4 parallels vv. 5-6.[5] There is consensus that vv. 4/5-6 compare and contrast the divine appointments of Aaron and Christ. However, there is a confusing lack of agreement on the way in which the details of vv. 1-3 parallel those of vv. 7-10.[6] This wide variety of interpretations suggests that one should be cautious in pressing the correspondences between these verses.[7] Nevertheless, the following analysis is convincing because of the way in which it elucidates this passage and does full justice to the particulars of the text.[8] While vv. 4/5-6 compare and contrast these priests

whose ineffectiveness is about to be described in the following verses. In this regard Kurianal, *Jesus Our High Priest,* 49-83, is correct, though he fails to see that vv. 1-4 provide the basis for a typological relationship between the Aaronic high priest and Christ.

3. See Ellingworth, 271. Thus the present tense in vv. 1-4 has nothing to do with whether or not the Jerusalem priesthood is still functioning (Weiss, 303; Braun, 131).

4. Ellingworth, 271.

5. Vanhoye, *La structure littéraire,* 108-13. Cf. Michel, 214-15, esp. n. 1 on 214.

6. Michel, 214-15, thinks that both show the humanity of the high priests. Gottfried Schille, "Erwägungen zur Hohepriesterlehre des Hebräerbriefes," *ZNW* 46 (1955): 105, thinks that these verses show how both high priests are taken from among men and how both are beset with weakness. Egon Brandenburger, "Text und Vorlagen von Hebr. V 7-10," *NovT* 11 (July 1969): 220-22, thinks that v. 7 corresponds to vv. 2-3, showing the human weakness of the high priests and their need to offer sacrifices for themselves, and that vv. 8-10 correspond to v. 1, showing that both are taken from among men. Theodor Lescow, "Jesus in Gethsemane bei Lukas und im Hebräerbrief," *ZNW* 58 (1967): 235, sees two points of comparison in these verses: the sacrificial service mentioned in v. 1 corresponds to Jesus' offering of prayers in v. 7, the ability of the old high priest in v. 2 to "deal gently" (μετριοπαθεῖν), since he himself is beset with weakness, is paralleled by Jesus' learning obedience through suffering (ἔπαθεν) in v. 8. Johnson, 142, thinks that the author elaborates various characteristics of the OT high priest in vv. 1-3 but then applies only one of them to Christ in vv. 7-9, especially "his intense identification with the weakness of those he represents" (144).

7. Ellingworth, 271.

8. This analysis develops further the insights of Christian Maurer, "'Erhört

with reference to their divine appointment, vv. 1-3/7-10 compare and contrast them in regard to their effectiveness (vv. 2a, 9), their humanity and its relationship to sin (vv. 2b, 8), and their sacrifices (vv. 3, 7). Each point of comparison is also a contrast that substantiates the ineffectiveness of the old and the superiority of the new.[9] Verse 1 introduces this comparison/contrast which concludes with the divine proclamation of Christ's effective high priesthood in v. 10. The chart below delineates the vital chiastic comparison between vv. 2-3 and vv. 7-9.

Old High Priest	Category of Comparison/ Contrast	New High Priest
2a He is able to deal gently with those who are ignorant and going astray.	*Effectiveness*	9 And having been perfected, he became to all who obey him the Source of eternal salvation,
2b because he himself is also beset with weakness.	*Humanity*	8 Although being One who is Son, he learned obedience through what he suffered.

Wegen der Gottesfurcht,' Hebr 5,7," in *Neues Testament und Geschichte: Historisches Geschehen und Deutung im Neuen Testament, Oscar Cullmann zum 70. Geburtstag,* ed. Heinrich Baltensweiler and Bo Reicke (Zürich: Theologischer Verlag, 1972), 275-84. Maurer is also correct in maintaining that the correspondences between the two high priests demonstrate the superiority of the latter.

9. Vanhoye is correct in arguing for the chiastic structure of this passage, but his insistence that the author's purpose is only to show the similarity between the two high priests and not the superiority of the new is belied by his own exegesis of vv. 7-10, which speaks of the perfection of Christ as effective Savior (Vanhoye, *Old Testament,* 133-37). Indeed, it is because of this superiority that Vanhoye is able to discuss "new perspectives" on Christ's priesthood. Thus he is forced to make statements like this: "Although his purpose has been to show the continuity between the Old Testament priesthood and the mystery of Christ, he has not in fact been able to avoid allowing some new perspectives to appear" (138). Perhaps he does not intend to avoid them. Bénétreau, 1:203-4, on the other hand, is correct in his contention that this passage moves toward a climax — the proclamation of the Son as the Source of salvation. He is mistaken, however, in denying the concentric or chiastic parallels between 5:1-4 and 5:5-10. These parallels serve to show the superiority of the new High Priest as well as the ways in which he fulfills the priestly role. Thus, while the two halves are chiastically parallel, they are not equal. The use of chiasm in this passage mirrors the chiastic tendencies of the entire book. In this passage the insufficient ministry of the old high priest (vv. 1-3) is followed by the sufficient ministry of the New (vv. 7-10). The turning point between the two is the proclamation of the Son's high priesthood (vv. 4-6). So the negative examples in chapters 3 and 4 are followed by the positive examples in chapters 11 and 12. In between is the sufficiency of Christ's high priesthood (chapters 7–10).

3 Because of this he must
offer for sins on his own
behalf as well as on behalf
of the people.

Sacrifice

7 In the days of his flesh he
offered both prayers and
petitions to the one who
was able to save him out of
death with loud cries and
tears, and he was heard because of his godly fear.

The chiastic development of this comparison/contrast is integral to the argument. The ineffectiveness of the old high priest (v. 2a) introduces the description of his humanity (v. 2b) and sacrifice (v. 3) because they are the cause and evidence of that ineffectiveness. The effectiveness of Christ (v. 9) climaxes the description of his sacrifice (v. 7) and humanity (v. 8) because he has been made fully adequate as High Priest through them. The pastor would move his hearers from "every high priest" (v. 1) to the "high priest according to the order of Melchizedek" (v. 10); from a high priest who offered for himself (v. 3) to one who offered himself (v. 7); from a high priest who was "beset with weakness" (v. 2b) to one who "learned obedience" (v. 8); from a high priest who can merely "deal gently" (v. 2a) to one who is "the Source of eternal salvation" (v. 9). The pastor varies the use of participles and finite verbs in each half of this comparison in order to highlight the superiority of the new High Priest and the ineffectiveness of the old.[10] The fundamental contours of Christ's high priesthood here delineated lay the foundation for the author's elaboration of this priesthood in 7:1–10:18.[11]

1 It is clear that "every high priest" refers to the priests descended from "Aaron" (v. 4) and not to Christ. Only they are "taken from among human beings."[12] The Son had to assume human "blood and flesh" (2:14). Only

---

10. Thus, the pastor describes the old high priest's sinful humanity that made his ministry ineffective and his sacrifice that substantiated his sinfulness with finite verbs: "since even he himself is beset (περίκειται) with weakness" (v. 2b), "and on account of this he must (ὀφείλει) offer a sacrifice for himself for sins" (v. 3). However, he describes the new High Priest's obedient humanity and his resultant effective ministry with finite verbs: "he learned (ἔμαθεν) obedience" (v. 8); "he became (ἐγένετο) the Source of eternal salvation" (v. 9). Thus the pastor moves from the ineffective ministry of the old high priest, described by a participle (μετριοπαθεῖν δυνάμενος τοῖς ἀγνοοῦσιν καὶ πλανωμένοις, "being able to deal gently with those ignorant and going astray"), to the effectiveness of the new, described by a finite verb. Bénétreau's attempt (1:203-4) to structure the passage according to finite verbs misses this distinction in the use of participles and finite verbs.

11. Weiss, 302-3.

12. ἐξ ἀνθρώπων λαμβανόμενος ("taken from among human beings") is best taken as an attributive participle: "Every high priest who is taken from among human beings," rather than as adverbial, "Every high priest is taken from among human beings." The above contention, however, is not negated even if the participle is adverbial.

the Aaronic high priest offers "gifts and also sacrifices." The Son offered one sacrifice "once for all" (9:28; cf. 10:5-10).

Nevertheless, the pastor's unprecedented emphasis on the humanity of this typical Aaronic high priest shows that he is planning to compare and contrast this priest with the high priesthood of the incarnate Son.[13] Otherwise there would be no reason for him to make the obvious assertion that "every high priest" was taken "from among human beings."[14] Only in Hebrews is the high priest described as "on behalf of" or "for human beings." Compare "for the people" and "for the nation" in John 11:50-51.[15] The pastor uses these expressions because he is going to compare and contrast Aaron with a new High Priest who assumed humanity in order that he might share the human condition of the people of God (2:14-18).[16] Thus while the OT and Jewish tradition emphasized the dignity of the high priest and his relationship to God, Hebrews focuses on his identification with humanity in order to establish a pattern for the incarnation and suffering of the new High Priest.[17]

Furthermore, this general description of the Aaronic high priest announces the ways enumerated above in which vv. 2-9 will compare and contrast the old and new high priests: the pastor compares (1) their effectiveness in dealing with sin ("for sin"; cf. vv. 2a, 9); (2) their humanity ("taken from among human beings" . . . "on behalf of human beings," vv. 2b, 8); (3) their sacrifices ("in order that he might offer gifts and sacrifices," vv. 3, 7),[18] and their divine appointment ("appointed on behalf of human beings in things pertaining to God," vv. 4, 5-6).

13. According to Weiss, 302-3, the author of Hebrews has used Jewish tradition to craft this description of the Aaronic high priest in such a way as to provide a basis for presenting by comparison and contrast what he would say about the high priesthood of Christ.

14. From what other source would one get a high priest? There is no indication within the context that the pastor is combating speculations about angelic priestly ministry.

15. Ellingworth, 273, and Braun, 130-31.

16. This approach is in accord with the pastor's immediate interest in the perseverance of the people of God. He is convinced that the Son became the human Jesus and died for all humanity (2:10).

17. In addition, the phrase "being able to deal gently with those who are ignorant and going astray" finds little or no parallel in Jewish tradition. Weiss, 304, thinks the author has added this phrase to emphasize the humanity of the old priest in anticipation of the humanity of the new.

18. Although a distinction was sometimes made between the terms δῶρον, "gift," and θυσία, "sacrifice," Hebrews appears to use them interchangeably. See Heb 8:3-4; 9:9; 11:4. Attridge, 143, n. 85; Ellingworth, 274-75; Koester, 285. Together they form a comprehensive description of sacrifices, which the pastor describes as "for sins" (Bénétreau, 1:205, n. 2; Bruce, 119). Ellingworth, 274-75, agrees that "for sins" qualifies both "gifts" and "sacrifices."

2 Verse 1 ends with "for sins." Verse 2a introduces the first point of comparison/contrast by describing the Aaronic high priest's inadequacy to address human sinfulness. Although Christ is able to "sympathize" (4:15) with and deliver his people from their sinful "weakness," the Aaronic high priest can only "deal gently" (NIV) with the sinner. He can do no more than restrain his anger against the offender.[19] He knows what it is like to fall into temptation and thus can be understanding toward others when they succumb. He has no ability to deliver them from sin and remove the barrier that separates them from God.

This description of his impotence is reinforced by the depiction of those to whom he ministers as "those who are ignorant and going astray."[20] This expression describes one group of people[21] and may imply that they are "those who are going astray through ignorance."[22] In Heb 9:7 the pastor will remind his readers that the OT sacrifices were only for sins committed in ignorance.[23] Thus the pastor may be limiting the ministry of the old high priest by saying that he could restrain his anger only against those who committed sin without knowledge.[24]

However, Heb 3:10 portrays the wilderness generation as willfully ignorant and going astray. "Those who are ignorant and going astray" describes the tendency of the people of God under the old high priest's ministry.[25] By contrast, Christ has become "the Author of eternal salvation" not to those who are "going astray" but to "those who obey him" (v. 9). Their successful obedience substantiates the effectiveness of his ministry.

Verse 2b introduces the second point of comparison/contrast between the Aaronic high priest and this new High Priest. The humanity of the Aaronic high priest is evidenced by his debilitating "weakness" — "he himself is beset with weakness." "Beset" can also be translated "clothed" or "burdened."[26] This description stands in contrast to the many sources that de-

---

19. Lane, 1:116-17. Rissi, "Menschlichkeit," 40-41; Riggenbach, 125; and W. Michaelis, "συμπαθής, συμπαθέω," *TDNT* 5:935-36 note the difference in the objects of συμπαθῆσαι, "sympathize," in 4:15 and μετριοπαθεῖν, "restrain one's anger," in 5:2. The first deals with the "weakness" itself; the second only with the people "going astray." For a similar use of μετριοπαθεῖν see Philo, *Abraham* 257, and Josephus, *Ant.* 12.128 (cited in Johnson, 143).

20. ". . . to 'be ignorant' and 'to err' are two expressions that tend to diminish the guilt" (Vanhoye, *Old Testament,* 119).

21. As demonstrated by the fact that this phrase translates two substantive present participles, ἀγνοοῦσιν καὶ πλανωμένοις, joined by one article, τοῖς. See Ellingworth, 276.

22. See Bruce, 120. But Ellingworth, 276, thinks this interpretation unlikely.

23. For an exception see Lev 6:1-7.

24. Cf. Riggenbach, 126.

25. Bénétreau, 1:207.

26. For περίκειται as "clothed" or "completely covered with" see Herodotus

scribe the Aaronic high priest as clothed in splendor.[27] Since, according to
v. 3, the old high priest had to sacrifice for his own sins, this "weakness" included sinfulness.[28] Thus the burden of this sinful weakness limited his ministry to only "restraining his anger" against the erring. As a sinner he could
make allowance for the sins of others. Hebrews affirms the full humanity of
Jesus, but it never says that he was "clothed" or "burdened" with "weakness."[29] Such weakness, including sinfulness, did not determine his life or
impinge upon the effectiveness of his ministry.

This affirmation that the old high priest was "beset with weakness" is
at the heart of vv. 2-3. His sinful "weakness" is the cause of his ministry's inadequacy as described in v. 2a and the reason why he had to offer sacrifice
for himself as affirmed in v. 3.[30] As we will see below, v. 8 stands at the heart
of vv. 7-9. While the Aaronic high priest's humanity may be described as
"clothed," "burdened," or determined by "weakness," Christ's is described by
the clause: "He learned obedience through what he suffered." His human life
was not determined by sinful weakness but by the practice of godly obedience. This sinful "weakness" identifies the Aaronic high priest with our human sinfulness but sets him in contrast to the one tempted without sin
(4:15).[31]

1.171; Josephus, *Life* 334; and 4 Macc 12:2 (cited by Johnson, 143). For "burdened," see
Mark 9:42; Acts 28:20; and Ellingworth, 277.

27. Koester, 286-87, comments: "Many sources spoke of the glorious vestments
worn by Israel's high priest in order to accent the priest's authority (Exod 28; Sir 45:6-7;
Philo, *Moses* 2.109-35; Josephus, *Ant.* 3.151-87), but what the priest wears according to
Hebrews is 'weakness' (Vanhoye, *Old Testament,* 139)." Vanhoye, *Old Testament,* 139,
suggests that what the author thinks about Christ may have caused this change in his conception of the old high priest.

28. Bénétreau (1:207) argues that this weakness is "not yet sin," but admits that it
is the lack of power to resist sin and do good. This seems to be a distinction without a difference. In any case, this being "beset with weakness" implies that he is a sinner.

29. Williamson's affirmation that "like the priests of Judaism Jesus too was 'beset
with weakness'" ignores the way this phrase is used in the immediate context (Williamson, "Sinless," 6). Thus, *pace* Schille, "Hohepriesterlehre," 105, the pastor's failure to attribute "weakness" to Christ is no accident (cf. Rissi, "Menschlichkeit," 41-45; Maurer,
"Gottesfurcht," 283). Johnson, 137, finds twelve characteristics of priesthood in 5:1-4
which "in one way or another will also be ascribed to Christ." However, his sixth, seventh,
and eighth characteristics do not apply to Christ but serve to contrast him with the old:
"(6) dealing gently with ignorant and wandering, (7) sharing their weakness, (8) offering
gifts for himself." His statement on p. 143 would seem to belie the application of these
characteristics to Christ: "The high priest can deal moderately with those who sin in this
way, for he does himself as well."

30. See ἐπεί ("because") at the beginning of v. 2b and δι' αὐτήν ("because of this")
at the beginning of v. 3.

31. Weiss, 306.

3 This verse introduces the third element of the comparison/contrast between the Aaronic high priest and the Son as High Priest. Both offered sacrifices for sin, as every high priest must (v. 1). However, the role played by sacrifice in their ministries was very different. The OT instructs the high priest to make two sacrifices, one for himself (and his house) and one for the people.[32] The pastor's concern is with the former. He wants his hearers to remember the Aaronic high priest's need to offer sacrifice for his own sin. A more literal rendering of this verse would run: "And on account of this it was necessary, as for the people, thus also for himself to offer for sins." The "as"/"so also" construction focuses the hearers' attention on the second clause. This high priest had to make an offering "for himself" that was for his "sin."[33] In order to make this point clear we have reversed the clauses in our translation above: "Because of this he must offer for sins on his own behalf as well as on behalf of the people." Furthermore, it was because he was "beset with weakness" that he had to make this offering.[34] Thus the Aaronic high priest's sacrifice for himself (v. 3) is clear evidence of his sinfulness (v. 2b) and therefore of his insufficiency (v. 2a).[35] There is no reason, then, to think that the all-sufficient new High Priest would have need to make such an offering for himself.[36] The contrasting way in which v. 7 describes Christ's effective self-offering for others will be explained below. Thus the description of the old high priest in vv. 1-3 reveals the inadequacy of

---

32. Although the mention of this double sacrifice may anticipate the pastor's later reference to the Day of Atonement (9:11-14), he shows no particular concern with that occasion in this verse. The OT high priests offered sacrifices for themselves on other days besides the Day of Atonement. See Lev 4:3-12; 9:7-14; 16:6, 11; 17:24; and *Yoma* 4:2–5:7; Philo, *Drunkenness* 129; *Moses* 2.153; *Heir* 174; *Spec. Laws* 1.229 (cited in Ellingworth, 277).

33. This emphasis on offering for himself is shown by the fact that his sacrifice is mentioned last, while in the OT it was required to be offered first (Ellingworth, 277).

34. *Pace* Riggenbach, 127, and Michel, 218, ὀφείλει, "it is necessary" (v. 3), does not indicate obligation under the law per se, but obligation incurred because of the "weakness" (v. 2) of the old high priest (Weiss, 306). Ellingworth, 277-78, notes that this verb is not used in Leviticus. Furthermore, the law is always mentioned in the context when this verb has a legal connotation (cf. John 19:7).

35. The pastor returns to this mark of his insufficiency in 9:7. For the way in which Christ transcends this necessity to offer for himself see on 7:27 and 9:14 below.

36. Those who try to find a parallel way in which Christ offered a sacrifice for himself fail to recognize the function and significance of the old high priest's offering for himself. Cf., for instance, Jürgen Roloff, "Der mitleidende Hohepriester: Zur Frage nach der Bedeutung des irdischen Jesus für die Christologie des Hebräerbriefes," in *Jesus Christus in Historie und Theologie: Neutestamentliche Festschrift für Hans Conzelmann zum 60. Geburtstag,* ed. Georg Stecker (Tübingen: Mohr, 1975), 156, who thinks that Jesus offered "prayers and petitions" for himself in v. 7 because he, like the Aaronic high priest, was characterized by "weakness."

the old order. This inadequacy will be confirmed by the description of the old tabernacle and its ritual in 9:1-10.

4 Verse 4 introduces the fourth point of comparison/contrast — a legitimate high priest is not self-appointed but is "called by God."[37] The pastor anticipated this need for divine authorization in v. 1 when he affirmed that "every high priest" was "established" by God.[38] His hearers would have accepted this necessity of divine appointment as a self-evident principle.[39] They were very familiar with the Scriptures asserting the divine establishment of Aaron's priesthood.[40] The pastor, however, must give biblical substantiation for the Son's divine call to such an office. This he will do in vv. 5-6.

There are several terms of note in v. 4. The pastor underscores the dignity of the high priesthood by referring to it as "this honor." This reverence for the high priesthood is reinforced by the statement of v. 5 that Christ did not "glorify" himself to become High Priest. Note the conjunction of "honor" and "glory" in 2:7, 9. It was not unusual to refer to the high priesthood with such respect.[41] Nevertheless, the conjunction of these terms may anticipate the fact that Christ enters into the full exercise of his high priesthood when he sits down at "the right hand of the throne of the majesty in heaven" (8:1; cf. 1:3). Furthermore, the word "called" is particularly appropriate for the way in which the pastor will affirm Ps. 110:4 as God's direct address to the Son establishing him as High Priest.

5-6 As noted above, vv. 1-4 begin with "every high priest" and climax in "Aaron." Verses 5-10 begin with "thus also Christ," and climax in, "a high priest forever, according to the order of Melchizedek." The general description of the old high priest gives way to a narration of this new High Priest's saving work.[42] "Thus also" introduces the comparison and contrast between the two.

37. Vanhoye, *Old Testament,* 120, points out, in contrast to Spicq (2:110) and others, that there is no shift here from the humility to the glorification of the high priest. The whole point is that this priest must be appointed by God — he cannot himself assume priesthood.

38. καθίσταται in v. 1 is a divine passive: "has been established" by God.

39. This necessity of divine appointment is based solely on Scripture and takes no account of the sordid way in which the contemporary high priesthood had been seized, bought, and sold (Weiss, 306-7; Ellingworth, 280; cf. Josephus, *Ant.* 15.2.4; 20.9). The pastor might have been thinking of Korah's attempt to usurp the priestly dignity as recorded in Numbers 16 (esp. v. 5). See Ellingworth, 280.

40. Cf. Exod 28:1; 29:4-9; Lev. 8:1-2, 5; Num 3:10; 16:1–18:32.

41. Compare Josephus, *J.W.* 4.149, 164; Philo, *Spec. Laws* 1.42; *Moses* 2.225, cited by Johnson, 144.

42. Thus the change from the present tense of general description, which dominates vv. 1-4, to the aorist, which characterizes vv. 5-10.

The pastor introduced the sonship of Christ in 1:1-3 and his high priesthood in 2:17-18. He brought the two together in 4:14, "Since we have a great high priest, . . . the Son of God."[43] In Heb 5:5-6 the pastor offers Scriptural support for merging Christ's high priesthood with his sonship. The same God who declared him Son (Ps. 2:7), also declares him High Priest (Ps 110:4).

Hebrews joins three key oracles of God directed to Christ: Ps 2:7; Ps 110:1; and Ps 110:4. The first is God's declaration of his sonship; the second, of his exaltation; and the third, of his priesthood. The pastor united the first two in chapter 1: "You are my Son, today have I begotten you" (Ps 2:7 in Heb 1:5); "Sit at my right hand until I make your enemies a stool for your feet" (Ps 110:1 in Heb 1:13). He unites the first and third in Heb 5:5-6: "You are my Son, today have I begotten you" (Ps 2:7 in 5:5) and "You are a priest forever, according to the order of Melchizedek" (Ps 110:4 in 5:6). The one whom God addressed as Son (and invited to his right hand) he also addresses as Priest "forever."

We have already noted the messianic character and widespread Christological application of Ps 2:7 and Ps 110:1.[44] The writer of Hebrews builds on this Christian consensus when he discerns the divine oracle proclaiming Christ's priesthood in Ps 110:4. He can join this verse to Ps 2:7, although it comes from "another place," because both are God's oracles to the Son.[45] The "one who spoke" (aorist participle) in Ps 2:7 also "speaks" (present tense) the proclamation of Ps 110:4. The historical present "speaks" adds vividness and puts emphasis on the divine affirmation of the Son's priesthood without implying that God's speech was continuous or that this second declaration occurred at a different time.

At this point the pastor uses Ps 110:4 to substantiate the divine authorization of Christ's high priesthood. His priesthood, like Aaron's, was legitimate.[46] However, the pastor's ultimate purpose in joining Ps 110:4 with Ps 2:7 is to demonstrate that the Son's priesthood is founded on his sonship.[47]

---

43. These two titles begin and conclude the pastor's description of Christ in 4:14. Thus they encompass the whole.

44. See the comments on 1:5, 13.

45. Thus the pastor has much more warrant for joining these verses than mere verbal analogy based on the fact that both make "you are" statements. The indefinite way of referring to the human source of this quotation as "another place" only highlights its divine origin (Weiss, 308, n. 26). Compare Acts 13:35; *Barn.* 15:2; *1 Clem.* 8:4; 29:3; and 46:3.

46. Most scholars would translate the introductory formula at the beginning of v. 6: "As (καθώς) also in another place he says." Attridge, 145-46, argues that καθώς has causal force — "Since also in another place he says." Ps 110:4 is the reason the pastor can say that Christ did not make himself high priest.

47. Many commentators underscore the importance of the pastor's linking priest-

When he explains "forever" and "according to the order of Melchizedek" in 7:1-25, it will become clear that this High Priest is effective only because he is the eternal Son of God.[48] It is through his high priesthood that he procures redemption and enters into his inheritance as Son (see on 1:1-3). Thus God's declaration that the One who is Son is a "priest forever, according to the order of Melchizedek" (1) insures Christ's priestly legitimacy alongside that of Aaron (5:4-6); (2) exposes Aaron's priesthood as ineffective and antiquated (7:11-14); and (3) affirms the sufficiency of the ultimate High Priest because he is Son (7:15-25).

The association of Ps 110:4 with Ps 2:7 and Ps 110:1 suggests that God proclaimed him High Priest at his exaltation.[49] Although he may have been High Priest during his earthly life, he did not enter into the full exercise of that office until "he sat down at the right hand of the Majesty in heaven" (8:1; cf. 1:3).[50] As the reader will see below, Hebrews understands Christ's sacrifice by analogy with the Day of Atonement sacrifice (9:11-14), with the sacrifice of priestly consecration (5:7-10; 9:23-24; 10:5-10), and with the covenant-establishing sacrifice (9:15; 10:15-18).[51] The first requires him to be High Priest before his self-offering. The second emphasizes the fact that he enters into the fullness of his priesthood through his offering and subsequent exaltation.[52] The third clarifies the benefits now available to God's people through this effective High Priest.

---

hood and sonship by joining these Pss 2:7 and 110:4: "The citation of the two texts . . . serves to link the key christological motifs of Son and High Priest" (Attridge, 145-46). "The purpose of vv. 5f. is to bind together the titles of Son and (high) priest as being equally conferred on Christ by God, as scripture attests" (Ellingworth, 281). Weiss, 308, argues that the author develops his hearers' confession of Jesus as the Son of God in terms of high priesthood. Both have the same divine authorization. Bénétreau (1:208-10), however, is mistaken when he argues that the joining of these two references identifies Christ as both the High Priest (Ps 110:4) and Davidic Messiah (Ps 2:7). Ps 2:7 may have been messianic, but the author of Hebrews uses it to affirm Christ's eternal sonship (1:5-6).

48. Riggenbach, 128-29.

49. For substantiation that God's declaration of sonship (Ps 2:7) was at the exaltation see the comments on Heb 1:5 above.

50. On the Son's entering into the full exercise of his sonship at the exaltation see on Heb 1:1-5 above.

51. Cf. Vanhoye, *Old Testament,* 142: "His unique offering is totally sufficient: it is at the same time a sacrifice of priestly consecration for himself and a sacrifice of expiation for the sins of all mankind, a sacrifice which is the basis of the Covenant and a sacrifice of thanksgiving."

52. Thus the pastor's theological vision embraces a high priesthood that begins on earth but reaches its fulfillment after Christ's exaltation. There is no need to assume a combination of various conflicting traditions about an earthly and a heavenly high priesthood. See Weiss 309-10.

7-10 In vv. 1-3 the pastor has painted the picture of a high priest whose ministry was limited by his own sinfulness and was therefore ineffective. In vv. 7-10 he describes the Son who has been set apart for a fully effective high priesthood through complete obedience. This offering of total submission to God unto death is his sacrifice of priestly consecration. As vv. 1-3 anticipate the contrast between Christ and the old high priest in 9:1-14, so vv. 7-10 anticipate the perfect obedience of the Son described in 10:5-10.

Verses 7-10 are one long relative clause describing the "Christ" of v. 5 whom God has just addressed as Son and Priest in vv. 5-6: "Who in the days of his flesh. . . . having been proclaimed by God High Priest according to the order of Melchizedek." This relative clause narrates the actions of this Christ and the events through which he has become effective as Savior. Since it is very difficult to render this construction in smooth English, most translations have divided this relative clause into two (NRSV, NIV) or three (NASB) complete sentences.[53] In fact, the Greek grammatical structure invites us to give each verse separate attention. Verse 7 derives cohesion from two closely related aorist participles — "having offered" and "having been heard." Verses 8 and 9 each center around a finite verb — "he learned obedience," "he became the Source of eternal salvation." The story reaches its climaxes in v. 10 with the aorist participle "having been declared" by God a high priest of Melchizedek's order. The translation given above renders v. 7, v. 8, and vv. 9-10 as three separate sentences. Nevertheless one must not forget that the whole is a description of the Christ whom God has just addressed as Son and Priest. The elevated language of this passage has suggested to some that the pastor may have been dependent on an early Christian hymn or confession.[54]

---

53. A literal translation might run something like this: "who in the days of his flesh prayers and petitions to the one able to save him from death with loud cries and tears having offered, and having been heard because of his godly fear; although being one who is Son, he learned obedience through what he suffered; and having been made perfect, he became to all who obey him the Source of eternal salvation; having been declared by God High Priest according to the order of Melchizedek."

54. See studies by Brandenburger, "Vorlagen," 190-224; Gerhard Friedrich, "Das Lied vom Hohenpriester im Zusammenhang von Hebr 4,14–5,10," *TZ* 18 (March/April 1962): 95-115; Lescow, "Gethsemane," 215-39; Schille, "Hohepriesterlehre," 81-109; Jukka Thurén, "Gebet und Gehorsam des Erniedrigten (Hebr. V, 7-10 noch einmal)," *NovT* 13 (April 1971): 136; Ulrich Luck, "Himmlisches und irdisches Geschehen im Hebräerbrief: Ein Beitrag zum Problem des 'historischen Jesus' im Urchristentum," *NovT* 6 (July 1963): 192-215; and Heinrich Zimmermann, *Die Hohepriester-Christologie des Hebräerbriefes* (Paderborn: Ferdinand Schöningh, 1964), 1-36. There is no consensus on the content of the supposed underlying hymn or confession. The only line upon which all the above agree is ἐγένετο αἴτιος σωτηρίας αἰωνίου, "he became the Source of eternal salvation." The vocabulary of this passage is no more distinctive than that of many other passages in Hebrews. The author has demonstrated himself quite capable of an elevated po-

However, a closer analysis shows that he has carefully formulated these verses for his own purposes.[55]

7 In agreement with most English translations we have rendered the two aorist participles of this verse as finite verbs: "In the days of his flesh he offered . . . and was heard," instead of "having offered" and "having been heard."[56] Nevertheless it is important to remember that by using participles in v. 7 the pastor has put emphasis on the finite verbs of vv. 8 and 9: "he learned obedience," "he became the Source of eternal salvation."

The way in which the pastor has conjoined these two participles in the Greek sentence reflects the bond he would establish between their meanings:[57] the first refers to Christ's sacrifice, the second to its acceptance by God. We might expect the pastor to say that the Son offered "himself" or "his own blood" (9:14) instead of "prayers and petitions." This way of speaking has caused some to doubt that this verse was intended as a description of Christ's sacrifice.[58] However, the affirmation in v. 1 that "every high priest"

---

etic style characterized by participles and relative clauses. Furthermore, he here addresses his favorite themes — the eternal Son, his suffering, and his obedience. For further evaluation see Thorleif Bowman, "Der Gebetskampf Jesu," *NTS* 10 (January 1964): 266; Gareth Lee Cockerill, "The Melchizedek Christology in Heb. 7:1-28" (Ph.D. diss., Union Theological Seminary in Virginia, Richmond, 1976), 338-52; R. Deichgräber, *Gotteshymnus und Christushymnus in der Frühen Christenheit: Untersuchungen zu Form, Sprache und Stil der frühchristlichen Hymnen* (WUNT; Göttingen: Vandenhoeck & Ruprecht, 1967), 174; Ellingworth, 284-85; and Braun, 140-144.

55. Maurer, "Gottesfurcht," 278. See also Weiss, 303, 311, n. 36.

56. In order to make this and the following verses independent sentences, I have used "he" in place of the relative pronoun ὅς, "who," found in the Greek text (cf. NASB). The ESV, NIV, and NRSV have inserted "Jesus" as the subject of this sentence. This is a reasonable choice, since the pastor often uses "Jesus" when referring to the Son's earthly life and suffering. Nevertheless, the antecedent of the relative pronoun is "Christ" (v. 5). Since Hebrews appears to use the names and titles of Christ with some precision, it seemed best not to insert a designation for him when omitted by the author.

57. The pastor delays the first participle until the end of its clause but gives the second at the beginning of its clause, thus joining the two: προσενέγκας καὶ εἰσακουσθείς, "having offered and having been heard." One might suggest a chiasm: qualifiers, participle; participle, qualifiers — except for the fact that the qualifiers of the first participle are so much more extensive than the simple ἀπὸ τῆς εὐλαβείας, "because of his godly fear," that qualifies the second.

58. Both Attridge's and Riggenbach's rejections of the sacrificial significance of v. 7 seem to arise at least partly from misunderstanding. Attridge, 149, appears to think that admitting a parallel between Christ's sacrifice in v. 7 and the old high priest's in v. 3 would imply that Christ offered for himself. He cites Montefiore, 97; Buchanan, 254; Rissi, "Menschlichkeit," 37; Thurén, "Gebet und Gehorsam," 144; K. Nissilä, *Das Hohepriestermotiv im Hebräerbrief: Eine exegetische Untersuchung* (Schriften der Finnischen Exegetischen Gesellschaft 33; Helsinki: Oy Liiton Kirjapaino, 1979), 92; and

offers sacrifice, the parallel description of the old high priest's sacrifice in v. 3, and the use of the word "offered" all substantiate the sacrificial intention of this verse.[59] The most important thing to observe is the way in which the pastor uses every phrase to emphasize the complete and utter dependence of the incarnate Son upon God. Thus this verse anticipates the concluding description of Christ's sacrifice in 10:5-10.[60] The graphic portrayal of the Son's abandonment to God in 5:7 finds expression in his declaration, "Here am I, I have come to do your will" (10:9).[61] This doing of God's will is the sacrifice that does away with all previous sacrifices. The description of Christ's sacrifice in 9:11-14 as "himself" and "his own blood" must be understood within the framework of these two passages (5:7-10; 10:5-10).

This verse is not about the Son's becoming human (2:14, 17) but about what happened "in the days of his flesh."[62] The pastor is describing the eternal Son's time on earth when he was subject to all the frailty and limitation characteristic of humanity.[63] "Flesh" contrasts the finitude and mortality

---

Bowman, "Gebetskampf," 268. Cf. Riggenbach, 131. This misunderstanding, however, misses the point, established above, that the pastor is both comparing and contrasting the two priesthoods. The pastor relates the old high priest's offering for his own disobedience as evidence of his ineffectiveness. The new, however, was effective because he offered himself in complete obedience. Anyone who looks for a reference to Christ's offering for himself will seek in vain. See Ellingworth, 288.

59. "To offer" (προσφέρειν) is used for sacrifice in Heb 5:7; 8:3; 9:7, 14; 10:1, 2, 8, 11, 12. The related noun, προσφορά, is used of Christ's sacrifice in 10:10, 14. See Friedrich, "Lied," 95-97. *Pace* Weiss, 314, the fact that "offer" can be used for "offering" prayers as well as sacrifices facilitates rather than contradicts its sacrificial significance in this passage. Among recent commentators, both Koester, 298-99, and Johnson, 146, agree that 5:7 describes Jesus' high-priestly offering. See also Nissilä, *Hohepriestermotiv,* 92.

60. Bénétreau, Attridge, and Weiss, along with many who doubt the sacrificial significance of v. 7, miss the connection with Heb 10:5-10. Cf. Vanhoye, *Old Testament,* 125. This connection from the larger context gives strong reinforcement to the evidence already provided by the sacrificial significance of "to offer" (προσφέρειν) and by the parallels between vv. 1, 3, and 7.

61. Cf. Rissi, "Menschlichkeit," 41-45, and Maurer, "Gottesfurcht," 283.

62. Thus Roloff, "Der mitleidende Hohepriester," 152, and others are in error when they import the preexistence–humiliation–exaltation schema from Phil 2:6-11 into this passage. The pastor certainly assumes the incarnation here, but he says nothing about the preexistent act of obedience by which he became incarnate. God's declaration of sonship and priesthood in vv. 5-6 did not occur in the Son's preexistence but at his exaltation. Verses 7-8 describe the obedient course of his human life. This earthly obedience is integral to both the theological development and pastoral purpose of Hebrews. It is by this obedience that Christ becomes the "Source" of salvation and thus the one who enables the obedience of his people. His obedience is also their example and encouragement. See Weiss, 321-27.

63. Vanhoye, *Old Testament,* 124.

of humankind with the eternity of God. The pastor is not speaking of a heavenly obedience but of an abandonment to God that occurred when the Son was experiencing all of the impairment of a humanity like our earthly humanity.

The pastor uses two parallel expressions to describe the offering of the Son and the manner of its presentation. The Son offered "prayers and petitions." He did so "with loud cries and tears." Occasionally "prayers and petitions" were linked in Hellenistic Judaism.[64] One can also find expressions similar to "with loud cries and tears."[65] The fusion of two similar terms within each of these expressions intensifies their effect. The joint use of these intensified expressions redoubles the emphasis on the desperate need of the one offering and of his utter dependence on God and ensuing faithful obedience (cf. 12:1-3).

The pastor emphasizes "the One who was able to save him out of death" by framing it with the parallel phrases "prayers and also petitions," and "with loud cries and tears." His intentional use of this description suggests that he has more in mind than the prevention of Christ's death. This is the God who could raise the dead (see on 11:19, 35).[66] He could save Christ not only "from" but "out of" death.[67] This description of God further underscores the utter dependence of the Son, living under the conditions of mortal "flesh," upon the God who can deliver from death.

Yet the pastor does not say the God "who is able to save out of death" but the God who is able to "save him" out of death. This wording strongly suggests that the "prayers and also petitions" were offered "with loud cries and tears" in anticipation of the Son's passion. This description of the Son's offering is reminiscent of the laments of the Psalter in which the innocent sufferer entreats God for deliverance from impending death.[68] Nor is it any

64. Philo, *Cherubim* 47; *Embassy* 276. Cf. Job 40:22 (LXX).

65. For similar expressions see 2 Macc 11:6; 3 Macc 1:16; 5:7, 25; Philo, *Heir* 19.

66. Hughes, 183-84.

67. Attridge, 150, argues convincingly that the phrase ἐκ θανάτου means "out of death," that is, out of the realm or power of death. He says that this is the normal understanding of σῴζειν ἐκ (cf. John 12:27; 2 Cor 1:10; Jude 5; and Jas 5:20). Preservation from impending death would be more accurately described by σῴζειν ἀπό (cf. Matt 1:21; Acts 2:40; Rom 5:9). See Westcott, 126.

68. *Pace* August Strobel, "Die Psalmengrundlage der Gethsemane-Parallele Hebr. 5,7ff," *ZNW* 45 (1954): 252-66, it is difficult to find the background for this language of suffering in a particular psalm. There is some justification, however, for arguing that the anguish of the righteous sufferer evident in many psalms is reflected in these "prayers and also petitions" with "loud cries and tears" (Attridge, 148-51). Weiss, 312-13, thinks the author has taken traditional language often used for the righteous sufferer's entreaty and used it to portray Christ's Gethsemane suffering. Thus this description is independent of the tradition found in the Gospels.

surprise that many have found in this intense struggle before impending death a reference to Christ's agony in Gethsemane[69] or to the cry of dereliction from the cross.[70]

Reference to Gethsemane is suggestive without being definitive. On the one hand, almost any reader familiar with the passion tradition would be reminded of Christ's agony in the garden. On the other hand, the wording of this verse finds no close parallels in the synoptic accounts. Thus it would be a mistake to restrict Christ's "prayers and also petitions" with "loud cries and tears" to that one event "in the days of his flesh." The pastor could have made such a reference unmistakable had he so desired. It is better to see this entire verse as a depiction of the utter dependence upon God that characterized the Son's earthly life and came to its climax in Gethsemane and on the cross.[71] This understanding does not compromise the sacrificial nature of the Son's death (9:14). His death was not only the climax of his earthly obedience, it was the offering of his obedient humanity to God.[72] By thus accomplishing God's will, he offered the all-sufficient sacrifice.

The pastor does not tell his hearers the object of the Son's "prayers and also petitions" offered in anticipation of his death to the God who could deliver him. Many have tried to supply this lack. Some have suggested that he prayed for escape from the cross, or for deliverance from the fear of death so that he might do the will of God, or that he might be saved through resurrection.[73] We might be closer to grasping the pastor's intention, however, if

69. See Spicq's comment: "Hebrews certainly refers to the agony of Gethsemane, whether it comments on the Gospel accounts or is informed by other sources" (2:113, translation mine). Hughes, 182-83, argues that "loud cries and tears" depict Christ's Gethsemane agony not just in the face of death but because he is bearing the sins of the world and wrestling with the powers of evil.

70. Vanhoye, *Old Testament,* 125, esp. n. 26.

71. Within the Synoptic Gospels Gethsemane is seen as the climax of the Son's life of obedience to the Father's will, also affirmed at the beginning of his ministry at the temptation in the wilderness. Weiss, 312, argues that the author of Hebrews uses the incident in the garden as paradigmatic of Jesus' earthly life. See also Rissi, *Theologie,* 67-68.

72. Thus it is not necessary to follow Vanhoye, *Old Testament,* 126-30, by limiting the "offering" in v. 7 to the passion in order to preserve the sacrificial significance of Jesus' death.

73. The first of these suggestions is eliminated by the fact that Jesus' prayer was answered. Obviously God did not save him from going through the experience of crucifixion. For a full catalogue of suggestions as to the content of Jesus' prayers see Attridge, 150, nn. 159-64. Swetnam's suggestion that the Son prayed to die even though he was Son is very unconvincing (J. Swetnam, "The Crux at Hebrews 5,7-8," *Bib* 81 [2000]: 347-61; J. Swetnam, "The Context of the Crux at Hebrews 5,7-8," *Filología Neotestamentaria* 14 [2001]: 101-20). The supposed allusions to Psalm 22 are too subtle for the readers to discern. Furthermore, this interpretation requires taking "although he was a Son" with what

we do not try to discern what he has not revealed.[74] By describing the intensity of Jesus' prayer without specifying its object the pastor only strengthens his description of the Son's total dependence upon the Father, who will determine the way in which these prayers are answered.[75]

The outcome of the Son's having offered "prayers" is described by the next participle, "having been heard." The God to whom he had directed his "petitions" gave a favorable answer.[76] There can be no doubt that God's reply pertained to the "death" from which God was able to save him. How did God deliver him from that death? The answer to this question is closely tied to the way one interprets the following prepositional phrase. There are two prominent suggestions: "from fear" and "on account of his godly fear."[77]

The first implies that God heard his prayer and answered by delivering him "from fear" of death so that he was able to do God's will. Those who hold this view often argue that 5:7 should be interpreted in light of 2:14-15.[78] The incarnate Son delivers God's people from the fear of death (2:15) because he himself has been delivered from that fear (5:7).[79] However, the word these interpreters translate "fear" in 5:7 is different from the term used in 2:15.[80] In accord with contemporary usage, Hebrews employs the word used in 5:7 to

---

goes before: "and having been heard because of his godly fear although he was a Son." *Pace* Swetnam, "The Crux at Hebrews 5,7-8," 353, there is no reason to believe that the usage here should conform to the other four NT occurrences of this phrase, where it goes with the preceding main verb. The pastor's familiarity with the LXX might point to the influence of the Greek Bible, where it sometimes goes with the following main verb. This is especially true since the preceding verb is a participle.

74. Cf. Vanhoye, *Old Testament,* 126.

75. Vanhoye, *Old Testament,* 126-30. Thus the Son did not actually pray for the resurrection, although his prayer was answered in the resurrection/exaltation. He may have offered "prayers and supplications" for himself, but by his submission he was obtaining our salvation at the same time (Vanhoye, *Old Testament,* 130-31). Bénétreau, 1:215, dismisses Vanhoye's interpretation on the basis that v. 7 refers to Gethsemane alone.

76. The verb used for "hear" is εἰσακούειν, which implies God's favorable response (Matt 6:7; Acts 10:31; Sir 34:26). When used of humans in relation to God it intimates a hearing that leads to obedience (Deut 1:43; 9:23; Sir 3:6; 39:13). See Johnson, 146.

77. Koester, 289-90. The phrase in question is ἀπὸ τῆς εὐλαβείας. In the first instance above, the preposition ἀπό has the sense of separation and is translated "from"; εὐλαβείας is rendered "fear." In the second, ἀπό is translated causally and εὐλαβείας as "godly fear" or "reverence/piety." The only drawback to this second interpretation is that elsewhere Hebrews does not use ἀπό in a causal sense.

78. Michael Bachmann, "Hohepriesterliches Leiden: Beobachtungen zu Hebr 5:1-10," *ZNW* 78 (1987): 257-59

79. On the contrary, we have argued when commenting on these verses that the Son saves from the fear of death by removing sin.

80. Compare φόβος in 2:15 with εὐλαβεία in 5:7.

mean "godly fear," "reverence," or "piety" in 11:7 and 12:28.[81] Nowhere else does the expression "heard from" mean "heard and delivered from."[82] Furthermore, there is a certain incongruity in affirming that the God "who was able to save him out of death" only saved him from the fear of death.[83]

The preferred interpretation is the one followed by most English translations: "because of [his] godly fear." "Godly fear" is admirably suited to the context because it is an apt way of referring to the Son's obedience resulting from his utter dependence on God. The incarnate Son's life of God-honoring obedience culminating in and offered up by his death was his self-offering. It was also the reason God gave his offering ultimate acceptance — "he was heard." God confirmed that he had heard and accepted the Son's offering by inviting the Son to sit down at his right hand (cf. 10:11-14). His session in the place of heavenly authority implies both resurrection and exaltation.

8 As stated in the comments on v. 2b above, this verse is central to vv. 7-9. Many translations make one sentence of vv. 8-10 (cf. NRSV, NIV, TNIV). It is better, however, to make v. 8 an independent sentence (cf. ESV, NASB) because it relates as much to what has gone before as to what follows.[84] Verse 8 provides a concrete explanation of the "godly fear" mentioned at the end of v. 7 and describes the means by which, according to v. 9, the priest of Melchizedek's order "has been perfected."[85] By this arrangement the pastor puts the obedience which characterized the Son's human life in clear contrast to the sinful "weakness" which determined the course of the

---

81. For εὐλάβεια as "godly fear" see Luke 2:25; Acts 2:5; 22:12; and Philo, *Cherubim* 29; *Heir* 22.

82. Koester, 289, citing Vanhoye, *Old Testament*, 127.

83. The chief difficulty with saying that God delivered him from "the fear of death" is that the description of God as "'the one who was able to save him from death'" "gives the strong impression that he prayed for deliverance" (Koester, 288). Paul Andriessen and A. Lenglet, "Quelques passages difficiles de l'Épître aux Hébreux (5,7; 7,11; 10,20; 12,2)," *Bib* 51 (1970): 209, miss the point when they say that ἀπό is always used to show the cause and not the motive. His "godly fear" is not the motive for his being heard by God but its cause. Furthermore, "godly fear" is more than a motive — it is his entire life of obedience. Their view that the phrase should be translated "after his fear" also requires "although he was a son" to be taken with what goes before. Nor does the meaning it gives to εὐλάβεια accord well with its other uses in Hebrews. Andriessen and Lenglet ("Quelques passages," 208) support their hypothesis by the unconvincing claim that εὐλάβεια refers to fear of punishment in 11:7 and 12:28.

84. In fact, the aorist participles of v. 7, προσενέγκας καὶ εἰσακουσθείς, "having offered and having been heard," are formally dependent on the finite verb of v. 8, ἔμαθεν, "he learned." The NKJV seems to interpret these participles as temporal qualifiers of the verb in v. 8, "when He offered . . . and was heard." We have translated them as circumstantial participles and thus allowed them to assume the indicative character of the verb they qualify.

85. Attridge, 147.

old high priest. Notice the contrast between the active verb describing Christ's obedience, "he learned obedience," and the passive describing the old high priest's sinfulness, "he was beset with weakness" (v. 2b).

The pastor's astounding contention, implicit in the opening verses of chapter 1, comes to expression in this verse: the eternal Son of God procures our redemption through his earthly obedience. Up until now he has put great emphasis on the majesty and grandeur of the eternal Son.[86] Thus it was appropriate for the author to contrast the Son's exalted status with the humble obedience of his earthly sojourn: "Although he was Son" (NIV, NRSV, NASB).[87] A literal rendering of the present participle with which this verse begins would be "Although being Son." The pastor emphasizes the quality of sonship by omitting the definite article before "Son" (cf. Heb 1:1). Thus his meaning is well expressed by the phrase, "Although being One who is Son." Christ's sonship did not cease while he was learning "obedience." When the pastor speaks of the human Son he is always referring to the eternal Son who has assumed humanity.[88]

The Aaronic high priest's life was "beset" and determined by human "weakness," including sinfulness. The life of this High Priest, however, was characterized by the fact that "he learned obedience through what he suffered." The educative value of suffering was a common theme in ancient literature.[89] Thus at one level the pastor identifies the incarnate Son with the common lot of humanity. There was nothing common, however, about the "obedience" that he "learned" or the way in which he learned it. He did not learn to be obedient by suffering for his disobedience, as other humans do. The hearers/readers have already been told that he was "without sin" (see the comments on 4:15 and 5:2). The pastor is going to affirm that he completely fulfilled the will of God (10:5-10). Rather, he learned or experienced what it was like to be perfectly obedient though that obedience elicited unrelenting

86. See Heb 1:2, 5, 8; 3:6; 4:14; 5:5.
87. Attridge, 152, Koester, 290; Lane, 1:120-21; Johnson, 147; and Bénétreau, 1:216, along with most commentators, argue that "although" goes with what follows. In arguing that the phrase "although he was a Son" should go with the previous verse, deSilva, 193, ignores the way in which the author has already stressed the Son's majesty (see the references in the previous note) for what he will later say about suffering being the mark of true sonship in 12:4-11.
88. In the same way, when he speaks of the exalted Son, he is always referring to the eternal Son who became incarnate and through his obedient sacrifice has been exalted. Thus, those who would speak of the exalted Son without reference to his preexistence or incarnation distort the message of Hebrews.
89. See Herodotus, *Hist.* 1.207; Aeschylus, *Agamemnon* 177; Sophocles, *Trachiniae* 143; Aesop, *Fables* 134.1-3; 223.2-3; and many times in Philo (*Flight* 138; *Dreams* 2.107; *Spec. Laws* 4.29; *Heir* 73; *Moses* 2.55, 280). Citations in Johnson, 147.

antagonism from the unbelieving world (12:1-3).[90] Because he persevered in the kind of obedient dependence on God depicted in v. 7 even unto death, his obedience was full and complete.[91] It became richer with each act of obedience culminating in the cross. The Son's obedience revealed a dependence on God's power and assurance of his promises that was the antithesis of the wilderness generation's faithless disobedience (3:18; 4:11).

Vanhoye would distinguish between the absolute submission of the Son in v. 7 and the obedience he learned in v. 8.[92] The first focuses on the cross, the second on his life of obedience that anticipated the cross. There is a certain justice in his contention. The intense description in v. 7 brings the reader to the climax of the Son's earthly life when he faced and experienced the cross. The learning in v. 8 certainly took place during the course of his incarnate life. Nevertheless, a radical distinction is unnecessary. Verse 7 depicts a submission that climaxes his life of obedience to the Father. The suffering through which he came to experience the fullness of obedience in v. 8 cannot exclude the cross.[93] As stated above, Hebrews sees Christ's death as both the climax of his life of obedience and the offering up of that life to God. The Son's complete obedience in v. 8 clarifies the nature of his sacrifice in v. 9 and of the "godly fear" that made it effective.

9 "Having been perfected" describes the result of the Son's obedience in vv. 7-8 as the cause of his becoming "the Source of eternal salvation" in v. 9.[94] Yet the passive reminds the hearers that this perfecting is the work of God. His life of obedience unto death was the offering accepted by the God who "heard" (v. 7). It resulted in God's invitation to sit at his right hand as the only effective Mediator of salvation.[95] The pastor does not focus on the effectiveness of Christ's sacrifice in itself. His concern is with what the Son has become through his life of obedience offered up to God on the cross. Salvation is not in a sacrifice but in a Savior. The eternal Son of God who was without defect has become "perfected" as the Savior of humankind.[96] Thus

---

90. "Thus to say that Jesus 'learned' obedience means that he practiced obedience" (Koester, 290).

91. He maintained the unity of his will with that of the Father (Riggenbach, 137; cf. Rissi, "Menschlichkeit," 43-45).

92. Vanhoye, *Old Testament*, 126-30.

93. *Pace* Bénétreau, 1:216, it is impossible to exclude the cross from the obedience the Son learned through "suffering."

94. Thus the aorist participle τελειωθείς, "having been perfected," gives the means or the cause of the main verb: "he became" the Source of salvation. See Johnson, 148. In fact, his "perfecting" is almost synonymous with his becoming the fully adequate Savior.

95. In agreement with Johnson, 148. *Pace* Koester, 290, who thinks that this "having been perfected" refers only to the exaltation/session.

96. "It is thus, the perfection of his life leading up to the perfection of his death, that

this is a being perfected of vocation. We have already argued, however, that the Son enters into the fullness of his sonship as heir of all things through redemption (see on 1:1-3). Thus there is a sense in which his sonship is perfected through the earthly obedience, self-offering, and subsequent session by which he became the all-sufficient High Priest. Only thus does he enter into its full exercise and expression as the ultimate revelation of God as well as the "Source" of salvation. "Source" (NIV, NRSV, NASB) is a better translation than "author" (KJV) or "cause" because it encompasses both the past and present work of the Son. He not only brought this salvation into being, but as the exalted High Priest he is the "Source" from which it is continually received (4:14-16; 8:1; 10:19-25). Salvation cannot be separated from the Savior. As the one who "has been perfected" as Savior through obedience he has entered God's presence and is thus able to "perfect" God's people by cleansing them from sin so that they too can enter (cf. 7:18-19; 10:14)

The hearers are now in a better position to understand what the pastor meant in Heb 2:10 when he said that it was fitting for God to "perfect" the one who would bring God's people to their ultimate destiny through "suffering." It has now become clear that the role of suffering was to bring obedience to its completion. Only through the suffering that culminated in the cross could the Son's submission to the Father be complete. Furthermore, this passage confirms what has already been said in the comments on 2:10 above: the pastor takes advantage of the various nuances available for the expression "having been perfected." By what he has done culminating in his session, the Son has reached his goal.[97] He did not achieve this goal through a process of growth in moral perfection, but he did achieve it through the consistent obedience of his earthly life. Finally, this "having been perfected" was achieved by his becoming the exalted High Priest. The pastor can hardly have been insensitive to the OT's use of the term "to perfect" in relation to priestly consecration.[98]

The Son became the "Source of eternal salvation" only through his in-

---

he became the source of eternal salvation" (Hughes, 188, italics original). "'Once made perfect' announces the validation by God of the perfect obedience that Jesus rendered as the priestly representative of the people" (Lane, 1:122). See Peterson, *Perfection,* 96-103.

97. *Pace* deSilva, 197-99, and others, there is no reason to limit this perfecting to nothing more than reaching a goal. deSilva seems to forget that it is not suffering but the obedience honed by suffering through which he is perfected. Nor is it completely correct to separate the suffering of believers (12:5-11) from their "perfection" (deSilva, 198, n. 48). Though both the Son and believers must endure suffering, it accentuates the obedience of the One but brings the others to a more complete obedience. See also Peterson, *Perfection,* 73; Anthony A. Hoekema, "Perfection of Christ in Hebrews," *CTJ* 9 (1974): 33-37; Attridge, 86-87.

98. Vanhoye, *Old Testament,* 133, notes that the verb τελειοῦν is used in the Pentateuch exclusively for priestly consecration. He argues that one so knowledgeable of the Greek Bible as our author could not have missed this significance.

carnate obedience. Yet this description is a strong affirmation of his deity, as evidenced by the fact that Philo can call God the "source of salvation."[99] As noted above, it is as exalted High Priest and Savior that the Son enters into the full exercise of his divine sonship. This salvation is "eternal," ultimate, and fully effective because its "Source" is God. It has been provided by the eternal Son, who offered himself "by the eternal Spirit" (9:14) and who "remains forever," exercising an inviolable high priesthood (7:24) that provides complete salvation (7:25). The Son provides permanent access to life in fellowship with God.

It is no surprise, however, that this salvation is for "those who obey him." The Son has become this Savior through obedience and, as yet-to-be-explained but already affirmed (4:16), he provides access to God's throne for the people of God and thus to the grace necessary for perseverance in obedience until final entrance into God's presence (12:25-29). Such obedience is characteristic of those who live under the New Covenant (10:15-18). His salvation is not for those "ignorant and going astray" (v. 2). For this reason the pastor would awaken his hearers from lethargy (2:1-4, 5:11–6:20) and draw their full attention to Christ's provision. This provision is both means and motivation for emulating the faithful (11:1-40) and shunning the example of the disobedient (3:7–4:11).

10 Verses 7-9 have been a description of the One God addressed as "a priest forever according to the order of Melchizedek" (v. 6, quoting Ps 110:4). Thus it is no surprise when v. 10 concludes this section by declaring that the Son has "been designated [by God] as high priest according to the order of Melchizedek." When quoting and expounding Ps 110:4 in 5:6 and 7:1-25, the pastor retains the simple "priest" of the psalm. However, he cannot refrain from using *high* priest at the climax of this description of fully sufficient priesthood. He will reintroduce this subject in 6:20 using the same expression. The one and only priest of Melchizedek's order is, by his very nature, *High* Priest.[100]

There is no reason to separate God's public declaration of the Son's Melchizedekian high priesthood in Ps 110:4 from the invitation to God's right hand in Ps 110:1 (cf. 1:3; 1:13). God made open proclamation of both his sonship and high priesthood at the exaltation (Pss 110:4 and Ps 2:7 in Heb 5:5-6).[101] As the following chapters will show, it is as "high priest forever according to the order of Melchizedek" exalted to the right hand of God that he

---

99. *Spec. Laws* 1.252.

100. Spicq, 2:120.

101. προσαγορευθείς, "having been declared," is parallel to καλούμενος, "being called," in v. 4. It appropriately describes God's public declaration of the Son's high priesthood.

will function as "the Source of eternal salvation." By the sacrifice of his obedient life unto death the eternal Son has been consecrated as eternal High Priest. When the pastor returns to the subject of priesthood in chapter 7, he will show how divine sonship makes the difference between the high priest described in vv. 2-4 and the one portrayed in vv. 7-10. God's declaration in Ps 110:4 justifies the end of the old priesthood and establishes the permanency and effectiveness of the new.

The pastor, then, is about to present a vision of salvation according to which the people of God are cleansed from sin and enabled to enter God's presence through the work of their exalted High Priest seated at God's right hand.[102] He urges them to enter through prayer and worship on a regular basis both to enjoy what is theirs and to obtain the grace for perseverance. His great concern is that they persevere until ultimate entrance into the presence of God at Christ's return (9:28; 12:26-29). Thus the obedience of the Son by which he became the adequate Savior not only atoned for their sin but provided for their obedience (9:14; 10:15-18). The pastor, however, is concerned that his hearers are condoning a certain spiritual lethargy and complacency that will prevent their appropriating the glorious significance of these truths and thus keep them from achieving the all-important perseverance necessary for final salvation. Thus before going further he must address this laxity in 5:11–6:20 so that they might truly grasp and appropriate what he has to say. He would not have them be "ignorant" of Christ's sufficiency and thus "go astray" (v. 2a).

B. DO NOT BE UNRESPONSIVE BUT GRASP WHAT CHRIST HAS PROVIDED (5:11–6:20)

In accord with the custom of ancient orators the pastor postpones further discussion of Christ's high priesthood until 6:20 in order to regain his hearers' attention and rouse them to appropriate action.[1] His concern, however, is with spiritual inertia more than with wandering thoughts.[2] He has tried to

102. Hebrews' presentation of the work of Christ also complements the ways in which other NT writers use the imagery of Tabernacle and Temple. For Hebrews God's people enter the heavenly sanctuary of his presence through the work of Jesus their High Priest. In John Jesus' "body" is the new sanctuary in which God dwells and through which people come into fellowship with him (John 2:21-22). For Paul the church as the "body of Christ" is the new temple infilled by the Spirit of God (1 Cor 3:16-17). Each of these approaches provides a different perspective on the intimacy with God that Christ has provided for his people.

1. For ancient orators' use of such "digressions" to regain their hearers' attention see deSilva, 209-19 and Koester, 306-7 (cf. Braun, 149). Koester (307) estimates that it would have taken about fifteen minutes to deliver Heb 1:1–5:10.

2. While deSilva's caution (210-11, esp. n. 1) against using Heb 5:11-14 as a pre-

whet their appetite and arouse their curiosity by giving them a foretaste of the great benefits that are theirs through Christ's priestly ministry. He now turns to shame (5:11–6:3), warning (6:4-8), consolation (6:9-12), and assurance (6:13-20) in order to awaken them from complacency and direct them to the path of persevering faith. He would bring them back to his main topic with a renewed determination to comprehend its significance and appropriate its benefits as the adequate and only means of such perseverance. Thus although the pastor temporarily defers discussion of Christ's high priesthood, this section is no diversion. It is integral to the overarching concern of this sermon that the hearers appropriate God's adequate provision for endurance in obedient faith until the end.

We can feel the impact of the pastor's argument best if we divide this unit into four smaller sections — 5:11–6:3; 6:4-8; 6:9-12; and 6:13-20.[3] With consummate skill he uses the negative emotions of shame (5:11–6:3) and fear (6:4-8) to prepare his hearers for comfort (6:9-12) and assurance (6:13-20).[4] The pastor balances the shame aroused by his accusations of spiritual immaturity (5:11–6:3) with comfort drawn from God's dependability in remembering their "work" and service (6:9-12). He offsets dire warnings against apostasy (6:4-8) with the assurance of God's faithfulness to the promise given to Abraham and his heirs (6:13-20). He would move his hearers from spiritual immaturity (5:11–6:3) and its tragic consequences (6:4-8) to perseverance (6:9-12) in imitation of faithful Abraham (6:13-20).[5]

---

cise diagnosis of the hearers' spiritual situation has some merit, this description of their state and the following exhortations cannot be reduced to mere rhetoric. The pastor is burdened about real spiritual lethargy (Bénétreau, 1:221). Cf. Weiss, 327.

3. Bénétreau, 222, and Johnson, 152, are representative of those who divide 5:11–6:3 into two sections, 5:11-14; 6:1-3. In the first the pastor shames his hearers for their immaturity; in the second he urges them to go on to maturity. We have kept the two together for several reasons. First, the theme of immaturity/maturity clearly unites these verses and separates them from the following description of apostasy (6:4-8). Second, the exhortation in 6:1-3 is based on the description of the hearers' condition in 5:11-14 (note διό, "therefore," in 6:1 and the argument below). Third, the parallel description of the hearers in 6:9-12 also concludes with exhortation (6:11-12).

4. Attridge, 166-67, fails to see that the major turning point is between vv. 8 and 9 because he tries to find a chiastic structure in this passage. He argues that the apostasy of 6:4-8 balances the faithfulness of 6:9-12, but that there is no parallel between 5:11–6:3 and 6:13-20. In fact, the description of the hearers' immaturity in 5:11–6:3 parallels the positive description of their conduct in 6:9-12. Both of these passages are second person plural address followed by first person plural exhortation (compare the impersonal third person of 6:4-8). As above in the text, 6:4-8 parallels 6:13-20. Thus the pastor turns from negative to positive between vv. 8 and 9.

5. The pastor often follows a strategy of turning his hearers from what he would have them avoid to the life he would have them emulate. Thus he would deter them from

The pastor states the main point of 5:11–6:20 in 6:12. By reviving the term "dull" (5:11) he climaxes the warning of 5:11–6:8 against unresponsiveness to God's word, only to urge imitation of the faithful as the opposite of such unresponsiveness.[6] Verses 13-20 reinforce his plea by demonstrating the certainty of God's promise to those who are faithful. This promise is verified by the oath of the One who cannot lie and certified by its fulfillment in the high-priestly ministry of Christ. Thus the pastor brings his hearers back to this high priesthood as the indisputable demonstration of divine faithfulness and the fully adequate means of perseverance. He has aroused their curiosity about this truth, shamed them for their dullness in grasping it, caused them to fear lest they neglect it, and assured them that this promise is theirs because of God's faithfulness — if they will persevere in obedience.

Just as this exhortation prepares the hearers to embrace the discussion of Christ's high priesthood in 7:1–10:18, so the exhortation of 10:19–12:3 draws out the implications of that priesthood for perseverance. In both the pastor follows a similar sequence: description of the hearers' spiritual condition (5:11–6:3; 10:19-25), warning against apostasy (6:4-8; 10:26-31), expression of confidence (6:9-12; 10:32-39), and examples to emulate (6:13-20; 11:1–12:3). However, the new situation of the hearers intensifies — in sharpest terms — the urgency of the exhortation in 10:19–12:3. Those once accused of being "dull in hearing" (5:11–6:3) have now been exposed to God's only adequate provision for salvation — the high-priestly ministry of Christ (10:19-25). Furthermore, a multitude of witnesses makes the way of persevering faith absolutely clear (11:1–12:3).

---

following the disobedient wilderness generation in 3:7–4:11 before urging them to follow those characterized by "faith and patience" (6:12) in 11:1–12:3. His purpose in explaining the privileges now theirs in Christ (7:1–10:18) is to move them from the former to the latter. This strategy does not prevent him from concluding the main section of his sermon with a strong reprise of previous warnings (12:25-29).

6. Thus νωθροί, "dull" or "sluggish" (5:11/6:12), forms more than a mechanical inclusion around 5:11–6:12. Yet it would be a mistake to separate 5:11–6:12 from 6:13-20 on the basis of this inclusion, as Lane, 1:133-35, and others have done. Such separation neglects the way in which the exhortation to imitate the faithful in 6:12 is substantiated by 6:13-20. Thus it risks missing the key importance of this verse. One need not deny the unity of 5:11–6:12 and 6:13-20 just because one function of the latter is transition back to the topic of priesthood (cf. deSilva, 209-10). Nor can one make a clean break between 5:11–6:12 and 6:13-20 by arguing that the former is hortatory, while the latter is expository (pace Lane, 1:133-35). Note the "we have" in 6:19-20 characteristic of other hortatory passages (4:14-16; 10:19-25) and the third person description in 6:4-8 so uncharacteristic of the hortatory. Even Weiss, 328, who would separate the two, admits that 6:13-20 is completely subordinate to the hortatory context. Furthermore, pace Weiss, 328-29, the language of Hellenistic moral philosophy is largely confined to 5:11–6:3.

1. Reverse Your Unnatural Regression (5:11–6:3)

11 *Concerning which we have an extensive message, but it is diffi-cult to explain because you have become dull of hearing.* 12 *For al-though you ought to be teachers on account of the time, you again have need of someone to teach you the basic elements of the beginning of the words of God; you have become those who have need of milk rather than solid food.* 13 *For everyone living on milk is unskilled in the word of righteousness, for he is immature.* 14 *But solid food is for the mature, for those who on account of their mature state have their senses trained for the discrimination of both what is appropriate and what is evil.*

6:1 *Therefore, let us leave the elementary Christian message and let us go on to maturity, not laying again a foundation of repentance from dead works and faith in God,* 2 *of teaching about washings and laying on of hands, of resurrection of the dead and eternal judgment.* 3 *And this we will do, if indeed God permits.*

5:11–6:3 The pastor must defer further discussion of Christ's high priest-hood because his hearers are "dull of hearing." This dullness of hearing is ex-plained in 5:12 as an inexcusable regression into spiritual immaturity. By contrasting such immaturity (5:13) with spiritual maturity (5:14) the pastor demonstrates the repulsiveness of return to the former and the great desirabil-ity of attaining the latter. Thus, in 6:1-3 he exhorts his hearers to leave their immaturity and their fixation on what is elementary and go on to the spiritual maturity/perfection that is in accord with and brought about by Christ's high priestly ministry.

11 "Concerning which" might be translated "concerning whom" as a reference to "Christ" in v. 5 or to "Melchizedek" in v. 10.[1] Nevertheless, the broader context favors the more general "concerning which" in reference to the Son's high priesthood according to Melchizedek's order soon to be ex-plained in 7:1–10:18.[2]

"We have an extensive message, but it is difficult to explain" is a smooth rendering of the Greek text. A wooden translation helps recover its significance: "much to us the word and difficult to explain." The term "word" is central and emphatic.[3] This "word" is the "salvation" so much greater than

---

1. Johnson, 154, thinks περὶ οὗ, "concerning whom," refers to "Christ" or "the Messiah" introduced in v. 5. Ellingworth, 299, opts for Melchizedek in v. 10.

2. Lane, 1:135-36; Spicq, 1:142; Weiss, 330; cf. Ellingworth, 299.

3. πολὺς ἡμῖν ὁ λόγος καὶ δυσερμήνευτος λέγειν. ὁ λόγος, "the word," is definite and is preceded by one adjective and its complement, πολὺς ἡμῖν, "much to us," and fol-lowed by a second adjective and its complement, δυσερμήνευτος λέγειν, "difficult to ex-

"the word" God spoke through angels (2:1-4). Christ's high priesthood is nothing less than the ultimate "word" or message from God addressed to his people and requiring their response. As the pastor will demonstrate, it is based on God's word in Ps 110:4 and prefigured by the God-established priesthood described in the God-inspired OT. No expression could better emphasize the divine origin and consequent urgency of obedience than "the word." It was failure to heed God's "word" that condemned the wilderness generation (4:2), and it is God's "word" that penetrates all and holds all accountable (4:12-13). The "much" that the pastor will say about Christ's high priesthood (7:1–10:18) and its centrality in his argument underscore the importance and finality of this "word."[4]

Although Christ's high priesthood might be "difficult to explain" because of its complexity, the main reason for this difficulty is the spiritual state of the hearers: "because you have become dull (sluggish) of hearing."[5] The catastrophe of the wilderness generation (3:7–4:11) gives the phrase "dull in hearing" a particularly ominous sound. That generation refused to "hear" with obedience. The expression translated "in hearing" is plural and could also be rendered "in the ears." Dullness "in the ears" may lead to wilderness-generation hardness "of heart" (3:12, 15) and thus to ultimate loss. The perfect tense verb translated "you have become" implies that, while they once were receptive, they have now become and are in a state where they fail to attend, grasp, and heed God's message as they should. "Dullness in hearing" betokens not merely a passive inability but an active resistance to God's word.[6] The pastor's accusation confronts modern believers whose sensitivity

---

plain." Most English versions obscure this emphasis on "word" by the translation "we have much to say" (NIV, NASB, RSV, NRSV, ESV).

4. Lane, 1:135-36, shows how this phrase, "much to us the word," was a common literary device for designating something the writer felt important. Contrast the "much" (πολύς) the pastor has to say about this "word" (λόγος) with the "word" (λόγος) "of the beginning of Christ" (τῆς ἀρχῆς τοῦ Χριστοῦ) in 6:1.

5. For the causal sense for ἐπεί, "because," see Ellingworth, 300-301. Paul Andriessen, "La communauté des 'Hébreux,' était-elle tombée dans le relâchement?" *NRTh* 96 (1974): 1054-66, has argued that this word means "otherwise" and that the pastor nowhere gives evidence that he thinks his hearers "dull," "sluggish," or immature. David G. Peterson, "The Situation of the 'Hebrews' (5:11–6:12)," *Reformed Theological Review* 35 (1976): 14-15, has shown that where Hebrews uses ἐπεί as "otherwise" (9:26; 10:2), the context makes this meaning clear. "Otherwise" does not fit the context of 5:11 (cf. 2:14; 4:6; 5:2; 6:13; 9:17; and 11:11). "Otherwise" fits poorly with the following perfect tense verb. Moreover, the exhortations in 2:1-4; 3:7–4:11, etc., appear to substantiate the sluggishness affirmed in this passage.

6. *Pace* Thompson, *Christian Philosophy,* 29. "Dull in hearing" is much more than "intellectual inertia." Such mental sluggishness is of a piece with spiritual dullness, as evidenced by the listeners' slowness to hear and obey. "Dullness in hearing" describes

to God's voice has been dulled either by the fear of disadvantage or the complacency of ease.

With this accusation and its elaboration in the following three verses the pastor would shame his hearers into heeding his message.[7] Their inattentiveness to God's word, subsequently described as spiritual regression (v. 12), is real, but, as vv. 9-12 (cf. 10:32-34) would indicate, not complete. The pastor earnestly desires them to respond with, "We are not like the spiritual babies you have described (v. 13); we are and we want to be like those you describe as spiritually mature (v. 14)."[8]

12 Every word in this verse stresses the unnaturalness and thus the culpability of this refusal to hear. Many subsequent spiritual leaders can identify with the pastor's frustrated expectations expressed in the opening participial phrase: "Although you ought to be teachers on account of the time."[9] Anyone who has been a believer as long as the recipients of Hebrews should be able to instruct those new in the faith.[10] But instead, "you again have need for someone to teach you."[11] In Greek the first word of this phrase is "again" — they had once been taught but now need re-teaching. Emphasis is also put on "you" — it is none other than "you," the hearers, who need this redundant instruction. Furthermore, they need this instruction in the most elementary tenets — "the basic elements of the beginning of the words of God." This description stands in stark contrast to those under the New Covenant who no longer need to teach a brother or sister, saying, "know the Lord" (8:11).[12]

It would be both speculative and misleading to identify these "basic elements" with precision and use them as an objective barometer of the recipients' spiritual state. The pastor is intentionally exaggerating in order to goad his hearers to action. The word we have translated "basic elements" indicates instruction in the most elementary principles.[13] "Of the beginning of

---

resistant hearers in Heliodorus, *Aethiopica (Ethiopians)* 5.1.5 and Epictetus, *Diatr.* 1.7.30 (cited in Johnson, 155).

7. See Koester, 308.

8. See Lane, 1:136-37; Attridge, 158.

9. The participle ὀφείλοντες is certainly concessive, "Although being obligated," "Although you ought."

10. It was common in antiquity to arouse people by telling them that they should by now be teachers (examples in Moffatt, 70). Thus there is no reason to believe that the pastor is referring to a particular office of "teacher" (Bénétreau, 1:223; *pace* Donald Guthrie, 134). Cf. Weiss, 331-32.

11. For τινά as the indefinite "someone" instead of the interrogative, τίνα, "which" or "what basic elements," see Riggenbach, 141-42.

12. Koester, 301. However, this reference to lack of need for teaching under the New Covenant does not play a prominent part in the pastor's thinking. He makes no mention of it in his summary of New Covenant benefits (10:15-18).

13. For στοιχεῖα as "basic elements" of instruction see Xenophon, *Mem.* 2.1.1. In

the words of God" intensifies the rudimentary nature of this instruction. The expression "words of God" encompasses both what God has now said in his Son (1:1-3) and all that he has revealed in the OT Scripture (Acts 7:38; Rom 3:2).[14] If that is true, then "the beginning" of the "words of God" may refer to initial instruction in OT faith. This instruction is more fundamental than "the word of the beginning of Christ" in 6:1.[15] The recipients of Hebrews need to relearn their A B C's.[16] The pastor has no interest in describing the content of these teachings. He emphasizes their primitiveness by overstatement in order to move his hearers to action.

The figurative expression at the end of v. 12 underscores the shamefulness of their condition: "and you have become those who have need of milk rather than solid food."[17] The perfect tense of the verb translated "you have become" reinforces the perfect of v. 11. They once were more mature, but they now need the milk of infants rather than the food of adults. They are guilty of a disgraceful regression. This type of language came from contemporary philosophical and pedagogical tradition that pictured education as nurture.[18] The pastor, however, is not concerned with a series of steps leading

---

Diogenes Laertius, *Lives* 7.56, and Philo, *Prelim. Studies* 149-50, it is used for the letters of the alphabet (Johnson, 155). See Bénétreau, 1:224.

14. Attridge, 159; cf. Bénétreau, 1:224. "Words" reminds the hearers that they are accountable before God's revelation (4:12-13). Cf. Johnson, 155; Koester, 301, 309.

15. Hughes, 190, n. 23, and Weiss, 332, represent those who miss the pastor's rhetorical intention by identifying these "basic elements" with the elementary teachings of Christ in 6:1. Noel Weeks, "Admonition and Error in Hebrews," *WTJ* 39 (1976): 76, errs in the opposite direction by making the teachings of 6:1 no more than those referred to in this verse. Koester, 309, supported by Johnson, 155, has speculated that the author was referring to a proper Christological understanding of 2 Sam 7:14; Ps 2:7; and Ps 110:1. However, the context would indicate that these "basic teachings" were something even more primitive.

16. Cf. Calvin, 68.

17. Many translations render this verse smoothly by the use of an infinitive: "And you have come to need milk, not solid food." However, the Greek finite verb γεγόνατε ("you have become") is followed by a participial phrase: χρείαν ἔχοντες ("need having"). The participle might be taken as modal, "you have become as having need." However, the "as" unduly weakens the analogy. The full force of the pastor's thought is retained by a substantive translation: "you have become those who have need."

18. Terms such as νωθροί ("dull," v. 11); γάλα ("milk," v. 12), στερεὰ τροφή (vv. 12, 14, "solid food"); ἄπειρος (v. 13, "inexperienced"); νήπιος ("immature," v. 13); τέλειος ("perfect," v. 14); ἕξιν ("mature state," v. 14), and γυμνάζω ("to exercise," v. 14) are drawn from this philosophical environment (see Thompson, *Christian Philosophy*, 35-37). However, Spicq, 2:142, is right when he says, "These first four verses [5:11-14] contain many ideas and expressions current in the philosophical language of the first century, particularly those of Stoic moralism, but the inspiration is fundamentally biblical" (translation mine).

from immaturity to maturity. He is using these two extremes to shame the hearers into heeding his instruction.[19] Conduct that might be appropriate for a child is infantile and offensive in an adult.

The pastor intentionally softens the blow by shifting from the second person plural of accusation in v. 12 to the more impersonal third person of description in vv. 13-14.[20] He would shame them because they have begun to show symptoms of the milk drinkers described in v. 13, in order that they might take their rightful place among those described in v. 14 as living on "solid food."

13 Regression is shameful. Furthermore, immaturity is disadvantageous because "everyone who lives on milk" (NRSV, RSV, ESV; cf. NIV, TNIV) is "unskilled in the word of righteousness." In Hellenistic moral philosophy the expression "word of righteousness" referred to "reasoning about what was right."[21] It was the ability to discern and follow a correct course of action. Furthermore, this understanding fits nicely with the contrasting description of the mature in v. 14 as able to discern "what is appropriate and what is evil." However, the broader context of Hebrews suggests that the pastor has more in mind. Since God "speaks" his revelation (1:1-3, etc.), it can be called his "word" (2:2; 4:2, 11; 5:11). This "word of righteousness" is more than reasoning about what is right. It is the revelation of Christ's high priesthood as the means by which the pastor's hearers will be able to follow the "righteous" (10:38; 11:4, 7) of chapter 11 and thus persevere in faithfulness.[22] This deeper meaning informs the first. It is only by grasping and ap-

---

19. Lane, 1:137; Attridge, 159; Koester, 309. Thompson, *Christian Philosophy,* 39, argues that, under the influence of Platonic *paideia,* Hebrews affirms that one passes from lower to higher to the highest studies. The highest pertain to heavenly things. H. P. Owen, "The 'Stages of Ascent' in Hebrews V.11–VI.3," *NTS* 3 (1957): 243-53, finds the three stages of development characteristic of Platonic/Stoic philosophy in Hebrews. Both neglect two important aspects of Hebrews' thought. First, the pastor uses this language only to shame his hearers for their unnatural immaturity. Second, Hebrews does not see the Christian life as progress toward but as perseverance in the "perfection" that comes through Christ's high priesthood. The pastor would have his hearers understand the benefits of this priesthood not because they are the goal but because they are the *sine qua non* of the Christian life. Owen's argument is undone by his own admission that Hebrews skips the supposed stage one, the acquiring of rudimentary knowledge, and combines two and three — the practice that brings maturity and the acquisition of advanced knowledge (248, 250, 252).

20. Riggenbach, 143-46, draws attention to the importance of this shift.

21. For examples of this usage see Koester, 302, and Johnson, 156.

22. See Lane, 1:137-38; Ellingworth, 307; George Guthrie, 202-3; Osborne, "Arminian," 109; and Bénétreau, 1:226. Cf. also Bénétreau, 1:226. In the second century Polycarp referred to obeying "the word of righteousness" as practicing the kind of endurance that led to martyrdom (*Phil.* 8.1–9.1, cited by Lane, 1:138).

propriating Christ's high-priestly ministry (4:14-16; 10:19-25) that the recipients of Hebrews will be able to discern and follow the right course of life marked out for them by the faithful (11:1-40) and by Jesus (12:1-3).[23]

Although the pastor accuses his hearers of having regressed to the place where they needed "milk," he stops short of describing them directly as "those who live on milk." Nevertheless, this description strikes them uncomfortably close to home. He intends their faces to burn with shame when he says that milk drinkers are unskilled in discerning and following the correct course of action because they are only "infants." Thus he would turn them from such behavior to the maturity so aptly depicted in v. 14.

14 On the other hand, if those who live on milk are infants, then the "solid food" of Christ's high-priestly ministry is for "the mature."[24] In Greek this verse begins with the "mature," and it is about them the pastor would speak. Unlike "unskilled" infants, they are those "who on account of their mature state have their senses trained for the discrimination of both what is appropriate and what is evil." With the terms translated "mature state" and "senses trained" the pastor once again draws on the language of the moral philosophers for his own purposes.[25] The spiritual senses of the mature have been trained by exercise in the life of faith. Their constant practice of dependence on God and trust in his promises through the power available from Christ's high priesthood have brought them to this place of maturity. As the mature they are able to discern and follow what is true and conducive to a life of faithful obedience while detecting and spurning every hindrance.[26] The athletic flavor of this language is well suited to the pastor's concern with the endurance of believers.

The adjective here used as a noun for "the mature" might be translated "the perfect." It comes from the same root as the verb "to perfect" used both for Christ's having been perfected in 2:10 and 5:9 (see above) and for

23. *Pace* Hughes, 191-92, and others, reference to Christ as our righteousness decontextualizes the expression "word of righteousness" by putting it in a forensic context foreign to Hebrews. Hughes also misidentifies the "word of righteousness" with the elementary Christian teachings.

24. Riggenbach, 143.

25. John A. L. Lee, "Hebrews 5:14 and ἕξις: A History of Misunderstanding," *NovT* 39 (1997): 151-76, has shown conclusively that there is no basis for translating ἕξις as "exercise." This word was a favorite of the philosophers, and the evidence is overwhelming that it should be translated "state" or "condition" in Heb 5:14, denoting the good state or condition of the mature. We have adopted Lee's translation, "mature state" (166). His study confirms the opinion of many previous commentators and has won broad support (see, most recently, O'Brien, 210).

26. The Greek word is κάλος, not ἀγαθός, and implies not only what is morally right but what is appropriate in God's sight. See Hughes, 193. "It is precisely the discernment of the good or evil course, of the noble and the base, and of the proper evaluation of advantages and disadvantages that is at risk among the wavering" (deSilva, 213).

Christ's perfecting of believers in 10:14 (cf. 10:1; 9:9), 11:40, and 12:23.[27] The Son, as explained above, has been "perfected" as our "Source of eternal salvation," the one who through his self-offering brings the faithful into the presence of God. As will be demonstrated below, he "perfects" believers by cleansing their sin and giving them access to God's presence so that they can receive persevering grace until their final entrance into the heavenly homeland (11:40; 12:23). Nevertheless, there are two reasons for translating these expression in 5:14 and 6:1 as "the mature" and "maturity" instead of as "the perfect" and "perfection": first, "the mature" stands in contrast to those who are immature infants in 5:11-13. Second, Christ's "perfecting" of the faithful is the precondition for, and thus a necessary part of, their attaining this maturity. "The mature" have attained this stability of character and constancy of obedience by their constant appropriation of Christ's "having perfected" them. They grow strong in the life of faith by regularly availing themselves of the cleansing from sin and access to God that he provides.

The contrasting description of the "mature" in v. 14 intensifies the shame and folly of return to the "immaturity" of vv. 11-13. This description also portrays the beauty of the life the pastor would have his hearers pursue. Thus the exhortation of 6:1 flows naturally from vv. 11-14. Regression into immaturity and fixation with elementary teaching result in loss. Maturity, and the advanced teaching about Christ by which it is fostered, are eminently desirable for perseverance. "Therefore, . . . let us go on to maturity."[28] There is no contradiction between the pastor's statement that his hearers have come to "need milk" and his insistence on feeding them "solid food." One weans infants by feeding them adult fare.[29] Thus, the pastor would wean his hearers — ancient and modern — by feeding them the solid food of the "great salvation" (2:3) provided by Christ our High Priest and challenging them to maturity by its regular appropriation.

6:1a The exhortation, "Let us go on to maturity," is central to the first three verses of chapter 6. The participles which precede and follow this main verb, "having left behind" and "not laying again," clarify its meaning and derive from it the character of exhortation.[30] A literal translation of the

---

27. τελείων is the genitive plural of the adjective τέλιος (-α, -ον) used substantively for "the mature" (people). Its lack of an article puts emphasis on the quality of maturity, "those who are mature." The same adjective is translated "the perfect" in the KJV of 1 Cor 6:2 (cf. Eph 4:13). The verb used in 2:10; 5:9; 10:14; 11:40; and 12:23 is τελειόω, "to perfect." Cf. τελειοτής, "perfection" or "maturity," in 6:1 below.

28. διό ("therefore") at the beginning of 6:1 has full inferential force.

29. Compare Epictetus, *Diatr.* 2.16.39: "Are you not willing, at this late date, like children, to be weaned (ἀπογαλακτισθῆναι) and to partake of more solid food (τροφῆς στερεᾶς)" (cited by Johnson, 156).

30. "Having left behind (ἀφέντες) the word of the beginning of Christ," and "not

opening participial phrase might be, "having left behind the word of the beginning of Christ." We have translated it smoothly as an exhortation in order to bring out its hortatory character: "Let us leave the elementary Christian message."

Koester has suggested that the term translated "leave behind" was used as a technical term for finishing one point of a discussion in order to engage the next.[31] Thus he translates "granting the basic message of Christ, let us go on. . . ."[32] The pastor may have been influenced in his choice of this term by its use in the contexts Koester suggests. Nevertheless, the pastor has more in mind for his hearers than transition. They must leave their preoccupation with this elementary material if they would attend to his teaching that is both for the mature and produces maturity. A closer look at what the pastor says shows why this is true.

As indicated above, "the elementary Christian message" is more literally "the word of the beginning of Christ." Most translations take both "of the beginning" and "of Christ" as qualifying "the word."[33] "Of the beginning" shows its elementary nature. "Of Christ" describes its content. The pastor is not referring to the teaching about Christ in the Gospels or to what Christ taught. He is concerned with basic Christian teachings like those listed later in this and the following verse.[34] This teaching is not false, but it is insufficient for perseverance in faith because it does not reveal the full sufficiency

---

building (καταβαλλόμενοι) again the foundation of. . . ." The first is aorist active, the second present middle. Both are nominative, plural, masculine modifying the first person plural subject of φερώμεθα, "let us go on," to maturity.

31. Koester, 303, citing Epictetus, *Diatr.* 1.16.9; 4.1.15; Plutarch, *Mor.* 423C; 793A. Cf. Westcott, 142.

32. Koester, 300.

33. This understanding is sustained by the Greek word order. Both genitives, τῆς ἀρχῆς, "of the beginning," and τοῦ Χριστοῦ, "of Christ," are in the attributive position, coming between the article τόν, "the," and the noun λόγον, "word": "the of-the-beginning, of-Christ word."

34. τοῦ Χριστοῦ, "of Christ," is a genitive of description (Ellingworth, 311-12; Bénétreau, 1:229). In light of the teachings to follow, the adjective "Christian" best represents its intended meaning. J. C. Adams, "Exegesis of Hebrews VI.1f," *NTS* 13 (1966-67): 378-85 (followed by Attridge, 162), argues that "of Christ" is a subjective genitive and that the pastor is referring to what the earthly Jesus taught. The pastor's teaching for the mature, on the other hand, is about the significance of what Jesus did in providing salvation, about his "work." This position is untenable. The teachings of Christ were highly valued. As remembered in the Gospels, they had much to do with his "work." Furthermore, such things as "baptisms and laying on of hands" were not central to Jesus' preaching. Those, like Spicq, 2:146, who attempt to identify these teachings with "the basic elements of the beginning of the words of God" in 5:12 miss the ironic character of the pastor's argument in 5:11-14.

of Christ as the only Savior.[35] In every generation there are those who profess
the rudiments of the Christian faith without grasping the reality of Christ or
pursuing the course of persevering faith. They follow their own way, recognizing neither their privileges nor their peril. Believers must embrace all that
Christ is and has done for them. Thus the pastor urges his own, "Let us go on
to maturity," by appropriating the "perfection" provided by Christ so that we
can persevere until the end. This maturity is not an ideal or a distant goal but
the norm expected of a believer and the only means of perseverance.[36]

The advanced teaching of 7:1–10:18 is, then, both for the mature and
the means of producing maturity. The pastor will "move on to maturity" by
instructing his hearers in this teaching. They are to move on by embracing
this anticipated instruction.[37] The pastor would inform them about the eternal
Son who through his self-offering has been "perfected" as his people's high
priest "forever" (7:28) and thus has "perfected" (10:14) those availing themselves of his high-priestly ministry. The benefits of this ministry include inward cleansing and access to God (9:14; 10:19-25), mediation of timely
grace (4:14-16), and the transformation provided by the Christ-established
New Covenant (10:16-18). Only by appropriating these benefits can those
who profess faith in Christ enter this life of Christian maturity and persevere
therein.

The present middle subjunctive, translated "let us go on," might also be
understood as a passive: "Let us be carried (or moved) on to maturity."[38] The
pastor desires that they allow themselves to be moved by the power of God
through a proper appropriation of Christ's high-priestly ministry. Attridge argues that classical parallels make reference to the passive unnecessary.[39]
However, the divine passive is in full accord with "if God permits" at the end
of v. 3. Though the pastor would urge his hearers to vigorous action, that action itself is possible only by yielding to the power of a gracious God.

6:1b-2 "Not laying again a foundation" begins a participial phrase
that continues to the end of v. 2. With this phrase the pastor reinforces the ex-

35. So Johnson, 158.
36. The author's use of ἐπὶ τὴν τελειότητα, "for the purpose of (this) perfection"
(cf. BDAG, 366, 11), instead of εἰς τὴν τελειότητα or πρὸς τὴν τελειότητα, is in accord
with his urgency that this "maturity" can and must be obtained.
37. Bénétreau, 1:228, correctly attributes double reference to the term τελειότητα
("maturity"): "on the one hand the fullness characteristic of the maturity of an adult; on
the other, the fullness of a teaching that communicates all the wealth of revelation" (translation mine).
38. φερώμεθα, first person, plural, present, passive or middle, subjunctive of
φέρω. Among others, Hughes, 194; Westcott, 143; Montefiore, 104; and Spicq, 2:146,
prefer the passive.
39. Attridge, 162-63, n. 97. Cf. also Bénétreau, 1:228, who prefers the middle.

hortation of v. 1a to "leave the elementary message about Christ." He also initiates a subtle shift from his hearers to himself as the primary actor. He wants them to leave their preoccupation with these teachings, but he is also affirming that he is not going to go back and re-teach them these basic fundamentals.[40] By listing these teachings the pastor removes possible distractions and focuses his hearers on the instruction for the mature he is about to present.

Clarity requires comment on both the structure of this participial phrase and the Jewish nature of the pastor's language. The direct object of the participle "not laying again" is the noun translated "foundation." Three pairs of genitive qualifiers describe this "foundation": (1) "of repentance from dead works and faith in God"; (2) "of teaching about washings and the laying on of hands"; (3) "of resurrection of the dead and of eternal judgment."[41] The

---

40. This shift of reference to the pastor and his future activity is in agreement with the change from the initial aorist participle, ἀφέντες, "having left," to the present participle, καταβαλλόμενοι, "laying." We agree with Bénétreau, 1:238-39, that the pastor uses participles with care. Nevertheless, his suggestion that the difference in tense between these two participles justifies distinguishing the teachings listed in vv. 1b-2 as Jewish from the basic Christian teaching of v. 1a is unjustified. Furthermore, the metaphor of laying a foundation fits well with the idea of teaching. Compare 1 Cor 3:10; Philo, *Cherubim* 101; *Names* 211; *Spec. Laws* 2.110; *Dreams* 2:8; and Epictetus, *Diatr.* 2.15.8 (cited in Attridge, 163, n. 104).

41. The first pair consists of two genitives each qualified by a prepositional phrase: μετανοίας ἀπὸ νεκρῶν ἔργων ("of repentance from dead works"); καὶ πίστεως ἐπὶ θεόν ("and of faith in God"). The second, of two genitives each qualified by a second genitive: βαπτισμῶν διδαχῆς ("of teaching of baptisms"); ἐπιθέσεώς τε χειρῶν ("and of laying on of hands"). The third, of two genitives, the first qualified by another genitive, ἀναστάσεως τε νεκρῶν ("of resurrection of the dead"), and the second by an adjective, καὶ κρίματος αἰωνίου ("and of eternal judgment"). See Koester 310-11. Thus one could lay out the structure of these verses as follows:

> not laying again a foundation
>> of repentance from dead works and of faith in God
>> of teaching of washings and of laying on of hands
>> of the resurrection of the dead and of eternal judgment.

There are two alternate ways of arranging the structure of these phrases. First, some would take "of the resurrection of the dead and of eternal judgment" as qualifying "teaching" (Riggenbach, 148-49; Weiss, 336). Then one would lay out these verses as follows:

> not laying again a foundation
>> of repentance from dead works and
>> of faith in God
>> of teaching of washings and of laying on of hands
>>> of the resurrection of the dead and of eternal judgment.

Second, some would follow those manuscripts that have the accusative (διδαχήν) for "teaching" instead of the genitive (διδαχῆς). See Lane, 1:140; Attridge, 163; Hughes, 196;

first pair is given emphasis and distinction by its initial position, by the structure of these verses, and by the fundamental nature of its content. It would receive even greater emphasis if we were to accept either of the two alternate arrangements of this text given in the previous footnote.

There is a balance between the first pair, which describes the basis and beginning of the Christian life, and the third, which pertains to its outcome.[42] The second pair has caused commentators much consternation because of the difficulty in identifying both the religious rituals to which the author refers and the significance he would give them. The pastor wants his hearers to cease their preoccupation with these teachings because such teachings alone are not adequate for the perseverance of God's people. However, they are foundational and assumed, if not always developed, in the teaching for the mature to follow.[43]

The Jewish character of the language used to describe this basic Christian teaching demonstrates its continuity with God's OT revelation.[44] The pastor has already made it clear that there is one people of God through-

---

and Montefiore, 105. This rendering joins "foundation" (θεμέλιον) and "teaching" (διδαχήν) as the compound direct object of the participle καταβαλλόμενοι ("laying"). Attridge identifies the "foundation" as the initial preaching of the gospel but the "teaching" as subsequent instruction for new believers:

> not laying again a *foundation* of repentance from dead works and of faith in God
> *teaching* of washings and of laying on of hands
> of the resurrection of the dead and of eternal judgment.

Both of these alternate arrangements find support from the way in which the last two pairs are bound together by a semi-chiastic structure: βαπτισμῶν διδαχῆς ("teaching of washings") balancing κρίματος αἰωνίου ("eternal judgment"); and ἐπιθέσεως τε χειρῶν ("laying on of hands") paralleling ἀναστάσεως τε νεκρῶν ("resurrection of the dead"). They may also be supported by the initial location of βαπτισμῶν ("washings") before διδαχῆς ("teaching"). Cf. Westcott, 145-46. The accusative alternate reading is, however, unlikely. The UBS[4] gives the genitive διδαχῆς an "A" rating (see *TCGNT*, 596). Despite Ellingworth's reservations (313-14), the genitive is supported by scribal probability, by the balance of external evidence, and by the likelihood that the pastor intends to emphasize the "foundational" nature of all of these teachings.

42. According to Koester, 311, "The six items listed in 6:1-2 span the journey of faith from initial repentance to final judgment."

43. The pastor's first reason for using the term "foundation" was to continue his emphasis on the elemental nature of these teachings and thus on their insufficiency (Bénétreau, 1:230). However, the term also implies that these teachings were basic to more advanced instruction, as witnessed by its use among the philosophical schools (deSilva, 216, n. 10; cf. Thompson, *Christian Philosophy*, 30).

44. Note Ellingworth's comment (313) that this "list contains nothing distinctively Christian, and of course nothing exclusively Jewish [in contrast to Christianity, not to paganism]."

out history. God spoke to the "fathers" of present believers (1:1-3). The Son became incarnate in order to bring the people of God, which was already in existence, to its intended goal (2:5-18). Along with those Moses brought out of Egypt, present believers are part of God's "house" (3:1-6). They stand in continuity with the wilderness generation and risk loss of the same eternal goal (3:7–4:11). The faithful who come after Christ continue the line of those who lived before (11:1-40), all of whom will reach their final goal through Jesus. Thus this unity of God's people throughout history is confirmed by the fact that the incarnate and exalted Son is the indispensable fulfillment of that history. To reject him is to reject the whole history of God's relationship with his people. Thus it was natural for the author of Hebrews to describe basic Christian teaching with Jewish terminology. Furthermore, it was appropriate to describe those who have fallen away from Christ in terms appropriate for idolatrous and therefore apostate Israel (cf. Acts 7:35-43).[45]

In light of these considerations it is no surprise that the author describes conversion to Christ with terms appropriate for those who show "repentance" from the "dead works" of idolatry and turn to "faith" in the "God" of Israel.[46] "Dead works" are works of unbelief that lead to eternal loss, like those evidenced by the wilderness generation.[47] The continuity of God's people is substantiated by the way Hebrews always describes "faith" as "faith in God." Faith is living in the assurance of God's promises for the future and of

45. This explanation for the Jewish character of the basic teachings described in these verses is superior to either of the two mutually contradictory alternatives. Some, like Ellingworth, attribute the Jewish character of this language to the fact that the author of Hebrews was "a Jewish Christian writing mainly to readers in the same tradition" (Ellingworth, 313). Others contend that the readers were originally Gentiles who needed this basic "Jewish" teaching before they could come to Christ. Weiss (337-39) argues that there was much commonality between Jewish and Christian preaching to Gentiles. Braun (160) thinks that Hebrews is referring to his hearers' earlier conversion to Judaism. See the critique of this position in both Koester (305) and Bénétreau (1:231-32). The first of these alternatives reduces the use of Jewish-sounding language in 6:2-3 to habit. The second does not adequately account for the author's widespread custom of describing Christians in ways appropriate for God's OT people.

46. The term "repentance" (cf. 6:6; 12:17) fits well with conversion because it "suggests a once-for-all, definitive turning" (Johnson, 158, citing J. K. Solari, "The Problem of Metanoia in the Epistle to the Hebrews" [Ph.D. diss., Catholic University of America, 1970]).

47. Cf. 9:14 and Attridge, 164. Cf. also Koester, 305. "Dead works" describe the actions of those separated from the "living God" (cf. Spicq, 2:147). Bénétreau, 1:231, suggests sin in general which leads to death. The pastor is not thinking of the external regulations of the Levitical cult (*pace* Lane, 1:140). There is no contextual support for understanding these works as works of human self-justification (*pace* Donald Guthrie, 138). deSilva's (217) suggestion of works "without value or life or honor" is also forced.

his power for the present (see 11:1-6). The difference for those living after Christ is that his high-priestly ministry has moved from future promise to present power. By using language appropriate for those who lived before Christ the pastor puts the situation of contemporary believers in historical perspective and emphasizes the seriousness of apostasy and faithfulness. He also makes it clear that there is no possibility of finding refuge in the Old Covenant apart from Christ. He invites not only his first hearers but believers of all time to identify with this one people of God and thus to be reshaped by the Christ who fulfills its history.

No doubt the first readers knew what the pastor meant by "teaching about baptisms/washings and the laying on of hands." Modern commentators must attempt what the pastor says he is not going to do — explain what these terms mean. It is attractive to argue that the pastor was referring to the baptism and subsequent laying on of hands that followed conversion in Acts 8:17 and 19:6. On this interpretation the conversion indicated by "repentance from dead works" and "faith in God" is confirmed by these rites. The word for "baptism," however, is plural, is used for Jewish "washings" in 9:10, and is not the normal word used for baptism in the NT, though Josephus uses it for the baptism of John.[48] One of the best suggestions is that the pastor uses the plural because he is referring to teachings that distinguish Christian baptism from various OT or contemporary Jewish washings.[49] The laying on of hands was used for healing (Mark 1:41; 6:5), blessing (Mark 10:13-16), and commissioning (Acts 6:6; 13:3; 1 Tim 4:14; 5:22; 2 Tim 1:6), as well as for the imparting of the Spirit in conjunction with baptism (Acts 8:17-19; 9:17-18; 19:5-6).[50]

Finally, "resurrection of the dead and eternal judgment" refer to the destiny for which those who have repented from "dead works" and turned to God in faith have prepared. Many who were loyal to the OT also believed in

---

48. The NT normally uses βάπτισμα for both the baptism of John (Mark 1:4; Matt 3:7; Luke 3:3; Acts 19:3) and for Christian baptism (Rom 6:4; Eph 4:5; Col 2:12; 1 Pet 3:21). The word used here in Hebrews, and in Josephus, *Ant.* 18.117, for John's baptism, is βαπτισμός.

49. Hughes, 199-202; Ellingworth, 315; Attridge, 164; and Bénétreau, 1:233-34. Apollos's experience (Acts 18:24-28) shows that the same person could have undergone proselyte baptism, John's baptism, and Christian baptism (Johnson, 159; Spicq, 2:148). Justin, *1 Apol.* 62, condemns the continuation of Jewish washings. This understanding is much more likely than a reference to triple immersion (*pace* Braun, 160-61, critiqued by Bénétreau, 1:234), or distinction between inward and outward cleansing (*pace* deSilva, 218).

50. *Pace* Braun, 161-62, it is unlikely that the pastor is critiquing OT sacrifices on which people placed their hands. Nor is it likely, as Lane, 1:140, contends, that the pastor develops his understanding of Christ's high priesthood from the imposition of hands in priestly ordination.

resurrection and judgment even if they had not accepted Christ. For the pastor and his hearers, however, these events find their fulfillment in him. The exaltation of Christ assumes his resurrection (13:20-21), and his session at God's right anticipates the coming final Judgment when all his "enemies" will be put "under his feet" (1:13; cf. 12:25-29). The dead will be raised (11:35), and this judgment will occur at Christ's return (9:23-28).

The pastor's anticipated teaching for the mature about Christ's high priesthood is not a systematic development of these foundational teachings. He says little or nothing, for instance, about "washings" or "laying on of hands." Nevertheless, his advanced teaching is vitally related to these fundamental truths. The fully adequate high-priestly ministry of Christ is the only way that those who have repented of "dead works" and turned to God in faith can persevere so that they receive "salvation" (9:28) and enter God's "Unshakable Kingdom" (12:25-29) at the resurrection when Christ returns in judgment. Nothing could be more important to all who accept these foundational truths than the means of such perseverance.

3 The pastor tactfully associated himself with his hearers in v. 1 when he urged them, "Let us go on to maturity." The hearers were still included when he spoke of "not laying again a foundation" of elementary teaching. The "we" of v. 3 ("this we will do") is clearly an authorial "we."[51] The pastor is affirming that he will not re-teach the foundational truths but that he will expound teaching that is both for the mature and fosters maturity. Yet the very fact that he still uses "we" invites his hearers to join him. "This we [the hearers] will do" — that is, embrace your teaching for the mature. "If God permits" is no mere pious addition. This statement reminds the hearers that both the presentation and the appropriation of this teaching about Christ's high priesthood are dependent upon God's grace and power.[52] "If God permits" also anticipates the following warning against apostasy (vv. 4-8). Those to whom God gives opportunity must not presume upon his grace.

2. Avoid the Danger of Apostasy (6:4-8)

4 *For it is impossible to renew again to repentance those who have once been enlightened,* 5 *who have also tasted the heavenly gift, and have become partakers of the Holy Spirit, and have tasted both the good word of God and the powers of the coming age,* 6 *and who have fallen away. Renewal is impossible because they are re-crucifying for themselves the Son of God and holding him up to public disgrace.* 7 *For land that drinks the rain that often falls upon it and produces*

51. Bénétreau, 1:237.
52. Hughes, 206. Cf. Attridge, 165, and Bénétreau, 1:237.

fruit useful to those for whom it is farmed receives a blessing from God. 8 But if it produces thorns and thistles, it is unprofitable and subject to a curse. Its destiny is to be burned.

The tension suggested by "if God permits" at the end of v. 3 becomes explicit with the first word of v. 4 in the Greek text — "impossible." Verses 4-8 vigorously reinforce the exhortation in vv. 1-3 by showing the dire consequences of refusal to "go on to maturity" (v. 1).[1] Persistence in a state of spiritual regression, accompanied by the refusal to appropriate the pastor's teaching about Christ's high priesthood, leads to ultimate loss without possibility of restoration. The pastor would not be issuing this warning had his hearers come to this terrible end. His exhortation is not counsel of despair but a timely wake-up call. Yet in these verses he makes clear what he anticipated in 2:1-4 and graphically portrayed in his description of the wilderness generation (3:7–4:11) — persistence in neglect of God's salvation springs from and reinforces unbelief. Thus it can lead to a definitive rejection of God's grace and the resultant irrevocable loss of his eternal blessings. The pastor issues this warning so that his hearers will realize their need of and embrace his teaching on Christ's high priesthood through which they can escape this fate. The warning in 10:26-31 concludes the pastor's teaching on this subject. It is, therefore, even more forceful because it is based on the full disclosure of the benefits provided by Christ as High Priest and "Source of eternal salvation" (5:9).

This small section is composed of two parts. Verses 4-6 describe the people for whom repentance is impossible. Verses 7-8 clarify their condition by likening them to unprofitable land.

4-5 Though "impossible" is the first word of v. 4, it is best to postpone discussion of its nature until the pastor's description of its cause in v. 6. One Greek article joins five aorist substantive participles in a unified description of those for whom repentance is impossible. In the translation above these participles have been rendered as three relative clauses. Because the first participle is emphasized by pride of place and by the qualifying "once," it has been given its own relative clause: "those who have once been enlightened."[2] The next three participles are in apposition to this first participle, reinforcing and elucidating its significance: "who have also tasted the heavenly gift, and have become partakers of the Holy Spirit, and have tasted both the good word of God and the powers of the coming age."[3] The final participle,

---

1. deSilva, 219. γάρ, "for," shows that vv. 4-8 provide motivation for vv. 1-3.
2. "Those" before this first relative clause indicates that all three relative clauses describe the same people.
3. Although the other participial phrases are linked by καί, the second is linked to

at the beginning of v. 6, stands in opposition to the others, "and who have fallen away."

"Those who have once been enlightened" is a reference to conversion. Eph 1:18 speaks of spiritual enlightenment, and the term was used in the second century as a description of baptism.[4] The aorist tense and the qualifying "once" affirm the definitive nature of the way those described have experienced divine enlightenment. "Once" anticipates the impossibility of the apostate's re-conversion by hinting at the irrepeatability of this event.[5] This term echoes in the reading of the following participles emphasizing the reality and finality of the experiences described.[6]

The next three participles can describe nothing less than the blessings experienced by the converted.[7] By recounting what these people have

the first only by a postpositive τε (γευσαμένους τε τῆς δωρεᾶς τῆς ἐπουρανίου, "and having tasted of the heavenly gift"). If καί is the major connective, then the second through fourth participles expand the first. Cf. Osborne, "Arminian," 111-12. The internal use of τε in the fourth phrase (θεοῦ ῥῆμα δυνάμεις τε μέλλοντος αἰῶνος, "the word of God and the powers of the coming age") establishes a balance between the fourth and second phrases. The contrasting nature of the fifth participle has caused Bénétreau, 1:244, to take the last καί as adversative: "but have fallen away" (καὶ παραπεσόντας).

4. Ellingworth, 319. There is no suggestion of baptism itself in the immediate context. Compare λαβεῖν τὴν ἐπίγνωσιν τῆς ἀληθείας ("to receive the knowledge of the truth") in 10:26 (Moffatt, 78). Yet these believers were, no doubt, baptized at the time of their conversion. Thus the usage of this term here prepared for its later use as a technical term for baptism (Weiss, 343). The pastor's use of "enlightened" is distinct from its usage at Qumran and in the Gnostic writings (Weiss, 342).

5. Spicq, 2:150. ἅπαξ, "once," describes the finality of heart cleansing in 10:2, of death in 9:26, and of the last Judgment in 12:26-27. Cf. also 9:7, 27, 28. The related ἐφάπαξ ("once for all") is used in 7:27; 9:12; and 10:10 to affirm the unrepeatable finality of Christ's saving work. See Koester, 313.

6. Bénétreau, 1:242; Spicq, 2:150; Weiss, 347; Randall C. Gleason, "A Moderate Reformed View," in Four Views on the Warning Passages in Hebrews, ed. Herbert W. Bateman IV (Grand Rapids: Kregel, 2007), 352. Although the following participles need not refer specifically to the event of conversion, as Bénétreau (1:242) and Johnson (162-63) contend, they do describe the blessings received in conversion and enjoyed by the converted. See Ellingworth, 319; Weiss, 341.

7. Lane, 1:141-42. Roger Nicole and Wayne Grudem have argued that these participles describe those not yet fully converted. V. D. Verbrugge has tried to avoid the implications of these participles describing the converted by arguing that the author is concerned with communal, not individual, apostasy. See R. Nicole, "Some Comments on Hebrews 6:4-6 and the Doctrine of the Perseverance of God with the Saints," in Current Issues in Biblical and Patristic Interpretation, ed. G. Hawthorne (Grand Rapids: Eerdmans, 1975), 355-64; Wayne Grudem, "Perseverance of the Saints: A Case Study from the Warning Passages in Hebrews," in Still Sovereign: Contemporary Perspectives on Election, Foreknowledge, and Grace, ed. Thomas R. Schreiner and Bruce A. Ware (Grand Rapids: Baker, 2000), 133-82 (a reprint from The Grace of God, the Bondage of the Will,

"tasted," the first and third frame the central and most important affirmation: they "have become partakers of the Holy Spirit."[8] The pastor has already affirmed that his hearers experienced the Holy Spirit at their conversion (2:4). Hebrews bears witness to the common NT affirmation that salvation comes to those who are "partakers of Christ" (3:14) through the indwelling of the Spirit (see Rom 8:9).

The metaphor "taste" is important because it demonstrates that those described have not just been taught about these realities but have truly experienced them.[9] The pastor underscores the magnitude of their spiritual privilege by drawing on both spatial and temporal imagery — "the heavenly gift" and "the powers of the coming age." In between he affirms that they have tasted "the good word of God." "The heavenly gift" can be nothing less than God's gift of "such a great salvation" in Christ (cf. 2:3).[10] This gift comes from heaven (see 3:1) and gives God's people entrance to the divine presence. "Gift" underscores the divine generosity.[11] The "good word of God" by which the worlds were created (11:3) is the same word that has revealed God's great gift of salvation (1:1-4).[12] The term "good" describes what is ap-

1995); and V. D. Verbrugge, "Towards a New Interpretation of Hebrews 6:4-6," *CTJ* 15 (1980): 61-73. McKnight, "Warning Passages," 45-48, has shown the weakness of their arguments. Even Randall C. Gleason, "The Old Testament Background of the Warning in Hebrews 6:4-8," *BSac* 155 (1998): 62-69, agrees that these participles describe true believers. "If this passage were found in Romans 8, we would all hail it as the greatest description of Christian blessings in the entire Bible" (Osborne, "Arminian," 112). See also Gareth Lee Cockerill, "A Wesleyan Arminian Response to a Moderate Reformed View," in *Four Views on the Warning Passages in Hebrews,* ed. Herbert W. Batemann IV (Grand Rapids: Kregel, 2007), 272-80.

8. Rissi, *Theologie,* 5, argues that the preceding and following blessings are received through the Spirit.

9. The normal meaning for the metaphorical use of "taste" in the LXX and the NT (Acts 10:10; 1 Pet 2:3) is not to sample but to fully experience (Bénétreau, 1:242-43). "It is not merely a matter of 'instruction' *(logos)* that apostates reject, but of actual experience. The aorist tense of the participles therefore is significant: they *were* once-for-all enlightened, they *did* taste, they *had* been made partakers! The 'falling away' is not from an external teaching but from the experience that the hearers have themselves had" (Johnson, 162).

10. This gift encompasses their whole present experience of salvation (cf. Riggenbach, 155). Bénétreau, 1:242, cautions the interpreter against making the "heavenly gift" more specific than the evidence allows. He cites Braun, 166, as giving a list of such overly specific proposals: baptism, the eucharist, the Holy Spirit, pardon for sins, Christ himself, etc.

11. Spicq, 2:151.

12. Hebrews makes no distinction between ῥῆμα, the term here used for "word," and its synonym, λόγος (2:1; 4:2, 11; 5:11, etc.). See Ellingworth, 321; Spicq, 2:152; and Attridge, 170. Attridge cites Philo, *Flight* 137 and *Alleg. Interp.* 3.169, 174-75, as illustra-

propriate, pleasing, and beneficial.[13] God's "word" is "good" because it is the faithful fulfillment of God's promised salvation.[14] Those described have "tasted" the quality of its goodness because they have experienced his faithfulness. The pastor's presentation of Christ's high-priestly ministry is meant to reinforce and enrich the hearers' experience of these blessings by deepening their understanding.

Through God's good word these people have experienced the "powers of the coming age."[15] By reserving mention of "the coming age" until the end of v. 5 the pastor sets future reward in direct contrast to "having fallen away" at the beginning of v. 6. Much is at stake. This is the age of salvation, inaugurated by Christ's commencement of his high-priestly work, but not fully entered until his return (9:27-28), when his enemies will be made his footstool (1:13). The "powers" or miracles that the hearers experienced at their conversion (2:4), as well as their participation in the Holy Spirit, betoken the inauguration of this coming age.[16] This age is characterized by the transforming power of the New Covenant (10:15-18). Furthermore, the pastor reserves mention of the "coming age" until last in order to direct his hearers toward the goal he would have them pursue. The magnitude of their privilege climaxes in this affirmation that they experience the reality of nothing less than the coming age of salvation.

Thus the imagery of "taste" is doubly fitting. It affirms that those described have truly experienced a salvation that consists of all the blessings God has generously made available to his people in Christ.[17] Yet it leaves room for the fact that these privileges are a "taste" of the fulfillment to come.[18] Hebrews clearly affirms, with the rest of the NT, both the present re-

---

tive of the synonymous use of these terms. God's word is never abstract theory but is always truth addressed to the human situation (cf. Weiss, 344-45).

13. The word is καλός rather than ἀγαθός. It comes first in the clause, after the initial καί ("and"), for emphasis.

14. deSilva, 224, makes reference to τὰ ῥήματα τὰ καλά in Josh 21:45 and 23:15, where this term refers to God's promises that have been fulfilled.

15. Cf. Weiss, 344.

16. Ellingworth, 321. The pastor is certain that his hearers are part of the same people of God to which the exodus generation belonged (see on 3:1–4:11). However, *pace* D. Mathewson, "Reading Heb 6:4-6 in Light of the Old Testament," *WTJ* 61 (1999): 219-20, the use of δυνάμεις ("miracles" or "powers") does not establish a parallel with the miracles of the exodus. See the discussion of σημεῖα καὶ τέρατα ("signs and wonders") and δυνάμεις at 2:4. The "powers of the age to come" is a clear reference to what Christ has provided.

17. See deSilva, 244.

18. In v. 4 the object of "taste" (γεύομαι) is the "heavenly gift" (τῆς δωρεᾶς τῆς ἐπουρανίου) in the genitive case. In v. 6, however, "word" (ῥῆμα) and "powers" (δυνάμεις) are in the accusative. In the NT "taste" (γεύομαι) usually takes its object in the genitive

ality and future consummation of salvation.[19] The cumulative effect of these participles is to emphasize the comprehensive nature of the spiritual benefits received and thus the greater obligation to honor God by perseverance in faithful obedience. "God's salvation and presence are the unquestionable reality of their lives."[20]

No doubt the pastor wants his hearers to keep the fate of the wilderness generation in mind, for they are, as indicated above, his paradigmatic example of apostasy. Nevertheless, attempts to show that these participles describe the pastor's hearers in terms that identify their experience with that of the wilderness generation are unconvincing.[21] This warning plays the unique

---

(Matt 16:28; Mark 9:1; Luke 9:27; John 8:52; Heb 2:9). BDF §169, 3, suggests that the genitive signifies "eat one's fill," while the accusative implies, "eat some of it." If so, the pastor is saying that they have eaten their fill of "the heavenly gift" but have had only a taste of God's "good word" and the "powers" of the coming age." However, such a subtle distinction is unlikely (Ellingworth, 320).

19. It is gratuitous, then, to argue that, because Hebrews sees salvation as future, the people here described were not truly converted (cf. deSilva, 221). Such a position ends up affirming that none can fall from salvation because none are saved until Christ's return. Those who argue this way neglect the great privileges provided for believers through Christ's high priesthood — "forgiveness" (10:17), a "cleansed" conscience (9:14; 10:22), God's law on their hearts (10:16), access to God through Christ to receive what is needed for perseverance (4:14-16; 10:19-25; 12:22-24). For refutation of this position see David A. deSilva, "Hebrews 6:4-8: A Socio-Rhetorical Investigation (Part 1)," *TynBul* 50 (1999): 33-57.

20. Lane, 1:142.

21. For such attempts see Weeks, "Admonition," 78-79; Gleason, "Moderate Reformed," 343-44; Gleason, "OT Background," 74-78; and Mathewson, "Heb 6:4-6," 209-25. Cf. also M. Emmrich, "Hebrews 6:4-6 — Again! (A Pneumatological Inquiry)," *WTJ* 65 (2003): 83-95, and *Pneumatological Concepts,* 56-64. When speaking of "once having been enlightened" the pastor is hardly thinking of the "enlightenment" brought by the pillar of fire in the wilderness. The experience of the Holy Spirit described in 6:5 is far from the limited experience of Bezalel or of the elders in Num 11:16-30. Having "tasted the heavenly gift" or "the good word of God" is hardly parallel to "tasting" manna. One cannot draw significant theological conclusions from such very tenuous OT allusions. The accumulation of unconvincing arguments does not lead to a convincing conclusion. For critique see deSilva, 222, esp. n. 28; deSilva, "Hebrews 6:4-8, Part 1," 44, n. 24; and Cockerill, "Wesleyan Arminian," 424-25. In spite of all the immediate contextual evidence to the contrary, Weeks and Mathewson use the above hypothetical parallels to argue that the experience of those described in 6:4-8 was no more that of true believers than was the experience of the wilderness generation. Gleason, on the other hand, argues that the judgment of 6:6 was no more than the temporal judgment inflicted on those who sinned at Kadesh. We have already demonstrated that the wilderness generation had truly experienced God's grace and that, according to Hebrews, their loss was eternal. Gleason's position also falls prey to the fact that virtually all OT judgment, whether on professed believers or unbelievers, is described in temporal terms. For critique of the way he handles the wilderness generation see Cockerill, "Wesleyan Arminian," 420-24.

role of preparing the hearers for the pastor's teaching about Christ's high priesthood. Thus instead of drawing on OT examples, it anticipates the great benefits of that priesthood by focusing on the magnificent splendor of the privileges the hearers have experienced in Christ.[22]

6 The final aorist participle introduces an abrupt and shocking change by describing the same people who have been genuinely converted as having "fallen away."[23] Thus it is evident why the pastor has used the third person plural of general description instead of addressing his hearers with the personal "you" or embracing them in an inclusive "we." While they have experienced the salvation described by the first four participles, they may yet escape the fate of those described by the fifth as having "fallen away."[24] The pastor issues them a most timely warning.

By affirming the impossibility of renewing the repentance of those here described, the pastor leaves no doubt that they "have fallen away" into apostasy.[25] If this participle were conditional, then the pastor would be describing the genuinely converted who might fall. The substantive is much more powerful: it describes the genuinely converted who have fallen.[26] Those portrayed here have, like the wilderness generation, turned "away from the living God" (3:12). Like Esau, they have become "profane" (12:16). The

22. Mathewson, "Heb 6:4-6," 210-11, argues that the presence of OT examples in the other warning passages makes their presence here more likely. Such *a fortiori* argument is questionable. Even on Matthewson's interpretation, the OT example in this passage is not nearly as clear as the examples in 2:1-4; 3:7–4:11; 10:26-31; 12:14-17. Furthermore, neither 4:12-13 nor 12:25-29 invokes OT examples in support of the warning given. Mathewson neglects the unique purpose of this passage as described in the text above.

23. Attridge, 171.

24. Riggenbach, 157.

25. "This is not a matter of faults and errors, in other words, but of apostasy, of making a deliberate choice not to participate in the gift once given" (Johnson, 161). It the LXX of Ezek 14:13; 15:8; 18:24; and 20:27 the verb παραπίπτω ("fall away") and the related noun παράπτωμα are used together to describe unfaithfulness to God's covenant. In these contexts they translate the Hebrew verb and noun meaning "to be unfaithful"/"unfaithfulness," derived from the root מעל. See also Wis 6:9. The related noun παράπτωμα is used five times of Adam's "offense" or fall (Rom 5:15 [twice], 17, 19, 20). The same term is used to describe Israel's "fall" from God through unfaithfulness in Rom 11:11-12. Gal 5:4 and 2 Pet 3:7 use the related verb ἐκπίπτω to describe falling from God's grace (Cockerill, "Wesleyan Arminian," 275, n. 41).

26. John A. Sproule, "Παραπεσόντας in Hebrews 6:6," *GTJ* 2 (1981): 327-32, has shown conclusively that παραπεσόντας, "having fallen away," is not conditional but is the fifth of five substantive participles joined by the article τούς. Although he does not draw conclusions from this fact, he seems to think that it weakens the threatening nature of the passage. In fact, as per the text above, it reinforces the text's foreboding character. See Cockerill, "Wesleyan Arminian," 275.

aorist tense of this participle affirms the completeness of the apostasy described and suggests that it culminated at a definite point in time.[27] The pastor is not referring to sin in general but to a repudiation of Christ and surrender of one's confession that sunders all connection with him.[28]

The two present participles of v. 6, "re-crucifying" and "exposing to public shame," give the reason why it is impossible to restore such people to repentance and thus clarify the nature of apostasy: Renewal is impossible because they are re-crucifying for themselves the Son of God and holding him up to public disgrace.[29] The word we have translated "re-crucify" or "crucify again" is a form of the simple Greek term "to crucify" with a prefix that can mean "up" or "again."[30] In contemporary Greek this compound verb appears to have been a more intensive form of the word for "crucify."[31] Perhaps the idea of "up" fit well with raising one "up" on a cross.[32] However, the translators of the ancient versions and the Church Fathers understood it to mean "crucify again" or "afresh." Its context in Hebrews supports their interpretation.[33] By "crucifying" Christ "again" these apostates have not subjected Christ to renewed suffering, but they have severed themselves from what Christ accomplished "once for all" (9:12; 10:10).[34] Their blatant disloyalty is also like crucifixion in that it holds Christ "up" and exposes him to the public shame deserved by none but the worst criminals.[35] Those who abandon

27. deSilva (225, n. 34) argues that Hebrews' emphasis on "drifting away" (2:1; cf. 3:13; 4:1) and "falling short" (12:15) precludes reference to a "decisive moment" of apostasy. He fails to see that drifting can lead to such a moment. Israel's rebellion at Kadesh-Barnea (3:7–4:11) was the conclusion of such a process. See Lane, 1:142; Hughes, 218, n. 68.

28. Weiss, 345-46.

29. Riggenbach, 157.

30. Compare the word used here, ἀνασταυρόω, with σταυρόω, "to crucify." ἀνα is the prefix in question.

31. For ἀνασταυρόω as simply "to crucify" see Josephus, *J.W.* 1.97; 2.75, and the examples cited by Koester, 315.

32. Johnson, 161.

33. The parallel πάλιν ("again") earlier in this verse makes "re-crucify" or "crucify again" more likely. By "re-crucifying" the one who offered himself "once for all" the apostates cut themselves off from the only sufficient source of salvation (cf. also 9:25-28). See esp. Ellingworth, 324. Thus the pastor probably used ἀνασταυρόω over σταυρόω, not merely from a predilection for more sophisticated terminology, but because of this possible aspect of its meaning.

34. Thus with Koester, 315, and Riggenbach, 158 (but *pace* Ellingworth, 324-25, and Lane, 133), ἑαυτοῖς, "for/to themselves," is more than a dative of disadvantage — "to their own loss." "Those who have crucified Christ 'to themselves' have terminated their relationship with him (Moffatt)" (Koester, 315).

35. παραδειγματίζω, the word used here for exposing Christ to disgrace, was often used for punishments that made an example of the victim. Koester, 315, cites the fol-

Christ out of shame expose him to great shame. This language is all the more forceful because the pastor does not speak of crucifixion elsewhere in this sermon.[36]

Thus the primary explanation for the impossibility of the apostates' restoration is not to be found merely in the hardening of their hearts but in the magnitude of the salvation they have rejected and the finality of their rejection.[37] They have definitively turned from God's final, once-for-all, provision in Christ which was the climax of all that God had previously done. Where, now, can they go for deliverance?

God, however, is the author of this salvation. Thus Koester is right to locate the ultimate source of this impossibility in the character of God.[38] Remember, the last words of v. 3 were "if God permits" and the first word of v. 4 was "impossible." In 2:10 the pastor spoke of what was "fitting" in relation to God. He uses the stronger language of impossibility here because of the warning nature of this passage. This divine impossibility is not a limitation on God's power but, like v. 18 below, a description of his character.[39] In fact, the parallel statement in v. 18, that it is "impossible" for God to lie, confirms this interpretation of v. 6. The danger of apostasy is based on the first of these divine impossibilities, the assurance of God's provision on the second. One might express the pastor's thought in this way: "What God has done in

---

lowing examples of such usage: Polybius, *Histories* 2.60.7; 29.29.5; Plutarch, *Mor.* 520b; Num 25:4; and Ezek 28:17.

36. The author's affirmation that Jesus "endured the cross" (σταυρός) in 12:2 is the only other place he comes close to crucifixion language.

37. Lane, 1:142; Ellingworth, 323; Attridge, 169; deSilva, 225; Weiss, 346-49; and Johnson, 163-64. Koester, 319-20, contends that it is the definitiveness of their rejection rather than the greatness of what was rejected that makes renewal impossible. However, to set these two causes in opposition is to oversimplify Hebrews. The rejection of those described in 6:4-6 is so definitive because in rejecting Christ they have rejected the great, all-sufficient, climax of God's plan. That is why the description of Christ's high priesthood reinforces the impossibility of restoration (see 10:26). Their possession of fulfillment in Christ distinguishes them from the wilderness generation to which Koester refers in support of his position. However, even that generation's fall was definitive because refusal to enter the land was rejection of that which was the goal for which they had been brought out of Egypt and the climax of their pilgrimage.

38. Koester, 312-13, 322. In light of 2:1-4, 3:7–4:11, and 10:26-31, it is impossible to reduce "impossible" to "impossible for men (but not for God)." See Bénétreau, 1:241; Hughes, 212-13; Braun, 164.

39. Nevertheless, the pastor may have hesitated to directly affirm the impossibility of God's bringing restoration. The faithfulness of God — and thus his inability to lie — is part of the bedrock of biblical faith (6:18). A direct assertion that it was "impossible" for him to restore the apostate might have been mistaken as a limitation on his power and thus as inappropriate. The pastor would do nothing that might distract his hearers from following his argument.

275

Christ is the grand and glorious, all-sufficient means of salvation. It fulfills all that he has done before, and brings his promises to fruition. How, then, could we expect him to provide an alternate way of salvation for those who so definitively and publicly spurn his most gracious provision?"[40]

Nevertheless, careful attention to the present tense of these two participles reminds us of not only the cause but also the effect of such apostasy in the life of the apostate.[41] Drifting, neglect, and obstinate resistance to trusting God may lead to a definitive point of apostasy, but the postapostate life is also a continual "re-crucifying of the Son of God and holding him up to public shame." This would imply that, in accord with the example of the wilderness generation, apostates do not seek repentance. If the pastor had extended his discussion of that generation, he could have described their postrebellion persistence in disobedience. Thus unconcerned persistence in disobedience is characteristic of the apostate for whom restoration is impossible. Those anxious for their own condition can be reassured, because the apostate would be unmoved by the pastor's warning.[42]

For fear of the Canaanites the wilderness generation repudiated God's promise, rejected his provision, and thus fell "away from the living God" (3:12). The intimidation of unbelieving society appears to have been leading

40. deSilva, 244, argues that understanding Hebrews from the perspective of the ancient patron/client relationship leaves room for God to restore such apostates. Hebrews is instruction to clients. Such instruction warned clients to expect their benefactor to cease bestowing benefits once and for all if they refused to render due gratitude and loyalty. On the other hand, instruction to patrons encouraged them to continue giving even if they did not receive due honor. Thus these client-directed threats to the recipients of Hebrews do not limit the generosity of God, their Patron. This argument is fascinating, but unconvincing, because it tends to reduce Hebrews to no more than instruction for clients. It does not take sufficient account of the eschatological magnitude of what those who turn from Christ reject.

41. In spite of the arguments put forward by J. K. Elliott, "Is Post-Baptismal Sin Forgiveable?" *BT* 28 (1977): 330-32, it would be inaccurate to mollify the harshness of this verdict by construing the present participles as temporal: they cannot repent "so long as they are re-crucifying for themselves the Son of God." The entire context has the urgency of finality. This interpretation ignores the way in which the impossibility of restoration is proportionate to the rejection of the greatness of Christ's provision. The following parable of the land and the examples of Esau (12:14-17) and the wilderness generation (3:7–4:11) forbid such a reduction. The present tense shows that the lives of those who have thus apostatized continue to heap shame on their former Savior (see Hughes, 218, n. 68). Koester, 315, and Bruce, 149, are correct in arguing that a temporal interpretation reduces these participles to a truism hardly worth stating.

42. The pastor had no intention of establishing a standard by which the church could determine if a person could be reunited to fellowship. Thus the use of this passage by the ancient church in the controversy over the readmission of those who had denied Christ under persecution was inappropriate. See Weiss, 347.

the pastor's hearers to a similar fate. They were in danger of rejecting "the heavenly gift" now theirs through Christ and losing confidence in the fulfillment of God's promise anticipated by their experience of "the powers of the coming age." The pastor will explain Christ's high-priestly ministry in order to expand their understanding of, and renew their confidence in and commitment to, these blessings. His words are a warning to believers of every age pressured by rejection from the unbelieving world and enticed by its offer of immediate, though temporary, gratification.

7-8   The pastor enables his hearers to see the judgment of the apostate by drawing a picture. They could almost feel the timely rain falling gently on fertile ground. Such was the abundance of grace received from the Lord. It was only natural for those who farmed such land to expect a "useful" harvest. How right it is for God to expect faithful obedience in response to his grace. "Will receive a blessing from the Lord" goes beyond the picture because fruitful land needs no further blessing.[43] Thus by introducing this statement the pastor makes his point clear: those who respond to God's grace with faithfulness will receive his ultimate "blessing." The pastor looks forward to the confidence he will express in his hearers below (vv. 9-12), and anticipates what he will say about God's promise of blessing to Abraham (6:13-14). The covenant language of "blessing" and "curse" is here intended in terms of eternal gain or loss.[44]

It is important to observe that v. 8 assumes but does not repeat the phrase "land that drinks the rain often coming upon it" from v. 7. Both verses are about the *same* piece of land. Thus the pastor is not contrasting two parcels of "land," but two "harvests" from the same land. He envisions the possibility of land that produces a useful harvest "bringing forth thorns and thistles." Thus, with most translations, the participle that begins v. 8 should be taken as conditional, "if it brings forth thorns and thistles." The apostasy of those who give every evidence of being faithful is possible.

The omission of this phrase also allows the pastor to concentrate in v. 8 on the unprofitable production and subsequent fate of the land. "Thorns and thistles" are a most appropriate contrast to the "useful" harvest of v. 7. The punishment of the apostate, introduced in v. 4, climaxes in the lengthy description of the land's fate: it is "worthless and subject to a curse; its destiny is burning."

The word translated "worthless" also contrasts nicely with the "use-

---

43. In the OT fruitful land is the blessing given to the obedient.

44. Under the Old Covenant God's "blessing" was "life" lived in the abundance of the Promised Land. The "curse" was destruction and exclusion from the land and its blessings. The pastor, however, has discerned that the true goal of the promise is the Heavenly Homeland (11:8-10, 13-16). See the comments on 4:1-11 above.

ful" of v. 7. In the NT this term always refers to those who have turned away from God's grace.[45] Within this context "worthless" probably reflects the sentence passed at the final Judgment.[46] The translation given above, "subject to a curse," expresses the intent of the more literal, "near to a curse."[47] The phrase is an ominous affirmation of the curse's inevitability, and gives no hope that it can be avoided.[48] The fate of those likened to this grace-repudiating land is sealed by the final relative clause: "Its destiny is burning." "Burning" betokens nothing short of eternal judgment.[49] The pastor has brought his hearers from the freshness of rain, at the beginning of v. 7, to the heat of judgment. Here he concludes his warning.

The recipients of Hebrews were enriched in their hearing of this parable by their knowledge of the OT. The pastor evokes many traditional concepts and expressions, but he does not seem to be drawing the context for his picture from any particular OT passage. The ideas of this passage are closest to those of the Song of the Vineyard in Isa 5:1-7. The land, like the vineyard, represents God's people. God's building and care of the vineyard, like the often falling rain on the land, represent God's grace. Both "vineyard" and "land" refuse to bring forth the expected harvest, and suffer judgment. However, in Hebrews the inappropriate harvest is only potential and thus reinforces the possibility of apostasy and the urgency of the warning. The only significant verbal parallel between these two passages is the mention of "thorns" in Isa 5:2, and "thorns and thistles" in Heb 6:8.[50]

Many have noted the echoes of Deut 11:26-28 in Heb 6:7-8.[51] Moses promised the people that, if they would "hear" God's commands, they would receive a "blessing" (cf. Heb 6:7). If they refused to "hear," they would receive a "curse" (cf. Heb 6:8). Remember the importance of "hearing" in 3:1–4:11, and the pastor's accusation at the beginning of this larger section that

45. Rom 1:28; 1 Cor 9:27; 2 Cor 13:5-7; 2 Tim 3:8; Tit 1:16.

46. Ellingworth, 328. This interpretation follows the etymology of ἀδόκιμος: α-privative, meaning "not," and δόκιμος, meaning "approved."

47. Compare the NRSV: "on the verge of being cursed."

48. Attridge, 173; Ellingworth, 328; and Hughes, 223-24; but pace Riggenbach, 161.

49. Heb 10:27; 12:25-29. Riggenbach, 160, cites Isa 8:18-19; 10:17; 33:12; Mal 4:1; Matt 13:30, 40-42; and John 16:6 as examples of judgment by fire. Pace Montefiore, 110, there is no evidence that the pastor is thinking of a burning off in order to foster new growth (deSilva, 233).

50. See ἀκάνθας, "thorns," in Isa 5:2, and ἀκάνθας καὶ τριβόλους, "thorns and thistles," in Heb 6:8. ὑετός, "rain," is used in both passages, but in very different ways. On the differences in language see deSilva, 229. Still, similarity of ideas was likely to remind the pastor's Scripture-literate hearers of Isaiah. See Hughes, 223.

51. deSilva, 232; Allen, *Deuteronomy*, 127-34. Cf. Lane, 1:143; Ellingworth, 326-27.

those receiving his sermon were "dull of hearing" (5:11). The "thorns and thistles" that evoke God's curse in Heb 6:8 are reminiscent of the "thorns and thistles" given as part of his curse in Gen 3:17-18.[52] It is less likely, but possible, that the hearers remembered Sodom and Gomorrah, those cities in a well-watered plain (Gen 13:10) that were the premiere example of God's judgment by fire (Gen 19:24; Deut 29:22-25). Mathewson's attempt to establish a connection between the "land that drinks rain" in this passage and the Promised Land in Deut 11:11 is even more unlikely.[53] The imprecision of these allusions suggests that the pastor is not evoking the specific context of any of these passages. However, these Scriptural echoes fill this parable with language characteristic of the covenant — the language of obedience and disobedience, blessing and cursing, life and death. All of this reinforces the eternal consequences of apostasy, because Hebrews, as noted above, understands these promised blessings to be of eternal proportions. The more immersed one is in the language of Scripture, the more one will be aroused to alarm and challenged to obedience by the pastor's warning against squandered grace.

3. Shun Apostasy and Embrace the Community of the Faithful (6:9-12)

> 9 *But we are persuaded in your case, beloved, of things that are better and pertain to salvation, even if we thus speak.* 10 *For God is*

---

52. Since this combination of terms, ἀκάνθας καὶ τριβόλους, "thorns and thistles," occurs only once elsewhere in the LXX (Hos 10:8), it is very likely that this expression is an echo of the Genesis passage, which refers to "thorns and thistles" as part of God's curse on the "land." In fact, τρίβολος, "thistles," occurs only four times in the LXX — Gen 3:18; 2 Kgs 12:31; Prov 22:5; and Hos 10:8.

53. Mathewson, "Heb 6:4-6," 221-22. Compare Heb 6:7, γῆ γὰρ ἡ πιοῦσα τὸν ἐπ' αὐτῆς ἐρχόμενον πολλάκις ὑετόν, "for the land that drinks the rain that often comes upon it," and Deut 11:11, ἡ δὲ γῆ εἰς ἣν εἰσπορεύῃ ἐκεῖ κληρονομῆσαι αὐτήν, γῆ ὀρεινή καί πεδεινή? ἐκ τοῦ ὑετοῦ τοῦ οὐρανοῦ πίεται, "But the land into which you are going to inherit it, a land of mountains and plains. From the rain of heaven it will drink." These two quotations share only three scattered words (underlined above). These words are separated by a number of varying expressions, they do not come in the same order, and two of them, ὑετόν/ὑετοῦ ("rain") and πιοῦσα/πίεται ("drink"), occur in different grammatical forms. The contexts of the keyword γή ("land") are distinctly different. In Hebrews the land represents God's unfaithful people who suffer judgment. In Deuteronomy, enjoyment of the land will be the reward given the people for faithfulness. Thus it is very unlikely that the pastor intends his hearers to identify the "land" of Heb 6:7 with the Promised Land of Deut 11:11. Such an association is at least as doubtful as "the allusions/echoes from the wilderness generation" proposed by Mathewson "for vv. 4-6" and discussed above. Instead of putting those allusions, which Mathewson admits were not "entirely convincing" (222), "on firmer footing" (222), it confirms their dubious nature.

not unjust to forget your work and the love which you demonstrated
for his name by having ministered to his saints and by ministering to
them. 11 *But we yearn for each of you to demonstrate the same zeal for*
the full assurance of faith until the end, 12 *in order that you might not*
become dull, but might become imitators of those who through faith
and patience are inheriting the promises.

The pastor's stern warning that his hearers abandon their shameful spiritual regression (5:11–6:3) lest they fall and suffer God's final judgment (6:4-8) renders them anxious for the hope now granted them. He assures them that they are not (yet!) identified with the apostates he has just described, and urges them to participate diligently in the community of those who, like Abraham, persevere through faith (6:9-12). Provision for that perseverance is made certain, as it was for Abraham, through the faithfulness of God, which has now been fulfilled in the high priesthood of Christ (6:13-20).

Thus awakened, the hearers are ready to grasp that priesthood (7:1–10:18) and its benefits (10:19-25) as the only means of perseverance. After another warning (10:26-31), intensified by the magnitude of Christ's priesthood, the pastor will again express his confidence in them (10:32-36) and provide a comprehensive list of those to be imitated, who, like Abraham, have persevered by faith (11:1–12:3).

9 The pastor assures his hearers that they are not among the apostates just described and then, in v. 10, affirms the grounds for this confidence. He draws them to himself by resuming the first and second person plural, abandoned since v. 3: "But *we* are confident concerning *you*" (italics added). Only here does he address them as "beloved." This expression is not only a term of endearment, but an affirmation of their unity with the pastor as part of God's people.[1] Moreover, he is confident in their case of "things that are better and pertain to salvation." What comfort for those whose ears are still blistered from the "curse" and "burning" of v. 8. These "better" things are the "blessing" of v. 7 soon to be certified in vv. 13-20.[2]

Hebrews uses the term "better" for the absolute excellence of the eternal destiny God has for the faithful, and the exclusive sufficiency of his provision for their attaining thereunto.[3] This understanding of "better" is reinforced by the coordinate expression: "pertaining to salvation."[4] The hearers

1. Riggenbach, 161.
2. Cf. Lane, 1:144.
3. See pp. 33; 98, n. 66; and 118, n. 4.
4. Note how one article joins both the adjective κρείσσονα, "better," and the participle, ἐχόμενα, "having" — τὰ κρείσσονα καὶ ἐχόμενα σωτηρίας, literally "things better and having salvation." Spicq, 2:157, contrasts "having salvation" with "subject to a curse" (κατάρας ἐγγύς) in v. 8.

began to sense the magnitude of this salvation with the "so great" of 2:3, and its singular quality with the "eternal" of 5:9. Here in 6:9 the pastor uses "salvation" in a most comprehensive way: contrast with the fate of the apostates directs the hearers' attention to the final enjoyment of salvation at Christ's return (9:28; cf. 12:25-29). The pastor, however, would not omit the present experience of salvation (4:14-16), and especially Christ's provision for both its present experience and future enjoyment (5:9). It is this provision that flows from Christ's high-priestly ministry. Thus the pastor expresses confidence that Christ's provision for present and future enjoyment of God's blessing is available for the hearers. Nothing need keep them from perseverance.

The hearers would never have grasped the importance of the pastor's confidence in them had he not made them aware of their danger. Thus he concludes his affirmation of confidence with a reminder of his warning: "Even though we are speaking thus."

10   The pastor's confidence is founded on two of his favorite themes: the faithfulness of God and the corresponding faithfulness due from God's people.[5] With an emphatic double negative he asserts: "For God is not unjust to forget your work."[6] God's faithfulness is beyond question, as vv. 13-20 will certify.

Signs of his hearers' faithfulness provide the second foundation for assurance: their "work" encompasses the full scope of their past faithful conduct (cf. 10:32-34). The pastor becomes more specific with "the love which you demonstrated for his name by having ministered to the saints and by ministering to them" (cf. 13:1-6). Their service to other believers has demonstrated their love for God.[7] They have even risked their own security by supporting those subjected to persecution (10:33-34). The use of both aorist and present participles makes it plain that their past demonstration of love continues into the present.[8] We need not wonder at the pastor's mention of love for God instead of his favorite themes of faith and obedience.[9] Mention of this love (evidenced by their service) allows him to affirm the sincerity of their

5. Johnson, 165.

6. Here "forget" means "neglect" or "overlook" (Luke 12:6; cf. esp. Heb 13:6, 11). For *litotes,* emphasis by understatement or negation, see Johnson, 165.

7. εἰς τὸ ὄνομα αὐτοῦ is literally "unto his name." We follow Ellingworth, 331, who suggests either "with regard to him" or "to his account" (see MM, 451) instead of the popular translation: "for his sake" (NRSV; ESV). For ἅγιοι, "saints," as believers in general see 3:1; 13:24; and compare Rom 16:2; 1 Cor 16:1, and many other passages (Riggenbach, 164; Weiss, 354).

8. The two participles, διακονήσαντες (aorist, "having ministered") and διακονοῦντες (present, "ministering"), are instrumental. This love for God is shown "by having ministered" and "by ministering."

9. Johnson, 165, calls the pastor's mention of love "unexpected."

faith. They lack, however, something necessary for their perseverance in that faith — a firm grasp on the reality of God's promises for the future and his provision for their attainment. The pastor is intent on supplying this lack.

11 Therefore, although the pastor has no doubt about the faithfulness of God, he dare not take the positive aspects of his hearers' conduct for granted. Such conduct is motivation for, but no guarantee of, future perseverance. Thus his assurance that they are not among the apostate in vv. 9-10 is a prelude for his exhortation, in this and the following verse, that they vigorously identify with those who persevere through faith.

Nothing shows the writer's pastoral heart like the intensity of his longing revealed in this verse, and the comprehensiveness of his concern, which reaches to each individual in the community — "we desire," "we long for" (REB), "we yearn for" "each of you."[10] This warning does not spring from self-importance or hostility, but from the deepest desire for his hearers' eternal salvation. He urgently desires them to "demonstrate the same" intensity of "zeal," evidenced in v. 10. The object of this zeal is now described as "for the full assurance of hope." The compassionate ministry of v. 10 may have evidenced their love for God and thus their faith. Nevertheless, if that faith was to endure, they needed to be just as zealous to live with "full assurance" in the reality of the things for which they hoped. Furthermore, they must demonstrate or maintain that assurance "until the end." Then they will be granted final entry into God's "Unshakable Kingdom" (12:28) with the return of Christ (9:28) at the Judgment (12:25-29). The pastor would have them fervent to live with complete confidence that these eternal blessings are as certain as the unchanging promises of God.[11] If they keep their eyes focused with certainty on the ultimate blessings God has promised, they will be able

10. Cf. "it is our earnest wish" (J. B. Phillips, *The New Testament in Modern English*). Hughes, 227-28.

11. Such confidence is what the pastor means by τὴν πληροφορίαν τῆς ἐλπίδος, "the full assurance of hope." Although etymology and the use of its cognate verb suggest the idea of "fullness," πληροφορία always means "full confidence" or "assurance" in nonbiblical Greek (Gerhard Delling, "πληροφορία," *TDNT* 6:310-11). This meaning is well suited to the context of Heb 6:11, and is confirmed by the parallel πληροφορία πίστεως ("full assurance of faith") in 10:22. Cf. Koester, 317; Weiss, 355-56. Under the influence of 10:22, a few mss (I *pc* a*) have substituted πίστεως ("faith") for ἐλπίδος ("hope") in 6:11. This substitution suggests that πληροφορία was understood as "full assurance" in both places. However, Bruce, 150; Attridge, 176; and Johnson, 167, opt for "fullness" or "fulfillment." On this interpretation the prepositional phrase, πρὸς τὴν πληροφορίαν τῆς ἐλπίδος ("for the fullness of hope"), gives the purpose of the infinitive ἐνδείκνυσθαι ("to demonstrate"), rather than the object of σπουδήν ("zeal," "diligence"). "Show diligence for the fulfillment of hope" — cf. "show this same diligence . . . in order to make your hope sure" (T/NIV). That is, be diligent so that you will obtain the things for which you hope.

to persevere. They will be undeterred by hardship or by the rewards offered for compromise. If they want to see examples of life lived with such conviction, they have only to await the saga of those who "through faith and patience" (v. 12) inherit God's promises (11:1-40). Verses 13-20 demonstrate that such "full assurance" is warranted because God's promises are founded on the constancy of the divine character.

12 The pastor describes what such confidence will help them avoid in order that he might announce what it will enable them to become. It will prevent them from becoming "dull."[12] The pastor initiated this larger section with an accusation that his hearers were "dull of hearing" in order to provoke their denial (5:11), which he now accepts. If they are not "dull" or resistant to God's word, then let them show confidence in God's promises (v. 11) in order that they might not become "dull" and unresponsive to the divine voice.[13] Thus with consummate skill the pastor who awakened them in 5:11-14 to their danger of resisting God's revelation concludes his warning against that peril with one final caution in order that he might direct them in the proper path.

The hearers will follow that path by becoming "imitators of those who through faith and patience inherit the promises." Nothing could be further from dullness or resistance to God's word than "faith and patience." This pair of terms was often used to describe Abraham, and it thus anticipates his appearance in the following verses.[14] He was certainly the example par excellence of such faith, as his prominent inclusion in the roll call of the faithful will indicate (11:1-40). Nevertheless, the plural clearly anticipates all of the faithful in that honored list. They are those who persevered in obedience despite resistance because they believed in the certainty of God's promised reward and the availability of his power and provision. Those unresponsive and resistant fall into the company of the apostate wilderness generation (3:7–

12. Thus taking γένησθε, "you became," as ingressive aorist: "in order that you might not begin to be dull." Such dullness is the opposite of the "zeal" described in v. 11 (O'Brien, 233).

13. *Pace* Ellingworth, 333, the pastor avoids redundancy of style by allowing this one word "dull" to evoke the earlier phrase, "dull of hearing" (5:11). This understanding is confirmed by the fact that those "dull of hearing" are the direct opposite of "those who through faith and patience inherit the promises."

14. Lane, 1:145, citing *Jub.* 17:7; 19:1-9. The terms used here are πίστις ("faith") and μακροθυμία ("patience"). The pastor introduces the examples of chapter 11 in 10:36 with πίστις, "faith," and ὑπομονή, "endurance." μακροθυμία and ὑπομονή are closely related terms (Col 1:11; 1 Tim 1:16; 2 Tim 3:10; Rom 2:4-7; 2 Cor 6:4-6; and Jas 5:10-11). The pastor begins with the traditional μακροθυμία, but replaces it with his term of choice, ὑπομονή. μακροθυμία ("patience") is well suited to Abraham's waiting for God to fulfill his promise of a son, but ὑπομονή ("endurance") is better suited to the pastor's concern for perseverance through difficulties. Thus ὑπομονή, and its cognate verb ὑπομονέω ("endure"), are important terms in Hebrews (10:32, 36; 12:1, 2, 3, 7).

4:11). However, those who practice "faith and patience" join the company of those "inheriting the promises."

"Inheriting the promises" is charged with the language of covenant and Promised Land. The promises of God are richly manifold, and the present tense suggests reference to the way in which God's faithful have inherited what he has promised throughout the ages.[15] Yet, as the pastor will make clear, God's "promises" focus on his promise to Abraham of a people who would inherit blessing in the Promised Land.[16] This promise, as demonstrated in 3:7–4:11 and confirmed by 11:1-40, is fulfilled in God's faithful people inheriting the eternal heavenly homeland through his Son. Thus after concluding his warning against unresponsiveness to the divine invitation (5:11–6:8), the pastor states his major concern for his hearers by urging them to assume their place as part of this faithful people destined for an eternal inheritance. His invitation extends to all who will hear. In vv. 13-20 he will ground this exhortation/invitation in the certainty of the promise made by a God who cannot lie.

4. Trust God's Promise Verified by God's Oath (6:13-20)

> 13 For when God made a promise to Abraham, since he had no one greater by whom to swear, he swore by himself, 14 saying, "If I will not certainly bless you and certainly multiply you." 15 And thus, by having been patient, Abraham obtained what was promised. 16 For human beings swear by someone greater, and for them an oath is the end of every controversy for confirmation. 17 Because God was desirous of demonstrating the unchangeable character of his plan most convincingly to the heirs of the promise, he mediated it with an oath. 18 He did this in order that through two unchangeable things, in both of which it was impossible for God to lie, we might have strong encouragement, we who have fled for refuge to take hold of the hope laid before us. 19 We have this hope as an anchor of the soul, sure and indeed steadfast and entering into the inside of the veil, 20 where the forerunner on our behalf has entered in, Jesus, according to the order of Melchizedek having become high priest forever.

Verse 12 ends with the word "promises." If the hearers would persevere through "faith and patience," they must be assured that the promises undergirding their faith are valid. The pastor spares no effort in certifying the reliability of these divine commitments. He turns naturally to the promise God

15. Ellingworth, 333.
16. Cf. Riggenbach, 166-67.

made Abraham as embodying all his promises, and then hurries to the time when God reinforced that promise with an oath (vv. 13-14). The validity of this promise is ascertained by the testimony of Abraham (v. 15), by the oath of God (vv. 16-17), by the indisputable truthfulness of God's character (v. 18), and by its fulfillment in the privilege given the faithful of entering God's presence through their "forerunner," who has become "High Priest forever" (vv. 19-20).

Abraham's receipt of promised blessings (v. 15) anticipates the hearers' reception of promised blessings through Christ's high priesthood (vv. 19-20). The following chapters reveal the magnitude of their privileges granted through his priestly ministry (7:1–10:18). Furthermore, God's unshakable oath to Abraham foreshadows the certainty and sufficiency of Christ's high priesthood because that priesthood has also been established on the oath of God (7:20-22).

13-14   As noted above, God's promise to Abraham of a great nation that would inherit the Promised Land encompasses all of God's promised blessings. This promise was first issued in Gen 12:1-3, 7 and then dramatically reinforced in Gen 15:1-21. God's subsequent command to sacrifice Isaac, the initial fulfillment and future agent of this promise, put Abraham's "faith and patience" to its greatest test (Gen 22:1-19). No wonder God responded to Abraham's obedience by confirming his promise with an oath.[1] Verse 14 quotes this oath from Gen 22:17: "If I will not certainly bless you and certainly multiply you."[2] The oath character of this proclamation is made certain by God's words of introduction in Gen 22:16: "By myself I have sworn." From this statement the pastor also draws the deduction that God swore by himself "because he had no one greater by whom to swear." Verse 16 below reveals the value of this statement.

15   Abraham is a witness to the surety of the divine promise and an example to those who would obtain it. The fact that "he obtained" what God had promised bears witness to the faithfulness of God. The pastor is referring to Abraham's receiving more than a reconfirmation of the promise, but less than the heavenly homeland. Mere reconfirmation would not bear the weight of Abraham's testimony.[3] His entrance into the homeland through Christ and

---

1. Johnson, 169.

2. Literally, "If not blessing I will bless you, and multiplying I will multiply you." In Gen 22:17 God's oath ends with "I will multiply your seed" instead of "I will multiply you." The pastor keeps the focus on Abraham without altering the meaning by paraphrasing "you" for "your seed." This paraphrase also facilitates reference to Isaac's birth as the initial fulfillment of the promise (Riggenbach, 169).

3. Ellingworth, 338-39, is certainly correct when he says that ἐπέτυχεν, "he obtained," is too strong a word to mean that Abraham merely received the renewal of the promise. *Pace* Lane, 1:151.

in company with Christian believers (11:39-40) is an article of faith to be affirmed, not a testimony to the surety of God's promise.[4] The validity of this
testimony rests on Abraham's having received fulfillment of God's promise
during his earthly life according to the clear text of Scripture. After great patience Abraham received the promised son in Gen 21:1-17.[5] Through this son
God would "multiply" Abraham so that his descendants would become the
promised people who would inherit the Promised Land. After offering this
son in obedience Abraham received him from God a second time (Gen 22:1-
19).[6] God's oath, quoted in v. 14 (from Gen 22:17), comes after Abraham's
offering and thus confirms not only the promise of God but the faithfulness
of Abraham.

Thus, although the pastor's main concern in this verse is Abraham's
testimony to the integrity of the divine promise, he cannot resist suggesting
Abraham as an example for emulation.[7] That is why he reminds us that Abraham obtained this promise "by having been patient." He demonstrated what
it meant to continue in obedience while waiting long for God to give what he
had promised. "Having been patient" reminds those who confess Christ of
their invitation to join those who "through faith and patience inherit the
promises" (v. 12). It anticipates the pastor's description of Abraham and others in 11:1-40 as those who enter the heavenly homeland "through faith and
endurance" (10:32, 36). That history of the faithful will expand the exemplary nature of Abraham's "patience."

16   The pastor reminds his hearers of two generally accepted facts in
order to clarify the significance of this oath and of the one who swore it. The
first fact supports the affirmation of divine integrity in v. 18; the second, the
reason for God's use of the oath in v. 17. First, "human beings swear by
someone greater." They certify their own integrity by invoking someone of
greater integrity as well as of greater power. Thus the fact that God "swore by
himself" (v. 13) shows that his integrity is unsurpassed and supports the pastor's affirmation in v. 18 that God "cannot lie." Second, an "oath" is the ultimate arbiter for the "confirmation" of every dispute among human beings.
Thus by using an oath, as v. 17 affirms, God spoke the language understood
by his human people.

17   Verse 17 describes the motivation for God's oath; v. 18, its purpose. The unchangeable character of God's provision for salvation is at the

4. Attridge, 179-80.
5. So Koester, 326; Riggenbach, 170; Weiss, 361; Ellingworth, 338-39; O'Brien,
236; Bruce, 153; and many others.
6. Hughes, 231. The pastor will make it clear in 11:17-19 that Abraham's willingness to offer Isaac was the greatest demonstration of his faith in the trustwhiness and
power of God.
7. Cf. Weiss, 359.

heart of both verses. The pastor would move his hearers by the wonder of the divine motivation that they might participate in the divine purpose.

The pastor uses every resource at his disposal to show the lengths to which God has gone in order to assure his people that his promise of salvation is absolutely reliable. Although God's integrity was beyond question, he condescended to use an oath, the means by which unreliable human beings affirm their truthfulness.[8] He stooped so low because he was so "desirous" to convince them. The participle here translated is causal, "Because God was desirous" (cf. T/NIV), not merely temporal, "When God desired" (NRSV, ESV). "Was desirous" emphasizes the intensity of the divine yearning by bringing out the significance of the present participle missed by the simple "desired." Furthermore, God wished to demonstrate the absolutely "unchangeable character" of his promise "most convincingly." This expression comes near the beginning of the Greek sentence for emphasis, but it qualifies "demonstrating" and thus underscores the thoroughness of this demonstration.[9] The pastor climaxes his description of the divine provision for assurance with the words "mediated by oath." "Mediated" here carries the significance of "guaranteed."[10] By concluding with the word "oath" the pastor leaves this word ringing in his hearers' ears as a reminder of God's assurance and an anticipation of the oath by which the Son is made "Guarantor" of the New Covenant (Ps 110:4 in Heb 7:20-22). The "unchangeable character" of God's promise is appropriate for a plan based on that "Guaran-

---

8. "ἐν ᾧ at the beginning of this verse means "in regard to which" or "because of which," referring back to God's oath — "because of the significance of the oath" for human beings God makes use of it (Ellingworth, 340-41; cf. Spicq, 2:161). Compare Philo's discussion of God's oath (*Abraham* 273). We have begun our translation of this verse with "thus" to show that the pastor is referencing God's oath. For God's great condescension in using an oath see Chrysostom, quoted in Heen and Krey, 92.

9. περισσότερον, "even more," takes on particular coloring from the word it modifies. Translations that understand the infinitive ἐπιδεῖξαι as "show" take περισσότερον as "even more clearly" (NRSV). The whole tenor of the context, however, seems to indicate that one should understand ἐπιδεῖξαι as "demonstrate, prove." If so, then περισσότερον should be rendered "more convincingly" (ESV) or "most convincingly." Though comparative in form, this expression draws superlative force from the context. Weiss, 362, n. 15, along with the KJV and NASB, takes περισσότερον with the following participle βουλόμενος ("desiring"), for example, "desiring even more" (NASB). Weiss, however, acknowledges the possibility of taking περισσότερον with ἐπιδεῖξαι. We have translated the Greek infinitive ἐπιδεῖξαι as an English gerund, "demonstrating."

10. Spicq, 2:160-61; Montefiore, 115; Riggenbach, 173; and Weiss, 362, n. 16. Cf. Philo, *Spec. Laws* 4.31. Compare μεσιτεύω, "mediate," "confirm," with μεσίτης, "mediator." Jesus is not only the mediator of the new and better covenant (κρείττονος, "better," 8:6; καινῆς, "new," 9:15; νέας, "new," 12:24), but, by God's oath, he is its "guarantor" (ἔγγυος, 7:20-22).

tor's" "inviolable" priesthood (7:24) and effected by the "eternal spirit" (9:14).[11]

God did all of this so that Abraham's descendants, called "the heirs of the promise" (cf. 11:9), might be certain of his promised salvation. All who put their faith in Christ join the pastor's hearers as "heirs" of God's blessings backed by such divine assurance.[12] Yet as "heirs" they must persevere to receive their promised inheritance. Verse 18 affirms that it is for this purpose alone that their gracious God stoops to such lengths in order to assure them.

18 God's purpose in certifying his promise with an oath was the encouragement of his people in perseverance. God's oath and his promise were the "two unchangeable things" by which he substantiated the "unchangeable character" of his gracious plan of salvation.[13] In relation to both of these things "it was impossible for one who is God to lie." As in v. 4 above, this "impossible" is an affirmation of God's character, not a limitation on his power. The basis for assurance in God's plan and provision for salvation is the absolute integrity of his character communicated powerfully through promise and oath. The pastor is guilty of no exaggeration when he affirms that such assurance is "*strong* encouragement" for perseverance.

By "in order that we might have strong encouragement" the pastor includes his hearers and all subsequent believers among the people of God who are given encouragement through the divine promise and oath. When God's people identify themselves as those "who have fled for refuge to take hold of the hope laid before [them]" they embrace all that the pastor has said about the present peril and promise of their existence.[14] As those who "have fled

11. The adjective ἀμετάθετον appears nowhere else in the NT and is used here in the neuter substantively: "unchangeableness" or "unchangeable character." This translation by the ESV (compare NRSV, "unchangeable nature") is certainly better than that by the NIV/TNIV, "unchanging nature." Compare ἀμετάθετον with ἀπαράβατον ("inviolable") as a description of Christ's priesthood in 7:24.

12. The pastor is not speaking of Abraham's physical descendants (Weiss, 172). See on 3:1-6 above. It is obedient response to the word (promise) of God that constitutes the people of God and defines the descendants of Abraham.

13. The "promise" incorporates the entire series of God's promises to Abraham (Gen 12:2-3, 7; 13:14-17; 15:5-7, 13-16; 17:4-8, 19), while the oath refers to the climax of God's promise in the oath God swore to Abraham after the sacrifice of Isaac (Gen 22:16-17). So Ellingworth, 335, and Koester, 328. For the unlikely suggestion that the reference is to Ps 2:7 and Ps 110:4, or to the two oaths of God in Gen 22:16-17 and Ps 110:4, see Lane, 1:152. Nor is it likely that the "two unchangeable things" are God's "word" and Christ's "entrance," as suggested by Johnson, 171.

14. The NRSV and ESV understand the infinitive phrase κρατῆσαι τῆς προκειμένης ἐλπίδος ("to take hold of the hope laid before us") as qualifying παράκλησιν ("encouragement") rather than the participle καταφυγόντες ("having fled for refuge"): "In order that we who have taken refuge might be strongly encouraged to seize the hope set

for refuge" they have rushed from danger in search of a place of safety.[15] They have run from the fate of the wilderness generation, of the apostates described in 6:4-8, and of all who have yielded to the pressure and enticement of the unbelieving world. They seek safety in the heavenly sanctuary and dwelling place of God (12:22-24), the heavenly homeland that is their destiny. The pastor may have chosen the term "fled for refuge" because of its common use for seeking sanctuary in a temple.[16] The infinitive "to take hold of" puts emphasis on the present without excluding the future.[17] The hearers are to hold continually to the reality of the future hope that is theirs in order that they might finally take hold of that hope at the end of their pilgrimage (9:28; 12:25-29). Such entrance is the goal "laid before" them by God through the high-priestly work of Christ. In the coming chapters the pastor will explain how the present privileges that are theirs in Christ provide for present entrance into God's presence in order to receive the grace needed for "holding on" to this "hope" (4:14-16; 10:19-25). At one and the same time, this description of God's people reminds them of the danger of the faithlessness from which they have fled, the ultimate eternal goal they pursue, and the necessity of faithful endurance if they would succeed. By its urgency it prepares them to receive the soon-to-be-described, all-sufficient provision for

---

before us" (NRSV). On the other hand, the NASB takes the infinitive κρατῆσαι ("to lay hold") as a modal qualifier of the participle καταφυγόντες ("having fled for refuge"), "We who have fled for refuge in laying hold of the hope. . . ." The urgency of the pastor is best expressed by taking the infinitive phrase as expressing the purpose of the participle, "having fled for refuge to take hold of the hope laid before us." See the discussion in Attridge, 182-83; Lane, 1:148j, 153; Ellingworth, 343-44; and O'Brien, 240, n. 182.

15. Gen 19:20; Exod 21:14; Lev 26:25; Num 25:25-26; cf. Deut 4:42. There is no reason to follow Ellingworth's (344) contention that the pastor uses καταφυγόντες ("having fled for refuge") for seeking safety but not for flight from danger. One can hardly do one without the other. The pastor intends both.

16. See 1 Kgs 1:50; 2:28; Euripides, *Iphigeneia at Aulis (Iphigeneia aulidensis)* 911; Herodotus, *Hist.* 2.113; 5.46; and Tacitus, *Ann.* 3.6 (cf. Koester, 328). καταφεύγω is also used for fleeing to the cities of refuge in Num 35:25-26 and Philo, *Spec. Laws* 3.130.

17. See Ellingworth, 344, for lists of those who understand both "take hold of" (κρατῆσαι) and "laid before" (προκειμένης) as referring to the present or to the future. "The tension between present and future [in this verse] is not merely a matter of lexical ambiguity: it lies at the heart of the situation which the writer addresses (cf. 12:22, προσεληλύθατε)" (Ellingworth, 344). One must not forget that Hebrews normally uses "hope" in the objective sense of the things for which God's people hope (Lane, 1:153; cf. Attridge, 183). "Laid before us" is best understood as confirming the future, eschatological reality of the things hoped for. Yet those who now "take hold" of this future hope live their lives in the present with confidence in its reality. Thus in this verse the pastor would not sever the future final fulfillment of this hope from present subjective confidence in its certainty (see Weiss, 365-66; Koester, 329; cf. O'Brien, 240).

attaining this goal. The pastor longs for God's people to live as "those who have fled for refuge to take hold of the hope laid before [them]."

19 Verse 18 ended with the word "hope." The pastor enables his hearers to grasp the significance of this certain hope for their lives by painting three pictures in vv. 19-20. The first picture is drawn from sailing, the second from a journey or race, the third, and most important, from high-priestly entrance into the Most Holy Place on the Day of Atonement.[18] Thus the pastor brings his now eager hearers to his exposition of the high-priestly work of Christ deferred since 5:10. This high priesthood, the fulfillment of the divine promise, is the ultimate ground of hope and God's fully adequate provision for its attainment.

Even in the present "we" as the people of God "have" God's certain verification of the things for which we hope as a precious possession that functions "as an anchor of the soul." "Of the soul" signals the pastor's metaphorical use of "anchor." "Soul" designates the essential person that transcends death (10:39; 13:17).[19] Thus this anchor is a means of eternal, not temporal, security. Just as a well-placed anchor prevents a ship from drifting into danger, so God has given his people this sure hope as a means of avoiding eternal loss. The certainty of the hope represented by this anchor is affirmed in the strongest terms by the mutually reinforcing adjectives "sure" and "steadfast."[20]

The believer's hope is as unshakable as an unmoving anchor. It also, however, moves forward "entering into the inside of the veil."[21] "Inside of the

18. Cf. Johnson, 172.

19. Hughes, 235. Heb 13:2; cf. Matt 10:28; 16:26; Luke 9:24; 12:19-20; John 12:27; 2 Cor 1:23; 12:15; Phil 1:27; 1 Thess 2:8.

20. ἀσφαλῆ τε καὶ βεβαίαν, "sure and indeed steadfast." Although these two words modify ἄγκυραν ("anchor"), they affirm the certainty of the ἐλπίδος ("hope," v. 18) represented by the anchor (Attridge, 183-84). They also occur together in the LXX of 2 Sam 8:2. βεβαίος is a favorite of Hebrews (2:2; 3:6, 14; 9:17). See βεβαίωσις, "confirmation," in 6:16 and βεβαιόω, "to confirm," in 2:3; 13:9. For the anchor as a metaphor of stability see Plato, *Laws* 961C; Artemidorus, *Onir.* 2.23; and Philo, *Sacrifices* 90; *Cherubim* 13 (cited in Johnson, 172).

21. We have taken the participle εἰσερχομένην ("entering into") as modifying the relative pronoun ἥν at the beginning of the verse, and thus qualifying ἐλπίδος ("hope," v. 17), which is the antecedent of that relative pronoun, instead of modifying ἄγκυραν ("anchor"). Notice how τε καὶ binds the two adjectives that modify ἄγκυραν ("anchor") closely together (ἀσφαλῆ τε καὶ βεβαίαν, "steadfast and also sure"), and separates them from the following participle, εἰσερχομένην ("entering into"). This construal makes much better sense than mixing the nautical and priestly imagery by having an unmoving anchor suddenly enter into the Most Holy Place. Riggenbach, 176; Ellingworth, 345; O'Brien, 241; Otfried Hofius, *Der Vorhang vor dem Thron Gottes: Eine exegetisch-religionsgeschichtliche Untersuchung zu Hebräer 6,19f und 10,19f* (WUNT 14; Tübingen: Siebeck, 1972), 87, n. 226 (cited in O'Brien), but *pace* Spicq, 2:164-65, and Weiss, 367, n. 38.

veil" can refer to nothing but the dwelling place of God in the Most Holy Place of the Tabernacle that contained the Ark of the Covenant.[22] The pastor uses this expression for the true heavenly dwelling place of God to which the faithful now have access.[23] He normally uses the aorist of completed action when he speaks of Christ's once-for-all entrance into the heavenly Most Holy Place.[24] Thus the present participle "entering into" reminds the hearers of what the pastor has said (4:14-16) and anticipates what he will say (10:19-25) about their present privilege of preliminary entrance into God's presence. Their High Priest provides this entrance as a foretaste of that ultimate hope and the means of receiving grace for persevering unto its attainment. The language of stability was incomplete without the language of motion forward. If God's people would avoid drifting, they must enter in.

20 The pastor leaves no doubt as to the source from which believers have received this wonderful privilege of entrance into God's presence. He immediately describes that heavenly sanctuary as the place "where a forerunner on our behalf has entered in, even Jesus." The term translated "forerunner" has the smell of the race track.[25] It echoes "pioneer" from 2:10, and could mean "advanced guard," "guide," or "precursor."[26] It fits well with the imagery of fleeing for refuge and of pilgrimage to the Promised Land. However, the phrase "on our behalf" indicates that the pastor has deliberately chosen the term "forerunner" to affirm that his entrance opens the way for the

---

22. The phrase ἐσώτερον τοῦ καταπετάσματος, "inside the veil," occurs only four times in the LXX — Lev 16:2, 12, 15 and Exod 26:33. In Exodus it describes the location of the Ark, but in the three Levitical verses it refers to the high priest entering the Most Holy Place on the Day of Atonement. Thus the entrance described in Heb 6:19-20 draws on Day of Atonement imagery. See Norman H. Young, "'Where Jesus Has Gone as a Forerunner on Our Behalf' (Hebrews 6:20)," *AUSS* 39 (2001): 165-73. Norman H. Young, "The Day of Dedication or the Day of Atonement? The Old Testament Background to Hebrews 6:19-20 Revisited," *AUSS* 40 (2002): 61-68, has successfully refuted Davidson's objections to his position (Richard M. Davidson, "Christ's Entry 'within the Veil' in Hebrews 6:19-20: The Old Testament Background," *AUSS* 39 (2001): 175-90; Richard M. Davidson, "Inauguration or Day of Atonement? A Response to Norman Young's 'Old Testament Background to Hebrews 6:19-20 Revisited,'" *AUSS* 40 [2002]: 69-88).

23. There is no contradiction in the pastor's use of the Most Holy Place as a description of both God's heavenly dwelling place (9:24) and the coming age (9:6-10), for the latter is the full realization and triumph of the former. Cf. Koester, 330.

24. Ellingworth, 347. If the participle were aorist, we might identify the "anchor" directly with Christ himself. As it is, the author establishes a more indirect analogy between the "anchor" and Christ. The certainty of the anchor is provided by the fully adequate High Priest (v. 20). See Attridge, 183-84.

25. This is the runner who wins the race (Pollux, *Onom.* 3.30.248, cited by Koester 330; cf. 12:1-3).

26. See Johnson, 173.

faithful to follow.[27] In contrast to the present tense of v. 19, the pastor uses the aorist, "has entered," in anticipation of what he will say about Christ's finished work and once-for-all entrance and session at God's right. As is his habit, the pastor maintains suspense by reserving the identity of this "forerunner" until the end, "even Jesus." The incarnate One who lived on earth has entered God's presence and opened the path for the faithful to follow.

From his first mention of "entering inside the veil" (v. 19), the pastor has evoked the memory of Aaron's entry into the Most Holy Place on the Day of Atonement. By calling Christ "forerunner," he has made Christ superior to Aaron, for none could follow Aaron into the inner sanctum of the earthly sanctuary. Thus the stage is set for return to the subject of Christ's priesthood according to Melchizedek's order proclaimed in Ps 110:4 and postponed since 5:10: "having become High Priest forever according to the order of Melchizedek."

Although the above translation of v. 20b is awkward, it reveals the pastor's emphases. Just as in 5:10, he has substituted "High Priest" for the simple "Priest" of Ps 110:4. This term has been given greater emphasis by its relocation near the end of the sentence. Although the pastor will revert to "priest" when expounding the psalm oracle in chapter 7 below, the contrast with Aaron and the unique once-for-all character of this priest fully justify his being called "High Priest."[28] Thus he resumes this term in 7:26 and then describes this "High Priest" in 8:1–10:19 as the one who offered a once-for-all sufficient sacrifice before being seated once-for-all at God's right hand.

The pastor has also singled out the expression "forever" by moving it to the end of the sentence. Thus the "forever" of eternity contrasts with the incarnate "Jesus" at the end of v. 19. This relocation not only emphasizes "forever," but signals the pastor's intention to explain the significance of this term in 7:1-25:[29] the priest according to Melchizedek's order is priest "forever" because he is nothing less than the eternal Son of God.[30] As we will see, the Son's eternity is the premise for, and never to be separated from, the

27. For "on our behalf" cf. 2:9; 7:25; 9:7; 10:19-20. The omission of the article before πρόδρομος, "forerunner," may indicate that the pastor is focusing on the "quality" of being a "forerunner" for others.

28. Note the way in which he introduced this whole section on Christ's high priesthood with the emphatically redundant "great high priest" of 4:14.

29. The pastor ends 3:15 with "rebellion" and then describes its nature in 3:16-19; he ends 6:12 with "promises" and verifies their integrity in 6:13-20; he concludes 6:18 with "hope" and elaborates upon it in 6:19-20.

30. Attridge, 185, affirms the importance of the author's reserving "forever" until the end of v. 20 and the fact that its significance is explained in chapter 7. However, he thinks its primary reference is to Christ's eternal priesthood rather than to the eternal sonship that makes his priesthood sufficient.

discussion of his incarnation, obedience, sacrifice, exaltation, and session in 8:1–10:18. This "forever" at the end of 6:20 anticipates the absolute nature and full sufficiency of the high priesthood it introduces. Without further ado, the pastor explains that priesthood to his hearers.

C. OUR HIGH PRIEST'S LEGITIMACY AND ETERNITY (7:1-28)

Hebrews 7:1-28 is the long-anticipated exposition of Ps 110:4 (Heb 5:5-6, 10; 6:20).[1] This psalm verse is God's declaration of the Son's priesthood. It builds upon his address to his Son, found in Heb 1:5-14, and brings that address to its climax. The pastor's exposition of Ps 110:4 is crucial because it shows how this psalm provides divine/Scriptural substantiation for the superiority of Christ's high priesthood. It also demonstrates how this divine word affirms the eternity of this new priest as the bedrock of his unlimited effectiveness.[2] Furthermore, Ps 110:4 substantiates the pastor's priestly understanding of "sit at my right hand" in Ps 110:1 (Heb 1:4, 13). Thus Heb 8:1–10:18 continues the story of chapter 7 by showing how the one "according to the likeness of Melchizedek" (7:15) has "sat down at the right hand of the majesty in the highest" (1:3d) by "making purification for sins" (1:3c) as God's fully efficient High Priest (8:1-2). This relationship between 7:1-28 and 8:1–10:18 has been announced in Heb 6:20. Chapter 7 explains the significance of the Son's becoming "a High Priest forever after the order of Melchizedek" (6:20b). Heb 8:1–10:18 reveals the significance of such a high

---

1. Attridge, 187; Ellingworth, 350; Spicq, 2:205; Weiss, 371-72; G. Sowers, *The Hermeneutics of Philo and Hebrews: A Comparison of Interpretation* (Richmond: John Knox, 1965), 123-24; and esp. Leschert, *Hermeneutical Foundations*, 212-15. *Pace* Joseph A. Fitzmyer, " 'Now This Melchizedek . . . ,' " *CBQ* 25 (July 1963): 305, who thinks that Gen 14:18-20 is the primary text. There is no evidence to sustain Davila's contention that because of the widespread use of Ps 110:1 Christians were aware of a "Melchizedek tradition at least to some degree" (James R. Davila, "Melchizedek, the 'Youth,' and Jesus," in *The Dead Sea Scrolls as Background to Postbiblical Judaism and Early Christianity* [Leiden: Brill, 2003], 267; cf. D. W. Rooke, "Jesus as Royal Priest: Reflections on the Interpretation of the Melchizedek Tradition in Heb 7," *Bib* 81 [2000]: 84). The way in which Hebrews introduces the fourth verse of this psalm and argues for its significance belies Davila's hypothesis.

2. The importance of the eternity of the Son in this chapter is demonstrated by the way the pastor introduces and concludes this chapter with "forever," εἰς τὸν αἰῶνα (6:20; 7:28; cf. Weiss, 372). P. Pilhofer, "KREITTONOS DIATHEKES EGGYOS: Die Bedeutung der Präexistenzchristologie für die Theologie des Hebräerbriefs," *Theologische Literaturzeitung* 121 (1996): 319-28, makes it clear that this "eternity" includes the Son's preexistence.

priest's entrance into the heavenly Most Holy Place as the "Forerunner" of the people of God (6:20a). Furthermore, Heb 8:1-2 joins what follows to what has gone before.[3] Thus Heb 8:1–10:18 builds the edifice of the Son's high priesthood on the exposition of Ps 110:4 in Heb 7:1-28.

Hebrews 7:1-28 is unified by the exposition of Ps 110:4, by the sustained contrast between Melchizedek and the Priest of his order with Levi/Aaron and the priests of their order, and by verbal inclusion.[4] This chapter is easily divided into three major sections.[5] In vv. 1-10 the pastor interprets Ps 110:4 in the light of Abraham's encounter with Melchizedek in Gen 14:14-27. In this section he demonstrates the superiority of Melchizedek to the Levitical/Aaronic priesthood. In vv. 11-25 he expounds this psalm in reference to the priest of Melchizedek's order, whom it anticipates, and shows how that all-sufficient Priest accomplished what the sons of Aaron could never have done.[6] Verses 26-28 return to the term "high" priest (cf. 6:20) and introduce 8:1–10:18, with its theme of Christ's once-for-all sacrifice and subsequent session. Nevertheless, v. 28 reminds the hearers that the one who is "perfected forever" by offering this sacrifice and accepting the divine invitation is the eternal "Son" described in 7:1-25. Verses 26-28 are not only a literary transition from chapter 7 to chapters 8 through 10 but the pastor's affirmation that these last three chapters tell the story of the one described in chapter 7.[7]

Verses 1-10 can be conveniently subdivided into vv. 1-3 and vv. 4-10.[8]

3. See the comments on these verses below.

4. Vanhoye, *La structure littéraire,* 125, points out the occurrence of "Melchizedek" and "met" in vv. 1 and 10 and "perfection" and "having been perfected" in vv. 11 and 28. The term "Son" in v. 3 anticipates "Son" in v. 28.

5. Bénétreau's analysis (2:19-20) of this chapter on the basis of classical rhetoric (6:20, thesis; 7:1-4, the facts; 7:5-25, argument; 7:26-28, conclusion) obscures the role played by Ps 110:4 and Gen 14:17-24 and the transitional nature of 7:26-28.

6. Weiss, 407, argues that ὁρκωμοσία ("oath," vv. 20, 28) forms an inclusion joining vv. 20-25 with vv. 26-28. However, v. 28 resumes the whole of vv. 11-25. Note νόμος ("law") in vv. 12 and 20 and νενομοθέτηται ("received the law") in v. 11. Weiss, however, expounds vv. 20-22 and 23-25 as subunits, just as we do below.

7. Vanhoye, *La structure littéraire,* 137-52, fails to see the way vv. 26-28 announce themes to come and thus joins these verses with vv. 11-25. See the criticism in John Bligh, "The Structure of Hebrews," *Heythrop Theological Journal* 5 (1964): 173. On the other hand, Delitzsch, 1:325-27, 2:1-6, represents those who fail to see the connection with vv. 1-25.

8. Westfall's attempt to make 7:1-3 part of 6:13-20 is unconvincing (Westfall, *Discourse Analysis,* 159-62, 169). First of all, 6:20 reintroduces Ps 110:4 and the subject of Christ's high priesthood rather than the subject of Melchizedek. We have already noted the use of "high priest" and the way this verse ends with "having become a high priest forever." Furthermore, *pace* Westfall, 160, οὗτος ("this"), in 7:1, is not a demonstrative pro-

In the first of these subdivisions the pastor recalls the desired details from Abraham's encounter with Melchizedek, which he then explains in the second. Verses 11-25 are appropriately arranged according to the phrases of Ps 110:4: "according to the order of Melchizedek" (vv. 11-19); "the Lord has sworn and will not repent" (vv. 20-22); and "you are a priest forever" (vv. 23-25).[9] The pastor begins by showing his hearers, both ancient and modern, how the encounter in Genesis 14 enlightens their understanding of this important psalm.

1. Melchizedek Is Greater than Levi (7:1-10)

1 *For this Melchizedek, King of Salem, Priest of God Most High, met Abraham as he was returning from the slaughter of the kings and blessed him,* 2 *to whom also Abraham apportioned a tithe from all. First his name is translated "King of Righteousness"; then also he is "King of Salem," which means "King of Peace."* 3 *Without father, without mother, without genealogy; having neither beginning of days nor end of life; made like the Son of God; he remains a priest forever.*

4 *See, then, how great this one is, to whom even Abraham gave a tithe from the spoils, Abraham the patriarch.* 5 *And those from the sons of Levi receiving the priestly office have an ordinance according to the law to collect the tithe from the people, that is, their brothers and sisters, although they also have come out of the loins of Abraham.* 6 *But the one not reckoning his genealogy from them has received tithes from Abraham and has blessed the one who has the promises.* 7 *Now without any contradiction the inferior is blessed by the superior.* 8 *And here dying men received tithes, but there one about whom it is witnessed that "he lives."* 9 *One might even say that through Abraham Levi, the one receiving tithes, paid tithes,* 10 *for he was still in the loins of his father when Melchizedek met him.*

---

noun that refers back to Μελχισέδεκ (Melchizedek) in v. 20, but a demonstrative adjective that intensifies ὁ Μελχισέδεκ in 7:1 — "now this Melchizedek" (οὗτος ὁ Μελχισέδεκ). This phrase in 7:1 introduces the Melchizedek of Gen 14:17-24. The exposition of this passage unites 7:1-10. Verse 11 returns to the interpretation of Ps 110:4 cited in 6:20. θεωρεῖτε, "see," in 7:4 introduces the pastor's interpretation of the material cited from Gen 14:17-24 in vv. 1-3.

9. In vv. 11-19 the pastor explains what "according to the order of Melchizedek" is not (vv. 11-14) before he explains what it is (vv. 15-19). Note the inclusions τελείωσις/ἐτελείωσεν ("perfection"/"perfected") and νενομοθέτηται/νόμος ("have received the law"/"law") in vv. 11 and 19 (Ellingworth, 370; deSilva, 268 n. 15).

At last the pastor will explain "this Melchizedek" of Ps 110:4, reintroduced in Heb 6:20.[1] Who was he? Although we have made vv. 1-2a, 2b, and 3 separate sentences, in Greek they are one long description of Melchizedek. The pastor uses a cluster of participles, adjectives, nouns of apposition, and a relative clause until he comes to the main verb at the very end: "he remains a priest forever." It is as if, after whetting his hearers' curiosity by delay, he would tell them everything about Melchizedek in one breath. Yet this flow of data provides an overload that will take the rest of the chapter to explain.

It is natural for the pastor to make use of the only Scriptural appearance of Melchizedek in order to answer the question of his identity. Thus he does not mechanically join Gen 14:14-27 to Ps 110:4 in accord with the rabbinic rule of verbal association merely because both passages contain the words "Melchizedek" and "priest."[2] Nor is he particularly concerned with Melchizedek's being the first priest mentioned in Scripture.[3] Rather, the Genesis passage provides a legitimate basis for showing Melchizedek's superiority to Abraham and thus to the Levitical priestly order.[4] By demonstrating the superiority of Melchizedek, Gen 14:14-27 supports the witness of Ps 110:4 to the superiority of the Priest Melchizedek foreshadows (see on 7:11-12 below). Furthermore, as demonstrated below, the role Melchizedek plays in Genesis enables the pastor to explain the ultimate priesthood affirmed by the psalm as derived from the eternal nature of its priest.

1-3 *"He remains a priest forever."* In vv. 1-2a the pastor recollects the information from Gen 14:14-27 that is important for his argument. He gives Melchizedek's name and two titles, "King of Salem," "Priest of the Most High God." He reminds his hearers of two incidents that occurred at this meeting — Melchizedek "blessed" Abraham, and Abraham "apportioned" to Melchizedek "a tenth of everything."[5] The pastor makes no men-

---

1. γάρ ("for") shows clearly that the pastor is explaining Ps 110:4, cited in 6:20 (Weiss, 373).

2. Note Leschert's comment: "But whereas the rabbis often employed this rule of interpretation artificially, here Genesis 14 is the true historical background of Ps 110:4" (Leschert, *Hermeneutical Foundations,* 218-19).

3. *Pace* Fred L. Horton Jr., *The Melchizedek Tradition: A Critical Examination of the Sources to the Fifth Century a.d. and in the Epistle to the Hebrews* (SNTSMS 30; Cambridge: Cambridge University Press, 1976), 170. See the critique of Horton in Gareth Lee Cockerill, "The Melchizedek Tradition, a Review," *Int* 31 (July 1977): 329, and Joseph A. Fitzmyer, "The Melchizedek Tradition, a Review," *CBQ* 39 (July 1977): 437.

4. Mikeal C. Parsons, "Son and High Priest: A Study in the Christology of Hebrews," *EvQ* 60 (1988): 214, n. 204; Leschert, *Hermeneutical Foundations,* 204.

5. Hebrews uses ἐμέρισεν, "apportioned," instead of the LXX, ἔδωκεν, "he gave." Neither Josephus nor Philo uses ἐμέρισεν when describing this episode in Genesis 14 (Attridge, 188 n. 28). This observation supports the assertion of Ellingworth, 356, and

tion of Melchizedek's giving Abraham "bread and wine" because it did not facilitate demonstration of Melchizedek's superiority.[6]

2b The significance of these two events must await discussion in vv. 4-6. The pastor's first concern is with the meaning of Melchizedek's name and titles. Other contemporary sources understood "Melchizedek" as "King of Righteousness," but only Philo rendered "King of Salem" as "King of Peace."[7] No doubt the pastor knew that the conjunction of these terms was suggestive of the Messiah, who would bring righteousness and peace.[8] He allows this dormant Messianic significance to heighten the greatness of Melchizedek in anticipation of what he will say in v. 3, but makes no further use of these terms or their implications in the subsequent argument of this chapter.[9] In order to explain "you are a priest forever after the order of Melchizedek," he focuses on Melchizedek's premier title, "Priest of the Most High God," which he interprets in v. 3.[10]

Moffatt, 91-92, that the author of Hebrews chose this word to emphasize the fact that Abraham paid a tithe to Melchizedek.

6. Nor did the pastor feel the need to explain it away as if it detracted from Melchizedek's position. Much ancient and medieval interpretation of Genesis understood this "bread and wine" as a type of the eucharist and used it as a defense of the priesthood and Mass (Bruce G. McNair, "Luther, Calvin and the Exegetical Tradition of Melchizedek," *RevExp* 101 [2004]: 750-54). Although Luther and Calvin rejected this interpretation (McNair, "Luther, Calvin," 751-53), Jonathan Edwards, *A History of the Work of Redemption* (first published Edinburgh: W. Gray, 1774; Edinburgh: Banner of Truth Trust, 2003), 60, retained a place for this typology in his Reformed theology: "The bread and wine [presented by Melchizedek] signified the same blessings of the covenant of grace, that the bread and wine do in the sacrament of the Lord's supper. So that, as Abraham had a seal of the covenant in circumcision that was equivalent to baptism, so now he had a seal of it equivalent to the Lord's supper."

7. For "Melchizedek" as "King of Righteousness" or "Righteous King" see Josephus, *Ant.* 1.180; Philo, *Alleg. Interp.* 3.79-82; *Tg. Neof.* 1; and *Targum Pseudo-Jonathan;* Fitzmyer, "'Now This Melchizedek . . . ,'" 311-13, and Str-B 3:692-93. However, only in the passage from Philo cited above is "King of Salem" interpreted as "King of Peace." In the *Genesis Apocalypse,* Josephus, and the Targums "Salem" is identified with Jerusalem. See Fitzmyer, "'Now This Melchizedek . . . ,'" 313-14. In later rabbinic literature this identification was made on the basis of Ps 76:3 (Str-B, 3:693). See also Martin McNamara, "Melchizedek: Gen 14,17-20 in the Targums, in Rabbinic and Early Christian Literature," *Bib* 81 (2000): 1-31, esp. p. 11.

8. Bénétreau, 2:30-31, summarizes the Messianic significance of these terms. For the joining of "righteousness" and "peace" with Messianic significance see Isa 9:6-7; 11:1-9; 32:16-18; *4 Ezra* 13:37-39; and *T. Levi* 18:2-4 (deSilva, 266, n. 4). Koester has shown how "King of Righteousness" and "King of Peace" are appropriate for the larger argument and parenetic purpose of Hebrews (Koester, 347-48).

9. *Pace* Rooke, "Reflections," 88-89.

10. See Héring, 57; Gerd Theissen, *Untersuchungen zum Hebräerbrief* (Studien zum Neuen Testament 2; Gütersloh: Gerd Mohn, 1969), 23-24; and Windisch, 59.

3 Many have noted the unusual vocabulary and poetic style of this verse. It can be construed as a poem of four lines:

Without father, without mother, without genealogy;
having neither beginning of days nor end of life;
made like the Son of God;
he remains a priest forever.

There is no need, however, to assume that the pastor is quoting from a hymn to Melchizedek.[11] He has proven himself capable of an elevated literary style and demonstrated his ability to use a wide variety of sophisticated terminology. These lines also appear to be from his hand because without residue they are important for his argument in the following verses.[12] If this were a hymn to Melchizedek, it would presume that the readers were familiar with speculations about Melchizedek as a heavenly being. In that case one would expect the pastor to demonstrate the Son's superiority to such a figure. Furthermore, there is no evidence for such speculations in Philo,[13] the Qumran writings,[14] or other Second Temple

11. Attridge, 189-90. For others who have found a hymn here see Rooke, "Reflections," 87-89, esp. n. 24. Rooke cites me as affirming a hymn in this verse, a position I no longer hold. See also Koester, 349-50.

12. On the appropriateness of Heb 7:3cd to the argument of Hebrews see Paul J. Kobelski, *Melchizedek and Melchiresha'* (CBQMS 10; Washington, DC: The Catholic Biblical Association of America, 1981), 120-21; Fitzmyer, "'Now This Melchizedek . . . ,'" 316, n. 48; Leschert, *Hermeneutical Foundations,* 210-12; and Attridge, 189-90. The exposition below will demonstrate the importance of v. 3ab.

13. Philo's treatment of Melchizedek in *Alleg. Interp.* 3.79-82; *Prelim. Studies* 99; and *Abraham* 235 provides no evidence for such a speculation. Philo believed Melchizedek to be a human being. He allegorized such terms as "priest," "king," "righteousness," and "peace" in the Genesis account of Melchizedek in the same way that he allegorized those terms in other passages. There is no distinction between the way Philo allegorizes Melchizedek and what he does with the Levitical priests (Koester, 340). There is absolutely no basis for Longenecker's contention that for Philo Melchizedek was "mainly the manifestation of the eternal logos" (Richard N. Longenecker, "The Melchizedek Argument of Hebrews: A Study in the Development and Circumstantial Expression of New Testament Thought," in *Unity and Diversity in New Testament Theology,* ed. Robert A. Guelich [Grand Rapids: Eerdmans, 1978], 177). For extensive treatment of the Philonic Melchizedek passages see Gareth Lee Cockerill, "Melchizedek without Speculation: Hebrews 7:1-25 and Genesis 14:14-24," in *A Cloud of Witnesses: The Theology of Hebrews in Its Ancient Context,* ed. Richard Bauckham et al. (LNTS 387; T&T Clark, 2008), 134-36.

14. 11QMelchizedek (11Q13) has been the primary Qumran document cited in support of a contemporary Melchizedek speculation. Most scholars agree that this document uses the name Melchizedek for the angel called Michael, "Angel of Truth," and "Prince of Light(s)" in other Qumran writings. For the extensive literature on this docu-

sources.[15] Subsequent mainstream Jewish interpretation often identified the Melchizedek of Gen 14:14-24 and Ps 110:4 with Shem, and Salem, his city, with Jerusalem.[16]

---

ment see the notes in Cockerill, "Melchizedek without Speculation," 136-41. 4Q401 (4QShirShabb[b]) may refer to Melchizedek as a heavenly priest (Carol Newsom, *Songs of the Sabbath Sacrifice: A Critical Edition* [Harvard Semitic Studies; Atlanta: Scholars Press, 1985], 133-34). 4QAmram[b] (4Q544); and 4QBer[f] (4Q280) appear to refer to Michael's evil counterpart, often called "Belial," as "Melchiresha'," "King of Wickedness." I have argued elsewhere that the use of this parallel name for Michael's antithesis and the fact that "Melchizedek" is written as two words in 11QMelchizedek (מלכי, "king"; צדק, "righteousness") suggest that the people of Qumran coined the name "King of Righteousness" for Michael by analogy with the other names they gave him, "Angel of Truth" and "Prince of Light(s). "King of Righteousness" was particularly appropriate for Michael's function in 11QMelchizedek as the one who brings about the "righteousness" of God by establishing God's eschatological kingship. Thus there is no more reason to speak of a "Melchizedek" ("King of Righteousness") speculation than of an "Angel of Truth" speculation. That the people of Qumran would understand "Melchizedek" as "King of Righteousness" is substantiated by the fact that Hebrews, Philo (*Alleg. Interp.* 3.79-82), Josephus (*Ant.* 1.180; *J.W.* 6.438), who knew Hebrew, and the admittedly later Targums (see McNamara, "Melchizedek," 3, 21 and Fitzmyer, "'Now This Melchizedek . . . ,'" 309-13) understand "Melchizedek" in this way. I know of no witness to any other understanding of this name in the Second Temple period. Furthermore, there is no reason to believe that 11QMelchizedek is describing the biblical person named "Melchizedek." This document makes no reference to Psalm 110 or to Gen 14:14-27. When the people of Qumran did refer to the Melchizedek of Genesis in the *Genesis Apocalypse,* they wrote his name as one word. See Gareth Lee Cockerill, "Melchizedek or 'King of Righteousness,'" *EvQ* 63 (October 1991): 305-12, and Cockerill, "Melchizedek without Speculation," 136-41. The fragmentary condition of 11QMelchizedek renders any conclusion about its nature and contents tentative. This inconclusiveness is demonstrated by the fact that two recent scholars have presented cogent cases for diametrically opposite interpretations of 11QMelchizedek, both of which differ from the majority view: Paul A. Rainbow, "Melchizedek as a Messiah at Qumran," *BBR* 7 (1997): 179-94, has argued that 11QMelchizedek presents Melchizedek as the human royal messiah anticipated at Qumran. Franco Manzi, *Melchisedek e l'angelologia nell'Epistola agli Ebrei e a Qumran* (AnBib 136; Rome: Pontifico Istituto Biblico, 1997) has argued that 11QMelchizedek uses "Melchizedek" as a title for Yahweh, the God of Israel. Both agree that "Melchizedek" is a title and should be translated "King of Righteousness." Both affirm that 11QMelchizedek is no witness to speculation about the biblical Melchizedek as a heavenly being.

15. Davila, "The 'Youth,'" 253-54, n. 10, argues that "Other, roughly contemporary, Jewish traditions accept his [Melchizedek's] angelic status and his high priesthood." However, the only source he can cite, in addition to Philo and Qumran, is *Slavonic Enoch,* a document of uncertain antiquity, as Davila admits (261, n. 10). Nor is there evidence of such speculation from an earlier period, as P. J. Nel, "Psalm 110 and the Melchizedek Tradition," *Journal of Northwest Semitic Languages* 22 (1996): 11, and others have suggested. Nel argues that by Hebrews' use of Ps 110:4 "Christ was legitimized as Priest ac-

The resonance of "without father, without mother, without geneal-ogy" is evident in English. The first two expressions could be used in antiq-uity to describe those who were orphans, illegitimate, or whose genealogy was unknown. Nevertheless, they were also used as descriptions of deities and eventually of the eternal, uncreated deity.[17] The third term, "without ge-nealogy," appears to be the pastor's creation by analogy with the first two.[18] It serves his purpose well, for it facilitates his emphasis on the fact that both Melchizedek and the priest after his order lacked priestly, that is, Levitical/Aaronic, genealogy. Nevertheless, the pastor is concerned with more than ge-nealogy. When these three words are taken together and understood in con-junction with the following line, "having neither beginning of days nor end of life," there can be no doubt that they describe eternal, uncreated Deity.[19] Neyrey's collection of parallel examples from contemporary sources demon-

cording to the priesthood of Zion that existed for ever in terms of Yahweh's (El Elyon) eternal connection with the cult of Zion." However, he must admit that "the historical evi-dence of an El Elyon cult in Jerusalem is as yet very sparse" and "evidence does not con-firm the worship of a god Zedek in Zion" (Nel, "Tradition," 5-6).

16. See McNamara, "Melchizedek," 11 and Joseph A. Fitzmyer, "Melchizedek in the MT, LXX, and the NT," *Bib* 81, no. 1 (2000): 66, n. 19. This united voice of later Jew-ish (and also Christian) interpretation belies Bodinger's suggestion that Melchizedek was already a heavenly being in Gen 14:14-22 and Ps 110:4 (M. Bodinger, "L'énigme de Melkisédeq," *Revue de l'histoire des religions* 211 [1994]: 297-333, esp. 309, 313). See Aschim's critique of Bodinger (Anders Aschim, "Melchizedek the Liberator: An Early In-terpretation of Genesis 14?" in *SBL 1996 Seminar Papers* [Atlanta: Scholars Press, 1996], 254, n. 53).

17. ἀπάτωρ, "without father," was used of the gods Hephaestus (Pollux, *Onom.* 3.26), Pan (*Scolia* on Theocritus, *Idyls* 1.3/4) and Horus (Karl Preisendanz, ed. and trans., *Papyri graecae magicae. Die griechischen Zauberpapyri* [2nd ed., 2 vols.; Stuttgart: B. G. Teubner, 1973-74], 1:5, 282), denoting the unusual circumstances of their birth. See also Nonnos, *Dionysiaca* 41.53 (with ἀμήτωρ). Pseudo-Athanasius, *Dialogues on the Trinity* 11.19, applies this term to God. From even earlier times ἀμήτωρ, "without mother," was used of Athena (Pallas Athena, Pallas), who was "born" from the head of Zeus split open with an axe (Euripides, *Phoenician Maidens* 666; Pollux, *Onom.* 3.26; Julian, *Orations* 5.166, 439; 7.230; and Nonnos, *Dionysiaca* 36.21-22). A later Christian writer, Lactantius, quotes the non-Christian source Trismegistus as applying both ἀπάτωρ and ἀμήτωρ to God because he was born from no one (*The Divine Institutes* 4.13). Attridge, 190, cites the *Apocalypse of Abraham* 17:9 as applying both to God. See Cockerill, "Melchizedek Chris-tology," 42-48, for a full discussion of these terms. See also Westcott, 172.

18. MM, 3.

19. O'Brien's (248-49) attempt to restrict this description of Melchizedek in v. 3 to the perpetuity of Melchizedek's priesthood rather than to the "eternity" of his person is unconvincing. He must reduce "without beginning of days or end of life" to the level of "without genealogy." His statement regarding "he lives" of v. 8 betrays the weakness of this approach: "as far as the biblical record goes Melchizedek is *without . . . end of life* (Heb. 7:3)" (O'Brien, 253, italics original).

strates with certainty that the first two lines of v. 3 describe deity that is eternal because it has neither beginning nor end.[20]

Furthermore, these two lines provide the rhythm for the following argument. The first beat of this rhythm comes from the first line understood in the more limited sense of "without" priestly "genealogy." This lack of priestly descent is important for Melchizedek in vv. 4-10, and for the priest of Melchizedek's order in vv. 11-14. The second beat is the pastor's affirmation of the unoriginate and unending deity of the one described. This deity is implicit in the first line, but confirmed and made explicit by "having neither beginning of days nor end of life" in the second. The author makes limited application of this aspect of his argument to Melchizedek in v. 8, but full application to the priest after Melchizedek's order in vv. 15-19 and 23-25. The priest after Melchizedek's order is not only without Aaronic genealogy but he is also, "according to the likeness of Melchizedek," eternal. The first beat enables the pastor to deny this priest's Levitical ancestry; the second empowers him to affirm this priest's eternal nature and priesthood "according to the likeness of Melchizedek."

It is important to remember that these two lines do not describe the Son of God himself, but the Melchizedek of Genesis 14 as the one who foreshadowed him.[21] In fact, any attempt to apply the first line to Christ results in considerable awkwardness. How can the one Hebrews regularly describes as "Son" or "Son of God" be called "without father"? How can one whose incarnation is so vehemently affirmed be described as "without mother"? Lack of clarity about the identity of the one described has led many throughout the history of interpretation to affirm that the Son was "without father" in relation to his humanity and "without mother" in relation to his deity.[22] This arti-

20. J. H. Neyrey, "'Without Beginning of Days or End of Life' (Hebrews 7:3): Topos for a True Deity," *CBQ* 53 (1991): 439-55; cf. Weiss, 376-77, and sources there cited. When used, as here, with a Jewish background and as part of the exegesis of Scripture, such language clearly describes the one of whom it is predicated as included within the one true God (Bauckham, "Divinity," 28-32).

21. The inappropriateness of applying "without father, without mother, without genealogy" directly to the Son is no evidence for a hymn to Melchizedek (*pace* Weiss, 380-81), but of the author's sensitivity to the Genesis text.

22. Gottfried Wuttke, *Melchizedek, der Priesterkönig von Salem: Eine Studie zur Geschichte der Exegese* (BZNW 5; Giessen: Alfred Töpelmann, 1927), 44-45, esp. 45, n. 1. See also Bruce Demarest, *A History of Interpretation of Hebrews 7,1-10 from the Reformation to the Present Day* (Beiträge zur Geschichte der biblischen Exegese 19; Tübingen: Siebeck, 1976), 11, and Heen and Krey, 104-6. Such inappropriate application has led Vanhoye to the speculative assertion that the resurrection was a new beginning of the Son's human nature without father or mother. This interpretation is in accord with his unconvincing argument that "priest according to the order of Melchizedek" refers to the Son's exaltation rather than to his eternity. See Vanhoye, *Old Testament,* 156-67.

ficial solution is unnecessary if one remembers that the writer is talking about Melchizedek, not Christ. These terms fit easily with the way Melchizedek appears in Genesis 14 without any indication of parentage, origin, or end.

With "made like the Son of God" in v. 3c the pastor asserts that Genesis 14 has described Melchizedek in such a way that he foreshadows the Son.[23] While the particular terminology at the beginning of v. 3 might be inappropriate for a description of the Son, it is well suited to describe the Genesis Melchizedek as an anticipation of the Son's eternity. Melchizedek's "eternity" is a reflection of the Son's eternity in order that Melchizedek might be a pattern for and anticipation of the Son in his uncreated and everlasting nature (see vv. 15-19 below).[24] There is no hint that the pastor feared that Melchizedek's "eternity" would make him the Son's rival and thus no apologetic diminishing Melchizedek.[25] Thus any compelling understanding of the "eternity" of Melchizedek in this passage must explain how Melchizedek's "eternity" anticipates, but does not rival, the eternity of the Son.[26]

It is necessary to examine the final line of v. 3 before further consideration of how the pastor understood the "eternity" of Melchizedek. "He remains a priest forever" is the climax of these three verses.[27] Since the "priest of the Most High God" in Genesis 14 "remains a priest forever," he antici-

---

23. "Scripture itself has drawn Melchizedek in such a fashion as to enable the reader to see a likeness between him and Jesus the Son of God" (Johnson, 177). Thus we give the perfect passive participle, ἀφωμοιωμένος, its full force as a divine passive, "having been made like the Son of God," rather than reducing it to adjectival status, "like the Son of God." See Bénétreau, 2:31-32; Ellingworth, 358-59; and O'Brien, 249.

24. Cf. Weiss, 378.

25. Horton, *Melchizedek,* 155.

26. This situation confirms the argument above that Hebrews is not dependent on speculation about a heavenly Melchizedek. Any actual heavenly being great enough to foreshadow the Son's eternity would also be his rival. Any too small to be his rival could not foreshadow his eternity (see Horton, *Melchizedek,* 164). *Pace* Davila, "The 'Youth,'" 253, there is no anti-Melchizedek apologetic in Hebrews, and thus no evidence that the recipients of this sermon believed in Melchizedek's eternal priesthood. Ellingworth gives one of the clearest articulations of the way in which the argument of Hebrews necessitates parity between the eternity of Melchizedek and the eternity of the Son. Still, he fails to see how this parity prohibits Hebrews' dependence on speculation about a heavenly Melchizedek (Paul Ellingworth, "'Like the Son of God': Form and Content in Hebrews 7:1-10," *Bib* 64 [1983]: 255-62).

27. μένει ("he remains") is the main verb in the long Greek sentence that makes up vv. 1-3. ἐμέρισεν ("he apportioned," v. 2a), in the relative clause "to whom Abraham apportioned a tenth of all," is the only other finite verb. ἐμέρισεν is fundamental to the comparison between Melchizedek and Abraham in vv. 4-10; μένει, to the contrast between the Son and the Levitical priests in vv. 11-25.

pates the one God addressed in Ps 110:4 with "you are a priest forever."[28] Furthermore, since the first half of v. 3 has described this person from Genesis in terms appropriate for eternal deity, the hearers cannot easily reduce "he remains a priest forever" to mere perpetual priesthood.[29] They were aware that the word translated "remains" was often used to describe the permanence of God.[30] The Melchizedek who is described as "without genealogy" (v. 3a) and without beginning or end (v. 3b) is also described as one who "remains an eternal priest" (v. 3d). He foreshadows the one after his order who is without priestly genealogy (vv. 11-14), has "indestructible life" (vv. 15-19), and exercises an "inviolable" priesthood because he "remains" (vv. 23-25). The pastor passionately desires his hearers to persevere in obedience through the adequacy of this priest anticipated in Scripture by Melchizedek. The "eternity" of the priest after Melchizedek's order is fundamental to the quality of his priesthood, which cannot be reduced to mere perpetuity.

There have been numerous suggestions for the way in which the pastor understood the "eternity" of Melchizedek: Melchizedek was an angelic or heavenly being; Melchizedek was a copy of the true heavenly high priest just as the Tabernacle was of the heavenly Temple; or Melchizedek was a preincarnate appearance of the Son of God.[31] Some argue that the writer of Hebrews follows Hellenistic/rabbinic practice by basing his understanding of Melchizedek on the silences of the Genesis text.[32] This commentary has

---

28. Weiss, 377, says "he remains" is used in a "free citation" of Ps 110:4. εἰς τὸ διηνεκές, "forever," in v. 3 is an elegant stylistic variant of εἰς τὸν αἰῶνα, "forever," in Ps 110:4. See Ellingworth, 359; Johnson, 177. Vanhoye's attempt to make εἰς τὸ διανεκές less than εἰς τὸν αἰῶνα because Melchizedek was only "like" the Son is unconvincing (Vanhoye, *Old Testament,* 153).

29. *Pace* Bénétreau, 2:32.

30. See Weiss, 377-78, and note 7:23; 10:34; 12:27; and 13:14. *Pace* Weiss, however, the use of this term does not necessarily indicate a distinction between the real and the material world like that found in Philo. For more on μένει ("remain") see the pastor's exposition of "you are a priest forever" in vv. 23-25, with comments.

31. See the references cited by Bruce Demarest, "Hebrews 7:3, a Crux Interpretum Historically Considered," *EvQ* 49 (1977): 148-49, 156-57, 161; McNair, "Luther, Calvin," 748; A. T. Hanson, *Jesus Christ in the Old Testament* (London, 1965), 70-71; and Heen and Krey, 98-100. See Rissi, *Theologie,* 89, for the argument that Melchizedek was a copy of the heavenly High Priest.

32. Bruce, 159-60; Lane, 1:165-67; Westcott 199, n. 1; etc. This exegetical principle affirmed that what was not recorded in Scripture did not exist — at least for exegetical purposes. This principle is often expressed by the Latin phrase, *quod non in Torah, non in mundo,* "What is not in the Torah, is not in the world." When Philo used the silences of Scripture in his allegorical interpretations, he was not denying the actual existence of that about which Scripture was silent. For instance, in *Drunkenness* 59–60, Philo allegorizes Sarah as "the virtue-loving mind." Scripture makes no mention of her mother. Thus she is

already demonstrated the inadequacy of the first suggestion above. There is no evidence of contemporary belief in a heavenly Melchizedek. Nor would such a heavenly/angelic Melchizedek have been suitable as a precursor of the Son's eternity.[33] The second suggestion fares little better. Aaron, not Melchizedek, is the earthly copy of the true high priest.[34] As for the third, it is difficult to imagine that the pastor would describe the preincarnate Son as "without father." Furthermore, the pastor makes a clear distinction between what God spoke in the prophets and what he has now spoken in his Son (1:1-4).[35]

Finally, the pastor does not base his presentation of Melchizedek merely on the fact that Genesis gives no account of Melchizedek's origin, genealogy, or decease. He is drawn from Ps 110:4 to Genesis 14 because of the unique role attributed to Melchizedek by many aspects of the Genesis text.[36] Furthermore, it is this unique role that makes Melchizedek's lack of recorded parentage significant. The literal encounter between Melchizedek and Abraham is also very important for his argument. If readers would understand Heb 7:3, they must follow the pastor's lead by attending to the distinct role and unusual figure of Melchizedek in Genesis 14. Even recent commentaries on Hebrews neglect Melchizedek's place in the larger context of the Genesis account.[37]

"without mother" (ἀμήτωρ; cf. Heb 7:3a) in that the "virtue-loving mind" is not descended from "perceptible" and ever-changing "matter." Philo is not denying that the Sarah who married Abraham had a mother. On the other hand, the rabbis seem to have denied the existence of something until its mention in Scripture. See the examples in Str-B 3:693-95: there was no old age until its mention in regard to Abraham (Gen 18:1; 24:1); no sickness prior to its affirmation in regard to Jacob (Gen 48:1); no war before its first recorded occurrence in Genesis 14, etc. They appear to have searched for the origin of everything in the sacred text. Thus it is questionable whether they distinguished between reality and what was claimed "for exegetical purposes," as Bruce, 159, n. 18, seems to suppose.

33. The description of Melchizedek of Heb 7:1-10 is derived from Scripture and patterned on the Son of God. Melchizedek's being the concrete historical figure who met Abraham is essential to the pastor's argument. See Pfitzner, 108.

34. Melchizedek's very appearance in Genesis puts him outside the old earthly order of tabernacle, priesthood, and the law that sustained them. He is the one who, according to Ps 110:4, foreshadows the Son's priesthood, not the one whose priesthood the Son fulfills. See Bénétreau, 2:27-30.

35. It is true that the pastor sees various OT passages as conversation between God and his Son (Ps 2:7; 2 Sam 7:14; Pss 110:1; 110:4; and 40:6-8; in Heb 1:5, 13; 5:5-6; 10:5-10). Yet this conversation always pertains to the Son's incarnation, exaltation, session, second coming, etc.

36. See Cockerill, "Melchizedek without Speculation," 141-44, for a more extensive discussion of the role of Melchizedek in Genesis.

37. Cf. Johnson, 176.

Wenham has shown that the appearance of Melchizedek is integral to the Abraham/Lot narrative initiated in Gen 13:1–14:24 and continued in Gen 18:1–19:38.[38] This narrative is preceded by God's promise of blessing to Abraham (12:1-9) and the subsequent threat to the promise by Pharaoh (12:10-20). It is followed by the parallel threat from Abimelech (20:1-18) and the fulfillment of the promise in the birth of a son (21:1-7). The chapters between these two sections (15:1–17:27) anticipate God's visit to Abraham in chapter 18 by focusing on the promise of a Son. In this narrative Lot is the foil of Abraham.[39]

Genesis 13:1–14:24 contrasts the choice of Lot to seek blessing in Sodom with Abraham's commitment to trust the promise of God. Genesis 18:1–19:38 exposes the consequences of their choices.[40] The contrast between Abraham and Lot finds its counterpart in the contrast between Melchizedek and the King of Sodom. The text establishes many parallels between the two kings.[41] However, the abrupt appearance of Melchizedek between the King of Sodom's entrance (14:17) and his speech (14:22) anticipates the antipathy between the two. This antipathy is confirmed by Abraham's contrasting responses.[42] By giving the tithe Abraham acknowledges God's blessing mediated through Melchizedek. He then refuses wealth from the King of Sodom (Gen 14:23).

Now we are in a position to perceive Melchizedek's unique role in Genesis. He is identified as a human being like the King of Sodom, yet he is neither Abraham's enemy nor his ally. He is above those who receive the

---

38. Gordon J. Wenham, *Genesis 1–15* (WBC 1; Dallas: Word, 1991), 304-7. Terence E. Fretheim, "The Book of Genesis: Introduction, Commentary, and Reflections," in *The New Interpreter's Bible* (Nashville: Abingdon, 1994), 438, concurs when he says that chapter 14 "serves as an integral part of the larger story of Lot and Abraham." See also N. M. Sarna, *Genesis* (Jewish Publication Society Torah Commentary; Philadelphia: Jewish Publication Society, 1989), 109. For a convenient summary and evaluation of many proposals concerning the tradition history of Genesis 14 see John A. Emerton, "Riddle of Genesis 14," *Vetus Testamentum* 21 (1971): 403-39.

39. Cf. George W. Coats, "Lot: A Foil in the Abraham Saga," in *Understanding the Word*, ed. James T. Butler, Edgar W. Conrad, and Ben C. Ollenburger (Journal for the Study of the Old Testament: Supplement Series 37; Sheffield: JSOT Press, 1985), 117.

40. For the numerous detailed parallels between Abraham in Genesis 18 and Lot in Genesis 19 see Cockerill, "Melchizedek without Speculation," 142. A comparison of the opening verses of these chapters in the Hebrew text is also instructive.

41. Cockerill, "Melchizedek without Speculation," 143.

42. Wenham, *Genesis 1–15*, 321. Wenham is incorrect, however, when he argues that Melchizedek and the King of Sodom are examples of how those who bless Abraham will be blessed (here by receiving the tithe) and those who curse Abraham will be cursed. The text does not identify the King of Sodom with those who curse Abraham. Wenham's understanding ignores the way this event fits into the story of Abraham and Lot.

promise, reject the promise, or oppose the promise.[43] He stands on the side of the Blesser, not the blessed. He abruptly appears in the narrative unannounced by genealogy or family connection. He dispenses and reconfirms God's blessing on Abraham, receives Abraham's homage, and then, just as abruptly, disappears from the text.[44] His appearance and actions are reminiscent of God's appearance to Abraham in Gen 18:1-15; of the Captain of the Lord's host's appearance to Joshua in Josh 5:13-15; and of certain appearances of the "Angel of the LORD."[45] Thus the pastor is able to discern in the unique role played by this character a foreshadowing of the eternal being of the Son. The pastor's commitment to a literal encounter between Abraham and Melchizedek and his concomitant assumption of Melchizedek's humanity frees him to use Melchizedek without fear that Melchizedek might become the Son's rival. Thus we have a Melchizedek adequate to foreshadow but unable to compete with the Son.

4-10 *Greater than the Levitical Priesthood.* The torrent of description in vv. 1-3 has left an overwhelming impression of Melchizedek's greatness. The pastor introduces this section in v. 4 by inviting his hearers to consider that greatness and its significance, "See how great this person is."[46] He also states the primary basis for affirming Melchizedek's primacy, "to whom Abraham gave a tithe from the spoil, Abraham the patriarch."[47] The pastor would demonstrate Melchizedek's overwhelming superiority to the Levitical priesthood. Thus his argument takes the form of two contrasts between Melchizedek and the sons of Levi, the first and most extensive in vv. 5-7, the second and more suggestive in v. 8.[48] In v. 9 he reaches his conclusion, which receives necessary qualification in v. 10. Melchizedek's blessing Abraham

43. Rabbinic and later Jewish interpretation appears to have attempted removal of the offense caused by Melchizedek's being outside the Abrahamic family by identifying him with Abraham's ancestor, Shem. See pp. 299-300, n. 16.

44. John D. Currid, *A Study Commentary on Genesis* (2 vols.; Webster, NY: Evangelical Press, 2003), 1:285, suggests that Melchizedek's abrupt entry was a timely intervention to forestall Abraham's accepting the offer made by the King of Sodom.

45. Gen 16:7-11; 21:17; 22:11-15; Exod 3:2; Num 22:22-35; Judg 6:11-22; 13:3-21. Except in Judg 2:1-4, the Angel of the Lord appears to individuals. Melchizedek's appearance was public.

46. πηλίκος (4 Macc 15:21; Gal 6:11) is used here as an exclamation ("how great!" see Ellingworth, 360), and is the key word in this section which emphasizes Melchizedek's superiority (Spicq, 2:185). It would be possible to translate this opening phrase as indicative, "You see how great this one [described in vv. 1-3] is" (Ellingworth, 360).

47. Thus Michel, 264, would take δεκάτη, "tithe," as the word most characteristic of this section.

48. Note καὶ οἱ μέν (v. 5) . . . ὁ δέ (v. 6), "and on the one hand those . . . but he." Compare καὶ ὧδε μὲν . . . ἐκεῖ δέ, "and here on the one hand . . . but there" (v. 8).

will also come to prominence in vv. 6b-7 as part of the first contrast. Verse 3a, "without father, without mother, without genealogy," provides background for the first contrast; v. 3b, "having neither beginning of days nor end of life," for the second. The pastor's Christological concern and orientation to Ps 110:4 set his discussion apart from rabbinic disputes about the relative superiority of OT persons.[49]

4 The pastor's recollection of the Genesis 14 encounter reached its climax in the relative clause of v. 2a above: "and to whom Abraham apportioned a tithe from all." The pastor now signals the importance of the tithe for his argument by repeating this clause in revised form (v. 4b). The word for "tithe" maintains its importance as the first noun of the Greek clause, despite the fact that it is the direct object. Every revision in the wording of the Genesis text highlights Melchizedek's excellence. The tithe is now described as "of the spoils" instead of "from all." This expression could denote the "first fruits" or the best of the "spoil" reserved for God.[50] The word "Abraham" has been moved forward in order to leave the concluding emphatic position for "the patriarch."[51] Melchizedek's superiority is demonstrated both by the quality of the gift he is offered and the dignity of the one who offers.[52] As "patriarch" Abraham is representative of both the Levitical priests who acknowledge Melchizedek's superiority through the tithe of their "father" (v. 9) and those from whom the Levitical priests collect tithe (v. 5).[53]

5-6 The pastor presents this grand contrast between the Levitical priests and Melchizedek in vv. 5 and 6. Verse 5 describes the Levitical priests in terms of (1) their genealogy, (2) their authority to collect tithes, and (3) the identity of those from whom they collect them. Verse 6 describes Melchizedek in terms of (1) his lack of genealogy, (2) the one from whom he collected tithes, and (3) his blessing Abraham. Melchizedek's blessing Abraham comes last because it is the crowning demonstration of the magnitude of his greatness and authority. This blessing contrasts sharply with the legally based authority of the Levitical priests, put earlier in v. 5 to show the limited sphere of their activity.

49. See Str-B 1:249-50, 774.
50. Spicq, 2:185; Weiss, 389. This verse reads ἐκ τῶν ἀκροθινίων ("of the spoils") instead of ἀπὸ πάντων ("from all," v. 2a).
51. We have repeated the word "Abraham" for clarity in our English translation.
52. Although Abraham is called πατήρ ("father") more than anyone else in the NT (Ellingworth, 361), this is the only place where he is called ὁ πατριάρχης ("the patriarch"). In fact, this word occurs only three other times in the NT: Peter refers to "the patriarch David" in Acts 2:29, and Stephen refers twice to the twelve sons of Jacob as "the patriarchs" in Acts 7:8-9.
53. Compare πατήρ, "father," in v. 9 with πατριάρχης, "patriarch," at the end of v. 4.

The concluding description in v. 3a above, "without genealogy," provides the context for this contrast.[54] The Levitical priests are described by a phrase that binds their priesthood closely with their descent: "those from the sons of Levi receiving the priestly office."[55] Their genealogy is doubly emphasized by the word "from," probably to be understood as "descended from," and by the word "sons."[56] The legitimacy of the OT priestly office was totally dependent on genealogical integrity. On the other hand, Melchizedek is described as "the one whose genealogy was not reckoned from them [the sons of Levi]." Despite this lack, however, no one less than Abraham acknowledged the legitimacy of his priesthood. His priesthood rested on divine authority that transcended genealogy.

The word here translated "priestly office" is more concrete than the synonym used for the institution of "priesthood" in vv. 11, 12, and 24 below. The first of these words was common in the canonical books of the LXX, while the second was used by the apocryphal books, Philo, and Josephus.[57] This distribution would suggest that the two were largely synonymous.[58]

---

54. Compare ἀγενεαλόγητος ("without genealogy," v. 3), ἐκ τῶν υἱῶν Λευί ("from the sons of Levi," v. 5) and μὴ γενεαλογούμενος ("not reckoning his genealogy from them," v. 6).

55. οἱ μὲν ἐκ τῶν υἱῶν Λευί τὴν ἱερατείαν λαμβάνοντες. The article οἱ joins both the prepositional phrase ἐκ τῶν υἱῶν Λευί and the participial phrase τὴν ἱερατείαν λαμβάνοντες as a description of one group of people. See MHT, 3:260. The author uses "sons of Levi" instead of "sons of Aaron" to facilitate connection with Abraham, Levi's "father." Anyone with the OT mastery demonstrated by the author of Hebrews was certainly aware that according to Lev 18:21 and Num 18:26-28 the Levites collected tithes from the people and the Levitical priests from the Levites. This practice was in force as late as Neh 10:38-39. The pastor does not address such details in the present argument because by doing so he would distract his hearers from the main point. His description of "those from the sons of Levi receiving the priesthood" is sufficient. He is talking about the Levites who were priests. They collected tithes from all other Israelites either directly or through other Levites. See Delitzsch, 1:340-43, 397-98. There is no need to explain this usage by reference to contemporary practices according to which the priests collected the tithes directly (see Josephus, *Life* 80; *Ant.* 20.181, 206-7) or to arbitrarily emend the text (see Ellingworth, 364).

56. It is possible to take ἐκ, "from," as derivative (Westcott, 175) or partitive (Spicq, 2:186): either as "those descended from the sons of Levi who receive the priesthood" or "those from (that part of) the sons of Levi who receive the priesthood." The parallel with Melchizedek in v. 6 supports the former. Ellingworth, 362, is correct when he argues that the derivative sense of ἐκ would have been clearer if the pastor had just written ἐκ Λευί, "from Levi," instead of ἐκ τῶν υἱῶν Λευί, "from the sons of Levi." However, this omission would have lost the emphasis on descent inherent in the use of "sons."

57. ἱερατεία, "priestly office," here in v. 5, but ἱερωσύνη, "priesthood," in vv. 11, 12, and 24 below. ἱερατεία occurs in Luke 1:9; ἱερωσύνη, nowhere else in the NT. See Michel, 265, esp. n. 4.

58. See Riggenbach, 188, n. 16.

Nevertheless, since the pastor uses both, he may have chosen the more concrete term here in accord with his emphasis on the concrete, external, legal nature of the OT priesthood. Those who receive this priestly office "have an ordinance" that gives them authority "to collect tithes."[59] This ordinance was "according to the law," that is, it was part of and based on the whole Levitical religious system.[60] It granted, but also circumscribed, their authority. Their authority to collect tithes was no more intrinsic to their persons than was their priestly office. All was based on physical descent and legal ordinance.

Furthermore, Levitical priestly authority was limited by those from whom they could collect tithes. They received tithes from "the people" of God, that is, their own "brothers and sisters." They received these tithes from them "although they also" had "come out of the loins of Abraham." When God wanted to emphasize that Abraham's heir would be his physical descendant, he described that descendant as one who "would come out of" Abraham's "loins" (Gen 15:4).[61] Thus the pastor uses this very graphic Semitic phrase to reinforce what he has said about the physical descent of the Levitical priesthood and to minimize the difference between those priests and the ones from whom they received tithes.[62] All can now be subordinated to Melchizedek through Abraham, whose name is the last word of v. 5.

Thus Melchizedek's superiority is clearly demonstrated by the fact that he received tithes from this Abraham, the "patriarch" and representative

---

59. The present tense of ἔχουσιν, "have," followed by the present infinitive ἀποδεκατοῦν, "to tithe," is the present of general description. The use of the present here neither confirms nor denies the continuation of the temple ritual at the time of writing. For ἀποδεκατόω used in reference to collecting tithes see the LXX of 1 Sam 8:15, 17 and Neh 10:37.

60. See Riggenbach, 189, n. 21. Hebrews distinguishes between ἐντολή, "a specific commandment" or "ordinance," and νόμος, "the law as the sum of its commandments" (Lane, 1:168). This interpretation takes κατὰ τὸν νόμον, "according to the law," as qualifying ἐντολήν, "ordinance." See Bleek, 2, 2:232. Since Hebrews understands the law primarily in terms of priesthood, tabernacle, and sacrifice, "according to the law" implies "according to the whole Levitical religious system" (Cockerill, "Melchizedek Christology," 68, 105-7). Joslin's attempt to limit νόμος ("law") in this verse to the specific law establishing the Aaronic priesthood is without support (Barry C. Joslin, *Hebrews, Christ, and the Law: The Theology of Mosaic Law in Hebrews 7:1–10:18* [Milton Keynes: Paternoster, 2008], 139, n. 26). See on vv. 11-12 and 18-19 below.

61. In Gen 15:4, however, the LXX reads ὅς ἐξελεύσεται ἐκ σοῦ, "the one who will come out of you," omitting ὀσφύς, "loins," but retaining the verb (ἐξέρχομαι, "to come out") used in Heb 7:5. See also the LXX of Gen 35:11, cf. 2 Chr 6:9.

62. On the Semitic nature of this phrase see Riggenbach, 188, n. 15. Reference to "loins" anticipates what v. 9 will say about Levi being in Abraham's "loins" when Abraham paid the tithe.

of both the Levitical priests and those from whom they collected tithes. The pastor will draw the appropriate conclusion from this fact in v. 9. However, he cannot fail to mention the greatest thing that Melchizedek did according to the Genesis record. Melchizedek "blessed Abraham."

The pastor prevents his hearers from missing the significance of this act by describing Abraham as the one who "has the promises" (cf. 6:13-20). As the original recipient of God's promises Abraham has a unique place in the economy of God, far above the Levitical priests with their "ordinance."[63] God promised Abraham a great people who by faith would inherit the heavenly homeland (4:1; 10:36; 11:9, 11, 13, 17) through the redemption provided by Christ (cf. 6:19-20). Melchizedek blessed the one who had received such promises of blessing. Thus he is closely identified with the God who issues the blessing rather than with Abraham and all of his descendants who receive it. The verbs "tithe" and "bless" are both perfect tense, suggesting the definitive and lasting character of Melchizedek's superior authority demonstrated in this passage from Genesis.[64]

7 To prevent misunderstanding the pastor adds, "without any contradiction the inferior is blessed by the superior."[65] Nevertheless, various interpreters have offered "contradiction" to this statement. Attridge points to the many places where the lesser in status blesses the greater (Job 31:20; 2 Sam 14:22; 1 Kgs 1:47) and to the numerous occasions where human beings bless God.[66] He contends that this evidence demonstrates the fallacy of those, like Michel, who think this statement is a traditional cultic rule.[67] Whether or not this was a traditional formula, the pastor's logic is sound within the present context. Melchizedek has pronounced a priestly blessing on Abraham (cf. Num 6:33). Within the context of the Genesis passage a priestly blessing certainly attests the superiority of the one who blesses.[68]

63. Michel, 266, esp. n. 4. The promises of God are certain of fulfillment (6:13-18), while, as the pastor will show, the "law" with its "ordinances" perfects nothing (vv. 18-19 below).

64. See A. T. Robertson, *A Grammar of the Greek New Testament in the Light of Historical Research* (3d ed.; New York: Hodder & Stoughton, 1919), 895-96, in reference to Heb 7:6, 9, 11, 13, 16, 20, 23. See also Bruce, 163, n. 32; Westcott, 177; Spicq, 2:186; and Ellingworth, 365.

65. The neuter singular of τὸ ἔλαττον ("the lesser" or "the inferior") and τοῦ κρείττονος ("the greater" or "the superior") puts emphasis on the quality of the persons involved. BDF, §138; Spicq, 2:186; MHT, 3:21. Cf. Heb 9:5.

66. Attridge, 196.

67. Michel, 266. The traditional nature of this formulation is supported by Philo's use of "blessing" in *Spec. Laws* 1.142.

68. Ellingworth, 366. Cf. O'Brien, 253, who distinguishes between εὐλογέω as "blessing" and as "praise." An inferior may "praise" a superior, but it is a superior who "blesses" an inferior.

8   The pastor follows this first contrast with one much greater. Receiving "tithes" becomes nothing more than the formal means of association. Concern with genealogy fades. The one superior to the Levitical priests is not only "without genealogy" (v. 3a). He is one who has "neither beginning of days nor end of life" (v. 3b), and thus the one about whom Scripture attests that "he lives." The one just identified so closely with the God who blesses is now described in terms appropriate for the "living God."[69]

Everything is done to heighten this contrast between the "eternity" of Melchizedek and the mortality of the Levitical priests. They are described not merely as "mortal" but as "dying human beings."[70] The pastor pictures the whole succession of Levitical priests continually and repeatedly dying and thus anticipates what he will say about their futility in v. 23 below.[71] He puts this description early in the sentence so that it establishes the strongest contrast with the last word of this verse, "he lives."

"It is witnessed," however, by God in Scripture that this other person who collected tithes, "lives."[72] The source of this "witness" can be nothing other than Gen 14:17-24 interpreted with the assistance of the proclamation of an eternal priesthood after Melchizedek's order in Ps 110:4.[73] The unique role played by Melchizedek in the Genesis passage, as described above, attests the fact that "he lives." In light of v. 3b, "he lives" cannot be reduced to unending priesthood but must be an affirmation of life without beginning or end.[74] This interpretation is substantiated by its similarity to descriptions of the "living" God referenced above. By refraining from further comment the pastor allows this affirmation of Melchizedek's "eternity" to be suggestive of

---

69. See, in Hebrews alone, Heb 3:12; 9:14; 10:31; 12:22.

70. The use of ἄνθρωποι, "human beings," is reminiscent of what the pastor said in 5:1-4 about these priests' being taken ἐξ ἀνθρώπων ("from human beings") and having ἀσθένεια ("weakness"). It anticipates the contrast in v. 28 between those who are merely ἄνθρωποι ("human beings") and the eternal υἱός ("Son").

71. MM, 62, and Ellingworth, 367.

72. For μαρτυρούμενος as a divine passive see Michel, 267; Ellingworth, 368; and compare v. 17 below.

73. Genesis 14 is clearly the primary text of this witness because it is the text about Melchizedek himself. Thus we would hesitate to say, with Ellingworth, 368, that the Scriptural witness points backward to Genesis and forward to Ps 110:4. See Westcott, 178.

74. See Delitzsch, 1:345-46. Windisch's contention (63) that v. 8 refers only to the last half of v. 3b, μήτε ζωῆς τέλος ἔχων ("nor end of life having"), and not to the first, μήτε ἀρχὴν ἡμερῶν ("neither beginning of days"), is both artificial and tendentious. Weiss, 391, and others like him, blunt the force of this verse when they import a contrast between the heavenly and the earthly borrowed from Philonic dualism. The pastor is not identifying Melchizedek with the heavenly world but describing him in terms appropriate for God alone.

what he will say about the Son in vv. 15-19 and 23-25 below.[75] In v. 9 the pastor draws the obvious conclusion from his first and more extensive contrast in vv. 5-7.

9-10 The pastor introduces v. 9 with a classical idiom found nowhere else in the Greek Bible.[76] This idiom can be appropriately translated "One might even say" (NRSV/ESV; cf. "And, so to speak," NASB). It signals the pastor's conclusion. It also indicates that "in the loins of his father" is a figure of speech. This introductory phrase, however, is not an admission, as some have suggested, that the pastor's ideas fit the context poorly or that his exegesis is artificial.[77] He has no hesitation about what he is going to say.[78] The logical conclusion of the contrast in vv. 5-6 is that Melchizedek is superior to the Levitical priests because Levi, representing his descendants, paid tithes to Melchizedek, through Abraham his father and representative. The pastor uses "in the loins of his father" to emphatically assert this representative role for "the patriarch" (v. 4). However, Abraham's authority to represent his descendants is based on more than physical descent. By divine choice his descendants were the heirs of the promises God had given him.[79] Thus this historical encounter between Melchizedek and Abraham clinches the superiority of Melchizedek over the Levitical priests.[80]

There are two ways in which this Melchizedek who was superior to the Levitical priests anticipates the priest after his order (Ps 110:4): he does "not reckon his genealogy" from the Levitical priests (v. 6; cf. v. 3a), and "he

75. While Héring, 58, may be correct when he says that the author "was already thinking about the new High Priest," he is still describing Melchizedek.

76. But this phrase, ὡς ἔπος εἰπεῖν, occurs fairly often in Philo (*Creation* 13; *Planting* 158; *Drunkenness* 51) and Josephus (*Ant.* 15.387). Michel, 268, n. 1, citing Bleek, 2, 2:343-46.

77. *Pace* Michel, 267-68; Pfitzner, 107; and Attridge, 197. But see Bénétreau, 2:36, and Weiss, 392.

78. See Héring, 59; Spicq, 2:187; and Lenski, 221.

79. Westcott, 178, is worth quoting at length on this point: "The descendants of Abraham were included in him, not only as he was their forefather physically, but also because he was the recipient of the divine promises in which the fullness of the race in its manifold developments was included. And Levi includes his descendants in his own person just as he was himself included in Abraham."

80. From the time of Augustine older commentators discussed the question of whether Christ was not also in Abraham's "loins" when he met Melchizedek (see Kuss, 56; Calvin, 93-94). If the author of Hebrews had considered this question, he probably would have answered with Ps 110:1, 4: Christ was a descendant of Abraham, but as the eternal Son he was much more. See Riggenbach, 191, n. 22; Bleek, 2, 2:348. This question reminds one of the way in which Jesus used Ps 110:1 to challenge the view that the Messiah was merely the Son of David and not also the Son of God (Matt 22:41-46 and parallels).

lives" (v. 8; cf. v. 3b). Having established these facts, the pastor brings this section to a close with the words he used at the beginning: "Melchizedek" and "met" (vv. 1, 10). He is now ready to return to his exposition of Ps 110:4 and thus to the Priest after Melchizedek's order.

2. The Priest in "the Likeness of Melchizedek" Displaces Aaron (7:11-25)

> 11 *If, then, there had been perfection through the Levitical priesthood, for on the basis of it the people have received the law, what need would there have been for a different priest to arise according to the order of Melchizedek and not one designated according to the order of Aaron?* 12 *For a change of the priesthood is of necessity a change of the law.* 13 *For the one about whom these things are said has taken part in a different tribe, from which no one has ever attended to the altar.* 14 *For this is clearer because our Lord arose from the tribe of Judah. Moses has said nothing about priests in regard to that tribe.* 15 *And this is exceedingly yet more clear, if a different priest arises according to the likeness of Melchizedek,* 16 *who has not come to be priest according to the law of fleshly ordinance but according to the power of an indestructible life.* 17 *For it is attested that "you are a priest forever, according to the order of Melchizedek."* 18 *For on the one hand the abolition of the foregoing ordinance has become a reality because of its weakness and uselessness* 19 *(for the law has perfected nothing); on the other hand is the bringing in of a better hope through which we draw near to God.*
>
> 20 *And according to how much not without an oath — for they have become priests without an oath,* 21 *but he with an oath through the one saying to him, "The Lord has sworn and will not change his mind: You are a priest forever."* 22 *According to this much he has become the Guarantor of a better covenant — he, even Jesus.* 23 *And on the one hand many have become priests because by death they have been prevented from continuing.* 24 *But he, because he "remains" forever, has a priesthood that is inviolable.* 25 *Therefore he is able even to save completely those who come to God through him, because he is always living to make intercession for them.*

The pastor returns to Ps 110:4, cited in 6:20, equipped with the insights gained from his exploration of Genesis 14.[1] He expounds this psalm phrase

---

1. μὲν οὖν marks the resumption of the train of thought initiated in 6:20 (Riggenbach, 194, n. 25).

by phrase, beginning with "according to the order of Melchizedek" in vv. 11-19. His explanation of this phrase lays the foundation for all that follows by showing why this new priest replaces the old. He then explains "the Lord has sworn and will not change his mind" in vv. 20-22, climaxing with the key phrase, "you are a priest forever," in vv. 23-25.

Verse 3 is even more important for vv. 11-25 than it was for vv. 4-11. Verse 3a, "without father, without mother, without genealogy," provides the background for vv. 11-14; v. 3b, "having neither beginning of days nor end of life," for vv. 15-19; and v. 3d, "he remains a priest forever," for vv. 23-25. Even v. 3c, "made like the Son of God," prepares for the pastor's crucial interpretation of "according to order of Melchizedek" in v. 15 as "according to the likeness of Melchizedek." Only vv. 20-22 escape direct dependence on v. 3. At last the pastor reveals the significance of the priest according to Melchizedek's order for the salvation of God's people. He desires above all that his hearers fully embrace this priest and enjoy his blessings.

11-19 *"According to the order of Melchizedek."* A proper understanding of this phrase shows why the priesthood has been changed. The pastor's argument moves from negative to positive. He begins by explaining that the Priest of Melchizedek's order was not "according to the order of Aaron" (vv. 11-14). This Priest, like Melchizedek (v. 6), was "without" Aaronic "genealogy" (v. 3a). Then he explains the significance of the new Priest's being "according to the likeness of Melchizedek" (vv. 15-19). The Priest of Melchizedek's order is eternal like the one who "lives" (v. 8) and has "neither beginning of days nor end of life" (v. 3b). God's ordination of a new Priest without Aaronic genealogy meant that the old priesthood had been changed (vv. 11-12); the new Priest's divine eternity meant that the former priesthood had been "abolished" as a means of approaching God and replaced by a priesthood capable of providing such access (vv. 18-19).[2]

11 The pastor states his premises in v. 11, describes their implications in v. 12, and then supports them in vv. 13-14. By describing the OT priesthood as "Levitical," he provides a smooth transition between what he has said about the sons of "Levi" in vv. 4-10 and the key phrase of vv. 11-14: "not according to the order of Aaron" (cf. "without genealogy" in v. 3a; "one not reckoning his genealogy from them" in v. 6).[3]

The pastor begins with the psalm itself apart from its fulfillment. His main premise is contained in the contrary-to-fact conditional clause of v. 11ac: "If there had been perfection through the Levitical priesthood," why was there need for another priest to arise "according to the order of

2. Weiss, 393, has a good description of the unity and significance of this section.
3. The fact that there is no known pre-Christian occurrence of the term λευιτικός ("Levitical") suggests that the pastor may have coined this term.

Melchizedek" and not "designated according to the order of Aaron?"[4] Ps 110:4 reveals that God appointed a priest of a different order and confirmed his appointment by an oath.[5] By this oath God himself established the "need" for a different priesthood and thus implied the ineffectiveness of the old.[6] Although the pastor's experience of Christ may have led him to this insight, the logic of his argument rests solely on the OT text.

Access to the presence of God is the "perfection" unattainable under the Levitical priesthood. The purpose of priesthood was to enable the worshiper to approach God (cf. vv. 18-19 below). As noted above, the LXX uses the language of perfection to describe priestly consecration.[7] By this consecration the Levitical priests were authorized to approach God and to mediate access for others through offering sacrifice for sin. The pastor is careful to show that the Levitical priesthood did not attain the ultimate goal of priesthood because its priests were mere human beings subject to death and encumbered with sin (see 5:1-3; 7:11-14; 9:1-10). The pastor's choice of the term "perfection" may be indebted to the LXX, but he also finds it useful for other reasons. First, its moral connotations are appropriate because the "perfection" of which he speaks includes the removal of sin. Second, the Greek term, like the English "perfection," is useful for expressing the ultimate. Only the Son, not the Levitical priests, could provide ultimate access to God through a definitive removal of sin.[8]

"For a different priest to arise" anticipates "if . . . a different priest arises" in v. 15.[9] "Different" in both verses indicates that the Priest like Melchizedek is a "different" kind of priest.[10] The expression translated "to

4. Εἰ᾽ μὲν οὖν τελείωσις διὰ τῆς Λευτιτικῆς ἱερωσύνης ἦν ("If then perfection had been through the Levitical priesthood") must be taken as a condition contrary to fact despite the absence of the particle ἄν normally employed by Hebrews (cf. 4:8; 8:4, 7; 11:15). Cf. Weiss, 394.

5. Compare the pastor's argument from Jer 31:31-34 in Heb 8:6-13.

6. Cf. Bénétreau, 2:38.

7. For a discussion of the way Hebrews uses the language of perfection see the comments on 2:10. Cf. also 5:9. Lane, 1:181, denies the priestly connotation of "perfection" because he does not think the author of Hebrews would completely deny the privilege of approaching God to OT people (cf. 10:1; 11:6). This is a misunderstanding. The OT faithful certainly worshiped God and the priests were "perfected" so that they could approach God in the ritual of the Tabernacle or Temple. The OT priests, however, were not "perfected" in the sense that Christ is "perfected" as our Savior and thus able to bring us into God's heavenly presence. See the comments on 11:39-40.

8. Cf. O'Brien, 257.

9. Compare ἕτερον ἀνίστασθαι ἱερέα, "a different priest to arise" (v. 11), with ἀνίσταται ἱερεὺς ἕτερος, "a different priest arises" (v. 15).

10. For "a different" (ἕτερον) priest instead of merely "another" (ἄλλον) priest see Bruce, 165, n. 45; and Spicq, 2:188-89.

arise" is often used for the coming of a great leader.[11] It distinguishes the Priest like Melchizedek from those whose priesthood is based on "descent" and who are merely "designated" priests according to the order of Aaron.[12] For the messianic connotations of this term see on v. 14 below.[13] This first use of "different" inaugurates the discussion of what it means for this priest to be without Aaronic descent (vv. 11-14); the second use of this term in v. 15 introduces what it means for him to be "in the likeness" of Melchizedek.

The major premise of v. 12 is found in v. 11ac: God's promise of a new priest has exposed the insufficiency of the old. The parenthetical statement in v. 11b is the minor premise: "For on the basis of it [the Levitical priesthood] the people have received the law."[14] The perfect tense of "have received the law" implies the resultant state of living under the law once received. Thus, although the law given at Sinai established the priesthood, living under that law was based on and dependent upon its perpetual functioning.[15]

Some would render this phrase as follows: "For concerning it [the Levitical priesthood] the people have received the law (or laws)."[16] This translation, however, is not as contextually appropriate. The pastor is not referring to the specific part of the law that established and regulated the priest-

11. See 1 Macc 2:1; 14:41; Acts 7:18. Compare the English phrase, "a new king arose."

12. Thus ἀνίστασθαι, "to arise," contrasts with οὐ λέγεσθαι, "not . . . to be designated." This contrast appears purposeful because the pastor usually abbreviates the second half of a contrast, leaving the hearers to supply the necessary words from the first (7:8, 16, 20b-21, 23-24). Here he expects hearers to supply ἱερέα but prevents them from supplying ἀνίστασθαι by his use of λέγεσθαι. See Cockerill, "Melchizedek Christology," 87-88.

13. See Num 24:17; Jer 23:5; Zech 3:8; 6:11-12. The "great priest" of Heb 10:21 is reminiscent of Zech 3:8. Heb 3:6 refers to the Son's being over God's house; Zech 6:11-12 describes the "Branch" who will "arise" and rebuild God's house. Cf. Matt 2:2. See Ellingworth, 373.

14. "For the people have received the law (νενομοθέτηται) on the basis of it (ἐπ' αὐτῆς, referring to the priesthood)." For support of this translation, see, among others, Spicq, 2:189; Attridge, 220, n. 30; Ellingworth, 372; Johnson, 185; Michel, 270; Moffatt, 96; and Mitchell, 145.

15. See Ellingworth, 372. Cf. O'Brien, 258.

16. "For the people received the law [or "laws," νενομοθέτηται] concerning it (ἐπ' αὐτῆς)." See H. W. Hollander, "Hebrews 7:11 and 8:6: A Suggestion for the Translation of Nenomothetetai Epi," BT 30 (1979): 244-47, followed by Lane, 1:174, n. b.; Weiss, 395; and Koester, 353. Lane supports this position with two examples from Philo. The clearest of these examples is found in Spec. Laws 2.35: ταῦτα μὲν ἐπ' ἀνθρώπων, ἐπὶ δὲ κτηνῶν τάδε νομοθετεῖται, "these regulations were laid down by the law (νομοθετεῖται) concerning human beings (ἐπ' ἀνθρώπων), but those concerning livestock (ἐπὶ κτηνῶν)." This parallel is not exact because the subject is impersonal (cf. ὁ λαός, "the people," in Heb 7:11 with ταῦτα, "these," in Philo). Spec. Laws 1.235 is less clear because the verb is active and the preposition ἐπί is followed by the dative.

hood. He is speaking about the law as a whole and its dependence upon the priesthood. Before the advent of Christ God's people could not live under the law without the priesthood as a means of approaching God through atonement. Thus the fate of the priesthood and that of the law were inextricably bound one to the other.[17]

12 Both "for" and "of necessity" show that the pastor is making a logical deduction from v. 11.[18] His thought can be expressed in syllogistic form: The prophecy of another priesthood in Ps 110:4 affirmed the insufficiency of the Aaronic priesthood and thus implied it was to be changed. Life under the law was dependent on the functioning of the Aaronic priesthood. Therefore, "a change of the priesthood"[19] is necessarily a "change of the law."[20] Thus the pastor would substantiate from the OT alone, without reference to Christ, that the prophesied change of priesthood anticipated a radical alteration in the relationship between the law and the people of God. This contention would shock those like Philo or the Pharisees who held that the law was eternally immutable.[21] And yet, as will become evident in the following verses, the pastor is convinced that fulfillment in Christ reveals what the law was always intended to be — not a means of approaching God but a God-instituted type and foreshadowing of the sufficient means of atonement and approach that would be provided by Christ.[22]

17. The importance of the association between "law" and the Levitical "priest-hood" is reinforced by the way the pastor comes back to this theme in v. 28. Cf. ἱερωσύνης and νενομοθέτηται in v. 11 with ὁ νόμος and ἀρχιερεῖς in v. 28. Some would see evidence for a pre-A.D. 70 date in the author's insistence that life under the law depends on a functioning priesthood. His unswerving attention to the OT text and lack of reference to contemporary events make it difficult to evaluate such evidence.

18. On γάρ, "for," see Riggenbach, 195, n. 45; on ἐξ ἀνάγκης, "of necessity," see Michel, 270, who compares this verse with 2 Cor 9:7. Philo often uses this expression to denote logical necessity (Bruce, 164, n. 37, citing Spicq, 1:42).

19. For euphony we have rendered the genitive absolute μετατιθεμένης γὰρ τῆς ἱερωσύνης ("the priesthood being changed") by "a change in the priesthood." The oracle of Ps 110:4 demonstrates that this change of priesthood is a condition of fact (Attridge, 200-201, n. 34).

20. Joslin, *Hebrews, Christ, and the Law,* 143-48, argues that the "cultic" (i.e., the priesthood, sacrifice, and all that pertains to them) but not the moral part of the law has been changed. One must not lose sight, however, of the intrinsic relationship between the priestly/sacrificial system and the entire law as outlined in the text above. By fulfilling the "cultic" aspects of the law and exposing their typological nature Christ has actually radicalized the need for obedience to the law's moral demand (2:1-4; 10:26-31, and comments).

21. Sowers, *Hermeneutics,* 98-99, n. 27. See Joslin's discussion of contemporary Jewish attitudes toward the law (Joslin, *Law,* 23-90).

22. See "The Sermon's Use of the Old Testament" in the Introduction to this commentary, esp. pp. 52-54.

13 The argument of vv. 11-12 depends on this new Priest's being a "different" kind of priest who could not be subsumed under the Aaronic order. The pastor makes it clear that the priest prophesied in Ps 110:4 was a "different" kind of priest because "he has taken part" in a "different," that is, a non-priestly, tribe.[23] He uses a picture to emphasize the nonsacerdotal character of this tribe: "from which [tribe] no one has ever attended to the altar." This phrase brings to the fore the central aspects of priesthood — sacrifice and approach to God. It anticipates the pastor's description of the priestly ritual in 9:1-10. The perfect tense "has ever attended" is emphatic — no one from the tribe of this new priest has ever performed this central function of priesthood.[24] This verb is never used elsewhere for approaching an altar.[25] The pastor may have selected it for the sake of euphony because it is derived from the same root as the verb translated "has taken part."[26]

The pastor has not yet referred to the identity of this new Priest "concerning whom these things are said" in Ps 110:4.[27] His argument rests on the psalm alone apart from its fulfillment. Yet he uses the verb "has taken part" deliberately in anticipation of the one who will fulfill this psalm. First, since this verb is never employed for physical descent, it distinguishes this priest from one dependent on genealogy. Second, it recalls the incarnation of the Son, who "took part" in human "blood and flesh" (2:14).[28] The perfect tense of "has taken part" asserts the reality of this par-

---

23. Compare "a different (ἑτέρας) tribe" (v. 13) with "a different (ἕτερον/ἕτερος) priest" (vv. 11, 15) and see the comment on v. 11 above.

24. The perfect tense of both μετέσχηκεν ("has taken part") and προσέσχηκεν ("has attended") is supported by B, ℵ, D, and most manuscripts. 𝔓[46] has the aorist for both of these verbs. A few other manuscripts attest the aorist rather than the perfect for προσέσχηκεν. The perfect is certainly to be preferred.

25. The use of this verb, προσέχω, in Heb 2:1 for "pay attention" is much more typical of its general use. Thus we have translated it here in 7:13 as "no one has ever attended to an altar."

26. See Ellingworth, 376. Compare not only μετέσχηκεν ("he has taken part") and προσέσχηκεν ("he has attended"), but the entire phrases, φυλῆς ἑτέρας μετέσχηκεν ("he has taken part in another tribe") and ἀφ' ἧς οὐδεὶς προσέσχηκεν ("from which no one has ever attended . . ."). There is balance between the sound of φυλῆς and of ἀφ' ἧς; a bit less between ἑτέρας and οὐδείς.

27. Robertson, *Grammar,* 721, says that οὗτος is implied before ἐφ' ὅν, "this one [the priest according to Melchizedek's order] about whom." "The one about whom these things were spoken" is not, as Michel, 270-71, seems to think, a circumlocution for Christ. The pastor is not yet speaking of Christ. On the basis of the psalm alone, the "one about whom it spoke," whoever that might be, took part in "a different tribe."

28. Compare the perfect μετέσχηκεν, "he has taken part," with the aorist μετέσχεν in 2:14. Ellingworth, 375, quotes Westcott: "It is not said simply that He was born of another tribe: [it is implied that] He was of His own will so born."

ticipation in a different tribe and thus also anticipates application to the Son in v. 14.[29]

14 The argument of v. 13, based on Ps 110:4 alone, becomes "still exceedingly more clear" because it receives historical verification by the coming of Christ in fulfillment of the psalm.[30] The pastor evidences his veneration for Christ by calling him "our Lord" and thus reserves the implications of the word "Jesus" for v. 19.[31] However, he is not yet openly concerned with the eternal quality of this new priest. His sole interest in this verse is that "our Lord" about whom Ps 110:4 spoke came "from Judah."[32] The pastor does not describe Christ as "from David" in accord with common NT practice, because he is not arguing that the Son is the royal messiah.[33] He uses the more general "from Judah" in order to substantiate Christ's non-Levitical origin (cf. "sons of Levi," v. 5; "Levi," v. 9; "Levitical priesthood," v. 11).

There is no way, however, that the pastor can describe even the earthly origin of "our Lord" in terms totally appropriate for other priests. Thus most versions are in error when they read "descended from Judah" (NIV/TNIV) or "was descended from Judah" (RSV/NRSV/ESV). This meaning for the underlying Greek term does not occur in the LXX, the papyri, or Classical Greek.[34] This term means "arise," not "descend." It was often used for the "rising" of the sun, a star, or light.[35] The pastor appears to have chosen this

29. On the perfect tense of μετέσκηκεν see Delitzsch, 1:353, and Riggenbach, 197, n. 47. The perfect tense here emphasizes certainty more than the continual participation advocated by Lenski, 225-26.

30. Spicq, 2:192. Thus we have understood πρόδηλον ("all the more clear") as referring to the argument of v. 13, and ὅτι as adverbial, "because," instead of "that." Despite the way in which this understanding differs from many translations, it seems to be required because it allows πρόδηλον to be comparative and to anticipate περισσότερον ἔτι κατάδηλον ("exceedingly more clear") in v. 15. The argument of v. 13 becomes "clearer" because Christ has come from the non-Levitical tribe of Judah (v. 14). This argument becomes "exceedingly yet still clearer" when one realizes the eternal quality of this new priest (vv. 15-17). On the other hand, if one takes ὅτι as "that" introducing a noun clause, then it is Christ's descent from Judah that has become "clear" (cf. TNIV, "For it is clear that our Lord descended from Judah"). πρόδηλον becomes a rather weak affirmation of something the author can assume is commonly shared by his hearers.

31. See the comments on v. 19 below. The pastor also refers to the incarnate Jesus as "our Lord" in 2:3. Compare also "our Lord Jesus" in 13:20. Cf. Lane, 1:183.

32. Thus the words ἐξ Ἰούδα, "from Judah," come first in the ὅτι clause: "that (ὅτι) from Judah (ἐξ Ἰούδα) arose our Lord." Cf. Spicq, 2:190.

33. See references to Davidic descent in Acts 2:29-36; Rom 1:3; 2 Tim 2:8; and Rev 22:16. Only the birth narratives of Matthew (cf. Matt 2:6) and Luke refer to descent from Judah.

34. See LSJ, 123; MM, 38.

35. Matt 4:16 (quoting Isa 9:1); 5:45; 13:6; Mark 4:6; 16:2; Jas 1:11; and 2 Pet 1:19.

word deliberately in imitation of the Balaam oracle in Num 24:17. "Our Lord has arisen from Judah" echoes "a star shall arise from Jacob."[36] Even when referring to Christ's human ancestry the pastor must distinguish him from those whose priesthood was dependent on their genealogy. They may have descended from a particular tribe, but he, even in his incarnation, "arose." He receives no authority from his ancestry. The perfect tense is also significant. He "has arisen" at a particular place and time, and his rise is still in effect. Although this term refers to his human origin, it is appropriate for one who has taken his seat at God's right hand (1:3, 13; 8:1-2).[37] Since the Son fulfills all OT prophecies, the pastor has no hesitancy in applying the Balaam oracle to him.

36. Compare ἐξ Ἰούδα ἀνατέταλκεν ὁ κύριος ἡμῶν ("from Judah has arisen our Lord") with ἀνατελεῖ ἄστρον ἐξ Ιακωβ ("a star shall arise from Jacob") in Num 24:17. The parallel phrase in Num 24:17 is "a scepter shall arise out of Israel," which the LXX has rendered, "a human being shall arise out of Israel" (καὶ ἀναστήσεται ἄνθρωπος ἐξ Ισραηλ). Several observations should be made about this passage. In its original context the "star" and the "scepter" referred to a person (or persons?). The LXX's translation of "scepter" as ἄνθρωπος, "human being," confirms this interpretation. The "star" was someone of great importance. Thus this verse uses ἀνατέλλω to speak of a great leader's arising "from Jacob" just as Heb 7:14 uses this verb to speak of "our Lord" arising "from Judah." Furthermore, in the parallel clause the LXX uses ἀνίστημι, "arise," the same word that Hebrews uses for the "arising" of the "different priest" (ἱερεὺς ἕτερος) in vv. 11 and 15. Thus the verbal parallels between Hebrews and Num 24:17 plus their common use of these two verbs (ἀνατέλλω and ἀνίστημι) in reference to the coming of a great person strongly suggest that the wording of Hebrews has been influenced by Numbers. The Messianic significance of this oracle may be attested by the parallel use of ἀνατέλλω, "arise," in Mal 4:1-2 (in the LXX 3:19-20) and the Messianic significance of the cognate noun ἀνατολή ("branch") in Jer 23:5; Isa 11:1; Zech 3:8; and 6:11-12. 1QM 11, 4-6; 4QTestimonia; CD 8:18-21; and T. Jud. 24:1 recognize the Messianic character of Num 24:17. See Joachim Gnilka, "Die Erwartung des messianischen Hohenpriesters in den Schriften von Qumran und im Neuen Testament," RevQ 2 (1960): 399-402; F. F. Bruce, Biblical Exegesis in the Qumran Texts (Grand Rapids: Eerdmans, 1959), 45-47; and M. De Jonge, The Testaments of the Twelve Patriarchs: A Study of Their Text, Composition and Origin (2nd ed.; Van Gorcum's Theologische Bibliotheek; Assen: Van Gorcum, 1975), 89-96. For further discussion see Bruce, 165-66, nn. 42, 46; O'Brien, 260-61; and Cockerill, "Melchizedek Christology," 97.

In light of these observations there should be no surprise that Hebrews alludes to this passage. The fourth Balaam oracle (Num 24:15-19), in which Num 24:17 occurs, is, like Deut 32:43 (Heb 1:6), part of a prophecy for the future. Thus it can be associated with such passages as Ps 2:7-8; Ps 110:1, 4; and 2 Sam 7:14 (see Heb 1:5, 13; 5:5-6; 6:20; etc.). Although the author of Hebrews allows these Messianic echoes to "remain very much in the background" (Attridge, 201), they are in full accord with his conviction that the Son fulfills all OT expectations.

37. However, pace Johnson, 186-87, ἀνίστημι ("arise") in vv. 11 and ἀνατέλλω ("arise") in v. 14 refer to the earthly origin of the Son from Judah, and not to his exaltation. The use of ἀνίστημι in v. 15 is more ambiguous.

Although the pastor cannot disguise this new Priest's uniqueness even when describing his human origin, he reserves discussion of his eternal quality until the next verse. Christ's tribal origin confirms what the pastor has already said on the basis of Ps 110:4 alone — the new priest of Ps 110:4 was not from the priestly tribe of Levi and thus could not trace his genealogy from Aaron. He came from the tribe of "Judah." The next clause might be rendered more literally, if somewhat more woodenly, as follows: "in regard to which tribe concerning priesthood Moses has said nothing." The way in which the pastor puts "tribe" and "concerning priesthood" together emphasizes the incongruity of "Judah" and "priesthood." Since "Moses," in giving the law, said "nothing" about a priest from Judah, then such a priest has no place in the old priestly system. Thus, as stated in v. 12 above, the change of priesthood means a change in the whole system dependent upon its functioning. The coming of Christ from the tribe of Judah clinches all that the pastor has already established on the basis of Ps 110:4.

15   In vv. 11-13 the pastor has argued that the prophecy of a non-Aaronic priest was enough to substantiate the "change" of the old priesthood and law. In v. 14 he mentioned the coming of "our Lord" from "Judah," but only to substantiate the non-Levitical character of the tribe to which he belonged. He can restrain himself no longer. He begins to describe the eminently superior quality of the Son as Priest like Melchizedek. The Son is not merely lacking in Aaronic genealogy (v. 3a), but he is, "like" Melchizedek, one "without beginning of days or end of life" (v. 3b). The quality of the Son as Priest makes both the extent and certainty of this change in priesthood and law "exceedingly yet more clear."[38] Since the extent of the "change" is proportionate to the quality of the new, it can be nothing less than an "abolition" (v. 18) of the old as a means of approaching God and a "bringing in" of the new (v. 19).[39]

"If according to the likeness of Melchizedek there arises a different (kind of) priest" implies no uncertainty. This condition of fact is in accord with the logical style of the passage and serves to gain the hearers' assent and

---

38. περισσότερον ἔτι κατάδηλόν ἐστιν. περισσότερον ("exceedingly") is a comparative adverb (Riggenbach, 198, n. 51; BDF §102, 1; cf. Heb 6:1), as is κατάδηλον ("more clear"). The force of the whole is redoubled by the use of these two comparatives (Robertson, *Grammar*, §63). ἔτι also heightens the degree (MHT, 3:29) over the πρόδηλον ("clearer") of v. 14.

39. Compare v. 12 — "The priesthood having been changed (μετατιθεμένης), of necessity a change (μετάθεσις) of the law occurs" — with v. 18 — "the abolition (ἀθέτησις) of the foregoing ordinance" (v. 18). Joslin, *Law*, 141-53, fails to give ἀθέτησις ("abolition"; "setting aside") its full force because he fails to see that the eternal character of the new Priest necessitates the complete removal of the old *as a means of approaching God*.

involvement. "Different" and "likeness" are the key words in this statement. The pastor intentionally changes "according to the order of" to "according to the likeness of."[40] Since "according to the order of" followed by the name of a priest occurs only in Ps 110:4, this phrase has an enigmatic quality.[41] From v. 11 above the hearers know that "according to the order of Aaron" means "according to genealogical descent from Aaron." Since, however, this new Priest is not authorized by genealogy, he is a priest "according to the likeness of Melchizedek." The pastor prepared for this statement in v. 3c by describing the "eternal" Melchizedek of that verse as "made like the Son of God." This new priest is "different" in kind from the Levitical priests but "according to the likeness" of Melchizedek.

16 This verse consists of a relative clause in which the pastor explains once and for all what it means for this new Priest to be "not according to the order of Aaron" but "according to the order of Melchizedek." He is "different" from the Aaronic priests in that he has not become priest "according to a law of fleshly ordinance." He is "according to the likeness" of Melchizedek in that he has become priest "according to the power of an indestructible life."[42] "According to" now means "because of."[43] The cause and final authority of these priesthoods is what makes the difference.

Although the pastor does not say "the" law, he is referring to the whole Pentateuchal legal system. The omission of the definite article puts emphasis on the quality of this law as a system based on nothing more than a "fleshly ordinance."[44] By "fleshly ordinance" the pastor is referring to the rule that established priesthood on the basis of human ("fleshly") descent.[45] However, vv. 18-25 will show how all three of these words "law," "ordinance," and "fleshly," intimate the inadequacy of this old order. How can a

---

40. *Pace* Ellingworth, 378, this replacement is far more than a stylistic variant. Cf. Vanhoye, *Old Testament*, 162.

41. τάξις, the word here translated "order," could be used for "position" or "office" as well as for priestly "descent." See LSJ, 1756, III; MM, 625; and BDAG, 989, 3-4. It is noteworthy that Hebrews is the only reference given by the foregoing sources as an example of priestly "descent."

42. The perfect, γέγονεν ("has become"), in v. 16a, is implied in v. 16b. This one "has become" already and continues to be "a priest by the power of an indestructible life."

43. Ellingworth, 378.

44. Westcott, 184; Michel, 272; W. Gutbrod, "νόμος," *TDNT* 4:1078; BDF §167.

45. See Weiss, 400, n. 104. σαρκίνης ("made of flesh") is preferred over the alternate σαρκικῆς ("pertaining to the flesh"). It has the best manuscript support. Furthermore, it fits the context better than the alternative, although a scribe would be more likely to substitute σαρκικῆς because it is the most common Pauline word (Rom 15:27; 1 Cor 3:3; 9:11; 2 Cor 1:12; 10:4). σαρκικός even occurs as an alternative in the two places where Paul probably used σάρκινος (Rom 7:14; 1 Cor 3:1). σαρκίνης best expresses the idea that this "ordinance" referred to actual physical descent.

mere "ordinance" compete with the "oath" of God (vv. 20-21)? What does such a "law" have to offer when contrasted with a "better hope" (v. 19) or a "better covenant" (v. 22)? How can a priesthood based on the mere mortal humanity implied by "fleshly" be equal to one based on the divine life (vv. 16b, 24)? Such a priesthood could draw on nothing but human weakness and was circumscribed by human frailty (cf. 5:1-3).

By contrast, the priest "according to the likeness of Melchizedek" has become a priest "according to the power of an indestructible life." "Power" contrasts with "law"; "life," with "ordinance"; and "indestructible," with "fleshly."[46] This new priesthood is based on nothing less than the power of the eternal God. The pastor has carefully prepared his readers to understand what he means by "indestructible life."[47] He opened this sermon by describing the eternal Son as sovereign creator and judge of all (1:1-14). In v. 3b he described the one "made like the Son" as having "neither beginning of days nor end of life." In v. 8 that same Melchizedek foreshadows the Son in that "he lives."[48] Thus it would be impossible for the first hearers of this sermon to understand "indestructible life" as anything less than the eternal life of God shared by the eternal Son.[49] "Indestructible" contrasts with "fleshly" as "immortal" with "mortal." Nothing but the divine life can be called "indestructible." The assertion that the Son's priesthood was "without genealogy" (v. 3a) has paled into insignificance by contrast with this great declaration. Furthermore, it must be emphasized that this "indestructible life" is not a description of but the basis and cause of his all-effective priesthood. Being "according to the likeness of Melchizedek" says nothing about his being a priest "in the realm of the eternal and unchanging."[50] It says everything about his being a Priest by the power of God's own eternal life.

Numerous interpreters have argued that, since the incarnate Son died, he did not enter into this "indestructible life" until his resurrection, exaltation, or session.[51] However, the context of Hebrews gives no support to this

46. Michel, 272; see Héring, 60.

47. The term ἀκατάλυτος, "indestructible," only occurs once in the LXX, 4 Macc 10:11, where it refers to "indestructible sufferings." Here it is probably a more specific description of ζωή αἰώνιος ("eternal life"). See John 3:16; 11:25; Michel, 272; and Cockerill, "Melchizedek Christology," 109-10.

48. There is no justification, in light of Heb 1:1-4, and especially in light of 7:3b, "without beginning of days or end of life," to follow Ellingworth, 379, and reduce "he lives" to "he still lives." As noted above, "he lives" is intentionally parallel to descriptions of "the living" and eternal God.

49. Neyrey, "True Deity," 450. See also Philip E. Hughes, "The Blood of Jesus and His Heavenly Priesthood in Hebrews, Part II: The High-Priestly Sacrifice of Christ," *BSac* 130 (1973): 208.

50. *Pace* Attridge, 202, referencing Thompson, *Christian Philosophy*, 122.

51. Koester, 355; Johnson, 188; deSilva, 271; Michel, 272; Héring, 60; O'Brien, 264; and Barnabas Lindars, *The Theology of the Letter to the Hebrews*, ed. J. D. G. Dunn

position. The pastor has unambiguously and emphatically affirmed the divine eternity of the Son (1:1-14). If there is a contradiction in affirming that the one who always had the "indestructible life" of God offered himself in death, it is a contradiction inherent in the incarnation.[52] The pastor uses this term deliberately to affirm that the death experienced by the incarnate Son could not destroy the "indestructible life" of God that was his.[53] His exaltation was not his deification but his "perfection" (5:9; 7:28) as the Savior of God's people.[54] The eternal Son's possession of "indestructible life" provides a solid basis for contrasting him with the priests of the old order whose life was very "destructible" (vv. 22-25). The foundation of his priestly effectiveness is the eternal life of God in his own Person. The pastor invites his hearers to put full confidence in the one who possess this "indestructible life."

17 This understanding of "indestructible life" is confirmed by v. 17 in two ways. First, the phrase "it is attested that" establishes a clear parallel between the Son and Melchizedek as described in v. 8. Just as God bore witness in Genesis 14 that Melchizedek "lives" (v. 8), so he bears witness in Ps 110:4 to the "indestructible life" of the one Melchizedek foreshadowed.[55] Second, this witness in Ps 110:4 affirms that the Son is "like" this Melchizedek who "lives" and has "neither beginning of days nor end of life" (v. 3b). It is important to remember that when the pastor chooses his own terms he chooses expressions that affirm the eternity of this new Priest and the one who foreshadowed him — "having neither beginning of days nor end of life" (v. 3); "he lives" (v. 8); "indestructible life" (v. 16). It is only the expression given him by the psalm, "a priest forever," that might have implied no more than life without end. Certainly the pastor intends the recipients of his sermon to hear "a priest forever" in light of these other terms he has cho-

---

(New Testament Theology; Cambridge: Cambridge University Press, 1991), 78, hold this position. For support of "indestructible life" as the divine life of the eternal Son see Westcott, 185; Montefiore, 125-26; Spicq, 2:193; and esp. Neyrey, "True Deity," 450. Compare Williamson, *Philo and Hebrews,* 447, and Hughes, "Sacrifice," 208.

52. "Is it any more difficult to think of the Son as having 'indestructible life' in Himself and yet dying than to think of Him as 'without beginning of days' and yet 'arising from Judah'?" (Cockerill, "Melchizedek Christology," 111). See Alexander Nairne, *The Epistle of Priesthood: Studies in the Epistle to the Hebrews* (2nd ed.; Edinburgh: T&T Clark, 1913), 170.

53. According to Lane, 1:184, the pastor uses "indestructible" to show that Jesus' "life was not destroyed by the death suffered on the cross."

54. The heroes of antiquity cited by Neyrey were accorded divinity because of their benefaction to humanity. The eternal Son, however, was exalted because of his incarnate obedience (10:5-10) in order that he might grant benefaction to God's people. See Neyrey, "True Deity," 449-50.

55. "For" indicates that this witness attests the "indestructible life" predicated of the Son in v. 16.

324

sen and of his description of the eternal Son in chapter 1. As suggested above, the pastor's thought might be best expressed by the translation "you are an eternal priest." This priest is superior because he has not only unending life but a different kind of life, the very eternal life of God.[56] Thus God's witness to his Son, "you are an eternal priest," attests the divine eternity of the Son as the bedrock of his fully effective priesthood. This understanding of the Son's "indestructible life" is confirmed by the conclusion of the pastor's argument in vv. 23-25. In those verses the pastor reveals the benefit that flows from a Priest who is the eternal Son of God.

18-19   The pastor brings the argument of vv. 11-19 to its logical conclusion by affirming the removal of the old as a means of approaching God (vv. 18-19a) and the institution of the new as the effective agency of drawing near to him (v. 19b).[57] The prophecy of another priest in Ps 110:4 was enough to demonstrate the required "change" of the Levitical system (v. 12). When, however, one sees the divine quality of this new priest in comparison to the temporal human character of the old, it is obvious that the "change" (v. 12) suffered by the "foregoing ordinance" has been its "abolition," or complete removal as a competent means of atonement.[58] Verses 18-19a affirm the "abolition" of this old system that was founded on "a law or fleshly ordinance" (v. 16a). Verse 19b describes the corresponding "institution" of the new system based on "the power of an indestructible life" (v. 16b).

The "ordinance" that established the old system's priesthood on the basis of "fleshly" descent was "foregoing" (v. 18). It was provisional, temporary, and transitory, but also typical of the permanent and effective yet to come.[59] The revelation of the effective new Priest has demonstrated the reason for the "abolition" of the old: it was removed "because of its weakness and uselessness." These two terms are joined by one article and describe the opposite of the "perfection" (v. 11) brought by the new.[60] This ordinance had

---

56. See the discussion of εἰς τὸ παντελές ("to the uttermost") in v. 25 below.

57. Cf. Weiss, 400.

58. Thus the μετάθεσις ("change") of the priesthood and law in v. 11 can now be expressed by the much stronger terms, first negatively, the ἀθέτησις ("abolition") of the old in v. 18; then positively, the ἐπεισαγωγή ("bringing in"; "establishing") of the new in v. 19b. Cf. Moffatt, 97. In Heb 9:26 ἀθέτησις, "abolition," refers to the cancellation of sins through Christ's self-offering. In the papyri this term is often used for the cancellation of debts (Michel, 273; MM, 12; G. Adolf Deissmann, *Bible Studies: Contributions Chiefly from Papyri and Inscriptions to the History of the Language, the Literature, and the Religion of Hellenistic Judaism and Primitive Christianity,* 2nd ed., trans. Alexander Grieve [Edinburgh: T&T Clark, 1909], 228-29).

59. See the examples of προάγω in BDAG, 864; MM, 537. While the pastor is emphasizing the removal of the old as a means of salvation, he would not forget its continuing validity as a type (Attridge, 203). See Westcott, 186-87; Delitzsch, 1:356-57.

60. The two words, ἀσθενές ("weakness") and ἀνωφελές ("uselessness"), joined

"weakness" because it depended for its fulfillment on mortal men, who, by implication, were sinful (4:15; 5:2; see on 7:28 below).[61] Thus it was characterized by "uselessness" because it could not provide cleansing from sin and bring anyone into God's presence. As noted above, the specific "ordinance" establishing the Levitical priesthood was integral to the functioning of the whole law. Thus it was not a part of the law but the whole that has been abolished as a way of approaching God, though not as a foreshadowing of what has come in Christ.

The pastor who began by saying, "If perfection were through the Levitical priesthood" (v. 11), can now affirm beyond doubt that "the law perfects nothing." This proclamation of the law's obsolescence makes it clear that the whole system has been abolished. The quality of the new Priest has put the law's complete ineptitude as a means of relating to God beyond all doubt. The use of the aorist tense for "did not perfect" puts the now-abolished Levitical system of atonement in the past. That whole system of approaching God did not achieve God's purpose for priesthood because it did not cleanse God's people from sin (9:11-14) and thus could not enable them to "draw near" to God.[62] However, the pastor's very argument for its ineffectiveness assumes that it remains valid as a Scriptural type now fulfilled in Christ.

This abolition of the old has been effected by the establishment of the new as described in v. 19b.[63] "Bringing in" contrasts with "abolition"; "better," with "foregoing"; and "hope," with "ordinance." "Bringing in" or "introduction" denotes the permanent establishment of the new.[64] This hope is "better" just as Christ's sacrifice (9:23) and priestly ministry (8:5) are "better," and thus the covenant (8:6) he guarantees is "better" (7:22; 8:6) because it is based on "better" promises (8:6). The pastor uses "better" to describe a binary relationship between the new and the old. Simply put, the old did not work; the new does. It actually enables the faithful to "draw near to God."

---

by this article, are adjectives used here as abstract nouns (BD §263, 2; Robertson, *Grammar*, 763).

61. Cockerill, "Melchizedek Christology," 116.

62. Michel, 273. See also Peterson, *Perfection,* 127-28.

63. Although ἐπεισαγωγή can be used for the "bringing in" of something new in addition to the old (MM, 231), here it describes the "bringing in" of the new in place of the old (Spicq, 2:194; Moffatt, 98). See Josephus, *Ant.* 11.196, where the new wife brought in replaces the old.

64. Contrast the noun used here for "bringing in" or "institution," ἐπεισαγωγή, with the participle used to modify "ordinance" above, προαγούσης, "foregoing." The pastor, ever a master of word sounds, uses two words based on the root ἄγω to contrast the transitoriness of the old with the permanent establishment of the new.

The pastor would incite his hearers to perseverance by introducing this new arrangement for approaching God as a better "hope."[65] "Hope" looks toward the eternal reward. This new provision in Christ provides not only present but ultimate entrance into God's presence. As "hope" it is as sure as the promises of God (6:11, 18) for those who persevere in faith.[66] With such a glorious "hope" guaranteeing both present and ultimate access to God, who would not want to persevere? None need imitate the wilderness generation and fall by the way (3:7–4:11). All can join the company of the faithful (11:1–12:3). Although the pastor will soon begin to describe this same reality as the "better covenant" (v. 22), he wants his hearers to remember that it is an unshakable "hope" all-sufficient for their perseverance.

It is easy for contemporary readers influenced by a secular world to miss the grand significance of "through which we draw near to God." The priestly context of Hebrews reflects the LXX use of "draw near" in Exodus, Leviticus, and Ezekiel. In these books it is used to describe both priests (Exod 19:22; Lev 21:21; Ezek 40:46; 42:13; 43:19; 44:13; 45:4) and people (Exod 3:5; 24:2; Lev 10:3) when they approach God in worship.[67] Restoration of fellowship with God has been the divine purpose and the often-unrecognized longing of humanity since its loss in Eden. The pastor will make it clear in the following chapters that faithful believers have a direct access to God unexperienced even by the high priests before Christ (cf. 11:39-40). They have an access that, by perseverance, will culminate in their eternally dwelling with him (cf. 12:22-29). All God's people have the high-priestly privilege of entrance into the heavenly Most Holy Place, though only Christ is the High Priest who mediates this privilege.[68] "Drawing near" refers to ". . . the relationship with God through Christ that displaces the cult of the old order."[69] This relationship is enjoyed in many ways but particularly through prayer and worship.

Finally, it is important to remember that the pastor is not engaging in

---

65. Spicq, 2:194. Every other occurrence of ἐλπίς ("hope") in Hebrews is part of an encouragement to perseverance (3:6; 6:11, 18; 10:23). See also 11:1.

66. Cf. Michel, 209-10, 273.

67. Although ἐγγίζω, "to draw near," followed by πρός with the accusative is normal, the dative used in Hebrews is also possible (Exod 19:22; Lev 10:3).

68. The pastor refers to believers with priestly language, especially in chapter 13. However, the suggestion of Olaf Moe, "Der Gedanke des allgemeinen Priestertums in Hebräerbrief," *TZ* 5 (1948): 163-65, and Scholer, *Proleptic Priests,* 201–7, that Hebrews understands Christ as High Priest and believers as priests, must be taken with a caveat. While believers have the priestly privilege of access, only Christ has performed the priestly function of atonement, and only he performs the priestly function of mediating that atonement to the faithful.

69. Attridge, 204.

speculation when he describes the replacement of the old by the new and truly effective. He has shown that this replacement is Scripturally established. He describes it as an experienced reality. He invites his hearers to participate in the "drawing near" to God that he enjoys. Since the new actually achieves God's purpose in the lives of his people, the ineffective old is now of use simply as a type of what was to come. Thus the replacement of the old by the new is an exegetically established and existentially experienced fact. This radical displacement of the old Levitical system by the all-sufficient priesthood of Christ is foundational for all that the pastor will say about Christ's sacrifice, priesthood, and covenant in chapters 8 through 10.

In vv. 20-25 the author makes pastoral application of what he has said by describing the wonderful benefits of this new Priest and the way he has provided for God's people to "draw near." This application, however, is exposition of the remaining phrases of Ps 110:4. In vv. 11-19 he has explained "according to the order of Melchizedek." In vv. 20-22 he will explain "the Lord has sworn and will not change his mind." Then in vv. 23-25 he will conclude all he has said in vv. 11-19 by focusing on the key phrase from Ps 110:4, "you are an eternal priest." His euphoria is contagious as he waxes eloquent about this great Priest and the wonderful benefits of his ministry.

20-22 *"The Lord has sworn and will not repent."* The opening line of v. 20, "And according to how much not without an oath,"[70] is resumed by the opening line of v. 22, "according to this much he has become the Guarantor of a better covenant — he, even Jesus." One might paraphrase as follows: "And in proportion to how significant it was that he did not become a priest without an oath" (v. 20a), "to that degree he has become the Guarantor of a better covenant — he, even Jesus" (v. 22a). The first statement gives the cause and substantiates the magnitude of the second:[71] "Since he has become priest by the divine oath, he has become the Guarantor of a better covenant."

20-21a By beginning this verse with "according to how much," instead of "according to which," the pastor has underscored the magnitude of the Son's having been made Priest by the divine oath.[72] He uses the double negative, "not without an oath," to affirm the reality of this oath in the most emphatic way.[73] This double negative also anticipates the contrast between the Son and the Levitical priests who were "without an oath" (v. 20b). It is this contrast that will reveal the degree of importance indicated by "how

---

70. The ellipsis in "according to how much . . . not without an oath" is to be filled from the following parenthesis, "he has become priest" (Riggenbach, 203-4; Westcott, 188).

71. Robertson, *Grammar,* 966-67; Ellingworth, 383. See Spicq, 2:195; and Riggenbach, 203-4, n. 56.

72. καθ᾽ ὅσον rather than καθ᾽ ὅν.

73. Ellingworth, 383.

much." Simply put, "they [the Levitical priests of Aaron's order], on the one hand, have become priests without an oath, but he, on the other hand, with an oath." This contrast makes the inherent binary nature of the relationship between the old priesthood and the new Priest absolutely clear. The difference between the two is a difference in kind, not in degree. They were not, but the Son is. The word order and economy of style evident in these verses allows the emphasis to fall on the phrases "not without an oath" (v. 20a); "without an oath" (v. 20b); and "with an oath" (v. 21a). The magnitude of the Son's having been made priest by the divine oath breaks all bounds. One cannot put a limit on the "how much" of this verse.

21b   Verse 21 makes it clear that the oath in question is found in Ps 110:4. "The Lord has sworn" is reinforced by "and will not change his mind." The word used here for "oath" is more solemn than that used in 6:13-20.[74] In that passage the pastor established the certainty created by a divine oath. This oath, however, given directly by God, "the one speaking," to the eternal Son, is more majestic and of greater moment than the oath given mortal Abraham. The first was given to a human being by way of concession in order to guarantee what God would do in the future. By this second oath God has already established the exalted Son as "Guarantor" of the "better" covenant's effectiveness.[75] The faithful can be absolutely certain of entering God's presence and receiving grace for perseverance (4:14-16) through their Guarantor. They can be certain that those who persevere in faithful obedience will enter God's eternal "rest" (4:1-11). He is Guarantor that God's promise for the future is certain and his power for the present is real and available for the people of God.

22   Thus this "oath" is the reason why "of a better covenant he has become Guarantor, even Jesus." This translation reflects the word order of the Greek text. The pastor calls the "better hope" a "better covenant" in anticipation of Jer 31:31-34 (Heb 8:6-13). By beginning this clause with his characteristic "better" he reminds the hearers of the unsurpassable quality of this new arrangement for approaching God. "Covenant" is appropriate because it is broad enough to encompass the whole arrangement God has made for people to relate to him without the negative connotations the pastor finds in "law" and "ordinance."[76] By using "covenant" the pastor emphasizes the fact that this ar-

---

74. Compare ὁρκωμοσία in 7:20-21 with ὅρκος in 6:16. Michel, 274; cf. Ellingworth, 383. 1 Esd 8:93 and Ezek 17:18-20 are the only places this term occurs in the LXX. Cf. Josephus, *Ant.* 17.163 and MM, 458.

75. This statement assumes that God's words in Ps 110:4 are directed to the Son at his exaltation, just as those found in v. 1 of this psalm were so directed. See on 1:3, 13 and 5:5-6 above.

76. Thus E. Grässer, *Der alte Bund im Neuen: Exegetische Studien zur Israelfrage im Neuen Testament* (WUNT 35; Tübingen: Mohr/Siebeck, 1985), 99, mistakenly identi-

rangement is God's gracious gift.[77] "Covenant" establishes an expectation that the Son will be called "Mediator."[78] The surprise created by "Guarantor" calls attention to the pastor's purposeful use of this important term.[79] Since the unalterable oath of God has established the Son as Priest, he is not merely the "Mediator," but the "Guarantor" of God's "better covenant."[80] On the basis of God's own oath the Son absolutely guarantees that God's people can be cleansed of sin and come into God's presence because he is the one at God's right who mediates these benefits.[81] Chapters 8 through 10 explain all that the Son has done in order to become the "Guarantor" that this new "covenant" or arrangement for approaching God is truly effective and thus "better."[82]

---

fies "covenant" with "law." Hebrews always uses "law" in a negative sense. This first introduction of "covenant" is positive.

77. J. Behm, "διαθήκη," *TDNT* 2:124-34, defines διαθήκη ("covenant") in the LXX as the freely given ". . . ordinances, or dispositions of the sovereign will of God, which declare both His demands and His saving purposes" (127). This understanding of διαθήκη was continued in the Apocrypha and Pseudepigrapha and was known by Philo, though he is influenced by contemporary Hellenism. In the papyri διαθήκη occurs exclusively as "testament" or "will" (MM, 148-49). See Cockerill, "Melchizedek Christology," 126.

78. Attridge, 208, substantiates the pastor's purposeful use of ἔγγυς ("guarantor") by noting that it is not normally associated with covenant language.

79. *Pace* Ellingworth, 388, ἔγγυς ("guarantor") is not a mere synonym for μεσίτης ("mediator") that the pastor has used because of euphony with ἐγγίζομεν ("we draw near") at the end of v. 19. As we have seen, the pastor is a word-smith sensitive to the impact made by the sound of words. He may well have been aware of this euphony coming appropriately at the end of two sections of his thought, but such similarity of sound cannot account for his choice of ἔγγυς. προσέρχομαι ("come to," "approach," v. 25) would have been just as appropriate in v. 19. Thus, if anything, it is more likely that he used ἐγγίζομεν at the end of v. 19 in anticipation of ἔγγυς at the end of v. 22. He uses ἔγγυς to express the certainty created by the oath. If μεσίτης ("mediator") in 9:15 takes some of the significance of ἔγγυς, as Ellingworth suggests, it is because the pastor has used ἔγγυς here to prepare for that later reference. Just as he uses ἔγγυς to establish a context for understanding Christ's mediatorial work, so ἐλπίς ("hope," v. 19) establishes a context for understanding the future orientation of the new διαθήκη ("covenant").

80. Cf. Weiss, 408, who thinks that the unchangeable divine oath underlies not only the priesthood ("you are a priest") but also the eternity ("forever") of the Son. However, Heb 1:1-14 makes it clear that the pastor does not base the Son's eternity on Ps 110:4. Yet this verse is in accord with the Son's eternity because it establishes and confirms the eternal Son as the eternal and thus ultimate "Priest."

81. Bruce, 171, n. 70, argues that the God-man guarantees the New Covenant to God by fulfilling its requirements as a human being; and to human beings, by fulfilling its requirements as the Son of God. The pastor is, however, primarily concerned with his assuring the effectiveness of this covenant for the people of God (Westcott, 189; Lenski, 237; and Delitzsch, 1:368-69). It is important to note that the text does not say "he guarantees" but he is, in himself, the "Guarantor" — for all and any.

82. Cf. Bénétreau, 2:43.

The pastor hints at the direction of this explanation, however, by ending this verse with the name "Jesus." He opened this chapter by speaking of "one made like the Son of God" (v. 3), and he will conclude with "a Son perfected forever" (v. 28). He has identified this new Priest of Ps 110:4 with the eternal Son of 1:1-14 exalted to God's right hand according to Ps 110:1. When he referred to the Son's advent in v. 14, he called him "our Lord." Thus when he says in v. 22, "he has become Guarantor of a better covenant," his hearers are thinking of the Son — until the last word — "Jesus." The exalted Son at God's right (8:1) is the eternal Son who through his obedient life and self-offering as Jesus (cf. 6:20) "has become" the one who guarantees the effectiveness of this new way of approaching God.[83] He has achieved the effective priesthood inherent in his divine sonship only through his incarnation and death.[84]

Thus the superiority of the New Covenant is founded on God. It is effective because the Son shares God's eternal life and because he has been established by God's oath as its "Guarantor." As eternal Son and Guarantor he gives God's people all the reason they could possibly need to persevere through faith in the availability of God's power and the certainty of his promises (see 11:1-6).[85]

The hearers are anxious for more about this "better covenant" and what Jesus has done to guarantee its effectiveness. The pastor will not disappoint their expectations in the chapters that follow. However, he must first conclude his exposition of Ps 110:4 by expounding its key affirmation: "You are a priest forever."

23-25 *"You are a priest forever."* This clause is the most important part of Ps 110:4. The pastor has already drawn on its implications in his explanation of "according to the order of Melchizedek" in vv. 11-19 above (particularly in vv. 15-19). He has reminded his hearers of its importance by citing it at the end of v. 21. There are two reasons, however, for his reserving formal comment on this statement until the conclusion of his exposition. First, the argument of vv. 11-19 was necessary before his hearers could properly understand his explanation. Second, this statement expresses the main point he would leave with all who will listen. All those who would persevere in faith and obedience must avail themselves of this "inviolable" priesthood exercised by Jesus the Son of God (v. 25).

The pastor's return to this clause also shows how closely he has followed the plan anticipated by v. 3. In vv. 11-14 he showed how this Priest

---

83. The perfect tense of "has become" (γέγονεν) in v. 22 indicates that he became and continues to be the Guarantor.

84. See Weiss, 409-10.

85. See Westcott, 189; Delitzsch, 1:368-69.

"according to the order of Melchizedek" was "without [Aaronic] genealogy" (v. 3a); in vv. 15-19 he showed how this Priest was "like" Melchizedek because he had "neither beginning of days nor end of life" (v. 3b). Now in vv. 23-25 he explains the significance of "he remains a priest forever" (v. 3d). His "eternal" life (v. 3b; vv. 15-19) is the basis of his "inviolable" priesthood (v. 3d, vv. 23-25). This observation exposes once again the fallacy of all attempts to reduce the teaching of this chapter to the perpetual or unending priesthood of the Son. The pastor clearly intends to affirm that both the quality and duration of his absolute priesthood are founded on the eternity of his person.

23-24   The pastor concludes his exposition of the psalm with one final comprehensive contrast between the old priesthood (v. 23) and the new (v. 24), from which he draws his final conclusion in v. 25.[86] This contrast takes the form of a chiasm in which the limited scope of the old priesthood is followed by the reason for its limitation; but the reason for the new priest's superiority precedes the all-sufficient scope of his priesthood:[87]

"And on the one hand many have become priests (v. 23a)
    because by death they have been prevented from continuing
        (v. 23b).
    But he, because he remains forever (v. 24a),
has a priesthood that is inviolable (v. 24b)."

As is his habit, the pastor ends with the payoff, in this case, Christ's "inviolable priesthood."

"Many have become priests" attests their ineffectiveness. The perfect "have become" encompasses the whole long history of the Aaronic priesthood. The pastor, who has said much about genealogy, remembers the extended succession of these priests. However, extended succession has merged into multiplicity. The long line has become a crowd. The greatness of their number made necessary by their mortality shows that every one of them individually and all of them together were inadequate. Multiplicity meant that their priesthood was founded on nothing more than human weakness. They are a "great cloud of witnesses" to the inability of the old to bring people into God's presence. This multiplicity also sets the stage for what the pastor will say about Christ's "once-for-all" sacrifice and entrance into God's presence (7:27; 9:12; 10:10). The reason for this multiplicity and thus their

86. For the contrast between vv. 23 and 24 note καὶ οἱ μέν ("and those on the one hand) . . . ὁ δέ ("but he"). For v. 25 as the logical conclusion note ὅθεν ("therefore").

87. Attridge, 209. Ellingworth, 389, fails to see that ἀπαράβατον ἔχει τὴν ἱερωσύνην ("he has an inviolable priesthood") parallels πλείονές εἰσιν γεγονότες ἱερεῖς ("many have become priests").

ineffectiveness is stated simply as "because by death they were prevented from continuing." The pastor focuses on the frailty indicated by their mortality in order to contrast the Son's eternity. He is aware, however, that human priesthood is also limited by sin (see on 5:1-3 above and v. 28 below).

24   Christ has an effective priesthood "because he remains forever." It is informative to compare the term used above for the old priesthood's inability to "continue" and the one used here for the new's "remaining." Although the first term is built on the second, it could be used for "continuing in office," and that is the way in which the pastor uses it here.[88] The term used for "remain," however, is characteristically used by the Greek OT for God and things pertaining to God,[89] such as the new heaven and earth or the new Jerusalem (Isa 66:22; Zech 14:10). Compare its use in Heb 10:34; 12:27; and 13:14. Thus the pastor does not say that Christ "continues" in the office of priesthood, but simply and absolutely that he himself "remains."[90] "Forever" is the only qualification added to this infinitive. Thus there can hardly be any question that "to remain" describes the eternal character of the Son's person affirmed in the opening chapter of Hebrews.[91]

Thus this use of "to remain" confirms what we have said above about "without beginning of days or end of life" (v. 3b); "he lives" (v. 8); and "indestructible life" (v. 16). When the pastor chooses his own words to describe the Son or his precursor, he uses terms that affirm imperishable eternity past and future. The same is true of "ever living" in v. 25 below. This strongly suggests that his thought is not limited to eternity future even when he uses the words of the psalm, "You are a priest forever." It is not merely the duration but also the eternal quality of the one who exercises this priesthood that is crucial. Thus the use of "to remain" confirms our suggestion above that "you are a priest forever" should be understood as "you are an eternal priest," or perhaps, even better, "You are a priest who is eternal."[92] Christ's continu-

88. Compare παραμένειν ("to continue [in office]") in v. 23 with μένειν ("to remain") in v. 24. For examples of παραμένειν as "continue in office" see Weiss, 415, n. 157; Braun, 218-19; MM, 458; and F. Hauck, "παραμένω," TDNT 4:587-88. Josephus uses this term for priests continuing in office (Ant. 9.273).

89. See θεὸς μένων καὶ ζῶν εἰς γενεὰς γενεῶν ἕως τοῦ αἰῶνος ("God remaining and living unto generations of generations forever") in Dan 6:27 LXX. See also F. Hauck, "μένω," TDNT 4:575-76. Neyrey, "True Deity," 445-46, has collected many examples of similar terms used in the broader Hellenistic world to describe the eternal, uncreated, and imperishable gods or God.

90. Attridge, 209.

91. Attridge, 209. Though Attridge missteps when he says that Hebrews uses μενεῖν ("to remain") here to develop the "contrast between the earthly and the heavenly, the temporal and the eternal," there is nothing here about "the earthly and the heavenly."

92. Although Neyrey has shown clearly from contemporary parallels that Hebrews describes the Son as eternal deity past and present in chapter 7, he misses this dis-

ing perpetual exercise of the priestly office is, of course, also very crucial to the author's pastoral concern. His hearers must persevere into the future, and he wants them to know that the eternal Son will always be there as their High Priest. If, however, he were not "eternal," that priesthood would do them no more good than the Aaronic one.

Because he is eternal, his priesthood is powered by the eternity of God and not by the frailty of mortal humanity. Thus "he has a priesthood that is inviolable."[93] The term translated "inviolable" does not appear before Hellenistic Greek, where it occurs in Epictetus, the Stoics, Plutarch, the Hermetic Writings, Josephus, Philo, and the papyri.[94] In these sources it always means "unchangeable," "permanent," or "inviolable."[95] It never means "not passing to another" — the reduced sense that many interpreters would give it in Hebrews.[96] Furthermore, the normal meaning is well suited to the context of Hebrews. The pastor has gone far beyond talking about genealogy and descent. He has just spoken of a priest who, like God, "remains."[97] As the eternal Son of God, he has the permanent, final, and absolute priesthood.[98]

25 With "therefore" the pastor expounds the implications of Christ's final and absolute priesthood for his hearers:[99] "he is able to save completely those who come to God through him." The pastor has chosen the phrase translated "completely" with intention.[100] His purpose is to emphasize that

---

tinction between the terms the author chooses and those given him in the psalm, "You are a priest forever." Thus the statement made by him on the basis of the psalm verse is unnecessary: "Yet it must be quickly noted that the author of Hebrews seems considerably more interested in Jesus' imperishability and eternity in the future than he is in his eternity in the past." See Neyrey, "True Deity," 452.

93. The emphasis given to ἀπαράβατον ("inviolable") by its initial position is best expressed by translating it as a relative clause. See Robertson, *Grammar,* 656, 789. See Heb 5:14.

94. See ἀπαράβατος in BDAG, 97; MM, 53.

95. E. K. Simpson, "The Vocabulary of the Epistle to the Hebrews, II," *EvQ* 18 (1946): 187-90. See also Weiss, 416, n. 159, and Paul Ellingworth, "The Unshakable Priesthood: Hebrews 7.24," *JSNT* 23 (1985): 125-26.

96. Spicq, 2:197; Montefiore, 128; Hughes, 268-69; and Moffatt, 99, among others. This interpretation was common among the Church Fathers. For criticism of this position, see Bénétreau, 2:43-44, and O'Brien, 273.

97. See Attridge, 210.

98. Cockerill, "Melchizedek Christology," 133-34.

99. For the significance of ὅθεν ("therefore") see Michel, 276; Lane 1:189; and Heb 2:17; 3:1; 7:25; 8:3; and 9:18.

100. Compare εἰς τὸ παντελές ("to the very end") with comparable expressions the pastor normally uses for "forever" — εἰς τὸν αἰῶνα (1:8; 5:6; 6:20; 7:17, 21, 24, 28) and εἰς τὸ διηνεκές (7:3; 10:1, 12, 14).

the "eternal priest" has an absolute priesthood and thus can save to the full-est, to the most complete extent. The "law perfected nothing" (v. 19), but the one with the "inviolable" priesthood can save, one might say, to the Nth de-gree.[101] "Completely" is the most common use of this expression in later Greek.[102] The pastor would be thoroughly puzzled by those of his interpret-ers who try to reduce this term to "forever," or who attempt to separate "for-ever" from "completely."[103] Eternal or final salvation and perseverance in faith and obedience through the complete provision of Christ are "one and in-separable."[104] Christ is able to save so "completely" that his people are able to persevere until the end and thus be saved "forever." The pastor knows of no final or "forever" salvation that is not the result of perseverance through the completed work of Christ. That is why he is so eager and urgent that his hearers persevere in faith and obedience. He earnestly desires them to avail themselves of Christ's ability to save them "completely."

This strong desire is the reason why the pastor describes this complete salvation as being for "those who come to God through him." The term trans-lated "come to" is very close in meaning to the word translated "draw near" at the end of v. 19.[105] Both "come to" and "draw near" are used in the LXX for the approach of both priests and people to God in worship. However, the Greek OT uses the word we have translated "come to" in one way when it re-fers to priests, in another when to the people of God. The priests "come to" the altar, veil, or Holy Place. The people, however, only "come to," "before" God or "before" the Lord, for they cannot approach the altar itself.[106] Christ has saved so completely, however, that he has done away with this distinc-tion. The faithful need not come "before" God or his altar but directly to God

---

101. The pastor may have been influenced in his choice of εἰς τὸ παντελές ("com-pletely," "to the uttermost," in the KJV) because παντελές and the words he uses for "per-fect" (τελείόω, 7:19) and "perfection" (τελείωσις) share the same root. Such association only reinforces the interpretation given above.

102. Thus εἰς τὸ παντελές was equivalent to παντελῶς ("completely," "fully," "wholly"), and was used by Philo and Josephus in this sense. See BDAG, 754; Bleek 2, 2:398; Gerhard Delling, "παντελής," *TDNT* 8:66-67.

103. Ellingworth, 391; Weiss, 416; Moffatt, 100; Montefiore, 129; Windisch, 67; and MM, 477, among others.

104. Thus Johnson, 194; Michel, 275; Dods, 316; Delitzsch, 1:371; and O'Brien, 274, affirm the meaning "completely" without excluding "forever." Attridge, 210, agrees, but his statement that "the very ambiguity of the phrase probably appealed to our author" shows he has not grasped how "completely" and "forever" are bound together in the pas-tor's thought. It is usually those who fail to see that the Son's eternity is central to the pas-tor's argument who miss the significance of this term.

105. Here προσέρχομαι; in v. 19, ἐγγίζω.

106. For προσέρχομαι of priests see Lev 9:7-8; 21:23; and 22:3; for its use of peo-ple approaching "before" God see Exod 16:9 and Lev 9:5.

himself through Christ and the sacrifice he has offered.[107] The pastor implicitly invites his hearers to join those who take advantage of all Christ has done by thus coming to God through him. All that the pastor will say about Christ's high priesthood from now until 10:18 is aimed at encouraging and enabling them to do so. Thus in 10:22 he makes this invitation explicit: "come with a true heart in full assurance of faith."[108] However, "those who come to God through him" also contains a germ of warning. If the hearers cease to thus draw near, they will forfeit these benefits (cf. 10:26-31).

The pastor concludes with a final affirmation of Christ's competence by freshly restating the burden of v. 24: "Because he is always living to make intercession for them."[109] The participle "living," like "to remain" above, is often used to describe God (Heb 3:12; 9:14; 10:31; 12:22; cf. 4:12; 10:20). It is intensified by the use of "always,"[110] and harks back to the "indestructible life" of v. 15, the "he lives" of v. 6, and the "having neither beginning of days nor end of life" in v. 3. The pastor concludes his exposition of this psalm by affirming once again that the Son's effective priesthood is founded on his sharing the eternal life of the "living" God.

The pastor describes Christ's present, enduring, postsacrificial ministry as intercession for "those who come to God through him." The priestly categories the pastor has been using make it natural for him to speak of intercession, even if he uses this term in an unusual way.[111] Christ does not perpetually petition God on behalf of his people.[112] His sacrifice has been accepted, and he has taken his seat in the place of all authority at the Father's

---

107. It is true that in secular Hellenistic Greek προσέρχομαι was often followed by τῷ θεῷ, "to God," in the dative case, just as in Hebrews (J. Schneider, "προσέρχομαι," *TDNT* 2:683-84). Nevertheless, in light of the way the pastor is influenced by the LXX, this deviation from its usage appears significant.

108. The expression in 10:22 is προσέρχομαι, the same word that we have translated "come to" in 7:25.

109. This participle, ζῶν, "living," is probably causal (MHT, 3:154-58; BDF §418, 1). A literal translation of the phrase would be, "Always living to make intercession for them."

110. On the significance of πάντοτε ("always") see Robertson, *Grammar,* 300.

111. Hay calls the eternal intercession of the Son "somewhat of a 'foreign body'" in Hebrews' theology (David M. Hay, *Glory at the Right Hand: Psalm 110 in Early Christianity* [Society of Biblical Literature Monograph Series 18; Nashville: Abingdon, 1973], 132). He suggests that the pastor uses ἐντυγχάνειν, "to intercede," of Christ because it was a traditional formulation. Cf. Bruce, 174; Michel, 277. Although this term is a bit awkward, Christ's present eternal ministry as High Priest is at the very heart of the pastor's thought and pastoral concern (cf. 8:1). For an extended discussion of ἐντυγχάνειν see Cockerill, "Melchizedek Christology," 138-43.

112. This is the normal meaning of ἐντυγχάνειν followed by περί or ὑπέρ (BDAG, 341, 1, a).

right hand "once-for-all" (10:11-15).[113] However, when the recipients of Hebrews hear that Christ "intercedes" for them, they will be encouraged by
knowing that he represents them before God.[114] They will also remember that
God is the ultimate source of their "great salvation" (2:3) revealed and made
effective in his Son. When they draw near and receive the "mercy and timely
help" (4:15) that Christ so freely gives, they will not forget the ultimate giver.
Christ's intercession results in his providing cleansing for sin, access to God,
and grace to overcome all temptation and opposition (4:14-16; 10:19-25; cf.
2:18; 5:2, 7).[115] The pastor concludes this section by reminding his hearers
that the eternal Son is there for them and that he is always ready to enable
their perseverance.

3. This Priest Is Exactly the Kind of Priest We Need (7:26-28)

> 26 For such a high priest would be precisely fitting for us — cov-
> enant keeping, without evil, without blemish, having been separated
> from sinners and having become higher than the heavens, 27 who does
> not have daily need, as those high priests, to offer sacrifice first for
> his own sins, then for the sins of the people. For this he did once for
> all by offering himself. 28 For the law established human beings hav-
> ing weakness as high priests, but the word of the oath, which came af-
> ter the law, a Son having been perfected forever.

The pastor has just described the great benefit that accrues to God's people
because their Priest is the eternal Son of God. He can restrain himself no longer from breaking into a grand description of all the ways in which this High
Priest is precisely appropriate for God's people and their needs. These final
verses of chapter 7 join the insights gained from the exposition of Ps 110:4
with themes introduced in 2:17-18; 4:14-16; and 5:1-10 and further developed in 8:1–10:18. These verses form one of those pregnant passages in Hebrews that combines summary and announcement; integration of the pastor's
thought with application of the truth (cf. 4:14-16; 10:19-25). The pastor
would have his hearers engage this High Priest so suited to their predicament.
He would renew their attention so he can continue his explanation of that
High Priest's effectiveness in order that they might persevere through this
High Priest's aid.

The unity of this section is beyond question. It opens with what is
clearly an introductory phrase and is followed in 8:1 by a similar phrase in-

---

113. Spicq, 2:198; Bruce, 175.
114. Weiss, 419.
115. Ellingworth, 392.

troducing the next section. The term "high priest," abandoned since 6:20 in deference to Ps 110:4, occurs in each verse and bounds the whole with an inclusion.[1] The appropriateness of this High Priest announced in the opening line is the theme throughout. Each of the three verses forms a subunit. Verse 26 describes this High Priest with a series of three adjectives followed by two participial phrases. The relative clause of v. 27 continues this description. Although v. 28 begins a new sentence, it is joined to v. 27 in that both contrast the new and old high priests. Verse 26 describes the sinlessness and exaltation of this high priest; v. 27 his once-for-all sacrifice in contrast with the multiple sacrifices of the old; v. 28 the appointment of the Son as High Priest by divine oath in contrast to the appointment of humans as high priests by the law. The themes of v. 26 have been well announced in previous passages (1:3, 13; 4:14-16; 5:5-10); v. 27 introduces the main theme of 8:1–10:18. Verse 28 integrates the thought of 7:1-25 into this larger context and brings all to a grand conclusion with the final word, "having been perfected."

26 The poetical character of this verse rivals that of v. 3. It falls naturally into four lines:

> For such a high priest would be precisely fitting for us —
> covenant keeping, without evil, without blemish,[2]
> having been separated from sinners and
> higher than the heavens having become

The word translated "such" almost always refers to what has preceded, the exceptions being the few times it is followed by a correlative pronoun.[3] "Who," at the beginning of v. 27, might have such correlative force

---

1. Note the contrast between ἡμῖν καὶ ἔπρεπεν ἀρχιερεύς ("a high priest is appropriate for us") in v. 26 and ἀρχιερεῖς ἔχοντας ἀσθένειαν ("high priests having weakness") in v. 28.

2. Compare this line, ὅσιος, ἄκακος, ἀμίαντος, with v. 3c above, ἀπάτωρ, ἀμήτωρ, ἀγενεαλόγητος ("without father, without mother, without genealogy"). There is no concrete evidence, however, that the pastor is quoting from a hymn. These lines are closely integrated with his theology. Weiss, 420, lists those who find a hymn here in n. 173; those who do not in n. 174.

3. Fifty-one of the fifty-six times that τοιοῦτος occurs in MG, 954-55, it clearly refers to what has gone before. In the remaining five instances it is followed by a correlative — ὁποῖος in Acts 26:29; ἥτις in 1 Cor 5:1; ὡς in Phlm 9; and ὅς in Heb 7:27; 8:1. The question is whether ὅς is too far from τοιοῦτος to have correlative force. Compare τοιοῦτον ἔχομεν ἀρχιερέα, ὅς ("we have such a high priest, who . . .") in 8:1. Delitzsch, 2:2; Michel, 278; and Ellingworth, 393, think τοῦτος refers to the previous material; Héring, 62-64; Robertson, *Grammar,* 710; Bruce, 176-77; and Windisch, 68-69, think the following. Westcott, 193; Dods, 317; and Kuss, 65, opt for both. See Cockerill, "Melchizedek Christology," 148-50.

even though there is considerable distance between the two words. As v. 28 shows, the pastor would certainly include the preceding description of the eternal Son as Priest in these verses. Nevertheless, his focus is on the once-for-all sacrifice of v. 26, which he will expound in the following chapters. As we will see below, the way in which he ends this section with "having been perfected" confirms this focus.

"Such a high priest [as the one we are describing] would be appropriate for us."[4] The pastor has no doubt as to the suitability of this High Priest.[5] He uses the tendential imperfect, which we have translated "would be," to appeal to his hearers. "Such a high priest would be precisely fitting [would he not?]." This High Priest is exactly suited to the need of "us," we who are God's people. His people need cleansing from sin so that they can enter the divine presence. They need grace for perseverance in obedience. He can give both. He is suited to meet these needs first of all because he himself is without sin.

His sinlessness, so clearly affirmed in 4:15, is the burden of the three adjectives in the first line of this verse. One might use the term "holy" or "pious" for the first adjective, but we have translated it as "covenant keeping" in line with its use in the LXX.[6] The LXX uses this term in the plural, usually followed by "of God," to designate the community of Israel (Pss 149:1-2; 79:1-2; 132:9, 16) and especially those in Israel who maintained their covenant relationship with God and others (Pss 12:1; 18:26; 32:6).[7] Thus this word does not describe some speculative, preincarnate holiness but the faithfulness of the incarnate Son in his relationship to the Father as he learned

---

4. καί ("and") emphasizes ἔπρεπεν ("it is fitting") (Michel, 277-79; Westcott, 193). We have translated καί as "precisely" (Robertson, *Grammar,* 1181). This opening statement is the controlling statement for vv. 26-27 (Lane, 1:191). "It is fitting" not only denotes the logical conclusion of the pastor's discussion but also indicates its pastoral appropriateness (Weiss, 420-21).

5. πρέπω ("fitting") denotes what is fitting or proper in the light of certain circumstances or a particular relationship; with regard to the position or nature of the persons involved (BDAG, 861; MM, 534; LSJ, 1461, III, 4; cf. Matt 3:15; 1 Cor 11:13; 1 Tim 2:10; Tit 2:1). See the comments on Heb 2:10.

6. "Holy" runs the risk of not distinguishing this term, ὅσιος, from the more common word for "holy," ἅγιος. In the LXX ὅσιος is used to translate חסיד, but never קדוש (= ἅγιος, "holy"), or צדיק (= δίκαιος, "righteous"). In older English "pious" meant one who kept one's responsibilities to God, family, etc. In that sense it was very close to ὅσιος. "Pious," however, has been spoiled by its modern usage for superficial godliness. ὅσιος is rare in the NT, being used of the Messiah in Acts 2:27; 13:34 (both in dependence on Psalm 16); of God in Rev 15:4; 16:5 (cf. Deut 32:4; Ps 144:17 in the LXX); and twice of human beings (1 Tim 2:8; Tit 1:8; see also 1 Tim 1:9; 2 Tim 3:2). See F. Hauck, "ὅσιος," *TDNT* 5:491-92.

7. Cockerill, "Melchizedek Christology," 153-56.

what it meant to be an obedient human being.[8] The second adjective, "without evil," also follows the usage of the LXX, where the term describes one who is "innocent" or "untouched by evil."[9] The exalted Son has lived an obedient human life and so can be declared "untouched by evil."[10]

The final adjective in this series, "blameless" or "pure," occurs three other times in the NT (Heb 13:4; 1 Pet 1:4; and Jas 1:27) and five times in the later books of the LXX (Wis 3:13; 4:2; 8:19-20; 2 Macc 14:26; and 15:34). Both in these references and in extrabiblical sources it is usually applied to things (Heb 13:4; 1 Pet 1:4; Jas 1:27; Wis 4:2; 8:19-20; 2 Macc 14:26; 15:43) rather than, as here, to persons (Wis 3:13). In both biblical and nonbiblical Greek it can refer to blamelessness in general (cf. Jas 1:27). It can also be used for sexual purity (Heb 13:4; Wis 3:13; 4:2; 8:19-20), and especially for cultic purity (2 Macc 14:26; 15:34; Josephus, *J.W.* 6.99).[11] In these last three references it describes the purity of the Temple. Philo uses this term to describe the wife of the high priest in *Flight* 114 and the high priest himself in *Flight* 118 and *Spec. Laws* 1.113. In Philo's allegorical interpretations the cultic or ritual purity of the high priest and his wife represent moral purity.[12] *T. Jos.* 4:6 is a good example of the way in which the cultic use of "blameless" is employed figuratively for moral purity: "those who approach God" are to do so "with a pure heart and a blameless mouth."[13] Thus it was most appropriate for the pastor to conclude his description of the sinlessness that qualified Christ as High Priest with this term. The one who kept God's covenant without disobedience through every kind of temptation was "un-

---

8. Delitzsch, 2:2.

9. Compare the usage of ἄκακος ("without evil") by Philo in *Spec. Laws* 3.119; *Virtues* 43; *Creation* 156, 170. For a discussion of these passages see Cockerill, "Melchizedek Christology," 157, n. 440. Rom 16:18, the only other NT passage that uses ἄκακος, has little relevance for Hebrews, since the word there has the alternate meaning, "simple."

10. W. Grundmann, "ἄκακος," *TDNT* 3:482, contends that we should take ἄκακος in the active sense of "one who does no evil" because the following adjective, ἀμίαντος, "blameless," is passive. His position does not give due weight to the overwhelming evidence from LXX usage.

11. The cultic context of ἀμίαντος is reinforced by the way in which the LXX uses the related verb μιάνω for cultic pollution (F. Hauck, "μιαίνω, μίασμα, μιασμός, ἀμίαντος," *TDNT* 4:644-47).

12. That is, "freedom from passion, from sense-perception, from degeneration, from the ties of this life" (Cockerill, "Melchizedek Christology," 160)

13. "The verb προσέρχομαι (cf. v. 25 above) is used to describe "those who draw near to God" in *T. Jos.* 4:6. In this passage καθαρός describes the "pure" heart and ἀμίαντος the "blameless" mouth. καθαρός and ἀμίαντος are often used together, particularly in passages drawing on cultic imagery (cf. 2 Macc 14:36; Josephus, *J.W.* 6.99; Philo, *Flight* 119). They also occur together, but without clear cultic association, in Jas 1:27.

touched by evil" and thus "blameless," and therefore qualified to be the kind of High Priest we need. Taken together, these three adjectives make it very clear that this now-exalted High Priest is sinless because he lived a completely obedient human life.[14]

"Having been separated from sinners" is an appropriate transition between the affirmation of this High Priest's sinlessness in the previous line and his exaltation in the next. When the word translated "having been separated" is followed by the preposition "from," it almost always refers to local separation and not just to difference.[15] This phrase is not merely saying that Jesus is "different" from sinners.[16] He has been separated from them by the exaltation.[17] This understanding is also in harmony with the use of the perfect tense. Jesus was separated from sinners at the exaltation and remains separated.[18] Yet the very fact that the pastor describes Christ's exaltation as having been separated "from sinners" shows that it was his final triumph over sin.[19] Through his obedience he overcame the opposition he endured from "sinners" (12:3) and has become triumphant.[20] He continues to be this one who was victorious over sin so that he can aid those now facing its fierce opposition (12:4; cf. 4:14-16; 10:19-25). The exaltation may have separated him from sinners, but it opened the way for fellowship with "those who draw near to God through him" (7:25).[21]

14. See Michel, 279; Spicq, 2:201; Attridge, 213.
15. The verb is χωρίζω followed by the preposition ἀπό. Conversely, when it signifies difference it is almost never followed by ἀπό (Cockerill, "Melchizedek Christology," 163-69).
16. As advocated by Westcott, 195; Lenski, 244; and Buchanan, 128.
17. Michel, 280; Delitzsch, 2:4; Spicq, 2:201; Riggenbach, 210-11; Montefiore, 130.
18. Reduction of this phrase to a description of Jesus' sinlessness requires one either to affirm that at a particular time Jesus became sinless or to exclude any sense of past action from this perfect participle, κεχωρισμένος ("having been separated").
19. Under the influence of Strack and Billerbeck, many commentators make reference to the high priest's being sequestered in a special part of the Temple seven days before the Day of Atonement in order to ensure ritual purity (Str-B 3:696). However, this separation of the Aaronic high priest is of little relevance. He was separated to ensure his ritual purity. Christ has been exalted on the basis of his moral purity and has actually entered the presence of God. Cf. Attridge, 213.
20. Michel, 279; Delitzsch, 2:4; Riggenbach, 211; Montefiore, 130; Moffatt, 101.
21. Ellingworth, 394, misses this distinction when he says, "But this kind of distance from sinners does not entail inability to help them (cf. 4:15; 5:7f)." Hebrews uses the word "sinners" for those who oppose Jesus. Jesus has come to help God's people, "those who draw near to God through him." Of course, this distinction does not mean that God's people were totally without sin, nor does it exclude the conversion of "sinners." This perspective is in accord with the pastor's purpose of enabling the perseverance of those who already belong to God.

"Having been separated from sinners" describes that *from* which Christ has been exalted, and "having become higher than the heavens" indicates that *to* which he has been exalted. The first describes the exaltation as Christ's final triumph over sin. The second underscores the dazzling heights he has attained. "Higher than the heavens" identifies him closely with God, to whom the psalmist declares, "Be exalted above the heavens" (Pss 57:5, 11; 108:5).[22] Hebrews shows no interest in contemporary speculations about intermediary "heavens" between earth and the dwelling place of God.[23] The Son shares the eternal life of God and has joined him in the place of highest exaltation. The aorist tense of "having become" underscores the reality of this event. The pastor is assuring his hearers of the reality and magnitude of Christ's exaltation before describing the sacrifice through which he attained it. The faithful "draw near to God" through the exalted Son. He alone is their source of help.

27 The pastor continues to describe the High Priest who is eminently suitable for the needs of God's people. This Priest's triumph over sin and his exaltation, described in the last verse, provide the context for understanding the High Priest "who" has offered himself. At last the pastor explicitly introduces the self-offering of the Son. He has been preparing for this moment from the beginning of his sermon. With rising anticipation he has described the Son as making "purification for sins" (1:3), "tasting death" for all (2:9), and "offering loud cries and tears" (5:7-8). His hearers must grasp the eternity, sinlessness, and exaltation of this High Priest before they can comprehend the significance of his self-sacrifice. As with these other aspects of his priesthood, the significance of this self-sacrifice becomes clear only by contrast with the old. The pastor has already reminded his hearers of the Aaronic high priest's double sacrifice (5:2-3) to facilitate this comparison. The significance of Christ's sacrifice is the central theme in each of the three parts of the following section (8:1-13; 9:1-22; 9:23–10:18). The pastor continues to bring its significance into clearer focus.

The sufficiency of Christ's sacrifice is shown by explicit contrast with the double and perpetually repeated sacrifice of the old high priests. This new High Priest "does not have daily need, as those high priests, to offer sacrifice first for his own sins, then for the sins of the people." Although the pastor is referring to the double offering of the old high priests on the Day of Atonement, the term we have translated "daily" (or "day by day") is not a reference

22. Bénétreau, 2:47.
23. Weiss, 422. See Michel, 311-12, for discussion of the supposed intermediate "heavens" through which Christ had to pass. The idea that Christ had to overcome hostile forces in these heavens is totally foreign to Hebrews. See the further discussion in Cockerill, "Melchizedek Christology," 170-71.

to that Day. It is an emphatic expression for "regularly" or "repeatedly" that the pastor uses to put strong emphasis on the old high priests' need for repeated sacrifice in contrast to the Son's "once-for-all" self-offering. The pastor was well aware that the high priest offered these double Day of Atonement sacrifices annually.[24] Just as the multiplicity of priests exposes their insufficiency (7:23-25), so the multiplicity of their sacrifices reveals their ineffectiveness (9:25–10:4).

The pastor's first intention is to deny Christ's need for "daily" sacrifice.[25] However, he is also denying Christ's need to offer "for himself." In 5:3 the grammatical structure emphasized the old high priest's need to offer for himself.[26] Here the structure puts emphasis on the fact that Christ had no need to make such an offering. Indeed, 5:3 has already argued that the Aaronic high priest's necessity to offer for himself demonstrated his insufficiency. Thus when the pastor says, "For this he did," he is referring to Christ's sacrifice "for the people."[27]

The second half of this verse describes the sacrifice of Christ with an economy of words that draws the hearers' attention to the essentials. "For this he did" — offer sacrifice for the people; "once for all" — not repeatedly but definitively and finally; "by offering himself" — not "for himself."[28] This verse ends with the self-offering of Christ so central to the following chapters.

28 Properly understood, this final verse summarizes all that the pastor has said about this new High Priest. The themes from 7:1-25 are integrated

---

24. Weiss, 424-25. Thus there is no need here to take καθ' ἡμέραν, "daily," or "day by day," as "every day of atonement" (Str-B 3:696-700). Nor is there need to speculate that the author is following an alternate interpretive tradition according to which the high priest offered daily sacrifices (deSilva, 275; Attridge, 214), or that he has fused the daily sacrifices with those of the Day of Atonement (Bénétreau, 2:48). The accurate knowledge he displays in 9:7 and 25 shows clearly that there is no need to accuse him of making a mistake (Johnson, 195).

25. This fact is demonstrated by the position of καθ' ἡμέραν ("daily") immediately after ἔχει ("he has") and before ἀνάγκην ("need").

26. Note the structure of 5:3, "as (καθώς) for himself . . . thus also (οὕτως καί) for the people."

27. Note the way τῶν τοῦ λαοῦ ("for the [sins] of the people") is isolated from τῶν ἰδιῶν ἁμαρτιῶν ("for his own sins") by θυσίας ἀναφέρειν ("sacrifice to offer") and put immediately before τοῦτο γὰρ ἐποίησεν ("for this he did"). Bruce, 178; Westcott, 197; Spicq, 2:203; and Attridge, 214 agree that τοῦτο, "this," refers only to the last phrase of the previous clause.

28. Thus taking the participle ἀνενέγκας ("having offered up") as instrumental. The aorist tense of this participle is in accord with the "once-for-all" nature of this sacrifice, as is the aorist of ἐποίησεν, "he did." This aorist contrasts with the present tense used to describe the old high priests' need for perpetual sacrifices and is in accord with the aorist of 1:2, God "has spoken" (Weiss, 425).

with the other aspects of his priesthood summarized in vv. 26-27. The contrast established in 7:20-22 between the "oath" and the "ordinance"/"law" provides the obvious framework for this concluding contrast between the old high priests and the new. However, this verse also brings to a final conclusion the contrast between a priesthood based on "genealogy" (vv. 3a, 4-9, 10, 11-14) and one based on "the power of an indestructible life" (vv. 15-19, 23-25).

"For the law established human beings having weakness as high priests." The pastor has reserved the expression "having weakness" for the end of this verse in the Greek text because it bears the burden of his thought. The "law," as we have seen, established priests on the basis of genealogy. They were merely "humans" because their priesthood was based on human ancestry; thus they had all the "weakness" of humans. With the expression "humans having weakness" the pastor includes the sinfulness of the old priests affirmed in 5:1-3 with their mortality described in 7:1-25.[29]

"The word of the oath" stands in sharp contrast to "the law." This "oath" is a direct "word" spoken by God with all the power, effectiveness, and permanence of his speech (see on 4:12-13). "A Son perfected forever" is the exact opposite of mere "human beings having weakness." All of the pastor's contrasts between the old and the new come to focus in these two descriptions. The "Son" is one and only; the "human beings" are many. The "Son" is eternal; "human beings" are dying.[30] The Son "has been perfected forever";[31] human beings are described as "having weakness."

"Having been perfected forever" requires further comment. We have already said much about this term in relation to 2:10; 5:8-9; and 7:11, 19. The pastor will make its meaning even clearer in the following chapters. It stands here in direct contrast to the sinfulness of humanity implied by the term "having weakness." The eternal Son, however, "has been perfected" as our Savior by offering his life of complete obedience to God on the cross (4:15; 5:8-9; esp. 10:5-10) resulting in his exaltation.[32] The effect of that self-

29. Compare ἀνθρώπους . . . ἔχοτας ἀσθένειαν ("human beings . . . having weakness") in 7:28 with ἐξ ἀνθρώπων ("from human beings," 5:1) and περίκειται ἀσθένειαν ("beset with weakness," 5:2). See the comments on these verses. Ellingworth, 397, would limit "weakness" to being "subject to sickness and death" because he does not understand 5:2 properly. Also, Hebrews never attributes "weakness" to Christ.

30. The lack of an article before both ἀνθρώπους ("human beings") and υἱόν ("Son") emphasizes the comparative quality of each (Robertson, *Grammar,* 794, j).

31. With Bénétreau, 2:49, "forever" qualifies "having been perfected" and not an implied "established."

32. Weiss, 427, correctly sees his "having been perfected" as taking place at the exaltation (5:8-9); however, it cannot be separated from his sacrifice by which it was accomplished. It might be better to say that his "having been perfected" was completed at his exaltation.

offering continues in his Person equipping him as the all-sufficient Savior. By his sacrifice he is consecrated and remains the only High Priest able to cleanse sins and thus bring God's people into his presence. This understanding implies no deficiency in the eternal Son. Yet by his having been perfected as the Savior of God's people through his incarnate obedience, he has fulfilled what was inherent in his sonship and provided the ultimate revelation of God (see on 1:1-4). Thus the phrase "a Son perfected forever" affirms his eternal sonship, incarnation, human obedience, self-offering, exaltation, and present session at God's right as the "Source of eternal salvation" (5:9). It is as the "Son perfected forever" that he is a High Priest so suited for his people's needs.[33]

As noted above, the self-offering of Christ, announced at the end of v. 27, is central in each of the three parts of the next major section (see 8:3-5 in 8:1-13; 9:11-15 in 9:1-22; 9:25–10:15 in 9:23–10:18). However, in a deeper sense, 8:1–10:18 explains the last word in the Greek text of chapter 7, for it is by his self-offering that he has "been perfected forever" as the Savior of God's people.[34] His sufficiency is the means by which we, as the people of God, are enabled and inspired to persevere in obedience.

D. OUR HIGH PRIEST'S ALL-SUFFICIENT SACRIFICE: A SYMPHONY IN THREE MOVEMENTS (8:1–10:18)

The story of chapter 7 continues. Heb 7:1-28 reveals who this High Priest has always been — the eternal Son of God. Heb 8:1–10:18 discloses what he has now become through his self-offering — a High Priest "perfected forever" (7:28) and thus "the Source of eternal salvation" (5:9). Only the eternal Son could become such a High Priest, one adequate for human need, and only by so doing could he fulfill his sonship. The pastor would have his hearers grasp the implications of who this High Priest *now* is — the sum of what he has al-

---

33. Contrary to Johnson, 185-86, these other aspects of the Son's "having been perfected" do not negate the cultic connotation of this word, discussed above, for priestly consecration. Rather, they are taken up into this cultic connotation, giving it a deeper meaning. Johnson, 186, is certainly correct, however, that the moral purity of the Son is his obedience to the Father and is not a matter of Philonic superiority of the inner (moral) to the physical (ritual).

34. Note the emphatic position of τετελειωμένον, "having been perfected," at the end of the sentence. εἰς τόν αἰῶνα, "forever," echoes Ps 110:4 (6:20; 7:17, 21). In light of the argument in 7:1-25, it describes not only the perpetuity of Christ's "having been perfected," but the "eternal" degree or quality of that perfection. There is no need to take this phrase as qualifying an understood καθίστησιν, from the previous line, as does Héring, 64. (See Moffatt, 102.)

ways been and what he has now become. He is the eternal Son who through his obedient, incarnate life offered himself in death and is now seated at God's right hand fully able to meet their deepest need.[1]

The Son has become this effective High Priest only by the offering of himself as an all-sufficient sacrifice for sin. In 7:27 the pastor announces his intention to discuss this long-anticipated theme (1:3; 5:7-9).[2] All that he has said up to this point provides the foundation necessary for its explanation. By delaying its consideration he has awakened the curiosity of his hearers: "When are you going to explain the significance of Christ's self-offering?" In these chapters he satisfies their desire: by his sacrifice the Son has atoned for sin, entered the heavenly Sanctuary as High Priest, and established the New Covenant. Thus, he uses the themes of sanctuary, covenant, and sacrifice to disclose the full magnitude of the Son's self-offering.[3]

A careful preview will assist the contemporary reader in negotiating this richly rewarding section. Thus, we will begin with a structural overview of 8:1–10:18 followed by a synopsis of each main subdivision (8:1-13; 9:1-22; 9:23–10:18).[4] Next, we will summarize the use of the principal OT citations in this section. Our preview will conclude with a description of the relationship between the three important themes of sanctuary, sacrifice, and covenant.

The artistry of the pastor's presentation is like a symphony in three movements (8:1-13; 9:1-22; 9:23–10:18) developing these three themes — sanctuary, sacrifice, and covenant.[5] Each movement begins with the theme of

---

1. The pastor's concern with the high priest "we" now "have" is better served by understanding the relationship between 7:1-28/8:1–10:18 as what he "was"/what he "has become" instead of what he "was"/what he has "done" (as per James Swetnam, "Form and Content in Hebrews 7–13," *Bib* 55 [1974]: 335; Grässer, *Bund*, 105; and others).

2. Harold W. Attridge, "The Uses of Antithesis in Hebrews 8–10," in *Christians among Jews and Gentiles: Essays in Honor of Krister Stendahl on His Sixty-Fifth Birthday,* ed. G. W. E. Nickelsburg and G. W. MacRae (Philadelphia: Fortress, 1986), 3.

3. Thus Lane, 2:257, "In this extended section the themes of covenant, sacrifice, and ministry are developed in concert." Bénétreau, 2:51, notes the importance of Christ's sacrifice in chapter 8 for the renewal of the covenant and the designation of the true sanctuary. M. Gourgues, "Remarques sur la 'structure centrale' de l'épître aux Hébreux: A l'occasion d'une réédition," *RevBib* 84 (1977): 32-33, says that the "sacrificial cult" is the "middle term" between the terms "covenant" and "ministry" (sanctuary) in 9:1-28. Others have recognized the importance of these themes in chapters 8 through 10.

4. The unity of 8:1–10:18 is widely accepted. See Attridge, "Uses," 3.

5. Some, like Vanhoye, *La structure littéraire,* 137-72 (cf. Bénétreau, 2:51, 96), have taken 8:1–9:28 as one section and 10:1-18 as a second. Guthrie, *Structure,* 106, 117, on the other hand, separates 8:1-13 (Guthrie takes 8:1-2 as a "direct intermediary transition" and then makes 8:3-6 and 8:7-13 separate sections) from 9:1–10:18. Such disagreement is not surprising since, as Gourgues, "Remarques," 26-37, has pointed out, formal

sanctuary (8:1-2; 9:1-10; 9:23-24) and ends with covenant (8:7-13; 9:16-22; 10:15-18). At the center of each is the ever-expanding theme of sacrifice (8:3-6; 9:11-15; 9:25–10:14). The pastor appeals to his hearers through the growing beauty of his presentation as well as the cumulative cogency of his argument. When the author as conductor has finished his symphony, he would leave his hearers overwhelmed with the magnitude and wonder of this High Priest and ready at all cost to persevere through the benefits he affords. The pastor makes this purpose clear in the encore that follows (especially 10:19-25).

A summary of each of these movements confirms their boundaries and reveals their interrelationships. The first (8:1-13) lays a Scriptural foundation. Even before their fulfillment, Ps 110:1 and Jer 31:31-34 meant that the Son would not serve as High Priest in the earthly tabernacle or mediate the Old Covenant. The very prophecy of the New Covenant meant that the Old was obsolete. Thus, the Son's sacrifice would be different from that of the old priests, suited to both heavenly sanctuary and New Covenant. How would it be different? The second movement (9:1-22) begins to answer this question by showing how the OT descriptions of sanctuary and covenant betray their insufficiency and point to the adequacy of Christ's sacrifice. The third movement (9:23–10:18) completes this answer by expounding the full glory and effectiveness of ministry in the heavenly sanctuary (9:23-24), of the New Covenant (10:15-18), and especially of Christ's sacrifice (9:25–10:14),[6] which occupies the major portion of this movement and reaches its pivotal point in 10:5-10.[7]

---

literary indicators of structure are not as prominent in 8:1–10:18 as in many other parts of Hebrews. Thus Vanhoye's argument that προσφέρειν, "to offer," establishes an inclusion between 8:3 and 9:28 is undone by the fact that the same word occurs in 8:4; 9:7, 9, 14, 25; 10:1, 2, 8, 11, and 12 (Vanhoye, *La structure littéraire,* 43; see Gourgues, "Remarques," 29). Nor is Χριστός in 9:11, 24, and 28 cause for inclusions between 11/28 and 24/28 (*pace* Vanhoye, *La structure littéraire,* 148-49). Furthermore, Weiss, 429-30, has shown the many linguistic connections both between 8:1-13 and 9:1-28 and between 9:1-28 and 10:1-13. Westfall points out the continuity of cultic vocabulary throughout 8:1–10:18 (Westfall, *Discourse Analysis,* 228). For critique of Vanhoye see Gourgues, "Remarques," 28-31 and Attridge, "Uses," 1-3. Gourgues himself divides this larger unit into 8:1-13; 9:1-28; and 10:1-18, as have many others. Justification for ending the second section at 9:22 and adding 9:23-28 to 10:1-18 will be given below. For a more extensive analysis of the structure of this section see G. L. Cockerill, "Structure and Interpretation in Hebrews 8:1–10:18: A Symphony in Three Movements," *BBR* 11 (2001): 179-201.

6. Bénétreau, 2:96, recognizes clearly that 10:1-18 is the summit of this section and not merely its summary, as some have suggested. As noted above, we would begin this final section at 9:23 instead of 10:1.

7. Thus, *pace* Vanhoye, Heb 10:5-10, not 9:11-14, is the ultimate explanation of Christ's sacrifice. Vanhoye thinks that 9:11-14 is at the center of the chiasm he has found in

347

The pivotal significance of 10:5-10 is supported by the pastor's use of the OT. In the first movement (8:1-13) he introduces the Scriptures that affirm Christ's priestly ministry in the heavenly sanctuary (Ps 110:1) and his role as Mediator/Guarantor of the New Covenant (Jer 31:31-34). However, he reserves Ps 40:6-8, the passage that shows the significance of Christ's sacrifice, until the heart of the third movement, found in 10:5-10. His interpretations of Ps 110:1 and Jer 31:31-34 frame this crucial explanation of Ps 40:6-8.[8]

Before listening to this symphony it is helpful to know how each of the three themes relates to the self-offering of Christ. Christ's self-offering is, first of all, at the center of each movement (8:3-5; 9:11-15; 9:23–10:14, especially 10:5-10), the great once-and-for-all "Day of Atonement" sacrifice that removes sin. However, when sin is removed, there is no hindrance to approaching God. Thus Christ's self-offering is also a sacrifice of high-priestly consecration that authorizes him to enter God's presence in the heavenly Sanctuary on behalf of God's people (cf. 8:1-2; 9:1-10; 9:23-24). Furthermore, when sin is taken away, the forgiveness and obedience promised by the New Covenant become a reality. Thus Christ's offering is a covenant-making sacrifice that establishes him as the Mediator of a new and effective way to approach God (cf. 8:7-13; 9:16-22; 10:15-18).[9] By definitively removing sin

---

8:1–9:28 (Vanhoye, *La structure littéraire,* 140-45, 161). Cf. Weiss, 430, citing both Vanhoye and L. Dussaut, *Synopse structurelle de l'épître aux Hébreux* (Paris: Cerf, 1981), 73.

8. Those who attempt to structure Hebrews according to its use of primary OT citations — such as Psalm 8; Psalm 95; Psalm 110; Jeremiah 31 and/or Psalm 40 — sometimes miss the subtlety of their inner relationship. For a summary of such proposals see J. R. Walters, "The Rhetorical Arrangement of Hebrews," *Asbury Theological Journal* 51 (1996): 59-70. In addition to his own proposal Walters refers to those of Caird, Lohse, Bruce, and Nauck. Walters opts for Jeremiah 31 as the dominant passage in this section, though others give this honor to Psalm 40. Attridge overstates the case when he likens the exposition of Jeremiah 31 in this section to that of Psalm 95 in 3:1–4:12 (Attridge, "Uses," 5). O'Brien, 287, also describes Jer 31:31-34 as the central text of Heb 8:1–10:18. Although there can be no doubt that Jer 31:31-34 receives more attention in this section than Ps 40:6-8, the latter is the keystone at the pinnacle of the pastor's argument. The pastor argues from Ps 110:1 and Jer 31:31-34 to Ps 40:6-8.

9. In describing Jesus' death Hebrews uses "Yom Kippur (Leviticus 16), the Red Heifer (Numbers 19), the institution of the covenant (Exodus 24), and the ordination of the priests (Leviticus 8)" (Daniel Stökel Ben Ezra, *The Impact of Yom Kippur on Early Christianity: The Day of Atonement from Second Temple Judaism to the Fifth Century* [WUNT 163; Tübingen: Mohr Siebeck, 2003], 187). However, Hebrews uses the red heifer only in describing the limitations of the old sacrifice. The above quotation is cited in Felix H. Cortez, "From the Holy to the Most Holy Place: The Period of Hebrews 9:6-10 and the Day of Atonement as a Metaphor of Transition," *JBL* 125 (2006): 529. Cortez shows many ways in which 9:6-10 anticipates the themes yet to be developed. However, he gives no evidence that contradicts the clear indication in 9:11-14 that Christ's sacrifice has provided the atonement only anticipated by the annual Day-of-Atonement sacrifice.

through his great Day-of-Atonement sacrifice, he now ministers all benefits to God's people as their heavenly High Priest and the Mediator/Guarantor of a new and "better" covenant. Everything depends on recognizing who he is, being joined to him by faith, and thus appropriating the blessings only he affords.

1. First Movement: The New Promised (8:1-13)[1]

The pastor introduces the basic themes and their Scriptural foundation.[2] Ps 110:1 makes it clear that the Son ministers as High Priest in the heavenly sanctuary (8:1-2). The promise of Jer 31:31-34 shows that he is Mediator of a New Covenant (8:7-13). Since his sacrifice was fitting for such a sanctuary and covenant, it must have been different from and superior to that of the Aaronic priesthood (8:3-6). Furthermore, God's promise of a New Covenant demonstrates the ineffectiveness of the Old. The central theme of sacrifice is muted in this first movement, increases in the second, and crescendos to dominate the third as the pastor comes to his grand finale.

a. A Minister of the Sanctuary and True Tent (8:1-2)

> 1 *Now this is the main point of the things being said: we have such a high priest who has sat down at the right hand of the throne of the Majesty in the heavens,* 2 *a minister of the Sanctuary and the true Tent that the Lord, and not any human being, has pitched.*

Although these verses are integral to the pastor's argument in vv. 1-13, they also introduce this entire section and bind it to what has gone before.[1] The pastor's declaration that "we have such a High Priest who has sat down at the right hand of the Majesty in the heavens" is "the main point of the things being said."[2] The present participle translated "the things being said" encompasses all that the pastor has written and has yet to write.[3] This affirmation

---

1. The section headings for each of these movements are taken, sometimes with adaptation, from Cockerill, "Structure and Interpretation in Hebrews 8:1–10:18," 182, 185, 190.

2. Heb 8:1-13 provides "an elaborate statement of the points about to be made" (Swetnam, "Hebrews 7-13," 335).

1. Cf. Guthrie, *Structure,* 106, who describes 8:1-2 as a "Direct Intermediary Transition."

2. Williamson, *Philo and Hebrews,* 126-29, argues cogently that "main point" means the "crown" of the pastor's argument, what he has been coming to and what he will develop in the following section.

3. See Weiss, 431, n. 10, citing Braun, 227, concerning ἐπὶ τοῖς λεγομένοις, "of

that we have a High Priest who has sat down at God's right hand is the conclusion of what has gone before. Its significance will be explained in chapters 8 through 10. It is at the core of the author's pastoral purpose: he would have his hearers avail themselves fully of this High Priest "we have" (compare 4:14-16; 10:19-25 with 8:1) so that they might persevere in faith.[4] By his depiction of both the benefits of Christ's high priesthood (10:19-25) and the perils of its neglect (10:26-39), the pastor would move his hearers from the disobedience described in 3:7–4:11 to the faithful endurance depicted in 11:1-40.[5]

1 It should be no surprise that the weight of the phrase "Now we have such a High Priest" falls on the following relative clause, "who has sat down at the right hand of the throne of the Majesty in the heavens."[6] From the third verse of the first chapter the pastor has been preparing for the time when he would be able to openly proclaim the high-priestly significance of God's invitation, recorded in Ps 110:1, for the Son to sit down at his right hand. By attributing the Son's session to his "making purification for sins" (1:3) he has already anticipated its priestly character. Furthermore, Ps 110:4, introduced in 5:5-6 and expounded in 7:1-28, has provided Scriptural substantiation for the priestly nature of the heavenly session described in Ps 110:1.[7]

The pastor has also clarified the identity of this High Priest who has sat down in heavenly authority. After all, it was the eternal Son of 1:1-2 who "sat down at the right hand of the Majesty in the highest" according to 1:3. The series of quotations in chapter 1 began with the eternal Son of Ps 2:7// 2 Sam 7:14 and concluded with that Son seated at God's right hand according to Ps 110:1. Ps 110:4 not only demonstrated the priestly nature of his session but proved that the "priest after the likeness of Melchizedek" was effective because he was the eternal Son of God.

---

the things being said." Unfortunately O'Brien, 287-88, emphasizes the way in which 8:1-2 introduces what follows to the neglect of how these verses tie what follows to what has gone before. See the introduction to Heb 4:14–10:18 on pp. 218-20 above.

4. See Weiss, 428-29.

5. *Pace* Koester, 375, Bénétreau, 2:52, and others who would make Christ's high priesthood the main theme of only the central section of Hebrews. Those who hold this position fail to grasp its significance for the author's overall pastoral purpose.

6. τοιοῦτον ("such") is probably correlative with ὅς ("who"). See Attridge, 217; Westcott, 213; and Spicq, 2:234. See also the comments on 7:26 above.

7. For a concise statement of the way Hebrews has used Ps 110:4 to interpret Ps 110:1 see Andrew T. Lincoln, "Hebrews and Biblical Theology," in *Out of Egypt: Biblical Theology and Biblical Interpretation,* ed. Craig Bartholomew et al. (Scripture and Hermeneutics Series 5; Grand Rapids: Zondervan, 2004), 317. Cf. Weiss, 431-32; George Guthrie, 279. Thus it is a bit misleading to say that the author "resumes" the theme of the Son's session (cf. Ellingworth, 400). All that he has been saying in chapter 7 enables him to explain the significance of the Son's session (cf. Lane, 1:200ab).

Thus when the pastor says, "We have such a High Priest who has sat down at the right hand of the throne of the Majesty in the heavens," he assumes his hearers have grasped the priestly character of this session and the eternal sonship of the one who has sat down. However, they still await with anticipation the pastor's explanation of how the Son's self-offering was the means of his heavenly session as all-sufficient High Priest. In the following chapters the pastor will develop the many hints that he has already provided. That most seminal verse, Heb 1:3, spoke of Christ "making purification for sins." According to Heb 2:5-18, Psalm 8 showed the necessity of the Son's identification with humanity and subsequent death for his session and for the efficacy of his priesthood. Heb 5:1-3, 7-10 put the Son's human obedience and suffering in contrast to the sacrifice of Aaron. Finally, Heb 7:27-28 has just announced that this High Priest has "offered himself" "once for all" and subsequently "been perfected forever." The pastor is now ready to explain the climactic and pivotal significance of the exalted Son's self-offering through which he has become the "Source of eternal salvation" (5:9) to all who heed him.

Thus the "High Priest who has sat down at the right hand of the throne of the Majesty in the heavens" is not a reference limited to exaltation or session. It is a comprehensive description of the present reality available for the faithful: the one who is seated in the place of all authority as the only effective High Priest is the eternal Son who achieved his position by offering his obedient, incarnate life up in death as an effective sacrifice for the sins of humanity. The pastor's burden is for his hearers to realize that this is the High Priest "we have" (4:14-16; 10:19-25) and to appropriate his benefits. Thus the pastor is guilty of no exaggeration when he says that this High Priest is the "main point" of his message.

Note the pastor's increased emphasis on the exalted place of the Son's session. In Ps 110:1 God invited the Son to "sit at my right hand." At the climax of the prologue the pastor insisted that the Son had sat down at the right hand "of the Majesty in the highest" (1:3). At this crucial point in his argument (8:1) he expands this description: the Son has sat down at the right hand "of the throne of the Majesty in the heavens." He does not add "throne" out of deference to contemporary speculations about a throne in the heavenly temple but in order to magnify the divine authority and sovereignty of the Son's position.[8] "In the heavens" underscores this exalted station because it is more emphatic than the singular "in heaven" would be. The pastor affirms the "main point" of his message with all of the intensity at his command. At

---

8. Cf. the use of "throne" in 1:8-9. Attridge, 217, provides a number of references from later literature in which the heavenly throne was a standard feature of the heavenly temple.

the same time he has carefully chosen these expressions to further other concerns. "In the heavens" anticipates the "heavenly" (v. 5) locus of the Son's high-priestly ministry affirmed in the next verse. "Throne" reminds his hearers that this "throne" has been made a "throne of grace" (4:16) for them through the one who has now sat down at its right. The pastor would ever draw his hearers' eyes to this High Priest at God's right hand because he is the only high priest able to meet their need (7:26-28).

2 In v. 2 the pastor draws a conclusion from the Son's high-priestly session that is important for his immediate argument as well as for the further development of his thought. Since the Son has sat down as High Priest at God's right hand, he can be called "minister of the Sanctuary and the true Tent that the Lord, and not any human being, has pitched." The term "minister" enhances the dignity and authority of this High Priest.[9] Both the LXX and other Jewish literature contemporary with Hebrews use this term and its cognates for priests or priestly service.[10] In the Hellenistic world "ministers" were "public servants" or benefactors who contributed to the community's well-being.[11] The priestly service of this "minister" provides untold benefit for the people of God by, as the following chapters will reveal, bringing them into the very Sanctuary in which he serves. As minister of the heavenly "Sanctuary" he is far above God's angelic "ministers" (1:7, 14) sent to do God's bidding.

The OT provides the foundation for identifying the heavenly dwelling place of God as the "true" Sanctuary replicated by the earthly Tent established by Moses (sometimes called the Tabernacle) or the Temple.[12] The Son's session at God's right as High Priest evokes this vista of heaven as the divine Sanctuary. The simplicity of Hebrews' vision shines by comparison to more elaborate ancient speculations. The OT itself may bear witness to the conception prevalent in antiquity that earthly temples were copies of the Uni-

---

9. The pastor omits the definite article before λειτουργός ("minister") in order to emphasize this High Priest's quality as "minister of the Sanctuary and true Tent." He shares this ministry with no other.

10. λειτουργός ("minister") is used of priests in Isa 61:6; Sir 7:30 and of those who serve in God's house but not necessarily as priests in Ezra 7:24; Neh 10:39 (40). For related uses of λειτουργεῖν ("to minister") see Exod 28:35; 39:30; and for λειτουργία ("ministry") see Exod 37:19; Num 8:22. For the use of λειτουργός for priests in literature roughly contemporary with Hebrews see *Letter of Aristeas* 95; *T. Levi* 2:10; 4:2; Philo, *Alleg. Interp.* 3.135; *Dreams* 2.231 (Attridge, 217, n. 16).

11. Johnson, 198.

12. Cf. Pss 11:4; 18:7; 29:9; Isaiah 6; Mic 1:2; Hab 2:20 (Riggenbach, 221). Riggenbach admits that much other literature enlarged and furnished this heavenly Sanctuary in many ways, but contends that Hebrews uses it only to explain the true heavenly high priesthood of Christ.

verse, which was the true Temple. The outer parts of the Tent may have represented earth and sky, while the Most Holy Place depicted the heavenly dwelling place of God.[13] Both Josephus and Philo accept this vision of the Universe as God's Temple.[14] Philo, however, develops it in his own Platonic way: the physical Universe is God's sanctuary accessible to the senses and a copy of his heavenly sanctuary that was accessible only to the mind.[15] There were also speculations in Second Temple Judaism that might suggest that the two-part earthly Tent was a copy of a two-part Tent Sanctuary in heaven.[16]

The pastor wastes no time indulging in speculations about the visible universe as the outer parts of God's Temple. Despite many protestations to

---

13. G. K. Beale, *The Temple and the Church's Mission: A Biblical Theology of the Dwelling Place of God* (New Studies in Biblical Theology 17; Downers Grove: InterVarsity Press, 2004), 29-59. See also Aelred Cody, *Heavenly Sanctuary and Liturgy in the Epistle to the Hebrews* (St. Meinrad, IN: Grail Publications, 1960), 9-46, who argues that the idea of a heavenly Sanctuary is Semitic in origin.

14. In *Ant.* 3.123 (cf. 180-81) Josephus calls the Tabernacle an "imitation and representation of the cosmos" (εἰς ἀπομίμησιν καὶ διατυπῶσιν τῶν ὅλων). Philo describes the Universe as the Temple of God in "the highest and truest sense" with heaven as its sanctuary, the stars as its votive offerings, and the angels as its priests. God has also ordained the one Temple made "with hands" as a place of worship (*Spec. Laws* 1.66-67). Thus Philo can give parts of the Temple cosmic significance. For instance, the material for the veil, curtain, and covering represents the four elements of the universe (earth, air, fire, water) in *Moses* 2.88. He says some hold the Cherubim to be the two hemispheres, but he prefers to understand them as God's creative and kingly power (*Moses* 2.98). However, in *Cherubim* 23–26 he understands the Cherubim before the gate of the Garden of Eden as the two hemispheres. The candlesticks are the sun, and the lights are the planets (*Moses* 2.102-3).

15. Thus, in *Planting* 50 the whole world is God's sanctuary "in the realm of sense perception," a copy of the original and made ὑπὸ χειρῶν θεοῦ ("by the hands of God"). Again in *Heir* 75 Philo refers to two sanctuaries, the world represented by the sense-perceived order and the world discovered by the mind. In *Dreams* 1.185-87 he clarifies the relationship between these two "sanctuaries." The sensible world, as God's "house," is the "gate" of the true "heaven" because, by contemplating this sensible world, one's mind can comprehend the eternal forms that constitute that true "heaven." There is nothing about the Tabernacle in these references. However, in *Prelim. Studies* 116–17, the Tabernacle is, in line with the above references, representative of both the world of our senses and of a house perceived by the mind. In *QE* 2.90-96 he appears to take a different approach, though the text is not always clear. The inner part of the Tabernacle represents the invisible world perceived only by the mind, and the outer part represents the world perceived by the senses. This last usage is hardly "Philo's favorite temple symbolism," as claimed by George W. MacRae, "Heavenly Temple and Eschatology in the Letter to the Hebrews," *Semeia* 12 (1978): 185. On the relationship between Heb 8:1-5 and Philo see Mackie, *Eschatology and Exhortation,* 158-64, and Williamson, *Philo and Hebrews,* 142-46, 157-59, 557-65.

16. See *1 En.* 14:10-20 and *T. Levi* 3:2-4 (Attridge, 222) and the Qumran references cited by MacRae, "Heavenly Temple," 183-84. Cf. Mitchell, 160-62.

the contrary, he has little in common with Philo. The Sanctuary of Hebrews is not a heavenly sanctuary of eternal ideas perceived only by the mind through contemplation of the visible universe or the earthly Tent. The pastor speaks of the "place" of God's presence already entered by the incarnate and exalted Son, who gives entrance to all who persevere through faith and obedience. Unlike Philo, Hebrews never refers to the physical world using Tent imagery.

Many have suggested that the pastor's use of both "Sanctuary" and "Tent" betrays affinity with those who understood the earthly Tent as a copy of a two-part Tent in heaven.[17] According to this interpretation, the "Sanctuary" is the Most Holy Place entered only by the high priest and the "true Tent" is the whole structure encompassing both the outer Holy Place and the inner Most Holy Place. However, the larger context in Hebrews suggests that the "true Tent" and "the Sanctuary" refer to the same reality.[18] Contemporary examples of speculation about a two-part heavenly Temple are vague and show little connection with Hebrews.[19]

"The Sanctuary" is the primary expression the pastor uses to describe the place Christ has entered as High Priest on our behalf. The interpreter who would understand Hebrews must carefully note the two ways in which the pastor identifies this place. First, "the Sanctuary" is "heaven itself" (9:24). This assertion alone would appear to exclude a two-part Temple in heaven.[20] Second, this "Sanctuary" is clearly "the Most Holy Place" of God's presence

17. Attridge, 218, 222-23; Michel, 310-11; Sabourin, *Priesthood,* 199-203; Hofius, *Vorhang,* 56-57; Nissilä, *Hohepriestermotiv,* 156-57; Loader, *Sohn und Hoherpriester,* 163; Albert Vanhoye, "'Par la tente plus grande et plus parfaite (He 9:11),'" *Bib* 46 (1965): 4; and P. Andriessen, "Das grössere und vollkommenere Zelt (Hebr. 9,11)," *BZ* 15 (1971): 87-88.

18. So O'Brien, 288, n. 10. However, *pace* Lane, 1:200-201e, and others, the use of the feminine singular ἥν ("which") in reference to the feminine singular σκηνῆς ("Tent," "Tabernacle") is no argument for the identity of "Tent" (σκηνῆς) and "Sanctuary" (τῶν ἁγίων). Verse 2 would be as grammatically appropriate if the "Tent" included the "Sanctuary" as it would be if the two were identical. See Attridge, 218, n. 22.

19. As noted above, Attridge, 222, mentions *1 En.* 14:10-20 and *T. Levi* 3:2-4. However, in the first, though Enoch sees a two-house complex, outer and inner, with God on the throne in the inner, it is not called a Temple. In *The Testament of Levi* there is a lower heaven where angels dwell and a higher in which they exercise a priestly ministry in God's presence. Neither of these clearly depicts a two-part heavenly sanctuary as a model for the earthly. Several Qumran documents appear to describe a Tabernacle in heaven with an angelic liturgy but without clearly distinguishing the Holy Place from the Most Holy Place. See MacRae, "Heavenly Temple," 183-84.

20. It is very difficult to believe, as MacRae, "Heavenly Temple," 186-88, would assert, that the pastor is thinking of the earthly Tabernacle as a copy of a multipart heavenly Sanctuary in 9:23 and then of heaven itself as the Sanctuary in 9:24.

"behind the veil" (6:19).[21] Thus the Tent into which Christ has entered consists only of a Most Holy Place which is heaven itself. This interpretation is confirmed by the fact that Hebrews offers no conceivable purpose for a heavenly "Holy Place" anterior to a heavenly Most Holy Place.[22] According to 9:1-10, the ritual conducted in the Holy Place of the earthly Mosaic Tent demonstrated the impossibility of access to God under the old system. Once the Son has entered the very presence of God, there could be no purpose for such a preliminary compartment of the heavenly Tent.[23] Thus Hebrews employs the term "Sanctuary" in accord with its most common LXX usage to describe the whole Tent/Temple.[24] However, this Temple, in which God truly dwells, is "heaven itself" and consists of naught but a Most Holy Place.

Preoccupation with the above question has obscured the pastor's real reason for introducing this topic by joining these two terms. He often uses pairs of words for rhetorical effect.[25] In this instance he employs both terms

21. See τὰ ἅγια or the genitive τῶν ἁγίων, "Sanctuary," for the heavenly Most Holy Place in 8:2; 9:12, 24; and 10:19. The same term is used in 9:25 and 13:10 for the Most Holy Place entered by the Aaronic high priest in contrast to the heavenly Most Holy Place.

22. Some argue that "through a greater and more perfect Tabernacle" in 9:11 is a reference to an outer compartment of the heavenly Temple. However, the very elusiveness of this statement only reinforces the fact that an outer part of the heavenly Sanctuary plays no part in the thought of Hebrews. See Riggenbach, 220-21. According to Riggenbach, any seeming distinction between an outer and inner part of the heavenly Sanctuary in 9:11 is more of "word" than of "fact" (221). See the further discussion on 9:11 below.

23. Hughes's comment (289) is compelling: "In fact, throughout these chapters our author's perspective does not include the concept of a holy place above, as distinct from the holy of holies, precisely because, now that the curtain between the two has been abolished and the way opened up by him [Christ] for all into the heavenly holy of holies which is the sanctuary of God's presence, the distinction no longer exists."

24. A. P. Salom, "Ta Hagia in the Epistle to the Hebrews," AUSS 5 (1967): 60-61, has analyzed the 170 times ἅγια/ἅγιον, "Sanctuary," is used for the Tabernacle or Temple in the Greek OT. In 142 instances this term refers to the Tabernacle/Temple as a whole. More than two thirds of these 142 are in the plural, ἅγια, as in Hebrews. When the term is used specifically of either the outer Holy Place or inner Most Holy Place, it is usually singular, as in the Leviticus 16 description of the Day of Atonement (Lev 16:2, 3, 16, 17, 20, 23, 27). See Salom, "Ta Hagia," 62. According to Cosaert, the usage of ἅγια in Second Temple literature conforms to LXX usage (Carl P. Cosaert, "The Use of ἅγιος for the Sanctuary in the Old Testament Pseudepigrapha, Philo, and Josephus," AUSS 42 [2004]: 91-103). His findings show that ἅγια is used 44 times in this body of literature for the Sanctuary as a whole but never, by itself, for the Most Holy Place. Twenty-four of these occurrences are found in Josephus's account of the Jewish war for independence.

25. Koester, 376, reminds us that Hebrews likes to use pairs of words: compare "transgression and disobedience," 2:2; "glory and honor," 2:9; "grace and mercy," 4:16; "gifts and sacrifices," 5:1; 8:3; "ignorant and erring," 5:2; "prayers and supplications," 5:7; and "faith and perseverance," 6:12; with "the Sanctuary and true Tabernacle," 8:2.

because each makes a distinct contribution to the following argument. "Sanctuary" designates the place entered as the very presence of the holy God of Israel.[26] This term was commonly used in the LXX to distinguish both the Tent and Temple of the true God from pagan shrines described by more customary words for "temple."[27] On the other hand, "Tent" provides an opportunity for asserting the superiority of this heavenly Sanctuary by contrasting it with the OT "Tent" established as the place of worship by Moses. The fact that the pastor must qualify "tent" when referring to the heavenly reality — "true" Tent (8:1); "greater and more perfect" Tent (9:11) — shows that its primary referent is the Mosaic structure.[28] We might say that "Sanctuary" is a close-up of the inside entered by Christ; "Tent" is a wide-angle photograph of the outside for comparison with the Mosaic pattern.[29]

The term "true" before "Tent" anticipates the pastor's initiation of this contrast with the Mosaic shrine in v. 5 below. Furthermore, this "Tent," which was "pitched" by no human being but by the Lord himself, is certainly superior to the tent pitched by Moses.[30] "True" does not condemn the Mosaic Tent as "false."[31] Nor does it identify this "Tent" with Philo's invisible heavenly sanctuary accessible only to the mind.[32] This "Tent" described in Hebrews is "true" because it is the place where the salvation accomplished by Christ brings eternal fellowship with God.[33] The Mosaic Tent which, although it may have anticipated, did not effect God's promised salvation, was only a transient sketch of this heavenly Tent.

Thus, Westcott was correct both (1) to recognize a difference in the

---

26. Cf. 9:12, 24, 25; 10:19; 13:11.

27. Compare τὰ ἅγια/τὸ ἅγιον with ἱερόν ("temple") and ναός ("temple," "sanctuary"). See Salom, *"Ta Hagia,"* 64 and cf. Koester, 375.

28. See ἀληθινῆς ("true") in 8:2 and μείζονος καὶ τελειοτέρας ("greater and more perfect") in 9:11. σκηνή without a qualifying adjective is used for the Mosaic Tent in 8:5; 9:8, 21; and 13:10. The pastor also uses σκηνή with the meaning of "tents" in 11:9 to describe the transitory earthly dwelling place of the patriarchs in contrast to their permanent home in the "city with foundations" made by God. Cf. Riggenbach, 220-21.

29. Bénétreau, 2:53, is not far off when he suggests that the first, τῶν ἁγίων, "sanctuary," emphasizes the nearness to God described in v. 1 and the second, σκηνή, "tabernacle," anticipates this High Priest's sacrifice.

30. God "pitched" the tents of Israel in Num 24:6, and the "heavens" (sometimes thought of as a "tent") in Isa 42:5. Noted in Koester, 376.

31. Contrast the Gospel of John where "truth" is the opposite of falsehood (John 8:32); the "true" light, of darkness (John 1:9); and the "true" God, of a false god (John 17:3).

32. Philo calls the sanctuary that is the world of ideas the "truly" (ἀληθῶς) invisible order in *Heir* 75. This is the closest he comes to calling this invisible sanctuary "true" (*Planting* 50; *Dreams* 1.185-87; *Prelim. Studies* 116–17).

33. Lane, 1:206.

connotation of "Sanctuary" and "Tent," and (2) to deny any "local distinction" in the heavenly reality to which they refer.[34] The pastor's effective use of these terms depends both on their diverse connotations and their common referent.

This understanding of "Sanctuary" and "Tent" both confirms and is confirmed by our structural analysis of this "symphony" (8:1–10:18). The use of "Tent" in 8:2 anticipates the frequent use of this word to describe the inadequacy of the old "Tent" in the Sanctuary section of the second movement (9:1-10). On the other hand, the Sanctuary section of the third movement, 9:23-24, defines the "Sanctuary" as "heaven itself." This identification is anticipated by the way in which the Greek text of Heb 8:1 ends with "in the heavens" and 8:2 begins with "of the Sanctuary."[35]

b. A Different Sacrifice (8:3-6)

3 *For every high priest is established to offer gifts and sacrifices. Therefore it was necessary for this one to have something to offer.* 4 *Now if he were on earth, he would not be a priest at all, because there are those who offer gifts according to the law.* 5 *They minister in a pattern and shadow of the heavenly, as Moses was solemnly commanded when he was about to complete the Tent: For he said, "See that you make all according to the copy shown you on the mountain."* 6 *But now this High Priest has obtained a ministry that is as much superior to theirs as the covenant of which he is Mediator is better, a covenant that has been legitimately established on better promises.*

Sacrifice was such an integral part of Temple worship that mention of the Son's ministry in the "true Tent" led naturally to consideration of his self-offering in sacrificial terms.

3 The pastor has stated his major premise in vv. 1-2: the Son has been installed as High Priest in the heavenly Sanctuary at God's right hand. In v. 3 he introduces his minor premise: "For every high priest is appointed to offer gifts and sacrifices." The first premise is based on Ps 110:1 and 4; the second is inherent in the biblical definition of high priesthood (see 5:1). Thus, the pastor does not offer his hearers gratuitous speculation but biblical

34. Westcott, 214. See also Riggenbach, 220-31; Moffatt, 105; Spicq, 2:234; Michel, 288; Hughes, 289; Lane, 1:200e; Ellingworth, 402.
35. See ἐν τοῖς οὐρανοῖς, τῶν ἁγίων λειτουργός, literally, "in the heavens, of the Sanctuary a Minister." With ἐν τοῖς οὐρανοῖς ("in the heavens") in 8:1 compare ἐν τοῖς οὐρανοῖς ("in the heavens"), τὰ ἐπουράνια ("the heavenly things") and αὐτὸν τὸν οὐρανόν ("heaven itself") in 9:23-24.

interpretation. "Gifts and sacrifices" anticipates the repetitive and thus ineffective sacrificial ministry of the Aaronic high priests (9:28–10:4).[1]

With "therefore it was necessary" the pastor introduces two conclusions from these premises:[2] a preliminary conclusion in v. 3b, and a more comprehensive conclusion in vv. 4-5. According to v. 3b, if the Son is a High Priest and high priests offer sacrifice, then "it was necessary for this one to have something that he might offer." "Something" is intentionally general.[3] The pastor establishes the fact of Christ's offering without describing its superior quality. Yet he anticipates its once-for-all character (9:25–10:4) by using a singular noun ("something") and an aorist verb ("that he might offer") in contrast to the present tense of repeated action appropriate for other high priests.[4] This "something" will be described in the second movement as offering "himself without blemish to God" (9:14) and in the third as "the offering of the body of Jesus Christ once for all" (10:10).[5]

4-5 The pastor's second deduction points even more clearly toward the superiority of this sacrifice. "This one" is not only a High Priest; he is High Priest in the "heavenly" Sanctuary. Therefore, the sacrifice he offers

1. See on δῶρά τε καὶ θυσίας ("gifts and sacrifices") in 5:1.

2. Compare ὅθεν ("therefore") in 8:3 with 2:17; 3:1; 9:18; and esp. 7:25. Six of the fifteen NT occurrences of this word are in Hebrews. Compare ἀναγκαῖον ("necessary") with ἐξ ἀνάγκης ("of necessity") in 7:12 and ἀνάγκη ("necessity") in 9:23. These terms underscore the logical and rhetorical nature of the pastor's argument.

3. Thus, the pastor does not intend his readers to fill this "something" with content. Riggenbach, 222-23, is overly subtle in his insistence that this "something" does not refer to Christ's death per se but to his self-presentation in the heavenly Sanctuary that validated his self-offering in death. Spicq, 2:235, seems to have a similar view. In light of the further developments in 9:11-14 and 10:5-10, it is unnecessary to insist that this sacrifice had to take place "in" the heavenly Sanctuary. It pertained to the heavenly Sanctuary and brought about Christ's entrance as high-priestly representative of his people.

4. Koester, 377; Lane 1:201-2; cf. Hughes, 291; Bruce 182, n. 20; Bénétreau, 2:54, n. 1. Compare the aorist of προσενέγκῃ ("that he might offer") with the present προσφέρειν ("to offer").

5. Vanhoye contends that "to offer gifts and sacrifices" (8:3) and "gifts and sacrifices are offered" (9:9) stand in contrast to "he offered himself" (9:14) and "offer himself" (9:25). He uses these observations to support his theory that 8:1–9:10 is chiastically parallel to 9:11-28 (Vanhoye, *La structure littéraire,* 139). However, the progress from "something" to "himself" to "the body of Christ," outlined above, is more significant for grasping the pastor's thought. The pastor also indicates the crescendoing nature of his argument by the way he refers to Christ in the sacrifice section of each movement. Compare no designation for Christ in 8:3-6 with "Christ" (9:11)//"the blood of Christ" (9:14) in 9:11-15 and "Christ" (9:28)//"through the offering of the body of Christ" (10:10) in 9:25–10:14. For critique of the way Vanhoye uses the names of Jesus in this section to support his chiastic structure see Cockerill, "Structure and Interpretation in Hebrews 8:1–10:18," 184, n. 22.

must be appropriately different from those offered in the earthly sanctuary, and his ministry must be of a superior order. The pastor carries forward the logic of his argument with a condition contrary to fact: "Now if he were on earth [instead of in the heavenly Sanctuary], he would not be a priest at all [much less a high priest], because there are those who offer gifts according to the law." "Gifts" evokes "gifts and also sacrifices" from v. 3 (cf. 5:1), yet the use of this word alone without a coordinating "sacrifices" may reflect the inferior nature of the sacrifices given in the Mosaic Tent. In chapter 7 (see esp. 7:11-12, 18-19) the pastor has already shown the ineffectiveness of the priestly ministry that was "according to the law."

5a The pastor would illuminate the magnitude of this heavenly High Priest and his all-sufficient ministry. To achieve this end he affirms both the inferiority of those priests who "ministered in a pattern and shadow of the heavenly" and their positive function as precursors of the heavenly High Priest. On the one hand, every word underscores the inferiority of their ministry. The term for "ministered" distinguishes these priests from the great "minister" of the "Sanctuary and true Tent" described in v. 2.[6] Taken together, "pattern and shadow" underscore the derivative and merely symbolic nature of the earthly Tent.[7] "Of the heavenly" implies "of the heavenly Sanctuary." Omission of this last word, however, allows the emphasis to fall on the "heavenly" character of this Sanctuary and thus exposes the solely representative character of its ephemeral copy. The pastor will show how this ministry was ineffective when he describes the earthly Tent and its rituals in 9:1-10. The inability of the old to remove sin only anticipates and highlights the all-sufficiency of the new.

Moreover, the terms "pattern and shadow" also affirm the positive function of the old as outline or blueprint of the "heavenly." The term translated "pattern" never means "copy," but is always the "pattern" from which

---

6. The pastor uses the verb λατρεύω for the "ministry" of earthly priests here in 8:5, and also in 9:6 and 13:10. He employs this term for the worship of Old Covenant people in 10:2, and uses the related noun, λατρεία, for the worship of the old Tabernacle in 9:1. Although he can use λατρεύω for the worship of New Covenant people (9:14; 12:28), he never uses it for the ministry of Christ. On the other hand, Hebrews never dignifies the priests of the earthly Tabernacle by calling them λειτουργοί, "ministers," the term used for Christ in 8:2, or by describing their ministry as λειτουργία (8:6). See Ellingworth, 406. The reserving of λειτουργός for Christ owes something to the dignity associated with this word in the Hellenistic world (see p. 352, nn. 9, 10, and esp. 11) and cannot be adequately explained by reference to the LXX, as Weiss, 432, n. 16, would contend. The very fact that λατρεύω is similar in meaning to λειτουργέω, the verb cognate with λειτουργός (Koester, 377), makes this distinction in usage significant.

7. However, the positive function of these terms described below is obscured if we take them as a hendiadys, "shadowy sketch," as Lane, 1:201i, suggests.

something else is made.[8] The pastor's use of "shadow" for the anticipation of the new in 10:1 confirms the anticipatory character given to this term in the immediate context by association with "pattern."[9] This is no "pattern" of eternal ideas or "shadow" of a timeless ministry that has always gone on in the heavenly Sanctuary. This "pattern and shadow" anticipated the ministry inaugurated by the exaltation of the Son and now available for God's people.[10] With the words "pattern and shadow" the conductor anticipates the next movement of his symphony in which he will reveal how this "pattern" points to its fulfillment and reveals its own shadowy inadequacy (9:1-14).

5b The pastor knows that the Mosaic Tent was a "pattern and shadow" on the basis of Exod 25:40. Just as Gen 14:17-24 brought clarity to Ps 110:4 in Heb 7:1-10, so Exod 25:40 sheds light on this extended exposition of Ps 110:1. To properly understand the Son's high-priestly session in the heavenly Tent the pastor must probe the nature of the OT Tent. If one would understand the old Tent, one must examine the Scriptural account of God's instructions for its assembly. Thus, the pastor turns to the time when "Moses was about to construct the Tent." Moses was "solemnly instructed" by God in Exod 25:40: "see that you make all according to the copy given you on the mountain."[11] Both the inferior nature of the old Tent and its anticipation of Christ's ministry were established by God's solemn instruction to Moses.[12] The pastor probably adds "all" from the preceding verse, Exod 25:39. By this addition he anticipates the way he will use the details of the old Tent and its ritual in 9:1-14 to demonstrate both its inferiority and the way in which it an-

---

8. L. D. Hurst, "How 'Platonic' Are Heb. Viii. 5 and Ix. 23f.?" *JTS* 34 (1983): 157-63. Cf. BDAG, 1037. Weiss, 436; Braun, 232; and Thompson, *Christian Philosophy*, 106, overlook the full connotation of the word ὑπόδειγμα ("pattern") when they assume that it only denigrates the earthly sanctuary. Hebrews' use of this word is not influenced by Philo. Philo uses ὑποδείγμα only four times. In three of these instances he uses it in the sense of a moral example (*Posterity* 122 is the only exception). See Hurst, "'Platonic,'" 157.

9. "Shadow" was widely used by contemporaries in a general and nontechnical sense (Hurst, "'Platonic,'" 163-64).

10. Williamson, *Philo and Hebrews*, 157-59; L. D. Hurst, *The Epistle to the Hebrews: Its Background of Thought* (SNTSMS 65; Cambridge: Cambridge University, 1990), 13-17.

11. The word translated "copy" (τύπον) is not used here as a technical term and thus should not be translated "type." Riggenbach, 225, says that v. 5b can substantiate v. 5a only if τύπος here means something like "copy" or "model." The "copy" that Moses saw was constituted a pattern for his work by the fact that he was told to copy it (Ellingworth, 408).

12. Lane (1:201j) calls κεχρημάτισται ("solemnly instructed") a "narrative perfect," but this perfect emphasizes the lasting relevance of the warning. None should consider the Tabernacle either more or less than a "copy and shadow."

ticipated the work of Christ.[13] As "pattern and shadow" "the tabernacle was a rough reminiscence intended to suggest the idea of the original and to train the people of God to appreciate the heavenly reality itself."[14] Thus "pattern and shadow" underscore both the insufficiency of the old as a means of salvation and its typological character as anticipation of the new.

A comparison of the ways in which Philo and Hebrews explain Exod 25:40 exposes the great difference in their approaches to Scripture. They have little in common beyond the fact that both use this verse when discussing the nature of the Mosaic Tent and its relationship to the heavenly reality upon which it was patterned.[15] As indicated above, Philo understood the heavenly world of ideas perceivable only to the mind as the Temple of God. Thus, in Exod 25:40 God instructed Moses to reproduce in sensible form this pattern of ideas accessible only through contemplation (*Moses* 2.74-75).[16] By contemplating the Tent one could comprehend this world of ideas. Philo provides several examples of how the Tent revealed this world inaccessible to the five senses. According to *Drunkenness* 132–33, the inner sanctuary of the Mosaic Tent which none but the high priest could see represented divine virtue, while the altar, which all could see, represented human virtue as a copy of the divine.[17] According to *Heir* 112–13, the whole Tent was an image of

---

13. See also Exod 25:9; 26:30; and 27:8. Cf. Num 8:4. D'Angelo, *Moses*, 205-22, and deSilva, 282, suggest that the pastor has included "all" because the details of the old priestly system foreshadow fulfillment in Christ. They fail to adequately note the use of these details for demonstrating the ineffectiveness of the old order.

14. Lane, 1:206.

15. *Pace* Moffatt, xxxiii-xxxiv; Héring, 66; Sowers, *Hermeneutics,* 107. See Ronald Williamson, "Platonism and Hebrews," *SJT* 16 (1963): 415-24; Williamson, *Philo and Hebrews,* 142-46; Ellingworth, 408; and especially the extended discussion in Hughes, 293-95. Gilbert claims that Exod 25:40 in Heb 8:5 was "a happy opening by which the Platonic speculation enters our epistle" (G. H. Gilbert, "The Greek Element in the Epistle to the Hebrews," *American Journal of Theology* 14 [1910]: 528, cited in deSilva, 283). If so, very little speculation took advantage of this "opening."

16. One might say there were three "Temples" in Philo: the world of ideas perceived only by the mind, the world accessible to the senses, and the Tabernacle. See references and discussion in nn. 14 and 15 on p. 353. The Tabernacle was an image of both of these other "Temples" (*Prelim. Studies* 116–17). Thus, Philo could allegorize the parts of the Tabernacle as parts of the cosmos perceptible to the senses. However, in his discussion of Exod 25:40, it is the Tabernacle's role as a concrete copy of the world of ideas that is in view.

17. *Pace* Attridge, 223, n. 95, this distinction between "altar" (βωμός) and inner "tabernacle" (σκηνή) is hardly support for a two-part heavenly Sanctuary in Hebrews. *Worse* 160–61 shows how natural it was for Philo to allegorize the Tabernacle as human and divine "virtue." In this passage the Tabernacle (σκηνή) of Witness (Exod 33:7) set up outside the camp represents human virtue (ἀνθρώπου ἀρετή) as a copy of divine virtue (τῆς θείας ἐκείνης).

wisdom. Philo does not use Exod 25:40 to assert the inferiority of the earthly Tent but to affirm its usefulness as a means of contemplating the world of ideas. This role for the Tent does not antiquate its rituals nor preclude one from participation in their performance.

The author of Hebrews shows no affinity for the approach followed by Philo. The Tent is no copy of the world of ideas.[18] Rather, it prefigures the "place" of God's presence that Christ has entered and the heavenly high-priestly ministry upon which he has embarked. Moreover, it reveals its own inadequacy as a means of approaching God (see 9:1-10). Thus, continued participation in the old Tent's services would be a denial of Christ's sufficiency. In summary, the Tent provides no help in comprehending an ethereal world of ideas but enables the pastor to explain the all-sufficient saving work of Christ.

6 The pastor brings the argument of vv. 3-5 to its conclusion and then supports that conclusion with Jeremiah's prophecy of the New Covenant in vv. 7-13.[19] Verse 6a contrasts with v. 4: "Now if he were on earth, he would not be a priest at all" (v. 4). "But now" in these last days when God has fulfilled his promises, the Son "has obtained" a "superior ministry" (v. 6a) appropriate for the heavenly Sanctuary.[20] The excellency of this ministry grows clearer with each succeeding movement of this symphony. All that the pastor says about the inadequacy of the old is counterpoint for the excellency of the new.[21]

The word translated "has obtained" suggests the "achievement, success, and victory" through which Christ has entered upon this "more excellent" high-priestly ministry by the sacrificial offering of himself.[22] This ministry is ever available to enable the perseverance of those who appropriate it by drawing near to God through this High Priest.

What is the difference between a high-priestly ministry appropriate

---

18. Nor is it a copy of the Universe.

19. Vanhoye, *La structure littéraire,* 140-41, identifies "minister" (λειτουργός) in v. 2 and "ministry" (λειτουργίας) in v. 6a as an inclusion. By introducing vv. 7-13 in support of v. 6a, v. 6b provides a smooth transition between these sections (Koester, 378).

20. The δέ of v. 6 sets up a contrast with the μέν of v. 4. See Lane, 1:208 (cf. Ellingworth, 409). This contrast shows that v. 6 should be joined to vv. 3-5. Furthermore, νυνὶ δέ ("but now") is inferential (Hughes, 295), indicating that v. 6a is the logical conclusion of vv. 3-5. However, νυνί ("now") is also temporal (Koester, 378; Bénétreau, 2:57-58; and Ellingworth, 408-9): Christ has obtained this "most excellent ministry" in these "final days" (1:2; cf. 9:26) of fulfillment. This is the priest we "now" have.

21. Vanhoye, *La structure littéraire,* 139, 143-44, ignores the importance of v. 6 and thus misses the pastor's emphasis in this section on the excellency of Christ's priesthood. Thus he argues that 8:1–9:11 does nothing but demonstrate the inferiority of the old priesthood and sacrifice. See Gourgues, "Remarques," 29-30.

22. Hughes, 296, n. 16.

for the heavenly dwelling place of God and one confined to its earthly representation? To what degree is Christ's ministry superior to that of the OT Tent? The pastor answers in v. 6b: to the degree that "the covenant of which he is Mediator is better, a covenant which has been legitimately established on better promises."[23] This is no speculative answer about the relative values of the heavenly and the earthly. As the "Mediator" of the "better covenant" he provides the benefits described in the "better promises" of Jer 31:31-34 upon which this New Covenant is "legitimately established."[24] These benefits are the ultimate mark of the New Covenant's superiority.[25] They are so magnificent that further explanation must await the climax of this symphony in 10:15-18. Because the New Covenant provides these benefits — unobtainable through the Old — the New is "better," that is, effective.

The association of the terms "mediator" and "covenant" invites comparison with Moses (cf. 9:16-22). Because Moses established the Old Covenant, he was its "mediator" (Philo, *Moses* 2.166; cf. Heb 9:16-22). However, this heavenly High Priest is far superior to Moses. Not only has he established the New Covenant, but he also continues to make its benefits available. Thus he is not merely its "Mediator" but the "Guarantor" of its perpetual effectiveness (7:22).[26]

c. A Better Covenant (8:7-13)

7 *For if that first [covenant] had been blameless, there would have been no occasion for a second to be sought.* 8 *For finding fault with them he says: "Behold days are coming," says the Lord, "when I*

23. The clause which begins with ὅσῳ ("by how much") supports the previous clause: his ministry is superior to the degree that he has become "Mediator of a better covenant." Elsewhere in Hebrews ὅσος is always the supporting clause (1:4; 3:3; 7:20, 22; 10:25). Thus the NRSV is mistaken when it reverses the role of these clauses: "But Jesus has now obtained a more excellent ministry, and to that degree he is the mediator of a better covenant."

24. ἐπί followed by the dative case ἐπαγγελίαις ("promises") means "on the basis of" (BDF §235, 2; Gutbrod, "νομοθετέω," *TDNT* 4:1090; Lane, 1:201q). κρείττονος διαθήκης ("better covenant") and κρείττοσιν ἐπαγγελίαις ("better promises") have shorn νενομοθέτηται ("was legitimately established") of the negative overtones it received in 7:11 by association with νόμος ("law") and ἐντολή ("ordinance").

25. Spicq, 2:239, locates the superiority of these promises in their certainty, effected only through the work of Christ. However, their superiority is also in what they promise, their content, which the Old Covenant did not provide.

26. Bénétreau, 2:58; cf. Weiss, 441-42. Thus Christ is "Guarantor" because, as a result of his effective once-for-all self-sacrifice, he now sits at God's right hand mediating the New Covenant benefits. His ministry as "Guarantor" is not based on his having become the "Testator" of a "new will" or "testament," as suggested by Riggenbach, 227.

will complete a new covenant with the house of Israel and the house of Judah. 9 It will not be like the covenant that I made with their fathers in the day when I took them by the hand to lead them out of the land of Egypt; because they did not remain in my covenant, and so I showed no concern for them," says the Lord. 10 "For this is the covenant that I will covenant with the house of Israel after those days," says the Lord: "I will put my laws in their minds, and inscribe them upon their hearts; and I will be their God, and they shall be my people. 11 And they will not teach each his neighbor and each his brother, saying, 'Know the Lord,' because all shall know me, from the least unto the greatest of them. 12 For I will be merciful toward their unrighteous deeds, and their sins I will remember no more." 13 By saying "new" he makes the first obsolete. What is becoming obsolete and growing old is on the verge of passing away.

The pastor quotes these "better promises" from Jer 31:31-34 with no commentary beyond the introductory and concluding statements in Heb 8:7-8a and 13. This Jeremiah passage divides naturally into three parts — v. 31; v. 32; vv. 33-34.[1] In v. 31 (Heb 8:8) God announces that he is going to establish a "new" covenant. The rest of the passage clarifies the nature of this newness, first negatively (v. 32) and then positively (vv. 33-34). In v. 32 (Heb 8:9) God says that the New Covenant will not be like the one he made with his people when he brought them out of Egypt. Verses 33-34 (Heb 8:10-11) contain God's "better promises" that describe what the New Covenant will be like. It will overcome the sin problem that deterred God's people from persevering under the first covenant. With the thrice-repeated "says the Lord" Jeremiah makes it quite clear that these are the words of God himself. Hebrews concurs. Thus, God is the one who both finds fault with the Old Covenant and promises the New.[2] Hebrews shows no evidence of being influenced by or offering polemic against the view of the New Covenant held at Qumran (CD 6:19; 8:21; 9:33-34).[3]

It is these "better promises" of vv. 33-34 (Heb 8:10-11) that support

1. George Guthrie, 281-82.
2. Weiss, 445.
3. For the people of Qumran "to enter the new covenant" was equivalent to entering the Qumran community. Their "new covenant" was a restoration of the old, which included a renewed earthly Temple and ritual. No reference to Jer 31:31-34 has been found in their extant writings. See the excursus in Hughes, 303-4; cf. Bénétreau, 2:63-64; Bruce, 193-94; and Weiss, 446. The Last-Supper traditions recorded in Luke 22:20 and 1 Cor 11:25 also speak of a "new" covenant without reference to Jeremiah (cf. Weiss, 445-46). The pastor's use of Jer 31:31-34 is in full agreement with the way he uses other Scripture (see the discussion on pp. 45-46 in the Introduction to this commentary; cf. Weiss, 446).

the pastor's affirmation in Heb 8:6. They illuminate the superiority of the New Covenant and thus the fathomless magnitude of Christ's high-priestly ministry in the heavenly dwelling place of God. The pastor, however, postpones giving further attention to these promises until the conclusion of his symphony in 10:15-18. The intervening exposition of Christ's high-priestly ministry is his explanation that clarifies their significance.[4] Thus the tension created by introducing these promises is not released until the chords of this symphony find harmonious resolution in that concluding passage.

The pastor's immediate commentary in vv. 7-8a and 13 focuses on the inadequacy of the first covenant as evidenced by Jer 31:31-32, quoted in Heb 8:8-9. The opening comments in vv. 7-8a concentrate on the failure of the first covenant as described in v. 32 of the Jeremiah passage (Heb 8:9). The concluding remarks in v. 13 use the newness of the second covenant affirmed in v. 31 (Heb 8:8) as conclusive evidence for the antiquated nature of the old. Thus, with consummate skill the pastor uses "new" to form an inclusion around the whole passage (vv. 8, 13) and to bring home his intended message — the inferiority and outdated nature of the Old Covenant.[5]

7-8a   The pastor again avails himself of the contrary-to-fact condition so characteristic of his argument: "For if that first had been blameless, there would have been no occasion for a second to be sought."[6] In 7:11 the mere prophecy of a priest after Melchizedek's order demonstrated the inadequacy of the old. Here the divine promise of another covenant, apart from its fulfillment, proves that the Old is not "without blame." It is true that the pastor shows a preference for Greek words that begin with alpha-privative like the term translated "blameless" or "without blame."[7] It is also true that the Old's failure to be "blameless" will be augmented by the declaration in v. 13 that it is "obsolete." Furthermore, "blameless" is used in anticipation of "for finding fault with them he says" in v. 8a.[8] However, describing the Old Cov-

---

4. France, "Biblical Expositor," 259, 264-65; Joslin, *Law,* 190-92, esp. n. 68; 226-27; cf. G. B. Caird, "Exegetical Method of the Epistle to the Hebrews," *Canadian Journal of Theology* 5 (1959): 44-51, and Walters, "Rhetorical," 59-70; but *pace* Weiss, 446, and Grässer, 2:101.

5. Vanhoye, *La structure littéraire,* 143, is followed by many (cf. Bénétreau, 2:59) in noting this inclusion. *Pace* Riggenbach, 229, vv. 7-13 are no "excursus."

6. For contrary-to-fact conditions cf. 4:8; 7:11; 8:4, 7; 10:2; 11:15.

7. With ἄμεμπτος ("without blame") compare ἄκακος ("without evil") and ἀμίαντος ("without blemish") in 7:26; ἀπάτωρ, ἀμήτωρ, ἀγενεαλόγητος ("without father, without mother, without genealogy") in 7:3a; and ἀθέτησις, ἀσθενές, ἀνωφελές ("abolition," "weakness," "uselessness") in 7:18. The pastor's fondness for words beginning with alpha-privative matches his penchant for argument based on conditions contrary to fact.

8. The adjective ἄμεμπτος ("blameless") in v. 7 is cognate with the participle μεμφόμενος ("finding fault") in v. 8.

enant as not "blameless" is less forceful than the pastor's earlier denunciations of the old priesthood as incapable of providing "perfection" (7:11) and
as characterized by "weakness and uselessness" (7:18).[9] This difference
might be accounted for by the fact that the ineffectiveness of the old order
rested on the insufficiency of its priesthood.

Nevertheless, there may be another reason for this restraint in describing the inadequacy of the Old Covenant. The words with which the Jeremiah
passage is introduced, "for finding fault with them he says" (v. 8a), point directly to God's criticism of the wilderness generation in Jer 31:32 (Heb
8:9).[10] It is their failure that evidences the insufficiency of the Old Covenant.
The pastor would not describe the deficiency of the Old Covenant in such a
way as to relieve the wilderness generation of responsibility for their disobedience. It is not their inability to obey but their refusal to obey that demonstrates the insufficiency of the first covenant to adequately transform the human heart.[11] The faithful in 11:1-38 demonstrated the possibility of
obedience before Christ's advent even though they could not experience

---

9. Thus not "blameless" is, in this context, a way of restraining criticism of the
Old Covenant rather than, as Bénétreau, 2:59, has asserted, "a vigorous way of affirming
that the criticisms [of the Old Covenant] are justified."

10. Although the manuscript evidence is fairly evenly divided between the accusative αὐτούς and the dative αὐτοῖς, TCGNT, 597, gives the accusative a "B" rating as
"almost certainly correct" because it is the more difficult reading. Since the participle
μεμφόμενος, "finding fault," can take either the accusative or dative as object, there need
be no difference in meaning: μεμφόμενος γὰρ αὐτούς/αὐτοῖς λέγει, "for finding fault with
them, he says." On the other hand, the dative offers the possibility of taking αὐτοῖς,
"them," as the indirect object of λέγει: μεμφόμενος γὰρ αὐτοῖς λέγει, "for finding fault, he
says to them." Lane, 1:202s; Hughes, 298-99; Johannes L. P. Wolmarans, "The Text and
Translation of Hebrews 8:8," ZNW 75 (1984): 139-44, and others who accept the dative
as original, argue that this "finding fault" (μεμφόμενος) was not with the people but with
the covenant that, according to v. 7, was not "without blame" (ἄμεμπτος). However, desire for superficial logical consistency and the propensity to use a dative with λέγει ("he
says") probably account for the change from the accusative αὐτούς to the dative αὐτοῖς
(Attridge, 225, n. 2; cf. Ellingworth, 415). In fact, in the opening verses of the quotation
from Jeremiah God does "find fault," not with those to whom his speech is addressed but
with the wilderness generation (vv. 8-9). Furthermore, the pastor does not use a dative of
indirect object when introducing the words of Scripture elsewhere (2:6, 12; 3:7, 15; 4:3,
7; 6:14; 9:20; 10:5, 15; 12:5, 26; see Koester, 385). See the comments in the text above
for the significance of God's "finding fault" with the people rather than directly with the
Old Covenant. The accusative is to be preferred, but on either reading God is finding
fault directly with the people and thus only indirectly with the old way of approaching
God.

11. Note God's warning, "do not harden your hearts" (μὴ σκληρύνητε τὰς καρδίας
ὑμῶν, 3:8) as the wilderness generation did, for they "always go astray in heart" (ἀεὶ
πλανῶνται τῇ καρδίᾳ, 3:10).

cleansing from sin and reach their goal by entering God's presence apart from the fulfillment he would provide (11:39-40).

The following verses will show that the "occasion" for "seeking" or "desiring" a second was the failure of God's people to persevere under the first. The prophecy from Jeremiah shows that their gracious God is the one seeking such an occasion for a covenant that will overcome their disobedience.[12]

9 The "fathers" of God's people, with whom he made the first covenant, are to be identified with the "fathers" to whom his word was addressed of old (1:1-2). Since God made this covenant with them "in the day" of his "taking them by the hand to bring them out of Egypt," they can be none other than the rebellious wilderness generation described in 3:7–4:11. How gracious God was to take "them by the hand" and effect such a great deliverance. The Christian believers to whom Hebrews was addressed are their spiritual descendants, the present people of God.[13] The inadequacy of God's first covenant has been exposed by the fact that this privileged generation "did not remain" in it. These words encapsulate the continued rebellion that climaxed at Kadesh-Barnea. They poignantly express the pastor's concern: he wants his hearers to persevere in faith, to "remain" through the efficacy of a High Priest who "remains" (7:3, 24) in order to receive an eternal inheritance that "remains" (10:34; 12:27; 13:14). By implication, the promised New Covenant will be one that provides resources that enable his people to "remain." The last line of Jer 31:32 (Heb 8:9) summarizes the consequences suffered by that rebellious generation (cf. 3:16-19) with an understatement all the more ominous for its brevity: "and so I [God] showed no concern for them." Nothing could contrast more sharply with God's former deliverance through "taking them by the hand."[14]

This passage from Jeremiah provides an ideal transition between the pastor's warning against imitation of the disobedient wilderness generation in 3:7–4:11 and his exhortation to imitate the faithful in 11:1–12:3. While the disobedience of the former exposes the inadequacy of the Old Covenant (vv.

12. Literally, ἐζητεῖτο τόπος, "an occasion was being sought" by God (divine passive, Ellingworth, 412; cf. O'Brien, 296).

13. "God's words concern 'the house of Israel' and 'the house of Judah,' but Hebrews brings the oracle to bear on the listeners' situation, since they belong to God's 'house' (Heb 3:6)" (Koester, 389).

14. The LXX's "and so I showed no concern for them" (κἀγὼ ἠμέλησα αὐτῶν) differs from the standard translation of the Hebrew, which reads "for I was a husband to them" (Koester, 391). The pastor uses the same word when he says that God "showed no concern" (ἠμέλησα) for those who would not persevere that he used when warning his hearers against "neglecting" (ἀμελήσαντες) the "great salvation" (2:3) provided by Christ (Koester, 390). God will "show no concern" for those "neglecting" his provision.

8-9; Jer 31:31-32), the faithfulness of the latter anticipates the resources for obedience and fellowship with God available through Christ in the promised New Covenant (vv. 10-11; Jer 31:33-34). Even those faithful who lived before Christ will not "be made perfect" apart "from us" (11:39-40) and the fulfillment Christ has now achieved (12:1-3). Thus, those the pastor addresses have all the more reason to be faithful than the best examples he could muster from the OT era.

There is only one pair of variations from the standard LXX text of Jer 31:31-34 that may be significant.[15] Greek Jeremiah uses the usual word for "make" or "ordain" a covenant with reference to the New Covenant in Jer 31:31, 33 and the Old in 31:32. This word is cognate with the word "covenant" and so could be translated, "I will covenant a covenant."[16] However, Hebrews uses a stronger word for God's establishing the New Covenant in Jer 31:31 (Heb 8:8), and a weaker when speaking of his establishing the old in Jer 31:32 (Heb 8:9). According to v. 8, God will "accomplish," "fulfill," "perfect," or "complete" the New Covenant.[17] This expression is closely related to the pastor's favorite terms — "perfect" and "perfection."[18] On the

15. In the references below we have maintained the numbering of the Hebrew and English Old Testaments. However, in the LXX this New Covenant passage occurs in Jer 38:31-34 instead of 31:31-34. Hebrews substitutes λέγει ("he says") for its synonym φησίν ("he says") before κύριος each time it occurs — once each in Jer 31:31, 32, and 33 (Heb 8:8, 9, and 10). This substitution is not surprising since Hebrews normally uses λέγει for God's speaking (1:1-2, 6, 7; 2:5, 12; 3:15; 6:14; 7:21), but see φησίν in 8:5. Hebrews uses the compound κἀγώ ("and I") for the καὶ ἐγώ in Jer 31:32. Instead of the literal rendering of the Hebrew, διδοὺς δώσω ("putting I will put") in Jer 31:33, Hebrews has simply διδούς ("putting"). Hebrews has ἐπιγράψω ("I will write upon") in v. 10 for the simpler γράψω ("I will write") in Jer 31:33. Some manuscripts of Hebrews read γράψω, probably under the influence of the LXX text, and some of Jeremiah read ἐπιγράψω, perhaps influenced by Hebrews (Ellingworth, 417). Finally, Heb 8:11 abbreviates the ἀπὸ μικροῦ αὐτῶν καὶ ἕως μεγάλου αὐτῶν, "from the least of them even until the greatest of them" in Jer 31:34 to ἀπὸ μικροῦ ἕως μεγάλου αὐτῶν, "from the least until the greatest of them." For other variations in the manuscript tradition see Weiss, 445. These stylistic variations have no semantic significance.

16. Thus, in Jer 31:31 διαθήσομαι ("I will covenant") . . . διαθήκην ("a covenant").

17. συντελέσω ("I will fulfill or perfect") . . . διαθήκην ("a covenant"). The use of this word accounts for the change from Jeremiah's dative τῷ οἴκῳ Ισραηλ καὶ τῷ οἴκῳ Ιουδα, "with the house of Israel and the house of Judah" (Jer 31:31) to Hebrews' ἐπί with the accusative, ἐπὶ τὸν οἶκον Ἰσραὴλ καὶ ἐπὶ τὸν οἶκον Ἰούδα (Heb 8:8), without change of meaning.

18. Compare the word used here, συντελέσω ("I will fulfill, perfect"), with τελειόω ("to perfect") in 2:10; 5:9; 7:19; 9:9; 10:1, 14; 11:40; 12:23; τελείωσις ("perfection") in 7:11; εἰς τὸ παντελές ("to the uttermost," "completely") in 7:25; τελειωτής ("perfecter") in 12:2; and τέλος ("end") in 3:14; 6:8, 11; 7:3. Cf. Mitchell, 168; O'Brien, 297.

other hand, v. 9 uses the general word for "make" — not the "first covenant which I covenanted" but simply "the first covenant which I made."[19] By this slight paraphrase the pastor anticipates the sufficiency of the new. God will "fulfill" or "perfect" the New Covenant so that it will accomplish what was lacking in the first covenant, which he merely "made."[20]

10-12 This second half of the Jeremiah passage outlines the interlocking benefits of the New Covenant that address the deficit of the Old — a willing obedience springing from God's laws written on the heart, intimate fellowship with God, and the removal of sin.[21] The fulfillment of God's promise that this covenant would be established "after these days" has been inaugurated by the High Priest at God's right hand who has come "at the end of these days" (1:2). The pastor cites this Jeremiah passage in full for several reasons in addition to those clearly stated in vv. 7-8 and 13. First, he would arouse his hearers' interest in and desire for these New Covenant blessings. Second, he lays a solid foundation for his discussion of the Son's high-priestly sacrificial ministry to follow.[22] It is that ministry which makes these New Covenant benefits a reality and clarifies their nature and quality. Thus it is no surprise that he returns to this Jeremiah passage in 10:15-18 at the conclusion of his treatise on the Son's effective high-priestly sacrifice. In those verses he will excerpt the crucial parts of this New Covenant passage with the confidence that his hearers will understand their significance. We reserve further comment on these benefits until consideration of 10:15-18 in order to take advantage of the pastor's intervening explanation.

13 In his introductory comment (vv. 7-8a) the pastor affirmed that the mere promise of a "second" covenant implied the inadequacy of the "first." This inadequacy was substantiated by the way God "found fault" with the wilderness generation who received the "first" covenant. The pastor now carries this argument a step further by returning to the word "new" in the first verse from Jeremiah quoted in v. 8 above. "By saying 'new,'" that is, by the

---

19. Compare Jer 31:32: τὴν διαθήκην ("the covenant"), ἣν διεθέμην ("which I covenanted") with Heb 8:9: τὴν διαθήκην ("the covenant"), ἣν ἐποίησα ("which I made").

20. See Kenneth J. Thomas, "The Old Testament Citations in the Epistle to the Hebrews," *NTS* 11 (1965): 310.

21. Forgiveness or the removal of sin anticipates and opens the way for God's law written on the heart. See Joslin, *Law*, 190-92; France, "Biblical Expositor," 259, 264-65; and Fred A. Malone, "A Critical Evaluation of the Use of Jeremiah 31:31-34 in the Letter to the Hebrews" (Ph.D. diss., Southwestern Baptist Theological Seminary, 1989), 175, 193.

22. Following Ellingworth, 417-18; France, "Biblical Expositor," 259, 264-65; and Joslin, *Law*, 191, n. 68. *Pace* Grässer, 2:101 (cf. Weiss, 446), who appears to think that the Jeremiah passage is quoted merely to establish the antiquity of the Old Covenant without regard for the actual quality of the New.

very act of declaring this covenant "new" and "not like" the earlier covenant, God "made the first obsolete."[23] He branded it as "old," out of date and thus inferior to the "new." Furthermore, "that which is becoming obsolete and growing old is on the verge of passing away."[24] The pastor is speaking from Jeremiah's point of view. As soon as God promised a "new" covenant, the Old was "near to passing away."[25] Since the New has come in Christ, the Old is no longer "near to" but *has* definitively passed away as a way of relating to God. This assertion is a fitting transition to the impotence of the old Tent and priestly service as described in 9:1-10. The Old Covenant continues only as a type of the New. It was always intended to have this typological function.

Thus the heavenly Sanctuary, in which, according to Ps 110:1, this High Priest exercises his ministry (vv. 1-2), and the "new" covenant of Jer 31:31-34, which he administers (vv. 7-13), both demonstrate that his sacrifice must have been different from and superior to those offered in the earthly Tent (vv. 3-6). The first movement of this symphony ends with the audience eager to behold the nature of this difference.

2. Second Movement: The Old Antiquated; the New Foreshadowed (9:1-22)

In this second movement the pastor revisits the themes of the first but reverses their emphases. In the first his orchestra played the themes of "sanctuary" (8:1-2) and "covenant" (8:7-13) in a major key, but the central theme of "sacrifice" in minor (8:3-6). The pastor boldly affirmed that Christ was "Minister" in the heavenly Sanctuary and "Mediator" of the New Covenant. On the other hand, he did little more than deny that Christ's sacrifice was like the sacrifices offered "according to the law" by the priests who ministered in the earthly "pattern and shadow" of the heavenly Sanctuary (8:3-6). In the second movement, however, we hear "sanctuary" and "covenant" in a minor key but "sacrifice" in major. The pastor/conductor describes the old sanctuary (9:1-10) and the establishing of the Old Covenant (9:16-22) in order to expose their insufficiency and their preparatory character. On the other hand he vigorously affirms the unfathomable efficacy of Christ's sacrifice offered "according to the eternal Spirit" and thus able to "cleanse the conscience" (9:11-15). In the first

23. While the distinction between καινός, "new" and superior (8:13; 9:15), and νέος, "new," young, and recent (12:24), may have been disappearing (Bénétreau, 2:65), the very passage quoted from Jeremiah shows that this "new" covenant is superior because it is "not like" the first covenant. The pastor is aware of this superiority in 8:13 even if he postpones its discussion until 10:15-18.

24. Compare 1:11.

25. Ellingworth, 419; Attridge, 229; and O'Brien, 303. Thus, *pace* Gordon, 113-14, and others, this is no reference to the imminent destruction of the Jerusalem Temple.

movement he looked ahead at how the OT prophecies (Ps 110:1 and Jer 31:31-34) proclaimed Christ "Minister" of the heavenly sanctuary and 'Mediator' of the New Covenant. In the second he looks back at the Pentateuchal descriptions of the earthly sanctuary (9:1-10) and the founding of the Old Covenant (9:16-22) in order to expose them as preparatory but inadequate. The first focuses on the heavenly Sanctuary and New Covenant character of Christ's ministry in order to distinguish his sacrifice from the sacrifices of the earthly sanctuary and Old Covenant. The second focuses on the inadequacy of the old sanctuary and Covenant in order to highlight the all-sufficient quality of Christ's sacrifice. Thus this interplay of major and minor keys, of positive and negative emphases, begins to bring the theme of "sacrifice" into prominence. The sacrifice of Christ will attain overwhelming predominance in the conductor's third and final symphonic movement yet to come (9:23–10:18).

a. Limitations of the Earthly Sanctuary (9:1-10)

1 *On the other hand, then, the first covenant was having regulations for worship and an earthly sanctuary.* 2 *A Tent had been prepared, the first, in which were the lampstand and the table and the presentation of bread. This Tent was called the Holy Place.* 3 *But after the second curtain was a Tent called the Most Holy Place,* 4 *having an incense altar covered with gold and the Ark of the Covenant covered all over with gold, in which were a golden jar containing manna and Aaron's rod that budded and the tablets of the covenant.* 5 *Above the Ark were the Cherubim of Glory overshadowing the mercy seat. Concerning these things we cannot now speak in detail.* 6 *When these things had been prepared, the priests regularly entered the first Tent in order to fulfill their service,* 7 *but into the second once a year the high priest alone not without blood which he offered for himself and for the people's sins of ignorance.* 8 *By this the Holy Spirit is showing that the way into the Sanctuary was not yet revealed while that First Tent still had validity.* 9 *That Tent was a parable for the time then present. In relation to that Tent gifts and sacrifices were offered which were not able to perfect the worshipers in regard to their conscience.* 10 *Those gifts and sacrifices pertained only to food and drink and various washings, regulations of the flesh, established until the time of correction.*

The unity of 9:1-10 is beyond question.[1] In v. 1 the pastor announces his topic as the "regulations for worship" and "earthly sanctuary" of the First

---

1. Note the inclusion formed by δικαιώματα, "regulations," in vv. 1 and 10 (Vanhoye, *La structure littéraire*, 144-45). The pastor shows the unity of the whole by us-

Covenant.[2] Verses 2-5 describe this sanctuary, and vv. 6-7 the First-Covenant worship appropriate for such a sanctuary. Verses 8-10 conclude by unveiling the significance of this sanctuary and liturgy as intended by the Holy Spirit.[3] The structure of the earthly sanctuary (vv. 2-5) is determinative for its worship (vv. 6-7). Both structure and liturgy have a twofold significance: First, they demonstrate the impossibility of approaching God through the old sanctuary. Second, they anticipate the "new and living way" (10:20) of approach to God through Christ.

Several features of the pastor's description reveal the impossibility of approaching the divine Presence through the "earthly sanctuary." The text emphasizes the distinction between and the impenetrable boundary separating the Holy Place from the Most Holy Place. The Holy Place with its repetitious worship is a graphic reminder that access was not available before Christ.[4] On the other hand, by emphasizing the majesty of the Most Holy Place the pastor anticipates the way in which its liturgy foreshadows Christ's entrance into God's heavenly presence as described in vv. 11-14.[5] The details used in describing this "earthly sanctuary" keep the hearers from forgetting its earthly, and therefore limited, character.

1 During its tenure that "First" and inadequate Covenant "was having an earthly sanctuary," that could also be called a "Tent" (v. 2).[6] Contrast Christ's entry into "the Sanctuary and true Tent" as recorded in 8:2. A comparison of these expressions reveals the importance of the word "earthly." Just as the pastor never uses "Tent" for the heavenly reality without a qualifying description,[7] so he never uses "Sanctuary" for the earthly copy without qualification — "an earthly sanctuary" (9:1); "a sanctuary made by hand" (9:24). Furthermore, the pastor has emphasized the adjective "earthly" by locating it in the predicate position after the noun "sanctuary." His meaning is

---

ing λατρεία ("worship") and κατασκευάζω ("prepare") in vv. 1-2 and then by repeating them at the crucial transition point in v. 6 (Weiss, 449).

2. For δικαιώματα as "regulations" see the examples given in Attridge, 231, n. 15.

3. Westcott, 242; cf. Lane, 2:217; Attridge, 231.

4. See Koester, 400; but *pace* Vanhoye, *Old Testament,* 181, who thinks that the Holy Place was "a rough sketch of the 'new and living way' that Christ was to inaugurate (10:20)."

5. Note μέν in v. 1 and δέ in v. 11 — "on the one hand," "on the other" (Johnson, 218; Koester, 393; Weiss, 449). The pastor contrasts the insufficiency of the old (vv. 1-10) with the full sufficiency of the fulfillment in Christ (vv. 11-14).

6. εἶχε, "was having," the imperfect tense of ἔχω, is in accord with the continuous existence of "the earthly sanctuary" up until the time of its supersession by Christ (see Weiss, 450, n. 4; Riggenbach, 237; Moffatt, 112). If καί is retained in v. 1, it underscores the parallel nature of the Covenants. Both Covenants have a sanctuary and regulations for worship (Westcott, 243; cf. Moffatt, 112).

7. See "true Tent" (8:2) and "greater and more perfect Tent" (9:11).

well rendered by a translation such as the following: the First Covenant had "the Sanctuary, but it was earthly," or "the Sanctuary that was indeed earthly."[8] This "sanctuary" is severely limited because it is part of the temporal, created universe and thus can provide no access to the Creator, who is beyond his creation.[9] Contrast the opening section of the next and final movement where the Sanctuary entered by Christ is nothing less than "heaven itself."[10]

An additional comparison between 9:1 and 8:2 is also instructive. The pastor uses the singular when he refers to the "earthly sanctuary," but the plural in 8:2 and elsewhere in reference to the Sanctuary entered by Christ.[11] This contrasting use of the singular is in accord with the inferiority of the earthly sanctuary. The singular also shows that the pastor thinks of this sanctuary as one structure despite his reference to first and second tents in vv. 2-3 below.

2 This is the "Tent" that "had been prepared" by Moses (cf. 8:5) in the wilderness under God's direction.[12] The pastor is anxious to point out the division between the two parts of this "earthly sanctuary" in order to demonstrate the limitations revealed by the first and the significance of the second as foreshadowing Christ's work. Although he knows that there is one "earthly sanctuary," which he calls a "Tent," he describes it as if its two parts were two separate "Tents" — a "First" and a "Second."[13] Thus he brings this

---

8. Instead of putting "earthly" (κοσμικόν) in the attributive position, "the earthly sanctuary" (τὸ κοσμικὸν ἅγιον or τὸ ἅγιον τὸ κοσμικόν), the pastor has used the predicate position, τὸ ἅγιον κοσμικόν (Riggenbach, 238-39; Moffatt, 113; Westcott, 244; cf. Lane, 2:219; Hughes, 306).

9. The pastor follows neither Josephus nor Philo in his use of this word κοσμικός, "cosmic," "pertaining to the cosmos," "earthly." With this adjective Josephus (*J.W.* 4.324) affirmed that the ministry of the priests had "cosmic" or "universal significance." According to Philo (*Moses* 2.108; cf. 2.48), those who worship rightly partake of "the eternal life of . . . the whole kosmos" (Koester, 402).

10. In 9:23-24 see τοῖς οὐρανοῖς τούτοις ("these heavens") and τὰ ἐπουράνια ("the heavenly things") as well as αὐτὸν τὸν οὐρανόν ("heaven itself").

11. Thus, see the plural with the article, τὰ ἅγια or τῶν ἁγίων, in 8:2; 9:8, 12; 10:19, but the singular with the article, τὸ ἅγιον, in 9:2. The plural without the article is used in 9:24 for the χειροποίητα . . . ἅγια, "the sanctuary made by hand," and for the Holy Place and the Most Holy Place in 9:2-3.

12. Compare χειροποίητα ("made by hands") in 9:24. Westcott says that the aorist κατεσκευάσθη, "has been established," shows that "the writer is considering the Mosaic system in its divine constitution" (243).

13. There is no indication that the pastor is influenced by cosmic speculations that understood the "first" Tent as the created universe and the "second" as heaven (Weiss, 450). Nor is there reason to believe that he is following an exegetical tradition that understood the Mosaic shrine as composed of two separate tents. Heb 8:5; 9:21; and 13:10 dem-

distinction to "the strongest possible expression."[14] The impenetrable barrier between the two is vital to his argument.

The pastor refers to the seven-branched "lampstand" described in Exod 25:31-40 and 37:17-24 (cf. Exod 40:4, 24). The lamps on this lampstand were kept perpetually burning before the Lord. Exod. 25:23-30 (cf. 39:36; 40:23) describes the "table" upon which the "presentation of the bread" was renewed each week after the old loaves were consumed by Aaron and his sons (Lev 24:9). Since the OT locates the "lampstand" and the "table" with its "bread" in the outer section of the Mosaic Tent, it is no surprise that the pastor identifies this first "Tent" as the "Holy Place."[15]

3 "After the second curtain" continues the pastor's emphasis on the division between the Holy and Most Holy Places.[16] Verse 2 described the contents of the First Tent and then identified it as the "Holy Place." Verses 3-4 call the Second Tent the "Most Holy Place" before describing its furnishings. Thus "after the second curtain" comes at the central emphatic position created by the chiastic relationship between these two descriptions.[17] This

---

onstrate clearly that the author knew there was one Tent with two parts (Otfried Hofius, "Das 'erste' und das 'zweite' Zelt: Ein Beitrag zur Auslegung von Hbr 9 1-10," *ZNW* 61 [1970]: 271-72). See also Weiss, 453.

14. Riggenbach, 240. Cf. Vanhoye, *Old Testament*, 184. Josephus, *J.W.* 5.184, 186, provides an interesting parallel to the pastor's use of σκηνή ("Tent") in Heb 9:2-7. Josephus uses ἱερόν ("Temple") for the whole Temple, τὸ πρῶτον ἱερόν ("the first Temple") for the outer court open to the Gentiles, and τὸ δεύτερον ἱερόν ("the second Temple") for the inner court reserved only for Jews. See Lane, 2:219.

15. In accord with LXX usage, the pastor uses ἅγια and ἅγια ἁγίων to distinguish between the outer "Holy Place" and the inner "Most Holy Place" of "the earthly sanctuary" (τὸ ἅγιον κοσμικόν). This use of these words without articles is distinct from his normal use of τὰ ἅγια (with the article; 8:2; 9:8, 12, 24; 10:19) for the heavenly Sanctuary entered by Christ. 𝔓46 reverses these two terms in 9:2, 3, reading ἅγια ἁγίων in v. 2 for "the Holy Place" but ἅγια in v. 3 for the "Most Holy Place." A, the original hand of D, and some Vulgate manuscripts conform to 𝔓46's ἅγια ἁγίων in v. 2, but none follow 𝔓46's ἅγια in v. 3. Attridge (230, 233-34) argues that the reading of 𝔓46 was original. He claims that the usage of ἅγια ἁγίων for the Holy Place corresponds to the multiplicity of rituals performed there. Furthermore, ἅγια for the "Most Holy Place" is in agreement with the use of τὰ ἅγια elsewhere for the heavenly Most Holy Place entered by Christ. This suggestion conforms to Attridge's contention that the τὰ ἅγια Christ has entered is not "heaven itself," as we have suggested above, but the inner sanctuary of a two-part heavenly Temple. However, the external evidence for this alternate reading is very weak. There is no reason to think that the original recipients of Hebrews would have understood ἅγια ἁγίων ("Holy of Holies" or "Most Holy Place") as indicative of the multiple rites repeatedly performed in the Holy Place.

16. "Second" distinguishes this "veil" from the curtain that separated the "First" tent or Holy Place from the outer court (Exod 26:36; Bénétreau, 2:68).

17. Ellingworth, 422.

emphasis on the distinction between the Holy and Most Holy Places and the barrier separating them serves the immediate purpose of disclosing the lack of access to God under the old system. In the larger picture it highlights the magnitude of the barrier breached by Christ (10:20).

4 The pastor has crafted every detail of this description to express the beauty and majesty of the Most Holy Place in anticipation of its role as foreshadowing the high-priestly ministry of Christ. Verse 4a describes the two articles of furniture as "golden": "having a golden Altar of Incense and the Ark of the Covenant covered all over with gold."[18] In Greek "golden" and "gold" are the first and last words of this statement. The pastor focuses our attention on the Ark. Verse 4b describes its contents, and v. 5 climaxes with the Cherubim over the Mercy Seat, the place of atonement above the Ark.

Two interrelated questions surround the term translated "Altar of Incense." First, the underlying Greek word could be used for "censer" as well as for "Incense Altar." Second, according to the OT text, the Altar of Incense was located in the Holy Place, not the Most Holy Place. Some would solve both questions by arguing that Hebrews is referring to the censer that the high priest took into the Most Holy Place on the Day of Atonement (Lev 16:12-13).[19] Thus, by speaking of a censer in conjunction with the Ark the pastor draws his hearers' attention to that great Day now fulfilled by Christ. Riggenbach, in particular, contends that the author was far too conversant with the OT to mistakenly locate the Altar of Incense in the Most Holy Place. He knew that the high priest sprinkled the blood of the sacrifice on this altar (Exod 30:10) and took coals of fire from it (Lev 16:12-13) before entering the Most Holy Place.

Others argue that the Greek word refers to the Altar of Incense and that the author is following an exegetical tradition that located the Altar of Incense within the Most Holy Place.[20] After all, the instructions for building this altar are given separately from the instructions for other furnishings.[21] Furthermore, some OT passages associate the Altar of Incense closely with the Ark and the Most Holy Place.[22] Several other writings roughly contempo-

18. The Altar of Incense was about three feet (.8 meter) high and about one and one half feet (.5 meter) in length and width (Exod 30:1-6). The Ark of the Covenant, on the other hand, was about three and three-fourths feet (1.1 meters) long and two and one-fourth feet (.7 meter) in both width and height. See Kistemaker, 237, 293.

19. See esp. Riggenbach, 241-46, followed by Bénétreau, 2:69.

20. Attridge, 232-37.

21. The instructions for the construction of the Ark of the Covenant, the Table, and the Lampstand are given in Exodus 25, but those for the Altar of Incense are delayed until Exodus 30.

22. "Thus Exodus 30:6 says it was to be placed 'before the veil that is by the ark of the testimony' (cf. 40:26), and Exodus 40:5 requires it to be situated 'before the ark of

rary with Hebrews may bear witness to a tradition locating the Incense Altar within the inner sanctuary.[23] Those who espouse this position argue that the author could not have omitted something so important as the Altar of Incense.

It seems clear that the pastor is referring to the Altar of Incense and not to a censer.[24] Both Philo and Josephus bear witness to this meaning for the underlying Greek term.[25] Furthermore, the description would be incomplete if the author omitted what was arguably the second most important article of furniture in the Mosaic sanctuary. We would expect him to make use of exegetical traditions available to him. He was not, however, the mere hapless victim of an exegetical tradition that located the incense altar within the Most Holy Place.[26] Riggenbach is correct in his contention that one so schooled in the OT would not misplace this altar. Rather, the author draws on those OT

---

the testimony,' without even mentioning the curtain. In the description of Solomon's temple, indeed, the altar of incense is spoken of as 'belonging to the inner sanctuary' (1 Ki. 6:20; 22)" (Hughes, 310).

23. Attridge, 235, refers to 2 Macc 2:4-8; Bar 6:7; and Rev 8:3 as attesting an exegetical tradition that located the Incense Altar in the Most Holy Place. However, he is forced to admit the ambiguity of these passages. Although they associate the Incense Altar with the Most Holy Place, they do not necessarily locate it within that sanctuary. Dependence on these passages borders on explaining the unclear by the unclear. At the very least their lack of clarity should caution us against insisting that Hebrews has located the Altar of Incense within the Most Holy Place.

24. So, most recently, Mitchell, 174; Gordon, 116; and O'Brien, 308-9.

25. See θυμιατήριον as "Altar of Incense" in Philo, *Heir* 226; *Moses* 2.94; Josephus, *J.W.* 5.218; *Ant.* 3.147, 198, but as "censer" in 2 Chr 26:19; Ezek 8:11; and 4 Macc 7:1. The LXX uses (τὸ) θυσιαστήριον (τοῦ) θυμιάματος, ("altar of incense") in Exod 30:1, 27; Lev 4:7; 1 Chr 6:49 (cf. Luke 1:11) and the closely related τὸ θυσιαστήριον τῶν θυμιαμάτων ("altar of incenses") in 1 Chr 28:18; 2 Chr 16:16, 19. These expressions represent a literal translation of the Hebrew. See (τὸ) θυσιαστήριον (τοῦ) θυμιάματος and מזבח מקטר קטרת in Exod 30:1. The Greek θυσιαστήριον ("altar") is equivalent to the Hebrew מזבח ("altar"); the Greek θυμιάματος ("of incense"), to the Hebrew מקטר קטרת ("of the burner of incense"). See Westcott, 247. Symmachus and Aquila insert θυμιατήριον into the text of Exod 30:1 without removing θυσιαστήριον — θυσιαστήριον θυμιατήριον θυμιάματος (literally, "altar incense altar of incense").

26. The various features Attridge, 232-37, attributes to exegetical tradition are not found together but are located in diverse sources. This fact demonstrates that the author of Hebrews is not slavishly following a given exegetical tradition. Even when drawing from others, he selects what suits his purpose. Thus Hebrews agrees with both Philo (*Heir* 226; *Moses* 2.161-64) and Josephus (*J.W.* 1.7.6; 5.5.5; *Ant.* 3.6.6-8) in describing the lampstand before the table, although the OT follows the reverse order. However, neither Philo nor Josephus associates the Incense Altar with the Most Holy Place. Sometimes there are no known parallels to the way Hebrews describes these furnishings. No other available source separates the "presentation of the bread" from the Table as in Heb 9:2. See Hughes, 313-15.

passages cited above that connect this altar with the Most Holy Place. In making this connection he joins his contemporaries, also cited above, who made a like association. Note the difference between the way he locates furniture "in" the Holy Place but speaks of the Most Holy Place as "having" the Incense Altar and the Ark of the Covenant.[27] He does not "relocate" this altar within the inner sanctuary but closely associates it with the Most Holy Place in accord with its function.

Westcott reminds us that just as the Altar of Sacrifice was important for entrance into the Holy Place, so the Incense Altar was crucial for entrance into the Most Holy Place.[28] On the Day of Atonement the high priest could not enter that inner sanctum without filling his censor with coals of fire from this altar (Lev 16:12-13). He sprinkled the blood of the sin offering on the horns of the Incense Altar as well as on the Mercy Seat or Place of Atonement above the Ark (Exod 30:10; Lev 16:15).[29] Thus the pastor has associated the Incense Altar with the Most Holy Place in accord with its function and his own purposes.[30] By making this connection he magnifies the Most Holy Place and anticipates its role as foreshadowing Christ's entering "heaven itself" (9:24) in fulfillment of the Day of Atonement. However, that fulfillment will denude its earthly type of all magnificence.

The pastor focuses his hearers' attention on the Ark by enumerating its contents. Its most important objects were "the tablets of the covenant" on which the Ten Commandments were engraved. According to Exod 25:16 and Deut 10:1-5 these tablets had been deposited in the Ark by Moses. The presence of the "jar containing manna and Aaron's rod that budded" is suggested by God's command to put these objects in the Most Holy Place as recorded in Exod 16:32-34 and Num 17:10-11.[31] Some rabbinic sources agree that these items were in the Ark itself.[32] Later reference to the tablets bearing the Ten Commandments as the only contents of the Ark may have suggested that

27. Westcott, 247. Moffatt, 115, disagrees with this distinction between "in which" (ἐν ᾗ) and "having" (ἔχουσα), but cites Delitzsch, Zahn, Peake, and Seeberg in its support. While "having" could denote location, the contrast with "in which" suggests a broader meaning in this context. In v. 1 the pastor has just referred to the "First Covenant" as "having" (εἶχε, imperfect of the same verb used for "having" in v. 4) a sanctuary and regulations for worship. Bruce, 201, is too quick to call this distinction "special pleading." See A. Ito, "Concerning the θυμιατήριον (Heb 9:4) [in Japanese]," *Exegetica* 10 (1999): 149-65.

28. Westcott, 247.

29. See Bruce, 201-2. Furthermore, when regular priests offered incense on this altar, they were as close as they ever came to the Most Holy Place.

30. See the brief discussion in Gordon, 116.

31. Hughes, 315, refers to Delitzsch as saying that the presence of these items within the Ark was a natural deduction from the OT language.

32. Lane, 2:221.

something else had once also been located therein.[33] If the Ten Commandments were the foundation of God's covenant, manna was evidence of his
provision, and the rod symbolized his choice of Aaron as priest. Only in the
LXX of Exod 16:33 is the "jar of manna" described as "golden." Philo picks
up this description in *Prelim. Studies* 100. Our author, who has emphasized
the gold covering of both Altar and Ark, would not miss the chance to call
this jar "golden" and thus increase his emphasis on the majesty of the Most
Holy Place.

5   The pastor climaxes his description not with what was within but
with what was "above" the Ark — "the Cherubim of Glory overshadowing
the Mercy Seat." The Cherubim were two figures made of gold whose wings
overshadowed the "Place of Atonement" or "Mercy Seat" covering the Ark
(Exod 25:10-22; 37:1-9). They were Cherubim of "Glory" because it was between them that the "Glory" of the divine presence dwelt among God's people (cf. Exod 25:22).[34] This was the earthly "throne" of God (1 Sam 4:4;
2 Sam 6:2; Pss 80:2; 99:1). It was the place where the high priest came annually on the Day of Atonement to sprinkle sacrificial blood before the "Mercy
Seat" in atonement for sin (Lev 16:1-19). The pastor concludes his description of the "earthly sanctuary" by focusing his hearers' eyes on this place of
atonement in anticipation of fulfillment in Christ (vv. 11-14). As High Priest,
the Son has made atonement sufficient for entrance into the true heavenly
presence of God where he now sits with all authority at the right hand of the
divine "throne." Through his ministry this "throne" has now become a
"throne of grace" (4:16) for God's people, a true "Mercy Seat." The pastor
has brought his hearers from the Incense Altar to the Mercy Seat. His description mirrors the high priest's annual entrance from initial approach to
crowning act of atonement. These foreshadowings anticipate their all-
sufficient fulfillment in Christ.

The pastor has accomplished his purpose. He has emphasized the
"earthly" and thus preliminary character of the Mosaic sanctuary. He has
demonstrated the great separation between the Holy and the Most Holy
Places. He has shown the corresponding splendor of the latter in anticipation
of the way it foreshadows Christ's entrance into Heaven itself.[35] Thus he
would not sidetrack his hearers from these important issues by speaking "of
these things in greater detail."[36] He proceeds immediately to the ministries

---

33. See 1 Kgs 8:9; 2 Chr 5:10; and Hughes, 315.
34. Thus "Cherubim of Glory" does not mean "glorious Cherubim" but the
"Cherubim" between whom the "Glory" of God dwelt. See Koester 396, REB. So also
Kistemaker, 240; Westcott, 249.
35. Cf. Koester 402.
36. For the rhetorical use of such phrases as "we are not now able to speak in detail" compare 2 Macc 2:20-32; Philo, *Heir* 221.

appropriate to these two parts of the "earthly sanctuary" (vv. 6-7) and to their significance (vv. 8-10, 11-14).

6-7 "When these things had been prepared" introduces the age that began with Moses and established the "earthly sanctuary," an age that was characterized by repetition of the Levitical rituals.[37] Verse 6 describes the ministry of the "priests" in the "First Tent"; v. 7, that of the "high priest" in the "Second." Everything in v. 6 emphasizes the continuous, repetitive nature of the priests' ministry and its consequent limitation to "the First Tent." The LXX uses the term here translated "regularly" to describe the routine lighting of the lamps in the Holy Place (Exod 27:20), the daily offering of incense (Exod 30:8), and the regular presentation of the bread (Exod 25:30).[38] The verbs "enter" and "perform" are iterative present emphasizing the repetitive character of these liturgical acts. The ministers of the "First Tent" repeatedly "enter" to "perform" their ministry. The pastor refrains from further description of these rituals so that the weight of his words might fall on their repetition.

The pastor has carefully chosen the verbs translated "enter" and "perform." He distinguishes these priests from Christ by using a word for "enter" that differs from the word used for Christ's entrance into the heavenly Sanctuary.[39] "Perform" is regularly used for executing religious rituals.[40] Nevertheless, the pastor uses this verb with subtle irony. In other contexts this word has the connotation of bringing to completion.[41] These priests are continuously performing rituals that are never completed and that never get them further than "the First Tent." They never achieve even symbolic access into the divine Presence. Thus, the pastor lays a firm foundation for demonstrating the ineffectiveness of the ministry on which the First Covenant was established.

37. The perfect participle κατεσκευασμένων, "having been prepared," refers to the "abiding system" that resulted from the "historical foundation" of the Mosaic sanctuary at Sinai described by the aorist form of the same verb (κατεσκευάσθη) in v. 2 (Westcott, 250; cf. Riggenbach, 247).

38. See διὰ παντός, for "repeatedly" or "regularly" in Exod 25:30; 27:20; and 30:8. See Dennis Hamm, "Praying 'Regularly' (not 'Constantly'): A Note on the Cultic Background of διὰ παντός at Luke 24:53, Acts 10:2, and Hebrews 9:6, 13:15," *ExpTim* 116 (2004): 50-52.

39. Heb 9:6 uses εἰσίασιν (εἴσειμι) for the priests' entrance into the Holy Place. Elsewhere Hebrews uses εἰσέρχομαι for Christ's entrance into the Most Holy Place (see 9:12, 25; cf. 6:19-20). Although εἰσέρχομαι had largely replaced εἴσειμι in Hellenistic Greek, εἴσειμι was used for the high priests entering the Most Holy Place in Exod 28:29, 35 and in Josephus, *J.W.* 5.5.7 (see Ellingworth, 433).

40. Herodotus, *Hist.* 2.63; 4.26; Philo, *Dreams* 1.214-15; Josephus, *Ant.* 4.123; 9.273.

41. See BDAG, 383 and the comments on the use of ἐπιτελέω in 8:5 above.

Every feature of ministry in "the Second" Tent as described in v. 7 also demonstrates the insufficiency of the First Tent's rituals to provide access. "Only" the "high priest" enters. None can "draw near to God" through him (cf. 7:25). He enters only "once a year." His annual entrance indicates both the limitation of his access and its repeated, and therefore inconclusive, nature. His entrance is also limited in that it is "not without blood," and he must "offer" this blood both "for himself" and for the "people's sins of ignorance."[42] There is little distinction between "sins of ignorance" and "sins."[43]

However, the pastor also describes this ministry of the old high priest on the Day of Atonement because, as vv. 11-15 will show, it is the pattern for Christ's high-priestly ministry. The old high priest's entrance "once a year" into the "Second Tent" of the "earthly sanctuary" was inconclusive, but it was symbolic of Christ's entrance "once for all" (vv. 11-14) into "heaven itself" (9:24).[44] His entering "not without blood" anticipated Christ's entrance "through his own blood" (v. 12; cf. vv. 15-23). Finally, the old high priest's offering for himself and for the sins of the people anticipated Christ's obedient offering of himself for the people (7:27; 9:11-14; 10:5-10).

8 The pastor begins to explain the significance of the priests' ministry in the "earthly sanctuary" as just described in vv. 6-7. As always, the Scripture is of immediate relevance. Thus, "the Holy Spirit" as the inspirer of Scripture is even now "revealing" the inadequacy of the old order through the biblical description of its limitations. The pastor claims no esoteric divine

---

42. Hebrews uses the term προσφέρω, "offer," for Christ's sacrifice on the cross (9:14, 25, 28; 10:12; see also the cognate noun προσφορά, "offering," in 10:10, 14), and, in this verse, for the high priest's presentation of blood in the Most Holy Place (v. 7). This last usage is striking because it lacks OT precedent. Thus it appears that the pastor is drawing a parallel between Christ's self-offering on the cross and the high priest's presentation of the blood: "the repeated entrance followed by a repeated blood sprinkling in the old order is now in the new age a once-for-all sacrifice-cum-sprinkling followed by a once-for-all entrance" (Norman H. Young, "The Gospel according to Hebrews 9," *NTS* 27 [1981]: 209; see also 207-9).

43. Compare "sins of ignorance" (ἀγνοήματα) with "sins" (ἁμάρτιαι). See Weiss, 455, n. 28. Moffatt, 117, notes that the LXX of Judg 5:20; Sir 23:2; Tob 3:3; and 1 Macc 13:39 use the two terms together. If there is any difference, "sins of ignorance" may refer to the perversity of the people in their refusal to know God's law: "but they did not know (ἔγνωσαν) my ways" (Heb 3:10). The pastor does not use this term in reference to the "unintentional" (ἀκούσιος) sins described in Lev 4:1–5:19 and Num 15:22-31 (*pace* Attridge, 239). He does not believe that the old high priest's offerings atoned for unintentional sins but Christ's for all sins (*pace* Ellingworth, 435; Gordon, 117-18). Instead, he states clearly that the former brought only the ceremonial cleansing "of the flesh," while the latter effected cleansing of the "conscience" or "heart" (9:13-14).

44. Weiss, 454-55. Compare "once a year" (ἅπαξ τοῦ ἐνιαυτοῦ) with "once for all" (ἐφάπαξ) in 9:12.

disclosure. What he has to say is drawn from the plain biblical description of the old order understood in light of its fulfillment.[45]

Above all else, this description of ministry in the "earthly sanctuary" reveals that "the way into the [heavenly] Sanctuary had not yet been disclosed while that First Tent still had validity." It is important to clarify the referents of both "Sanctuary" and "First Tent." That "Sanctuary" refers not to the earthly Most Holy Place but to the heavenly "Sanctuary" in which Christ is a "minister" (8:2).[46] "First Tent," however, refers to the first part of the Mosaic shrine, the Holy Place,[47] rather than to the entire Mosaic structure as temporal precursor of the "true" (8:2), "greater and more perfect Tent" (9:11).[48] There are several weighty reasons for preferring this interpretation.[49] First, in the immediate context the pastor has consistently used "first"/

45. Bruce, 208; Vanhoye, *Old Testament,* 186, and others affirm that 9:8 refers to the Spirit's work in inspiring Scripture (cf. Riggenbach, 249). However, Emmrich, "Pneuma in Hebrews," 63-64, contends that this verse refers to the Spirit's giving a new revelation through Scripture in light of Christ's coming. The two other references to the Spirit as the source of Scripture (3:7; 10:15) do not support Emmrich's conclusion. Since the pastor regularly paraphrases Scripture, his paraphrases of Psalm 95 in 3:7-11 are no indication that these words, spoken by the "Spirit" (3:7), are a "new oracle" of God (*pace* Emmrich, "Pneuma in Hebrews," 57-58). Psalm 95 is relevant to the hearers because they, like the wilderness generation, are part of the one people of God. The pastor cites Jeremiah 31 in 10:15-18 as Scriptural support for the conclusion reached in 10:14. The Holy Spirit who inspired Scripture now "bears witness" to the veracity of what he inspired (10:15). The present participle δηλοῦντος, "revealing," is not indicative of new revelation but underscores the pastor's sense of the immediacy of Scripture (cf. 1:6, 7; 2:11-12; 3:7; 5:6; 7:21; 8:8; and 10:5). The Spirit who inspired Scripture enables the pastor to understand the meaning inherent in the text from the beginning (cf. Koester, 397; Lane, 2:223; and Attridge, 240; cf. O'Brien, 312).

46. Riggenbach, 249.

47. See Westcott, 252; Moffatt, 118; Riggenbach, 249; Buchanan, 144; Ellingworth, 437; Attridge, 240; George Guthrie, 299-300; deSilva, 297, 302; O'Brien, 313; Vanhoye, *Old Testament,* 185-86; Theissen, *Untersuchungen,* 69; Hofius, *Vorhang,* 61; Loader, *Sohn und Hoherpriester,* 163-64; Laub, *Bekenntnis,* 193. "The Holy Place portrays a barrier space separating the people of God from the presence of God" (George Guthrie, 300).

48. For the temporal understanding see Hughes, 323; Kuss, 115; Héring, 74; Michel, 307; Bruce, 208-9; Kistemaker, 243-44; Schierse, *Verheissung,* 30-34; Cody, *Heavenly Sanctuary,* 145; and Peterson, *Perfection,* 133.

49. According to Steve Stanley, "Hebrews 9:6-10: The 'Parable' of the Tabernacle," *NovT* 37 (1995): 385-99, the "First Tent" refers to both the Holy Place and the whole earthly sanctuary: as the earthly Holy Place ("First Tent") was to the earthly Most Holy Place ("Second Tent"), so the whole earthly sanctuary, including both parts ("First Tent"), was to the heavenly Sanctuary ("Second Tent"). This suggestion betrays a fundamental misunderstanding because it makes the distinction between the old order/earthly sanctuary and the new order/heavenly Sanctuary one of degree instead of kind. Note Stan-

"First Tent" and "second" to distinguish the earthly "Holy Place" from the earthly "Most Holy Place" (vv. 2, 3, 6, 7). Second, the pastor could hardly call an "earthly sanctuary" the "First Tent" since it did not precede the eternal heavenly Sanctuary of which it was a copy (8:4-5). He can refer to the Old and New Covenants as "first" and "second" (8:7, 13) because they followed one another in temporal sequence, but he cannot use this language for their respective sanctuaries. Furthermore, the identification of the First Tent with the Holy Place makes good sense of what the pastor has said. The First or Old Covenant was a covenant of the Holy Place. Thus in vv. 2-5 the pastor emphasized the impenetrable barrier between the Holy Place and the Most Holy Place. In v. 6 the rituals of the First Covenant were confined to the Holy Place, where they were endlessly repeated without providing access to anything more. They could not even penetrate the boundary between the earthly Holy Place and the Most Holy Place. The high priest's annual entrance into the Most Holy Place, described in v. 7, was only "the exception that proved the rule."[50] He went "alone," only "once a year," and only into the earthly Most Holy Place. OT religion might have been oriented toward the Most Holy Place, but it was confined to the Holy Place.[51] This very fact showed its inability to bring people into God's presence and its nature as foreshadowing a fulfillment to come. By contrast, the New Covenant has no Holy Place but only the Most Holy Place that is "heaven itself" (9:24).

With this understood, it becomes clear why the pastor says that the way into the true heavenly "Sanctuary" was not even "made known" or revealed as long as the Holy Place and its rituals were in force.[52] If the outer "Tent" could not even give access to the inner "Tent," what would give access to heaven itself?[53]

---

ley's statement in n. 42 on p. 397: "The term 'better' implies that the old did have some value, albeit a lesser value, and 9:11 uses the comparative forms μείζωνος and τελειοτέρας, indicating that the old had the positive qualities of greatness and perfection (perfection understood in a relative sense)." Compare this statement with 7:19: "For the law perfects nothing." It is true that both have value, but they differ in kind rather than degree. The old has typological value; the new, salvific. Thus it would be impossible for the first part of the old sanctuary to have the same relationship to the second as the whole would have to the heavenly Sanctuary.

50. Attridge, 240.

51. In this sense there is truth in Westcott's statement: "Thus the outer sanctuary was the representative symbol of the whole Tabernacle as the place of service" (252).

52. BDAG, 940, 1, suggests that στάσις may mean *place* or *position* rather than existence. This understanding makes better sense of the context in Heb 9:1-10, as long as the First Tent had *place, position,* or *validity.* Hughes (322, n. 71) and Lane (2:216t) support this understanding.

53. Koester (397) is surprised that the text says "was not manifested" because he fails to note that it was the way into the *heavenly* Sanctuary that was hidden. Cf. Vanhoye,

9a   The pastor calls this "First Tent" a "parable" for "the present time."[54] How could a Tent whose every feature demonstrated the impossibility of access to God be a "parable" for "the present time" of fulfillment in Christ? The First Tent is not a parable of the present as the time before the greater, final access to God that will be available after the Judgment (9:28; 12:25-29).[55] The pastor is at pains to emphasize the marvelous access believers now have (4:14-16; 10:19-21) as reason and resource for perseverance. Thus Attridge suggests that the First Tent was an "inverse parable" — lack of access under the old points to access through the new.[56] Ellingworth proposes that the Holy Place was a "parable" of the situation that existed "until the present time."[57] Others suggest that it was a "parable" with relevance "for the present time" and disclosed only in the present age.[58] Many, however, have followed a simpler and more direct interpretation: The Holy Place was not a type anticipating the time of fulfillment, but a "parable" or symbol of "the time then present" during the period of its validity.[59] In any case, the First

---

Old Testament, 186: "A tent which leads to another tent is obviously not the way to the true Sanctuary. But no other way was known." However, as in the text above, we would alter Vanhoye to read: "A tent which did not even lead to another tent is obviously not the way to the true Sanctuary."

54. τῆς πρώτης σκηνῆς ("the first tent") is the antecedent of the feminine singular ἥτις ("which") at the beginning of v. 9. The pastor is careful about agreement between pronouns and their antecedents (cf. 2:3; 8:6; 9:2; 10:9, 11, 35; 12:5; Young, "Gospel," 201; George Guthrie, 300). Thus, there is no reason to think that ἥτις has been attracted to the feminine by παραβολή (*pace* Hughes, 323-25, esp. n. 73). It is "the First Tent" in particular and not everything the pastor has said in general that is a "parable."

55. Riggenbach, 249-51, cites those who hold such a position. deSilva, 302, proposes a variation on this theme: as the Holy Place covered the Most Holy Place, so in the present age the physical universe hides the true heavenly dwelling place of God. This position is based on the doubtful assumption that cosmic speculations about the Mosaic shrine are determinative for Hebrews' thought. Nowhere does Hebrews suggest that the "Holy Place" represents the created universe. Furthermore, any proposal that understands the "First Tent" as a "parable" for limitations on access to God still in force is inadequate because it must take this statement as a parentheses devoid of connection with vv. 9b-10. Verses 9b-10 diagnose the problem of the First Tent as the inadequacy of its sacrifices. The present time, however, is the time characterized by Christ's all-sufficient sacrifice.

56. Attridge, 241-42, takes the εἰς of εἰς τὸν καιρὸν τὸν ἐνεστηκότα as an adverbial accusative of reference — "in reference to the present age."

57. Ellingworth (440-41) takes the εἰς of εἰς τὸν καιρὸν τὸν ἐνεστηκότα as "until" instead of "for" and makes καιρόν an adverbial accusative showing extent of time — "until the present time."

58. See William Manson, *The Epistle to the Hebrews* (London, 1951), 132 (cited in Bruce, 209); Emmrich, "Pneuma in Hebrews," 64-66, and Riggenbach, 249-50.

59. George Guthrie, 300. Thus παραβολή ("parable") is not a technical term for a

Tent or Holy Place represented the situation before Christ when there was as yet no provision for direct access to God. This situation has come to an end with the fulfillment brought by Christ at the "time of correction" (v. 10), as described in vv. 11-15 below.[60]

Although the pastor uses the Holy Place as a "parable" of the situation before Christ, he stops short of designating the Most Holy Place a parable for the age inaugurated by Christ. We have seen that the annual repetition of the high priest's entrance into this inner sanctum highlighted the inability of the rituals done in the Holy Place to provide access into the divine Presence. Nevertheless, in vv. 11-14 below the pastor will demonstrate that this same annual entrance also foreshadows the "once-for-all" entrance of Christ into God's true presence.

9b-10   The repetitious rituals of the earthly Holy Place demonstrate clearly that the way of access into "heaven itself" (9:24) was neither open nor disclosed under the Old Covenant. The pastor is now going to show why such access was unavailable. The ineffective sacrifices offered "in relation to that Tent" were its undoing.[61] The combination "gifts and sacrifices" embraces all the offerings of the First Tent and thus condemns them all to futility.[62] They were not able to perform the essential purpose of sacrifice: they could not "cleanse the worshiper in regard to conscience" no matter how many

---

"type" that foreshadows the future (*pace* Weiss, 458). "The parable suggests thoughts: the type points to a direct fulfillment" (Westcott, 253). See Stanley, " 'Parable,' " 390-91.

60. However, we cannot press "the (then) present time" and the "age of correction" into the mold of the two ages of Jewish apocalyptic, as Ellingworth, 440-41; Vanhoye, *Old Testament,* 186-87; Koester, 398; and O'Brien, 314-15, have done. Hebrews may exhibit features of this two-age approach, but it does not describe the era of the Old Covenant per se as an age characterized by the lack of God's presence and the dominion of evil. Hebrews conceives of the Old Covenant age as a time that foreshadowed and typified the fulfillment that would come in Christ. God was active in that time of foreshadowing (1:1-2), and obedience was possible (11:1-40). Thus, it is inaccurate to speak of the times of the Old and New Covenants as overlapping (*pace* Koester, 398; O'Brien, 314-15, and others). With fulfillment in Christ the time of foreshadowing has come to an end. See the section entitled "The Pastor and the Heavenly/Futuristic Eschatology of Apocalyptic Writings" on pp. 25-28 of the Introduction to this commentary.

61. Taking καθ' ἥν, "according to which," as referring to τῆς πρώτης σκηνῆς, "the First Tent" (Riggenbach, 252; cf. Lane and Weiss). However, Koester, 398, is correct when he argues that there would be little difference in meaning if this phrase were taken as referring to παραβολή (as argued by Attridge, 241, and Stanley, " 'Parable,' " 397).

62. As noted above, all the "gifts and sacrifices" pertained to the First Tent or Holy Place because they did not provide access into the second. Stanley's suggestion that the lesser sacrifices were to the Day-of-Atonement sacrifice as all the sacrifices together were to Christ's sacrifice introduces needless complexity unsupported by the text (Stanley, " 'Parable,' " 398).

times they were offered. The "conscience" is to "flesh" (v. 10) as the inner person is to the outer.[63] It is the worshiper's inner being or true self, the "heart."[64] As the wilderness generation has demonstrated, the essence of the human predicament is an "evil heart of unbelief" not only burdened with guilt but dominated by the proclivity to sin and rebellion (3:12-14).

The sacrifices of the First Tent could not touch this need, for they "pertained only to the realm of food and drink and various washings."[65] "Only" is emphatic. These sacrifices could produce nothing more than the kind of purity that came from observing dietary laws and ceremonial washings.[66] The sacrifices of the First Tent belonged to the same sphere as these ceremonial regulations and provided the same kind of cleansing — outward and ceremonial. Thus the First Tent's "regulations for worship" (9:1) can be described as "ordinances of the flesh." They are external, ceremonial, temporal, and weak.[67] They were devoid of divine power and thus unable to change the heart or transform the person.[68] They were appropriate only for a priesthood based on "a fleshly commandment" (7:16). Thus they were valid and "incumbent upon" God's people but only "until the time of correction" when Christ "arrived as High Priest of the good things that have come" (v. 11).[69] The word translated "correction" can refer to the abrogation of a

63. Weiss, 460.

64. Lane, 2:225, says, ". . . the 'conscience' is directed toward God and embraces the whole person in his relation to God (9:9, 14; 10:2, 22; 13:18)." συνείδησις ("conscience") describes an awareness of sin before God in writers such as Plutarch, Philo, and Josephus as well as in the NT (cf. Heb 9:14; 10:2, 22; 13:18).

65. These sacrifices could not cleanse κατὰ συνείδησιν, "in respect to the conscience," but ἐπὶ βρώμασιν καὶ πόμασιν καὶ διαφόροις βαπτισμοῖς, "in relation to the realm of food and drink and various washings." The change from κατά to ἐπί is purposeful. These sacrifices did not cleanse the worshipers in regard to food and drink, but they "related to" (cf. NASB) the same outward sphere as the regulations concerning food, drink, and ritual washings (Ellingworth, 443; Riggenbach, 252-55; cf. Bénétreau, 2:75, and Koester, 399, 406). Westcott, 254, cites 1 Thess 4:7; 1 Cor 9:10; 2 Cor 9:6; Gal 5:13; Eph 2:10; 2 Tim 2:14 in support of ἐπί as expressing "accompanying circumstances or conditions." He also invites comparison with Heb 9:15, 17; 8:6; and 10:28.

66. This description includes the laws of purity regulating everyday life as well as those pertaining to the food and drink offerings at the Mosaic sanctuary. See the references in Koester, 399, 406. It was natural to refer to the Levitical code as regulating "food and drink," as evidenced by references in the *Letter of Aristeas:* περί τε τῶν βρωτῶν καὶ ποτῶν ("concerning both food and drink," 128); διὰ βρωτῶν καὶ ποτῶν ("through food and drink," 142); ἐπὶ τῶν βρωτῶν καὶ ποτῶν ("in regard to food and drink," 158). Cited by Moffatt, 119.

67. Koester, 399-400.

68. Attridge, 231.

69. It is better to take this present participle ἐπικείμενα as middle, "incumbent upon," instead of making it a divine passive, "laid down" (by God), as argued by

law and its replacement by a better.[70] The pastor is referring to the time described in vv. 11-15 when Christ "corrected" the Old Covenant by establishing the New.[71]

It is essential that the modern reader grasp the intrinsic relationship between lack of cleansing and the inability to enter God's heavenly presence. Only those who have been forgiven and cleansed from sin so that they now live in faithful obedience are able to enjoy such communion with our holy God. The pastor uses this description of inadequate sacrifices to prepare his hearers for what he will say about Christ's all-sufficient sacrifice in vv. 11-15.[72] By his obedient sacrifice Christ can "cleanse" the conscience (9:14) from the impurity of sin and write God's laws on his people's hearts as promised in the New Covenant (10:15-18).[73] Thus, Christ's obedience empowers the faithful to live in obedience and in fellowship with God (see 10:5-10).[74] As believers we come through him to God's "throne" in order to find grace for living this life of faithfulness (4:14-16; 10:19-25).

b. The All-Sufficiency of Christ's Sacrifice (9:11-15)

11 *But Christ has arrived as High Priest of the good things that have come through the greater and more perfect Tent not made with*

Bénétreau, 2:76. Thus ἐπικείμενα, "incumbent upon," is equivalent to ἐχούσης στάσιν, "having legal standing," in v. 8 (Hughes, 325, n. 75). Both expressions are legal terms describing a system that is "in force."

70. For examples of διόρθωσις ("correction") in this sense see Attridge, 243, n. 165; cf. Bénétreau, 2:76. Compare the μετάθεσις ("change") of 7:12 and the stronger ἀθέτησις ("abolition") of 7:18.

71. With Riggenbach, 255-56, the "time of correction" refers to the event of Christ's coming, not to the present time of salvation subsequent to his coming. Cf. Weiss, 461-62.

72. The fact that this section describes only the inadequacy of the old system in the Mosaic Tent to achieve access prevents giving it the definitive place claimed by Cortez, "Transition," 527-47. Cortez shows some valid connections between this section and what follows. However, his argument does nothing to remove the clear way in which 9:11-14 describes Christ's sacrifice as the fulfillment of the Day of Atonement sacrifice. The pastor's use of other images and typologies detracts nothing from the central importance of this analogy.

73. Lane, 2:225. Attridge's acknowledgment (242) that Christ's cleansing includes the inscribing of God's law on the heart as promised in the New Covenant seems inconsistent with his restriction of this cleansing to the guilt of sin.

74. "Thus, although the perfecting of believers does not involve a moral development in our writer's perspective, it has its proper outworking in a life of obedience to God's will and perseverance in hope. The cleansing of the conscience leads to a decisive change in a person's heart with respect to God and enables that person to serve God as he requires." Peterson, *Perfection*, 140.

hands, which is not of this creation. 12 *He entered <u>once for all</u> into the Sanctuary <u>not by means of the blood of goats and calves but by means of his own blood, having obtained eternal redemption.</u> 13 For if the blood of goats and bulls and the ashes of a heifer sprinkled on the participants sanctify for the purification of the flesh,* 14 *<u>by how much more will the blood of Christ, who through the eternal Spirit offered himself blameless to God, cleanse our conscience from dead works to serve the living God!</u>* 15 *And on account of this he <u>has become Mediator of a New Covenant, so that, since a death has occurred for redemption of the transgressions committed under the First Covenant,</u> those who have been called might receive the promise of eternal inheritance.*

The opening words, "But Christ," show that these verses stand in sharp contrast with vv. 1-10. The "earthly sanctuary" (9:1) provided no access to God "but Christ."[1] However, it is also important to note the transition from the theme of "sanctuary" to "sacrifice." In vv. 1-10 the pastor described the "earthly sanctuary" in order to show that no access to God was possible through its ministrations. Only in vv. 9b-10 did he reveal that the sacrifices of the "earthly sanctuary" were the reason access was unavailable. This insufficiency of the old sacrifices anticipates the adequacy of Christ's sacrifice, which is the burden of vv. 11-15.

This central section (9:11-15) in the second movement (9:1-22) of the pastor's great symphony (8:1–10:18) is his most thorough description of Christ's work in the sacrificial categories established by the Old Covenant.[2] One has only to note the predominance of "blood," "self-offering," and "cleansing."[3] Christ has entered the true heavenly sanctuary (v. 11) because his sacrifice has done away with the sin before which the Old Covenant was impotent (vv. 12-14). Furthermore, by this sacrifice's effective removal of sin it has made him the Mediator of the "New Covenant" (v. 15). The pastor has anticipated what he has to say here in many places.[4] He will more fully reveal the significance of these sacrificial categories in 10:5-10 at the heart of his third and final symphonic movement. There he will clearly disclose the ultimate secret of Christ's effective self-offering.

Virtually all commentators are agreed on the unity of vv. 11-14. Verse 15, however, has close ties with both the preceding and following verses. On

1. δέ ("but," "on the other hand") in v. 11 indicates sharp contrast. It is probably the complement of μέν ("on the one hand") in v. 1 above (Johnson, 218; Koester, 393; Weiss, 449).

2. Weiss, 471.

3. Weiss, 472.

4. Weiss, 463, n. 3, compares 9:11 with 4:14; 9:12 with 2:17; 5:1; 7:27; and 8:2; finally, 9:13-14 with 4:16; 7:25; and 10:22.

the one hand, v. 15 draws a concluding inference from vv. 11-14 — "on account of" the fact that Christ has offered the atoning sacrifice of vv. 11-14 "he has become Mediator of the New Covenant."[5] Thus v. 15a completes the description of Christ's fully sufficient sacrifice given in vv. 11-14. This statement in v. 15a is also the mirror image of 8:6: according to 9:15a Christ's high-priestly sacrifice is the cause of his becoming Mediator of the New Covenant; according to 8:6 his being Mediator of the "Better Covenant" gives evidence of his superior priestly ministry (cf. 7:12). In fact, these verses appear to play an analogous role in the first and second movements of the pastor's symphony: both conclude the sacrifice section (8:3-6; 9:11-15) and provide transitions to the covenant section (8:7-13; 9:16-22).

The integrity of vv. 11-15 and vv. 16-22 is also suggested by the chiastic relationship between them. Note how vv. 11-14 and 18-20 are bound together by the frequent occurrence of "blood," while vv. 15 and 16-17 are joined by the repeated use of "covenant" and "death."[6]

On the other hand, as will become evident below, vv. 16-17 use covenantal terms to explain "since a death has taken place for redemption of the transgressions committed under the First Covenant" (v. 15b). The repetition of "covenant" and "death" noted above underscores the explanatory role of vv. 16-17. Furthermore, this explanation is reinforced by the description of the First Covenant's inauguration in vv. 18-22.

Neglect of these ties between vv. 16-22 and v. 15 would certainly lead to misunderstanding the pastor's concerns. However, in light of the considerations presented above, it is best to take v. 15 as the conclusion to the description of Christ's sufficiency in vv. 11-14.[7]

---

5. The way in which Hebrews establishes Christ's mediatorship on his sacrifice indicates that διὰ τοῦτο ("on account of this") should be taken with what goes before instead of what follows. The parallel often cited from Xenophon, *Cyr.* 2.1.21 offers no evidence to the contrary (Gabriella Berényi, "La portée de διὰ τοῦτο en He 9:15," *Bib* 69 [1988]: 108-12). See also Weiss, 474-76; Braun, 272; Lane, 2:241; Johnson, 239; Kistemaker, 254; Westcott, 263; Spicq, 2:261; S. W. Hahn, "A Broken Covenant and the Curse of Death: A Study of Hebrews 9:15-22," *CBQ* 66 (2004): 420; and John J. Hughes, "Hebrews IX 15ff. and Galatians III 15ff.: A Study in Covenant Practice and Procedure," *NovT* 21 (1976-77): 33. *Pace* Westfall, *Discourse Analysis,* 205, 207. O'Brien, 327; Lane, 2:241; and Ellingworth, 459-60, also affirm the close connection between v. 15a and vv. 11-14.

6. Note αἷμα ("blood") in vv. 12, 13, 14, 18, 19, 20, 21, and 22. Note especially δι' αἵματος τράγων καὶ μόσχων ("through the blood of goats and calves") in v. 12 and τὸ αἷμα τῶν μόσχων ("the blood of calves") in v. 19. See also αἱματεκχυσίας ("shedding of blood") in v. 22. Vanhoye, *La structure littéraire,* 152, notes the recurrence of "blood" in vv. 18-22 but thinks διαθήκη and its related verbal forms in vv. 15 and 16-17 indicate that v. 15 should be joined to these verses.

7. The position taken above on the unity of v. 15 with vv. 11-14 is more nuanced than that argued in Cockerill, "Structure and Interpretation in Hebrews 8:1–10:18," 188.

11 The pastor has finished describing the repetitious sacrifices of the Old Covenant that brought no access to God. He turns now to the present time of fulfillment with a definitive statement of Christ's achievement: "Christ has arrived as High Priest of the good things that have come."[8] The participle translated "has arrived" is technically dependent upon the main verb of v. 12, "entered in." However, the force with which the pastor affirms the contrasting reality of Christ suggests that this participle be taken as coordinate with that main verb; thus, we have made v. 11 a separate sentence. Nevertheless, one must not forget that the pastor's main emphasis is on v. 12. As concerned as he is to contrast what Christ has achieved in v. 11 with its ineffective predecessor (9:1-10), he has reached the place in his sermon where his main burden is to explain how Christ has accomplished this achievement, which he does initially in v. 12 and more comprehensively in vv. 13-14.[9]

Christ has returned to God's presence, but in a new capacity — as "High Priest" of God's people.[10] His earthly life of obedience and suffering has been completed on the cross, and he has now fulfilled the divine invitation to sit at God's right as the savior of humanity (8:1-2; 1:3, 13).[11] Thus, he has entered into his role as the enthroned Son of God awaiting the consummation (see on 1:1-3). His arrival in this high-priestly office at the Father's right hand is an established fact, and the benefits he now provides, here called "good things," are available for the people of God.

It is difficult to decide between the alternate readings, good things "that have come" and good things "to come."[12] The manuscript evidence for

---

8. Note the pastor's strategic use of Χριστός ("Christ"). He uses it here in 9:11 to introduce this crucial central section of the second movement and to underscore the contrast with vv. 1-10 (see Weiss, 462-63). He also uses it in 10:10 to conclude the final explanation of Christ's sacrifice, found in 10:5-10. Thus, the pastor introduces his initial (9:11-15) and concludes his final (10:5-10) explanation of Christ's death with "Christ." Cf. Ellingworth, 448. Johnson, 233, thinks that the pastor uses "Christ" here to show that he is speaking of the "messianic priest." This suggestion, however, lacks substantiation. Hebrews appears to use "Christ" as a general designation that neither emphasizes nor excludes the deity implied by "Son" or the humanity underscored by "Jesus." For "Christ" see on 3:6, 14; 5:5; 6:1; for "Jesus," 2:9; 3:1; 4:8, 14; 6:20; 7:22.

9. Contrast 1:3, where Christ's achievement, his session at God's right, was affirmed by a finite verb (ἐκάθισεν, "he sat down"), and the means, purification for sins, by a participle (ποιησάμενος, "having made").

10. There can be no doubt that the pastor is speaking of Christ's arrival in heaven (Attridge, 245; Ellingworth, 448-49; Weiss, 464; Koester, 407, 412; O'Brien, 319; and Mackie, *Eschatology and Exhortation,* 91). The noun ἀρχιερεύς, "high priest," clearly qualifies the manner of his arrival. See Ellingworth, 449.

11. "Arrived" reminds the hearers that the Son did not seize this priesthood for himself (5:4-6; Koester, 412).

12. γενομένων, "having come"; and μελλόντων, "about to come," or "to come."

389

both readings is of near-equal quality.[13] Those who espouse the reading "to come" think that a scribe was influenced to write the aorist participle "have come" by the preceding aorist participle "arrived."[14] Those who champion "have come" argue that scribal alteration has occurred under the influence of 10:1.[15] If the pastor intended "have come," he was referring primarily to the benefits of cleansing from sin and access to God described in v. 14 as the achievements of Christ's self-offering for the succor of the faithful. If he wrote "to come," he was thinking chiefly about the "heavenly homeland" (11:1-8) that is their goal. The fact that "good things" can be used in the OT as a description of the Promised Land favors this second interpretation.[16] Nevertheless, the pastor concentrates in this section on the present effectiveness of Christ's work. This emphasis accords best with the reading "good things" that "have come." Of course, present cleansing from sin and future entrance into the heavenly homeland are one inseparable whole. The pastor earnestly desires the second for his hearers and urgently presses the first upon them as the only adequate means for its attainment. Thus the phrase "good things that have come" focuses on present cleansing from sin and access to God available for the faithful without excluding ultimate entrance into the "heavenly homeland" opened by these present blessings.

"Through the greater and more perfect Tent not made with hands, which is not of this creation" distinguishes Christ from those priests who served in the "earthly sanctuary" (9:1) and human-made "Tent" (9:2).[17] By making v. 11 a separate sentence the translation given above takes this phrase as qualifying "has arrived" instead of the finite verb in v. 12, "entered." Hebrews often uses some expression to describe the place of Christ's session (see 8:1-2; 9:23). "Through the greater and more perfect Tent" fits well with the idea of arriving. Furthermore, v. 12 has its own indicator of location, affirming that Christ has "entered into the Sanctuary."

"Greater" and "more perfect" affirm the absolute superiority of this

13. Though γενομένων, "having come," has a slight advantage in diversity of evidence: (𝔓46), B, D*, 1739, Itᵈ, syrᵖ, ʰ, ᵖᵃˡ, Origen, etc. See *TCGNT,* 598.
14. Riggenbach, 256-57; Montefiore, 151. The participle παραγενόμενος, "having arrived," is a compound form of the participle γενομένων, "having come."
15. Lane, 2:229b; Hughes, 327; Bénétreau, 2:76-77; Weiss, 464, Gordon, 119; most recent commentaries. See τῶν μελλόντων ἀγαθῶν, "the good things about to come" or "the good things to come," in 10:1. In that verse, however, the author is speaking from the point of view of the Old Covenant, not the New.
16. See ἀγαθά, "good things," in Exod 3:8; 10:12; Num 14:7; and Deut 1:25; 8:1. Cf. Ellingworth, 450. Bénétreau, 2:76-77, identifies these "good things" with "the world to come" (1:6; 2:5), though he would probably include present as well as future benefits within this description.
17. See κατεσκευάσθη ("constructed") in v. 2 and compare 8:4-5.

"Tent."[18] It can be nothing less than the Sanctuary Christ has entered, the ultimate dwelling place of God. As noted in the discussion of 8:2 above, the pastor uses "tent" to establish typological continuity between the old and the new. Thus, he uses "true" (8:2) and "greater and more perfect" when using "Tent" for the Sanctuary entered by Christ. When one approaches this heavenly reality, it is "the greater and more perfect Tent" through which Christ has passed, penetrating to the very throne of God; when one enters, it is the "Sanctuary" (v. 12) in which he has taken his seat at God's right hand. As described in 9:1-10, the Old Covenant was a religion of the Holy Place confined to its boundaries and excluded from the Most Holy Place. In the New there is no need for a heavenly "Holy Place" since Christ brings his people into the very presence of God. Thus any suggestion that "the greater and more perfect Tent" represents a heavenly "Holy Place" is nothing more than a vestigial remnant from the parallel the pastor has drawn between Old Tent and the New.[19] Since this "Tent" is "not made with hands, that is, not a part of this creation," it can be nothing other than the Tent that "God, not man, built," called the "true Tent" in 8:2. By thus stressing the heavenly location of Christ's ministry, the pastor affirms its unique effectiveness in bringing God's people into his presence.[20]

Some have attempted to identify this "greater and more perfect Tent" through which Christ "arrived" as the physical heavens through which he passed on his way to the "Sanctuary" in which God dwells.[21] However, the

18. τελειοτέρα, "more perfect," reminds the hearers that Christ has obtained τελειότης, "perfection," or access to God, which the faithful enjoy in this heavenly "Tent." See Ellingworth, 450. Koester, 413, is misguided when he takes these terms as true comparatives and thus asserts that "the Mosaic sanctuary had a degree of greatness and perfection." According to 7:19, "the law made nothing perfect." This "Tent" is "greater and more perfect" in the same sense that Christ's sacrifice was "better" (κρείττοσιν, 9:23) because it provided what the old could not, a way to live in fellowship with God under a "better" (κρείττονος) Covenant (7:22). See Attridge, 247.

19. Following Ellingworth, 447-48; cf. also Davidson, 174; but *pace* Lane, 2:236-38; Attridge, 247-48; and O'Brien, 320, who think that this "greater and more perfect tent" is the outer part of a two-part heavenly sanctuary instead of a reference to heaven itself. However, even Attridge (247-48) concludes by saying, "Hebrews will finally be concerned not so much with a realistically conceived heavenly journey made by Christ as with the significance of entry into the realm where God is truly worshiped." Philip E. Hughes, "The Blood of Jesus and His Heavenly Priesthood in Hebrews, Part III: The Meaning of the 'True Tent' and 'the Greater and More Perfect Tent,'" *BSac* 130 (1973): 313-14, agrees that the effective work of Christ leaves no room for a heavenly Holy Place distinct from the Most Holy Place.

20. This "Tent" is superior not merely, as Koester, 413, suggests, because "heaven is superior to earth," but because heaven is the place where God dwells.

21. See Riggenbach, 258; Andriessen, "Zelt," 76-92; and Peterson, *Perfection*, 143-44. Cf. also the discussions in Héring and Spicq.

physical heavens are part of the creation (1:10-12; 12:25-27), while the "Tent" under consideration is "not of this creation." Andriessen has attempted to overcome this objection by positing an "intermediate" heaven populated by angels and located between the visible heavens and the dwelling of God.[22] However, the fact that angels appear along with the faithful in God's presence according to 12:22-24 has forced Andriessen to say that Christ has done away with this distinction.[23] Thus his position falls under the same judgment as the previous — both a heavenly Holy Place and an intermediate heaven are superfluous to the argument of Hebrews.[24] Furthermore, it is unlikely that the pastor would use "true" (8:2) and "greater and more perfect" to describe any "heaven" less than the dwelling place of God.[25]

Others have argued that "the greater and more perfect Tent" is a metaphor for the body of Christ.[26] They contend that "through the greater and more perfect Tent" is parallel to "by means of his own blood" in v. 12. Both phrases begin with the same Greek preposition, which can be used locally for passing "through" or instrumentally to express "by means of." Furthermore, since this preposition is obviously instrumental in the second phrase, "by means of" his own blood, it must be instrumental in the first.[27] Those who

22. Andriessen, "Zelt," 76-92.

23. See Andriessen, "Zelt," 91-92. Andriessen's argument that Christ has a present ministry in the heavenly Holy Place as well as the Most Holy Place is contrary to Hebrews' assertion of Christ's session. Furthermore, his suggestion that the heavenly Holy Place is the present place where the people of God dwell is in plain contradiction to the assertions of Hebrews that believers have continual access to the very presence of God (4:14-16; 10:19-21). See the criticism of Andriessen in Vanhoye, *Old Testament*, 191-92.

24. Riggenbach, 258-59, agrees that the author of Hebrews believes Christ has entered heaven as a whole. Thus although he thinks "tent" refers to an intermediate heavens, he concedes that the author uses this expression only by analogy with the old.

25. Cf. Montefiore, 153.

26. Hughes, "Tent," surveys the different ways in which the "true Tent" of 8:2 and the "greater and more perfect Tent" of 9:11 have been understood as Christ's "body": his human body (Owen, Bengel, Calvin, Chrysostom, etc.), his body the church (Cornelius à Lapide; Westcott), or the human person (Ambrose; Gregory of Nazianzus; F. F. Bruce). One must also add the eucharistic body of Christ (J. Swetnam, "'The Greater and More Perfect Tent': A Contribution to the Discussion of Heb. 9:11," *Bib* 47 [1966]: 91-106).

27. The question is whether διά followed by the genitive case should be understood as local or instrumental — a reference to motion "through" or to "by means of." Those like Young ("Gospel," 202-3), who insist on the instrumental, make much of the parallel between "through [διά] the greater and more perfect Tent" in v. 11 and "by [διά] his own blood" in v. 12. Although Lane (2:229c, 236-38) defends the local significance of διά, he lays out the chiastic parallels between vv. 11 and 12 with clarity: [A] διὰ τῆς μείζονος καὶ τελειοτέρας σκηνῆς ("through the greater and more perfect Tent"); [B] οὐ χειροποιήτου, τοῦτ᾽ ἔστιν οὐ ταύτης τῆς κτίσεως ("not made with hands, that is, not of this creation"); [B¹] οὐδὲ δι᾽ αἵματος τράγων καὶ μόσχων ("not by means of the blood of goats and calves"); [A¹]

hold this position argue that the pastor would not vary his usage in such close quarters — "by means of the greater and more perfect Tent"; "by means of his own blood." Thus "Tent" here is used for the body of Christ in line with the way tent/temple imagery is used elsewhere in the NT.[28] Christ has entered into the Sanctuary "by means of his body" and "by means of his own blood."

This position is inadequate for several reasons. First of all, the pastor is free to use a preposition in various ways within the same context. Note his use of the same preposition found here in 13:15.[29] Second, one can hardly say that Christ's "body" was "not of this creation" unless one is speaking only of the glorified body of Christ.[30] Third, those who have espoused this interpretation have been unduly influenced by the use of tent/temple imagery elsewhere in the NT. The pastor has supplied no contextual clues that would enable the recipients to hear "greater and more perfect Tent" as a metaphor for Christ's body. Instead, he expects them to identify this "Tent" with the "true Tent and Sanctuary" in which Christ ministers (8:2).

12 In v. 11 the pastor affirmed Christ's arrival in heaven as the High Priest who has provided the blessings of salvation (cf. 8:1-2) unavailable under the Old Covenant (9:1-10). In v. 12 he addresses his main concern in this passage — the means by which Christ has entered God's presence as effective High Priest: "by means of his own blood." In accord with his habit, the pastor underscores the effectiveness of Christ's "own blood" by contrasting it with the "blood" of the old animal sacrifices.[31] The shedding of blood is the offering of one's life, for "the life of the flesh is in the blood" (Lev 17:11; cf. 17:14). The shed blood of "goats and calves" represented the lives of those who offered them poured out in death. Thus, when the pastor would explain Christ's death by analogy with the sacrifices of the Old Covenant, he describes it as Christ's "own blood."[32] His shed "blood" is his willing offering

---

διὰ δὲ τοῦ ἰδίου αἵματος ("but by means of his own blood"). Young's defense of the instrumental is linked with his argument that "the greater and more perfect Tent" is a reference to the whole new order by which Christ has brought salvation (Young, "Gospel"). The immediate context gives little indication that the pastor intends such a metaphor. This interpretation fits poorly with the parallel reference to the "true Tent" in 8:2.

28. See John 1:14; 2:19-22; Mark 14:58; 15:29; 1 Cor 6:19; 2 Cor 6:16; 2; Eph 1:22-23. See also Hughes, "Tent," 313.

29. Weiss (465, n. 12) and Bénétreau (2:77, citing Braun) also mention 2:14-16; 10:20; and 13:21-22. The parallels between vv. 11-12, outlined above by Lane, provide this passage with cohesion and a pleasing rhythm. However, they afford no basis for insisting that the first use of διά conform to the two following — especially since the object of the first διά is a place, but of the second and third, a thing.

30. As argued by Vanhoye, "Tent." See also Vanhoye, *Old Testament,* 189-96, for a summary in English. This position also suffers from a lack of clear contextual support.

31. ἰδίου, "his own," is stronger than αὐτοῦ would have been (Spicq, 2:257).

32. Riggenbach, 260-61, n. 19. Weiss, 467, agrees that Christ's "blood" refers to the

of his life through death on the cross. It was by means of this self-offering alone that he entered the heavenly presence of God. Heb 10:5-10 below will make this understanding of the blood of Christ absolutely clear.

The aorist verb translated "entered," along with the aorist participle in the phrase "having obtained eternal redemption," underscores the "once-for-all" character of Christ's entrance and thus the ultimate effectiveness of his "blood." His sacrifice was accomplished on the cross and was the means of his entrance into heaven as High Priest.[33] Christ's superiority is shown by the way he breaks the pattern established by the old high priests on the Day of Atonement. After shedding the blood on the altar, those high priests carried it into the Most Holy Place, where they stood sprinkling it on the Mercy Seat above the Ark. Their offering with its limited ceremonial cleansing was incomplete without this ritual.[34] The pastor, however, is careful to avoid giving the impression that Christ carried his blood into heaven.[35] Christ entered heaven "by means of his blood" shed on the cross.[36] Instead of sprinkling blood on the Mercy Seat representing God's throne he took his seat at the right of that throne, demonstrating the effectiveness of his shed blood (10:11-14).

Thus the aorist participial phrase, "having obtained eternal redemption," should not be taken as subsequent to Christ's entrance or as describing its purpose, as in the NRSV: "he entered . . . thus obtaining eternal redemp-

---

giving up of his life as an offering in death. See Johnson, 237, and O'Brien, 321. Note the association of Christ's blood with his death in the traditions of the Last Supper (Matt 26:28; Mark 14:24; Luke 22:20; 1 Cor 10:16; 11:25, 27). The NT often associates blood with Christ's death (Matt 27:24-25; John 19:34; Acts 20:28; Rom 3:25; 5:9; Eph 1:7; 2:13; Col 1:14, 20; 1 Pet 1:2, 9; 1 John 1:7; Rev 1:5; 5:9; 7:14; 12:11; 19:13). For a thorough refutation of Westcott's argument (294) that shed "blood" represents the life of the victim made available for others see Philip E. Hughes, "The Blood of Jesus and His Heavenly Priesthood in Hebrews, Part I: The Significance of the Blood of Jesus," *BSac* 130 (1973): 99-109, and Leon Morris, "The Biblical Use of the Term 'Blood,'" *JTS* 3 (1952): 216-27, esp. 223, 227.

33. Stökel Ben Ezra, *Yom Kippur,* 189.

34. See on 9:7 above, where the verb προσφέρω, "offer," is used of the high priest's carrying the blood into the Most Holy Place.

35. Thompson, *Christian Philosophy,* 108, says, "The language throughout Chap. 9 indicates that the blood of Jesus was actually offered in the heavenly tabernacle." However, neither he nor Mitchell, 185, who affirms the same position, provides *any* support for this statement. The NRSV, "with his own blood," is misleading. The pastor intentionally uses διά ("by means of") his own blood instead of μέτα ("with") or ἐν ("in," "with"). See Riggenbach, 260; Bruce, 212-13; O'Brien, 321; and Gordon, 120. Walter Edward Brooks, "The Perpetuity of Christ's Sacrifice in the Epistle to the Hebrews," *JBL* 89 (1970): 205-14, argues that Christ has carried his blood into the Sanctuary, where he continually offers it before the throne of God. For a thorough refutation of this position see Hughes, "Blood," 99-109, and Hughes, "Sacrifice," 195-212.

36. See O'Brien, 321 n. 89, *"by virtue of . . .* his death he entered the heavenly sanctuary" (italics original).

tion."[37] This phrase gives the means or cause of his entrance, "he entered . . . by obtaining eternal redemption" on the cross. From the beginning (1:3) the pastor has affirmed that Christ's atoning work was the means of his session (cf. 9:15 and 10:5-10). Christ's sacrifice on the cross and his session at God's right must be neither separated nor confused.[38] If the first is the means of the second, the second is the confirmation and consummation of the first. The pastor would have his beleaguered hearers keep their eyes on the High Priest at God's right as the one with all authority to administer the much needed benefits obtained through his self-offering (8:1-2).

This "eternal redemption" provides something more that the "purification of the flesh" (9:10) available under the old sacrificial system. The word used for "redemption" signifies the paying of a price in order to obtain freedom from bondage for those redeemed.[39] The Greek OT often uses the verb form of "redemption" to speak of Israel's deliverance from Egypt.[40] Oppression under Pharaoh had prevented God's people from serving him in the Promised Land. Long ago God had "redeemed" them from that bondage. Christ has now obtained a "redemption" that delivers them from something far deeper and more insidious. He has provided for their liberation from the corruption of sin that prevents fellowship with God in the heavenly homeland, and thus from the fear of death and judgment endemic to humankind (2:14-15).[41] That first redemption was temporal in both the benefits it provided and their duration. This second is "eternal" in its effectiveness, benefits, and duration. The price of "eternal redemption" was costly beyond measure, for it could be procured by nothing less than the "once-for-all" self-offering of the eternal Son of God.[42] The pas-

---

37. *Pace* Johnson, 237; Koester, 406; and Attridge, 244. The aorist participle εὑράμενος, "having obtained," denotes action logically, if not temporally, prior to the main verb "entered." Hughes, 328, n. 84, has clearly demonstrated that Christ obtained this redemption by his sacrifice before and in order to enter God's presence. See Hughes' excursus, "The Blood of Jesus and His Heavenly Priesthood," 329-54; and Hughes, "Sacrifice," 210. Cf. Ellingworth, 452-53.

38. Thus we would heed Riggenbach's warning (259-62) not to separate the two but avoid Koester's (415) confusion of the two as both part of Christ's sacrifice.

39. See λύτρωσις ("redemption") in Lev 25:29, 48; Pss 48:8; 110:9; 129:7 (Johnson, 236).

40. Exod 6:6; 13:15; 15:13; Deut 7:8; 9:26; 13:5 (Johnson, 236). See also Ellingworth, 453, and Pss. 59:1; 77:15.

41. *Pace* Weiss, 468, n. 21. This "eternal redemption" certainly includes forgiveness for sins, but, in light of v. 14 below, it should not be limited to forgiveness in a narrow sense, as O'Brien's discussion of this subject (322) might suggest.

42. The finality of a "once-for-all" sacrifice results in the finality of an "eternal redemption" (Weiss, 468; Riggenbach, 262). It was possible only for one who was the eternal Son to obtain such "eternal" redemption (Johnson, 236).

tor's great concern is that his hearers avail themselves of this great provision that is theirs in Christ.

13 The pastor has already established the fact that the sacrifices of the Old Covenant could not cleanse the heart and bring God's people into his presence (vv. 9-10 above). In vv. 13-14 he avails himself of his beloved less-to-greater argument in order to show their lasting value as a type or anticipation of the true cleansing available through the blood of Christ. Verse 13 gives the "lesser" part of the argument: "if the blood of goats and calves"; v. 14, the greater: "how much more the blood of Christ." The blood of animal sacrifices "cleansed for the purification of the flesh." Those sacrifices provided a ritual purification that permitted God's people to participate in the worship of the Mosaic Tent and in the community life of the people of God.[43] Thus, they were an appropriate anticipation of the inner purification provided by Christ that entitles God's people to live in his presence.[44] There is little comparison between Hebrews' criticism of the Levitical ritual and the condemnation of the Temple by the people of Qumran. The Qumran community condemned the Jerusalem Temple because its ritual was incorrectly executed. On the one hand, Hebrews exposes the inability of the Levitical system to achieve its purpose even when correctly practiced.[45] On the other, it affirms the Scriptural record of the Old as an abiding anticipation or type of Christ's sacrifice.

"Goats and calves" (v. 12) and "goats and bulls" (v. 13) would draw the hearers' minds once again to the great double Day of Atonement sacrifice (see 5:1-4; 6:19-20; 7:27; and 9:8-10). On that day the high priest offered a "calf" for himself and a "goat" for the people (see Lev 16:11-19). Yet the pastor has reversed the order, for the calf was sacrificed before the goat. In this verse he has also used "bull" instead of the word "calf" found in the Leviticus 16 instructions for the Day of Atonement.[46] Thus, while he evokes the Day of Atonement, he expands his reach in order to include all the old sacrifices as under the sentence of impotency.

The "washings" in v. 10 above anticipated the pastor's introduction of

43. Riggenbach, 263-65.

44. "The death of Christ accomplishes this cleansing from sins (1:3) and liberation from sinful impulses (9:14: νεκρὰ ἔργα, which defile as contrasted with those done in the service of God). It thus gives access to holiness and enables man truly to live in the presence of God." Friedrich Hauck and Rudolf Meyer, "καθαρός, καθαρίζω, καθαίρω, καθαρότης," *TDNT* 3:426.

45. Thus it is strange when Witherington, 269, says that Hebrews' criticism of the old system was "less severe" than that voiced against the Temple by such sources as 1QpHab 12:8-9; *T. Mos.* 6:1; and *Sib. Or.* 4.8.27.

46. Ellingworth, 454. Heb 9:13 uses ταῦρος ("bull"); Heb 9:12 and Lev 16:11-19, μόσχος ("calf").

the purifying water mixed with the "ashes of a heifer" as described in Num 19:1-10. According to Numbers 19 it was not Aaron, the high priest, but his son Eleazar who supervised the production of these ashes. Eleazar was directed to sprinkle the heifer's blood toward the "Tent of Meeting" and then to see that the body was properly burned. Since Eleazar succeeded his father as high priest, it was not unreasonable for Hebrews to assume, along with both Philo (*Spec. Laws* 1.267) and Josephus (*Ant.* 4.4.6), that the high priest was in charge of producing these ashes.[47] The heifer's ashes mixed with water and sprinkled on the unclean held a central place in the Levitical purification rituals. Thus, by associating this ritual with sacrifices offered for sin the pastor helps his hearers realize that the whole sacrificial system was restricted to outward purification.[48] It could do nothing more for them than point to the true inward purification necessary for approaching God.[49]

14 But, if outward cleansing was available through those rituals, "how much more" (v. 14) is true inward cleansing available through "the blood of Christ."[50] The main clause of this verse declares what Christ's "blood" can do: "cleanse our conscience from dead works to serve the living God." The relative clause indicates why his blood is thus effective: "who through the eternal Spirit offered himself blameless to God." The pastor is not referring to the physical substance of Christ's blood per se but, as noted above, to his offering of himself in obedience to God as an "unblemished sacrifice" (see 10:5-10).[51]

First of all, Christ's sacrifice was effective because it was offered "through the eternal Spirit."[52] The debate as to whether the "eternal Spirit" is

47. Later rabbinic tradition asserted that the water produced with these ashes was used to purify the high priest before the Day of Atonement. However, *pace* W. Horbury, "The Aaronic Priesthood in the Epistle to the Hebrews," *JSNT* 19 (1983): 51-52, who is followed by Stökel Ben Ezra, *Yom Kippur,* 188, there is no indication that Hebrews was drawing on a tradition that already associated these two rituals.

48. O'Brien, 323; cf. Mitchell, 183. Although ῥαντίζουσα ("sprinkling") agrees with the feminine singular σποδός ("ashes"), it is probably also meant to qualify the αἷμα ("blood") of "bulls and goats" (Ellingworth, 455).

49. Thus, Weiss, 469, is correct in asserting that the water-of-purification ritual was introduced to strengthen the typological relationship between old and new — ritual cleansing/inner cleansing. See Lane, 2:239. Hughes's suggestion (462-63) that the author may have mentioned this ritual because it was practiced at Qumran is gratuitous.

50. The pastor does not compare the blood of animals to the blood of a human being or a martyr (cf. 4 Macc 6:29; 17:22), but to the blood of Christ, the obedient incarnate Son of God (Koester, 415).

51. O'Brien, 323, citing Michel, 314; Lane, 2:240; Ellingworth, 456; Peterson, *Perfection,* 138.

52. Albert Vanhoye, "Esprit éternel et feu du sacrifice en He 9, 14," *Bib* 64 (1983): 263-74; followed by Weiss, 473, and Koester, 415, thinks "eternal Spirit" is the ty-

the Holy Spirit or Christ's divine nature has often diverted interpreters from the pastor's main point — Christ's sacrifice is based on the power of God.[53] The pastor is probably using this term in reference to the Holy Spirit, but without diminution of all that he has said about the Son's eternal being. References to the Holy Spirit in 2:4; 3:7; 6:4; and 9:8 (cf. 10:15) prepare readers to hear "eternal Spirit" as a description of the same reality. A few late manuscripts read "Holy Spirit" in this verse, confirming the expectation created by previous passages.[54] Jewish tradition associated the Holy Spirit with the atoning work of the high priest.[55] Thus there need be no surprise when the pastor refers to the Holy Spirit in this context. One must ask, however, why the pastor chooses to describe the Holy Spirit as "eternal Spirit?"[56] Omission of the definite article in Greek (literally, "through eternal Spirit") puts emphasis on the "eternal" quality of the Spirit thus displayed.[57]

---

pological fulfillment of the "perpetual fire" (see Lev 6:5-6) upon which the old sacrifices were burned. For critique see M. Emmrich, "'Amtscharisma': Through the Eternal Spirit (Hebrews 9:14)," *BBR* 12 (2002): 18; Attridge, 250. The pastor has hardly given his hearers sufficient contextual clues to make this identification.

53. Advocates of Christ's divine nature include Westcott, 262; Riggenbach, 266-67; Moffatt, 124; Spicq, 2:258-59; Montefiore, 154-55; and Hughes, 358-59. Bruce, 216-17; Lane, 2:240; Ellingworth, 456-57; Weiss, 472-73; Witherington, 270-71; George Guthrie, 312; Emmrich, "'Amtscharisma,'" 22-25; Vanhoye, "Esprit Éternel"; and many others identify the "eternal Spirit" with the Holy Spirit. A few, such as Bénétreau, 2:82, and Johnson, 238, appear to take "eternal Spirit" as Christ's own spirit. Taken this way, the phrase reinforces the voluntary nature of Christ's "blameless" obedience. As Bénétreau himself admits, this position is difficult to reconcile with the use of "eternal." Westcott, 262, almost joins this last position to the first when he argues that Christ's "eternal Spirit" (his divine nature) includes his more limited "human" spirit (cf. Attridge, 251). *Pace* Grässer, 2:159, there is nothing to indicate that "the eternal Spirit" who was the means of Christ's effective offering is a synonym for "the heavenly realm" in which his sacrifice was supposedly offered. See critique in Emmrich, "'Amtscharisma,'" 22, n. 25.

54. The Latin Vulgate also reads "Holy Spirit" (Hughes, 358).

55. See Emmrich, "'Amtscharisma,'" 17-32. Emmrich is able to show that Jewish tradition affirmed the necessity of the Holy Spirit for the work of the high priest as well as for the office of prophet or king. However, he has not been able to demonstrate close verbal or conceptual connection between Hebrews and any of these Jewish sources.

56. Compare the pastor's purposeful description of the Holy Spirit as the "Spirit of Grace" in 10:29.

57. The omission of the definite article before "eternal Spirit" (πνεύματος αἰωνίου, instead of τοῦ πνεύματος αἰωνίου, "the eternal Spirit") is no objection to the Holy Spirit as the referent of this phrase. The pastor uses the definite article before "Holy Spirit" in 3:7; 9:8; and 10:15 when the Holy Spirit is the subject of the sentence. He uses the article with the direct object "Spirit of Grace" in 10:29. However, he omits the article in 2:4 and 6:4, where "Holy Spirit" is the genitive qualifier of a noun. The grammatically subordinate place of "through the eternal Spirit" in 9:14 is closer to these two passages.

Furthermore, "eternal" evokes all that the pastor has said about the eternal being of the Son in chapters 1 through 7. Heb 7:1-25 has made it clear that the Son's effective priesthood is based on his eternal sonship, for he has become priest "by the power of an indestructible life" (7:16).[58] "By means of the eternal Spirit" perfectly complements all the pastor has said about Christ's eternal sonship as the foundation of his priesthood. The pastor, who often speaks of the exalted and preincarnate Son as eternal, here refers to the role of God's Spirit in the Son's incarnate life. It was "through the eternal Spirit" that he lived a "blameless" life, offering himself up in death.[59] This reference to the work of the Spirit in Jesus' earthly life is in accord with the Gospel tradition.[60] It is no denial that while incarnate he continued to be Son (5:8; 10:5-10), but it is an affirmation of the true humanity he then assumed. Unlike many commentators, the pastor would drive no wedge between the Son and the Holy Spirit. Rather, he would emphasize in every way possible that Christ's High Priesthood, including his sacrifice, was made effective by the "eternal" power of God rather than by the weakness of mortal, sinful humanity ("flesh").[61] Thus Christ was able to achieve an "eternal redemption" (v. 12).[62]

58. While "by the power of an indestructible life" in 7:16 does not refer directly to Christ's self-offering, it does refer to his becoming the all-sufficient (High) Priest (cf. γέγονεν, "he has become"). Since entering into his effective high priesthood and his self-offering are co-terminus (5:7-10; 7:26-28), this phrase is, *pace* Emmrich, clearly relevant to our understanding of "by the eternal Spirit" in 11:14. Emmrich seems to be so afraid of reading later Christological developments back into Hebrews that he fails to grasp what Heb 7:1-25 is affirming. It is the eternal nature of the Son and not merely the unending duration of his priesthood that qualifies him as effective (High) Priest. See Emmrich, "'Amtscharisma,'" 20–21. Ellingworth, 457, and Attridge, 251, evidence a similar fear that prevents them from acknowledging Hebrews' clear affirmations of the Son's deity.

59. *Pace* Riggenbach, 267, and many others, it is not likely that the pastor is thinking primarily of Christ's resurrection when he says he offered himself "by means of eternal Spirit." If Christ's sacrifice was his life of obedience culminating in the cross (see also 10:5-10), then it would be natural to say that he accomplished this "by means of the eternal Spirit." This interpretation fits well with the following adjective "blameless." There is nothing in the context about resurrection.

60. "The statement in Hebrews is a logical deduction from the gospel portrait of Jesus" (Donald G. Guthrie, *New Testament Theology* [Downers Grove, IL: InterVarsity Press, 1981], 568), cited by Kistemaker, 251-52.

61. An important aspect of the pastor's thought is lost if "eternal" is reduced to mere "eschatological," as suggested by Werner Bieder, "Pneumatologische Aspekte im Hebräerbrief," in *Neues Testament und Geschichte* (Festschrift for O. Cullmann), ed. H. Baltensweiler and B. Reicke (Tübingen: Mohr-Siebeck, 1972), 251-60, cited in Emmrich, "'Amtscharisma,'" 22, n. 26. The "eternal salvation" (5:9) that Christ brings is "eschatological" in the sense that it is God's final and fully sufficient salvation. It is this, however, because it is based on the power of the eternal God.

62. The use of αἰώνιος ("eternal") in v. 14 is particularly appropriate because of

The second reason for Christ's successful sacrifice is an extension of the first: it was "through the eternal Spirit" that Christ offered himself "blameless" or "without fault." According to Jewish tradition cited by Emmrich the Holy Spirit sanctified the Jewish high priest so that he could enter the Most Holy Place.[63] Although there was nothing from which the Holy Spirit could purge the sinless Christ, the Spirit, in conjunction with his deity as the eternal Son, empowered him to live a life of complete conformity to the divine will and thus to make his all-sufficient self-offering and enter God's presence on our behalf. The word used for "without fault" or "blameless" was often used to describe the "goats and bulls" of the Old Covenant as without physical blemish.[64] By his incarnate obedience Christ offered himself without moral blemish in a final act of obedience on the cross.[65] The pastor is not referring to a timeless holiness but to the blamelessness that Christ achieved during his earthly life and which he continues to possess at God's right hand.[66] The importance of his incarnate obedience was anticipated in 5:6-10 and will be fully explained in 10:5-10. Thus the blamelessness here affirmed anticipates that climactic description of the reason for Christ's effectiveness given in 10:5-10 at the heart of the third and final movement (9:23–10:18) of the pastor's grand symphony (8:1–10:18) in praise of Christ's self-offering.

The main clause of v. 14 is the pastor's most definitive statement thus far of the benefits brought by Christ: the blood of Christ "cleanses our conscience from dead works to serve the living God." It is natural for the pastor to describe the cleansing power of Christ's death in that cleansing is native to the world of sanctuary, sacrifice, and priesthood. By cleansing God's people from sin the blood of Christ delivers them from the wrath of God, enables them to enter the true Sanctuary of God's presence, and empowers them to walk in obedient fellowship with him.[67] Hebrews makes it clear that God's

---

its occurrence in v. 12 ("eternal redemption") and its pending reuse in v. 15 ("eternal inheritance"). Cf. also 5:9 and 13:20.

63. Emmrich, "'Amtscharisma,'" 25-27.

64. See ἄμωμον, "without blemish," in Exod 29:1; Lev 1:3; Num. 6:14; 19:2; and Philo, *Dreams* 1.62; *Sacrifices* 51 (Lane, 2:240; Johnson, 238).

65. ἄμωμον, "without blemish," was also used for the moral integrity of human beings in Pss 17:23, 30; 36:18; Prov 11:5 (Lane, 2:240; Johnson, 238).

66. Ellingworth (458) is correct in saying that this word refers to the moral purity of Christ which is the basis of his effective sacrifice and not to something he obtained in heaven, although he of course maintains this purity there. See also Hughes, 357, n. 4; Lane, 2:240.

67. William G. Johnsson, "Defilement/Purification and Hebrews 9:23," in *Issues in the Book of Hebrews,* ed. Frank B. Holbrook (Silver Spring, MD: Biblical Research Institute, 1989), 79-103, esp. 88-89. See also William G. Johnsson, "Defilement and Purga-

people receive the benefit of this cleansing in union with their High Priest who sits at God's right hand as the "source of eternal salvation" (5:10; cf. 4:14-16; 10:19-25).

Three phrases describe the nature of this cleansing — the first describing what is cleansed, "our conscience"; the second, that from which it is cleansed, "dead works"; and the third, the positive result of this cleansing, "to serve the living God." First, this is not a cleansing of the body or of the "flesh" but of the "conscience." The pastor uses "conscience" when he would speak of removing sin from the "heart," that is, from the inner reality of the faithful.[68] Any cleansing that does not deal with the hardened, "evil unbelieving heart" (3:12; cf. 3:8-10) will not suffice. "Cleansing" the conscience and "perfecting" (v. 9 above) the conscience refer to the same reality. The first word emphasizes the removal of sinful pollution; the second, the readiness of the cleansed heart to approach God. Second, this cleansing is "from dead works." By "dead works" the pastor is not referring to the rituals of the Old Covenant but to the sin from which those rituals could not cleanse the inner person.[69] The Old Covenant rituals had no power to cleanse from "an evil, unbelieving heart" (3:12) and the resulting disobedience so characteristic of such a heart (3:7–4:11). Such "dead works" that spring from a refusal to trust God are the equivalent of idolatry and thus result in falling "away from the living God" (3:12).[70] Mention of the "living God" leads to the third phrase used to describe the cleansing provided by Christ: this cleansing purges the true inner person of believers so that they can "serve" or obey "the living God."[71] Thus, the "dead works" so purged will be replaced by God's "laws" (10:15-18) written on the heart, empowering the cleansed for obedient living. Christ's sacrifice achieves a true inner moral and spiritual transformation that results in an obedient life in reliance on God.

15 "On account of" the effective sacrifice offered by Christ described in v. 14, "he is" now "the Mediator of [the] New Covenant." This sacrifice is the death that "has occurred for redemption of the transgressions based on the First Covenant." By cleansing the inner being of the worshiper, Christ's sacrifice brought an end to the sacrifices that could cleanse nothing

---

tion in the Book of Hebrews," Ph.D. dissertation (Vanderbilt University, 1973); and Peterson, *Perfection*, 140. This last reference is cited approvingly by O'Brien, 326.

68. "'Conscience' (συνείδησις) is the human organ of religious life embracing the whole person in relationship to God. . . . It is the point at which a person confronts God's holiness" (Lane, 2:240-41).

69. Attridge, 252; Ellingworth, 459; and Gordon, 121-22; cf. deSilva, 307, but *pace* Johnson, 239; Lane, 2:240; and others.

70. On "dead works" and idolatry see deSilva, 307.

71. λατρεύειν, "to serve" or "to worship," is used for all God's people and not just for the service of priests (cf. 9:9; 10:1; 12:28). Riggenbach, 269; Attridge, 252.

but the "flesh" (9:10). Thus, by establishing an effective way of approaching God, he terminated the Old Covenant as a way of salvation and inaugurated the New that it typified.[72] His self-offering became a sacrifice of covenant inauguration. He is no mere go-between, but a Mediator who, on the basis of his all-sufficient self-offering, guarantees (7:22) the benefits provided to all "those who draw near to God through him" (7:25). He functions now as Mediator for beleaguered believers, enabling them to obtain their promised "eternal inheritance."[73]

"Transgressions based on the First Covenant" does not limit the effectiveness of Christ's sacrifice to offenses committed before his coming or before the hearers became believers.[74] The Old Covenant may not have been able to cleanse the heart, but it did expose the true nature of sin as unbelief and disobedience springing from an evil heart.[75] Apart from Christ the condemnation of the broken covenant described in 8:7-13 continues to threaten the people of God. God's people who come after Christ are endangered by the same unbelief and disobedience that characterized the wilderness generation (3:7–4:11; 8:8-9). Christ's coming has only intensified the condemnation of the Old Covenant on those who reject God's grace (2:1-4). The pastor uses "transgressions" to underscore the deliberate character and thus the seriousness of these disobedient acts.[76] Christ's death provides "redemption" from "the consequences and . . . power" of these transgressions.[77] His self-offering cleanses God's people from sin so that they can escape the condemnation of the broken Old Covenant and receive the promised inheritance that it anticipated.[78]

Christ exercises his present ministry both as High Priest at God's right hand and as Mediator of the New Covenant. His high priesthood and his

72. "The new internal and spiritual relation of man to God established by Christ involved of necessity a New Covenant" (Westcott, 263). "Thus the death of Christ appears under a twofold aspect. His blood is the means of atonement and the ratification of the Covenant which followed upon it" (Westcott, 264). Cf. Riggenbach, 270.

73. *Pace* Ellingworth, 461, within the immediate context this "eternal inheritance" is something to be received in the future (note the aorist subjunctive of λάβωσιν, "take," "receive") through the present mediation of Christ.

74. The way Spicq, 2:261-62, restricts these "transgressions" to the pre-Christ era seems to limit Christ's mediatorial work to the past. See also Koester, 417.

75. ἐπὶ τῇ πρώτῃ διαθήκῃ means "on the basis of the first covenant"; contrast ἐπ' αὐτῆς, used for the Aaronic priesthood in 7:11 (cf. 9:10, 17) (Johnson, 239)

76. Rather than the "outward" and "legal" aspect of these offenses, as advocated by Johnson, 239.

77. Westcott, 264. *Pace* Ellingworth, 461, the immediate context forbids locating this "redemption" in the future. The pastor has just described the benefits that Christ's death has already provided and called them "eternal redemption" in v. 12 above.

78. Cf. Lane, 2:241-42.

mediatorship are two sides of the same coin. We might say that as High Priest he does what the Old Covenant could not do by cleansing the heart from sin. As Mediator he undoes what the Old did, by removing the condemnation pronounced on the sinner. Yet the two cannot be separated because the New Covenant he mediates results in God's law written on the cleansed hearts of his people (10:15-18). Priesthood and covenant are inseparable (7:11).

"Those who have been called" describes God's people in this world.[79] The divine promise to Abraham (11:8) was a "heavenly calling" (3:1) that invited the people of God to join him in his heavenly abode. The life of the "called" is to be a life of faith and obedience appropriate for those offered such a destiny. All who persevere through the mediation of Christ will attain this "eternal inheritance." However, those who imitate the unbelief of the wilderness generation will fail to reach that final destination.[80] God's people once experienced "redemption" from Egypt so that they could "receive" their "inheritance" in the Promised Land. Christ has now provided a "redemption" that opens the "eternal inheritance" in the heavenly homeland (11:10, 13-16) for all the faithful (11:1-40). No one needs to go the way of unbelief (3:7–4:11), for Christ is the Mediator and High Priest who removes condemnation and provides cleansing so that his people can persevere until entrance into that final, "eternal," heavenly "inheritance" promised them.[81]

c. Freed from the Condemnation of a Broken Covenant (9:16-22)

16 *For where there is a covenant, of necessity the death of the one making the covenant must be borne. 17 For a covenant becomes valid on the basis of death, since it never is in force when the one making the covenant is alive. 18 Therefore, the First Covenant was not inaugurated without blood. 19 For when all the ordinances according to the law had been spoken by Moses to the whole people, he took the blood of goats and bulls, with water and with scarlet wool and hyssop, and sprinkled both the book itself and all the people, 20 saying: "This is the blood of the covenant that God has completed for you." 21 And the tent and all the utensils of worship he likewise sprinkled with blood. 22 And almost everything is purified with blood according to the law, and without the shedding of blood there is no release.*

79. Thus the perfect tense of the substantive participle οἱ κεκλημένοι, "those who have been called," indicates that they have been called and continue to live in the effect of that calling — that is, as the "called ones." See Riggenbach, 271-72, and Spicq, 2:261. They are "the 'called-elect' of all time" (Bénétreau, 2:86).

80. "And 'those who have been called' are not distinguished as a separate population from those who may have transgressed under the Sinai covenant" (Johnson, 240).

81. See Hughes, 367.

In the covenant section (8:7-13) of the opening movement of this symphony the pastor quoted the New Covenant prophecy from Jer 31:31-34. According to that passage, God condemned those who broke the Old Covenant and promised that he would institute a New and effective Covenant. In 9:16-22 the pastor shows how Christ removes the condemnation engendered by the Old. In 10:15-18, the final covenant section, he will enumerate the blessings of the promised and now fulfilled New.[1]

The pastor has shown that Christ's death brings genuine inner cleansing from sin. By providing this cleansing it does away with the Old Covenant as a means of approaching God because that Covenant was unable to purify its adherents from sin. Thus by providing for genuine cleansing, Christ's death inaugurated the New Covenant as an effective way of coming into God's presence (9:11-14) and established him as its "Mediator." Thus his death provided "for redemption from transgressions committed under the First Covenant" (9:15). As noted above, that First Covenant's condemnation of sin has only been intensified for those who reject Christ. Verses 16-17 explain how Christ's sacrifice procured this liberation according to the terms of that First or Old but broken Covenant. Verses 18-22 verify this liberation through a description of the First and Old Covenant's inauguration.

16-17 Many English translations use "testament" or "will" in vv. 16-17, but revert to "covenant" in vv. 18-22 (NKJV, NIV, NRSV).[2] The Greek term in question was used for one's last "will" or "testament" in the world contemporary with Hebrews, but for "covenant" in the Greek OT.[3] Elsewhere Hebrews always employs the OT meaning (7:22; 8:6, 8, 9, 10; 9:4, 15, 20; 10:16, 29; 12:24; 13:20). Those who select "will" for vv. 16-17 do so because of the statement in v. 17 that the one making a "will" must die for the "will" to be confirmed. Covenants, they contend, do not require the death of their maker. On the other hand, the effectiveness of a last will or testament requires the maker's decease. After all, such play on the alternate meanings of a term was characteristic of the kind of rhetorical style evidenced by Hebrews.[4] One must question, however, if the pastor would use such wordplay at the expense of the conceptual unity that pervades his sermon.[5]

---

1. For extensive bibliography on the theme of covenant see Bruce, 221-24, nn. 115-33.

2. Bénétreau, 2:85-87; Moffatt, 127-28; Spicq, 2:260, 262; Wilson, 158; J. S. Wiid, "The Testamental Significance of διαθήκη in Hebrews 9:15-22," *Neotestamentica* 26 (1992): 149-56; Montefiore, 156-57; and Johnson, 240. Montefiore and Johnson appeal to the language of inheritance in support of "testament," but inheritance language is at home in a "covenant" environment (Bruce, 223).

3. See διαθήκη in BDAG, 228.

4. Cf. Attridge, 255; deSilva, 308-9.

5. On the conceptual unity of Hebrews see Hahn, "A Broken Covenant," 425-26.

Furthermore, there are many reasons for maintaining the translation "covenant" used in the preceding (v. 15) and following (vv. 18-19) verses.[6] First, the statement that a "will" had no force while its maker was alive does not describe contemporary practice. The will-maker could arrange for its provisions to go into effect while he lived.[7] Second, the terms Hebrews uses for "confirm" and "have force" would have been appropriate for the establishing, but not the execution, of a will.[8] Third, "will" does not fit what Hebrews says about Christ's death: he does not transfer an inheritance to others by his death. He enters his inheritance, which he then shares with his "brothers and sisters."[9] In fact, the translation "will" fits very poorly with the larger context and conceptual world of Hebrews.[10] Finally, the close syntactical connection of vv. 16-17 with both v. 15 and vv. 18-22 prohibits this change in meaning.[11]

Most defenders of the translation "covenant" have argued that the pastor is speaking of covenant sacrifices that represented the death of the covenant-maker.[12] By these sacrifices the covenant-maker invoked the curse of death upon himself for covenant violation.[13] While better than the above proposal, this solution also has its problems. It would seem artificial for the pastor to say that a covenant "is never in force while the covenant-maker lives" if he were truly referring to a sacrifice that symbolized the covenant-maker's potential death.[14] Furthermore, not all covenants were established by sacrifice.

In a truly ground-breaking study Scott Hahn has presented an interpretation that removes this artificiality and shows how "covenant" fits admirably in both the immediate and wider contexts.[15] Verses 16-17 are not de-

---

6. See the definitive defense of "covenant" instead of "will" for διαθήκη in John J. Hughes, "Hebrews IX 15ff and Galatians III 15ff.: A Study in Covenant Practice and Procedure," *NovT* 21 (1976-77): 27-66. His arguments are summarized and augmented in Hahn, "A Broken Covenant," 416-26.

7. Hughes, "Hebrews IX 15ff," 61-63; Hahn, "A Broken Covenant," 418.

8. Hughes, "Hebrews IX 15ff," 43-47; Hahn, "A Broken Covenant," 417-18.

9. Hahn, "A Broken Covenant," 421-22. See 1:3; 2:9; 9:11-12; 10:10-13.

10. Hahn, "A Broken Covenant," 421-25. "The mediation of both covenants is primarily cultic, the sacred realm of liturgy not the secular realm of law" (Hahn, "A Broken Covenant," 424).

11. Hughes, "Hebrews IX 15ff," 33-34, 63; Hahn, "A Broken Covenant," 420-21.

12. Lane, 2:242-43; Westcott, 265-66; George Guthrie, 313; G. D. Kilpatrick, "Διαθήκη in Hebrews," *ZNW* 68 (1977): 263-65.

13. See also L. Lincoln, "Translating Hebrews 9:15-22 in Its Hebraic Context," *Journal of Translation and Textlinguistics* 12 (1999): 1-29.

14. For an evaluation of this position see Hahn, "A Broken Covenant," 426-31.

15. Hahn, "A Broken Covenant," 426-36. See also Scott W. Hahn, "Covenant, Cult, and the Curse-of-Death: Διαθήκη in Heb 9:15–22," in *Hebrews: Contemporary Methods — New Insights,* ed. Gabriella Gelardini (Biblical Interpretation Series 75; Atlanta: Society of Biblical Literature, 2005), 65-88.

scribing how one establishes a covenant but what must be done when a covenant is broken. These verses explain how the "death" spoken of in v. 15 provides for "redemption from the transgressions committed under" that First — and now broken — Covenant.[16] Thus we might gloss v. 16, "For where there is a [broken] covenant, the death of the covenant-maker must be borne."[17] God's people are the "covenant-maker" who broke God's First Covenant.[18] Thus they have invoked the covenant curse upon themselves and are subject to death. The pastor speaks generally of what is true concerning "a covenant" in order to reinforce his argument. What he says, however, is patterned on the broken Sinai Covenant that is his main concern. Thus his thought does not move primarily from covenant in general (vv. 16-17) to the Sinai Covenant in particular (vv. 18-22). Instead it moves from the fate of those who broke the Sinai Covenant to the anticipation of that fate foreshadowed by its inauguration.

"Be borne" is a much more natural translation of the underlying Greek term than the translations advocated by those who render the text with "testament" or "will."[19] Nevertheless, at first glance this phrase appears awkward: why did the pastor say "the death of the covenant-maker must be borne" instead of "the covenant-maker must die"? As usual, the pastor has chosen his words with deliberate care. He affirms the necessity of the death resultant from the covenant curse, but he does not say by whom it must "be borne." Indeed, the death that has "occurred" (v. 15) for redemption from First Covenant violation is the death of the incarnate Son of God that frees the condemned people of God from the covenant curse. He has "borne" the death resultant from their sin just as God's Servant in Isa 53:4 "bore" the sins of God's people through his suffering.[20] This interpretation is strengthened

16. Hahn, "A Broken Covenant," 431. Thus, these verses are an explanation of θανάτου γενομένου, "a death having occurred" (v. 15), or, as above, taking the participle as causal, "because a death has occurred."

17. ὅπου in v. 16 reinforces the general reference to covenant, "wherever" (Ellingworth, 463). But see Hahn, "A Broken Covenant," 432, who argues for a causal significance here on the basis of Heb 9:16; 10:18 (cf. 1 Cor 3:3; 4 Macc 14:11, 14, 19; BDAG 576a, def. 2b).

18. Hahn, "A Broken Covenant," 433.

19. Hahn, "A Broken Covenant," 432. Most interpreters espouse a translation something like the NRSV's "be established." Attridge, 256, confesses the difficulty felt by virtually all who accept such a translation when he admits that "the sense of φέρεσθαι is somewhat uncertain." Hahn's comment is telling: "The idiosyncrasy of the phrase is demonstrated by the way lexicographers treat it as a special case, being unable to produce analogous citations" (Hahn, "A Broken Covenant," 419). He references BDAG 855b; LSJ, 1923a; and L&N 1.§70.5.

20. See φέρω ("bring," "bear") in Heb 9:16 and Isa 53:3-4. See Hahn, "A Broken Covenant," 433.

by the way v. 28 below echoes Isa 53:12 when it says that Christ offered himself once "to bear the sins of many."[21]

Verse 17 confirms this interpretation of v. 16: "For a [broken] covenant becomes valid on the basis of deaths." Until the curse of a covenant falls on the covenant breakers, the validity of the covenant is in question. A covenant that is broken is proven authentic only by the deaths of those who broke it and thus invoked its curse.[22] Verse 17b confirms 17a by stating the same thing in negative terms, "since it [a broken covenant] never has force when the covenant maker is living." "It is not *in force* until it is *enforced*."[23]

18 The pastor confirms his argument based on breach of the Old Covenant (vv. 16-17) by describing its inauguration (vv. 18-22).[24] According to vv. 16-17, the sacrificial death of Christ provided "redemption" from the consequences that ensued from that breach. According to vv. 18-22 the blood that inaugurated the Old Covenant invoked those consequences upon the sinner. "Not without blood" has the force of understatement. The following description will show how thoroughly that "First Covenant" was "inaugurated" with sacrificial blood.[25]

19 None can doubt that the pastor is describing the institution of the

21. See ἀναφέρω for "bearing" sin in Heb 9:28 and Isa 53:11, 12. Isa 53:1-12 shares other significant terms with Heb 9:15-22: θάνατος ("death," Heb 9:15, 16; Isa 53:8, 9, 12); κληρονομία ("inheritance," Heb 9:15; Isa 53:12); καθαρίζω ("cleanse," Heb 9:22-23; Isa 53:10); λάος ("people," Heb 9:19; Isa 53:8). See Hahn, "A Broken Covenant," 433, n. 75.

22. Hahn, "A Broken Covenant," 433-34. The plural, "on the basis of deaths," would be a very awkward and unusual way of referring to the time of a will maker's death (Hughes, "Hebrews IX 15ff," 44). O'Brien, 332, agrees with Hahn that vv. 16 and 17b refer to the death of the covenant maker brought about by the breaking of the covenant. Yet he thinks "on the basis of deaths" in v. 17a refers to the sacrificial animals by which a covenant was inaugurated and which symbolized the fate of the covenant maker if the covenant was broken. If one accepts this revision of Hahn's thesis, then "covenant" would mean "broken covenant" in v. 16; "covenant" in v. 17a; and "broken covenant" again in v. 17b. There is, however, no reason why the pastor should not have been thinking of the "deaths" of the disobedient wilderness generation as well as of other covenant breakers.

23. Hahn, "A Broken Covenant," 434. Cf. Ezek 17:15: "Can he break the covenant and yet escape?"

24. Hahn, "A Broken Covenant," 434, argues that ὅθεν, "therefore," "that is why," shows the close connection between vv. 18-22 and vv. 16-17. When vv. 16-17 are rightly understood, there is no reason for ὅθεν to refer back to v. 15, as Ellingworth, 465-66, contends, especially since, as Ellingworth admits, Hebrews habitually uses ὅθεν in reference to what immediately precedes.

25. ἐγκεκαίνισται refers to the inauguration of the Old Covenant in this verse and to the inauguration of the New in 10:20. The perfect tense reminds us that the inauguration of the Old Covenant is permanently recorded in Scripture (Ellingworth, 466, citing Riggenbach and Michel).

Sinai Covenant that Moses proclaimed "to the whole people." However, Hebrews underscores the solemnity of this occasion by adding features from other passages not found in the description of its inauguration according to Exod 24:3-8. Moses uses not only the blood of "calves" but the blood of "bulls and goats, with water and scarlet wool and hyssop." Since "water and scarlet wool and hyssop" occur in other passages dealing with purification, they were a natural addition.[26] Their presence emphasizes the fact that the whole covenant is included in its inauguration.[27] The textually uncertain "goats" has probably been added by assimilation to v. 12 above. Omission by conformity to Exod 24:5 is unlikely since so much else is included that is absent from the Exodus account.[28]

Several features of this solemn description emphasize the way in which the blood binds the people to obey the covenant stipulations. First, note how the passive voice of the initial genitive absolute puts stress on the oral proclamation of these stipulations: "When every ordinance according to the law had been spoken by Moses." The "whole people" gave their assent and were thus committed to obey "every ordinance" (cf. 3:7–4:11).[29] Second, Hebrews says that Moses sprinkled the "book," containing these same stipulations, and the "people," instead of the "altar" and the "people" as in Exodus. The text is emphatic when it says that Moses sprinkled "the book itself." The pastor may have assumed that Moses laid the "book" on the altar. Nevertheless, by this paraphrase he indicates that the blood bound the people, on pain of death, to obey the stipulations proclaimed and now written in the "book."[30]

20 Moses' words confirmed the significance of his actions. The way the pastor paraphrases this text from Exod 4:8 emphasizes the importance of the blood in establishing the Old Covenant. Compare Hebrews and Exodus: "This is the blood of the covenant which he has completed for you, even God" (Heb 9:20); "Behold, the blood of the covenant which the Lord has covenanted for you" (Exod 4:8 LXX). The pastor signals this emphasis by substituting "This is the blood of the covenant" for "Behold, the blood of the covenant." He says that God has "completed" this covenant for them.[31] Finally, Hebrews reserves the word "God" for the final emphatic position in

26. Hughes, 376, citing Delitzsch. Water was used in the purification of lepers (Lev 14:5-9) and of cultic officials and people (Num 19:7-10). For scarlet wool see Lev 14:4; for hyssop, Lev 14:4-5; Num 19:6; Ps 51:7; and John 19:29. See Ellingworth, 468.

27. Hughes, 376.

28. *Pace* Ellingworth, 468, and others.

29. Note how Moses warns the people in Deut 32:45-47 to obey "all the words" he has declared to them. Cf. Ellingworth, 467.

30. Westcott, 266.

31. Hebrews uses the stronger ἐνετείλατο, "complete," in place of the LXX διέθετο, "make a covenant." See on the related συντελέσω in 8:8 above.

the sentence.[32] The pastor will not let his hearers escape from the sacrificial blood that invoked the curse of death on covenant breakers.

Furthermore, there are interesting parallels between the words and actions of Moses at Sinai and those of Christ at the Last Supper as recorded in Matt 26:27-28 (cf. Mark 14:13-14). Moses "took" the "blood" and "sprinkled the people, saying, "this is the blood of the covenant." Christ "took" the "cup" and "gave it to his disciples, saying, . . . for this is my blood of the covenant."[33] Furthermore, "without the shedding of blood there is no release" (v. 22) may echo the blood "which is poured out for many for the forgiveness of sins" in Matt 26:28.[34] Although the hearers may not have been attuned to pick up these clues, it is possible that the pastor used these similarities to suggest a parallel between God's establishing the Old Covenant through Moses and Christ's establishing the New.[35] Of course the relative clause in Hebrews, "which he has completed for you, even God," describes the "covenant"; while the equivalent participial phrase in Matthew, "which was poured out for many for the forgiveness of sins," describes Jesus' blood. The blood of the Old brought condemnation for disobedience; only the blood of the New brought true "release" (Heb 9:22).

21-22 The pastor has been building his case that the pervasive role of sacrificial blood in the Old Covenant anticipated the cleansing power of Christ's blood. The high priest could not enter "without blood" (9:7). The Old Covenant was not established "without blood" (9:18). At its inauguration Moses not only sprinkled the "book" and "all the people" with blood but also the "Tent" and even "all its utensils for ministry," some of which were described in vv. 2-5 above.[36] The pastor omits mention of the oil of dedica-

---

32. The LXX puts κύριος ("Lord") right after διέθετο ("was made"), but Hebrews substitutes ὁ θεός, "God," and withholds it until the end of the sentence. See Lane, 2:245, and Ellingworth, 469-70, for other suggestions concerning the altering of these words.

33. The parallels are even more striking in Greek: λαβὼν τὸ αἷμα . . . πάντα τὸν λαὸν ἐρράντισεν, 20 λέγων? τοῦτο τὸ αἷμα τῆς διαθήκης (Heb 9:19b-20). καὶ λαβὼν ποτήριον . . . ἔδωκεν αὐτοῖς λέγων? . . . τοῦτο γάρ ἐστιν τὸ αἷμα μου τῆς διαθήκης (Matt 26:27-28).

34. Compare τὸ αἷμα . . . ἐκχυννόμενον εἰς ἄφεσιν ἁμαρτιῶν ("the blood . . . poured out for the forgiveness of sins") in Matt 26:28 and χωρὶς αἱματεκχυσίας οὐ γίνεται ἄφεσις ("without shedding of blood there is no release") in Heb 9:22. αἱματεκχυσία ("shedding of blood") is compounded from the words used in Matthew for αἷμα ("blood") and ἐκχέω/ἐκχύννω ("pour out"). See BDAG, 26-27, 312. The word translated "forgiveness" in Matthew is the same word we have translated "release" in Hebrews (ἄφεσις).

35. Ellingworth, 469. See Hughes, "Hebrews IX 15ff," 52-57. Cf. Spicq, 2:264; Michel, 317-18; Grässer, Bund, 111-12; Theissen, Untersuchungen, 72-75. Bénétreau, 2:88, shares Braun's doubts as to this allusion.

36. καὶ . . . δέ mark the continuity with v. 19 and may indicate emphasis, "moreover; what is more" (Ellingworth, 470).

tion described in Exod 40:9-11 and Lev 8:10-11 as irrelevant to his argument. The widespread use of blood in rituals associated with the Tent made it easy for him and his hearers, in agreement with Josephus (*Ant.* 3.206), to assume that blood was also used in the dedication of the Tent and its contents.[37] Thus he concludes his evidence for the role of blood in the Old Covenant by saying that "almost everything" associated with that Covenant and its Tent "is purified by blood according to the law" (v. 22a). The few exceptions to this statement only establish the general rule.[38]

This Old Covenant precedent and pattern allows the pastor to make a definitive statement that permits no exception: "without the shedding of blood there is no release" (cf. Lev 17:11). He has already told his hearers that the blood of the old sacrifices does no more than purify the "flesh" (9:13). He will soon tell them what they already anticipate: animal blood cannot "take away sin" (10:4; cf. 10:18). Thus the pastor is no longer focused on the way things were "according to the law." His statement goes beyond later rabbinic discussion on the necessity of blood.[39] The blood that brings this "release" can be nothing less than the shed blood of Christ.[40]

The terms translated "shedding of blood" and "release" are crucial. Though "shedding of blood" occurs here for the first time, it appears to be derived from a phrase used in the LXX both for the killing of humans and animals (Gen 37:22; Lev 17:4; and Num 35:33) and for the pouring out of the remaining sacrificial blood at the base of the altar (Exod 29:12; Lev 4:7, 18, 25, 30, 34; 8:15; 9:9). The pastor's use is based on the first of these senses, since he employs this term as a powerful description of Christ's death.[41] The blood that inaugurated the Old Covenant invoked the curse of death on covenant violators. There is no "release" from that curse apart from the shed blood of Christ.

The term we have translated "release" is normally followed in the NT

37. See references in Hughes, 377.
38. For example, water in Lev 15:10; fire in Num 31:22-23 (Montefiore, 158).
39. See the following tractates of the Babylonian Talmud, *b. Yoma* 5a; *b. Zebaḥim* 6a; *b. Menaḥot* 93b; and cf. Philo, *Spec. Laws* 1.205.
40. See Ellingworth, 472-73.
41. Compare αἱματεκχυσίας, "shedding of blood," with αἷμα ἐκχεῖν, "to shed, pour out blood." Since this phrase was used for pouring the remaining blood at the base of the altar, T. C. G. Thornton, "The Meaning of αἱματεκχυσία in Heb. IX.22," *JTS* 15 (1964): 63-65, has argued that Hebrews uses αἱματεκχυσίας in reference to the application of the blood to the altar. However, Norman H. Young, "Αἱματεκχυσία: A Comment," *ExpTim* 90 (1979): 180, has shown that the pouring of the blood on the base of the altar was distinct from sprinkling the atoning blood on the altar. Even the rabbinic tractate Thornton cites in support of his argument maintains this distinction (*b. Zebaḥim* 36b, 51ab). The pastor's focus is on the death of Christ, not the application of his blood to a heavenly altar.

by the qualifying phrase "of sins" and translated by "forgiveness" (Matt 26:28; Mark 1:4; Luke 1:77; 3:3; 24:47; Acts 2:38; 5:31; 10:43; 13:38; 26:18; Col 1:14; cf. Eph 1:7). The immediate context and the way Hebrews uses this term without qualifier (cf. 10:18) demand a more comprehensive interpretation.[42] The pastor has been discussing cleansing as well as release from the consequences of covenant violation. The blood of Christ frees God's people from sin, both by cleansing their hearts from its taint and dominion and by releasing them from its condemnation.[43] The pastor has clearly affirmed in v. 15 that Christ's death, which brought cleansing, established him as Mediator of the New Covenant. This assertion suggests that, once cleansed from sin, God's people are no longer subject to the covenant curse on disobedience.[44] However, one cannot exclude the idea that by his death Christ not only cleansed but took upon himself the penalty due his people for breach of covenant.[45]

The pastor leaves the music of the word "release" ringing in his hearers' ears. This term sets the stage for 9:23–10:18, the third and final movement of the pastor's symphony. In 10:5-10 he will unveil the secret of how Christ's death provides such deliverance. Then he will conclude by describing the exalted Christ (10:11-14) as mediating the benefits of this deliverance (10:15-18).

The three movements of the pastor's symphony in praise of Christ's self-offering each end with a covenant section: 8:7-13; 9:(15)16-22; 10:15-18. The first covenant section described both God's condemnation of his people for breach of the First Covenant (8:7-9) and his promise of a New Covenant (8:10-13) characterized by obedience. The second covenant section, which we have just investigated, addresses the concern raised by the breach of the Old Covenant. It reveals how Christ has removed the condemnation incurred by that breach. The third and final covenant section will describe the benefits of the New Covenant mediated by Christ.

3. Third Movement: The New Explained (9:23–10:18)

We have likened the pastor's explanation of Christ's sacrificial death in 8:1–10:18 to a grand symphony in three movements. In each movement the pastor/conductor plays his familiar themes of sanctuary, sacrifice, and covenant.

---

42. Cf. "release" in Luke 4:18.
43. See Johnsson, "Defilement," 324-29, cited in Lane, 2:246-47. There is no "release" "without the shedding" of *Christ's* "blood" (Pfitzner, 132).
44. "By expiation, appeasing the divine wrath, one is liberated from slavery to sin and the condemnation it entailed" (Spicq, 2:265).
45. "He, as their substitute, paid the covenant penalty of death due them" (Hughes, "Hebrews IX 15ff," 48).

We have seen how the pastor uses the first and third of these themes to bring out the grandeur of the second — Christ's great all-sufficient sacrifice. In the first movement, 8:1-13, entitled "The New Promised," the pastor played the themes of sanctuary and covenant in a major key but left sacrifice in a minor. He demonstrated in 8:1-2, 7-13 how the OT promises of heavenly sanctuary (Ps 110:1) and New Covenant (Jer 31:31-34) anticipated Christ's entrance into the heavenly sanctuary and assumption of his role as Mediator of the New Covenant. However, he said nothing more about sacrifice than that the sacrifice offered by a person ministering in such a sanctuary as Mediator of such a covenant must be different from the sacrifices appropriate for the Mosaic Tent. Thus, he prepared the hearers for the ever more complete descriptions of Christ's sacrifice in the following movements (9:1-22; 9:23–10:18).[1]

In the second movement, "The Old Antiquated; the New Foreshadowed," 9:1-22, the pastor played the themes of sanctuary (9:1-10) and covenant (9:16-22) in a minor key but sacrifice in a major (9:11-15). He postponed discussing the promises of entrance into the heavenly sanctuary and establishment of the New Covenant in order to consider the Pentateuchal descriptions of the Old. Those descriptions betrayed the inadequacy of the Old to bring people into God's presence and thus showed the necessity of Christ's shedding his blood for "release" from the sin that barred access to God. In Heb 9:11-15 the pastor gave the most definitive description of Christ's all-sufficient sacrifice yet offered his hearers — Christ's sacrifice was a divinely empowered life of obedience unto death that cleansed God's people from sin and enabled them to live in obedience.

The third movement, 9:23–10:18, brings this grand symphony to its finale.[2] The pastor expounds the full significance of God's promises.[3] He plays all three themes — sanctuary, sacrifice, and covenant — in a

---

1. Guthrie, *Structure,* 121, entitles 9:1–10:18 "The Superior New Covenant Offering" and then divides it into three sections, 9:1-10; 9:11-28; and 10:1-18. However, the superiority of Christ's offering is more clearly elucidated by the division suggested above.

2. There is widespread agreement that 10:1-18 forms a unit divisible into four subsections, vv. 1-4, 5-10, 11-14, and 15-18 (Westfall, *Discourse Analysis,* 219). Most also recognize a paragraph break between 9:22 and 23 (Westfall, *Discourse Analysis,* 208, 210, 218). However, the climactic nature of 9:22 (cf. 10:18) and the return to the theme of sanctuary in 9:23-24 (cf. 8:1-2; 9:1-10) indicate that the new section should begin with 9:23. Furthermore, the contrast in 9:24 supports the contrast in 9:23. Verses 25-28 return to the theme of the "once-for-all" sacrifice of Christ and thus should be joined with 10:1-4. See Cockerill, "Structure and Interpretation in Hebrews 8:1–10:18," 191-98, esp. 191-92.

3. Westfall is right when she argues that 10:1-18 is not a mere summary or recapitulation of what has gone before. See Westfall, *Discourse Analysis,* 229. The pastor has introduced new material. However, *pace* Westfall, new material does not preclude 9:23–10:18 from being the conclusion of this central section on Christ's high priesthood.

crescendoing major key. Against the counterpoint of the old he expounds the grand superiority of the new. The pastor succinctly describes the true nature of the sanctuary entered by Christ (9:23-24) and the essence of the New Covenant's provision (10:15-18). The theme of sacrifice, so muted in the first movement, swells to overwhelming predominance — three verses in the first movement (8:3-5), five in the second (9:11-15), eighteen (9:25–10:14) in this the third.

This final grand expose of Christ's sacrificial death can be further subdivided into three parts: 9:25–10:4; 10:5-10; and 10:11-14.[4] The first (9:25–10:4) gives definitive evidence for the sole effectiveness of Christ's sacrifice. The central subsection (10:5-10) is crucial because it fully discloses *the reason* for the all-sufficiency of Christ's sacrifice — the "blameless" (9:14) incarnate obedience unto death of no one less than the eternal Son of God. The third subsection (10:11-14) describes what Christ has become and done for the benefit of his people as a result of his sacrifice. The by now familiar Ps 110:1 and 4 (1:3, 13; 5:5-6; 6:20; 7:1-25; 8:1-2) provide the foundation for the first and third subsections. In the central subsection the pastor introduces Ps 40:6-8 in order to explain the incarnate obedience of the Son.

He puts great emphasis on this second subsection (10:5-10) and the Son's obedience described therein by making it the chiastic center of this sacrifice section. Notice the way in which the first subsection, 9:25–10:4, moves from new high priest to old; the second, 10:11-14, from old to new: Christ offered himself "once-for-all" (9:25-28) in contrast to the repeated offerings of priests under the Old Covenant (10:1-4); the old priests continually stood (10:11), while Christ has permanently taken his seat at God's right (10:12-14). However, as important as 10:5-10 may be, the pastor turns his hearers' gaze back to the place where he began in 8:1-2 — the High Priest seated at God' right hand (10:11-14) who has offered the definitive sacrifice (10:14) and thus mediates the benefits of the New Covenant (10:15-18). It is by drawing near through this High Priest alone that believers will be able to persevere (10:19-25).

The comments below will show how 9:23-24, the "sanctuary section," anticipates the third and concluding "sacrifice" subsection (10:11-14). In a similar way, the opening "sacrifice" subsection (9:25–10:4) anticipates the "covenant section" (10:15-18) with which the entire symphony concludes. The pastor has skillfully woven his material together for maximum impact on his hearers.

---

4. Ellingworth, 489, says that 10:1-4, 5-10, and 11-14 form a "triptych" of three paragraphs of which the second, vv. 5-10, holds the central position. Our analysis would agree, except that we begin the first unit at v. 25: 9:25–10:4; 10:5-10; 10:11-14.

At the end of the second movement the pastor anticipated what he was about to say concerning the sufficiency of Christ's death: "without the shedding of [Christ's] blood there is no release" (9:22). The corollary at the end of the third assumes that sufficiency: "where there is release" provided by Christ "there is no longer" need to keep presenting any other "offering for sin" (10:18). Only his sacrifice will do and, when it has been offered, there is no need for another.

a. Sanctuary: "In the Presence of God for Us" (9:23-24)

> 23 Therefore it was[1] necessary for the pattern of the things in the heavens to be cleansed with these sacrifices, but the heavenly things themselves with better sacrifices than these. 24 For Christ has not entered into a sanctuary made with hands, a representation of the true Sanctuary, but into heaven itself, now to appear before the face of God on our behalf.

Note the definitive change of vocabulary and theme in 9:23-24. Those listening to this sermon no longer hear of "covenant" and "blood," so important in vv. 16-22, but of "in the heavens," "heavenly things," and "heaven itself."[2] The pastor completes what he began in the first movement of his symphony with his description of Christ at God's right hand "in the heavens," which he declared to be his main theme (8:1-2).[3] He boldly affirms that the one described in 8:2 as "a minister of the Sanctuary and true Tent" has entered the "Sanctuary" that is nothing less than "heaven itself."[4] He began by arguing that Christ's sacrifice was something other than the offerings appropriate for the Mosaic Tent because Christ never served in that Sanctuary (8:3-5). He now daringly proclaims that Christ's sacrifice is of all-surpassing excellence because it has procured en-

---

1. A literal translation of the Greek text would be, "Necessary therefore on the one hand the pattern of the things in the heavens to be cleansed by these." A smooth English translation must supply a verb, either "It is necessary" (cf. NEB, NJB, Braun, Attridge) or "it was necessary" (NRSV, NIV, REB, Lane). See Ellingworth, 475-76.

2. *Pace* Vanhoye, *La structure littéraire,* 154-55, these words referring to "heaven" are not catchwords that bind vv. 16-23 with vv. 24-28. They occur nowhere else in vv. 16-28. Their true significance is in showing the unity of vv. 23-24. George Guthrie, 314-15, treats vv. 23-24 as a unit in his commentary, though not in Guthrie, *Structure,* 121.

3. Compare ἐν τοῖς οὐρανοῖς, "in the heavens"; τὰ ἐπουράνια (v. 23), "the heavenly things"; and αὐτὸν τὸν οὐρανόν (v. 24), "heaven itself," with ἐν τοῖς οὐρανοῖς (8:1), "in the heavens." Note also ἀντίτυπα τῶν ἀληθινῶν, "copies of the true," in 9:24 and τῆς σκηνῆς τῆς ἀληθινῆς, "the true Tent," in 8:2.

4. See ἅγια in 9:24 and τῶν ἁγίων in 8:2. Compare χειροποίητα, "made by hand," in 9:24 with οὐ χειροποιήτου, "not made by hand," in 9:11.

trance into "heaven itself" and is thus appropriate for the Sanctuary in which God truly dwells (9:23-24). He will set himself the task of describing the excellent nature of this sacrifice in 9:25–10:14. These two short verses that comprise the sanctuary section of this third movement plant seeds that reach full fruition in 10:11-14. Christ's entrance "into heaven itself now to appear before the face of God on our behalf" (9:24) becomes "he sat down forever at the right hand of God" (10:12). The "better" sacrifice necessary for Christ's entrance into such a sanctuary (9:23) becomes the "one sacrifice" by which he "has perfected forever those being made holy" (10:14).

23 The pastor contrasts the cleansing of the Mosaic sanctuary, or "pattern of the things in the heavens" (v. 23a), with the cleansing of the Sanctuary entered by Christ, described as "the heavenly things themselves" (v. 23b). The first half of his contrast is beyond doubt: vv. 16-22 have verified that "it was necessary" for that preliminary sanctuary "to be cleansed by" animal sacrifices.[5] After all, "according to the law" almost everything was cleansed by blood (v. 22), including the "Tent" (v. 21) that served as sanctuary.[6] Careful attention must also be given to the way the pastor describes each of these sanctuaries. By portraying the old sanctuary (described in 9:1-10) as "the pattern of the things in the heavens" he affirms both its inferior status and its typological relationship to the Sanctuary now entered by Christ.[7] By describing that ultimate Sanctuary as "the heavenly things themselves" he puts emphasis on its heavenly quality.[8]

These descriptions of the Old and New Sanctuaries effectively turn this contrast into an argument from lesser to greater: since the "pattern" was cleansed by animal sacrifices, then the far greater "heavenly things" must be cleansed by proportionately and therefore definitively "better sacrifices." The undisputed necessity of the lesser cleansing demonstrates the necessity of the qualitatively greater. If the hearers would know the definitive superiority of these "sacrifices," they must continue listening to what the pastor will say about Christ's sacrifice in 9:25–10:14.

---

5. ἀνάγκη, translated here "necessarily," denotes logical necessity just at it did in v. 16 at the introduction of the last section.

6. The οὖν, "therefore," that opens v. 23 shows that the pastor is drawing an inference from the previous discussion, especially from v. 22. καθαρίζεσθαι, "to be cleansed," in v. 23 picks up καθαρίζεται, "are cleansed," in v. 22a; and τούτοις, "by these," in 23 refers to the sacrifices/rituals κατὰ τὸν νόμον, "according to the law," in v. 22a. It is unclear why Ellingworth (477) thinks that τούτοις refers to the old tabernacle and its vessels.

7. For ὑποδείγματα as "pattern" see the comments on 8:5. On the positive typological significance of this term see Ellingworth, 475.

8. There is no reason to take the very general phrase αὐτὰ τὰ ἐπουράνια ("the heavenly things themselves") as a reference to the heavenly archtypes characteristic of the Platonic worldview (Ellingworth, 477).

This verse evokes two questions in the minds of many modern readers: (1) Why must "the heavenly things" be cleansed? (2) Why does the pastor say better "sacrifices" (plural) when he is obviously referring to the sacrifice of Christ, which he unquestionably affirms as offered "once for all" (9:25–10:4)?

An answer to the second question is not only easier but gives some direction for addressing the first. The pastor uses the plural, "better sacrifices," because he is drawing a parallel with the various sacrifices of the Old Covenant and establishing a general principle before discussing the "better sacrifice" of Christ.[9] Thus, he also refers to the "heavenly things" as being purified by analogy with the necessary cleansing of the earthly "pattern" described in vv. 18-22 (cf. Lev 16:16-19).[10] Christ's sacrifice cleanses the heavenly Sanctuary by analogy with the way in which animal sacrifices cleanse the "pattern." Furthermore, since cleansing was prerequisite to entering the Mosaic Tent, the cleansing of the heavenly appears to have been accomplished by the "once-for-all" sacrifice of Christ which procured his high-priestly entrance.[11]

Those who contend that Hebrews is dependent on the radical heavenly/earthly dichotomy characteristic of Platonic dualism have the most difficulty explaining how the heavenly world required cleansing.[12] Riggenbach, however, reminds us that it was the sins of the people and not its earthly character that polluted the Mosaic sanctuary.[13] Their sins formed a barrier that prevented them from coming into God's presence and exposed them to his wrath. If sin erected a barrier forbidding entrance into the sanctuary that was a "pattern," how much more did it bar the way into the "true" Sanctuary in which God dwells. Lane is correct when he says, "The writer conceived of defilement as an objective impediment to genuine access to God."[14] Thus by cleansing the heavenly Sanctuary Christ removed this otherwise impregnable barrier and the accompanying threat of judgment. The pastor is not merely

9. See Riggenbach, 283.

10. See Spicq, 2:266.

11. Thus, the pastor is describing the completed work of Christ, not the continual cleansing of God's people as they approach the sphere of fellowship with God (*pace* David J. MacLeod, "The Cleansing of the True Tabernacle," *BSac* 152 [1995]: 70-71).

12. On the other hand, Michel, 323-24, following Bleek, suggests that this cleansing refers to Satan's being cast out of heaven, a theme popular in apocalyptic literature (12:7-9; cf. Luke 10:18; John 12:31). "Had the author wanted to introduce Satan at this point, he surely would not have been so obscure" (MacLeod, "Tabernacle," 68).

13. Exod 30:10; Lev 16:16, 19; Riggenbach, 283.

14. Lane, 2:247. Cf. Cody, *Heavenly Sanctuary*, 81-91; Johnsson, "Defilement," 256-61; Bénétreau, 2:92; Koester, 421; and Cockerill, "Structure and Interpretation in Hebrews 8:1–10:18," 192 n. 50.

repeating what he said about Christ's sacrifice cleansing the "conscience" (9:14), and the heavenly Sanctuary is no mere metaphor for human interiority.[15] The sacrifice of Christ has made an "objective" difference in the relationship between God and his people.[16] A new possibility of genuine fellowship with God is now open to them. By cleansing the heavenly Sanctuary of the barrier erected by sin, Christ has inaugurated his ministry as High Priest at God's right hand in that Sanctuary.[17] When God's people look toward him, they no longer face the barrier of their sin but find their High Priest (10:21), through whom their consciences are cleansed.

24 The pastor must clarify the excellence of the Sanctuary Christ has entered before he can describe the grandeur of the sacrifice appropriate for its cleansing. He tells his hearers what this Sanctuary is not (v. 24a) in order for them to understand the full significance of what it is (v. 24b). Christ did not enter a "sanctuary made with hands" (cf. 9:11) like the one erected by Moses (8:3-5) and described in 9:1-10. He did not enter a mere "representation of the true" Sanctuary (cf. "true Tent" in 8:2),[18] a fragmentary and di-

---

15. As suggested by Attridge, 260-62 (cf. Montefiore, 160), on the basis of a supposed Philonic/Platonic background of the pastor's thought. Not only is this Platonic frame of reference doubtful, but it is questionable whether Plato dissolved transcendence into interiority. Attridge's suggestion sounds more modern or existentialist than Platonic. For critique of this position see Johnsson, "Defilement," 94-95. Bruce, 228-30, and others have suggested that "the heavenly things themselves" is a reference to the church as the Body of Christ. However, the pastor shows no knowledge of the temple-equals-the-people-of-God imagery used elsewhere in the NT (see comments on "the greater and more perfect Tent" in 9:11 above). It seems clear that he identifies "the heavenly things themselves" and "heaven itself" as the "place" of God's dwelling and the ultimate destiny of God's people (11:8-10, 16; 12:22-29). See the thorough discussion of this issue in Hughes, 379-81.

16. "That the entrance to the sanctuary has been made possible not alone by the purification of those who are to enter, but also by an act of consecration in the heavenly Sanctuary itself, is the way in which not only the *subjective* but also the *objective* significance of the Atonement is brought to expression in the cultic terminology of Hebrews" (N. A. Dahl, "'A New and Living Way': The Approach to God according to Hebrews 10:19–25," *Int* 5 [1951]: 404).

17. Some would solve the perceived difficulty of heaven's cleansing by translating καθαρίζεσθαι in v. 23 as "inaugurate" instead of "cleanse" (Ellingworth, 477, Spicq, 2:267; and Dunnill, *Covenant,* 232). See 1 Macc 4:36-59 and Exod 29:36; Lev 8:15. It is true that the pastor has just described the inauguration of the Mosaic Tent in 9:18-22. However, "a dedication by means of sacrificial blood would still involve the notion of cleansing and atonement" (MacLeod, "Tabernacle," 69). See Johnsson, "Defilement," 95-96.

18. ἀντίτυπα, translated here as "representation," may mean simply "copy," or it may have the connotation of "prefiguration," a "copy" that anticipates the reality to come. The parallel with ὑποδείγμα, "pattern," in the previous verse (cf. 8:5; compare σκιά,

vided "pattern of the heavenly things" (9:23). There can be no doubt — he entered "heaven itself." The singular "heaven" with the intensive "itself" is an unmistakable description of the place where God dwells.[19] In fact, the divine presence is what makes the Sanctuary Christ has entered the "true" Sanctuary.

The pastor cannot pass by this opportunity of directing his hearers to the purpose of Christ's entrance and the benefits that accrue to them. Christ did not enter to resume his preincarnate heavenly life. He entered "to appear to the face of God on our behalf." One who has appeared "to" or "before the face of God" has received divine acceptance and favor.[20] Christ has received God's ultimate favor and acceptance not for himself but "on our behalf." The "now" of this verse determines the life of the faithful. Christ is "now" in God's presence on our behalf ministering the benefits of God's favor (enumerated below, in 10:19-25). To "appear to the face of God on our behalf" is a powerful description of Christ's present High Priestly ministry.[21]

The pastor turns now to the sacrifice by which Christ "entered" "once

---

"shadow"/"foreshadow" in 8:5; 10:1; Hurst, *Background,* 17-19) suggests "prefiguration." However, the emphasis of the immediate context on the qualitative difference between the Sanctuaries suggests "copy" ("qualitative" difference is more accurate than "spatial" difference, *pace* Ellingworth, 479). Hebrews' use of this word is no indication of dependence on Platonic thought. Neither Plato nor Philo used it to describe the "world of sense perception" in contrast to "the heavenly realm of ideas." That meaning of the term is not found before Plotinus (*Enn.* 2.9, 6; see Hurst, *Background,* 17-19). In 1 Pet 3:21, the only other NT occurrence, the ἀντίτυπος is the reality prefigured by the τύπος ("type"). "Representation" (Lane, 2:248) maintains the contextual emphasis on inferiority without evoking the Platonic nuance that might be implied by "copy."

19. This statement is definitive evidence that the pastor is not dealing with a two-part heavenly Sanctuary. *Pace* Attridge, 263, in the immediate context "heaven itself" clearly contrasts this sanctuary with the "representation of the true" and not with lower heavens. So Riggenbach, 284-85.

20. Koester, 422; Lane, 2:248. Compare ὀφθήσομαι τῷ προσώπῳ τοῦ θεοῦ, "I shall appear to the face of God" (Ps 42:3, cf. 17:15), with ἐμφανισθῆναι τῷ προσώπῳ τοῦ θεοῦ, "to appear to the face of God," in Heb 9:24. BDAG, 325, 1, gives the meaning of ἐνμθανίζω as "to make visible" and lists Heb 9:24 as an example of the passive used in the active sense of "to appear." However, the first example of this usage given, Philo, *Alleg. Interp.* 3.101, refers to God revealing himself and could be understood as a true passive: μὴ γὰρ ἐμφανισθείης μοι δι' οὐρανοῦ ἢ ὕδατος . . . , "For I would not have you be manifested to me through heaven or water . . . [but directly through yourself]." Most of the other references in this category also refer to a supernatural appearance (Josephus, *J.W.* 47; *Ant.* 1.223; Wis 17:4; Matt 27:53). Christ's appearance in heaven "to the face of God" is clearly a real but extraordinary event. The pastor's point is his appearance to, and acceptance by, God, not his appearance in heaven to the eye of faith (Ellingworth, 480-81).

21. Attridge, 263.

for all." By this sacrifice he has "made purification for sins" (1:3a) so that he could "take his seat" at God's right hand (1:3b) on our behalf, where he now mediates the benefits of his atoning work to his people (4:14-16; 10:19-25).[22] If the hearers would know what kind of sacrifice could achieve such results, let them read on. The pastor brings closure to his description of Christ's self-offering in 9:25–10:14, the sacrifice section of this third and final movement of the pastor's symphony.

b. Sacrifice — "Once for All" (9:25–10:4)

> 25 Not that he might offer himself often, as the high priest goes into the Most Holy Place year after year with blood other than his own; 26 because then it would have been necessary for him to have suffered many times since the foundation of the world. But now he has appeared once for all at the climax of the ages for the abolition of sin through the sacrifice of himself. 27 And just as it is appointed to human beings to die once for all, and after this, judgment, 28 so also since Christ has been offered once for all in order to bear the sins of many, he will appear a second time without reference to sin for the purpose of bringing salvation to those awaiting him.
>
> 10:1 For because the law has only a shadow of the good things to come, not the reality itself of those things, it was never able to perfect those drawing near by the same sacrifices which are offered continuously year after year. 2 Because then would they not have ceased being offered, since those worshiping would no longer have had any consciousness of sin if they had been cleansed once for all? 3 But by those sacrifices there was a memorial of sin year after year. 4 For it is impossible for the blood of bulls and goats to take away sin.

In this passage the pastor presents the "once-for-all" character of Christ's high-priestly sacrifice as definitive evidence of its full sufficiency. These verses are knit together by the contrast between Christ's "once-for-all" sacrifice (9:25-28) and the repeated annual sacrifices of the old order (10:1-4).[1] "Year after year" in 9:25 links vv. 25-28 to the description of the Aaronic

---

22. Attridge, 263-64, affirms correctly that Christ's intercession is based on his sacrifice. However, he misunderstands Hebrews when he says that "Christ's sacrificial death is not an act distinct from his entry into God's presence." Beginning with Heb 1:3 Christ's sacrifice has been the basis for his entrance.

1. Cf. Lane, 2:258: "The writer juxtaposes the single, unrepeatable nature of Christ's offering (9:28) and the perpetual repetition of the sacrifices prescribed by the law (10:1)."

sacrifice in 10:1-4, which was offered "year after year" (10:1, 3).[2] On the other hand, "once for all" in 10:2 contrasts this repeated sacrifice with the sacrifice of Christ offered "once for all" according to 9:26, 27, 28.[3]

The coherence of these verses deserves further refinement: Heb 9:25-26 and 10:1-3 exhibit the contrasting functions of these "once-for-all" and repeated sacrifices. The first does away with sin (9:26b);[4] the second shows that sin yet continues (10:3).[5] Heb 9:27-28 and 10:4 contrast the resultant impact of these sacrifices on the lives of God's people. The first prepares them for eternity; the second has no power to alter their situation.[6] The impotency of the old in 10:4 anticipates by contrast the definitive description of Christ's obedient self-offering in vv. 5-10.

Heb 9:25–10:4 is also an integral part of 9:23–10:18, the third "movement" of this symphony. As noted above, Heb 9:23-24 (the "sanctuary" section) planted seeds that come to fruition in 10:11-14 (the final part of the "sacrifice" section). So 9:25–10:4 (the opening part of the "sacrifice" section) produces a harvest in 10:15-18 (the "covenant" section).[7] The old sacrifices are nothing more than a "reminder" of sins (10:3), for they are unable to "take" them "away" (10:4). On the other hand, the New Covenant bears witness that Christ's sacrifice provides a full "release" from sins (10:18) because God "remembers" (10:17) them no more.

25 The pastor provides smooth transition from the topic of sanctuary to sacrifice by pairing the self-offering of Christ (v. 25a) with the en-

---

2. See κατ' ἐνιαυτόν, "annually" or "year by year" (Ellingworth, 482), in 9:25 and 10:1, 3. The translation "year after year" brings out the Aaronic sacrifice's perpetual repetitiveness, so important to the pastor's argument.

3. See ἅπαξ, "once" or "once for all," in 9:26, 27, 28 and 10:2.

4. *Pace* Riggenbach, 285, the pastor's main thesis is found in v. 26b and not v. 25.

5. Thus 10:2-3 is not a parenthesis, as in Lane's translation (2:253). Rather, v. 3 is the climax of the argument of vv. 1-3, just as v. 26b is the climax of 9:25-26.

6. For further justification of the unity of 9:25–10:4 see Cockerill, "Structure and Interpretation in Hebrews 8:1–10:18," 193-94. Westfall, *Discourse Analysis,* 215-19, followed by O'Brien, 335, argues that vv. 23-28 should be taken with vv. 15-22. The transition between vv. 22 and 23 is smooth. Moses' sprinkling of the "Tent" and all associated with it (v. 22) anticipates the "sacrifices" by which the "pattern" was "cleansed" (v. 23). Yet return to the "pattern" in vv. 23-24 evokes the description in 9:1-10, the previous sanctuary section. On the distinct vocabulary of vv. 23-24 see pp. 414-15 above. Westfall, *Discourse Analysis,* 217, gives her case away when she says in regard to vv. 23-28: "Therefore, the fact that Christ appeared to do away with sins by the sacrifice of himself is the most prominent information in the paragraph." This theme clearly ties these verses with the previous sacrifice section, 9:11-14 (15), rather than with 9:15-22.

7. One might diagram these relationship using italics and bold as follows: *Heb 9:23-24;* **Heb 9:25–10:4**; Heb 10:5-10: *Heb 10:11-14;* **Heb 10:15-18**. This arrangement underscores the centrality of Heb 10:5-10.

trance of the old high priests into the earthly Most Holy Place (v. 25b).[8] The sacrifice theme will occupy his attention not only to the end of this subsection but through 10:14. Verse 25 establishes two points of contrast between Christ and those high priests, indicated by the words "not often"/"year after year" and "himself"/"blood other than his own." The structure of the sentence gives prominence to the first of these contrasts — "Not that he might offer . . . often, . . . as the high priest goes into the Most Holy Place year after year." The pastor's immediate concern is the "once-for-all" character of Christ's sacrifice. He will not return to the "blood" of animal sacrifices until 10:4 in order to contrast it with Christ's sacrifice of "himself" in 10:5-10. Thus he skillfully anticipates the theme of the following section.

Only in contrast to Christ's self-offering would one call the offerings by which the old high priests entered the Most Holy Place "blood other than his own."[9] In Greek this expression almost puts these sacrifices in the category of "strange" blood or sacrifices unclean and thus unfit to be brought before the Lord.[10] Thus this description anticipates all the pastor will say about their impotency.

26 The opening statement of this verse shows how absurd the repetition of Christ's sacrifice would be: "Because then it would have been necessary for him to have suffered many times since the foundation of the

---

8. The pastor has no intention of identifying Christ's self-offering with his entrance into heaven (Young, "Gospel," 209). Christ's offering is his death on the cross (Lane, 2:249). παθεῖν, "to suffer," in v. 26 refers to his death (Ellingworth, 484). Note how vv. 27 and 28 pair the self-offering of Christ with the death of humanity. Heb 10:5-10 makes it clear that Christ's offering was his life of obedience climaxing with his submission to death on the cross. See Westcott, 273-74, and Wilfrid Stott, "The Conception of 'Offering' in the Epistle to the Hebrews," NTS 9 (1962): 64, n. 2. Christ's suffering, death, and entrance into heaven form "a single course" that happened "once for all" (Weiss, 489). However, his self-offering on the cross is the basis of his entrance into heaven, and that entrance brings his offering to fulfillment, thus demonstrating its effectiveness. See Riggenbach, 286, and the comments on 9:12 above.

9. The ἐν in ἐν αἵματι ἀλλοτρίῳ may denote means, "by [means of] blood of another," like διά in v. 12 above; or accompanying circumstance, "with the blood of another" (Ellingworth, 481). Christ enters heaven by means of his self-offering on the cross. As noted in the comments on v. 12 above, the fact that the old high priest carries the blood into the earthly Most Holy Place only indicates the insufficiency of his sacrifice.

10. Compare ἐν αἵματι ἀλλοτρίῳ, "with blood not his own" (or "with blood pertaining to another"), with the frequent use of θεοὶ ἀλλότριοι, "strange" or "foreign gods" in the Greek OT (Gen 35:2, 4; Deut 31:16, 18, 20; 32:12, 16; Josh 24:14, 20, 23; Judg 10:16; 1 Sam 7:3; 1 Kgs 9:9; 2 Chr 28:25; 33:15; 34:25; Pss 43:20; 81:9; Hos 3:1; Mal 2:11; Jer 1:16; 5:19; 7:6, 9, 18; 11:10; 13:10; 16:11; 19:4, 13; 22:9; 25:6). Compare also the expression πῦρ ἀλλότριον, "strange fire," used to describe unauthorized fire offered in censers before the Lord (Lev 10:1; 16:1; Num 3:4; 16:37; 26:61).

world."[11] This statement clearly identifies the sacrifice of Christ with his suffering and death.[12] If repetition had been necessary, Christ, who has existed since before "the foundation of the world" (1:10-12),[13] would have had to offer himself in death many times by now. However, we know for a fact that he has not done this: "But now he has appeared once for all at the climax of the ages for the abolition of sin by the sacrifice of himself."

Every expression in this statement underscores the definitive nature and continuing effectiveness of Christ's sacrifice. "But now" indicates that the pastor is contrasting fulfillment in Christ with the arrangements for approaching God before he came. Christ has not appeared repeatedly because he dealt with sin "once for all."[14] He has not come "often from the foundation of the world," but "at the climax of the ages."[15] Christ himself has brought the ages to their God-intended consummation and climax (cf. 1:2).[16] He has

11. ἐπεί is causal, "because." Both here and in 10:2 it appears to precede the final "then" clause of a contrary-to-fact condition (Lane, 2:233k). The imperfect ἔδει, "it would have been necessary," indicates this counterfactual significance even though the author has neglected to use the normal contrary-to-fact particle ἄν, which was sometimes omitted in Hellenistic Greek (Ellingworth, 483). To compensate for the missing "if" clause, ἐπεί should be translated "because otherwise." This expression is shorthand for something like, "Because if repeated sacrifices had been necessary."

12. Weiss, 489, points to the alternate reading of 1908 s a that substitutes ἀποθανεῖν, "to die," for παθεῖν, "to suffer."

13. ἀπὸ καταβολῆς κόσμου, "from the foundation of the world" (Matt 13:35; 25:34; Luke 11:50; Rev 13:8; 17:8; cf. πρὸ καταβολῆς κόσμου, "before the foundation of the world," in Eph 1:4; 1 Pet 1:20; John 17:24), is a designation for the beginning of time taken from Jewish tradition (As. Mos. 1:14) and implying that God founded the world (Weiss, 489-91). Thus it implicitly affirms the sovereignty of God over his creation.

14. Pace Johnson, 244, this is no contrast between the Platonic "one" and "the many." The "many" earthly sacrifices are not the dim reflection of "one" heavenly sacrifice existing from eternity. It is the one sacrifice of Christ on the cross that brings the "many" sacrifices to an end.

15. ἐπὶ συντέλεια τῶν αἰώνων, "at the end of the ages," is a variation of a common apocalyptic formula denoting the end of time (Gerhard Delling, "συντέλεια," TDNT 8:64-66). See (ἡ) συντέλεια (τοῦ) αἰῶνος, "the end of the age," in Matt 13:39, 40, 49; 24:3; 28:20. The use of the plural "ages" (αἰώνων) in contrast with both "from the foundation of the world" and the "once-for-all" offering of Christ makes it clear that the pastor is not referring to a period of time at the end but to the climactic event of the ages (Delling, TDNT 8:64-66; cf. BDAG, 974). Christ's sacrifice is the climax of the ages because it has brought the plan of the one who founded the world to its fulfillment (cf. Bruce, 231).

16. By being "made perfect" as our high priest (τετελειωμένον, 7:28) and source of salvation (τελειωθείς, 5:9) the Son "has perfected" (τετελείωκεν) God's people so that they can come into God's presence (10:14). Thus he has brought about the climax or "perfection" (συντέλεια) of the ages. See the comments on συντελέω, "complete" or "perfect," in 8:8. Cf. Koester, 422.

achieved this consummation by nothing less than the abolition of sin.[17] It is sin that has separated humanity from God and bedeviled human life with destruction, fear of death, and judgment (2:14-15). Many had longed for the time when sin would be destroyed. Christ's coming has made that deliverance a reality.[18]

The pastor has chosen his words carefully in order to describe the complete destruction of sin by Christ. Note the singular "sin" instead of "sins." Christ has done away with sin as a principle and force, as a source of pollution and separation from God.[19] Christ's appearing has not merely restrained or weakened sin but produced its "abolition." The term translated "abolition" is the same legal term used in 7:18 for the "abolition" of the "former commandment" and its attendant priestly system.[20] In fact, one might argue that it is by the "abolition" of sin that Christ has abolished the old priestly system that could not deal with sin. This term, however, does not denote a mere change on the law books.[21] The "abolition" of sin is more like the "abolition" of slavery. Sin is no longer in force and thus no longer determines the lives of its once-victims. This removal of sin dominates the history of the world, for it has happened "once for all" at the "climax" of history and will need no further attention even at Christ's return (v. 28).[22] Christ's "abolition of sin" reinforces the interpretation of the "cleansing" of the "heavenly

17. εἰς ἀθέτησιν [τῆς] ἁμαρτίας, "for the abolition of sin," is a final clause denoting the purpose of Christ's appearing (Weiss, 492).

18. If Christ's sacrifice was truly the "climax" of the ages, then it also dealt with the sin that occurred before his coming but subsequent to the "foundation of the world" (v. 26). See Riggenbach, 287. Thus, the faithful of chapter 11 are ultimately saved through Christ (11:39-40). In the immediate context, however, the pastor is concerned with his hearers and their deliverance from sin.

19. With the singular [τῆς] ἁμαρτίας, "of sin," contrast Christ's atoning "for sins" (plural) in 1:3; 2:17; 9:28; 10:1. The idea of sin as a principle is reinforced if the article τῆς, missing in some manuscripts, is original. See Westcott, 276; Riggenbach, 288. *Pace* Ellingworth, 483, it was natural for the pastor to return to the plural in v. 28a because he is speaking of the "sins" of "many."

20. ἀθέτησις, "abolition," "removal," cf. 7:18, is the opposite of βεβαίωσις, "confirmation," in 6:16 (MM, 12; Weiss, 492, n. 67). Compare ἄφεσις, "release," in 9:22 and 10:18. "Sin is vanquished, shewn in its weakness, 'set at naught' (Mk vii.9; Gal. iii.15)" (Westcott, 275).

21. Ellingworth, 482-83, seems to downplay the parallel with 7:18 and the legal sense of this term because he mistakenly equates "legal" with a mere change in the written code.

22. "It [sin] will never be able to regain its power, having been vanquished once for all by the blood of Christ. This inaugurates a purified universe (8:10-12). Thus the sacrifice of Calvary dominates the history of the world, from its origins until the end of time" (Spicq, 2:269). Cf. Bénétreau, 2:93.

things" (9:23) given above.[23] Christ has made provision so that sin need no longer determine the lives of God's people and exclude them from his presence. The way in which Christ has so definitively dealt with sin surpasses the grandest hopes of the devout who lived before his coming.[24]

Christ's objective removal of sin has subjective consequences for the lives of the faithful, which they must appropriate if they would persevere in faith.[25] He has made a way for the cleansing of their consciences from sin and for them to be made new by the inscription of God's law on their hearts (10:15-18) so that they can "serve the living God" (9:14). Thus cleansed and empowered, they are no longer debarred from his presence. They receive these benefits as they draw near to God through Christ (4:14-16; 10:19-25), who makes available all that is necessary for them to persevere in faith (11:1-40) and avoid falling through unbelief (3:7-19).

With obvious appropriateness and intentionality the pastor has used the perfect tense "he has appeared" to affirm the lasting effect of Christ's definitive self-offering accomplished at his first coming.[26] As always, he draws his hearers' attention to the adequate Christ at God's right hand (8:1-2) and to their ultimate destiny (12:22-24). The one who appeared on earth to accomplish our salvation has not disappeared, for he now, as a result of his self-offering, sits at God's right hand on our behalf visible to the eyes of faith (2:8-9).[27] In vv. 27-28 the pastor directs his hearers' gaze forward to the climax of history at Christ's return. This future orientation is both theologically sound and pastorally essential. From a theological perspective, if Christ's saving work was truly the "climax of the ages," then it must also determine the future and the ultimate outcome of history. From the pastoral point of

---

23. "The cancelling of sin must in this context have primary reference to the purging of the 'heavenly things' mentioned in v. 23" (Lane, 249).

24. What Hebrews has described goes far beyond the anticipations of the last times in the following passages, cited by Michel, 326; Weiss, 492; Ellingworth, 483; and others: "In his priesthood sin shall cease and lawless men shall rest from their evil deeds, and righteous men shall find rest in him" (*T. Levi* 18:9; *OTP,* 1:795). "And he himself (will be) free from sin, (in order) to rule a great people. He will expose officials and drive out sinners by the strength of his word" (*Pss. Sol.* 17:36; *OTP,* 2:668). "He will lead them all in holiness [some manuscripts read "equality"] and there will be no arrogance among them, that any should be oppressed" (*Pss. Sol.* 17:41; *OTP,* 2:668).

25. Lane, 2:249.

26. Ellingworth, 484.

27. "Appeared" does not refer to Christ's appearance before God in heaven (*pace* Weiss, 491) but to his appearance to humanity, first of all in the incarnation (Koester, 422, citing Grässer). Yet the pastor would keep the whole work of Christ from his past definitive sacrifice to his present intercession before his hearers (cf. Ellingworth, 483). Similar phrases in 1 Pet 1:20 and 1 Tim 3:16 suggest that Hebrews may be using common Christian tradition (Ellingworth, 483).

view, focus on the ultimate destiny of God's people is strong motivation for endurance until the end.

The pastor is consumed by this concern that his hearers persevere. Thus once he has convinced them that Christ's atonement is effective, he would keep their eyes fixed on the all-sufficient Christ at God's right (8:1-2) and on their final destiny. Note how the pastor draws his hearers' eyes to the exalted Christ in 10:11-14, toward the conclusion of this great symphony on Christ's sacrifice. In the following chapters he will hold their gaze upward and forward.

The expression "he has appeared" also reminds us that, as our High Priest and Savior, Christ fully reveals God and thus accomplishes his vocation as the eternal Son (cf. 1:1-3).[28] The way to God, not yet revealed under the Old Covenant (9:8), has been fully disclosed in him.

27 Since Christ's "once-for-all," finished work has provided for both the present condition and future destiny of humanity, it is the perfect antidote for the universal human predicament. The way in which his finished work is described in v. 28 shows that it corresponds appropriately to human need as described in v. 27.[29] The pastor has already exhibited the common condition of mankind as living under the pall of death (2:14-15).[30] Human beings fear death and especially the judgment that follows. There is a disturbing finality to both — "it is appointed for human beings to die *once for all,* and after this, judgment" (italics added). The pastor leaves "judgment" without an article in Greek in order to emphasize the fearsome quality of this post-death event. He has no doubt that his hearers believe in judgment; it was part of elementary Christian teaching (6:2). The parallel with Christ's return in v. 28 suggests that the judgment coming "after" death is the final Judgment described in 12:26-29.[31] Although v. 27 makes no mention of sin, correspon-

---

28. Weiss, 490, notes the connection between "he has appeared" and revelation, although he does not develop it in the same way as the commentary above.

29. Note the correlatives at the beginning of vv. 27 and 28 respectively: καθ' ὅσον . . . οὕτως, "just as . . . so." The validity of Christ's work is substantiated by its correspondence to the human situation (see Riggenbach, 288). Compare the similar constructions in 3:3 and 7:20 (Ellingworth, 485).

30. The mortality of humanity was a common theme in the ancient world. Compare 4 Macc 8:11 and Josephus, *J.W.* 5.355. See further references in Weiss, 493, and Ellingworth, 486. Ellingworth, however, is correct when he says that this reference to death and subsequent judgment "strike[s] a distinctively biblical note."

31. Ellingworth, 486; Westcott, 277; *pace* Attridge, 265. Elsewhere the pastor never mentions an immediate postmortem judgment. *Pace* Wilfried Eisele, *Ein unerschütterliches Reich: Die mittelplatonische Umformung des Parusiegedankens im Hebräerbrief* (BZNW 116; Berlin and New York: Walter de Gruyter, 2003), 84-85, the second coming of Christ is not an individual "coming" of Christ to each believer at death. Christ's second coming is as concrete and universal an event as his first coming with which it is parallel.

dence with v. 28 makes it quite clear that sin is the cause of death, and especially of subsequent condemnation at the final Judgment.

28 Christ's second coming to bring final salvation for his people is the ultimate proof that his sacrifice was "once for all," unrepeatable because absolutely sufficient. As noted above, anticipation of this joyous second coming is also the ultimate motivation for perseverance. The very structure of this sentence undergirds this future orientation: Verse 27 used the finite verb "appointed" to put stress on human death and left the verb to be implied in the description of future judgment. Verse 28, however, reverses this emphasis. As important as Christ's once-for-all offering is, the pastor relegates it to the opening causal participial clause, "Since Christ has been offered once for all in order to bear the sins of many." With the main verb he focuses his hearers on the coming salvation: "he will appear a second time without reference to sin for the purpose of bringing salvation to those awaiting him."[32] Christ's "once-for-all" self-offering is so definitive that his second coming will be totally "without" reference to the sin problem. This thorough removal of sin at his first coming (v. 26) paved the way for him to bring full and final "salvation" for its beneficiaries at his second. The "salvation" he will bring is nothing less than entrance into the heavenly homeland (11:10-16) and reception of the "unshakable kingdom" (12:25-29).

The pastor's use of "Christ," absent since v. 11, signals the climactic nature of this verse. Just as humans die "once" or "once for all" due to sin, so Christ "was offered once for all"[33] to "bear" the sins "of many." We noted above the way in which this phrase echoes what Isa 53:12 says about the Suffering Servant who offers himself for "the sins of many."[34] "Of many" contrasts with "once for all" and signifies not the limitation but the vast extent

32. εἰς σωτηρίαν, "for salvation," describes the purpose of ὀφθήσεται, "he will appear," rather than the object anticipated by τοῖς αὐτὸν ἀπεκδεχομένοις, "those who await him" (Ellingworth, 487-88). Christ will appear "to those who await him" for the purpose of their "salvation," rather than, "Christ will appear to those who are waiting for him" to bring their "salvation." εἰς σωτηρίαν, "for salvation," is reserved until the end of the sentence for emphasis.

33. The passive, προσενεχθείς, "having been offered," "was offered," strengthens the analogy between Christ's death and the death of human beings (Riggenbach, 289; Ellingworth, 483). Strictly speaking, this is not a divine passive (Westcott, 277; *pace* Bénétreau, 2:95), for Hebrews never says that Christ was offered by God. Yet the passive does remind us that he offered himself in accord with the divine will (10:5-10; Riggenbach, 289; Ellingworth, 483). The fact that human beings die only once also makes the thought of his repeated dying ridiculous (Hughes, 387).

34. Compare εἰς τὸ πολλῶν ἀνενεγκεῖν ἁμαρτίας, "in order to offer for the sins of many," with καὶ αὐτὸς ἁμαρτίας πολλῶν ἀνήνεγκεν, "and he offered up for the sins of many" (LXX of Isa 53:12).

and grandeur of what Christ has done.[35] The pastor adds "bear" to the variety of terms employed to stress the thoroughness with which Christ does away with sin. This term suggests that by his self-sacrifice Christ took sins as a whole upon himself — not just their deserved punishment.[36] Thus, he is able to deliver not merely from punishment but from the pollution and dominion of sin.[37] It also reminds us that salvation is not separate from the Savior. His people have deliverance from sin only by being joined to him as their High Priest and Brother who took their sins upon himself.

For "those who await him"[38] his future appearing will bring "salvation" instead of the condemnation from final Judgment dreaded by all humanity (see on 2:14-18). Just as the high priest returned and blessed the people after offering his sacrifice on the Day of Atonement, so Christ will return with the blessing of ultimate salvation.[39] His return will be the final confirmation of his sacrifice's "once-for-all" effectiveness.[40] Nevertheless, unlike those awaiting the return of Aaron's sons (cf. Sir 50:5-10), those who await Christ need have no hesitancy about the adequacy of his sacrifice.[41]

10:1-4   These verses contrast the regular repetition of the old sacrifices with the "once-for-all" character of Christ's sacrifice as described in 9:25-28.[42] That continual repetition betrayed their inadequacy to deal with sin. They had no future but to foreshadow the work of Christ by continually reminding God's people of their sinfulness. On the other hand, as noted above, the "once-for-all" sacrifice of Christ has so definitively dealt with sin that it provides final salvation and determines the ultimate future of God's

---

35. πολλῶν, "many," is not in contrast to "all," but to "one" (Hughes, 388).

36. ἀνενεγκεῖν (second aorist active infinitive of ἀναφέρω), by analogy with Isa 53:11, 12, means "bear" in the sense of "take upon oneself" (Spicq, 2:270; Ellingworth, 487; BDAG, 75, 4). "The burden which Christ took upon Him and bore to the cross was 'the sins of many,' not, primarily or separately from the sins, the punishment of sins" (Westcott, 277).

37. "His bearing of sin implies the removing of sin from others, and the consequent liberation of those who enter into the benefits of his self-oblation" (Bruce, 232).

38. ἀπεκδέχομαι is normally used in the New Testament of those who wait eagerly for the Christian hope because they are ready for it (Rom 8:19, 23, 25; 1 Cor 1:7; Phil 3:20).

39. Lane, 2:250-51; Hughes, 388-89; Westcott, 276; Spicq, 2:270-71. Bruce, 232, quotes the description of the return of the high priest Simon the Just on the Day of Atonement as found in Sir 50:5-10.

40. Lane, 2:251.

41. Bénétreau, 2:94-95.

42. Thus γάρ, "for," at the beginning of 10:1, indicates that 10:1-4 supports 9:25-28 (see Ellingworth, 492). οὐδέποτε δύναται, "was never able" (v. 1), and ἀδύνατον γάρ, "for it is impossible" (v. 4), form an inclusion unifying this section (Weiss, 499) and setting it in contrast to the description of Christ's sufficiency in 9:25-28.

people. These verses are no return from the future salvation in 9:28 to present salvation.[43] They describe a system that could not produce salvation but could only anticipate the future by being its opposite and thus by showing the need of what was to come.

10:1 The last word in the Greek text of 9:28 was "salvation"; the first word in 10:1 is "shadow." The pastor has just said that the "once-for-all" sacrifice of Christ effectively provides for future ultimate salvation (Heb 9:28). By contrast, "the law has only a shadow of the good things to come and not the reality itself of those things." This principle is fundamental to the pastor's interpretation of the OT throughout his sermon. The "law" is the whole OT system of Tent, priests, sacrifices, purification rituals, and the like, seen as a way of expunging sin and approaching God. The pastor has been continually hammering away at its inability to achieve this purpose (5:1-4; 7:11-28; 9:1-10). Still, the law was a "shadow," an intimation, a pattern (5:1-10; 9:11-14; etc.) given through Moses (3:5) that made comprehensible the "reality itself" yet to come.[44] In fact, the very ineffectiveness of the old system was part of the way in which it exposed human need and pointed forward to the new.

The pastor's use of the terms translated "shadow" and "reality" betrays the distance between his worldview and the Platonic dualism espoused by Philo.[45] Philo uses both words almost synonymously to describe things in the created world as temporal, transitory copies of the eternal world.[46] Thus in translations of Philo's works the second of these terms is usually rendered not by "reality" but by some term such as "image." The pastor, however, contrasts these two terms.[47] The first is not a somewhat deceptive reflection of

---

43. *Pace* Ellingworth, 488, it is a misnomer to use "realized eschatology" for this description of sacrifices that did not produce salvation.

44. "Without the cultus, Hebrews would not have a canvas on which to paint the portrait of Christ — the eternal high priest who has sacrificed himself for the forgiveness and cleansing of God's covenant people" (Joslin, *Law,* 254).

45. Weiss, 501, and somewhat begrudgingly Attridge, 270, admit the distance between the use of these terms in Hebrews and Philo. Weiss, 501-2, deconstructs Braun's advocacy of Platonic dualism as the source of Hebrews' usage by pitting Braun's statements against each other. Contrast, "The background of 10:1 is near Plato" with "This terminology is foreign to normal Greek usage."

46. See σκιά ("shadow") and εἰκών ("image") in Plato, *Republic* 509E-510E; Philo, *Alleg. Interp.* 3.96; *Decalogue* 82; *Migration* 12; *Heir* 72. At times εἰκών may be used somewhat more positively than σκιά to denote a clearer rather than a "shadowy" copy of heavenly realities (see Bruce, 235, n. 10, citing Plato, *Cratylus* 306E, and Philo *Moses* 1.51). However, εἰκών is still a "copy" and not the "reality" itself, as here in Hebrews.

47. The contrast with σκιάν, "shadow" — introduced by οὐκ ("not") plus the intensive αὐτήν ("itself," "the reality itself") — indicates that εἰκών should be translated as

the eternal but a divinely ordained, though imperfect, anticipation and foreshadowing of God's full salvation to come.[48] The second is used for the "reality" of that salvation itself manifested in Christ.[49]

Thus the "good things" yet "to come" from the Old Covenant point of view are the "good things that have come" in Christ (9:11) plus that final salvation to be received at his second coming (9:28) though provided for by his first. He has made cleansing from sin and access to God available for the faithful as means for perseverance. He has also opened the way for those who do persevere to enter God's presence finally, "once for all," at the Judgment. What "good things" could be better than the saving work of Christ past, present, and future?

Because of its merely anticipatory nature, the law could never provide salvation for the people of God.[50] Compare the smooth translation given above, "by the same sacrifices which are offered continuously year after year," with a more literal rendering: "year after year by those same sacrifices which are offered continuously."[51] The pastor emphasizes the repetitive nature of these sacrifices by sandwiching them between "year after year" and "continuously." Both the word "same" and the present continuous tense of

---

"reality" instead of the more usual "image" (Lane, 2:260; cf. Attridge, 270). 𝔓⁴⁶ removes this contrast by omitting οὐκ αὐτήν, thus identifying εἰκών with σκιά: "for since the law has a shadow (σκιά) of the good things to come, the image (εἰκών) of the things." The generally received reading is well supported. Desire to remove the unusual contrast between these terms may have given rise to the variant. Lane, 2:254b, argues that the very structure of this sentence implies a contrast. However, even if the alternate reading were original, these terms would still not be used for temporal "copies" of eternal things as in Philo. Ellingworth, 490, is mistaken when he says that Philo contrasts these two terms in *Dreams* 1.7 and *Alleg. Interp.* 3.96. The latter of these two references reads, . . . τῆς εἰκόνος, ἣν σκιὰ νυνὶ κέκληκεν, ". . . of the Image, to which the title of Shadow has just been given" (Coleson and Whitaker, LCL).

48. See Lane, 2:253-54a, 259; Ellingworth, 490-91; cf. Weiss, 500.

49. Koester, 431. An attempt to discern a three-way distinction between "shadow," "image" of the reality, and the "reality" itself is oversubtle and unsupported by the rest of Hebrews (Ellingworth, 490). See the discussion in Hughes, 390, n. 48.

50. The participial phrase that opens this verse is causal: "Because the law has a shadow . . . and not the reality . . ." (cf. RSV, NRSV, ESV, etc.).

51. εἰς τὸ διηνεκές probably qualifies the preceding verb, προσφέρουσιν ("offer"), as in 7:3, instead of the following verb δύναται ("is able"), as in 10:11-12 (Ellingworth, 492; *pace* Westcott, 303-4). Thus "which are offered continuously" instead of "is not able to perfect forever." This phrase is used for "forever" elsewhere in the Greek Bible but for "continuously" in other literature. The previous use of this phrase to describe the duration of the Son "forever" (7:3) only makes its use for the perpetual offering of the old sacrifices more pungent. Ellingworth (492) cites Bleek, Riggenbach, Spicq, Moffatt, Héring, Buchanan, Hughes, Braun, Attridge, and Lane in support of the former position; Westcott, Peake, Michel, Montefiore, and Morris of the latter.

the verb for "offer" sustain this emphasis. The repetitive character of these sacrifices shows definitively that they are not able to "perfect" the worshiper. To "perfect" something is to bring it to its intended goal. The parallel with v. 2 shows clearly that the goal envisioned for these sacrifices was cleansing from sin and the resultant access to God's presence.[52] Since these sacrifices were repeated over and over again, it is obvious that they did not achieve this goal. As noted above, the Greek OT describes the consecration by which the OT priests were authorized to "approach" God as their being "perfected."[53] The pastor envisions the whole people of God as being "perfected" through such a definitive cleansing from sin that they are authorized to enter the true heavenly dwelling place of God.[54] Hebrews could hardly be more emphatic: the law "is never able" to provide such perfection, no matter how long its sacrifices are perpetuated.[55]

2 In 9:26 the pastor used a contrary-to-fact condition to substantiate the non-repetitive, and thus definitive, character of Christ's sacrifice affirmed in 9:25. In 10:2 he uses a similar construction to substantiate the inability of the old sacrifices to "perfect" those who approach God as affirmed in 10:1: "Because" if those sacrifices had been able to bring perfection, "would they not have ceased being offered, since those worshiping would no longer have had any consciousness of sin if they had been cleansed once for all?" The concluding conditional participial phrase, "if they had been once for all cleansed," compensates for the lack of an opening "if" clause. The cleansing in question is the true inner cleansing of the person effected by Christ according to 9:14. The pastor reserves the perfect participle, translated "if they had been cleansed," for the end of the sentence in order to conclude with a strong emphasis on the purpose of sacrifice and the inability of the old to achieve that purpose. The perfect tense of this participle suggests a definitive cleansing that determines the subsequent lives of the cleansed.[56] Absence of this continuing effect belies the ability of the old sacrifices to truly cleanse.

52. Compare the final τελειῶσαι, "to perfect," at the end of v. 2 with ἅπαξ κεκαθαρισμένους, "once having been cleansed," at the climax of v. 3.
53. See the comments on 2:19; 5:9; 7:19, 28.
54. Peterson, *Perfection*, 146-47.
55. According to Ellingworth, 491, the plural, δύνανται ("they are [never] able"), has a bit better textual support than the singular accepted by the UBS⁴/NA²⁷ text, δύναται (the law "is [never] able"). The plural is perhaps the more difficult reading because it leaves the singular ὁ νόμος ("the law") hanging. On the other hand, such awkward construction would not be characteristic of Hebrews. The plural verb προσφέρουσιν ("they are offering"), may have influenced a scribe to alter the singular to a plural (Ellingworth, 491-92).
56. κεκαθαρισμένους, "having been cleansed." See Lane, 2:255i.

430

It is tempting to render the word translated "consciousness" as "conscience," the meaning it has in 9:14. "Consciousness," however, is the more common meaning and is appropriate by contrast with "reminder" in the next verse: instead of removing all "consciousness of sin" the old sacrifices provide a perpetual "reminder" of sin.[57] The sacrifices of the Mosaic system left worshipers "conscious" not merely of guilt but of sin, and especially of its pollution that demanded cleansing.

3 The pastor began the main clause of v. 1 with the Greek expression translated "year after year." He concludes v. 3 with the same term. Thus, this entire discussion of the repetitive and thus insufficient character of the old sacrifices is enclosed by these two uses of this expression. Verses 2 and 3 are two sides of the same coin, explaining the complementary implications of this continuous repetition: the perpetual offering of these sacrifices demonstrates their inability to remove sin (v. 2); consequently, they become a continual "reminder" that sin still remains (v. 3).[58] The annual cycle of sacrifices climaxing with the Day of Atonement became an outward, visible, continuous "memorial" to sin forcing people to live their lives with the awareness of their inability to be free from its pollution.[59] Philo (*Moses* 2.107; *Planting* 108; *Spec. Laws* 1.215) taught that the offerings of the unjust brought only a reminder of sin because of the character of the person offering.[60] Hebrews teaches that all Old Covenant sacrifices were a memorial to sin because of the impotency of the sacrifices themselves. However, when the "conscience" (9:11) has been cleansed by the sacrifice of Christ, the faithful are no longer "conscious" (10:2) of sin. Furthermore, God himself no longer "remembers" their sin (8:12 and 10:17, quoting Jer 31:34). Sin no longer dominates their lives, nor does it prevent their access to God. One can hardly avoid recalling Jesus' words of institution — "do this in remembrance of me" (Luke 22:19). The old sacrifices were a "reminder" of sin's continuing dominion. The

57. See συνείδησις in BDAG, 967; Ellingworth, 494; Lane, 2:255j. If one translates συνείδησιν as "consciousness," then the following ἁμαρτιῶν is an objective genitive, "consciousness of sin." If one takes συνείδησιν as "conscience," then the following genitive must be descriptive — "sinful conscience."

58. Note the ἀλλ', "but," that joins vv. 2 and 3.

59. Westcott, 305, argues that the pastor is not thinking exclusively of the Day of Atonement but is referring "to the whole sacrificial system of the Law, completed in a yearly cycle." On the character of these sacrifices as an outward "memorial" to sin see Weiss, 504 (cf. Bruce, 237).

60. At least in *Planting* 108 Philo is speaking of a "remembrance" (ὑπόμνησις) by God rather than by the sinner. In the other references it is not clear who remembers the sins. Hebrews uses ἀνάμνησις, "memorial," instead of the ὑπόμνησις employed by Philo. Bénétreau, 2:98, n. 1, rightly criticizes those like Héring, Spicq, and Moffatt who find an allusion to the remembrance of sin brought by the offering of jealousy as described in Num 5:15.

Lord's Supper is a reminder of its definitive removal.[61] Thus, the impotency of the old anticipated the sufficiency of the new.

4 The inability of the old sacrifices to cleanse from sin was demonstrated by their perpetual repetition. However, the reason for their impotence was that they consisted of nothing more than "the blood of bulls and goats."[62] The eye of the Greek reader or ear of the Greek listener was struck by the first word of this verse — "impossible."[63] Many had condemned the sacrifices of the wicked and hypocritical.[64] The pastor categorically condemns the saving efficacy of all Old Covenant animal sacrifices *in toto*. Spicq rightly describes the sharpness of this statement as "almost brutal."[65] Those sacrifices could not "take away" sin and thus remove its pollution and dominion from human life.[66] How could the blood of mere animals purge the human heart of the pollution brought by disobedience?

The pastor established the necessity of the "shedding of blood" for the "remission" or "removal" of sin at the conclusion of the last movement in 9:22. He now affirms that the "blood of bulls and goats" was not sufficient for that task. Nothing less than Christ's "own blood" (9:12, 14) offered "once for all" (9:26) would do. In the following section, vv. 5-10, the

---

61. The repetition of the old was a remembrance of guilt, the "once-for-all" offering of the new a remembrance of grace (Hughes, 394).

62. The alternate reading τράγων καὶ ταύρων ("goats and bulls") instead of ταύρων καὶ τράγων ("bulls and goats") is probably assimilation to 9:13 (Ellingworth, 498).

63. ἀδύνατον γάρ resumes the οὐδέποτε δύναται of v. 1.

64. See 1 Sam 15:22-23; Hos 6:6; Isa 1:10-12; Mic 6:6-9; Jer 6:20; 7:21-23; Ps 40:7-10. This criticism continued in Hellenistic Judaism: *Letter of Aristeas* 234; Philo, *Planting* 107–8, *Moses* 2.108, *Spec. Laws* 1.271-72; Josephus, *Ant.* 6.141-43. Yet such tradition always considered the offerings necessary (Weiss, 505, n. 32).

65. Spicq, 2:303. Ellingworth (497-98) misses the radical nature of this statement when he says that Hebrews goes little further than the critiques of sacrifice in the prophets and contemporary Judaism. Thus he mistakenly argues that the old sacrifices atoned for unintentional sin, Christ's sacrifice for intentional sin, with no sacrifice for sin after baptism. Hebrews clearly says that the old sacrifices provided nothing more than outward, ritual cleansing (9:13). They could do nothing for actual sin but remind sinners of the way it dominated their lives.

66. ἀφαιρεῖν (present infinitive of ἀφαιρέω), "to take away," is similar to περιελεῖν in v. 11 (aorist of περιαιρέω) and an appropriate companion for other words the pastor uses for the complete removal of sin: ἀθέτησις, "abolition" (9:26); ἀνενεγκεῖν (aorist of ἀναφέρω), "to bear" (9:28); and ἄφεσις, "release" (10:18). "ἀφαιρεῖν is used of taking away sins only in Rom. 11:27 — Isa. 27:9; cf. Sir. 47:11, but it occurs frequently in this sense in the OT, with a variety of words for wrongdoing and shame (Nu. 14:18, ἀφαιρῶν ἀνομίας καὶ ἀδικίας καὶ ἁμαρτίας; cf. Lv. 1:17; Is. 6:7, 17:9; Je. 11:15; Ezk. 45:9)" (Ellingworth, 498). The pastor is referring to the removal of sins with their attendant guilt, pollution, and dominion over the person.

432

pastor explains why the blood of Christ succeeded where animal blood failed. He would have his hearers comprehend what he meant when he said that "through eternal Spirit" Christ "offered himself blameless to God" (9:14).

c. Sacrifice — "To Do Your Will, O God" (10:5-10)

5 *Therefore, as he was coming into the world, he says: "Sacrifice and offering you did not desire, but a body you have prepared for me.* 6 *With whole burnt offerings and sin offerings you were not pleased.* 7 *Then I said, 'Behold, I have come, in the scroll of the book it has been written concerning me, to do, O God, your will.'"* 8 *Saying above that "sacrifices and offerings and whole burnt offerings and sin offerings you did not desire, nor were you pleased with them" — which were offered according to the law.* 9 *Then he said, "Behold, I have come to do your will." He abolishes the first in order that he might establish the second.* 10 *By which will we are made holy through the offering of the body of Jesus Christ once for all.*

These verses contrast the incarnate Son's obedience unto death with the impotent shed blood of animals just mentioned in v. 4.[1] Thus the "blood" of Christ is nothing less than his obedient human life offered on the cross.[2] The pastor's interpretation of Ps. 40:6-8 shows that the incarnate Son of God "learned obedience" (5:8) by following the path of unbroken submission to the will of God. That obedience unto death was the source of his being "made perfect" (5:9) as our Savior. Thus, it was the means by which "we have been made holy" (10:10).[3]

Psalm 40:6-8 is quoted in 10:5-7 as Christ's affirmation of obedience on the eve of his incarnation. By using this psalm the pastor asserts the incarnate obedience of the one he has already described as the eternal Son of God.

---

1. Riggenbach, 299.

2. See the discussion of the significance of Christ's blood in Hughes, "Blood," 99-109, and the definitive argument that his sacrifice was offered on earth in Hughes, "Sacrifice," 195-212. "The blood of Christ is not understood here materially: how could it be? It denotes the offering up in death of a life wholly dedicated to the will of God, a life characterized by unspotted holiness" (F. F. Bruce, "'A Shadow of Good Things' [Hebrews 10:1]," in *The Time Is Fulfilled: Five Aspects of the Fulfillment of the Old Testament in the New* [Grand Rapids: Eerdmans, 1978], 86).

3. Thus this section brings clarity to 5:7-10 as well as to 9:14. D. Hamm, "Faith in the Epistle to the Hebrews: The Jesus Factor," *CBQ* 52 (1990): 285, notes that δεήσεις ("prayers") and εἰσακουσθείς ("having been heard") in Heb 5:7 echo the opening verse of Psalm 40.

Verses 8 and 9a respectively give the negative and positive implications of this psalm-attested obedience — summarized at the end of v. 9 as "he takes away the first in order that he might establish the second." The argument reaches a grand climax in v. 10 with the pastor's final description of Christ's obedience and the benefits that accrue therefrom for the faithful.[4]

5a Heb 10:1-4 climaxed in the assertion that animal sacrifices provided no atonement. "Therefore" it was proper for Christ to pronounce God's displeasure upon them and replace them with the offering of his "body."[5] "As he was coming into the world," or, perhaps, "as he was about to come into the world," pinpoints the eve of the incarnation as the occasion when Christ spoke these words.[6] This expression echoes the "Behold, I have come" from v. 7 of the psalm quoted in 10:5 below.

The pastor has shown his hearers how God's promises of sonship (Pss 2:7; 110:1; cf. Heb 1:5, 13; 5:5-6) and priesthood (Ps 110:4; cf. Heb 5:5-6; 6:20; 7:1-25) to David and his descendants find their ultimate fulfillment in Christ. Thus David's words of response in Ps 22:22 and Ps 40:6-8 find their truest significance as the Son's response to the Father.[7] The first of these references has become the Son's expression of praise at the exaltation (Heb 2:12); the second, his declaration of submission to God at the incarnation (10:5-7). In the first he affirmed his humanity as a means of identifying with God's sinful people; in the second, as the sphere of his unbroken loyalty to God. His very assumption of humanity was an act of obedience that climaxed in the cross. By thus accomplishing the will of God, his obedience did away with all the sacrifices of the Old Covenant.

5b-7 The Son's superior obedience was prefigured by the imperfect obedience of David, expressed in Ps 40:6-8.[8] The standard LXX text pro-

---

4. The offering of Christ's body in v. 10 is "the author's goal in the Christological interpretation of this psalm" (Weiss, 507).

5. On διό, "therefore," see Ellingworth, 499; Attridge, 273, n. 59. We cannot give unqualified assent to Weiss's assertion (507) that the impotence of animal sacrifices in v. 4 was a "Christologically grounded judgment." The pastor may not have perceived their lack without Christ. However, he argues that this lack is evidenced by what is said in the OT text itself: first, those sacrifices were offered by sinful priests (5:1-3; 9:7-10); second, they pertained to an earthly Tent and could provide only ritual cleansing (9:1-14); and third, they had to be repeated (10:1-4).

6. While "coming into the world" may have been a Jewish way of referring to birth (Str-B 2:358), the pastor is describing the Son's incarnation (Riggenbach, 300; Michel, 336; Koester, 432; and Kistemaker, 274). See John 1:9; 6:14; and especially 11:27, where "the one who is coming" is virtually a title for Jesus (Ellingworth, 500; cf. Attridge, 273, n. 63). Lane, 2:262, calls this phrase distinctly "incarnational" language.

7. For other aspects of Psalm 40 that find echoes in Hebrews' portrayal of Jesus see Johnson, 250-51.

8. Riggenbach, 304-5.

vides a literal rendering of this psalm.[9] However, the version quoted by Hebrews differs from this literal translation in several ways that facilitate its application to Christ's perfect obedience. First, Hebrews uses the word "body" instead of "ears" in Ps 40:6: "a body you have prepared for me" instead of "ears you have prepared for me." Second, Hebrews has the plural, "whole burnt offerings," at the beginning of v. 6 instead of the singular "whole burnt offering" found in most manuscripts of Ps 40:6b.[10] Third, Hebrews reads "you were not pleased" instead of "you did not request" at the end of v. 6: "With whole burnt offerings and sin offerings you were not pleased."[11] Finally, in the last line of this quotation Hebrews reads, "to do, O God, your will" instead of "to do your will, O my God, I have resolved" (Ps 40:8).[12] Hebrews has omitted "my," put "O God" before instead of after "your will," and terminated the quotation before the words "I have resolved."

The most striking difference between Hebrews and the LXX text is the use of "body" instead of "ears." The editors of the standard LXX believe that the Old Latin bears witness to an original Greek text "ears you have fashioned for me," despite the fact that the major Greek manuscripts read "a body you have fashioned for me."[13] However, it is difficult to believe that the pastor could have introduced a change of this nature into a text with which his readers were familiar without raising questions in their minds.[14] Nor is the argument that scribes have conformed the texts of the major LXX manuscripts

---

9. Alfred Rahlfs, ed., *Psalmi cum Odis* (vol. 10 of *Septuaginta Vetus Testamentum Graecum Auctoritate Academiae Scientiarum Gottingensis editum;* Göttingen: Vandenhoeck & Ruprecht, 1979), 143. In the LXX Ps 40:6-8 is Ps 39:7-9.

10. Compare the singular, ὁλοκαύτωμα ("whole burnt offering"), found in most witnesses to the LXX text of Ps 40:6b, with the plural, ὁλοκαυτώματα ("whole burnt offerings"), found in Heb 10:6. Codex Alexandrinus is one prominent manuscript that has the plural in Ps 40:6b.

11. Compare ᾔτησας "you requested," with εὐδόκησας, "you were pleased with."

12. Compare the τοῦ ποιῆσαι ὁ θεὸς τὸ θέλημά σου of Hebrews with the τοῦ ποιῆσαι τὸ θέλημά σου, ὁ θεός μου, ἐβουλήθην of the psalm.

13. See ὠτία, "ears," instead of σῶμα, "body," in Rahlfs, *Septuaginta Gottingensis,* 143. For argument defending this reading see Pierre Grelot, "Le texte du Psaume 39,7 dans la Septante," *RevBib* 108, no. 2 (2001): 210-13, and Karen H. Jobes, "Rhetorical Achievement in the Hebrews 10 'Misquote' of Psalm 40," *Bib* 72 (1991): 387-96. Sinaiticus, Vaticanus, and Alexandrinus all read σῶμα. Riggenbach, 301, n. 27, argues that the infrequent use of ὠτία ("ears") in the LXX makes its appearance here very unlikely. According to his investigations, the LXX normally uses οὖς, ὠτός for "ear" (180 times) instead of the diminutive ὠτίον, ὠτίου (only sixteen times). Furthermore, outside of Sirach and a variant of Isa 55:3 ὠτίον is only used in the singular.

14. Ellingworth's statement made in reference to the plural ὁλοκαυτώματα ("whole burnt offerings") is more appropriate concerning σῶμα: "Nowhere does the author base an argument on a text which he has significantly changed" (501).

to Hebrews convincing.[15] They did not consistently change these manuscripts to reflect other differences in the way Hebrews cites this psalm.[16] It is possible that "body" was a textual corruption of "ears."[17] It is more likely, however, that "body" represents an alternate translation of the original text.[18] The Hebrew of this verse presents several difficulties that may have puzzled LXX translators. It could be translated "ears you pierced for me" or "ears you dug for me."[19] "Ears you prepared for me" fits the context well. God has prepared "ears" for the speaker in order to hear and obey God's word. However, it is probable that another translator took "ears" as a metaphor in which the part stood for the whole, "ears" for the entire "body," which God "prepared" as a vehicle of obedience. The pastor builds his argument on this version of the text with which he and his hearers were familiar.[20] He could have built his case on the more literal translation which would have been in full agreement with the obedience of the Son.[21] However, "body" allowed him to tie this obedience more readily to the incarnation and final offering of Christ's "body" on the cross.

The rest of these changes were probably made by the pastor and demonstrate his ability in using style to communicate his message. By introducing the second and third variations from the standard LXX mentioned above, he has achieved a balance of sounds that makes the passage more pleasing to the hearers' ears and easier to remember.[22] At the same time these changes

15. *Pace* Grelot, "Le texte du Psaume 39,7 dans la Septante," 210-13, and Jobes, "'Misquote,'" 387-96.

16. Alexandrinus does have the plural, ὁλοκαυτώματα, "whole burnt offerings," found in the Heb 10:6 citation of the psalm.

17. An original LXX ὠτία ("ears") may have become σῶμα ("body") through a misreading that mistook the final sigma of ἠθέλησας ("you did not desire") at the end of the previous line for the beginning of ὠτία. Thus ὠτία would become σωτια and then became σῶμα. Such mistakes could easily occur when copying an exemplar without space between words. See Koester, 433, citing Bleek.

18. See Heb 10:30, where the pastor uses a version of Deut 32:35a that differs from the received LXX (Lane, 2:295; Attridge, 295). See also the comments on Heb 1:6 above.

19. Peter C. Craigie, *Psalms 1–50* (WBC 19; Waco, TX: Word, 1983), 313, n. 7a.

20. So Lane, 2:255m; Bruce, 240; Ellingworth, 500; Riggenbach, 301; F. Schröger, *Der Verfasser des Hebräerbriefes als Schriftausleger* (BU 4; Regensburg: Pustet, 1968), 174; and many others.

21. ". . . if the Hebrew wording had been reproduced literally by the Greek translator, it would have served [the author's] purpose equally well, for the ears are the organs of hearing, and hence of obeying" (Bruce, "'A Shadow of Good Things' [Heb 10:1]," 84). See Attridge, 274.

22. See Jobes, "'Misquote,'" 387-96, and Karen Jobes, "The Function of Paronomasia in Hebrews 10:5-7," *TJ* 13 (1992): 181-91. She has shown how the last three

reinforce the truth he would have them grasp. The plural "whole burnt offer-ings" (v. 6) fits well with Hebrews' emphasis on the multiplicity, and thereby inability, of the old sacrifices.[23] "You were not pleased with" (v. 6b) is a stronger expression of the divine displeasure than "you did not request." It has the advantage of avoiding any possible misunderstanding because at one level God had "requested" these sacrifices in the Mosaic law.[24] Finally, the adaptations in the last line of the quotation (v. 7) allow it to end with an em-phatic "your will."[25] The omission of "I have resolved" also makes "to do your will" the complement of "come": "I have come . . . to do your will," in-stead of "I have resolved to do your will."[26] Thus this final line as recorded by Hebrews makes it clear that the purpose of the Son's becoming human was to do the will of God.[27]

"The scroll of the book" anticipated Christ's obedience and self-offering just as much as it did his session at God's right as High Priest (Ps 110:1, 4) and Mediator of the New Covenant (Jer 31:31-34).[28] The psalmist's

---

syllables of the plural ὁλοκαυτώματα ("whole burnt offerings") in v. 6a (LXX 7a) achieve phonetic assonance with σῶμα δέ ("but a body") in Ps 40:5c. Furthermore, οὐκ εὐδόκησας ("you were not pleased with") later in v. 6 achieves a similar effect with οὐκ ἠθέλησας ("you did not desire") at the end of v. 5b. Because of the adaptations in the last line of this quotation the σου (τὸ θέλημα σου, "your will") at the end of this line balances the ἐμοῦ (περὶ ἐμοῦ, "concerning me") at the end of the previous. Jobes contends that the author of Hebrews is responsible for substituting σῶμα ("body") for ὠτία ("ears"). However, it is more likely that he changed ὁλοκαύτωμα ("whole burnt offering") into ὁλοκαυτώματα ("whole burnt offerings") to achieve phonetic assonance with a σῶμα that was already in his text. After all, according to Jobes, he changed οὐκ ᾔτησας ("you did not request") into οὐκ εὐδόκησας ("you were not pleased with") in order to conform to οὐκ ἠθέλησας already present at the end of v. 5b. The textual evidence makes it very unlikely that the LXX manuscripts have been conformed to Hebrews (Koester, 433).

23. However, Ellingworth, 500-501, thinks that the LXX text received by He-brews already had the plural, as does Codex Alexandrinus, a manuscript with which He-brews is often in agreement.

24. Attridge, 274.

25. *Pace* Ellingworth, 501, who thinks the author has deemphasized this phrase by moving it.

26. The pastor's interpretation below shows clearly that he took the clause "in the scroll of the book it is written concerning me" as parenthetical: "Behold, I have come (in the scroll of the book it is written concerning me) to do your will" (Attridge, 274; Ellingworth, 501; Riggenbach, 303; cf. NKJV, NASB, NIV, and NRSV). *Pace* Lane, 2:263, who would make "to do your will" the complement of "it is written concerning me" — "it is written concerning me to do your will."

27. The omission of "my" before "God" ("O God" instead of "O my God") does little more than streamline the quotation. In the light of "your God" in 1:9, the pastor could have had no objection to the Son's referring to God as "my God."

28. The literal meaning of κεφαλίς, found in the phrase ἐν κεφαλίδι βιβλίου ("in

"book" was probably the Pentateuch, especially the "book" of Deuteronomy that contained the law concerning kingship (Deut 17:14-20).[29] In light of Christ's incarnation, however, this "book" expands to encompass the entire OT.[30] The whole has become an anticipation or prophecy fulfilled by his coming to do God's will.[31]

8 The pastor divides this psalm into two parts in order to bring out its significance. The first is signaled by the phrase "saying above" at the beginning of v. 8; the second is introduced by "then he said" at the beginning of v. 9.[32] The first describes what has been abolished, the second what has been established. The pastor begins each part of his interpretation by rearranging selected phrases from the psalm and concludes each with an interpretive comment. His emphasis is on the positive second part of his interpretation: the animal sacrifices of the old are declared invalid in order to make way for Christ's affirmation of his willing self-sacrifice.[33] Thus the interpretive comment at the end of v. 9 is summative for the whole: "he abolishes the first in order that he might establish the second."

The pastor returns to Ps 40:6, the first part of the psalm quoted "above" in vv. 5b-6. Every feature of his interpretation underscores God's radical rejection of all OT sacrifices as means of atonement. First, the pastor produces a comprehensive description of OT sacrifices by bringing together all four expressions from the first and third lines of the quotation — "sacrifices," "offerings," "burnt offerings," and "sin offerings."[34] Furthermore, he strengthens the all-encompassing nature of this description by making all the terms for sacrifice plural, although "sacrifices" and "offerings" were singular in his quotation of the psalm above. He does not exploit the distinctions between these four terms but brings them together to encompass the totality of

---

the scroll of the book"), is "knob." It was the knob at the top of the stick around which the scroll was wrapped. It is used here as a figure of speech for the scroll itself. Thus "the scroll of the book" means "the book in scroll form" (Bruce, 242, n. 44). See Ezek 2:9; 3:1-3; 2 Esd 6:2, cited by Koester, 433.

29. Attridge, 275; Hughes, 397-98.

30. Lane, 2:263; Attridge, 275; Hughes, 397-98; Bénétreau, 2:101.

31. Riggenbach, 302; Schröger, *Der Verfasser,* 175. The OT is "a prophecy for the Messiah" (Michel, 337) or a "Christbook" (Weiss, 509, n. 45).

32. ἀνώτερον ("above") "was a common way of referring to something earlier in a document (Josephus, *Ant.* 19.212; *Ag. Ap.* 2.18). Yet here it marks an antithesis in the two portions of the psalm" (Koester, 434). See also Michel, 338; Weiss, 507; and Ellingworth, 503.

33. Compare the present participle, λέγων, "saying," at the beginning of v. 8, with the emphatic perfect indicative, εἴρηκεν, "he has said," at the beginning of v. 9 (Ellingworth, 503).

34. θυσίας ("sacrifices"), προσφοράς ("offerings"), ὁλοκαυτώματα ("burnt offerings"), and περὶ ἁμαρτίας ("sin offerings," literally, "for sins").

OT sacrifices under the rubric of atonement.[35] Thus it was appropriate that the psalm list concluded with "sin offerings."

He demonstrates the totality of God's rejection by combining "you did not desire" and "you were not pleased with," taken from the same part of the psalm. Thus by the words of this psalm Christ affirmed God's total rejection of all OT sacrifices as means of purification from sin. The interpretive statement at the end of v. 8 only makes the radical nature of this repudiation more pungent: the sacrifices God has completely rejected were none other than those "offered according to the law."[36] Thus the pastor sets the provisions of the law in sharpest contrast with Christ's performance of God's "will." This relative clause also reminds the hearers of the intrinsic connection between these rejected sacrifices and the entire Old Covenant system of Tent, priests, and purifications (see on 7:11-16).[37]

The New Covenant prophecy of Jeremiah showed that God had "found fault" with the Old Covenant (8:7-8a). The persistent disobedience of the people betrayed its ineffectiveness (8:9). The description of the Tent established by the Old Covenant revealed the impotency of its sacrifices (9:1-10). The continual repetition of those sacrifices demonstrated their incapacity to remove sin (10:1-4). Thus, at his coming Christ pronounced God's rejection of the old sacrificial system as a way of approaching God and sealed this pronouncement by his own obedience (Ps 40:6-8). The coming of Christ makes it clear that God has rejected that whole system, not because it was practiced with hypocrisy, but because it was fundamentally unable to bring the remission and removal of sin. Thus this repudiation of the old as a means of atonement (but not as a type of what was to come) goes far beyond the prophetic criticism of those who practiced the OT rituals with insincerity.[38]

---

35. For distinctions between these words and the Hebrew words they often translate see Attridge, 274, or Ellingworth, 502.

36. Kistemaker, 279, suggests that the indefinite relative αἵτινες ("which") can be concessive: Cf. "though they are required by the law of Moses" (NLT) instead of "which are offered according to the law." αἵτινες refers to all of the sacrifices mentioned above, though its grammatical antecedents are θυσίας ("sacrifices") and προσφοράς ("offerings"), the two nouns in the list that the pastor uses elsewhere. This relative clause is no parenthesis or distraction from the argument (Ellingworth, 504). Although κατὰ νόμον ("according to law") may echo the legal and therefore ineffective (cf. 7:19) character of these sacrifices (Westcott, 312), it also identifies them as part of the Mosaic law. It would be wrong to make too great a distinction in this passage between κατὰ νόμον ("according to law") and κατὰ τὸν νόμον ("according to the law") (Ellingworth, 504).

37. Vanhoye, *Old Testament,* 216-17.

38. See Jer 7:21-23; Isa 1:12-17; Hos 6:6; Amos 5:21. "What was in the prophetic texts an attempt to safeguard the integrity of the sacrificial system becomes in Hebrews a declaration of the inefficacy of the system itself" (deSilva, 320). Ellingworth, 497-98, misses the radical nature of this rejection. He simply misreads the text of Hebrews when

9 By making several slight modifications in the wording of the second part of the psalm (40:7-8), the pastor sharpens Christ's declaration of submission to the "will" of God. With an economy of words worthy of his literary skill he adapts the opening phrase of Ps 40:7 to serve as its introduction: "Then I said" becomes "Then he said." "Then" calls attention to what is important. The change from the simple aorist ("I said") to the perfect (also translated here simply as "he *said*") highlights the significance of what follows.[39] The pastor would rivet his hearers' attention on Christ's affirmation of perfect obedience. By omitting the parenthetical clause, "in the scroll of the book it has been written concerning me," and the vocative, "O God," he removes distractions without distorting meaning: "Behold, I have come . . . to do . . . your will." The first omission leaves no doubt that the Son became incarnate for the purpose of accomplishing God's will. The second produces a directness and economy of statement that allows the sentence to end with a strong "to do your will."

The hearers are now ready for the pastor's strongest assertion that the old has been removed and the new instituted as a means of atonement: Christ "abolishes the first in order that he might establish the second" (v. 9b). It would have been difficult for the pastor to have found words stronger than "abolish" and "establish." Both were often used in contemporary sources for the annulling and promulgating of laws.[40] Furthermore, the neuter singulars "first" and "second" are all-encompassing. At the end of v. 8 the pastor reminded his hearers how integral the sacrifices enumerated

---

he argues that the OT sacrifices dealt with "accidental *pollution*" while Christ's sacrifice deals with "deliberate *sin*" (Ellingworth, 498, italics added). The contrast is not between "accidental" and "deliberate" but between outward ceremonial "pollution" and the sin that taints the heart, the essence of the human person (9:11-14). The OT sacrifices dealt with ritual pollution and were a pointer to Christ's sacrifice which atones for *all* sins.

39. See Westfall, *Discourse Analysis,* 227. The NA[27] edition of the Greek NT does not italicize τότε εἴρηκεν ("then he said") and thus excludes it from the psalm quotation. UBS[4] italicizes τότε ("then") but leaves εἴρηκεν ("he said") unitalicized, no doubt because Ps 40:7 uses the first person aorist εἶπον ("I said") instead of the third person perfect εἴρηκεν. Nevertheless, it is clear that the pastor's τότε εἴρηκεν is dependent on the psalm's τότε εἶπον ("then I said"). See Ellingworth, 504. It would be awkward in this context to express the difference between these two tenses in English translation.

40. "Ἀναιρεῖ is the strongest negative statement the author has made or will make about the OT cultus" (Ellingworth, 504). For examples of ἀναιρέω, "abolish," used for the annulment of laws see Koester, 434; Michel, 338, n. 2; and BDAG, 64, 1. The strength of this word is demonstrated by its frequent use for "kill" or "destroy" (BDAG, 64, 2). ἵστημι (στήσῃ), "establish," was used for making (Gen 6:18; 17:7; Exod 6:4) and adhering to (1 Macc 2:27; cf. Rom 3:3, 31) covenants (BDAG, 482, 3). Compare the cognate noun στάσις, "validity," in 9:8. The sacrifices prescribed by the law could not "take away" (ἀφαιρεῖν, 10:4) sin, so Christ "abolished" (ἀναιρεῖν) them (Koester, 439).

"above" were to the whole Mosaic system. Thus, Christ's repudiation of those sacrifices was an annulment of that whole "first" system as a means of access to God. He ratified that annulment by his complete incarnate submission to God's will, climaxing in his self-offering on the cross. That same obedience has established the "second" or new way of approaching God through Christ. The natural antecedent of "the second" is the "will" of God accomplished by Christ in his earthly obedience. Still, the whole New Covenant arrangement for cleansing and entrance into God's presence through Christ's obedience is the "will" of God established by his perfect submission.[41] The obedience of Christ is key to all Hebrews has to say about the rejection of the Old Covenant and priesthood as a way of approaching God and the establishment of the new. The Old was and remains only a type of the New.

Thus, it is no surprise that the twofold way in which the pastor has used this psalm to substantiate the rejection of the old and the establishing of the new corresponds to his interpretation of Jeremiah's New Covenant prophecy.[42] Jeremiah first condemns the Old Covenant as obsolete (Jer 31:31-32). He then describes the virtues of the New (Jer 31:33-34) as a covenant under which God's laws will be inscribed on his people's hearts so that they do his will. When the pastor first cited this passage from Jeremiah in 8:7-13, he focused on the abolition of the old. When he again recalls this prophecy — in 10:15-18 at the conclusion of this great symphony — it will be to remind his hearers of the forgiveness and heart obedience established by the new. The obedience of Christ described in Ps 40:6-8 is the means by which the old, ineffective system is removed (Heb 10:8) and the new system of heart obedience is established (Heb 10:9). Thus this psalm is the turning point that enables the pastor to move from his initial explanation of Jer 31:31-34 in 8:7-13 to his final reiteration of this prophecy in 10:15-18.[43]

---

41. It is important to remember that Hebrews rejects the sacrifices of the Mosaic system in favor of Christ's sacrifice, not the need of sacrifice per se (Vanhoye, *Old Testament*, 218). Nor is this a rejection of "material" sacrifices in favor of an internal or "spiritual" sacrifice. Christ's willing obedience was carried out in his "body." Furthermore, the old system continues to be, what it always has been, a type and foreshadowing of the adequate means of atonement effected by Christ.

42. "This comment [the final statement in v. 9] reminds us of the author's interpretation of the Jer 31:31-34 passage in Heb 8:13" (Johnson, 252).

43. Thus, the bond forged between Ps 40:6-8 and Jer 31:31-34 is one of theological congruence rather than mere "verbal analogy." However, this congruence is sustained by the verbal analogies suggested by George H. Guthrie, "Hebrews," in *Commentary on the New Testament Use of the Old Testament*, ed. G. K. Beale and D. A. Carson (Grand Rapids: Baker Academic, 2007), 977. Guthrie notes that both passages use "behold" (ἰδού), and that both refer to God (θεός), sin (ἁμαρτία), something "written," and the inter-

441

The pastor's twofold interpretation of Ps 40:6-8 also corresponds to his explanation of Christ's high-priestly session foretold in Ps 110:1, 4. At the beginning of this symphony Christ's session was implicit evidence for rejection of sacrifices offered by the Levitical priests: since Christ ministered in the heavenly sanctuary, his sacrifices must have been different from (greater than) theirs (8:3-5). At symphony's end his high-priestly session is the result of his "one" all-sufficient sacrifice (10:11-14). It is, however, Ps 40:6-8 in Heb 10:8-9 that explains how Christ has nullified the old sacrifices (10:8) and taken his high-priestly seat at God's right hand (cf. 10:9) by making "purification for sins" (1:3). We conclude, then, that Psalm 40 is the vital link that completes the pastor's argument and integrates his use of these other key OT passages. This OT prophecy reveals the means by which Christ has atoned for sin, entered into his high priesthood at God's right hand, and become Mediator of the New Covenant. Thus it is the heart and unifying center of 8:1–10:18, the symphony in praise of Christ's sacrifice.

The obedience of the Son as depicted in this psalm also reaches beyond this central section of Hebrews. The Son's submission to God's will depicted in Ps 40:6-8 contrasts sharply with the disobedience of the wilderness generation as described in Ps 95:7-11 (Heb 3:7–4:11). Furthermore, his complete obedience qualifies him to be the climactic example of faithful endurance in 12:1-3.

10 The incarnate Christ's perfect accomplishment of God's "will" is the source of our holiness.[44] Every feature of this verse emphasizes the key importance of this fact. First, note the pastor's use of pronouns. There has been no first person plural subject since 8:1, and there will be none again until 10:22. At the commencement of this symphony on Christ's sacrifice (8:1–10:18) the pastor announced his topic as "*we* have such a high priest" (8:1). After concluding this symphony he will exhort his hearers: "let *us* draw near with true hearts . . ." (10:22). "*We* have been made holy" is the key that joins this opening assertion with the concluding exhortation. It is only because "*we* have been made holy" through the obedience of this High Priest (8:1) whom *we* have that *we* can "draw near" (10:22) to God with confidence.[45]

---

nalization of the law. He admits that in the case of Psalm 40 the pastor terminates the quotation just before the reference to the law's internalization.

44. ἐν ᾧ θελήματι, "by which will," is "God's will as done by Jesus" (Ellingworth, 505).

45. In 8:1–10:18 the pastor reserves the first person plural for affirmation of the benefits received by "we" the people of God. His usage confirms the division of this "symphony" into three movements: "The New Foretold" (8:1-13); "The Old Antiquated"/"The New Foreshadowed" (9:1-22); "The New Explained" (9:23–10:18). As noted above, in the first movement the pastor used OT prophecies to indicate that something better was coming, without describing its quality. Thus, after the introduction in 8:1, he had no occa-

Second, the pastor uses the perfect tense, "we have been made holy," in order to affirm the definitive nature and abiding effectiveness of the purification from sin that Christ has provided through his obedience.[46] One cannot reduce this holiness to a legal standing, nor can one identify it with perfection of life. Christ has set his people apart for God by cleansing them from the pollution and dominion of sin (9:14) so that they can enter the divine presence where they receive the "mercy" of continual cleansing and the "grace" for perseverance in obedience (4:16).[47] The pastor will give further explanation of the continuing effects of Christ's cleansing in vv. 11-18 before exhorting his hearers to continue availing themselves of these benefits in vv. 19-25.

Third, the pastor brings this section to its climax with a clear description of the obedience by which Christ fulfilled the "will" of God: "through the offering of the body of Jesus Christ."[48] The Son identified with humanity

---

sion to describe the benefits that "we" receive. In the second, the pastor describes the inadequate and anticipatory nature of the old Tent (9:1-10) and Covenant (9:16-22), but begins to describe the superiority of Christ's sacrifice in 9:11-15. Thus, he says that Christ's blood "cleanses *our* conscience from dead works" (9:14, italics added). The third and final movement describes the full glory of the new. Thus, the pastor uses the first person plural at crucial points in all three sections of this movement (sanctuary, 9:23-24; sacrifice, 9:25–10:14; covenant, 10:15-18): Christ has "entered heaven itself to appear before the face of God for *us*" (9:24); "the Holy Spirit bears witness to *us*" (10:15), and, at the center of all, "*we* are made holy" (10:10, all italics added). Thus, use of the first person plural confirms the importance of 10:5-10 as the heart of this symphony.

46. See Weiss, 511. The perfect periphrastic, ἡγιασμένοι ἐσμέν ("we have been made holy") allows the pastor to bring the noun for "will" and the perfect passive participle translated "having been made holy" into the closest conjunction: θελήματι ἡγιασμένοι. Thus, he joins Christ's obedience and our sanctification.

47. The term for "make holy" (ἁγιάζω) is closely related to cleanse/purify (καθαρίζω). The pastor introduces this term in 2:11 where the Son is described as "the one who makes holy" and his people as "the ones who are being made holy." While this term may denote consecration to God (BDAG, 10, 2), it is a consecration brought about by cleansing from sin. This is evidenced clearly by its use in 9:13, where the old sacrifices "make holy" for the "cleansing of the flesh" in contrast to Christ who by his sacrifice "cleanses" the conscience. Hughes, 395, confirms this interpretation: ". . . in the terminology of this epistle sanctification, involving the purging away of sin and access into the holy presence of God himself, is synonymous with the whole experience of salvation (see commentary above on 2:11)." Bénétreau, 2:102, agrees with Hughes, whom he names saying that this holiness consists of purification from sin and restoration to the sphere of divine favor.

48. διὰ τῆς προσφορᾶς τοῦ σώματος ("through the offering of the body") gives specificity to ἐν ᾧ θελήματι ("by which will") at the beginning of the verse. See Spicq, 2:306. Spicq is not quite correct, however, when he calls the "will" of God the "efficient" cause (following ἐν) and Christ's sacrifice the "instrumental" cause (following διά). As

by taking the "body" that God had prepared for him (v. 5). In the complete humanity that he assumed with that body he lived a life of uncompromising obedience that culminated in his obedient offering of himself in death on the cross.[49] His obedience was from the heart, but it took concrete form in human life and climaxed with his willing self-offering of that life.[50]

Finally, this sentence ends with a most emphatic "Jesus Christ once for all." Every term in this expression contributes to its climactic nature. In the earlier part of this sermon the pastor used "Jesus" when he wished to emphasize the humanity of the Savior.[51] However, this name has not yet appeared in the symphony on Christ's sacrifice (8:1–10:18). The pastor has reserved it for this moment when he reveals that the key to that sacrifice is the human obedience of the Son. The pastor/conductor's use of "Christ" marks progression within this symphony from anticipation to fulfillment. Thus the first movement, 8:1-13, which deals with the prophecies of what was to come, does not mention "Christ." Nor does "Christ" occur in the opening (9:1-10) and closing (9:16-22) sections of the second movement, which describe the insufficiency and typological nature of the old. However, when the pastor begins to describe the sufficiency of Christ's sacrifice in the central section (9:11-15) of the second movement he uses "Christ" twice (9:11, 14). With "Christ" (9:24) the pastor introduces the grand description of fulfillment that comprises the third movement (9:23–10:18). As noted above, his presentation of Christ's sacrifice in this third movement is divided into three subsections — 9:25–10:4; 10:5-10; and 10:11-14. The pastor uses "Christ" at the high point of the first of these subsections (9:28), and then finally here, in 10:10, at the conclusion of his definitive explanation of why Christ's sacrifice is effective. Furthermore, this is the first time that the pastor has used the combined expression, "Jesus Christ," which he will use again only in 13:8, 21.

The word translated "once for all" is the final and thus climactic Greek word in this verse. It is a stronger form of the word translated "once for all" in the pastor's defense of the unrepeatable nature of Christ's sacrifice

---

noted above, the "will" of God to which reference is made is the "will" of God fulfilled by Christ.

49. By offering his "body" (σῶμα) Christ offered the life of obedience that he had "learned" (5:6-8) in one final act of obedience. His human body was the vehicle of his obedient life and the means of offering it to God on the cross. Thus, his earthly obedience was both preparation for and an essential part of that final act of sacrifice. See Westcott, 313; Ellingworth, 499; and Hughes, 399. Christ's obedience was as integral to his sacrifice as physical perfection was to the sacrifices of the Old Covenant (see the comments on 9:14).

50. Attridge, 276.

51. See the comments above on 2:9; 3:1; 4:14; 6:20; and 7:22.

(9:25–10:4).[52] The pastor has reserved this more forceful term for the introduction of key points at crucial junctures in his argument: in 7:27 he used it to introduce the "once-for-all" character of Christ's sacrifice; in 9:12, the "once-for-all" nature of Christ's entrance into heaven resulting from his sacrifice; and finally, in 10:10, the "once-for-all" sanctification obtained by his obedient sacrifice. Although "once for all" comes at the end of the verse for emphasis, it qualifies the verb "we have been made holy" near the beginning. The pastor is not merely reasserting the "once-for-all" nature of Christ's sacrifice. He is saying that its "once-for-all" character has provided a "once-for-all" and thus sufficient sanctification of the people of God.[53] The benefit derived from Christ's sacrifice is as definitive as the sacrifice itself.[54]

Christ came to make the already existing people of God "holy" by cleansing them from the pollution and dominion of sin so that they would have true access to God.[55] This cleansing is "once for all" in that it is completely adequate without need of supplement or repetition. Those who embrace what Christ has done through faithful obedience continue in this cleansing as part of the persevering people of God. However, as the pastor makes abundantly clear, the full sufficiency of this cleansing work is no guarantee of, but the strongest motivation for, perseverance. Repudiation of Christ through faithlessness and disobedience results in severance from this sanctified people. Thus the author expresses his pastoral concern by repeatedly urging his hearers to persevere by making use of the cleansing work of Christ to continue in faithful obedience (10:19-31). By his obedience Christ makes their obedience possible.

The offering of "his own blood" (9:12) has been explained in these verses as the eternal Son's offering of his perfectly obedient human life in a final act of obedience on the cross. The following verses continue to flesh out what Christ has become through his once-for-all sacrifice and the benefits

---

52. Compare the more emphatic ἐφάπαξ, "once for all," in 7:27; 9:12; and 10:10 with ἅπαξ, "once," or "once for all" in 9:26, 27, 28; and 10:2.

53. Thus ἐφάπαξ goes with the verb ἡγιασμένοι ἐσμέν ("we are made holy"), as argued by Bénétreau, 2:102; Braun, 299; Michel, 339; and Weiss, 511; and not with the noun προσφορᾶς ("offering"), as Lane 2:256v; Hughes, 399; Héring, 96; Spicq, 2:306; Koester, 434; and others contend. ἐφάπαξ is normally used with a verb (7:27; 9:12). That the pastor used it to describe the offering of Christ in 7:27 (where it qualified the verb ἐποίησεν, "he did") does not require that he use it in the same way here. After all, in 9:12 he used it for Christ's entrance into heaven. He achieves the greatest emphasis by putting ἡγιασμένοι ("made holy") right after θελήματι ("will") and reserving ἐφάπαξ for the final position. ἡγιασμένοι ἐσμέν is still the closest verb.

54. "The offering of Jesus was complete, involving his entire somatic existence. Therefore, the 'cleansing' accomplished by Jesus was complete" (Johnson, 253).

55. See the comments on 2:10-18.

made available therefrom for his people. As a result of his self-offering he has taken his seat at God's right as his people's fully sufficient High Priest (10:11-14) and has become the Mediator of the New Covenant that provides forgiveness and power for obedience (10:15-18).[56] The pastor would ever fasten the gaze of his hearers on this exalted High Priest and Mediator as their only sufficient source of needed grace.

d. Sacrifice: "He Sat Down Forever" (10:11-14)

> 11 *And every priest has stood day after day ministering and frequently offering the same sacrifices which are never able to take away sin.* 12 *But this one by having offered one sacrifice for sin has sat down forever at the right hand of God,* 13 *in the meantime eagerly waiting until his enemies are put under his feet.* 14 *For by one sacrifice he has perfected forever those who are being made holy.*

The pastor concludes his grand symphony on Christ's all-sufficient sacrifice by returning to the topic announced at the beginning: "we have such a High Priest who is seated at the right hand of the throne of the Majesty in heaven" (8:1; cf. 1:3, 13). In the intervening chapters he has demonstrated the full sufficiency of the sacrifice through which this High Priest has taken this exalted position and is thus able to succor his own. From the beginning it has been the pastor's goal to fix his hearers' gaze on none other than this exalted Son seated at God's right (1:1-3; 2:5-9), for no one else can bring them to their heavenly homeland.

Hebrews 9:23-24, the opening "sanctuary" section of this third movement, established the background for these verses by reintroducing the relationship between Christ's sacrifice and session. Christ's entrance "into heaven itself to appear in the presence of God for us" (9:24) has become, "he sat down forever at the right hand of God" (10:12). The "better" sacrifice necessary for his entrance (9:23) is one by which "he has perfected forever those who are being made holy" (10:14).

Each part of this concluding sacrifice section (9:25–10:14) plays an important role in finalizing the pastor's argument. Heb 9:25–10:4 establishes the finality of Christ's sacrifice. Heb 10:5-10 is the crucial explanation of why Christ's sacrifice was effective. Heb 10:11-14 is the climactic description of what Christ has done and become through this sacrifice so that he can empower the faithful for present perseverance.[1] These concluding verses re-

---

56. See Attridge, 279.

1. Ellingworth, 507, notes this shift from focus on Christ's once-for-all sacrifice itself to focus on the present time in which Christ sits at God's right hand.

veal the full significance of the divine invitation (given in Ps 110:1; cf. Heb 1:3, 13) to "sit at my right hand." They are no mere summary or recapitulation but a conclusion that brings the impact of all that has been said home to the hearers.[2]

The pastor makes one final contrast between the old priests and the new: according to 10:11, the ineffectiveness of the old is exposed by their perpetual standing throughout their ministry. On the other hand, according to 10:12-14, in his preeminent position as High Priest permanently seated at God's right hand the Son possesses all authority necessary to assist the faithful.

11 If Heb 9:25–10:4 was implicitly based on Ps 110:1, 4; Heb 10:11-14 is the final explanation of that psalm's significance. We noted above the chiastic parallel between these two sections. The former contrasts the "once-for-all" sacrifice of Christ (9:25-28) with the vain repetition of the old sacrifices (10:1-4); the latter contrasts the perpetual standing of the old priests (10:11) with the definitive session of Christ (10:12-14) through his "one offering." Thus, it is not surprising that this description of the Aaronic priests' ineffectiveness in v. 11 evokes many images familiar from 10:1-4. Compare "day after day," "never able to take away sins," and "frequently offering the same sacrifices" with "year after year," "never able to perfect those approaching," and "the same sacrifices which were offered perpetually" in 10:1.[3] Nevertheless, the changes are significant. The pastor has broadened his purview to include "every priest" and not just the high priest. He is no longer limiting himself primarily to the annual Day-of-Atonement sacrifice, but is explicitly including the ministry of the outer Holy Place so characteristic of the Old Covenant (see 9:6). His vision encompasses other nonsacrificial duties performed "ministering day by day." The "same sacrifices" are not merely repeated in perpetuity but they are "frequently" offered. He pictures the priests of that system piling up sacrifice after sacrifice as hard as they can go, but all in vain, for they can never reach their goal. They can never sit because their job is not done. The repetitious inadequate sacrifices of 10:1-4 demonstrate the inadequacy of the priesthood.

The contrast with v. 12 is near chiastic in structure. Thus, "every priest has stood daily" in v. 11a contrasts with "he has sat down forever at the right hand of God" in v. 12b. "Ministering and offering the same sacrifices

---

2. Attridge, 279, misses the import of this passage when he argues that it is a mere résumé or summary of what has gone before.

3. Compare the κατ' ἐνιαυτόν ("year by year"), ταῖς αὐταῖς θυσίαις ("the same sacrifices"), and οὐδέποτε δύναται . . . τελειῶσαι ("never able to perfect") of 10:1 with καθ' ἡμέραν ("day by day"), τὰς αὐτὰς . . . θυσίας ("the same . . . sacrifices"), and οὐδέποτε δύνανται περιελεῖν ("can never remove utterly") as given in Lane 2:266.

which are never able to take away sins" in v. 11b parallels "having offered one sacrifice for sins" in v. 12a.[4] The main contrast is between the first and last members of this chiasm, the old priests' perpetual standing and Christ's definitive session.[5] Although the pastor has not introduced this contrast before, it is inherent in the invitation to sit at God's right hand found in his theme verse, Ps 110:1. He has saved it until now so that he can show how Christ's session was made possible by, and is the crowning result of, his all-sufficient self-sacrifice.

Since the old sacrifices were offered perpetually (10:1-4), it was obvious that "every priest has stood." The perfect tense of this verb is emphatic, signifying the continual state of those priests. We can grasp its significance by rendering the sentence "every priest has always stood."[6] Within the OT context there was nothing unusual about this fact. To "stand" before a king was to be his servant. To "stand" before God was an expression normally used to describe the honor of serving as a priest.[7] The significance of this "standing" becomes clear only in light of Christ's session promised in Ps 110:1 and described in Heb 10:12. His session shows that they continued standing because their sacrifices never achieved the goal of true atonement. It was vain to continuing doing the same thing but expect differing results. Thus, a perpetually standing priest was an ineffective priest.

When the pastor says that those sacrifices could not "take away sin," he assumes that Christ's sacrifice could. Thus he joins "take away" to other expressions used to underscore the definitive removal of sin achieved by Christ (cf. 9:22, 26; 10:4 [cf. 10:18]).

12 "But this one" refers to Christ, mentioned in 10:10, and initiates the contrast with v. 11. The present participles in v. 11b described the perpetual manner of the old priest's standing: "ministering and frequently offering the same sacrifices" (v. 11b). The parallel aorist participial phrase with

---

4. With πᾶς μὲν ἱερεὺς ἔστηκεν καθ' ἡμέραν ("every priest has stood daily," v. 11a) compare οὗτος δὲ . . . εἰς τὸ διηνεκὲς ἐκάθισεν ἐν δεξιᾷ τοῦ θεοῦ ("but this one . . . has sat down forever at the right hand of God," v. 12b). With λειτουργῶν καὶ τὰς αὐτὰς πολλάκις προσφέρων θυσίας, αἵτινες οὐδέποτε δύνανται περιελεῖν ἁμαρτίας ("ministering and offering the same sacrifices which are never able to take away sins," v. 11b) compare μίαν ὑπὲρ ἁμαρτιῶν προσενέγκας θυσίαν ("having offered one sacrifice for sins," v. 12a).

5. Note that the only finite verb in v. 11 is ἔστηκεν, "has always stood," and in v. 12 ἐκάθισεν, "has sat down."

6. "The verb ἔστηκεν, though perfect in form, has, as is normal, the force of a present: he 'has taken his stand' and therefore 'is standing.' Hence ἕστηκα is described as a present perfect by J. H. Moulton, Blass-Debrunner, and Nigel Turner" (Hughes, 400, n. 63).

7. "In the OT, to stand in God's presence was considered an honour; but the exalted Jesus sits as a sign that he shares the authority of God himself" (Ellingworth, 508).

which v. 12 begins is instrumental: "By having offered one sacrifice for sins." Christ's sacrifice is finished. It is not the manner of his session but its effective means and cause. Although the pastor's focus is now on Christ's session, he will not allow his hearers — ancient or modern — to disconnect this session from the sacrifice that made it possible. The main verb of the sentence expresses the point of contrast with the old priests: this one "has sat down at the right hand of God forever." While the pastor used the perfect tense in the last verse when he wanted to emphasize that the old priest "has always stood," he uses the aorist here to emphasize the finality of Christ's session: this one "has taken his seat."[8] Christ's session "forever" contrasts with "every" priest's standing "daily."[9] The phrase translated "forever" underscores the definitive character of Christ's session, as well as affirming its permanence. There is a certain appropriate irony in the pastor's using this same phrase for the "perpetual" vain repetition of the old sacrifices in 10:1 and the permanent and eternal session of Christ "forever."[10]

It is true that Christ's session confirms God's complete acceptance of his sacrifice as fully sufficient for cleansing the pollution and dominion of sin. The sufficiency of his sacrifice, however, has already been well established. Thus, the pastor's main concern at this point is to present Christ's sac-

8. Cf. Vanhoye, *Old Testament,* 174.

9. Many translations (NIV, NRSV, NASB, NKJV) and interpreters (Bruce, 244, n. 57; Westcott, 314; Peterson, *Perfection,* 148-49) mistakenly take εἰς τὸ διηνεκές ("forever") with the participle προσενέκγας ("having been offered") since it qualifies the verb it follows in 7:3 and 10:1. However, the parallel between εἰς τὸ διηνεκές ("forever") and καθ᾽ ἡμέραν ("daily") shows clearly that εἰς τὸ διηνεκές ("forever") goes with ἐκάθισεν ("he has sat down") just as καθ᾽ ἡμέραν ("daily") qualifies ἕστηκεν ("has always stood"). See Riggenbach, 308; Bénétreau, 2:103; Braun, 301; Michel, 340-41; Attridge, 280; Ellingworth, 509-10; and Weiss, 512-13. Furthermore, since the phrase ὑπὲρ ἁμαρτιῶν προσενέκγας ("having been offered for sin") comes between μίαν ("one") and θυσίαν ("sacrifice"), it is closely bound to the latter and consequently separated from εἰς τὸ διηνεκές. Finally, this is the climax of the pastor's interpretation of the first and fourth verses of Psalm 110. His whole purpose has been to explain God's invitation to "sit" at his right in v. 1 in light of God's declaration of perpetual priesthood in v. 4. Thus, as a result of his offering Christ "has sat down" as High Priest "forever." The pastor has already used εἰς τὸ διηνεκές ("forever") to explain the εἰς τὸν αἰῶνα ("forever") of Ps 110:4 in Heb 7:3. Here, as in 7:3 and 10:1, the pastor uses this phrase to qualify the main thought expressed by the finite verb. Weiss, 512-13, however, seems to think that the pastor has put this phrase between the participle and finite verb to create an intentional ambiguity. A "forever" sacrifice leads to a "forever" session.

10. See εἰς τὸ διηνεκές in both verses. With the iterative present, ἃς προσφέρουσιν, "which they offer" (10:1), εἰς τὸ διηνεκές signifies perpetual repetition, "continuously" or "perpetually." However, with the aorist ἐκάθισεν, "he has sat down" (10:12), εἰς τὸ διηνεκές affirms the finality of an action not subject to change: "He has sat down forever."

rifice as the instrument or cause of his definitive session rather than his session as confirmation of his sacrifice.[11] This interpretation is substantiated by the syntax of this verse: the instrumental participle, "having offered," gives the means or cause of the assertion made by the main verb: "He has sat down." It is also confirmed by the overall direction of the pastor's argument. At the beginning of this symphony the pastor told his audience that his main point was the High Priest "we" now have, "who has sat down at the right hand of the throne of the Majesty in heaven" (8:1). He has explained the significance of Christ's sacrifice in order to demonstrate the sufficiency of the one now seated at God's right hand. The pastor earnestly desires his hearers to keep the gaze of faith and obedience fixed on this one.

13 God's invitation given to his Son in Ps 110:1a has been fulfilled: "Sit at my right hand." His promise in Ps 110:1b still awaits consummation: "until I make your enemies a footstool for your feet." Thus, since the Son has definitively taken his seat at God's right hand, the place of all authority, he is now "eagerly waiting until his enemies be made a footstool for his feet."[12] This statement extends the contrast with "every priest" initiated above. They "stood," vainly performing perpetual sacrifices but never able to obtain their goal. He has definitively "sat down" and awaits with expectation the final consummation fully assured by the potency of his sacrifice. The pastor makes no further comment on Christ's eager expectation of the consummation. The time envisioned is obviously the occasion of Christ's second coming, when we will "see all things subjected to him" (2:8). At that time Christ's enemies will suffer irrevocable judgment (12:25-29), but he will bring final salvation for those who, like himself, "eagerly await" his coming (9:28). The pastor earnestly desires his hearers to grasp Christ's present situation because it determines their own. Christ has sat down in the place of ultimate authority with all the resources necessary to enable his people to persevere in faithful obedience until the final anticipated denouement. Until then, he practices a ministry of "intercession," which consists in his mediating grace adequate for and appropriate to the needs of the faithful (4:14-16). The pastor would have his hearers look up to their High Priest at God's right hand and press forward in anticipation of Christ's return.

14 "For" shows that this description of Christ's offering is given to support the definitive nature of the seat he has taken at God's right hand in

11. *Pace* Guthrie, "Hebrews," in *Commentary on the New Testament Use of the Old,* 978, who says, "Specifically, the psalm verse serves here to emphasize the sacrifice of Christ as decisive."

12. ἐκδεχόμενος, "eagerly awaiting," indicates eager expectation (cf. 7:28; 11:10; Ellingworth, 510) without the least anxiety about the outcome, for Christ waits in triumph (Hughes, 402).

anticipation of the final Judgment.[13] Verse 11 affirmed that those ineffective, perpetually repeated offerings were "never able to take away sins." Verse 12 says merely that Christ's "one sacrifice" was "for sin." The pastor does not abandon this part of his argument without making the significance of "for sin" clear. The better his hearers understand the efficacy of Christ's sacrifice, the more confidence they will have in the position of supreme authority he now holds. However, by postponing this description of Christ's sacrifice until now, the pastor is able to conclude this section with a definitive statement of the benefits available for the faithful through Christ. At the conclusion of the opening part of this sacrifice section the pastor announced the uselessness of animal sacrifices to deal with sin (10:4). At the conclusion of this third and final part he affirms the potency of Christ's sacrifice to do all that is necessary in order to bring God's people into his presence.

The hearers know that Christ's consecration through obedience to high priesthood at God's right hand was his perfection as Savior (5:9-10; 7:28; cf. 2:10). Thus, it comes as no surprise that by that same obedience this heavenly High Priest "has perfected" his people by cleansing them from disobedience so that they might enter God's presence.[14] The obedience by which he was "perfected" as Savior, able to cleanse and sustain, also "perfected" them as the cleansed, able to obey through his sustenance. He enters heaven as their representative; they, as those for whom he has provided entrance.

"He has perfected" is in emphatic contrast with the inability of the old sacrifices to deal with sin (10:1, 11).[15] This expression describes from Christ's point of view what "we have been made holy" (10:10) meant for the viewpoint of the faithful.[16] Both expressions refer to a cleansing from the pollution of sin that enables people to come into God's presence. The first may put emphasis on the privilege of access to God;[17] the latter, on consecra-

13. Peterson, *Perfection,* 149; Riggenbach, 308. Cf. Weiss, 513.

14. See Vanhoye, *Old Testament,* 219-22. Vanhoye, however, overstates the case for the parallel between the "perfection" of Christ and of believers when he says: "In 10:14 the participation of all believers in the priesthood of Christ is therefore affirmed" (220). He corrects this overstatement on 222, where he admits that mediation, "the most specific characteristic of the priesthood," belongs to Christ alone. Thus, "The only priest, in the full sense of the term, is Christ himself."

15. Riggenbach, 309.

16. Weiss, 514, notes the parallel between τετελείωκεν ("he has perfected") in v. 14 and ἁγιασμένοι ἐσμέν ("we have been made holy") in 10:10.

17. Riggenbach, 309, suggests that, in 10:1 and 14, where "perfecting" (τελειόω) refers to the effect of sacrifice, "the thought seems to be mainly about the perfecting of the relationship with God." So also Peterson, *Perfection,* 151-52, who describes this having been perfected as "The *consummation* of man in a direct and lasting personal relationship with God . . ." (italics original).

451

tion to God through the removal of sin. The pastor has used the perfect tense with both of these expressions to put emphasis on the continuing effect of that past act of cleansing or perfection. When he used "forever" to qualify the aorist verb translated "he sat down," it emphasized the definitive and unrepeatable nature of Christ's session. When he uses that same expression here with the perfect, it denotes the continuing ultimate validity of the effect achieved by Christ's perfecting his people.[18] Christ's own are a "perfected" or "cleansed" people. This "perfecting" is of such a quality that it will never need renewal or supplementation, any more than Christ's session might need repetition. Nothing more need be done for God's people to be delivered from sin and brought into God's presence. It is for this reason that the pastor urgently exhorts his hearers to persevere in their identification with the faithful people of God. To fall away in apostasy is to separate oneself from this people whom Christ has "perfected" and thus to abandon the only cure for sin that brings access to God.

The description of God's people as "those who are being made holy" emphasizes this need for continual participation in the benefits available to Christ's "perfected" and "cleansed" people. The sanctifying work of Christ is not only definitive (10:10), but continuous (2:10). Thus, the present tense of "being made holy" is not timeless, iterative, or progressive, but simply continuous. If the pastor wished to describe the state of his hearers, we would expect the verb "to be perfect."[19] There is nothing in the context that suggests the repeated entering of people into the state of holiness as they are converted.[20] Nor has the pastor been discussing the progress of believers in moral perfection.[21] He is describing the continuous reception of grace from Christ, "the one who makes holy" (2:11).[22] Reception of this grace enables God's people to receive necessary forgiveness and live a life of faithful obedience (4:14-16) so that they can continue in fellowship with the people of

18. Peterson, *Perfection,* 149.

19. Bruce, 247; George Guthrie, 329; and O'Brien, 357, contend that "those who are being made holy" is a timeless description. This interpretation reduces this statement to near tautology: "he has perfected those who are holy."

20. *Pace* D. Guthrie, 208.

21. Bénétreau, 2:105, seems to think that "those who are being made holy" refers to progress in sanctification. Cf. Michel, 341.

22. Compare 2:11, where Christ is ὁ ἁγιάζων, "the one who makes [them] holy." See Lane, 2:268. We agree with Attridge's (281) statement that the present tense of τοὺς ἁγιαζωμένους, "those who are being made holy," "nuances the relationship suggesting that the appropriation of the enduring effects of Christ's act is an ongoing present reality." *Pace* O'Brien, 357, Attridge is not talking about progressive sanctification, but about continuous dependence on the benefits of Christ's high priesthood for perseverance. While ἁγιάζειν ("to make holy") may imply separation to God (Bruce, 247), it is a separation that includes "cleansing" (καθαρίζειν) from sin (see 9:13-14; 10:29; 13:12).

452

God once-for-all "perfected" by Christ.[23] The pastor does not want his hearers to forget that their continued holiness, expressed in faithful obedience, is totally dependent on the benefits regularly and perpetually received from their High Priest seated at God's right hand. Thus, his great concern is that his hearers "draw near" to receive these benefits from the Son enthroned with all authority for their succor. This final statement makes the benefits of the "high priest" we now "have at the right hand of the throne of the Majesty in heaven" (8:1) abundantly clear. Thus the pastor draws his grand symphony toward its conclusion.[24] However, before its end he attests the all-sufficiency of this High Priest by a final reprise of Jeremiah's New Covenant prophecy in vv. 15-18 below.

e. Covenant — "Where There Is Release" (10:15-18)

> 15 And the Holy Spirit bears witness to us. For after having said, 16 "This is the covenant that I will covenant with them after those days," the Lord says: "I will put my laws upon their hearts, and upon their minds I will inscribe them; 17 and their sins and their lawless deeds I will no longer remember." 18 And where there is release from these, there is no longer a sacrifice for sins.

In Heb 8:7-13, near the beginning of this symphony, the pastor referred to the New Covenant promise in Jer 31:31-34 from the vantage point of its time of issue. He concludes this great symphonic section on Christ's high priesthood and sacrifice (8:1–10:18) by reexamining this promise in light of its fulfillment. The intervening sections have shown how Christ's high-priestly work has made the provisions of Jeremiah's promise a present reality.[1] The very issuing of that promise in Jeremiah's time indicated the imminent demise of the Mosaic system (8:13). That same promise, now fulfilled, is the ultimate attestation to the sufficiency of Christ's sacrifice and high-priestly ministry.[2]

---

23. "The writer locates the decisive purging of believers in the past with respect to its accomplishment and in the present with respect to its enjoyment" (Lane, 2:267).

24. Weiss, 514, describes v. 14 as a "statement of the goal" of 10:1-18. This verse corresponds to the statement of the pastor's main point in 8:1-2 and is thus the goal of 8:1–10:18. In fact, one might claim it as the goal of the pastor's entire explanation of Christ's high priesthood.

1. Koester's statement (441), "The effects of the new covenant are not fully realized, of course," is misleading. The New Covenant is not to be equated with the fullness of blessing at Christ's return. It is adequate provision for perseverance. To deny its present realization would be to deny the adequacy of Christ's sacrifice.

2. One may call this return to Jeremiah 31 an inclusion (Guthrie, "Hebrews," in *Commentary on the New Testament Use of the Old*, 978-79), but it is no mere mechanical

The inadequacy of the Old Covenant was confirmed by the way in which the persistent disobedience of God's ancient people rendered it invalid, as described in the prophecy's first two verses (Jer 31:31-32). Thus, the pastor need not cite those verses again. He is now interested in the description of the New Covenant blessings in the last half of the prophecy (vv. 33-34). These now-fulfilled blessings not only attest the adequacy of Christ, but clarify what he has done and is doing for his own. This concluding covenant section is meant to fix "once for all" the hearers' trusting attention upon their all-sufficient High Priest at God's right (8:1).

15 The Scriptural conversation between God and his Son begun in 1:5-14 and concluded in 10:5-10 has demonstrated the full sufficiency of the Son as High Priest and sacrifice.[3] The Holy Spirit also "bears witness to us" concerning this reality.[4] By introducing the concluding quotation with this phrase the pastor brings this symphony (8:1–10:18) to an appropriate conclusion and anticipates the urgent exhortations that follow (10:19–12:29). First, by attributing Jeremiah's New Covenant promise to the Holy Spirit the pastor underscores its divine authority as Spirit-inspired Scripture. These are indeed words that "the Lord" himself "says" (v. 16a; cf. 8:8).[5] Thus, he concludes this whole composition (8:1–10:18) by affirming in the strongest way that the adequacy of Christ's sacrifice and high-priestly session (vv. 11-14) rest on divinely inspired biblical attestation. Second, however, the Holy Spirit "bears witness to us" in the present through this now-fulfilled Scriptural promise urgently calling the people of God to faithful action.[6] "Bear witness" underscores the solemnity of the Spirit's address.[7] It was the Holy Spirit who addressed God's people in Psalm 95 with urgent warning lest they imitate the disobedient wilderness generation (Heb 3:7). It is the Holy Spirit who bears "witness" to them now through Jeremiah in anticipation of the following exhortations to join the faithful (11:1–12:3) through availing themselves of all

---

device. The pastor's return to this New Covenant passage is integral to the progress of his argument. Cf. Bruce, 248: "In Heb. 8 the oracle of Jer. 31:31-34 was quoted in order to prove the obsolescence of the old economy; now it is quoted again in order to establish the permanence of the era of 'perfection' inaugurated under the new covenant. 'God has spoken in his Son'; and he has no word to speak beyond him." One might add, "until the Judgment" (12:25-29). See also Attridge, 281, and Lane, 2:268.

3. See pp. 45-46 in the Introduction to this commentary. See also the introductions to 1:1–2:18 (pp. 85-86) and 4:14–10:18 (pp. 218-20).

4. O'Brien, 358.

5. Cf. Riggenbach, 311.

6. Thus ὑμῖν ("to us") includes both the pastor and his hearers within the contemporary people of God to whom the following exhortations apply (Lane, 2:268; cf. Ellingworth, 512).

7. Riggenbach, 309-10.

Christ has done (10:19-39).[8] The disobedience of God's people in Jer 31:31-32 recalled the unfaithful wilderness generation. The benefits of the new described in Jer 31:33-34 look forward to a life of Christ-empowered obedience in imitation of those who were faithful (11:1-40). There is no gap between the authoritative inspiration of Scripture and its impact on "us," the contemporary heirs of those to whom it was spoken.

"After having said" suggests that a phrase such as "then he said" should follow partway through the quotation. Several late manuscripts and early translations into other ancient languages supply such a statement at the beginning of v. 17: "After having said" that in the New Covenant he would write his laws on his people's hearts (v. 16b), "then he said" that he would no longer remember their sins (v. 17).[9] This structure separates the two New Covenant blessings described and makes the first preliminary to the second. On this understanding it is primarily the second, God's no longer remembering sins, that demonstrates the "removal" of or "release" from sin affirmed in v. 18.

It is more likely, however, that "the Lord says" at the end of v. 16a is the dividing point. We have already noted in v. 7 above how the pastor used a slightly adapted phrase from the quotation of Ps 40:6-8 to introduce the second part of the quotation. This understanding of "the Lord says" joins the two New Covenant blessings: "After having said" that this is the covenant he would make (v. 16a), "the Lord says" that he will write his laws on his people's hearts (v. 16b) and no longer remember their sins (v. 17). This arrangement requires no speculative textual emendation and makes good sense of the pastor's thought.[10] It is true that God's refusal to remember sin has the final

8. Emmrich, "Pneuma in Hebrews," 60-63, correctly draws a parallel between the Spirit as the one who directly addresses God's people with Scripture in both 3:7 and 10:15. However, *pace* Emmrich, the fact that Hebrews paraphrases the Jeremiah passage to facilitate its application is no evidence that attribution to the Holy Spirit makes this prophecy a new oracle separate from that given Jeremiah. The pastor regularly paraphrases OT quotations not attributed to the Holy Spirit. Furthermore, the pastor believes that Scripture once addressed to the people of God is relevant to the contemporary people of God. Thus, he has no need for such a device to contemporize its message. There is no reason to think that his hearers would have accepted the authority of Jeremiah except for their belief in its Scriptural authority. See the footnote on 9:8.

9. See ὕστερον λέγει ("later he says"), or τότε εἴρηκεν ("then he said") at the beginning of v. 17 in manuscripts 104, 323, 945, 1739, 1881, and 1505 respectively. It is unnecessary, with Lane, 2:256-57dd, to posit a primitive corruption of the text that a later copyist attempted to restore. Although Ellingworth, 514, does not think the text has been corrupted, he argues that the καί at the beginning of v. 17 indicates that the quotation should be divided at this point. Westcott, 316; Spicq, 2:310-11; and Bénétreau, 2:106, are among those who also think "he said" should be supplied at the beginning of v. 17.

10. Johnson, 254; deSilva, 326; Braun, 304; Weiss, 516; Attridge, 281, n. 44, and many others.

and climactic position. If God does not remember sins, what possible use could any additional sacrifice have? However, God's refusal to remember sins cannot be separated from his writing his laws upon the hearts of his people. God no longer takes account of their sins because the blood of Christ has "cleansed their conscience from dead works to serve the living God" (9:14) with hearts ready to do his will. Both God's writing his laws on his people's hearts and his no longer remembering sins constitute the "release" effected by Christ's one offering (v. 18).

16a The pastor emphasizes the opening of v. 16, "*This* is the covenant that I will covenant with them" (italics added), by separating it from what follows with the phrase "the Lord says." He has now come to his conclusion and would bring the truth home to his hearers. Therefore, it was natural for him to substitute "with them" for "with the house of Israel," which he retained in his previous quotation of this passage (cf. 8:10). As has been evident at every turn, the pastor sees one people to whom God has spoken first by prophets and now by a Son (1:1-2). God's promise to Abraham and all that he did in establishing this people through Moses have now been fulfilled in the Son perfected forever as heavenly High Priest. Thus, his hearers are constituted the continuation of that people through the redeeming word of God. In fact, all of us who receive God's word in Christ are more than its continuation, for we live during the time "after those days" in which God promised that he would establish his New Covenant. We are the privileged heirs who live in the time of fulfillment. How important perseverance is for those who have received such benefits.

16b With an authoritative "the Lord says" the pastor begins his summary of the benefits brought by the New Covenant promised in Jeremiah and fulfilled by Christ. He has selected the first (Jer 31:33b; Heb 8:10b) and last (Jer 31:34d; Heb 8:12b) benefits enumerated in that promise as most directly attesting the effectiveness of Christ's sacrifice in removing sins. There can be no doubt that he affirmed the reality of the intervening description of how God's people would "know" him (Jer 31:33c-34c; Heb 8:10c-12a). After all, it is only through Christ's sacrifice and under the New Covenant that his people have direct access to God's presence. However, the disobedience of God's people, their refusal "to remain" in God's Covenant, was part of what kept them from an intimate knowledge of God under that first administration.[11] Thus, the first benefit of the New Covenant, affirmed here in v. 16b, is that God would deal with this problem by inscribing his "laws" on his people's hearts. God himself will now do what he urged his people to do in Deut 6:6-9 — put his laws on their hearts so they will be willing and able to obey.

11. Even the faithful under the Old Covenant only looked forward to the intimacy with God now provided by Christ (11:39-40).

This writing of God's laws on the hearts of the faithful is the result of their "conscience" being "cleansed from dead works to serve the living God" (9:14).

The general import of God's writing his laws on the heart is clear: people with such hearts are characterized by the "willing obedience that Christ embodied" (10:5-10).[12] Can we be more specific about the "laws" that the pastor had in mind? Elsewhere Hebrews normally uses the singular "law" to describe the old system as ineffective and no longer valid (7:5, 12, 16, 19, 28; 8:4; 9:22; 10:1).[13] It is, therefore, unlikely that the pastor would refer to the New Covenant as a "new" or "Christologized" "law."[14] It is not the "law" as a sacrificial system but God's "laws" that he has written on his people's hearts. The context of Hebrews suggests that the pastor's meaning in this verse is close to that of Jeremiah whom he quotes. It is true that when Jeremiah spoke of God's "laws," his frame of reference could be nothing but the Mosaic Covenant. It was not, however, a failure to keep the sacrifices and ceremonies that prevented the ancient people of Israel or the people of Jeremiah's day from "remaining" in God's covenant. Jeremiah (Jer 7:1-15), in accord with other prophets, soundly condemned his contemporaries for trusting in the performance of such rituals while abandoning their allegiance to God and mistreating their neighbors. As noted elsewhere (2:1-4; 10:26-31; 12:18-24), fulfillment in Christ has not removed but intensified the moral demand of the law. Thus it was those fundamental "laws" that demanded the loyalty to God and love of neighbor that God would inscribe on his people's hearts. This interpretation is confirmed by the rejection of the old sacrifices in favor of the obedience of Christ as described in 10:5-10. The obedience envisioned is not mere conformity to any list of laws, no matter how long, but to the greatest commandments (Deut 6:4-5; Lev 19:18). It is a total willing and passionate obedience to the whole will of God. This obedience is both modeled on and made possible by the obedience of Christ that established this New Covenant (10:5-10). It is indeed "appropriate" (see on 2:10) that his obedience should result in the obedience of God's people.

Jeremiah wrote, "in their minds . . . and upon their hearts" (8:10). The pastor has reversed the order, "upon their hearts . . . and upon their minds," in accord with the prominence he gives to the word "heart" as a description of the true person (3:8, 10, 12, 15; 4:7, 12; 8:10; 10:16, 22 [twice]; 13:9).[15]

---

12. Attridge, 281.

13. The pastor refers to the "law" as a historical entity in 10:28. Cf. 9:22.

14. *Pace* Joslin, *Law*, 243-44. Cf. Westfall, *Discourse Analysis*, 224, who refers to "the shadow law of sacrifices" and "the law of voluntary obedience."

15. Hebrews quotes Jeremiah without change in 8:10: εἰς τὴν διάνοιαν αὐτῶν ("in their minds") and ἐπὶ καρδίας αὐτῶν ("upon their hearts"). In 10:16, however, the pastor not only reverses these two expressions but changes the εἰς ("in") of εἰς τὴν διάνοιαν

These references disclose the prevalence of "heart" in the exhortation against imitating the wilderness generation (Heb. 3:7–4:13). As noted above, that generation embodied those whom Jeremiah described as not "remaining" in God's covenant because of disobedience. The New Covenant expects much more than outward conformity — it envisions transformation of the person.

17 The pastor strengthens this final and climactic statement from Jeremiah in several ways. First, he omits the previous line of the Jeremiah quotation, "for I will be merciful to their unrighteous deeds," but adds "their lawless deeds" to this final line, quoted in v. 17: "their sins and their lawless deeds I will remember no more."[16] There is no reason to distinguish between "sins" and "lawless deeds" as if the first were accidental and the second intentional (cf. 5:2; 9:7). Both Jeremiah and Hebrews are concerned with nothing less than the intentional breach of God's moral law that excluded one from the benefits of the Old Covenant. The addition of this phrase adds emphasis to the totality of God's remission. It also binds this second benefit of the New Covenant closely to the first: God will not remember the "lawless deeds" of those upon whose hearts he has inscribed his "laws" (v. 16b).

Second, the pastor has underscored this statement by changing the tense and voice of the verb "I will remember no more." In 8:12 he retained the aorist subjunctive used in the Greek text of Jeremiah. Here he exchanges it for the equivalent but stronger future indicative.[17] God says definitively that he will no longer remember all of their former misconduct no matter how "lawless" it may have been. In light of what the pastor has said about the "abolishing" (9:26) and "taking away" (9:27-28) of sin, it would be a mistake to unduly circumscribe God's no longer remembering sin. The pastor is saying more than that God will no longer "remember their sins and their lawless deeds" against them. The removal of sins from the divine memory is the strongest possible way of affirming their total abolition.

18 On one level this final verse is an explanatory note. The pastor wants his hearers to understand how the Jeremiah passage attests the full sufficiency of Christ's sacrifice, just described in v. 14 at the climax of his argument. The complete removal of sin attested by Jeremiah excludes all other offerings and shows that Christ's must have been completely successful. At the same time, however, this verse is a powerful conclusion to the whole

αὐτῶν to the ἐπί ("upon") of the now first expression, ἐπὶ καρδίας αὐτῶν. This change only underscores the intentional emphasis put on ἐπὶ καρδίας αὐτῶν ("upon their hearts").

16. Compare ταῖς ἀδικίαις αὐτῶν ("their unrighteous deeds") in 8:12a with τῶν ἀνομιῶν αὐτῶν ("their lawless deeds") in 10:17b.

17. Compare the aorist μνησθῶ in οὐ μὴ μνησθῶ ἔτι (8:12) with the future indicative μνησθήσομαι in 10:17 (οὐ μὴ μνησθήσομαι ἔτι). This change is intentional (see Attridge, 281; Guthrie, in *Commentary on the New Testament Use of the Old*, 979); *pace* Ellingworth, 514, who makes no distinction between these expressions.

symphony. The removal of sin effected by Christ's sacrifice is so complete that it clears all rivals from the field. The sufficiency of Christ's sacrifice in v. 14 may have been reason to follow the instructions of 10:19-25 and draw near to God through him. However, his sacrifice's exclusion of any other in v. 18 is a most urgent cause to heed the warnings against apostasy in 10:26-31.[18]

"Where there is release from these" refers to Christ's sacrifice that provides freedom from the "sins" and "lawless deeds" mentioned in v. 17. "Where" also has causal significance: since "release" from disobedience has been effected by Christ's offering, "there is no longer" any other "sacrifice for sins."[19] English versions normally render the term we have translated "release" by "forgiveness" throughout the NT.[20] The LXX, on the other hand, regularly uses this term in the broader sense of "release."[21] In the present context we cannot restrict "release" to a mere forensic or legal "forgiveness." The pastor is not dealing with a verdict given in court but with cleansing provided in a sanctuary. By his sacrifice Christ "cleanses the conscience" of his people "from dead works to serve the living God" (9:14). Christ's own obedience has produced a covenant in which he has written his laws on his people's hearts so that they too can live in obedience (10:16). God's grand climactic declaration that he has blotted their sins from his memory affirms that he has done away with sin in the broadest sense.[22] The cessation of sacrifice implies purification (cf. 1:3) as well as forgiveness.

The pastor has long anticipated his use of "release" in this concluding statement to encompass all that God has done in Christ to free humanity from sin. He ended the second movement of his symphony by saying that there was no "release" without the shedding of blood (9:22). He then made it clear that animal "blood" could not "take away" sin (10:4). Christ alone has provided the "release" that makes all other sacrifices superfluous. The pastor's hearers have now heard his symphony in praise and explanation of Christ's sacrifice. It is by this sacrifice that the eternal Son has taken his seat forever at God's right hand as the only High Priest able to bring God's people into the divine presence. They now know why they should follow those introduc-

---

18. Cf. Weiss, 517, who argues that οὐκέτι ("no longer") in v. 18 is the foundation for the fact that no "sin offering" remains for the apostate (v. 26).

19. Ellingworth, 515 (citing BDF §456, 3), rightly contends that here ὅπου, "where," is as much logical as local, giving the circumstances that will result in what is described in the main clause.

20. Matt 26:28; Mark 1:4; Luke 1:77; 3:3; 24:47; Acts 2:38; 5:31; 10:43; 13:38; 26:18; etc. But contrast Luke 4:18.

21. Rudolf Bultmann, "ἀφίημι, ἄφεσις, παρίημι, πάρεσις," in *TDNT* 1:510.

22. See Lane, 2:269, citing Johnsson, "Defilement," 349-51. See also O'Brien, 359-60.

tory exhortations of 4:14-16 to hold firm and to draw near through this High Priest. In light of this deepened understanding the pastor will renew those exhortations with greater detail and urgency in the following verses (10:19-25). He will follow them with proportionately dire warnings lest they turn away from this High Priest seated at God's right hand (10:26-31) in order that his hearers might maintain their place (10:32-39) among the faithful people of God (11:1-40)

III. A HISTORY OF THE FAITHFUL PEOPLE OF GOD FROM CREATION TO CONSUMMATION (10:19–12:29)

This history of God's faithful people is the counterpart to the history of the disobedient in 1:1–4:11, particularly 3:7–4:11. The pastor urges his hearers to shun the company of the disobedient. He calls them to take their place in this history of those who persevere in faith and obedience. He begins this section (10:19-39) by showing his hearers how perseverance as part of God's faithful people is dependent upon the work of Christ just described in 4:14–10:18. Then he narrates this history from creation (11:1-7) to its pivotal point in Christ (12:1-3), and then to its consummation at the Judgment (12:25-29). He would have them identify with the history of the faithful before Christ (11:1-40), whose lives define the nature of persevering faith. Christ is both the greatest example of such endurance and the one who makes the way of faith possible (12:1-3). Then the pastor addresses the present experience of God's people (12:4-24) both in suffering (12:4-13) and joy (12:18-24), before turning their attention to the final Judgment (12:25-29). The introduction to this commentary has already demonstrated the chiastic relationship between the individual sections of 1:1–4:16 and 10:18–12:29 (pp. 63-70). We will explore those relationships and their significance more fully in the exposition below.

A. THE LIFE OF PERSEVERING FAITH AND THE HIGH PRIESTHOOD OF THE SON (10:19-39)

It is important to recognize both the unity and the transitional character of this section. There is no hard break between the full sufficiency of Christ described in 4:14–10:18 and the life of faith and endurance exemplified by the people of God throughout history, as narrated in 11:1–12:29. The pastor forges the closest bond between the two. He passionately desires his hearers to take their place as part of God's faithful people through appropriating the high-priestly work of Christ (12:1-3). He assures them that even those who lived before Christ will enter God's eternal blessing only by the Jesus who suffered and is now enthroned as High Priest at God's right hand (11:39-40). The pastor forges three links in the chain that joins the people of faith (11:1–12:29) to Christ their High Priest (4:14–10:18) — link one, vv. 19-25; link two, vv. 26-31; and link three, vv. 32-39.[1] The first two "links" have close ties with the preceding description of Christ's high priesthood; the third introduces the history of the faithful that follows.[2] In 10:19-25 the pastor urges his hearers to draw near to God through Christ's high-priestly provision in order to persevere in faithfulness. In 10:26-31 he warns them against joining those who repudiate Christ's high-priestly work and suffer the dire consequences of their repudiation. Both of these "links" access the work of Christ in order to encourage the type of faithful endurance introduced in 10:32-39. In this final "link" the pastor assures his hearers that they are not like the apostates whom he has just described in 10:26-31 (cf. 3:7-19); they belong to

1. For the division of this section into vv. 19-25; 26-31; and 32-29 see Vanhoye, *La structure littéraire*, 172-81; Guthrie, *Structure*, 117, 127, 131; and Westfall, *Discourse Analysis*, 239-40, 243-49. Compare UBS[4], NA[27], NRSV, ESV, NIV, NASB, and NKJV. Vanhoye also divides between vv. 32-35 and 36-39. Cf. NIV's division between vv. 32-34 and 35-39.

2. Some would join 10:19-25 to 4:14–10:18 (Koester, 454; cf. Guthrie, *Structure*, 117, 136, 144; Westfall, *Discourse Analysis*, 238-44). Others recognize that 10:26-31 also applies the preceding discussion of Christ's high priesthood (cf. Lane, 2:279, 290-91; Attridge, 19; Buchanan, 1-2, 92; Vanhoye, *La structure littéraire*, 173-82) and that 10:32-39 introduces the following chapter. They would include both vv. 19-25 and 26-31 with the previous section, but join vv. 32-39 to 11:1-40 (Thompson, 200-201; C. Rose, *Die Wolke der Zeugen: Eine exegetisch-traditionsgeschichtliche Untersuchung zu Hebräer 10,32–12,3* [WUNT 60; Tübingen: Siebeck, 1994], 34). Both of these suggestions recognize important features of the text but fail to fully grasp its essential unity as a bond joining the preceding and following sections. This second way of segmenting the text (vv. 19-25 and 26-31 with the previous section, vv. 32-39 with the following) gives too little weight to the contrast between the faithfulness of the hearers in vv. 32-34 and the apostasy of unbelievers in vv. 26-31. Furthermore, vv. 35-39 extend the exhortations to perseverance found in vv. 23-25. The first way of dividing the text given above (vv. 19-25 with the previous section) rests on the obvious parallels between 10:19-25 and 4:14-16. However, as the exposition below will show, 4:14-16 is tailored to bring the hearers into Christ's high priesthood, but 10:19-25 is shaped in order to direct them from that high priesthood to faithful endurance. This purpose is best served by recognizing the relationship that 10:19-25 has with what has gone before, but at the same time letting it begin the introduction of what is to follow. All of these features of the text are best accounted for when one takes 10:19-39 as the chain that joins the life of faith described in the following section with the work of Christ expounded in the preceding. Rose, *Die Volke*, 24-25, is correct when he insists that the author's exhortation to faithfulness cannot be separated from the high-priestly work of Christ.

the people of faith whom he will now describe in 11:1-40. The transitional nature of this section becomes clear only when one recognizes both the unity of 10:19-39 and the affinity of the first two "links" (vv. 19-25; 26-31) with what has gone before and the third (vv. 32-39) with what follows.

Both the unity of this section and the way in which it introduces what follows are reinforced by the clear parallels between 10:19-39 and 5:11–6:20, the exhortation with which the pastor aroused his hearers for the "solid food" of 7:1–10:18.[3] In both, the hearers' present situation (5:11-14; 10:19-25) exposes them to the danger of apostasy (6:1-8; 10:26-31). However, the pastor is confident, on the basis of their past behavior (6:9-12; 10:32-39), that they will join the company of those who persevere through faith (6:13-20; 11:1–12:3). Incitement to such perseverance has always been the pastor's goal. However, in that preparatory exhortation his purpose was to awaken them from lethargy in order that they might grasp the magnitude of Christ's high priesthood as the only sufficient resource for perseverance. He now urges them forward to vigorous perseverance based on appropriation of the benefits provided by their High Priest.[4] Thus, he directs them not just to Abraham (6:13-20), but to the grand panoramic history of God's faithful people in 11:1-40. The hearers are now able to comprehend and appropriate the privileges that are theirs in Christ.

The way in which Heb 10:19-39 builds on the exposition of Christ's high priesthood in 4:14–10:18 is substantiated by the many parallels between 10:19-25 and 4:14-16, the opening paragraph of that previous section.[5] In fact, the trail that the pastor blazes from the high priesthood of Christ (5:1–10:18) to the grand history of God's faithful in 11:1-40 is the mirror image of the path he took from the unfaithful people of God in 3:7-19 to Christ's high priesthood (5:1–10:18).[6] He brought his hearers to Christ's high priesthood by urging them not to join the unfaithful who perished (3:7-19), but to pursue what the unfaithful lost (4:1-11) because his hearers, too, were accountable

---

3. Wayne Gordon McCown, "Ο ΛΟΓΟΣ ΤΗΣ ΠΑΡΑΚΛΗΣΕΩΣ: The Nature and Function of the Hortatory Sections in the Epistle to the Hebrews" (Th.D. diss., Union Theological Seminary in Virginia, 1970), 50, 69, 158, 299, quoted by Lane, 2:279-80.

4. Thus 5:11-14 describes their present inadequacy, but 10:19-25, the privileges they now have in the all-sufficient Christ.

5. Wolfgang Nauck, "Zum Aufbau des Hebräerbriefes," in *Judentum–Urchristentum–Kirche: Festschrift für J. Jeremias,* ed. Walther Eltester (Berlin: Verlag Alfred Töpelmann, 1960), 200-203; Guthrie, *Structure,* 79-82; and Westfall, *Discourse Analysis,* 237-39. See the comments on 4:14-16 above, and the comparison of these passages in the exposition of 10:19-25 below.

6. See "The Sermon's Rhetorically Effective Structure," subsection entitled "Heb 3:1–4:13 and Heb 10:19–12:3: On Pilgrimage to the Promised Home," pp. 65-67 in the Introduction to this commentary.

before the word of God (4:12-13). Thus, they should enthusiastically avail themselves of the benefits provided by their High Priest (4:14-16). After explaining Christ's high priesthood (5:1–10:18) he reverses the order by urging them first to take full advantage of Christ's high priesthood (10:19-25), for they are now more accountable because of what Christ has provided (10:26-31), so they should pursue the goal promised the faithful (10:32-39) by taking their place in the history of God's faithful people who persevered to the end (11:1-40).[7] A diagram of this progression is given below. "A¹" is parallel to "A"; "B¹" to "B"; etc. "E," "Christ's All-Sufficient High Priesthood," is at the center. Although the arrangement is chiastic, going from "A" back to "A¹," the argument is not circular. The pastor's emphasis is on the last half. Notice how much more attention he gives the faithful people of God in 11:1-40 than he gave the unfaithful in 3:7-19. Thus we have arranged these passages in ascending order. He would turn his hearers away from the unfaithful to the faithful through the provision of their High Priest. He would detach them from the pressures and pleasures of this life in order to fix their gaze on their heavenly goal where even now Christ sits at God's right hand to give them aid.

(A¹) Join the Company of the Faithful of Old (11:1-40).
(B¹) Pursue the Blessing Promised the Faithful (10:32-39).
(C¹) You are More Accountable Because of This High Priest (10:26-31).
(D¹) Avail Yourselves of This Great Priest (10:19-25).
(E) Christ's All-Sufficient High Priesthood (5:1–10:18).
(D) Embrace This Great High Priest (4:14-16).
(C) You Are Accountable before the Word of God (4:12-13).
(B) Pursue the Blessing Lost by the Faithless Generation (4:1-11).
(A) Avoid the Company of the Faithless Generation (3:7-19).

Christ their High Priest is the all-sufficient resource for escaping the fate of the unfaithful and joining the victorious faithful. The urgency of obedience is all the clearer because the "word" of God that the hearers have received is nothing less than the astounding revelation of Christ's full sufficiency to save. Thus, the pastor would use the grand description of Christ's high priesthood just completed to turn all who will heed from disobedience to faithfulness, from sluggishness to perseverance, from ultimate loss to eternal blessing in God's presence.

7. Guthrie, Structure, 136, shows the parallels between 3:7-19 and 11:1-40; 4:3(?)-11 and 10:32-39; 4:12-13 and 10:26-31. He confirms his argument by showing the parallel between 3:1-6 and 12:1-2. See on 12:1-2 below.

1. Avail Yourselves of This Great Priest (10:19-25)

19 *Therefore, brothers and sisters, since we have authorization for entrance into the Most Holy Place by means of the blood of Jesus, 20 an entrance which he inaugurated for us, a way new and living through the veil, that is, [through] his flesh; 21 and since we have a Great Priest over the house of God, 22 let us keep drawing near with true hearts in fullness of faith, having allowed our hearts to be sprinkled from an evil conscience and our bodies to be washed with pure water. 23 Let us hold the confession of the hope firm, for the One who has promised is faithful; 24 and let us pay attention to each other for the provoking of love and good works. 25 We will accomplish this by not continuing to abandon the assembling of ourselves together, as is the habit of some, but by continually exhorting one another, and all the more as we see the Day approaching.*

The similarities between this admonition and the exhortation in 4:14-16 extend to the arrangement of material. Both describe the privileges we "have" through Christ's high priesthood (10:19-21; 4:14a, 15) and then what we should do in light of these privileges (10:22-25; 4:14b, 16). However, when the earlier exhortation was given, the hearers as yet had no comprehensive knowledge of Christ's high-priestly ministry. Thus, the pastor fed them in small portions, dividing the privileges afforded by Christ's accomplishments and resulting exhortations into two pairs — privilege (4:14a), exhortation (4:14b); privilege (4:15), exhortation (4:16). The pastor's exposition of Christ's high priesthood has provided the "solid food" (5:12) of the mature. Thus, he begins this exhortation in 10:19-25 with a comprehensive description of the benefits Christ's priesthood provides (vv. 19-21), followed by a more complete exhortation to take advantage of those privileges (vv. 22-25). This comprehensive description is introduced by a causal participle translated "since we have" (v. 19). The first of these benefits is described in vv. 19-20, the second (closely related) benefit, in v. 21. Thus the translation above has added a second "since we have" at the beginning of v. 21 for clarity. The exhortation in vv. 22-25 consists of three hortatory subjunctives: "Let us draw near with true hearts in fullness of faith" (v. 22); "Let us hold the confession of the hope firm" (v. 23); and "Let us pay attention to each other for the provoking of love" (v. 24).[1] Thus, by enjoining faith, hope, and

---

1. Weiss, 520; Riggenbach, 313; and most commentaries (cf. Vanhoye, *La structure littéraire,* 175-77) recognize the structural arrangement of this passage as based on the causal participle ἔχοντες ("having," v. 19), followed by three hortatory subjunctives: προσερχώμεθα ("let us draw near," v. 22); κατέχωμεν ("let us hold fast," v. 23); and κατανοῶμεν ("let us pay attention," v. 24).

love, these three exhortations encompass the totality of the Christian life.[2] In 10:32–12:29 the pastor will urge his hearers to persevere by faith in light of the assured hope awaiting the people of God. In 13:1-17 he will describe the love that is to characterize their common life.[3]

The order in which the pastor presents the accomplishments of Christ and the privileges they provide reflects the different purposes of these two passages (4:14-16; 10:19-25). As we have seen, Heb 4:14-16 introduces the section on Christ's high priesthood (5:1–10:18). That passage moved from Christ's exaltation (4:14a) to his humiliation (4:15) in order to focus attention on the means by which Christ had become all-sufficient High Priest through incarnate obedience, as described in 5:1–10:18. On the other hand, 10:19-25 moves from humiliation (10:19-20) to exaltation (10:22). Thus, the pastor leaves his hearers focused on the ever-relevant result of Christ's incarnate obedience — a High Priest seated at God's right hand. As such he is the one who is able to empower the endurance necessary for joining and emulating the soon-to-be-described faithful of old (11:1-40). Furthermore, in 4:14-16 the pastor urged his hearers to steadfastness (4:14b) before inviting them to draw near (4:16) because he was about to show them Christ's high priesthood as sufficient means for approaching God. In 10:19-25, however, he reverses this order (draw near, v. 22; steadfastness, v. 23) so that he can leave them attending to the steadfast endurance for which that drawing near is the means. By ending with steadfastness he again anticipates the examples of faithful perseverance in 11:1-40. Thus, the very order in which the pastor presents the accomplishments of Christ, the privileges these accomplishments provide, and the resulting exhortations, demonstrates the fact that both 4:14-16 and 10:18-25 introduce their respective sections (4:14–10:18; 10:19–12:29). Moreover, the way in which both of these passages unite Christ's incarnation and exaltation reminds the reader that the all-sufficient, exalted High Priest can never be separated from the one who was obedient "in the days of his flesh" (5:7).

19 "Therefore" ties this whole section closely with the teaching about Christ's high priesthood in 5:1–10:18.[4] The opening causal participle, translated "since we have," shows clearly that the benefits of this high priesthood, summarized in vv. 19-21, provide the resource and motivation for the exhorta-

2. Westcott, 322; Spicq, 2:314; Vanhoye, *Old Testament,* 222-27; Lane, 2:280.

3. Lane, 2:280 (cf. Swetnam, "Hebrews 7–13," 333-48), contends that "faith" anticipates 11:1-40; "hope," 12:1-13; and "love," 12:14–13:2. The pastor, however, does not make such a clear distinction between "faith" and "hope." His exhortations to love clearly begin at 13:1. *Pace* Westfall, *Discourse Analysis,* 244-53, the exhortation toward love and mutual concern, which comes third in this list, does not introduce the theme of 11:1–12:2.

4. Ellingworth, 517; see Lane, 2:282; Michel, 343; Scholer, *Proleptic Priests,* 125 (cited by O'Brien, 362, n. 104).

tions in vv. 22-25. The benefits described are distilled directly from the teaching of the previous chapters. By addressing his hearers as "brothers and sisters" (3:1, 12), the pastor reminds them that they are in fact part of the "household of God" (3:6) whom Christ owned as his "brothers and sisters" (2:11) and affirmed as God's "children" (2:10-18). This reminder prepares them for the exhortation to mutual encouragement with which this section ends (vv. 24-25).

Verses 19 and 20 complement and correspond to one another. In v. 19 the pastor describes the most fundamental privilege that God's people now have: "authorization for entrance into the Most Holy Place by means of the blood of Jesus." In v. 20 he reinforces the grandeur of this privilege by describing how it was provided by Christ. The terms translated "authorization" and "entrance" underscore the magnitude of this right of access now available for the faithful. "Authorization," often rendered by "boldness," was used for the right of free speech exercised by those who were citizens in the assembly of a Greek city.[5] The objective nature of this "boldness" is confirmed by the fact that it has been provided by Christ. It is parallel to that other great objective privilege now possessed by God's people — a "Great Priest" (v. 21) over God's house.[6] The pastor is not merely concerned with a feeling of confidence. He is concerned with the basis for such confidence in the "authorization" or "right" of entry now provided by Christ's all-sufficient sacrifice.[7] By what Christ has done he has "empowered" God's faithful to enter God's presence.[8] At the same time, the word translated "entrance" can refer to the "right of entrance" or to the place of entrance, the "entryway." This last meaning is suggested by the use of "a way fresh and living" below. "We" have "authorization" of the "entryway" into the very presence of God. The way to God that was not even revealed under the old system (cf. 9:8) is now fully open to the people of God. God's own enter freely and continuously in prayer, repentance, and supplication to receive the "mercy" of needed forgiveness plus the "grace" for victorious living and perseverance (4:16). They need not "slink" into his presence. This privilege is fully compatible with the climactic declaration in v. 14 that Christ "has perfected" those "being made holy." As noted on that verse, Christ's "perfecting" is his making capable of entrance into God's presence through cleansing by his sacrificial death.[9]

As the discussion of Christ's high priesthood has made so clear, this

---

5. deSilva, 336. For παρρησία ("boldness") as the mark of a clear conscience see Philo, *Heir* 5–21. See also the discussion in Thompson, *Christian Philosophy*, 32-33.

6. O'Brien, 362-63.

7. Weiss, 520-21; cf. Lane, 2:274b; Ellingworth, 517; Scholer, *Proleptic Priests*, 126; Vanhoye, *Old Testament*, 222-23; and, most recently, Thompson, 202.

8. Weiss, 520-21, calls this boldness "Ermächtigung" ("empowering").

9. Scholer, *Proleptic Priests*, 185-200, has shown clearly that Christ's "perfecting" his own refers to their present privilege of access to God.

right of entrance was procured only by means of the cleansing "blood of Jesus" (9:11-15). The pastor maintains the appropriate sacrificial imagery though he has explained Jesus' "blood" as shorthand for his willing earthly obedience climaxing in his self-offering in death on the cross (10:5-10). The High Priest at God's right hand cannot be separated from the earthly obedience of the fully human "Jesus."[10] The name "Jesus" anticipates the reference to "flesh" in the next verse.

20 The relative pronoun with which v. 20 begins in Greek refers back to the Greek word for "entrance" in v. 19.[11] The translation above makes this reference clear by adding the words "an entrance" at the beginning of v. 20. The pastor wants his hearers to more fully grasp the vital significance of the nature and origin of this entrance into God's presence. Just as Moses "inaugurated" the earthly Tent of worship with animal blood (9:18), so Christ "has inaugurated" this way of entrance into the heavenly Most Holy Place with his own blood (v. 19).[12] The underlying Greek term has been translated as both "inaugurate" and "consecrate" ("dedicate"). It is misleading to affirm one of these meanings to the exclusion of the other. "Inaugurate" reminds the hearers that Christ has established something totally "new."[13] "Consecrate" prevents them from forgetting that he established access into God's presence by nothing less than the high-priestly sacrifice of himself.[14] By this sacrifice he provided cleansing from sin, thereby establishing the New Covenant, taking his seat at God's right hand as High Priest, and inaugurating a new way of access to God. This "way" is "new" in fact and in quality. It did not exist before it was inaugurated and thus opened by Christ. It has a "fresh" new character.[15] This is not the same old barrier but a "new"

10. See Westcott, 319; Weiss, 521-22.

11. ἥν ("which") is feminine singular, in agreement with εἴσοδον ("entrance"). See Westcott, 319.

12. According to 9:18, the first Tent "was inaugurated" (ἐγκεκαίνισται) not "without blood" (χωρὶς αἵματος). Note the close proximity in 10:19-20 between "by means of his blood" (ἐν τῷ αἵματι Ἰησοῦ) and "which he inaugurated" (ἣν ἐνεκαίνισεν).

13. Koester, 443, reminds us that ἐνκαινίζω ("inaugurate," "consecrate") contains the adjective καινός, meaning "new." καινός, however, is not the same word used for "fresh" or "new" (πρόσφατον) in this verse.

14. ἐνκαινίζω is used for inauguration and ratification through consecration in Deut 20:5; 1 Kgs 8:63; 2 Chr 7:5; and 1 Macc 4:36, 54; 5:1 (cited by Johnson, 256). The cultic connotation of this term used in contexts such as these demonstrates that "it was by his blood, and not simply by his ascent, that Christ opened (or, rather, consecrated) the entrance to the sanctuary as 'a new [fresh] and living way through the curtain'" (N. A. Dahl, "A New and Living Way," *Int* 5 [1951]: 403-4). Furthermore, this opening of the way to God was "a cultic act of consecration, identical with the ratification of the new covenant" (Dahl, "A New and Living Way," 405).

15. Lane, 2:274f, 283; BDAG, 886.

entrance that provides the people of God with access into his presence. Ever "fresh," it will never, like the Old Covenant, become antiquated or out of date (8:13). Thus it is rightly called a "living" way. It leads to life in the presence of the "living" God (10:31) rather than to some "dead" end.[16] Yet "living" emphasizes the quality of this road as well as its destination. This road is not merely "enduring"; rather, it is a way of access provided and guaranteed by the "living" God himself.[17] Christ offered himself "by the eternal Spirit" of God (9:14); he "lives" (7:8) and is a High Priest by "the power of an indestructible life" (7:16). He "remains forever" with an "inviolable" priesthood (7:24). Thus this way is provided by the ever "living" and thus eternal Son of God (1:1-14), incarnate, obedient, and now seated at God's right hand.[18] It is not dependent on mortal humanity or clogged by human sinfulness. As certainly as disobedience to the "living" word brings condemnation (4:12-13), so pursuit of the "living" way leads to life. The Tent that Moses "inaugurated" (9:18) with animal blood demonstrated that access to God was neither revealed nor available (9:8) under its ministrations. The "way new and living" "inaugurated" by Christ with his own "blood" is a sure means of entering the divine presence.

Few expressions have bedeviled Hebrews commentators more than "through the veil, that is, his flesh." In Heb 6:20 (cf. 9:3) the "veil" was analogous to the curtain before the Most Holy Place of the Mosaic Tent, and thus representative of the barrier that kept mankind from approaching God.[19] Christ himself has passed through that barrier as the "Forerunner" and representative of his people (6:20). Thus, it would be natural for the hearers to understand the "veil" of 10:19-20 as the same barrier: by passing through this barrier/"veil" their "Forerunner" has made a "new and living way" for his

16. Ellingworth, 519; cf. Lane, 2:275g, 283-84.

17. Certainly, with Weiss, 523, this is an "enduring" way. If, however, that was all the pastor wanted to say, a form of μένω ("remain," "endure," 7:3, 24; 10:34; 12:27; 13:14; cf. 7:23) would have been more appropriate than ζῶσαν, "living."

18. However, Westcott, 318-19; Bruce, 250; Spicq, 2:315-16; and others go beyond the evidence when they identify this way with Christ himself, citing John 14:6 as a parallel. See Ellingworth, 518. *Pace* Vanhoye, *Old Testament*, 225, esp. n. 37, the "new and living way" cannot be equated with Christ's resurrected body.

19. For "the veil" as that which prevented entrance into God's presence see Weiss, 523; Riggenbach, 315; Spicq, 2:316. *Pace* Braun, 307-9; Käsemann, *Wandering*, 209-10; Schierse, *Verheissung*, 36-37; and Grässer, *Glaube*, 110-11, this "veil" cannot be traced to Philo's veil that divided the world of sense from the world of ideas (*Moses* 2.74-76) or from the Gnostic "cosmic, demonic barrier" between the earthly and heavenly worlds. There is no evidence for a "school tradition" using this concept in (Christian) Gnostic circles. Furthermore, the references to such a barrier in the *Gospel of Philip* are probably dependent on Hebrews. Hebrews says nothing about the Redeemer breaching such a barrier. See Weiss, 524; Koester, 444; and Ellingworth, 519.

followers.[20] However, the pastor immediately associates this veil with Christ's "flesh." The Son's assumption of "flesh" (2:10; 5:7), however, is no barrier, but is integral to his procuring salvation by his self-offering and thus to his role as the ultimate revelation of God.

One cannot deny that "his flesh" appears to be in apposition to, and thus identified with, "the veil." Both "veil" and "flesh" are in the genitive case, separated only by the phrase "that is."[21] Elsewhere in Hebrews "that is" always identifies two words or phrases in the same case with one another (2:14; 7:5; 9:11; 11:16; 13:15). Furthermore, in all the above examples save 7:5, the word following "that is" is identified with the nearest preceding substantive of the same case.[22] Thus, there appears to be tension between 6:20 and this verse. In 6:20 (cf. 9:3) the "veil" was the barrier through which Christ, and his people, must pass in order to enter the heavenly Most Holy Place. Here the "veil" is identified with Christ's flesh. How can the "flesh" that Christ assumed in order to procure access to the divine presence (2:14; 5:17) be identified with the "veil" that separated humanity from God?[23]

Some attempt to solve this problem by reminding us that within the OT the "veil" was both the barrier that separated God's people from his presence and the point of contact between them. Thus, Bruce sees no contradiction between the "veil" as a barrier in 6:20 and the "veil" as Christ's flesh, through which we have access to God's presence in 10:20.[24] While this may be so, the pastor has deliberately created this tension in order to impact his hearers.[25] By his reference to the "veil" penetrated by Christ in 6:20, and his

---

20. Philo distinguished between the curtain before the Holy Place and the one before the Most Holy Place by using κάλυμμα for the former (*Moses* 2.101) but καταπέτασμα, as here, for the latter. See Bruce, 199, n. 14; 250, n. 87. Cf. also Philo, *Giants* 53, "the inmost curtain" (τὸ ἐσωτάτω καταπέτασμα).

21. διὰ ("through") τοῦ καταπετάσματος ("the veil"), τοῦτ᾽ ἔστιν ("that is") τῆς σαρκὸς αὐτοῦ ("of his flesh").

22. See N. H. Young, "Τοῦτ᾽ ἔστιν τῆς σαρκὸς αὐτοῦ (Heb. x.20): Apposition, Dependent or Explicative?'" *NTS* 20 (1973-74): 101-4. In Heb 7:5 there is no ambiguity concerning the referent of the word in apposition. The factors noted in the text above make it unlikely that "flesh" should be taken as a genitive qualifier of the accusative noun "way": "a new and living way [that consists] of his flesh." Westcott, 319-21, is the classic advocate of this view. See also Spicq, 2:316.

23. The pastor cannot mean that human "flesh" in general is this barrier, for he is speaking specifically of Christ's "flesh." Furthermore, there is no basis in Hebrews for Käsemann's distinction between Christ's "body" as the instrument of, but his "flesh" as a hindrance to, salvation (Käsemann, *Wandering*, 225-26).

24. Bruce, 252. Such positive assessment of the "veil" in 10:20 comes close to identifying it with the "new and living way" (Johnson, 257).

25. Thus, as Young, "Τοῦτ᾽ ἔστιν," 101-4, suggests, the solution is to be found in the pastor's rhetorical intent, not in speculation. Such speculation is evidenced by those

typological use of the Tent and its "veil" in 9:1-10, he has emphasized its nature as a barrier. His general use of Day of Atonement imagery has done nothing to lessen this impression. It is thus likely that his first, as well as his modern, hearers were shocked when he said, "through the veil, that is, his flesh." The pastor brings the barrier that separated humanity from God and the means by which that barrier was removed into closest proximity. It is almost as if he had said that Christ's incarnate obedience ("his flesh") has transformed the once-horrible barrier into a "way new and living."

Comparison with v. 19 does not remove the shock value of this statement, but it does suggest that the pastor may not have intended a simple identification between the "veil" and Christ's "flesh." It also confirms that "his flesh," in tandem with "his blood" (v. 19), represents the means by which he has achieved salvation for the people of God (cf. 2:14; 5:7). The three phrases, "for entrance," "into the Most Holy Place," and "by means of the blood of Jesus," in v. 19 correspond respectively to "a way new and living," "through the veil," and "[through] his flesh" in v. 20.[26] As noted above, v. 19 describes these realities from the viewpoint of what God's people "have"; v. 20 presents them from the perspective of their establishment by Christ. Thus, "the Most Holy Place" that is the destiny of God's people is parallel to "the veil" that Christ breaches in order that they might enter that destiny. The parallelism between "by means of the blood of Jesus" and "his flesh" suggests that the preposition before "the veil" should be repeated before "his flesh" — "through the veil, that is, through his flesh."[27] The Greek preposi-

---

who argue that the "veil" represents Christ's "flesh" in 6:20 as well as in 10:20. While he was on earth, Christ's "flesh" was "the veil" that "hid" God, but when he passed through his flesh by his death it revealed the way to God (Attridge, 286-87; Johnson, 257; and esp. Dahl, "A New and Living Way," 405; cf. Bénétreau, 2:111). Westcott, 319-20, describes, but then rejects, this view. The pastor, however, provides no clue that would enable his hearers to identify the "veil" of 6:20 with Christ's flesh. Furthermore, the "veil" not only hid but blocked entrance into God's presence. It was typified by the Mosaic Tent (9:3) and thus existed before the incarnation.

26. εἰς τὴν εἴσοδον ("into the entrance," v. 19) parallels ὁδὸν πρόσφατον καὶ ζῶσαν ("a way new and living," v. 20); τῶν ἁγίων ("of the Most Holy Place," v. 19) parallels διὰ τοῦ καταπετάσματος ("through the veil," v. 20), and ἐν τῷ αἵματι Ἰησοῦ ("by the blood of Jesus," v. 19) parallels [διὰ] τῆς σαρκὸς αὐτοῦ ("[through] his flesh," v. 20). In addition to Young, "Τοῦτ' ἔστιν," 202; Otfried Hofius, "Inkarnation und Opfertod Jesu nach Hebr 10, 19f," in Der Ruf Jesu und die Antwort der Gemeinde: Festschrift Jeremias, ed. E. Lohse (Göttingen: Vandenhoeck & Ruprecht, 1970), 132-43; and J. Jeremias, "Hebräer 10:20: τοῦτ' ἔστιν τῆς σαρκὸς αὐτοῦ," ZNW 62 (1971): 131. See Lane, 2:275-76j, and Koester, 443-44.

27. Hofius, "Inkarnation und Opfertod," 132-43; Jeremias, "τοῦτ' ἔστιν," 131. Cf. Spicq, 2:316 and Young, "Τοῦτ' ἔστιν," 202. διά ("through" or "by," when followed by a noun in the genitive) is the preposition in question.

tion, like the English "through," can be used both locally and instrumentally. It can refer to passing "through" a place. It can also describe the means "through" which something is done. Thus while "through the veil" is local, "through his flesh," in parallel with "by the blood of Jesus," describes the means by which Christ has "inaugurated" a "new and living way" through the veil.[28] Together "blood" and "flesh" (cf. 2:14) describe the earthly obedience, suffering, and self-offering by which Christ has opened the way to God. Nevertheless, as noted above, the pastor has deliberately compacted this expression for effect, utilizing the ambiguity of the preposition "through," and closely identifying the means by which Christ has provided entrance into God's presence with the barrier that separated humanity from God. When the faithful hearers of today approach God they find no barrier — only the incarnate, now exalted High Priest mentioned in the next verse. This expression may be "a daring, poetical touch," to cite Moffatt's oft-quoted phrase, but it is given with intentional pastoral purpose.[29]

The imagery of Christ the High Priest "consecrating" a "way" into the Most Holy Place fits smoothly with Christ the Pioneer, who opens the way for the faithful (11:1-40) to persevere until entrance into the heavenly homeland. Thus this terminology anticipates the urgency of faithful perseverance that dominates the remainder of Hebrews (10:32–12:29).

21 The pastor uses "Great Priest" without an article for the alternate expression "High Priest" in order to let the full eminence and superiority of this Priest impact his hearers.[30] After beginning with "great high priest" in 4:14, this conclusion has the force of understatement. The pastor would have his hearers feel that "Great" is hardly adequate to express the magnitude of the Priest he has described for them. This is the Priest who has provided "such a great salvation" (2:3) by opening the "way new and living" for the members of God's household to enter the divine presence. They enjoy this great privilege because they are part of the household over which he presides (cf. 3:6).

The mission of the Son for the people of God has found its fulfillment

---

28. For two different uses of the same preposition in close proximity, see the comments above on 9:11-12 and the examples there given. The fact that the second διά ("through") must be supplied before τῆς σαρκὸς αὐτοῦ ("his flesh") causes hesitation before giving it a different significance (Young, "Τοῦτ' ἔστιν," 100-104). Yet on any interpretation "through his flesh" cannot have the literal local sense of "through the veil" (cf. Attridge, 286). The difference in objects is also significant — "veil" or "curtain" is a place that can be passed through; "flesh" is not.

29. Moffatt, 143.

30. See the LXX of Lev 21:10 and Num 35:25, 28, where it uses this more literal ἱερεὺς μέγας ("great priest") instead of ἀρχιερεύς ("high priest"). Westcott, 321. See the comments on 4:14.

in this "Great Priest." The intervening chapters have shown how the one called "Son over the House" of God in 3:6 has become the "Great Priest" over that "House."[31] God has spoken his final word in the eternal Son by providing salvation through the incarnate, obedient Great Priest now seated at his right. Thus, as Great Priest God's Son becomes "heir of all things" (1:2) and brings the other members of God's House into "glory" (2:10). What privileges could association with the powerful households of this world, however influential in unbelieving society, afford in comparison to this?[32] How urgent that the members of the divine household take advantage of what is theirs lest they become separated from this glorious "House" (cf. 3:6, 14) and lose the privileges it affords. For the members of this household the eternal Son who has become such a Priest is the most important reality that directs the course of their lives. Thus, it was most fitting that this Priest should be the main point of the pastor's sermon (8:1-2).

As we have seen, the pastor both introduces and concludes his exposition of Christ's high priesthood with exhortations to persevere (4:14; 10:23) and to draw near (4:15a; 10:22). However, returning full circle to consideration of the "house of God" enables him to cap this concluding exhortation with a now-strengthened reprise of his earlier concern for mutual encouragement (cf. 10:24-25 with 3:13-14). It is only as part of God's household and in union with its other members that God's people can draw near and persevere. Therefore, it is both the natural expression of their filial bond in Christ and vital for the well-being of the whole that each be concerned for the perseverance of the others. Even as the pastor would sever his hearers from the rebellious "house" in the wilderness (3:7-19; 8:8; cf. Jer 31:1), so he would have them persevere as God's faithful "house," soon to be epitomized by the obedient of 11:1-40. If participation in God's house entails the privileges of 10:19-25, separation exposes one to the dire consequences of 10:26-31.

22 Our "Great Priest" over God's house has provided access into the very presence of God. Thus, it is only appropriate that the pastor begin his exhortation by urging his hearers to "draw near." Such regular and continuous "drawing near" through prayer and worship is vital because life in God's presence is the essence, means, and end of their existence as the people of God.[33] Their present continuous drawing near (4:16; 7:25; cf. 11:6) is the

31. There is no reason to take God's "House" in 10:21 as anything other than what it was in 3:6 (Weiss, 527; Bénétreau, 2:111): the whole people of God for whom Christ is High Priest (cf. Westcott, 321). *Pace* Spicq, 2:316, the "House of God" is not a reference to the heavenly Sanctuary.

32. "Identifying the community with 'the house of God' (10:21) also offers listeners the dignity of belonging to God's own household in a society dominated by prestigious households" (Koester, 449).

33. Lane, 2:286-87. Dahl, "A New and Living Way," 408, is correct to emphasize

472

means of perseverance until they enter his presence finally and forever (12:25-29).

The manner in which God's people are invited to "draw near" is described by two prepositional phrases: "with true heart" and "in fullness of faith." The means of approach, by two closely related perfect participles: "having our hearts sprinkled from an evil conscience" and "having our body washed with pure water."[34] As the hearers have already seen in relation to the wilderness generation, an "evil heart" is by definition a heart of "unbelief" that "turns away" from the living God in disobedience (3:12). The "true" heart is not only sincere. It is attuned to God and ready to obey him.[35] It is a heart that has been examined by the word of God (4:12-13); a New Covenant heart upon which God has written his laws (Jer 31:33). Thus, the person with a "true heart" is characterized by the "fullness of faith" or the "full assurance (conviction) of faith."[36] Such people live with a robust confidence in God's promise for the future and sturdy reliance on his power for sustenance in the present. The people of the wilderness generation were completely devoid of faith. The soon-to-be-described faithful (11:1–12:3) live by the "fullness of faith." Such "fullness of faith" is based on the proven faithfulness of God and results in obedient surrender to his gracious purposes.[37] The pastor urges his hearers to "draw near" to God with such obedient confidence and singleness of purpose.

The pastor describes the means by which one can thus approach God with two perfect participles that are permissive middles, "having the heart sprinkled from an evil conscience" and "having the body washed with pure water." The perfect tense refers to a past act of purification that remains valid and enables the worshiper to enter God's presence. As we would expect, the pastor uses the language of the Old Covenant. "Sprinkling" from an "evil conscience" recalls what he has said contrasting the effectiveness of Christ's sacrifice with the sprinkled blood of animal sacrifices.[38] The washing of the

---

that this "drawing near" includes both private and community worship. Hebrews gives no indication, however, that the primary reference is to approaching God through the eucharist.

34. The articles τάς ("the") before καρδίας ("hearts") and τό ("the") before σῶμα ("body") suggest the possessive: "our hearts," "our body."

35. Lane, 2:276n.

36. Rissi, *Theologie*, 99. It makes little difference whether one translates πληροφορία "fullness" (Lane 2:276o) or "full assurance" (Ellingworth, 523).

37. Cf. Westcott, 322; George Guthrie, 343; Lane, 2:286. "If πληροφορία τῆς ἐλπίδος [6:11, "fullness of hope"] is the goal of the Christian, πληροφορία πίστεως ["fullness of faith"] is the condition or means of it" (MacRae, "Heavenly Temple," 193).

38. With Heb 9:14 compare Heb 9:19, Num 19:13, and Ps 50:9. Rissi, *Theologie*, 99.

"body" requisite to entrance into the true Most Holy Place echoes the fact that Aaron had to "wash all his body with water" (Lev 16:4) before entering its earthly prototype.[39] Yet the all-effective sacrifice of Christ has moved this language from the realm of ritual purification to the sphere of personal transformation. The pastor finds appropriate vocabulary in Ezekiel's promise of inner cleansing (Ezek 36:25-27), a passage closely related to Jeremiah's New Covenant promise (Jer 31:31-34 cited in Heb 8:7-13; 10:15-18).[40] Ezekiel promised that God would "sprinkle" them "from all their iniquity" with "pure water" and give them a "new heart." Compare the way in which Hebrews speaks of "hearts sprinkled from an evil conscience" and bodies washed "with pure water."[41]

Thus, the contrast between "heart" and "body" is no contrast between reality and ritual. The pastor is talking about an inner transformation of the "heart" expressed in the changed conduct of the "body." The "heart sprinkled from an evil conscience" is not merely a forgiven heart. It is a heart freed "from dead works to serve the living God" (9:14); it is the "true heart" that lives in obedient trust, the "new heart" promised by Ezekiel; the heart upon which God has written his laws as anticipated by Jeremiah

39. With λελουσμένοι τὸ σῶμα ὕδατι καθαρῷ ("having the body washed with pure water") compare λούσεται ὕδατι πᾶν τὸ σῶμα αὐτοῦ ("he shall wash all his body with water") in Lev 16:4. Cf. also Exod 29:4. Dahl, "A New and Living Way," 406-8; Bénétreau, 2:115-16; Moffatt, 146. P. J. Leithart, "Womb of the World: Baptism and the Priesthood of the New Covenant in Hebrews 10.19-22," *JSNT* 78 (2000): 50-51, claims that by giving God's people the right of priestly entrance, this "washing" (which he identifies with baptism) has taken the place of ordination and thus made all God's people priests. In fact, God's people are "now in the position of the High Priest" (Leithart, "Womb of the World," 62). This last statement reveals the fallacy of his argument. It was not the priests of the old order but the high priest whose function typified entrance into the divine presence. Yet Hebrews is clear that Christ is the only sufficient High Priest. Priesthood consists not merely of entrance but of atonement and mediation.

40. Rissi, *Theologie,* 100; cf. Attridge, 289.

41. Compare the underlined wording in Heb 10:22 with the underlining in Ezek 36:25-26a.

Heb 10:22: προσερχώμεθα μετὰ ἀληθινῆς καρδίας ἐν πληροφορίᾳ πίστεως ῥεραντισμένοι τὰς καρδίας ἀπὸ συνειδήσεως πονηρᾶς καὶ λελουσμένοι τὸ σῶμα ὕδατι καθαρῷ

("Having hearts sprinkled from an evil conscience and having bodies washed with pure water").

Ezek 36:25-26a: 25 καὶ ῥανῶ ἐφ' ὑμᾶς ὕδωρ καθαρόν, καὶ καθαρισθήσεσθε ἀπὸ πασῶν τῶν ἀκαθαρσιῶν ὑμῶν. . . . 26 καὶ δώσω ὑμῖν καρδίαν καινήν

("And I will sprinkle upon you pure water, and you will be purified from all your uncleanness . . . 26 and I will give you a new heart").

(10:16b).[42] The "body" washed with Ezekiel's "pure water" represents the life of obedience that is the expression of a "heart" cleansed from "an evil conscience" and inscribed with God's law (10:15-18).[43] The washed "body" of the faithful is the vehicle of obedience, just as the "body" God prepared for his Son was the context for the Son's faithfulness (10:5-10).[44]

As permissive middles, the perfect participles "having our hearts sprinkled" and "having our bodies washed" describe the work of God in the believer's life made real through human cooperation. Thus, we have translated them, "having allowed our hearts to be sprinkled from an evil conscience and our bodies to be washed with pure water." Many would identify the past act implied by these perfect participles with the hearers' conversion. This identification has led some to suggest that "having the bodies washed with pure water" is a reference to the act of baptism.[45] Although this language may have reminded some of their baptism, it is doubtful that baptism was the pastor's primary referent.[46] He makes no explicit connection with that event.[47] His emphasis is on the present state of his hearers. Although the pastor is addressing the converted, it is clear by his own exhortations that they have not always had the "fullness of faith" he desires for them. The perfect participles indicate that not only having been, but continuing to be, cleansed is prerequisite for entrance into the divine presence. Indeed, these participles share the hortatory character of the main verb, "Let us have hearts

42. "In our particular passage, then, the author would not only say that we need no longer have a bad conscience because of our past sins. He would probably say as well that we have been made free from an evil attitude of mind, a consciousness full of evil inclination" (Dahl, "A New and Living Way," 408). Dahl cites 1 Pet 3:21 as a parallel.

43. Thus the cleansing of "heart" and "body" represents complete cleansing that changes motive, attitude, and behavior. See Bénétreau, 2:116.

44. Rissi, *Theologie*, 99.

45. See Bruce, 255; Attridge, 289; Lane, 2:287; Weiss, 530; Spicq, 3:217; Ellingworth, 523-24; Vanhoye, *Old Testament*, 228; Dahl, "A New and Living Way," 408; and Peterson, *Perfection*, 155. Even on this view, however, the pastor is not distinguishing the "washing" of baptism as an outward Christian ritual from "sprinkling" as inward cleansing (see Spicq, 2:317; Bruce, 255). The two expressions both refer to the "event" of baptism when cleansing was experienced. This approach interprets the clear reference to cleansing in both "sprinkling" and "washing" by the supposed allusion to baptism in "washing" (Bénétreau, 2:114).

46. Rissi, *Theologie*, 100, rightly contends that the text is using OT imagery rather than referring to baptism. See also George Guthrie, 344, 348; Bénétreau, 2:115-16; O'Brien, 367-68.

47. Those who argue for a reference to baptism implicitly acknowledge this fact. They assume that the hearers would have made this connection because they had themselves been baptized (Moffatt, 144; Westcott, 323; Spicq, 2:317; Weiss, 530; Attridge, 289; Lane, 2:287; and Dahl, "A New and Living Way," 406-8).

sprinkled from an evil conscience and bodies washed with pure water." The pastor is urging his hearers to fully appropriate the cleansing provided by Christ so that they can continually "draw near." While this "drawing near" finds clear expression through prayer and worship, it encompasses the entire orientation of the life of faith. Thus, the life characterized by "fullness of faith," to which the pastor is about to turn, is a life of drawing near to God through appropriation of Christ's high-priestly work.[48]

23 Encouragement to persevere follows the invitation to "draw near." The two are intimately related. Drawing near to God through Christ is the means of perseverance. Perseverance is necessary for final entrance into the divine presence at Christ's return (12:25-29). Thus the present practice of drawing near to God reaches its anticipated goal through perseverance.[49] Therefore, the pastor urges his hearers, "Let us continue holding the confession of the hope firm."[50] Perseverance in faithful living is dependent on an adequate grasp of Christ and his sufficiency. As noted in the comments on 3:1 and 4:14, "confession" probably refers to a summary of Christian doctrine that affirmed Christ's sonship and was known and used by the hearers.[51] The pastor's teaching on Christ's high priesthood has reinforced this confession and perhaps contributed to its further development by demonstrating Christ's complete adequacy and unique indispensability for the salvation of the hearers. The sufficiency of what Christ has already done guarantees his return for the full "salvation" (9:28) of those anticipating his arrival. Thus

48. Weiss, 528, sees clearly that the pastor encompasses the whole life of faith within the parameters of "draw near." He is mistaken, however, when he deduces from this fact that the pastor is no longer using "draw near" in terms of priesthood and worship. The opposite is true: the whole life of faith is now enclosed within the context of approach to God through Christ the High Priest. Heb 13:1-17 will show that the life of drawing near to God through faith expressing itself in love is the "sacrifice" of praise that pleases God.

49. Thus, in agreement with Dahl, "A New and Living Way," 409, when the hearers draw near, they partake proleptically of their ultimate entrance.

50. The pastor strengthens the theme of endurance. Compare the following: "If we hold (κατέχω) the boldness and boasting of our hope" (3:6); "If we hold (κατέχω) the beginning of our reality firm until the end" (3:14); "Let us hold (κρατέω) to the confession" (4:14; cf. 6:18); and "Let us continue to hold (κατέχω) the confession of the hope firm" (10:23). There is little more than stylistic difference between κρατέω in 4:14 and κατέχω in this verse (see the comments on 4:14).

51. Thus the usage of ὁμολογία in this passage parallels its usage in 4:14 and draws on the foundation laid in 3:1. See Ellingworth, 525, and Laub, *Bekenntnis*, 10-13. Since, however, the reference to baptism in v. 19 is less than clear, the contention that the pastor is referring to a fixed baptismal confession remains speculative. For those who advocate such a position see, among others, Dahl, "A New and Living Way," 410; G. Bornkamm, "Das Bekenntnis im Hebräerbrief," *Theologische Blätter* 21 (1942): 56-66; Westcott, 323; Spicq, 2:318; and Braun, 313.

this "confession" of Christ's full adequacy is, above all things, an affirmation of trust in that assured "hope" of glory at his return.[52] As such, it is sufficient basis and motivation for the endurance advocated in chapters 11 and 12. The heroes of faith in 11:1-40 persevere in anticipation of this "reward" (11:26). Since, then, this "confession" has doctrinal content, it is better to render the underlying Greek word as an adjective, "firm," rather than as an adverb, "without wavering."[53] The hearers are to continue holding the confession itself with all that it says about the adequacy of Christ "firm," without loss or diminution.[54] They hold it "firm" not merely by verbal affirmation but by drawing daily on Christ's provision and by conducting themselves as those expecting to enjoy the final "hope."

With incisive brevity of expression, the pastor concludes this verse by giving the ultimate motivation for such perseverance in reliance upon God — "faithful is the One who has promised." God himself has promised, backing it with an oath (6:13-20; 7:20-22, 28), and repeatedly proved himself true. The revelation of his faithfulness has reached a climax in the high priesthood of his Son. Thus, God's people have the most certain guarantee that if they persevere they will receive what God has promised. On the other hand, this statement lays a foundation for the warning to follow in 10:26-31: those who turn aside are doing nothing less than denying the faithfulness of God. Fur-

---

52. The pastor is not merely speaking of a "hopeful confession" but of a "confession" that has reference to a specific hope (see Lane, 2:276q; Michel, 347). Ellingworth, 525, takes τῆς ἐλπίδος ("of the hope") as an appositive genitive identifying the content of the confession.

53. Johnson, 259; Attridge, 289; Braun, 313; Weiss, 532, n. 46; Bruce, 256; deSilva, 340; Bénétreau, 2:115-17; and others argue that ἀκλινῆ is an adjective, "firm," agreeing with ὁμολογίαν ("confession") rather than an adverb, "unwaveringly," qualifying κατέχωμεν ("let us continue to hold"). Attridge cites the similar usage of βέβαιος ("firm") in 3:6, 11 and refers to Philo, *Spec. Laws* 2.2; *Heir* 87, 95; *Rewards* 30, where ἀκλινῆ is used as an adjective synonymous with βέβαιος. While the lack of an article before ἀκλινῆ does not require it to be adverbial (*pace* Koester, 445), it does make the adjective predicate. Thus, "hold the confession firm" or "hold the confession unshaken" is a better translation than "the secure confession of hope" (Johnson, 259) or "the confession of hope, the confession that is secure" (deSilva, 340). See Bénétreau's insightful comments (2:115-17). ἀκλινῆ ("firm," "unwaveringly") is used only twice in the LXX (4 Macc 6:7; 17:3) and nowhere else in the NT. However, it is often used by Philo for the immutability of God (*Alleg. Interp.* 2.83; *Confusion* 96; *Names* 176; *Posterity* 23) or the stability of God's friends (*Giants* 49, 54; *Abraham* 170). Lane, 2:288-89, takes ἀκλινῆ as adverbial, qualifying κατέχωμεν ("let us continue to hold"), because he denies the objective sense of ὁμολογίαν ("confession").

54. Such an interpretation does not obligate us to follow Braun, 313, who thinks the author is advocating a rigid adherence to the formulas of a received confession (see the critique in Attridge, 289).

thermore, this emphasis on the faithfulness of God clarifies the relationship between "faith" and "hope." Since "faith" is in a God "who has promised," it is always directed toward the "hope" of what he has promised. Thus, such reliance on God is expressed by living a life of "faithfulness" in anticipation of receiving that "hope." Faithful obedience is the only appropriate response to divine faithfulness.

24 We noted the significance of this third exhortation in the introduction to 10:19-25 (pp. 464-65). It is most appropriate for those who draw near through Christ in anticipation of receiving God's promised reward to encourage one another in the life of love. Thus, the pastor brings these exhortations to a climax with, "Let us give attention to one another for the provoking of love and good works."[55] Such mutual concern, in turn, creates and sustains a community conducive to perseverance in a hostile world. It is only right that those called to give full attention to Christ as all-sufficient Savior and example of perseverance (3:1; 12:2-3) should give such caring attention to God's people. The hearers are, after all, members of the "house of God" over which Christ is both "Son" (3:6) and "Great Priest" (10:21). The pastor once charged them to show mutual concern lest "an evil heart of unbelief" cause them to be separated from that "house" in imitation of the wilderness generation (3:12-14). He now urges them to "give attention to one another for the provoking of love and good works" as those who participate with the faithful of all time (11:1-40) in the glorious fellowship of the people of God (12:22-24).

Translations like the NRSV (cf. RSV; ESV; T/NIV; NASB) are misleading: "Let us consider how to provoke one another to love and good works." The pastor would draw his hearers' attention first to their sisters and brothers rather than to the act of provoking: "Let us give attention *to one another* for the provoking of love and good works" (italics added).[56] "Provoke" adequately expresses the negative connotation of the underlying Greek term.[57] Thus, with intentional irony the pastor underscores his exhortation: as forcefully as some "provoke" others to anger, God's people should "provoke" one another to "love and good works." This love is no mere sentimentality but an orientation of the heart that expresses itself in appropriate action.[58] Such "good works" are the opposite of the "dead works" (9:14) from

55. Here in 10:19-25, where the pastor is urging his hearers to appropriate the benefits of Christ's high priesthood, this exhortation to mutual concern is vital. It would, however, have been rhetorically inappropriate in 4:14-16, where he was whetting their appetites for his teaching on that subject.

56. deSilva, 341.

57. Lane, 2:276s; Koester, 445. See 1 Cor 13:5; Acts 15:39; 17:10. This predominantly negative connotation is valid even if there were occasionally other examples of its positive use (cf. Johnson, 259, citing Xenophon, *Mem.* 3.3.13).

58. Johnson, 259, calls "love and good works" a hendiadys.

which Christ has cleansed the believer. They are works of goodness beneficial and pleasing to those who receive them and appropriate and acceptable in the eyes of God.[59] In 13:1-6 the pastor will describe these works as deeds of brotherly love, hospitality, concern for the suffering, sexual purity, and generosity. The pastor's hearers have practiced such conduct in the past (6:10). He would have them continue to encourage one another in this behavior, for it is the full expression of the community life appropriate for God's people.[60]

25 How do God's people "provoke" each other to such works of love? The pastor answers with two instrumental participles: first, by "not abandoning" the meetings where Christians gather for worship and fellowship; second, by "exhorting" one another. In order to make this long sentence more manageable and to show the relationship of the participles to the previous exhortation we have begun this verse by adding, "We will accomplish this by." Nevertheless, the reader must not forget that these participles share the admonitory force of the exhortation in v. 24: the pastor is urging his hearers not to "abandon" meeting together and to "exhort" one another.

The first, negative concern is prerequisite to the second and positive: those who absent themselves from God's people can do nothing to "provoke one another to love and good works." Thus the pastor begins with, "by not abandoning our [own] assembly." Those who thus "abandon" other believers leave them in the lurch and thus deprive their brothers and sisters of needed support. The temptation to abandon God's people may have been due to fervor dulled through the passage of time, by "neglect" (2:3; cf. 10:32) and "sluggishness" (5:11-14).[61] One need not posit a date late in the first century to account for such loss of enthusiasm. Perhaps the hearers were discouraged because Christ had not yet returned.[62] However, it also appears that disapproval and rejection from an unbelieving society played a significant part in the hesitancy of some to continue their identification with those who believed in Jesus (10:32-34; 12:4-11). The pastor will give examples of those who braved such resistance and persecution in 11:1-40. Whatever the cause, then or now, such abandoning of God's people has tragic results.

---

59. Bénétreau, 2:117. The pastor uses καλός ("good," "beautiful," "appropriate") rather than ἀγαθός ("good"). Westcott, 325, provides an extensive list of references contrasting καλὰ ἔργα ("good," "beautiful," "appropriate works") and ἀγαθὰ ἔργα ("good works").

60. "The totality of Christian conduct willed by God is summarized in these few words" (Bénétreau, 2:117).

61. Weiss, 534, n. 56, cites comparative exhortations in *Did.* 16:2; *Barn.* 4:10; and *Herm. Sim.* 9.6.3, though these sources postdate Hebrews. He also notes similar concerns in Judaism (Str-B 3:743).

62. Bruce, 259.

What were they "abandoning"? The word translated "assembly" is an unusual term that can be used for the process of "assembling" (2 Thess 2:1) or for the group that has assembled, that is, an "assembly" (cf. 2 Macc 2:7).[63] This word is followed by the intensive "ourselves," which can be taken as an objective genitive, "the assembling of ourselves," or a possessive, "our [own] assembly."[64] The latter is more concrete and sharpens the pastor's concern that the hearers regularly identify with the gathering of God's faithful. Some have suggested that "our own" suggests conflict with another assembly, perhaps Jewish or even heretical.[65] There is, however, little else in the context that would sustain such a contrast.[66] The pastor is speaking of the "assembly" that is proper for those who profess faith in Christ. They must not abandon the Christian assembly when it has gathered for worship and for the mutual encouragement enjoined by the pastor. The word "synagogue," to which this word for "assembly" is related, was used with this connotation in the Apostolic and Post-Apostolic Fathers.[67] In addition, by using a word similar to "synagogue" the pastor strengthens his emphasis on the unity of his hearers with God's faithful people of all time. On the other hand, both the noun used here in Hebrews (2 Macc 2:7; 2 Thess 2:1) and its related verb (Mark 13:27; Matt 23:37) are employed by Scripture for the final "assembly"/"assembling" of God's people at the last Judgment. Thus it is an apt designation for the meetings of those who enjoy the end-time blessings brought by Christ and participate in the fellowship of the heavenly city (12:22-24) even as they "see the Day [of Judgment] drawing near."[68] Those who habitually abandon this assembly when it has gathered for worship risk exclusion from the community of the faithful, and thus forfeiture of the ultimate salvation that Christ provides for his own.

63. Cf. BDAG, 382. With the noun ἐπισυναγωγή compare the related verb ἐπισυνάγω in Matt 23:37 (cf. Luke 13:34); Matt 24:31 (Mark 13:27); and Luke 17:37.

64. Ellingworth, 529, notes that ἑαυτῶν could be either "ourselves" in dependence on the previous cohortative, κατανοῶμεν ("let us give attention to"); or "yourselves," in dependence on the following βλέπετε ("you see"). The former, however, is to be preferred, especially since the participles ἐγκαταλείποντες ("abandoning") and παρακαλοῦντες ("exhorting") both qualify the previous verb.

65. Koester, 446, and Spicq, 2:319, suggest contrast with Jewish assemblies; Moffatt, 148, with various heretical groups influenced by the mystery religions. See Wolfgang Schrage, "συναγωγή, ἐπισυναγωγή, ἀρχισυνάγωγος, ἀποσυνάγωγος," TDNT 7:843, nn. 11-15.

66. Cf. Ellingworth, 529; Bruce, 257-58; and Riggenbach, 323, n. 6.

67. Schrage, TDNT 7:840, 4, Compare ἐπισυναγωγή ("assembly") with συναγωγή ("synagogue").

68. Weiss, 533-34. In light of 1:13; 2:5-10; 9:27-28; 10:38-39, there is no reason, pace Eisele, Ein unerschütterliches Reich, 89-90, to understand this approaching "day" as the day of one's death rather than the Day of Judgment. It appears to be the same "Day" for all.

The pastor's concern is urgent because such abandonment has become "the custom" or habit of part of the congregation he is addressing. Instead of such desertion, provoke each other to loving works by "continuing to exhort" one another. The word "exhort," used without a qualifier, encompasses the full range of meaning available for this term — "rebuke," "warn," "encourage," "comfort." The pastor wants his hearers to do for each other what he has done for them in this "word of exhortation" (13:13) with which he has addressed them. They must encourage and warn each other by reminding each other of the sufficiency of Christ and the magnitude of the privileges to be gained or lost by drawing near to God through him.

The privileges now available in Christ (vv. 19-21) are both the guarantee of future blessing and the means of attaining it at Christ's return (9:25-28). Thus it is no surprise that the pastor directs his hearers' attention to this future "hope" as motivation for perseverance and assures them that "the One who has promised" is "faithful" (v. 23). We can feel added urgency in his voice when, at the end of this final exhortation, he urges them to "exhort" one another "all the more as we see the Day approaching." Warning joins hope as motivation for perseverance. The time of full salvation is also "the Day" of judgment.[69] The intensity of their mutual concern should increase as they "see" this day "drawing near." Those who "see" Jesus seated at God's right hand with the eyes of faith (2:9) also see his approaching return with those same eyes.[70] "As you see the Day approaching" provides a smooth transition to the warning that follows in vv. 26-31.

2. You Are More Accountable Because of This High Priest (10:26-31)

26 *For if we persist in willfully sinning after we have received the knowledge of the truth, there no longer remains a sacrifice for sin.* 27 *Instead, there is a certain terrifying prospect of judgment and a fury of fire about to consume the adversaries.* 28 *Anyone who has set aside*

---

69. It was common in early Christianity to use expressions like "the Day" (1 Thess 5:4; 1 Cor 3:13), the "Day of God" (2 Pet 3:12; Rev 16:14), or the "Day of the Lord" (1 Cor 1:8; 5:5; 1 Thess 5:2; 2 Thess 2:2; 2 Cor 1:14; 2 Pet 3:10) in reference to the Judgment. Such usage had OT precedents (cf. Amos 5:18-20; 8:9-14; Isa 2:12-22; Zeph 1:12-18; Joel 1:15; 3:14; Zech 14:1). ἐγγίζω, the verb used here for "drawing near," occurs in Rom 13:12 of "the Day," in Jas 5:8 of the Lord's second coming, and in 1 Pet 4:7 of the "end of all things." Cf. Luke 21:8, 20, 28.

70. Bruce, 259; Spicq, 320, and others think that the pastor may have been referring to certain ever-more-visible signs of the end, like the persecutions described in Jesus' Olivet Discourse or the impending destruction of Jerusalem. Westcott, 326, goes so far as to say, "The beginning of the Jewish war was already visible to the Hebrews." The pastor, however, provides no clear reference that would substantiate these speculations.

the law of Moses dies without mercy on the basis of two or three wit-
nesses. 29 Of how much worse punishment do you think any person
will be considered worthy who has trampled under foot the Son of
God, accounted the blood of the covenant by which he was sanctified
profane, and insulted the Spirit of grace? 30 For we know the one who
has said, "Vengeance is mine, I will repay," and again, "God will vin-
dicate his people." 31 It is a terrifying thing to fall into the hands of the
living God.

The mention of foreboding judgment in 10:25 has ushered those the pastor addresses into the dire warnings of this section. While this warning passage reminds us of 6:4-8, it plays a significantly different role.[1] That earlier warning was tailored to rouse the hearers from lethargy so that they would grasp the pastor's teaching on Christ's high priesthood. The pastor has now instructed them in the full sufficiency of their High Priest. This he did in 7:1–10:18 when he served them the "solid food" (5:12, 14) of the mature. His summary in 10:19-22 boiled these benefits down for easy digestion. Thus, the pastor raises the alarm lest his hearers abandon the now-explained salvation provided by Christ's priesthood. The urgency of his concern has increased in direct proportion to the way in which the magnitude of this provision has become clear: there is no other way of salvation if one abandons the all-sufficient sacrifice of Christ. This different purpose is reflected in the pastor's use of participles. The earlier warning began with four substantive participle phrases describing the privileged people of God (6:4-5).[2] Those privileges have been made patently clear in the intervening chapters. Thus the pastor climaxes this concluding warning with three such phrases describing the enormity of the offense perpetrated by those who abandon Christ and the privileges he bestows (v. 29).[3]

Furthermore, the pastor demonstrates his urgency by exchanging the

---

1. Note the parallels with 6:4-8. Both passages refer to those who have experienced the Christian life (6:4-5; 10:26) and then apostatized (6:6; 10:29). Both recognize that renewal is impossible (6:4, 6; 10:26), for the curse of the covenant is imposed on the apostates (6:8; 10:27). See Lane, 2:291.

2. τοὺς ἅπαξ φωτισθέντας ("those who have once been enlightened"); γευσαμένους τε γῆς δωρεᾶς τῆς ἐπουρανίου ("and have tasted the heavenly gift"); καὶ μετόχους γενηθέντας πνεύματος ἁγίου ("and have become partakers of the Holy Spirit"); καὶ καλὸν γευσαμένους ῥῆμα θεοῦ δυνάμεις τε μέλλοντος αἰῶνος ("and have tasted the good word of God and the powers of the coming age").

3. ὁ τὸν υἱὸν τοῦ θεοῦ καταπατήσας ("the one who has trampled under foot the Son of God"); καὶ τὸ αἷμα τῆς διαθήκης κοινὸν ἡγησάμενος ("and accounted the blood of the covenant common"); καὶ τὸ πνεῦμα τῆς χάριτος ἐνυβρίσας ("and insulted the Spirit of grace").

impersonal speech of 6:4-8 ("if they fall away") for the intensely personal: "For if we" who have this experience of God's blessing and knowledge of his truth "persist in willfully sinning."[4] If rejection or acceptance of that which anticipated fulfillment in Christ could lead to ultimate loss (3:7–4:11) or result in eternal blessing (11:1-40), how much more surely will the rejection of the fulfillment itself have eternal consequences.

The pastor may use this appeal to fear followed by words of encouragement (10:32-34) in accord with the rhetorical practices of his day as described in various ancient sources.[5] However, his warnings are more than empty rhetoric. The sufficiency of Christ is real, and the consequences of abandoning Christ's provision are tragic. The pastor recounts these realities because they provide valid and compelling motivation for perseverance. He has no intention of establishing norms for church discipline whereby a congregation could discern and thus excommunicate an apostate. Nor does he wish to cause sensitive believers anxiety over the possibility that they have irrevocably fallen. The apostate whom he is describing would be unmoved by his warnings (see on v. 29 below).

Verse 26a is a conditional genitive absolute, "For if we persist in willfully sinning after we have received the knowledge of the truth." Verses 26b-27 set forth the consequences of persistence in willful disobedience. Verses 28-29 support these consequences by contrasting the lesser punishment of one who rejected the law of Moses with the greater of one who repudiates Christ. The pastor adds Scriptural support in v. 30 before concluding with a solemn warning in v. 31.

26a "For if we persist in willfully sinning after we have received the knowledge of the truth" describes the course of action the pastor would have his hearers shun. The term translated "willfully," located at the beginning of the Greek sentence for emphasis, indicates the willing, intentional, involvement of the transgressor (cf. Phlm 14; 1 Pet 5:2). The present tense of "sin" suggests persistent disobedience — "persist in sinning."[6] Furthermore, the pastor is speaking of sin "after we have received the knowledge of the truth." Thus, this sin is intentional, persistent, and informed. In the ancient world both Jews and non-Jews commonly distinguished between intentional and unintentional sin or evil.[7] Thus, despite the opinion of some interpreters, it is an oversimplification to explain this distinction in He-

---

4. Compare "If we neglect . . ." in 2:3.

5. See the comments on 6:4-8 and Thompson, 124.

6. Koester, 451; Bénétreau, 2:119-20; Ellingworth, 532; and many others (cf. Kistemaker, 293). The implied negative with the present conditional participle ἁμαρτανόντων, "sinning," may imply the cessation of action that had been in progress — "Do not continue sinning after receiving. . . ."

7. See Koester, 451, for non-Jewish sources.

brews by the contrast in Num 15:22-31 (cf. Deut 17:12-13) between "unintentional" sin for which sacrifice was available and sin "with a haughty hand" for which it was not.[8] In the first place, Hebrews neither cites Num 15:22-31 nor echoes its terminology.[9] In the second, one did not have to persist in the "sin with a haughty hand" to forfeit the benefits of atonement (Num 15:30). Furthermore, the OT elsewhere provides sacrifices for some intentional sins (Lev 6:1-7). Philo echoes this ambiguity by the way he both affirms and denies atonement for intentional sins in different contexts.[10] These and other sources may be helpful in understanding the general context in which Hebrews discusses this issue of willful or intentional sin. Nevertheless, it is clear that the distinction made by Hebrews must be understood within the context of the pastor's argument rather than as an unadapted derivation from another source. The pastor is speaking of that laxity, drifting, and neglect of both spiritual things (2:1, 3; 5:11–6:1; 6:12) and the Christian community (3:12-13) about which he has been warning his hearers from the beginning. Such activity can no longer be covered with the veil of ignorance or unintentionality. The pastor has exposed it for what it is. His exposition of Christ's high priesthood, the "knowledge of the truth," has shown the seriousness of such neglect by describing the ultimate value of the thing neglected. This neglect is not in itself apostasy. However, persistence in such laxity and neglect can lead to ultimate rejection of Christ and the "great salvation" he provides. Such a rejection would parallel Israel's sin at Kadesh-Barnea. Verse 29 below describes just such a final rejection of salvation. Thus, we can agree that this now-willful persistence in neglect of what Christ has provided — perhaps because of fatigue, the attractions of the unbelieving world, or its hostility — is the polar opposite

8. Spicq, 2:322, is representative of many who take this OT distinction as a primary source for understanding Hebrews.

9. Num 15:22-31 uses ἀκουσίως (15:24, 28, 29) and words from the same root to describe sinning "unintentionally." Compare the ἑκουσίως ("willfully," "intentionally") used in Heb 10:26. However, Numbers describes the opposite of such unintentional sin as sin ἐν χειρὶ ὑπερηφανίας ("with a haughty hand").

10. In *Posterity* 8–11 Philo uses ἑκούσιος/ἀκούσιος to distinguish between sinful acts that are voluntary and involuntary. He contrasts Adam being driven out by God and Cain going out "willingly." Adam received another seed, Seth, showing that involuntary sin could receive healing. For Cain, however, there was no remedy, demonstrating that sin committed with "desire and forethought" (βουλῇ καὶ προμηθείᾳ) incurs woes "forever" (εἰς ἀεί). On the other hand, according to *Spec. Laws* 2.196, the Day of Atonement provides remission for both voluntary and involuntary sins (ἁμαρτημάτων ἑκουσίων τε καὶ ἀκουσίων). Furthermore, in *Spec. Laws* 1.234-38 the voluntary (ἑκούσιος) sins against people in Lev 6:1-7 are equivalent to involuntary sins (ἀκούσιος) against God, because both require the same sacrifice. Cf. also *Unchangeable* 48; *Alleg. Interp.* 3.141; and *Cherubim* 75.

of "drawing near" (v. 22) to God through Christ.[11] The latter leads to perseverance, the former to perdition.

Thus, at this point in the argument of Hebrews, the pastor is not referring primarily to the conversion or baptism of his hearers when he speaks of the time they "received the knowledge of the truth."[12] He is not merely repeating what he said about their "being enlightened" in 6:4. He is using this familiar expression, "the knowledge of the truth" (cf. 1 Tim 2:4; 2 Tim 2:25; 3:7; and Titus 1:1), to encompass all that he has just said about the fully sufficient Christ. He has presented this teaching on Christ's high priesthood so that they would understand the magnitude of the gospel they received when they first believed. The word used for "knowledge" betokens both the grasping and appropriation of what is known.[13] Attention to what the pastor has said has changed the situation of the hearers. All who have listened to the pastor's message recognize the danger of persisting in that now-willful neglect of what Christ has provided. They see the tragic consequences of abandoning the faithful community that lives by his provision. They both share the privilege and bear the responsibility of those who comprehend the truth.

26b-27 The pastor describes the terrible loss suffered by those who repudiate Christ. For them "there no longer remains a sacrifice for sin." As we have seen, the grand symphony in praise of Christ's sacrifice (8:1–10:18) has demonstrated that his self-offering alone provides release from sin and access to God. That symphony concluded just a few verses ago with the ringing affirmation that Christ's all-sufficient sacrifice had done away with any other sacrifice "for sin" (10:18). Thus, those who repudiate what Christ has done are left without remedy, recourse, or hope. The pastor has made this statement most emphatic by beginning the Greek sentence with "no longer" and bringing it to a conclusion with "sacrifice."[14] The plural "for sins" is comprehensive: Christ's sacrifice excludes any other sacrifice for any sin.[15]

We have seen that the assured hope of final salvation (9:28) at Christ's

---

11. Thompson, 208, 211.

12. *Pace* Spicq, 2:322; Ellingworth, 532-33; Weiss, 537-39, and Johnson, 261. Weiss does refer to a baptismal confession of Jesus as the Son now augmented by the author's teaching on Christ's high priesthood.

13. ἐπίγνωσις, "knowledge" (10:26a), is more solemn than γνῶσις and refers to both the intellectual grasp and the experience of the truth. See Ellingworth, 532-33; Attridge, 293.

14. A literal rendering of the Greek word order would be, "No longer for sins remains there a sacrifice."

15. Hebrews uses the plural περὶ ἁμαρτιῶν ("for sins") although the OT usually described the "sin offering" by the singular, περὶ ἁμαρτίας (cf. 10:18). This difference, according to Ellingworth, 533, implies not merely that there was "no further sin offering" but that there was "no further sacrifice to take away sin."

485

return is the hallmark of the faithful and strong motivation for their perseverance. Christ has removed their fear of judgment (2:14-15) and replaced it with joyful, if awe-filled, anticipation of their place in God's "Unshakable Kingdom" (12:22-29). Those who have repudiated Christ, however, have exchanged this blessed hope for "a certain terrifying prospect of judgment." The indefinite "certain" emphasizes the magnitude of this terrible fate.[16] "Prospect" is a better translation than "expectation."[17] This judgment is not merely what they expect. It is what lies before them whether or not they anticipate its arrival.

In Greek v. 27 begins appropriately with the word we have translated "terrifying." Note its use in 12:21 for the terrifying nature of the God who judges from Sinai. In the following clause the pastor uses the imagery of the prophets in general and of Isa 26:11 in particular to make the terror of this judgment all the more palpable: "a fury of fire about to consume the adversaries."[18] The fire of judgment is like a beast, ravenous to devour its prey.[19] In Isa 26:11 the prophet pronounced judgment on God's idolatrous people. Thus, by echoing this prophecy the pastor suggests that repudiation of Christ by those who have embraced him is equivalent to the idolatry of God's ancient covenant people.[20] Those who have thus repudiated Christ have become his "adversaries." They have abandoned the "house" of God on its way to final salvation (3:6, 14; 10:21) and taken their place with the "enemies" to be subjugated under his feet at his return (1:13; 10:13). Their condemnation has been anticipated by the judgment on Korah and those who rebelled against Moses in Num 16:35; 26:10.[21] Johnson has aptly grasped the pastor's intention in these verses: "Those who fear God through obedience need fear noth-

---

16. For the indefinite τις ("a certain") as emphatic see Ellingworth, 534, and compare Acts 8:9 and Jas 1:18.

17. Morris, 108-9; Ellingworth, 534.

18. Note the parallel between the underlined words in "a fury of fire about to devour the enemies" (πυρὸς ζῆλος ἐσθίειν μέλλοντος τοὺς ὑπεναντίους) in Heb 10:27 and "Fury will seize an undisciplined people, and now a fire will devour the enemies" (ζῆλος λήμψεται λαὸν ἀπαίδευτον, καὶ νῦν πῦρ τοὺς ὑπεναντίους ἔδεται) in Isa 26:11. See also Ps 78:5, "will your fury burn like a fire" (ἐκκαυθήσεται ὡς πῦρ ὁ ζῆλός σού) and the reference to the world being consumed "by the fire of [God's] fury" (ἐν πυρὶ ζήλους) in Zeph 1:18; 3:8. God's judgment was commonly associated with "fire" (Matt 3:10-12; 5:22; 7:19; 13:42; 25:41; John 15:6; 1 Cor 3:13; 2 Thess 1:8; 1 Pet 1:7; 2 Pet 3:7; Rev 17:16; 18:8; 20:14).

19. The "fire" has the ζῆλος, "zeal," "ardor," of such an animal. See BDAG, 427, 1. Ellingworth, 535, suggests that, in the phrase "zeal of fire," "of fire" is a genitive of apposition: "zeal that is fire."

20. Cf. Weiss, 539.

21. Lane, 2:293.

ing else (13:6) but those who do not must fear an awesome judge because they have become his 'enemies.'"[22]

28-29 The pastor has described the magnitude of Christ's high priesthood and the resulting salvation that it provides (cf. 2:3). Thus, he can effectively use his beloved less-to-greater argument (2:1-4; 9:13-14) to underscore the magnitude of the punishment due one who has repudiated Christ. Verse 28 gives the lesser case: "Anyone who has set aside the law of Moses dies without mercy on the basis of two or three witnesses." Idolatry was the supreme rejection of the Mosaic law, punishable by death "without mercy" or exception (Deut 13:8) on the authority of "two or three witnesses" (Deut 17:6).[23] The Greek sentence begins emphatically with the participle translated "who has set aside the law of Moses." Just as definitively as Christ "set aside" the Aaronic priesthood (7:18), and just as thoroughly as his sacrifice did away with sin (9:26), so the idolater "has set aside" the law of Moses and severed himself from it.[24] "Anyone" makes this statement comprehensive — it brooks no exceptions. The verse ends with the iterative present "dies" — such idolaters always die.[25] If idolatry can be used as the lesser case, then the greater case, repudiation of Christ, must be equivalent to a total abandonment of God and his provision for salvation, resulting in separation from the household of faith.

Verse 29 presents the greater case — those who repudiate Christ. What could be "worse" than the capital punishment administered according to the Mosaic law? Nothing less than the punishment of eternal loss. The faithful may endure God's formative "discipline" (12:4-11), but final retributive judgment is the fate awaiting the apostate at the last Day.[26] Just as the

---

22. Johnson, 262.

23. Deut 17:2-6 describes the death penalty due to one who breaks the covenant through idolatry. Deut 13:6-10 prescribes the same penalty for one who entices someone else to commit idolatry. The requirement of two or three witnesses is drawn from Deut 17:6; "without mercy" summarizes the instructions of Deut 13:8. The pastor appears to evoke Deut 17:2-6 in its entirety with its prohibition against idolatry (Johnson, 264; Attridge, 295; cf. Westcott, 329).

24. This term (here the participle ἀθετήσας) was often used for rejecting God or his law (Mark 7:9; Luke 7:30; 10:16; John 12:48; Gal 2:21; 1 Thess 4:8; cf. Ezek 22:26). Compare this participle with the related noun ἀθέτησις used in 7:18 for the "abolition" of the "former commandment" and in 9:26 for the "setting aside"/"annulling" of sin.

25. Lane, 2:277dd. Ellingworth, 537, suggests that the present signifies the permanent record of the Scriptural injunction.

26. For τιμωρία ("punishment") as retributive see Aristotle, *Rhet.* 1369B, and the uses in Euripides, *Orestes* 400, 425; Wis 19:13; 2 Macc 6:12, 26; 4 Macc 4:24 (Johnson, 264). Thus, such punishment must not be confused with the παιδεία ("discipline") of Heb 12:7-11 that marks the true children of God. The later is temporal and corrective; the former, final and retributive.

provision of Christ is "better" because it leads to ultimate salvation, so the punishment of those who reject Christ is "worse" because it consists in ultimate perdition. The God by whom such people "will be considered worthy" of eternal retribution is none other than the God who pronounced judgment on the OT idolater.[27] With "do you think" the pastor appeals to his hearers' sense of justice and propriety in support of God's verdict: after hearing 7:1–10:18, could anyone really contest this judgment on those who have rejected Christ and all that he has done to provide entrance into the heavenly homeland?[28] By using the death penalty imposed by the Mosaic law as the lesser part of his argument, the pastor is not denying that the faithfulness or disobedience of OT people had eternal consequences. We have already seen that he believed that God's OT people would be subject to both eternal loss stemming from unbelief (3:7–4:11) and eternal blessedness based on faith (11:1-40). He does not rescind that view here by referring to the punishment for idolatry as death. He merely uses the literal statement of the OT as a basis for substantiating the severity of the apostate's fate.

The pastor allows no ambiguity concerning the magnitude and finality of the repudiation (i.e., of Christ's provision) that he describes here. Thus, the weight of these verses rests on the description of the apostate and his offense at the conclusion of v. 29. The pastor joins three culminative aorist participial phrases with one article to create a comprehensive description of this person: the one "who has trampled under foot the Son of God, accounted the blood of the covenant by which he was sanctified profane, and insulted the Spirit of grace."[29] This description of the apostate from Christ makes "setting aside," the participle used in the lesser case above, however forceful in itself, pale by comparison. The pastor draws on the entire panorama that he has been presenting since the beginning of his sermon. Thus, the first participle echoes all that he has said in the opening chapters of Hebrews about the Son of God, eternal, exalted, and the ultimate agent of both revelation and salvation.[30] This theme continues into chapter 7. The pastor has no more majestic description in his repertoire than the full ex-

27. ἀξιωθήσεται, "will be considered worthy," is a divine passive (Ellingworth, 539). See McKnight, "Warning Passages," 35-36.

28. Ellingworth, 538.

29. ὁ . . . καταπατήσας . . . καὶ . . . κοινὸν ἡγησάμενος . . . καὶ . . . ἐνυβρίσας, "the one who . . . tramples . . . and . . . considers common . . . and . . . insults. . . ." All three participles are, of course, substantive.

30. Weiss (540) contends that "Son of God" must have come from the community's confession because there is nothing that anchors it in the immediate context. This contention, however, is without merit. As noted in the text above, the pastor has prepared for this use of "Son of God" by everything that he has said about the "Son" in previous chapters.

pression, "Son of God."[31] By his repudiation of Christ the apostate "has trampled under foot," and thus shown great disdain for, no one less than the one whom God himself has "exalted" as Savior to the place of all authority at his right hand (1:3; 13; etc.), the very "Son of God."[32] It may be no surprise that the apostate who was previously described as "crucifying the Son of God again" and "exposing him to contempt" (6:6) can also be described as trampling him "under foot."[33] Yet the incongruity of trampling the God-exalted One is meant to shock the hearers and to elicit their repudiation of such Christ-rejection. At the Judgment God will make all such "enemies" who have "trampled" the Son "a footstool" under his feet (1:13, quoting Ps 110:1).[34]

The second participle, "having accounted the blood of the covenant profane," recalls what the pastor has said about Christ's high priesthood, first mentioned in 2:17-18 but more fully introduced in 4:14–5:10. The pastor's grand symphony on the adequacy of Christ's sacrifice in 8:1–10:18 is still resounding in his hearers' ears. It was that sacrifice alone, described as nothing less than "his own blood" (9:14), that has taken away sin, providing access to God and establishing a New Covenant of heart obedience. By repudiating Christ the apostate has "accounted" the very "blood" of Christ that had provided for his salvation, the very "blood" that established the New "Covenant," a "common" or "profane" thing. That is, he has treated Christ's "blood" as if it were no different from any other blood, and thus desecrated it.[35] The pastor makes it clear that this "blood" of Christ was the very blood by which the apostate had been "sanctified" at his conversion, when his sin had been removed and he had been given access to God.[36] The contrast between "common"/"profane" and "sancti-

31. This is only the fourth time the pastor has used the full expression "Son of God" (4:14; 6:6; 7:3). Cf. Johnson, 264.

32. For trampling underfoot as an expression of utter contempt and disdain see esp. Matt 5:13; 7:6 (cf. Mic 7:10; Isa 26:6; Pss 56:2-3; and Dan 8:10). Homer (*Iliad* 4.157) uses this expression for the scorning of oaths, and Plato (*Laws* 714A; *Gorgias* 484A) for disdain toward laws (Johnson, 264).

33. Thompson, 209.

34. Mackie, *Eschatology and Exhortation,* 128.

35. Hebrews' use of κοινός cannot be restricted to the meaning "common" or "ordinary" (Aristotle, *Rhet.* 1355A). The contrast with "by which he was sanctified" shows that it must also include the more specific connotation of "unholy," "desecrated," or "defiled" (Ellingworth, 540-41). κοινός often had this latter significance in Judaism and the NT (*Letter of Aristeas* 315; Josephus, *Ant.* 12.112; Mark 7:2; Acts 10:14, 28; Rom 14:14; Rev 21:17; see Johnson, 265). By considering Christ's blood as nothing more than "ordinary" blood, the apostate has desecrated it. The translation "profane" best encompasses both "common" and "defiled."

36. The aorist tense of ἡγιάσθη ("sanctified") shows that the pastor is referring to a definite past event (Westcott, 331), the initial act by which the hearers were cleansed

fied" is intentionally crafted to intensify the shock administered by the previous statement.[37] The pastor wants his hearers to feel revulsion and thus to respond with, "Oh no, that is not us, we are not going to be like that."

Thus, the first of these participles, "has trampled," describes the apostates' rejection of all that the pastor has taught about the eternal, exalted Son of God in the opening chapters of Hebrews. The second, "has considered common," describes all that has previously been said about Christ's priesthood and especially about the sufficiency of his sacrifice in 8:1–10:18. The apostate has rejected both the "divine person" of the Son and "the work of redemption which he has accomplished" through his incarnation.[38] This description of apostasy, however, reaches its climax with "has insulted the Spirit of grace." The pastor has been preoccupied with the full sufficiency of Christ. Still, it is clear that he agrees with the rest of the NT in affirming the gift of the Spirit as the special privilege bequeathed to the faithful through the work of Christ. At the heart of his earlier description of the converted, he presented believers as those who "have become partakers of the Holy Spirit" (6:4; cf. 2:4). Thus, rejection of the Spirit is so serious because it is repudiation of the presence and power of God in one's own life. Such rejection is tantamount to kicking God out.[39] The word rendered "insulted" means to show haughtiness or arrogance toward someone.[40] The pastor's emphasis is not so much on the offense taken by the Spirit as on the brazen insolence of the apostate.[41] The apostate has rejected with haughty disdain the very One who is not only gracious but has administered the "grace" of God to his life.[42]

---

from sin and thus given access to God through Christ at their conversion. Cf. Morris, 107. While their conversion was no doubt accompanied by and included baptism, there is no reason, *pace* Weiss, 540, to think that the pastor is referring specifically to baptism as distinct from conversion as a whole. *Pace* Theissen, *Untersuchungen,* 60-61 (cf. Hughes, 423; Montefiore, 179), the aorist tense makes reference to the eucharist unlikely.

37. Lane, 2:294, calls this contrast "rhetorically forceful."

38. Hughes, 422-23.

39. If possible, what the pastor is describing is even worse than the sin against the Holy Spirit described in Matt 12:31-32; Mark 3:28-30; and Luke 12:10, because the person he is describing has actually been a "partaker of the Holy Spirit" (6:4).

40. BDAG, 342, translates ἐνυβρίζω as "insult," "outrage." It refers to the manifestation of ὕβρις — "arrogance," "insolence," "pride" — toward someone. While this verb is not used elsewhere in the NT, such ὕβρις is characteristic of those who assert themselves against God's will (1 Macc 3:20; 2 Macc 8:17; 3 Macc 6:12; cf. Rom 1:30; 1 Tim 1:13) and deserve his judgment (Prov 16:18; cf. Isa 13:11). Even the Greeks recognized the propriety and indeed the inevitability of punishment upon those who showed ὕβρις, especially toward the gods (see references in Koester, 453).

41. "The emphasis is not on the Spirit becoming 'outraged' (NRSV) but on the sinner's *hybris* or outrageous behavior (NIV; NAB[2]; NJB; REB)" (Koester, 453).

42. "One cannot make a more striking contrast than the contrast between ὕβρις

The pastor shocked his hearers when he spoke of one who "has trampled" the exalted Son of God. He increased the voltage when he described this person as having considered the very "blood" of Christ by which he had been "sanctified" as "common" or "unclean." It is almost more than his hearers can bear when he adds that this person has treated the Holy Spirit, the very presence and power of God in the believer's life, the gracious administrator of God's grace, with arrogant insolence. One can almost see the pastor's hearers raising their arms to hide their faces from the blinding judgment of God on such a person.

It is misleading to take the aorist participles we have translated "has trampled," "has considered," and "has insulted" as summarizing a persistent attitude.[43] They describe the climax to which uncorrected laxity and neglect of God's provision in Christ will lead. Disassociation from the worshiping assembly of God's people is both a symptom and a further cause of such neglect. Those who persist in such laxity and neglect due to inertia, the threats or promises of an unbelieving society, or any other reason, are headed for such a destiny. They may approach it gradually, but, if unchecked, they will come to the point of definitively, willfully, and indeed probably publicly repudiating the One whose cleansing power they once experienced. Thus, with this description of the apostate the pastor would dissuade any of his hearers from following this path lest they suffer the dire consequences awaiting them at its end. Let all who are aroused to concern by the force of his warning take heed, yet let them also take comfort. Those in whom the pastor's words evoke concern have not come to such a destiny, for the ears of those who have arrogantly insulted the "Spirit of grace" are deaf to his pleas. The two quotations from Deuteronomy in v. 30 appropriately reinforce the pastor's warnings because they pronounce God's judgment, heretofore reserved for idolaters and covenant breakers, on those who repudiate Christ.

30 This judgment on those who repudiate Christ is in accord with the holy character of God established by the history of his dealings with his people. The pastor reminds his hearers that they know this God and his holy character when he says, "We know the one who has said. . . ." He substantiates the holy character of God by drawing two quotations from the Song of Moses, found in Deut 32:1-43 (cf. Heb 1:6). Moses sings this Song to the covenant people of God as they are about to enter the Promised Land. The number of allusions to this passage in the NT attests its popularity in early

---

["hubris," "arrogance"] and χάρις ["grace"]" (Spicq, 2:325; cf. Mackie, *Eschatology and Exhortation*, 128; O'Brien, 379-80). The genitive "of grace" expresses that which comes to expression through the Spirit (Westcott, 331; cf. "spirit of slavery" in Rom 8:15, and esp. "Spirit of wisdom" in Eph 1:17).

43. *Pace* Lane, 2:294.

Christianity.[44] As noted in comments on 1:6 above, this Song also appears as the second "Ode" attached to the Psalter in the LXX. In this Song Moses first reminds the people of God's great grace toward them. He then predicts God's judgment on their future unfaithfulness. He concludes by proclaiming God's ultimate vindication of his people through the pronouncement of judgment on their enemies who reject God. Thus, this Song is admirably suited to substantiate God's holy character. The pastor draws his first supporting quotation from God's declaration of judgment on the nations who have rejected him in Deut 32:35a: "Vengeance is mine, I will repay." This reading differs from both the LXX and the received Hebrew text, though it is attested by Paul in Rom 12:19 and supported by several of the Targums.[45] In this succinct pronouncement God both affirms his right to judge the ungodly and promises that he will indeed do so. God will judge those who turn away from Christ once for all as he did the idolatrous nations who refused to acknowledge him.[46]

Just as the pastor used the phrase "and again" to separate Isa 8:17 and Isa 8:18 in Heb 2:13a-b, so he separates Deut 32:35a from Deut 32:36a in Heb 10:30a-b. "Vengeance is mine, I will repay" (Deut 32:35a in Heb 10:30a); "and again," "The LORD will judge/vindicate his people" (Deut

44. For other references to the Song of Moses see Rom 10:19 (Deut 32:21); 1 Cor 10:20, 22 (echoing 32:16-17); Rom 15:10 (32:43); Phil 2:15 (echoing 32:5); Heb 1:6. Cf. Deut 32:28 in CD 5:17. For use in Jewish apologetic see Justin, *Dial.* 20, 119, 130. Bruce, 264, nn. 149, 150.

45. Compare "Vengeance is mine, I will repay" (ἐμοὶ ἐκδίκησις, ἐγὼ ἀνταποδώσω, Heb 10:30; Rom 12:19) with "On the day of vengeance I shall repay" (ἐν ἡμέρᾳ ἐκδικήσεως ἀνταποδώσω, Deut 32:35 LXX) and "Vengeance is mine, and recompense" (לִי נָקָם וְשִׁלֵּם; Deut 32:35 MT). Cf. J. Proctor, "Judgement or Vindication? Deuteronomy 32 in Hebrews 10:30," *TynBul* 55 (2004): 76. The emphasis in Hebrews and Romans is on the initial ἐμοί ("mine") — "mine" is vengeance (Spicq, 2:325). *Targum Onqelos* ("Before me is punishment, and I will dispense it"); *Targum Neofiti* ("Vengeance is mine, and I am he who will repay"); and *Targum Pseudo-Jonathan* ("Punishment is before me, and I will repay") support the reading found in Hebrews and Romans. *Fragmentary Targum* is closer to the MT: "Vengeance and retribution are his" (Proctor, "Judgement or Vindication?" 77).

46. ἐκδίκησις "vengeance," is used for exacting vengeance for a wrong and is often associated with God (Exod 7:4; 12:12; Num 31:2; 33:4; Judg 11:36; 2 Sam 4:8; Pss 17:47; 93:1; Luke 18:7-8; Acts 7:24). ἀνταποδίδωμι ("I will repay") and its related noun ἀνταπόδοσις ("repaying") are often used for God's "paying back" the punishment due wrongdoers (Lev 18:25; Deut 32:6, 41, 43; Judg 1:7; Pss 7:4; 30:23; 40:10). Johnson, 266. Randall C. Gleason, "The Eschatology of the Warning in Hebrews 10:26-31," *TynBul* 53 (2002): 97-120, has argued that the author of Hebrews is encouraging his hearers to leave Jerusalem so that they will not suffer the judgment that God will bring in its soon-to-occur destruction by the Romans. For a definitive refutation of his position see Mackie, *Eschatology and Exhortation,* 129-32.

32:36a in Heb 10:30b). The first Isaiah quotation duplicated 2 Sam 22:3; the second Deuteronomy quotation duplicates Ps 135:14. Thus, by this separation the pastor emphasizes the second quotation and allows it to speak with a double voice.[47] Both Deut 32:36a and Ps 135:14 attest the fact that "The LORD will judge/vindicate his people." The Hebrew reads, "The LORD will vindicate his people." The larger context makes it clear that the LXX should be understood in the same way even though the Greek word used can mean either "vindicate" or "judge."[48] This verse from Deuteronomy and its duplicate in the psalm do not declare that God will "judge" his people but that he will "vindicate" them by bringing judgment on their enemies. Despite the opinion of many commentators and translators, the original intention of these OT passages is well suited to its context in Hebrews and admirably serves the pastor's purpose. First, the pastor would establish the holy character of God. Such holiness consists in both God's judgment on the wicked ("Vengeance is mine, I will repay") and his vindication of the righteous ("The LORD will vindicate his people"). Vindication is the necessary corollary of judgment. Second, within this context "The LORD will vindicate his people" continues the threat initiated by "Vengeance is mine, I will repay." The pastor has been warning his hearers that abandoning Christ means exclusion from the people of God. Thus, God's vindicating his own will mean judgment on those who have severed their relationship with his people by turning from Christ.[49] At the same time, this second quotation anticipates the words of comfort to follow in vv. 32-34 and the exhortation to persevere in vv. 35-39. Those who persevere despite the opposition of the unbelieving world can take comfort in the fact that God will vindicate them. Thus this second quotation from the Song of Moses both clinches the pastor's warning and anticipates the encouragement to follow. As is so often the case in Hebrews, the pastor prepares his hearers for what is to come even while he concludes his present argument (cf. the comments on 10:25 above).[50]

47. See Ellingworth (542), who confirms that "and again" puts emphasis on the second quotation and especially on "his people." Thompson (209) notes that the author uses "and again" to join the first lines of Deut 32:35 and Deut 32:36 for rhetorical effect.
48. Although κρίνω usually means "judge"; Pss 7:9b; 25:1; 34:24; 42:1; 53:3; 71:4; 81:3; 134:14 (Deut 32:36); Prov 31:8, 9; and Isa 51:22 attest the meaning "vindicate." Cf. also T. Jud. 24:6 and Proctor, "Judgement or Vindication?" 71-73.
49. Note Westcott, 332: "The two quotations establish two facts with regard to the divine judgment. It will carry with it strict requital; and it will extend to all those who stand to God as His people." We would modify the last part of this statement as follows: "and it will fall on all those who abandon the people of God."
50. Thus, we agree with both Swetnam and Proctor (cf. also Hughes, 425) that κρίνει should be understood as "vindicate" rather than "judge" — but for different reasons. See J. Swetnam, "Hebrews 10,30-31: A Suggestion," Bib 75 (1994): 388-94; and

31   The pastor could not have concluded this warning with a stronger assertion of "the awesome majesty and holiness of the living God."[51] Before beginning his Grand Exposé of Christ's high priesthood, he warned his hearers that they were fully accountable before God because they were completely and absolutely exposed by his "living and active" word (4:12-13). He has now shown that the full sufficiency of Christ their High Priest is the content of that divine word. Thus, by explaining the sufficiency of Christ, he has enabled God's word to do its work — they now have no excuse. If those so exposed reject God's "living word," they will experience that most "terrifying thing" — falling "into the hands of the living God." Just a few verses after the above quotations from the Song of Moses (Deut 32:1-43) God referred to himself as the one who "lives" and thus, in contrast to the idols, brings judgment on those who repudiate him (Deut 32:40-41). Those who have rejected Christ do not stand before human witnesses (v. 28) but before the "living God," from whose judgment there is no appeal.

The pastor begins this concluding verse in Greek with the same word he used at the beginning of v. 27 — "terrifying." The prospect of judgment described in v. 27 was so "terrifying" because it meant "falling into the hands of the living God."[52] What could be more terrible for the person who has fallen "away from the living God" (3:12) by rejecting God's full provision in

---

Proctor, "Judgement or Vindication?" 65-80. When we recognize that Deut 32:36a both clinches the pastor's warning and anticipates his encouragement, it is unnecessary to follow Swetnam's suggestion that the words of comfort begin with "and again" at the middle of v. 30 instead of at the beginning of v. 32. His argument that φοβερόν ("terrifying") at the beginning of v. 31 should be taken positively as "awesome" is unconvincing. Proctor uses the first person plural in vv. 26 ("if we sin") and 30 ("we know") to disassociate these verses from the "impersonal" way of speaking in vv. 27-29 so that he can interpret v. 30 in light of the comfort in vv. 32-34. Such disassociation is hardly permissible. Certainly, "if we sin willfully" in v. 26 implies that there will be a "certain fearful prospect of judgment" (v. 27) *for us*. For further criticism of Proctor, see Mackie, *Eschatology and Exhortation,* 128-29. The approach we have advocated necessitates neither rearrangement nor unnatural division of the text. The fact that the Targums understand Deut 32:36a as vindication substantiates the interpretation given above as much as it supports either Swetnam or Proctor. It is questionable, however, whether we can argue that the Targums represent an interpretive tradition also shared by Hebrews, since they simply take the OT text at its face value and interpret it in a literal, forthright fashion. Attridge, 296, is clearly unjustified when he says: "As usual in Hebrews, the original context does not determine the application of the text."

51. Lane, 2:296.

52. φοβερόν ("terrifying") at the beginning of v. 31 forms an inclusion with the same word, φοβερά, at the beginning of v. 27 (Weiss, 542). The terror of God's judgment introduced in v. 27 is now fully described. This term occurs nowhere else in the NT, except in Heb 12:21 (cf. Westcott, 332).

Christ than to "fall into" this same God's "hands" and thus be completely at his disposal?[53] It is true that falling into God's hands could be used to describe throwing oneself upon his mercy (2 Sam 24:14; 1 Chr 21:13; cf. Sir 2:18). However, those who have repudiated Christ have cut themselves off from God's great, all-sufficient mercy in his Son. To fall into God's hands after rejecting his mercy is, indeed, the most "terrifying" thing. The apostate finds only retribution in the place where the penitent hopes for mercy.[54] What more could the pastor say to bring the consequences of repudiating Christ vividly before his hearers' eyes? Thus he has come to the point where warning must be balanced with encouragement lest they fall into despair. It takes both warning and encouragement to sustain perseverance.

When the pastor said "if we sin willfully" in v. 26, he made it clear that apostasy was a possibility for his hearers. Nevertheless, since v. 28 he has been speaking impersonally of the one who apostatized under the law of Moses and the one who does the same under the New Covenant. He wants his hearers to recoil with "we have not fallen into that situation" and to rebound in the opposite direction. Thus, in vv. 32-39, the concluding section of this exhortation, he reassures them that he is confident they have not apostatized (vv. 32-34) and encourages them to join the examples of faithfulness and endurance soon to be described in chapter 11 (vv. 35-39). His is no counsel of despair but an urgent exhortation that they grasp the hope set before them.

3. Pursue the Blessing Promised the Faithful (10:32-39)

32 *Remember the earlier days during which, after your enlightenment, you endured a great contest of sufferings.* 33 *You endured this contest, on the one hand, by being made a public spectacle through insults and also tribulations; on the other, by having become partners of those who lived this way.* 34 *For you showed sympathy to the prisoners, and you accepted the seizure of your property with joy, because you were aware that you yourselves have a better reward and one that endures.* 35 *Do not throw away your boldness, which has great reward.* 36 *For you have need of endurance, so that, when you have done the will of God, you might receive the promise.* 37 *For yet in a very little while the coming one will come and will not delay.* 38 *And my righ-*

53. For "falling into the hands of" as coming under the complete power of someone see Judg 15:18; Sir 8:1; Susanna 23; Luke 10:36; cf. Deut 32:39; 2 Macc 6:26; 7:31; and Acts 13:11.

54. Thus, the fact that falling into God's hands usually refers to reliance on his mercy (see Ellingworth, 543) is no evidence that this passage should be interpreted as words of comfort (*pace* Swetnam, "Suggestion," 390). The use of such a phrase to describe the judgment of apostates only emphasizes the terror of their situation.

teous one shall live by faith; but if he should draw back, my soul has no pleasure in him. 39 *We, however, are not of drawing back for destruction but of faith for the preservation of the soul.*

Heb 10:32-39, the third and final part of the pastor's exhortation (10:19-39) linking what follows to the preceding description of Christ's high priesthood, provides a smooth transition to the following description of the heroes of faith (11:1-40). The pastor has urged his hearers to draw near and persevere through the privileges now theirs in Christ (vv. 19-25), and warned them of dire peril if they refuse (vv. 26-31). He now reassures them that he does not believe they belong to the company of those who refuse (vv. 32-35), and thus urges them to occupy their rightful place as part of God's obedient people (vv. 32-39) who endure in and through faithful reliance upon him. He turns their attention to the history of this faithful people in 11:1-40.

In 4:1-11 the pastor urged his hearers to pursue the eternal destiny that had been forfeited by the unfaithful wilderness generation, whose fate was described in 3:7-19. In this passage (10:32-39) he urges them to maintain their identity with the faithful people of God, whose style of life and promised destiny he will describe in 11:1-40. The history of the disobedient wilderness generation was short and without a future. The history of the obedient people of God, on the other hand, stretches from creation (11:3) to consummation (12:25-29) and leads to glorious life in the presence of God through the exalted Jesus (12:1-3). Thus, he would focus their gaze upward on the all-sufficient Christ at God's right hand (8:1-2; 12:1-3) and forward to their heavenly homeland (11:13-16, 26) and ultimate goal (12:25-29). In this way he would encourage them — despite hardship — to endure by relying on the promises and power of God.

32 The pastor follows his dire warning against apostasy in vv. 26-31 with a reminder of his hearers' sterling faithfulness during the "earlier days" right after their conversion.[1] We can sense their deep relief when he tells them that their initial faithfulness suggests that they are not among those who fall away — despite their recent regression, laxity, and neglect of divine things. The pastor's warning was no counsel of despair, but rather his way of awakening them from their sluggishness (5:11-14) lest they fall. He reminds them of the "great contest of sufferings" they endured after their initial conversion. It was natural in the context of the first century for the pastor to

---

1. The aorist verb φωτισθέντες, "having been enlightened," refers "to the saving illumination of the heart and mind mediated through the preaching of the gospel" (Lane, 2:298) at their conversion (cf. 6:4) rather than to their baptism as distinct from the conversion event (Bénétreau, 2:123). This verb is a divine passive — they were "enlightened" by God (Ellingworth, 545).

speak of their sufferings as an athletic "contest." Athletic competition was an important part of the Greek emphasis on excellence of body as well as mind. Furthermore, it was common for contemporary philosophers to liken the virtuous life to an athletic "contest" that required discipline and was shaped by the endurance of suffering.[2] The Stoics, in particular, were fond of using such imagery to describe the pursuit of the good life.[3] Philo and other Jewish writers influenced by the Greek philosophical tradition made abundant use of this athletic metaphor.[4] The ease with which Paul uses the language of sports demonstrates its wide familiarity in popular culture (1 Cor 9:24-27; Phil 1:27; 3:12–4:3; 1 Thess 2:2; 2 Tim 4:6-8). Furthermore, the status given victorious athletes in the contemporary world made this way of speaking a most effective way to encourage a suffering minority by turning their present shame into a badge of honor. By enduring the very abuse and shame heaped on them by an unbelieving world, they win the honor and glory of a victor's crown.[5]

Jewish authors such as the writer of 4 Maccabees had already described those who endured suffering for loving God and rejecting idolatry as victorious athletes (4 Macc 17:11-16).[6] Pagan moralists may have urged the virtuous person to endure hardship in order to perfect character without regard for reward.[7] The pastor, however, and his Jewish predecessors, urged endurance out of devotion for God in anticipation of "incorruptibility in longlasting life."[8] In Hebrews loyalty to Christ has replaced the devotion to the law enjoined by 4 Maccabees as the expression of love for God. Christ alone is the one who has opened the way to an eternal inheritance more glorious than any earthly trophy. He alone gives grace to persevere in this race. The

2. See N. C. Croy, *Endurance in Suffering: Hebrews 12:1-13 in Its Rhetorical, Religious, and Philosophical Context* (SNTSMS 98; Cambridge: Cambridge University Press, 1998), 43, and the references cited in Thompson, 217-18.

3. Epictetus, *Diatr.* 1.24.1; 3.15.1-7; 3.22.51; 3.24.113; 4.4.30; Seneca, *Ep.* 1.7.1; 34.2; 109.6 (cited by Thompson, 217).

4. *Alleg. Interp.* 1.98; 3.14, 72; *Migration* 27; *Sobriety* 65 (cited by Thompson, 217).

5. deSilva, 361-64; Koester, 464-65.

6. Both Hebrews and 4 Macc 17:11-16 use ὑπομονή ("endurance"). Heb 10:32 uses ἄθλησις for "contest." 4 Macc 17:11-16 uses the related ἀθλητής ("prize fighter," "athlete"), ἐναθλέω ("bear up bravely under"), and ἀθλοθετέω ("offer a reward").

7. F. Hauck, "ὑπομένω, ὑπομονή," *TDNT* 4:582. "Where a philosopher would say that true good is discerned by reason, . . . Hebrews would say that it is given through the promises of God and discerned by faith" (Koester, 466).

8. The translation of ἀφθαρσία ἐν ζωῇ πολυχρονίῳ (4 Macc 17:12) in Albert Pietersma and Benjamin G. Wright, eds., *A New English Translation of the Septuagint, and the Other Greek Translations Traditionally Included under That Title* (New York and Oxford: Oxford University Press, 2007), 540.

faithful of old who went on pilgrimage to the eternal City (11:1-40) acknowledged that they were aliens in this sinful world (11:9-10). Thus, their children must endure the shame heaped on aliens and run the race with perseverance in order to win eternal glory (12:1-13).

Hebrews' use of the terms translated "endurance"/"endure" demonstrates the way in which the pastor has adapted the Greek athletic and philosophical tradition for his own purposes. In the Greek OT this word group had the connotation of expectant waiting upon God.[9] In the realm of Greek moral philosophy it described the endurance of hardship and suffering without relief or reward.[10] In Hebrews, however, the faithful endure hardship because they are waiting expectantly for the indescribable reward of God's "Unshakable Kingdom" (12:25-29).

This "contest" was "great" in both intensity and duration.[11] It lasted throughout "the earlier days" and was characterized by many "sufferings" more fully described in the following verses. The words translated "sufferings," "tribulations," and "reproaches" (v. 33) were often used by NT writers to describe the trials of believers.[12] The pastor's concern in the following chapters is that his hearers' initial enthusiasm become the kind of long-term obedience exemplified by the faithful of 11:1-40.

33-34b The four statements in these verses reveal the nature and magnitude of the "sufferings" endured by the hearers after their conversion. In v. 33 the pastor uses two instrumental participles to describe the manner in which his hearers have endured this suffering: "on the one hand, by being made a public spectacle through insults and also tribulations"; "on the other, by having become partners of those who lived this way." In v. 34 he uses two complete clauses: "For you showed sympathy to the prisoners"; "and you accepted the confiscation of your property with joy." These four statements stand in chiastic relationship to one another:[13]

"You endured a great contest of suffering" (v. 32b)

A "on the one hand, by being made a public spectacle through insults and also tribulations" (v. 33a);

B "on the other, by having become partners of those who lived this

9. Hauck, "ὑπομένω, ὑπομονή," *TDNT* 4:584.

10. Hauck, "ὑπομένω, ὑπομονή," *TDNT* 4:582.

11. Westcott, 333; Spicq, 2:328. πολύς in this context has both the connotation of "much," "extensive" (BDAG, 848, 2, a, ℵ) and "great" (BDAG, 849, 3, a).

12. Cf. πάθημα ("suffering"), θλῖπις ("tribulation"), and ὀνειδισμός ("reproach") in 1 Pet 1:6; Jas 1:2, 12; Matt 5:11-12. Weiss, 544, following W. Nauck, "Freude im Leiden: Zum Problem einer urchristlichen Verfolgungstradition," *ZNW* 46 (1955): 68-80, esp. 72, thinks this language representative of an early Christian "persecution tradition."

13. Lane, 2:299.

way" (v. 33b).
B¹ "For you showed sympathy to the prisoners" (v. 34a),
A¹ "and you accepted the seizure of your property with joy" (v. 34b).

The fourth statement (v. 34b) gives specificity to the sufferings directly endured by the hearers as described in the first (v. 33a). The third (v. 34a)
shows how the hearers have identified with suffering believers as stated in
the second (v. 33b). The final statement (v. 34c) shows why they have been
able to endure: "because you were aware that you yourselves had a better
possession and one that endures."

The pastor is not making a distinction between one group of his hearers that suffered for their faith (v. 33a) and another that sympathized with the
sufferers (v. 33b).¹⁴ A straightforward reading of the text suggests that those
who sympathized with their imprisoned comrades also suffered by losing
their property. The pastor has another reason for mentioning both suffering
and identification with those who suffer — he wishes to emphasize the latter.
Throughout this sermon he has been concerned that his hearers not fail to
identify with the people of God. Their lethargy and apparent fear of disfavor
from the surrounding world has weakened this identification to the point
where some are no longer participating in the worship and fellowship of the
community (10:24-25; cf. 3:12-13). In the following chapter the pastor will
urge them to identify with the faithful people of God who have gone before
them — even if it involves the kind of suffering described in 11:35b-38. Thus
it is no surprise that the pastor makes this issue of identification with God's
people the heart of his chiasm (vv. 33b-34a).

We turn first to the sufferings they have borne, as described in vv. 33a
and 34b. "By being made a spectacle" underscores the public nature of their
persecution, with all of the shame attendant thereto.¹⁵ They were made such a
spectacle by means of "reproaches" or insults, verbal abuse, mockery, scorn,
and false accusation (cf. Ps 69:7, 9; Jer 15:15; 20:8) as well as by "tribulations" consisting of such physical suffering as the beatings and deprivation
that often accompanied imprisonment (cf. Rom 5:3; 8:35; 12:12; 2 Cor 1:4,

14. *Pace* Koester, 459; Lane, 2:299; Weiss, 545; Riggenbach, 331-32; and
Vanhoye, *La structure littéraire,* 179. See Ellingworth, 546, who affirms that τοῦτο μέν/
τοῦτο δέ ("on the one hand"/"on the other") is a classical idiom showing correspondence
between the two clauses (Ellingworth, 546).
15. θεατριζόμενοι, "being made a spectacle," is related to the word θέατρον,
"spectacle," "theater." Compare 1 Cor 4:9, in which Paul says that he and his coworkers
"have become a spectacle (θέατρον) to the world." Sometimes Jews (Philo, *Flaccus* 74–
75, 84–85, 95, 173; Josephus, *Ag. Ap.* 1.43) or Christians (Acts 19:29) were denounced
publicly in theaters (Koester, 459). The present tense of θεατριζόμενοι is in accord with
the duration of their earlier time of persecution and adds vividness to its description.

8; 2:4; 4:17; 6:4-5; 7:4; 8:2, 13). Even the unconvicted might suffer such beatings from officials (Acts 16:22-23) as well as from the mob (Acts 18:17; Heb 11:37).[16] As Moses bore the "reproach" of Christ before his coming (11:26), so those addressed by the pastor have borne and are called to continue bearing "reproach" with Christ (13:13; cf. 12:1-3).

It is difficult for modern readers to feel the full fury of the shame and public ostracism experienced by these first-century believers. They were demonized and depersonalized as many minorities have been throughout history. On the one hand, early followers of Jesus ran afoul of their Jewish colleagues because of their insistence that Christ was the fulfillment of God's promise to Israel and thus the sole means of salvation.[17] On the other hand, their non-Jewish neighbors began to despise them because they refrained from the worship of idols and participation in other immoral practices associated with pagan society. Since virtually every civic, social, and family event involved such practices, those who followed Christ seemed to be tearing at the very fabric of society. When writing to the Corinthian church Paul had to deal with something so fundamental as buying meat in the market or attending a dinner party, because in both cases the food involved had been offered to idols (1 Cor 10:23-30). Most people in society had not been able to understand why Jews abstained from such practices. Now, however, those who followed Christ were urging everyone to abstain. The Roman historian Tacitus, born in the middle of the first century, expressed the feeling of many when he called the church a "deadly disease" (*Ann.* 16.5) and accused Christians of "hatred of the human race" (*Ann.* 15.44).[18] Our ignorance concerning the time when the persecution described in these verses occurred does not prevent us from grasping the urgency of the pastor's concern for faithful endurance amid suffering.[19]

16. Koester prefers the translation "denunciations" because Roman officials depended on citizens to "denounce" those who broke the law (C. R. Koester, "Conversion, Persecution, and Malaise: Life in the Community for Which Hebrews Was Written," *Hervormde Teologiese Studies* 61 [2005]: 238-39).

17. Note how Paul persecuted those who followed Jesus (Acts 8:1-3) and then how he in turn after his conversion was persecuted by his fellow Jews at such places as Thessalonica (Acts 17:1-9), Corinth (Acts 18:12-17), and finally Jerusalem (Acts 21:27-36).

18. On Jews and Christians under the Roman Empire see Koester, "Conversion, Persecution, and Malaise," 243, and the literature there cited.

19. It is clear that the pastor is referring to a particular time of persecution in his hearers' past (Koester, 464; cf. Bruce, 267-68, but *pace* Grässer, 3:58-65). Yet the available knowledge precludes identification of this persecution with persecutions known from other sources (Bruce, 267-70; Bénétreau, 2:124; Riggenbach, 333-34; etc.). The fact that the community who received Hebrews had suffered no martyrdoms (12:4) precludes reference to persecutions in Jerusalem after the stoning of Stephen in A.D. 33 (Acts 8:1-3), under Herod

The pastor has reserved the confiscation of property until last, anticipating the description of destitution at the climax of chapter 11 (11:37-38). Such loss of property meant exclusion from society and from the means of providing a livelihood. "Seizure" expresses the violence of the underlying Greek term.[20] Confiscation was often accompanied by imprisonment or exile. It might be carried out by a hostile mob or by the judicial action of civic officials (Eusebius, *Hist. eccl.* 3.17).[21] Officials were only too ready to punish those condemned by the mob.[22] In fact, seizure of property was a common first-century experience for those in disfavor with greedy authorities, and it left its victims isolated and without resources.[23] The pastor wants his hearers to know that such marginalization is a normal way for the people of this unbelieving world to treat the faithful who pursue the eternal destiny prepared by God (see 11:37-38). The "great cloud of witnesses," whose story is told in 11:1-40, saw this apparently shameful "spectacle" of destitution from the glorious perspective of eternity. The pastor would have his hearers share this point of view.

As noted above, the pastor's main concern is revealed in vv. 33b-34a — the hearers have not shied away from suffering by silently disassociating themselves from those persecuted because of their faithfulness to God. Instead, they "became partners of those who lived this way."[24] It is not merely that they identified with those who were suffering. They identified with those who were actively and faithfully enduring suffering. They were no spectator fans but became "partners" who entered into and endured the sufferings of those with whom they partnered.[25] One concrete expression of this partner-

---

Agrippa I in A.D. 44 (Acts 12:2), after the stoning of James the Just in A.D. 62 (Josephus, *Ant.* 20.200), or in Rome under Nero in A.D. 64-65 (Tacitus, *Ann.* 15.44.6). Nor is there positive evidence that would identify these sufferings either with the expulsion of Jews from Rome under Claudius in A.D. 49 (Seutonius, *Claud.* 25.4) or with the confiscation of the resources of wealthy Christians under Domitian in A.D. 81-95 (*pace* Weiss, 545-46).

20. Johnson, 271, and the references there cited.

21. For plundering during outbreaks of violence see Josephus, *J.W.* 3.177; 4.168; 4 Macc 4:10; Polybius, *Histories* 4.17.4 (cited by Koester, "Conversion, Persecution, and Malaise," 240, n. 10).

22. See Philo, *Flaccus* 54, 76–77; Josephus *J.W.* 2.275; 305-6; 4.335.

23. On first-century punishments in the Roman world see B. Rapske, *The Book of Acts and Paul in Roman Custody* (Grand Rapids: Eerdmans, 1994), 10-20 (cited in Koester, "Conversion, Persecution, and Malaise," 239).

24. Johnson, 269-70, is correct when he takes ἀναστρεφομένων as middle, "those who conducted themselves thus," rather than as passive, "those so treated" (Attridge, 200, n. 27).

25. See BDAG, 553, 1, a, β. As Christ became a partaker of human suffering by sharing the human condition (2:14), so these faithful became "partners" (κοινωνοί) with suffering believers.

ship was their showing "sympathy to the prisoners." The verb "showed sympathy" (see on 4:15) implies not mere feeling but concrete assistance. Those imprisoned for their faith and awaiting further punishment would have no one to provide them with the necessities of life except other followers of Christ.[26] When their fellow believers provided these things, they identified themselves and became subject to the same harassment. It would have been normal for those imprisoned to have already lost their property. Thus, it is no surprise that those who identified with them by ministering to their needs should have their "property" seized. Being mindful of those imprisoned for their faith is an integral part of the faithful endurance that the pastor enjoins (cf. 13:3).

34c The pastor uses the causal participle with which he ends this verse to express his main point: "because you were knowing that you yourselves have a better possession and a heavenly one."[27] Because of this knowledge, the hearers had not merely acquiesced to the seizure of their property, but they had actually "welcomed" its confiscation "with joy."[28] What did their material possessions matter when they had something so much more valuable? According to Heb 11:1-40, the faithful people of God have always lived by this principle. Moses, for instance, exemplified this point of view when he "considered the reproaches of Christ greater riches than the treasures of Egypt," because he "looked toward the [eternal] reward" (11:26). The faithful described in 11:37-38 could live in temporal destitution because their very destitution was evidence of eternal wealth.

The pastor has used the aorist tense to narrate the past event of their great contest of suffering. Here, however, he has deliberately chosen the present continuous tense of the participle — "knowing." He does not say "because you knew" but "because you were knowing," or, more smoothly, "because you were aware." This conviction concerning their eternal reward was not an event. It was, and is, the normal, continuous attitude of those who live the life of faith. Furthermore, their orientation to this eternal reward had not been speculative but intensely personal. "Yourselves" is emphatic. They did not merely believe that the eternal reward existed. They were confident that they themselves had such an abiding possession.

Three contrasts demonstrate the all-surpassing value of this heavenly

26. On Christians caring for their imprisoned brothers and sisters see Phil 2:25; 4:14-18; Lucian, *Peregr.* 12–13; Ign. *Eph.* 1:2; *Magn.* 2; *Trall.* 1–2; *Phld.* 11:1-2; Tertullian, *Mart.* 1 (Koester, 460).

27. Ellingworth, 548.

28. The phrase "with joy" confirms the fact that προσεδέξασθε means "welcome" (Luke 15:2; Rom 16:2; Phil 2:29) and not just "accept" (Johnson, 271). For joy amid persecution, see Matt 5:11-13; Acts 5:41; 2 Cor 6:10; 7:9; 8:2; Phil 2:17; Col 1:24; 1 Thess 1:6; and 1 Pet 4:14.

possession: first, the substantive present participle used for the possessions that have been seized is plural; the noun used for the better "possession" is singular. This "possession" is *the* "possession" worth having.[29] Furthermore, the use of the participle for earthly possessions is in accord with their transitory nature: "the things [then/now] existing." Second, this possession is "better." As indicated elsewhere, Hebrews uses "better" to denote the qualitative superiority and ultimate nature of the redemption brought by Christ, along with its present and future effects. His salvation is "better" because it truly brings people into the heavenly homeland of God's presence, which is indeed a "better" possession.[30] Third, in contrast to the temporal nature of what was seized, this "possession" is "enduring." The word translated "enduring" is last in the Greek sentence for emphasis and is the description of the heavenly possession par excellence. We have tried to express this emphasis by the translation, "a better possession and one that endures." The pastor has used this term to describe the eternal character of Christ's person, and thus the ultimate nature of his priesthood (7:24; cf. 7:3). He will use it to describe the eternal and indestructible City established by God.[31] Words like "enduring" or "lasting" are not fully adequate to express the pastor's intention. This "possession" is not merely "more lasting" (NRSV) but is eternal in quality and indestructible in nature because it is nothing less than life in the presence of the eternal God. It will transcend the Judgment and the destruction of all things temporal (12:27). It is that "rest" (3:7–4:11), heavenly "homeland" (11:13-16), and "City with foundations" (11:10; 12:22) promised as the ultimate destiny of the faithful. The pastor uses the word "possession" to emphasize the fact that the faithful even now "possess" this eternal destiny — if they will only persevere. It is a truly "great reward" (v. 35).

35 The imperative in v. 35 is the linchpin of this passage: "Do not throw away your boldness, which has great reward." This exhortation shows why the pastor has been describing their past faithfulness in vv. 32-34: "Do not throw away" the "boldness" that you evidenced when tested by trials after your conversion. You endured those trials because you knew you had an eternal "possession." "Let me remind you," says the pastor, "that the maintenance of

---

29. Compare the plural τῶν ὑπαρχόντων, "property," "things existing," with the singular ὕπαρξιν, "possession." Cf. Weiss, 546. ὕπαρξιν is without the article because the pastor would emphasize its superior quality.

30. Hebrews uses "better" (κρείττων) to describe Christ and his work (1:4; 9:23; 12:24), the salvation he provides (7:19, 22; 8:6), and, as here, the ultimate destiny of God's people. All that God has prepared for his people is "better" (11:40) because it is eternal life in fellowship with God in the "better" country (11:16) for those who enjoy the "better" resurrection (11:35) and the "better" things of salvation (6:9).

31. The participle μένουσαν, "enduring," "remaining," occurs again in 13:14. Cf. μένει ("he remains") in 7:3 and μένειν ("to remain") in 7:24.

that boldness is the key to receiving this 'great reward.'" In vv. 36-39 the pastor explains what he means by maintaining their "boldness." His key word is "endurance." Those who endure opposition until the end, trusting in God's provision through Christ, maintain their "boldness" and thus receive the "reward."

In 4:16 and 10:19 the pastor used the word we have translated "boldness" to describe the right or privilege of entrance into God's presence given to those who draw near through Christ. Here in 10:35 he appears to be encouraging his hearers to practice the "boldness" or courage of persistently professing Christ before a hostile world (cf. 3:6). The two, however, are closely intertwined.[32] Only those who make use of their privilege in approaching God and are thus assured, if they persevere, of his acceptance at the end, can be "bold" before the opposition of unbelieving society. To "throw away" (see Mark 10:50) such "boldness" as if it were worthless would be a great mistake. Indeed, the maintaining of this "boldness" will result in "great reward."[33] The pastor puts no article before this term because he would emphasize its overwhelming greatness — not "a great reward" or even "the great reward," but "great reward" — reward great beyond reckoning. They faced and still face a "contest" that is "great" — intense in degree and seemingly long in duration (v. 32). If they maintain their boldness, however, they will receive a "reward" that is "great" because eternal, both in degree and duration.[34] Furthermore, this blessing has been made possible only through the "great salvation" (2:3) provided by Christ. Those who remain faithful can be sure of receiving this "reward" because of God's character — he is a "rewarder" of those who seek him (11:6).[35]

36 The opening words of this verse provide the clearest expression of the author's pastoral concern for his hearers: "you have need of endurance." It is for this reason that he sought to forestall their drifting (2:1-4) and awaken

32. deSilva, 365-66; Bruce, 271; and others distinguish between παρρησία as confidence in approaching God (4:16; 10:19) and as courage before unbelievers (10:35; cf. 3:6). Weiss, 546-47, emphasizes the relationship between the two uses of this term. Cf. Ellingworth, 551.

33. In agreement with Bénétreau, 2:124-25, the pastor is thinking of the final recompense at journey's end.

34. On the balance between "great reward" (μεγάλην μισθαποδοσίαν) and "great contest" (πολλὴν ἄθλησιν, v. 32) see Johnson, 272. Compare also "such a great salvation" (τηλικαύτης ἀμελήσαντες σωτηρίας) in 2:3. Among NT books only Hebrews uses the term μισθαποδοσία ("recompense," "reward"). In 2:2 it was used for the "recompense" or punishment of those who neglected what God has done in Christ. Here, in 10:35, and in 11:26, it describes the ultimate "reward" of the faithful. The very use of this term mirrors what the pastor would accomplish in his hearers. He would move them from threat of eternal loss (2:2) to possession of eternal gain (10:35; 11:25).

35. The term "rewarder" (μισθαποδότης) in 11:6 is related to the word Hebrews uses for "reward" (μισθαποδοσία) in 2:2; 10:35; and 11:26.

them from lethargy (5:11-14). It is for this that he explained the great high-priestly work of Christ (4:14–10:18) as both motivation and adequate resource for endurance. Every warning and every promise has been crafted to encourage endurance and forestall discouragement engendered by opposition or by the dulling effect of time. Those who endure persist in a life of faith and obedience despite opposition from the unbelieving world. Thus, the pastor can describe the person who has endured to the end as one who has "done the will of God."[36] Although his hearers now have an "enduring possession," it is then, and only then, that they "will receive" what God has promised. There is no smell of merit about this doing of God's will. To do his will is merely to continue in the obedience that comes from living in reliance on Christ and the salvation that he has provided by his own obedience to the divine will (10:5-10).[37]

It will be helpful at this point to note the relationship between "faith," "obedience," and "endurance." In what follows the pastor will use "faith" (11:1-40) and "endurance" (12:1-11) to describe the way of life he desires for his hearers.[38] We noted above the importance of "unbelief" and "disobedience" in the description of the faithless wilderness generation (3:7–4:11).[39] In the following description of the positive counterpart to that generation (11:1-40) the expression "by (through) faith" has taken the place occupied by both of these negative terms. As the opening verses of chapter 11 will show, to live "by faith" is to live as if God's promise of future reward is sure and his power for present victory is real. By thus defining faith as a way of life rather than as a mental act the pastor encompasses obedience within the life of faith. "Endurance" is persistence in this life of faith despite hardship and persecution. One can also say that the life of faith is a life of endurance through reliance on God. Those who lived "by faith" according to 11:1-40 exemplified the "endurance" enjoined in 12:1-13.

The goal of this life of enduring faith is that "you might receive" the eternal reward that God has promised.[40] The faithful before Christ (11:1-40) did not "receive" (11:39) this reward before his coming or apart from him.[41]

---

36. The aorist tense of ποιήσαντες, "having done," refers to the completion of the life of faith. Cf. Koester, 461.

37. Weiss, 548; Riggenbach, 335.

38. See πίστις ("faith") in 10:38, 39; 11:1, 3, 4, 5, 6, 7, 8, 9, 11, 13, 17, 20, 21, 22, 23, 24, 27, 28, 29, 30, 31, 33, 39; ὑπομονή ("endurance") in 10:36; 12:1; and ὑπομένω ("to endure") in 12:2, 3, 7.

39. Note ἀπειθέω ("disobey") in 3:18; ἀπείθεια ("disobedience") in 4:6, 11; and ἀπιστία ("unbelief") in 3:12, 19.

40. The pastor is not referring to the reception of the promise itself but to what has been promised (Hughes, 433, n. 32; Lane, 2:303).

41. The pastor uses κομίζομαι (middle) in 10:36 and 11:39 when he refers to receiving the "promise" (ἐπαγγελίαν, singular) of eternal blessing. Cf. 11:19. See κομίζεσθαι

For both those who precede and those who follow Christ, this goal is attainable only through his saving work. No wonder the faithful must keep their eyes on Jesus (12:1-3).

37 The pastor substantiates his urgent call for enduring faith and introduces the examples that follow by recalling the words of Hab 2:3b-4. He finds support in these verses for both the life of faith and the closely related need for endurance. God spoke clearly through Habakkuk concerning the life of faith when he declared: "My righteous one will live by faith." God warned against the failure to endure when he said, "If he should draw back, my soul has no pleasure in him." The opening line of the quotation (". . . the coming one will come . . .") provides motivation for endurance by affirming the imminent coming of the Lord, and thus of the time when the faithful will receive "the promise" (v. 36).[42] The pastor has been preparing for this quotation since 10:19, and he will clarify its meaning by the examples that follow.[43] They are given both to show how the "righteous" before God persevere "by faith" and to encourage the recipients of Hebrews to follow in their footsteps.

It is clear that the pastor quotes this passage with Scriptural authority as the very word of God, yet he uses no formula of introduction and appears to rearrange the text more freely than usual in order to clarify its meaning.[44] Thus, in order to understand what he is saying one must compare his quotation with the text as given in the context of Habakkuk. We begin with the quotation of the last line from Hab 2:3 in Heb 10:37.

In Hab 2:2 God tells the prophet to "write" down the "vision" that he will give him concerning God's final judgment on the wicked Chaldeans now

---

μισθόν in 2 Macc 8:33. On the other hand, he uses ἐπιτυγχάνω (6:15), λαμβάνω (11:13), and τυγχάνω (11:33) when referring more generally to the reception of God's "promises" (plural). It is not surprising, however, that some manuscripts, including ℵ, have κομίζομαι in 11:13. Although the object of this verb is the general plural, "promises," it appears to encompass the promise of eternal reward. Weiss, 548 (esp. n. 21), claims that κομίζεσθαι ("receive") is a technical term in early Christianity for experiencing the reward of the end time (2 Cor 5:10; Col 3:25; Eph 6:8; as also 1 Pet 1:9; Heb 11:39).

42. Affirmation that the Lord would soon return is not indication that the hearers were discouraged by a delay in Christ's second coming (cf. Weiss, 549).

43. One is reminded of the way Heb 4:14–6:20 prepared for the exposition of Ps 110:4 in Heb 7:1-25, although in this case the OT passage was cited much earlier (5:5-6) and expounded line by line. Cf. Koester, 464. The pastor's use of Hab 2:3-4 is, perhaps, more suggestive, less controversial, and not in need of as much clarification. See "The Rhetorical Shape of Hebrews and Its Use of the Old Testament," pp. 72-76 in the Introduction to this commentary.

44. Spicq, 2:331, and Riggenbach, 335-36, are less than convincing when they suggest that the pastor used no formula because the quotation was familiar. His audience was certainly familiar with many of the Scriptures that he used a formula to introduce. "My soul" leaves no doubt that God is the speaker.

ravaging the world. In v. 3 he assures the prophet that this "vision" has its "appointed time." Thus, though it might seem to delay, it will surely come. Hebrews picks up the last line of v. 3, which, rendered literally from both Greek and Hebrew, reads as given in the left column below. The wording in Heb 10:37 is given to the right for comparison:

Hab 2:3	Heb 10:37
For yet . . . <u>wait for it/him</u>.	For yet <u>in a very little while,</u>
for coming it/he will come and	the coming one will come and
will not delay.	will not delay

This comparison highlights three features of the text that require comment. First, note the use of "it/him" and "it/he" in the translation of Habakkuk. This translation reflects the ambiguity as to whether it is the "vision" itself (i.e., its fulfillment), the "appointed time" of the vision, or the person who will fulfill the vision that comes in a timely manner. It is natural to read the Hebrew text as describing the coming of the "vision." However, in v. 3 the Greek translators have used a feminine word for "vision" but masculine forms for the "appointed time," for the pronoun ("it/him"), and for the participle ("coming"). Thus, the translator of the Oxford Septuagint renders Hab 2:3 as follows: "For there is still a vision for an appointed time, and it [the appointed time] will rise up at the end and not in vain. If it should tarry, wait for it, for when it comes, it will come and not delay." In a footnote the translator tells us that the occurrences of "it" in this verse refer to the "appointed time."[45] Yet use of the masculine pronoun and participle suggests that a person is coming to execute judgment and thus fulfill the vision.[46] Furthermore, it was not impossible for the Greek translator to read the Hebrew original in this way. Thus, many have argued that the LXX already understood the coming deliverer as the Messiah who would execute God's judgment on the ungodly.[47] In the larger context of Habakkuk the coming One is the Lord himself.[48]

---

45. Pietersma and Wright, *A New English Translation of the Septuagint,* 808.

46. O. Palmer Robertson, *The Books of Nahum, Habakkuk, and Zephaniah* (Grand Rapids: Eerdmans, 1990), 172-73; O'Brien, 389. See R. Gheorghita, *The Role of the Septuagint in Hebrews* (WUNT 2/160; Tübingen: Siebeck, 2003), 216-18, for a discussion of whether or not the LXX translator intended to heighten the eschatological or Messianic significance of the Hebrew text.

47. Lane, 2:304; Bruce, 273; Bénétreau, 2:127-28; Spicq, 2:332, and others. Bruce, 273, is so thoroughly convinced that the LXX is Messianic that he can write: "Our author, then, is but dotting the i's and crossing the t's of the Septuagint interpretation when he applies Hab 2:3b to the second coming of Christ." The "coming" one was a designation of the Messiah (Matt 3:11; 11:3; 21:9; Mark 11:9; Luke 7:19; 19:38; John 1:15, 27; 11:27; Koester, 462).

48. Gheorghita, *Septuagint,* 223; O'Brien, 389.

The second and third important features that arise from this comparison make it clear that the author of Hebrews attributed Messianic significance to this verse. The promised coming of the Lord with earth-shaking judgment on the Chaldeans has become a foreshadowing of Christ's return and the final Judgment (12:25-29).[49] In the second place, then, note the phrases underlined in Hab 2:3 and Heb 10:37 as given above: the pastor omits the phrase "wait for him" from Habakkuk although the verb translated "wait for" comes from the same root as "endurance" in v. 36 and might have suited his purpose well.[50] In place of "wait for him" the pastor writes: "in a very little while." These words echo Isa 26:20, a passage that speaks even more clearly of God's final Judgment.[51] The pastor uses this phrase in accord with Isaiah's intention to encourage his hearers as they waited for their deliverance at the Day of Judgment. This expression underscores the certainty of God's coming vindication as well as the relatively brief time that it will be necessary to endure.[52]

The third important feature arising from this comparison of Heb 10:37 with Hab 2:3b finalizes the identification of the coming deliverance with Christ and his anticipated denouement at the second coming. We have already noted that the pastor omitted "him" (in "wait for him") from the earlier part of

49. See the discussion in Gheorghita, *Septuagint,* 220-23, cited and affirmed by O'Brien, 389.

50. Cf. Hughes, 435, n. 38.

51. *Pace* Guthrie, "Hebrews," in *Commentary on the New Testament Use of the Old,* 982, the author of Hebrews does not join Isa 26:20 to Hab 2:3-4 on the basis of verbal analogy. The two Greek texts do not even use the same words for "coming." The author joins them because they both deal with the same theme — the imminent arrival of God's coming Judgment. See Hughes, 434; Gheorghita, *Septuagint,* 182.

52. In Isa 26:20 the prophet urges those addressed to hide themselves for "a very little while," until God's judgment on the wicked has passed. T. W. Lewis, "'And If He Shrinks Back . . .' (Heb. 10:38b)," *NTS* 22 (1975-76): 88-94, has argued on the basis of this allusion to Isaiah that those addressed by Hebrews were applying this verse to themselves. Instead of boldly professing Christ, as the pastor would encourage them to do, they were "hiding" until the end. However, in the absence of other evidence, the reference to Isaiah is too elusive to sustain this thesis. Kistemaker, 302, even questions whether the pastor is intentionally referring to Isa 26:20. It is true that Isaiah 26:9-20 (entitled προσευχὴ Ἰσαίου, "prayer of Isaiah") was also the fifth ode attached to the psalms and used in the prayers of the early church (Lane, 2:303-4). When, however, one considers the absence of an introductory formula and the brevity of the reference, inclusion in the prayers of the church need mean no more than that the language of the Isaiah passage was familiar and ready to hand in contexts speaking of judgment. The pastor's other exhortations make it clear that his hearers were not hiding but were in danger of denying Christ and severing their relationship with the community of his followers (e.g., 6:4-8; 10:26-31). The pastor's positive use of this allusion is no indication of misuse by his hearers. For further criticism of Lewis's suggestion, see Rose, *Die Volke,* 57-59.

Hab 2:3. In its place he has added an article making the participle substantive — "the coming one." This phrase is clearly a Messianic title.[53] The judgment anticipated by Habakkuk finds fulfillment in the final Judgment at Christ's return. That Judgment was promised in the pastor's key verse — Ps 110:1 (Heb 1:3, 13; cf. 8:1-2; 10:11-14; 12:1-3).[54] It will be described as the great climax of history in Heb 12:25-29 at the conclusion of his main discourse (cf. 9:27-28). As Habakkuk had to wait in faith for God's vindication, so the pastor's hearers must wait for final vindication at Christ's return.[55]

38   A look at the way in which the pastor has arranged his quotation of Hab 2:4 clarifies the Messianic significance of this passage, already evident from his use of Hab 2:3b, and confirms "the coming one" as a reference to the return of Christ. It also brings the meaning of v. 4 into closer accord with the underlying Hebrew text. Compare the translations of Hab 2:3b-4 (LXX) and Heb 10:37-38 given below:

Hab 2:3b-4	Heb 10:37-38
3 For yet . . . wait for him.[56] for coming he will come and will not delay.	37 For yet in a very little while, the coming one will come and will not delay
4 *If he should draw back, my soul has no pleasure in him.* **But the righteous one shall live by my faith.**	38 **But my righteous one shall live by faith,** *but if he should draw back, my soul has no pleasure in him.*

Italics and boldface have been added to the two clauses in Hab 2:4/Heb 10:38 to show the way in which they have been reversed. This change clarifies

53. For "the coming one" as a reference to Jesus see Matt 3:11; Luke 7:19; John 1:9; 3:31; and 6:14. For the Messianic significance of this expression, see the references given above. ἥκω ("arrive") is used in reference to Christ's second coming (Matt 24:50; Luke 12:46; 13:35; Rom 11:26; Rev 2:25; 3:3; Koester, 463). Eisele, *Ein unerschütterliches Reich,* 112, argues that this verse does not refer to the second coming. Since the faithful enter their reward at death, it refers to Christ's coming to each believer at that time. There is no evidence, however, that Hebrews locates entrance into salvation at the point of death. It would be much more natural to say that believers go to Christ at death rather than that he comes to them. Thus, this interpretation is without precedent in other sources and without support in either the immediate or larger context of Hebrews.

54. See "The Rhetorical Shape of Hebrews and Its Use of the Old Testament," pp. 72-76 in the Introduction to this commentary.

55. According to Spicq, 2:332, the life of the Israelites rescued from the Chaldean threat was "a type of the eternal life" that the pastor's hearers "are tempted to abandon."

56. Here the Greek pronoun has been translated unambiguously as "him" on the assumption that the LXX translator intended and the author of Hebrews understood this verse as referring to a person.

the identity of both the "coming" one and the one who "draws back." It establishes a clear contrast between drawing "back" and living "by faith." First, it makes Hab 2:4a, "if he should draw back, my soul has no pleasure in him," refer unambiguously to "my righteous one" who lives by faith in Hab 2:4b, rather than the "coming one" of Hab 2:3b. Second, by clarifying the identity of the "coming one," this reversal brings the syntax of these verses into accord with the broader context. This "coming one" is not merely the Messiah, whose identity is confirmed by the fact that he does not "draw back,"[57] but the Lord himself.[58] Third, this change establishes a clear contrast between the righteous person who "lives by faith" and the erstwhile righteous person who "draws back" and experiences the ultimate of divine displeasure.[59] This contrast is closer to the intention of the original Hebrew text.[60] The prophet Habakkuk compared two kinds of people — the wicked (2:4a, "his soul is puffed up with pride, it is not right in him") and the righteous (2:4b, "my righteous one shall live by faith").[61] The pastor contrasts two alternatives for the righteous — they can live "by faith"; they can "draw back" from faith.[62] Those who '"draw back" are indeed the wicked; they are "puffed up with self-sufficiency" and are "therefore blind to the need of trustful and patient endurance."[63] This contrast between living "by faith" and "drawing back" is fundamental to the pastor's concern for his hearers. If the wilderness generation embodied those to be avoided because they "drew back" (3:7–4:11), the heroes of chapter 11 represent those to be emulated because they persevered in living "by faith." The

---

57. If one understands the "coming one" in the unreordered clauses of Hab 2:3-4 (LXX) as a potential Messianic figure, then "if he turn back" might be taken as evidence that a particular Messianic claimant was false. See T. W. Manson, "The Argument from Prophecy," *JTS* 46 (1945): 129-36, esp. 134 (followed by Lane, Bruce, and Bénétreau). There is no other convenient way to understand this verse as it stands in the LXX as Messianic (cf. Riggenbach, 336-39).

58. See Gheorghita, *Septuagint,* 213-18, 221-24, cited in O'Brien, 390, n. 249. There is no way to coherently understand "if he draw back" as a reference to the Lord himself, who surely will not "draw back."

59. Note the adversative καί, "but," at the beginning of the second half of Heb 10:38.

60. The translation of Hab 2:4a is difficult, as the translator of the LXX discovered. See Guthrie, "Hebrews," in *Commentary on the New Testament Use of the Old,* 982, and the sources he cites. For suggestions on the Hebrew text used by the Greek translator and the way he construed his text, see Bruce, 272-73, n. 195.

61. Westcott, 337, says that Hab 2:4a, "His soul is puffed up with pride; it is not right within him," refers to the Chaldeans. Note, however, *Targum Pseudo-Jonathan:* "Behold, the wicked say to themselves, 'None of these things is happening'; but the righteous will be established by their truth" (Bruce, 272, n. 194).

62. Lane, 2:305; Bénétreau, 2:128.

63. Hughes, 436.

pastor's hearers have much in common with those addressed by Habakkuk. They, too, must endure suffering while they wait patiently in the confidence that God will fulfill his promise.

Finally, this reversal of clauses allows Hab 2:4b, "but my righteous one will live by faith," to become the centerpiece of the quotation. This affirmation anticipates the description of the "righteous" (11:4) who, according to 11:1-40, lived by faith, and who are now, through Christ, in God's presence (12:23).[64] It is instructive to compare the forms that this statement takes in the standard Hebrew text and in the Septuagintal tradition: (1) "the righteous one shall live by *his* faith" (MT). (2) "The righteous one shall live by *my* faith" (LXX B, the standard LXX text). (3) *My* righteous one shall live by faith (LXX alternate reading found in A, C, and the manuscripts grouped with C). Italics have been added to show the variation in the identity and location of the pronoun "his"/"my." The original translation of the Hebrew text into Greek is probably represented by the standard LXX text. It is easy to see how the translator would have mistaken the *vav* of the Hebrew text ("his") for a *yod* ("my").[65] The Hebrew text refers to the "faith" of the righteous person ("his faith"); the standard LXX to the "faithfulness" of God ("my faithfulness"). However, the total impact of this verse is little altered: "the righteous person will live by his faith [in God]"; "the righteous person will live by [trusting in] my [God's] faithfulness." The pastor follows the alternate LXX reading: "My righteous one shall live by faith." In fact, he is likely responsible for making "my" qualify "righteous one" instead of "faith" and that the LXX alternate reading arose under the influence of Hebrews.[66] By making this alteration the pastor has brought the text into line with the original Hebrew — both refer to the "faith" of the righteous person.[67] It is this kind of "faith" that the pastor wants from his hearers; it is this kind of faith that the godly of 11:1-40 exemplify.

This statement is pregnant with meaning. In the first place, the pastor means that the "righteous" person will conduct his life by trusting in the va-

---

64. In 1QpHab 8:1-3 "the righteous shall live by his faith" is applied to "all the doers of the law in the house of Judah, whom God will save from the place of judgment because of their toil and their faith in the Teacher of Righteousness" (Bruce, 274, n. 202). Thus, the people of Qumran also gave this passage an eschatological interpretation by applying it to faith in their "Teacher of Righteousness." On Paul's use of "the righteous shall live by faith" in Rom 1:17 and Gal 3:11, see Koester, 467-68, and Bruce, 274-75.

65. Compare *vav* (ו) with *yodh* (י), "by his faith" (באמונתו) with "by my faith(fulness)" (באמונתי).

66. D. A. Koch, "Der Text von Heb. 2.4b in der Septuaginta und im Neuen Testament," *ZNW* 76 (1985): 76-78, 84-85.

67. Cf. Guthrie, "Hebrews," in *Commentary on the New Testament Use of the Old*, 983.

lidity of God's future promise and the reality of God's present power, as did the faithful in the next chapter. To be "righteous" is to live with such trust in God's promise and power. To live with such trust is to be "righteous."[68] However, the pastor would also say that the "righteous" will obtain eternal life by such perseverance in dependence upon God's promise and power.[69] The reader must not forget that the faith the pastor enjoins is thoroughly rooted in his understanding of Christ.[70] The righteous trust in the promise that God has made available through Christ and in God's power for perseverance provided by Christ's all-sufficient sacrifice. The faith of the righteous who lived before Christ (11:1-40) anticipated what faith now enjoys. By putting "my" with "righteous one" the pastor has also emphasized the bond between God and the one who depends upon him.

39 Thus, the prophecy from Habakkuk both reinforces the pastor's call for endurance (issued in v. 36) and focuses the hearers' attention on the people of faith, toward whom the pastor would direct them in v. 39. In v. 39 the pastor applies the two alternative courses of action outlined in v. 38 to the lives of his hearers. In v. 38 he began with those who "live by faith" before speaking of those who "draw back." In v. 39 he reverses the order by beginning with those who are characterized by "drawing back" and concluding with those who are characterized "by faith."[71] Just as "faith" was made the centerpiece of the quotation from Habakkuk, so it is given the final and emphatic position in this verse and chapter. The pastor ends with what he would illustrate in chapter 11 and what he would inculcate in his hearers. There can be no doubt that the destiny of those characterized by "turning back" will be eternal "destruction" at the Judgment, when the "one who is coming" arrives. The pastor, however, would conclude this section by assuring his hearers that they are, and he wants them to be, part of those characterized by "faith," and not participants in those characterized by "drawing back." He adds warmth to

---

68. Cf. Riggenbach, 338.

69. Lane, 2:307; Riggenbach, 338. Rose, *Die Volke*, 70-77, argues that in Hebrews "will live by faith" refers primarily if not solely to obtaining eternal life by faith. He notes the parallel between "will live by faith" and "through faith for the preservation of the soul." Since "preservation of the soul" stands in contrast to "destruction," it is obviously a reference to eternal life. He also supports this position by noting the way in which "the righteous one will live by faith" was used in Jewish tradition to refer to eternal life. Nevertheless, "will live by faith" also refers to a course of life or conduct that is the opposite of "turning back." The examples below will show how the pastor uses this phrase in both senses.

70. Weiss, 551.

71. The genitives ὑποστολῆς ("of turning back") and πίστεως ("of faith") describe what marks the two classes of people. Compare χαρᾶς ("of joy") and λύπης ("of grief") in 12:11. Westcott, 338, cites 1 Thess 5:5; 1 Cor 14:33; Luke 9:55; and Acts 9:2 as other examples of this usage.

his encouragement by using the inclusive "we" — "you and I." Yet he does nothing to diminish the force of his implied warning.

It is a mistake to pass the expression "for the preservation of the soul" off as a reversion to Hellenistic (i.e., dualistic) eschatology or as a mere borrowing from classical sources.[72] Furthermore, it is a serious misreading of the text to identify this "preservation of the soul" with the "spirits of the righteous made perfect" and now in God's presence (12:23).[73] The pastor has chosen this expression because it is most appropriate both for the immediate context and for the present stage of his argument. It is important to note that this "preservation of the soul" is the opposite of the "destruction" that will occur at the last Judgment when the "coming one" arrives.[74] Thus, it can refer to nothing that anyone living or dead has yet experienced. The pastor has chosen this phrase because of its minimalism. All it really says is that those "of faith" will be preserved from the "destruction" of that final Judgment.[75] The use, then, of this minimal description arouses anticipation and gives the pastor room over the next several chapters to build up a positive description of what the people who live "by faith" will receive at the Judgment — "a City with foundations" (11:10); a "better" and "heavenly" country (11:16); the "reward" greater than Egypt's treasures (11:26); a "better resurrection" (11:35b); and, finally, the "Unshakable Kingdom" (12:28). It is true that the faithful, both living and dead, already experience God's "city," the "heavenly Jerusalem" (12:22-24). Yet Hebrews is clear that this reality will be received in its fullness as the "Unshakable Kingdom" at the Judgment (12:25-29). The pastor who begins by speaking of the Judgment as the time when the faithful will escape destruction by the "preservation of the soul" climaxes by describing it as the time when they will receive the "Unshakable Kingdom." An appropriate positive equivalent for the "preservation of the soul" might be the "better resurrection" (11:35b) necessary for participation in this Kingdom.[76]

In vv. 36-39 the pastor has skillfully introduced his hearers to the "history of the faithful people of God" (11:1–12:29) with whom he would have them identify. He wants them to be part of that people who endure

---

72. *Pace* Weiss, 552, who cites various non-Christian sources (n. 36) in support of his contention that Hebrews has here adapted "Hellenistic" eschatology. Attridge, 304, calls this expression "classical," citing Xenophon, *Cyr.* 4.4.10 and Isocrates, *Epistulae* 2 in n. 104. There is no indication here that the pastor is separating body from soul.

73. *Pace* Koester, 463.

74. This contrast with "destruction" shows clearly that "preservation" (BDAG, 804, 1) is the appropriate translation of περιποίησιν rather than, *pace* Johnson, 274, "obtain" (BDAG, 804, 2). Cf. Spicq, 2:333; Riggenbach, 339; and Luke 17:33.

75. Thus, taking ψυχή ("soul") as "the seat and center of life that transcends the earthly" (BDAG, 1099, 2, d).

76. See the comments on 11:17-19, 35.

through faith until the return of Christ at the judgment. The themes of this section structure this history. Note the following sequence of themes and the sections in the following discourse where they are developed:

"endurance" (v. 36) — 12:1-13
"judgment" (v. 37) — 12:25-29
"faith" (v. 38a) — 11:1-40
"judgment" (v. 38b) — 12:25-29
"faith" (v. 39) — 11:1-40

The pastor begins with the "endurance" he would inculcate. He then features by its central and concluding position the "faith" that is the means and practice of endurance. Thus, he is ready to identify his hearers with the past faithful, whom he discusses in 11:1-40, trusting that they will claim these faithful as their own. Such faith is foundational to the pastor's call (in 12:1-13) for his hearers to endure as the present people of God. Just as he has interspersed this introduction with the theme of judgment, so these discussions of faith and endurance often refer to reward and punishment in anticipation of that end (12:25-29). Thus, with great skill he has prepared his hearers, ancient and modern, for what follows, and yet he has reserved a special surprise for 12:18-24. Just at the point where he turns from the present endurance of God's people (12:1-13) to their future judgment and destiny (12:25-29), he gives a beautiful picture of the privileges the redeemed enjoy in God's presence through Christ's high priesthood and mediation.[77] This picture partakes of both present and future. The present is not merely a time of discipline and endurance (12:1-13), but of joy in God's presence as part of God's redeemed from all time. And yet this picture in 12:18-24 is also a window through which we can peak at what it will be like to live in the "Unshakable Kingdom" granted the faithful at the Judgment (12:25-29).

B. THE PAST HISTORY OF THE PEOPLE OF GOD UNTIL THE COMING OF JESUS (11:1–12:3)

In Heb 10:36-39 the pastor invited his hearers to take their rightful place in the history of God's faithful people. From 11:1 through 12:29 he reinforces this invitation by narrating that history so that they might understand the part they

---

77. The pastor uses the warning example of Esau in 12:14-17 to introduce the present blessedness of the faithful in 12:18-24. The contrasting description of judgment in 12:18-21 reinforces the beauty of the blessedness described in 12:22-24. See the comments on these verses below.

have been called to play.[1] His graphic narrative is like a grand mural, beginning with creation (11:3) and concluding with consummation at the final Judgment (12:27). The pastor wants his hearers to be aware of their heritage, so he begins by describing the history of the faithful before the incarnation (11:1-40). He accomplishes several objectives in this part of his story. First, the lives of the ancient faithful clarify the nature of the faith that the pastor would have his hearers emulate. Second, the perseverance of those who have gone before serves as motivation for perseverance in the present. Third, the faithful of old provide an alternate society that counters the baleful influence of the unbelieving world in which the hearers live. It is no surprise that the major turning point in this grand panorama is the coming of Christ (12:1-3).[2] The history of the past faithful reaches its grand finale in him. By his obedient perseverance he became both the ultimate example of endurance and the one sufficient to enable the faithful — whether they lived before or after his coming — to reach the goal of their pilgrimage (11:39-40) and cross the finish line of their race (12:1-3). Thus, this mention of Christ assumes all that the central section of Hebrews has said about his effectiveness as Savior. It is the centerpiece of the pastor's history of the faithful just as the final Judgment (12:25-29) is its goal. With this return to Jesus in 12:1-3 the pastor completes what he began in 3:1-6. Thus we can expand the chiastic relationships enumerated in the previous section by enlarging the diagram there given as follows:

(A[1]) Keep Your Eyes on Jesus, Seated at God's Right Hand (12:1-3).
(B[1]) Join the Company of the Faithful of Old (11:1-40).
(C[1]) Pursue the Blessing Promised the Faithful (10:32-39).
(D[1]) You Are More Accountable Because of This High Priest (10:26-31).
(E[1]) Avail Yourselves of This Great Priest (10:19-25).
(F) Christ's All-Sufficient High Priesthood (5:1–10:18).
(E) Embrace This Great High Priest (4:14-16).
(D) You are Accountable before the Word of God (4:12-13).
(C) Pursue the Blessing Lost by the Faithless Generation (4:1-11).
(B) Avoid the Company of the Faithless Generation (3:7-19).
(A) Consider Jesus, a Son over the House of God (3:1-6).

1. Rhee, *Faith in Hebrews,* 180-81, recognizes the unity of 11:1–12:29. However, because he has not noted the transitional nature of 10:19-39, he does not see the close connection between this history and the exposition of Christ's high priesthood in 7:1–10:18. Thus, despite his insistence on the Christological nature of faith in Hebrews, he fails to see how closely the "faith" of 11:1-40 is related to the high-priestly work of Christ.

2. While deSilva, 377, argues that 12:1-3 is the conclusion to the list of testimonies in 11:1-40, he also recognizes its significance for what follows. Westfall, *Discourse Analysis,* 242-43, 264, rightly includes 12:1-2 (we would add v. 3) with both the preceding and following sections.

1. Join the Company of the Faithful of Old (11:1-40)

Those who would accurately interpret this great catalogue of heroes must do so from two vantage points: first, they must grasp the beauty, distinct literary style, and unity of this passage;[1] second, they must always remember that this roll call of the faithful is, as we have argued above, an integral part of the pastor's sermon.[2] The pastor has not made use of a preexisting Jewish or Jewish-Christian example list as earlier commentators sometimes suggested.[3] While such lists occurred in other writings, there is no evidence that they circulated independently or constituted a distinct literary form in antiquity.[4] Careful comparison with lists in these other sources confirms the uniqueness of Heb 11:1-40 while providing valuable insight into its interpretation. Like Greco-Roman orators, the pastor praises heroes of the past in order to encourage a particular course of action. However, Greek and Roman speakers preferred to use only a few examples chosen from the recent past. They were concerned with encouraging a course of action, but not with establishing community solidarity by retelling the history of a people.[5] For these reasons, as Eisenbaum has demonstrated, Heb 11:1-40 is much closer to the longer Jewish lists found in Sirach 44–50, Wisdom 10, and the Covenant of Damascus.[6] Sirach 44–50, for instance, retells Biblical history using an extensive catalogue of heroes in order to glorify the nation of Israel and its

1. See Vanhoye, *La structure littéraire,* 183; and Michael R. Cosby, *The Rhetorical Composition and Function of Hebrews 11 in Light of Example Lists in Antiquity* (Macon, GA: Mercer University Press, 1988), 88-89. Cf. Westfall, *Discourse Analysis,* 247; Guthrie, *Structure,* 87-88.

2. Weiss, 553-54; A. Vanhoye, *Structure and Message of the Epistle to the Hebrews* (Subsidia Biblica 12; Rome: Editrice Pontifico Instituto Biblico, 1989), 29-30.

3. Such as Windisch, 98-99; Michel, 422-23; or Gottfried Schille, "Katechese und Taufliturgie: Erwägungen zu Hbr 11," *ZNW* 51 (1960): 112-31.

4. "The number of example lists of famous people in the literature of antiquity that have been cited as parallels to Hebrews 11 is actually quite modest, and they are of sufficiently different composition and function that it is doubtful that their authors were following a set pattern when composing them" (Cosby, *The Rhetorical Composition and Function of Hebrews 11,* 12). For a summary of such lists, see Thompson, 226-27.

5. Because of his focus on the Greco-Roman world, Croy, *Endurance,* fails to grasp the character of 11:1-40 as a community-forming historical narrative. He is also misled when he argues that Hebrews follows the Greco-Roman pattern of using examples only as a supplement following logical discourse (cf. Croy, *Endurance,* 70-76). This assertion misses the parallel between 11:1-40 and 3:7-19. It also obscures chapter 11's unique contribution to the pastor's sermon.

6. Eisenbaum, *Jewish Heroes,* 56-57. Eisenbaum is mistaken, however, when she says that Hebrews follows the Greco-Roman example in mitigating the esteem shown to the chosen heroes (Eisenbaum, *Jewish Heroes,* 84). For her comparison of these two kinds of lists and their relationship to Hebrews, see Eisenbaum, *Jewish Heroes,* 73-84.

institutions. With this history Sirach would cement Jewish community identity in a hostile world. Like Sirach, Heb 11:1-40 narrates a history. It is not, however, a history of Israel, per se, nor is it written to glorify Israel's national institutions. It is a history of the people of God who have been called into being and sustained by the word of God, now fulfilled in Christ (1:1-4). Thus, this history is written in accord with all that has been said about the sole sufficiency of Christ and the way he has fulfilled and antiquated those OT institutions.[7] These heroes have a faith that anticipates God's future, made available through his Son. Thus, the pastor reinforces community solidarity: by their loyalty to Christ his hearers take their place with God's people of all time. As the exegesis that follows will show, this Christocentric perspective has determined both the shape of Heb 11:1-40 and its details. Thus, while the pastor may have used traditional material, it is clear that he has not edited a preexisting list. In this chapter he masterfully adapts for his own purposes the practice of praising great people of the past in order to retell the history of God's people, reinforce community identity, and encourage a particular course of action.[8]

While these people lived before Christ, the pastor has no need to demean their faith or belittle their achievement.[9] They sustained the greatest difficulties by means of their genuine faith and thus receive, through Christ

---

7. The evidence that Eisenbaum gives to support her contention that Hebrews presents a "denationalized" (Eisenbaum, *Jewish Heroes,* 3, 7) version of Israel's history substantiates this affirmation. While she does not develop the significance of Christology for Heb 11:1-40, she does acknowledge its role: "The author's understanding of Christology and the new covenant . . . cause him to value the heroes of the Jewish Bible for reasons different from those that had traditionally been employed" (Pamela M. Eisenbaum, "Heroes and History in Hebrews 11," in *Early Christian Interpretation of the Scriptures of Israel: Investigations and Proposals,* ed. C. A. Evans and J. A. Sanders [JSNTSup 148; Sheffield: Sheffield Academic Press, 1997], 394).

8. Cosby has emphasized that Hebrews, along with other such example lists, used the praise of past heroes (epideictic rhetoric) in order to encourage the action exemplified by these heroes (deliberative rhetoric). See Michael R. Cosby, "The Rhetorical Composition of Hebrews 11," *JBL* 107 (June 1988): 257-73 as well as his full-length book cited on p. 516, n. 1. Yet, as Eisenbaum, *Jewish Heroes,* 56-59, has so clearly demonstrated, the Jewish lists with which Hebrews has the closest affinity were also used to reinforce community identity. However, *pace* Eisenbaum, *Jewish Heroes,* 87, there is no tension between inculcating community solidarity and encouraging faith. The latter, properly understood, finds its expression in the former.

9. *Pace* Eisenbaum, *Jewish Heroes,* 84, and many places. Eisenbaum's attempt to demean the OT personages in Hebrews appears to be the result of her contention that Hebrews considers the narrative of the OT less authoritative than the OT "oracles" used as direct quotes. See the section on Hebrews' use of the OT in the Introduction to this commentary (pp. 41-59).

(12:1-3), the greatest reward — entrance into God's eternal city (12:22-24). Furthermore, in various ways these heroes of faith foreshadow or anticipate the course by which their "Forerunner" (6:20) will open the way for them to reach this goal. Those heroes most closely prefigure Christ through whose obedience born of faith God's people are delivered from death (cf. vv. 7, 17-19, 28). Such correspondences are not contrived by the pastor and are left largely without comment. They arise from the intrinsic relationship between the way Christ has provided salvation and the way his people appropriate it. It should be no surprise that those who live "by faith" reflect the course of the "Pioneer and Perfecter of the faith" (12:2) by which they live.

No part of Hebrews is more difficult to categorize as doctrinal exposition or hortatory exhortation than this chapter.[10] It is totally lacking in the second person plural imperatives and hortatory subjunctives so characteristic of exhortation. Thus it reminds us of the close bond between the pastor's doctrinal exposition and exhortation. He presents the truth in order to persuade and exhorts his hearers so that they will understand the practical significance of the truth presented.[11]

It is important to remember that these heroes of faith elucidate the meaning of Hab 2:4, "my righteous one will live by faith" (Heb 10:38). This chapter falls into two major sections — vv. 1-31 and vv. 32-40.[12] In vv. 1-31 the pastor lists individual examples of faithful people from the creation and Abel (vv. 3-4) to the fall of Jericho and Rahab (vv. 30-31). An instrumental "by faith" introduces each example. Verses 32-40, on the other hand, amass great deeds of faith without identifying the individual who performed each. One "through faith" covers the entire section. These verses provide an intense review of the time between the conquest and the coming of Christ. Furthermore, vv. 1-2 distinguish themselves as an introduction to the whole,

---

10. Guthrie, *Structure,* 40, categorizes chapter 11 as exhortation, while Vanhoye, *La structure littéraire,* 51, 59, considers it doctrinal, though he recognizes that the pastor's parenetic purpose is near at hand. Cf. Westfall, *Discourse Analysis,* 242. Rose, *Die Volke,* 80-81, argues that 10:32-39 and 12:1-3 are exhortation, while 11:1-40 is theological. Rhee, *Faith in Hebrews,* 28, agrees, labeling 10:19-39, 12:1, and 13:1-21 "exhortation," but 11:1-40 "exposition."

11. See Guthrie, *Structure,* 144-45.

12. This structural analysis of Heb 11:1-40 has been presented in Cockerill, "The Better Resurrection (Heb. 11:35)," 215-34. This analysis also finds a large measure of support in Cosby, "The Rhetorical Composition of Hebrews 11," 257-73; Alan D. Bulley, "Death and Rhetoric in the Hebrews 'Hymn to Faith,'" *Studies in Religion* 25 (1996): 410-12; Bénétreau, 2:132; Attridge, 307; and Westfall, *Discourse Analysis,* 248-50. Lane, 2:320-23, and Vanhoye, *La structure littéraire,* 183-95, affirm the same divisions except that they do not formally separate vv. 1-2 as an introduction. However, Ellingworth, 561, argues persuasively for the introductory character of these verses. Guthrie, *Structure,* 131, does not subdivide 11:1-40 into smaller units.

while vv. 39-40 provide a conclusion.[13] Verses 3-31 can be further subdivided into three smaller sections — vv. 3-7, 8-22, and 23-31 — each of which makes its own contribution to the whole. Verses 3-7 give examples from the primeval history (Genesis 1–11), vv. 8-22 from the time of Abraham and the patriarchs (Genesis 12–50), and vv. 23-31 from the era that began with Moses and ended with the conquest (Exodus-Joshua). Since the primeval history sets the pattern for the whole, we will include vv. 3-7 with the introduction in vv. 1-2.

a. From Creation to Noah: The Foundations of Faith (11:1-7)

1 *Now faith is the reality of things hoped for, the evidence of things not seen.* 2 *For by it the people of old were attested.* 3 *By faith we understand that the worlds were ordered by the word of God, so that what is seen has not come into being from the things that appear.* 4 *By faith Abel offered to God a better sacrifice than Cain, through which he was attested as righteous by God's bearing witness in regard to his gifts. And through this he still speaks, although he has died.* 5 *By faith Enoch was translated so that he did not see death, and he was not found because God translated him. For before his translation he had the attestation that he pleased God.* 6 *But without faith it is impossible to please him. For it is necessary for the one coming to God to believe that he is and that he is a rewarder of those who diligently seek him.* 7 *By faith Noah, having been warned concerning things not yet seen, moved by godly fear, prepared an ark for the salvation of his household, by which he judged the world and became an heir of the righteousness that is according to faith.*

Heb 11:1-7 makes appropriate use of the primeval history found in Genesis 1–11 to disclose the basic structure of faith. Verses 1-2 introduce this chapter with a definition of faith (v. 1) and an affirmation of its importance in the lives of the godly of old, who will be discussed below (v. 2). Verses 3 and 6 clarify this definition by giving the object or content of faith. They enclose the first two examples of faith, Abel and Enoch (vv. 4-5). By complementing each other, these two faithful men set the parameters for the rest of this history by demonstrating both the struggle and the triumph of faith. The pastor uses the example of Noah in v. 7 to direct his hearers toward the goal of faith and to provide a smooth transition to the heroes discussed in the following verses. This opening section of the grand history of the faithful is meant to

---

13. Notice how vv. 1-2 begin with "now faith is" (ἔστιν δὲ πίστις) and vv. 39-40 are introduced with a second "through faith" (διὰ τῆς πίστεως; cf. διὰ πίστεως in v. 33).

impress upon all who will hear the necessity of living by faith if they would please God.

1 The pastor begins with a carefully crafted definition of faith designed to stimulate the perseverance of his hearers in a life of obedience through dependence upon God — "Now faith is the reality of things hoped for, the evidence of things not seen."[1] Faith is oriented toward both the future, hoped-for realization of God's promised reward (vv. 9, 11, 13, 26, 39-40) and the present, but unseen, reality of God's existence, providence (v. 6), fidelity (v. 11) and power (v. 19).[2] There is no reason to argue that, while the future hope is based on biblical categories, the "things not seen" are derived from Platonic dualism.[3] Belief in the present power and faithfulness of God was the common heritage of all who accepted the OT.[4]

Many English versions translate the first part of this verse "Now faith is the assurance of things hoped for" (NASB; cf. T/NIV). However, this subjective understanding of the word translated "assurance" has little support in contemporary usage. "Reality" (HCSB) is more in line with linguistic evidence (see the comments on 1:3; 3:14).[5] The philosophers used this term to

---

1. The question as to whether this verse should be called a "definition" is inconsequential (Braun, 337). The pastor highlights the essential characteristics of faith that he would emphasize for his hearers' — and our — benefit (Thompson, 229; cf. Koester, 479). Thus, Eisenbaum, *Jewish Heroes,* 143, has appropriately described this statement as a "*rhetorical* definition" (italics original). For a survey of the use of such "definitions" in other relevant literature, see Rose, *Die Volke,* 93-96.

2. It is a mistake to make "things not seen" equivalent to the "things hoped for" and then to identify both with the future "promised blessings" yet to be experienced at the Judgment (*pace* Rose, *Die Volke,* 130-35; Braun, 339). It is true that the "things hoped for" already exist and are therefore an unseen reality. However, when the pastor speaks of "things not seen," he is thinking primarily about the power of God available for the people of God in the present. "Things hoped for" is reserved for future reward. This understanding is confirmed by the subsequent examples, who both experience God's power in the present and anticipate receiving his promised blessings in the future. It corresponds to the Christology of this sermon — Christ is at God's right hand, administering the benefits of his sacrifice in the present (8:1-2). He will usher God's people into final salvation at his second coming (9:28). Furthermore, it is in accord with the pastor's two fundamental exhortations: "draw near" to receive the benefits of Christ's work in the present (4:16; 10:22); "hold fast" in order to receive final salvation in the future (4:14; 10:23). Brawley's position stands under the same criticism (Brawley, "Discursive Structure," 81-98).

3. *Pace* Thompson, 231.

4. Thus it is surprising that Attridge, 311, identifies this "unseen" reality as God, his power and faithfulness, but still attributes it to Platonic influence. Furthermore, Hebrews substantiates belief in the unseen world on the basis of the biblical doctrine of creation (v. 3).

5. For ὑπόστασις as "reality" see Attridge, 305; Spicq, 2:337; O'Brien, 399; Helmut Köster, "ὑπόστασις," *TDNT* 8:587; BDAG, 1040, 1b. Köster, however, mistakenly

distinguish "reality" from mere "appearance."[6] It was also used for the "guarantee" or "title deed" to property in the business transactions of ordinary life.[7] We probably understand this statement best, however, if we remember that "faith" refers to a way of life and not to mere theoretical belief. Thus, one might paraphrase, "Faith is living in accord with the reality of things hoped for," or "faith is living as if the things hoped for are real." This interpretation is eminently appropriate for the immediate context: Abraham conducted his whole life on the assumption that the heavenly "homeland" (vv. 13-16) and permanent City (v. 10) were real; Moses lived for the eternal "reward" (v. 26). The pastor would have his hearers conduct themselves as if the promised "Unshakable Kingdom" (12:25-29) were real rather than in pursuit of worldly goods. It is true that such a life of faith does not bring the future, hoped-for salvation into existence. It is, however, the means the pastor would have his hearers pursue in order that this final salvation might become a reality for them. Perseverance in such faith is also the guarantee of future enjoyment. Thus, this understanding of the opening clause is in perfect accord with the author's pastoral concern that his hearers live by faith in order to receive what God has promised. Such faith is no meritorious act, but simply utter dependence upon the living God.[8]

Faith is also "the evidence of things not seen." Subjective renderings like "the conviction of things not seen" (NASB; cf. T/NIV) are even more inappropriate as translations of this term. Faith is the objective "evidence" or "proof" (HCSB) of unseen reality.[9] How does faith "prove" the unseen reality of God, his power and faithfulness? As the examples of this chapter show, through trust in God the faithful experience his power in their lives and receive his approval. Thus, they confirm his reality. The pastor offers these examples of faith and the way God demonstrated his power in their lives as evidence for the reality of God and his present activity on his people's behalf.[10]

---

attributes this "reality" not to faith but to the things hoped for and thus interprets this passage in terms of Platonic dualism. Cosby, *The Rhetorical Composition and Function of Hebrews 11*, 38-40, is correct in arguing that ὑπόστασις ("reality") should be understood in light of the author's rhetorical purpose and the close connection between 10:39 and 11:1. He errs, however, in thinking that an objective sense of ὑπόστασις is inconsistent with these factors.

6. See Artemidorus, *Onir.* 3.14; Aristotle, *De mundo* 395A (cited in Johnson, 277).

7. See BDAG, 1041, 4. deSilva, 383, citing David A. Worley Jr., "God's Faithfulness to Promise: The Hortatory Use of Commissive Language in Hebrews" (Ph.D. diss., Yale University, 1981), 87-92, thinks the translation "title deed" appropriate in light of the temporal property lost by the hearers according to 10:32-34.

8. Hughes, 440.

9. See ἔλεγχος ("proof") in BDAG, 315, 1; Lane, 2:329; cf. O'Brien, 399-400.

10. Johnson, 280.

He would also have his hearers live "by faith" that they might experience this power themselves and know this confirmation. During the earthly lives of the OT faithful the high priesthood of Christ was part of the "things hoped for." For all who live since Jesus, his high priesthood is the very present expression of the real but "unseen" power and faithfulness of God to save.[11] Thus, the faith enjoined by the pastor is profoundly Christ-centered. Both those who lived before his coming and those who come after enter the heavenly homeland only through him (11:39–12:3). If the pastor's hearers would live "by faith," they must persist in "drawing near" to God through Christ (4:14-16; 10:19-25).[12]

2 "By this" kind of faith defined in v. 1 "the people of old were attested" by God.[13] The term we have translated "people of old" or "elders" is a respectful way of honoring the examples of faith that follow. Like the wilderness generation described in 3:7–4:11, they were among the "fathers" to

11. K. Backhaus, "Das Land der Verheissung: Die Heimat der Glaubenden im Hebräerbrief," *NTS* 47 (2001): 184-85, gives too little attention to the Christology of Hebrews when he argues that both those who lived before and those who come after Christ stand in exactly the same position in relationship to the promise — its fulfillment is future. His assertion that "Jesus does not fulfill the promise but makes it certain" is misleading. The blessings Christ bestows, as described in 4:14-16 and 10:19-25, include but are much more than mere assurance.

12. Grässer, *Glaube,* is able to denude the "faith" of Heb 11:1-40 from its Christological focus only by isolating this chapter from the rest of Hebrews and by failing to see how the reorientation of the OT faithful toward the heavenly homeland necessitates the work of Christ. On this reorientation see the work of Pamela Eisenbaum cited above. Hamm, "Jesus Factor," 270-91, has clearly established the importance of Christ for the faith enjoined by Hebrews. Some of the arguments for the Christocentric nature of faith in Hebrews provided by Rhee, *Faith in Hebrews,* are substantial, but others are weak. His work is marred by an undue use of chiasm and by a rigid insistence that each hortatory section depends on the previous expository section. Thus he fails to note one of the strongest arguments for his case — the transitional role played by 10:19-39 (Rhee, *Faith in Hebrews,* 154-78). This passage establishes the Christological focus of faith by linking the teaching on faith in 11:1–12:29 with the Christology of 7:1–10:18. Only by drawing near to God through Christ, their High Priest, in reliance on his sole sufficiency (7:1–10:18), could the hearers successfully live the life of faith enjoined in 11:1–12:29. Once one realizes that the high-priestly work of Christ *is* the word that God has spoken and now speaks through him (see the comments on 1:1-4), every exhortation to faith in God and his word is then, for those who live after Christ, an exhortation to faith in him. For further criticism of Grässer see Graham Hughes, *Hebrews and Hermeneutics: The Epistle to the Hebrews as a New Testament Example of Biblical Interpretation* (SNTSMS 36; Cambridge: Cambridge University Press, 1979), 137-42; Rose, *Die Volke,* 77-79; and Rissi, *Theologie,* 105.

13. ἐν ταύτῃ is instrumental, referring to the faith described in v. 1 (Attridge, 314).

whom "of old" God spoke (1:1).[14] Unlike that generation, they lived "by faith" and thus received divine approval at the end of their lives rather than exclusion from the divine "rest."[15] The Scriptural record is testimony to this ultimate divine acceptance.[16] Their "attestation" by God is also their validation as examples worthy of emulation by the pastor's hearers if they too would receive that ultimate divine commendation. Thus, from the beginning the pastor anticipates the conclusion of this history at the Judgment (12:25-29). In various ways these "people of old" described in the following verses elucidate and enrich the meaning of "by faith."[17]

3 This verse initiates the roll call of those who lived "by faith" from the beginning of Genesis to the conquest of Jericho. It was appropriate for this list to begin with creation since it is the first part of a history that climaxes with the consummation (12:25-29). Yet we must not let the natural way in which the pastor introduces this topic blind us to the fundamental significance of his assertion: "the worlds [ages] were ordered by the word of God."[18] These words take the hearers back to the first chapter of Genesis. There God created the physical world and arranged its parts in a harmonious whole by merely speaking his word.[19] But the term translated "worlds" also means "ages."[20] It is by the word of God that the "ages" of the world have

14. See Rose, *Die Volke,* 28.

15. ἐμαρτυρήθησαν is a cumulative aorist, affirming the final witness of God to all the faithful who will be described in the following verses. See Lane, 326g. The use of the verb μαρτυρέω in vv. 4 and 5 suggests that ἐμαρτυρήθησαν (a divine passive; cf. 7:8, 17; 10:15; 11:2, 4, 5, 39) should be translated in the normal way, they were "attested" or "approved" by God because of their faith. Baugh's suggestion that the elders were "testified" to by God concerning "the invisible objects of hope" is less than convincing (S. M. Baugh, "The Cloud of Witnesses in Hebrews 11," *WTJ* 68 [2006]: 118).

16. See Lane, 330.

17. Eisenbaum, *Jewish Heroes,* 141. Yet Eisenbaum, *Jewish Heroes,* 144-46, suggests that πίστει ("by faith") is little more than a rhetorical device that gives cohesion to the great variety of examples in this chapter. This variety, however, is important. The pastor does not force all of these heroes into one mold. His understanding of faith is coherent but not simplistic or monochromatic. As we will see, he uses the various ways in which these heroes are described in the biblical text to elucidate the various facets of faith.

18. Other example lists from antiquity, such as Wisdom 10 and Sirach 43–50 (if we include chapter 43 in this list of heroes) mention the creation. See Rose, *Die Volke,* 85, 158.

19. Spicq, 2:340, suggests that τοὺς αἰῶνας ("the worlds," "the ages") refers to the different parts of the created universe — firmament, earth, heavenly bodies. κατηρτίσθαι ("to arrange," "to order") indicates their arrangement by God. The perfect γεγονέναι ("have come into being") affirms their continued existence as God's creation. "What was striking to the Israelite in regard to creation was less its existence than its harmony, its finality, and the wisdom that it revealed" (Spicq, 2:340).

20. For αἰών in the temporal sense, "age," see Heb 1:8; 5:6; 6:5; 7:17, 21, 24, 28;

been ordered and will be brought to their climax (cf. 1:2). The next phrase brings out the significance of these facts — "so that what is seen has not come into being from things that appear."[21] "What is seen" is singular, describing the whole created order. It has not come into being from any "things that appear" or have the quality of visibility. This affirmation is the foundation of the faith exemplified in this chapter — it is not the visible world of daily experience but God and his word that constitute ultimate reality. His word is ultimate because it is the means of creation. Thus, it is also the means of redemption (see the comments on 1:1-4) and final Judgment (12:25-29). To live "by faith," then, is from beginning to end to live in accord with the word of God.[22]

It is possible to take the negative "not" with "things visible" instead of with "has come into being," resulting in the following translation: "so that what is seen has come into being from things that are not visible."[23] This rendering invites commentators to further identify the "things that are not visible." The pastor is hardly referring to the Platonic world of ideas, as some have suggested.[24] In this chapter it is God (11:27), his existence, providence (11:6), fidelity (11:11), and power (11:19), along with the heavenly city he has prepared (11:9-10), that constitute invisible reality. Furthermore, it is still the "word" of God that is "the most obvious element of" the "transcendent world."[25] This identification of the "word of God" with "things not seen" is

---

9:26; 13:8, 21. The spatial connotation "world" is dominant in 6:5, 20 (Johnson, 279). Rose, *Die Volke,* 157, is guilty of overinterpretation when he tries to make this verse a reference to the present age/visible world and to the age-to-come/invisible world.

21. εἰς with the articular infinitive (τὸ . . . γεγονέναι, "have come into being") shows result (Attridge, 315).

22. See Rose, *Die Volke,* 158-59.

23. Does μή ("not") go with the infinitive γεγονέναι ("have come into being") or with the participle ἐκ φαινομένων ("from things that appear")? The first is followed by the NASB: "so that what is seen was *not* made out of things which are visible" (cf. NKJV, NIV, italics added); cf. Lane, 2:326-27, who calls this rendering more natural. It allows the writer to put μή early for emphasis and delay γεγονέναι until the end for the same reason. The second is represented by the NRSV: "so that what is seen was made from things that are *not* visible" (italics added; cf. REB). Attridge, 315; Spicq, 2:341; and Ellingworth, 568, follow this interpretation.

24. Attridge, 316, and Thompson, 232 (following Braun, Grässer, and Weiss), associate this term with Platonism. Yet Attridge, 311, is the one who affirms that God, his power, providence, fidelity, etc., constitutes the unseen reality. Koester, 474, notes insightfully that Hebrews fails to consistently posit the connectedness between heavenly patterns and earthly realities that we would expect from a document rooted in Platonic dualism.

25. Attridge, 316; cf. Koester, 474; Hughes, 452; Rose, *Die Volke,* 156-59; and Johnson, 280.

confirmed by the way Ellingworth has shown that the two expressions are mirror images of each other in the chiastic structure of this verse.[26] Thus, this alteration in translation leaves the basic interpretation of this verse unchanged — people who live by faith live in accord with the word of God rather than by the values of the visible world. They live confident of God's power in the present and relying upon his promise for the future. The divine word is the agent of the first and the guarantee of the second.

The pastor is pursuing no abstract philosophical discussion of God's existence. He is concerned about God's place in his hearers' lives. Thus, he begins this verse with "by faith *we* know" (italics added). This turn of phrase accomplishes several important objectives. First, the inclusive "we" brings the pastor and his hearers close together. Second, this manner of speaking embraces the hearers from the outset within the company of the faithful, whom the pastor would have them emulate and with whom he would have them identify.[27] Finally, by speaking thus, the pastor affirms that they also are committed to the fundamental principle that underlies the life of faith. "We," like these heroes of faith, have come to this understanding of God's word through our own trust in God and experience of his power.[28] Thus, at the very beginning the pastor calls his hearers to testify to themselves. They are not of "those who turn back" (10:39) but of those who persevere through trusting in God's promise and power. They are not to live as if this visible world were the ultimate reality, the final source of happiness, approval, gain, or loss. They know better. They are to live as if the unseen God and his power are the ultimate reality — which they are. The pastor will not address them again in the first person plural until he reaches the climax of his list and urges them, "Let us run the race laid before us" (12:1) in imitation of this "cloud of witnesses" now behind us. Then he will direct their vision to the exalted Jesus (12:2), who alone enables them to reach the goal.

4-5 Abel and Enoch establish a pattern for all the heroes who follow.[29]

---

26. Ellingworth, 568: (A) κατηρτίσθαι ("were ordered"); (B) τοὺς αἰῶνας ("the worlds"); (C) ῥήματι θεοῦ ("by the word of God"); (C1) μὴ ἐκ φαινομένων ("from things that do not appear"); (B1) τὸ βλεπόμενον ("what is visible"); (A1) γεγονέναι ("has come into being"). If μὴ ("not") is taken with γεγονέναι ("has come into being"), then this chiastic relationship would demonstrate that ῥήματι θεοῦ ("by the word of God") is the opposite of ἐκ φαινομένων ("from things that appear"). Cf. O'Brien, 402.

27. Koester, 480. Rose, *Die Volke,* 158, argues that "we" includes not only author and hearers but the heroes of faith in the following verses. Faith in the creation and in the final fulfillment of God's promised salvation unites both those who come before Christ and those who come after (cf. 11:39-40).

28. νοοῦμεν ("we understand") is perfective present, indicating a state of understanding reached by our experience of God's power through faith (Ellingworth, 570).

29. According to O'Brien, 403, n. 50, "these first two examples form a pair in

Taken together, they anticipate Christ's example of suffering and triumph (12:1-3). Sometimes, as in the case of Abel, people suffer for their faith without temporal deliverance. At other times, as in the case of Enoch, God brings great deliverance in response to faith. For most, the life of faith is a mixture of suffering and triumph. Thus, Abraham lived as an alien in the Promised Land but also experienced God's power, especially through the birth of Isaac (vv. 8-19). Moses suffered ill-treatment with the people of God and endured the wrath of the king, but also experienced God's mighty deliverance from Egypt (vv. 23-29). In some lives God's great deliverance is the dominant experience. Thus, Enoch anticipates those enumerated below in vv. 32-35a, through whom God accomplished mighty deeds of deliverance including temporal resurrection. But Abel anticipates the final examples at the end of this chapter, vv. 35b-38, who suffer in this life without reprieve in order to obtain the "better resurrection."[30] However, it is important to note that Enoch's translation surpasses the temporal deliverance experienced by all those in this chapter whom he typifies. Even those who were brought back to life eventually died. From the beginning the pastor would assert that God's power to deliver transcends death. Every temporal deliverance provides assurance of ultimate deliverance in the "better resurrection" (11:35b) because it bears witness to the faithfulness and power of God. The pastor would prepare his hearers to suffer and die for their loyalty to Christ, in imitation of Abel, by assuring them that God's power transcends death, as demonstrated by Enoch. He is a God "who raises the dead" (v. 19).

In a more profound sense, however, every person who lives by faith identifies with both Abel and Enoch. All, like Abel, will die without receiving the fullness of what God has promised. All, like Enoch, are promised triumph over death. Heb 12:1-3 will make it clear that this victory is assured to the faithful by Christ's experience to the ultimate degree of both Abel's suffering and Enoch's deliverance.[31] Innocent Abel died for his faith — Christ "endured the cross, despising the shame." Enoch was "translated" — Christ

---

the account of Heb. 11: explicit mention is made of the divine commendation of both (vv. 4, 5), there is a common interest in the death of each (vv. 4, 5), and the accounts describe their responses of faith in God without specific reference to the spoken word of God (as in Noah's case) or the promise of God (as for Abraham, Isaac, and Jacob). Lane, 2:335."

30. Victor Rhee's chiastic understanding of Heb 11:1-40 is somewhat forced (see Victor Rhee, "Chiasm and the Concept of Faith in Hebrews 11," *BSac* 155 [July-September 1998]: 327-45). Yet he recognizes the chiastic relationship between (A) suffering Abel (v. 4); (B) triumphant Enoch (v. 5); and (B[1]) the examples of triumph in vv. 33-35a; (A[1]) the examples of suffering in vv. 35b-38. On the chiastic structure of 11:1-31, see below and Cockerill, "The Better Resurrection (Heb. 11:35)," 215-34.

31. Thus, it is not, as Spicq, 2:342-43, suggests, merely Abel (11:4) and Christ (12:1-3) that frame this section, but Abel/Enoch (11:4-5) and Christ.

"has sat down at the right of the throne of God." He is both the "Pioneer" and "Perfecter" of faith (12:2).[32]

Abel (Gen 4:2-8) was not a major figure in Jewish literature and plays virtually no part in other lists of past heroes.[33] Yet some considered him to be the first martyr (4 Macc 18:11). Since he comes right after the creation, he was the pastor's natural choice for an opening example that would encourage the faithful who suffer without relief in this life. Nor is it surprising that the pastor refers to his sacrifice, since little else is recorded about him in Scripture: "By faith Abel offered a better sacrifice than Cain." God's acceptance proved that Abel's sacrifice was offered "by faith" and was thus "better" than Cain's.[34] The pastor adds "by God bearing witness in regard to his gifts" in order to make it very clear that it was through his "sacrifice" that he received divine attestation as "righteous."[35] It was traditional to speak of "righteous Abel."[36] However, the use of this term to describe his approval by God demonstrates that he initiates the roll call of God's "righteous one[s] who live by faith" as described in the quotation from Habakkuk in Heb 10:37-38 above.

It is clear, then, that God attested Abel as righteous not after his death but after his sacrifice while he was still alive. Furthermore, it is "through this," that is, through his act of faith in offering this sacrifice, that Abel "still speaks" to the people of God.[37] Thus, Koester is correct when he says that the author of

32. Thus there is no need to speculate, as does Eisenbaum, *Jewish Heroes,* 147-51, on why the pastor chose to use Abel and Enoch.

33. Thompson, 232. See also the chart in Rose, *Die Volke,* 85.

34. For speculation about the moral qualities of Cain and Abel, see Josephus, *Ant.* 1.52-59. No doubt the pastor believed that Abel's sacrifice was accepted because Abel acted in accord with the conviction that God's promise of future reward was sure and his power in the present was real. When *Targum Neofiti* 21-23 and *Targum Pseudo-Jonathan* 5 comment on Gen 4:8, they describe Cain and Abel in the field arguing over a future judgment, a Judge, rewards for the righteous, and punishment for the wicked. Abel affirms all of these things. Cain denies them and then kills Abel. See Rose, *Die Volke,* 160-78. Yet the pastor makes no use of such speculations. He waits until the Scriptural text gives him warrant to describe the following heroes of faith as those who believe in God's future City, etc.

35. δι' ἧς, "through which," probably refers to the closer feminine noun, θυσίαν ("sacrifice"), rather than to the more distant πίστει ("faith"). See Attridge, 316. There is, however, little difference in meaning since his "sacrifice" was the expression of his "faith." I have taken the genitive absolute, μαρτυροῦντος ἐπὶ τοῖς δώροις αὐτοῦ τοῦ θεοῦ, as instrumental, "by God's bearing witness in regard to his gifts." τοῖς δώροις ("gifts") is equivalent to θυσίαι ("sacrifice"). See 5:1; 8:3-4; 9:9.

36. For Abel as "righteous," see Josephus, *Ant.* 1.53; *Ascen. Isa.* 6:8; *T. Iss.* 5:4 (cited in Johnson, 281). Cf. Matt 23:35; 1 John 3:12.

37. δι' αὐτῆς ("through this") is feminine, referring not merely to his "faith" (πίστει; *pace* Rose, *Die Volke,* 162), but to his faith expressed through his "sacrifice" (θυσίαν). It is Abel himself, through Scripture, who speaks (Moffatt, 164; Lane, 2:335; cf.

Hebrews does not speculate about Abel's heavenly existence.[38] Nor does Abel speak from heaven. It is through his act of faith recorded in Scripture that he "still speaks." Still, by adding the phrase "although he has died," the pastor deliberately raises a question: "How could Abel by his faith be a witness to the faithfulness of God if his death ended it all?"[39] If that were true, why would anyone want to emulate such an example? The pastor probably believes that Abel is one of those "spirits of the righteous made perfect" now in the heavenly city (12:23). Yet because of his commitment to base his sermon on Scripture he makes no effort to use the example of Abel to answer this question. Thus the example of Abel and his innocent death forces the hearers to ask: "Does not the validity of faith depend on God's power to transcend death?"[40] "Must he not be a God who raises the dead?" (See the comments below on 11:19, 35b.) The example of Enoch that immediately follows will confirm that this is true. These same considerations mean that Abel exemplifies one meaning for "my righteous one will live by faith" (Heb 10:38/Hab 2:4): "my righteous one lives," that is, conducts his or her life, "by faith." It is left for Enoch and others to show that "my righteous one lives," that is, receives eternal life, "by faith."

The pastor has been careful to use a different word for "better" when describing Abel's sacrifice than he used for Christ's.[41] However, this combination of obedience, sacrifice, and innocent death clearly anticipates the work of Christ. "Righteous" Abel presented a sacrifice that was pleasing to God because offered in faith. In a similar — but greater — way, the sinless Son of God offered a sacrifice that was pleasing because of his perfect obedience (10:5-10). He is the "righteous one" par excellence. As noted above, Abel anticipates Christ's obedient death; Enoch, his triumphant exaltation.

O'Brien, 403-4), not (*pace* Attridge, 317; Ellingworth, 573; Spicq, 2:343; cf. Johnson, 281) Abel's blood. The pastor uses the same word for "speak" (λαλέω) in 12:24, where he is referring to Christ's blood "speaking" a better word than Abel's. However, the use of this common word is no indication that 11:3 is a reference to Abel's blood. The LXX of Gen 4:10 uses βοάω, "cry out," in reference to "the voice" of Abel's blood. *Pace* Spicq, 2:343, and Bénétreau, 2:138, Abel's "speaking" is no type of Christ's intercession. Abel speaks not to God but to "us" as a witness to faith.

38. Koester, 476, comparing Hebrews with the speculations in *L.A.E.* 40.

39. Cf. Hughes, 457. Weiss's statement, though cautious and very modern sounding, attests this fact: "The specially emphasized contrast between 'dead' and 'yet-speaking' thus signifies here at least that faith in the end also bears in itself a power that overcomes death" (Weiss, 577).

40. Thus, with Koester (482), Abel's speaking means that "death is not the end of his story." The pastor refrains from saying that Abel is the first example of one who lives beyond the grave (see Attridge, 317), though that is what he intends his exposition to suggest.

41. Compare πλείονα, here certainly to be taken as qualitative, "better" (Ellingworth, 571; Lane, 335), with κρείττοσιν θυσίαις ("better sacrifices") in 9:23.

The account of Enoch in Gen 5:21-24 begins typically enough by giving his age at the birth of his firstborn (v. 21) and the number of years he lived after that birth (v. 22). However, the Scriptural text then makes two statements about him that distinguish him from all others.[42] It is these two statements that catch the attention of the author of Hebrews. First, Genesis describes the course of his life: he "walked with God" (v. 22, repeated for emphasis in v. 24a). Then it describes the unusual end of his life: "and he was not, for God took him" (v. 24b). The LXX renders the first of these statements as "he pleased God"; the second by, "and he was not found because God translated him." Hebrews begins with the LXX version of Enoch's remarkable end. The pastor interprets the meaning of Enoch's being "translated" in v. 5a and then quotes the biblical text as support in v. 5b. First, Enoch can be included in this list because his "translation" was "by faith." He was "translated" because he lived in obedient dependence upon God's power and promises.[43] Second, the pastor clarifies what is intimated by the biblical text in both Hebrew and Greek — this "translation" meant that "he did not see," that is, he did not experience "death." Enoch's being taken by God was a "translation" that bypassed the death incumbent on all (cf. 2:14-15).[44] In v. 5b the pastor quotes Gen 5:24b in support of this interpretation: "and he was not found because God translated him."[45] The pastor assumes his hearers will include Enoch along with Abel among the "righteous."[46] Abel is the paradigmatic example of "my righteous one who lives," that is, conducts his earthly life, "by faith." Enoch, however, is the corresponding example of "my

42. On the vast amount of speculation about Enoch, who was taken up to God without death, see Johnson, 282-83. The pastor sticks close to the Genesis text in the LXX and shows little, if any, influence from such speculations.

43. Spicq, 2:344, thinks that this should be translated "by, in exchange for, because of his translation" he pleased God. This understanding fits poorly, with both the Genesis text and the immediate context in Hebrews. Enoch's translation is not the cause of his pleasing God but its attestation.

44. The OT text was also understood as Enoch's bypassing death in Philo, *Names* 38; *QG* 1.86; Josephus, *Ant.* 1.85; and *Jub.* 4:23. It is true that Enoch, along with all of the other faithful who lived before Christ, was not "perfected" and thus did not enter into the presence of God before, or at least apart from, the coming of Christ (11:39-40). The pastor does not tell us where Enoch was from the time he bypassed death until the coming of Christ any more than he tells us where the other heroes of faith were between their deaths and the coming of Christ. See the comments on vv. 39-40 below. This fact, however, does not take away from the fact that Enoch bypassed, that is, overcame, death.

45. Heb 11:5b quotes Gen 5:24b (LXX) verbatim, καὶ οὐχ ηὑρίσκετο ὅτι μετέθηκεν αὐτὸν ὁ θεός (underlining added), only substituting διότι for the synonym ὅτι (underlined above). In this context both Greek words mean "because."

46. For Enoch as "righteous" see *T. Levi* 10:5; *T. Dan* 5:6; *T. Benj.* 9:1; cf. Wis 4:4, 7, 16; *1 En.* 1:2; 12:1; *Jub.* 10:17 (cited by Koester, 476).

righteous one who lives," that is, obtains eternal life, "by faith."[47] Both are necessary for an adequate understanding of what it means to live in dependence on God.

How can the hearers know that Enoch lived "by faith"? The brief biblical text does not use "by faith" to describe him any more than it used "by faith" in conjunction with Abel. The pastor assumes that Abel acted "by faith" because God accepted his "gifts." The hearers can be sure that Enoch acted "by faith" because the biblical text says twice that "he pleased God." In v. 6 the pastor will make it clear that no one can please God without living in reliance on his present power and in confidence of his future promise. Indirectly addressing any lingering doubt in the hearers' minds, this argument reinforces the fact that Abel acted by faith. Abel must have pleased God if God received his sacrifice. Although the pastor could have supported his premise on the basis of the Hebrew text, "Enoch walked with God" (Gen 5:23, 24a), he found the LXX rendering, "Enoch pleased God," felicitous for his purposes. The perceptive Greek translator wished to bring out the significance of this praise used only of Enoch, for no other patriarch of Genesis is described as "walking with God."[48] Certainly one who walked with God pleased him.

Enoch's translation may anticipate all of the other triumphs of faith in this chapter, but it also surpasses them. Thus, it both points to and pales before the Christ whom it typifies. Enoch did not experience death. The Son of God experienced the bitterness of death to the full in order that he might conquer death for all (2:9; 5:7-10; 9:14; 10:5-10; 12:1-3).

6 According to Hab 2:4 (Heb 10:38), God's "soul was not pleased" with someone who "turns back." On the other hand, God is pleased with those who "live by faith." Therefore the pastor affirms: "For without faith it is impossible to please God." This statement is important for the argument. It confirms the faith of Abel and Enoch — they pleased God; therefore, they must have been people of faith. It plays an even greater role in the author's pastoral concern for his hearers: if they would please God, they must be people characterized by this kind of faith. How vital it is to understand the nature of this faith. Thus, the pastor would confirm and augment the "definition" he gave at the opening of this chapter by describing the object of faith: "for the one who comes to God must believe that he is and that he is a rewarder of those who diligently seek him." The significance of this statement becomes clearer when its elements are viewed as the mirror image of v. 1:

---

47. The author of Hebrews says that Enoch did not "see death" in order to show that faith transcended death. He is not combating ancient Jewish speculations that Enoch was "taken" by God in death because he became godless. *Pace* Rose, *Die Volke,* 184, 190.

48. Spicq, 2:343-44; cf. Hughes, 457.

A. "Faith is the reality of things hoped for" (v. 1a)
B. "the evidence of things not seen." (v. 1b)
B[1]. "The one who comes to God must believe that he is" (v. 6b)
A[1]. "and that he is a rewarder of those who diligently seek him."
(v. 6c)

Once again the pastor emphasizes both the present and future orientations of faith. Believing that God "is" clarifies what the pastor meant by "things not seen" in v. 1b. As argued above, those unseen "things" are God, his power, and his fidelity. The people of faith live as if God "is" and is powerfully active on behalf of the faithful in the present.[49] Furthermore, they live with confidence in the future when they will receive the "things hoped for" because God is "a rewarder of those who diligently seek him."[50] Those translations that read "he rewards" (NRSV) instead of "he is a rewarder" diminish the pastor's message: the faithful live with anticipation of receiving what God has promised because of their absolute confidence in the character of God (cf. 6:13-20). Faith rests securely on his faithfulness and power. This God-centered perspective is in complete harmony with the rest of Scripture and confirms the understanding of faith given above. Notice how the pastor begins in v. 1 with "things hoped for" and concludes in this verse with "God is a rewarder."[51] He misses no chance to fix his hearers' attention on the ultimate Goal — where Christ is enthroned at the right hand of God (12:1-3).

The pastor makes it clear that this belief in the reality of God and the certainty of his promises is far more than speculation or mental assent. Thus, in Greek this statement begins with an emphatic "to believe." It is addressed to the one "who draws near to God" in worship and service. The promised salvation is only for those "who diligently seek" God.[52] With all of these terms the pastor calls his hearers to faith as a way of life. They are to act as if God is real and his promises are certain. Thus, there can be no disjuncture between faith and obedience (v. 8; see on 3:18-19). Nor can there be any waffling about their commitment to Christ, who has become for them the present power of God, fully sufficient for their perseverance, and the one through whom they will receive what God has promised.

---

49. *Pace* Rose, *Die Volke*, 186-89, the pastor is not concerned with the theoretical existence of God, as were the Stoics (see references in Rose).

50. Spicq, 2:345.

51. The last two words in the Greek text of v. 6 are μισθαποδότης γίνεται ("he is a rewarder"). One could translate these words "he becomes a rewarder" for those who seek him. He is not such a rewarder for those who do not.

52. The participle τοὺς ἐκζητοῦσιν, "those who diligently seek [him]," describes "a singular determination to devote oneself to the service of God. It implies the recognition that human action has to demonstrate its integrity before God." Lane, 2:338.

7   Noah is the next major godly person in the Genesis narrative so familiar to the pastor's hearers. They know that Noah, like Abel and Enoch, was both "righteous" (Gen 6:9; 7:1) and pleasing to God (Gen 6:9).[53] And yet the pastor employs v. 6 to separate Noah from these two earlier examples because he would use Noah to emphasize the future orientation of faith. As noted above, v. 6 ends with the words "is a rewarder." Noah lived as if God was "a rewarder," as if his promise — or in this case his warning — for the future was sure: "Having been warned [by God] concerning things not yet seen." Those "things not yet seen" were the coming universal judgment of the flood that anticipated or typified the final Judgment at the end of history (12:25-29; cf. 1 Pet 3:20). God's promise of eternal blessing can be understood only in light of his warning against ultimate judgment. Throughout the rest of this history the pastor describes the promised hope of the faithful in the most positive terms as a heavenly home (11:13-16); an eternal City (11:9-10; 12:22-24); a great "reward" (11:26); and an "Unshakable Kingdom" (12:28). However, by beginning (11:7) and ending (12:25-29) with judgment, he will not let his hearers forget that from which God has delivered them. God promises his own deliverance from eternal judgment (9:28) so that they can enjoy life in the promised eternal City (vv. 9-10). The pastor would motivate his hearers by focusing their attention on the promised blessing without letting them forget the threat of judgment.

It is quite appropriate to describe Noah's response to God's warning as his being "moved by godly fear."[54] As noted on 5:7 above, such "godly fear" is the full recognition — by the way one lives — of God's awesome sovereign power and faithfulness. Noah came to such a recognition of God "by faith," that is, by believing both in God's "promise" of a flood and in his fearsome power to bring it about. His "godly fear" became fully real in his obedience — "he built an ark." From Noah the hearers learn that true faith leads to an inner recognition of and complete surrender to God that expresses itself in humble obedience. Thus, Noah fills in the nature of the faith outlined by the pastor's descriptions of Abel and Enoch and establishes a context for the following examples of those who live "by faith." The "godly fear" (5:7) through which Christ has provided salvation is replicated in the lives of God's people "by faith."

53. See also Ezek 14:14, 20. Jewish tradition often describes Noah as "righteous" (Sir 44:17; Wis 10:4; *Jub.* 5:19; 10:17; Philo, *Worse* 105; *Posterity* 48.173-74; *Giants* 5; *Agriculture* 2; *Prelim. Studies* 90; *Migration* 125; *Abraham* 46). See Rose, *Die Volke*, 193-94.

54. Lane, 2:327v. The aorist passive participle εὐλαβηθείς, "having been moved by godly fear," is causal. The NRSV mistakenly weakens this participle immeasurably when it reduces it to "respected the warning." This translation also masks the connection with the godliness of Jesus in 5:7.

This emphasis on future judgment enables the pastor to use Noah as proof that God will deliver his "righteous one" from the Judgment "by faith." Close attention to the text shows that Noah "condemned the world" and "became an heir of righteousness" by being delivered from the universal judgment of the flood. Noah built an "ark for the salvation of his household." We can understand this salvation as either the purpose or the result of his building the ark. The next phrase, "through which," is crucial. The word for "which" is feminine, and thus probably refers to the closest feminine antecedent — "salvation," or possibly to the feminine noun for "ark" a bit earlier in the Greek sentence. "Ark" and "salvation" are so closely related that the decision between them is not crucial. It is through the "salvation" from the flood provided by the "ark" that Noah both "condemned the world" and "became an heir of the righteousness that is according to faith."[55] This condemning "of the" unbelieving "world" did not take place through the preaching of Noah.[56] He did not "become an heir of the righteousness that is according to faith" while he was building the ark. These two expressions refer to the condemnation of the world and the deliverance of Noah at the time of universal judgment by the flood. The "godly fear" by which Noah was moved is the appropriate response of all the faithful before the Judgment (12:28).

Attention to the text of Genesis confirms this explanation as representing the pastor's intention. As we have seen above, the pastor describes Abel as "righteous" because of the way he conducted his life. The first verse of the Noah account in Genesis — Gen 9:6 — calls Noah "righteous."[57] Yet the pastor does not use this term to describe him. Instead, Hebrews says that he "became an heir of the righteousness that is according to faith" through the deliverance provided by the ark. A careful comparison of terminology

55. Thus, agreeing with Rose, *Die Volke,* 201, that the relative clause beginning with δι᾽ ἧς continues through κληρονόμος.

56. In 2 Pet 2:5 Noah is called a "preacher of righteousness." In other sources he preaches to his contemporaries, calling them to repentance (*Sib. Or.* 1:125-36, 150-98; *1 Clem.* 7:6; Clement of Alexandria, *Stromateis* 1.2.1). For more on the use of Noah in other literature, see Johnson, 285-86 (referencing Weiss), and Rose, *Die Volke,* 197-99. Since the author of Hebrews focuses on Noah's act of faith in building the ark, it is not, *pace* deSilva, 391, surprising that he makes nothing of this tradition about Noah's preaching. Furthermore, the pastor usually stays close to the biblical text when describing these heroes of faith. Cf. Koester, 477.

57. Noah was often called "righteous" (δίκαιος) in Jewish tradition (cf. *L.A.B.* 3:4; *Sib. Or.* 1:280; Philo, *Worse* 105; *Posterity* 48; Rose, *Die Volke,* 193-94). Gen 6:9 also describes Noah as "perfect" (τέλειος). However, in the terminology of Hebrews, being made "perfect" is reserved for those who, through Christ, have been so cleansed that they can come into the presence of God. See the comments on 11:39-40. Thus, it would have been confusing for the pastor to describe any of these faithful as "perfect." See Johnson, 284.

shows that the pastor is thinking of Gen 7:1. In that verse, the time of universal judgment through the flood is at hand. Noah has demonstrated his obedience because the ark is ready. God is speaking to Noah: "You and all your household, go into the Ark, because I have seen that you [singular, referring to Noah] are righteous before me in this generation." Noah became "an heir of the righteousness that is by faith" at this point in time when God declared him "righteous" and delivered him from impending universal judgment. Reference to Gen 7:1 is confirmed by the fact that this is the only place in the account of Noah that refers, as does Heb 11:7, to Noah's "household."

Mention of Noah's "household" reminds the hearers of the "household" of God, over which Christ is Son (3:1-6). This link between Noah and Christ is strengthened by the entire phrase "for the salvation of his household." The Genesis account does not describe Noah's deliverance as "salvation." Thus, by using "salvation" and "household" together the pastor establishes a connection between the "salvation" from the flood Noah provided for his "household" through faithful obedience and the "salvation" (9:28) Christ will provide for God's "household" (3:6) at the final Judgment. We have seen that Abel, by his innocent death, foreshadows the suffering of Christ; and Enoch, by his "translation," the exaltation of Christ to God's right hand. In light of the fact that Noah was the agent by which his "household" (= God's people) was delivered, he is an even clearer premonition of Christ's delivering his own at the Judgment (9:28).[58] It is worth noting that the pastor began this sermon by founding all three of these events (suffering, exaltation, second coming) on Ps 110:1 (Heb 1:3, 13) and Ps 8:4-6 (Heb 2:5-9). His teaching on Christ's high priesthood (4:14–10:18) is his explanation of their significance. Through the first two of these events Christ has become the "Pioneer and Perfecter of the faith" (12:2) who will come again "for salvation" (9:28) at the third.

The pastor would have his hearers leave this section on the primeval history with a richer understanding of "my righteous one will live by faith" (Hab 2:4/Heb 10:38). Abel demonstrated that "my righteous one" will conduct his or her life "by faith" even in the face of suffering or death. Enoch proved that "my righteous one" will overcome death "by faith." Noah shows conclusively that "my righteous one" need have no fear of the Judgment "by faith." It is "by faith" that the righteous will finally enter the "Unshakable Kingdom" (12:28) at the consummation of all things. From beginning to end a life of obedience in reliance on God's promises and dependence on his power is the key to pleasing God.

---

58. Baugh, "Cloud of Witnesses," 127-28.

b. Abraham, Faith at Its Best: Perseverance in an Alien World (11:8-22)

8 *By faith Abraham obeyed as soon as he was called to set out for a place that he was going to receive as an inheritance. And he set out, although he did not know where he was going.* 9 *By faith he sojourned in the land of promise as in a strange land, dwelling in tents with Isaac and Jacob, who were fellow heirs of the same promise.* 10 *For he was continually looking forward to the City that has foundations, whose architect and builder is God.* 11 *By faith even Sarah herself, although barren, received power for the disposition of seed, even though she was past the season for child bearing, since she considered that the one who had promised was faithful.* 12 *Therefore, from one man, who was indeed dead, there came into being as many as the stars of heaven in multitude and as the sand along the seashore without number.*

13 *These all died according to faith, although they had not received the promises. However, they had seen them from afar, greeted them, and confessed that <u>they were aliens and transients on earth.</u>* 14 *For those who say such things show that they are diligently seeking <u>a place where they are citizens.</u>* 15 *And if they had been mindful of that place from which they had come, they would have had opportunity to return.* 16 *But now they fervently long for a better, that is, a heavenly place. Therefore, <u>God is not ashamed to be called their God, for he has prepared for them a City.</u>*

17 *By faith Abraham offered Isaac when he was being tested. And he who had received the promises was ready to offer the only begotten,* 18 *he to whom it had been said that "in Isaac will your seed be called."* 19 *He did this because he reckoned that God was able to raise from the dead. Therefore, he received him as a type.*

20 *By faith Isaac blessed Jacob and Esau concerning things to come.* 21 *By faith Jacob, as he was dying, blessed each of the sons of Joseph and worshiped on the top of his staff.* 22 *By faith Joseph, as he was coming to an end, remembered the exodus of the children of Israel and gave instructions concerning his bones.*

The pastor has appropriately chosen Abraham (vv. 8-22) and Moses (vv. 23-31) to be the centerpiece examples of the next two sections. According to Scripture they were the two most important persons in establishing the people of God. God gave Abraham the promise of a redeemed people living in a promised place of blessing. God fulfilled that promise through Moses and Joshua (Josh 23:14). However, in 4:1-11 the pastor has already demonstrated that the conquest under Joshua was not the true fulfillment God had in mind. Something much greater would be made available through Christ.

535

As the recipients of God's "promises" (11:9; cf. 7:6), Abraham and his "fellow heirs" (v. 9), Isaac and Jacob, appropriately set the standard for all the faithful. In earlier days there had been people who lived "by faith" (vv. 1-7). However, God's people came into existence as a defined entity through God's promises to these three patriarchs.[1] Although the pastor pursues four examples from Abraham's life (vv. 8-12, 17-19) and three from his "fellow heirs" (vv. 20-22) in chronological order, he has carefully arranged this material to accomplish his purposes. The first two examples (v. 8, vv. 9-10) pertain to God's promise of a home, and thus envision the destiny of God's people; the third (vv. 11-12), to his promise of a son, thus speaking to that people's origin. The pastor uses these three examples to reinforce what he has already said about faith in vv. 1-7. The first two (vv. 8-10) substantiate the pastor's conviction that "faith is the reality of things hoped for" (v. 1a). Abraham and his "fellow heirs" conducted their lives according to the conviction that the permanent, hoped-for "City" promised by God was real and attainable. The third (vv. 11-12) substantiates the pastor's assertion that "faith is the proof of things not seen" (v. 1b). By faith Sarah experienced the real but unseen power of God in the present through the birth of Isaac.

The pastor also uses these three examples to expand his hearers' understanding of faith by identifying the future reality that faith "hopes for" (v. 1a) and attesting the "unseen" divine power upon which it depends. The first two examples (vv. 8-10) make it clear that the "place" (v. 8) God had promised Abraham was ultimately not the earthly land of Canaan but "a City that has foundations, whose architect and builder is God" (v. 10). This City is the future "hoped-for" object of his people's faith (v. 1a). The third example (vv. 11-12) makes it plain that no one but God raises up a people for himself, and that his power to do so transcends death. This is the power, though often "unseen" (v. 1b), upon which his people depend as they make their way toward the promised City. It is necessary for the pastor to provide additional insight into both the destiny of faith and its sustaining power before going further. In vv. 13-16 he clarifies the relationship of the faithful to the heavenly "City" established by God as their true home. The location of these verses is strategic because the perspective they provide on the heavenly home is foundational to all that follows. The pastor is then free to use the fourth example from the life of Abraham (vv. 17-19) to make a definitive affirmation of

---

1. Eisenbaum, *Jewish Heroes,* 166, makes a distinction foreign to Hebrews when she says that "Abraham, Isaac, and Jacob are not the founding fathers of Israel," but "the ancestors of an elite group." Hebrews agrees with the OT that Abraham, Isaac, and Jacob are "the founding fathers" of the people of God. That people has always consisted of those who have faith in God's promises, which are now fulfilled in Christ. Hebrews never makes a contrast between the people of God and ethnic Israel.

God's power over death — by sacrificing Isaac, Abraham affirmed his faith in a "God who is able to raise from the dead." The God who has provided a heavenly "City" will raise his people from the dead so that they can enjoy it.

The pastor has given multiple indications that mark the importance of Abraham's faith in the resurrection (vv. 17-19). The sacrifice of Isaac through which Abraham affirms this faith is the fourth and climactic example drawn from his life. This event is centrally located between the pastor's explanation of the heavenly City (vv. 13-16) and the examples of Isaac, Jacob, and Joseph, who were seeking that city (vv. 20-22). They also believed in a God whose power transcended death. When we have finished analyzing the structure of 11:1-40 below, we will see that vv. 17-19 and resurrection faith are central to this entire chapter.[2]

The pastor returns to the picture, first introduced in 3:7–4:11, of God's people on pilgrimage to the heavenly home where they are natives and citizens. H. B. Partin has developed a useful paradigm of religious pilgrimage drawn from an analysis of pilgrimages in various world religions.[3] According to this paradigm, there are four characteristics of such journeys: (1) They begin with a definite departure from home and from the normal life of the one going on pilgrimage. (2) They pursue a definite destination — they are not mere wanderings. (3) This destination has religious significance. (4) The journey is often beset with hardship. The pastor will help his hearers endure this hardship by transforming the pilgrim journey into the race of faith in 12:1-13. William Johnsson has shown how the pilgrimage paradigm brings clarity to the heroes of faith 11:1-40.[4] No one illustrates this pattern of pilgrimage better than Abraham.

8 Indeed, no list of heroes could exclude him.[5] Although other writers often ignored his "call" (Gen 12:1-9), the pastor finds this event a most fitting place to begin.[6] Abraham's response illustrates the first three charac-

---

2. See also Cockerill, "The Better Resurrection (Heb. 11:35)," 215-34.

3. H. B. Partin, "The Muslim Pilgrimage: Journey to the Center" (Ph.D. diss., University of Chicago, 1969).

4. Johnsson, "Pilgrimage Motif," 239-51. For an interpretation of Hebrews for people of Muslim background using this paradigm see Gareth Lee Cockerill, *Guidebook for Pilgrims to the Heavenly City* (Pasadena: William Carey Library, 2004). Cf. Gareth Lee Cockerill, "To the Hebrews/to the Muslims: Islamic Pilgrimage as a Key to Interpretation," *Missiology* 22 (1994): 347-59; and Gareth Lee Cockerill, "Building Bridges to Muslims: A Test Case," in *Contextualization and Syncretism: Navigating Cultural Currents,* ed. Gailyn Van Rheenen (Evangelical Missiological Society 13; Pasadena: William Carey Library, 2006), 323-43.

5. Cf. 1 Macc 2:52; 4 Macc 16:20; Sir 44:19-21; Rom 4:3; Gal 3:6; Jas 2:21.

6. Thompson, 234. For fanciful stories about the circumstances of Abraham's leaving Mesopotamia, see David A. deSilva and Victor Matthews, *Untold Stories of the*

teristics of pilgrimage outlined above: he made a definitive break with his former life when he "set out" in response to God's promise (characteristic one).[7] He went in pursuit of a definite, if unknown, "place" (characteristic two). This place had great significance because God had promised it to him "as an inheritance" (characteristic three). His action also demonstrated the kind of faith described in vv. 1 and 6 above: he obeyed because he trusted God's promise calling him "to set out for a place that he was going to receive as an inheritance" (cf. vv. 1a, 6d).[8] Furthermore, he depended upon God's power to sustain him on the way (cf. vv. 1b, 6c). The quality of this faith is further demonstrated by the fact that "he did not know where he was going." The pastor emphasizes the immediacy of Abraham's response. In Greek the initial "by faith" is followed immediately by the present participle "being called" and the aorist verb "he obeyed." This construction is appropriately translated, "as soon as Abraham was called he obeyed."[9] There was no hesitation or procrastination. What a contrast with the people of the wilderness generation, who repeatedly expressed their unbelief through disobedience.[10] The pastor would remind his hearers of the need to respond promptly to their own "heavenly calling" (3:1). By concluding the primeval history with Noah's "godly fear" (v. 7) and beginning his presentation of Abraham with obedience, the pastor sets the direction for all of the following heroes.[11] Faith

---

Bible (Lincolnwood, IL: Publications International Ltd., 1998), 34-48 (cited in deSilva, 393, n. 43). The brief references in Philo to Abraham's departure from Mesopotamia are concerned with his turning from idolatry or with the return of the soul to God (see *Migration* 43–44; *Heir* 90–101; *Virtues* 211–19).

7. The aorist infinitive ἐξελθεῖν, "to go out," is best understood as ingressive, "to set out." The same thing is true for the indicative form of this verb (ἐξῆλθεν) later in the verse, "and he set out." See the NRSV.

8. The infinitive phrase ἐξελθεῖν εἰς τόπον ὃν ἤμελλεν λαμβάνειν εἰς κληρονομίαν ("to set out for a place that he was going to receive as an inheritance") is the object of the participle καλούμενος ("being called") — "called to set out for a place that he was going to receive as an inheritance" (NKJV, NIV, NRSV, REB). Some interpreters would connect this infinitive phrase with ὑπήκουσεν ("he obeyed") — "he obeyed by setting out for a place that he was going to receive as an inheritance" (NASB; Lane, 2:349). It would be awkward, however, to complete the meaning of ὑπήκουσεν ("he obeyed") with an infinitive, even though the infinitive immediately follows. The pastor has refused to put this infinitive phrase between καλούμενος and ὑπήκουσεν because he does not want to dilute the immediacy of Abraham's obedience — as soon as he was "called" he "obeyed" (see below).

9. καλούμενος ("being called") is a present participle, followed by the aorist verb ὑπήκουσεν ("he obeyed). "As Abraham was called he obeyed" (Lane, 343a).

10. Compare the parallel between "those who disobeyed" (τοῖς ἀπειθήσασιν) and "unbelief" (ἀπιστίαν) in 3:18, 19.

11. Eisenbaum, *Jewish Heroes,* 156, is mistaken when she says that the term "obey" is of little importance for this list because it occurs only here. First, she neglects the significance of the place it does appear — at the very beginning of the first example

is *living* as if God's power for the present is real and his promise for the future is secure (vv. 1, 6).

By using "place" for Abraham's God-directed destination instead of "land" the pastor prepares his hearers for the fact that this "inheritance" is not the earthly Promised Land but an eternal dwelling place.[12] In fact, he never uses the word "land" for the eternal destination of God's people. In v. 9 Abraham dwells in the earthly "land of promise" as an "alien" land. By v. 13 the word translated "land" has assumed its broader meaning — "earth" — and is a description of the place where the faithful live as strangers.

9 Abraham not only "set out," leaving his earthly homeland, but he also lived by choice as a stranger and alien in this world (v. 9), because he anticipated God's permanent "City" to come (v. 10).[13] The word translated "sojourned" is used by Genesis to describe Abraham's living in the Promised Land as temporary and without ownership or the rights of a citizen.[14]

---

from Abraham's life. Second, she fails to see that, although the term is not used, the following heroes of faith do in fact obey. Furthermore, one must not forget that the pastor has recently referred to the completion of the life of faith as "when you have done the will of God" (10:36), nor neglect the contrast with the wilderness generation noted above. On faith as obedience, see Hamm, "Jesus Factor," 289.

12. Lane, 349. Some MSS have attempted to correct this indefiniteness by adding the article before place, τὸν τόπον, "the place" (see ℵ², D², 1739, 1881, etc.). Cf. Koester, 484. While this "inheritance" is indeed "the fullest fellowship with God" (Backhaus, "Das Land der Verheissung," 173), one must be careful not to denude it of all locality, as Backhaus seems to do.

13. Eisenbaum has emphasized the "marginalization" of God's people in this chapter (Eisenbaum, *Jewish Heroes,* 3, 142, and many places in between). It is important, however, to note that they were not mere victims. Their marginal status in relation to the world was the result of their own choice. However, her contention that the author has "denationalized" biblical history is more problematic. It assumes that he began with a list of heroes that glorified the nation of Israel (cf. Sirach 44–50), and that he intentionally rewrote that history to degrade Israel. The truth is, however, that the author never refers to ethnic Israel. Thus, Eisenbaum's statement introducing this section on Abraham is simply mistaken: "Now the author moves into a period when the heroes are not just distinguished from generic humanity, but from the would-be nation of Israel" (Eisenbaum, *Jewish Heroes,* 153). See also her "profile" of a "hero" on pp. 178-85.

14. See παροικέω ("sojourn") in Gen 17:8; 24:37; 26:3; 35:27; 37:1. Note also Abraham's affirmation of his status as a πάροικος καὶ παρεπίδημος ("resident alien and transient") in the land (Gen 23:4; cf. Heb 11:13 below). In Gen 28:3-4 the land is called the "land of your sojourning " (τὴν γῆν τῆς παροικήσεώς σου). The pastor uses κατοικέω later in this verse when he speaks of Abraham's "dwelling" in tents. Although this word usually denoted a more settled existence, it is used along with παροικέω in Gen 26:2-3. Furthermore, the addition of ἐν σκηναῖς ("in tents") shows that Hebrews is using both terms to emphasize the patriarch's temporary, alien status (Rose, *Die Volke,* 212-13). Lane's contention (2:344c) that παρῴκησεν means "migrated to" instead of "sojourned in"

There is a touch of irony in the way the pastor refers to the place of his sojourning as "the land of promise." By using this term he acknowledges the role played by this land in the OT. Yet, it is almost as if he had said "the supposed land of promise," for, as Scripture shows, Abraham lived there as in a "strange" or "alien" land. Furthermore, it is a matter of record that Abraham, along with Isaac and Jacob, the two generations that followed him, lived as nomads in nothing more permanent than "tents."[15] Those who pursue such a pilgrimage do not, as it were, build their homes in this world. Hebrews uses the aorist tense, "he sojourned" or "he dwelt as a stranger," not because Abraham's sojourn was short, but because he completed it by enduring to the end. By deciding to journey toward the eternal "City" in answer to God's call, Abraham, Isaac, and Jacob chose to be strangers and aliens in the unbelieving society of this world. They lived their lives with a different point of reference. This alien status willingly embraced by the patriarchs makes sense of the hostility that the faithful endure at the hands of an unbelieving world (vv. 23-27, 35b-38; cf. v. 4 above). That world would force the people of faith to conform to the accepted standard and adopt a this-worldly point of view. Thus, Abraham's alien status sets the stage for the hardships that are the fourth and final characteristic of pilgrimage given above.

The pastor mentions Isaac and Jacob in order to reinforce what he has said about Abraham. According to Scripture, God specifically passed the Abrahamic promise of land and progeny on to them (cf. Gen 26:33; 28:3-4, 23-25; etc.). Thus, in a unique way they were "fellow heirs of the same promise" and join him as the prototypical example of faith. The pastor will exploit this relationship in vv. 20-22 below.

10 The fact that Abraham spent his whole life as a temporary resident, without citizenship in the supposed "land of promise," shows that the "place" (v. 8) he anticipated was "a City that" had "foundations, whose architect and builder" was "God" — the same God who called him to "set out" from his home. Abraham endured this life as a stranger and alien, "for he was continually looking forward to" this eternal destination.[16] The imperfect tense

---

is contradicted by this second phrase (Ellingworth, 583). For the use of this terminology as a self-definition of the faithful in a hostile world, see 1 Pet 1:17; 2:11, and references in Backhaus, "Das Land der Verheissung," 174.

15. The lives of Abraham, Isaac, and Jacob overlapped. Abraham was 100 when Isaac was born (Gen 17:17; 21:5) and he lived until he was 175 (Gen 25:7-8). Since Isaac was 60 when Jacob and Esau were born (Gen 25:26), Abraham would have been 160 at their birth, with fifteen years yet to live. Thus, commenting on Gen 25:29, *Targum Pseudo-Jonathan* says, "On the day when Abraham died, Jacob cooked a mess of pottage and went in order to comfort his father." See Rose, *Die Volke,* 218.

16. ἐξεδέχετο is better understood as "was looking forward to" (NIV/REB) than

of this verb indicates that such anticipation was habitual and implies that it was motivation for endurance. Because the God-established permanent City is the first description within this chapter of the goal pursued by the faithful, it sets the direction for what follows. Its importance is substantiated by the way the pastor draws his history to a close, bringing his hearers to "the City of the living God, the heavenly Jerusalem" (12:22-24; cf. 3:14). This imagery reminds them of the way Scripture describes Jerusalem past and future as a city firmly established by God.[17] The permanence of this city is evidenced by its "foundations." Those who now dwell in "tents" (v. 9) because they are strangers in this world will enjoy its unfading durability. Although this city can be described as "heavenly" (12:24), it does not derive its enduring nature merely from its location. It is permanent and utterly superior to the cities of this world because its "architect and builder is God."[18] Earthly cities are the transient work of mortal, sinful human beings (cf. 7:23-25; 8:7; 9:24). The words translated "architect" and "builder" are very similar in meaning. "Architect" could be used for the "designer" who planned a building project; "builder," for one who completed it.[19] By using both the pastor insists that this city is permanent and superior because from conception to completion it is the work of God. These two words would hardly have been appropriate if the pastor had wished to describe God as the source of some "heavenly" noumenal world of ideas. In fact, both were used in Hellenistic Judaism to describe him as the creator of the physical universe.[20] This God-established "City" is a true "place" (v. 8). It is, in fact, identical to the "rest" that God has prepared for his people (4:1). Thus, we may assume, on the basis of 4:3-6, that it was established by God on the seventh day of creation. It is his own "rest" that already exists and that he has intended from the beginning for his people to share. It will be revealed at the Judgment as an "Unshakable Kingdom" when all that is merely temporal passes away (12:25-29). In fact, since the coming of Christ the faithful, both living and dead, have preliminary access to this City (12:22-24). The importance of this pilgrimage is demonstrated by the significance of its destination.

---

as "was looking for" (NASB). Abraham was not searching for, but anticipating, an eternal City (Lane, 2:351).

17. Lane, 2:352. See Pss 46:4-5; 48:8; 87:1-3, 5; Isa 14:32; 33:20; 54:11; Rev 21:14, 19; cf. *4 Ezra* 10:27.

18. Lane, 2:344h, rightly, takes the relative clause beginning with ἧς as causal — the City has foundations, is permanent, *because* its architect and builder is God.

19. For τεχνίτης ("architect") see BDAG, 1001; for δημιουργός ("builder") see BDAG, 223.

20. Philo uses τεχνίτης ("architect") in reference to God as creator of the world in *Creation* 135; *Names* 29–31; cf. Wis 13:1) and δημιουργός ("builder") with the same significance in *Creation* 18, 146 (cf. Josephus, *Ant.* 1.155). See Williamson, *Philo and Hebrews,* 48-51; Koester, 487; and Lane, 2:353.

11-12   Faith is living as if God's promise for the future is sure and his power in the present is real (vv. 1, 6). Verses 8-10 have emphasized that Abraham lived as if God's promise for the future was sure. God would fulfill his promise of an eternal City. In vv. 11-12 Sarah depends upon and receives God's power in the present. God had also promised Abraham many descendants who would join him in inheriting this permanent, God-built "City." But, as yet, he did not have the son through whom those descendants would come. By trusting God Sarah received the power to conceive and bear that son — Isaac. This event confirmed Abraham and Sarah in their faith because it gave "evidence" (v. 1b) of the reality and faithfulness of God. As we will see, the way the pastor describes the birth of Isaac implies that God exercises power over death on behalf of his own — a reality already affirmed by the "translation" of Enoch in v. 5. This intimation of God's death-transcending power will be made more explicit when the pastor declares that by sacrificing Isaac Abraham affirmed his faith in "a God who is able to raise from the dead" (vv. 17-19).

"By faith even Sarah herself, although barren, received power for the disposition of seed." There has been much controversy over whether Sarah or Abraham is the subject of this sentence. One would presume that Sarah is the subject because the words "even Sarah herself" occur in the nominative case immediately after the initial "by faith."[21] Those who insist on Abraham remind us that he is the subject of the three previous verses (vv. 8-10) and that he is also the "one" who is the source of many descendants in the following verse (v. 12).[22] The chief reason, however, for rejecting Sarah as subject is the fact that "for the disposition of seed" ("for the sowing of seed") invariably describes the male function in procreation.[23] Some who take Abraham as the subject argue that "Sarah, herself barren," should be taken as a nominative concessive, "although Sarah herself was barren [Abraham] received power. . . ."[24] Others add an iota subscript, making "Sarah" dative, "Abraham, with Sarah herself, received power. . . ."[25]

---

21. καί before αὐτὴ Σάρρα ("Sarah herself") is intensive — "even Sarah herself." For Sarah as subject, see Westcott, 360-61; Moffatt, 171; Spicq, 2:348-49; Hughes, 470-71; Montefiore, 193-94; Johnson, 291-91; Vanhoye, *La structure littéraire,* 186; and J. Harold Greenlee, "Hebrews 11:11 — Sarah's Faith or Abraham's?" *Notes on Translation* 4 (1990): 37-42.

22. Thompson, 236; Koester, 488; Attridge, 324-26; Braun, 358-59; Bruce, 294-96; Lane, 2:353-54; Ellingworth, 586-88; Weiss, 586-99; Riggenbach, 357-60; Michel, 395-97; Rose, *Die Volke,* 228-31.

23. For this use of καταβολὴ σπέρματος see Philo, *Creation* 132; *Cherubim* 49; Epictetus, *Diatr.* 1.13; Lane, 3:253-54; and BDAG, 515, 2.

24. See Thompson, 236; Koester, 488; Lane, 2:353-54; Rose, *Die Volke,* 228-31.

25. Attridge, 324-26; Braun, 358-59; Bruce, 294-96; Ellingworth, 586-88; Weiss,

There are, however, excellent reasons for taking Sarah as the subject, in accord with the natural use of the nominative case. First, the pastor and his hearers, who were very familiar with the OT, knew that Abraham had no problem with the "disposition of seed." He successfully impregnated Hagar fourteen years before the birth of Isaac (Gen 16:4, 15-16). He fathered other children after the death of Sarah (Gen 25:1-4). Although the OT mentions Abraham's age in conjunction with his childlessness, it puts the main emphasis on Sarah.[26] The opening genealogy of the Abraham narrative sets the tone for what is to follow by introducing Sarah as "barren" (Gen 11:30). It is because she does "not bear" children for Abraham that she offers him Hagar (Gen 16:1). As the story progresses, Sarah reaches the age beyond which women are able to conceive (Gen 18:11; cf. 17:18-19). The narrative of Genesis focuses on what God is going to do through her. First, Abraham thinks that his steward will be his heir (Gen 15:1-6). Then, after God tells him that his own physical descendant will inherit the promise (Gen 15:4), he assumes that the son of Hagar will be his heir (cf. Gen 17:18). Finally, God tells him that the heir will be born from aged, barren Sarah (Gen 17:16). Abraham will know that this birth is by the power of God. Furthermore, by using Sarah as the subject the pastor introduces an element of surprise that makes this example all the more powerful. Sarah, who had the problem and bore the shame, who gave Abraham Hagar as a substitute for her own inadequacy, and who laughed at God's promise (Gen 18:11-13) — she was the one who "by faith" received "power." Moreover, the use of Sarah in this passage corresponds with the pastor's larger arrangement. We will show below that the first example of Abraham's faith (v. 8) corresponds to the third example from the Moses section (v. 27); the second from Abraham (vv. 9-10), with the second from Moses (vv. 24-26); the third from the Abraham section (vv. 11-12), with the first from Moses (v. 23). The first example from the Moses section is not about the faith of Moses but about the faith of his parents; the third from the Abraham section is not about the faith of Abraham but the faith of his wife.[27] The pastor introduces these others who were closely related to Abraham and Moses in order to strengthen the testimony of these two great heroes. It was not merely Abraham, but also Sarah who

---

586-88; Riggenbach, 356-60; Michel, 395-97; O'Brien, 415. Thus αὐτὴ Σάρρα ("Sarah herself") becomes αὐτῇ Σάρρᾳ ("with Sarah herself"). However, no known manuscript has this iota subscript. Cf. Koester, 488.

26. Abraham was one hundred when Isaac was born (Gen 18:11-12; Rom 4:19; Heb 11:12); Sarah was ninety. Abraham mentions his age in Gen 17:17; Sarah mentions it in 18:12.

27. When we observe these relationships, we can no longer agree with Rose, *Die Volke*, 229, who contends that Abraham must be the subject of v. 11, so that the four examples from Abraham's life would parallel the four from Moses'.

had faith; not merely Moses, but also his parents. God's people are a people who live "by faith."

The only substantive objection to Sarah's being the subject comes from the phrase "for the disposition of seed." No one has been able to present convincing evidence that this phrase could be used to describe the woman's part in procreation.[28] However, as Johnson has shown, this sentence can be understood without undue stress as Sarah's receiving "power" to receive Abraham's "disposition of seed"[29] "By faith even Sarah herself, although barren, received power for the [reception of Abraham's] disposition of seed, although she was also beyond the season of childbearing." This interpretation gives Sarah's example maximum force. The pastor magnifies the obstacles to faith by affirming that Sarah was both "barren" and "beyond the season of childbearing."[30] By doing this, he embraces Sarah's story, which began by

28. Some have argued that ancient sources describe not only men but also women as having "seed" (P. W. van der Horst, "Sarah's Seminal Emission: Hebrews 11:11 in Light of Ancient Embryology," in *Greeks, Romans, and Christians: Essays in Honor of Abraham J. Malherbe,* ed. D. L. Balch, E. Ferguson, and W. A. Meeks [Minneapolis: Fortress, 1990], 287-301; cf. J. Irwin, "The Use of Hebrews 11:11 as Embryological Proof-Text," *HTR* 71 [1978]: 312-16). This may well be so (Gen 3:15). Yet there is no evidence that the combined phrase καταβολὴν σπέρματος was used for women's role in procreation (Ellingworth, 586). Some have suggested that εἰς καταβολὴν σπέρματος be translated as "for the establishment of a seed [i.e., posterity]" (Bénétreau, 2:145; Hughes, 473). καταβολή by itself could mean "establishment," and σπέρμα alone could refer to a "posterity." However, when brought together these two words form an idiom that cannot be reduced to its parts (Ellingworth, 586-87; Koester, 487).

29. Johnson, 291-92. He argues that if Abraham were the subject, an infinitive phrase, καταβολεῖν σπέρμα ("to plant seed") "would have been a more natural complement to 'receiving a power'" than εἰς καταβολὴν σπέρματος ("for the disposition of seed," "for the planting of seed"). See also Moffatt, 171: Sarah received power from God "for Abraham the male to do the work of generation upon her." Attridge, 325, n. 53, cites Chrysostom, *PG* 63:162; Ps.-Oecumenius, *PG* 119:408B; Theophylact, *PG* 125:34CD; and Augustine, *Civ.* 16.26, as holding this view.

30. στεῖρα ("barren") is absent from a number of manuscripts ($\mathfrak{P}^{13vid}$ ℵ A D² 33 Maj). It appears alone in $\mathfrak{P}^{46}$ D* Ψ; prefaced with a definite article in D¹ 6 81 1241s 1739 1881; and accompanied by οὖσα ("being") in P 104 365 1505. Those who affirm Sarah as the subject of this sentence (Spicq, 2:349; Moffatt, 171) or make Sarah dative (Attridge, 326; Bruce, 294-96) often argue that σπεῖρα was a scribal addition intended to remove the awkwardness of a woman's receiving power "for depositing seed." Moffatt, 171, suggests that it arose by dittography with Σάρρα (ΣΑΡΡΑΣΤΕΙΡΑ). The use of this term in Gen 11:30 to describe Sarah would, according to these interpreters, make its addition natural. On the other hand, στεῖρα occurs as early as $\mathfrak{P}^{46}$ and is confirmed by the original of D. It fits most appropriately with the author's intention in this verse. It is possible that its omission was an early scribal error. Both its omission in some manuscripts and the addition of the article and οὖσα in others may have arisen because σπεῖρα seemed awkward. See Koester, 487; *TCGNT,* 602.

describing her barrenness (Gen 11:30) and drew to a climax just before Isaac's birth by declaring that she was now also past the time when women are able to have children (Gen 18:11). However, by trusting God and his promise she received "power" from him to overcome these difficulties. She received this power "since she considered that the one who had promised was faithful." Sarah's giving Hagar to Abraham (Gen 16:1-4) and laughing at God's promise (Gen 18:12) are no objection to applying this statement to her. The pastor is certain that she could not have received such "power" unless she had trusted God. Thus, he asserts that she overcame all such hesitancy by faith. It remains to explain why the pastor would have used this phrase, "the disposition of seed," if the above interpretation is correct. Why did he not simply say that Sarah received power to conceive or to bear Isaac? A probable answer is close at hand. By using this phrase the pastor leaves no doubt that Sarah is bearing the "seed" promised to Abraham (cf. v. 19). Her action is linked inextricably to the promise that God would multiply Abraham's seed. Thus, the pastor can refer in v. 12 to Abraham as the "one" through whom numerous progeny have come to be.

Verse 12 magnifies the power and faithfulness of God by comparing it with human impotence. "Therefore," through the birth of Isaac a vast multitude "came into being" from only "one" man, and he was "indeed dead." While a copyist would expect "were born," the alternate reading, "came into being," better serves the pastor's intention because it puts the emphasis on God's power and agency.[31] This multitude was brought into being by God from "one" man, Abraham (the pronoun "one" is masculine), who was "indeed dead" and totally impotent to produce children with Sarah.[32] The number of Abrahamic descendants, however, was as vast as God had promised in Gen 22:17b, which the pastor now quotes: "as the stars of the heaven in multitude and as the grains of sand along the seashore without number." By add-

31. In my judgment ἐγενήθησαν ("came into being," $\mathfrak{P}^{46}$ A D* K P 6 33 81 104 326 365 1175 etc.) has somewhat better external attestation than ἐγεννήθησαν ("were born" or "were begotten," ℵ D² Ψ *Byz*), though both are well represented in the manuscript tradition (see Ellingworth, 590). However, as explained in the text above, ἐγενήθησαν has much stronger support from internal evidence. ἀφ' ἑνός, "from one," denotes source but not agency — "came into being [by God] from one man [Abraham]."

32. καὶ ταῦτα is an emphatic classical expression, "and indeed" (Ellingworth, 590). The perfect participle, νενεκρωμένου, "having been dead," emphasizes the present condition of Abraham at the time he begat Isaac. Due to Sarah's barrenness and age he had absolutely no human prospect of begetting a child with her (Hughes, 476). It is possible that the pastor also considered Abraham's age a problem. If so, then the children he bore after Sarah's death (Gen 25:1-6) would also have been the result of divine intervention, though none of them were "the" child of promise. The oft-suggested translation "as good as dead" unduly weakens the impact the pastor would make on his hearers (deSilva, 398).

545

ing the words "in multitude" and "without number" to the text of Gen 22:17 the pastor underscores the fact that Abraham's God-given descendants are beyond counting. He has borrowed "in multitude" from Moses' reference to this same promise found in Exod 32:13.[33] "Without number" was suggested by God's first promise of many descendants (Gen 15:5).[34] The pastor has separated the attributive adjective "without number" from "sand," the noun it modifies, and given it prominence by putting it at the end of the Greek sentence. He leaves "without number" ringing in the ears of his hearers — such is God's faithfulness and power. Abraham and Sarah experienced the birth of Isaac as God's token of this coming multitude "without number." However, the pastor's hearers are reminded of God's faithfulness because they can see the fulfillment of this promise. The rest of this chapter is filled with representatives of that innumerable multitude. They are the people of God throughout the ages who live by faith in the promise given to Abraham, but now fulfilled in Christ (6:13-20).[35] Thus both this "great cloud of witness" (12:1) and the recipients of Hebrews are among their ranks.

It is obvious that God's promise to Abraham given in Gen 22:17 immediately after the sacrifice of Isaac has great importance. The pastor quoted Gen 22:17a in Heb 6:14. Here he quotes Gen 22:17b in anticipation of the sacrifice of Isaac, soon to be discussed in vv. 17-19 below. The rest of this chapter will bring out the full significance of God's promise of many descendants. The God who brought such a multitude from one who was "indeed dead" is a God whose power and plans for his people transcend death. The birth of Isaac anticipates what Abraham will attest by the sacrifice of Isaac — God is a "God who is able to raise from the dead" (11:19).

13-16   We have already demonstrated the importance of these verses

33. τῷ πλήθει ("in multitude") from Exod 32:13 may have been suggested by πληθύνων πληθυνῶ τὸ σπέρμα σου ("multiplying I will multiply your seed") in Gen 22:17a. The pastor has also used the neuter word for "stars" (τὰ ἄστρα) found in Exod 32:13 rather than the masculine of Gen 22:17 (τοὺς ἀστέρας). Furthermore, the words for "stars" and "sand" are nominative in order to fit into the syntax of Heb 11:12 instead of accusative as they were in Gen 22:17b.

34. Compare "without number" (ἀναρίθμητος) with God's command in Gen 15:5 for Abraham to "count" (ἀρίθμησον) the stars if he is able to "number" (ἐξαριθμῆσαι) them.

35. It is a mistake to import a Pauline distinction between the "literal" and "spiritual" "seed" or descendants of Abraham into Hebrews. The pastor never contrasts those who believe in Christ with ethnic Israel. Thus, he has no need for such a distinction. The people of God are — and always have been — his people because they hear the word of God and respond "by faith" (cf. 1:1-4). In the case of the birth of Isaac, God used physical descent to perpetuate the people of faith. Thus, the "seed" Sarah received in v. 11 was, *pace* Swetnam, *Jesus and Isaac,* 117-18, the physical seed of Abraham from which Isaac was born.

and their strategic location within this chapter. The goal pursued by Abraham, Isaac, and Jacob is the goal pursued by all the people who lived "by faith" in the promises God had given to them. Therefore, by clarifying the relationship of Sarah and these patriarchs to the eternal "City" (v. 10) and to the society of their earthly sojourn, the pastor establishes the pattern for all the examples of faith who follow. Thus, these verses provide further insight into both the goal pursued by the faithful in this chapter and the character of the "marginalization" they incur as the people of God because they have chosen the way of faith.[36] The pastor could go no further without drawing his hearers more fully into this vision of reality.[37]

This explanation in vv. 13-16 finds its complement in vv. 39-40.[38] If the hearers would understand the nature God's people, who live by faith in his "promises," they must begin with the patriarchs who first received those promises. That explanation, however, is incomplete without Christ, who is the fulfillment of the Abrahamic promises (cf. 6:13-20). Thus, after completing this roll call, the pastor will explain the relationship of the faithful of old to contemporary believers in light of all that Christ has done (vv. 39-40). Then he will be able to show both how Christ is the greatest example of perseverance, and how he has provided the way for all those who live "by faith" — both before and after his coming — to enter the "City" God has prepared for them (12:1-3). The pastor's deep concern is that his hearers identify with the faithful of the past by fully embracing the advantages that are theirs through Christ but were unavailable during the lives of their predecessors.

13 "These all died according to faith" refers specifically to Abraham, Sarah, Isaac, and Jacob, who have been mentioned in the last five verses.[39] The pastor's description is crafted with their experiences in mind.[40]

---

36. In a sense it is true, as Eisenbaum, *Jewish Heroes,* 160-61, says, that these verses highlight the "marginalization" theme. However, to put the stress on marginalization is to emphasize an effect of the pastor's main point rather than the main point itself — these people of faith are native to the heavenly home God has prepared for them.

37. The way in which the perspective of these verses is integrated with the examples of this chapter precludes its being an editorial addition to a preexisting list, as suggested by some (cf. Rissi, *Theologie,* 106, 109; Rose, *Die Volke,* 247; and Weiss, 556-57). On this integration, see pp. 514-19 above and Cockerill, "The Better Resurrection (Heb. 11:35)," 215-34. Note O'Brien's (418) comment: ". . . the eschatological perspective that is specially emphasized in the case of the patriarchs is ultimately the viewpoint from which the whole chapter is to be understood (so v. 39)."

38. On the relationship between vv. 39-40 and vv. 13-16, see Rose, *Die Volke,* 247.

39. See Rose, *Die Volke,* 248-49.

40. For instance, it was Abraham, Sarah, and Abraham's "fellow heirs" who first received God's promises and "left" (v. 14) the land of their birth. Thus, Rhee, *Faith in Hebrews,* 185-86, is mistaken when he would apply "all these" to the other heroes of this

Verses 1-7 have shown that God has had faithful people from the beginning. Yet Abraham, who received God's "promises" (7:6; 11:17), and his "fellow heirs" (v. 9), were in a unique sense the progenitors of the people of God. They determined the way of life for all the faithful referred to in v. 39 at the end of this catalogue as "these all." The "these all" of v. 13 established the course for the "these all" of v. 39.[41] "According to faith" interrupts the refrain, "by faith," with which the pastor has been introducing each new example. Since dying is not something people choose to do, the pastor cannot describe it as an action done "by" means of "faith." The manner of their deaths, however, was "according to faith."[42] They kept their course to the end, trusting in God's promises and in his power. The three following participial phrases describe their degree of participation in "the promises" of God by the time they died.[43] The first and primary participial phrase is negative, and should probably be taken as concessive; the second two are positive. First, then, "although they had not received the promises." They completed the life of faith, but at the time of their deaths they "had not" yet "received" what God had promised. Instead they had endured hardship in anticipation of fulfillment to come. The pastor makes this point in order to fortify his hearers and all other believers for such endurance.

It is crucial that one identify the content of these "promises." The following verses make it clear that the heavenly "City" is the main promised but not-yet-received reality under immediate consideration. Elsewhere, however, when the pastor speaks of the final hope of believers he uses the singular "promise" (4:1; 6:17; 9:15; 10:36; 11:9, 39). He normally reserves the plural to describe situations in which the multiple nature of what was promised is clear: Abraham received the "promises" of land, a son, posterity, and blessing (7:6; 11:17). The New Covenant was based on the "promises" of forgiveness, God's law on the heart, and an intimate knowledge of God (8:6). The

---

chapter. Nevertheless, because of the role played by Abraham and his "fellow heirs," their faith and the perspective established by vv. 13-16 is determinative for the whole chapter, especially for those who follow. They also lived in anticipation of the fulfillment of the promise made to Abraham.

41. Rissi, *Theologie,* 109, sees this connection with v. 39.

42. Ellingworth, 592-93. Compare κατὰ πίστιν ("according to faith"), indicating the manner of their death, with πίστει ("by faith"), describing the means by which an action was carried out. "These believers of the past did not allow the crisis of death to invalidate the principle of faith" (Hughes, 477, n. 44).

43. 1. μὴ λαβόντες τὰς ἐπαγγελίας ("not having received the promises"); 2. ἀλλὰ πόρρωθεν αὐτὰς ἰδόντες ("but having seen them from afar"); 3. καὶ ἀσπασάμενοι ("and having greeted [them]"). The fourth participial phrase, καὶ ὁμολογήσαντες ὅτι ξένοι καὶ παρεπίδημοί εἰσιν ἐπὶ τῆς γῆς ("and having confessed that they were aliens and transients on the earth") describes their relationship to the world in light of their relationship to the "promises" of God.

heroes of faith received many "promises" of temporal deliverance (10:36). The closest parallel to our present text is the pastor's exhortation to his hearers (in 6:12) that they become "imitators of those who through faith and patience are inheriting the promises." Both in that passage and here (in 11:13) the plural magnifies the abundance of what God has promised. Yet from Abraham's vantage point God's "promises" included not only a place of inheritance but also a great nation whom God would bring into that inheritance lest the promise of heritage be meaningless. We have already noted how vv. 8-10 addressed the issue of inherited home-place, and vv. 11-12, the concern for descendants. By the time of Moses, the next great exemplar of faith, the company of Abraham's faithful descendants had become a reality. Only in Christ would the means of its inheritance become clear. Thus, there is a fullness in this promise that comes to focus in the singularity of entrance into the promised heavenly City. The other parts of the promise pertain to establishing a people of God and bringing them to that destination. The pastor's point here is that Abraham, Sarah, Isaac, and Jacob lived by faith although they did not reach this ultimate goal of God's promises during their lifetimes.

The next participial phrase confirms this interpretation: with the eyes of faith "they had seen" the fulfillment "from afar" at the time of death. "From afar" includes, but must not be limited to, mere temporal distance.[44] Abraham, Isaac, and Jacob did not have access to what had been promised. Compare this sense of distance with all that the pastor has said about Christ's opening the way for his people to "draw near" to God (4:14-16; 10:19-25) and with the grand description of the faithful "who have come" to "the City of the living God" (12:22). The pastor also speaks of final entrance into God's blessings as temporally near for those who live after Christ — "for the coming one will come and will not delay" (10:37). At Christ's soon return all things will be put under his feet (1:13; 2:5-9). Abraham, Sarah, Isaac, and Jacob, like all those who lived before Christ, had neither the privilege of access available since Christ's coming nor the hope of his imminent return with the ultimate access it would bring. Yet, despite these limitations, it is important not to forget in what way they did participate in what God had promised. They did "see" its certain reality and future fulfillment with the eyes of faith.[45] When the pastor recounted the story of the unbelieving generation in 3:7–4:11, he used the language of "hearing" (3:7, 15, 16; 4:2, 7). However, as Noah (v. 7) has already demonstrated, the people of faith hear and obey the

44. Ellingworth, 593; Lane, 2:356, and others emphasize the temporal nature of this expression.

45. *Pace* Rose, *Die Volke*, 249-52, there is no reason to believe that Hebrews has been influenced by Jewish tradition about Abraham seeing the heavenly Jerusalem during the night vision of Genesis 15.

word of God because they "see." "By faith" they "see," that is, they give their full attention to and live in accord with, both the "unseen" present power of God and the not yet visible future fulfillment of his promises. Note vv. 23, 26, and 27 below. By keeping their eyes on God's promised eternal blessings, Abraham, Isaac, and Jacob set the pattern for God's people. It is living by this "vision" that makes them people of faith and sustains their perseverance.

The next participial phrase, "and greeted [what God had promised]," does not gainsay what we have said. This is the greeting of travelers who can see home, as these people could see the promised eternal City with the eyes of faith, but who do not yet enjoy its comfort. The pastor's point is that these people of faith acknowledged this heavenly destination as their own while still alive in the world. By so doing they "confessed that they" were "aliens and transients on the earth." To "sojourn" in "an alien land" (v. 9) is one thing. To intentionally embrace this lifestyle by "confessing" one's status is another. The pastor is referring to Abraham's description of himself in Gen 23:4 as a "resident alien and transient."[46] The term used by the LXX of Gen 23:4 for "resident alien" is related to the verb translated "sojourn" in v. 9 above and was a technical term for those who lived in a country without the rights of citizenship.[47] If anything, the alternate word used by Hebrews, which we have translated simply as "aliens," is even more forceful.[48] The second term, "transients," found in both Hebrews and Gen 23:4 (LXX), is closely related to both "resident alien" and "alien." It describes those whose stay in a place is temporary.[49] Abraham and his descendants were ready to confess both that "this world" was "not [their] home" and that they were "just passing through." When the pastor's hearers maintain their "confession" of the full sufficiency of Christ, they join the faithful of the past in "confessing" that they are citizens of the world to come, and thus only temporary aliens in this world. Such people should not be surprised if they lack

46. Compare the ξένοι καὶ παρεπίδημοι ("aliens and transients") of Hebrews with the πάροικος καὶ παρεπίδημος ("resident alien and transient") of Gen 23:4 (LXX). For the translation of παρεπίδημοι as "transients" see Koester, 489.

47. BDAG, 779.

48. In T. Levi 6:9 Abraham is called an "alien" (ξένος). Attridge, 330, thinks ξένοι ("alien") may be a bit stronger than πάροικος ("resident alien"). For ξένος as the opposite of πολίτης ("citizen") see Philo, Posterity 109; Josephus, Ant. 11.159; Life 372 (cf. συμπολίτης in Eph 2:19). The close relationships between all three of these words, ξένος ("alien"), πάροικος ("resident alien"), and παρεπίδημος ("transient"), is demonstrated by the way they are often combined. Thus, with ξένοι καὶ παρεπίδημοι here (cf. Acts 17:21) compare ξένοι καὶ πάροικοι in Eph 2:19 and παροίκους καὶ παρεπιδήμους in 1 Pet 2:11 (Gen 23:4 [LXX]). See additional references for these combinations in BDAG, 684, 2a; 779, 2.

49. Cf. 1 Pet 1:1-2; MM, 493.

the protection of citizens and are persecuted by those who consider here and now their home.[50] "On earth" represents the same Greek word used for the "land" of promise in v. 9. However, the contrast with "heavenly" (v. 16) suggests that "on earth" is more appropriate here.[51] The supposed "land of promise" was no more than the place of Abraham's earthly sojourn as he awaited his true home. The pastor, however, would not have us attribute this earthly alienation to some form of Platonic dualism.[52] The people of faith are not "strangers" on earth because they belong by nature to heaven. They are aliens here because they have affirmed their faith in God, chosen to obey his heavenly calling, identified with his people, and committed themselves to live for the heavenly "City."[53] If one would enjoy eternal citizenship in this city, one must forgo the benefits of those who are at home in the present world.

14-16a   With almost syllogistic precision the pastor explains what promised good these people of faith hope to obtain. Verse 14 provides his major premise; v. 15, the minor premise; and v. 16a, the conclusion. The author is substantiating what he said in v. 10 — the people of faith are anticipating the "City" that God has prepared for them. These verses also portray how intensely they pursued these promises. Verse 13 has described the limitations imposed on Abraham and those who first received God's promise and, by implication, on all the faithful who lived before Christ. They experienced neither final entrance into the eternal City nor the present participation in that reality made available through Christ. They lived simply with the conviction that these promises of access into the eternal City would be fulfilled in the future. Even so, they pursued this goal with vigor. The pastor expects nothing less from his hearers.

The pastor begins v. 14 with the main premise of his argument: "Those who say such things" as Abraham did in Gen 23:4, when he confessed himself to be "a resident alien and a transient" on earth, show "that they are diligently seeking a place where they are citizens." We have rendered one Greek word by the phrase "a place where they are citizens." It is unfortunate that many English translations have used the term "homeland" for this word. "Homeland" suggests the term "Promised Land" — an expression the pastor avoids using for this heavenly reality. The Greek word in question is derived from the word for "father" and does not contain the word for "land." It denotes the place where people belong, where they are "at

50. On the privileges of citizens over "strangers" or foreigners see Philo, *Flaccus* 54.

51. Spicq, 2:350; NIV, NKJV, NRSV, REB, NASB.

52. *Pace* Backhaus, "Das Land der Verheissung," 175.

53. Philo spoke of human souls becoming aliens when they entered the body (*Dreams* 1.181; *Cherubim* 120; *Confusion* 77–79. In Hebrews, however, it is "by faith" that one becomes a stranger on earth. See Koester, 489.

home," where their family is, where they are natives, where they are citizens.[54] The pastor consistently describes this "home place" of the faithful as a City (11:10, 16; 12:22-24; 13:14). The city is the place of community, as the description in 12:22-24 will make abundantly clear. In the ancient world loyalty to one's place of birth and citizenship was a cardinal virtue.[55] A life banished from one's city was considered by many to be hardly worth living. Thus, the pastor's hearers feel what he says when he speaks of the people who live "by faith" and are thus self-confessed aliens in this world, "diligently seeking" the place where they are citizens and natives.

The pastor uses the same word for "diligently seeking" that he used for the pursuit of God in v. 6. It is a strong word reserved until the end of the Greek sentence for emphasis.[56] The path pursued "by faith" is no course of passive indolence. Because these heroes who lived "by faith" were aliens on earth, most anxious to reach their home, they "'diligently sought" it by persevering in the life of faith and obedience.

Let us restate the pastor's major premise: since Abraham and company were self-confessed aliens in Canaan, the "so-called land of promise" was not their home. Verse 15 provides the minor premise: The place they left before coming to Canaan was not their true home, for "if they had been mindful of that [native] place from which they had come, they would have had opportunity to return." The pastor establishes his point by using a condition contrary to fact. Abraham and those associated with him had, indeed, not been "mindful" of the earthly home where they had once been citizens. They no longer considered it their native place. That is why they did not return to it and save themselves the trouble of "diligently seeking" some other place.

"But now" at the beginning of v. 16 introduces the pastor's conclusion:[57] The destiny promised the faithful was neither Canaan, the supposed "land of promise" (v. 9), nor the city they had abandoned when they answered God's call. Therefore, it must have been that "such people" of faith as Abraham and his "fellow heirs of the same promise" Isaac and Jacob were

---

54. Note the two meanings given for πατρίς, πατρίδος by BDAG, 788-89: "a relatively large geographical area associated with one's familial connections and personal life, *fatherland, homeland*" (italics original); "a relatively restricted area as locale of one's immediate family and ancestry, *home town, one's own part of the country*" (italics original). It is unclear why BDAG lists Heb 11:14 under the first of these meanings when the context shows that Hebrews is talking about a "city" (Heb 11:10, 16). Compare this term with πατήρ, πατρός, "father."

55. See Josephus, *J.W.* 1.434. Cf. 2 Macc 8:21; 13:14; Philo, *Planting* 146; *Drunkenness* 17; Josephus, *Ant.* 12.304. Cited by Koester, 490.

56. Lane, 2:358 (*pace* Ellingworth, 596), argues correctly that ἐπιζητοῦσιν ("they were diligently seeking") is stronger than uncompounded ζητοῦσιν would have been.

57. Attridge, 331; Ellingworth, 598. Cf. νῦν δὲ ("but now") in 8:6; 9:26; 12:26.

"ardently desiring a better, that is, a heavenly place" where they could live as citizens in their home "City." "Better" has been used throughout Hebrews to describe both the fully sufficient and effective work of Christ in cleansing God's people from sin and the permanent and eternal blessings made available through that work.[58] It is used in this latter sense here and reinforced by the addition of "heavenly" at the end of the sentence. The English word "heavenly" can be misleading. The pastor is not using this word to mean "wonderful." He is not describing this city as "ethereal." He has no concern with an abstract world of "ideas." This "City" is, we might say, "more real" than anything we now know because it has been established by the living God as the permanent place of his own abode with his people. It is "better" in kind, for it is the only place where his people will enjoy full fellowship with God and enter his "rest" (4:1-11). God's people have received the "heavenly call" (3:1) extended to Abraham (11:8) inviting them to this "heavenly" City.

These people who live "by faith" were not only "diligently seeking" this heavenly home city, they were also "ardently desiring" it. This pursuit was no mere hobby or pastime. It was much more than insurance against damnation while they attended to their own affairs. It was the passion and the main business of life because its object was the only true source of blessing and "rest."[59]

16b-c   In the opening section of this chapter (vv. 1-7) the pastor made it clear that faith was prerequisite for divine approval (v. 6). It is those who live with the conviction that God's promise is certain and his power is real who receive divine commendation. This truth found its most profound expression in the lives of father Abraham and his "fellow heirs" (v. 9) Isaac and Jacob. They have been described as those "diligently seeking" and "fervently desiring" the "better," "heavenly" City established by God because it was truly their native place, the repository of their citizenship. Their whole lives were oriented and directed toward God and his promise. "Therefore," says the pastor with great emphasis, "God" not only was, but "is not ashamed of them to be called their God."[60] God declares himself to be, and is perpetu-

---

58. See some form of κρείττονος ("better") in 1:4; 6:9; 7:19, 22; 8:6; 9:23; 10:34; 11:35, 40; 12:24.

59. One is reminded of Mary L. Demarest's hymn in Scots dialect entitled "My Ain Countrie":

"I am far frae my hame, an' I'm weary aftenwhiles,
For the langed for hame bringin', an' my Father's welcome smiles;
An' I'll ne'er be fu' content, until mine een do see
The gowden gates o' Heav'n an' my ain countrie.

60. αὐτῶν ("their") at the end of the Greek sentence is emphatic — "God *of them*" (italics added; see Ellingworth, 599). The two occurrences of θεός ("God") together in the

ally known throughout Scripture as, the God of "Abraham, Isaac, and Jacob" (Gen 28:13; Exod 3:6). They "confessed" themselves to be strangers in this world because they were seeking him (v. 13). Therefore, he is "not ashamed" to "confess" himself as their God.[61] Thus, the pastor holds up the way in which Abraham, Isaac, and Jacob responded to the promise of God as the model and paradigm for all those who live by faith and receive the divine approval. The pastor "fervently desires" that his hearers follow the patriarchs' example, joining the train of God's people in the life lived "by faith." The use of the word "ashamed" may indeed have reminded the hearers of something even more astounding than the fact that God was not "ashamed" to be known as "the God of Abraham, Isaac, and Jacob": the Son of God had not been "ashamed" to identify with God's people by taking on their humanity in order to redeem them (2:11). To accuse the pastor of advocating works righteousness would be to completely misunderstand his intention and to import forensic categories alien to his thought.[62] God showers his approval on those who abandon themselves to him in utter trust, nor is his approval an empty accolade. "For he has [already] prepared . . . a City" for such people. The object of their diligent seeking and fervent desire is real, and they will experience it. The pastor need do no more than end with the simple word "City." None can fail to see that this "City" is God's own divine "rest" prepared for his own from the beginning (3:7–4:11); a "City" that is permanent because established by him (v. 10); the true home of his people promised long ago to Abraham.

17-19 The story of Abraham's walk with God began with his call (v. 8) but reached its climax in the sacrifice of Isaac (Gen 22:1-18). Through this event God brought Abraham's faith to its final "test" (Gen 22:1).[63] By obedience to the divine command Abraham became a person totally aban-

---

middle, framed by the two pronouns referring to the faithful (αὐτούς, "them"; αὐτῶν, "of them," "their"), emphasize that God himself is not ashamed of them!

61. For parallels between "be ashamed" (ἐπαισχύνω) and "confess" (ὁμολογέω) see Mark 8:38; Luke 9:26; Rom 1:16; 2 Tim 1:8, 12, 16; Heb 2:11.

62. Ellingworth, 598, falls into this trap when he refuses to relate the διό ("therefore") in v. 16b to what goes before for fear of affirming works righteousness. The entire book of Hebrews teaches that God commends the life of faith. It also corrects a false notion of what that life is. True faith is never mere mental assent. It cannot be separated from and will always be expressed by obedience, just as it was in these great heroes of faith. Ellingworth's attempt to make this διό refer to what follows in v. 16c is awkward and leaves no room for the γάρ that introduces that following statement.

63. Josephus, *Ant.* 1.223, 233, describes God's command to offer Isaac as a test. *Jub.* 17:15–18:16 attributes the agency of this test to an evil being rather than to God (17:15-16; 28:9, 12). Both Sir 44:20 and 1 Macc 2:52 refer to Abraham as "faithful" (πιστός) "in testing" (ἐν πειρασμῷ), though neither specifically mentions the offering of Isaac. See Rose, *Die Volke,* 234-35.

doned to God. The abundance of attention given to the "Binding of Isaac" in ancient Jewish literature confirms the importance of this event.[64] Thus the pastor is in complete accord with the Genesis account when he uses Abraham's willingness to offer his son as the final and greatest example of his trust in God. As we have come to expect in this chapter, the pastor's exposition pays close attention to the OT text and is free of legendary accretion. He affirms the sacrifice of Isaac in v. 17a; explains how it was a test in vv. 17b-18; and concludes in v. 19 by describing what this sacrifice revealed about Abraham's faith.

17a "By faith Abraham offered Isaac when he was being tested." The pastor put the verb "offered" right after the initial "by faith" in the Greek sentence in order to emphasize that Abraham's obedience was an expression of his trust in God.[65] It is instructive to examine the verb tenses of this verse. "Offered" is perfect indicative; "was being tested" is a present participle. The perfect tense of "offered" underscores the fact that Abraham's act of obedience was complete; he did not actually have to take Isaac's life.[66] It also affirms the abiding validity of this act of obedience.[67] The continuous nature of the participle "was being tested" reminds the hearers that this test was not merely a single moment. Gen 22:1-18 describes in considerable detail the process by which Abraham arose, set out on his journey, and then proceeded with the sacrifice until God's intervention before the knife could fall. Faith perseveres until the end.

17b-18 In order to explain how God's command was a test of Abraham's faith, the pastor gives further information about both father Abraham and son Isaac: "And he who had received the promises was offering the only begotten, he to whom it had been said that 'in Isaac will your seed be called.'" This relatively smooth English translation masks the fact that in Greek this statement begins with a shocking "and the only begotten," or "and the one and only." The pastor emphasizes the unique position of Isaac, whom God describes in Gen 22:2 as "your beloved son."[68] Abraham also had Ishmael. How-

64. Sir 44:20; Wis 10:5; 2 Macc 2:52; 4 Macc 16:20; *Jub.* 18:1-9; Josephus, *Ant.* 1.222-36; Philo, *Abraham* 167–207; and one tractate from the Mishnah, *m. 'Abot* 5:3.
65. πίστει ("by faith") προσενήνοχεν ("he offered").
66. Lane, 2:361. See Grässer, 3:145; Thompson, 238. Rose's contention that Hebrews thinks Abraham actually killed Isaac is without validity (Rose, *Die Volke*, 235-44). The fact that προσφέρω is the normal word for "sacrifice" and that κομίζω was used elsewhere for receiving resurrection life has nothing to do with whether or not the sacrifice of Isaac was literally carried through. Rose cites ancient tradition in witness that others thought Abraham actually sacrificed Isaac. However, the sources he cites are ambiguous, of questionable age, and without demonstrable relationship to Hebrews.
67. Ellingworth, 600.
68. Hebrews uses τὸν μονογενῆ ("only begotten" or "only") in place of the τὸν

ever, at God's command, he had just sent Ishmael away (21:1-11). Furthermore, Isaac was the "only" son born by the promise of God. Thus, Abraham is described as "the one who had received the promises" (v. 17b).[69] Verse 18 gives the specific part of the "promises" under consideration: Abraham was the one "to whom it had been said [by God] that 'in Isaac your seed will be called.'"[70] It was not merely that God asked Abraham to sacrifice one so long awaited and so dearly loved. God asked him to sacrifice the very one through whom God himself had promised to multiply his descendants and make him a great nation. The pastor's use of the imperfect tense, "was offering," serves two purposes. First, it reminds the hearers that Abraham was not required to complete this sacrifice. Thus, we have translated it "was ready to offer" (or "was about to offer").[71] However, it also reminds the hearers that Abraham carried out the entire process, from the time he rose in the morning and prepared for his journey until he raised the knife above Isaac. The immediacy and the persistence of Abraham's obedience are marked characteristics of the Genesis text. He did not delay when God called him to leave his home (v. 8). He did not fail to persevere in obedience when God ordered him to sacrifice Isaac.

19 "Having reckoned" at the beginning of v. 19 introduces a causal participial phrase showing why Abraham was willing to sacrifice Isaac: "He did this because he reckoned that God was able to raise from the dead." How could Abraham explain these two facts: God had promised him many descendants through Isaac; God commanded him to offer this very Isaac as a sacrifice? Abraham came to the conclusion that if he obeyed God's command God could still fulfill his promise because "God is able to raise from the dead."[72] The infinitive "to raise" is the present of general statement, not the aorist appropriate for a specific act.[73] If Abraham believed God could raise Isaac in order to fulfill his promise, then he must have believed that God could raise the dead in general. The Greek word order emphasizes the significance of this

---

ἀγαπητόν ("beloved") found in the LXX of Gen 22:2. The pastor may be following an alternate Greek translation, since Aquila used μονογενής in Gen 22:2 (cf. Symmachus in Gen 22:12 and Josephus, *Ant.* 1.222). Elsewhere the LXX uses μονογενής for the same Hebrew word that occurs in Gen 22:2 (see μονογενής for יחיד in Judg 11:34; Pss 21:20; 24:16; 34:17).

69. Lane translates ὁ τὰς ἐπαγγελίας ἀναδεξάμενος as "he who had accepted the promises" (2:343) on the basis of the papyrii, which use ἀναδέχομαι of accepting responsibility (2:361).

70. Taking πρὸς ὅν ("to whom") as referring to Abraham (Ellingworth, 601). The pastor does not direct his hearers' eyes to Isaac but to Abraham.

71. Following the NRSV. Cf. Thompson, 238.

72. The aorist form of λογισάμενος, "reckoned," indicates that Abraham came to a conclusion about God on the basis of these facts. See Lane, 2:362.

73. Furthermore, ἐγείρειν ("to raise") has no specific object, indicating that it refers to more than Isaac alone. See Ellingworth, 603.

truth by putting the phrase "from the dead" first, and maintains a certain suspense by reserving "God" until the end.[74] While the hypothetical raising of
Isaac may have been only a temporal resurrection like that described below in
v. 35a, Abraham's faith was in a God who is "able to raise from the dead" in
the "better resurrection" of v. 35b.[75] The faith Abraham demonstrated when he
offered Isaac made sense only if he believed that God could raise the dead.
What is true of Abraham the patriarch is true for all the people of faith in this
chapter. It only makes sense that the God who created the world (v. 3) could
raise the dead.[76] It is only logical that the one who brought Isaac into being
from one "indeed dead" (v. 12) could raise the dead. Abel's faith (v. 4) was
without vindication if God could not raise the dead. Furthermore, since all the
faithful die, they will enter the God-made "City" only through the "better resurrection" (v. 35b). The pastor wants his hearers to realize that all those who
imitate Abraham and live "by faith" in the "promises" God gave him live in
the confidence that God will raise those who live "by faith."[77] Those who obey
out of such reliance upon God are the "righteous" who, "by faith," will "live"
by attaining the "better resurrection" (cf. 10:38; 11:4). The analysis of the rest
of this chapter below will confirm the central importance of these verses and
of faith in the God who raises the dead.

Some versions render the final clause of this verse as follows: "From
thence he received him figuratively speaking" (NIV/NRSV/ESV). Compare
the translation given above: "Therefore, he received him as a type." There are
two differences between these renderings: the first has "from thence," the second, "therefore"; the first has "figuratively speaking"; the second, "as a type."
The second translation is to be preferred for several reasons. Both "therefore"
and "type" reflect the way Hebrews uses these terms elsewhere.[78] Abraham's
receiving Isaac as a type of the resurrection of the righteous is in accord with
the pastor's concerns. As we have seen, he began to intimate that those who
live "by faith" have a destiny beyond death in vv. 4-5. Without such a destiny

---

74. ἐκ νεκρῶν ("from the dead") ἐγείρειν δυνατὸς ὁ θεός ("God").

75. For such faith in a resurrection to eternal life, see 2 Macc 7:9-14, 28-29, and
the other references to resurrection faith in contemporary Judaism cited by Weiss, 598-99.

76. The mother of the Maccabean martyrs in 2 Maccabees 7 uses faith in God's
creation of the world from nothing as motivation for confidence in his power to raise the
dead (O. Hofius, "Eine altjüdische Parallele zu Röm. IV. 27b," NTS 18 [1971-72]: 93-94).

77. The comprehensive statement "God is able to raise from the dead" could also
include the resurrection of the wicked. The pastor does not deny such a resurrection; however, his concern in this chapter is with the hope of those who live "by faith." They are the
ones who will attain to the "better resurrection" of v. 35b. His business is to urge his hearers on so that they will be among the number who attain this goal.

78. For ὅθεν (11:19) as "therefore" see 2:17; 3:1; 7:25; 8:3; 9:18. Compare ἐν
παραβολῇ ("in a parable," "in a figure," "in a type") in 11:19 with παραβολή ("type") in 9:8-9.

they could not inherit the promised God-established "City" (vv. 10, 13-16). Abraham's faith that "God is able to raise from the dead" suggests that Isaac, who embodies the many faithful descendents promised to Abraham, typifies their resurrection.[79] The pastor did not have to explain that Isaac was not literally raised from the dead. The hearers knew that Abraham had not actually taken his life. One might say that Isaac's "figurative" resurrection "typified" the future literal resurrection of those who live by faith.[80] A type is normally less than the greater reality it typifies.[81] God's promise of a heavenly City and of a people who would inherit it necessarily included their resurrection.

Some would also argue that Isaac was a type of Christ's death and resurrection.[82] After all, readers familiar with the Gospel of John can hardly help thinking of Christ when the pastor speaks of Abraham's "offering" the "only begotten."[83] However, there are two important factors that make this further typology unlikely. First, the pastor is describing the people of faith who lived before Christ and is concerned that they, "by faith," transcend death so that they can inherit God's promised "City." Second, the pastor's focus is on Abraham. He is the one who exercises faith by the sacrifice of Isaac.[84] Therefore, if anyone in vv. 17-19 foreshadows Christ, it must be Abraham. Abraham's obedient offering of his son with the assurance that God would, if necessary, raise him from the dead may foreshadow Christ's obedient self-offering in anticipation of the "joy" that would be his at God's right hand (cf. 12:2). Thus, Abraham, like Noah (see on v. 7), foreshadows the One soon to be described as "the Pioneer and Per-

---

79. Lane, 2:362-63; Attridge, 335; Braun, 371; Weiss, 598; Koester, 492.

80. So O'Brien, 425.

81. Rose, *Die Volke,* 235-44, neglects this fact when he attempts to substantiate Isaac's literal resurrection by arguing that he was a type of the resurrection.

82. Bénétreau, 2:148-49, Spicq, 2:353-54, and esp. Swetnam, *Jesus and Isaac,* 122-23, 128.

83. See μονογενής ("only begotten," "one and only") in John 1:14, 18; 3:16, 18; 1 John 4:9. However, one must be cautious in deriving a Christological connotation from this combination of μονογενής ("only begotten") and φροσφέρω ("offer"). First, as Eisenbaum, *Jewish Heroes,* 162, points out, Isaac was called μονογενής by Josephus and in Aquila's translation of the OT. Hebrews could easily be dependent on these or other sources. Second, the pastor does not develop these themes (cf. Koester, 492). There is no reason, *pace* Weiss, 598, to explain this lack of development by reference to a Jewish source. The pastor develops no Christology from this combination of terms either because he sees no Christological significance in them or because his purpose lies elsewhere. In either case this combination of terms provides little support for an Isaac/Christ typology.

84. In his attempt to make Isaac a type of Christ's death and resurrection, Swetnam, *Jesus and Isaac,* 122-23, 128, overlooks this focus on Abraham. However, Spicq, 2:354, betrays the centrality of Abraham when he says, "It is remarkable that our author does not exploit the Messianic traits of the figure of Isaac but exalts only the merits of his father." As noted above, this fact is not so "remarkable" in light of the pastor's purpose in this section.

fecter of the faith" (12:1-3) by his own obedient act of faith. It is the intrinsic relationship between living "by faith" and Christ's own obedience, by which he established the way of faith, that makes these connections between the ancient faithful and Christ almost inevitable. They are not the pastor's main concern, but they reflect the wholeness and consistency of his understanding of salvation.

20-22   In vv. 9-10 the pastor affirmed that "Isaac and Jacob" were "fellow heirs" with Abraham of the permanent, God-established "City." Verses 13-16 described the significance of Abraham, Sarah, Isaac, and Jacob's relationship to that "City" and to the "promises" of God. They lived as self-confessed "aliens and transients" on earth because the "City" established by God was their true home and place of citizenship, the place they were "diligently seeking" by faith out of ardent desire. In vv. 20-22 the pastor shows how the lives of Isaac, Jacob, and Joseph illustrate the pilgrim way of life described in vv. 13-16.[85] By framing vv. 17-19 with these two parallel passages, the pastor again highlights the resurrection faith of Abraham. Only those who have faith in a "God who is able to raise from the dead" (v. 19) persevere in this pilgrim way with the hope of entering the eternal "City."

The prominence of the "promises" of God in vv. 13-16 is continued in this passage through an emphasis on "blessing." As we will see, Isaac blessed Jacob, and Jacob blessed the sons of Joseph by passing on to them the Abrahamic "promises." Furthermore, Joseph "remembers" the promise of "the exodus" first given to Abraham. Thus, these examples continue the emphasis on faith as living with the certainty that God will fulfill his promises. These people are confident that by faith they will attain "the things hoped for" (v. 1a), including the eternal "City." In the meantime they are sustained by relying on the "unseen" but real power of God (v. 1b). As "fellow heirs" with Abraham of God's "promises" (v. 9), Isaac and Jacob form a natural pair. The pastor acknowledges this by the way he binds them together. Both of them bless their descendants. The Greek word order makes Jacob a mirror image of Isaac: A. "concerning things to come"; B. "blessed"; C. "Isaac Jacob and Esau"; C[1]. "Jacob . . . each of the sons of Joseph"; B[1]. "blessed"; A[1]. "and worshiped on the top of his staff." This description begins and ends with eyes fixed on the future. By remembering God's promise of the "exodus" Joseph continues this future emphasis while providing a smooth transition to the examples of Moses that follow.

20   Gen 27:27-40 and 28:1-5 record Isaac's blessing of "Jacob and Esau." "Concerning things to come" occupies the initial emphatic position in the Greek sentence. Translations such as the NRSV's "for the future" rob this substantive participle of its force. Isaac blessed them not just in reference to

---

85. On the close relationship between these and the previous examples see Ellingworth, 604; Lane, 2:364.

the future but concerning the "things" that God was going to do in the future. "Things to come" fits well with other descriptions of God's final salvation.[86] In the immediate context, however, this expression is broad enough to encompass all that God would do through Christ's first and second comings, with particular emphasis on entrance into the heavenly "City." It is important to remember (as affirmed in Gen 28:4) that, when Isaac blessed Jacob, he passed on to him nothing other than the promise God had given Abraham — the promise of a people, a home, and a blessing for the world. It may seem strange that the pastor mentions Esau along with Jacob. His appearance provides balance for "each of the sons of Joseph" in the next verse.[87] Yet one as deliberate as the author of Hebrews must have had more in mind. By associating him here with the people who lived by faith, the pastor prepares for the way he will use him as a warning in 12:14-17. Only one who was once part of God's faithful people could be a warning against apostasy.[88] Thus, mention here qualifies Esau to be the foil of the faithful in 12:14-17 and a final warning of the fate awaiting those who turn away. The pastor anticipates this ominous role by the fact that Esau does not pass on the blessing to anyone.

21 "By faith" Jacob (v. 21) bestowed this blessing on each of the sons of Joseph (Gen 48:1-22). The pastor is still, by implication, referring to the blessing "concerning things to come." The participle that we have translated "as he was dying" is crucial. The period of Jacob's dying began with his giving instructions about his burial (Gen. 47:27-31), continued through his blessing of Joseph's sons (48:1-22) and his own twelve sons (49:1-28), and concluded with his last charge and death (49:29-32). The pastor, however, does not tell us that

---

86. Compare περὶ μελλόντων ("things to come") with 1:4; 2:5; 6:5; 9:11; 10:1; 13:14 (Attridge, 335-36).

87. It is more likely that Esau was added to balance the two sons of Joseph in the next verse than that the two sons of Joseph were added, as Lane, 2:365, suggests, to balance Jacob and Esau. Spicq's contention (2:355) that Isaac showed his faith by discerning God's will that Jacob be blessed above Esau is naught but speculation.

88. Rose, *Die Volke,* 253-58, goes beyond the evidence when he argues that according to Hebrews Isaac passed the blessing of Abraham on to Esau as well as to Jacob. Isaac did conclude the blessing given Esau on a more positive note (Gen 27:40). Yet Isaac specifically passed on the blessing of Abraham to Jacob (Gen 28:4). Furthermore, according to Hebrews Esau's impiety consisted in the selling of his "birthright" (12:16; Gen 25:29-34), which subsequently prevented him from receiving the desired blessing (12:17; cf. Gen 27:27-40). The pastor's intentions are more modest. He can mention Isaac's blessing of Esau because it is recorded in the OT. He does so simply to identify Esau with the people of faith. The pastor does not mention what *Targum Pseudo-Jonathan* says about Esau's selling of his birthright. According to this source, cited by Rose, *Die Volke,* 253-58, Esau denied life in the world to come when he traded his birthright to Jacob. Such a denial makes him an opponent of those who believe in a "God who is able to raise from the dead" and anticipate life in the "City" that God has established.

Jacob was dying in order to identify this event. He does so in order to show that Jacob's faith transcended his death. He looked beyond his death to God's fulfillment of his promises. Thus his testimony reinforces the pastor's contention that faith transcends death because "God is able to raise from the dead" (v. 19). There need be no mystery about why the pastor chose Jacob's blessing of Joseph's sons (Gen 48:1-22) over Jacob's blessing of his own sons (Gen 49:1-28).[89] He wanted to demonstrate that God's promise to Abraham had been passed on through the generations. The blessing of Joseph's sons in Gen 48:1-22 made this transmission much clearer than the account of Jacob's blessing his own children (Gen 49:1-28).[90] First, Jacob blessed Joseph's sons in the name of the God of Abraham. Second, he said they would be called by his name and by the names of his fathers Abraham and Isaac. Third, he transmitted to them the promise given Abraham and Isaac of numerous progeny who would inherit the promised place of blessing (see Gen 48:15-16). Thus the pastor links Jacob to Isaac as the channel through which God has passed on his promise through the patriarchal blessings. Mention of Jacob's "dying" leads naturally to Joseph's concern with burial in the following verse.

The pastor concludes the Jacob example in v. 21 by citing Gen 47:31: Jacob "bowed in worship over the top of his staff." The standard Hebrew text reads: "bowed himself on the head of his bed." The LXX translation followed by Hebrews differs in two ways. First, the Greek word for "bowed in worship" brings out a possible, but not necessary, meaning of the Hebrew word for "bowed." Second, a slight change in vowel pointing allowed the LXX translator to read "staff" instead of "bed."[91] Thus according to Gen 47:31 (LXX) Jacob "bowed in worship over the top of his staff" just before he blessed Joseph's sons. Even as he died Jacob worshiped God leaning on the pilgrim's staff, indicative that he was a stranger in this world bound for the eternal City.[92] This pair of examples began with "things to come" (v. 20) and ends with a pilgrim's staff of one on the way to inheriting those "things."

---

89. Spicq, 2:355, misses the obvious when he says, "It is astonishing that the blessing of the twelve patriarchs (Gen 49) should be omitted."

90. Cf. Koester, 500. Eisenbaum, *Jewish Heroes*, 142, has suggested that Hebrews omitted reference to the other patriarchs because of their prominence in settling the land and in the institutions of Israel. This suggestion overlooks the reason demanded by the context of Hebrews in favor of Eisenbaum's hypothesis that Hebrews is intentionally "denationalizing" the history of Israel.

91. The Hebrew text has the following four consonants המתה. These consonants can be pointed הַמִּטָּה ("bed," MT) or הַמַּטֶּה ("staff," LXX).

92. See Lane, 2:365. If, as Attridge, 335-36, contends, the "staff" had no significance, then there would have been no reason for the pastor to include this quotation from Gen 47:31 (LXX). Rose, *Die Volke,* 260-61, refers to Gen 32:11 as an indication that Jacob's staff was the sign of his pilgrimage.

22   The recipients of Hebrews would not be surprised by the use of Joseph as this section's final example of faith drawn from the account of Abraham and his family in Genesis 12–50. The pastor has just mentioned Joseph in v. 21. His life far surpassed those of all the other sons of Jacob as an example of one who lived by trusting in God.[93] Since the pastor has just mentioned the death of Jacob, it was natural for him to go to the closing verses of Genesis that describe Joseph's last act (Gen 50:24-26). This description of Joseph's faith in the concluding verse of the Abraham section (Heb 11:22) has a beauty born of rhythm and brevity that effectively recalls the Genesis account and impresses the pastor's desired truth upon his hearers. "By faith Joseph" links it to the larger catalogue of examples. "Concerning the exodus of the children of Israel he remembered" is paralleled by "concerning his bones he gave command."[94] "He gave command" at the end of the verse sounds like the word translated "as he was coming to an end" at the beginning.[95] These two words give this incident a ring of finality appropriate for the last example from the era of Abraham and his immediate descendants.

"As he was coming to an end, Joseph remembered the exodus of the children of Israel." Joseph's recollection at the end of Genesis formed a bridge to the account of the exodus in the opening chapters of the following book. The pastor also concludes this section with Joseph in order to direct his hearers to the examples from Moses' life that follow (11:23-29).[96] Joseph, however, is far more than a convenient means of transition. His example brings several of the pastor's main concerns in this section to a crisp climax. First, "as he was coming to an end" Joseph exercised faith in God's future. The pastor found the word we have translated "was coming to an end" in the last verse of Genesis. He has chosen it because, if anything, it is even more final than the word used for Jacob's "dying" in v. 21 above.[97] Joseph's earthly life was "coming to an end," but he had a faith that did not come "to an end." His faith transcended death because "God is able to raise from the dead" (v. 19). Second, "he remembered the exodus of the children of Israel."[98] Long

---

93. Note how the author of Genesis contrasts the faithfulness of Joseph in Gen 39:1-23 with the faithlessness of Judah in 38:1-26.

94. περὶ τῆς ἐξόδου τῶν υἱῶν Ἰσραὴλ ἐμνημόνευσεν ("concerning the exodus of the children of Israel he remembered"); περὶ τῶν ὀστέων αὐτοῦ ἐνετείλατο ("concerning his bones he gave command").

95. τελευτῶν ("as he was coming to an end"); ἐνετείλατο ("he commanded").

96. See Rose, *Die Volke,* 262-63.

97. Gen 50:24-26 uses both ἀποθνῄσκω ("die," Gen 50:24; cf. the participle ἀποθνῄσκων describing Jacob in Heb 11:21) and τελευτάω ("come to an end"; Gen 50:26) in reference to Joseph's death. The pastor has chosen the latter, τελευτῶν ("as he was coming to an end"), for effect.

98. Most translations render ἐμνημόνευσεν as "he made mention" (NKJV, NASB,

ago during the night vision of Gen 15:7-21 God had promised Abraham that after much suffering his descendants would be brought out of a strange land (Gen 15:13-14; cf. 46:4). Joseph had a faith that remembered, believed in, and acted upon the promises of God. Because he believed this promise, "he gave command concerning his bones." Since the hearers were familiar with Genesis, they needed nothing more than this brief statement to remind them of what Joseph had ordered. So confident was Joseph in God's promise of deliverance from Egypt that he instructed the "children of Israel" to take his bones with them when this event happened.[99] Rose suggests that the writer of Hebrews thinks Joseph believed that the Promised Land was the place where the resurrection would take place.[100] This suggestion lacks credibility because it does not cohere with the pastor's general attitude toward Canaan. With the exception of 11:9, he never uses the expression "Promised Land" or "land of promise." In 11:9 he uses this term only to affirm that said land was not the fulfillment of God's promise. Joseph gives this command because he wants to continue his identity with the people of God even after his death.[101] He will go with them and inherit the future that God has for them — including the resurrection of his "bones."[102] The pastor would have his hearers remember God's promises, believe that his promises transcend death, and persist in their identity with the people of God so that they might enter into the final inheritance promised by God.

NRSV; cf. Ellingworth, 608). Johnson, 296; deSilva, 405, n. 69; and Koester, 493, however, are correct when they suggest that Joseph "remembered" God's promise of the exodus given his great-grandfather Abraham in Gen 15:13-16. In Gen 50:24 Joseph reminds his brothers that God "swore" to give them the land (cf. *T. Jos.* 20:1).

99. τῶν υἱῶν Ἰσραήλ ("the sons of Israel") in Heb 11:22 recalls the υἱοὺς Ἰσραηλ ("sons of Israel") in Gen. 50:25. In Genesis the reference is obviously to Joseph's brothers whom he made swear to take his "bones" with them in the exodus. However, in Heb 11:22 the pastor is referring to the exodus of the whole nation. Thus I have chosen the translation "children of Israel."

100. Rose, *Die Volke,* 264-66.

101. Thus, Jacob's burial in Canaan (Gen 50:4-14) would not have suited the pastor's purposes. It is not the land but the people of God with whom Joseph identifies.

102. It is likely that with the mention of Joseph's "bones" the pastor is thinking of Joseph's resurrection in light of the emphasis this chapter puts on God's power over death (see esp. vv. 5, 17-19, and 35). According to Max Wilcox, "The Bones of Joseph: Hebrews 11:22," in *Scripture: Meaning and Method,* ed. Barry P. Thompson (Hull: Hull University Press, 1987), 126, some Jewish interpreters believed that the "visitation" of God to which Joseph referred in Gen 50:24-26 was not only the exodus but also "the final liberation of Israel at the hand of the Second Redeemer." Cited in Rhee, *Faith in Hebrews,* 193. Note Koester's comment, "Joseph's confidence of being taken to the promised land after his death reinforces the hope that the believer's final rest will be in the place that God has promised (Heb. 12:22-24)" (Koester, 500; cited with approval by O'Brien, 427).

c. Moses, Faith under Stress:
A Story of Resistance and Triumph (11:23-31)

> 23 *By faith Moses, when he was born, was hidden three months by his parents, because they saw that he was a beautiful child, and they did not fear the edict of the king.* 24 *By faith Moses, when he was grown, refused to be called a son of Pharaoh's daughter,* 25 *but chose rather to suffer ill treatment with the people of God than to have the temporary advantage of sin.* 26 *He did this because he considered the reproach of Christ greater riches than the treasures of Egypt, for he was continually looking toward the reward.* 27 *By faith he abandoned Egypt, having not feared the wrath of the king, for he endured as seeing the Unseen One.* 28 *By faith he established the Passover and the application of blood, in order that the destroying one might not touch their firstborn.*
>
> 29 *By faith they passed through the Red Sea on dry ground, which when the Egyptians attempted they were swallowed up.* 30 *By faith the walls of Jericho fell because they had been encircled for seven days.* 31 *By faith Rahab the prostitute was not destroyed with those who disobeyed because she welcomed the spies with peace.*

The pastor parallels the seven examples of faith in the Abraham section above with seven in this Moses section. Four examples from the life of Moses (vv. 23-29) parallel the four from Abraham's life (vv. 8-12, 17-19); three from those associated with or following Moses (vv. 30-31) parallel the three from the patriarchs who succeeded Abraham (vv. 20-22). In each series the faith of the main character reaches its climax in the fourth example. In each the fourth is the centerpiece of the seven.[1] This section, however, is no mere repeat of the previous. Faith has entered a new era. One part of God's promise has begun to assume a clearer shape. Abraham's descendants have become a great people. Clearly, to live by the faith of Abraham is to identify with the people of God. However, the Mosaic era was not the era of fulfillment. The hearers already know that the deliverance initiated by Moses and completed by Joshua was not the ultimate realization of God's promise. The pastor has made this fact clear, both in his discussion of the wilderness generation in 4:1-11 and in his explanation of the patriarchs' sojourn in vv. 13-16 above. This Mosaic epoch, however, was a time when God's people experienced his power in unprecedented ways. Thus, without losing sight of faith's focus on the future ultimate fulfillment of God's promise (v. 1a), these verses emphasize the reality of his "unseen" power to sustain the faithful in the

---

1. Cockerill, "The Better Resurrection (Heb. 11:35)," 226-27.

present (v. 1b). Furthermore, these verses also make it clear that the self-confessed alienation of the patriarchs (vv. 9-10, 13-16) leads to opposition from and persecution by the unbelieving world.[2] Such opposition requires courage and perseverance, the theme of 12:1-13. The courage required by the resistance of Egypt and its "king" to the people of God has become the occasion for the manifestation of God's power on behalf of his own. The first three examples from Moses' life (vv. 23-27) demonstrate the courageous perseverance of faith in the face of opposition.[3] Thus, these examples focus on the fourth characteristic of pilgrimage given above — the necessity of hardship on the way to the journey's goal. Moses' endurance anticipates the way the pastor will urge his hearers to run the race with "endurance" in 12:1-13.[4] The three examples from the lives of those who follow Moses illustrate God's great power on behalf of his own (vv. 29-31). The fourth example from Moses' life (v. 28) is the transition point between the two.

Although the pastor appears to pursue the events of Moses' life in simple chronological order, his arrangement and description are as carefully crafted for effect as they were in the Abraham section.[5] In addition to the observations above, it is also crucial to note how the first three examples from Moses' life form a reverse parallel with the first three examples from the Abraham section.[6] The deliverance of the baby Moses from death in order to achieve the purposes of God in v. 23 parallels the God-promised birth of Isaac in vv. 11-12 from one "indeed dead." The opposition of the world against Moses in vv. 24-26 is the corollary of the patriarchs' alienation described in vv. 9-10.[7] Finally, Moses' departure *from* Egypt in v. 27 parallels Abraham's departure *for* the "place" of God's promise in v. 8. This arrangement is well suited for the pastor's purpose of inculcating courage in the face of opposition. He introduces this theme of courage in v. 23 through the deci-

2. It is no doubt true, as D'Angelo, *Moses,* 33-34, contends, that the pastor describes Moses' courage both in light of his hearers' situation and in anticipation of what he will say about Jesus in 12:1-3. The same, however, could be said for his description of all the heroes of faith in this chapter. The Maccabean martyrs were a natural source of language to describe the courage and suffering of God's people (D'Angelo, *Moses,* 32-34). Note especially the use of καρτερέω ("endure") in v. 27 and καρτερία ("endurance') as the distinctive virtue of the martyrs (4 Macc 9:9, 30; 10:11; 16:14).

3. Thus, Koester, 507, entitles 11:23-27, "Faith in the Face of Adversaries."

4. The pastor uses καρτερέω for Moses' endurance in v. 27, reserving ὑπομονή/ὑπομένω ("endurance"/"endure") for resuming the athletic metaphor in 12:1-13.

5. For this reason the pastor omits mention of the things most important in other lists, such things as the miracles of Moses, the details of the exodus event (Wis 10:16-17; Sir 45:1-5), and Moses' role as lawgiver (Eisenbaum, *Jewish Heroes,* 167).

6. See the discussion in Cockerill, "The Better Resurrection (Heb. 11:35)," 228.

7. Rose, *Die Volke,* 283, notes this parallel, but fails to show how the hostility endured by Moses builds upon the alienation experienced by Abraham.

sion of Moses' parents, while at the same time reminding his hearers of God's power over death. It is this power of God that forms the basis for courage. The description of Moses' courageous decision in vv. 24-26 follows naturally. The opposition he faced is only what those people should expect who, like Abraham and his associates (vv. 9-10), live in sinful society as citizens of heaven. By concluding with Moses' abandonment of Egypt in v. 27 he brings this courage to its highest pitch. The faith by which God's people "set out" for the heavenly home (v. 8) necessitates a definitive rejection of both the allurement and hostility of an unbelieving world. Thus the first three examples of this Moses section fortify the hearers, enabling them to resist intimidation by "seeing" God's future reward and present power with the eyes of faith.

23 Moses' heritage of faith began at his birth (Exod 2:1-10). The pastor could hardly speak of Moses' life without mentioning the wonderful account of his preservation "when he was born." He skillfully establishes unity with the following examples by making Moses the subject of this sentence. Nevertheless, the verb is passive, "he was hidden." His parents are the true, celebrated heroes of faith.[8] First, the pastor gives their act of faith: Moses "was hidden" by them "for three months." The duration of their act highlights its significance and underscores their perseverance.[9]

Next, the pastor shows why this was an act of faith by explaining the reason for their action: they acted in faith "because they saw that the child was beautiful." The unusual word translated "beautiful" is the only term the pastor has borrowed from the account of Moses' birth in Exod 2:1-10 (LXX). Stephen used this term in Acts 7:20 to affirm that Moses was "beautiful" to God. Jewish tradition employed this expression to underscore the extraordinary status of Moses.[10] One is reminded of the way the pastor used "only begotten" to describe Isaac's God-given role in v. 17. Moses' parents "saw," as the NIV says, that Moses "was no ordinary child."[11] They acted not merely from parental affection, but from the realization that God had a special purpose for Moses. They could see what the unbelieving could not see: both God's power at work in his birth and his God-intended role in the "hoped for" future fulfillment of God's promises.[12] Their faith was another illustration of

---

8. ὑπὸ τῶν πατέρων ("by his parents") denotes agency.

9. Cf. Philo, *Moses* 1.9: "His parents resolved, as far as was in their power, to disregard the command of the king" (cited in deSilva, 406).

10. Philo uses this term, ἀστεῖον, to describe the "good character" of those who are willing to reject pleasure and wealth rather than depart from God's way (*Alleg. Interp.* 3.23; *Posterity* 101; and *Good Person* 72). Cf. Koester, 501.

11. Cf. deSilva's translation (405) of ἀστεῖον as "gifted."

12. Lane, 2:370; Spicq, 2:356-57. In Jewish *Haggadah*, Moses' parents had been informed of his role in delivering Israel through a dream given to Miriam his sister (Rose,

the faith described in v. 1, and thus an extension of the faith exercised by the ancients (vv. 1-7) and the patriarchs (vv. 8-22). The pastor begins this Moses section by emphasizing that God's people walk "by faith" because they can "see" and thus keep their eyes on both God's future promises and his present power (cf. vv. 26, 27 below).

Finally, the pastor affirms the opposition they overcame. Because they could thus see God at work, they acted contrary to the world's expectations, expressed in the "edict" of the king of Egypt, condemning Hebrew male children to death. Since their deed was an act of obedience born of faith, "they were not afraid" of this king though he held them in slavery. This verb is probably ingressive aorist, "they did not begin to fear," or, rather, "they did not give in to fear."[13] They were "not intimidated" (REB) by the king. Thus, the pastor begins to build his case for courage and perseverance in the face of opposition and suffering. By his own courageous acts (given below) Moses was but following the lead of his parents. The pastor would encourage his hearers both to see God at work in Christ, now seated at God's right hand (8:1-2; 12:1-3), and to resist the intimidation of those around them.

In both this first example from the Moses section and the third from the life of Abraham (vv. 11-12) the action of faithful parents gave life to a child whom God would use to fulfill his promise.[14] Thus, as he moves into the Mosaic era the pastor will not let his hearers forget that God's power transcends death — he is, indeed, a God who "is able to raise from the dead" (v. 19). This knowledge is essential if one would exercise the courage required by faith. Isaac's parents waited upon God because they knew by faith that God would fulfill his promises. Moses' parents braved opposition because they could see "by faith" that God's hand was at work. The pastor would call God's people to a trust in God that enables them to be both patient in the face of seeming delay and brave in the face of opposition.

24-26   If the first example of Mosaic faith occurred "when he was born" (v. 23), the second occurred "when he was grown."[15] He affirmed his parents' obedience as his own. Verse 24 describes Moses' act of faith at his

---

Die Volke, 270-74). According to Hebrews, however, Moses' parents "saw" his potential for God's plan with the eyes of faith.

13. See Lane, 2:370, on ἐφοβήθησαν ("they were not afraid").

14. The fact that Abraham was νενεκρωμένου, "dead" (v. 12), shows that the birth of Isaac, like the deliverance of the baby Moses, was an instance of God bringing life out of death.

15. Compare μέγας γενόμενος ("when he had become big"; "when he was grown") with γεννηθείς ("when he was born") in v. 23. The pastor, as is his custom, sticks close to the OT text, avoiding the speculations about Moses' upbringing so prominent in other sources (Josephus, *Ant.* 2.223-53; Philo, *Moses* 1.23-31; *Jub.* 47:9; *L.A.B.* 9:19; Artapanus, *On the Jews,* frag. 3, cited in Johnson, 299).

maturity. The participle in v. 25 clarifies the nature and difficulty of this act. The concluding participle in v. 26 reveals the reason for Moses' action with the hope that those who hear this message will follow suit. When he was old enough to make his own choice Moses "refused to be called a son of Pharaoh's daughter."[16] As Abraham has shown, faith is first of all a response to God's call. It is choosing to follow God by obedience in pursuit of God's eternal reward. The corollary, however, of answering God's call is the rejection of the unbelieving world. The pastor uses the faith of Moses to emphasize this truth by telling us what Moses "renounced."[17] This verb is culminative aorist, affirming that Moses' decision was complete. He rejected totally, once and for all, the exalted status of being "a son of Pharaoh's daughter."[18] After narrating the birth of Moses, at which time he became "a son of Pharaoh's daughter" (Exod 2:1-10), the OT recounts his killing of the Egyptian (Exod 2:11-12), by which he severed his ties with Pharaoh. Jewish sources often glossed over or omitted this act through apparent embarrassment.[19] Hebrews, however, sees this event for what it was — Moses' definitive rejection of Egyptian privilege.[20]

25 The pastor's vision, however, reaches beyond Moses' initial act of renunciation by describing what Moses affirmed in its place. The aorist participle, "having chosen," is coordinate with the culminative aorist verb "renounced": "but chose rather to suffer ill treatment with the people of God than to have the temporary advantage of sin."[21] Moses provides the pastor

16. Both Philo (*Moses* 1.13) and Josephus (*Ant.* 2.232-33) assume that Moses was heir to the throne of Egypt. Josephus, *Ant.* 2.33, recounts a legend of the young Moses trampling the crown of Egypt offered him by his adopted mother's father. However, what Hebrews says about him does not go beyond the OT text. He was raised by Pharaoh's daughter as her own (Exod 2:1-10) and, whether or not he was the heir to Egypt's throne, he was heir to its wealth and pleasures.

17. Ellingworth (611) translates ἠρνήσατο as "renounce." He says that the author may have chosen this word because of its use in relation to "denying" Christ — Matt. 10:33; Acts 3:13; 1 John 2:23; 2 Pet 2:1; Jude 4.

18. υἱός ("son") is left without an article to put emphasis on the quality or status of sonship.

19. Pseudo-Philo (*L.A.B.* 9:16–10:1) and Josephus (*Ant.* 2.254-56) omit Moses' act of killing. Josephus (*Ant.* 2.254-56) and Philo (*Moses* 1.43-46) explain his flight from Egypt as escape from a royal plot on his life. Artapanus (*On the Jews,* frag. 3) combines the killing and the plot — Moses killed an assassin sent by the king to eliminate him. See Johnson, 299.

20. This identification of the rejection of Pharaoh by Moses and the killing of the Egyptian is confirmed by the way Heb 11:24 takes the words μέγας γενόμενος ("when he was grown") from Exod 2:11 (Lane, 2:370 n.).

21. The pastor is concerned about the definitive nature of Moses' act. Thus the translation of ἑλόμενος as "having chosen" is preferable to the REB's "preferring." Ac-

with his first clear opportunity in this roll call of the faithful to emphasize another crucial aspect of faith — those who live by faith identify with God's people. The pastor could hardly have made this point in his earlier examples because during their times the people of God had not fully taken shape. Joseph's final instructions (v. 22), as we have seen, suggest this identification. Moses shows how fundamental this choice is. The need to identify with God's people is the corollary of the Son of God's own complete identification with them through assuming their humanity (2:5-18). Salvation is available only to those who are part of that fellowship of people with whom the Son identified in order to provide their redemption.[22]

As noted above, the second example of Abraham's faith (vv. 9-10) provides the springboard for this second example from Moses' life. By answering God's call to pursue a heavenly home, Abraham lived as a stranger in the world of those who sought only temporal reward. Moses' public identification with God's own required courage because it exposed him to the ire of those who lived according to the goals and standards of the unbelieving world. If there was ever a person who, at great cost, identified with the people of God, it was Moses. At God's command he returned to Egypt in order to be the agent of God's deliverance (Exod 3:1–4:34), and thus endured "ill treatment with" God's people under Pharaoh's yoke. The pastor may have used the phrase "endured ill treatment with" because it reminded him of a related expression used for the ill-treatment of God's people by the Egyptians in Exod 1:11 (LXX) and Gen 15:2 (LXX; cf. Acts 7:6, 19). Furthermore, he speaks of both the past faithful (11:37) and his hearers (13:3) as suffering "ill treatment."[23] By suffering at the hand of the unbelieving world, they too have

---

cording to Lane, 2:368, this word is a true middle, showing personal involvement in the choice. It is used for choosing God in Josh 24:15, and choosing to do what God wants (followed by an infinitive) in Deut 26:17-18.

22. Eisenbaum has argued that Hebrews "denationalizes" the history of Israel by omitting mention of "Israel" and her national institutions in this chapter. However, in place of this national identity she tends to overemphasize the individualism of these heroes. The pastor may not mention Israel, but he is concerned about the community of God's people, and it is crucial that his heroes identify with that community. Eisenbaum notes that Moses identifies with the "people of God," but overlooks the communal significance of this act (Eisenbaum, *Jewish Heroes,* 167). Abraham and the patriarchs are concerned about their descendents; Moses' establishing the Passover evokes memory of God's people; it is God's people who cross the Red Sea; and Rahab identifies with them by receiving the spies with "peace." Eisenbaum goes well beyond the text when she says that "Moses is no more an Israelite than he is an Egyptian" (Eisenbaum, *Jewish Heroes,* 171). While Hebrews fails to call Moses an "Israelite," it clearly affirms that he is *not* an Egyptian. This overdone emphasis on individualism occurs throughout Eisenbaum's work. See particularly her conclusion (Eisenbaum, *Jewish Heroes,* 226).

23. Compare συγκακουχεῖσθαι (from συγκακουχέω), "endure ill treatment with,"

identified with the people of God. By using "people of God" for the belea-guered Israelites, the pastor reminds his hearers that there is one people of God throughout history.[24] Those who follow Christ become part of the same "house" in which Moses was a "steward" (3:1-6).

Johnson has suggested that "advantage" is a more contextually appro-priate rendering of the underlying Greek word than the "pleasure" followed by most translations.[25] The pastor is not speaking primarily about "sinful pleasures" in the sense of illicit sensual enjoyment or excess. Any "advan-tage" Moses acquired through continuing his identification with Egypt would have been "sin" because it would have kept him from identifying with the people of God.[26] Such an abandonment of God's own would have been equivalent to the apostasy against which the pastor has repeatedly warned his hearers (3:7-4:11; 6:4-8; 10:26-31). Legitimate things become "sin" for the pastor's hearers if they entice them to sever their relationship with Christ and the community he has redeemed. Still, as the contrast with "ill treatment" demonstrates, this "advantage" would certainly have been pleasurable. The pastor can use this term for the "advantage" Moses would have enjoyed and at the same time evoke the luxury of Egypt.[27] The pastor puts the Greek word translated "temporary" first in this clause to remind his hearers that this plea-surable advantage, though real, would have been short-lived.[28] Thus, as Mo-

---

and κακουχούμενοι/κακουχουμένων (11:37; 13:3 from κακουχέω), "enduring ill treat-ment." The latter lacks the prefix συγ ("with"). συγκακουχέω is used only here in the NT. See the various forms of κακόω in Exod 1:11 (LXX) and Gen 15:2 (LXX). This term also means "to mistreat."

24. See Attridge, 340, n. 34, referring to Heb 4:9; 8:10; cf. 10:30; 13:12. Ellingworth, 612, speaks from our vantage point when he says, "Nowhere does the author express more strongly his sense of the continuity between Israel and the Christian com-munity." The author of Hebrews simply does not conceptualize the people of God before Christ and his people after Christ as two different communities that need to be identified.

25. See Johnson, 300. For ἀπόλαυσις as "advantage" see Xenophon, *Mem.* 2.1.33; Plato, *Timaeus* 83A.

26. Michel, 409; Weiss, 605; deSilva, 408.

27. Josephus, *Ant.* 4.42, uses ἀπόλαυσις ("pleasure") for Moses' rejecting the "en-joyment" of the good things Egypt afforded. However, this term is not particularly charac-teristic of such descriptions in Hellenistic sources.

28. πρόσκαιρος ("for a time") is also used of the temporal safety that the Maccabean martyrs would have received if they had denied their faith (4 Macc 15:2, 8, 23). Several other terms in this section echo the accounts of these martyrs. Thus the mar-tyrs were asked to "deny" (ἀρνήομαι) their Jewish religion, the same word used in v. 24 for Moses' denying his status as a son of Pharaoh's daughter. A verb related to ἀπόλαυσις ("pleasure," v. 25) is used when the king invites the Maccabean martyrs to deny their faith and "enjoy" his friendship (4 Macc 8:5; cf. 5:8). See Ellingworth, 612, and Lane, 2:371-72.

ses will demonstrate in v. 26, such earthly advantage, no matter how great, is of no value to those who walk "by faith." The pastor would arm his hearers against both the "advantage" by which the unbelieving world seeks to allure them, and the "ill treatment" by which it would coerce them to abandon the people of God, whom he has now redeemed through his incarnate Son.

26 Moses rejected the "temporary advantage" of v. 25 in favor of suffering because he "reckoned" (i.e., accurately calculated) the vast superiority of the divine reward.[29] The pastor spares nothing in his description of the way Moses calculated this reward's superlative worth because he would have his hearers follow Moses' example. The vast value of the "treasures of Egypt" was legendary, yet Moses refused to compare Egypt's treasures with God's promised reward. Instead, he compared the best Egypt had to offer with the "reproach of Christ." Moses "reckoned" that even the "reproach of Christ" was "greater wealth" than "the treasures of Egypt." The Greek word order underscores the pastor's emphasis. Note how "greater riches" and "the reproach of Christ" surround "the treasures of Egypt" in the middle of the sentence.[30] To be identified with Christ is itself of supreme value even when it brings "reproach."[31] Furthermore, the "reproach of Christ" is the mark of those who will inherit the eternal reward (cf. 12:4-11). The last part of v. 26 tells us why Moses made, and how he sustained, this value judgment: "for he kept on looking toward the reward." Like Noah, he lived in pursuit of "things not yet seen" (v. 7). Like Abraham, he "saw" God's promised City (v. 13). He had his parents' vision into the things of God (v. 23). He firmly believed in a God who was the "rewarder" of the faithful (v. 6). The imperfect tense of "look" is important.[32] The habit of his life was to "keep on looking toward" the eternal "reward." Perpetual attention to the reward is key to courageous perseverance in the face of opposition.

We must give special attention to the striking way in which the pastor

---

29. Just as Sarah "reckoned" (ἡγήσατο, v. 11), and Abraham "considered" (λογισάμενος, v. 19), so Moses "reckoned" (ἡγησάμενος). The pastor appeals to his hearers' sense of what is reasonable. These people had compared both the costs and the rewards of living "by faith" and decided that such a life was by far the most advantageous course. Such calculations can be made only "by faith" — only by those who keep their eyes on God's promises and power.

30. μείζονα πλοῦτον ("greater riches") . . . τῶν Αἰγύπτου θησαυρῶν ("than the treasures of Egypt") τὸν ὀνειδισμὸν τοῦ Χριστοῦ ("the reproach of Christ").

31. "If Greco-Roman writers said that virtue is its own reward, even when it entails suffering (Silius Italicus, *Punica* 13.663; Diogenes Laertius, *Lives* 3.78), Hebrews says that one's relationship with Christ is its own reward, even when it entails suffering" (Koester, 503).

32. According to Ellingworth, 615, the imperfect of ἀπέβλεπεν ("was looking") denotes repeated action. Cf. Thompson, 242; Grässer, 3:172.

571

calls the suffering endured by Moses for his identification with God's people "the reproach of Christ." This usage is fully compatible with the pastor's teaching throughout Hebrews. There is and always has been only one people or "household" of God. Both Christ and Moses function in relation to this "household" — Moses as "steward" within God's "house"; Christ as "Son" over it (3:1-6). As God's Son Christ identified with God's "household" by assuming the humanity of its members in order to procure their redemption and bring them to their God-intended goal (2:5-10). He is, then, the means by which the faithful who live both before and after his coming reach their eternal destination (11:39-40; 12:22-24). Thus, it is no stretch of the imagination to say that those who identify with God's people identify with Christ (as either promise or fulfillment), whether they live before or after his coming. Therefore, the suffering they endure because they have identified with God's own they endure for identification with Christ. The sufferings that mark them as part of the people of God correspond to his suffering for the redemption of God's people (cf. 12:1-11; 2:5-10). The pastor, then, would describe Moses' sufferings as "the reproach of Christ" in order to encourage his hearers to endure "the reproach of Christ," incurred because they too have identified with God's people and suffer rejection by an unbelieving world.[33]

The pastor's language, however, suggests not only that Moses' sufferings were "the reproach of Christ," but that Moses recognized their similarity to Christ's sufferings and knew they were endured out of loyalty to him. This knowledge formed the basis of his calculation — he knew that his suffering was worth more than the treasures of Egypt because it was indeed "the reproach of Christ." We have already seen that through the divine revelation Moses received as "steward" in God's house he was a "witness to the things that would be said" by God in Christ (3:5; cf. 1:1). Thus, there is no need to assume that the pastor thinks Moses received some special vision apart from Scripture.[34] Moses knew that by his sufferings he identified with "the Christ" who was to come.[35] His

33. It is doubtful whether "the reproach of Christ" has been influenced by Pss 68 or 88:51-52, as some have suggested (deSilva, 410, though very tentatively). D'Angelo, *Moses,* 48-53, does not advocate the influence of these psalms, though she suggests the possibility thereof. A review of the evidence as she presents it demonstrates the weakness of this hypothesis. Furthermore, the suggestion that Moses suffered "reproach as an anointed one" is without substantiation. The pastor gives no clue that Χριστοῦ should be taken in such a generic sense. Such an understanding robs this expression of its potency to encourage the endurance of the pastor's hearers. Furthermore, Moses is not known in Jewish tradition as "an anointed one."

34. As suggested by D'Angelo, *Moses,* 95-149; Eisenbaum, *Jewish Heroes,* 169; and Attridge, 341.

35. The "reproach" Moses suffered was "the reproach of the coming Messiah with whom he was united by faith" (Hughes, 497). See John 5:46.

hearers are fully aware of who that Christ is. Thus, the pastor would have them imitate Moses' value judgment and joyfully embrace "the reproach of Christ." With Abraham the emphasis was on endurance through time in an inhospitable world; with Moses, on courage in the face of suffering inflicted by an unbelieving world.[36] Furthermore, if Moses suffered shame for Christ, then one cannot escape such shame by abandoning Christ for Moses. If one abandons the fulfillment of the promise in Christ, then one can find no solace in either the promise itself or those who anticipated its fulfillment.

The pastor's hearers could not have missed the parallels between Moses and Christ even if the pastor had not called Moses' sufferings "the reproach of Christ." The pattern of obedient suffering followed by (anticipated) triumph is much clearer than it was in the combined example of Abel/Enoch (vv. 4-5) above. Moses willingly identified with the people of God and endured great "reproach" in anticipation of the divinely promised "reward" (v. 26). Christ incurred great suffering by identifying with the people of God (2:5-18). "For the joy set before him he endured the cross, despising the shame" (12:2). As the first great example of one who endured suffering for Christ, Moses anticipates Christ's climactic example of enduring suffering in obedience to the will of God — "consider the one who has endured such opposition by sinners against himself" (12:3). However, the pastor has reserved Moses' role in delivering God's people until v. 28.[37] When we reach that verse we will see that he, like Noah and Abraham before him, clearly anticipated Christ as the "Pioneer and Perfecter of the faith" (12:2).

27 Moses' faith-born courage reaches its apex in this third example. The climactic nature of Moses courageously abandoning Egypt is demonstrated by the magnitude of this act of faith and by the intensity of the opposition overcome. It is confirmed by the grandeur of his motivation. Notice the growing magnitude of these acts of faith. First, Moses was "hidden" by his parents — a secret act (v. 23). Then he "refused" his privileged place in Egyptian society (v. 24). Now we are told that he "abandoned" Egypt altogether.[38]

---

36. Rose, *Die Volke,* 283, affirms the parallel between Abraham in 11:9-10 and Moses in 11:24-26. In both, faith persists through "strangeness in expectation of the eschatological blessings of salvation." He does not see, however, what Moses' example adds to Abraham's. Self-confessed "strangeness" or "alienation" has become courage in the face of persecution inflicted by an unbelieving world.

37. To be fully true, Hughes's declaration (493) that Moses is here "a notable type of Christ in his role of deliverer" must await v. 28. Rose, *Die Volke,* 281-83, writes as if the author's interest in using Moses as an example of faith excludes all Christological implications. While it is true that the pastor's interest in vv. 23-26 is primarily the exemplary character of Moses' behavior, neither he nor any other NT writer knows any such hard-and-fast division between the exemplary and the Christological.

38. Taking κατέλιπεν ("he abandoned") as culminative aorist.

Consider the opposition overcome: his parents were not intimidated lest their disobedience of the "king's decree" be discovered (v. 23); he was willing "to suffer ill treatment with" the people of God (v. 25); now we are told that he was not intimidated by "the wrath of the king" directed at his open rebellion. Confirmation comes from the increasingly greater descriptions of motivation: his parents "saw" God's purposes in his birth (v. 23); he "was continually looking to the" God-promised "reward" (v. 26). We are now told that he saw more than the reward — he endured "as seeing the Unseen One" himself.

According to Exodus, Moses fled to Midian (Exod 2:13-15) after killing the Egyptian (Exod 2:11-12). This flight, however, could hardly be what the pastor is referring to when he says that Moses "abandoned Egypt, not intimidated by the wrath of the king." Exod 2:14 says clearly that Moses was "afraid." It is true that some Jewish tradition found ways to explain away Moses' fear on this occasion.[39] Unlike the pastor, however, those traditions were not using this event as the climactic example of Moses' courage.[40] To have attempted to do so without addressing Moses' fear would hardly have been convincing to people familiar with the OT. Moreover, such an argument would be inconsistent with the pastor's habitually careful use of the OT text. Furthermore, the pastor is speaking of an event commensurate to Abraham's total break with the land from which God called him in v. 8 above. Nothing would be adequate short of Moses' final departure from Egypt at the head of God's people.[41] Both Philo and Josephus speak of the Exodus as Moses' "abandoning" Egypt.[42] Throughout the whole process of deliverance from Egypt — repeated interviews with Pharaoh, invoking of the plagues, and final crossing of the Red Sea — he was in no way "intimidated by the wrath of the king."[43] It would be artificial to constrain the pastor to a rigid chronology by insisting that this event could not be the final departure from Egypt because it preceded the establishing of the Passover in v. 28 and the crossing of the Red Sea in v. 29.[44] Those two

39. Philo (*Moses* 1.49-50; *Alleg. Interp.* 3.14), Josephus (*Ant.* 2.254-56), and Artapanus (*On the Jews,* frag. 3.19) eliminate the motive of fear from Moses' flight to Midian. See Johnson, 302.

40. In my judgment those like Weiss, 608-9, who think Hebrews dependent on such traditions, overlook this fact.

41. Westcott, 373; Héring, 105; Riggenbach, 373; Montefiore, 204; Kistemaker, 339-40; and O'Brien, 433-34.

42. See κατελίπω ("abandon") for the exodus in Josephus, *Ant* 2.318; 4.78; and Philo, *Moses* 1.149.

43. Thus Spicq, 2:359, argues that Moses' abandoning Egypt includes all his interviews and discussions with Pharaoh recorded in Exod 5:1–15:21. Cf. Rose, *Die Volke,* 284-87.

44. Rose, *Die Volke,* 284-87. *Pace* Attridge, 342; Moffatt, 182; Bruce, 312-13; Hughes, 497-98; Weiss, 608; and Braun, 382.

events are specific aspects of the whole described in v. 27.[45] The pastor gathers all of this under the rubric of Moses' "abandoning" Egypt as the most economical way to emphasize the courage of Moses expressed through this departure. In fact, the pastor may be consciously countering Moses' fear in Exod 2:14: "You may remember," he says by implication, "Moses' fear when he fled to Midian, but I tell you, he returned and abandoned Egypt at the head of God's people, unintimidated by the king's anger."[46]

This interpretation is confirmed by the reason given for Moses' fearless faith in the following statement: "For he endured as seeing the Unseen One." Since this "seeing" is described as the continuous habit of Moses' life, the pastor cannot be referring specifically to any of Moses' visual experiences of God.[47] Furthermore, since he is using Moses as an example to be emulated, Moses' vision of God must be something available to all who live "by faith."[48] Nevertheless, the pastor has purposefully reserved discussion of this aspect of faith until he came to Moses. He feels free to make this statement because of the way Scripture describes Moses as "seeing" God at the burning bush (Exod 3:4), on Mount Sinai (Exod 19:20; 24:9-11; 34:27-35), and at other times when Moses saw God "face to face" as one talks to his friend (Exod 33:11; Num 12:1-16; Deut 34:10).[49] The flight to Midian, however, occurred before the burning bush, which was the first of these experiences.[50] It would, then, have been surprising if the pastor had described that flight as the time when Moses abandoned Egypt because "he endured as seeing the Unseen One."

This reference to Moses "seeing the Unseen One" is too brief to determine to what degree the pastor may have been familiar with the discussion of Moses' visionary experiences in Jewish tradition.[51] In any case, his affirmation that Moses sees the "Unseen One" is not speculation, but is thoroughly

45. Rose, *Die Volke,* 284-87.

46. Only in this way could the pastor be giving a "summary of Moses' departures from Egypt," as Koester, 504, D'Angelo, *Moses,* 62, and Eisenbaum, *Jewish Heroes,* 170, suggest. There is no reason to believe that he sees any positive value in Moses' initial flight to Midian beyond the fact that it gave God the opportunity to call him.

47. *Pace* D'Angelo, *Moses,* 56, who thinks Hebrews is referring to the burning bush; and Eisenbaum, *Jewish Heroes,* 170, who includes Moses' repeated visual experiences.

48. See Spicq, 2:359.

49. Thus, we can agree with D'Angelo's contention that Moses' visual experiences set him off from the other examples (D'Angelo, *Moses,* 35) only in that they gave the pastor opportunity to bring out an aspect of faith that is common to all.

50. Rose, *Die Volke,* 284-87, argues that Moses did not actually see God at the burning bush, but from then on he lived "as one seeing the invisible."

51. See, for instance, Sir 45:5; Philo, *Moses* 1.158; *Alleg. Interp.* 3.100; *Rewards* 27.

integrated into the understanding of faith that the pastor is communicating to his hearers.[52] As noted above, "faith" is living as if God's "hoped-for" promise of future salvation is certain (v. 1a) and as if his "unseen" power is available to sustain the faithful in their present perseverance (v. 1b).[53] We have already seen that those who live "by faith" do so because, with the eyes of faith, they "see" the fulfillment of God's future promise. Thus Noah was "warned of things not yet seen" (v. 7); Abraham and those associated with him "saw" the God-built eternal city (v. 13); Moses himself "kept looking toward the reward." Moses, however, demonstrates that people who live by faith are also able to "endure" persecution and suffering because with the eyes of faith they can "see" the "Unseen One" at work in the present. They are confident that "God is" (v. 6). By faith they know that God's power is available to enable their perseverance even when his presence is not apparent (cf. v. 1b).[54] This reality, so singularly demonstrated by Moses, was anticipated by his parents, who could "see" God at work in his birth. While assurance of God's promise may motivate the faithful, it is confidence in his power for the present that enables them to persevere in the face of persecution and hardship. Such endurance is the opposite of the apostasy against which the pastor has repeatedly warned his hearers.[55]

"As seeing the Unseen One"[56] more accurately conveys the pastor's intention than the weaker possibility, "as if he were seeing the Unseen One."[57]

---

52. Attridge, 343, agrees that Hebrews is not concerned with Moses' visionary experiences in themselves, but with Moses' faith. Thus, the author of Hebrews has used this material about Moses to expand and bolster his teaching on this subject. Philo, on the other hand, has developed traditions about Moses' visionary experiences in accord with philosophical speculation. See also Lane, 2:376; Weiss, 610; Koester, 504; and O'Brien, 434.

53. See also the comments on vv. 3 and 6 above.

54. Weiss, 610, also draws a connection between Moses' vision of the "Unseen One" and the "unseen" power of God in v. 1b.

55. καρτερέω, the word used here in Heb 11:27 for "endure" or "persevere," is the opposite of ἀποστῆναι, "to turn aside," in Sir 2:2-3. It is synonymous with other words used for "endure"/"endurance" in Hebrews (μακροθυμέω, 6:15; μακροθυμία, 6:12; ὑπομένω, 10:32; 12:2-3; and ὑπομονή, 10:36); and the opposite of words used to describe apostasy (ὑποστέλλω, "draw back," 10:38; ὑποστολή, "drawing back," 10:39). Hebrews uses καρτερέω ("endure," "persevere") for the endurance of suffering in anticipation of God's future reward in accord with the usage of this verb and its related noun in 4 Macc 9:8-9, 30; 10:9-11; 15:14. The pastor has little in common with the Hellenistic idea of "endurance" as self-control (D'Angelo, *Moses*, 32).

56. Westcott, 373-74; D'Angelo, 95-149; Attridge, 342-43. D'Angelo, especially, assumes this position because she thinks Hebrews is referring directly to Moses' visionary experiences.

57. Moffatt, 181; Spicq, 2:359; Michel, 411; Braun, 383.

To be sure, Hebrews is not arguing that Moses saw God with his physical eyes. Such a statement would be, as Williamson contends, a self-contradiction.[58] Moses was "seeing" with the eyes of faith the "One" who cannot be seen with physical eyes. The present tense of the participle "seeing" shows that the pastor is describing the perennial habit of Moses' life — he endured "as continually seeing" by faith "the Unseen One."[59] The aorist tense of "he endured" signals the fact that Moses persevered in obedience until the end. Only such a continuous vision of God's presence and power will enable the faithful to persistently "endure" the hardship of the present. In the following examples the pastor will remind them of some of the ways in which God's great power was manifest in Moses' life and the lives of those who followed him. He gives this reminder in order to encourage them during times when God's power is not visible to physical eyes. The pastor began preparing for the application of this visionary theme to his hearers long ago, when he spoke of what "we see" by faith (2:9). He will bring it to a climax in 12:1-3 when he encourages his hearers to "look unto the Pioneer and Perfecter of the faith, Jesus."

The pastor invokes these three examples from the life of Moses in order to stimulate the courage necessary to continue living in dependence on God in the face of shame, rejection, and persecution. These examples complement his concern in the opening Abrahamic examples above. The alienation depicted in those examples has become stout resistance. The need to wait in faith for God to act has become the need to endure ill treatment as one waits. Faith looks not only to the future promises, but also to the present reality of God's power. We have noted above how the first Mosaic example (v. 23) parallels the third Abrahamic example (vv. 11-12); and the second Mosaic (vv. 24-26), the second Abrahamic (v. 10). The way in which this third example from the life of Moses (v. 27) parallels the first from Abra-

58. Williamson, *Philo and Hebrews,* 475-77. Williamson would argue that Moses endured "by faith" "as if he were seeing God," while we would contend that Moses endured "by seeing God with the eyes of faith." In the final analysis, the two amount to much the same thing. Williamson, however, is overly cautious because he is distinguishing Hebrews from Philo. We would certainly agree that Hebrews has little, if any, affinity with Philo's descriptions of Moses as actually seeing the unseen God (*Alleg. Interp.* 3.100-107) or the invisible world of ideas through contemplation (*Spec. Laws* 4.192; *Moses* 1.158). Hebrews is not dealing in philosophical speculation. The author of Hebrews, however, is not concerned with distinguishing himself from Philo. He wishes to state his point in the most powerful way.

59. Lane, 2:376, calls Moses' seeing God "a fixed habit of spiritual perception." However, Lane, 2:375-76, is probably mistaken when he renders ὁρῶν ἐκαρτέρησεν, "he continued to see," instead of "as seeing he endured." This interpretation not only faces syntactical problems (Ellingworth, 616-17), but also fits less readily with the author's driving pastoral concern that his hearers endure (cf. 10:32-39; 12:1-3, 4-11).

ham's life (v. 8) illustrates the complementary purposes of these two sets of examples. In both examples under consideration, the person involved goes from one country to another. However, in the case of Abraham, the focus is on the country to which he is going; in the case of Moses, the one he is leaving. Compare "to set out" (11:8) with "he abandoned" (11:27). Abraham is going to a place he will receive as an "inheritance." Moses is leaving the place of "ill-treatment." Abraham trusts God although he does not "know" where God is taking him. Moses trusts despite "the wrath of the king." Abraham is waiting for God to fulfill his promises. Moses is depending on the "unseen" God for deliverance in the present without forgetting his promise of future "reward." The pastor focuses his hearers on the reward before urging them to brave the resistance.

The complementary nature of these two lists of three is also illustrated by the fact that it is the third example from Abraham's life (vv. 11-12) that is longest and most significant, but the second from Moses' (vv. 24-26). Abraham must have the kind of faith that waits for God to fulfill his promises in the future. Thus, it was appropriate for his series to conclude with the birth of Isaac as evidence that God is faithful to his commitments in the end. On the other hand, Moses must have faith to endure contemporary mistreatment and persecution. Thus, it was the second example describing the time of difficulty before he was delivered from Egypt that was most useful.

This chiastic relationship between vv. 23-27 and vv. 8-12 reveals even more clearly the central position and crucial importance of Abraham's faith in a God "who raises the dead," as described in vv. 17-19. We have already seen that the lives of Isaac, Jacob, and Joseph in vv. 20-22 illustrate the alien existence of the faithful as described in vv. 13-16. Thus, we can see that vv. 17-19 are at the center of the following chiasm:[60]

A. 11:8
    B. 11:9-10   Faith That Awaits the Promises of God.
        C. 11:11-12
            D. 11:13-16
                E. 11:17-19 Faith in a God "Who Raises the Dead."
            D^1. 11:20-22
        C^1. 11:23
    B^1. 11:24-26   Faith That Endures through the Power of God.
A^1. 11:27

There are some resemblances between the four remaining examples from the Moses section (vv. 28-31) and the four examples from the primeval

60. On the chiastic structure of Heb 11:8-27, see Cockerill, "The Better Resurrection (Heb. 11:35)," 228-29.

history (vv. 3-7), although the correspondences are not as exact as those above.[61] Nevertheless, it is clear that Abraham's faith in a God "who raises from the dead" is central to the kind of faith the pastor desires his hearers to emulate, and to the destiny of the people of God with whom they must identify. Only a God "who raises the dead" is adequate to bring his people into the "City" he has prepared for them and to sustain or deliver them amid present tribulation.

28 The pastor has used the first three examples from Moses' life to build a compelling case for endurance amid persecution, shame, and hardship inflicted by the unbelieving world. At great cost Moses identified with the people of God and persevered amid such suffering. He did so "by faith" that God was real and active on behalf of his own, even when God's activity was invisible to human eyes (cf. v. 1b). The three examples of those associated with Moses as described in vv. 29-31 complement this message. "By faith" they experienced deliverance through the very visible mighty power of God in the present. Thus, their testimony encourages the people of God even when God's power is not so evident. The fourth example from the life of Moses (v. 28) is the point of transition from the three examples of hardship to the three of deliverance. It brings resolution to Moses' suffering by introducing the first in the series of mighty deliverances to follow.

Moses himself, who had braved such suffering, experienced the mighty power of God when "by faith" he "established the Passover and the application of blood." In most contexts the verb here rendered "established" is translated "do" or "make." The pastor, however, uses the perfect tense, for he is describing more than Moses' "doing" or "celebrating" the Passover.[62] Moses established it for all time as a memorial to the faithfulness of God. The pastor has not used the perfect indicative since he declared that Abraham "offered" Isaac "by faith" in v. 17. Both the "Binding of Isaac" and the Passover stand as great monuments to God's trustworthiness. It is not hard to see how Moses' establishing of the Passover was "by faith." God's instructions concerning the institution and celebration of this feast are found in Exod 12:1-20. According to Exod 12:21-22, Moses followed those instructions. Moses believed God's word that he was going to destroy the "firstborn" of Egypt, so he obeyed God's instructions in order to preserve the "firstborn" of God's own people. As a result of this obedience he indeed experienced God's

---

61. Cockerill, "The Better Resurrection (Heb. 11:35)," 231.

62. πεποίηκεν τὸ πάσχα could mean "kept the Passover." However, the larger context and the perfect tense of ποιέω suggest that the pastor is referring to Moses' establishing the Passover as the νόμιμος αἰώνιος, "perpetual ordinance," of Exod 12:14, 17. See Ellingworth, 617. Weiss, 611, agrees, noting the predominance of aorist verbs in this chapter.

"unseen" power in the present. The destruction of the firstborn of Egypt was the greatest of the ten plagues (Exod 7:1–11:10; 12:29-32) and God's greatest act in delivering his people save the crossing of the Red Sea (Exod 14:1-31) described in the next verse. The establishment of the Passover, however, embodies something even greater than the destruction experienced by Egypt — the preservation of God's own "by faith" amid such destruction. The pastor included "the application of blood" because it was the blood on the doorpost that was necessary "in order that the destroyer might not touch their firstborn."[63] The angel of death who "struck down" the firstborn of Egypt would not even "touch" the firstborn of God's people.[64] The word "firstborn" is neuter plural and therefore comprehensive. All the firstborn, both human and animal, were saved from death by the "application of blood." Yet it is hard to escape the impression that the pastor is thinking of the "firstborn" as representative of the people of God in its entirety (cf. 12:23).[65]

Those who have persevered to this point in the pastor's catalogue of the faithful are not surprised that he draws no Christological implication from "the application of blood." He has made much of the blood of Christ (see especially 9:14) and will speak of the "blood of sprinkling" in 12:24. We have, however, seen numerous possible Christological applications left undeveloped in the previous verses of this chapter (vv. 4, 5, 7, 17-19). It appears that the author suggests these possibilities but leaves them without further explanation because he does not want to divert his hearers from the need for faithful endurance that is the main concern in this chapter.[66] Nor does he wish to dilute the typological relationships that he has already established in the central part of his sermon (4:14–10:18).[67] Nevertheless (as noted when commenting on vv. 4-5, 7 and 17-19), the obedience of the faithful, by which they participate in salvation, corresponds to and reflects the obedience by which Christ has provided salvation (cf. 10:5-10). We have now come to the third and final place where this occurs: "by faith" Noah obeyed God and provided for the salvation of "his household" (v. 7); "by faith" Abraham offered the "only begot-

---

63. Ellingworth, 618. It is possible to take τὰ πρωτότοκα ("the firstborn") as the object of the substantive participle ὁ ὀλεθρεύων ("the one destroying") or of θίγῃ ("touch"): "in order that the one destroying the firstborn might not touch them" or "in order that the one destroying might not touch their firstborn." The second assumes that the pastor has put τὰ πρωτότοκα ("the firstborn") directly after ὁ ὀλεθρεύων ("the one destroying") for emphasis. See Weiss, 611.

64. Exod 12:12 speaks of the destroyer not "smiting" (πατάξαι) the Israelites, but here the angel does not even "touch" (θίγῃ) them.

65. Weiss, 611.

66. Cf. Bénétreau, 2:158.

67. Thus, Bruce, 314-15, suggests, that development of a Passover typology might have detracted, at least rhetorically, from the pastor's Day of Atonement typology.

ten" and received him back as from the dead (vv. 17-19); and now, "by faith" Moses established the Passover and thus delivered the "firstborn" from death (v. 28). As we have seen, the second and central of these three events makes one of the primary emphases of this chapter clear: God's salvation includes resurrection from the dead. The first and third foreshadow the deliverance from the Judgment that accompanies the resurrection. The third reminds the hearers that this deliverance is accomplished only through the "blood."

The literary or structural relationship among these three examples of faith should by now be apparent. We have already noted that Abraham's offering of Isaac in vv. 17-19 and Moses' establishing the Passover in v. 28 are each the fourth and climactic example of the respective hero's faith.[68] Furthermore, we have demonstrated above that Abraham's offering Isaac in vv. 17-19 is at the center of a chiasm extending from v. 8 through v. 27 (v. 8/v. 27; vv. 9-10/ vv. 24-26; vv. 11-12/v. 23; vv. 13-16/vv. 20-21). We can now extend this chiasm to Noah's building the ark in v. 7 and Moses' establishing the Passover in v. 28.[69] In both verses the obedience of the main character expressed in building the "ark" or establishing the "Passover" results in the deliverance of God's people from judgment on the wicked. From beginning (11:7) to end (11:28) God's salvation provides for the deliverance of his people from judgment and death through the power of the resurrection (11:17-19).

The three final examples of faith (vv. 29-31) do not show such striking parallels with the three at the beginning of this chapter (vv. 3-5). Nevertheless, one can hardly deny the centrality of the resurrection faith attested in 11:17-19, nor can one reject the significant connections between Noah's building the ark (v. 7), Abraham's offering Isaac (vv. 17-19), and Moses' establishing the Passover (v. 28).

29-31   These verses continue the emphasis of the Moses section (vv. 23-31) on the second aspect of faith, confidence in God's real — though often "unseen" — power in the present (v. 1b).[70] The pastor would encourage his hearers by reminding them of how marvelously the "unseen" God demonstrated his power on behalf of Moses and his successors during their earthly lives. He emphasizes the magnitude of what God has done in several ways. First, his field of vision now encompasses the whole people of God. God promised Abraham that this numerous people would come into being (v. 12). Moses identified with them (v. 25) and delivered them through the

---

68. The fourth example from Abraham's life (11:17-19) and the fourth from Moses' (11:28) are related by "faith in salvation from death" (11:17-19) and "faith in deliverance from death" (11:28).

69. Cockerill, "The Better Resurrection (Heb. 11:35)," 231.

70. The blessings these people received by faith were both earthly deliverances and victories over powerful enemies.

Passover (v. 28). It is not one or two people but this great body of the faithful who attest the power of God. Second, by giving these examples in abbreviated form the pastor quickens his pace and increases emotional intensity. These three "by faith's" come in rapid succession. The more ponderous descriptions of alienation (vv. 8-11; 13-16; 20-22) and persecution (vv. 23-27) have become ringing declarations of triumph. The three final examples of the Abraham section (vv. 20-22) described those who waited long with patience. These three at the end of the Moses section give a sense of rapid movement from one triumph to another despite the fact that the events they describe spanned more than forty years. Finally, in the first two of these final examples the pastor puts more emphasis on the event itself and its magnitude than on the persons who experienced it. All of these changes in style underscore the magnitude of God's power to deliver and anticipate the even more rapid, compact, inclusive, and intensive description of God's deliverances in vv. 32-35a.

The people whom Moses led out of Egypt provide the first two examples of faith, and Rahab supplies the third. The pastor passes by the entire wilderness period in silence because, as he has already shown in 3:7–4:11, the wilderness generation was no example of faithfulness. Perhaps he does not name this generation in v. 29 because of this their subsequent unbelief. Instead, he allows the subject to be implied from the context of the previous verse and the third person plural verb, "they passed through." However, the omission of the names of the people who exercise faith in both vv. 29 and 30 serve several purposes. First, as noted above, this omission anticipates the shift from the person who exercises faith to the events achieved through or suffered by faith in vv. 32-38. The pastor does not make this change, as Eisenbaum suggests, in order to depersonalize faith, but rather to put emphasis on the extent of its results. Second, the omission of names in vv. 29 and 30 puts great emphasis on the mention of Rahab in the concluding example of this section (v. 31).

29 Whatever their subsequent conduct, when "they passed through the Red Sea on dry ground" (v. 29) the soon-to-be wilderness generation acted "by faith." God provided deliverance for them, but they had to appropriate it by enacting their trust through obedience. Exod 14:15-31 tells their story. They began by fearing the pursuing Egyptians (14:10-14) but ended by fearing the God who had delivered them from and destroyed those Egyptians (14:31).[71] One could hardly blame them for their initial hesitancy, but the fact that they walked into the sea in obedience to God's word demonstrated their faith.[72] Two expressions in this verse underscore the magnitude of God's act.

71. See Lane, 2:377.
72. Bruce, 316; Rose, *Die Volke,* 267. The Israelites' faith was not demonstrated by pious entreaty but by obedience.

First, in Greek the phrase translated "on dry ground" indicates that the land was indeed dry — God did such a thorough job that they did not have to wade. Second, "the Egyptians were swallowed up when they attempted to do the same." The term "swallowed up" is an intensive verb taken from Exod 15:4 that emphasizes the complete destruction of the pursuing Egyptians.[73] They were "engulfed." The deliverance of the righteous included the destruction of the wicked who oppressed them just as it did in both the flood (v. 7) and the Passover (v. 28).[74] These judgments anticipate the final Judgment (12:25-29). God's mighty deliverance of those who live "by faith" carries an implicit warning for the rebellious.

30 God's deliverance of his people through the Red Sea was the final and greatest demonstration of his power in the exodus. When one turns to the Conquest, no event is either so compelling or so demonstrative of faith as the fall of mighty Jericho: "By faith the walls of Jericho fell because they had been encircled for seven days" (see Josh 6:1-27). Although Jericho was a mighty city, its walls fell through no human stratagem. Their collapse was due to the direct power of God in response to the people's persistent faith, demonstrated by their persevering until they had encircled the walls for seven days at God's instruction.[75] Its fall is an indirect reminder that no earthly city is permanent.[76] The children of the wilderness generation were not disobedient as their parents had been. Nevertheless, by using the passive voice the pastor allows them to recede into the background while he puts all emphasis on the mighty power of God. He has already given his hearers many examples to follow. He would now impress them with the magnitude of God's power on behalf of his own. The pastor will continue this emphasis on the mighty manifestations of God's power in vv. 32-35a without neglecting the exemplary character of the people who did them. One might wonder why the pastor makes no mention of Joshua here. There are several possible reasons. First, the fall of Jericho did not occur merely in response to Joshua's faith but in response to the faith of all those who circled the city. It was not an individual act like Abraham's setting out in response to God's call (v. 8) or Moses' refusing to identify with Egyptian privilege (v. 24). This collective act of faith precedes the many acts of faith performed by the faithful in vv. 32-38. Furthermore, the pastor would not find Joshua rhetorically effective because his life was so closely bound to the earthly Promised Land. It is much easier for the pastor to

---

73. The pastor uses an aorist form of καταπίνω, "swallow." The prefix κατα makes it an intensive form of πίνω ("drink"). See Ellingworth, 620.

74. "It is almost as if, in the author's estimation, the absence of faith on the part of the pursuing Egyptians was what accounted for their destruction (cf. on v. 31)" (Gordon, 165). Cf. O'Brien, 436, citing Attridge, 344, and Bruce, 316.

75. On the seven days as indicative of the people's persistence, see Weiss, 612.

76. deSilva, 415.

address those on their way to the heavenly "home" or "City" from the vantage point of Abraham or Moses, who were also anticipating entrance into God's heritage. To be sure, in vv. 32-38 the pastor will refer to many faithful who lived in the Promised Land, but he does not refer to them in relationship to that land. It would be all but impossible to discuss Joshua's exploits without mention of the earthly Promised Land. No doubt the pastor believed that Joshua's life attested many examples of faith, but it did not serve his cause to discuss them.[77]

These great miracles at the Red Sea and Jericho dwarf the power of God experienced by the patriarchs and anticipate the great deliverances soon to be narrated in vv. 32-35a. As noted above, what God did through Moses and his successors was not the ultimate fulfillment of his promises, but it was the greatest demonstration of his power to deliver the faithful in the OT. Thus, it is at first surprising to find that the final example in this series concerns the private individual Rahab and introduces no new miracle. As we will see, however, by introducing Rahab at this point the pastor concludes this section with what is perhaps his clearest and most powerful example of one who lived "by faith." If his hearers will imitate Rahab's faith, he will ask no more.

31 There are at least four factors that make Rahab a most appropriate conclusion not only to the Moses section but to the discourse in vv. 1-31.[78] First, she is a very clear example of the kind of faith described in vv. 1, 3, and 6 and extolled throughout this chapter. Because she believed both that God's power was real and his promises were certain, she was confident that he would give his people the land. She acted on this faith "by welcoming the spies with peace." By describing the other citizens of Jericho as "those who were disobedient" the pastor indicates that Rahab's accepting the spies was an act of obedience to God's word.[79] Second, by calling Rahab "the prosti-

---

77. Eisenbaum's contention that Joshua is omitted because he was too closely tied to national Israel is too simplistic and insensitive to the contours of Hebrews' argument (Eisenbaum, *Jewish Heroes,* 171-73). Joshua was no more closely associated with ethnic or national Israel than were Abraham or Moses. It is the pastor's conviction that God's promise to Abraham is fulfilled through Christ in a heavenly home that makes Joshua rhetorically ineffective or at least inefficient, though not theologically problematic. For this reason Hebrews deprives Joshua of the attention he receives in such works as Josephus, *Ant.* 5.1-120, and Pseudo-Philo, *L.A.B.* 20:1-3. See Johnson, 303.

78. Rahab is prominent in Christian writings (Matt 1:5; Jas 2:25; *1 Clem.* 12:1), though absent from Jewish hero lists (Thompson, 243). See Eisenbaum, *Jewish Heroes,* 173. Weiss's contention, 612, that she must already have been a remarkable example of faith in Jewish tradition because she is mentioned in *1 Clement,* Hebrews, and James is puzzling, since these are Christian sources. Furthermore, *1 Clement* is demonstrably dependent on Hebrews. See the references on p. 34, n. 144 in the Introduction to this commentary.

79. By calling the other citizens of Jericho "those who disobeyed," the pastor im-

tute" the pastor makes it clear that one does not become or persevere as a part of God's people because of previous merit or birth.[80] A believing Canaanite is saved, while the unbelieving, "disobedient" Canaanites perish just like the disobedient wilderness generation (3:18). Third, although it required no miracle, Rahab "did not perish." Thus, she continues the theme of receiving life through faith, initiated in vv. 5-6, brought to a climax in vv. 17-19, and sustained through all the verses since. The pastor began with Abel, who died for his faith (v. 4). He brings this section to its climax with Rahab, who "did not perish."[81] Finally, "by faith" she, like Moses (v. 25), identified with the people of God. She did this when "she welcomed the spies with peace." "Peace" is the last word in the Greek of v. 31. "Peace" was the normal greeting exchanged by God's own.[82] By accepting these spies, she practiced the "peace" appropriate for the common life of God's people (13:20-21), a "peace" the pastor urges his hearers to pursue (12:14).[83] With such a clear example of faith in mind, the pastor can conclude this chapter by emphasizing the power of God (vv. 32-35a) to sustain the faithful in suffering (vv. 35b-38).[84]

d. The Rest of the Story — A "Better Resurrection" (11:32-38)

32 *And what more shall I say? For time would fail me if I tried to recount the stories of Gideon, Barak, Samson, Jephthah, David, and also Samuel and the prophets,* 33 *who through faith captured kingdoms, established righteousness, obtained promises, shut the mouths of lions,* 34 *quenched the power of fire, escaped the edge of the sword,*

---

plies that they had received the word of God just as Rahab had received it. They, too, had heard about all that God had done for his people (Josh 2:9-11). See Bénétreau, 2:160, quoting Donald Guthrie, 242. Note Attridge's (338, n. 6) comment on the inferior textual reading, "those who did not believe" (NKJV): "The variant is probably a scribal correction to make the text more thematically consistent, but it diminishes the subtle complexity of the motif of faith."

80. Perhaps the pastor's hearers would have thought, "if even a prostitute acted 'by faith' it would be shameful for us to do less" (Koester, 505, referencing Chrysostom). Jewish sources tended to explain away Rahab's prostitution by calling her an "innkeeper" (Josephus, *Ant.* 5.8; Targum on Josh 2:1) and making her a model of hospitality (see rabbinic references in Johnson, 304).

81. See the discussion in Cockerill, "The Better Resurrection (Heb. 11:35)," 231.

82. Bénétreau, 2:160; citing Bruce, 315, n. 213.

83. See Koester, 505-6.

84. Thus *pace* Eisenbaum, *Jewish Heroes,* 166, the "real body of our text" does not end "with Rahab." The very intensity of the following section shows that the pastor has been preparing for it all along. Only when the pastor has brought his hearers to a full understanding of the nature of faith as exemplified in Rahab is he free to concentrate on the urgency of perseverance amid suffering.

were made strong out of weakness, became powerful in battle, put to flight the armies of aliens. 35 Women received their dead by resurrection. But still others were tortured, refusing release in order that they might obtain a better resurrection. 36 But others received trial of mockings and beatings, and even of bonds and of prison. 37 They were stoned, they were sawn in two, by murder of sword they died; they went about in sheepskins, in goatskins, destitute, afflicted, mistreated, 38 of whom the world was not worthy, in deserts wandering and in hills and caves and holes of the earth.

The pastor concludes this chapter with a swift but massive recounting of faith from the judges until just before Jesus. He alters his style so that the accelerated descriptions of triumphant faith in vv. 28-31 can reach full throttle in both the triumphs and trials of faith in vv. 32-38. First, instead of discussing each person who acted by faith he begins with an open-ended list of people typical of what he will say (v. 32). One "through faith" (v. 33) has replaced the individual "by faith's" as a cover for all. Then in the following verses the results achieved by anonymous acts of faith replace the enumeration of individuals. Each result achieved by faith — whether of triumph or endurance — is in the plural, implying that many people were involved with each. The pastor trusts that these events will be compelling because they suggest names to his hearers' minds, but he intends each event to be more inclusive than any number of names the hearers might recall.[1] Thus, within the next seven verses the pastor implies that many times more people have lived "by faith" than those enumerated above.[2] He clarified the nature of the faith he would commend by the detailed examples of vv. 1-31. This clarification culminates in the example of Rahab (v. 31). In this final section, he would intensify the motivation of his hearers to maintain their place among God's faithful people. He has now focused clearly on the fourth characteristic of pilgrimage — hardships along the way. Thus, he describes faith's momentous triumphs as encouragement amid its horrendous trials. In this way he lays a solid foundation for his transformation of the pilgrim's journey into a marathon, a long race finished only through endurance (12:1-13). He reminds his hearers of

1. Since Rose is attempting to analyze the traditions that the author may have used, he goes to great lengths in identifying the people involved in these triumphs and sufferings (Rose, *Die Volke*, 306-22). Cf. also Koester, 511-16. Such a thorough identification of these people runs the risk of giving the impression that one has definitively identified to whom the pastor is referring, and thus of skewing the impression he would make of an open-ended, innumerable host of the faithful.

2. "Clearly, the impression the rhetor wishes to leave with his audience is that there exists an inexhaustible supply of examples of faith and faithfulness to God in their spiritual heritage" (Bulley, "Death and Rhetoric," 412).

the vast host of faithful with whom they are associated. With this rapidly changing imagery he leaves his hearers overwhelmed and breathless before the accumulated mass of testimony presented to their senses. In addition, the pastor uses this grand company of witness to impress upon his hearers that they live at the climax of God's plan and, thus, to prepare them for the introduction of Christ's example in 12:1-3.[3]

Verse 32 introduces this section and initiates the pastor's change of style. The triumphs of faith described in vv. 28-31 find their conclusion in the collage of victories celebrated in vv. 33-35a. These victories are followed by an equally graphic collage of the faithful who suffer without temporal deliverance in vv. 35b-38.[4] The pastor, who began with the suffering of Abel (v. 4) and the triumph of Enoch (v. 5), concludes with a great picture of triumph followed by one of suffering. At the heart and center of the previous section the pastor established the importance of reliance on the God "who is able to raise from the dead" (v. 19). At the center of this section in v. 35 he builds on that truth: God raises his own to a "better resurrection" that is nothing short of ultimate victory over death (see 2:14-15).[5] This assurance of Enoch-like triumph over death through the resurrection (v. 5; vv. 33-35) enables the faithful to endure Abel-like suffering for loyalty to Christ (v. 4; vv. 36-38).

32   The pastor begins this section with a deliberative question: "And what more shall I say?"[6] This question has a double edge that strengthens the force of the argument both ways. First, it implies that the evidence already given is sufficient (cf. REB, "Need I say more?"). Second, it introduces the overwhelming amount of concluding evidence that follows. "For time would fail me if I tried to recount" has a similar effect. Not only are the examples already given sufficient, but the examples that could be added are so numerous that there is no time to explain them in detail. The following list of names, "Gideon, Barak, Samson, Jephthah, David, and also Samuel and the prophets," is both suggestive and open ended. The first five names are joined without conjunction. The first four summarize the period of the judges that cli-

---

3. By bringing chapter 11 to a climax in this way the pastor leaves "the audience with the distinct impression that they stand at the peak of salvation history: all of the lives of the faithful have been building up to this moment" (Bulley, "Death and Rhetoric," 413).

4. Lane, 2:382-90, and Braun, 390, recognize the introductory character of v. 32 and correctly divide between vv. 33-35a and 35a-38. For an explanation of the chiastic relationship between vv. 33-35a and 35a-38, see Cockerill, "The Better Resurrection (Heb. 11:35)," 220-23. Spicq, 2:362, notes the division between v. 35a and v. 35b. Attridge (347) recognizes the introductory character of v. 32, but misses the division in the middle of v. 35.

5. Cockerill, "The Better Resurrection (Heb. 11:35)," 232-33.

6. Attridge, 347, and Thompson, 243-44, citing Philo, *Sacrifices* 27; Josephus, *Ant.* 20.11.1.

maxed in the reign of David. With "and also Samuel and the prophets" the pastor recognizes the close bond between David and Samuel.[7] By putting Gideon (Judg 6:12-24; 7:1–8:3) before Barak (Judg 4:6-11), Samson (Judges 13–16) before Jephthah (Judges 11), and David (1 Sam 16:11–1 Kgs 2:10-12) before Samuel (1 Sam 1:20–25:1), the pastor has departed from the chronological order of the OT. This reordering indicates that in the following verses he is not as concerned with the chronological as with the typical and the representative.[8] The reversal of David and Samuel establishes David in the most prominent position as the link between the judges before him and the prophets and others who followed him.[9] Thus, the pastor acknowledges David's place along with those of Abraham and Moses in the OT text. It is also appropriate to place Samuel after David in order to honor him as the first of the prophets and to link him with his successors in that office. Just as there were seven examples each in the Abraham and Moses sections, so this concluding section begins by listing seven typical of the acts of faith that follow — six actual names and then a group of people, "the prophets." The open-ended character of this final category confirms the representative nature of the whole list. In some ways, however, the six names appear to be more appropriate for the triumphs of faith in vv. 33-35a. With "but others" in v. 35 and again in v. 36 the pastor expands his horizon far beyond these he has listed.

33-35a   "Who through faith" introduces the nine examples of triumph in vv. 33-34 that climax in the tenth and greatest example recorded in v. 35a. These nine each contain a third person plural aorist verb, and in each but the ninth and final this verb is first in the sentence.[10] Both in structure and content these nine statements divide naturally into three sets of three — v. 33abc; vv. 33d-34ab; and v. 34cde. In the first set the verbs are followed by direct objects;[11] in the second, by direct objects with genitive qualifi-

---

7. Of these six names, only David and Samuel occur in other such lists (Thompson, 244).

8. This emphasis on the representative is quite probably the purpose behind the pastor's altered order (cf. Ellingworth, 623), though most think this reordering of little significance. See Lane, 2:382-83, and Attridge, 347-48.

9. Thus the pastor is hardly insulting David, as Eisenbaum, *Jewish Heroes,* 175, suggests, especially in light of the great deeds narrated in the following verses. His reasons for saying nothing directly about David's establishing the kingdom are much like those suggested above for his omission of Joshua's conquest of the land.

10. Many commentators recognize this structural feature. See Lane, 2:385-87; Attridge, 347; Michel, 415. Vanhoye, *La structure littéraire,* 192, and Bénétreau, 2:161-62, among others, have shown how these three sets of three statements in vv. 33-34 climax in v. 35a.

11. Heb 11:33abc: κατηγωνίσαντο βασιλείας ("they conquered kingdoms"),

ers;[12] in the third a passive verb and an intransitive verb are followed by a statement in which the direct object is put first.[13] The first set describes political successes; the second, deliverances from death; the third, military victories.[14] This orderly structure is a triumphant march of faith culminating in the restoration of the dead in v. 35a.[15]

Note the political successes in v. 33abc: "conquered kingdoms; established righteousness [carried out justice], obtained promises." It is easy to see how these statements have been suggested by the names listed in v. 32. David, especially, conquered kingdoms and "established righteousness" by practicing justice (2 Sam 8:15; 1 Chr 18:14). Barak, Gideon, and David were all promised and received victory.[16] This section pictures the establishment of a just political order pleasing to God as envisioned by the Mosaic covenant and intended through the establishment of the Davidic throne.

The second and central of these three sections focuses on deliverance from certain death: "shut the mouths of lions, quenched the power of fire, escaped the edge of the sword" (vv. 33d-34ab). Thus, the pastor gives prominence to a theme important in the examples of Enoch (v. 5), Noah (v. 7), Abraham (vv. 11-12, 17-19), Moses (vv. 23, 28), and Rahab (v. 31) above. By faith Daniel "shut the mouths of lions" (Dan 6:1-28) and his three friends "quenched the power of fire" (Dan 3:1-30; cf. 1 Macc 2:59-60; 4 Macc 16:21-22). These two events were closely associated in Jewish tradition, just as they are in the mind of every Sunday school pupil.[17] Many people "es-

---

ἠργάσαντο δικαιοσύνην ("they established righteousness"), ἐπέτυχον ἐπαγγελιῶν ("they obtained promises").

12. Heb 11:33d-34ab: ἔφραξαν στόματα λεόντων ("shut the mouths of lions"), ἔσβεσαν δύναμιν πυρός ("quenched the power of fire"), ἔφυγον στόματα μαχαίρης ("escaped the edge of the sword").

13. Heb 11:34cde: ἐδυναμώθησαν ἀπὸ ἀσθενείας ("were made strong out of weakness"), ἐγενήθησαν ἰσχυροὶ ἐν πολέμῳ ("became powerful in battle"), παρεμβολὰς ἔκλιναν ἀλλωτρίων ("put to flight the armies of aliens").

14. For this analysis of vv. 33-35a see Cockerill, "The Better Resurrection (Heb. 11:35)," 220-21.

15. Thus, it is hardly appropriate to argue that the "haphazard order" of the first part of this list leads to a "chaotic reading of history," indicating that "Israel's history is no longer teleologically directed" (Eisenbaum, *Jewish Heroes*, 175). As noted above, the pastor is not narrating the history of national Israel per se (as Eisenbaum elsewhere admits), but the history of the people of God. As we will see, the style of vv. 35b-38 is more "chaotic" in order to demonstrate the present condition of suffering often endured by God's people.

16. Lane, 2:386, and Koester, 513. "Received promises" refers to provisional receiving of what God promised, in such things as victories over enemies (Judg 4:6-9, 14; 6:16; 7:9; 2 Sam 5:19), not to the reception of "the" promise (see on 10:36; 11:39-40).

17. Lane, 2:386.

caped the edge of the sword." One has only to think of David (1 Sam 17:45-47), Elijah (1 Kgs 19:1-3), Elisha (2 Kgs 6:26-32), and Jeremiah (Jer 26:7-24). If the first two descriptions add vividness, this third is inclusive of many.

There seems to be a progression in the final three: "were made powerful out of weakness, became strong in battle, put to flight the armies of aliens" (v. 34cde). Note the movement from passive, to intransitive, and finally to an active verb: they were "made powerful out of" their human "weakness" by God; thus they "became strong in battle" so that they were able to "put to flight the armies of aliens." Many biblical examples could be included under this description. One thinks particularly of Gideon as one who was strengthened so that he put foreign armies to flight (Judg 6:1–8:35). The hearers might have recalled the victories of the Maccabees (1 Macc 3:17-25; 4:6-11, 30-33). The pastor signals the end of his three sets of three by putting the direct object first in the last of these statements, literally: "the armies put to flight of aliens," thus reaching a penultimate climax. The progression in this section builds momentum for the grand climax in v. 35a. At the same time, by ending this verse with the term "aliens" the pastor anticipates the suffering of the faithful in an "alien" world, soon to be described in vv. 36-38.[18]

The routing of huge foreign armies may have been the greatest triumph of faith in the nine, but there was something even greater: "women received their dead by resurrection." The hearers would have thought immediately of the sons of the widow of Zarephath (1 Kgs 17:17-24) and the Shunammite (2 Kgs 4:18-37). The restoration of the dead is indeed greater than all that has gone before because it cannot possibly be achieved by human power. Thus, this grand series of the many triumphs of faith highlights victory over death, both by the prominence given to escape from death in its central section (vv. 33d-34ab) and by the restoration of the already dead here at its climax.

35b However, all of these victories, including escape from death and even the restoration of the dead to mortal life, are insufficient in themselves. They are given to encourage the suffering faithful, reminding them that God has power over death and demonstrating that he will not break faith with his obedient people. He is the God who translated Enoch so that he did not experience death (v. 5). Abraham knew that he was the God "who is able to raise from the dead" (v. 19). He who has often delivered his people from death (vv. 7, 28, 31, 33d-34ab) is the God of the "better resurrection," from which there is no return to death. This "better resurrection" is made possible through the "better sacrifice" (9:22-23) of Christ, which has established the

---

18. Compare "of aliens" (ἀλλοτρίων) at the end of v. 34d with Abraham's dwelling in the "land of promise" as an "alien" (ἀλλοτρίαν) land in v. 9.

"better covenant" (7:22), and delivered the faithful from the fear of death through the removal of sin (2:14-18; 9:26-28). All of God's people, regardless of how many times they have experienced his temporal deliverance, anticipate this resurrection, for it belongs to those whose home is the "City" that has been established by God (vv. 9-10) and therefore will not be shaken by the Judgment (12:25-29). Thus, while resuscitation to mortal life (v. 35a) may be the climax of the temporal deliverances enumerated in vv. 33-34, the assured promise of a "better resurrection" is the foundation and premise that empowers God's people to suffer for their loyalty to Christ, as recounted in vv. 36-38.[19]

All those who live "through faith" anticipate the resurrection, but not all suffer torture on account of their faith. "But others" distinguishes this group from those who enjoyed great triumphs in vv. 33-34, and especially from those who "received their dead by resurrection" in v. 35a. These "others" are the martyrs (cf. 2 Macc 6:18–7:42) and confessors, all those who "were tortured" in the attempt to make them deny their faith. Verses 36-38 suggest some of the gruesome means of torture the pastor may have had in mind. These "others" could have escaped this torture by denying their faith and found "release," but they did not in order that through perseverance "they might gain" the promised resurrection to eternal life in the eternal City.[20] All that the pastor has said in this chapter has been to fortify his hearers with such courage and to prepare them for the kind of circumstances he now describes.[21]

36-38   The pastor begins v. 36 with a second "but others."[22] This

---

19. Restoration to mortal life in v. 35a anticipates the banishment of death through the "better" resurrection to eternal life in v. 35b (Lane, 2:389). The following statement by Rhee, "Hebrews 11," 340, needs refinement: "The chiastic structure of verses 32-38 implies that faith manifested in the outer sections (vv. 32-34, 36-38) was based on the hope of resurrection in the center section (v. 35)." It would be more accurate to say that the victories of the first part of this chiasm (vv. 33-34) build up to the "better resurrection" in v. 35, which sustains faith amid suffering in the last half (vv. 36-38).

20. ἐτυμπανίσθησαν οὐ προσδεξάμενοι τὴν ἀπολύτρωσιν ("were tortured because they refused to be released," v. 35b) naturally leads one to think of martyrdom. However, this phrase is broad enough to include all of the sufferings described in vv. 36-38. All of these people endured the type of suffering that was their lot rather than surrender their faith. Johnson, 308, refers to the aged scribe Eleazar, who was tortured on the rack rather than save his life by renouncing God's law. The word used here for "torture" (τυμπανίζω) is related to the word used in 2 Macc 6:28 for the "rack" (τύμπανον) upon which he was stretched.

21. Weiss, 614.

22. The pastor appears to use ἕτεροι δέ ("but others") at the beginning of v. 36 as a stylistic variant of ἄλλοι δέ ("but others") in the middle of v. 35. See BDAG, 399, 1b8; cf. L&N §58.36; 58.37.

repetition of "but others" serves several purposes. First, by making some distinction between those who suffer for their faith in the following verses and those tortured in v. 35 the pastor increases the number of those who endured such opposition. His hearers should not be surprised if they find themselves among this company who suffer for their faith. Second, "but others" makes it clear that he is not talking about the same people who were described in vv. 33-35a.[23] While many people, such as Moses above, experience both suffering and triumph through faith, the pastor would prepare his hearers for what lies ahead by having them consider these two groups in separation. It is crucial, however, to remember that the "through faith" of v. 32 applies to this entire section. Both groups, though their experiences were very different, lived "through" the same "faith" in God's power and promises.

This diverse collection can, like vv. 33-34 above, be divided into three subsections: v. 36, v. 37a, and vv. 37b-38.[24] The first and third each center around one finite verb qualified in different ways — "received trial" in v. 36; "went about" in v. 37b. Verse 37a, the second subsection, contains three finite verbs reminiscent of the three groups of three statements that constitute vv. 33-34. In fact, these three subsections of vv. 36-38 are the mirror image of the three subsections in vv. 33-34: contrast the severe punishment described in v. 36 with the military triumphs of v. 34cde; the cruel deaths described in v. 37a with the deliverances from death in vv. 33d-34ab; and, finally, the total exclusion from society imposed on the faithful in vv. 37b-38 with the establishment of just rule in v. 33abc. The pastor paints the situation of the pilgrim in this unbelieving world at its worst, preparing to urge his hearers to brave these difficulties by becoming athletes who run the race of faith "with endurance" to the finish line in 12:1-13.

36 The verb "received trial" stands at the center of the Greek text of this verse: "of mockings and beatings they received trial, and even of bonds and of prison." Heb 10:32-35 and 13:3 suggest that the recipients of Hebrews may already have endured this type and degree of persecution. The pastor begins with what they have experienced in order to prepare them for what may be coming. "Beatings" were one of the favorite punishments of the ancient world. By their public nature such beatings were intended to be shameful and were usually accompanied by the "mockings" of a leering crowd. "Beatings"

---

23. Rose, *Die Volke,* 312-22, seems to miss this point when he suggests some of the same names as examples of those who suffer as he did above for those who triumphed. Of course these events might bring to mind some of the same people — but we must remember that the author is intentionally being suggestive by the omission of names.

24. For this analysis of vv. 36-38, see Cockerill, "The Better Resurrection (Heb. 11:35)," 221-22.

and "mockings" recall 2 Macc 7:1, 37; 9:11 and 2 Macc 7:7, 10 respectively. Those suffering "beatings" were often also restrained with "bonds" and confined in "prison." No doubt the hearers would recall their own earlier suffering and that of their friends, as well as the biblical accounts of Jeremiah (Jer 20:2, 7; 29:26; 37:15; 1 Kgs 22:27) and others. "Received trial" implies that these people suffered such things as a trial or testing of their faithfulness to God and his promise. Such punishment by society is the antithesis of the military conquests described in the third subsection of the catalogue of triumphs above (v. 34cde). The people the pastor is now describing were not delivered "out of weakness" (v. 34c). The hearers have already entered the lists of the faithful by enduring such experiences (10:32-34). Let them be prepared to persevere in the face of what follows, assured that the God who has given others such great victories is "able to raise from the dead" (v. 19) into a "better resurrection" (v. 35b).

37a   The central subsection of the catalogue of triumphs above described three ways in which the faithful were delivered from death (vv. 33d-34ab). This parallel subsection describes three ways in which they were martyred for their faith.[25] In both subsections the pastor uses three finite aorist verbs. However, in this description of martyrdom the first two verbs are passive and the third intransitive, denoting the impotency of the victims.[26] Our English translations of necessity mask the crisp directness of these statements: "they were stoned to death" is one word in Greek, as is "they were sawn in two." Contrast "by murder of the sword" with "escaped the edge of the sword" in v. 34b. With a careful, economic choice of words the pastor brings the pain and violence of these deaths before his hearers' eyes. The finality of their earthly suffering is reinforced by the way the pastor ends this sentence in Greek with the word translated "they died." According to 2 Chr 24:21, Zechariah, son of Jehoiada, was stoned to death. Legend has it that Jeremiah (*Liv. Pro.* 2:1) was stoned in Egypt and that Isaiah was sawn in two (*Mart. Isa.* 5:1-11; *Liv. Pro.* 1:1; cf. Susanna 59).[27] The pastor would prepare his hearers to brave death rather than deny Christ. Still, a martyr's death is

25. The threefold parallel with vv. 33d-34ab is an additional reason for omitting ἐπειράσθησαν ("they were tried"), which many manuscripts have in various places in this verse. See *TCGNT,* 603-4. Even the inclusion of this word, however, would not invalidate the parallels between vv. 36-38 and 32-34. As the first (v. 36) and, especially, the third (vv. 37b-38) subsections show, the pastor intends to create a certain discord in contrast to the glorious triumphant march of vv. 33-34.

26. ἐλιθάσθησαν ("they were stoned") and ἐπρίσθησαν ("they were sawn in two") are passive. Although ἀπέθανον ("they died") is intransitive, "by murder of the sword" shows that their deaths were by the agency of another and thus reinforces this sense of impotency.

27. See deSilva and Matthews, *Untold Stories,* 98-114.

over and done with. He appears to reserve his greatest concern for the exclusion from society described in vv. 37b-38.[28]

37b-38   In the opening subsection of the triumphs of faith above,
God's people established his righteous rule on earth (v. 33abc). Here, by contrast, they are unjustly but totally excluded from and by unbelieving society.
The pastor has been preparing for this final subsection from the beginning of
the chapter. First, he has made it clear that God's own live "by faith" in his
assured promise of an eternal, God-prepared City (vv. 9-10, 13-16). Thus,
exclusion by earthly society is worth the goal. Second, those who live for this
eternal City naturally, as did Abraham and those associated with him, confess that they are "aliens and transients" (v. 13), out of step with unbelieving
society. Thus, they should not be surprised when, like Moses, they suffer "ill
treatment" because they refuse to conform to the temporal values of this unbelieving world (vv. 23-27). Furthermore, they are able to endure this ill
treatment because they also live "by faith" in God's present power to deliver
and sustain them. After all, God is a God "who is able to raise" his people
"from the dead" (vv. 17-19) to a "better resurrection" (v. 35b). In fact, according to v. 33abc, the parallel opening subsection of this final part of the
chapter, God has demonstrated his power over the very forces of society now
excluding his own. Thus, the entire chapter is preparation for the pastor's

hearers to face the total banishment from human society depicted in these final verses. Such ill treatment is to be expected by God's faithful. It is well
worth enduring because God's "hoped-for" eternal City is real (v. 1a). It can
be endured because he is real (v. 6) and his power, though often "unseen," is
available to sustain his own even in such circumstances (v. 1b).

The pastor's concern to prepare his hearers for such experiences is
also evidenced by the fact that he has developed this final section more thoroughly than any other part of either the catalogue of triumphs (vv. 33-34) or
collection of sufferings (vv. 36-38). The hearers will strain in vain to catch
the regular cadence created by the three sets of three sentences in the catalogue of triumphs above (vv. 33-34). This is no triumphal parade. The very
meandering style that the pastor has adopted for this section communicates
the homeless wandering of those described. "They went about" is the finite
verb used to depict their condition. This verb is a global aorist, describing the
totality of their final state of existence on earth. Two prepositional phrases
and four present participles describe the destitute manner of their wandering,
deprived of the necessities of life — clothing, food, and shelter — but abundantly supplied with suffering. First, the two prepositional phrases reveal

28. While vv. 35b-38 as a whole may describe the situation of the hearers (Weiss,
614), the pastor is primarily concerned with the situation he describes in vv. 37b-38. See
Cockerill, "The Better Resurrection (Heb. 11:35)," 223.

their lack of proper clothing: they went about "in sheepskins and in goat-skins." Society had excluded them from the resources necessary for proper attire and left them to wear whatever they could find. However, such skins were also the distinctive garb of the prophets.[29] Thus, the very poverty forced upon them by unbelieving society identified them with the faithful people of God. The first participle, "being destitute," describes their poverty, in partic-ular their lack of food. The next two, "being oppressed" and "being ill treated" or "tortured," underscore the belligerence of society and the painful treatment that drove these faithful from "civilized" life. One is reminded of the afflictions of Elijah and Elisha (1 Kgs 17:2-16; 19:1-19; 2 Kgs 1:3-15; 2:23; 4:1-2, 8-12, 38-43; 8:1-2) and of the Maccabean patriots and martyrs (2 Macc 5:27).[30] The fourth and final participle, "wandering," brings this de-scription to its climax. What could be worse than being deprived of clothes and food? Nothing but loss of shelter — banishment from house and home and the support network they sustain. These exemplars of faithfulness went about "wandering" in places totally excluded from human society — "in deserts and in mountains and caves and holes of the earth." These were the places of the destitute and persecuted (Judg 6:2; *Pss. Sol.* 17:17). Here David had fled from Saul (1 Sam 23:14). It is here that the faithful Maccabees sought shelter (1 Macc 2:28, 31; 2 Macc 5:27; 10:6). Here people would take refuge from the destruction of the Temple. Such banishment from home and society was considered a fate worse than death.[31] And yet, how appropriate that the pastor should end here. It is no surprise that the people who live "by faith" in God's promise of an eternal City, and thus confess themselves as "aliens and transients" (v. 13) on earth, should be driven from their earthly homes.

We have intentionally reserved the relative clause, "of whom the world was not worthy," for our final comments on this verse. The pastor has inserted this clause just before describing the unbelieving world's complete exclusion of those who live by faith in God's power and promises.[32] God's evaluation of the unbelieving world precedes and has precedence over the fi-nal verdict of that world on his own. God has determined that the unbelieving world is "unworthy" of his suffering people. Thus, his people need not suc-cumb to the unbelieving world's judgment that they are "unworthy" to partic-

29. See 1 Kgs 19:13, 19; 2 Kgs 2:8, 13-14; *Liv. Pro.* 22:5; cf. Zech 13:4; Matt 7:15; and *1 Clem.* 17:1. See also Lane, 2:391; Thompson, 245; and Koester, 515.

30. Lane, 2:391.

31. Lane, 2:391-92.

32. ὁ κόσμος refers to unbelieving human society (see Lane 2:392), not, as has been suggested by some (e.g., Spicq, 2:36; Westcott, 381), to the physical world. Compare the world's rejection of the faithful as unworthy and Noah's condemnation of that same world (v. 7). Cf. Weiss, 623-24.

ipate in its life. The pastor is certain of this fact because it is only those who live by faith who have the divine approval (v. 6). Complete condemnation by those whom God rejects does naught but confirm the totality of divine acceptance. When unbelieving society excludes God's own, it affirms that they really are "aliens and transients" (v. 13), on their way to God's permanent City.

In summary, the pastor has carefully crafted this chapter to incorporate his hearers into the history of God's faithful people. He uses the primeval narrative of Genesis 1–11 to show them the fundamental nature of faith (vv. 1-7): faith is living as if God's future promises are certain and his present sustaining power is real. Only those who pursue this life of faith are pleasing to God. Like Abel, those who live "by faith" may suffer, but, like Enoch, they will be delivered from death and, like Noah, they will escape the Judgment. From Abraham and those associated with him (vv. 8-22), the hearers come to realize that God's promises referred to a heavenly City and to a people who would live by faith and thus enter that City as their true home. Since, like Abraham, God's people pursue the promised eternal City, they, like him, are aliens in this world who must patiently await God's fulfillment. However, the birth and sacrifice of Isaac show them that the God who calls and sustains his people has power even over death. They can trust him and his power although they cannot "see" him (cf. vv. 1b, 6). Furthermore, alienation from the world begets persecution by the world. Thus, they are urged to emulate Moses, maintaining their identity with the people of God by practicing courage and perseverance in the face of persecution without turning their eyes away from the eternal reward (vv. 22-27). The hearers are given further assurance of God's "unseen" but real sustaining power in the present and his ultimate authority over death (v. 35b) by his mighty deliverances in the lives of Moses (v. 28), those who succeeded him (vv. 29-31), and the great hosts of the faithful described in vv. 33-35a. Thus, those who live "by faith" are ready to obey God and identify with his people, even if it means the alienation, persecution, and banishment from society described in vv. 35b-38. They refuse to surrender their faith in God's promise and power, forfeit the resurrection, and lose their place in the eternal City.

e. "They without Us . . ." (11:39-40)

> 39 Even though these all were attested through their faith, they did not receive the promise, 40 because God had prepared something better for us, so that they might not be perfected apart from us.

Everything that the pastor has said in this chapter assumes that both the faithful of old whom he has enumerated and his hearers who live after Christ are members of the one people of God. They are heirs of the same divine promise. By the real but unseen power of God they endure the same sufferings because they share the same faith in God's power and promises. Therefore, it is natural for him to urge upon his hearers the imitation of God's people who lived "by faith" before Christ. They must maintain their place with the ancient faithful in the "household" of God. However, the pastor has not forgotten the fulfillment brought by Christ the High Priest of God's people, now seated at God's right hand (7:1–10:18). Thus, he would clarify more fully how the faithful of old relate to the faithful who live in the time when they can enjoy the privileges afforded by Christ's high-priestly ministry (4:14-16; 10:19-25). His appeal for faithfulness gathers strength as he anticipates turning his hearers' gaze back up to Jesus, the "Pioneer and Perfecter of the faith" (12:1-3).

39 "Even though all these were attested through their faith, they did not receive the promise." With this statement the pastor brings to expression a tension that has been an underlying current from the beginning of this history of God's people before Christ. How can it be that God's ancient people received his approval but did not receive what he had promised? Verse 2 above is the key to the first half of v. 39; v. 13, to the second.[1] If, then, we would understand "even though all these were attested through their faith" (v. 39a), we must look at "by [faith] the people of old were attested" in v. 2. Both "all these" in v. 39 and the "people of old" in v. 2 refer to the faithful of this chapter. Thus, from the beginning of this chapter to the end, the pastor has maintained that these heroes received divine approval (v. 6) "through their" deeds of "faith."[2] God himself attests this fact in Scripture. And yet, "they did not receive the promise" (v. 39b). We turn to v. 13: "these all died although they had not received the promises."[3] Verse 13 made it clear that God had promised to establish a people whom he would bring into his own eternal City by faith. However, "all" of these people, from Abraham, Isaac, and Jacob to the end of this chapter, did not enter that City during their earthly lives.[4] Throughout their earthly sojourn they confessed themselves "aliens and transients" on the earth who had not as yet entered their home. They could only see it "from afar." Those, however, who live after Christ can

---

1. For connections between vv. 39-40 and vv. 1-2, 13-16 see Rose, *Die Volke,* 323.

2. The phrase διὰ τῆς πίστεως repeats the διὰ πίστεως of v. 33. The addition of the definite article, τῆς ("the"), indicates that the pastor is referring to the faith he has narrated, the acts of faith of these people. Thus, it is legitimate to translate this phrase "through their faith" instead of just "through faith."

3. On the use of the plural "promises" see the comments above on v. 13.

4. It is true that "these all" in v. 13 refers to Abraham and those associated with him — Sarah, Isaac, and Jacob. However, as noted in commenting on that verse, the pastor uses this description of Abraham to demonstrate what is true for all who follow him.

"draw near" (4:14-16; 10:19-25). In a few verses the pastor will describe them as "having come to" this heavenly City (12:22-24). The pastor makes no statement about what the faithful of old experienced after their deaths. He does affirm that, although they were approved by God, they did not receive the promise of the eternal City. They could not begin to enjoy the privileges of that abode during their earthly sojourn because they could not yet avail themselves of the benefits provided by Christ.[5]

40 This is exactly what the pastor means when he says that they could not begin to participate in that City "because God has provided something better for us."[6] In Greek "for us" is put second for emphasis, right after "God," the first word in the sentence. This "something better" can be nothing less than the cleansing from sin and restoration to God that are the present possession of the people of God through the work of Christ — the "better covenant" (7:22; 8:6) and the "better hope through which we draw near to God" (7:19) because Christ's better sacrifice (cf. 9:22-23) has removed our sin.[7] The pastor has already described contemporary believers who have been fitted for access to God through cleansing from sin as being "made perfect" (10:14).[8] The faithful of old could not experience this being "made perfect" through cleansing from sin "without us" because Christ had not yet come. The pastor's implication is that now, since Christ has come, all the faithful experience this cleansing from sin and access to God through Christ.[9] Thus, the pastor forges the strongest bond between God's people before and after Christ: in order to attain the promised eternal city, "we" need their persevering faith; "they" need the benefits that are "ours" through Christ.

As noted above, the perfecting of believers in 10:14 referred to their being cleansed from sin through Christ so that they could draw near to God and thus enter the divine presence. Many interpreters, however, contend that here in 11:40 and in 12:23 the perfecting of believers refers to their final entrance into God's presence in the eternal City at the climax of their pilgrim-

---

5. Thus, we would not quite agree with Eisenbaum that the "promise" of this verse is "salvation effected [by] Christ" (Eisenbaum, *Jewish Heroes,* 177). It is, however, entrance into God's City that has been made available through the "salvation effected [by] Christ."

6. τοῦ θεοῦ . . . προβλεψαμένου ("God . . . having provided") is a causal genitive absolute. Rose, *Die Volke,* 325.

7. Attridge, 352. By identifying these "better things" with final salvation, Rose clouds the difference between those who came before Christ and contemporary believers. Rose, *Die Volke,* 325-26.

8. See the comments on 10:14 (cf. 2:10; 5:9; 7:19, 28; 9:9; 10:1).

9. "The clear implication of this statement is that the faithful from Abel to the Maccabean martyrs will share in this same access to God" (Johnson, 310) provided by Christ.

age.[10] Thus, one can speak of a "cultic" perfection in 10:14 and an "eschatological" perfection in both 11:40 and 12:23.[11] However, the meaning of "perfected" in 10:14 is the simplest explanation of both 11:40 and 12:23. When Christ "has perfected" believers by cleansing them from sin, he has made them fit to enter God's presence.[12] It is this the same work of Christ that fits his own for present entrance through Christ (4:14-16; 7:25; 10:19-25), for future entrance at death (12:23), and for ultimate entrance into the presence of a holy God at the Judgment (12:25-29) when Christ returns (9:28-29). The difference between the faithful before Christ and those who live after is that the former did not enjoy this privilege of access to God during their lifetimes. Since Christ has come, however, both the faithful who lived before his coming and those who live after enjoy access to the heavenly City.[13] Those who are alive draw near through prayer and worship (4:14-16; 7:25; 10:19-25). Those who lived before Christ and those who have died since he came are among "the spirits of the righteous" who have been "made perfect" through the work of Christ and thus dwell in the heavenly City (12:23) awaiting the return of Christ and the Judgment (9:28-29; 12:25-29).[14]

10. Lane, 2:393, Riggenbach, 383, and deSilva, 416, 424, who translates "in order that they might not be perfected without us" as "in order that they should not arrive at the goal apart from us." Many Church Fathers held to this position (Heen and Krey, 206-8). This being "perfected" in 11:40 is, according to this interpretation, the final reception of what God has "promised" (Rose, *Die Volke,* 324, 331-32; Peterson, *Perfection,* 157; O'Brien, 447).

11. See Rose, *Die Volke,* 330-32, and Hofius, *Katapausis,* 161, n. 359.

12. *Pace* Loader, *Sohn und Hoherpriester,* 39-49, it is not death but the work of Christ through which the faithful are "perfected" and thus authorized to enter God's presence.

13. Thus, these verses in no way demean the OT faithful, as Eisenbaum, *Jewish Heroes,* 177-78, maintains. Not only do those faithful now share the privileges of those who live after Christ, but they succeeded in enduring throughout their earthly lives without them. Note Koester's apt statement: "Some take this to mean that previous generations of Israel are allowed to share in the salvation given to Christians (Bengel; Braun) and others understand it to mean that Christians are allowed to share in the promises given to Israel (H.-F. Weiss). Neither approach is apt, since Hebrews emphasizes the unity of God's people over the generations, with all sharing in the realization of the promises together. At the resurrection 'all will come equally into the inheritance of eternal glory and will be joined at the same moment to their Head' (Erasmus, *Paraphrase,* 252)" (Koester, 520). In light of the argument in the text above we would maintain that they need not wait until their resurrection, but all instead begin to participate in the work of Christ from the time of his first coming.

14. Hebrews, however, gives no basis for speculation on where the OT faithful were after their deaths but before Christ. Answering this question is irrelevant to the pastor's purpose and would contribute nothing to the edification of his hearers. Attempts to fill this gap easily lead to speculation that distorts the pastor's thought, as evidenced by the discussion in Rose, *Die Volke,* 328-32.

In fact, 12:23 could not refer to ultimate entrance into God's City. It clearly describes the righteous dead before the Judgment, which is recounted in 12:25-29. Both ultimate entrance into the eternal City and Christ's provision for cleansing from sin were part of the future promise for which the faithful of old waited during their lifetimes. Final entrance into that City remains a future promise. The provision of Christ, however, is the power of God in the present for all the faithful whether they lived before or after his coming. Indirectly the pastor would shame his hearers: "The faithful of old persevered during their lifetimes without the privileges you have in Christ. You, therefore, are without excuse."

The pastor has used the term "perfected" in order to remind his hearers of the one who has provided this perfection. He has been waiting with anticipation for the climax of this list, when he will turn their eyes to "the Pioneer and Perfecter of" the common "faith" shared by the faithful of all time — "Jesus" (12:1-3).

2. Keep Your Eyes on Jesus, Seated at God's Right Hand (12:1-3)

> 1 Therefore, because we ourselves have such a great cloud of witnesses surrounding us, let us lay aside every hindrance and sin that so easily clings to us, and let us run with endurance the race set before us. 2 Let us run looking unto the Pioneer and Perfecter of the faith, Jesus, who for the joy set before him endured a cross, despising the shame, and has taken his seat at the right hand of the throne of God. 3 For consider the One who endured such opposition from sinners against himself, in order that you might not become weary, giving up in your souls.

According to 11:1-40, many, many have persevered in the life of faith. The pastor reintroduces the terms "endure" and "endurance" from 10:36-39 and builds his exhortation to perseverance on the accumulated weight of these examples. Thus, in vv. 1-2 he urges his hearers to respond to the examples he has given by running the race "with endurance" while keeping their eyes on Jesus who "endured."[1] Although this section flows smoothly into the next, v. 3 should be kept with vv. 1-2.[2] In v. 3 the pastor continues the hortatory

---

1. We have divided the one long Greek sentence that makes up vv. 1-2 into two by placing a period at the end of v. 1 and adding a second "Let us run" at the beginning of v. 2.

2. NIV, TNIV, NASB, Nestle[27] and UBS[4] (revised); Weiss, 631; Vanhoye, *La structure littéraire*, 196-98; Rhee, *Faith in Hebrews*, 224-32; and Rose, *Die Volke*, 334-35. Note also the change from present tense in v. 3 to past in v. 4, and the fact that v. 4 is joined to v. 5 by the conjunction καί (Croy, *Endurance*, 192-93). Some would limit this

style of vv. 1-2 by drawing further attention to the example of Jesus given in the previous verse. In v. 4 he returns to the indicative of description as he moves from the suffering of Christ to that of his followers.

In these verses the pastor brings to fruition what he first set in motion long ago in 3:1-6. In that passage he clearly established the unity of contemporary believers with those Moses led out of Egypt, and, by implication, with all the people of God who lived before Christ. All are part of the one "household" of God over which Christ is "Son." This enabled the pastor to urge his hearers to persevere, and thus avoid the fate of the wilderness generation he was about to describe in 3:7-19. This unity of the people of God throughout time is the basis upon which he now urges them to run the race set before them in response to the faithful cloud of witnesses just described in 11:1-40. Furthermore, in 3:1-6 he affirmed that Christ was uniquely "faithful" to God as a Son over his household. However, he drew no lesson from the Son's faithfulness because he had not yet given it content. The intervening description of Christ's high priesthood in 4:14–10:18 has made the unique faithfulness of the Son abundantly clear. He fulfilled his faithfulness by living a life of complete obedience unto death in order to procure the salvation of God's people (5:7-10; 9:11-14; 10:5-10). That faithfulness received absolute divine confirmation through his session at God's right hand (10:11-14). Now, therefore, the pastor is ready to affirm not only that the Son is "faithful," but that he is "the Pioneer and Perfecter of the faith, Jesus."

This phrase has more than a structural resemblance to "the Apostle and High Priest of our confession, Jesus" in 3:1. As Apostle, the Son provided the ultimate revelation of God through his high-priestly work, by which he cleansed God's people from sin and thus brought them into God's presence. By so doing he has become the Pioneer and Perfecter who has both initiated and completed the way for the faithful to enter God's presence. All this he accomplished by becoming the incarnate, now-exalted "Jesus." Thus, in 12:1-3 the full weight of the pastor's appeal presses upon his hearers — the apostate people they must shun (3:7–4:13); the full sufficiency of Christ that is theirs to embrace (4:14–10:25); the faithful whom they can claim as their own (11:1-40); and now, once again, Christ who is both fully sufficient to bring them to faith's goal and the ultimate example of endurance under suffering (12:1-3).

---

opening section to vv. 1-2 (REB, RSV, NRSV, ESV, NKJV; Guthrie, *Structure,* 132; Westfall, *Discourse Analysis,* 264, 275-76; Lane, 2:405). Others would extend it to include v. 4 (Koester, 534; Spicq, 2:382-90; Hughes, 525-27). Lane, 2:405, notes the transitional character of v. 4: ἁμαρτίαν ἀνταγωνιζόμενοι ("wrestling against sin") is reminiscent of ἁμαρτίαν ("sin") and ἀγῶνα ("race," "contest") in v. 1; yet v. 4 introduces the hearers' suffering, which is the subject of the following verses. It is best, however, for the reasons given in the text above, to take vv. 1-3 together.

1 The pastor has often urged his hearers to action because of the privileges they "have" in Christ (4:14-15; 6:18-19; 8:1; 10:19). Here he urges them forward because of the legacy they "have" from the witnesses of faith who have gone before. By initiating this sentence with "therefore" and with an emphatic "we ourselves," he redoubles the force of the causal participle: "therefore, because we ourselves have."[3] The hearers know that they are intimately and inseparably joined to the faithful who have gone before. Nor will the pastor let them forget the magnitude of the testimony he has amassed in his "such a great cloud of witnesses."[4] Even the term "cloud" underscores the unanimity of their testimony.[5] Nor can the hearers confine these witnesses to the dead past. They are even now "surrounding us." The pastor would have his hearers feel that they can reach out and touch these heroes who lived by faith. It is these faithful from the past whose approval is worth courting despite the sneer of the unbelieving world.

The pastor has chosen the term "witnesses" because it enables him to affirm that the heroes of old are both "witnesses" *to* and *of* God's contemporary people.[6] The first is in accord with all that he has said in 11:1-40. He affirms that the faithful of old are "witnesses" *to* contemporary believers of the power and faithfulness of God. The validity of their testimony is assured by divine attestation and approval (11:2, 6, 16, 39). Their lives clearly and forcefully demonstrate the "reality" of God's future promises and give "evidence" of his real but unseen power to deliver (11:1).[7] Their witness assures the hearers that any amount of rejection by the unbelieving world is worth the divine approval. However, in accord with the athletic imagery now resumed from 10:36-39, they are also "witnesses" *of* God's contemporary people. It is

3. Croy, *Endurance,* 168, argues that τοιγαροῦν ("therefore") is more emphatic than its more common synonyms used elsewhere in Hebrews — διό (3:7, 10; 6:1; 10:5; 11:12, 16; 12:12, 28; 13:12) and διότι (11:5, 23). Note also that the καί before ἡμεῖς is emphatic, "we ourselves."

4. τοσοῦτον, "such a great," emphasizes both the size and quality of the "cloud" of witnesses. Its position, early in the sentence and separated from the word it modifies, intensifies its force. See Croy, *Endurance,* 169, citing BDF, §473 (2).

5. νέφος, "cloud," is used in secular Greek, but not elsewhere in Scripture, to describe a group of people as a unity or a totality (see Lane, 2:408).

6. Attridge, 354-55, and Spicq, 2:384, recognize the pastor's choice of μάρτυς ("witness," "spectator") with both meanings in mind. Cf. Westcott, 393. Croy, *Endurance,* 58-62, gives a number of examples where μάρτυς ("witness") and θεατής ("spectator") are used together. Furthermore, in *Anacharsis* 11 Lucian appears to use μάρτυς because it can mean both "witness" and "spectator" (Croy, *Endurance,* 60-61). See also the examples given by deSilva, 428; Thompson, 247; and Attridge 354, nn. 18-19.

7. "This cloud [of witnesses] has borne witness to the reality of the invisible and the actuality of the future, in order to resume the ideas of 11:1" (Bénétreau, 2:169). Cf. Spicq, 2:384.

as if these heroes of old were in the stands watching the pastor's hearers run this race "by faith." They are "spectators," indeed, "fans." What an honor to have such "fans." In fact, it is less than fully accurate to say that the pastor "resumes" the athletic imagery of 10:36-39. Instead, he incorporates the entire history of those who have lived "by faith" (11:1-40) into this great contest pursued by the people of God. Their pilgrimage has now become a race of endurance to the finish. As noted above when commenting on 10:36-39, the pastor's hearers were accustomed to athletic contests and familiar with the metaphorical use of athletic imagery in moral discourse.[8] We also noted that use of this metaphor was crucial to the pastor's purpose. Suffering shame from the sinful world became a matter and source of great honor when it was seen as the endurance of an athlete in pursuit of victory. The pastor has transformed the pilgrimage lived "by faith" (11:1-40) into the race run "with endurance" in order to transform temporal shame into the means of eternal glory. The pastor's hearers will overcome the shame of the unbelieving world lest they suffer shame before the eyes of these great heroes of faith cheering them on from the sideline.[9] The pastor pours his whole heart and soul into this exhortation: "Let us run with endurance the race set before us."

Of course, unlike a race, all of those who "by faith" endure the opposition of the unbelieving world will win. Every metaphor has limitations. There are many ways, however, in which this metaphor is most useful. Thus, like athletes who would be successful, the hearers must "lay aside every hindrance" or "encumbrance."[10] "Every encumbrance" suggests the removal of excess weight or clothes in preparation for the impending contest.[11] Yet the expression is intentionally both general and comprehensive. The pastor wants his hearers to dispense with absolutely anything that will distract them from successfully running the race of faith. Indeed, if the runner refuses to put it aside, any such hindrance, though innocent in itself, becomes part of the "sin that clings so closely" and entangles the feet.[12] In order to

---

8. For the metaphorical use of athletic imagery in moral discourse, see Epictetus, *Diatr.* 1.24.1-3; 3.22.51-52; 3.25.2-5; Cicero, *Off.* 3.10.12 (Johnson, 315).

9. See deSilva, 426-27.

10. The participle ἀποθέμενοι ("laying aside") is hortatory, "let us lay aside," in accord with τρέχωμεν ("let us run"), the verb it qualifies. See Lane, 2:398d. For other uses of ἀποτίθημι ("lay aside") in the metaphorical sense of casting off burdens, see Rom 13:12; Eph 4:22-25; Jas 1:21; and 1 Pet. 2:1.

11. Lane, 2:409; Croy, *Endurance,* 63.

12. O'Brien's attempt (452) to distinguish between "hindrance" or "encumbrance" as inclusive of things that may not be sin but that might hinder various runners, and "sin" as that which hinders every runner, is unconvincing. The language of "hindrance" or "encumbrance" is drawn from the race; "sin" is its application to the lives of the hearers (see Weiss, 633).

avoid misunderstanding, the above translation omits the definite article before "sin." If one uses the article, it sounds as if one is referring to a particular "besetting" sin. However, the Greek article is used to describe sin in general, in totality, everything that is sin.[13] "Sin," as a potential reality, "clings so closely."[14] The pastor, is, however, particularly concerned with the "sin" of acquiescence to the discouragement that comes from unbelieving society's hostility and/or the pursuit of the advantages the unbelieving world offers to those who conform. Such acts betray a distrust of God's power and promises that may cause one to abandon the race and thus fall into apostasy.[15] On the one hand, the saints of old surround modern believers as fans, urging them on; on the other, the allure of the world's rewards and the hostility of unbelievers cling to the runners in order to retard their progress and turn them aside from the race.[16]

Getting rid of hindrances, though necessary, is preparatory to the pastor's main concern: "Let us run with endurance the race set before us."[17] The hearers would have immediately recognized "the race set before us" as the usual way of describing such a contest.[18] The pastor, however, has adopted this phrase for his own purposes: the life lived in obedience "by faith" has been determined and "set before us" by God himself. It has been established by Jesus the "Forerunner" (6:19-20), who alone has opened the way so that we can pursue this race to the end with success. This God-established race is a great privi-

---

13. "The word 'sin' (ἁμαρτία) is singular: it is sin considered in its totality as the refusal of God and his word" (Bénétreau, 2:170).

14. Although the exact meaning of εὐπερίστατον ("clings so closely"), which appears nowhere else in Scripture, is somewhat disputed, it probably refers to something that surrounds and threatens the Christian (Attridge, 355).

15. Rose, *Die Volke*, 336-37, referring to "sin" in Heb 3:12-14 and 11:24-26, defines "sin" here as the "temptation to apostasy." Cf. Weiss, 634: "'Sin' is that which, according to 3:12, leads Christians to fall away from faith in the end, it opposes them in unreconciled antagonism to their struggle of faith."

16. "The sin by which we are practically encircled answers to the cloud of witnesses with which God surrounds us for our encouragement" (Westcott, 394).

17. The word ἀγῶν ("race," "contest") adds to the athletic language of 10:32-39. Originally this term denoted the place where an athletic contest was held. It then came to be used for the contest itself (Attridge, 355). It was often used for a race, especially when following a verb for "run" (τρέχω/δραμοῦμαι/ἔδραμον). See references in Croy, *Endurance*, 63, n. 72.

18. Attridge, 355, calls τὸν προκείμενον ἡμῖν ἀγῶνα ("the race set before us") a "fixed classical expression" in which the participle is middle and descriptive but not passive, implying agency. Nevertheless, the parallel usage in v. 2 (the "joy set before" Jesus) shows that this occurrence in v. 1 is also a divine passive (Ellingworth, 639; Lane, 2:399; deSilva, 429). "God Himself has set our work and our prize before us as ἀγωνοθέτης [contestant]!" (Westcott, 394).

lege because it will take those who endure to the promised goal.[19] "Endurance" is the important thing. It is an exhausting race. The pastor's whole concern introduced in 10:36 is not just that they "run," but that they run "with endurance" to the end.[20] Such endurance is perseverance in a life of obedience through reliance upon God's promises and power, and this despite stiff opposition.[21] The pastor has substantiated this exhortation by offering the faithful of old as examples worthy of imitation and association and as heroes whose approval was worth winning. He fortifies this appeal in vv. 2-3 with his strongest argument: Jesus is both the source and greatest example of endurance.

2 In the opening comments on this section we have already shown how the pastor has been preparing for the introduction of "the Pioneer and Perfecter of the faith, Jesus," since 3:1-6. There can be no dispute about the importance and centrality of "looking unto" the person so described.[22] With this description the pastor joins the need for perseverance in the kind of faith depicted in chapter 11 with the full sufficiency of Christ the High Priest, as described in 4:14–10:18.[23] As the "Pioneer and Perfecter of the faith," Christ has become the fully sufficient Savior (4:14–10:18) who alone enables God's people to reach the goal of the way of faith (11:1-40). As demonstrated in the comments on 10:19-39 above, perseverance in faith (11:1–12:29) is founded upon the saving work of Christ (4:14–10:18). After examining "the Pioneer and Perfecter of the faith" more fully, we will be in a better position to examine the significance of "looking unto" him.

---

19. Thompson, 248.

20. Note the association of ὑπομονή with athletic imagery in Philo, *Good Person* 26; in the context of martyrdom recorded in 4 Macc 17:10, 12, 17; and in the other references recorded in Croy, *Endurance*, 63-65. See also on 10:36-39 above.

21. The need to pursue the moral life with "endurance" (ὑπομονή) was an important theme of contemporary Stoic philosophy (Croy, *Endurance*, 63-65, 174). However, the Stoic "endurance" of hardship in order to attain self-sufficiency (αὐτάρκεια) is vastly different from the God-oriented endurance advocated by Hebrews.

22. The importance of the phrase "looking unto the Pioneer and Perfecter of the faith, Jesus" is certain, even if Horning's chiasm putting it at the center of vv. 1-2 is problematic (Estella B. Horning, "Chiasmus, Creedal Structure and Christology in Hebrews 12.1-2," *BR* 23 [1978]: 40-41). See the evaluation of this chiasm in Croy, *Endurance*, 191-92. Gordon, 171, compares "looking unto . . . Jesus" and the exhortations to "look unto God" in passages such as 4 Macc 17:10. Such parallels certainly confirm the attribution of deity to the Son with which Hebrews began.

23. Rose's insistence that this verse be interpreted only within the immediate hortatory context is completely misguided (Rose, *Die Volke*, 338-39). To do so would be to ignore all of the ways in which the pastor has carefully developed his sermon to impact his hearers. It would also be to act as if the hearers had been stricken with amnesia after finishing chapter 10. In light of the pastor's larger argument "Pioneer and Perfecter of the faith" refers to the person and work of Christ as well as to his role as example (Weiss, 636-39).

All that the pastor has said about the full sufficiency of Jesus to atone for sin and bring the faithful into God's presence is encompassed in the all-inclusive phrase "the Pioneer and Perfecter of the faith."[24] It is important to note how the pastor has emphasized "faith" by the word order of this phrase. A literal rendering would run thus: "the of the faith Pioneer and Perfecter, Jesus."[25] Furthermore, by putting "of the faith" before the nouns "Pioneer" and "Perfecter" the pastor has shown that it qualifies both of them — Christ is both the Pioneer and Perfecter of "the faith." The pastor does not say "our" faith but "the faith."[26] He is referring to "the faith" just defined and exemplified in chapter 11. By his saving work Jesus is the Pioneer and Perfecter of "the" way of "faith" trod both by the saints of old and by contemporary believers.[27] Through him and what he has done the faithful of all time are able to persevere in obedience and reach the God-appointed goal of their pilgrimage.[28] The pastor's explanation of what it means to live "by faith" comes to its conclusion in this description of the one who makes the life of faith possible. Naught remains but to urge his hearers to persevere in living "by faith."

The intervening explanation of Christ's high-priestly ministry has enabled the pastor to expand his description of Christ as "the Pioneer of their salvation" (2:10) who would be "perfected" through suffering into "the Pioneer and Perfecter of the faith."[29] This latter phrase explains the fuller signifi-

---

24. *Pace* Thiessen, "Exodus," 366-67, the pastor does not give sufficient clues for his hearers to perceive that as ἀρχηγός ("Pioneer") Jesus is the true Joshua.

25. On the significance of the word order in τὸν τῆς πίστεως ἀρχηγὸν καὶ τελειωτὴν Ἰησοῦν ("the of the faith Pioneer and Perfecter, Jesus") see Lane, 2:412. Comparison with the twin phrase "the Apostle and High Priest of our confession" (3:1) confirms the importance of the location of "faith" in this phrase.

26. "The 'faith' of which the Apostle speaks is faith in its absolute type, of which he has traced the action under the Old Covenant" (Westcott, 395). In light of all that the pastor has done to affirm the continuity of the people of God and the validity of OT examples, it is unlikely that the definite article should be taken as indicating a possessive — "our" faith, in distinction from the faith of those who lived before Christ. However, see the discussion in Bénétreau, 2:172.

27. Hughes, 523, objects that Christ could not be the Pioneer and Perfecter of the faith of the ancients because their faith was "marred by sin and imperfection." This objection cannot be sustained for several reasons. First, they are now "made perfect" by being cleansed from sin through Christ, just as contemporary believers are so perfected through cleansing (11:39-40). Second, there is no other way of faith than the one of which Christ is Pioneer and Perfecter. To exclude the faithful of old from the way pioneered and perfected by him is to exclude them from the heavenly City altogether (12:22-24).

28. Bénétreau, 2:172-73, also takes "faith" in this general or absolute sense, and affirms that it has been made possible by the work of Christ.

29. Although Rose, *Die Volke,* 341, insists on interpreting "Pioneer and Perfecter" primarily within the immediate hortatory context, he cannot deny their soteriological significance. If Jesus suffers as "Pioneer," it is a suffering that anticipates the goal. If as "Per-

cance and intended direction of the former. As Pioneer of his people's salvation (2:10), Christ opened the way for their ultimate entrance into the presence of God by becoming their all-sufficient High Priest, able to cleanse them from sin.[30] This he did through his obedient self-offering, with all of the suffering it entailed. Since, then, he has been made fully competent ("perfected") as the one able to bring his people into God's ultimate presence by this suffering, he can be called "the Pioneer and Perfecter of the faith."[31] "Pioneer" and "Perfecter" are reminiscent of the words for "beginning" and "end" respectively.[32] He has not only initiated the opening of this way of faith but completed it by providing the only means for those who tread this road to reach journey's end. The way of faith is not under construction. It is open from beginning to end. Still, to speak of a "way of faith" separate from the Savior is misleading. As the "Pioneer and Perfecter," he himself is the way by which God's people both before and after his incarnation enter God's presence.

We have argued above (p. 270, n. 276; pp. 139-40) that the pastor uses "pioneer" when he is referring to Christ as the one who leads the pilgrim people of God into their ultimate destiny, but that he uses "high priest" when he would urge his hearers to draw near to God in the present for needed grace. The two, however, cannot be divorced from each other. Present entrance into God's presence is necessary for perseverance until final entrance. The work of Christ that opens the way for approaching God in the present is, as we have seen, the same work necessary for final entrance into the divine presence. "Pioneer and Perfecter of the faith," then, encompasses all that the Son of God has done as both Pioneer and High Priest. As "Pioneer and Perfecter" of the way "of faith" he is able to do everything necessary to succor the people of God in their daily pilgrimage, and thus to bring them into their ultimate destiny. The pastor has reserved this comprehensive term for 12:1-3, the high point of his appeal, and used it to invoke all that he has said about the

---

fecter" he has reached that goal, it is only as one who has suffered. The only other extant use of τελειωτής ("perfecter") not dependent upon this passage is found in Dionysius of Halicarnassus, *On Dinarchus* 1 (N. C. Croy, "A Note on Hebrews 12:2," *JBL* 114 [1995]: 117-19). The pastor obviously intends us to understand this word in connection with the rest of his "perfection" terminology.

30. See the commentary on 2:10 above.

31. *Pace* Bruce, 337, there is no hint in Hebrews that in some speculative way the preincarnate Christ "led all the people of God, from earliest times, along the path of faith." He is the "Pioneer" for those who lived before him because through his incarnate obedience he has opened the way for them to enter God's presence as well.

32. Compare ἀρχηγὸν καὶ τελειωτήν ("pioneer and perfecter") with ἀρχή and τέλος ("beginning" and "end"), used together in 3:14b and 7:3. See the discussion in Lane, 2:411.

full sufficiency of the Son of God as the Savior of his people. By concluding with the name "Jesus" he will not let his hearers forget that this salvation was procured through the incarnation of God's Son, or that the One sitting at God's right hand as their representative is the human "Jesus," in whom the eternal Son and the people of God are one.

Two additional issues must be addressed before leaving this climactic description of the Son of God. First, the "faith" of which he is the "Pioneer and Perfecter" is related to the "salvation" of which he is the "Pioneer" in 2:10 as response is related to provision.[33] The "salvation" that he has provided is what makes the response of "faith" effective. It is because of what he has done that those who persevere in living "by faith" will enter the heavenly City. The pastor began by talking about the "Pioneer" of the "salvation" that he went on to describe in the central part of his book. He concludes, most appropriately, by speaking of the "Pioneer and Perfecter" of the "faith" with which he urgently desires his hearers to respond.

Second, it is crucial to recognize that there is both continuity and discontinuity between the "Pioneer and Perfecter of the faith" and those who lived "by faith" in the previous chapter.[34] There is continuity because both the incarnate Son of God and the examples of 11:1-40 were obedient, and thus can be described as faithful to God. Both they and he "endured" despite opposition. Yet the pastor who describes Christ as the "Pioneer and Perfecter of the faith" is careful not to describe him as living "by faith."[35] His obedience and faithfulness were perfect. He never had to make a break with the unbelieving world as did the saints of old (Abraham, 11:8; Moses, 11:27; and Rahab, 11:31). Furthermore, he was not seeking entrance to the heavenly City on his own behalf but as the representative of God's people. Finally, as the one who provides entrance into God's presence he was a crucial part of the promise upon which they relied. Thus, to live "by faith" is to live in dependence on him.[36] He is, then, the premier example of one who endures in faithful obedience despite suffering. He cannot be described, however, as one who lived "by faith."

In the relative clause that begins with "who for sake of the joy set before

33. Bénétreau, 2:173, is correct when he says, "He [Christ] is the one who establishes the objective conditions of salvation offered to faith." He is misleading, however, when he says that "πίστις [faith] has become another term for salvation" (see Bénétreau, 2:173).

34. See Gordon, 172; Pfitzner, 177.

35. Spicq, 2:386, recognizes this fact when he says, "But, however, the Scripture does not speak of Christ as one who believes."

36. See the discussion of faith above in the comments on Heb 11:1-7, 13-16, and 39-40. Note Weiss's affirmation that faith in Hebrews is related to Christology and soteriology "not expressly in the sense that it is 'faith in Jesus' but rather in the sense of faith which is oriented in Jesus, the "Beginner/Leader and Perfecter of faith" (Weiss, 637). "Where it is a matter of the faith it is always a matter of the Christ" (Spicq, 2:386).

him" the pastor summarizes all that the "Pioneer and Perfecter" has done to procure the salvation of his people. Thus, this summary recalls what the pastor has already said about Christ providing atonement for sin and access to God through his humiliation, obedience, suffering, and final exaltation (4:1–10:18; especially 5:5-10; 9:11-15; 10:5-10). However, this time the pastor describes these events with different terms in order to show that by this suffering Christ has also become the source and supreme example of endurance. "Joy," "endured," "cross," and "despising the shame" all contribute to this purpose.[37] The procurement of salvation is the fulfillment of his sonship through earthly obedience (Heb 1:1-4). Thus, it is appropriately called the "joy" set before him by God as the goal of that obedience.[38] This "joy" that he has procured awaits those who endure at the consummation of their pilgrimage. It far outweighs anything that might attract or distract. Elsewhere the NT never says that Jesus "endured" the cross. Thus, it is clear that the pastor has chosen this term in order to encourage the endurance so needful for his hearers (10:39) in the face of suffering and shame from an unbelieving world. One could hardly mention the "cross" of Christ shorn of association with its redemptive significance.[39] However, the pastor uses "cross" in this context because it, like no other term, expresses the extreme shame born by Christ.[40] Jesus, however, "despised" this shame. He totally disregarded it and in no way allowed it to divert him from perfect obedience.

37. "This verse, therefore, is not merely a recital of Jesus' passion; it uses language that enhances his honor as a benefactor and the beneficiaries' awareness of debt" (deSilva, 433). Thus, it is very unlikely that the pastor is here quoting a creedal statement, as some have suggested (see Lane, 2:412-13).

38. Bénétreau, 2:174; cf. Westcott, 395-96. "For sake of (ἀντί) the joy that was set before him (προκειμένης)" is to be preferred over the alternate rendering, "instead of (ἀντί) the joy that was at hand (προκειμένης)." It is inconceivable that the pastor would have used "joy" (χαρά) for the "pleasure"/"advantage" (ἀπόλαυσις, 11:25) offered by the world to allure Christ from obedience. Pace Montefiore, 215, Chrysostom, and many of the Church Fathers, there is nothing in the context that suggests Jesus' preincarnate joy. Both he and those who emulate him "endure" in anticipation of future "joy" (cf. Weiss, 640). Furthermore, it was customary to speak of a prize being "set before" the athlete (Polybius, *Histories* 3.62; Pausanias, *Description of Greece* 9.2.6), or before those competing for virtue (Philo, *Rewards* 13; Josephus, *Ant.* 8.208). See Koester, 524, and Croy, *Endurance,* 66-67. Thus, the primary significance of προκειμένης ("set before") is temporal — the "joy" came after he "endured the cross." Esau, on the other hand (v. 16), surrendered his birthright "for the sake of" (ἀντί) food (Bruce, 339, n. 45). Croy, *Endurance,* 177-85, gives a thorough defense of this understanding of "joy" and answers the objections raised by P. Andriessen, "Renonçant à la joie qui lui revenait," *NRTh* 97 (1975): 424-38. See also the extensive discussion in O'Brien, 455-56.

39. Weiss, 638.

40. Lane, 2:414; Martin Hengel, *Crucifixion* (Philadelphia: Fortress, 1977), 22-63. See Deut 21:22-23. The absence of an article before σταυρόν ("cross") emphasizes the terrible nature of this type of death (Spicq, 2:388).

Notice how the pastor encases suffering within the arms of victory. He begins with "for the joy set before him" and ends with "at the right hand of the throne of God he has taken his seat." The pastor is well aware of the power of "shame" to deter his hearers. Thus, he follows Jesus' "despising shame" immediately with the glory of the exaltation. His hearers can also "despise" the shame of a mocking world because of their hope of glory. The pastor concludes by using the perfect tense, "he has taken his seat" (contrast the aorist in 1:3, 13; 8:1; 10:12), in order to remind his hearers that the Son's triumph as Savior "at the right hand of the throne of God" is completely and permanently effective.[41] The suffering, although necessary, was temporary. The triumph is forever.[42] Jesus is powerful as an example only because he has become the Savior who enables his own to sustain the same kind of suffering he endured. We saw how the entire roll call of the faithful was crafted to prepare God's people for the persecution and opposition described in 11:35b-38. The suffering by which Christ procured the salvation of God's people is a far greater example than the suffering through which they receive it.

God's faithful people have always been empowered for endurance by keeping their vision on the present power and future-oriented promises of God (11:1, 3, 6). Both Abraham and Moses were sustained by the vision of God's future reward (11:13, 26). Moses saw and drew strength from "the Unseen One" (11:27) during his earthly pilgrimage.[43] When all who live after Christ imitate these heroes of faith, they are "looking unto," and thus keeping their eyes upon, "Jesus" (2:9); "the Apostle and High Priest of" their "confession"; "the Pioneer and Perfecter of the faith"; the "High Priest who has sat down at the right hand of the throne of the Majesty in heaven."[44] When they keep their gaze on him, they are looking at their future goal in the heavenly City (12:22-24); the one who assures their access thereunto; and the present source of power for perseverance (4:14-16; 10:19-25).[45] He is the ful-

---

41. Ellingworth, 642. "At the right hand of the throne of God" combines something of the majesty of 8:1 ("at the right hand of the throne of the Majesty in heaven") with the specificity of 10:12 ("at the right hand of God").

42. "The suffering has come to an end, the glory endures forever" (Spicq, 2:388).

43. According to 4 Macc 17:10 the martyrs endure "looking to God" (εἰς θεὸν ἀφορῶντες; cited in deSilva, 431, n. 123).

44. The participle ἀφορῶντες (ἀπὸ ὁράω; "looking unto") implies that one should look away from this world to Jesus. It has the same import as ἀποβλέπω ("looking toward"), used in 11:26 of Moses' looking from present circumstances to the promised reward. The verb in this context carries the nuance of looking on the "unseen" and not letting one's life be determined by the "seen" (11:1, 3, 6, 27). The present tense of the participle indicates that this is to be the continuous occupation of God's people as they run the race.

45. Koester, 523, 536, refers to ancient runners looking at the guest of honor seated with distinction on a platform at the edge of the racetrack (Virgil, *Aeneid* 5.290). In

fillment of the promises anticipated by the faithful of old and the present power of God for the faithful of today. The fact that "we have such a High Priest who has sat down at the right hand of the throne of the Majesty in heaven" is indeed the "main point" (8:1) of the pastor's sermon.

3 We saw in v. 2 how the pastor described the saving work of Christ in such a way as to make his suffering an encouraging example and source of help for the beleaguered and threatened recipients of Hebrews. He now makes the importance of Christ's example explicit: "Consider the one who has endured such opposition of sinners against himself." It is true that the pastor would have them put their own sufferings in proper perspective by comparing them with Christ's. There is, however, something much more momentous afoot. He does not tell them to "consider" Christ's sufferings but to "consider" Christ himself who has suffered. Thus, this verse emphasizes the magnitude of his sufferings and the finality and continuing validity of his triumph in order to magnify him. It is fitting at this point to take some time and consider the magnitude of his sufferings. They are described as "such opposition."[46] "Opposition" is not used in the narrow sense of verbal conflict but in the most comprehensive way to include all the abuse and suffering he endured.[47] The word "opposition" also implies that this abuse was directed at Jesus personally by hostile persons. The personal nature of his sufferings is confirmed by "against himself."[48] Furthermore, this opposition was instigated and carried out by "sinful people."[49] They were not only against him, but they were also in

---

Hebrews, however, the faithful keep their gaze on Jesus, who has opened the way for them, and awaits them seated at the goal. *Pace* Johnson, 317, there is nothing that suggests the hearers are to keep their gaze on Jesus as he runs before them.

46. The position of τοιαύτην ("such") early in the sentence is emphatic. Compare τοσοῦτον ("so great") in v. 1 above. The pastor creates euphony and unity by putting ἀναλογίσασθε ("consider") at the beginning of this clause, while reserving its object, the similar-sounding ἀντιλογίαν ("opposition"), until the end.

47. Cf. Luke 2:34; Acts 28:22. See Lane, 2:415-16, and Hughes, 526, n. 121.

48. Lane (2:400u) and Ellingworth (643-44) adopt the plural reading, εἰς ἑαυτούς ("against themselves") instead of the singular, εἰς ἑαυτόν ("against himself") — Jesus "endured the opposition of sinners against themselves." The plural has stronger external attestation, including 𝔓13 and 𝔓46, but is difficult to construe. Other authors occasionally used such expressions to describe the self-destructive nature of wicked behavior (Moffatt, 198). However, such an interpretation seems out of place (Croy, *Endurance,* 189-90). This understanding of the plural reading fits poorly within the context (Bénétreau, 2:176, n. 1). It would only detract from the dominant emphasis on Jesus' suffering and introduce a concept elsewhere unattested in Hebrews. Thus, the plural is probably the result of a primitive scribal error. It is possible that someone felt this description of Jesus too harsh. See deSilva, 426, n. 111.

49. Jesus was betrayed into the hands of "sinful men" (Matt 36:45; Mark 14:41; Luke 24:7) and crucified by "lawless men" (Acts 2:23).

rebellion against God.[50] To abandon Christ would be to take one's place with them (10:26-31). The fact that this abuse was personal accords well with its shameful character. His sufferings were great, but he was triumphant. His victory is described by the perfect participle, "the one who has endured." The pastor is not now concerned with the triumph of resurrection, exaltation, or session at God's right. He asserts Christ's fully successful endurance of these sufferings without fail until the end. The perfect tense affirms that he is and continues to be such a person, one who has borne the full brunt of evil opposition with complete success.[51] Thus, the pastor would not have his hearers "consider" Christ merely or even primarily to put their own suffering in proportion. They are to "consider" Christ as the one who has been fitted by successful endurance of the worst to sustain them in whatever they face. "Consider" is a culminative aorist imperative.[52] They should come to the full realization of who he is. It is because he is one who has overcome that they need not "become weary, giving up in" their "very souls."

The pastor again invokes the image of the runner when he says "in order that you might not become weary, giving up in your souls."[53] This runner is in danger of giving up the race through extreme fatigue and discouragement.[54] A literal rendering of this clause might run as follows: "in order that you might not become weary in your souls giving up." "Might not become weary" is an ingressive aorist, followed by the present participle, "giving up" — in order that you might not enter a state of weariness that results in giving up. This phrase summarizes the pastor's concern with lassitude (2:1-4; 5:11-14) that leads to apostasy (6:4-8; 10:26-31; 12:14-17). "In your souls" emphasizes the depth of fatigue and discouragement. The race is not lost in the legs, but in the runner's inmost being. The phrase "in your souls" is often used with both the verb translated "become weary" and the one translated "giving up."[55] In the Greek sentence it comes between the two. If it is taken

---

50. "The opposite of the μάρτυρες [witnesses] who encourage the athlete (v. 1) are the ἁμαρτωλοί ("sinners") who would force them to give up (cf. 2 Macc 14:41)" (Spicq, 2:388).

51. On τὸν ὑπομεμενηκότα ("the one who has endured"), see Hughes, 526, n. 120.

52. On the significance of the second person plural aorist imperative ἀναλογίσασθε, "consider," see Lane, 2:415; Hughes, 526.

53. Although κάμνω ("become weary") and ἐκλύω ("give up") are not borrowed from the racetrack, they accord well with and extend the image of a race in this passage. See Croy, *Endurance*, 68.

54. See Attridge, 358, n. 80.

55. ἵνα μὴ κάμητε ταῖς ψυχαῖς ὑμῶν ἐκλυόμενοι ("in order that you might not become weary in your souls, giving up"). For ταῖς ψυχαῖς ("in your souls") with κάμνω (κάμητε, "become weary"), see BDAG, 506, 1; with ἐκλύω (ἐκλυόμενοι, "giving up," "being discouraged"), see BDAG, 306.

with the former, we have the translation, "lest you become weary in your souls, giving up"; if with the latter, "lest you become weary, giving up in your souls." A smooth English translation requires that we choose one or the other. However, by putting "in your souls" between the two the pastor could allow this phrase to qualify both. Its central location underscores his concern with the resilience of their inmost being. "The One who has endured" is able to sustain them, not primarily by removing the trials but by supplying the inner strength and fortitude they need. The pastor helps his hearers feel what he is saying by likening spiritual fatigue to a deep sense of physical exhaustion in order that they might draw upon the One who has endured. We have translated the participle with which this verse ends as "giving up." It can also be rendered "being discouraged." The pastor uses this word here in anticipation of its reoccurrence in Prov 3:11 quoted in v. 5 below: "do not become discouraged by his [God's] correction."[56]

C. THE PRESENT HISTORY OF THE PEOPLE OF GOD UNTIL THE CONSUMMATION (12:4-29)

The narrative of the past faithful (11:1-40), culminating in Jesus (12:1-3), who is both the example *par excellence* of endurance and the One who enables his people to endure, leads naturally to the present trials and privileges of the faithful. Heb 12:4-13 recounts the present suffering that must be endured by God's people; Heb 12:18-24, the present privilege they now enjoy through Christ. In the first of these passages the pastor reinforces the call to endurance by affirming that the trials incurred by the faithful are God's formative discipline marking them as his true children; in the second, he motivates his hearers with a grand picture of the privileges now theirs in Christ, a picture that is also a preview of ultimate blessedness. The pastor introduces this grand picture of privilege with a final example from the life of Esau against squandered privilege (12:14-17). Threat of eternal loss and promise of eternal gain come to a head with the description of the last Judgment in 12:25-29. Approval or disdain before the saints of old is mere prelude to judgment before the One "who is a consuming fire" (12:29). With this description of the Judgment the pastor concludes his history and rests his case for endurance.

The way in which 10:19–12:3 mirrors 3:1–4:16 has been discussed on pp. 65-67 above and in the introductions to the previous two sections — 10:19-39 and 11:1–12:3 (pp. 460-63, 514-15). Heb 12:4-29 continues this

56. Compare ἐκλυόμενοι ("being discouraged") at the end of v. 3 with ἐκλύου ("and do not become discouraged") in v. 5.

trend by mirroring 1:1–2:18. The suffering through which God's faithful sons and daughters receive salvation according to 12:4-13 reflects the suffering by which the Son provided salvation in 2:5-18. The apostasy of 12:14-17 springs from the neglect of 2:1-4. The contrast between Zion and Sinai in 12:18-24 corresponds to the contrast between God's word spoken through the Son and at Sinai in 1:5-14. Finally, God's earth-shaking word spoken at the Judgment in 12:25-29 will bring his word spoken in the Son (1:1-4) to its intended consummation. The exposition that follows will, where appropriate, illuminate the significance of these parallels. Below is an expansion of the diagram provided in the previous sections that gives the complete picture of how 10:19–12:29 is the mirror image of 1:1–4:16. See also the extensive discussion and diagrams on pages 60-70 in the Introduction. Yet one must not forget that these two images are not equal. The pastor's emphasis is on the positive direction toward which he would guide his hearers as described in this last part of the book, 10:19–12:29.

(A^1) God "Will Speak" Once More at the Final Judgment (12:25-29).

(B^1) God's Firstborn Enter His Presence through the Exalted Jesus (12:18-24).

(C^1) Don't Sell Your Birthright, as Esau Did (12:14-17).

(D^1) God's True Sons and Daughters Endure the Discipline of Suffering (12:4-13).

(E^1) Keep Your Eyes on Jesus, Seated at God's Right Hand (12:1-3).

(F^1) Join the Company of the Faithful of Old (11:1-40).

(G^1) Pursue the Blessing Promised the Faithful (10:32-39).

(H^1)You Are More Accountable Because of This High Priest (10:26-31).

(I^1) Avail Yourself of This Great Priest (10:19-25).

(J) Christ's All-Sufficient High Priesthood (5:1–10:18).

(I) Embrace This Great High Priest (4:14-16).

(H) You Are Accountable before the Word of God (4:12-13).

(G) Pursue the Blessing Lost by the Faithless Generation (4:1-11).

(F) Avoid the Company of the Faithless Generation (3:7-19).

(E) Consider Jesus, a Son over the House of God (3:1-6).

(D) The Crucial Importance of the Incarnate, Suffering Son (2:5-18).

(C) The Urgency of Attending to God's Son-Mediated Revelation (2:1-4).

(B) The Incomparable Majesty of the Eternal, Exalted Son (1:5-14).

(A) God Has Spoken through His Son (1:1-4).

1. God's True Sons and Daughters Endure the Discipline of Suffering (12:4-13)

4 You have not yet resisted unto blood in your struggling against sin. 5 And have you completely forgotten the exhortation that addresses you as sons and daughters? "My son, do not belittle the disci-

pline of the Lord, nor lose heart at his reproof. 6 *For whom the Lord loves he disciplines; and chastises every son or daughter whom he accepts." 7 Endure [these sufferings] as discipline, since God is treating you as sons and daughters. 8 For if you are without the discipline of which all have become partakers, then you are illegitimate children and not sons or daughters. 9 Furthermore, we have had our fathers according to the flesh as disciplinarians, and we respected them. How much more rather should we submit completely to the Father of Spirits, and live. 10 For on the one hand they disciplined us for a few days as seemed best to them; but he for benefit in order that we might come to share his holiness. 11 And all discipline for the time being does not seem to be of joy but of grief; but afterward it yields the peaceful fruit of righteousness to those who have been trained by it. 12 Therefore straighten the drooping hands and the enfeebled knees. 13 And make straight paths with your feet, so that what is lame may not turn aside but rather be healed.*

In vv. 4-13 the pastor quotes (vv. 5-6), interprets (vv. 7-11), and applies (vv. 12-13) Prov 3:11-12. One can hardly miss the change of topic and focus. In vv. 1-3 the pastor calls on his hearers to "look unto" Christ; in vv. 4-11 he directs their attention to God as their "Father." In vv. 1-3 he describes the suffering of Christ; in vv. 4-13 he explains the purpose of his hearers' suffering. In vv. 1-3 he uses the picture of a race; in vv. 4-11 he employs the language of education and of familial instruction. According to Weiss, vv. 1-3 deal with Christology while vv. 4-11 deal with rational explanation drawn from the tradition of Wisdom Literature.[1] However, to become fixated on these differences is to miss the unity and progress of the pastor's thought. To begin with, the transition from the athletic to the familial idiom betokens no great change. It was common for contemporary writers in the Hellenistic world to combine athletic and familial imagery in moral discourse.[2] Both the athletic and the young needed training in order to achieve success. Thus, the hearers would have perceived this combination as a natural blending rather than a mixing of metaphors. In fact, the athletic metaphor is perpetuated in vv. 4-11 by such terms as "struggling against" (v. 4) and "trained" (v. 11).[3] The exhortation in vv. 12-13 recalls both the race and the boxing match.

---

1. Weiss, 644-46.
2. See Croy, *Endurance,* 205, and references there cited.
3. In addition to the athletic connotation of ἀνταγωνίζομαι ("struggle") in v. 4, both αἷμα ("blood") and ἀντικαθίστημι ("oppose") suggest a boxing match. See Croy, *Endurance,* 69-70. Although γυμνάζω ("train") in v. 11 is a general word for "exercise," its etymological association with the gymnasium is obvious (Croy, *Endurance,* 70).

Furthermore, there is a clear correspondence between the suffering of God's "sons and daughters" in vv. 4-11 and the suffering of the Son described in vv. 1-3. In 2:5-18 the pastor affirmed that the Son assumed the humanity of God's "sons and daughters" (v. 10; cf. v. 14) in order to provide their salvation through suffering.[4] In 12:4-11 he declares that through suffering the "sons and daughters" receive this salvation, which the Son has provided. In 2:5-18 the pastor affirmed that "it was fitting" (2:10) for God to "perfect" the Son as the "Pioneer of their salvation" through suffering. In 12:4-11 he explains how appropriate it is for God's "sons and daughters" to suffer in light of his fatherly character. In the intervening chapters we have learned that the Son became "the Pioneer and Perfecter" of the way "of faith" through his persistent and total obedience to God despite suffering inflicted by those who would turn him aside (5:7-10; 9:11-15; 10:5-10). In 12:4-11 the pastor tells us that God's "sons and daughters" pursue that way of faith through persistent obedience despite the painful opposition of the world. It was necessary for the Son to suffer such opposition in order that his obedience might be total and complete (5:7-10). Such worldly opposition is now described as God's "discipline" by which his "sons and daughters" are hardened and confirmed in the way of obedience.[5] The cleansing from sin provided by Christ's obedience is the foundation for their obedience (9:14; 10:5-10, 15-18). The grace received by drawing near through him (4:14-16; 10:19-25) is its necessary daily resource. Thus, it is important to observe from the beginning that this divine "discipline" is not punishment for the sin from which Christ has cleansed them.[6] Nor is it merely "training" or "instruction" in a general sense.[7] It is God's use of opposition to fortify his "sons and daughters" in the way of obedience. That which marks the legitimacy of God's "sons and daughters" is a reflection of what demonstrated the legitimacy of his eternal Son.[8]

Comparison with Prov 3:11-12 in its original context and with Jewish

---

4. Weiss's contention (646) that this passage must be interpreted from the Jewish Wisdom tradition without reference to 2:5-18 is methodologically flawed. By thus isolating this passage from the larger context of the book, he reduces it to little more than an ad hominem argument.

5. "Discipline" in this comment and throughout the following paragraphs represents παιδεία in Heb 12:5, 7, 8, 11; likewise the verb "to discipline" translates παιδεύω in 12:6, 7, 10.

6. Thus, the translation of the CEV is particularly infelicitous: "When the Lord punishes you, don't make light of it" (12:5b).

7. Thus, by translating παιδεία as "instruction"/"education" and παιδεύω as "instruct"/"educate," Johnson, 313, 319-23, blurs the pastor's specific intention.

8. "When the author declares in 12:7 that 'God is treating you as sons,' he means also that 'God is treating you as God treated his own beloved Son'" (Johnson, 321).

and Hellenistic sources confirms the above interpretation of divine "discipline." It is clear that Prov 3:11-12 refers broadly to God's use of suffering as the "discipline" by which he shapes his children. The filial imagery itself suggests both correction or punishment for wrongdoing and positive instruction for living. Thus, we are not surprised that the writer of Proverbs includes both suffering that is punishment for sin and nonpunitive suffering within the scope of divine "discipline."[9] Furthermore, in light of the waywardness evidenced by God's people throughout Scripture, we would expect post-OT literature influenced by Hebraic thought to emphasize suffering as God's "discipline" by which he punishes or corrects sin.[10] On the other hand, under the influence of Stoic ideas of moral development it was normal for various Hellenistic writers to describe adversity as God's non-punitive "discipline" for character formation.[11] This difference is largely attributable to the OT belief in the holiness of God and the resulting greater emphasis on human moral impotence, the seriousness of sin, and the magnitude of its consequences. Furthermore, when comparing Hebrews with these other sources, it is important to note that the pastor has focused his interpretation of Prov 3:11-12 on one kind of suffering. He is concerned with suffering incurred out of loyalty to God's promise fulfilled in Christ.[12] Thus, it is no surprise that he is using this passage in regard to nonpunitive suffering.[13] Persecution because of devotion to Christ is neither the result of nor punishment for one's sin.

There is, then, a formal parallel between the way Hebrews describes God's use of nonpunitive suffering as "discipline" for character building and the writings of the Stoics.[14] The language of Hebrews would have had a familiar sound to hearers immersed in contemporary, Stoic-influenced Greco-

---

9. Note particularly his use of ἐλεγχόμενος ("being reproved," "being punished") in v. 5 (Prov 3:11) and of μαστιγοῖ ("he chastises") in v. 6 (Prov 3:12), both of which might imply punishment or correction for wrongdoing. Thompson, 254.

10. Croy, *Endurance,* 197-98.

11. See Seneca, *De providentia* 1.6; 2.6; 4.11-12, for παιδεία as nonpunitive "training" or "discipline" arising from God's love (Croy, *Endurance,* 196). Croy, *Endurance,* 197-98, cites Philo, Josephus, and 4 Maccabees as Jewish sources influenced by this Greco-Roman perspective.

12. Weiss (649) insists that the author includes all suffering in light of the Wisdom tradition from which he draws. However, this approach decontextualizes the passage. Even if the pastor is dependent on the Wisdom tradition, the exegete must determine how he has used that tradition.

13. Thus, the pastor does not use ἐλέγχω ("reprove") or μαστιγόω ("chastise") because they emphasize the punitive nature of the original text. Cf. Croy, *Endurance,* 198-99. *Pace* Weiss, 648-49, who wants to interpret παιδεία as "punishment" (in accord with the Wisdom tradition), though he admits that the suffering of the hearers is not the result of sin.

14. Croy, *Endurance,* 205.

Roman culture. The careful student of Hebrews, however, must pay close attention to its conceptual distinctiveness so as not to skew the import of the pastor's message.[15] The Stoics refer to all types of adversity as God's "discipline." Hebrews is referring primarily to opposition suffered because of loyalty to Christ. For the Stoics such "discipline" produces "self-sufficiency." For Hebrews it fortifies one's commitment to and habit of obedience. For the Stoics there is no reward beyond the "self-sufficiency" achieved. For Hebrews the obedience confirmed by "discipline" results in partaking of God's "holiness." The writer of Hebrews has clearly used this imagery for his own purposes. Comparison with other sources, then, is instructive as much for the differences it reveals as for the similarities.[16]

4 The pastor moves smoothly from Jesus' triumph over suffering (vv. 1-3) to the suffering faced by his hearers (vv. 4-13), and from Jesus' successful endurance (vv. 1-3) to their need for endurance (vv. 4-13). With "You have not yet resisted unto blood in your struggling against sin" he puts the limited nature of their sufferings in perspective. Clearly, the pastor is reminding his hearers that they have not yet suffered to the extreme.[17] Both "resisted" and "struggling" are reminiscent of a boxing match.[18] Such contests were often very bloody and sometimes resulted in death.[19] The pastor usually prefers the racetrack over the boxing match because the race is well suited to his emphasis on long-term endurance. Furthermore, he would not want to suggest that his hearers respond to their persecutors with the violence of a boxer. Nevertheless, he is not averse to using boxing when he wants to emphasize the strength of the resistance and its ability to inflict severe pain. Indeed, "unto blood" is reminiscent not only of the boxing match but of the Maccabean martyrs as well.[20] His hearers have not yet had to undergo the torture the martyrs

15. Croy, *Endurance,* 205-6 recognizes differences but fails to acknowledge their full extent and significance.

16. Although Croy, *Endurance,* is very helpful, his work is marred by giving Stoic and Greco-Roman parallels significance denied them by the context of Hebrews. Undue deference to these parallels is also behind Johnson's (313) mistranslation (in this context) of παιδεία and παιδεύω as "instruction"/"education" and "instruct"/"educate," respectively. Other commentaries, such as Thompson, 251-57, would have greater clarity if they recognized more fully the ways in which Hebrews differs from these proposed Greco-Roman parallels.

17. Montefiore, 217; Weiss, 646.

18. Lane, 2:417. ἀντικαθίστημι ("resist") and ἀνταγωνίζομαι ("struggle") occur nowhere else in the NT. ἀναγωνίζομαι is also reminiscent of ἀγῶνα, the word used for "race" in v. 1.

19. According to Bénétreau, 2.177, the boxers' gloves were inlaid with metal, making the sport particularly bloody.

20. Compare μέχρις αἵματος ("unto blood") and ἀνταγωνιζόμενοι ("struggling against") with ἀγωνίζεσθαι μέχρι θανάτου ("struggling unto death") in 2 Macc 13:1 (cf.

faced, nor have they died for the faith. Finally, with "resisted unto blood" (cf. 9:14) the pastor invokes a contrast between his hearers' sufferings and the suffering of Christ. "You have not yet resisted unto blood" as Jesus did on the cross. The shamefulness of the "cross" emphasized in v. 3 has given way to the violence and finality of the death it inflicted. The pastor is preparing his hearers "for what their imitation of Christ's endurance might ultimately involve."[21] While they have not yet endured bloody violence or death for their faith, they are currently engaged in "struggling against sin."[22] The present participle "struggling against" denotes an ongoing striving. "Sin" is the opponent. "Sin" was yielding to discouragement or anything else that would impede their race in v. 1. "Sin" was embodied in the "sinners" of v. 3.[23] "Sin" has become all those people and forces that exert pressure on the faithful to conform.[24] Thus, the pastor would use the ultimate example of Jesus' sufferings to fortify his hearers in the daily struggle against all that would turn them aside, and to prepare them for the isolation and deprivation that the unbelieving world can inflict upon the faithful people of God (11:36-38).[25]

5-6   With the mild rebuke of v. 4 the pastor attempted to rouse his hearers and silence their complaining by pointing to the lesser amount of suffering thus far allotted them.[26] He continues to provoke them by intensifying this tone of rebuke in his introduction to Prov 3:11-12: "And have you com-

---

Josephus, *J.W.* 2.141; *Ant.* 12.111; Phil 2:8, 30). The only other occurrence of ἀνταγωνίζεσθαι in the Greek Bible is in 4 Macc 7:14, where it is used of the martyrs' antagonist Antiochus IV Epiphanes. Note also the use of ἀγών in 4 Macc 11:20; 13:5; 15:29; 16:16; 17:11. See Lane, 2:418; Thompson, *Christian Philosophy,* 63-64; and Ellingworth, 646.

21. Attridge, 360.

22. Spicq, 2:390, is incorrect when he says: "The second aorist ἀντικατέστητε ["resisted"] evokes the precise event of persecution in a recent past." On the contrary, the pastor is referring to an event of resistance that has not yet occurred. However, Spicq is correct when he says: "the present participle ἀνταγωνιζόμενοι ["struggling against"] expresses a permanent spiritual disposition."

23. The pastor is referring to more than mere personal inward struggle against tendencies to sin; see Croy, *Endurance,* 194.

24. Lane, 2:418-19. In this context the pastor is not speaking about struggling against the "sin" of apostasy (*pace* Thompson, 253) itself, but against "sinners" and all that motivates and empowers them to persecute believers in the hope of eliciting compromise.

25. The way the pastor concludes the roll call of faith in 11:36-38 suggests that he is preparing his hearers for a protracted struggle against the total social ostracism described in that passage, rather than for martyrdom. Yet the death of Jesus and the possibility of martyrdom establish the context and parameters for all such suffering.

26. Croy, *Endurance,* 194, notes that the implied rebuke is pastoral and not severe. He argues that Lane, 2:419, goes too far when he says that the community's sufferings were "insignificant in comparison with those endured by Jesus."

pletely forgotten the exhortation that addresses you as sons and daughters?"[27] Only when they realize the little (by comparison) they have suffered, and the divinely established privilege they have neglected, will they grasp the full value of God's consolation. The perfect tense of the verb translated "completely forgotten" is important. One might paraphrase: "Have you truly been living without taking this message from God into account?" By expressing surprise at their oversight, the pastor both alerts them to their need and highlights the great importance he attaches to this passage of Scripture. Nowhere else in the OT is the faithful person so clearly called a "son or daughter" of God. No other passage so cogently expresses the filial character of God's "discipline." In fact, this passage may have been the pastor's authority for referring to God's people as the "many sons and daughters" whom Christ brings to "glory" in 2:10. He has, however, held this oracle in reserve until now so that he might use it effectively as the "encouragement" they need to brave persecution. In these verses God reminds them of who they are and why they suffer.[28]

It is Prov 3:11-12 in its character as "exhortation" or word of "consolation" that addresses the people of God as "sons and daughters."[29] What greater encouragement could the beleaguered people of God desire? Although this "exhortation" speaks of God in the third person, he is its true source. After all, he is the one who speaks through all Scripture. The word translated "addresses" is an intimate word suitable for God's engaging his own in conversation as his children.[30] Furthermore, the pastor has confirmed that the source of this message is God by adding "my" to the beginning of Prov 3:11 in the LXX — not just "son," but "my son."[31] Thus with "my son"

27. It is possible, with most translations, to take v. 5a as a statement: "You have completely forgotten the exhortation that addresses you as sons and daughters" (so Mitchell, 271). However, the question format is more in accord with the pastor's hortatory style (Lane, 2:397, 420; Johnson, 320; ESV; TNIV). It is also more tactful (Spicq, 2:392).

28. παράκλησις ("exhortation") can be used for a warning or, as in this case, for a word of encouragement. The pastor uses the same word in 13:12 to describe this entire sermon. Hebrews is indeed an "exhortation" that combines both warning and encouragement in order to promote perseverance.

29. "As sons," not "as if they were sons." "Those addressed *are* sons of God" (Weiss, 648, italics original; cf. O'Brien, 463).

30. Lane, 2:420, says, "The choice of διαλέγεται, 'speaks,' underscores the relational dimension that the writer intends to develop, since it views the utterance of the text of Scripture as the voice of God in conversation with his child" (cf. Gottlob Schrenk, "διαλέγομαι," *TDNT* 2:94; G. D. Kilpatrick, "διαλέγεσθαι and διαλογίζεσθαι in the New Testament," *JTS* n.s. 11 [1960]: 338-40; Michel, 438).

31. The MT includes this "my," but most interpreters doubt that Hebrews has corrected the LXX in conformity with the Hebrew (see Ellingworth, 648). Lane, 2:420, refers to McCullough, "Old Testament Quotations," 377-78.

God himself "addresses" every "son whom he accepts" (v. 6b).[32] We might paraphrase, "Through this exhortation God addresses you as sons and daughters." God himself assures his people of the filial relationship between them. That is why there was nothing unreasonable about the Son of God owning these same people as his "brothers and sisters" (2:11-12). He confirmed their status as God's children by taking on their "flesh and blood" in order that he might bring them to their inheritance as the "sons and daughters" of God (2:10-18). Thus, while this filial imagery is drawn from the sphere of human relationships, it is no mere figure of speech for which another could be substituted. The sonship/daughterhood of God's people has been established by God and confirmed by Christ. This relationship to their Father explains both their present struggle and their ultimate destiny. Well might the pastor be shocked at his hearers' neglect of this most relevant Scripture. All that he has been saying since chapter 2 assumes this divine declaration of God's filial relationship with his own.

The first two lines of this quotation need little explanation because they clearly express the pastor's concern for his hearers: "My son, do not belittle the discipline of the Lord nor lose heart at his reproof." These two negative exhortations are explained by the positive command at the beginning of v. 7. Do not "belittle" the persecutions as pointless or "lose heart" and be discouraged by their severity. Rather, "endure suffering as [divine] discipline" (v. 7a). God is not using the opposition of the unbelieving world to repay his children for their misconduct or, Stoic-like, for the general improvement of their character. He is using that opposition to confirm them in the obedience appropriate for sons and daughters worthy of his name. The quality of obedience is established by its costliness.

The second half of this quotation, found in v. 6, gives the reason why the pastor's hearers should not be disheartened by God's formative discipline manifested in worldly opposition: "For whom the Lord loves, he disciplines; and chastises every son or daughter whom he accepts." It is instructive to compare Hebrews' citation of the second half of this verse from the LXX with the translation of this psalm found in most English Bibles: "*and chas-*

---

32. Except for this "my son" at the beginning of the quotation from Prov 3:11-12, I have translated υἱός, "son," as "sons and daughters" (vv. 5, 7a, 8) or "son or daughter" (v. 7b) in order to show that this encouragement is for all of God's people. "My son or daughter," however, would mar the intimacy intended at the beginning of this quotation. On the one hand, this more inclusive translation is helpful. On the other, however, it obscures the father/son analogy intended by both the pastor and the author of Proverbs. This use of υἱός harks back to 2:10. The words used in this passage for "discipline" (παιδεία, vv. 5, 7, 8, 11), "to discipline" (παιδεύω, vv. 6, 7, 10), and "trainer" or "discipliner" (παιδευτής, v. 9) also remind the readers of 2:5-18 because they are cognate with παιδίον, "child" (2:13, 14), though παιδίον does not occur in this passage.

tises every son whom he accepts" (Hebrews); "*and as a father* every son in whom he delights" (Prov 3:12b NRSV). The italicized words represent a different but equally valid pointing of the Hebrew consonantal text.[33] "As a father" would have strengthened the pastor's emphasis on God's filial discipline. In the interpretation below the pastor does not cite the word "chastise" lest he suggest that God's discipline is punishment for sin. It is important, however, to note that "chastises" is the chiastic parallel of "disciplines": (A) "whom the Lord loves" (B) "he chastises"; (B[1]) "and disciplines" (A[1]) "every son or daughter whom he accepts."[34] This identification between the Lord's discipline and chastisement makes it easier to include the intense sufferings faced by the pastor's hearers under the rubric of divine pedagogy. Severe as it may be, this "discipline" comes from God's gracious fatherly love and distinguishes the recipient as a true "son or daughter" whom God "accepts" as his own.[35]

In vv. 7-11 the pastor shows how this psalm is indeed "consolation" for the beleaguered people of God. First, this divine discipline establishes their identity as legitimate "sons and daughters" (vv. 7-8). Second, it will bring eternal profit because of God's character as "father" (vv. 9-10). Similarity with human sonship supports the first; the superiority of God's fatherhood, the second. It is God's character as father that determines the nature of their sonship or daughterhood, the benefits received from his discipline, and the appropriateness of their response. Verse 11 concludes this interpretation by emphasizing the future benefits of present discipline.

7-8 The pastor begins by telling his hearers exactly what he wants them to do: "Endure [these sufferings] as discipline" or "for the sake of discipline."[36] All that follows is explanation of why they should follow this command. We have put "these sufferings" in brackets above to show that this phrase is not in the Greek text. Most translators have felt the addition of some such word or phrase necessary to make the pastor's meaning clear.[37] His ex-

---

33. The consonants of the first word in the Hebrew text of Prov 3:12b are וכאב, which the MT points as וּכְאָב, "and as a father," but which the text underlying the LXX appears to have pointed וִיַכְאִב, "and chastises."

34. See Lane, 2:421, for the chiastic structure of this verse: (A) ὃν γὰρ ἀγαπᾷ (B) κύριος παιδεύει; (B[1]) μαστιγοῖ δὲ (A[1]) πάντα υἱὸν ὃν παραδέχεται.

35. *Pace* Ellingworth, 650, παραδέχεται ("he accepts") is not primarily eschatological. The pastor is not saying that God will accept on the last day those whom he disciplines, but that such discipline is the mark of those whom he has already accepted. Compare the discussion of God's love for and chastening of his "sons" in Wis 12:20-22.

36. The NIV/TNIV takes εἰς παιδείαν as predicate accusative: "Endure hardship as discipline" (cf. REB; Lane, 2:397). The NRSV, as expressing purpose: "Endure trials for the sake of discipline" (cf. Ellingworth, 650).

37. The NIV/TNIV supplies "hardship"; the NRSV, "trials." These translations

pression is intentionally terse: "As discipline endure." By putting the phrase "as discipline" first in the Greek sentence the pastor drives home the point that their sufferings are to be received as God's formative "discipline" and appropriately endured for what they are. They should endure this suffering as God's discipline first of all because by this discipline "God is treating them as sons and daughters."[38] The word translated "sons and daughters" is without an article, emphasizing the filial quality of those described. Instead of being a reason for discouragement, such suffering, when understood as God's formative discipline, is an essential and most encouraging indication of their filial relationship with him. This assertion is supported by a generalization drawn from human experience: "For what son or daughter is there whom a father does not discipline?" It is of the very essence of sonship to be disciplined by a father. The pastor reinforces his point by stating its opposite in v. 8: "For if you are without the discipline of which all have become partakers, then you are illegitimate children and not sons or daughters." "Have become partakers" is perfect tense. All of God's true children have become partakers of and continue to experience his discipline.[39] Thus, the pastor tells his hearers that if they were living without such discipline they would be "illegitimate children," and emphatically "not sons or daughters" who are entitled to the protection, blessings, and inheritance of the father.[40] The pastor does not believe his hearers are illegitimate, so it would have been appropriate for him to have used a condition contrary to fact, which we might have translated, "For if you were without the discipline" experienced by all. However, he has used a condition of fact, "For if you are without the discipline . . ." in order to hone the keen edge of his warning.[41]

9 The similarity between human and divine sonship has demonstrated the appropriateness of God's corrective discipline for his true children. God, however, is far superior to any human father. The character of his fatherhood transforms our filial relationship into something much more than

---

are correct in taking ὑπομένετε as imperative, "endure," instead of indicative (cf. NASB: "It is for discipline that you endure"). The imperative is better suited to the hortatory context and parallels the introduction of Psalm 95 in Heb 3:12. See Attridge, 361.

38. This phrase in v. 7 ὡς υἱοῖς ὑμῖν προσφέρεται ὁ θεός ("God is treating you as sons and daughters") is parallel to the introductory formula in v. 5, ἥτις ὑμῖν ὡς υἱοῖς διαλέγεται ("that addresses you as sons and daughters").

39. The pastor's discussion of the faithful of old amply demonstrated this fact (11:10-12, 23-27, 35b-38). See O'Brien, 466.

40. For a detailed description of the ways in which the νόθος ("illegitimate child") lacked the rights of a legitimate son, see Spicq, 2:393-94. Ellingworth, 652, points out that νόθος is used in Wis 4:3, a passage that has many points of contact with Hebrews.

41. By insisting that this clause must be taken simply as a condition contrary to fact, Ellingworth, 651, dulls the force intended by the pastor.

its human counterpart. With "furthermore" the pastor introduces this new phase of his argument.[42] Both the response due God as Father and the benefits he gives far transcend what would be appropriate for a merely human father. The pastor uses two of his favorite less-to-greater contrasts (in vv. 9 and 10 respectively) to demonstrate this superiority. The second contrast depends on and develops the first.

The pastor contrasts "our fathers according to the flesh" (v. 9ab) with "the Father of Spirits" (v. 9cd). Verse 9 has four finite verbs, two for each half of the contrast: (1) "We have had fathers according to the flesh as disciplinarians" (v. 9a); (2) "and we respected them" (v. 9b); (3) "how much more rather should we submit completely to the Father of Spirits" (v. 9c); (4) "and live" (v. 9d). The first verbal clause emphasizes the limitation of human fathers (v. 9a). The second and third highlight the main point of comparison/contrast (v. 9bc). The fourth underscores the great benefit of submitting to the heavenly Father's discipline (v. 9d).

The first clause (v. 9a) is much longer than the second (v. 9b) because the pastor's main purpose in the first half of this contrast is to underscore the limitations of human fatherhood. "According to the flesh" emphasizes the weakness and mortality of our earthly fathers. "Flesh" carries no inherent authority. Thus, the pastor must add that "we had" them "as disciplinarians"[43] to justify the fact that "we respected them." The brief "we respected them" contrasts with the much longer "how much more rather should we submit completely to the Father of Spirits." This clause bears the main burden of the pastor's concern. If we respected our mortal, limited earthly fathers, then we should "submit completely" to one who is nothing less than "the Father of Spirits." The pastor does not use a hortatory subjunctive, "let us submit completely," but the more forceful future tense, "we will (must) submit completely."

The author of Hebrews has deliberately described God as "the Father of the Spirits" in contrast to "our fathers of the flesh."[44] This description accomplishes two seemingly disparate purposes at once. First, it emphasizes the absolutely superior character of God's fatherhood by echoing the phrase

---

42. For this use of εἶτα, "furthermore," "next," see BDAG, 295, 2. Ellingworth, 652, cites similar usage of εἶτα in Job 12:2; Wis 14:22; *Barn.* 13:2.

43. Although in the LXX παιδευτής is used for God as the punisher of Israel (Hos 5:2; *Pss. Sol.* 8:29), in Hellenistic writers it is used for "teacher," without the connotation of punishment (4 Macc 5:34; Rom 2:20). Croy, *Endurance,* 202.

44. It is clear that the pastor himself has formed this expression, "the Father of the spirits," both because of the way in which it contrasts with "our fathers of the flesh" and because of the important way it fits into his argument. Thus, Weiss's contention (652-53) that he must have taken it from tradition because of his reticence to use "father" for God (only here and in 1:5) is without cogency.

"God of the spirits." This description of God was used to affirm his transcendent majesty in 1QS 3:25; 2 Macc 3:24-25, and throughout *1 Enoch* 37–71.[45] On the other hand, Bruce is right when he says that the definite article "the" before "spirits" should be taken as a possessive pronoun — "the Father of our spirits."[46] A reference to God's universal "fatherhood" would only cloud the pastor's argument.[47] His whole point is that God addresses his own people as their Father.[48] He is absolutely superior as a "father," and he is *their* Father. He is the ultimate source of life both physical and eternal, and the one who would bring his own into his "glory" (2:10) and eternal "rest" (4:1).[49] There can be no question about complete submission to such a Father.[50] Submission will enable us to "live" in the "fullest sense" of that term.[51] The life lived in enjoyment of God's blessing envisioned by the writer of Proverbs has become the eternal life God has reserved for his own.[52] This "eternal life" is the inheritance of the faithful (10:38), who serve a "living God" (3:12; 9:14; 10:31) and will dwell in his eternal heavenly City (12:22) through the work of a High Priest who "always lives" (7:25) and has made "a new and living

45. Compare also the longer expressions found in Num 16:22; 27:16, "God of the spirits and of all flesh" (θεὸς τῶν πνευμάτων καὶ τῆς πάσης σαρκός); *1 Clem.* 59:3, "the benefactor/finder of spirits and God of all flesh" (εὐεργέτης/εὑρέτην πνευμάτων καὶ θεὸν πάσης σαρκός); *1 Clem.* 64:1, "Master of the spirits and Lord of all flesh" (δεσπότης τῶν πνευμάτων καὶ κύριος πάσης σαρκός). Weiss, 652-53, thinks these longer phrases and the shorter "God of spirits" come from different traditions. The shorter emphasizes God's transcendence. The longer imply that he is the giver of life. It is doubtful, however, if these two ways of describing God can be as hermetically sealed as he would contend. While "the Father of the spirits" emphasizes God's transcendence, the very word "Father" suggests that he is life-giving.

46. Bruce, 344, n. 80.

47. Montefiore, 220-21. Nor does the pastor intend to distinguish between earthly fathers from whom we get our body and the heavenly Father who gives us our spirit, as has been argued by some, such as Aquinas and Delitzsch (Hughes, 530-31).

48. The pastor has chosen to express the possessive with an article instead of a possessive pronoun in order to accomplish both of the purposes given above by this description of God.

49. Contrary to what some suggest, this contrast between God as "the Father of spirits" and "our fathers of the flesh" has nothing to do with a contrast between a heavenly noumenal world and the physical created world. It has everything to do with the common OT contrast between the eternal power of God and the weakness of mortal humanity. See Bénétreau, 2:179-80.

50. Weiss, 651, if "respect" was due "our fathers according to the flesh," then "complete" submission is due the "Father of spirits."

51. O'Brien, 467. Compare the contrast between "a law of fleshly ordinance" (νόμον ἐντολῆς σαρκίνης) and the "power of an indestructible life" (δύναμιν ζωῆς ἀκαταλύτου) in 7:16.

52. Ellingworth, 654. Note the future tense of ζήσομεν ("live").

way" (10:20) to their eternal destination. Submission to God's discipline is preparation for the eternal City. Thus the pastor continues to direct his hearers forward to the life that is and that is to come.

10 The pastor urges his hearers to the submission enjoined in v. 9 by contrasting the quality and purpose of the discipline exercised by human fathers (v. 10ab) and the divine Father (v. 10cd).[53] The lone finite verb of v. 10, "discipline," carries this theme. Yet in the Greek text this verb is qualified by four prepositional phrases, two for the first half of the contrast and two for the second: (1) "for a few days" (v. 10a); (2) "as seemed best to them" (v. 10b); (3) "for benefit" (v. 10c); and (4) "in order that we might come to share his holiness" (v. 10d).[54] The pastor's thought follows the pattern of v. 9. The first phrase emphasizes the limitation of human fathers (v. 10a). The second and third highlight the main point of comparison/contrast (v. 9bc). The pastor's emphasis is now on the fourth, which underscores the great benefit of the heavenly Father's discipline (v. 9d).

Because of their mortality our human fathers "according to the flesh" could discipline us for only "a few days." Through the heavenly Father's discipline, however, "we will live" forever (v. 9d). The pastor's main point comes to clearest expression in the two contrasting phrases: "as seemed best to them"; "for benefit." Even if well intentioned, the discipline of earthly fathers is limited by their judgment and prejudices. It is not necessarily in the best interests of those disciplined. God, however, has no such limitation, and his discipline is thus absolutely "for the benefit" of his own.[55] "For benefit" leaves the hearers asking, "What is this benefit?" The pastor has already told them that submission to God's discipline means that they will "live." He now adds: "that we might come to share his holiness." The faithful have already "been made holy" through the sacrifice of Christ.[56] Their sins have been cleansed (9:14) and God's laws have been written on their hearts, enabling them to obey (10:15-18). As they draw near through Christ in order to receive the resources he provides (4:14-16; 10:19-25), they are continually being made holy and empowered to persevere in obedience (10:14). The heavenly Father's discipline hardens them in obedience, thus confirming them in holy living. When they reach their final destination in the presence of God, his obedient sons and daughters will be confirmed in a charac-

---

53. Note the γάρ ("for") in v. 10.

54. English translation, of necessity, obscures the fact that in Greek each of these phrases is a prepositional phrase: πρὸς ὀλίγας ἡμέρας ("for a few days"); κατὰ τὸ δοκοῦν αὐτοῖς ("as seemed good to them"); ἐπὶ τὸ συμφέρον ("for the benefit"); and εἰς τὸ μεταλαβεῖν τῆς ἁγιότητος αὐτοῦ ("for the sharing of his holiness").

55. "But God is the perfect and permanent Educator" (Spicq, 2:395).

56. Thus, it is unclear why Attridge, 363, seems to identity this "holiness of God" in which they will come to share with the sanctification already provided by Christ.

ter like his.[57] Yet coming to "share in" God's "holiness" is more than the moral transformation necessary for fellowship with God. Those so transformed will participate in the very life of God through their intimate fellowship with him.[58] Those whom God brings to "glory" (2:10) and causes to enter his "rest" (4:1-11) will "come to share in his holiness." The "holiness" the faithful now enjoy in Christ is brought into closest relationship with its ultimate reward. We might paraphrase thus: "submit to the discipline of the Father of spirits" (v. 9c) "in order that through Christ you might be confirmed in a God-like character and thus share permanently in God's own eternal life." This reality of life with God exceeds the comprehension of both original hearers and modern readers.

11 The pastor concludes his discussion of Prov 3:11-12 by assuring his hearers that the present pain of God's fatherly discipline is well worth the future gain for which it prepares the children of God. The first half of this verse has the form of a general statement applicable to any area of life: "And all discipline for the time being does not seem to be of joy but of grief."[59] Moralists ancient and modern know that painful discipline is necessary for achievement. In the second clause, beginning with "but afterward," the pastor describes the benefits received in terms appropriate for the results that come from God's fatherly discipline — "the peaceful fruit of righteousness."[60] The gnomic or proverbial nature of this verse suggests that we should take "but afterwards" in a general sense rather than as a specific reference to the final Judgment. The pastor confirms this interpretation by describing the benefits of discipline as "the peaceful fruit of righteousness." This phrase appropriately describes benefits that the children of God begin to receive through God's discipline in this life. Many commentators think that the adjective translated "peaceful" and the genitive qualifier translated "of righteousness" function in essentially the same way.[61] The pastor, however, has very deliberately placed the word "righteousness" at the end of his interpretation of Prov 3:11-12. He introduced this long section on enduring persecution through persevering faith in 10:39 with Hab 2:4: "My *righteous* one will live by

---

57. Lane, 2:425.

58. Weiss, 655; Ellingworth, 655. Although coming "to share in his holiness" is more than moral transformation (cf. Bruce, 344), such transformation is the necessary condition for fellowship with God (Montefiore, 221). It is worth noting that the pastor uses ἁγιότης here for God's "holiness" but ἁγιασμός in 12:14 when speaking of the "holiness" necessary for the beatific vision.

59. Ellingworth, 655.

60. See Bénétreau, 2:181. Although Ellingworth, 656, thinks that ὕστερον ("afterward") probably has some eschatological overtones, he admits that the faithful begin to receive "peaceful fruit of righteousness" in this life.

61. Lane, 2:425.

faith." He began the roll call of the faithful with *"righteous"* Abel (11:4). Thus it is no surprise that he ends with "the peaceful fruit of *righteousness*" (italics added throughout). This arrangement of material suggests that "of righteousness" describes the source rather than the nature of this "fruit." To be "righteous" or to be in right relationship with God is indeed to persevere in obedience by faith despite opposition. It is God's fatherly discipline that perfects this righteousness and brings its "peaceful fruit" to maturity. Within the biblical context "peaceful" describes well-being and wholeness of relationships with God and with the family of the faithful.[62] This "peaceful fruit" only shines brighter amid the gloom of opposition. The euphoria felt by a successful athlete at the end of the race is nothing compared to the "peaceful fruit" matured through perseverance in obedience.[63]

The athletic metaphor that has been lying under the surface since the "no pain no gain" with which this verse began, becomes evident in the phrase "to those who have been trained" by God's discipline. The perfect tense of this substantive participle is important. This harvest comes only to those who have gone through the process of being trained and are in the state that results from that training. There is no other way to receive "the peaceful fruit" that comes from "righteousness" and thereby "partake of God's holiness" at the end of the race.

12-13 With these exhortations the pastor draws out the implications of vv. 1-11.[64] Since Jesus both enables and preeminently exemplifies endurance (vv. 1-3), and since persecution is God's fatherly discipline distinguishing his true children and preparing them for fellowship with him (vv. 4-11), the hearers should take courage (v. 12) and run straight for the goal (v. 13). We have noted how the fatherly discipline of vv. 5-11 is closely related to athletic training (v. 11). Thus, as the pastor began with the race (vv. 1-3) and the boxing match (v. 4), so he concludes with the boxing match (v. 12) and the race (v. 13).[65] As above, he uses boxing to describe the need for resistance to hostile opposition, a resistance that is required of those who would finish the race. Thus, the pastor calls on his hearers, who have not "resisted unto blood" (v. 4), to "straighten the drooping hands and the enfeebled

---

62. Spicq, 2:396, indicates that "peaceful fruit" signifies deliverance from outward troubles and peace with God.

63. According to Spicq, 2:396, when applied to the athletic contest εἰρηνικόν ("peaceful") evokes the idea of the rest and security of the athlete after running the course or coming through the bloody contest. He says that δικαιοσύνης denotes virtue, moral rectitude, union with God, and especially eternal blessedness.

64. Note the διό ("therefore") at the beginning of v. 12. See Spicq, 2:396.

65. Weiss, 658, says that the writer returns to the athletic sphere of v. 1. Montefiore, 222, refers to Philo, *Prelim. Studies* 164 and Sir 2:12 for similar descriptions of exhaustion.

knees."[66] In face of stiff opposition from the unbelieving world, the boxer has all but fallen — his hands have dropped and his knees have begun to buckle. The pastor calls on his hearers to straighten up, put up their proverbial dukes, and continue the fight. They must not surrender through discouragement to the tough resistance of a hostile, unbelieving world.

The pastor draws on the rich resources of the OT in his formulation of these exhortations. "Straighten the drooping hands and the enfeebled knees" recalls Isa 35:3-4;[67] "make straight paths for your feet" echoes Prov 4:26.[68] Both passages acquire a more profound significance through the work of Christ. In Isa 35:3-4 God called for "the drooping hands and enfeebled knees" to become strong because he was coming to deliver his people and take them back over a "holy way" (Isa 35:8) to "Zion" (Isa 35:10). In Hebrews, God has already come in Jesus and opened the "new and living way" (Heb 10:20) to the heavenly Zion (Heb 12:22). Thus God's people have much greater reason to reject discouragement.

Since Jesus has opened this way to "Zion," the pastor's hearers should resist the world in order to "make straight paths with" their "feet" to that heavenly City. In light of the quotation from Prov 3:11-12 above, it is no surprise that the pastor draws these words from the wise man's instructions to

66. παρειμένας ("drooping," from παρίημι) and παραλελυμένα ("enfeebled," "undone," from παραλύω) are perfect participles, emphasizing the present condition of extreme weakness and exhaustion felt by a boxer about to fall. See Spicq, 2:396.

67. The underlined portion of the text below highlights the similarity between the Greek of Heb 12:12 and Isa 35:3-4: Διὸ τὰς παρειμένας χεῖρας καὶ τὰ παραλελυμένα γόνατα ἀνορθώσατε (Heb 12:12, "Therefore the drooping hand and the enfeebled knees make straight"). ἰσχύσατε, χεῖρες ἀνειμέναι καὶ γόνατα παραλελυμένα, παρακαλέσατε, οἱ ὀλιγόψυχοι τῇ διανοίᾳ, ἰσχύσατε, μὴ φοβεῖσθε, ἰδοὺ ὁ θεὸς ἡμῶν κρίσιν ἀνταποδίδωσιν καὶ ἀνταποδώσει, αὐτὸς ἥξει καὶ σώσει ἡμᾶς (LXX Isa 35:3-4, "Be strong, you weak hands and feeble knees. Give comfort, you who are faint of heart and mind! Be strong, do not fear! Look, our God is repaying judgment; yes, he will repay; he himself will come and save us"). Hebrews substitutes παρειμένας ("enfeebled") for the closely related ἀνειμέναι of the LXX. In the LXX it is the "hands" (χεῖρες) and "knees" (γόνατα) rather than their owners who are addressed with the exhortation. Thus, they are in the vocative case instead of the accusative, and come before the participles that modify them. Cf. Sir 25:23.

68. The underlined portion of the texts below highlights the similarity between the Greek of Heb 12:13 and the LXX of Prov 4:26: καὶ τροχιὰς ὀρθὰς ποιεῖτε τοῖς ποσὶν ὑμῶν, ἵνα μὴ τὸ χωλὸν ἐκτραπῇ, ἰαθῇ δὲ μᾶλλον (Heb 12:13, "and make straight paths with your feet, in order that what is lame may not turn aside but rather be healed). ὀρθὰς τροχιὰς ποίει σοῖς ποσὶν καὶ τὰς ὁδούς σου κατεύθυνε (Prov 4:26, "Make straight tracks for your feet and straighten your ways"). The second person singular imperative of Proverbs, "make" (ποίει), has become the second person plural (ποιεῖτε) in Hebrews. Thus, the singular possessive adjective σοῖς ("your") has been replaced by the article τοῖς ("the") and the plural possessive pronoun ὑμῶν ("your").

629

his "son" in Prov 4:26. Yet through the work of Christ the pastor can see further down this path than the sage of old. The wise man was concerned that his "son" not turn aside; the pastor that his hearers persevere until the end. The wise man encouraged his "son" not to swerve from a life of moral rectitude because it was the way to enjoy the good "life" in this present world. The pastor urges his hearers as the "sons and daughters of God" to persevere in unfailing faithfulness in order to reach their goal in the eternal life of the heavenly City. The pastor's exhortation encompasses all that was in the wise man's words but puts them in eternal perspective.[69]

The instrumental "with your feet" is better suited to the context than a dative of indirect object, "for your feet."[70] To make straight paths "for your feet" would be to build a straight road to follow. To make straight paths "with your feet" is to walk in a straight line.[71] The road to the heavenly City has already been prepared by Jesus (10:19-25). If his hearers pursue their course straight to the heavenly City, they will by their example confirm this road for any who are "lame." The neuter singular "lame" makes this a very general expression. It refers to any in the community who are weak.[72] If the pastor's hearers "beat a straight path" to the heavenly City, then those who are weak will not be "turned aside" by their bad example but "healed" and enabled to persevere through the model thus established by their brothers and sisters.[73] The pastor's desire that his hearers show concern for the perseverance of all

69. *Pace* Grässer, 3:281, the path that the pastor would have hearers pursue until they reach their goal includes the moral rectitude of Prov 4:26. After all, "sin" is the impediment the runner must discard (12:1-2). See Koester, 530-31; O'Brien, 471, n. 141.

70. Lane, 2:427; *pace* Spicq, 2:396-97, and Westcott, 404-5. *Pace* Lane, the instrumental is also appropriate in the original context of Prov 4:26.

71. τροχιά is not restricted to a "path" or "road" but can be used for the course of life that one follows. See Prov 2:15 in both Brenton and the Oxford translation of the LXX. It is parallel to a person's "steps" (πορείας) in Prov 4:27b.

72. Attridge's claim (365) that the neuter "lame" refers to the weakness of the community as a whole rather than to individual members is, in Bénétreau's (2:184) words, "excessive."

73. For ἐκτραπῇ as "turn aside" see 1 Tim 1:6; 5:15; 6:20; 2 Tim 4:4. In 1 Tim 1:6 and 5:15 it refers to apostasy, as it does here in Hebrews. However, Attridge (365, n. 105) and many others (such as Bruce, 348; Ellingworth, 659-60; Lane, 2:428; and, among recent commentators, Mitchell, 274, and O'Brien, 471) contend that the medical meaning, "be put out of joint," is more appropriate here in light of the reference to being healed. However, Hughes is correct when he contends that "turn aside" is more suited to the imagery of the race: "The objection . . . that healing has no connection with straying is readily answered by observing that this is beside the point since it has a perfectly appropriate connection with lameness" (Hughes, 535). See also Weiss, 659, and those cited by Attridge, 365, n. 104 (Riggenbach, Spicq, Michel, and Buchanan). The passive may imply that God will be the one who heals them, thus enabling them to overcome their difficulties.

in their fellowship surfaces again, and will receive further attention in vv. 14-15 below.[74]

The pastor began this discussion of the present suffering of God's people by urging his hearers to "run the race set before them" (12:1). He ends by exhorting them to "make straight paths with their feet" (12:13) to the heavenly City. In order to run this race with endurance, they must resist opposition and discouragement by straightening their drooping hands and crumpling knees (12:12). After all, the opposition they have faced does not compare with what Jesus endured (12:3, 4). Furthermore, the suffering they are enduring for their faithfulness is God's fatherly discipline, demonstrating their filial relation to him and reinforcing their obedience in preparation for life in the heavenly City. The examples of the past (11:1-40) only reinforce the fact that running this race with endurance is to be the consuming concern of God's people in the present.

2. Don't Sell Your Birthright, as Esau Did (12:14-17)

14 *Together pursue peace and holiness, without which no one will see the Lord.* 15 *Pursue these goals by watching out lest anyone fall short of the grace of God; lest any root of bitterness springing up cause trouble and through it many be defiled;* 16 *lest there be anyone immoral or godless like Esau, who sold his own birthright for a single meal.* 17 *For you know that even afterward when he was seeking to inherit the blessing he was rejected, for he did not find a place of repentance, although he sought it [the blessing] with tears.*

Amid present suffering (12:1-13) the faithful find great joy in the privileges now theirs through Christ (12:18-24). The pastor, who has been addressing their sufferings with encouragement, introduces the description of their privileges in 12:18-24 with the warning of 12:14-17. Since the beginning of this history in 11:1 he has been urging his hearers to join the faithful of old in perseverance until they reach the heavenly City. He now warns them lest they disregard the "great salvation" (2:3) that is theirs in Christ and fall away. This emphasis on warning reaches its climax at the conclusion of the temporal history of God's people in the Judgment of 12:25-29. While suffering requires encouragement, privileges call for caution lest they be squandered.

This transition from the suffering/encouragement of vv. 1-13 to the

74. Cf. 3:12; 4:1, 11; 10:24 (Weiss, 660). Fixation on the opposition can engender this discouragement of weaker members of the community and lead to the "evil heart of unbelief" against which the pastor warned in 3:12.

631

privileges/warning of vv. 14-24 is mirrored in the structure of vv. 14-17.[1] Verse 14 consists of a second person plural imperative like those in vv. 12-13: "Together pursue peace and holiness, without which no one will see the Lord." The idea of pursuit echoes the imagery of the racecourse from 12:3, 13. One might argue that pursuing "peace" and "holiness" is the way to strengthen "drooping hands" and "enfeebled knees" (v. 12) and to "make straight paths with your feet" (v. 13).[2] On the other hand, the qualifying participle at the beginning of v. 15, "looking out," introduces three warnings that occupy the rest of this section — "lest anyone" (v. 15a); "lest any root" (v. 15b); "lest anyone" (v. 16).[3] Verse 17 explains the seriousness of the third and most somber warning. As we will see, this threefold warning is based on the threat of judgment for covenant violation in Deut 29:15-20, and thus anticipates the following contrast between Sinai (vv. 18-21) and Zion (vv. 22-24).

This crucial warning passage is, however, much more than a transition from 12:1-13 to 12:18-24. It is the climactic counterpart of 2:1-4 that brings the warning begun in that passage to final clarity and intensity in light of the intervening argument. The pastor began in 2:1-4 by cautioning against "drifting" and against "neglect" of God's provision for salvation in Christ. In the case of Esau that neglect has become outright disregard for the things of God

---

1. *Pace* Guthrie, who thinks that this transitional section is more closely related to what has gone before than to what follows. Guthrie finds a high-level cohesion shift between 12:17 and 12:18, but only a median-level shift between 12:13 and 12:14. However, the shifts he suggests in the topic, temporal, actor, subject, verb person, and verb number cohesion fields are inaccurate. First, the pastor abandons imagery that specifically refers to boxing or racing between vv. 13 and 14. Second, as noted in the text above, the shift from the promise of reward to the threat of loss occurs between vv. 13 and 14 and continues through 12:29. Third, comparison between believers under the New Covenant and God's people under the Old begins at v. 14, not at v. 18! The dependence of Heb 12:14-17 on Deut 29:15-20 makes this comparison clear. Fourth, the new actor, Esau, is related by his actions to those who disobey before Sinai (vv. 18-21). His rejection of his "birthright" (πρωτοτόκια) may connect him with the sonship of 12:1-13 (Guthrie, *Structure,* 145, n. 57), but it clearly anticipates Christians as "firstborn" (πρωτοτόκων) in 12:23. Fifth, the temporal reference is essentially present from 12:1 through 12:25. Note the hortatory subjunctive in 12:1 and the present or aorist second person plural imperatives in 12:3, 7, 12, 13, 14, 25. The second person plural perfect indicatives in 12:18 and 22 (προσεληλύθατε) offer no exception because they too describe the present situation of the hearers. Reference to Esau does not make the temporal frame of vv. 14-17 past any more than reference to Sinai or Moses gives a past reference to vv. 18-21. Finally, as is obvious from the previous point, the second person plural dominates 12:1-25. The only one of Guthrie's cohesion fields that really changes between vv. 17 and 18 is the spatial.

2. Cf. deSilva, 456.

3. Thus, the second person plural present imperative διώκετε ("pursue") in v. 14 is qualified by the participle ἐπισκοποῦντες ("seeing to it") at the beginning of v. 15. In turn, this participle introduces the three warning μή τις ("lest any") clauses in vv. 15 and 16.

and a positive preference for the things of this world. He is the foil of the faithful described in 11:1-40, both the embodiment of, and worse than, the disobedient wilderness generation of 3:7-19. While that generation was intimidated primarily by the threat of an unbelieving world (3:7-19), Esau was drawn into apostasy by his love for the world. It is especially instructive to compare him with that most courageous hero of old, Moses (11:24-26), and with "the Pioneer and Perfecter of the faith, Jesus" (12:1-3). Moses rejected the "temporary" pleasures and advantages of Egypt because he kept his eyes on the eternal reward; Christ endured the cross "for the sake of" eternal "joy"; but Esau despised the promise of eternal blessing "for the sake of" the earthly pleasure afforded by one meal. Esau shows us that persistent neglect of the things of God leads to a love for the transitory pleasures of this world that is perhaps more culpable than disobedience due to intimidation. The pastor's use of Esau as the ultimate example of apostasy is as strategic as was his use of Rahab (11:31) as the final example of faith. If she showed the irrelevance of one's background for faith, he shows that those who reject Christ return not to the God of Abraham, Isaac, and Jacob, but to the one who rejected that God.[4] Furthermore, in this crucial passage the pastor's long-standing concern that his hearers show mutual concern for the integrity and perseverance of the whole community reaches full bloom (cf. 3:12-14; 4:1-2; 10:24-25).

14 Nothing could reveal this concern for their common life more than the pastor's opening exhortation: "Together with all pursue peace and holiness, without which no one will see the Lord." This exhortation echoes Ps 34:15, and thus it has a familiar and authoritative ring in the hearers' ears.[5] "Holiness" has been given to them through the work of Christ (see the comments on 10:10, 14). They belong to God and have been cleansed from "dead works" (9:14) so that they can enter God's presence. His laws have been written on their hearts (10:15-18). The result of that holiness is the "peace," harmony, and wholeness of their common life that comes from living by faith in God's promises and power (cf. v. 11 above).[6] Still, both "peace" and "holiness" must be pursued. The hearers must not take these blessings for granted, but give diligence to preserve and cultivate them lest the harmony of their community be fragmented through rebellion. We might translate this present imperative: "keep on pursuing peace and holiness."[7] According to proper Greek grammar the phrase "with all" qualifies "pursue" and not "peace" —

4. See Gordon, 177.
5. Ps 33:14 in the LXX (MT 34:14) reads, ζήτησον εἰρήνην καὶ δίωξον αὐτήν ("let him seek peace and pursue it").
6. Thus, this "peace" and "holiness" are present realities rather than blessings received only at the end (deSilva, 459).
7. Johnson, 324.

"Together with all pursue peace" instead of "Pursue peace with all."[8] Popular Greek usage would allow this second interpretation, familiar to English readers.[9] However, the first is to be preferred not only because the pastor normally uses Greek with elegance and care, but because it fits most appropriately with his concern in the immediate context (cf. vv. 15-16) for the common life of the community. "Together with all [fellow believers] keep pursuing peace. . . ." The diligent quest to maintain their common harmony is the urgent and joint task of all.[10] The pastor puts great emphasis on the word "peace" by placing it first in the Greek sentence: "Peace keep pursuing together with all. . . ." "The church is the eschatological outpost of heaven and should be a dynamic reflection of that peace which is a mark of God's rule."[11]

The peace of the community must be maintained by diligent pursuit of the God-given, Christ-provided "holiness" that is its source.[12] Defilement through rebellion ruptures this wholeness and harmony. Perseverance in this God-given "holiness" is the only way to "see the Lord."[13] Although on earth the faithful of old did not enjoy the access to God now available through Christ, they kept the eyes of faith on the "invisible" God whose presence they

8. μετά ("with") followed by the genitive πάντων ("all") indicates accompaniment. Cf. 2 Tim 2:22. "Peace" with someone would normally be expressed by πρός, not μετά. See Lane, 2:438b; Ellingworth, 661-62.

9. For this second meaning, see μετὰ πάντων ("with all") in Rom 12:18 (cf. 1 Kgs 22:45 LXX). deSilva, 457-58, neglects the force of the immediate context when he opts for this interpretation.

10. Thus "with all" refers to all members of the believing community rather than to all people in general (Lane, 2:438b; Ellingworth, 662; Weiss, 661; Koester, 540). *Pace* deSilva, 457-58; Johnson, 323, Bruce, 348; Westcott, 405, and others who would extend the meaning of "all" to include the unbelieving world. It is true that in 1 Pet 3:11 the writer encourages persecuted believers to live in peace with unbelieving society. In Hebrews, however, the context indicates that the author is concerned with the harmony of the believing community. This is certainly true if we take "together with all" as qualifying "pursue." The pastor is not urging his hearers to join with unbelievers in pursuing peace (Ellingworth, 662).

11. O'Brien, 472.

12. "Within the community of faith, there is to be no separation of peace and holiness. If 'peace' binds the community together as the achievement of Christ, 'holiness' is that quality which identifies the community as the possession of Christ" (Lane, 2:450).

13. Some have suggested that ἁγιασμός ("holiness," 12:14) refers to a process of moral development since words ending in -μος often describe an action or process. However, "holiness" in Hebrews is always the gift of God through the work of Christ rather than a process of moral development (10:10, 14; cf. Lane, 2:450). Yet this action/process word is most appropriate in the immediate context. The "holiness" in question is not merely a one-time gift, but instead a continual living in the cleansing from sin and resultant access to God provided by Christ for the community of the faithful. This understanding is confirmed by the interpretation of vv. 15-16 given below.

would enter at journey's end. The faithful since Christ enjoy a present access to God, so beautifully described in vv. 22-24 below, but they still, by faith, keep their eyes fixed on "Jesus" at God's right hand (12:2; cf. 2:9; 8:1) in anticipation of final entrance into the divine presence, when the faithful of all time will "see" God.[14] The pastor's focus here on the ultimate vision of God fits well with his concern for perseverance.

15-16 For ease of reading we have divided the long sentence that runs from v. 14 through v. 16 by adding "Pursue these blessings" at the beginning of v. 15 — "Pursue these blessings by watching out. . . ." The hearers are to "pursue peace and holiness" by "watching out" lest that holiness be violated through the unfaithfulness of any member, and thus that peace be shattered.[15] These verses clearly show that the hearers are not called to "pursue" something they do not have, or even to perfect something they have already received. They "pursue" peace and holiness by diligently guarding what they have received through Christ from threat of loss.[16] This exhortation for the community to pursue peace and holiness becomes a warning for mutual vigilance.[17] Three "lest any" clauses in vv. 15-16 progressively reveal the nature and dire significance of that which threatens the peace and holiness of the community. The first two of these clauses echo warnings drawn from the example of the wilderness generation in 3:7–4:11.[18] Esau, who appears in the third clause, is a fitting companion for that disobedient congregation.

The pastor has drawn inspiration for vv. 15-17 from the warning against apostasy found in Deut 29:15-20. Deut 29:17 contains two "lest any"

---

14. In this verse "Lord" probably refers to God (7:21; 8:2, 8, 10, 11; 10:16, 30; 12:5, 6), though it could refer to Christ (1:10; 2:3; 7:14; 13:20). It makes little difference since Christ is seated at God's right hand (8:1, etc.). Cf. Attridge, 367.

15. ἐπισκοποῦντες ("watching out for") qualifies διώκετε ("pursue") and could thus be translated as an imperative itself (Lane, 2:451; Weiss, 662). It seems better, however to take it as instrumental, describing how one "pursues" peace and holiness. Such a rendering does not denude it of imperatival force — the pastor urgently desires his hearers to "watch out for."

16. ἐπισκοποῦντες μή ("watch that not") is "an expression of apprehension." The following subjunctives in vv. 15-16 denote that about which the author is concerned, and thus what he would have his hearers avoid. See Lane, 2:451; cf. Michel, 453; BDF §370(1).

17. Spicq, 2:399.

18. Compare μή τις ῥίζα πικρίας ἄνω φύουσα ἐνοχλῇ καὶ δι᾽ αὐτῆς μιανθῶσιν οἱ πολλοί (12:15b; "lest any bitter root springing up cause harm and through it many be defiled") with μήποτε ἔσται ἔν τινι ὑμῶν καρδία πονηρὰ ἀπιστίας ἐν τῷ ἀποστῆναι ἀπὸ θεοῦ ζῶντος (3:12; "lest there be in any of you an evil heart of unbelief in turning away from the living God") and μήποτε . . . δοκῇ τις ἐξ ὑμῶν ὑστερηκέναι (4:1; "lest any of you seem to have fallen short") with μή τις ὑστερῶν ἀπὸ τῆς χάριτος τοῦ θεοῦ (12:15a; "lest any of you fall short of the grace of God). Cf. Johnson, 324.

clauses like the three in Heb 12:15-17. The first clause in Hebrews has only a slight resemblance to the first Deuteronomy clause.[19] The second, however, is so close to Deut 29:17 LXX that it clearly substantiates the pastor's dependence upon this passage.[20] Deuteronomy contains no third "lest any" clause, but Deut 29:18-20 describes a person who deliberately flaunts the curses of the covenant against disobedience and goes his own way. God refuses to par-

---

19. Compare "lest any of you should come to lack the grace of God" (μή τις ὑστερῶν ἀπὸ τῆς χάριτος τοῦ θεοῦ, Heb 12:15) with "lest there be any among you man, or woman, or family, or tribe, whose heart has turned away from the Lord your God" (μή τίς ἐστιν ἐν ὑμῖν ἀνὴρ ἢ γυνὴ ἢ πατριὰ ἢ φυλή, τίνος ἡ διάνοια ἐξέκλινεν ἀπὸ κυρίου τοῦ θεοῦ ὑμῶν, Deut 29:17). Words identical in the Greek text of both passages are underlined.

20. Compare Heb 12:15b with both the LXX text of Deut 29:17b found in A (B corrected) and with the text as found in most manuscripts.

μή τις ῥίζα πικρίας ἄνω φύουσα ἐνοχλῇ (Heb 12:15b)
μή τίς ἐστιν ἐν ὑμῖν ῥίζα πικρίας ἄνω φύουσα ἐνοχλῇ (Deut 29:17 LXX, A text)
μή τίς ἐστιν ἐν ὑμῖν ῥίζα ἄνω φύουσα ἐν χολῇ καὶ πικρίᾳ (Deut 29:17 LXX, most manuscripts)
"lest any root of bitterness springing up cause trouble" (Heb 12:15b)
"lest there be among you any root of bitterness springing up cause trouble" (Deut 29:17 LXX, A text)
"lest there be among you any root springing up in gall and bitterness" (most manuscripts of Deut 29:17 LXX)

The text of Hebrews is in complete agreement with the A LXX text except for the omission of the underlined phrase ἐστιν ἐν ὑμῖν ("there be among you"). It has several other differences with the text found in most LXX manuscripts. These differences are represented by the second underlined phrase above, ἐν χολῇ καὶ πικρίᾳ ("in gall and bitterness"). First, instead of ἐν χολῇ ("in gall") Hebrews reads ἐνοχλῇ ("cause trouble"). Second, instead of the locative πικρίᾳ ("in bitterness") Hebrews has the genitive πικρίας ("of bitterness") qualifying ῥίζα ("root") — "root of bitterness." Weiss, 664-65, has contended convincingly that the text represented by the majority of LXX manuscripts is original and that Hebrews has adapted this passage by introducing all of these changes. The key to his argument is the fact that the phrase ἐστιν ἐν ὑμῖν ("there be among you") fits only very awkwardly with the following finite verb, ἐνοχλῇ ("cause trouble") in the A text of Deut 29:17. Thus the A manuscripts appear to represent a text that has been partially conformed to Hebrews by changing ἐν χολῇ ("in gall") to ἐνοχλῇ ("cause trouble") and by adjusting the significance of πικρία ("bitterness") but not yet by the omission of ἐστιν ἐν ὑμῖν ("there be among you"). Although under the influence of the LXX a few manuscripts of Hebrews read ἐν χολῇ ("in gall"), ἐνοχλῇ ("cause trouble") is certainly original because it is well suited to the context and to the author's purpose. The originality of ἐνοχλῇ ("cause trouble") in Hebrews is confirmed by deSilva's (457) observation that it is the opposite of pursuing peace just as being "defiled" is the opposite of holiness. It is possible that the τίς of Deut 29:17 should be translated as an interrogative ("who?") instead of as an indefinite ("any"). However, we have retained the translation "any" above for ease of comparison with Hebrews.

don this person, just as Esau finds no place of repentance. The "curses" (Deut 29:19) will fall on him, just as Esau fails to receive the "blessing" in Heb 12:17. Thus, the example of Esau introduced in the third "lest any" clause (found in Heb 12:16) parallels this Deuteronomic description of final condemnation on one who rejects God's covenant. In Deuteronomy Moses warns God's people that abandoning the covenant by turning from God to idols is apostasy. The pastor warns his hearers that abandoning the New Covenant by turning away from the work of Christ is the contemporary equivalent of such idolatry.

The two "lest any" clauses in Heb 12:15 reach a climax in the third "lest any" clause in v. 16: failure to appropriate God's grace leads to a rebellious attitude that results in open apostasy. The first clause, "lest anyone fall short of the grace of God," gives the cause of apostasy.[21] This is the "grace" of God provided by the high-priestly work of Christ, through which God's people are cleansed from sin, brought into God's presence, and enabled to live in victory despite opposition (cf. 4:16). This "grace" is nothing less than the "great salvation" of 2:3. Since the race of faith is not run in one's own strength, "falling short" of this grace is certain failure. One can "fall short" of Christ's provision from lassitude, from discouragement at the rigors of the race, or through attraction to the rewards of an unbelieving world.[22] However, such falling short of God's provision leads naturally to abandoning God and rejecting his grace. Thus, this phrase makes an appropriate transition from the theme of endurance to that of apostasy. These two are opposites without middle ground. To fail to endure inevitably leads to apostasy.

Nature abhors a vacuum. The absence of grace allows a "bitter root" or "shoot" to spring up in the community of God's people.[23] This poisonous "root" is either a rebellious person or the heart of unbelief and stubborn rebellion (3:12-13) that motivates such a person. Just as a few people turned the wilderness generation away from God, even so one such rebellious person may "cause" great "trouble." By example and influence he or she may lead "many" aside so that they become "defiled." In fact, with "the many" the pastor may fear for the defilement of the whole community, as was the case with the wilderness generation.[24] Such defilement is the stubborn, disobedi-

---

21. ὑστερῶν "falling short," may not be particularly common in descriptions of a race, but it has the idea of lagging behind or falling short of the goal (BDAG, 1043-44, 5). Thus it reminds us of the race imagery used earlier.

22. *Pace* Lane, 2:453; but see Ellingworth, 663.

23. Although Ellingworth, 664, prefers the translation "shoot," Riggenbach, 404, believes the author is thinking of a poisonous "root" that causes sickness or death.

24. It is true that the pastor uses "the many" here because he wants to show the possible extent of the damage caused by one rebellious person (Attridge, 368). Yet "the many" can be used as a designation for the whole community (see Matt 24:12; Rom 5:15,

ent, rebellious abandonment of the cleansing from sin provided by Christ. The person who causes such "trouble" is not far from "crucifying for themselves the Son of God afresh" (6:6). Thus, abandonment of the "holiness" provided by Christ shatters the "peace" of the believing community as well. No wonder the pastor urges his hearers ancient and modern to be on their guard against such a tragedy.

The warning of Deut 29:15-20 reached its climax in the description of one who flaunts God's covenant. In the same way, this warning in Hebrews climaxes with "lest there be anyone immoral or godless like Esau." With the double description "immoral" and "godless" Esau becomes the epitome of apostasy, surpassing even the wilderness generation. There is little disagreement over the meaning of "godless." Godlessness is the opposite of the "holiness" God's people are to pursue through the life of faith.[25] It is living without the "godly fear" (5:7; 11:7; 12:28) of the faithful. The godless person is one who has received the promise of God but lives as if God's power were not real and his promises of reward were invalid (see Heb 11:6). This is exactly what Esau did when he "sold his own birthright for a single meal" (Gen 25:29-34). His birthright as the "firstborn" was the promise given Abraham of a people and an eternal heavenly City (Heb 11:9-10, 13-16). He surrendered this promise for the merest pittance of this world's goods — "one" little "meal." Thus, he treated God's power as insufficient to meet his need and God's promise of future blessing as worthless. If the people who lived by faith in chapter 11 were the heroes, Esau is their antithesis. To abandon Christ would be to spurn the one who fulfilled the promise Esau disregarded.

The term "immoral" has generated much discussion. This expression is normally used to describe sexual misconduct. The OT, however, never accuses Esau of sexual immorality. The only related condemnation he receives is the displeasure of his parents for marrying several Hittite wives (Gen 26:34-35). It is true that later tradition often described him as sexually promiscuous, perhaps because of his polygamous relationship with these pagan women.[26] Nevertheless, as we have seen in our study of chapter 11, Hebrews

---

19; 12:5; cf. 1QS 6:8-21; 7:3, 10-16). Here and in earlier passages (3:12-13; 10:24-25) the pastor expresses his deep concern for the common life of the whole congregation. See Weiss, 662.

25. ". . . to be *bébelos* ("profane") means precisely to be unconcerned with the demands of God's holiness (Lev 10:10; 21:9; Ezek 4:14; 21:25; 22:36; 3 Macc 2:14, 17; Philo, *Moses* 2.158; *Alleg. Interp.* 1.62; Josephus, *J.W.* 6.271; *Ant.* 15.20; 1 Tim 1:9; 4:7; 6:29; 2 Tim 2:16)" (Johnson, 324).

26. On the immorality of Esau see *Gen. Rab.* 63:9, 12 (commenting on Gen 25:27, 29); *Jub.* 25:1-8; *Targum Pseudo-Jonathan* (on Gen 25:27); and Philo, *Virtues* 208; *Sobriety* 26; *Sacrifices* 120; *Alleg. Interp.* 3.2; and *QG* 4.242. See also Thompson, 259-60; Attridge, 369, esp. n. 48; and Lane, 3:454-55.

rarely draws on such tradition.[27] Furthermore, the pastor makes no further comment concerning Esau's sexuality. This has led some commentators to argue that only the adjective "godless" describes Esau.[28] The pastor warns against an "immoral person" and against a "godless person" like Esau. This interpretation, however, is unlikely. It leaves "immoral" hanging without further comment. The two terms "immoral" and "godless" appear elsewhere as a pair, so it would be arbitrary to separate them here without compelling reason.[29] Others have suggested that "immoral" is used figuratively for one disloyal to the covenant.[30] The OT often uses adultery and sexual unfaithfulness as a figure of speech for covenant disloyalty.[31] However, such language is normally used in reference to the nation as a whole rather than as a description of an individual.[32] Close attention to the way the pastor describes the sin of Esau provides a solution for this problem. The wilderness generation refused to trust God's promise and power because they were intimidated by the unbelieving world. Esau, however, abandoned God not out of fear but from desire. He wanted the pleasures of this world. Furthermore, he paid for that pleasure like one who hires a prostitute — one could say he sold himself for that pleasure. And what a little pleasure it was. Moses considered "the reproach of Christ greater than" all the vast "pleasures" and "advantages" of Egypt (11:26). Esau sold his eternal "birthright" for nothing more than "one meal." Therefore, it is likely that the pastor has used the term "immoral" for Esau because he was controlled by bodily desire and because he "sold" the eternal for a pittance of the temporal.[33] The unbelievably small amount for which he bartered the eternal attests the great disdain with which he treated the things of God. Nothing less than both "immoral" and "godless" sufficiently describes this arch-apostate.

17 "For you know" indicates that the hearers were well aware of Esau's story. Thus, the pastor uses the Genesis account to demonstrate that the

27. Bénétreau, 2:188.

28. Westcott, 407-8.

29. See Philo, *Spec. Laws* 1.102 (cited by Attridge, 369, n. 45, and referenced by O'Brien, 475).

30. Johnson, 324. Cf. Lane, 2:451.

31. See Deut 31:16; Num 14:33; Hos 1:2; Jer 2:20. Cf. Attridge, 369, n. 50. This analogy is not surprising since idolatrous worship often involved sexually immoral practices. Hughes, 540, reminds us: "Licentiousness is the destroyer of holiness."

32. Riggenbach, 405-6. However, Riggenbach's further contention that Esau was not in a covenant is no barrier to his conduct's being an example of covenant violation. He was heir to the promise of Abraham and the covenant God had made with him (cf. the comment on 11:20).

33. Riggenbach, 405-6, mentions the etymological meaning of πόρνος as one who sells himself for shameful purposes.

fate of this godless person was tragic and irreversible. The story begins with the sale of Esau's birthright, mentioned in v. 16 above and recorded in Gen 25:29-34. Because of this utterly godless act, he irrevocably forfeited his right "to inherit the blessing" that God had given Abraham and that was latter inherited by Isaac, Jacob, Jacob's children, Joseph's sons (Heb 11:20-22), and all the faithful who followed them.[34] Gen 27:1-40 records this failure. At the time when the blessing was given, he sought "to inherit" it, but he was "rejected."

The affirmation, "he found no place of repentance," is in accord with the pastor's earlier warnings (cf. 6:4-8; 10:26-31), and is crucial to his desire for the perseverance of his hearers. It is very unlikely that "repentance" should be reduced to "change," as some have suggested, arguing that Esau was not able to "change" Isaac's mind once Isaac had blessed Jacob.[35] "Place of repentance" is virtually a technical term that refers to the opportunity for repentance in a moral or religious sense.[36] Esau could not go back and undo what he had done when he sold his birthright to Jacob.[37] The godless and profane way in which he rejected the promise of God that was his birthright foreshadowed the way in which the pastor's hearers were in danger of definitively and publicly spurning the fulfillment of that promise in Christ. Such rejection of God's covenant excludes one from the means of salvation and thus the possibility of repentance.

It is important, however, to understand the next phrase, "although he sought it with tears." In Greek the word "it" is feminine and could refer either to "repentance" or "blessing," both of which are feminine, but not to the word for "place," which is masculine.[38] It is true that the word for "repentance" is closer.[39] Yet if the pastor were referring to repentance, one would

34. On the theme of "inheritance" see 1:2, 14; 6:17; 9:15; 11:7. The pastor assumes that Esau's failure to inherit in Gen 27:1-40 was the result of having sold his birthright in 25:29-34. This connection is logical, though not explicitly stated in the Genesis text. What would selling one's "birthright" mean but giving up the privileges of being the firstborn, including the blessing appropriate for that position? On this interpretation Isaac's intention to bless Esau in Gen 27:1-40 was illegitimate.

35. Spicq, 2:402, suggests this interpretation. Cf. Bénétreau, 2:189-90; Montefiore, 225-26. Although μετανοία ("repentance") can mean to change one's mind, there is no linguistic evidence of its being used of one person trying to change another's mind. See Lane, 2:440r; Ellingworth, 668.

36. For the phrase τόπος μετανοίας ("place of repentance") as a set expression meaning "opportunity to repent" see Wis 12:10; *1 Clem.* 7:5; *2 Clem.* 8:2; *4 Ezra* 7:82; 9:12 (cited, along with other references, in Lane, 2:440r). See also Koester, 533, and O'Brien 476, n. 163.

37. See Riggenbach, 409-10, and Moffatt, 212.

38. Thus, the pronoun αὐτήν ("it" — "though he sought it with tears") could refer to either εὐλογίαν ("blessing") or μετανοίας ("repentance"), but not to τόπον ("place"),

39. For this reason Attridge, 370, holds that "it" refers to "repentance." Attridge

expect the pronoun to agree with the masculine "place."[40] Furthermore, as Westcott notes, the word "seek" fits well with "blessing" but poorly with "repentance."[41] Esau did not seek a "place of repentance" with tears.[42] He sought the "blessing" with tears.[43] "It was his loss, not his profanity, that he mourned."[44] This understanding is in accord with the OT text, according to which Esau tries desperately to retrieve the blessing but says nothing of repenting of his own folly. It is also in accord with the earlier warning passages, which record nothing about an apostate seeking repentance (3:7-19; 6:4-8; 10:26-31). In fact, such people continue to "crucify the Son of God afresh" (6:6). In this Esau was much like the wilderness generation. After their rejection at Kadesh they did not repent — they just tried to go up and occupy the land on their own (Num 14:39-45). There can be no doubt, then, that those whom Hebrews describes as apostate have deliberately spurned and utterly rejected the grace of God, and have thus put themselves outside the benefits of Christ's sacrifice. They have been "rejected" by God.[45] Yet this rejection is reflected in a life of callousness that does not desire repentance or seek to turn from its rebellious ways. Thus, any who are truly concerned for their own salvation have not followed in the steps of Esau.

Thus, the pastor has answered the question posed in his opening exhortation: "How shall we escape if we neglect such a great salvation?" (2:3). If one who is a part of God's people neglects the provision Christ has made and falls short of the grace he provides, it is very easy for a rebellious, unbelieving heart to "spring up." This type of heart leads to open disobedience, distrust, and disregard for God — like that of Esau — and poses a great dan-

---

fails to see that Esau's seeking the "blessing" rather than a "place of repentance" is not only in accord with the OT account, but fits more appropriately with the other examples of apostasy in Hebrews and with the pastor's overall purpose.

40. Lane, 2:440t. There is no evidence that confirms Weiss's (666-68) assertion that Hebrews is drawing on an exegetical tradition that pictured Esau as seeking repentance.

41. Westcott, 409.

42. The LXX omits the reference to tears that is in the MT, but it does say that Esau "cried out with a loud cry and great bitterness" (Gen 27:34). *Jub.* 26:33; Josephus, *Ant.* 1.275; and Philo, *QG* 4.233, describe Esau as crying when he heard Jacob had received the blessing. Cf. Koester, 533.

43. Bruce, 351; Lane, 2:440t. Cf. NRSV, "though he sought the blessing with tears." Lane argues that the contrast is not between "seeking for" (ἐκζητήσας) and "finding" (εὗρεν) the place of repentance, but between "begging for" (ἐκζητήσας) the blessing and being "rejected" (ἀπεδοκιμάσθη).

44. Hughes, 541, n. 148, although Hughes thinks it makes little difference what the antecedent of αὐτήν ("it") might be.

45. Esau's rejection by Isaac was confirmation of his rejection by God (*pace* Mitchell, 278).

ger to the believing community. Those who follow such a course will indeed not "escape" the judgment of God.

3. God's Firstborn Enter His Presence through the Exalted Jesus (12:18-24)

18 *For you have not come to something that can be touched and to something that has been burning, to a fire, and to darkness, and to gloom, and to storm,* 19 *and to the sound of a trumpet, and to a voice of words, which those who heard begged that no word be added to them.* 20 *For they were not able to bear what was commanded: "If even an animal touches the mountain, it shall be stoned."* 21 *And so terrifying was the appearance that Moses said, "I am full of fear and trembling."*

22 *But you have come to Mount Zion, and to the City of the living God, heavenly Jerusalem, and to myriads of angels, a festal gathering,* 23 *and to the assembly of the firstborn enrolled in heaven, and to a Judge who is God of all, and to spirits of righteous people made perfect,* 24 *and to the Mediator of the New Covenant, Jesus, and to blood of sprinkling that speaks better than Abel.*

After each of his previous warnings (6:4-8; 10:26-31), the pastor assured his hearers of his confidence in their continued perseverance (6:9-12; 10:32-39). After the warning in 12:14-17, he hurries to assure them that they, unlike Esau, "have not come" into a state of judgment (12:18-21).[1] Through Christ "they have come" into a state of blessing (12:22-24) that anticipates their eternal destiny (12:25-29).

It is important to remember that there are two aspects to the pastor's contention that God's revelation on Sinai has been fulfilled in Christ. First, by providing an all-sufficient means of atonement Christ has shown the continuing validity of the old as a foreshadowing of this fulfillment, but done away with the practice of its sacrifices. Second, the judgment pronounced on sin by that first revelation continues valid with even greater intensity in light of this fulfillment in Christ.[2] The pastor, who has thoroughly established the first of these two related aspects, is concerned here almost solely with the second — with Sinai as a picture of judgment on those who have rejected

---

1. The γάρ ("for") in v. 18 connects vv. 18-24 with the warning of vv. 14-17 and with the example of Esau (Lane, 2:459; Weiss, 669; Pfitzner, 183; but *pace* Ellingworth, 670).

2. See the section entitled *Second, the Intensified Urgency of Obedience* on pp. 46-47.

Christ. He is not presenting Sinai (12:18-21) and Zion (12:22-24) as a simple contrast between the old and new religious orders, or between the times before and after Christ.[3] He is not arguing from a "lesser" Sinai to a "greater" Zion.[4] He is not describing Sinai as either the ineffective that foreshadows the effective,[5] or as an "earthly" copy of a heavenly reality.[6] The pastor is not pitting Judaism against Christianity.[7] As modern readers we will miss the pastor's intention and fail to grasp the effective way in which he has structured his argument if we do not see that he is describing two present possibilities for the professed people of God.[8] He is not concerned with old and new, before and after, but with belief and unbelief, with apostasy and faithfulness, with judgment and blessing. Sinai depicts the terrible exclusion of the apostate from the presence of God;[9] Zion, the present joy of the faithful in the divine presence. This grand contrast between Sinai and Zion brings to a con-

3. Lane, 2:461, is typical of those who make such a comparison when he says, "It should be recognized that the writer compares two covenants under the imagery of two mountains in order to contrast the distance that separated the worshiper from God under the old covenant with the unrestricted access to God under the new covenant" Cf. Mitchell, 284. Hughes, 542, speaks of "the contrast between the imperfect and the perfect, the temporary and the permanent. . . ."

4. *Pace* both Johnson (329) and Koester (549), who fall into this trap.

5. Failure to see this difference is the fatal flaw in Kiwoong Son's attempt to use 12:18-24 as the hermeneutical key to all the contrasts between the old and the new in Hebrews (Kiwoong Son, *Zion Symbolism in Hebrews: Hebrews 12:18-24 as a Hermeneutical Key to the Epistle* [Paternoster Biblical Monographs; Waynesboro, GA: Paternoster, 2005]).

6. As contended by Thompson, *Christian Philosophy,* 46; Thompson, 261-62; Johnson, 329; Weiss, 671; and others. There is no correspondence between the details of the Sinai and Zion descriptions. See Hughes, 545; Riggenbach, 414; and Lane, 2:461.

7. *Pace* Gordon, 179.

8. J. M. Casey, "Christian Assembly in Hebrews: A Fantasy Island?" *Theology Digest* 30 (1982): 332-33, is correct when she says that 12:18-24 presents the hearers "with two scenes — two options as it were. Will they choose Sinai or Sion?" Even Weiss, 672-73, admits that the author constructs the description of fearful exclusion in vv. 18-21 in order to highlight the glad acceptance of vv. 22-24. Hebrews, however, is not indulging in mere rhetoric. Verses 18-21 set vv. 22-24 in bold relief because they describe a genuine alternative. By making this statement Weiss unwittingly concedes that the relationship between these two descriptions is not one of less-to-greater or copy-to-original but of opposites.

9. However, the pastor is not describing Sinai without God, as Casey, "Christian Assembly," 332-33, contends (see also Weiss, 671, and Albert Vanhoye, "Le Dieu de la nouvelle alliance dans l'Épître aux Hébreux," in *Le notion biblique de Dieu,* vol. 41, ed. J. Coppens [Bibliotheca ephemeridum theologicarum lovaniensium 41; Gembloux: Duculot, 1976], 320-21). The awesome phenomena betoken his presence, but also his inaccessibility.

clusion the statement in 10:39 with which the pastor introduced this history of the faithful. Since the pastor's hearers do not belong to the apostates characterized by "drawing back for destruction" (10:39), they do not face the judgment depicted in vv. 18-21. They are, instead, among those who persevere in faithful obedience "for the preservation of the soul" (10:39), and thus "have come" to the Mount pictured in vv. 22-24.

Thus, the pastor's appeal for his hearers to persevere by appropriating the salvation Christ has provided reaches a climactic synthesis in this passage.[10] His previous warnings achieve full intensity in the picture drawn from Sinai (vv. 18-21); his words of encouragement culminate in the description of Zion (vv. 22-24).[11] Furthermore, it is Christ as Pioneer, High Priest, and Mediator of the New Covenant who, by his fulfillment of the old order, has provided access to the blessings of Zion for the people of God. By so doing he has also exacerbated the peril of Sinai. Thus, both the pastor's theological exposition and his exhortation are here forged into one powerful appeal.

Comparison with 1:5-14 confirms this interpretation of 12:18-24. In both passages God's people are gathered around a mountain to hear the voice of God.[12] In both, God's ultimate revelation in his eternal and now-exalted Son is compared and contrasted with his revelation at Sinai.[13] The first passage (1:5-14) laid a foundation for the pastor's argument; the second (12:18-24) brings it to a conclusion. The first (1:5-14) established the fact that God's revelation in his Son was superior because of the agent or medium of its disclosure. On the basis of this fact alone the pastor affirms that the judgment pronounced by the Sinai revelation was even more certain to fall on those who rejected its fulfillment in the Son (2:1-4). In the intervening chapters the pastor has described the content and quality of this revelation as the "great salvation" revealed and provided by the Son. Thus, in 12:18-24 he is able to describe with greater accuracy and intensity the nature both of that judgment

10. Many have noted the climactic significance of this passage (Schierse, *Verheissung*, 171-72; A. Vögtle, "Das Neue Testament und die Zukunft des Kosmos: Hebr. 12:26f. und das Endschicksal des Kosmos," *Bibel und Leben* 10 [1969]: 76; Ellingworth, 669; O'Brien, 477). For a fuller list of those affirming the climactic nature of this passage, see Son, *Zion Symbolism*, 78, n. 3.

11. See Casey, "Christian Assembly," 332-33, and cf. Lane, 2:448.

12. See the comments on 1:5-14 and on 2:1-4, the introduction to 12:1-29 above (pp. 613-14), and the discussion of the rhetorical shape of Hebrews in the Introduction to this commentary (pp. 60-70). See also Son, *Zion Symbolism*, 111-23, for connections between 12:18-24 and 1:5-14.

13. Son, *Zion Symbolism*, 98-102, argues that because these descriptions of Sinai and Zion both end with speaking they are symbolic of the two revelations announced in 1:1-4. See also O'Brien, 480. Yet, as is argued above, these two descriptions represent the first revelation not as it was in itself, but as the word of judgment that it continues to be after its fulfillment by the second.

on the disobedient (12:18-21) and of the privileges this salvation now affords the people of God (12:22-24). He began by affirming the past reality of God's revelation in the incarnation and exaltation of the Son (1:1-4). He concludes by affirming that God still "speaks" through the eternal, incarnate, and now-exalted Son. Those who reject this "heavenly calling" (3:1) through unbelief and disobedience face the judgment depicted by the Sinai of 12:18-21.

The pastor, then, is describing Sinai as it was and is *for those who reject the promise of salvation that Sinai and its related institutions foreshadowed.* For them Sinai is devoid of grace. The wilderness generation (3:7-19) did not experience this Sinai when they stood at the foot of the mountain. They experienced this Sinai of exclusion from God's presence at Kadesh-Barnea when they rejected the promise of God.[14] Contemporary believers will experience this Sinai if they reject the fulfillment of God's promise in his Son.[15]

These graphic descriptions of present reality anticipate the eternal destiny of the apostate and the faithful. It is, therefore, no surprise that the pastor reinforces his description of these two "mountains" with a description of the final Judgment in 12:25-29. Although he may have drawn on traditional materials for this grand vision of Sinai and Zion, the arrangement and use of these materials is distinctively his own.[16]

18-19a The phrases "for you have not come" in v. 18 and "but you have come" in v. 22 introduce the contrasting alternatives represented by Sinai (vv. 18-21) and Zion (vv. 22-24). The pastor's concern that his hearers

14. Thus, it is not surprising that the parallels suggested by Son, *Zion Symbolism,* 133-40, between 12:18-21 and the apostate wilderness generation of 3:7–4:11 are more convincing than the parallels he finds between 12:18-21 and many other passages.

15. For them "there no longer remains a sacrifice for sin. Instead there is a certain terrifying prospect of judgment and a fury of fire about to consume the adversaries" (10:26-27).

16. Lane, 2:447-48, 461. As an example of the traditional use of Sinai and Zion in Jewish literature see *Jub.* 4:26: "this mountain which you are upon today, Mount Sinai, and Mount Zion, which will be sanctified in the new creation for the sanctification of the earth." Cf. Gal 4:21-31. Thompson, *Christian Philosophy,* 44-47, argues that the pastor has reshaped an apocalyptic tradition that emphasized future judgment in terms of his own Platonic distinction between the spiritual and material worlds. Weiss, 673-75, on the other hand, thinks that he began with a tradition drawn from Hellenistic dualistic eschatology that affirmed a presently existing heavenly world. Into this tradition he has introduced apocalyptic eschatological elements that looked for the future coming of this world. Both of these approaches arbitrarily impose a supposed religious background upon both the specific language used by Hebrews and the larger context provided by the epistle itself. This combination of both present realized and future eschatology is native to both the biblical and apocalyptic traditions, and thus is no evidence of influence from Platonic dualism (see O'Brien, 484; and the Introduction to this commentary, pp. 24-34).

enter the presence of God (4:16; 7:25; 10:1, 22; 11:6) has come to fruition.[17] He uses the perfect tense to show that he is describing two possibilities that even now lie before the people of God, who have been redeemed by Christ but have not yet made final entry into the eternal City.[18] The pastor assures his faithful and obedient hearers that in their approach to God through Christ they do not stand before the first of these two alternatives, the place of terrifying judgment described in vv. 18-21.

The pastor's hearers could not fail to associate the description in vv. 18-21with God's self-revelation on Mount Sinai. Much of the graphic language in this passage is drawn directly from the familiar accounts of this event in the Greek OT.[19] In fact, the verb translated "have . . . come" echoes the word used for approaching Sinai in Deut 4:11. The hearers must, however, have been surprised at what the pastor has omitted from the OT's picture of this event, as well as what he has added to the inspired text. By careful selection, addition, and omission the pastor has presented Sinai as the dreadful place of judgment and of exclusion from God's presence. He creates this impression, first of all, by omitting any mention of God. Second, he uses neither "mountain" nor "Sinai" in his description.[20] The pastor is not so concerned with the specific place but with the awesome quality of this place. Thus, he calls this place "that which can be touched," a description not found in the OT, in order to affirm the reality of the terrible exclusion from God he is describing. As we will see below, his selection from the descriptions found in Exodus and Deuteronomy reduces this scene to impersonal but very *palpable* and frightening physical phenomena. The terror of the people and the dread of Moses make it clear that this is fear before the awesome judgment of God upon sin. The pastor would have his hearers feel and sense these awful phenomena and the exclusion from God that they betoken.

The pastor has constructed this description of the place of judgment

---

17. Heb 12:18 and 22 use the perfect προσεληλύθατε ("you have come"). The verses mentioned above (4:16; 7:25; 10:1, 22; 11:6) use a present tense of the same verb (προσέρχομαι, "I come to"). The usage of Hebrews reflects the way this term was employed for approaching God in worship. See Scholer, *Proleptic Priests,* 148-49.

18. Most commentators note the importance of the perfect tense, προσεληλύθατε ("you have come to"), though they give different explanations of its significance. See, for instance, Attridge, 372; Ellingworth, 671; and Weiss, 670. The explanation given above fits well with the overall interpretation of this passage advocated by this commentary.

19. As found in Exod 19:15-21; 20:18-21; Deut 4:11-12; 5:22-27; and 9:19. See Ellingworth, 671.

20. The unusual nature of this omission is confirmed by the fact that ὄρει ("to a mountain") occurs in the majority of manuscripts, attesting the need felt by copyists to supply this lack. Cf. Koester, 543. Riggenbach's contention (411-12) that ὄρει was omitted from the best manuscripts through a primitive scribal error is unconvincing.

with his usual care for the effective ordering of words. He begins with a substantive participle ("to something that can be touched"), followed by a participle and a noun ("to what has been burning, fire"), followed by three unqualified nouns ("to darkness, "to gloom," and "to storm").[21] The whole is brought to a conclusion by two nouns with genitive qualifiers ("to a sound of a trumpet," "to a voice of words"). The pastor uses no article before any of these descriptions in order to emphasize the terrifying quality of these phenomena and the situation they describe.[22] The way in which he has kept each of these brief descriptions separate by putting "and" between them produces a cumulative rhetorical effect as if each were piled on top of its predecessors.[23] With the two participles he appeals to his hearers' sense of touch; with the three unqualified nouns, to their sense of sight; and with the two final qualified nouns, to their sense of hearing. This sevenfold description is designed to overwhelm the pastor's hearers with the terror of this place of judgment. If possible, he would have them smell the horror of separation from God.[24]

The second participle, with its attendant noun, provides a smooth transition between the initial participle and the three following unqualified nouns.[25] As noted above, the pastor begins with "to something that can be touched" in order to emphasize the palpable reality of this scene of judg-

---

21. The only places where γνόφος ("darkness") and θύελλα ("storm," "whirlwind") appear in the Greek Bible are the descriptions of Sinai recorded in Deut 4:11 and 5:22-23. Deuteronomy uses the synonym σκότος ("darkness") for ζόφος ("gloom"). Thus it is not surprising that σκότος occurs in some manuscripts of Heb 12:18 (including 𝔓46, but not ℵ, A, D, or C).

22. Ellingworth, 672; Attridge, 371.

23. See Ellingworth, 672. The REB loses this rhetorical effect by making both participles modify πυρί — "to a tangible, blazing fire," and by making the following datives accompaniment — "they do not come to this tangible, blazing fire . . . with its darkness, gloom, and whirlwind." This makes the fire the central object of the picture.

24. According to Weiss, 672, the pastor describes Sinai as a "fear-engendering event."

25. ψηλαφωμένῳ is clearly a substantive participle — "to what can be touched." Interpreters are divided on how to construe the second participle, κεκαυμένῳ ("having been burning"), and its accompanying noun πυρί ("with/to fire"). Most English translations take the participle as parallel with the previous participle and therefore substantive — "to what has been burning." They render πυρί as an instrumental of manner: "to what has been burning with fire." Others take the participle as attributive and the noun πυρί as parallel to the following three nouns: "to a burning fire" or "to a fire that has been burning" (NRSV; NASB; Riggenbach, 411; Weiss, 668). However, as noted in the text above, the pastor has used this participle/noun combination in order to make a smooth transition from his initial participle to the following three nouns. We have tried to help the English reader see and hear this transition by taking the noun "fire" in apposition to the participle — "to what has been burning, fire."

ment.[26] It was appropriate for fire to be the next item due to its prominence at Sinai. For the same reason, it was fitting for the pastor to emphasize fire by using both a participle ("to what has been burning") and a noun ("fire"). This fire brought pain but no light — this was a place of "darkness," "gloom," and "storm."[27] "Gloom" is worse than "darkness," and "storm," than them all. Thus the pastor has moved from what can be "touched" through fire and darkness to awful tempest.[28]

Hebrews has deliberately reserved "to the sound of a trumpet and to a voice of words" until the end.[29] The Greek word order reveals the close relationship between this pair of expressions.[30] By far the most terrifying thing about Sinai was the voice of God himself, introduced by the awesome blast of a trumpet. Yet the terror of God's speaking is made all the more overwhelming by the impersonal nature of the description. The pastor does not

26. See Westcott, 410-11. Thompson, *Christian Philosophy,* 46 (Thompson, 261-62); Johnson, 329; Hermut Löhr, "Thronversammlung und preisender Tempel: Beobachtungen am himmlischen Heiligtum im Hebräerbrief und in den Sabbatopherliedern aus Qumran," in *Königsherrschaft Gottes und himmlischer Kult im Judentum, Urchristentum und in der hellenistischen Welt,* ed. M. Hengel and A. M. Schwemer (WUNT 55; Tübingen: Siebeck, 1991), 198; and others are led astray by reading Platonic assumptions into this text when they interpret "to something that can be touched" as indicative of the inferiority and unreality of the earthly material Sinai. The author of Hebrews is making a point diametrically opposed to their interpretation. He is using this expression to emphasize the *reality* of the judgment on sin and exclusion from God that he is about to describe. Thompson, *Christian Philosophy,* 45, surrenders his case when he admits that, although the author refers to the phenomena of Sinai as "that which can be touched," he "uses no terms suggesting intangibility for the Christian experience at Zion." How could he? Those realities are, if anything, more concrete than the earthly realities.

27. γνόφος ("darkness") and θυέλλα ("storm") occur nowhere in the Greek Bible except in the descriptions of Sinai recorded in Deut 4:11 and 5:22-23. Deuteronomy uses the synonym σκότος ("darkness") for ζόφος ("gloom"). Thus it is not surprising that σκότος occurs in some manuscripts of Heb 12:18 (including 𝔓[46], but not ℵ, A, D, or C).

28. Philo is troubled by the very concrete reality of the events at Sinai which the writer of Hebrews emphasizes. In *QE* 2.47 (commenting on Exod 24:17) he says that the fire was not real but only appearance. Philo also calls God's voice at Sinai the "invisible voice" (*Decalogue* 33). Thompson, *Christian Philosophy,* 47.

29. The "sound of the trumpet" (σάλπιγγος ἤχῳ) comes from Exod 19:16 (φωνὴ τῆς σάλπιγγος ἤχει μέγα). Both the sound of God's spoken voice and the sound of the trumpet were awesome, but the sound of the trumpet contained no intelligible content. φωνῇ ῥημάτων — "voice of words" — is also found in Deut 4:11 (cf. φωνὴ μεγάλη in Deut 5:22-23).

30. These last two features are associated structurally as well as conceptually. Note their chiastic arrangement: καὶ (A) σάλπιγγος, (B) ἤχῳ καὶ ; (B¹) φωνῇ, (A¹) ῥημάτων: (A) "of a trumpet," (B) "a sound"; (B¹) "a voice," (A¹) "of words."

say that God spoke but that they came "to a voice of words."[31] There is no access to God or fellowship with him at this place of judgment. In contrast to the description of Mount Zion below, those facing judgment "have not come to" persons but to awesome phenomena caused by the condemning presence of God. The pastor has minced no words in presenting his hearers with the condition of those who reject Christ.

19b-20 The response of the people showed how awesome was the terror of this impersonal "voice" that pronounced the judgment of God. Those "who heard" this voice "begged that no word be added to" the words already spoken. Immediately after God spoke the Ten Commandments in Deut 5:24-27 and Exod 20:19, the people requested that Moses intervene for them, and that they not hear the unmediated voice of God again. The term that the pastor has used for "begged" appears in the stronger sense of "refuse" in v. 25 below.[32] The intensity of the hearers' rejection reflects the degree of terror associated with the speech of God. Verse 20 cites the command that no one, "not even an animal," touch the mountain on pain of death, as reason for the people's request. This command was given in Exod 19:12-13 before God appeared on Mount Sinai, and reiterated in Exod 19:23-25, right before God spoke the Ten Commandments to the people. Thus, it is closely associated with those commandments. Hebrews refers to this specific instruction or command because it emphasizes the people's inability to approach God. The way the command is phrased by the pastor, beginning with "if even an animal," heightens this tension. Not only human beings, but even unwitting animals would suffer the death penalty if they touched the mount of God's disclosure.[33] Death by stoning meant that no one else had to touch the violator and suffer the same consequences. Thus, this verse concludes the previous description by making it clear that those who hear but reject the word of God cannot draw near the divine presence.[34]

31. Even in Deut 4:12 φωνῇ ῥημάτων ("voice of words") is used to emphasize that they heard God speak but could not see him.

32. Although many English translations render παρῃτήσαντο as "begged" here in 12:19 ("begged that no further," NIV, so also NRSV, NKJV, NASB; Ellingworth, 673; Lane, 2:462-63), many interpreters would translate it as "deny" or "refuse" (Spicq, 2:403-4; Thompson, 262; Koester, 543; Johnson, 327). If the stronger meaning is the author's intention, then the following μή, "that not," is pleonastic (BDF §429). Johnson, 327, notes that μή is missing from 𝕏 and a few other manuscripts, indicating that copyists took this term in the negative sense of "refuse" as in 12:25. We have retained the word "beg" in the translation above both because it is most natural with the following μή and because there is no indication that the pastor intended to contradict the OT text. On the other hand, we believe that he used such a strong word intentionally in order to emphasize how unbearable the people found God's voice. Translation into English forces upon us a choice that the pastor's hearers did not have to make.

33. Ellingworth, 674-75; Weiss, 673.

34. The γάρ ("for") of v. 20 refers to the whole preceding scene (Ellingworth, 674).

21 The pastor concludes by stating plainly what he has already made his hearers feel, see, and hear — the terror of the disobedient when approaching God: "so terrifying was the appearance." "The appearance" maintains the impersonal nature of the description and directs the hearers' minds to the phenomena already described. Then the pastor summons Moses, the very mediator of the Old Covenant, as witness: "I am full of fear."[35] At first sight this quotation appears to contradict Scripture. Were the phenomena on Mount Sinai so fearful that even Moses was helplessly afraid? According to the accounts in Exod 19:16-25; 20:21 (cf. Deut 5:5, 31) Moses went into God's presence. Then he reassured the people (Exod 20:20). This seeming contradiction is removed when we realize that Moses did not make this declaration of fear (Deut 9:19) until *after* the people worshiped the golden calf. Hebrews intensifies Moses' statement by adding "and trembling." Moses was afraid "because of the wrath and anger of God" against Israel's sin.[36] It was the sin of the people that made the Sinai revelation of a holy God so fearful.[37] The mediator's inadequacy is in accord with the Old Covenant's impotency to deal with sin.[38] The terror of Moses brings the description of this place of God's judgment to its climax.

22 The pastor's description of Zion is sevenfold, as was his description of the unnamed mount of judgment.[39] The similarity, however, goes no further. That mountain remained unnamed. This mountain is triply designated as "Mount Zion, and the City of the living God, heavenly Jerusalem." That mountain was replete with natural phenomena, both impersonal and dreadful. This mountain is filled with persons in fellowship with God. That

35. ἔκφοβος is the word here translated "full of fear." It is related to φοβερόν ("terrifying") used to describe the fearfulness of τὸ φανταζόμενον, the awesome "appearance" on Mount Sinai. φοβερόν has already been used for God's judgment in 10:26-31 (Lane, 2:463). Attempts to derive these words from Moses' experience at the burning bush (Hughes, 543), or from a Jewish homiletical tradition, are unnecessary. See Lane, 2:464.

36. Deut 9:19, διὰ τὴν ὀργὴν καὶ τὸν θυμόν ("on account of wrath and anger").

37. *Pace* Koester, 550, the author is not using a lesser-to-greater argument: if even God's most faithful servant was frightened, how much more others should be. Moses' fear indicates the inability of the rebellious to approach God because of the terrible sentence of judgment under which they stand.

38. Nevertheless, the pastor's emphasis is not on the inadequacy of the old, but on God's judgment of the disobedient.

39. Taking "Mount Zion, and the City of the living God, heavenly Jerusalem" as one, we have (2) "myriads of angels," (3) "the assembly of the firstborn," (4) "God," (5) "the spirits of the righteous," (6) "the Mediator of the New Covenant, Jesus," and (7) "the blood of sprinkling." Weiss, 674, is correct when he contends that unusual vocabulary and poetic style are no reason to believe that the author has here incorporated a preexistent piece of liturgy. *Pace* Theissen, *Untersuchungen*, 64-66; Grässer, *Glaube*, 182-83; Rissi, *Theologie*, 101-2; cf. Käsemann, *Wandering*, 54-55.

mountain was characterized by fear; this, by joy. The recipients of Hebrews are not rebellious and thus "have not come" to that place of God's judgment. They "have come to," stand before, and live in a different reality.[40]

By using three names to describe this place of blessed fellowship with God, the pastor reassures his hearers that it is a real "place." One description is incapable of adequately expressing its significance.[41] The pastor begins with "Mount Zion" in order to establish the contrast with the implied "Mount Sinai."[42] Furthermore, although Mount Zion stood for the entire city of Jerusalem, it was used to describe the Temple Mount and was uniquely associated with the Most Holy Place and the presence of God.[43] Let there be no mistake. The pastor is talking about the place where God's people dwell with him. By bringing God's people into the Most Holy Place, Christ has brought them to the true Mount Zion. The next two names for this place are set apart from "Mount Zion" and given due emphasis by the conjunction "even."[44] They are also closely joined to each other by the absence of a conjunction between them. "The City of the living God" confirms the fact that this is the place of God's presence.[45] As a "City" it is the place where the faithful will

40. See the comments on προσεληλύθατε ("you have come") in v. 18 above.

41. The following quotation from Johnson, 330, appears to reveal either an undue dependence upon Platonic dualism in interpreting Hebrews or a modern reluctance to accept the concrete reality of God's destiny for his people, or perhaps both: "I put quotation marks around the word 'place' as a reminder that this is entirely an imaginative evocation. If the author is truly speaking about entry into God's life, as I think he is, then there is no more *place* with God than there is *time*. Spiritual realities are by definition not local. Imagination is therefore also required of the reader" (Johnson, 330). Did not the author of Hebrews believe in the concrete reality of "the City with foundations, whose architect and builder is God" (11:9-10)? Can we really describe as "spiritual" in the sense of ethereal what is left after all that can be shaken has been removed (12:25-29)? Was the "home" Abraham sought (11:13-16) part of an "imaginative evocation"? I suggest that the writer of Hebrews believed that the "City of the living God" was more real or "concrete" than the present world. Our present understanding can go little further than this. Johnson's quotation above causes us to imagine a less real or concrete existence. The statement that "spiritual realities are by definition not local" is misleading and not in harmony with biblical faith in the bodily resurrection. Yet on 349 he can say, "In his imaginative evocation of their approach to God in 12:18-24, the author spoke of the City of the living God. *It is real.* But the author and his hearers are not yet there in their mortal bodies" (italics added).

42. Bénétreau, 2:194.

43. Ps 74:2; Isa 8:18; Joel 4:17, 21; Ps 2:6 (cf. Riggenbach, 414-15).

44. For the translation of καί as "even" instead of "and," see O'Brien, 483, n. 202.

45. This is the "living God" whom Christians worship (9:14) and from whom the author fears his hearers will fall away (3:12; 10:31). Christ brings access to him and to his City through the "new and living way" (10:20) and "by the power of an indestructible life" (7:16).

live as the society of God's people in fellowship with him.[46] This is the eternal "City that has foundations, whose architect and builder is God" (11:9-10). Those who persevere in faith are citizens of this City. Final entrance into this, their true home, is the goal of their earthly pilgrimage (11:13-16). The pastor has reserved the most comprehensive and evocative term until the end — this reality can be described as nothing less than "Jerusalem" — but not the earthly city.[47] This is the true "heavenly" Jerusalem foreshadowed by the earthly Jerusalem as the place where God dwells with his own.[48]

The reality described by these three names has always been the ultimate goal of the faithful (see the comments on 3:1–4:11). Since the exaltation of God's Son, Jesus, preliminary entrance thereunto has also been their ever-present privilege (4:14-16; 10:19-25). When the pastor has spoken of this reality as the ultimate goal, he has used the language of pilgrimage to the Promised Land. This goal is the "rest" that remains for God's people (3:7–4:11), the City God has established for them, and their heavenly "home" (11:1-40), into which Christ will lead them as their "Pioneer" (2:10; 12:1-3). When speaking of their present privilege he has called this reality the Most Holy Place (4:14–5:10; 7:1–10:25). Through his high-priestly work Christ has opened a "new and living way" through which they can enter daily into God's presence in order to find strength for perseverance until the end. It was natural to use the imagery of the Mosaic Tent and priesthood to describe this daily approach to God, since these were the means given in the OT for regular worship. Yet this high-priestly ministry of Christ is also the means through which all of God's people — past and present — will attain ultimate entrance at Christ's return (11:39-40; 9:28-29). When looking at the ultimate goal, the pastor has urged his hearers to persevere; when describing their present privilege, he has invited them to "draw near" in order to persevere. Even within the OT itself the imagery of Promised Land, Jerusalem, Zion, Temple, and Most Holy Place began to coalesce as representative of the ultimate hope of the people of God.[49] Here in 12:22-24 the pastor uses "Mount

46. "Mount Zion represents the strong divine foundation of the new Order, while the City of the Living God represents the social structure in which the Order is embodied" (Westcott, 413).

47. For Jerusalem as the "city of God" see Pss 48:9; 46:5; Ellingworth, 677.

48. Rev 3:12; 21:2, 10 describes the new Jerusalem as a present reality that will be the final abode of the blessed.

49. On the integral link between land, city, and Temple in Judaism see Peter Walker, "Jerusalem in Hebrews 13:9-14 and the Dating of the Epistle," *TynBul* 45 (1994): 50. Even before the exile Jerusalem had become the symbol and essence of God's promise of land (David E. Holwerda, *Jesus and Israel: One Covenant or Two?* [Grand Rapids: Eerdmans, 1995], 96). In the NT the Temple has become the quintessence of Jerusalem as it had become the embodiment of the land (W. D. Davies, *The Gospel and the Land: Early*

Zion, and the City of the living God, heavenly Jerusalem" to unite in one his description of the present preliminary privilege and future ultimate destiny of God's people.[50] His emphasis is on the present privilege — "you have come." Yet this is also his most comprehensive glimpse of the future that God has for his own.[51]

Impersonal, foreboding natural phenomena characterize life before Sinai. Life in the City of God is distinguished by joyful fellowship. The next five phrases describe the residents of the heavenly Mount Zion. First, the faithful have come "to myriads of angels, a festal gathering." Individual angels might be sent to serve (1:14), but multitudes of angels mark the presence of God. Long ago they attended his self-revelation on Sinai (Deut 12:12 LXX; Heb 1:5-14). Their innumerable company perpetually adorns God's heavenly court.[52] Thus, this numberless host marks nothing less than the heavenly dwelling place of God. As is fitting in this heavenly City, these angels in "a festal gathering" are engaged in joyful worship.[53] Whether the ex-

---

Christianity and Jewish Territorial Doctrine [Berkeley: University of California Press, 1974], 150-52; cf. Holwerda, *Covenant,* 107). The NT, however, is not concerned with Jerusalem as an earthly reality, but as the heavenly dwelling place of God and the destiny of God's people (James Calvin De Young, *Jerusalem in the New Testament: The Significance of the City in the History of Redemption and in Eschatology* [Kampen: Kok, 1960], 97-99, 116).

50. Thus, "Mount Zion" brings together the "Most Holy Place" entered by the faithful while on their journey, with the "City" that is their final destination. See Son, *Zion Symbolism,* 91-93; Beale, *The Temple,* 301-3 (cited by O'Brien, 483).

51. Thus this passage assumes both the present privileges available in Christ and the ultimate goal to which he gives access, as described throughout Hebrews (Bénétreau, 2:194; Ellingworth, 670-71). In my judgment it is misleading when Weiss, 674, says that the pastor has incorporated apocalyptic motifs into a Hellenistic dualistic eschatology as if such speculations were the source of the pastor's thought. Such an already/not yet eschatology is characteristic of the NT. Furthermore, it is artificial to divide sharply between those who believed in a heavenly Jerusalem to be revealed at the judgment (apocalyptic thought) and those who believed in a presently existing heavenly Jerusalem (Hellenistic dualistic thought). Most who believed in such a future revelation of the heavenly City also believed in its present existence (Rev 21:9–22:5). We agree with Weiss (675), however, in his opposition to Theissen, *Untersuchungen,* 8-88, who contends that the author of Hebrews is correcting his hearers' overrealized eschatology with a futuristic eschatology. Furthermore, M. Thiessen's contention that Hebrews envisions God's people between the literal exodus from Egypt and entrance into the heavenly promised land overlooks the Christology of Hebrews (Thiessen, "Exodus," 367-69). It is not the literal exodus but the work of Christ that puts God's people in their present position.

52. Attridge, 374-75 (esp. nn. 56 and 57); Lane, 2:467; cf. Dan 7:10 LXX; Rev 5:11; *1 En.* 1:9; 14:22. See also Thompson, 263.

53. πανηγύρει ("festal gathering") has the connotation of a joyful plenary gathering for worship (Ezek 46:11; Amos 5:21; Hos 2:14; 9:5; see also Josephus, *J.W.* 5.230).

pression "festal gathering" is descriptive of the angels, or joined to the following word "assembly," its occurrence here at the beginning of this section characterizes this entire description as a scene of joyful worship, in which the faithful join the angels in the praise of God.[54]

23 The faithful have also come "to the assembly of the firstborn who are enrolled in heaven."[55] The word "firstborn" is plural, and thus refers not to Christ (1:6) but to all the faithful people of God.[56] This is not a further

---

Ellingworth, 679; cf. Weiss, 679; Thompson 263. Thus its use here emphasizes the joyful worship of the heavenly City and reminds us of the festive "Sabbath rest" (σαββατισμός) that remains for God's people (4:9; Lane, 2:467). This term was also used to describe international festivals and athletic contests in the Greco-Roman world (Isocrates, *Panegyricus* 43, 46; Philo, *Embassy* 12; cited by Koester, 544). Thus, Spicq, 2:407, suggests that the angels are celebrating the triumph of Christ.

54. There are three main possibilities for the construal of μυριάσιν ἀγγέλων πανηγύρει καὶ ἐκκλησίᾳ πρωτοτόκων: 1. "to myriads of angels in festal gathering" (μυριάσιν ἀγγέλων πανηγύρει) "and to the assembly of the firstborn" (καὶ ἐκκλησίᾳ πρωτοτόκων); 2. "to myriads of angels" (μυριάσιν ἀγγέλων), "a festal gathering" (πανηγύρει), "and to the assembly of the firstborn" (καὶ ἐκκλησίᾳ πρωτοτόκων); 3. "to myriads of angels" (μυριάσιν ἀγγέλων), "to a festal gathering and assembly of the firstborn" (πανηγύρει καὶ ἐκκλησίᾳ πρωτοτόκων). In the first alternative the term πανηγύρει qualifies the "myriads of angels" as being "in festal gathering." In the second, it stands in apposition to the "myriads of angels" — "to myriads of angels, a festal gathering." In the third, it goes with "assembly" in reference to the "firstborn" — "to a festal gathering and assembly of the firstborn." Dumbrell argues for the third, contending that πανήγυρις is a more appropriate description of the people of God than of the angels (W. J. Dumbrell, "The Spirits of Just Men Made Perfect," *EvQ* 48 [1976]: 156-58). Weiss, 678-80, concurs, arguing that "festal gathering" (πανηγύρει) and "assembly" (ἐκκλησία) describe the cultic and political aspects of God's people, respectively. However, the first or second alternative fits best with the way the author appears to have separated each of these phrases with a καί ("and"). See Lane, 2:441-42jj, 468; Ellingworth, 678-79; Westcott, 414-15; cf. Riggenbach, 416. The second is to be preferred because it recognizes that "festal gathering" goes with the "myriads of angels" and yet suggests most clearly the festal tone of all in the heavenly City. Cf. the interpretation of κεκαυμένῳ πυρί ("to that which is burning, a fire") in v. 18 above. Cf. Attridge, 375.

55. This verse echoes the way God's people were described when he delivered them from Egypt. They were called the ἐκκλησία ("assembly," "congregation") in Deut 4:10 and 18:16 (cf. Acts 7:38). Deut 4:10; 9:10; and 18:16 call the time when God addressed them from Sinai ἡμέρα ἐκκλησίας ("the day of the assembly"). The title πρωτότοκος ("firstborn," singular) was given to the Israelites when God brought them out of Egypt in order to lead them to Sinai (Exod 4:22-23; cf. Jer 31:9; Sir 36:11). God's people are often described as registered in heaven (Exod 32:32-33; cf. Ps 69:29; Isa 4:3; Dan 12:1; Luke 10:20; Phil 4:3; Rev 3:5; 13:8; 17:8; 20:12; cf. *Jub.* 2:20; *1 En.* 47:3-4; 104:1; 108:3). Lane, 2:468; O'Brien, 485.

56. L. R. Helyer, "The *Prōtotokos* Title in Hebrews," *Studia Biblica et Theologica* 6 (1976): 15; Lane, 2:469; Hughes, 547-49; Bruce, 358-59; Westcott, 415; Attridge, 375.

reference to angels, as some have suggested.[57] The pastor could hardly call the angels "firstborn" without compromising his use of that term to distinguish Christ from the angels in 1:6.[58] Furthermore, it would make no sense to say that the angels were "enrolled in heaven."[59] It is the one faithful people of God spanning both Testaments whose names are enrolled in heaven, indicating the location of their citizenship.[60] There is no reason to restrict this assembly to those who lived before Christ.[61] Nor does the fact that their names are "enrolled in heaven" limit its membership to those now living on earth.[62] Heaven is the "home" of all the faithful and the place of their true citizenship (11:13-16). This is the great "assembly" or "congregation" of Christ's brothers and sisters before whom he praised God on the occasion of his exaltation (2:12). In their present worship they echo his praise and exalt in his triumph. The hearers join all the faithful, past and present, living and dead, in the presence of God on the heavenly Mount Zion. All God's sons and daughters (2:10-18) are the "firstborn" who share the inheritance of the Son and Firstborn *par excellence* (1:6).[63] They have refused to follow the example of Esau, who gave up his right to be "firstborn" because he desired the things of this world and despised the promise of God.[64] God's people may be excluded from the local assemblies and associations made up of citizens from the towns in which they live, but they are full members of the "assembly" of the heavenly City.[65] The pastor would have them know that through Christ they have come home to their own — to the witnesses that went before them (11:1-40); to the deceased leaders of their fellowship (13:7); and to all the faithful living in the world.[66]

Furthermore, "you have come," says the pastor, "to a Judge, God of

---

Spicq's objection (2:407) that this means Christians "have come" to Christians is of no force. The pastor is simply saying that his hearers join all the faithful by their coming to "Mount Zion."

57. *Pace* Käsemann, *Wandering,* 50; Spicq, 2:407-9, Montefiore, 231.

58. Cf. Löhr, "Thronversammlung," 200.

59. Lane, 2:468; Michel, 464; Dumbrell, "Spirits," 157.

60. Helyer, *"Prōtotokos,"* 15.

61. *Pace* Casey, "Christian Assembly," 329. The use of "firstborn" (singular) for the people of Israel as a whole in Exod 4:22-23 (cf. Sir 36:17) is no indication that the use of "firstborn" (plural) here should be restricted to those who lived before Christ (Riggenbach, 416).

62. *Pace* Riggenbach, 416; Michel, 464.

63. Attridge, 375.

64. Compare τὰ πρωτοτόκια ("birthright") in v. 16 above with πρωτοτοτόκων ("firstborn") in this verse.

65. See Koester, 551.

66. Lane (2:469) quotes Peterson (*Perfection,* 282), "'the ultimate, completed company of the people of God, membership of which is now enjoyed by faith.'"

all." It is most appropriate that God himself hold the central position in this list. He is the third of five persons or groups of persons described as present in the heavenly Jerusalem. His presence has been obvious from the beginning. He is the center of "the City of the living God." The innumerable angels are his attendants. The "assembly of the firstborn" has come into his presence to join the angels in worshiping him. He is what makes this place the "heavenly Jerusalem." Here the faithful will enter his "rest" (4:1-2). However, the pastor's description is striking — "to a Judge, God of all." Most English translations soften the force of this expression by rendering it "to God who is Judge of all." Why this emphasis on God as "Judge" in the midst of this joyous picture of life in his presence? Some have argued that it would be more in accord with the immediate context and with Hebrews' emphasis on the privilege of approaching God (4:14-16; 10:19-25) to take "Judge" in the positive sense of "Vindicator," "Redeemer," or "Deliverer."[67] However, the more natural translation "Judge" best represents the pastor's intentions for several reasons. First, by reminding his hearers that they have come to the ultimate and sovereign "Judge," he establishes the proper context for understanding the rest of this description of Mount Zion, especially the work of the Mediator and the benefits of his "blood" in v. 24. This joyful fellowship is not to be taken lightly. God has not relented in his holiness. This wonderful scene of blessing is possible only through the salvation he has provided in his Son. Second, by reminding his hearers that God is still the holy God of Sinai, he binds vv. 22-24 closely to the contrasting picture in vv. 18-21.[68] Finally, this understanding is in accord with the way the pastor has interwoven comfort and warning throughout his sermon. It is this combination that best represents the situation of God's people since the coming of Christ. It also provides the most compelling motivation for the perseverance of the pastor's hearers, both ancient and modern.

The "spirits of righteous people made perfect" is appropriately located between God the Judge and Christ the Mediator. They have been accepted as "righteous" before God the Judge because they have been "made perfect" through the mediation of Christ.[69] "Spirits of . . . righteous people" is an apocalyptic term for the people of God who have already died and await resurrection.[70] While "assembly of the firstborn" included the church militant and triumphant, the "spirits of righteous people made perfect" refers spe-

67. Weiss, 681; Attridge, 376, esp. n. 80; Riggenbach, 417-18.

68. Schierse, *Verheissung,* 173, n. 26, notes the importance of the theme of judgment throughout this section. Cf. also Delitzsch, 649, n. 114; Peterson, *Perfection,* 277, n. 98; and Löhr, "Thronversammlung," 201, n. 126.

69. See Lane, 2:470-72.

70. Hagner, 226; Riggenbach, 418; Attridge, 376. See *Jub.* 23:30-31; *1 En.* 22:9; 102:4; 103:3-4; *2 Bar.* 30:2 (cited in O'Brien, 487, n. 221, referencing Lane, 2:470).

cifically to the faithful people of God who have died.[71] Thus, this term encompasses people like the heroes of faith in 11:1-40 who lived before Christ, as well as the faithful who have died since his coming.[72] Those heroes were "righteous" (10:38) because they lived by faith, as epitomized by the first in their list, "righteous" Abel (11:4). When properly understood, the fact that the heroes of 11:1-40 could not be "made perfect without us" is no objection to their inclusion with those now "made perfect" (see the comments on 11:39-40).[73] They have been "made perfect" in the same way that contemporary believers "have been made perfect." Both have been cleansed from sin and thus brought into the presence of God through the work of Christ (7:19; 9:9; 10:1, 14).[74] In principle, the same cleansing enables the dead to live in God's presence on Mount Zion and the living to approach the throne of grace in prayer and worship (4:14-16; cf. 10:19-25). Since the exaltation of Christ the saints of old who did not enjoy access to that throne during their earthly lives dwell in the heavenly Jerusalem. The pastor, however, is not distinguishing between those who lived before Christ and those who come after. There is only one people of God. He is separating the faithful who have died from those still alive. All, of course, will enter into the destiny God has for his own in a deeper and final way at Christ's return (12:25-29; cf. 9:28).[75]

71. George Guthrie, 421. See also Gordon, 180. Koester, 546, notes that some sources believed the righteous entered heaven immediately after death (Wis 3:1); others, that their spirits were "specially preserved until the last judgment (*1 En.* 22:3-7; Rev 6:9; *4 Ezra* 7:99)." He is unduly skeptical, however, when he says, "Hebrews provides no clarity about a person's state between death and final judgment" (546; citing Peterson, *Perfection,* 162-65). Since the coming of Christ the righteous dead are with God in the heavenly Jerusalem awaiting the soon-to-be described last Judgment (12:25-29). The author of Hebrews is preaching, not speculating. He has neither occasion nor need to tell his hearers where the righteous dead were before the coming of Christ. Cf. Hermut Löhr, "Anthropologie und Eschatologie im Hebräerbrief: Bemerkungen zum theologischen Interesse einer früchristlichen Schrift," in *Eschatologie und Schöpfung: Festschrift für Erich Grässer zum siebzigsten Geburtstag,* vol. 89, ed. M. Evang, H. Merlkein, and M. Wolter (BZNW 89; Berlin and New York: De Gruyter, 1997), 194, n. 81.

72. Hughes, 550-51; Riggenbach, 418.

73. *Pace* Attridge, 376; Weiss, 681; Casey, "Christian Assembly," 329; Dumbrell, "Spirits," 154-59, and Silva, "Perfection," 69.

74. See the comments on 11:39-40. Cf. Lane, 2:471; Ellingworth, 680-81; and esp. Löhr, "Anthropologie," 194.

75. Thus Riggenbach, 418, is mistaken when he defines the being "made perfect" of the departed saints as their ultimate entrance into fellowship with God. Löhr may be correct when he says that 12:22-24 says nothing about a greater fulfillment of salvation yet to come. However, he is mistaken when he contends that the "spirits of the just made perfect" have thus entered into the final state of blessedness (Löhr, "Anthropologie," 192-93). The writer of Hebrews has made it clear that Christ will return for the "salvation" of his own (9:28). Christ's return is implicit in the pastor's use of Ps 110:1, first alluded to in

24 The pastor has held his hearers in suspense by postponing mention of "the Mediator of the New Covenant, Jesus" until the end of this description of Mount Zion. As is his custom, he puts great emphasis on the name "Jesus" by positioning it after the other terms used to describe Christ. This "Mediator," exalted at God's right hand, is still the same "Jesus" who lived an obedient human life, offering himself on the cross according to the will of God (10:5-10). God is at the center of this picture of Mount Zion and the recipient of worship from its human and angelic inhabitants. The "Mediator," however, comes at its climax because he is the one through whom God has made everything described in vv. 22-23 possible. As the "Mediator of the New Covenant" (7:23-25; 9:14-15; 10:15-18), he is able to cleanse the heart from sin, implant God's law within, and remove every barrier that has separated God's people from his presence.[76] This One, seated at God's right hand, is indeed the "main point" of the pastor's sermon (8:1-2) and the One worthy of constant attention by the people of God as they run the race of faith (12:1-3). If life on Mount Zion is the great benefit of the "New Covenant," those who reject this Mediator will suffer the judgment pronounced under the Old as portrayed in vv. 18-21. The former description of fearful separation from God ended with Moses, the mediator of the Old Covenant (v. 21; cf. 9:15-21), terrified before God's judgment on sin. This description of Mount Zion climaxes with "Jesus," the fully effective Mediator of the New, who is able to adequately deal with sin.

The work of this Mediator is summarized in the seventh and final description of that to which the hearers "have come" — "to blood of sprinkling that speaks better than Abel." "Better than Abel" is probably shorthand for "better than the blood of Abel."[77] Abel's blood "cried out" (Gen 4:10) for

---

1:3 and cited in 1:13. It is confirmed by his interpretation of Ps 8:4-6 in 2:8-9. He affirmed Christ's role in the consummation of all as early as 1:11-12. Furthermore, 12:22-24 leads naturally, as Löhr admits, into the description of the last Judgment in 12:25-29. Finally, the interpretation of 11:17-19 and 11:35 given above confirms the pastor's belief in the resurrection of the body. The pastor assumes that his hearers have heard what he has already said, and will hear his coming description of the last Judgment. As affirmed above, Heb 12:22-24 is a description of the present blessedness experienced by the people of God — both living and dead — that provides a glimpse into the final blessedness God has for his own.

76. The pastor called the covenant established by Christ κρείττων ("better") in 7:22; 8:6, καίνη ("new") in 9:15, and now νέας ("new") here in 12:24. He probably intends no technical difference between these last two near-synonymous words (Ellingworth, 681). Nevertheless, the use of three different terms to describe the New Covenant only serves to underscore its superior quality.

77. 𝔓46, supported by a few Latin manuscripts, makes this understanding explicit by reading τὸ Ἄβελ instead of τὸν Ἄβελ. τὸ is the accusative neuter article referring to αἷμα, blood, followed by Ἄβελ, now understood as a genitive: "the [blood] of Abel"

God's judgment to fall on the sin of guilty Cain.[78] The "blood" by which Jesus sealed the New Covenant (9:13-14; 18-21; 10:22) as its Mediator is blood that proclaims a "better" message of cleansing from sin and release from judgment. It invites the faithful into the presence of God. The pastor has already demonstrated that the New Covenant and the sacrifice of Christ are "better" than the Old Covenant and sacrifice because they provide what the Old only prefigured.[79] Here, however, he goes a step further. The "blood" of Christ addresses God's people with a "better" message than the blood of Abel because it provides salvation rather than condemnation. The God of Sinai (2:3; cf. 3:5) now speaks this word of invitation through the blood of Jesus. The present tense reminds the hearers that the God who procured these benefits once for all (through the incarnation of Christ) continually offers them (through the exalted Christ) to his people in their present distress.[80] Moses could do naught but tremble with fear at God's judgment on the sins of the people (v. 21). Jesus offers a complete remedy.

(Johnson, 328k). The "speaking" of Abel's blood is not to be identified with Abel's speaking in Heb 11:4. In 11:4 Abel testified to faith in a God who would raise the dead. Here in 12:24 his blood calls down condemnation on the guilty. Smillie's contention that "to the blood of sprinkling" is one thing and "to the one speaking better than Abel" is another cannot be sustained (G. Smillie, "'The One Who is Speaking' in Hebrews 12:25," *TynBul* 55 [2004]: 279-81). First of all, the pastor does not divide these two with καί ("and") as he does the other items in this series. Second, it is almost impossible to mention "blood" and "speaking" in context with Abel and not recall Abel's "blood" crying out from the ground in Gen 4:10.

78. Bruce, 361; Hughes, 552; Lane, 2:473; George Guthrie, 422; Weiss, 682-83; Riggenbach, 420; Westcott, 417; and most interpreters (cf. Spicq, 2:409-10). None of the other interpretations of Abel's blood adequately account for the context in Hebrews. Son, *Zion Symbolism*, 100-102, has suggested that Abel's blood represents the ineffective blood of the old sacrificial system. Attridge, 377, has proposed that Abel's blood had limited atoning power because Abel was the first martyr. His blood's limited ability to cleanse foreshadowed Christ's complete sufficiency to remove all sin. Spicq (2:409-10) appears to have some sympathy with this second proposal. According to Grässer, 3:324 (cited by Mitchell, 284), Abel's blood cried only from "the ground," but Christ carried his blood into the heavenly Sanctuary where he perpetually intercedes. The first suggestion fails because neither the account of Abel in Genesis nor the immediate context in Hebrews is concerned with the inadequacy of the old sacrifices. Hebrews has already settled that issue. The second suggestion fails because Hebrews affirms that Christ's blood alone can cleanse the conscience from sin (9:11-15). See further criticism of this second alternative in Bénétreau, 2:199, n. 1. Finally, Hebrews nowhere indicates that Christ carried his blood into the heavenly Sanctuary (see on 9:11-14). Nor is anything said here about Abel's blood crying from "the ground." The immediate context in Hebrews is concerned with God's judgment on sin. This emphasis is in full accord with what Genesis says about Abel's blood.

79. For the eschatological use of κρείττων see 1:4; 7:22; 8:6; 9:23.

80. Ellingworth, 683.

The pastor ends his account of the past and present history of God's faithful people, as he began, with the mention of righteous Abel (cf. 11:4).[81] All that remains is his awesome account of future Judgment in 12:25-29. And yet this grand description of the privileges now enjoyed by the people of God at "Mount Zion" has opened a window on the final blessedness God has for his own. The pastor has given his hearers this glimpse in order to encourage their perseverance by quickening their longing for what God has in store.

4. God Will Speak "Once More" at the Final Judgment (12:25-29)

> 25 See to it that you do not refuse the one who is speaking. For if those people did not escape when they refused the One who warns on earth, how much less shall we escape who turn away from the One who warns from heaven? 26 Then his voice shook the earth. But now he has promised, saying, "Once more I will shake not only the earth but also the heavens." 27 Now the "once more" shows the removal of the things that can be shaken as things that have been made, in order that the things that cannot be shaken might remain. 28 Therefore, since we are receiving a kingdom that is unshakable, let us be thankful. Through which let us serve God appropriately with godly fear and awe. 29 For indeed our "God is a consuming fire."

The pastor continues the theme of ultimate divine revelation with which he began in 1:1-4. God spoke by providing "such a great salvation" (2:3) through the incarnation and exaltation of the eternal Son (1:1-4). He now speaks from heaven offering that salvation to the faithful through the incarnate, but now exalted, Son (12:22-24). Those who refuse this offer will face condemnation when he speaks one last time at the final Judgment (12:25-29). God's self-disclosure at Sinai furnishes the pattern for each succeeding stage of divine revelation. God's word revealed in (1:1-4), and now offered from heaven through (12:18-24), the incarnate/exalted Son has both provided the fully sufficient salvation foreshadowed by Sinai and made it available for God's people in the present. God's earth-shattering word spoken at the Judgment will provide the ultimate condemnation and blessing anticipated by Sinai (12:25-29). The pastor began by arguing that God's revelation in "one who is Son" made the judgment of Sinai all the more certain on the disobedient (2:1-4). Since he has now described the full grandeur of the Son and the revelation/salvation he has provided, he can vividly describe the nature of that ultimate loss for those who reject Christ as well as the glory of the ultimate blessing for those who embrace him.

81. Cf. Lane, 2:474.

The pastor used one less-to-greater argument in his initial appeal to his readers (2:1-4). In this concluding appeal he uses two such arguments, one in v. 25 and one in vv. 26-27. The first makes the warning inherent in vv. 18-24 quite clear. If the wilderness generation who rejected the word that God spoke "on earth" at Sinai "did not escape" God's judgment, as depicted in vv. 18-21, how shall "we" who have the privileges of vv. 22-24 and have received God's invitation through his Son "from heaven" escape. The second (12:26-27) reinforces this appeal by contrasting the ultimate, earth-shattering word of God at the Judgment with his merely earth-shaking word at Sinai. The pastor concludes with an appeal for awe and gratitude at the "Unshakable Kingdom" the faithful will receive at this Judgment. The pastor's history of God's faithful people has reached its appropriate conclusion with this announcement of the final Judgment.[1]

25 "See to it that you do not refuse the one who is speaking" echoes the pastor's warning against imitating the wilderness generation: "See to it, brothers and sisters, lest there be in any of you an evil heart of unbelief in turning away from the living God" (3:12).[2] The pastor's main concern throughout this sermon has been that his hearers fully heed the voice of God, which that generation refused to "hear." The God who spoke on Sinai is the "one who is" now "speaking" to his people through his exalted Son.[3] He is offering the salvation provided by Jesus' "speaking" blood, just mentioned in v. 24. The OT as fulfilled in Christ is the vehicle of this revelation. Thus, the pastor's own exposition of Christ's sufficiency conveys this divine invitation to hearers and readers ancient and modern.[4] All who receive God's address stand ever accountable before the word of God (4:12-13).

The less-to-greater argument in v. 25bc updates the pastor's first such

1. The pastor anticipated this last Judgment in his description of Noah (11:7) at the climax of the opening section of this history (11:1-7). Noah escaped God's judgment and obtained "salvation" (σωτηρίαν) because of his faith. So the readers of Hebrews are to escape judgment by their faith and receive the "kingdom that cannot be shaken" (βασιλείαν ἀσάλευτον, v. 28). God's word to Noah was a warning (χρηματισθείς), just as God's speaking from Sinai and Zion is a warning (χρηματίζοντα, v. 25). The faithful are to be motivated by "godly fear" (εὐλαβείας, v. 28), just as was Noah (εὐλαβηθείς).

2. Johnson, 333-34.

3. God is "the one who warns on earth," "the one who is speaking" (from heaven), and the one who will speak "once" more at the Judgment (Hughes, 555; Lane, 2:475; Johnson, 334; Westcott, 418-20; Spicq, 2:410; O'Brien, 492). Lane, 2:475, shows this identity of speakers by a careful structural analysis of the text. This is not a contrast between speakers but between the "modes" of God's speech (Attridge, 380) or the "agents" of his speaking (Johnson, 334). The God who spoke at Sinai now speaks through his eternal Son seated at his right hand. See the fine discussion of this issue in Smillie, "'The One Who Is Speaking' in Hebrews 12:25," 283-87.

4. Smillie, "'The One Who is Speaking' in Hebrews 12:25," 291–92.

argument given in 2:2-3. A more detailed look at the similarities and differences between the two will be instructive. First, note the similarities. Both contrast the responsibility of those who heard God speak at Sinai with those who have received God's word in Christ. Both begin by describing the responsibility of the former with a condition of fact,[5] followed by a question that implies the proportionately greater responsibility of the latter.[6] However, the differences between these passages show how the pastor's intervening argument has made this final contrast much more forceful. First, 2:2 does not refer directly to the people who stood before Sinai. Heb 12:25b, however, refers directly to those who stood at Sinai as those who "refused him who warns on earth."[7] They began by "begging" God to cease speaking directly to them (v. 19), and then "refused" his word when told to enter God's promised "rest."[8] As a result of this rebellion, Sinai became for them the foreboding judgment depicted in 12:18-21 above (cf. 3:16-19). Their inability to "escape" this horrible judgment is far more foreboding than the pastor's initial almost sanitary affirmation that every transgression received a "just recompense" (2:2). Furthermore, the God "who warns on earth" has replaced "the word spoken by angels."[9] This phrase also evokes the frightful phenomena of vv. 18-21, and thus sharpens the warning's quality of foreboding. The pastor uses the present tense, the one "who warns," because Sinai has become the embodiment of God's perpetual warning that rejected grace leads to terrible judgment. By fulfilling everything anticipated in God's earlier revelation,

5. "For if the word spoken through angels proved valid, and every transgression and disobedience received a just reward" (2:2); "For if those people did not escape when they refused the One who warned on earth" (12:25).

6. "Then how shall we escape if we neglect such a great salvation?" (2:3); "How much less shall we escape who turn away from the One who speaks from heaven?" (12:25).

7. Ellingworth, 684, admits that "the broader context would suggest that ἐκεῖνοι [those] are the ἀκούσαντες [ones who heard] of v. 19." Thus, "those who refused the One who warned them on earth" refers to that prototype of all the disobedient, the wilderness generation (3:7-19), who stood before Sinai and later experienced its judgment because of their rebellion. Ellingworth, 684, however, misses the significance of his own observation because he fails to see that "those who heard" in v. 19 were transgressors.

8. The verb παραιτέομαι was used in v. 19, followed by an infinitive, in its weaker sense of "beg," "request" (BDAG, 764, 1b). The people "begged" that God not speak directly to them again. Here in v. 25, followed by a substantive participle denoting a person, it is used in the stronger sense of "refuse" or "reject" (BDAG, 764, 2bα). Do not "refuse" the one who is speaking. See Lane, 2:475. Their request not to hear more of God's word presaged their refusal to obey God's word. Cf. Hughes, 556; Johnson, 334; Weiss, 686; and Westcott, 418.

9. ἐπὶ γῆς "is slightly emphatic by its position; the normal order would be τὸν ἐπὶ γῆς χρηματίζοντα (BDF §474.5c, as in 𝔓⁴⁶ ℵ^c K L P Ψ)" (Ellingworth, 685).

Christ does not terminate that warning, but makes its consequences all the more certain.

The way in which God speaks through his Son is the second and most significant difference between 12:25 and 2:3-4. Heb 2:3-4 looks to the past. God's message "began to be spoken" by the incarnate Christ when he was on earth and was confirmed to us "by those who heard him." In 12:25c, however, God now speaks in the present from heaven through the exalted Son seated at his right hand. The pastor has explained how that Son, who was first attested to "us" by those who heard him, has become the all-sufficient, enthroned Savior. The Son has received this honor through his obedient human life and death, offering himself according to the will of God (10:5-10). It is through this Christ (cf. 8:1-2) — eternal, incarnate, obedient, exalted — that God now speaks "from heaven," offering salvation to his people in the present. The Sinai revelation that God gave "on earth" could not in itself bring God's people into his true heavenly presence. Through the work of Christ, however, God's address "from heaven" is a "heavenly calling" (3:1) that provides the access into his presence described in vv. 22-24 above.[10]

A third difference between 12:25 and that earlier exhortation reveals the depth of the pastor's concern for his hearers. "Neglect" of God's "great salvation" (2:3) has become not just a "refusal" but a definitive "turning away" from this "One [who speaks] from heaven."[11] The pastor minces no words, nor does he cushion his warning by saying "if we turn away." Instead he is very direct — "we who turn away."[12] He wants his hearers to respond in shock with "no, we are not those who turn away." As we saw when considering 2:3, this "neglect" was not wholly unintentional. The pastor reveals the awful reality hidden in such "neglect" and the very real consequences to which, if unchecked, it will lead.[13]

---

10. It is the work of Christ, and not some matter/spirit dualism, that makes this revelation "from heaven" superior to the on-earth Sinai revelation. Cf. Ellingworth, 685; Lane, 2:477.

11. Both ἀποστρέφομαι (v. 25b, "turn away") and παραιτέομαι (v. 25a, "refuse") refer to a deliberate, culpable rejection of God's address. Nevertheless, ἀποστρέφομαι is probably the stronger. "Refusal" has led to a definitive "turning away" (see Lane, 2:475; cf. BDAG, 123, 3; O'Brien, 492-94; Mitchell, 287). The pastor puts great emphasis on ἀποστρεφόμενοι by making it attributive ("we . . . who turn away," Attridge, 378, n. 4) and by reserving it for the end of the sentence. Though missing in 𝔓46, the article οἱ ("the") before this participle (οἱ . . . ἀποστρεφόμενοι, "[we] the ones who turn away") is probably original (*pace* Lane, 2:443ww).

12. The pastor, who often used conditional sentences in his earlier warnings, has reserved this more forceful substantive for the conclusion of his argument (Smillie, "'The One Who Is Speaking' in Hebrews 12:25," 288-89).

13. According to Weiss, 684-85, the possibility of the hearers "turning away" and suffering judgment shows that the Sinai theophany in vv. 18-21 is not merely a past event,

26 This second less-to-greater argument is divided between the "then" of Sinai, the "now" of the promise, and the "once more" of the judgment.[14] "Then" and "once more" bear the weight of the argument: "then" refers to the lesser shaking of the earth at Mount Sinai; "once more," to that much greater shaking at the Judgment. However, anticipation of this judgment is even "now," through God's promise, a reality that determines the lives of the faithful.[15] The embodiment of God's judgment on the disobedient in the Sinai of vv. 18-21 has become the anticipation of his final Judgment.

"Whose voice once shook the earth." The voice of the God who now speaks to us from heaven through his Son "once shook the earth" when he spoke on Mount Sinai. "Voice" recalls the awesomeness of Sinai (see on v. 19 above), where God's voice was heard though he was not seen nor was there access to his presence. The aorist tense of the verb translated "shook" and the particle "then" both point to the specific time when God not only spoke on Sinai but "shook the earth." "The earth" confirms this statement as a reference to Sinai and prepares for comparison with the shaking of "the earth" and "the heavens" below. The pastor has chosen a word for "shook" that is different from, though a close synonym for, the word used in the following quotation from Hag 2:6.[16] The LXX text of Exod 19:18 does not refer to the quaking of Mount Sinai. However, Ps 67:9 (MT 68:8) uses the same word found in Haggai to describe Sinai's trembling, and Judg 5:5 employs the word used by the writer of Hebrews. The pastor may have chosen to use this synonym because it was often used in the Greek Bible to describe God's judgment (2 Kgs 17:20; Ps 47 [MT 48]:6; Lam 1:8). It was also used to describe "the righteous as those who share in the unshakable character of God."[17]

God is the one who "has promised" this future Judgment through his words in Hag 2:6, which the pastor quotes as "once more I will shake not only the earth but also the heavens." The perfect tense of "has promised" indicates that God's promise, made in Scripture, remains valid. Indeed, the work of the Son, through whom God now speaks, confirms this divine pledge in anticipation of its fulfillment.[18] Thus the imminent fulfillment of this

---

but a present possibility for the pastor's hearers. Thus he confirms the interpretation of those verses given above.

14. The one whose voice shook the earth τότε ("then") has νῦν δέ ("but now") promised that he will ἔτι ἅπαξ ("yet once") again shake the earth and heaven.

15. God's future final Judgment has been promised by God through the prophet. Weiss, 687.

16. Compare ἐσάλευσεν ("shook," from σαλεύω) in 12:26a with σείσω ("I will shake," from σείω) in the Hag 2:6 quotation. See Josephus, *Ant.* 4.44; Matt 21:10; 27:51.

17. Lane, 2:481. See Pss 14 [MT 15]:5; 15 [MT 16]:8; 54 [MT 55:22]:23; 61 [MT 62:2]:3; 65 [MT 66]:9; 111 [MT 112]:6; 120 [MT 121]:3; 124 [MT 125]:1.

18. Spicq, 2:412.

promise of the consummation is determinative for the present existence of God's people. By calling this prophecy of judgment a "promise" the pastor has brought the art of combining warning and promise to perfection. The coming Judgment is obviously a warning — God's people need to be ready. And yet it is a promise of final salvation (cf. 9:28) to be anticipated with joy because only at the Judgment will God's people enter into the fullness of the "Unshakable Kingdom" God has for them.[19]

Hebrews quotes God's speech in the first clause of Hag 2:6, which runs in the LXX as follows: "Once more I will shake the heaven, and the earth, and the sea, and the dry land." According to Haggai, this shaking will be a judgment on the nations, in which the present world order will be overthrown and Jerusalem will be glorified as never before.[20] The pastor, however, knows that God's dwelling place in Jerusalem anticipates the heavenly Jerusalem. Thus, Haggai's prophecy looks forward to the final overthrow of this world order, when God's people will enter into the fullness of their final abode in the permanent, heavenly Jerusalem.[21] In order to bring out this significance, Hebrews has paraphrased Hag 2:6 by leaving out references to "the sea" and "the dry land"; by putting "the earth" before "the heavens"; and by setting these two in contrast ("not only," "but also").[22] Haggai intended "the heaven, and the earth, and the sea, and the dry land" to be all-inclusive. Hebrews intends "not only the earth but also the heavens" to be inclusive. Yet the effect of these changes introduced by Hebrews is to put emphasis on "the heavens," the last word in the verse. At first glance it would appear that by "the heavens" the pastor is referring to the higher part of the created universe, as in 1:10; 4:14; 7:26; 11:12.[23] In 1:10-12 he spoke of the Son as both creating and removing the "earth" and the "heavens." On this interpretation he would be saying little more than what Haggai intended. On the other hand, 11:13-16 has established a different perspective for these chapters. The faithful are strangers "on earth" because they have a "heavenly" home.[24] Furthermore, in 12:25 the pastor has just contrasted God's speaking "on earth" with his speaking "from heaven." The strong contrast formed by "not only" the

---

19. "The announcement of this final catastrophe of the world, however awful in itself, is a 'promise,' because it is for the triumph of the cause of God that believers look" (Westcott, 419).

20. Haggai 2:22-23 is very similar to vv. 6-7 and, therefore, reinforces this understanding of the text.

21. Spicq, 2:411-12.

22. For the use of this verse as descriptive of the final eschatological earthquake, see 2 Bar. 59:3 and 4 Ezra 6:11-17; 10:25-28 (cited by Thompson, 263).

23. So Mitchell, 288; Braun, 443; Weiss, 689-91; and Grässer, 3:331-35.

24. Note ἐπὶ τῆς γῆς ("on earth") in 11:13 and ἐπουρανίου ("heavenly") in 11:16. Cf. 9:24.

earth "but also" heaven suggests that the pastor is maintaining the same perspective here. God's final Judgment will shake not only the created order but even the heavenly dwelling place of God.[25] This contrast between God's shaking not only the "earth" but also "heaven" is a most forceful way of saying that this judgment is absolutely final.[26] This Judgment will occur "once more," and is thus as unrepeatable as Christ's sacrifice and session (v. 27).

27 The phrase "once more" is crucial to the pastor's understanding of God's promise in Hag 2:6. The hearers already know that the Son who came "once" to remove sin will return for the final "salvation" of his own (9:26-28). The God who has made provision "once for all" for the salvation of his people by speaking through his Son will speak "once more" — in a judgment so final that it will shake heaven and earth and bring God's own into the full enjoyment of that "salvation."[27] This is the time anticipated by Ps 110:1 (1:3, 13) when the Son's "enemies" will be "made a stool for" his "feet." It is the time when "all things" will be "subjected under his feet" (2:8; cf. Ps 8:8). The people of God now live in the "today" (3:7, 13, 15; 4:7) of opportunity between Christ's session and his return. The pastor has appropriately reserved his description of this climactic event for the end of this "history of the faithful people of God" (10:32–12:29).

Some have argued, on the basis of Platonic dualism, that a future Judgment is not the pastor's primary interest in this passage.[28] He is not truly

---

25. So Koester, 547.

26. Lane's attempt (2:480) to equate "heaven" with the New Covenant and "earth" with the Old cannot be sustained. The pastor is affirming the finality of this judgment, not merely the truism that God will judge the people of both covenants.

27. With the ἔτι ἅπαξ ("once more") of this verse compare the ἅπαξ ("once") of the Son's appearing (9:26) and sacrifice (9:28; 10:10) and the ἐφάπαξ ("once for all") of his sacrifice (7:27) and entrance into God's presence on our behalf (9:12). Cf. Michel, 473; Johnson, 335.

28. Weiss, 690-93; Thompson, *Christian Philosophy*, 45-51; Theissen, *Untersuchungen*, 108. Thompson thinks that the author began with a Jewish apocalyptic tradition that emphasized a coming final Judgment, but that he has reworked this tradition in terms of Platonic dualism. He wrongly attributes the devaluation of the Sinai revelation to this dualism rather than to the pastor's commitment to the finality of Christ. Weiss, on the other hand, believes the author has introduced futuristic elements from Jewish apocalyptic into a Hellenistic tradition that emphasized the ontological difference between the heavenly and earthly worlds. For instance, Weiss (693-94) thinks the expression "Unshakable Kingdom" has been derived from such apocalyptic speculation on future judgment (Dan 6:1, 29; 7:18; 2 Macc 4:7; 10:11; *Letter of Aristeas* 36; Josephus, *Ant.* 15.16), but he contends that it has lost its apocalyptic force by being integrated into the author's Hellenistic-dualistic eschatology (693-94). For both Weiss and Thompson the dualistic view is the author's primary frame of reference. Eisele, *Ein unerschütterliches Reich*, 133, goes further than either. He attempts to dissolve any reference to the temporal/eschatological when he

concerned with the "removal" or "destruction" of the temporal order at that time of ultimate accountability. Instead, the pastor contrasts the "change-ability" of the created order ("the things that can be shaken," "things that have been made") with the unchanging heavenly world that the faithful enter at death ("things that cannot be shaken").[29] The pastor, however, is neither a Platonist, nor is he indebted to Platonic dualism in this passage.[30] Those who hold this position rely heavily on their interpretation of the word we have translated "removal," to the neglect of both the immediate context and the broader concerns of Hebrews. It is true that this word can mean "change" or "transformation"[31] rather than "removal" or "destruction." It is used for Enoch's "translation" to heaven in 11:5. Perhaps more to the point, this term is used for the "change" of the priesthood from the order of Aaron to that of Melchizedek in 7:12. Yet, according to 7:18, this "change" is indeed an "abolition."[32] Thus, usage elsewhere provides no genuine support for translating this word as "changeability" rather than "removal." This interpretation ignores all of the other places given above where the pastor anticipates the return of Christ. It denies the force of "once more" (v. 27) as explained above.[33]

---

says, ". . . there exists a clear order of being which is characterized by the distinction between earth and heaven, the shakable *(Erschüttertem)* and the unshakable *(Unerschüttertem)*, the set aside *(Beseitigtem)* and enduring *(Bleibendem)*, the transient *(Vergänglichem)* and the intransient *(Unvergänglichem)*, the *changeable (Veränderlichem)* and the *unchangeable (Unveränderlichem)*" (italics added). Thompson can find only rather remote parallels in dualistic sources to τῶν σαλευομένων ("the things that can be shaken") and τὰ μὴ σαλευόμενα ("the things that cannot be shaken").

29. With the T/NIV we have taken τῶν σαλευομένων ("the things that are shaken") and τὰ μὴ σαλευόμενα ("the things that are not shaken") as potential: "the things that can be shaken," "the things that cannot be shaken." We have argued above that the "heaven" of v. 26 is indeed the true dwelling of God, that is, the home of the things "that cannot be shaken." This puts us in the position of saying that at the Judgment God will "shake" the "unshakable" heaven. The contradiction is only apparent. God will "shake" heaven in that it too is subject to his judgment. It is, however, "unshakable" in that it will withstand his judgment.

30. Attridge, 381; Lincoln D. Hurst, "Eschatology and 'Platonism' in the Epistle to the Hebrews," in *SBLSP* (Atlanta: Scholars Press, 1984), 41-74. The "things that cannot be shaken" have been described in vv. 22-24 and do not constitute an ethereal world of ideas. Furthermore, the pastor gives no indication that the "things that can be shaken"/ "things that have been made" are, in the Platonic sense, a copy of the unshakable realities. Nor does the pastor share the Platonic view that this created world is eternal (contrast 1:10-11 with Philo, *Decalogue* 58; cf. Bruce, 365).

31. BDAG, 639, 2, gives this meaning for μετάθεσις in Heb 12:27.

32. See the comment above on μετάθεσις at 7:12, a contrast to ἀθέτησις ("abolition") in 7:18.

33. Eisele, *Ein unerschütterliches Reich,* 118, admits that this "once-for-all," final shaking of the created order is parallel to Christ's "once-for-all" sacrifice. After this ad-

It overlooks the fact that the pastor has already described the eternal Son as the one who will bring the created order to an end (1:11-12). It does not acknowledge the resurrection of the dead as an important part of the pastor's future expectation (see the comments on 11:17-19, 35). It fails to recognize the appropriateness of the final Judgment here in 12:25-29 at the climax of the history of God's faithful (10:32–12:29).

It is probable that the pastor has not used a stronger term because he is not as concerned with the metaphysical demise of the created world as with its end as the context for the life of God's people.[34] He is not hostile toward creation. It will be removed when God shakes it because it consists of "things that have been made" by God. As part of the created order these "things" will be brought to an end when God has achieved his purposes for them (1:11-12). The creation "made" by God is also characterized by what humans make (8:5; 9:24), by human sinfulness, mortality, and weakness. It is the sphere that offers God's people no permanent home, the sphere in which they face opposition. It is also, however, the sphere in which Christ has achieved human redemption.

"The things that can be shaken" are not related to "the things that cannot be shaken" as "flesh" is related to "spirit."[35] These two realms are different because of their differing relationships to God.[36] He has made the first

---

mission, however, he proceeds to argue that the emphasis in this final, "once-for-all" shaking is not on the specific final temporal occurrence of this event but on "the final end of an ongoing process" (Eisele, *Ein unerschütterliches Reich,* 124). Hebrews knows nothing of such a process. The parallel with Christ's first coming forbids separating the temporal specificity and the eschatological finality of this event. Eisele, *Ein unerschütterliches Reich,* 124, admits the weakness of this argument by saying that "it is at least worth suggesting."

34. Thus, one might change Ellingworth's statement, "total annihilation probably lies beyond the author's horizon" (688) to something like "total annihilation is not what the author is emphasizing." The question as to whether the eternal abode of the blessed is heaven or a renewed earth would probably have seemed strange to the author of Hebrews. It is clear that the temporal passes away. On the other hand, this eternal abode is a "home," a "city," a true Mount Zion. It is "real" not in the abstract Platonic sense of a world of ideas, but in the concrete sense of those who have been raised from the dead. Since it is identified with the "rest" of God at the climax of creation, it is already in existence, just as the "Jerusalem" that comes down out of heaven from God in Rev 21:10 is already in existence. The "removal" of creation in Heb 12:27 reminds one of the way Rev 20:11; 21:1 refer to the heaven and earth fleeing away before the face of God (Bruce, 365). Cf. Rev 6:12-14; 18:18-20; 2 Pet 3:10; *1 En.* 60:1; *2 Bar.* 59:3.

35. *Pace* Attridge, 381. Though Attridge goes on to say, "All these things, Christ's priesthood and the eschatological inheritance of his followers, are unshakable and abiding *because they are grounded in the reality of God and God's immutable will*" (Attridge, 381-82, italics added).

36. "But for our author, the distinction is not between matter and spirit as such,

668

and will bring it to its consummation when he has achieved his purposes through it. It is not, however, his dwelling place. The heavenly City, on the other hand, is the place of his abode and the place of intimate fellowship with him.[37] As its "architect and builder" (11:10), he has established it on a permanent, enduring foundation.[38] A glance at the quotation from Gen 2:2 in Heb 4:4 will help to make this clear: "God rested on the seventh day from all his works." The Genesis text continues, "which he made," using the same word we find in Heb 12:26 for "the things that are made."[39] God "made" the world in six days, but it was by entering his "rest" at the climax of creation on the seventh day that he brought into being the eternal City that is the ultimate "rest" of the people of God. Thus, the Genesis account suggests that this "rest"/City is both beyond creation and creation's divinely intended goal (see the comments on 1:2-3). The essential difference, then, between what can be shaken and what cannot, lies in their respective relationships to God and his purposes.[40]

The pastor has given two unanswerable reasons why the people of God should "not refuse him who is speaking" (v. 25a). First, if God's judgment on those who heard him speak at Sinai was certain, his judgment on those who refuse his gracious word, spoken from heaven through the exalted

---

but between that which is created and that which participates in God. What 'remains' (*meine*) therefore is not the mental as opposed to the physical, but what 'receives a share in God's holiness' (12:10), as opposed to things that do not enter into the 'city of the living God'" (Johnson, 335-36). This quotation is the more significant because Johnson often attributes the contrast between the heavenly and the earthly in Hebrews to Platonic dualism.

37. "What cannot be shaken" refers to the "heavenly Jerusalem" as the "home" of God's people (11:13-16), God's eternal "rest" (3:7–4:11), and the "City whose architect and builder is God" (11:9-10). By implication, all who dwell within this city, and everything Christ has done to bring them thereunto, are also included within what cannot be shaken.

38. Compare μένουσαν πόλιν ("remaining city," "enduring city") in 13:14; ὕπαρξιν . . . μένουσαν ("remaining possession," "enduring possession") in 10:34 with ἵνα μείνῃ τὰ μὴ σαλευόμενα ("in order that what cannot be shaken might remain") here in 12:27. Cf. 7:3, 24. In the LXX μείνω ("remain") "is used frequently in reference to the enduring, unchangeable character of God, of reality like the new heaven and earth, and of persons who are rightly related to God (e.g., Ps. 102:25; Isa. 66:22; Zech 14:10 . . .)" (Lane, 2:482-83).

39. Compare ὧν ἐποίησε ("which he made") from Gen 2:2 with πεποιημένων ("things which have been made") in Heb 12:27 (cf. also ποιέω in 1:2 for God's creating). The perfect participle, πεποιημένων, implies that these things are established, they have been made and are still in existence. This word is used repeatedly in Gen 1:1-31 to describe God's creating the world (1:1, 7, 11, 12, 16, 21, 25, 26, 27, 31). In Gen. 2:4 God is described as the one who "made" (ἐποίησε) "the heaven and the earth" (τὸν οὐρανὸν καὶ τὴν γῆν).

40. O'Brien, 496. Cf. Lane, 2:482, but with different arguments.

Son, is much more certain (v. 25bc). Second, as he once caused Sinai to tremble, so he will shake "heaven and earth" at the final Judgment. That Judgment will leave those who have no part in the eternal City without a place to stand (vv. 26-27).

28 The pastor, however, would not let his hearers forget that Haggai's prophecy of the coming Judgment is for the faithful a promise (v. 26) of final entrance into the things "that cannot be shaken." Those who persevere in obedience are even now in the process of receiving the "Kingdom that is unshakable," which they will enter at Christ's return.[41] While God's people live in awe of this coming Judgment, they do not live in terror, for it will mean the final reception of what God has for them. The "Unshakable Kingdom" is the pastor's concluding depiction of the reality he has already described as the "rest that remains for the people of God" (4:3); "the City with foundations, whose architect and builder is God" (11:10); the heavenly "home" (11:13-16); "Mount Zion" and the "heavenly Jerusalem" (12:22); and "what cannot be shaken" by the final Judgment (12:27).[42] This sermon began with the enthronement of the Son at God's right hand (1:3). Thus it is fitting for the pastor to conclude by describing what the faithful are in the process of receiving as the "Unshakable Kingdom."[43] The idiom "to receive a kingdom" may mean to assume the rule over a kingdom.[44] In this instance, however, it refers to final and complete entrance into the permanent and unshakable rule of God. Things will be right only when God reigns from Zion. It is the reign of God that gives Mount Zion, the heavenly City and Home, its substance and identity. It is nothing less than the divine rule that establishes the ultimate peace, harmony, and holiness of the people of God (cf. 12:14). Only under his permanent rule is the fellowship of the people of

41. Notice how the pastor ends v. 27 in Greek with τὰ μὴ σαλευόμενα ("the things that cannot be shaken") and then begins v. 28, after the initial διό ("therefore"), by describing essentially the same reality as βασιλείαν ἀσάλευτον ("a Kingdom Unshakable"). The "things that cannot be shaken" (τὰ μὴ σαλευόμενα) probably includes the "Unshakable Kingdom" (βασιλείαν ἀσάλευτον), as well as those who will receive it and all Christ has done to provide it (see Lane, 2:484).

42. See O'Brien, 498; Son, *Zion Symbolism,* 195, n. 127.

43. Johnson, 336, reminds us that this emphasis on the enthronement of Christ shows that "Hebrews shares the common Christian understanding of the 'rule of God' *(basileia tou theou)* established through Jesus (Matt 4:17; 26:29; Mark 1:15; 14:25; Luke 4:43; 22:16; John 18:63; Acts 14:22; Rom 14:17; 1 Cor 6:9; Gal 5:21; Eph 5:5; Col 4:11; 1 Thess 2:12; 2 Thess 1:5; 2 Tim 4:1; Jas 2:5; 2 Pet 1:11; Rev 1:9)." For refutation of Stedman's contention that the "Unshakable Kingdom" is the millennial kingdom, compare Ray C. Stedman, *Hebrews* (Downers Grove, IL: InterVarsity Press, 1992), 14, 37, 123, 133, 144 with deSilva, 471-72, n. 69.

44. See 2 Macc 10:11 (cf. Thompson, 269). Cf. also Dan 7:18, where God's "holy ones" will receive and perpetually possess the "kingdom."

God "rest."[45] Thus, the submission of the faithful to the voice of God in the present is intrinsically related to their final state and place of blessedness in the Unshakable Kingdom where God's rule is all in all.[46]

The pastor brings his description of all that God has provided for his people through his Son to its climax in this "Unshakable Kingdom." The following exhortation expresses the ultimate response that he desires from his hearers in light of God's provision: "therefore, let us have gratitude."[47] In the

45. Cf. Ellingworth, 689-90.

46. The term "Unshakable Kingdom" may have been suggested to the author of Hebrews by Hag 2:6 and related passages. Compare the LXX translation of Hag 2:6-7 with the closely related Hab 2:21b-22a: "For this is what the Lord Almighty says, Once again *I will shake the sky and the earth and the sea and the dry land,* and I will *shake all the nations,* and the choice things of all the nations shall come, and I will fill this house with splendor, says the Lord Almighty" (Hag 2:6-7). "*I am shaking the sky and the earth and the sea and the dry land,* and I will *overthrow thrones of kings* and destroy power of kings of the nations . . ." (Hag 2:21b-22a). Note that in these passages God's shaking of sky (heaven), earth, sea, and dry land entails the shaking of the nations, the overthrowing of kings, and the bringing of the choice things of the nations to Jerusalem. Thus, it implies the establishing of God's rule. With these verses the prophet Haggai was encouraging God's people to rebuild the Temple. Thus, it would have been natural for the pastor to associate Psalm 96 LXX (97 MT) with Haggai because in the LXX this psalm bears the title, "When the house was being rebuilt after the captivity." Ps 96:9-10 reads, "Do obeisance to the Lord in his holy court; let *all the earth shake from before him.* Say among the nations, *'The Lord became king!'* Indeed, he set right *the world,* which shall *not be shaken.* He will judge peoples with forthrightness." In Haggai God said he would shake the earth. Here the psalmist calls on the earth to "shake from before" God. Then he declares, "'The Lord became king! Indeed, he set right the world (οἰκουμένη; cf. Heb 1:6; 2:5), which shall not be shaken.'" Taken together, these verses suggest that after judgment God will rule an unshakable dominion. The italics have been added to the quotations above for emphasis. See Lane, 2:485; Albert Vanhoye, "L'οἰκουμένη dans l'épître aux Hébreux," *Bib* 45 (1964): 248-53.

47. The word for "gratitude" (χάρις) in ἔχωμεν χάριν ("let us have gratitude") is the word translated "grace" elsewhere in Hebrews (2:9; 4:16; 10:29; 12:15; and 13:9). Indeed, ἔχωμεν χάριν ("let us have gratitude") here in 12:28 forms an inclusion with τῆς χάριτος τοῦ θεοῦ ("the grace of God") in 12:15 (Vanhoye, *La structure littéraire,* 209, cited by Ellingworth, 690). Spicq, 2:412-13, is representative of those who would translate χάρις as "grace" here in 12:28 as well: "let us have grace" (NKJV) so that we can live a life of obedience. However, the translation "gratitude" is to be preferred for several reasons. First, the pastor normally describes the benefits provided by Christ as something the faithful already "have" and upon which they should act (4:14-16; 10:19-25). In 4:16, which might be thought of as an exception to this statement, "grace" does not refer to these benefits in general but to God's specific help to meet a particular situation. Second, the fact that the pastor has used the term elsewhere with the meaning "grace" does not prevent his using it here in a different way. The hearers would not miss the inclusion formed by the use of this word in vv. 15 and 28, even if it has a different meaning in the later verse. Third, the combination ἔχωμεν χάριν is an idiom that normally means "let us have

earlier part of his sermon the pastor whetted their appetites through describing the magnitude of God's provision. He appealed to fear by warning them that rejection meant ultimate loss. The surest foundation, however, for a life of faithfulness is a profound sense of gratitude toward God for his goodness in offering his people unending fellowship with himself through his Son.[48] This gratitude is the means and basis for "serving God pleasingly with godly fear and awe." The word translated "serve" is also used for "worship."[49] The pastor has explained the work of Christ in priestly terms. Thus, the life of the faithful is a life of worship, a life of approaching God through Christ with the offerings of praise and good works, as chapter 13 will show. The pastor reinforces "godly fear" by adding "awe." Such "godly fear" is the recognition of the majesty of God, his authority over created human beings, and their ultimate accountability before him at the Judgment.[50] During his earthly life Jesus perfectly reflected such "godly fear" through his obedience (5:7-8). Such reverent recognition of God characterized Noah (11:7) and the other heroes of faith in chapter 11. Esau, on the other hand, was "godless" because he refused to recognize God's majesty and ultimate authority (12:16). This "godly fear" cannot be separated from the "gratitude" that the pastor desires. Only those with such "godly fear" can begin to appreciate the great goodness of God in providing salvation through his Son. On the other hand, grateful recognition of his blessings only heightens the awe and reverence with which God's people approach him. To live in such "gratitude" and "godly fear" is to live in the kind of obedience that flows from a heart on which God has written his laws (10:15-18). It is to live with full confidence in the reality of God's power for the present and in the certainty of his promises for the future — promises of both blessing and loss (11:1, 3, 6). Those who live this life truly "serve" God by approaching him with praise and the obedience of good works as described in the following chapter.[51]

29 In 4:13 the pastor affirmed that all were accountable before God. In 10:31 he declared that it was "a fearful thing to fall into the hands of the living God." Here in 12:29, this theme of God's judgment reaches its climax:

---

gratitude" (see BDAG, 1080, 5). This idiomatic combination and the immediate context are determinative. See deSilva, 473-76.

48. According to deSilva, 473, "let us have gratitude" becomes "the basic summons of the whole letter." It is the appropriate response to the "gift" of the "Unshakable Kingdom."

49. For λατρεύω as approaching God in worship or as priestly service, see 8:5; 9:1, 6, 9; 10:2; 13:10.

50. Lane, 2:487: "The life that is appropriate worship expresses fear and awe, because it recognizes the certainty of the promised eschatological shaking." See also Thompson, 269, and Weiss, 695.

51. Thompson, 269; deSilva, 469.

"For our God is a consuming fire."[52] In vv. 18-21 the pastor used the descriptions of God revealing himself at Sinai in Deut 4:11-12; 5:22-24 to underscore the awesomeness of God's judgment on the disobedient. He brings that theme to its highest pitch here by changing the "your" of Deut 4:15 to "our"; not "your God is a consuming fire," but "even our God is a consuming fire." By using "our" the pastor identifies with his hearers. At the same time, this change makes it clear that "our" God is the same God rejected by those whose judgment is depicted in vv. 18-21.[53] Such judgment is even more certain for those who turn away in apostasy from all God has done in Christ.[54] This statement is the pastor's final motivation for serving "God acceptably with godly fear and awe."[55] Yet it also reinforces his call for gratitude. Recognition of such potential judgment only heightens the awareness that God is good in providing not only a way of escape, but a way that his own can enjoy eternal fellowship with him.[56] In the following chapter the pastor will give specific instructions on how God's people are to live this life of gratitude and awe, both in relation to one another and to the unbelieving world.[57]

IV. INSTRUCTIONS FOR THE LIFE OF GRATITUDE AND GODLY FEAR (13:1-25)

Many modern readers are sensitive to the seemingly abrupt change in style at the beginning of chapter 13. After reaching the rhetorical high point of his appeal for perseverance in 12:25-29, the pastor adds a series of brief, diverse exhortations in 13:1-6. A further change in style occurs at v. 18, and even more clearly at v. 22, when the pastor adopts the intimacy of the first person singular and adds elements appropriate for the conclusion of a letter. Thus at first glance chapter 13 might appear to include a miscellaneous collection of materials that have little to do with one another or with the first twelve chapters of Hebrews.[1] Some have pointed out the difference in vocabulary evi-

---

52. See Thompson, 270. On "consuming fire" as an expression of God's judgment, see Ellingworth, 692, and Michel, 478. Cf. Isa 33:14; Deut 4:24; 9:3.

53. Note the emphasis achieved through the initial καί in v. 29: "*Even* our God is a consuming fire" (italics added).

54. Weiss, 696-97.

55. Note the γάρ ("for") at the beginning of v. 29.

56. See deSilva, 477.

57. Attridge, 379; Thompson 269; deSilva, 469.

1. According to the segmentation apparatus in the UBS[4] Greek text, one can find some Greek edition or modern language translation that makes a paragraph break after each of the following verses: 2, 3, 4, 5, 6, 7, 8, 9, 10, 14, 15, 16, 17, 19, 21, 22, 23, and 24.

denced by this chapter.[2] Others have contended that chapter 13 betrays a literary style inferior to the rest of the book.[3] These observations have led to the hypothesis that this final chapter or part thereof was added by a later hand.[4] Some have suggested that this happened when Hebrews was sent as a letter.[5] Others believe that this addition was made to apply the message of the first twelve chapters to a new situation, or to make Hebrews acceptable as a canonical book.[6] The objections to the authenticity of this chapter have, however, been adequately addressed by many.[7] The exposition below will show that the literary style of chapter 13 is as sophisticated as that evidenced by earlier chapters.[8] The pastor makes concrete application of the key themes developed in the earlier part of his sermon.[9] Furthermore, the diversity of vocabulary is no greater than that evidenced by other parts of Hebrews.[10] Thus

2. Most recently, A. J. M. Wedderburn, "The 'Letter' to the Hebrews and Its Thirteenth Chapter," *NTS* 50 (2004): 395-99.

3. C. C. Torrey, "The Authorship and Character of the So-Called 'Epistle to the Hebrews,'" *JBL* 30 (1911): 137-56.

4. The integrity of chapter 13 has been challenged by, among others, G. A. Simcox, "Heb. XIII; 2 Tim IV," *ExpTim* 10 (1898-99): 430-32; Torrey, "Authorship," 137-56; E. D. Jones, "The Authorship of Hebrews XIII," *ExpTim* 46 (1934-35): 562-67; Buchanan, 229-45, 267-68; and, most recently, Wedderburn, "The 'Letter' to the Hebrews and Its Thirteenth Chapter," 390-405.

5. Héring, 126, proposes that chapter 13 was added by Paul in order to recommend the Letter of Hebrews, written by his friend Apollos.

6. For the former suggestion see Wedderburn, "The 'Letter' to the Hebrews and Its Thirteenth Chapter," 403-5; for the latter, Buchanan, 229-45, 267-68.

7. See R. V. G. Tasker, "The Integrity of the Epistle to the Hebrews," *ExpTim* 47 (1935-36): 136-38; Floyd V. Filson, *"Yesterday": A Study of Hebrews in the Light of Chapter 13* (London: SCM, 1967); Jukka Thurén, *Das Lobopfer der Hebräer: Studien zum Aufbau und Anliegen vom Hebräerbrief 13* (Åbo: Akademi, 1973), 57-70; Albert Vanhoye, "La question littéraire de Hébreux XIII.1-6," *NTS* 23 (1977): 121-39; and esp. the thorough discussion in Lane, 2:495-507.

8. See Vanhoye, "Hébreux XIII.1-6," 121-27, esp. 127; Thurén, *Lobopfer, passim*. Nevertheless, Thurén's hypothesis that chapter 13 was composed before the rest of Hebrews and served as the inspiration for the earlier chapters cannot be sustained (Thurén, *Lobopfer,* 53-55, 108, 246-47). This chapter does not have the marks of an independent document. The exhortation to brotherly love in 13:1 is too limited to provide an introduction for the entire chapter. See Vanhoye, "Hébreux XIII.1-6," 130-32, 135-36. Chapter 13's diverse sections find their unity only as the "peroration" of the sermon begun in the previous chapters.

9. Filson, *"Yesterday,"* 27-84; Thurén, *Lobopfer.* Vanhoye, "Hébreux XIII.1-6," 128-30, compares love in 13:1-3 with 6:10; 10:24; 12:14; solidarity with prisoners in 13:2 with 10:34; 11:36; judgment in 13:4 with 6:2; 9:27; 10:30-31; and confidence in God's help in 13:6 with 2:18; 4:16. Weiss, 699, demonstrates that 13:10-14 assumes the Christological development of the central section and serves as warrant for the exhortations in 13:13 and 13:15.

10. Vanhoye, "Hébreux XIII.1-6," 129, shows that while 13:1-6 has sixteen words

it is clear that the thirteenth chapter of Hebrews is more than an "appendix" added after the pastor had finished with his main concerns.[11]

The recognition that Hebrews draws on the methods of Hellenistic rhetoric has helped interpreters put this chapter in proper perspective. It was customary in the ancient world for speeches to end with a *peroratio* in which the orator made a final attempt to move his audience in the desired direction.[12] This "peroration" was supposed to draw suggestively on the earlier part of the speech, using short exhortations and vivid imagery to arouse the hearers.[13] When viewed from this perspective, one can see clearly that Heb 13:1-17 is the pastor's "peroration." Verses 18-21 may be taken as part of this peroration or as the beginning of the letter ending that follows in vv. 22-25.[14] Without this "peroration" the pastor would not have been able to effectively conclude the appeal for perseverance through wholehearted reliance on Christ that he has so diligently pursued since the beginning of his sermon.

The pastor's exhortation in 12:28-29 to a life of "acceptable worship" characterized by profound gratitude and "godly fear" is the bond that unites chapters 1 through 12 with the verses that follow. Heb 12:28-29 is the pastor's richest description of the life of faith as it is lived by those who experience what God has done in Christ.[15] As such, these verses conclude and cul-

---

not found elsewhere in Hebrews, 12:18-21 and 12:14-17 each have fourteen words elsewhere absent from this book. Weiss, 698, suggests that the unique vocabulary of this chapter, with its "Paulinisms," is due to the author's use of traditional parenetic material. He reminds the reader that this traditional language of moral instruction has already been used in such places as 12:14. Furthermore, the terms used in 13:1-6 for "reminding" (μιμνῄσκομαι, 13:3; 2:6; 8:12; 10:17) and "remaining" (μένω, 13:1, 14; 7:3, 24; 10:34; 12:27; cf. διαμένω in 1:11) are characteristic of the earlier chapters.

11. *Pace* Spicq, 2:415; Montefiore, 237; and others.

12. See "The Sermon's Rhetorically Effective Structure," pp. 60-77 in the Introduction to this commentary, and esp. pp. 74, 76.

13. See Koester, 555-56.

14. Filson, *"Yesterday,"* 22-25, and Thurén, *Lobopfer,* 55-70, have attempted to show that the end of Hebrews reflects a literary structure common to other NT letters. Vanhoye, "Hébreux XIII.1-6," 132-34, however, has shown that, while these letter endings share many of the same themes or motifs, they do not represent a common literary form. On p. 132 he cites Thurén's own admission that, when compared with these other letters, the ending of Hebrews has many gaps, and that the author felt free to vary the order in which he considered the motifs common to others.

15. The life of faith is living as if God's promises for the future are certain and his power in the present is real (see on 11:1-7). This same life can be described as one that expresses the deepest, awe-filled gratitude for what God has done in Christ: delivering his people from judgment and providing them with the hope of an "Unshakable Kingdom" (12:28). The person who lives from such motives is certainly living in dependence on God's power and promises in the truest sense. Both descriptions are ways of depicting the person who lives as if God is God.

minate the pastor's appeal so ardently pursued in the previous chapters. Verses 28-29 also introduce the exposition and exhortations that follow.[16] In 13:1-17 the pastor describes the concrete form which this life of "acceptable worship" is to assume, and makes one last appeal for its pursuit in the face of an unbelieving world.

Thus, when properly understood, the material in this chapter can be appropriately divided into three sections — vv. 1-6; 7-17; and 18-25.[17] In vv. 1-6 four pairs of exhortations tell the hearers how to live the faithful life of gratitude and godly fear within the community of God's people. At the end of this section the pastor invites his hearers to join him in affirming the kind of trust in God through Christ that he has been urgently advocating throughout his sermon.[18] Verses 7-17 begin with a call to imitate past leaders and end with the urgency of submitting to present leaders.[19] In this section the pastor restates once again the appeal of the earlier chapters by exhorting his hearers to identify with Christ in his suffering and to offer the sacrifices of praise and good works. These sacrifices are the appropriate response to Christ's atoning sacrifice, and are thus to characterize the life of gratitude and godly fear.[20]

---

16. Lane, 2:497-98; O'Brien, 503; Thurén, *Lobopfer,* 234-35; and Filson, *"Yesterday,"* 28. Koester, 554-56, goes so far as to make 12:28-29 the introduction to 13:1-21 instead of the conclusion to 12:25-29. Westfall, *Discourse Analysis,* 295, *passim,* recognizes this dual role by including these verses both with what precedes and what follows.

17. These are the divisions suggested by Weiss, 700.

18. Although v. 7 begins with another second plural imperative, it should not be joined with vv. 1-6 for several reasons (*pace* Johnson, 337): v. 7 lacks the economy of style present in vv. 1-6; v. 6 is a fitting conclusion to what has gone before; and, finally, the mention of leaders in v. 7 forms an inclusion with v. 17. It is even less likely that vv. 7-9a should go with vv. 1-6, as Westfall, *Discourse Analysis,* 284, 295, suggests. Verse 9a is closely connected with vv. 9b-11.

19. Westfall's suggestion that the final section begin with v. 17 spoils the inclusion with v. 7 (Westfall, *Discourse Analysis,* 291-95). Vanhoye's attempt to include v. 18 with vv. 7-17 is awkward because of the close connection between vv. 18 and 19 (Vanhoye, *La structure littéraire,* 211-16). Lane, 499-500, following Guthrie, *Structure,* 134, makes a plausible case for including both vv. 18 and 19 with vv. 7-17. He argues that vv. 17-19, which refer to the recipients' present leaders and to the author himself, parallel vv. 7-9, which refer to their past leaders, to the finality of Christ, and to false teaching. These two sections frame vv. 10-16, which differs from them in that it develops exhortation based directly on Scriptural interpretation. Lane would also include the benediction in vv. 20-21 with what has gone before as a further development of the life of gratitude and godly fear. See also McCown, "Ο ΛΟΓΟΣ ΤΗΣ ΠΑΡΑΚΛΗΣΕΩΣ," 145-49, and Thurén, *Lobopfer,* 71. Attridge, 390, takes vv. 7-19 as a unit, but joins vv. 20-21 to vv. 22-25 as the letter ending. See the comments on vv. 18-25 below.

20. Thurén, *Lobopfer,* 74-90, 105-82, 187-245; Lane, 2:497-98; Weiss, 699; Koester, 557; Thompson, 276-77; and many others. Note the inclusion between εὐαρεστεῖται ὁ θεός ("God is well pleased," 13:16) and εὐαρέστως τῷ θεῷ ("well pleasing

After requesting the prayers of his hearers in vv. 18-19, he pronounces God's benediction upon them in vv. 20-21, and then adds (other) features characteristic of a letter ending in vv. 22-25.

A. THE COMMUNITY OF THE FAITHFUL AND THE LIFE OF GRATITUDE AND GODLY FEAR (13:1-6)

1 *Let brotherly love continue.* 2 *Do not forget hospitality, for through this some did not notice it when they showed hospitality to angels.* 3 *Remember those imprisoned as if you were imprisoned with them; those being tortured as you yourselves also being in a body.* 4 *Honored be marriage in everything, and let the marriage bed be undefiled, for the sexually immoral and adulterers God will judge.* 5 *Free from the love of money let your conduct be; be content in your present circumstances, for he himself has said, "I will never leave you, nor will I ever forsake you."* 6 *So let us confidently say: "The Lord is my Helper; I will not fear. What can a human being do to me?"*

The pastor uses four pairs of carefully crafted exhortations to urge upon his hearers the kind of community life appropriate for those who live in the gratitude and godly fear that are proper in light of what God has done in Christ (12:27-28).[1] First, "Let brotherly love continue. Do not forget hospitality" (vv. 1-2a). Second, "Remember those imprisoned as if you were imprisoned with them, those being tortured as you yourselves also being in a body" (v. 3). Third, "Honored be marriage in everything, and let the marriage bed be undefiled" (v. 4). Fourth, "Free from the love of money let your conduct be; be content in your present circumstances" (v. 5). The first, third, and fourth pairs have subordinate clauses, introduced by "for," that provide motivation for heeding the exhortations. Each exhortation of the second pair has a clause introduced by "as" that serves a similar purpose.[2] The first two pairs of exhortations use present imperatives; the second two use predicate adjectives and a present participle with imperatival force.[3] It is difficult to

to God," 12:28). Note also v. 21, εὐάρεστον ἐνώπιον αὐτοῦ, "what is well pleasing before him"). The hearers already know that it is only the people who live "by faith" who are able "to please" (εὐαρεστῆσαι, 11:6) God.

1. Marie E. Isaacs, "Hebrews 13.9-16 Revisited," *NTS* 43 (1997): 270-72.
2. Note γάρ ("for") in vv. 2b, 4b, and 5b; ὡς ("as") twice in v. 3.
3. Note the present imperatives μενέτω ("let . . . continue," v. 1), ἐπιλανθάνεσθε ("forget," v. 2), and μιμνήσκεσθε ("remember," v. 3); the predicate adjectives τίμιος ("honored," v. 4), ἀμίαντος ("undefiled," v. 4), and ἀφιλάργυρος ("free from love of money," v. 5); and the present participle used as an imperative (ἀρκούμενοι, "be content," v. 5).

represent the brevity, balance, and pungency of the original in English translation.

These four pairs of exhortations are an expansion of the "brotherly love" with which they begin. The first two pairs describe behavior that directly expresses this brotherly love — hospitality to strangers (v. 2), concern for the imprisoned, and aid for the persecuted (v. 3). The last two forbid conduct that violates brotherly love — sexual unfaithfulness (v. 4) and greed (v. 5).[4] "Love of money," in particular, is the antithesis of brotherly love. Trust in God is the immediate motivation for this last pair of exhortations. It is also a fitting conclusion because it reinforces the three previous pairs and ties together all four with the pastor's concern for perseverance in faith.

These exhortations draw on themes that are common in Christian and Jewish moral teaching. Nor are they without parallel in pagan sources.[5] However, the pastor's selection and careful combination of these themes are his own. They take on new meaning as the proper expression of awe-filled gratitude for the all-sufficient work of Christ. They are also integral to what the pastor has taught about the nature of God's people as his "household" (3:6), made up of his children, who are "brothers and sisters" of Christ and of one another (2:10-14). Thus, these exhortations cannot be dismissed as perfunctory repetition of moral platitudes.[6] The concluding Scriptural quotations

---

4. On the four pairs of exhortations in this passage, see Michel, 479. Thurén, *Lobopfer,* 208, 220-21, divides these exhortations into two pairs, as we have done, but separates the Scriptural citations in vv. 5b-6. He recognizes that the first pair enjoin conduct that expresses brotherly love by calling them "admonitions." He acknowledges that the second are concerned with behavior that violates brotherly love by calling them "warnings." Vanhoye is correct in criticizing Thurén for separating the Scriptural quotations (Vanhoye, "Hébreux XIII.1-6," 122). These quotations serve as the direct motivation for the final pair of exhortations. He is mistaken, however, in separating the last pair of exhortations with their motivation in vv. 5-6 from the third pair in v. 4 (Vanhoye, "Hébreux XIII.1-6," 123-24). As the exegesis below will show, these two pairs belong together both conceptually and structurally. He is also mistaken in objecting to Thurén's classification of the first two pairs as "admonition" and the second two as "warning" (Vanhoye, "Hébreux XIII.1-6," 122-23). The negative admonition in v. 2, "do not forget," is a reminder, not a warning. On the other hand, the two negative admonitions at the heart of vv. 4-5 are clear warnings: "let the marriage bed be undefiled," "let your conduct be free from the love of money" (notice the two alpha-privatives, ἀ-μίαντος ("undefiled"), ἀ-φιλάργυρος ("without love of money")). Furthermore, according to v. 4c, violators of the marriage bed are subject to God's judgment.

5. See Thompson, 272-73; Johnson, 339-44, and the notes on individual exhortations below for Jewish, Christian, and pagan parallels to these admonitions.

6. Isaacs, "Hebrews 13.9-16," 270-72; *pace* Weiss, 700-701, the traditional nature of these admonitions is no reason to deny their relationship to the concrete situation of the readers.

make it clear that obedience in these matters is the expression of a life lived in dependence on God's power and integrity.

1 The word for "brotherly love" is located prominently at the beginning of this verse. It not only announces the theme for the next five verses but also sets the tone for the entire chapter.[7] Outside of Christian literature this word is used almost exclusively for the natural bond that joins actual brothers and sisters and the mutual support that should characterize their relationships.[8] The pastor has already made it clear that those who respond to God's word are his "children," whom the Son owns as his "brothers and sisters" (2:10-18). They are joint members of the household of God under Jesus, the Son and High Priest (3:6; 10:21), and they are fellow heirs — with and through the Son — of the world to come (2:5). For this reason the pastor has felt free to call them "brothers and sisters" (3:1, 12; 10:19) and urged them to mutual concern for their spiritual welfare (10:25).[9] When, therefore, he exhorts them to let "brotherly love continue," he is not being sentimental, nor is he indulging in mere rhetorical flourish. He is urging them to live in accord with their relationship to God, now brought to fulfillment in Christ.[10] The use of the verb "continue" in the present imperative suggests that they continue their present practice of showing "brotherly love." Such brotherly love is not to be an occasional act but the ongoing habit and mark of God's people, who are destined to live in a City that "remains" (13:14).[11]

2 "Brotherly love" is paired with the second exhortation, "Hospitality do not forget."[12] Although this translation is a bit awkward, it brings out

---

7. Thompson, 277.

8. See the discussion of Aristotle, *Eth. Nic.* 1161b30-35, and Plutarch, *Mor.* 478C-E, 480B-C (cited by deSilva, 486-87). Cf. 4 Macc 13:23, 26; 14:1; Philo, *Embassy* 87; Josephus, *Ant.* 4.26; cited in Attridge, 385, n. 17. On "brotherly love" as a pattern for the Christian life, see Rom 12:10; 1 Thess 4:9; 1 Pet 1:22; 2 Pet 1:7.

9. Hughes, 562, along with many others, misses the fine nuance of Hebrews when he says "it is through union with him [Christ] that we participate in the grace of sonship." As we have seen in the analysis of 2:10-18, God's people were already his "children" before the incarnation. It is for this reason that the Son assumes their humanity in order to bring them into their destiny as God's "sons and daughters."

10. Cf. Rom 12:10; 1 Thess 4:9; 1 Pet 1:22; 2 Pet 1:7; *1 Clem.* 1:2; and Herm. *Mand.* 8:10. See Attridge, 385, n.18.

11. μενέτω ("let . . . continue") in 13:1 is the third, singular, present, active imperative of μένω while μένουσαν, ("remains") in 13:14 is the present participle of the same verb. "Brotherly love, then, that 'remains' has a future in the kingdom with God's Son who continues forever (12:27; 13:14)" (O'Brien, 506).

12. The wordplay on and close connection between φιλαδελφία ("brotherly love") and φιλοξενία ("hospitality") is, *pace* Weiss, 701, much more obvious and intentional here than elsewhere in traditional Christian parenesis (see Rom 12:10, 13; cf. also 1 Pet 4:8-9,

the emphasis put on "hospitality" by its position at the beginning of the sentence. This word order makes these first two exhortations parallel in structure and thus underscores the bond between them.[13] This bond is further strengthened by a deliberate play on words. The word for "brotherly love" is *philadelphia,* the same term used for the famous city by that name. *Phil* comes from the Greek word for "love," and *adelphia* from "brotherhood." The word used here for "hospitality" can be transliterated as *philoxenia.* Again the *phil* comes from the word for "love." *Xenia* alone means 'hospitality,' but it is related to the Greek word for "stranger." Thus, to the first hearers these two exhortations would have sounded something like, "Love of brother let it continue; love of stranger [or of "hospitality"] do not forget." They are not just to remember "hospitality" but the "love of hospitality."[14] This is no begrudging offer of kindness but a generous sharing of what one has. This second exhortation makes it clear that "brotherly love" extends to the whole people of God and is not just limited to those with whom we are familiar. The pastor may well have been thinking of visiting evangelists and other believers who would be in need of entertainment.[15] Verse 2b adds motivation for showing such hospitality: "For through this some did not notice it when they showed hospitality to angels."[16] "Through this" refers to the "hospitality" or "love of hospitality" mentioned in the previous clause.[17] The hearers might have thought of Abraham and Sarah in Gen 18:2-15, or of Lot in Gen 19:1-22.[18]

---

where the related adjective φιλόξενος ("hospitable") is associated with ἀγαπή, "love." φιλόξενος also occurs in 1 Tim 3:2 and Tit 1:8.

13. Compare the article/noun/imperative of ἡ φιλαδελφία μενέτω ("let brotherly love continue") with the same order in τῆς φιλοξενίας μὴ ἐπιλανθάνεσθε ("hospitality do not forget").

14. Lane, 2:511-12.

15. See Rom 12:13; 1 Tim 3:2; Tit 1:8; 1 Pet 4:9; cf. 1 Cor 16:5-6; Phlm 22; 3 John 5-10. For the virtue of hospitality in Hellenistic Judaism, see Philo, *Abraham* 114; Josephus, *Life* 142. See also Ellingworth, 694; deSilva, 487; and J. H. Elliott, *A Home for the Homeless: A Social-Scientific Criticism of 1 Peter, Its Situation and Strategy* (Minneapolis: Fortress, 1990), 146. Lucian, *Peregr.* 11–13, suggests that some may have taken advantage of Christian hospitality. See also the instructions in *Did.* 11:4-6 that prohibit an "apostle" from staying in the same home for more than one or two days.

16. This translation takes τινες ("some") as the subject of the third person plural second aorist ἔλαθον ("did not recognize," "did not take notice") and ξενίσαντες ("having entertained," "having shown hospitality") as temporal or circumstantial — "when they entertained" angels. This classical usage of λανθάνω ("not recognize," "not notice") in an adverbial sense with a complementary participle occurs nowhere else in the NT (Attridge, 386, n. 33).

17. The διά is instrumental, and ταύτης refers back to φιλοξενίας: "by means of practicing hospitality."

18. Both Philo, *Abraham* 107, 113, and Josephus, *Ant.* 1.196, understood the

Such hospitality brings unexpected benefits in terms of the fellowship it makes possible. The word order ties this motivational clause very tightly to the preceding exhortation that it substantiates.[19]

3 The second pair of exhortations specifically includes those being persecuted for their faith among the people to whom brotherly love is due. Thus, the pastor makes application of all he has said about the need for the faithful to endure suffering. "Remember" is a rhetorically appropriate counterpart to "do not forget" of the last verse. This imperative is given added force by being first in the sentence. The fact that the hearers must supply it again for the second of these exhortations only reinforces its impact on their consciousness. By "remember" the pastor means that they should minister to the needs of those who suffer for Christ. First, they are to remember "those in prison" just as if "imprisoned with them." The Greek sentence is powerful for its conciseness — "those in prison" translates a Greek article and noun, and "imprisoned with them" is a single participle.[20] Both noun and participle come from the same root. The pastor's primary reference is probably to those unjustly imprisoned for their faith. Thus, he would have his hearers continue their bold support of the persecuted, described in 10:33-34. While his hearers may not (yet) have been imprisoned, as God's faithful they are subject to such treatment, and thus they should minister to their brothers and sisters with the full sympathy of those who share their experience. The incarcerated endured great suffering because prisons were cramped, damp, dark, and filthy. Furthermore, those who kept them were often harsh and desirous of bribes. Prisoners were given no clothes and little if any food.[21] Thus to "remember" such prisoners was to supply their physical needs and provide them with moral support, even at the risk of exposing oneself to possible confinement.

The pastor reinforces this first exhortation with a second and more comprehensive one: remember "those being tortured as you yourselves also being in a body." By translating this substantive participle "those being tortured," we have followed the NRSV. "Tortured" represents the intensity of

---

three "men" who visited Abraham and Sarah in this passage as angels. For other examples of entertaining angels, see Judg 6:11-21; 13:3-10; and Tob 3:17; 5:4-16; 12:1-20.

19. φιλοξενίας ("hospitality") at the beginning is balanced by ξενίσαντες ἀγγέλους ("having entertained angels") near the end; ἐπιλανθάνεσθε (do not "forget") corresponds to ἔλαθόν τινες ("some did not notice"). See Lane, 2:507c.

20. τῶν δεσμίων ("those in prison"); συνδεδεμένοι ("imprisoned with them"). One might translate, "remember the prisoners as fellow imprisoned."

21. On the condition of prisons, see Koester, 564-65; C. S. Wansink, *Chained in Christ: The Experience and Rhetoric of Paul's Imprisonments* (JSNTSup 130; Sheffield: Sheffield Academic, 1996), 27-95; Rapske, *Book of Acts,* 195-225; and the primary sources cited in these references.

this term, which was used to describe the extreme deprivation of the faithful in 11:36-37 and, in a cognate form, Moses' sufferings for identifying with God's captive people in 11:25.[22] This translation makes it clear that the pastor's main concern is with fellow believers who are suffering for their faith. "As imprisoned with them" above was hypothetical; "as you yourselves also being in a body" is real.[23] The pastor could not have made this statement with greater forcefulness.[24] Being "in a body" represents vulnerability to suffering and abuse.[25] The hearers remember that Christ became human and assumed a body in order to identify with their vulnerability and redeem them through his suffering (2:14-16). The pastor's hearers feel the sufferings of the persecuted in their own bodies while he speaks. It would be a mistake, however, to limit the pastor's concern to those being persecuted because of their loyalty to Christ. "Brotherly love" extends compassion to all the suffering within the "household" of God (3:6), but it also overflows to those beyond. "Remember" is a present imperative. The hearers are to make this practical concern for the needs of the suffering a habitual part of their lives.

4 In vv. 4-5, as noted above, the pastor abandons the use of the present imperatives that characterized vv. 1-3 (i.e., "let it remain," v. 1; "do not forget," v. 2; "remember," v. 3). In vv. 4-5a he adopts a style characterized by the use of definite nouns qualified by predicate adjectives: note the noun "marriage" and the predicate adjective "honored" (v. 4); the noun "marriage bed" and the adjective "undefiled" (v. 4); the noun "conduct" and the one-word Greek predicate adjective translated by the English phrase, "free from the love of money" (v. 5). This predicate construction implies the missing third person imperative, "Let . . . be" — "Let marriage be honored."[26] The pastor concludes this series of four exhortations in v. 5b by employing a

22. Compare τῶν κακουχουμένων ("those who are tortured") in 13:3 with κακουχούμενοι ("suffering ill treatment") in 11:36-37 and συγκακουχεῖσθαι ("to suffer ill treatment with") in 11:25.

23. Ellingworth, 696. Those who supply "their," "as if you were in their bodies" (Attridge, 387, n. 42; cf. Koester, 558) would make this second "as" (ὡς) unreal like the first on the basis of Philo, *Spec. Laws* 3.161, which refers clearly to "their bodies." This suggestion, however, unduly weakens the pastor's statement and obscures the echo of Christ's assuming human corporeality and vulnerability (10:5-10; 2:14-18). See Bénétreau, 2:210-11.

24. καί ("also") strengthens the identity of the hearers with those suffering as does αὐτοί used as second person plural intensive, "yourselves." The present participle ὄντες ("being") also adds emphasis. See Lane, 2:508-9.

25. This is no reference to the people of God as the "body" of Christ or to the "body" as the source of moral evil (Ellingworth, 696).

26. Thus, the implied verb is not ἔστι(ν) ("is"), the third singular present indicative of εἰμι, but the third person singular imperative, ἔστω ("Let . . . be"). See Lane, 2:508i; Attridge, 387; Ellingworth, 697.

predicate participle with imperatival force: "being content." This brevity of style allows the pastor to speak with striking forcefulness. The shift from imperatives to nouns/predicate adjectives follows a shift in focus. The imperatives in the first two pairs of exhortations gave specific instructions for the practice of "brotherly love." These last two pairs of exhortations warn against sexual infidelity and greed, two types of conduct that violate and destroy "brotherly love."

The Greek text follows the order adjective ("honored"), noun ("marriage"); noun ("marriage bed"), adjective ("undefiled"): "Honored let marriage be . . . let the marriage bed be undefiled." This chiastic arrangement makes the impact of these two exhortations memorable and pungent by binding them closely together. The first is the most comprehensive: "Let marriage be honored." The pastor would have them do nothing that violates the marriage bond or belittles marriage, including both divorce and marital unfaithfulness.[27] The following "among all" or "by all" means none are exempt from this command — married or unmarried, young or old. It is possible that this expression should be translated "in every way."[28] Such an interpretation only extends the already comprehensive reach of this exhortation. By beginning with the covenant of marriage rather than with individual chastity, the pastor confirms the fact that sexual misconduct is not merely a matter of private concern but has implications for the common life of the people of God.

"And let the marriage bed be undefiled." This second exhortation makes the first more specific. The most fundamental way of honoring marriage is by not violating the marriage bed through sexual relationships outside of marriage.[29] The term "undefiled" is at home in the context of priesthood, sacrifice, and Tent.[30] "Defilement" is the opposite of holiness, of the

---

27. By "marriage" and "marriage bed" the pastor can be referring to nothing other than the bond between a man and woman established by God in the opening chapters of Genesis. There is absolutely no warrant for the following statement by Johnson (342): "We cannot conclude that the readers of Hebrews did not have or honor other expressions of sexuality beside marriage."

28. If πᾶσιν is taken as masculine, then ἐν πᾶσιν can be understood as local, "among all" (NKJV, NASB) or as instrumental of agency, "by all" (NIV, NRSV). There is little difference in meaning (Attridge, 387). If πᾶσιν is neuter, then the phrase is instrumental of manner, "in every way." None of the parallels Ellingworth (697) cites in support of this last interpretation is exact — ἐν παντί (v. 21), διὰ παντός (2:15), and κατὰ πάντα (4:15). The second (2:15) is a fixed idiom for "always" or "perpetually."

29. On the "marriage bed" as a euphemism for sexual intercourse, see Lev 15:21-26; Wis 3:13, 16.

30. Josephus, Ant. 2.55 uses the language of defilement for the marriage bed (cf. Gen 49:4; Wis 14:24; T. Reu. 1:6; Attridge, 387; Koester, 558; Johnson, 341). However, the pastor's use of ἀμίαντος ("undefiled") is most appropriate in light of his presentation of Christ as the High Priest who cleanses his people from the defilement of sin. The moral

cleansing from sin that allows God's people to enter his presence. The pastor has already used the example of Esau (12:16) to affirm the close relationship between sexual immorality and that disregard for God that is the fruit of unbelief and disobedience. Thus, sexual immorality is a breach of the New Covenant.[31] It is a violation of the life of faithfulness understood as the worship of God in gratitude and godly fear through the cleansing provided by Christ (cf. 12:28 above).[32] No wonder it incurs the judgment of Sinai and of the God who is "a burning fire" (12:29): "for the sexually immoral and adulterers God will judge."[33] The initial position of the words translated "the sexually immoral" and "adulterers" is emphatic. "Sexually immoral" comes immediately after the word "defiled" at the end of the previous clause. The first of these terms includes all who have sexual relations outside of the marriage bond.[34] The second focuses more closely on the unfaithfulness of married people. In Greek this sentence ends ominously with the word "God." The God who is "a consuming fire" (12:29), and no other, will judge such people (cf. 12:29).[35]

5 Greed often accompanies sexual immorality. Many writers of antiquity associated the two.[36] The conjunction of the seventh and eighth commandments made this connection common among Jewish authors.[37] Those who ignore the heavenly City and pursue the things of this life are often characterized by both. Thus, it was natural for the pastor to move from concern for sexual purity to warning against the love of money. The bond between these exhortations and the previous pair is shown by the way this first exhortation continues the definite noun/predicate adjective style: "conduct" (noun); "without love of money" (all one adjective in Greek). "Let your conduct be without love of money." The second exhortation is a predicate participle, "being content," that has imperative force: "be content with the things that are." The pattern of positive ("Let marriage be honored"), negative ("and

---

nature of this defilement is confirmed by the judgment of God, pronounced upon those who indulge in such behavior. Notice the word μιανθῶσιν ("be defiled") near the end of 12:15 and πόρνος ("sexually immoral") near the beginning of 12:16.

31. Attridge, 388.

32. "As in the case of Esau [12:16-17], to be subject to the sexual appetites is the epitome of an existence oriented to the present moment rather than to the unseen world" (Thompson, 279).

33. Cf. Sir 23:16-21.

34. For πόρνος in the sense of persons who commit any kind of sexual immorality, see 1 Cor 5:9-11; 6:9; Eph 5:5; 1 Tim 1:10; Rev 21:8; 22:15. Cf. Sir 23:16-21.

35. See Lane, 2:508l.

36. Luke 16:9-18; 1 Cor 5:1–6:11; Eph 5:3-5; Col 3:5; 1 Thess 4:3-7. Cf. also Philo, *Abraham* 133–34; and references in Attridge, 387, nn. 45-47.

37. See Lane, 2:517-18.

the marriage bed undefiled"), negative ("without love of money let conduct be"), positive ("be content") reinforces the cohesion among these exhortations.[38]

We have demonstrated the wordplay between "brotherly love" and "hospitality" in vv. 1-2. The pastor continues that wordplay with the single word that must be translated by the phrase "without love of money." As brotherly love was *philadelphia* and hospitality was *philoxenia* (see the comments on vv. 1, 2 above), so "without love of money" can be transliterated as *aphilargyros* — *a* meaning "without"; *phil* meaning "love"; and *argyros* meaning "money."[39] The syllable *phil* ("love") in this last word would remind the hearers of the opening exhortations in v. 1. The negative "without" is crucial. Greed or love of money is the opposite of brotherly love and hospitality. Greed prevents one from participating in the love of others by meeting their needs. Thus greed, along with sexual impurity, is sure to destroy the brotherly love of the community. In the second exhortation the pastor addresses the cause of greed — discontent with present circumstances: "being content with the things that are" (i.e., "with what you have"). The pastor's use of the participle "being content" is another example of his ability to say exactly what he intends with brevity of style. As a participle it qualifies the previous exhortation, giving the means or reason for rejecting the love of money. At the same time it has imperatival force and is legitimately translated, "be content."[40] The proper response to loss because of their faithfulness to Christ (10:34) is not a grasping greed but reliance upon God.[41] No exhortation is more appropriate for modern people living in an affluent society. For many, discontent has become a habit; they live in dissatisfaction with what they have and in vain anticipation of the next purchase.

---

38. Note also how the first word in the exhortation of v. 5, ἀφιλάργυρος ("without love of money"), echoes the alpha-privative from the last word of the exhortation in v. 4, ἀμίαντος ("without defilement"). Vanhoye recognizes this wordplay and the chiastic structure that binds vv. 4-5a (Vanhoye, "Hébreux XIII.1-6," 122), but then separates these two verses in his structural analysis of this section (Vanhoye, "Hébreux XIII.1-6," 122-24).

39. We are not suggesting that etymology is the primary guide to the meaning of ἀφιλάργυρος ("not love of money," v. 5), φιλαδελφία ("brotherly love," v. 1), and φιλοξενία ("love of hospitality," v. 2), but that the author of Hebrews is intentionally employing a wordplay by using these three terms. For the "love of money" (φιλαργυρία) as a fundamental vice see Luke 16:14, 2 Tim 3:2, and esp. 1 Tim 6:10: "The love of money is the root of every kind of evil." Cf. Philo, *Spec. Laws* 4.65, and the many secular sources cited in Johnson, 343.

40. Thus, *pace* Ellingworth, 699, it is misguided to argue that this participle has imperatival force and thus does not qualify the previous clause. The pastor avoids using a straight imperative, which he could easily have done, because he wants to do both.

41. Ellingworth, 698; deSilva, 491.

As motivation for maintaining the integrity of marriage, the pastor invokes the terrible judgment of God. It is the assured faithfulness of God that provides every reason to avoid the love of money and pursue a life of contentment. Divine steadfastness provides a much more certain foundation for contentment than Stoic appeals to self-sufficiency.[42] God himself has assured us of his faithfulness: "For he himself has said, 'I will never leave you, nor will I ever forsake you.'" This statement could not be more emphatic. The intensive "himself" has been added to show that the speaker is none other than God.[43] The intensive perfect, "he has said," shows that these words have abiding validity — God has said them, and they are still in effect.[44] The statement is doubled for emphasis: "I will never leave you"; "I will never forsake you." Furthermore, in Greek there are five negative particles, two in the first statement, one connecting the two statements, and two in the second.[45] With this firm declaration of divine faithfulness the pastor brings all of the OT quotations through which God has addressed his people to a grand conclusion. The God who has warned and exhorted his people through the OT assures them through this OT passage that he will never abandon the faithful. They can with assurance depend upon him rather than on the accumulation of uncertain earthly wealth.

Although these words do not occur in exactly this form in our OT, Philo (*Confusion* 166) also cites them as a Scriptural quotation. This fact suggests that a Greek version in this form was available to the writer of Hebrews. The pastor's argument depends on the hearers' recognition of this quotation as the actual words of Scripture.[46] The wording of this quote is very close to the statement of assurance that Moses gave Joshua in Deut 31:6: "He will never leave you, nor will he ever forsake you." Compare also Deut 31:8: "And the LORD who is going with you will not leave you, nor will he forsake you." God himself speaks such words of assurance to Joshua in Josh 1:5: "And as I was with Moses, so I will be with you, and I will not forsake you nor will I reject you."[47] Thus, it is likely that this quotation in Hebrews is an alternate transla-

---

42. "If Stoics counseled people to be content for the sake of self-sufficiency, Hebrews urges them to be content for the sake of serving others in the confidence that God will give them a future reward (Heb 10:35; 11:26)" (Koester, 559). See Attridge, 388, n. 62, for examples of pagan teaching on contentment; n. 63, for Christian.

43. On this use of αὐτός ("himself"), see Ellingworth, 699.

44. Lane, 2:519; Ellingworth, 699-700.

45. See οὐ and μή (both meaning "not") in the first statement, οὐδ' ("neither") connecting the two, and οὐ μή again in the second.

46. Ellingworth, 700.

47. The underlined words below highlight the similarities between Heb 13:5, Deut 31:6, 8, and Josh 1:5.

Heb 13:5: <u>οὐ μή σε ἀνῶ</u> οὐδ' <u>οὐ μή σε ἐγκαταλίπω</u> ("I will never leave you, nor will I ever forsake you").

tion of God's words of assurance to Joshua encouraging him to enter and take the Promised Land. The pastor has been urging his hearers to persevere until they enter the promised heavenly Home and City. The God who would not abandon Joshua on the eve of his entrance will not abandon them.[48]

6   With "So let us confidently say" the pastor invites his hearers to join him in the proper response to God's promise of faithfulness.[49] Throughout Hebrews God has addressed his people through OT Scripture. Here, in the closing verses of his sermon, he gives his hearers the words of Scripture through which they can appropriately answer the divine address by affirming their faithfulness.[50] Within the OT context this quotation from Ps 118:6 (LXX 117:6) is the trusting response of the faithful to God in the face of suffering and injustice at the hands of the unbelieving.[51] Thus it is a most fitting response for those who would follow in the footsteps of the OT heroes (11:1-40) through appropriation of the "great salvation" provided by Jesus (12:1-3) despite the intense opposition of an unbelieving world. The pastor invites his hearers to respond to his sermon by repeating this text with him as an expression of trust and gratitude: Let us confess our faith altogether: "The Lord is my Helper; I will not fear. What can any human being do to me?" Those whose lives are characterized by "godly fear" (12:28) need fear no human opposition. The God who promised Joshua, "I will be with you, and I will not

---

Deut 31:6: οὐ μή σε ἀνῇ οὔτε μή σε ἐγκαταλίπῃ (He will never leave you, nor will he ever forsake you").

Deut 31:8: οὐκ ἀνήσει σε οὐδὲ μὴ ἐγκαταλίπῃ σε ("He will not leave you, nor will he ever forsake you").

Josh 1:5: ἔσομαι καὶ μετὰ σοῦ καὶ οὐκ ἐγκαταλείψω σε οὐδὲ ὑπερόψομαί σε ("I will also be with you, and I will not forsake you nor will I reject you").

The above comparison shows that Heb 13:5 is identical to Deut 31:6 except for the substitution of οὐδ' οὐ for οὔτε between the clauses and for the first/third person variation.

48. There is little or no contextual reason for thinking that these words are addressed to Jesus, the supposed new Joshua (Lane, 2:519-20).

49. ὥστε ("so") shows that this is a response to what God has said. The infinitive λέγειν ("to say") with the first person plural subject ἡμᾶς ("we") is not merely a quotation formula (cf. Ellingworth, 700). It is hortatory, and thus an invitation: "let us say." The participle θαρροῦντας indicates how the hearers should respond to God by affirming this Scripture, "being confident," or, more smoothly, "confidently." Weiss, 707, notes how this verse ties this parenetic section back into the author's concern for perseverance in faith throughout the book. Verse 8 reprises the book's Christology.

50. See the section entitled "The Psalms and Related Passages — 'God has Spoken,'" pp. 45-47 in the Introduction to this commentary.

51. The pastor quotes Ps 117:6 in the LXX (118:6 in the MT) without variation except for the textually questionable καί ("and"), which appears between κύριος ἐμοὶ βοηθός ("the Lord is my helper") and οὐ φοβηθήσομαι ("I will not fear") in some manuscripts of Hebrews.

forsake you nor will I reject you" in Josh 1:5b also assured him, "No human being will be able to stand before you." Thus Moses could tell him, "Do not be afraid" (Deut 31:6-8).[52]

By explaining the high-priestly work of Christ the pastor has provided his hearers with a deeper understanding of what it means to confess, "The Lord is my Helper." Only through what God has done in Christ can they "draw near" and truly find "grace to help" them live victoriously in time of need (4:16).[53] Thus, the response of faith enshrined in Ps 118:16 is a suitable conclusion, not merely to Heb 13:5 but also to the pastor's concern throughout Hebrews that his hearers live with confidence in God's promises and power (11:1-6) as they have been and are yet to be fulfilled in Christ. God through Christ has furnished all the "help" that they need to reach the end of their pilgrimage and enjoy his presence forever. All who join the pastor in this response embrace his purpose in writing this sermon.

B. THE UNBELIEVING WORLD AND THE LIFE OF GRATITUDE AND GODLY FEAR (13:7-17)

> 7 *Remember your leaders, who spoke the word of God to you. Considering the outcome of their conduct, imitate their faith.* 8 *Jesus Christ, yesterday and today the same, and forever.* 9 *Do not be carried away with various and strange teachings. For it is good to confirm the heart with grace, not with foods, in which those who walk have not been profited.* 10 *We have an altar from which those who worship in the Tent do not have authority to eat.* 11 *For the blood of those animals is brought for sin into the Most Holy Place by the high priest. Their bodies are burned outside the camp.* 12 *Thus Jesus also, in order that he might sanctify the people through his own blood, suffered outside the gate.* 13 *Therefore, let us go out to him outside the camp, bearing his reproach.* 14 *For we do not have here an enduring city, but we are earnestly seeking one to come.* 15 *Through him, therefore, we continually offer a sacrifice of praise to God, that is, the fruit of lips confessing his name.* 16 *Do not forget doing good and sharing, for with such sacrifices God is well pleased.* 17 *Obey your leaders and submit to*

---

52. Compare οὐ φοβηθήσομαι ("I will not fear") with μὴ φοβοῦ ("do not fear") twice in Deut 31:6-8. Also compare τί ποιήσει μοι ἄνθρωπος ("What can a human being do to me?") in v. 6 with οὐκ ἀντιστήσεται ἄνθρωπος κατενώπιον ὑμῶν ("No human being will be able to stand before you") in Josh 1:5.

53. It is less likely, though possible, that the pastor thought of Jesus as the "Lord" who is "our Helper." Compare βοηθός ("helper") in this verse with βοηθεῖν ("to help") in 2:18 and βοήθεια ("help") in 4:16.

them, for they themselves watch carefully over your souls as those who will give account, in order that they might do it with joy and not with groaning. For this would be without profit for you.

The pastor has concluded his initial instructions on how to live together as the community of those who worship God with awe-filled gratitude for the "great salvation" (2:3) available through Christ. In vv. 7-17 he returns once more to his all-consuming concern that his hearers persevere in this life of faith by providing a brief reprise of his sermon. He would not have them subverted by fatigue, temporal benefit, or the disdain of an unbelieving world. In these verses, therefore, he brings all that he has said about the sufficiency of Christ and the testimony of the past faithful to bear on the immediate circumstances of his hearers' lives.[1]

The pastor frames this call for perseverance with exhortations to imitate the faithfulness of leaders past (v. 7) and to acknowledge the oversight of leaders present (v. 17). The abiding reality of Jesus Christ, asserted in v. 8, is the foundation for all perseverance. The deceptive nature of the false teaching in v. 9 that would impede his hearers' continued faithfulness is exposed by comparison with the benefits now theirs in Christ according to v. 10. In light of these benefits, it is only proper that they bear the "reproach of Christ" by going to him "outside the camp" and identifying with the sufferings through which he has redeemed them (vv. 11-13). As the constancy of Christ is the means of perseverance (v. 8), so the "enduring City" is its long-desired goal (v. 14). The present life is not to be characterized by false teachings or by the rituals of the Old Covenant, but by the "sacrifice" of praise and good works. It is only this kind of sacrifice that pleases God (vv. 14-16).

7   The pastor has urged his hearers to shun the disobedience of the wilderness generation (3:7–4:11) and warned them against the godlessness of Esau (12:14-17). He has urged them to imitate the "great cloud of witnesses" (12:1) from the past (11:1-40) who reach their eternal goal through Jesus (11:39-40), the ultimate exemplar of perseverance and source of grace (12:3). The lives of their now-deceased former leaders join those of the heroes of old recorded in God's word as both exemplars of endurance and witnesses to the faithfulness of God.[2]

It was natural to use the word translated "leaders" for those giving supervision to the church, since this word was a general term for civil or military authorities.[3] The pastor is speaking of the very people "who spoke the

---

1. Attridge, 391, calls this section "a forceful synthesis of the doctrine and paraenesis of the whole text." See also Isaacs, "Hebrews 13.9-16," 272-73.

2. See Bruce, 374-75.

3. The substantive participle ὁ ἡγούμενος was a general term for political (Deut

word of God to you." This "word" (2:2; 4:2, 12; 6:1) spoken by God (1:1, 2; 2:2, 3; 3:5; 4:8; 5:5; 11:4, 18; 12:24-25) could be nothing less than the "great salvation" (2:3) first preached by those who founded the church to which the hearers belonged. The pastor could bestow no greater honor on these founding leaders, nor could he attribute to them any greater source of authority. These leaders also exemplified faithful obedience to the very "word of God" that they proclaimed. The participial phrase, "considering the outcome of their conduct," is often translated as an imperative in line with the imperatives that open ("remember your leaders") and close ("imitate their faith") this verse — "consider the outcome of their conduct." It is important, however, not to miss the fact that this participle qualifies both the initial and concluding imperatives. First, it tells the hearers how they are to "remember" their leaders. The pastor is not referring to mere sentimental reminiscence. He wants them to remember these leaders by thinking about their conduct over the course of their lives and especially about its "outcome." The word translated "outcome" is probably not a reference to martyrdom but to the conclusion and total impact of the way of life pursued by these former leaders.[4] They were faithful amid difficulty to the end. Remembering them and "considering" the way that they persevered until the end is, then, motivation to "imitate their faith." In the original this phrase is literally "imitate the faith." As often in Greek, the definite article "the" is used to imply the possessive, "their." Nevertheless, these leaders are sterling examples of "the" way of "faith" pursued by the faithful of all time and made passable by Jesus (12:1-3). How important it is for the life of the church that its founders and leaders maintain their integrity.

8 The faithfulness of the community's past leaders was a response

---

1:13; Sir 17:17; 41:17) or military (1 Macc 9:30; 14:16) leaders. The related term προηγούμενοι was used as a technical term for church leaders in documents associated with Rome (*1 Clem.* 1:3; 21:6; Herm. *Vis.* 2.2.6; 3.9.7; Attridge, 391, n. 18). However, it is doubtful, *pace* Weiss, 710, whether ἡγούμενος already has the character of a title in Hebrews. Thus Weiss's attempt, 710-12, to locate the ecclesiastical development of the community addressed in Hebrews somewhere between the Pauline communities, where leaders were described by function rather than by title, and the hierarchy of postapostolic times, is purely speculative. See Weiss's discussion and the literature there cited. The pastor claims neither the apostolic authority of a Paul (Rom 1:1; Gal 1:1; etc.), nor the authority of ecclesiastical appointment (Phil 1:1; cf. 1 Tim 1:6), for either himself or these founding leaders of the community to which his hearers belonged. The authority of these leaders rests on the proclamation of God's word as fulfilled in Christ (1:1-4).

4. Hughes, 569, n. 18, reviews the usage of ἔκβασις ("outcome") elsewhere and comes to the conclusion that it should be understood as the "achievement" or "accomplishment" of their lives, the sum total of their daily living in faith until the end. Cf. Ellingworth, 703. "How they suffered, how they died, and how they found a place in the city of the living God (12:2; see also 11:4, 5, 7, 21, 22)" (Johnson, 345-46).

to and a verification of the faithfulness of "Jesus Christ," who is "yesterday and today the same, and forever." This truth about "Jesus Christ" is the message they preached and the antithesis of the false teachings described in v. 9.[5] The initial, emphatic "Jesus Christ" encompasses the fullness of who Christ is.[6] He is the eternal Son who became incarnate, lived an obedient human life, offered himself in obedience to God, and has now taken his seat at God's right hand (8:1-2). Thus, he has full authority to cleanse his people from sin and bring them into God's presence. The phrase "yesterday and today the same, and forever" echoes descriptions of God's eternity, and thus recalls both the direct (1:10-12; 7:16, 25) and indirect (7:3, 8) application of such language to the eternal Son of God.[7] The pastor intends his hearers to recall these earlier passages and thus to know that the constancy of "Jesus Christ" rests on the eternity of the Son of God.[8] Yet the way the Greek text joins "yesterday and today" and sets them off from "forever" suggests several further implications. First, the pastor would emphasize that the Jesus Christ who was available to the leaders of "yesterday" is just as adequate for his hearers "today."[9] Second, this structure puts "the same" at the very center of the verse. Jesus' perpetual effectiveness is both the expression and guarantee of God's faithfulness, so eloquently affirmed in vv. 5-6.[10] "We" must imitate the faith of those leaders because "we" can depend on God's faithfulness, made effective in Christ's High Priesthood, just as much as they could.[11] The pastor concludes with "and forever" in order to turn the eyes of his hearers ever forward to the "enduring City" (v. 14) guaranteed by "Jesus Christ." By joining the eternal Christ and the "enduring City" the pastor erects the strongest barrier against disobedience or pursuit of some alternate way of life.[12] "Jesus

5. O'Brien, 517.

6. See the comments on 10:10.

7. Koester, 560, likens this formula, "indicating that God was, is, and will be" to similar descriptions in various sources. See Rev 1:4, 8; 4:8; 11:27; 16:5 (Johnson, 346; Weiss, 715). "Forever" confirms the Son's eternal being (1:8), his perpetual priesthood (5:6; 6:20; 7:17, 21, 28), and the unchanging efficacy of the salvation he has accomplished (5:9; 9:12). See Johnson, 346.

8. See Bauckham, "Divinity," 34-36.

9. Ellingworth, 704. "Yesterday," as part of this formula underscoring divine perpetuity, refers to the indeterminate past. However, in light of v. 7, it also evokes the recent past or the hearers' deceased leaders. Cf. Riggenbach, 434-35. There is little contextual reason to identify "yesterday" with Christ's incarnation or suffering (*pace* Attridge, 393; Thompson, 281; Bruce, 375).

10. See Hughes, 570, citing Peter Lombard.

11. Thus, the perpetual effectiveness of Christ not only undergirds faith but, *pace* Weiss, 714-16, is its object — anticipated by those who lived before Christ, embraced by those who would live faithfully since.

12. Cf. Johnson, 346.

Christ yesterday and today the same, and forever," is an apt summary of God's word, received from their previous leaders and expounded by the pastor in this sermon.[13] It is, therefore, the antithesis of the "diverse and strange" teachings mentioned in v. 9.[14]

9 The pastor began by urging his hearers not to "drift away" through "neglect" of God's great salvation in Christ (2:1-4). He concludes by warning them not to allow themselves "to be carried away with diverse and strange teachings."[15] Instead, through Christ they are to move upward into God's presence and forward with perseverance. It is clear that these "diverse and strange teachings" are in some way associated with the "foods" mentioned later in this verse and with the people described in v. 10 as those "who worship in the Tent." Some have suggested that the pastor is not referring to aberrant doctrines that actually threatened his hearers. They contend that this general and, according to them, vague description is merely a traditional statement often inserted toward the end of letters.[16] With this reference to "teachings," "foods," and "Tent" worshipers the pastor is simply extending the contrast between the old and the new developed in the main part of his sermon.[17] It is much more likely, however, that the pastor is concerned with contemporary false teachings that are adversely affecting his hearers. The pastor emphasizes the word "teachings" by putting it at the beginning of the Greek sentence.[18] This interpretation of "diverse and strange teachings" as a contemporary reality is substantiated by the fact that "those who worship in

---

13. This phrase may have been a confession of faith drawn from the teaching of these early leaders (Lane, 2:502) and now adapted to the pastor's purpose within this immediate context (Weiss, 716-17).

14. On the progression — faithful leaders (v. 7); their teaching (v. 8); false teaching (v. 9) — see Lane, 2:526-28; Hughes, 570; Attridge, 392-93; and O'Brien, 517.

15. παραφέρεσθε ("do not allow yourselves to be carried away") is permissive middle. Cf. Col 2:6-8; Eph 4:14-16. For this expression in the context of being misled by error see Plato, *Philebus* 38D; *Phaedrus* 265D (Johnson, 346). Compare μήποτε παραρυῶμεν ("lest we drift away") in 2:1. This "being carried away" is also the opposite of τὴν τελειότητα φερώμεθα ("let us go on to maturity," "let us allow ourselves to be borne on to maturity") in 6:1. For other παρα-terms used in Hebrews with a negative connotation see παρακοή ("disobedience," 2:2); παραπικραίνω ("rebel," 3:16); παραπικρασμός ("rebellion," 3:8, 15); παραπίπτω ("fall away," 6:6); παραιτέομαι ("beg," "refuse," 12:19, 25).

16. Cf. Rom 16:17-18; 2 Thess 3:19-20; 1 Tim 6:20-21; Tit 3:9-11; Jas 5:19-20; 2 Pet 3:17; 1 John 5:16-17; Jude 22-23 (cited by Weiss, 717, n. 37).

17. Koester, 567; Thompson, 281-82; Johnson, 347; Weiss, 716-22; Isaacs, "Hebrews 13.9-16," 280-81; and D. Lührmann, "Der Hohepriester ausserhalb des Lagers (Heb 13,12)," *ZNW* 69 (1978): 178, represent those who follow this interpretation.

18. "Teachings diverse and strange do not be carried away with" is an awkward translation, but it represents the Greek word order and shows the emphasis put on "teachings."

the Tent" (v. 10) refers to people contemporary with the hearers rather than to people who lived before Christ.[19] True, the writer has admitted that the OT faithful did not yet have the privileges available to the followers of Christ (compare 10:19-25 with 11:13-16 and cf. 11:39-40). Yet he has never drawn such a sharp contrast between contemporary believers and OT people as he now asserts between "us" and "those who worship in the Tent."[20] He has consistently taught that the faithful who lived before Christ and those who live after are part of the one people of God (see on 2:11-18; 3:1-6; 3:7-4:11; 11:1-40). The radical contrast has not been between those who lived before and after Christ but between those who believed (11:1-40) and those who did not (3:7-19). Thus, the pastor is concerned with contemporary false teachings, contemporary "foods," and contemporaries who can be characterized as "those who worship in the Tent."[21]

It appears, then, that the writer is not merely extending his comparison/contrast between the old and the new, but applying it to a contemporary situation, in which some persisted in denying the obsolescence of the old despite the coming of Christ.[22] Such teachings acknowledged Christ but denied his complete sufficiency as the only Savior.[23] Thus, they tended to weaken the hearers' commitment to Christ in the face of opposition and to retard their separation from the relative safety of the synagogue and its practices. The very "diversity" of these teachings betrayed their error.[24] In fact, the word

19. This is no contrast between Christ and the OT priests; it is between "us" and the people "who worship in the Tent." See on v. 10 below.

20. The writer would have seen nothing wrong with "worshiping in the Tent" before the coming of Christ. Thus there is no reason to suppose that he was speaking of those who were unfaithful during that earlier era.

21. Weiss, 718-19, contends that the pastor has no specific false teaching in mind because he is concerned about "confirming the heart" of his hearers rather than correcting their thinking. Yet he admits that the "grace" by which hearts are confirmed has a Christological foundation (719).

22. The earlier chapters of Hebrews provide no support for the suggestion that the hearers were attracted by Gnostic or pagan mystical practices (Lane, 2:532-35; Attridge, 394-96; Hughes, 572-74). Hughes notes that since these teachings involved participation in "foods," they could not be Gnostic doctrines that taught abstention from food.

23. Lane, 2:532-35. Goulder, "Ebionites," 393-406, contends that Hebrews is a sustained apologetic against teachings like those held by the early Jewish Christians called Ebionites. According to the Ebionites Christ was an angel who came upon Jesus at his baptism and left before his crucifixion. N. H. Young, "'Bearing His Reproach' (Heb 13:9-14)," *NTS* 48 (2002): 253-55, attests the Jewish character of these teachings but puts more emphasis on social pressure to identify with the synagogue and less emphasis on the influence of aberrant beliefs. He envisions a situation in which the recipients of Hebrews have not yet made a clean break with their former congregation.

24. These teachings were "diverse" (ποικίλαις), while the gospel is one (Johnson,

translated "diverse" could be rendered "perverse."[25] These teachings may not have been unconventional or bizarre, but they were "strange" to the gospel of Christ.[26] The coming of Christ makes continued allegiance to what was anticipatory perverse.

If the pastor is truly refuting such false teachings, why wait until the end of his sermon to mention them?[27] In the first twelve chapters he has made no mention of aberrant teachings or teachers either Jewish or pagan. In fact, he has made no direct reference to contemporary Judaism at all.[28] The reading of Hebrews which we have thus far set forth suggests two factors which would account for the pastor's reserving this rejection of false teaching until the end. First, such delay was the most effective way to refute this error. In the first twelve chapters the pastor has carefully developed a consistent and full-orbed interpretation of the OT that shows how Christ has fulfilled the institutions of the Old Covenant, thus confirming their typological value but rendering their practice as a way of salvation obsolete. The Old Covenant foreshadowed the fulfillment to come both by its structure and by the obvious signs of its inadequacy contained within its own rituals. In the Scriptures God had promised this fulfillment in Christ. Thus, there has been no break in the divine plan to bring the one people of God, which was already in existence before Christ, into its heavenly destiny. These false teachings fall before such a consistent and thorough presentation of the way Christ fulfills the Old Covenant, just as the walls of Jericho fell before Joshua long ago. The pastor does not combat "diverse" teachings by diverse means. He is convinced that the best defense against error is a clear presentation of the truth. A second reason, however, for this delay may well have been that these false teachings were not at the center of his concern. He was burdened by his hearers' lassitude (2:1-4; 5:11-14), by their attachment to temporal rewards (12:14-17), and especially by the danger of their falling due to disgrace and persecution by an unbelieving society (11:1–12:13). There was, however, an

---

346). Compare the πολυμερῶς καὶ πολυτρόπως ("at various times and in various ways"), the very first words of this book, which the pastor used to emphasize the incompleteness — though not the perversity — of the old order.

25. BDAG, 842, 2b.

26. Attridge, 393; Ellingworth, 706; Young, "'Bearing His Reproach' (Heb 13:9-14)," 254-56.

27. This delay is one of the factors that has led some to believe that this is a stylized reference, rather than a real refutation of false teaching (see Koester, 567; Thompson, 281-82; Johnson, 347; Isaacs, "Hebrews 13.9-16," 280-81).

28. Writers like Young, "'Bearing His Reproach' (Heb 13:9-14)," 258-59, and esp. Goulder, "Ebionites," 393-401, greatly exaggerate the polemical character of chapters 1–12 because they fail to note both this lack of direct opposition to contemporary Judaism and the strong sense of continuity between the people of God past and present.

ideological component that could be used to justify their withdrawal from commitment to Christ because of these other factors. Thus, while it is a mistake to deny that this verse refers to false teachings that actually endangered the pastor's hearers, it is equally wrong to argue that the first twelve chapters of Hebrews are no more than a refutation of this teaching.[29] These earlier chapters are a grand presentation of Christ's sufficiency, meant to sustain the pastor's hearers against all odds.

The opposite of "allowing" oneself to be "carried away with strange teachings" is for "the heart to be confirmed by grace." The pastor's main concern has always been with the heart because it is the source of both rebellion and perseverance in obedience. His hearers do not have the "hardened," rebellious "hearts" of the wilderness generation (3:8, 12-15; 4:7). They have "true" hearts, cleansed by the blood of Jesus (10:22; cf. 9:11) and engraved with God's law (10:15-18). It is "appropriate" and necessary for such hearts "to be confirmed by grace," which they receive by regularly "drawing near" to God through their exalted High Priest (4:14-16; 10:19-25; cf. 2:16-18) who himself "died" for "all" according to the "grace of God" (2:9). The perpetual faithfulness of God (v. 5-6) expressed in the unchangingly effective high priesthood of Christ (v. 8) calls for hearts that are "confirmed" and faithful in their response. Those with such hearts are able to hold their confession "firm" to the end without "falling short" of God's grace (12:15).[30]

No such confirmation of "the heart" is achieved "by foods." The pastor intends the term "foods" to recall all that he has said about the old sacrificial system's inability to cleanse the heart from sin and sustain it in obedience (cf. 9:19).[31] Yet, in association with the false teachings mentioned above, it is likely that he is also making reference to Jewish ceremonial meals conducted throughout the Roman world but parallel to the sacrificial meals in the Temple (9:10).[32] Such contemporary Jewish rituals are of no more value

29. Goulder, "Ebionites," 393-406, falls into this error. Young, "'Bearing His Reproach' (Heb 13:9-14)," 243-61, is more balanced.

30. Compare βεβαιοῦσθαι ("to be confirmed") in this verse with βεβαίαν, used in 3:14 for holding the beginning of one's confession "firm" until the end.

31. Isaacs, "Hebrews 13.9-16," 281, and Johnson, 347, would limit "foods" to the sacrifices, etc. of the Old Covenant without reference to any contemporary practice. It is not clear why Johnson would translate "foods" as "dietary laws" if these foods are a metaphor for "foods" offered as sacrifices under the Old Covenant (Lev 3:1-17; 7:11-21; Ezek 44:30-31). It appears that his translation is determined by conflict over dietary laws mentioned elsewhere (Mark 7:1-8; Acts 10:1-11:30; 1 Corinthians 8-10; Rom 14:1-23; Rev 2:14, 20) rather than by the contextual concerns of Hebrews. Bruce, 377, tends to fall into the same error.

32. See the argument in Lane, 2:532-35. There is nothing in the context that suggests the pastor is referring to pagan sacrifices (*pace* Moffatt, 233). Gnosticizing teach-

695

in transforming the person than the already discredited sacrifices of the Old Covenant (9:11-14). Indeed, "those who walk in them," that is, whose conduct is based on these practices, "have not been profited" by the heart transformation available in Christ.[33] "Grace," on the other hand, leads to a confirmation of the heart that remains in effect and that was impossible to achieve through the outward rituals of the Old Covenant in either ancient or contemporary form.[34] The grace available through the high priesthood of Christ "confirms" and "steadies" the people of God so that they need not be "carried away" by false teachings.

10 The pastor gives no indication elsewhere that the heavenly Sanctuary has an "altar" or that Christ's sacrifice was offered therein (see on 9:11-15).[35] Nor is there any contextual support for identifying this "altar" with the eucharist, as some have tried to do.[36] "For we have an altar" recalls the high-priestly ministry of Christ that "we have" (4:14-16; 10:19-25), and reminds

---

ings usually required abstention from certain foods rather than participation in ritual meals (Hughes, 572-74; *pace* Bruce, 377). The pastor cannot be referring to the eucharist or the Lord's Supper since the meals he opposes belong to the old era (Attridge, 394-96; thus, *pace* Braun, 461-62, he is not combating a false or "magical" view of the eucharist). Lührmann, "Der Hohepriester," 178-80, suggests that "foods" represents not merely the "Jewish cult" but the earthly cult as contrasted to the heavenly. Hebrews acknowledges that the old sacrificial system was earthbound and dependent on mortal, sinful humanity. However, it never portrays the old as representative of anything but itself.

33. Note forms cognate with ὠφελέω ("to profit") in 4:2 and especially in 7:18 where the related term ἀνωφελές describes the "uselessness" of the "former commandment" to cleanse and bring into God's presence (cf. Lane, 2:535). *Pace* Riggenbach, 438, these "unprofitable" practices and Christ are mutually exclusive.

34. The perfect tense of βεβαιοῦσθαι ("to be confirmed," "to have been confirmed") is in accord with the continuing validity and effectiveness of this heart-confirming grace.

35. *Pace* Thompson, 282; Thompson, *Christian Philosophy,* 146; and Filson, *"Yesterday,"* 48-50; cf. Lührmann, "Der Hohepriester," 179. Isaacs, "Hebrews 13.9-16," 275, notes that even in the OT the altar of sacrifice was outside the sanctuary and the means of its entrance, a fact overlooked by Ronald Williamson, "The Eucharist and the Epistle to the Hebrews," *NTS* 21 (1975): 309.

36. *Pace* P. Andriessen, "L'eucharistie dans l'épître aux Hébreux," *NRTh* 94 (1972): 269-77; J. Swetnam, "Christology and the Eucharist in the Epistle to the Hebrews," *Bib* 70 (1989): 74-94. See the evaluation of this position by Williamson, "The Eucharist and the Epistle to the Hebrews," 300-312; Isaacs, "Hebrews 13.9-16," 277-80; Lane, 2:538-39; and Weiss, 723-29. The pastor, who has compared the old as outward ritual to the new as inner transformation (9:11-14), would hardly compare the "foods" of the old with the "food" of the eucharist. The first possible use of "altar" for the eucharist comes from Ignatius of Antioch (*Philadelphians* 4; cf. *Magn.* 7:2; *Trall.* 7:2; *Eph.* 5:2). However, one must also be skeptical of Williamson's speculative suggestion that the writer of Hebrews represented a noneucharistic Christianity.

the hearers that his once-for-all sacrifice on the cross is the continuous source of this heart-confirming grace.[37] The pastor uses the term "altar" to contrast the sacrifice of Christ with the "foods"/"false teachings" of v. 9 that bring no spiritual profit.[38] The fact that the faithful have these privileges represented by the "altar" is also the basis for his exhortation in v. 13 below that they identify with Christ and his suffering. Just as those who cling to the Old Covenant "eat" from the offerings they bring as an indication that they share in those offerings, so those faithful to Christ partake of the benefits derived from his sacrifice as they draw near through him (7:25; 4:14-16; 10:19-25). This imagery allows the pastor to set the privileges available through Christ in direct contrast to contemporary ritual practices that those who approach God through Christ must avoid.[39] It also allows him to emphasize the present reality of the benefits Christ provides through prayer and worship. Furthermore, this use of altar imagery is in accord with the pastor's description of praise, good works, and mutual concern as the "sacrifices" that please God (vv. 15-16).[40]

In light of 9:1-10 it was most appropriate for the pastor to refer to those who continued to worship according to the Old Covenant as "those who worship in the Tent."[41] We have already mentioned that he never uses the word "Tent" for the heavenly Sanctuary without adding a qualifier.[42] This is no contrast between Christ and the priests who ministered in the "Tent" but between "we" the recipients of Hebrews who have an "altar" and those who continue to worship according to the Old Covenant.[43] Those who continue to worship in

37. For "this altar" as a metaphor for Christ's suffering and death on the cross see Attridge, 396; Hughes, 575; Lane, 2:538; Montefiore, 244; Spicq, 2:425; O'Brien, 521; and Mitchell, 299.

38. Lane, 2:538; Ellingworth, 711; Weiss, 724.

39. See Spicq, 2:415.

40. See Attridge, 397.

41. The pastor is not referring to the Temple or to a literal "Tent" but to the "Tent" worship described in 8:5; 9:1-10. The words τῇ σκηνῇ ("the tent") without a preposition can be understood as a locative of sphere — those whose worship is in accord with the Tent-system of the old order. "Worship" (λατρεύω in 13:10) is used once for the ministry of priests (8:5), but four times for lay worshipers (9:9, 14; 10:2; 12:28).

42. "The true Tent" (8:1) and "the greater and more perfect Tent" (9:11).

43. The phrase "those who worship in the Tent" does not refer to the priests alone, nor does it refer to all who worship in a material, ritual, sacramental cult but, as stated above, to the people as a whole who continue to worship according to the Old Covenant since Christ has come. This position is substantiated in several ways. First, the pastor contrasts the priests with Christ (5:1-10; 7:10-25; 8:1–10:18), but "those who worship in the Tent" with his hearers who are followers of Christ (priests/Christ//"those who worship in the Tent"/the followers of Christ). See above on v. 9. Second, the metaphorical use of "eating" for receiving personal benefit from a sacrifice is analogous to the "peace" offer-

697

this way since Christ has come have "no right to" participate in the benefits brought by Christ. Thus, to (re)join these "Tent" worshipers or to refuse to separate from their practices would be fatal, because it would be to forfeit the cleansing provided by Christ and the ministration of the High Priest at God's right hand (8:1-2). This understanding of "those who worship in the Tent" confirms the identity of the hearers as "Jewish Christians" who wished to combine the now-superseded rituals of the synagogue with their commitment to Christ. It is important, however, to realize that "Jewish Christian" in this context is not an ethnic term. "Jewish Christian" is broad enough to include those many Gentiles who had adopted and felt comfortable with Jewish practices. This acculturation may have occurred after their conversion to Christ since many of their fellow believers were Jewish. However, one thinks particularly of Gentiles who had identified with the synagogue and been shaped by the OT Scriptures before their acceptance of Jesus as the Messiah.[44]

11 At first it seems as if the writer returns somewhat abruptly to the Day of Atonement sacrifices by paraphrasing the instructions found in Lev 16:27 for the disposal of the bodies of those sacrifices "outside the camp."[45] Yet the analogy described in vv. 11-13 demonstrates the radical difference between the "altar" located "outside the camp" and the altar of "those who worship in the Tent" (v. 10).[46] The LXX of Leviticus uses the active, "they shall burn them," because it is giving the priests direction. Hebrews employs the passive in order to focus on the sacrifices themselves — "their bodies shall be burned." The Pentateuch never uses the word here translated "ani-

---

ings (Lev 7:11-18) from which all could eat rather than to the sin offerings. Although the priests could eat the sin offerings of others (Lev 6:19, 22 [LXX 26, 29]; 7:6; 10:17-18; Num 18:9-10), neither priests nor people could eat their own sin offerings. Nor is the eating metaphor derived from the Day of Atonement sacrifices from which none could eat (*pace* Isaacs, "Hebrews 13.9-16," 281; Young, "'Bearing His Reproach' [Heb 13:9-14]," 246-47; and others). There is no indication that the pastor is using the inability of the priests to eat the Day of Atonement sacrifices as a type of their inability to "eat" from the "altar" that "we have" (*pace* Young, "'Bearing His Reproach' [Heb 13:9-14]," 246-47; L. Paul Trudinger, "The Gospel Meaning of the Secular: Reflections on Hebrews 13:10-13," *EvQ* 54 [1982]: 236; cf. Bruce, 378; Bénétreau, 2:221). Since Hebrews never uses the old earthbound sacrificial system as typical of all that is earthbound, it would be inappropriate to include all who participate in a material, ritual, sacramental cult among these "Tent worshipers" (*pace* Moffatt, 234; Lührmann, "Der Hohepriester," 178-80; and Braun, 463). Cf. O'Brien, 519, 522.

44. Young, "'Bearing His Reproach' (Heb 13:9-14)," 255-56; cf. Goulder, "Ebionites," 395, n. 6.

45. Ellingworth, 712, senses this apparent abruptness, but misses the connection between vv. 10 and 11-13 when he says that γάρ ("for") connects v. 11 only loosely with v. 10.

46. Weiss, 729.

mals" for the sacrifices of the Old Covenant. The pastor uses this term both as convenient shorthand for "the bull . . . and the goat" found in Leviticus and as a reminder that these sacrifices were mere animals in contrast to the self-offering of Christ.[47] A rather wooden rendering of Lev 16:27 as paraphrased in Heb 13:11 might run, "For animals, whose blood is brought into the Most Holy Place for sin by the High Priest, their bodies are burned outside the camp." At this point, both Leviticus (16:14-15, 18-19) and Hebrews (9:11-15) have already dealt with the blood. Their concern is with the disposal of the bodies. Thus both speak of the "blood" in a relative clause and of the "bodies" in the main clause. The pastor, however, is not finished with the "blood." In v. 12 he will use this contrast between the disposal of those bodies and the suffering of Jesus as his final argument for the insufficiency of the old "blood" and the effectiveness of the new.

12   The hearers already know that Jesus fulfilled and antiquated the Day of Atonement sacrifices (9:1-14). Since, therefore, the bodies of the animals sacrificed on that Day were burned "outside the camp" of wilderness Israel, it was appropriate for "Jesus also" to suffer "outside the gate" of Jerusalem. It is instructive to compare the two clauses of v. 12 with those of v. 11:

1. For animals, whose blood is brought for sin into the Most Holy Place by the high priest.	1. Thus Jesus also, in order that he might sanctify the people through his blood.
2. Their bodies are burned outside the camp. (v. 11)	2. suffered also outside the gate (v. 12)

Verse 11 begins with a relative clause identifying the animals whose bodies are "burned outside the camp" as those whose blood was brought into the Sanctuary. Verse 12 begins with a purpose clause asserting the effectiveness of Jesus' blood because he "suffered outside the gate."[48] The ineffectiveness of those sacrifices whose "blood" was carried into the earthly sanctuary was sealed by their bodies being burned "outside the camp."[49] Jesus' suffer-

---

47. ζῴων, the genitive plural of ζῷα ("animals"), replaces καὶ τὸν μόσχον . . . καὶ τὸν χίμαρον ("both the bull . . . and the goat") in Lev 16:27. ζῴων appears to be used absolutely in the genitive case, perhaps attracted to that case by the relative pronoun ὧν ("whose"). This word for "animals" is emphasized by being given a rather odd location, several words after this relative pronoun of which it is the antecedent — ὧν γὰρ εἰσφέρεται ζῴων τὸ αἷμα (literally, "of whom for is brought in of animals the blood . . ."; underlining added). By omitting the definite article before ζῴων the pastor emphasizes the "animal" quality of these sacrifices.

48. Cf. John 19:20: "the place where Jesus was crucified was near the city." The pastor may or may not be recalling a specific reference within the tradition used by the Gospels, but he is recalling the historical reality of Jesus' crucifixion (cf. 7:14).

49. It is not so much, as Lane, 2:540, and Hughes, 574-78, have suggested, that

ing "outside the gate" in his incarnate body (10:5-10) provided for cleansing, so that those who approach God through him can enter the true heavenly dwelling place of God. The place where they ended in defeat anticipated the place where he initiated his victory.[50]

"Outside the gate" cannot be a metaphor for the heavenly world, as some have suggested, because it is both the place where the incarnate "Jesus" "suffered" and the place where his followers will share his "reproach."[51] This is the place where Jesus "endured the cross, despising the shame" (12:2). Nor, however, is "outside the camp"/"gate" the created world per se. Inside and outside "the gate" are both conditions of life in this world. The first is the place of worldly security and acceptance for those who reject Christ. The second is the place of Christ's crucifixion and thus the place of rejection by the unbelieving world that despised him. The immediate context puts great emphasis on the area outside the "camp" and "gate" as the place of suffering and reproach. The pastor, however, could not have been oblivious to the fact that "outside the camp" was the place of greatest impurity, for which the old sacrifices could provide nothing more than temporary ritual cleansing. How-

---

the burning of these sacrifices outside the camp prevented the worshipers from eating them and thereby from partaking of their benefit. If anything, this burning reinforced the demonstration (in 9:1-10 above) that these sacrifices provided no true cleansing from sin and access to God. *Pace* Attridge, 397, the pastor is not alluding to the unavailability of Christ's body.

50. Thus, it is not necessary, with Bénétreau, 2:222, to explain the "tension" between the death of Jesus "outside the gate" and the burning of the sacrifices "outside the camp" as due to the partial nature of all biblical types. This disposal outside the camp both anticipated Jesus and demonstrated the ineffectiveness of the old sacrifices. Koester, 576, n. 480, correctly notes that the Day of Atonement sacrifice concluded with these burned bodies, Christ's began by his being taken outside the city.

51. Attempts by Thompson (283), Lührmann, "Der Hohepriester," 184, and others to identify the place of suffering and reproach with the heavenly world lead to numerous inconsistencies. This interpretation is usually bolstered by the way Philo explains Moses' setting up his tent "outside the camp" (according to Exod 33:7-10) as his leaving the material, temporal, bodily world in order to contemplate God and teach others about him (*Giants* 50–55). *Pace* Lührmann, "Der Hohepriester," 181-82, Philo's explanation of this passage is no witness to an interpretive tradition that saw "outside the camp" as a place of purity. Rather, what Philo says here is in complete accord with his normal methods of allegorical interpretation. The argument presented by Thompson and Lührmann is a classic example of interpreting an expression in Hebrews on the basis of its use in Philo rather than on the basis of its use in Hebrews. See Johnson, 349; Weiss, 734; and Bénétreau, 2:223-25. Furthermore, *pace* Ellingworth, 714, 717; Hughes, 578-83; Lane, 2:543-44; and those cited by Lane, there is little evidence for an allusion to Exod 33:7-10 in Heb 13:11-13. Aside from the phrase "outside the camp" (ἔξω τῆς παρεμβολῆς), which Hebrews borrows from Lev 16:27, there is no verbal or conceptual reminiscence of the Exodus passage. See Attridge, 399, n. 119.

ever, Jesus' fully sufficient self-offering "outside the gate" effectively removes the deepest impurity of the heart (9:11-15; 10:15-18, 29-25). This verse confirms the interpretation of 9:11-15 given above. Jesus' sacrifice did not take place in heaven. Hebrews indulges in no speculation about his carrying blood into the heavenly Sanctuary.

The clause "in order that he might sanctify the people with his own blood" would have reminded those first hearers of the sacrifice by which a covenant was established.[52] The pastor turns naturally from the Day of Atonement sacrifice to the sacrifice of covenant inauguration just as he did in 9:11-14/15. If Christ's death has atoned for sin, then it has established a New Covenant or way of approaching God. Any who continue to "worship" according to the stipulations appropriate for the earthly "Tent" are misled.

13 Verses 11-12 have shown that the "altar" (v. 10) the faithful "have" is "outside the gate" in the place where Christ "suffered." "Therefore," if we would enjoy its benefits, "let us go out to him outside the camp, bearing his reproach."[53] At every crucial point in his argument the pastor has directed his hearers to focus their attention on the exalted, all-sufficient Son of Ps 110:1, 4, and to enter God's presence through him (1:13; 4:14-16; 8:1-2; 10:19-25; 12:1-3).[54] In the last of these references (12:1-3) the pastor began to turn his hearers' attention toward the sufferings of Christ as explained in 8:1–10:18. He reminded them that the exalted One had achieved this position on their behalf only because he had "endured the cross, despising the shame," and encouraged them to follow suit.[55] In this final exhortation to perseverance, then, the pastor does not urge his hearers to draw near through the exalted one of Psalm 110, as we might expect. Instead, he pleads with them to take their place with the suffering Christ excluded from unbelieving society and covered with shame and reproach.[56] As his suffering was the means of his exaltation, so identifying with him in his suffering is the means by which his people enter God's presence through him. Drawing near to God through the exalted Christ and identifying with the reproach of the suffering

52. Cf. 9:18-20; 10:10, 14, 29; and Lane, 2:541, citing Andriessen, "L'eucharistie," 276.

53. Compare διό ("therefore") at the beginning of v. 12 with τοίνυν ("therefore") at the beginning of this verse.

54. See "The Rhetorical Shape of Hebrews and Its Use of the Old Testament," pp. 72-76 in the Introduction to this commentary.

55. When the pastor focuses on the suffering of Christ, he tends to think of him as sacrifice rather than as High Priest (Bénétreau, 2:221-22), though the two are so intimately connected that they can hardly be separated.

56. *Pace* Trudinger, "Gospel Meaning," 237, the pastor is not here calling the faithful to serve the world. He is calling them to bear the rejection of the world because of their faithfulness to Christ.

Christ are inseparably bound together.[57] Through the first God's people find grace for the second (4:14-16; 10:19-21; cf. 2:16-18). Through persevering in the second they will receive ultimate entrance into the first (11:1–12:29). The pastor, who has been encouraging them to "draw near" through the exalted One of the psalm, brings his sermon to an end by directing them to persevere in "going out" and identifying with the Christ of suffering and reproach.[58] It is for this that he has been fortifying the people of God. If the pastor's hearers remain unmoved after this powerful, long-prepared-for appeal, he has nothing more to say.

Thus "camp" refers metaphorically to the unbelieving social order that has rejected Christ. Several factors, however, suggest that by "camp" the pastor was referring specifically to the community of those who insisted on continuing to live by the Old Covenant even though it had been fulfilled in Christ.[59] Comparison with "those worshiping in the Tent" (v. 10) above and their "foods" (v. 9) supports this interpretation. Furthermore, the term "camp" is a reference to the "camp" of the wilderness generation, whose rebellion was amply described in 3:7-19. Rejection of Christ by their heirs is equivalent to the rebellion at Kadesh-Barnea.[60] If, therefore, the hearers would enjoy the fulfillment that Christ brings, they must separate themselves from the worship of the community that lives by the Old Covenant as if

57. "The location, 'outside the camp,' does not mark the place where Jesus now is; rather it signifies the manner in which the readers are to approach the exalted Christ" (Mitchell, 304).

58. The consistency of direction and careful arrangement of the pastor's exhortations to "go out" (ἐξερχώμεθα, 13:13; cf. 11:8 and κατέλιπεν, "abandon," in 11:27), to "go toward" (or "draw near," προσερχώμεθα, 4:15-16; 10:22; cf. 7:25), and to "go into" (various forms of εἰσέρχομαι in 4:1, 3, 6, and 11) provide further evidence of his consummate skill as a persuasive preacher. When the pastor presented his hearers with examples of the unfaithful, he urged them to "go into" that final "rest" forfeited by the disobedient (4:1, 3, 6, 11). On the other hand, when he urged them to follow the examples of the faithful, he encouraged them to "go out" (11:8; cf. 11:27) from the unbelieving world and bear its scorn. In between he directed their attention to the sufficiency of Christ as the means by which they could "go toward" or "draw near" to God for necessary grace (4:15-16; 7:25; 10:22). This arrangement has the salutary effect of focusing their attention first on the glorious goal to be attained and then on the all-sufficient means of attaining it before addressing the difficulties to be overcome. *Pace* Attridge, 398-99, who seems to think this variety of directions a bit bewildering.

59. See Attridge, 399; Hughes, 580.

60. Attridge, 399, contends that the "camp" has nothing to do with Jewish tradition but signifies "the realm of security and traditional holiness, however that is grounded or understood." This position strains such expressions as "those who worship in the Tent" (13:10) and is difficult to maintain in light of Hebrews' comparison of the old and new priesthoods, sacrifices, and covenants.

Christ had not come. This separation will incur the wrath of their former community, and perhaps the opposition of the larger society because the hearers no longer enjoy the protection and legitimacy of their previous associates. However, this specific reference to separation from the synagogue must not obscure the broader implications of the pastor's teaching. The heroes of chapter 11, for instance, did not hesitate to suffer alienation, shame, and abuse by separating themselves from unbelieving society in general. Thus Abraham "went out" (11:8) and lived as an alien (11:9) to the social order of his day. Moses "abandoned" the unbelieving world of Egypt (11:27) and suffered "the reproach of Christ" (11:26). By urging his hearers to "go out" to Christ, bearing "his reproach," the pastor invites them to join Jesus in such a way that they voluntarily become vulnerable to the kind of treatment from the unbelieving world described in 11:36-38. To bear the "reproach" of Christ is to bear the reproach of the unbelieving world because one publicly identifies with him. The faithful must not be "borne about" by false doctrine (v. 9), but they must "bear" the "reproach of Christ."[61]

14 The call to "go out . . . bearing reproach" in v. 13 is a call to join the faithful in chapter 11, who lived in anticipation of the "enduring City." Abraham embodied the anticipation of the faithful for this City "whose architect and builder is God" (11:10). Moses demonstrated clearly that those who attain it must abandon the unbelieving world and accept the "reproach of Christ" (11:26). In the same way, the heirs of their faith "go out" and "bear the reproach of Christ" in order to attain that "City."[62] The pastor uses the article with precision: "we do not have here *an* [any] enduring city," but we are earnestly seeking "*the* one that is coming" (italics added). "Here" in this world there is no such thing as an "enduring city." "Here" is only the "camp" of unbelieving society and the place of "reproach" with Jesus outside this "camp."[63] However, the City that is "coming" for the people of God is an "enduring" or eternal City because it is the "City of the living God" (12:22).[64] The faithful who lived before Christ "anticipated" their arrival at this City. Those who live

61. Compare παραφέρεσθε ("let yourselves be borne about," v. 9, from παραφέρω) and φέροντες ("bearing," v. 13, from φέρω).

62. γάρ ("for") at the beginning of v. 14 confirms the fact that the hope of the "enduring City" is strong motivation for bearing Christ's reproach as advocated in v. 13.

63. Ellingworth, 718-19, is misled when he says that ὧδε ("here") in v. 14 broadens the metaphorical meaning of "camp" from "the old cultic dispensation" to "this world in contrast to heaven." It is not a matter of broadening but of reference to two different things. The "camp" represents unbelieving society. "Here" is a reference to this present world.

64. On μένουσαν ("enduring") see the comments on μείνῃ ("might remain") in 12:27. Both words are forms of the μένω ("remain"). Even if ἐπιζητοῦμεν ("we are seeking") echoes ἐπιζητουμένη πόλις ("a city sought") in Isa 62:12, as Ellingworth, 719, sug-

after have even more incentive for "earnestly seeking" entrance thereunto.[65] The Jesus who suffered "outside the gate" of earthly Jerusalem has now taken his seat in this "enduring City" called "heavenly Jerusalem" (12:22).[66] By bearing "his reproach" and "drawing near" through him, the faithful have already begun to experience its reality (12:22-24).

The life of the faithful moves between the two poles of the privileges that "we" now "have" (v. 10) in Christ (cf. 4:14-16; 10:19-25) and the promise of the destiny that "we do not [yet] have" (v. 14). "Faith" itself is living as if God's power for the present (which "we" do "have" in Christ) is real, and his promises for the future (which "we do not [yet] have") are certain (11:1-6). As has been his custom throughout this sermon, the pastor would motivate his hearers by the wonderful privileges "we have" in Christ and by the great reward, the heavenly "City," that "we do not" yet "have" but fervently desire. Perseverance in the great privileges that "we do have" is the way to attain that wonderful promise that "we do not" yet "have."

15-16 The pastor has used both theme and style to weave these two verses together as a seamless robe. Notice the chiastic arrangement of verbs and their complements in the Greek text: (A) "let us offer" (B) "a sacrifice of praise"; (B[1]) "doing good and sharing" (A[1]) "let us not forget."[67] The first words in the Greek of v. 15 are "through him," referring to Jesus the mediator of these sacrifices. The last word in v. 16 is "God," the one who is pleased with these offerings. Thus the praise of v. 15 and the good works and mutual concern of v. 16 taken together constitute the sacrifices that are pleasing to God. These are the sacrifices appropriate for those who partake of Christ's "altar" (v. 10) and live in ardent expectation of the heavenly City (v. 14).[68]

gests, it is doubtful that the pastor intends to evoke that passage. A reference to πᾶς ὁ ζητῶν κύριον ("everyone seeking the Lord") in Exod 33:7 is even more tenuous.

65. Compare ἐξεδέχετο ("expect," "anticipate") in 11:10 with ἐπιζητοῦμεν ("earnestly seek") here in 13:14. "Seek to get" (BDAG, 302, 2) is a more appropriate translation for ἐπιζητοῦμεν in this verse than the "seek out, search for" under which BDAG lists this passage (302, 1). The pastor is not concerned with discovery of the eternal City but with earnest striving for entrance thereunto. Such striving is more than mere intense expectation (*pace* Lane, 2:523x; cf. Ellingworth, 719).

66. Lane, 2:548, cites De Young, *Jerusalem,* 108-9.

67. Note Lane's chiastic analysis of vv. 15-16: (A) Δἰ αὐτοῦ [οὖν] ἀναφέρωμεν θυσίαν αἰνέσεως διὰ παντὸς τῷ θεῷ ("through him let us offer a sacrifice of praise perpetually to God") (B) τοῦτ' ἔστιν καρπὸν χειλέων ὁμολογούντων τῷ ὀνόματι αὐτοῦ ("that is, fruit of lips that acknowledge his name"). (B[1]) τῆς δὲ εὐποιΐας καὶ κοινωνίας μὴ ἐπιλανθάνεσθε? ("do not forget doing good and sharing"), (A[1]) τοιαύταις γὰρ θυσίαις εὐαρεστεῖται ὁ θεός ("for with such sacrifices God is well pleased") (Lane, 2:504). Ellingworth, 719, misses the point here when he says, apparently on the basis of δέ in v. 16, that vv. 15 and 16 are not closely bound to each other.

68. Although οὖν ("therefore") in v. 15 is textually suspect, it is clear that believ-

The worship of the faithful does not consist of those rituals based on false teaching mentioned in v. 9 above. They are not to be "borne away" by those teachings, but to "bear the reproach" of Jesus and to "offer" the sacrifice of praise and good works "through" him.[69] Verses 15-16 are the positive counterpart to vv. 11-13. Within the context of the unbelieving world, the life of faith is best described as going out to Christ and bearing "his reproach" (vv. 11-13). When considered, however, in relation to God and the Christian community, this same life is most appropriately represented as the offering of praise and good works to God through Christ (vv. 15-16). These verses are the pastor's final description of the life of faith so forcefully advocated throughout his sermon.[70] Such sacrifices are not sacrifices for sin but sacrifices offered to God through the cleansing power of and in grateful response to the once-for-all, sin-removing sacrifice of Christ (cf. 12:28).[71] Thus, this replacement of animal sacrifices with praise and good works is not based on mere rational argument, as in some contemporary Jewish and pagan writers, but on the work of Christ.[72] The sacrifices of the Old Covenant were offered perpetually because they were never effective in removing sin (10:1-4). The sacrifices of praise and right living described in these verses are to be offered perpetually because Christ's obedient self-offering has effectively done away with sin.[73]

This understanding of these verses is confirmed by the pastor's defini-

---

ers offer this sacrifice of praise and good works in response to what they "have" in Christ, and in anticipation of that for which they hope.

69. Contrast δι' αὐτοῦ ("through him," i.e., Jesus Christ) with διὰ τοῦ ἀρχιερέως ("through the high priest") of v. 11. See Lane, 2:548. Thus δι' αὐτοῦ is mediatorial (Ellingworth, 720). The pastor gives cohesion to his train of thought by using three words based on the root φέρω ("bear," "carry"): παραφέρεσθε ("don't let yourselves be carried about," v. 9), φέροντες ("bearing," v. 13), and ἀναφέρωμεν ("let us offer," v. 15).

70. See Lane, 2:548; Spicq, 2:429.

71. See Lane, 2:549.

72. For moral virtue and praise as the sacrifices pleasing to God in Greco-Roman and Jewish piety, see Epictetus, *Enchiridion* 31.5; Apollonius of Tyana, *Letter* 26; Sir 34:18–35:11; *Pss. Sol.* 15:3; *T. Levi* 3:5-6; 1QS 9:4-5 (Johnson, 349). Yet these sources do not necessarily oppose the offering of animal sacrifices in principle (cf. 1QS 9:4-5). While Philo emphasizes the importance of thanksgiving and good deeds, he never suggests that the sacrificial ritual should cease (see *Migration* 89–93). Hebrews gives a thorough rationale for an understanding of sacrifice that is implicit elsewhere in the NT. Cf. Rom 12:1-2; Phil 2:17; 4:18; 1 Pet 2:5; John 4:24.

73. Compare διὰ παντός ("perpetually," "continuously," "continually") in 13:15 with the same expression in 9:6. διὰ παντός was often used in the LXX of the perpetual repetition of the sacrifice, but here of the permanent validity of the sacrifice of praise given in response to Christ's once-for-all sacrifice. Lane, 2:548-49, shows how the language of this verse is related to various OT and contemporary Jewish writings.

tion of the "sacrifice of praise" as "the fruit of lips that confess his name." Throughout this sermon he has been urging his hearers to persevere by maintaining their "confession" of Christ before an unbelieving world (3:1; 4:14; 10:23; cf. 11:13).[74] Now he affirms that the "fruit of lips confessing his name" is also the "sacrifice of praise" pleasing to God, and thus the ultimate act of worship.[75] "His name" may be a reference to God's "name," but it is probably a reference to the "name" of the "Son" of God (cf. 1:4).[76] In either case, to "confess his name" is to affirm and offer praise for the ultimate revelation of God in his Son.[77] In the OT God's people praised him by "confessing" his goodness revealed in his great acts of redemption. Now they praise him by "confessing" all that he has done in Christ as the ultimate fulfillment of those earlier blessings.[78] This kind of praise is an expression of "godly fear" (12:28) because it acknowledges God's rightful place in the lives of the faithful. Thus to maintain one's confession in the Son of God as all-sufficient High Priest is both the means of perseverance in this unbelieving world and the ultimate act of worship that is pleasing to the living God.

"Do not forget" takes the hearers back to v. 1, where they were en-

---

74. Compare ὁμολογία ("confession") in these verses with ὁμολογέω ("confess"), used here in 13:15 and in 11:13.

75. αἰνέσεως ("of praise") is an attributive genitive, defining the nature of this θυσίαν ("sacrifice"). See Lane, 2:549. In Lev 7:12-15; 2 Chr 29:31; 33:16 (LXX); and 1 Macc 4:56, animals offered in thanksgiving for what God has done are called "sacrifices of praise" (θυσία [τῆς] αἰνέσεως). In Ps 50:14, however, God tells his people to offer "a sacrifice of praise, and pay your vows to the Most High" instead of offering animal sacrifices (cf. Ps 50:23). This psalm verse is the only place in the Greek OT where θυσίαν αἰνέσεως ("sacrifice of praise") and θεῷ ("to God") are used together as they are here in Heb 13:15 (Lane, 2:549). Ps 50:14 in our English Bibles equals Ps 49:14 in the LXX. Hughes (583-84) thinks Heb 13:15 is referring to the Greek translation of Hos 14:2: "we will render the fruit of our lips." Compare the MT of this verse: "we will render the bullocks of our lips."

76. See Pfitzner, 201.

77. Thus Weiss, 741, is mistaken when he refuses to see a connection between "confessing" (ὁμολογέω, 13:15) his name and the "confession" (ὁμολογία) of the community (3:1; 4:14; 10:23).

78. The term here in Hebrews is ὁμολογέω ("confess"). The LXX uses the compound ἐξομολογέω followed by a dative referring to God with the meaning "praise" or "give praise to" — Pss 6:5; 7:17; 9:1; 17:49; 21:25; 27:7; 29:4, 9, 12; 32:2 (all of these references represent the LXX numbering). Thus some would translate Heb 13:15 as "the fruit of lips that praise his name" (BDAG, 709, 4c; see also Lane, 2:550-51, and Attridge, 400-401). This translation, however, misses the connection between ὁμολογέω ("confess") and ὁμολογία ("confession"). It also overlooks the fact that even within the OT God's people "praised" him by "confessing" his mighty and gracious acts of redemption. The TNIV translation is, on the other hand, most appropriate: "the fruit of lips that profess his name."

couraged not to "forget" the ministry of hospitality. One Greek article unites "doing good" and "sharing" as a grand description of the way the faithful are to treat each other.[79] "Doing good" suggests kind deeds.[80] "Sharing" encompasses the mutual concern already stressed by the pastor (10:24-25) as well as the sharing of material goods.[81] The combination of these two words creates a rich and comprehensive description of the mutual practice of doing good in every way to one another within the community of the faithful.[82] By this expression the pastor recalls in summary form the brotherly love, devotion to hospitality, ministry to the needs of the suffering, sexual integrity, and generosity born of trust in God that he enumerated in vv. 1-6. He uses the term "such sacrifices" to contrast both the good works of v. 16 and the praise of v. 15 with the animal sacrifices of old.[83] Generous treatment of others joins the praise of God as the sacrifices "with which God is pleased." Divine approval is the ultimate motivation for the life of faithfulness.[84] Attridge provides an apt summation of this passage: "Having a share in Christ's altar means finally to follow him on the road of suffering, to worship God through sacrifices of praise, and to devote oneself to loving service of other members of the covenant community."[85]

17 Perseverance in this life of faith is founded on emulation of the community's past leaders (v. 7) and sustained by submission to its present leaders (v. 17). The pastor, who began with encouragement to imitate the former, concludes with exhortation to submit to the latter. The opening clause of v. 17 contains this urgent exhortation: "Obey your leaders and submit [to them]." The rest of v. 17 gives the reasons why this submission is so urgent.[86]

We have put the words "to them" in brackets because they are absent from the Greek text. The words "obey" and "submit" surround the expression "your leaders" and thus emphasize their position as the recipients of submis-

---

79. A few manuscripts, including 𝔓[46], have a second article (τῆς, "the") before κοινωνίας ("sharing").

80. Weiss, 742, says that εὐποιΐα is equivalent to φιλαδελφία in v. 1. He also cites the following words as near synonyms: ἀγαθοποιΐα ("doing good"), 1 Pet 4:19; *1 Clem.* 2:2, 7; 33:1; 34:2; its equivalent verb, ἀγαθοποιεῖν ("to do good"), 1 Pet 2:15, 20; 3:6, 17; εὐεργεσία ("doing of good"), Acts 4:9; 1 Tim 6:2; *1 Clem.* 19:2; 21:1; 38:3; and ἀγαθοεργεῖν ("to do good"), 1 Tim 6:18.

81. Lane, 2:552.

82. Ellingworth, 721.

83. Weiss, 741. Cf. Ellingworth, 722.

84. γάρ ("for"), in "for with such sacrifices God is well pleased," shows that his pleasure is the motivation for this life.

85. Attridge, 391.

86. Weiss, 744, contends that this exhortation is more like the firm authority given to leaders in *1 Clem.* 1:3; 21:6; 37:2; *Did.* 15:2; 4:1 than the "respect" enjoined by Paul in 1 Thess 5:12. Such arguments are largely speculative.

sion. It would be a mistake to press the difference between these two imperatives.[87] The first term is passive, "be obedient to," and is often used of those who have been persuaded to obey rather than for obedience to constituted authority.[88] Thus, it is an appropriate response from those who hear to those who proclaim God's word. The second imperative, "submit to," is a more general expression that occurs nowhere else in the NT and demonstrates the breadth of the pastor's vocabulary.[89] The combination of these two terms stresses the need for faithful, thorough adherence to the oversight offered by their leaders. By using the present imperative, the pastor urges his hearers to continue with renewed enthusiasm the submission they have already been rendering. He would have them make such obedience and submission a lifelong habit.

The reasons the pastor gives for submission are inherent in the relationship between the people of God and their faithful leaders.[90] The pastor reminds his hearers of their leaders' task, of their leaders' character, and of the hearers' own ultimate good. First, the pastor turns to the ministry these leaders perform. They are charged with "watching over your souls," and thus guarding them from danger.[91] The pastor uses "watching over" to describe diligent care that has perseverance unto final blessedness as its goal.[92] "Your souls" clearly refers to the leader's concern for the eternal welfare of those in their charge as immortal, spiritual beings (see 10:39; 2 Cor 12:15).[93] Thus, the task these leaders are performing makes them eminently worthy of all submission. Furthermore, the manner in which they are carrying out this task shows the integrity of their character. They perform this oversight "as going to give an account." They do not carry out their oversight for personal gain,

---

87. Ellingworth, 723.

88. In order to distinguish πείθεσθε ("obey") from ὑπείκετε ("submit") and thus to avoid tautology, Johnson, 350a, translates πείθεσθε by "depend on" or "put trust" in (see Heb 2:13; 6:9). See Lane, 2:554-55, and the discussion in BDAG, 792, 3, a-c. Note the examples there presented.

89. BDAG, 1030, defines ὑπείκω as "to yield to someone's authority, yield, give way, submit."

90. γάρ ("for") introduces these reasons.

91. ἀγρυπνοῦσιν ("watch over") describes the leaders' "care for" the hearers (BDAG, 16, 2), but it also suggests vigilance against "threatening peril" (BDAG, 16, 1). The pastor has shown obvious concern lest his hearers fall away from Christ. See Lane, 2:555.

92. Lane, 2:55, points out that this word is always used in the NT in contexts which denote eschatological vigilance (Mark 13:33; Luke 21:36; Eph 6:18). See Ellingworth, 723, for the idea that ἀγρυπνοῦσιν ("watching over") suggests that these leaders are undershepherds of the "Great Shepherd" in v. 20.

93. "No separation of soul and body is implied, but the author's concern is clearly the spiritual good of the community" (Ellingworth, 723). Cf. Weiss, 745.

but as those who intend to give an account to God not only for themselves (4:12-13) but for the way they have conducted their ministry.[94] Their integrity is also substantiated by their deep concern for those under their care. It is because they have such concern that submission would enable them to do their work and give this account "with joy" and not "with groaning."[95] The word translated "groaning" and its related noun occur often in the psalms for the deep distress from which the psalmist cries out to God.[96] This expression depicts deep sorrow that arises like a groan from the depths of the one grieved.

Such grief on the part of leaders over the tragic fate of uncooperative hearers leads naturally to the pastor's final reason for submission: "For this would be without profit for you."[97] Because he has an unerring sense of what would be most effective, the pastor understates his case by replacing the language of judgment (cf. 10:30-31; 12:29) with the language of commercial transaction — "without profit."[98] Instead of wearing out his dire warnings by one more repetition, he forces his hearers to ask what this "without profit" might mean: refusal to submit to their leaders would result in the worst "bottom line" for them — eternal loss. In this skillful way the pastor puts the full weight of his sermon behind the local leaders of this community and strengthens their hands for the task before them. At the same time, he hands the care of this congregation, for whom he has expressed such concern, over to them, and indirectly reminds them of their responsibility before God.

94. It is possible to take the future tense of ἀποδώσοντες ("going to give") in ὡς λόγον ἀποδώσοντες ("as going to give an account") as a future of obligation: "as having to give an account" (Matt 12:36; Rom 14:12; 1 Pet 4:5). Lane, 2:556, however, argues that, following ὡς ("as"), this phrase implies intent. This understanding fits better with the pastor's emphasis on the integrity of the leaders' character as expressed in their ministry. The term λόγος ("word") is used here for the accountability of leaders as it is in 4:12-13 for the accountability of all believers.

95. "In order that with joy they might do this (τοῦτο) and not with groaning." τοῦτο ("this") probably refers to their "giving account" (Hughes, 587), rather than to their "keeping watch" (Ellingworth, 724), though the pastor makes no sharp distinction between the two.

96. For στενάζω ("to groan," "to sigh") and its related noun στεναγμός ("groaning," "sighing") see Job 23:2; Pss 6:6; 30:11; 37:9; 78:11 (these psalm references represent the LXX numbering); Rom 8:22-27; and 2 Cor 5:2.

97. Koester, 572; cf. Johnson, 351. Notice how στενάζοντες ("groaning") is followed immediately by ἀλυσιτελές ("unprofitable").

98. Lane, 2:556. Weiss, 746, misses the rhetorical impact of what the pastor says by attributing "without profit" to conditions within the immediate community life of the church rather than to the Judgment.

C. A SERMON SENT AS A LETTER (13:18-25)

18 *Pray for us, for we are persuaded that we have a good conscience, determining to conduct ourselves well in everything.* 19 *And I urge you to do this all the more in order that I might be restored to you soon.*

20 *And may the God of peace, the one who brought up from the dead the Great Shepherd of the sheep, by the blood of the eternal covenant, our Lord Jesus,* 21 *empower you in every good thing to do his will, doing in us what is well pleasing before him through Jesus Christ, to whom be glory for ever. Amen.*

22 *And I urge you, brothers and sisters, pay attention to this word of exhortation, for I have instructed you very briefly.* 23 *Know that our brother Timothy has been released, with whom, if he comes soon, I will see you.*

24 *Greet all your leaders and all the saints. Those from Italy greet you.*

25 *Grace be with you all.*

Comparison with 1 Peter and the letters of Paul demonstrates the typical nature of vv. 18-25.[1] The various issues addressed in these verses were the normal elements of a letter's end: request for prayer (vv. 18-19);[2] a blessing/benediction (vv. 20-21);[3] a final summative exhortation (v. 22); a note about future travel plans (v. 23); a final greeting (v. 24); and a concluding blessing (v. 25).[4] The solemn benediction in vv. 20-21 brings the final appeal of chap-

---

1. Hebrews parallels the ending of 1 Peter more closely than the endings of the Pauline letters (cf. Weiss, 760-61). Compare the blessing and ascription of praise in Heb 13:20-21 with 1 Pet 5:10-11. Compare the profession of brevity and the mention of Timothy in Heb 13:22-23 with the mention of Silas and a similar profession of brevity in 1 Pet 5:12. Both Heb 13:22-23 and 1 Pet 5:12 are the respective authors' final appeal for compliance with the messages they have sent. In Heb 13:24 and 1 Pet 5:13-14 both exhort the recipients to offer greetings and relay the greetings of others. Both texts conclude with a benediction (Heb 13:25; 1 Pet 5:14b).

2. 1 Thess 5:25 is the only inclusion of a prayer request within the closing of a Pauline letter. See, however, Rom 15:30; 2 Thess 3:1; and Col 4:3. Note also Phlm 22, where Paul expresses the hope that he will be restored to them in answer to their prayers.

3. Paul pronounces a blessing/benediction at the end of both 1 and 2 Thessalonians (1 Thess 5:23-24; 2 Thess 3:16). Neither of these blessings, however, ends with an ascription of praise to God and a concluding "amen" as do both Heb 13:20-21 and 1 Pet 5:10-11. For a simple ascription of praise to God with "amen" see Phil 4:20 (cf. Rom 16:25-27).

4. For the identical concluding blessing see Tit 3:15: ἡ χάρις μετὰ πάντων ὑμῶν ("grace with you all"). Col 4:18; 1 Tim 6:21; and 2 Tim 4:22 omit the πάντων ("all"): ἡ χάρις μετὰ ὑμῶν ("grace with you").

ter 13 to its conclusion and provides a fit ending for the entire book.[5] Thus the epistolary character of the subsequent material in vv. 22-25 is particularly clear.[6]

These final verses, however, are not a perfunctory following of tradition or a mere clone of other letter endings. As we would expect from one with such literary skill and such concern for his hearers, the pastor has carefully crafted these final verses to reinforce the message of his sermon. The integral way in which they are related to the rest of the letter belies the contention of some that they were added later, in total or in part, to claim Pauline authorship.[7] One who wanted to make such a claim would no doubt have reinforced the deception by adding an introduction at the beginning of Hebrews.[8]

The pastor, then, has ended what has appeared up until now to be a sermon as if it were a letter. The simplest explanation for this situation is that the author of Hebrews was not able to deliver his sermon in person, so he committed it to writing and sent it to be read to the congregation over which he was so gravely concerned. His letter ending, then, is no claim to Pauline authorship. However, by appending this ending he is associating his message with the other early Christian letters in our NT and claiming his place as a faithful interpreter of the message of Christ handed down through the apostles.[9] This letter ending also affords the opportunity to address several personal issues that would only have distracted from the body of his sermon. The information given demonstrates the intimate relationship between sender and recipients but is tantalizingly insufficient to establish with certainty their identity or location.

18-19 By this request for prayer and testimony to his own character and conduct, the pastor identifies closely with both the needs of his hearers and the life he has been exhorting them to live. While such deference at the

5. See Übelacker, *Appell,* 223-27. Hughes (588-89) thinks that the benediction in vv. 20-21, ending with the final "amen," is the true conclusion of the sermon. Weiss suggests that vv. 22-25 are even more personal in nature than vv. 18-21.

6. With his first person singular address, the requests for prayer, benediction, greeting, and final blessing Weiss, 747, says that the author has changed from the "speech" style evident until now to an "epistolary" style at v. 18. Vanhoye, *La structure littéraire,* 219, on the other hand, contends that the pastor passes from "the solemnity of the oratorical style" to "the simplicity of the epistolary style" at v. 22. Weiss also acknowledges the even more personal nature of vv. 22-25.

7. Grässer, 3:411-12, argues that vv. 22-25 were added later in order to conform Hebrews to the Pauline epistles. On the integration of these verses with the rest of Hebrews see Attridge, 405. In addition, the parallels with the endings of Paul's letters lack the exactitude of a forgery (Spicq, 2:434-35).

8. Koester, 582.

9. See the discussion in Weiss, 747.

end of a letter was a normal way of soliciting the recipients' favor, there is no reason to doubt the pastor's sincerity.[10] With "pray for us," he is asking for the same support from them that he has encouraged them to give one another.[11] His request is a reminder of the special need for prayer felt by those in places of leadership within the community of God's people. The pastor buttresses his appeal for prayer with a testimony to his own way of life: "For we are persuaded that we have a good conscience, in everything determining to conduct ourselves well." According to the grammatical structure of this sentence, "for" suggests that the integrity of the pastor's conduct shows he is worthy of their prayer.[12] He certainly desired their prayer for his continued perseverance. Yet the underlying implication of this statement is that the integrity of his life adds weight to the validity of his strong appeal for their faithfulness in the previous chapters.[13] His authority rests on his integrity as one who faithfully interprets and lives by the word of God, spoken first in the prophets and now in his Son (1:1-4). He offers himself as an example of one who has embraced Christ as the fully sufficient Savior and lived faithfully with the assured hope of God's promise for the future.[14] What he claims for himself he would have his hearers emulate.

In 6:9 the pastor affirmed his confidence in his hearers' future obedience in order to encourage their perseverance. He concludes in this verse by affirming confidence in his own conduct in order to strengthen his appeal. "We are persuaded" is a strong assertion, the very opposite of "we suppose."[15] A "good conscience" is the antithesis of an "evil conscience" (10:22) because it has been "perfected" (9:9) by being cleansed from sin by Christ

---

10. For appeal to one's own character, request for help, and deference as means of obtaining an audience's favor at the conclusion of an address, see deSilva, 509.

11. It would be natural for those who received a letter to understand περὶ ἡμῶν ("for us") in a closing prayer request as a reference to the writer and his associates. We know that Timothy, though temporarily absent (v. 23), was associated with the author. The switch to the singular in v. 19 confirms this understanding. See Ellingworth, 724-25. Without further contextual indication there is no reason that the hearers would have taken this term as inclusive of the leaders of their own local congregation mentioned in v. 17, as suggested by Lane, 2:556.

12. γάρ ("for") indicates that the hearers should pray for the pastor because he has a good conscience. Ellingworth, 725, argues that such an idea has little biblical precedent. Perhaps not, but it is in perfect accord with the pastor's larger concern that his hearers help each other to persevere. Note the connection between "conduct" and "conscience" in 2 Cor 1:12 and 1 Pet 3:16.

13. Weiss, 749.

14. See Attridge, 403.

15. πειθόμεθα ("we are persuaded") is the perfective use of the present tense of πείθω (Ellingworth, 725). This is the same word that was translated "obey" at the beginning of v. 17 (πείθεσθε).

(9:14). One so cleansed has a heart ready to obey because God has written his laws upon it (10:15-18). Thus it is the opposite of the hardened, rebellious, deceived heart of the wilderness generation (3:12-14). The following participial phrase well describes those with such a "good" conscience: "determining to conduct ourselves well in everything." The word we have translated as "determining" is closely related to the Greek word for "will."[16] Thus, this affirmation is appropriate for one who has asserted that Christ came to do God's "will" (10:5-10) and who is about to pray that God equip his hearers to perform the divine "will" (13:21). To conduct oneself "well" is to do what pleases God. The wholesome conduct of those cleansed by Christ is not something superimposed from without, but rather something pursued intentionally because it springs from a transformed heart and thus encompasses all of life.[17] This participial phrase might be taken as causal: we are sure we have a good conscience "because we are intentionally willing to conduct ourselves well in everything." A truly "good" conscience is demonstrated by "good" conduct.[18]

The pastor reinforces his appeal for prayer by adding a specific request: "I urge you to do this all the more in order that I might be restored to you soon" (v. 19).[19] His urgency is underscored by the fact that the word translated "all the more" comes first in the Greek sentence.[20] "In order that I might be restored to you soon" describes both the content of this prayer request and the reason for its urgency. He assumes his hearers know why he is delayed, and thus gives the modern reader no clue as to its cause. Reference to Timothy's "release" in v. 23 suggests that he may have been imprisoned

---

16. Compare the participle θέλοντες in v. 18, which we have translated "determining," with its noun cognate θέλημα ("will") in 10:7, 9, 10 and 13:21. Clearly the pastor means more than "desiring," a translation followed by various versions. Cf. Johnson, 353. The translation "willing to conduct ourselves well" would also be misleading because it might imply agreement but not intention (e.g., "He was willing to go if others were going").

17. The Patristic writers tended to take ἐν πᾶσιν as "among all people" (Ellingworth, 726), though most modern interpreters construe it as "in everything," "in every way." Spicq's argument (2:433) that "among all people" means among both Jews and pagans reads more into this expression than the context warrants.

18. The word for "good" (καλήν) conscience is from the same root as the word for conducting oneself "well" (καλῶς).

19. This is the author's first use of the first person singular, a usage continued in 13:22. Weiss, 746, says that until now he has used the "ecclesiastical we" when referring to himself.

20. Since περισσοτέρως, "all the more," is first for emphasis, it is closest to the verb παρακαλῶ ("I urge"; Ellingworth, 726). However, the pastor's habit of putting the word to be emphasized first suggests that it should be taken with ποιῆσαι, "to do." Thus, not "I urge you all the more to do this," but "I urge you to do this all the more."

for his faith. If so, then this request for their prayer reinforces his earlier call to identify with God's people by ministering to the imprisoned (13:3; cf. 10:33-34). The verb "restore" indicates the pastor's previous intimate association with his hearers, but it does not necessarily mean that he was a permanent member of their community any more than was Timothy, his hoped-for traveling companion.[21] By this request, the pastor both strengthens the bond of affection between himself and his hearers and reinforces the appeal of his sermon by the prospect of a personal visit.

20 The pastor, who has just requested urgent prayer for himself in vv. 18-19, offers a benediction for his hearers in vv. 20-21.[22] Yet he reinforces his identification with them by using the word "us" in v. 21b, thus extending the prayer to include his own enablement.[23] In v. 20 the pastor invokes and describes the God who blesses. In v. 21 he describes the blessing that he is entreating this God to bestow. The description of God in v. 20 ends with "the Lord Jesus Christ,"[24] while the description of the blessing in v. 21 has "Jesus Christ." What God has done in Christ is both his ultimate self-revelation and the all-sufficient provision for the salvation of his people.

It was most appropriate for the pastor to conclude by praying that God would enable his hearers to do all that he has been urging them to do through the Jesus whose sufficiency he has so aptly described.[25] It is no surprise that such a benediction would incorporate formulaic language of worship not used elsewhere in this sermon, such as "the God of peace" and "the Great Shepherd of the sheep." Yet, as will be demonstrated below, these expressions fit most appropriately with what the pastor has already said.[26] On the other hand, phrases like "by the blood of the eternal covenant" (8:6-13; 7:22; 9:14-15; 10:15-18) and "in order to do his will" (10:5-10) reflect not only the theology but also the wording of this sermon.[27]

The pastor fortifies the faith of his hearers by the way he describes the

21. *Pace* Johnson, 354. For ἀποκαθίστημι, "restore," as returning to one's former condition, see 2 Sam 9:7; Job 8:6; 2 Macc 11:25; Josephus, *Ant.* 15.195; Matt 12:13; 17:11; Mark 3:5; Luke 6:10; and Acts 1:6.

22. Lane, 2:560, suggests that the δέ in the first line of this benediction ties it closely to the prayer request in vv. 18-19.

23. Johnson, 354.

24. "Lord" is normal in statements about the resurrection (e.g., Rom 10:9; 1 Cor 12:3; Johnson, 355). See the use of "Lord" for Christ in Heb 1:10; 2:3; 7:14.

25. For similar benedictions, see Rom 16:20; Phil 4:9; 1 Thess 5:23; 1 Cor 13:11; 1 Pet 5:10.

26. After all, in 12:14 the faithful are to pursue "peace," and in 4:14/10:21 Jesus is called the "Great" (high) priest.

27. Weiss's comparison (752) with 1 Pet 5:12-14 shows both the traditional nature of this blessing and the way the pastor has adopted it for his own purposes.

God whose blessing he invokes. In his hands "the God of peace," though a traditional formula used in letter writing, becomes a reminder that this God has opened the way to fellowship with himself through the high-priestly work of Christ.[28] This restoration of fellowship is the basis for a life of peace and wholeness within the community of God's people (12:14).[29] Thus, this description of God reinforces the pastor's call for harmony and for submission to the community's godly leaders (v. 17).[30]

The pastor's focus on Ps 110:1 throughout this sermon, along with his concordant emphasis on Christ's bringing his own into God's presence, has led him to emphasize the exaltation/session of the Son. This final description of God as the God "who brought up" Jesus "from the dead" substantiates the fact that this emphasis on the exaltation was meant not to exclude but rather to include the resurrection of Christ. The pastor has made it clear that Christ has delivered his people from the fear of death (2:14-15) and that the faithful who seek the eternal City live in anticipation of the resurrection (see the comments on 11:1-40, esp. 11:17-19, 35). The use of the term translated "brought up" rather than the perhaps more common "raised" is in accord with the pastor's emphasis on exaltation without obscuring this expression as a reference to the resurrection.[31] It also recalls the OT description of God as "the one who brought you [Israel] up out of Egypt."[32] The ultimate description of God is not as the one who "brought up" Israel from Egypt but as the one who "brought up" Jesus from the dead. The hearers are fortified in the face of persecution by this reminder of Christ's resurrection.

"Great Shepherd of the sheep" evokes a host of OT associations. David, his royal successors, and the Messiah were described as God's "shepherds," charged with caring for his people.[33] The pastor's primary intention may have been to link Christ with Moses. Moses is the shepherd to whom the LXX of Isa 63:11 is referring when it describes God as "the one who brought

28. On the traditional nature of the expression "God of peace," see Attridge, 405. God shows that he both is "peace" and creates "peace" by raising Jesus from the dead (Weiss, 752-53).

29. Hughes, 588-89. Why Hughes thinks that it cannot also be an appeal for harmony and submission in the community is not clear.

30. Lane, 2:560; Attridge, 405.

31. The pastor uses ἀνάγω ("brought up") for Christ's resurrection rather than the more commonly used ἐγείρω (11:19). Yet ἀνάγω can also be used for Christ's resurrection (Rom 10:7). The pastor used the simple ἄγω for God's bringing "many sons and daughters to glory" in 2:10. See Attridge, 405-6. "From the dead" makes reference to the resurrection unambiguous. See Ellingworth, 729.

32. ὁ ἀναγαγών σε ἐκ γῆς Αἰγύπτων ("the one who brought you out of the land of Egypt," Ps 81:10) (Weiss, 755; cf. Lev 11:45; 1 Sam 12:6; Jer 2:6; 26:14).

33. See 1 Sam 16:11; Mic 5:2-4; Zech 11:4-17; Isa 40:11; 63:11; Ezek 34:1-31; and *Pss. Sol.* 17:40, cited by Johnson, 355.

715

up from the land the shepherd of the sheep."[34] Moses may have been "the shepherd" of God's "sheep" who led them toward the earthly Promised Land.[35] Jesus, however, is the "Great Shepherd" of God's people who leads them into the heavenly homeland.[36] As he was the "great" High Priest/Priest (4:14; 10:21) who brought removal of sin, so he is nothing less than "the Great Shepherd" who brings God's own to their true destiny.[37] Thus the term "Great Shepherd" enriches the pastor's use of "Pioneer" (2:10; 12:2) and "Forerunner" (6:20) as titles that describe Christ's leading God's own into their heavenly homeland. As "the Great Shepherd" he is not merely One who has opened the way but One who is ever present, "shepherding" his people toward their divinely promised goal by providing timely grace as they approach God through the One who is also their High Priest.[38]

Finally, this phrase reinforces all that the pastor has said about the eternal deity of the Son.[39] The OT describes God as the Shepherd greater than all others (Ps 23:1-6; Ezekiel 34).[40] When the pastor describes this "Great Shepherd" as the "Lord Jesus," his Greek-speaking hearers could hardly help recalling the opening verse of Psalm 23: "the LORD is my Shepherd." What assurance this description of the Christ as "the Great Shepherd" evokes by reminding the hearers that their Savior is none other than the eternal Son of God, who saves by the "power of an indestructible life" (7:16)!

34. Compare ὁ ἀναγαγὼν ἐκ νεκρῶν τὸν ποιμένα τῶν προβάτων τὸν μέγαν ("the One who brought up from the dead the Great Shepherd of the sheep") with ὁ ἀναβιβάσας ἐκ τῆς γῆς τὸν ποιμένα τῶν προβάτων ("the One who brought up from the land the shepherd of the sheep") in Isa 63:11. Emphasis on Christ's ascension may explain the pastor's substitution of ὁ ἀναγαγών ("the One who brought up") for Isaiah's ὁ ἀναβιβάσας ("the One who brought up"). See notes 31-33 above. The shorter ὁ ἀγαγών ("the One who led") occurs in Isa 63:12. See Lane, 2:560-62. Ellingworth, 728, accepts this reference to Isa 63:11, but Attridge, 406, thinks it faint.

35. Weiss, 755-57, sees a Moses typology here. The "great" shepherd is greater than the shepherd Moses. On Moses as shepherd see Philo, *Moses* 1.60; Str-B 1:755, 972; 2:209; 536 (cited in Weiss, 756, n. 35).

36. Spicq, 2:436.

37. Compare τὸν ποιμένα . . . τὸν μέγαν ("the great shepherd," 13:20); ἱερέα μέγαν ("great priest," 10:21); ἀρχιερέα μέγαν ("great high priest," 4:14).

38. Attridge, 406, grasps this nuance of present help when he suggests that the shepherd imagery has replaced the high-priestly imagery to emphasize Christ's present intercession. "The Great Shepherd," however, should be associated, as noted in the text above, with "Pioneer" and "Forerunner." "Great Shepherd" assures the hearers that he is presently leading them to the place he has already entered as "Forerunner."

39. Cf. O'Brien, 535.

40. Ezek 34:1-16 describes God as the one who will punish the unfaithful "shepherds" of his people. 1 Pet 5:4 affirms that faithful "shepherds" will receive their eternal reward at the return of Christ, the "Chief Shepherd" (ἀρχιποίμενος).

"Lord" emphasizes this Great Shepherd's sovereignty (see 1:10). "Our" reminds the hearers both that he is sovereign over them and that they belong to him as his sheep and household (3:6). As usual, the pastor's description climaxes with "Jesus," the One who assumed our humanity in order to provide for our salvation.

"By the blood of the eternal covenant" encapsulates the teaching of Hebrews on Christ's high priesthood and covenantal mediatorship. As noted in the comments on 9:11-15 and 10:5-10 above, Christ's "blood" refers to his faithful incarnate obedience, culminating in the offering of himself for sin with all of the suffering and shame his self-offering entailed. By this obedient self-offering he did away with sin, and thus established a "covenant" through which God's people could live in his presence. This covenant is "eternal" because it is effective and will never need replacing.[41] Furthermore, it is sustained by the eternal Son of God, who offered himself "by the eternal Spirit" (9:14) and is High Priest "by the power of an indestructible life" (7:16). "By the blood of the eternal covenant" is probably an instrumental of cause — because Christ offered himself in obedience to the divine will, God "brought" him "up" from death, thus signifying and sealing the effectiveness of his saving work.[42]

21 The pastor calls upon the God who has made this grand provision to put it into effect by equipping "you with every good thing" in order "to do his will."[43] "Every good thing" is a comprehensive description of all the "good things" (9:11; 10:1) brought by Christ's high-priestly ministry.[44] Thus, it includes cleansing from sin (9:14), a heart ready to obey (10:15-18), continual access into God's presence for succor in time of need (4:14-16),

41. See 5:9; 6:2; and 9:12, 14, 15 for other relevant uses of the adjective αἰώνιος ("eternal") in Hebrews. See Isa 55:3; 61:8; Jer 32:40; and Ezek 16:60; 37:26 for promises of an "eternal covenant." These references are listed in Attridge, 407, nn. 30, 31.

42. Compare "who brought up from the dead the Great Shepherd of the sheep, by the blood of the eternal covenant" (ἐν αἵματι διαθήκης αἰωνίου) with the LXX of Zech 9:11: "You also, by the blood of the covenant (ἐν αἵματι διαθήκης), have sent forth your prisoners from the pit that has no water." Lane, 2:562-63, argues that "by the blood of the covenant" is causal in Hebrews in accord with its causal use in this Zechariah quotation from which it is drawn. More pertinent, however, is the context of Hebrews. Beginning from Heb 1:3 Christ's self-offering has been presented as the cause of his saving effectiveness. For further discussion, see Lane, above; Weiss, 757; and Thurén, *Lobopfer,* 226.

43. καταρτίσαι ("equip") is the optative of wish appropriate for a prayer (Ellingworth, 730). The pastor uses the same word here for God's "equipping" his people to do his will as he did in 10:5 for God's "preparing" (κατηρτίσω) the body through which Christ accomplished the divine will. This double usage is appropriate, since it is the obedience of Christ that empowers the obedience of his people. See Johnson, 356, and O'Brien, 536.

44. Cf. Lane, 2:564.

and the promise of final entrance into the "Unshakable Kingdom" (12:28). God uses these "good things" provided by Christ's doing the "will" of God (10:5-10) to enable God's people "to do the will of God." The people who "do the will of God" are those who live as if God's saving power in Christ is available and his promise of entrance into the heavenly City is sure. God's equipping of his people to do his will is further defined as "doing in us that what well pleasing before him." This participial phrase reminds us that we do not and cannot live this type of life on our own. God does not "equip" his people in such a way that they no longer need him.[45] He is continually "doing" or "accomplishing" (NIV) this life in his people as they continually rely on him and draw near through their High Priest. This life of trust in God's power and promises (11:5-6), of filial awe and thanksgiving (12:28), of praise and brotherly love (13:15-16; cf. 13:1-6), is the only life that is "pleasing before him."[46] God's people are not swayed by the opinion of sinful society, but motivated by God's approval. By concluding with the comprehensive name/title "Jesus Christ" the pastor encompasses the totality of the eternal, incarnate, obedient, once-having-suffered-but-now-exalted Son. It is not only "through" or "by" him but "because of" him that God accomplishes his will in his people.[47] In this way the pastor concludes by reminding his hearers that perseverance is God's work. All of his exhortations for endurance are vain unless his hearers "draw near" and receive the grace available through Christ (4:14-16; 10:19-25).[48]

To whom is "glory" to be ascribed "forever"? The pastor is probably attributing glory to "the God of peace," who is the subject of these verses and the source of this blessing. The phrase, however, occurs immediately after the words "Jesus Christ," through whom God has accomplished such a "great salvation" (2:3). This ambiguity reflects the deity of the Son and his close association with God the Father. The pastor has been establishing this association from the opening words of this sermon as fundamental to all he would say.[49] Now, then, the pastor who began by affirming that God has revealed

45. By switching from the "you" plural of v. 20 to "us" in v. 21 the pastor includes himself among those "equipped" to do God's will.
46. "Romans 12:1-2 provides an especially close parallel: Paul tells his readers to offer their 'bodies as a living sacrifice, holy and acceptable to God, your spiritual worship,' and spells this out in terms of a renewal of the mind that enables them to do 'what is good *(agathon)* and acceptable *(euareston)* and perfect *(teleion)*'" (Johnson, 356).
47. The instrumental "through Jesus Christ" is comprehensive — means, manner, and cause (cf. Weiss, 759).
48. Thus, Weiss, 758-59, need not be surprised that an epistle urging endurance would conclude by reminding its recipients that such endurance is possible only by the work of God.
49. Ellingworth, 731; Lane, 2:565; Bruce, 389; Braun, 480; Thurén, *Lobopfer,*

himself through his Son (1:1-4), concludes by reaffirming that this disclosure is nothing less than the all-sufficient "great salvation" accomplished "through Jesus Christ." From beginning to end all is God's work in Christ. This truth has been the burden of his sermon. Glory is due "forever" to this God and to his Son, who has become the "source of eternal salvation" (5:9). With this blessing and ascription of praise the pastor brings his final appeal in chapter 13, and thus the whole sermon, to a fitting conclusion. Yet the following verses retain their importance. Even in these seemingly mundane matters so typical of a letter closing the pastor does what he can to encourage his hearers' wholehearted compliance with the will of God.

22 The style and content of vv. 22-25 are even more indicative of a letter closing than were vv. 18-21. Verse 22 shows clearly that the pastor's "word of exhortation" is complete. He now speaks simply of himself in the first person singular (vv. 22, 23). He is concerned with news (v. 23) and greetings (v. 24).[50] With "I *exhort* you, brothers and sisters, pay attention to my word of *exhortation*" (italics added) he indulges in one more wordplay.[51] "Brothers and sisters" strengthens his appeal by reminding the hearers of all he has said in 2:11-13 about their bond as children of God and brothers and sisters of whom Christ is not ashamed. "Word of exhortation" may well have been a common designation for a synagogue homily or sermon.[52] This phrase is a most apt description of Hebrews 1:1–12:29 or even 1:1–13:21.[53] The entire book has been an "exhortation" to perseverance in faith, characterized both by warning against the consequences of unfaithfulness and encouragement based on the sufficiency of Christ.[54] To call what he has written a "word" of exhortation is particularly appropriate in light of the oral style of his address and the way in which he presents the "word" of God as directly addressing his hearers. His exhortation joins with these OT quotations (cf. 12:5) as God's own appeal to those who will hear. Both "pay attention to"

230-33; and deSilva, 513 attribute this ascription of praise to God. Lane bases his judgment on a structural analysis of vv. 20-21. Attridge, 408, n. 43; Bénétreau, 2:235; Spicq, 2:437; Hagner, 251; and others argue that it applies to Christ. See 2 Tim 4:18; 2 Pet 3:18; Rev 1:6; *1 Clem.* 20:12; and *Mart. Pol.* 22:3. See Ellingworth, 731, for a further list of those who support each of these positions. Johnson, 356, suggests that the ambiguity is intentional.

50. For personal comments at the end of letters, see Rom 15:15–16:23; 1 Cor 16:1-21; Phil 4:21-23; Col 4:7-18; 1 Thess 5:26-28; 2 Thess 3:17-18; 2 Tim 4:19-22; Tit 3:12-15; Phlm 22-24; and 1 Pet 5:12-14.

51. "I exhort (παρακαλῶ) you, brothers and sisters, pay attention to my word of exhortation (παρακλήσεως)."

52. On the literary genre of Hebrews see pp. 11-16 in the Introduction.

53. Bénétreau, 2:236; Weiss, 762; Johnson, 357.

54. For παράκλησις ("exhortation") as inclusive of both strong appeal and encouragement see BDAG, 766.

and the claim to have written "briefly" were polite ways of showing deference, and thus of gaining the hearers' compliance.[55] The pastor's call to "pay
attention to" his message is his final appeal for his hearers to persevere by
heeding both the warnings and the encouragement that he has given them.
Even the claim to brevity, which might seem inappropriate for a book as long
as Hebrews, is meant to reinforce the sermon's message by implying that
there was much more that could have been said in its defense (cf. 9:5; 11:32).
"I have instructed you very briefly" confirms the epistolary character that
Hebrews now assumes, yet maintains the oral character of the address by
avoiding the usual word for "write."[56]

The specific details given in these verses are insufficient for modern
readers to identify either the author or the intended recipients. However, these
verses do remind us "of the remarkable way in which early Christian communities joined themselves together through networks of personal and written communication, even in circumstances that made such communication difficult."[57]

23 The opening verb of this verse is probably imperative, in accord
with the imperatives of vv. 22 and 24: "Know that our brother Timothy has
been released."[58] It is possible, however, that the pastor is recalling already
received news: "You know that our brother Timothy has been released." It is
probable that this reference is to Timothy the companion of Paul (Acts 16:1-
3; 17:14-15; 18:5; 19:22; 20:4), Paul's delegate to various churches (1 Cor
4:17; 16:10; Phil 2:19; 1 Thess 3:2, 6), the recipient of two letters from Paul
(1 Tim 1:1-3; 2 Tim 1:1-2), and Paul's associates in the writing of six letters
(2 Cor 1:1; Phil 1:1; Col 1:1-2; 1 Thess 1:1; 2 Thess 1:1; and Phlm 1). In the
opening of three of these letters, Paul gives himself a distinct title ("Paul, an
apostle of Christ Jesus," in 2 Cor 1:1 and Col 1:1; "Paul, a prisoner of Jesus
Christ," in Phlm 1) and refers to "Timothy, the brother."[59] In 1 Thess 3:2 he
speaks of "Timothy, our brother." The pastor has put even more emphasis on
"our brother" by locating it before Timothy's name: "our brother Timothy."[60]

55. For the conventional nature of "brief" see Lane, 2:568-69. Cf. 1 Pet 5:12;
Barn. 1:5. Hebrews should be distinguished from *Barnabas,* where this expression occurs
at the beginning of a letter twice as long as Hebrews, and from 1 Peter, where it concludes
a truly brief letter (deSilva, 513-14).

56. For ἐπιστέλλω as "inform/instruct by letter" see BDAG, 381. Cf. Josephus,
Ant. 12.50; 18.300; Acts 21:25; *1 Clem.* 62:1; MM, 245-46 (cited by Weiss, 762). The author of Hebrews never uses γράφω ("write"), γραφή ("writing"), or any word related to
this root.

57. Johnson, 352.

58. Weiss, 763, n. 66.

59. Τιμόθεος ὁ ἀδελφός, "Timothy, the brother" could, of course, signify either
"Timothy, my brother" or "Timothy, our brother."

60. The absence of ἡμῶν ("our") from τὸν ἀδελφὸν ἡμῶν Τιμόθεον ("our brother

The pastor does not claim to be Paul. Yet by thus calling Timothy "our brother," and by expressing his hope of seeing his hearers with Timothy, he clearly identifies himself with the network of people who were close to Paul.[61] This association strengthens the pastor's authority as a valid teacher of the "great salvation" that had its beginning in the Lord Jesus and "was confirmed to us by those who heard" (2:3).[62] By letting them know that he hopes to see them, the pastor both affirms his affection for them and reminds them that he will have opportunity to see if they have heeded his admonitions.

24   The way the pastor has framed his exhortation to "greet all your leaders and all the saints" is particularly appropriate. Special mention of "all your leaders" reinforces the exhortations to emulate their past leaders (v. 7) and submit to the oversight of those who are now faithfully directing the community (v. 17). "Saints" or "holy ones" was a common designation for followers of Christ.[63] Yet it is particularly useful here as a reminder of the cleansing from sin provided by Christ (2:11; 9:11-14; 10:10, 14, 29; 13:12) and the resulting holiness that the hearers are to pursue (12:14; cf. the comments on 3:1). Some suggest that this exhortation is evidence that those addressed were a smaller group within the larger community of those who followed Christ in a particular city. Thus, by "all" your leaders and "all" the saints the pastor is urging them to greet those outside their immediate fellowship.[64] The fact that he does not urge them to have this larger group read the entire letter or sermon is no objection to this position.[65] The pastor's sermon is directed to the situation of his immediate hearers. Other interpretations, however, are quite possible. The pastor may have been urging them to greet each other.[66] Or this may have been a way of sending his own greetings: "Greet all your leaders and all the saints" on my behalf. Note, particularly,

---

Timothy) in some manuscripts (א², D², Ψ) of Heb 13:23 may reflect the influence of 2 Cor 1:1; Col 1:1 and Phlm 1, where Timothy is simply called ὁ ἀδελφός ("the brother").

61. "If he comes quickly" (13:23) recalls 2 Tim 4:9 ("be diligent to come to me quickly").

62. Weiss, 763. For the proposal that Heb 1:1–13:21 was written by Timothy and that Paul appended vv. 22-25 as a note of recommendation, see John D. Legg, "Our Brother Timothy: A Suggested Solution to the Problem of the Authorship of the Epistle to the Hebrews," *EvQ* 40 (1968): 220-23.

63. Rom 1:7; 16:15; 1 Cor 1:2; 6:1-2; 14:33; 16:15; 2 Cor 1:1; 13:12; Eph 1:1; 6:18; Phil 1:1; 4:22; Col 1:2; 1 Thess 5:27; Phlm 7; etc.

64. Moffatt, 246; Spicq, 2:438; Lane, 2:570.

65. *Pace* Attridge, 409; deSilva, 514-15.

66. Compare ἀσπάσασθε ἀλλήλους ἐν φιλήματι ἁγίῳ ("Greet each other with a holy kiss") in Rom 16:16; 1 Cor 16:20; and 2 Cor 13:12; and ἀσπάσασθε ἀλλήλους ἐν φιλήματι ἀγάπης in 1 Pet 5:14 with ἀσπάσασθε πάντας τοὺς ἡγουμένους ὑμῶν καὶ πάντας τοὺς ἁγίους ("greet all your leaders and all the saints") in Heb 13:24.

Rom 16:3-15, where the second person plural imperative "greet" is repeatedly followed by the names of those whom Paul would greet. The people who are with the pastor and send their greetings are described as "those from Italy." This description could mean that the pastor was writing from Italy. This is the supposition of many of the subscripts that follow Hebrews in some manuscripts.[67] Alternatively, "those from Italy" may describe Italians living outside their homeland, thus suggesting that Hebrews is directed to people living in Italy, possibly Rome.[68] We can, however, agree with certainty that "the reference to Italy shows that the circle in which Hebrews originated included Christians who lived outside Palestine in the Greco-Roman world."[69] We must not be deterred by attempts to determine the specific referents of v. 24 from the fact that this sending and receiving of greetings reinforces the pastor's concern for mutual care among his hearers (3:12-13; 10:24-25; 13:1-6, 16) as those who truly are brothers and sisters in the household of God (cf. 3:6).

25 With "Grace be with you all" the pastor follows the normal practice of Pauline letters.[70] And yet, with this final statement the pastor offers a prayer that the fully sufficient "grace" of God, which he has resoundingly shown throughout this sermon to be available through the all-sufficient Christ (2:17-18; 4:14-16; 10:19-25; 12:15; 13:9), may be theirs in order that they might persevere in faith (12:1-13).

67. "To the Hebrews written from Rome" (A; P has "from Italy"); "To the Hebrews written from Italy through Timothy" (1739; 1881; many others); "To the Hebrews written from Rome by Paul to those in Jerusalem" (81); "To the Hebrews written by a Hebrew from Italy . . . through Timothy" (104); "The Epistle of Paul to the Hebrews written from Italy through Timothy" (probably 0285). See NA[27], 587.

68. Matt 21:11; Mark 15:43; John 1:44; 21:2; Acts 6:9, cf. 21:27; 14:18; and especially the reference to Priscilla and Aquila in Acts 18:2. Weiss, 765; Moffatt, 246-47; and Lane, 2:571, identify "those from Italy" as Italians living outside Italy. Spicq, 2:439, on the other hand, argues that if the writer were writing outside Italy he would send greetings from others and not merely from those with him who were from Italy.

69. Koester, 581.

70. Rom 16:20; 1 Cor 16:23; 2 Cor 13:13; Gal 6:18; Eph 6:24; Phil 4:23; Col 4:18; 1 Thess 5:28; 2 Thess 3:18; 1 Tim 6:21; 2 Tim 4:22; Tit 3:15; and Phlm 25.

INDEX OF SUBJECTS

INDEX OF NAMES

INDEX OF SCRIPTURE
AND OTHER ANCIENT TEXTS

738